STATE PROFILES

STATE PROFILES

THE POPULATION AND ECONOMY OF EACH U.S. STATE

10th Edition
2018

Edited by Hannah Anderson Krog

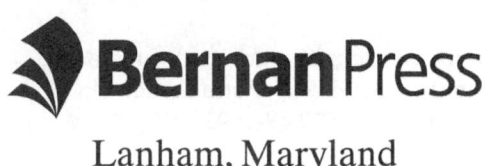

Lanham, Maryland

Published in the United States of America
by Bernan Press, an imprint of
The Rowman & Littlefield Publishing Group, Inc.
4501 Forbes Boulevard, Suite 200
Lanham, Maryland 20706

Bernan Press
800-865-3457
www.rowman.com/bernanpress

ISBN 13: 978-1-64143-275-7
E-ISBN: 978-1-64143-276-4

∞™ The paper used in this publication meets the minimum requirements of
American National Standard for Information Sciences—Permanence of
Paper for Printed Library Materials, ANSI/NISO Z39.48-1992.
Manufactured in the United States of America.

CONTENTS

LIST OF TABLES vii

PREFACE ix

USING THIS BOOK xi

UNITED STATES 1

RANKINGS. 3

    Alabama 15

    Alaska 25

    Arizona 35

    Arkansas 45

    California 55

    Colorado 65

    Connecticut 75

    Delaware 85

    District of Columbia 95

    Florida 105

    Georgia 115

    Hawaii 125

    Idaho 135

    Illinois 145

    Indiana 155

    Iowa 165

    Kansas 175

    Kentucky 185

    Louisiana 195

    Maine 205

    Maryland 215

    Massachusetts 225

    Michigan 235

    Minnesota 245

    Mississippi 255

    Missouri 265

    Montana 275

    Nebraska 285

    Nevada 295

    New Hampshire 305

    New Jersey 315

    New Mexico 325

New York 335

North Carolina 345

North Dakota 355

Ohio 365

Oklahoma 375

Oregon 385

Pennsylvania 395

Rhode Island 405

South Carolina 415

South Dakota 425

Tennessee 435

Texas 445

Utah 455

Vermont 465

Virginia 475

Washington 485

West Virginia 495

Wisconsin 505

Wyoming 515

NOTES AND DEFINITIONS **525**

INDEX **535**

LIST OF TABLES

The following tables are included for each state and the District of Columbia:

Table 1. Population by Age, Sex, Race, and Hispanic Origin
Table 2. Marital Status
Table 3. Households and Housing Characteristics
Table 4. Migration, Origin, and Language
Table 5. Median Income and Poverty Status, 2016
Table 6. Health Insurance Coverage Status for the Civilian Noninstitutionalized Population and Children Under 18 Years of Age
Table 7. Employment Status by Demographic Group, 2017
Table 8. Employment Status of the Civilian Noninstitutional Population Age 16 Years and Over
Table 9. Employment and Average Wages by Industry
Table 10. Employment Characteristics by Family Type
Table 11. School Enrollment and Attainment, 2016
Table 12. Public School Characteristics and Educational Indicators
Table 13. Reported Voting and Registration of the Voting Age Population, November 2016
Table 14. Crime
Table 15. State/District Government Finances, 2016
Table 16. State/District Government Tax Collections, 2017

PREFACE

Bernan Press is pleased to present the 10th edition of *State Profiles*, a publication that provides a state-by-state view of the United States. Topics covered include population composition by age, sex, race, and ethnicity; marital status; migration, origin, and language; households and housing; income and poverty; health insurance; employment; educational indicators; voting; crime; and other important aspects of the economy.

The publication's primary focus is on the 50 states and the District of Columbia, each of which possesses considerable differences in economic structure and demographics and has experienced various changes over time. Changes at the national level, including the diminished importance of agriculture and manufacturing and the growing influence of global trade, have resulted in today's information-based, service-providing economy. While national trends have laid the broad framework for change, each state has been affected differently. Cyclical fluctuations have also affected states in various ways during the nationwide recessions and the subsequent recovery periods. Recessions and recoveries spread unevenly among regions and states. Migration patterns have also reflected these changes, as states have experienced different influxes of workers from within the country and new residents from abroad.

Beyond the market forces, local and national government policies and expenditures on items such as education, health care, energy production and conservation, national defense, and homeland security have influenced economic circumstances.

The information provided in *State Profiles* aims to illuminate these trends. As such, the analysis and statistics are of interest not only to researchers and policy analysts but also to businesses seeking a broad basis for investments and expansion or relocation plans. The volume also profiles recent voting patterns, which will be of interest to political scientists.

DATA SELECTION

This edition of *State Profiles* generally continues the broad selection of information from previous editions. Most, but not all, of the data items have been updated through 2015, 2016, and even 2017, as demographic estimates from the U.S. Census Bureau became available.

As in the past, space constraints have influenced the amount of data presented for each state. The most meaningful and relevant data have thus been selected, analyzed, and highlighted. This edition expands upon the available information to include more detailed data on the demographics of each state, especially in regard to diversity of spoken languages and the foreign-born population. For most of the subjects addressed in this edition, further data are generally available from the source government agencies. Locations of sources of information are listed in notes and definitions at the end of the volume.

Although the editor has taken care to present accurate data, all statistical data are subject to a degree of error, resulting from sampling variability, erroneous reporting, and other causes. Many of the data are subject to subsequent revision.

The data in this book meet the publication standards of the federal agencies from which they were obtained. The responsibilities of the editor and publisher of this volume are limited to reasonable care in the reproduction and presentation of the data from the established sources.

Hannah Anderson Krog has edited the past four editions of *State Profiles*. She previously worked as an assistant editor for Bernan Press and is now a freelance writer and editor for several reference titles. She has a B.A. in journalism from the University of Maryland.

USING THIS BOOK: ORGANIZATION AND CONTENTS

STATE PROFILES 2018 PROVIDES:

- Rankings of states for key demographic and economic indicators
- A chapter for each state, complete with tables and figures that summarize and illustrate demographic and economic characteristics
- Notes and definitions to assist with interpreting the information contained in this volume

THE U.S. OVERVIEW. This short introduction to the demographics of the United States provides commentary on overall trends within the country.

THE STATE RANKINGS. The ranking tables that follow the national overview give state rankings by more than 30 characteristics, including population, demographic and age composition, income, per capita gross domestic product, homeownership, poverty, health indicators, education, and federal aid. These rankings provide the user with a quick analysis of the performance of each state in relation to the other states.

THE STATE CHAPTERS. The state chapters are the focus of this book. Each chapter follows a standard format and contains text highlighting the key features shown in the tables and figures. Some of these tables and figures contain references to the U.S. averages for the same characteristics.

Each of the state chapters is organized as follows:

Population. This table provides data on the state's total population and average annual population growth in comparison with the national average. It also shows the major population groups by sex, age, race, and ethnicity.

Marital status. The table shows the marital status for all men and women age 15 years and over.

Housing. This table showcases data pertaining to housing, such as number of households, types of households, housing characteristics, and median gross rent, mortgage, and monthly owner cost amounts.

Migration, origin, and language. This table provides statistics on residence one year ago, year of entry, place of origin, language spoken at home, and the native-born and foreign-born populations.

Income and poverty. Median household and family income and poverty rates by sex and age are contained in this table.

Health insurance coverage. This table provides information on health insurance, by type and coverage.

Employment. These tables illustrate each state's particular economic configuration. They exhibit employment status by detailed demographic group, labor force, participation rates, employment, unemployment, average wages and salaries by industry, and employment by family type.

Education. These tables provide the user with details on educational attainment, elementary and secondary school enrollment, student/teacher ratios, per student expenditures, and higher education enrollments.

Voter participation. Information is given on voter registration and voter participation in the 2016 presidential election, categorized by sex and race and ethnicity.

Crime. This table include the number and rates of violent and property crime.

Government finance. These tables provide data on revenues and expenditures by source for each state and the District of Columbia. In addition, tax information for each state/district is included.

NOTES AND DEFINITIONS. Each chapter relies on the same standard set of federal data sources. Since the basic data sources are common to all chapters, the main body of the volume contains few footnotes. Basic data and corresponding definitions and sources are identified in the notes and definition section at the end of the volume. It provides brief descriptions, methodologies, data availabity, information on calculations made by the editors, and references to additional sources of information.

Introduction

During the early 2000s, the United States experienced several economic fluctuations that had a great impact on the strength, size, and performance of its economy. The recession that began in March 2001 was concluded in a few months; however, the longer-lasting recession that began in December 2007 left a more serious impact on the country. The data in this book track the impact of that recession and subsequent recovery on the United States' economy over the past decade.

This edition of *State Profiles: The Population and Economy of Each U.S. State* creates a snapshot of the people and economy in each state and the District of Columbia. Each chapter (one per state/district) includes information on topics such as population, employment, marital status, crime, government finance, housing, education, and language.

Summary

The U.S. population grew 5.3 percent between 2010 and 2017. The District of Columbia experienced the largest population growth in the nation at 14.7 percent. The states with the largest population growth included Texas (12.1 percent), North Dakota (12.0 percent), Utah (11.8 percent), Florida (11.3 percent), Colorado (11.1 percent), Nevada (10.9 percent), Washington (9.9 percent), Arizona (9.5 percent), Idaho (9.3 percent), South Carolina (8.4 percent), Oregon (8.0 percent), and Georgia (7.4 percent). Three states' populations declined during that time period: Vermont (-0.3 percent), Illinois (-0.3 percent), and West Virginia (-2.1 percent).

Utah had the highest percentage of population younger than 18 years old in 2017, with 29.9 percent of its population in this age group, followed by Texas at 26.0 percent. The District of Columbia had the smallest percent of minors, at 17.9 percent, followed by Vermont at 18.7 percent. Florida had the highest percentage of people 65 years and older, with 20.1 percent of the population in this age group, followed by Maine at 19.9 percent. At 10.8 percent, Utah had the lowest percentage of senior residents, followed by Alaska at 11.2 percent and the District of Columbia at 12.1 percent.

In 2016, the median household income in the United States was $57,617. Maryland was the state with the highest median household income at $78,945, followed by Alaska ($76,440), New Jersey ($76,126), the District of Columbia ($75,506), and Massachusetts ($75,297). The states with the lowest median household incomes were Mississippi ($41,754), West Virginia ($43,385), Arkansas ($44,334), Louisiana ($45,146), and Alabama ($46,257). Some correlation to the percentage of residents with a bachelor's degree or more can be inferred, as Maryland, New Jersey, the District of Columbia, and Massachusetts rank in the top five states in this category. Mississippi, West Virginia, Arkansas, and Louisiana rank in the bottom five states in this category. The unemployment rate for the United States was 4.4 percent in 2017, which was down from 4.9 percent in 2016. Alaska had the highest percentage of unemployed residents in 2017 (7.2 percent), followed by New Mexico (6.2 percent) and the District of Columbia (6.1 percent). Hawaii (2.4 percent) and North Dakota (2.6 percent) had the lowest percentage of unemployed residents.

In the United States in 2016, 14.0 percent of the population lived below the poverty level. Mississippi, which had the lowest median household income, also had the highest poverty rate, with 20.8 percent of its residents below the poverty level. New Hampshire had the lowest poverty rate, at 7.3 percent. New Mexico had the highest rate of persons younger than 18 years of age below the poverty level (30.1 percent), followed by Mississippi (29.7 percent), Louisiana (28.6 percent), the District of Columbia (25.8 percent), and Kentucky (25.0 percent). The states with the fewest residents under 18 years of age below the poverty level included New Hampshire (7.9 percent), Hawaii (10.1 percent), Wyoming (11.1 percent), Utah (11.1 percent), and North Dakota (12.4 percent).

UNITED STATES RANKINGS

Population, 2017

Rank	State	Population
	United States......................	325,719,178
24	Alabama..........................	4,874,747
48	Alaska............................	739,795
14	Arizona...........................	7,016,270
32	Arkansas.........................	3,004,279
1	California........................	39,536,653
21	Colorado.........................	5,607,154
29	Connecticut......................	3,588,184
45	Delaware.........................	961,939
49	District of Columbia	693,972
3	Florida............................	20,984,400
8	Georgia...........................	10,429,379
40	Hawaii............................	1,427,538
39	Idaho.............................	1,716,943
6	Illinois............................	12,802,023
17	Indiana...........................	6,666,818
30	Iowa..............................	3,145,711
35	Kansas...........................	2,913,123
26	Kentucky.........................	4,454,189
25	Louisiana	4,684,333
42	Maine.............................	1,335,907
19	Maryland.........................	6,052,177
15	Massachusetts...................	6,859,819
10	Michigan.........................	9,962,311
22	Minnesota........................	5,576,606
34	Mississippi.......................	2,984,100
18	Missouri..........................	6,113,532
44	Montana..........................	1,050,493
37	Nebraska.........................	1,920,076
33	Nevada...........................	2,998,039
41	New Hampshire..................	1,342,795
11	New Jersey	9,005,644
36	New Mexico	2,088,070
4	New York.........................	19,849,399
9	North Carolina...................	10,273,419
47	North Dakota.....................	755,393
7	Ohio..............................	11,658,609
28	Oklahoma.........................	3,930,864
27	Oregon...........................	4,142,776
5	Pennsylvania.....................	12,805,537
43	Rhode Island.....................	1,059,639
23	South Carolina	5,024,369
46	South Dakota	869,666
16	Tennessee	6,715,984
2	Texas.............................	28,304,596
31	Utah..............................	3,101,833
50	Vermont..........................	623,657
12	Virginia...........................	8,470,020
13	Washington.......................	7,405,743
38	West Virginia.....................	1,815,857
20	Wisconsin.........................	5,795,483
51	Wyoming	579,315

Population, Percent Change, 2010–2017

Rank	State	Percent
	United States......................	5.3
38	Alabama..........................	1.9
27	Alaska............................	3.6
9	Arizona...........................	9.5
30	Arkansas.........................	2.8
18	California........................	5.9
6	Colorado.........................	11.1
48	Connecticut......................	0.2
15	Delaware.........................	6.9
1	District of Columbia	14.7
5	Florida............................	11.3
13	Georgia...........................	7.4
23	Hawaii............................	4.7
10	Idaho.............................	9.3
49	Illinois............................	-0.3
31	Indiana...........................	2.7
28	Iowa..............................	3.1
38	Kansas...........................	1.9
33	Kentucky.........................	2.4
28	Louisiana	3.1
45	Maine.............................	0.6
24	Maryland.........................	4.6
26	Massachusetts...................	4.5
43	Michigan.........................	0.9
21	Minnesota........................	5.0
47	Mississippi.......................	0.5
36	Missouri..........................	2.0
17	Montana..........................	6.1
22	Nebraska.........................	4.9
7	Nevada...........................	10.9
36	New Hampshire..................	2.0
34	New Jersey	2.3
41	New Mexico	1.1
35	New York.........................	2.3
14	North Carolina...................	7.3
3	North Dakota.....................	12.0
42	Ohio..............................	1.0
24	Oklahoma.........................	4.6
12	Oregon...........................	8.0
44	Pennsylvania.....................	0.7
45	Rhode Island.....................	0.6
11	South Carolina	8.4
16	South Dakota	6.5
19	Tennessee	5.7
2	Texas.............................	12.1
4	Utah..............................	11.8
49	Vermont..........................	-0.3
20	Virginia...........................	5.5
8	Washington.......................	9.9
51	West Virginia.....................	-2.1
40	Wisconsin.........................	1.8
32	Wyoming	2.6

Percent Population Under 18 Years Old, 2017

Rank	State	Percent
	United States......................	22.6
1	Utah..............................	29.9
2	Texas.............................	26.0
3	Idaho.............................	25.8
4	Alaska............................	25.0
5	Nebraska.........................	24.8
6	South Dakota	24.7
7	Kansas...........................	24.5
8	Oklahoma.........................	24.4
9	Georgia...........................	24.1
10	Mississippi.......................	23.9
11	Louisiana	23.7
12	Indiana...........................	23.6
12	Wyoming	23.6
14	Arkansas.........................	23.5
15	New Mexico	23.4
16	Minnesota........................	23.3
16	Arizona...........................	23.3
16	North Dakota.....................	23.3
16	Iowa..............................	23.3
20	California........................	22.9
20	Nevada...........................	22.9
22	Kentucky.........................	22.7
23	Illinois............................	22.6
23	Missouri..........................	22.6
25	Colorado.........................	22.5
25	Alabama..........................	22.5
27	Tennessee	22.4
27	North Carolina...................	22.4
29	Ohio..............................	22.3
29	Maryland.........................	22.3
31	Washington.......................	22.2
32	Wisconsin.........................	22.1
32	Virginia...........................	22.1
34	South Carolina	22.0
34	New Jersey	22.0
36	Michigan.........................	21.8
36	Montana..........................	21.8
38	Hawaii............................	21.4
39	Delaware.........................	21.3
40	Oregon...........................	21.1
41	New York.........................	20.9
42	Pennsylvania.....................	20.8
43	Connecticut......................	20.7
44	West Virginia.....................	20.4
45	Florida............................	20.0
45	Massachusetts...................	20.0
47	Rhode Island.....................	19.6
48	New Hampshire..................	19.3
49	Maine.............................	18.9
50	Vermont..........................	18.7
51	District of Columbia	17.9

Percent Population 65 Years and Over, 2017

Rank	State	Percent
	United States..............	15.6
1	Florida............................	20.1
2	Maine.............................	19.9
3	West Virginia..................	19.4
4	Vermont..........................	18.7
5	Montana.........................	18.1
5	Delaware........................	18.1
7	Pennsylvania..................	17.8
7	Hawaii............................	17.8
9	New Hampshire...............	17.6
10	South Carolina	17.2
11	Arizona...........................	17.1
11	Oregon...........................	17.1
13	New Mexico	16.9
14	Rhode Island	16.8
14	Connecticut	16.8
16	Michigan.........................	16.7
16	Iowa...............................	16.7
16	Ohio...............................	16.7
19	Arkansas........................	16.6
20	Alabama.........................	16.5
20	Missouri..........................	16.5
20	Wisconsin.......................	16.5
23	South Dakota	16.3
24	Massachusetts................	16.2
25	Tennessee	16.0
25	Kentucky........................	16.0
27	New York........................	15.9
27	North Carolina.................	15.9
29	Wyoming	15.8
29	New Jersey	15.8
31	Mississippi......................	15.5
32	Kansas	15.4
32	Idaho..............................	15.4
32	Minnesota.......................	15.4
32	Nebraska........................	15.4
32	Indiana...........................	15.4
37	Oklahoma.......................	15.3
37	Nevada...........................	15.3
39	Illinois............................	15.2
40	Washington.....................	15.1
41	Virginia...........................	15.0
41	North Dakota...................	15.0
43	Maryland.........................	14.9
43	Louisiana	14.9
45	California........................	13.9
46	Colorado	13.8
47	Georgia	13.5
48	Texas.............................	12.3
49	District of Columbia	12.1
50	Alaska	11.2
51	Utah...............................	10.8

Percent White Alone, 2017

Rank	State	Percent
	United States......................	76.6
1	Maine.............................	94.7
2	Vermont..........................	94.5
3	New Hampshire...............	93.6
3	West Virginia..................	93.6
5	Idaho..............................	93.2
6	Wyoming	92.8
7	Iowa...............................	91.1
8	Utah...............................	90.9
9	Montana.........................	89.1
10	Nebraska........................	88.6
11	Kentucky........................	87.8
12	North Dakota	87.5
13	Wisconsin	87.3
13	Colorado	87.3
15	Oregon...........................	87.1
16	Kansas	86.5
17	Indiana...........................	85.4
18	South Dakota	84.9
19	Minnesota.......................	84.4
20	Rhode Island..................	84.1
21	Missouri..........................	83.1
21	Arizona...........................	83.1
23	Ohio...............................	82.2
23	New Mexico	82.2
25	Pennsylvania..................	82.1
26	Massachusetts................	81.3
27	Connecticut	80.3
28	Washington.....................	79.5
29	Michigan.........................	79.4
30	Arkansas........................	79.3
31	Texas.............................	79.2
32	Tennessee	78.6
33	Florida............................	77.4
34	Illinois............................	77.1
35	Nevada...........................	74.6
36	Oklahoma.......................	74.3
37	California........................	72.4
38	New Jersey	72.1
39	North Carolina.................	70.8
40	Virginia...........................	69.7
40	Delaware........................	69.7
42	New York........................	69.6
43	Alabama.........................	69.2
44	South Carolina	68.5
45	Alaska	65.8
46	Louisiana	63.0
47	Georgia	60.8
48	Mississippi......................	59.2
49	Maryland.........................	59.0
50	District of Columbia	45.1
51	Hawaii............................	25.7

Percent Black or African American Alone, 2017

Rank	State	Percent
	United States......................	13.4
1	District of Columbia	47.1
2	Mississippi......................	37.8
3	Louisiana	32.6
4	Georgia	32.2
5	Maryland.........................	30.8
6	South Carolina	27.3
7	Alabama.........................	26.8
8	Delaware........................	22.8
9	North Carolina.................	22.2
10	Virginia...........................	19.8
11	New York........................	17.7
12	Tennessee	17.1
13	Florida............................	16.9
14	Arkansas........................	15.7
15	New Jersey	15.0
16	Illinois............................	14.6
17	Michigan.........................	14.1
18	Ohio...............................	12.9
19	Texas.............................	12.7
20	Connecticut	11.9
20	Pennsylvania..................	11.9
22	Missouri..........................	11.8
23	Nevada...........................	9.8
24	Indiana...........................	9.7
25	Massachusetts................	8.8
26	Kentucky........................	8.4
27	Rhode Island..................	8.2
28	Oklahoma.......................	7.8
29	Wisconsin	6.7
30	Minnesota.......................	6.5
30	California........................	6.5
32	Kansas	6.2
33	Nebraska........................	5.1
34	Arizona...........................	5.0
35	Colorado	4.5
36	Washington.....................	4.2
37	Iowa...............................	3.8
38	Alaska	3.7
39	West Virginia..................	3.6
40	North Dakota...................	3.1
41	New Mexico	2.5
42	Hawaii............................	2.2
42	Oregon...........................	2.2
44	South Dakota	2.1
45	New Hampshire...............	1.6
45	Maine.............................	1.6
47	Utah...............................	1.4
47	Vermont..........................	1.4
49	Wyoming	1.3
50	Idaho..............................	0.9
51	Montana.........................	0.6

Percent American Indian and Alaska Native Alone, 2017

Rank	State	Percent
	United States	1.3
1	Alaska	15.3
2	New Mexico	10.9
3	Oklahoma	9.2
4	South Dakota	9.0
5	Montana	6.7
6	North Dakota	5.5
7	Arizona	5.3
8	Wyoming	2.7
9	Washington	1.9
10	Oregon	1.8
11	Idaho	1.7
11	Nevada	1.7
13	California	1.6
13	Colorado	1.6
13	North Carolina	1.6
16	Utah	1.5
16	Nebraska	1.5
18	Minnesota	1.4
19	Kansas	1.2
19	Wisconsin	1.2
21	Rhode Island	1.0
21	Texas	1.0
21	Arkansas	1.0
21	New York	1.0
25	Louisiana	0.8
26	Michigan	0.7
26	Maine	0.7
26	Alabama	0.7
29	Delaware	0.6
29	Mississippi	0.6
29	New Jersey	0.6
29	District of Columbia	0.6
29	Illinois	0.6
29	Maryland	0.6
29	Missouri	0.6
36	South Carolina	0.5
36	Connecticut	0.5
36	Virginia	0.5
36	Iowa	0.5
36	Georgia	0.5
36	Florida	0.5
36	Massachusetts	0.5
36	Tennessee	0.5
44	Indiana	0.4
44	Hawaii	0.4
44	Vermont	0.4
44	Pennsylvania	0.4
48	Kentucky	0.3
48	New Hampshire	0.3
48	Ohio	0.3
51	West Virginia	0.2

Percent Asian Alone, 2017

Rank	State	Percent
	United States	5.8
1	Hawaii	37.8
2	California	15.2
3	New Jersey	10.1
4	New York	9.1
5	Washington	8.9
6	Nevada	8.8
7	Massachusetts	6.9
8	Virginia	6.8
9	Maryland	6.7
10	Alaska	6.5
11	Illinois	5.7
12	Minnesota	5.1
13	Texas	5.0
14	Connecticut	4.8
15	Oregon	4.7
16	District of Columbia	4.3
17	Georgia	4.2
18	Delaware	4.1
19	Rhode Island	3.7
20	Pennsylvania	3.6
21	Arizona	3.5
22	Colorado	3.4
23	Michigan	3.2
24	Kansas	3.1
24	North Carolina	3.1
26	Florida	2.9
26	Wisconsin	2.9
28	New Hampshire	2.8
29	Iowa	2.6
29	Nebraska	2.6
29	Utah	2.6
32	Indiana	2.4
33	Ohio	2.3
33	Oklahoma	2.3
35	Missouri	2.1
36	Tennessee	1.9
36	Louisiana	1.9
38	Vermont	1.8
39	New Mexico	1.7
39	South Carolina	1.7
41	Arkansas	1.6
41	North Dakota	1.6
41	Kentucky	1.6
44	Idaho	1.5
44	South Dakota	1.5
44	Alabama	1.5
47	Maine	1.2
48	Mississippi	1.1
49	Wyoming	1.0
50	Montana	0.8
50	West Virginia	0.8

Percent Native Hawaiian and Other Pacific Islander Alone, 2017

Rank	State	Percent
	United States	0.2
1	Hawaii	10.2
2	Alaska	1.4
3	Utah	1.0
4	Nevada	0.8
4	Washington	0.8
6	California	0.5
7	Oregon	0.4
8	Arkansas	0.3
8	Arizona	0.3
10	Idaho	0.2
10	Rhode Island	0.2
10	Oklahoma	0.2
10	Colorado	0.2
10	New Mexico	0.2
15	Missouri	0.1
15	Texas	0.1
15	District of Columbia	0.1
15	New York	0.1
15	North Carolina	0.1
15	Nebraska	0.1
15	Iowa	0.1
15	Kansas	0.1
15	Georgia	0.1
15	Virginia	0.1
15	Florida	0.1
15	Maryland	0.1
15	Alabama	0.1
15	New Jersey	0.1
15	Connecticut	0.1
15	Massachusetts	0.1
15	Wyoming	0.1
15	South Carolina	0.1
15	Tennessee	0.1
15	Delaware	0.1
15	Montana	0.1
15	Kentucky	0.1
15	South Dakota	0.1
15	Pennsylvania	0.1
15	Minnesota	0.1
15	North Dakota	0.1
15	Indiana	0.1
15	Illinois	0.1
15	Louisiana	0.1
15	Mississippi	0.1
15	Ohio	0.1
15	Wisconsin	0.1
47	New Hampshire	Z
47	Michigan	Z
47	Vermont	Z
47	Maine	Z
47	West Virginia	Z

Z = Value greater than zero but less than half of the unit shown.

Percent Two or More Races, 2017

Rank	State	Percent
	United States......................	2.7
1	Hawaii..............................	23.8
2	Alaska	7.4
3	Oklahoma..........................	6.1
4	Washington........................	4.7
5	Nevada..............................	4.3
6	California...........................	3.9
7	Oregon	3.8
8	Colorado	3.0
8	Virginia.............................	3.0
8	Kansas	3.0
11	Maryland............................	2.8
11	Arizona..............................	2.8
11	Rhode Island......................	2.8
11	Montana............................	2.8
15	District of Columbia	2.7
16	Delaware............................	2.6
17	New Mexico	2.5
17	New York............................	2.5
17	Utah	2.5
17	Minnesota..........................	2.5
21	Idaho................................	2.4
21	Michigan............................	2.4
21	Massachusetts	2.4
21	South Dakota......................	2.4
21	Connecticut........................	2.4
26	Missouri.............................	2.3
26	Ohio	2.3
26	North Carolina.....................	2.2
26	New Jersey	2.2
26	Nebraska............................	2.2
26	North Dakota.......................	2.2
32	Florida...............................	2.1
32	Wyoming............................	2.1
32	Georgia	2.1
32	Arkansas	2.1
32	Indiana..............................	2.1
37	Pennsylvania......................	2.0
37	Texas................................	2.0
37	Illinois...............................	2.0
40	Vermont.............................	1.9
40	Kentucky............................	1.9
40	Tennessee	1.9
40	Wisconsin	1.9
40	South Carolina	1.9
40	Iowa	1.9
46	Maine	1.8
47	West Virginia	1.7
47	New Hampshire....................	1.7
47	Alabama............................	1.7
47	Louisiana	1.7
51	Mississippi.........................	1.3

Percent Hispanic or Latino,[1] 2017

Rank	State	Percent
	United States......................	18.1
1	New Mexico	48.8
2	Texas................................	39.4
3	California...........................	39.1
4	Arizona..............................	31.4
5	Nevada..............................	28.8
6	Florida...............................	25.6
7	Colorado	21.5
8	New Jersey	20.4
9	New York............................	19.2
10	Illinois...............................	17.3
11	Connecticut........................	16.1
12	Rhode Island......................	15.5
13	Utah	14.0
14	Oregon	13.1
15	Washington........................	12.7
16	Idaho................................	12.5
17	Kansas	11.9
17	Massachusetts	11.9
19	District of Columbia	11.0
19	Nebraska............................	11.0
21	Oklahoma..........................	10.6
22	Hawaii..............................	10.5
23	Maryland............................	10.1
24	Wyoming............................	10.0
25	Georgia	9.6
26	North Carolina.....................	9.5
27	Virginia.............................	9.4
28	Delaware............................	9.3
29	Arkansas	7.6
30	Pennsylvania......................	7.3
31	Alaska	7.1
32	Indiana..............................	7.0
33	Wisconsin	6.9
34	Iowa	6.0
35	South Carolina	5.7
36	Tennessee	5.5
37	Minnesota..........................	5.4
38	Louisiana	5.2
39	Michigan............................	5.1
40	Alabama............................	4.3
41	Missouri.............................	4.2
42	Ohio	3.8
42	South Dakota......................	3.8
42	Montana............................	3.8
45	North Dakota.......................	3.7
45	New Hampshire....................	3.7
45	Kentucky............................	3.7
48	Mississippi.........................	3.2
49	Vermont.............................	1.9
50	Maine	1.6
50	West Virginia	1.6

[1] May be of any race.

Percent White Alone, Not Hispanic or Latino, 2017

Rank	State	Percent
	United States......................	60.7
1	Maine	93.3
2	Vermont.............................	92.9
3	West Virginia	92.2
4	New Hampshire....................	90.5
5	Montana............................	86.2
6	Iowa	85.7
7	Kentucky............................	84.6
7	North Dakota.......................	84.6
9	Wyoming............................	84.0
10	South Dakota......................	82.2
11	Idaho................................	82.0
12	Wisconsin	81.3
13	Minnesota..........................	79.9
14	Missouri.............................	79.5
15	Indiana..............................	79.2
16	Ohio	79.1
17	Nebraska............................	79.0
18	Utah	78.5
19	Pennsylvania......................	76.5
20	Kansas	75.9
21	Oregon	75.8
22	Michigan............................	75.2
23	Tennessee	73.9
24	Rhode Island......................	72.5
24	Arkansas	72.5
26	Massachusetts	72.2
27	Washington........................	68.7
28	Colorado	68.3
29	Connecticut........................	67.0
30	Oklahoma..........................	65.7
31	Alabama............................	65.6
32	South Carolina	63.8
33	North Carolina.....................	63.1
34	Delaware............................	62.3
35	Virginia.............................	61.9
36	Illinois...............................	61.3
37	Alaska	60.8
38	Louisiana	58.7
39	Mississippi.........................	56.7
40	New York............................	55.3
41	New Jersey	55.1
42	Arizona..............................	54.9
43	Florida...............................	54.1
44	Georgia	52.8
45	Maryland............................	50.9
46	Nevada..............................	49.1
47	Texas................................	42.0
48	New Mexico	37.5
49	California...........................	37.2
50	District of Columbia	36.8
51	Hawaii..............................	21.9

Birth Rate, 2016

Rank	State	Rate per 1,000 population
	United States......................	12.2
1	Utah	16.5
2	Alaska	15.1
3	North Dakota....................	15.0
4	District of Columbia	14.5
5	Texas.............................	14.3
6	South Dakota	14.2
7	Nebraska	13.9
8	Louisiana	13.5
9	Idaho.............................	13.4
9	Oklahoma........................	13.4
11	Kansas	13.1
12	Arkansas	12.8
13	Mississippi......................	12.7
14	Georgia	12.6
14	Hawaii	12.6
14	Iowa..............................	12.6
14	Minnesota	12.6
14	Wyoming	12.6
19	California........................	12.5
19	Indiana	12.5
19	Kentucky	12.5
22	Washington......................	12.4
23	Missouri..........................	12.3
23	Nevada...........................	12.3
25	Alabama..........................	12.2
25	Arizona...........................	12.2
25	Maryland.........................	12.2
25	Virginia...........................	12.2
29	Illinois	12.1
29	Tennessee.......................	12.1
31	Colorado	12.0
32	New Mexico	11.9
32	New York.........................	11.9
32	North Carolina...................	11.9
32	Ohio..............................	11.9
36	Montana..........................	11.8
37	South Carolina	11.6
38	Delaware.........................	11.5
38	New Jersey	11.5
38	Wisconsin........................	11.5
41	Michigan	11.4
42	Oregon	11.1
43	Florida............................	10.9
43	Pennsylvania....................	10.9
45	Massachusetts	10.5
46	West Virginia....................	10.4
47	Rhode Island....................	10.2
48	Connecticut......................	10.1
49	Maine	9.5
50	New Hampshire..................	9.2
50	Vermont..........................	9.2

Drug Overdose Death Rate, 2016

Rank	State	Age-adjusted rate per 100,000 population
	United States......................	19.8
1	West Virginia.....................	52.0
2	Ohio	39.1
3	New Hampshire..................	39.0
4	District of Columbia	38.8
5	Pennsylvania	37.9
6	Kentucky	33.5
7	Maryland.........................	33.2
8	Massachusetts	33.0
9	Delaware	30.8
9	Rhode Island	30.8
11	Maine	28.7
12	Connecticut......................	27.4
13	New Mexico	25.2
14	Tennessee.......................	24.5
15	Michigan	24.4
16	Indiana	24.0
17	Florida............................	23.7
18	Missouri..........................	23.6
19	New Jersey	23.2
20	Utah	22.4
21	Vermont	22.2
22	Louisiana	21.8
23	Nevada...........................	21.7
24	Oklahoma........................	21.5
25	Arizona...........................	20.3
26	North Carolina...................	19.7
27	Wisconsin	19.3
28	Illinois	18.9
29	South Carolina	18.1
30	New York.........................	18.0
31	Wyoming	17.6
32	Alaska	16.8
33	Virginia...........................	16.7
34	Colorado	16.6
35	Alabama..........................	16.2
36	Idaho.............................	15.2
37	Washington......................	14.5
38	Arkansas	14.0
39	Georgia	13.3
40	Hawaii	12.8
41	Minnesota	12.5
42	Mississippi.......................	12.1
43	Oregon	11.9
44	Montana..........................	11.7
45	California.........................	11.2
46	Kansas	11.1
47	Iowa..............................	10.6
47	North Dakota.....................	10.6
49	Texas.............................	10.1
50	South Dakota	8.4
51	Nebraska	6.4

Voting Population, 2016

Rank	State	Percent voted, total population
	United States......................	56.0
1	Maine	71.3
2	District of Columbia	68.7
2	Wisconsin........................	68.7
4	New Hampshire..................	66.9
5	Mississippi.......................	66.7
6	Minnesota	65.3
7	Montana..........................	65.2
8	Colorado	63.8
9	Wyoming	63.5
10	Nebraska	63.4
11	Missouri..........................	62.8
12	Virginia...........................	62.6
13	North Dakota.....................	62.1
14	Michigan	61.8
15	Massachusetts	61.7
16	North Carolina...................	61.6
17	Ohio	61.4
18	Vermont	61.0
18	Oregon	61.0
20	Iowa..............................	60.7
21	Washington......................	60.5
22	Pennsylvania....................	60.2
23	South Carolina	59.8
24	Louisiana	59.7
25	Alaska	59.4
26	Maryland.........................	59.2
27	Utah	58.9
28	Illinois	58.8
29	Idaho.............................	58.3
30	Kansas	58.0
31	Connecticut......................	57.5
32	South Dakota	57.3
33	Delaware.........................	57.2
34	Alabama..........................	56.4
35	Indiana	56.0
35	Arkansas	56.0
37	Georgia	55.7
38	Rhode Island....................	55.5
39	Kentucky	55.3
40	Nevada...........................	53.5
41	New Jersey	53.4
42	Arizona...........................	53.3
43	Oklahoma........................	53.2
44	Florida............................	52.9
45	Tennessee.......................	52.0
46	New York.........................	50.7
47	West Virginia....................	50.4
48	New Mexico	49.4
49	California.........................	48.2
50	Texas.............................	47.7
51	Hawaii	43.3

Percent of Persons 25 Years and Over with a Bachelor's Degree or More, 2016

Rank	State	Percent
	United States......................	31.3
1	District of Columbia	56.8
2	Massachusetts.....................	42.7
3	Colorado..............................	39.9
4	Maryland..............................	39.3
5	Connecticut..........................	38.6
5	New Jersey	38.6
7	Virginia................................	38.1
8	New Hampshire.....................	36.6
9	Vermont...............................	36.4
10	New York..............................	35.7
11	Washington..........................	35.1
12	Minnesota............................	34.8
13	Rhode Island........................	34.1
14	Illinois.................................	34.0
15	California.............................	32.9
16	Kansas.................................	32.8
17	Oregon.................................	32.7
18	Utah	32.6
19	Hawaii..................................	31.9
20	Nebraska..............................	31.4
21	Delaware..............................	31.0
21	Montana...............................	31.0
23	Pennsylvania........................	30.8
24	Georgia................................	30.5
25	North Carolina......................	30.4
26	Maine...................................	30.1
27	Alaska	29.6
27	North Dakota........................	29.6
29	Wisconsin	29.5
30	Arizona................................	28.9
30	South Dakota........................	28.9
30	Texas...................................	28.9
33	Florida.................................	28.6
34	Missouri...............................	28.5
35	Iowa....................................	28.4
36	Michigan	28.3
37	Idaho...................................	27.6
38	Ohio....................................	27.5
39	New Mexico	27.2
39	South Carolina	27.2
41	Wyoming..............................	27.1
42	Tennessee............................	26.1
43	Indiana................................	25.6
44	Oklahoma.............................	25.2
45	Alabama...............................	24.7
46	Nevada.................................	23.5
47	Kentucky..............................	23.4
47	Louisiana.............................	23.4
49	Arkansas..............................	22.4
50	Mississippi...........................	21.8
51	West Virginia........................	20.8

Violent Crime, 2016

Rank	State	Rate per 100,000 population
	United States......................	386.3
1	District of Columbia	1,205.9
2	Alaska	804.2
3	New Mexico	702.5
4	Nevada.................................	678.1
5	Tennessee............................	632.9
6	Louisiana	566.1
7	Arkansas..............................	550.9
8	Alabama...............................	532.3
9	Missouri...............................	519.4
10	Delaware..............................	508.8
11	South Carolina	501.8
12	Maryland..............................	472.0
13	Arizona................................	470.1
14	Michigan	459.0
15	Oklahoma.............................	449.8
16	California.............................	445.3
17	Illinois.................................	436.3
18	Texas...................................	434.4
19	Florida.................................	430.3
20	South Dakota........................	418.4
21	Indiana................................	404.7
22	Georgia................................	397.6
23	Kansas.................................	380.4
24	Massachusetts.....................	376.9
25	New York..............................	376.2
26	North Carolina......................	372.2
27	Montana...............................	368.3
28	West Virginia........................	358.1
29	Colorado..............................	342.6
30	Pennsylvania........................	316.4
31	Hawaii..................................	309.2
32	Wisconsin	305.9
33	Washington..........................	302.2
34	Ohio....................................	300.3
35	Nebraska..............................	291.0
36	Iowa....................................	290.6
37	Mississippi...........................	280.5
38	Oregon.................................	264.6
39	North Dakota........................	251.1
40	New Jersey	245.0
41	Wyoming..............................	244.2
42	Utah	242.8
43	Minnesota............................	242.6
44	Rhode Island........................	238.9
45	Kentucky..............................	232.3
46	Idaho...................................	230.3
47	Connecticut..........................	227.1
48	Virginia................................	217.6
49	New Hampshire.....................	197.6
50	Vermont...............................	158.3
51	Maine...................................	123.8

[1]Includes offenses reported by the Zoological Police and the Metro Transit Police.

Property Crime, 2016

Rank	State	Rate per 100,000 population
	United States......................	2,450.7
1	District of Columbia	4,802.9
2	New Mexico	3,937.1
3	Washington..........................	3,494.1
4	Alaska	3,353.0
5	Louisiana	3,297.7
6	Arkansas..............................	3,268.6
7	South Carolina	3,243.8
8	Georgia................................	3,004.5
9	Hawaii..................................	2,992.7
10	Oklahoma.............................	2,982.9
11	Arizona................................	2,978.4
12	Oregon.................................	2,964.4
13	Utah	2,951.5
14	Alabama...............................	2,947.8
15	Tennessee............................	2,854.1
16	Missouri...............................	2,799.1
17	Mississippi...........................	2,768.1
18	Delaware..............................	2,766.0
19	Texas...................................	2,759.8
20	Colorado..............................	2,740.7
21	North Carolina......................	2,737.5
22	Kansas.................................	2,695.5
23	Florida.................................	2,686.8
24	Montana...............................	2,683.5
25	Indiana................................	2,589.4
26	Nevada.................................	2,586.6
27	Ohio....................................	2,577.5
28	California.............................	2,553.0
29	North Dakota........................	2,295.9
30	Maryland..............................	2,284.5
31	Nebraska..............................	2,263.3
32	Kentucky..............................	2,189.7
33	Minnesota............................	2,133.3
34	Iowa....................................	2,086.0
35	Illinois.................................	2,049.0
36	West Virginia........................	2,047.2
37	South Dakota........................	1,980.6
38	Wyoming..............................	1,957.3
39	Wisconsin	1,933.3
40	Michigan	1,909.9
41	Rhode Island........................	1,898.7
42	Virginia................................	1,859.4
43	Connecticut..........................	1,808.0
44	Idaho...................................	1,744.2
45	Pennsylvania........................	1,742.7
46	Vermont...............................	1,697.4
47	Maine...................................	1,645.7
48	Massachusetts.....................	1,561.1
49	New York..............................	1,545.6
50	New Jersey	1,544.6
51	New Hampshire.....................	1,512.9

X = Not applicable.

State Government Employment, 2016 (Full-time equivalent employees)

Rank	State	State/Local employees per 1,000 residents
	United States......	13.4
1	Hawaii......	41.2
2	Alaska......	33.9
3	Delaware......	26.9
4	North Dakota......	25.6
5	Wyoming......	23.3
6	Vermont......	23.1
7	West Virginia......	22.8
8	New Mexico......	21.9
9	Arkansas......	20.8
10	Montana......	19.4
11	Kentucky......	19.2
12	Mississippi......	19.0
13	Utah......	18.6
14	Alabama......	18.5
15	Kansas......	17.9
16	Connecticut......	17.5
16	Oklahoma......	17.5
18	Rhode Island......	17.3
19	Washington......	17.1
20	Nebraska......	16.6
21	Oregon......	16.4
22	South Dakota......	16.2
22	Iowa......	16.2
24	South Carolina......	15.9
25	Louisiana......	15.8
26	Colorado......	15.7
27	Maine......	15.5
28	New Jersey......	15.4
29	Virginia......	15.0
30	Minnesota......	14.8
31	Michigan......	14.5
31	Massachusetts......	14.5
33	Missouri......	14.3
34	New Hampshire......	14.2
34	Maryland......	14.2
36	Idaho......	14.0
37	North Carolina......	13.6
38	Indiana......	13.4
39	Pennsylvania......	12.7
40	Wisconsin......	12.5
41	Georgia......	12.3
42	New York......	12.2
43	Ohio......	11.8
44	Tennessee......	11.7
45	Texas......	10.9
46	California......	10.5
47	Arizona......	10.3
48	Illinois......	9.7
49	Nevada......	9.4
50	Florida......	8.5
51	District of Columbia......	X

X = Not applicable.

Unemployment Rate, 2017

Rank	State	Unemployment rate
	United States......	4.4
1	Alaska......	7.2
2	New Mexico......	6.2
3	District of Columbia......	6.1
4	West Virginia......	5.2
5	Louisiana......	5.1
5	Mississippi......	5.1
7	Illinois......	5.0
7	Nevada......	5.0
7	Ohio......	5.0
10	Arizona......	4.9
10	Kentucky......	4.9
10	Pennsylvania......	4.9
13	California......	4.8
13	Washington......	4.8
15	Connecticut......	4.7
15	Georgia......	4.7
15	New York......	4.7
18	Delaware......	4.6
18	Michigan......	4.6
18	New Jersey......	4.6
18	North Carolina......	4.6
22	Rhode Island......	4.5
23	Alabama......	4.4
24	Oklahoma......	4.3
24	South Carolina......	4.3
24	Texas......	4.3
27	Florida......	4.2
27	Wyoming......	4.2
29	Maryland......	4.1
29	Oregon......	4.1
31	Montana......	4.0
32	Missouri......	3.8
32	Virginia......	3.8
34	Arkansas......	3.7
34	Massachusetts......	3.7
34	Tennessee......	3.7
37	Kansas......	3.6
38	Indiana......	3.5
38	Minnesota......	3.5
40	Maine......	3.3
40	South Dakota......	3.3
40	Wisconsin......	3.3
43	Idaho......	3.2
43	Utah......	3.2
45	Iowa......	3.1
46	Vermont......	3.0
47	Nebraska......	2.9
48	Colorado......	2.8
49	New Hampshire......	2.7
50	North Dakota......	2.6
51	Hawaii......	2.4

Employees on Nonfarm Payrolls, Percent Change, 2016–2017

Rank	State	Percent
	United States......	1.4
1	Idaho......	3.3
2	Nevada......	3.2
3	Utah......	2.9
4	Washington......	2.6
5	Arizona......	2.4
6	Colorado......	2.2
7	Florida......	2.1
7	Oregon......	2.1
9	California......	2.0
10	Georgia......	1.8
10	Texas......	1.8
10	South Carolina......	1.8
13	North Carolina......	1.7
14	Tennessee......	1.5
15	New Jersey......	1.3
15	Minnesota......	1.3
17	Massachusetts......	1.2
17	New York......	1.2
17	Michigan......	1.2
20	Missouri......	1.1
20	Pennsylvania......	1.1
22	Hawaii......	1.0
22	Indiana......	1.0
22	New Hampshire......	1.0
22	Alabama......	1.0
22	District of Columbia......	1.0
27	Arkansas......	0.9
27	Virginia......	0.9
27	Montana......	0.9
27	Maryland......	0.9
27	Rhode Island......	0.9
32	Ohio......	0.8
33	Maine......	0.7
33	Illinois......	0.7
35	Delaware......	0.6
35	Wisconsin......	0.6
35	Kentucky......	0.6
38	Oklahoma......	0.5
38	Mississippi......	0.5
38	South Dakota......	0.5
41	New Mexico......	0.3
41	Vermont......	0.3
43	Nebraska......	0.2
44	Connecticut......	0.1
44	Iowa......	0.1
46	Kansas......	-
47	Louisiana......	-0.1
48	West Virginia......	-0.3
49	North Dakota......	-0.9
50	Wyoming......	-1.0
51	Alaska......	-1.4

- = Zero or rounds to zero.

Per Capita Personal Income, 2017 (2017 Dollars)

Rank	State	Dollars
	United States....................	50,392
1	District of Columbia	76,986
2	Connecticut........................	70,121
3	Massachusetts...................	65,890
4	New Jersey	62,554
5	New York...........................	60,991
6	Maryland............................	59,524
7	California...........................	58,272
8	New Hampshire.................	57,574
9	Wyoming...........................	56,724
10	Washington........................	56,283
11	Alaska...............................	56,042
12	North Dakota.....................	54,643
13	Virginia..............................	54,244
14	Colorado............................	53,504
15	Minnesota..........................	53,043
16	Illinois...............................	52,808
17	Pennsylvania.....................	52,096
18	Hawaii...............................	51,939
19	Rhode Island.....................	51,503
20	Vermont.............................	51,114
21	Nebraska...........................	50,395
22	Delaware...........................	49,125
23	South Dakota.....................	48,281
24	Wisconsin..........................	47,850
25	Kansas..............................	47,603
26	Texas................................	46,942
27	Florida...............................	46,858
28	Oregon..............................	46,361
29	Iowa..................................	45,996
30	Ohio..................................	45,615
31	Michigan............................	45,255
32	Maine................................	45,072
33	Nevada..............................	44,626
34	Tennessee.........................	44,266
35	Indiana..............................	44,165
36	Montana............................	43,907
37	Missouri.............................	43,661
38	Louisiana	43,491
39	Oklahoma..........................	43,449
40	North Carolina...................	43,303
41	Georgia	43,270
42	Utah..................................	42,043
43	Arizona..............................	41,633
44	Arkansas...........................	40,791
45	Idaho.................................	40,507
46	South Carolina	40,421
47	Alabama............................	39,976
48	Kentucky...........................	39,393
49	New Mexico	39,023
50	West Virginia.....................	37,924
51	Mississippi.........................	36,346

Real Gross Domestic Product in Chained (2009) Dollars, 2017

Rank	State	Dollars (millions)
	United States.....................	16,721,499
1	California............................	2,386,388
2	Texas.................................	1,521,003
3	New York............................	1,294,571
4	Florida................................	836,056
5	Illinois................................	705,414
6	Pennsylvania......................	663,847
7	Ohio...................................	561,803
8	New Jersey	511,302
9	Georgia	478,966
10	North Carolina....................	459,287
11	Massachusetts....................	456,176
12	Virginia...............................	441,494
13	Michigan	440,341
14	Washington.........................	439,409
15	Maryland.............................	341,190
16	Indiana...............................	309,523
17	Minnesota...........................	305,627
18	Colorado	302,930
19	Tennessee	297,841
20	Wisconsin	282,043
21	Arizona...............................	277,725
22	Missouri..............................	263,103
23	Connecticut.........................	224,739
24	Oregon	212,573
25	Louisiana	207,854
26	South Carolina	189,102
27	Alabama.............................	182,843
28	Oklahoma............................	175,061
29	Kentucky............................	174,946
30	Iowa...................................	164,469
31	Utah...................................	141,111
32	Kansas...............................	138,185
33	Nevada...............................	134,347
34	District of Columbia	110,763
35	Arkansas............................	110,299
36	Nebraska............................	104,940
37	Mississippi..........................	96,824
38	New Mexico	86,904
39	Hawaii................................	75,473
40	New Hampshire...................	70,509
41	West Virginia.......................	67,827
42	Idaho..................................	62,567
43	Delaware............................	61,521
44	Maine..................................	52,797
45	Rhode Island.......................	51,195
46	North Dakota.......................	49,034
47	Alaska................................	47,059
48	Montana..............................	41,845
49	South Dakota.......................	41,748
50	Wyoming	35,391
51	Vermont..............................	27,959

Real Gross Domestic Product in Chained (2009) Dollars, Percent Change, 2016–2017

Rank	State	Percent
	United States......................	2.1
1	Washington........................	4.4
2	Colorado	3.6
3	Nevada	3.5
4	Arizona..............................	3.2
5	Utah..................................	3.1
6	California............................	3.0
7	Georgia	2.7
7	Idaho.................................	2.7
9	Massachusetts	2.6
9	Texas................................	2.6
9	West Virginia......................	2.6
12	Oregon..............................	2.5
12	Tennessee.........................	2.5
14	Michigan	2.3
14	North Carolina....................	2.3
14	South Carolina	2.3
17	Florida...............................	2.2
18	Indiana..............................	2.1
19	Virginia..............................	2.0
19	Wyoming	2.0
21	Minnesota..........................	1.9
21	New Hampshire..................	1.9
21	Ohio..................................	1.9
24	Kentucky	1.8
24	Pennsylvania	1.8
26	District of Columbia	1.7
26	Hawaii...............................	1.7
26	Wisconsin	1.7
29	Delaware	1.6
29	Rhode Island......................	1.6
31	Maryland............................	1.5
32	Maine................................	1.4
33	Alabama............................	1.2
33	Illinois...............................	1.2
35	Arkansas...........................	1.1
35	Missouri.............................	1.1
35	New York............................	1.1
35	Vermont.............................	1.1
39	North Dakota......................	1.0
40	New Jersey	0.9
41	New Mexico	0.8
42	Montana............................	0.6
42	Nebraska...........................	0.6
44	Iowa..................................	0.5
44	Oklahoma..........................	0.5
46	Alaska	0.3
46	Mississippi.........................	0.3
46	South Dakota	0.3
49	Kansas..............................	-0.1
50	Connecticut........................	-0.2
50	Louisiana	-0.2

Median Household Income, 2016

Rank	State	Dollars
	United States	57,617
1	Maryland	78,945
2	Alaska	76,440
3	New Jersey	76,126
4	District of Columbia	75,506
5	Massachusetts	75,297
6	Hawaii	74,511
7	Connecticut	73,433
8	New Hampshire	70,936
9	Virginia	68,114
10	California	67,739
11	Washington	67,106
12	Utah	65,977
13	Colorado	65,685
14	Minnesota	65,599
15	New York	62,909
16	Delaware	61,757
17	Illinois	60,960
18	North Dakota	60,656
19	Rhode Island	60,596
20	Wyoming	59,882
21	Vermont	57,677
22	Oregon	57,532
23	Nebraska	56,927
24	Pennsylvania	56,907
25	Wisconsin	56,811
26	Texas	56,565
27	Iowa	56,247
28	Nevada	55,180
29	Kansas	54,935
30	South Dakota	54,467
31	Georgia	53,559
32	Arizona	53,558
33	Maine	53,079
34	Michigan	52,492
35	Ohio	52,334
36	Indiana	52,314
37	Idaho	51,807
38	Missouri	51,746
39	Florida	50,860
40	North Carolina	50,584
41	Montana	50,027
42	South Carolina	49,501
43	Oklahoma	49,176
44	Tennessee	48,547
45	New Mexico	46,748
46	Kentucky	46,659
47	Alabama	46,257
48	Louisiana	45,146
49	Arkansas	44,334
50	West Virginia	43,385
51	Mississippi	41,754

Median Family Income, 2016

Rank	State	Dollars
	United States	71,062
1	District of Columbia	98,498
2	Maryland	95,336
3	Massachusetts	95,207
4	New Jersey	94,546
5	Connecticut	94,449
6	Alaska	88,604
7	Hawaii	86,768
8	New Hampshire	86,696
9	Minnesota	83,344
10	Virginia	83,306
11	Washington	81,234
12	Colorado	80,761
13	North Dakota	79,530
14	Rhode Island	77,940
15	New York	77,379
16	California	77,359
17	Illinois	76,950
18	Vermont	74,805
19	Delaware	74,251
20	Utah	74,181
21	Wyoming	73,574
22	Nebraska	73,488
23	Wisconsin	72,891
24	Iowa	72,351
25	Pennsylvania	72,313
26	Oregon	70,929
27	South Dakota	70,853
28	Kansas	70,792
29	Maine	68,277
30	Michigan	67,330
31	Texas	67,025
32	Ohio	66,722
33	Montana	66,288
34	Indiana	66,032
35	Nevada	65,384
36	Missouri	65,058
37	Georgia	65,018
38	Arizona	63,877
39	Idaho	63,182
40	North Carolina	62,289
41	Oklahoma	61,633
42	South Carolina	61,535
43	Florida	61,289
44	Tennessee	60,659
45	Alabama	59,764
46	Kentucky	59,023
47	Louisiana	57,490
48	New Mexico	56,802
49	West Virginia	56,703
50	Arkansas	55,484
51	Mississippi	52,672

Persons Below Poverty Level, 2016

Rank	State	Percent
	United States	14.0
1	Mississippi	20.8
2	Louisiana	20.2
3	New Mexico	19.8
4	District of Columbia	18.6
5	Kentucky	18.5
6	West Virginia	17.9
7	Arkansas	17.2
8	Alabama	17.1
9	Arizona	16.4
10	Oklahoma	16.3
11	Georgia	16.0
12	Tennessee	15.8
13	Texas	15.6
14	North Carolina	15.4
15	South Carolina	15.3
16	Michigan	15.0
17	Florida	14.7
17	New York	14.7
19	Ohio	14.6
20	Idaho	14.4
21	California	14.3
22	Indiana	14.1
23	Missouri	14.0
24	Nevada	13.8
25	Montana	13.3
25	Oregon	13.3
25	South Dakota	13.3
28	Illinois	13.0
29	Pennsylvania	12.9
30	Rhode Island	12.8
31	Maine	12.5
32	Kansas	12.1
33	Vermont	11.9
34	Iowa	11.8
34	Wisconsin	11.8
36	Delaware	11.7
37	Nebraska	11.4
38	Washington	11.3
38	Wyoming	11.3
40	Colorado	11.0
40	Virginia	11.0
42	North Dakota	10.7
43	Massachusetts	10.4
43	New Jersey	10.4
45	Utah	10.2
46	Alaska	9.9
46	Minnesota	9.9
48	Connecticut	9.8
49	Maryland	9.7
50	Hawaii	9.3
51	New Hampshire	7.3

Persons Under 18 Years Old Below Poverty Level, 2016

Rank	State	Percent
	United States......................	19.5
1	New Mexico	30.1
2	Mississippi...........................	29.7
3	Louisiana	28.6
4	District of Columbia	25.8
5	Kentucky..............................	25.0
6	Alabama...............................	24.5
7	West Virginia........................	24.0
8	Arkansas..............................	23.8
9	Arizona.................................	23.6
10	South Carolina	23.0
11	Georgia	22.9
11	Oklahoma.............................	22.9
13	Tennessee............................	22.6
14	Texas...................................	22.4
15	North Carolina	21.7
16	Florida..................................	21.0
17	Michigan...............................	20.7
17	New York..............................	20.7
19	Ohio.....................................	20.5
20	California..............................	19.9
21	Indiana.................................	19.5
22	Missouri...............................	19.2
23	Nevada.................................	19.1
24	Pennsylvania........................	18.5
25	Idaho....................................	17.7
25	Illinois..................................	17.7
27	Delaware..............................	17.4
28	Maine...................................	17.2
29	Oregon.................................	17.0
29	Rhode Island........................	17.0
31	South Dakota	16.9
32	Wisconsin.............................	15.7
33	Montana...............................	15.1
34	Iowa.....................................	14.8
34	Vermont...............................	14.8
36	New Jersey	14.6
37	Virginia.................................	14.3
38	Nebraska..............................	14.2
39	Alaska..................................	14.1
39	Kansas.................................	14.1
41	Washington...........................	13.7
42	Massachusetts.....................	13.6
43	Colorado	13.4
44	Connecticut..........................	12.9
45	Maryland...............................	12.7
45	Minnesota............................	12.7
47	North Dakota........................	12.4
48	Utah.....................................	11.1
48	Wyoming	11.1
50	Hawaii..................................	10.1
51	New Hampshire....................	7.9

Energy Consumption Per Capita, 2016

Rank	State	Million Btu
	United States......................	300.9
1	Louisiana	897.4
2	Wyoming	859.8
3	Alaska..................................	809.1
4	North Dakota........................	776.2
5	Iowa.....................................	488.6
6	Texas...................................	472.4
7	Nebraska..............................	455.2
8	South Dakota	444.8
9	Indiana.................................	422.4
10	West Virginia........................	419.0
11	Oklahoma.............................	417.2
12	Alabama...............................	397.8
13	Mississippi...........................	390.7
14	Kentucky..............................	383.8
15	Montana...............................	379.8
16	Kansas.................................	375.9
17	Arkansas..............................	353.6
18	South Carolina	333.3
19	Tennessee............................	332.6
20	Minnesota............................	327.0
21	New Mexico	320.2
22	Ohio.....................................	317.0
23	Idaho....................................	314.6
24	Wisconsin.............................	308.5
25	Illinois..................................	304.4
26	Pennsylvania........................	293.7
27	Missouri...............................	292.2
28	Maine...................................	291.6
29	Delaware..............................	287.0
30	Washington...........................	282.7
31	Virginia.................................	277.1
32	Michigan...............................	277.0
33	Georgia	275.3
34	Colorado	268.5
35	Utah.....................................	266.1
36	District of Columbia	254.5
37	North Carolina......................	251.4
38	New Jersey	247.2
39	Oregon.................................	239.2
40	Nevada.................................	231.1
41	Maryland...............................	225.6
42	New Hampshire.....................	225.4
43	Arizona.................................	212.9
44	Massachusetts.....................	208.5
45	Vermont...............................	206.4
46	Florida..................................	205.3
47	Connecticut..........................	201.8
48	California..............................	199.3
49	Hawaii..................................	198.0
50	New York..............................	184.6
51	Rhode Island........................	176.0

Homeownership Rate, 2017

Rank	State	Percent
	United States......................	63.9
1	West Virginia........................	75.1
2	Michigan	72.9
3	South Carolina	72.8
4	Minnesota............................	72.7
5	New Hampshire.....................	71.6
6	Vermont...............................	71.1
7	Maine...................................	71.0
7	Mississippi...........................	71.0
7	Utah.....................................	71.0
10	Wyoming	70.4
11	Kentucky..............................	70.1
12	Alabama...............................	70.0
12	Delaware	70.0
12	Indiana.................................	70.0
12	Iowa.....................................	70.0
16	Idaho....................................	69.9
16	Oklahoma.............................	68.9
18	Pennsylvania........................	68.6
19	Wisconsin.............................	68.0
20	South Dakota	67.8
21	Missouri...............................	67.6
21	Montana...............................	67.6
23	Virginia.................................	67.5
24	Tennessee............................	67.2
25	Maryland...............................	66.9
26	New Mexico	66.6
27	North Carolina	66.3
28	Connecticut..........................	66.1
28	Louisiana	66.1
28	Nebraska..............................	66.1
31	Kansas.................................	66.0
31	Ohio.....................................	66.0
33	Alaska..................................	65.5
34	Illinois..................................	65.4
35	Arkansas..............................	65.0
36	Arizona.................................	64.4
37	Florida..................................	64.1
37	New Jersey	64.1
39	Colorado	63.7
40	Washington...........................	63.6
41	Georgia	62.8
42	North Dakota........................	62.6
43	Oregon.................................	61.8
44	Texas...................................	61.7
45	Massachusetts.....................	60.0
46	Rhode Island........................	56.6
47	Hawaii..................................	55.9
48	Nevada.................................	55.0
49	California..............................	54.4
50	New York..............................	51.1
51	District of Columbia	40.3

One-Unit Detached or Attached Housing Units, Percent of Total Housing Units, 2016

Rank	State	Percent
	United States......................	68.6
1	Kansas	78.9
2	Iowa.................................	78.8
3	Indiana..............................	78.1
4	Nebraska...........................	78.0
5	Idaho................................	77.5
6	Michigan...........................	77.2
7	Delaware...........................	76.6
7	Pennsylvania......................	76.6
7	Utah	76.6
10	Oklahoma..........................	76.5
11	Missouri............................	75.0
12	Ohio.................................	74.8
13	Minnesota..........................	74.5
14	West Virginia......................	74.2
15	Maryland	73.9
16	Virginia.............................	73.6
17	Wyoming	73.4
18	Montana	73.2
19	Tennessee	72.9
20	Arkansas...........................	72.6
21	South Dakota	72.4
22	Alabama............................	72.3
23	Mississippi.........................	72.1
24	Colorado............................	71.1
24	Kentucky............................	71.1
26	Alaska...............................	70.9
26	Georgia.............................	70.9
28	Wisconsin	70.8
29	Arizona..............................	70.7
30	North Carolina.....................	70.2
31	Maine................................	70.0
32	Louisiana	69.8
33	New Mexico	69.5
34	Texas................................	69.1
35	Vermont.............................	68.9
36	South Carolina	68.8
37	New Hampshire....................	68.5
38	Oregon..............................	68.4
39	Washington.........................	67.6
40	Nevada..............................	67.2
41	North Dakota.......................	66.5
42	Illinois...............................	66.1
43	Hawaii...............................	65.9
44	Connecticut........................	65.1
45	California...........................	65.0
46	Florida...............................	64.6
47	New Jersey	63.4
48	Rhode Island.......................	57.6
49	Massachusetts	57.1
50	New York............................	46.9
51	District of Columbia	36.3

Percent of Population Not Covered by Private or Public Insurance, 2016

Rank	State	Percent
	United States......................	8.6
1	Texas................................	16.6
2	Alaska	14.0
3	Oklahoma..........................	13.8
4	Georgia.............................	12.9
5	Florida...............................	12.5
6	Mississippi.........................	11.8
7	Wyoming	11.5
8	Nevada..............................	11.4
9	North Carolina.....................	10.4
10	Louisiana	10.3
11	Idaho................................	10.1
12	Arizona..............................	10.0
12	South Carolina	10.0
14	New Mexico	9.2
15	Alabama............................	9.1
16	Tennessee	9.0
17	Missouri............................	8.9
18	Utah	8.8
19	Kansas	8.7
19	South Dakota	8.7
19	Virginia.............................	8.7
22	Nebraska...........................	8.6
23	Indiana..............................	8.1
23	Montana	8.1
25	Maine................................	8.0
25	New Jersey	8.0
27	Arkansas...........................	7.9
28	Colorado............................	7.5
29	California...........................	7.3
30	North Dakota.......................	7.0
31	Illinois...............................	6.5
32	Oregon..............................	6.2
33	Maryland	6.1
33	New York............................	6.1
35	Washington.........................	6.0
36	New Hampshire....................	5.9
37	Delaware...........................	5.7
38	Ohio.................................	5.6
38	Pennsylvania......................	5.6
40	Michigan...........................	5.4
41	West Virginia......................	5.3
41	Wisconsin	5.3
43	Kentucky............................	5.1
44	Connecticut........................	4.9
45	Iowa.................................	4.3
45	Rhode Island.......................	4.3
47	Minnesota..........................	4.1
48	District of Columbia	3.9
49	Vermont.............................	3.7
50	Hawaii...............................	3.5
51	Massachusetts	2.5

Traffic Fatalities Per 100 Million Vehicle Miles, 2016

Rank	State	Rate
	United States......................	1.16
1	South Carolina	1.88
2	Kentucky............................	1.69
3	Alaska	1.67
4	Mississippi.........................	1.63
5	Louisiana	1.53
5	New Mexico	1.53
7	Arkansas...........................	1.51
8	Alabama............................	1.49
9	Arizona..............................	1.44
9	Florida...............................	1.44
9	Montana	1.44
12	Idaho................................	1.43
12	Texas................................	1.43
14	Oklahoma..........................	1.40
15	West Virginia......................	1.37
16	Kansas	1.34
16	Tennessee	1.34
18	Oregon..............................	1.32
19	Georgia.............................	1.29
20	North Carolina.....................	1.26
21	Iowa.................................	1.25
21	Missouri............................	1.25
23	Nevada..............................	1.21
24	South Dakota	1.20
25	Delaware...........................	1.17
25	Wyoming	1.17
27	Pennsylvania......................	1.16
28	Colorado............................	1.15
29	North Dakota.......................	1.11
30	Maine................................	1.07
31	Nebraska...........................	1.05
32	Hawaii...............................	1.03
33	Michigan...........................	1.02
34	New Hampshire....................	1.01
35	California...........................	0.99
35	Illinois...............................	0.99
35	Indiana..............................	0.99
38	Ohio.................................	0.95
38	Wisconsin	0.95
40	Utah	0.94
41	Connecticut........................	0.92
42	Virginia.............................	0.90
43	Washington.........................	0.87
44	Maryland	0.86
45	Vermont.............................	0.85
46	New Jersey	0.78
47	District of Columbia	0.76
48	New York............................	0.75
49	Massachusetts	0.66
49	Minnesota..........................	0.66
49	Rhode Island.......................	0.66

ALABAMA

Facts and Figures

Location: Southeastern United States; bordered on the N by Tennessee, on the E by Georgia, on the S by Florida and the Gulf of Mexico, and on the W by Mississippi

Area: 52,420 sq. mi. (135,765 sq. km.); rank—30th

Population: 4,874,747 (2017 est.); rank—24th

Principal Cities: capital—Montgomery; largest—Birmingham

Statehood: December 14, 1819; 22nd state

U.S. Congress: 2 senators, 7 representatives

State Motto: *Audemus jura nostra defendere* ("We dare defend our rights")

State Song: "Alabama"

State Nicknames: The Yellowhammer State; The Heart of Dixie; The Cotton State

Abbreviations: AL; Ala.

State Symbols: flower—camellia; tree—Southern longleaf pine; bird—yellowhammer

At a Glance

- With an increase in population of 1.9 percent, Alabama ranked 38th among the states in growth from 2010 to 2017.

- Alabama's per capita personal income in 2017 was $39,976, ranking 47th in the nation.

- In 2016, Alabama had 18.5 full-time state government employees per 1,000 residents, a rate that ranked 14th in the nation.

- In 2016, 17.1 percent of Alabama residents lived below the poverty level, a percentage that ranked 8th in the nation.

- Alabama's violent crime rate in 2016 was 532.3 per 100,000 residents, compared to 386.3 for the entire nation.

- Alabama's median household income of $46,257 ranked 47th in the nation in 2016.

Table AL-1. Population by Age, Sex, Race, and Hispanic Origin

(Number, percent, except where noted.)

Sex, age, race, and Hispanic origin	2000	2010	2017 [1]	Average annual percent change, 2010–2017
Total Population..	4,447,100	4,779,736	4,874,747	2.0
Percent of total U.S. population	1.6	1.5	1.5	X
Sex				
Male..	2,146,504	2,320,188	2,359,836	1.7
Female	2,300,596	2,459,548	2,514,911	2.3
Age				
Under 5 years..	295,992	304,957	293,554	-3.7
5 to 19 years..	960,177	971,355	928,551	-4.4
20 to 64 years..	2,611,133	2,845,632	2,848,871	0.1
65 years and over	579,798	657,792	803,771	22.2
Median age (years)	35.8	37.9	39.0	2.9
Race and Hispanic Origin				
One race				
White..	3,162,808	3,362,877	3,374,131	0.3
Black..	1,155,930	1,259,224	1,308,214	3.9
American Indian and Alaska Native	22,430	32,903	34,108	3.7
Asian..	31,346	55,240	71,338	29.1
Native Hawaiian or Other Pacific Islander	1,409	5,208	5,239	0.6
Two or more races..	44,179	64,284	81,717	27.1
Hispanic (of any race)..	75,830	192,498	211,058	9.6

X = Not applicable.
[1] Population figures for 2017 are July 1 estimates. The 2010 estimates are taken from the 2010 Census.
- = Zero or rounds to zero.

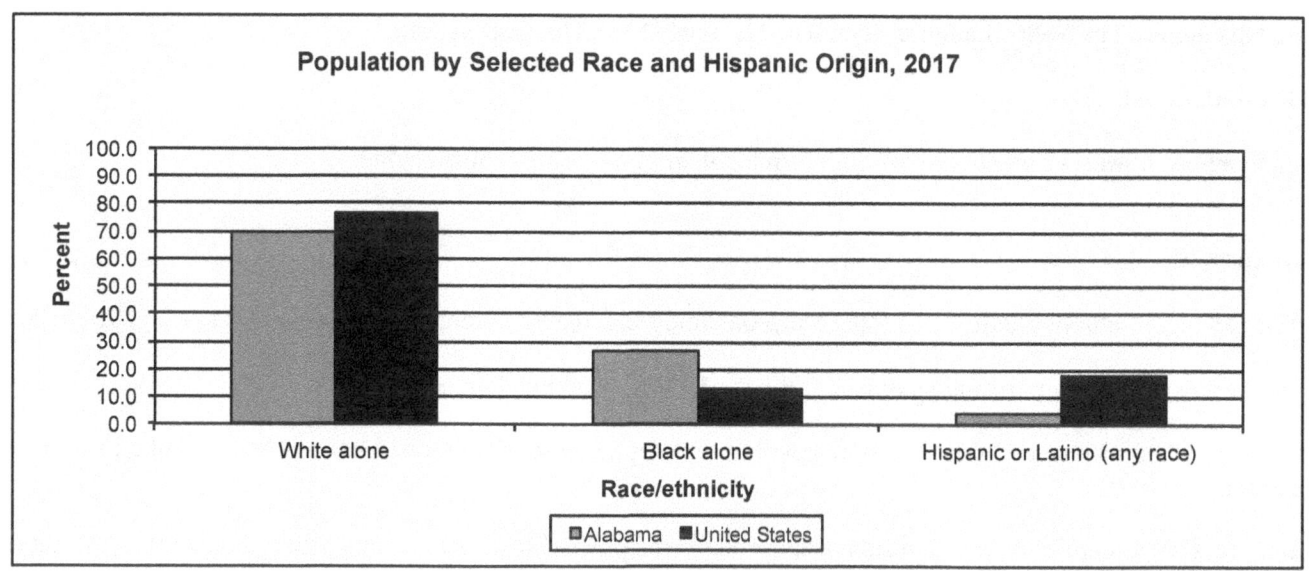

Table AL-2. Marital Status

(Number, percent distribution.)

Sex, age, and marital status	2000	2010	2016
Males, 15 Years and Over	1,666,798	1,844,661	1,894,579
Never married	26.7	32.5	34.1
Now married, except separated..	59.0	50.6	49.0
Separated..	1.8	2.5	1.9
Widowed..	2.8	3.0	3.2
Divorced..	9.8	11.4	11.8
Females, 15 Years and Over	1,847,401	2,004,450	2,067,543
Never married	21.4	26.1	28.2
Now married, except separated..	52.5	45.9	44.9
Separated..	2.5	3.1	2.7
Widowed..	12.4	11.2	10.9
Divorced..	11.2	13.6	13.3

Table AL-3. Households and Housing Characteristics

(Number, percent, dollars.)

Item	2000	2010	2016	Average annual percent change, 2010–2016
Total Households...	1,737,080	1,815,152	1,852,518	0.3
Family households.....................................	1,215,968	1,227,884	1,208,362	-0.3
Married-couple family.............................	906,916	868,946	864,330	-0.1
Other family..	309,052	358,938	344,032	-0.7
Male householder, no wife present............	62,586	79,308	81,060	0.4
Female householder, no husband present.....	246,466	279,630	262,972	-1.0
Nonfamily households..................................	521,112	587,268	644,156	1.6
Householder living alone..........................	453,898	511,708	568,566	1.9
Householder not living alone.....................	67,214	75,560	75,590	-
Housing Characteristics				
Total housing units.....................................	1,963,711	2,174,428	2,230,180	0.4
Occupied housing units	1,737,080	1,815,152	1,852,518	0.3
Owner occupied	1,258,705	1,272,846	1,268,138	-0.1
Renter occupied	478,375	542,306	584,380	1.3
Average household size................................	2.49	2.57	2.56	-0.1
Financial Characteristics				
Median gross rent of renter-occupied housing	447	667	743	1.9
Median monthly owner costs for housing units with a mortgage	816	1,130	1,126	-0.1
Median value of owner-occupied housing units.........	85,100	123,900	136,200	1.7

- = Zero or rounds to zero

Table AL-4. Migration, Origin, and Language

(Number, percent.)

Characteristic	State 2015	State 2016	State Percent change	U.S. 2015	U.S. 2016	U.S. Percent change
Residence 1 Year Ago						
Population 1 year and over	4,801,599	4,810,126	0.2	317,635,720	319,361,956	0.5
Same house	85.7	86.1	X	85.3	85.4	X
Different house in the U.S.	14.1	13.6	X	14.1	13.9	X
Same county	8.5	8.0	X	8.5	8.3	X
Different county	5.5	5.6	X	5.6	5.6	X
Same state	3.1	3.0	X	3.2	3.2	X
Different state	2.4	2.5	X	2.4	2.4	X
Abroad	0.2	0.3	X	0.7	0.7	X
Place of Birth						
Native born	4,689,007	4,699,671	0.2	278,128,449	279,388,170	0.5
Male	48.3	48.4	X	49.3	49.3	X
Female	51.7	51.6	X	50.7	50.7	X
Foreign born	169,972	163,629	-3.7	43,290,372	43,739,345	1.0
Male	52.1	49.2	X	48.6	48.5	X
Female	47.9	50.8	X	51.4	51.5	X
Foreign born; naturalized U.S. citizen..............	61,631	59,611	-3.3	20,697,103	21,238,372	2.6
Male	47.1	45.9	X	45.9	45.9	X
Female	52.9	54.1	X	54.1	54.1	X
Foreign born; not a U.S. citizen....................	108,341	104,018	-4.0	22,593,269	22,500,973	-0.4
Male	54.9	51.1	X	51.1	51	X
Female	45.1	48.9	X	48.9	49	X
Entered 2010 or later	20.7	23.5	X	15.6	18.6	X
Entered 2000 to 2009	34.6	36.9	X	27.9	26.7	X
Entered before 2000.................................	44.7	39.5	X	56.5	54.7	X
World Region of Birth, Foreign						
Foreign-born population, excluding population born at sea	169,972	163,629	-3.7	43,289,646	43,738,901	1.0
Europe	12.2	10.2	X	11.1	10.9	X
Asia	28.1	33.1	X	30.6	30.8	X
Africa	5.7	4.8	X	4.8	4.9	X
Oceania	0.6	0.4	X	0.6	0.6	X
Latin America	51.8	49.3	X	51.1	51	X
North America	1.6	2.3	X	1.9	1.8	X
Language Spoken at Home and Ability to Speak English						
Population 5 years and over..........................	4,573,857	4,576,657	0.1	301,625,014	303,328,961	0.6
English only	94.9	94.9	X	78.5	78.4	X
Language other than English.........................	5.1	5.1	X	21.5	21.6	X
Speaks English less than "very well"..............	2.2	2.1	X	8.6	8.6	X

NA = Not available.
X = Not applicable.
- = Zero or rounds to zero.

Table AL-5. Median Income and Poverty Status, 2016

(Number, percent, except as noted.)

Characteristic	State		U.S.	
	Number	Percent	Number	Percent
Median Income				
Households (dollars)..	46,257	X	57,617	X
Families (dollars)	59,764	X	71,062	X
Below Poverty Level (All People)	810,231	17.1	44,268,996	14
Sex				
Male	352,460	15.4	19,760,056	12.8
Female	457,771	18.6	24,508,940	15.2
Age				
Under 18 years...	265,901	24.5	14,115,713	19.5
Related children under 18 years...	262,862	24.3	13,805,435	19.1
18 to 64 years...	468,007	16.2	25,723,818	13.2
65 years and over	76,323	10.0	4,429,465	9.2

X = Not applicable.

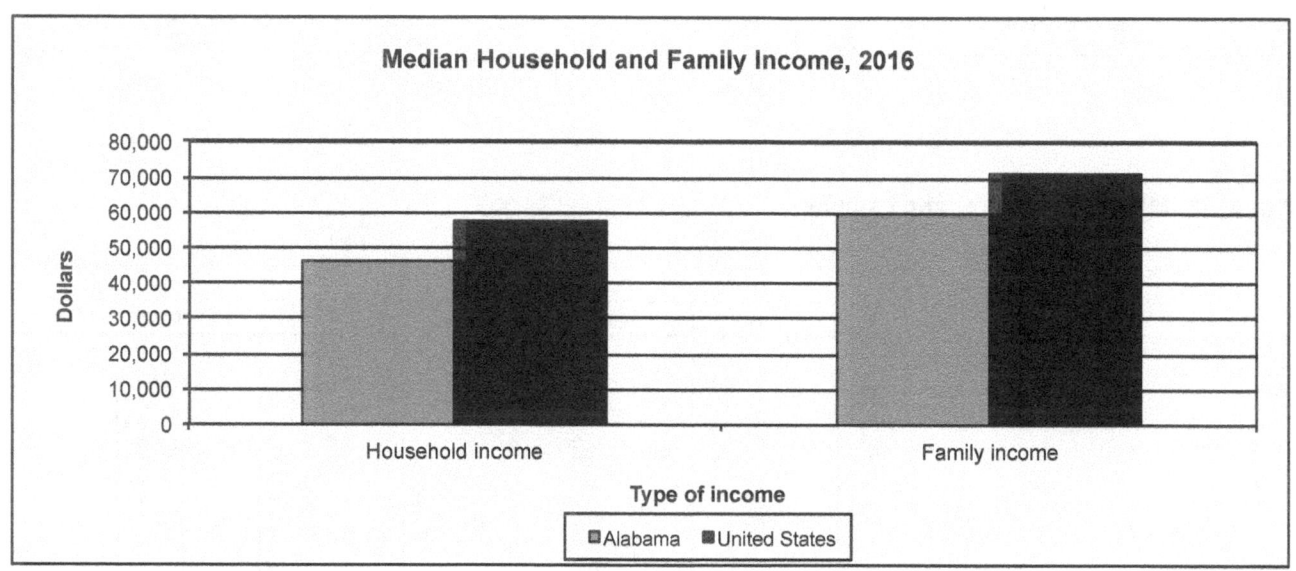

Table AL-6. Health Insurance Coverage Status for the Civilian Noninstitutionalized Population and Children Under 18 Years of Age

(Number; percent.)

Item	2008	2009	2010	2011	2012	2013	2014	2015	2016
Civilian Noninstitutionalized Population	4,574,185	4,616,028	4,702,769	4,720,067	4,741,698	4,755,381	4,767,383	4,781,070	4,782,529
Covered by Private or Public Insurance									
Number..	3,932,658	3,979,391	4,016,177	4,046,103	4,109,199	4,109,946	4,188,214	4,296,799	4,347,556
Percent...	86.0	86.2	85.4	85.7	86.7	86.4	87.9	89.9	90.9
Not Covered									
Number..	641,527	636,637	686,592	673,964	632,499	645,435	579,169	484,271	434,973
Percent...	14.0	13.8	14.6	14.3	13.3	13.6	12.1	10.1	9.1
Percent in the U.S. not covered................................	15.1	15.1	15.5	15.1	14.8	14.5	11.7	9.4	8.6
Children Under 18 Years of Age	1,119,732	1,124,227	1,133,638	1,122,125	1,123,000	1,107,844	1,106,847	1,106,716	1,098,052
Covered by Private or Public Insurance									
Number..	1,029,790	1,057,497	1,066,680	1,063,064	1,077,390	1,059,663	1,064,425	1,072,948	1,071,320
Percent...	92.0	94.1	94.1	94.7	95.9	95.7	96.2	96.9	97.6
Not Covered									
Number..	89,942	66,730	66,958	59,061	45,610	48,181	42,422	33,768	26,732
Percent...	8.0	5.9	5.9	5.3	4.1	4.3	3.8	3.1	2.4
Percent in the U.S. not covered................................	9.9	8.6	8.0	7.5	7.2	7.1	6.0	4.8	4.5

Table AL-7. Employment Status by Demographic Group, 2017

(Numbers in thousands, percent.)

Characteristic	Civilian noninstitutional population	Civilian labor force		Employed		Unemployed	
		Number	Percent of population	Number	Percent of population	Number	Percent of population
Total...	3,834	2,162	56.4	2,068	53.9	94	4.3
Sex							
Male...	1,811	1,146	63.3	1,096	60.5	50	4.4
Female..	2,023	1,016	50.2	973	48.1	44	4.3
Race, Sex, and Hispanic Origin							
White..	2,708	1,526	56.4	1,477	54.6	49	3.2
Male...	1,301	845	64.9	818	62.9	27	3.1
Female..	1,407	681	48.4	659	46.9	22	3.2
Black or African American..................	991	552	55.7	511	51.5	42	7.5
Male...	439	258	58.7	236	53.6	22	8.6
Female..	552	295	53.4	275	49.9	19	6.5
Hispanic or Latino ethnicity[1]..............	116	83	71.9	81	70.0	2	2.7
Male...	61	55	89.9	53	87.3	2	2.9
Female..	NA	NA	NA	NA	NA	NA	NA
Age							
16 to 19 years..................................	260	74	28.5	63	24.1	11	15.3
20 to 24 years..................................	320	219	68.4	206	64.3	13	6.0
25 to 34 years..................................	615	489	79.5	463	75.3	26	5.3
35 to 44 years..................................	573	427	74.6	412	71.8	16	3.7
45 to 54 years..................................	638	474	74.3	459	72.0	14	3.0
55 to 64 years..................................	667	358	53.6	347	52.0	11	3.0
65 years and over.............................	761	121	15.9	119	15.7	2	1.8

NOTE: Data in Table 7 are from the Current Population Survey (CPS) and do not match the estimates in Table 8. See notes and definitions for further information.
[1] May be of any race.
NA = Not available.

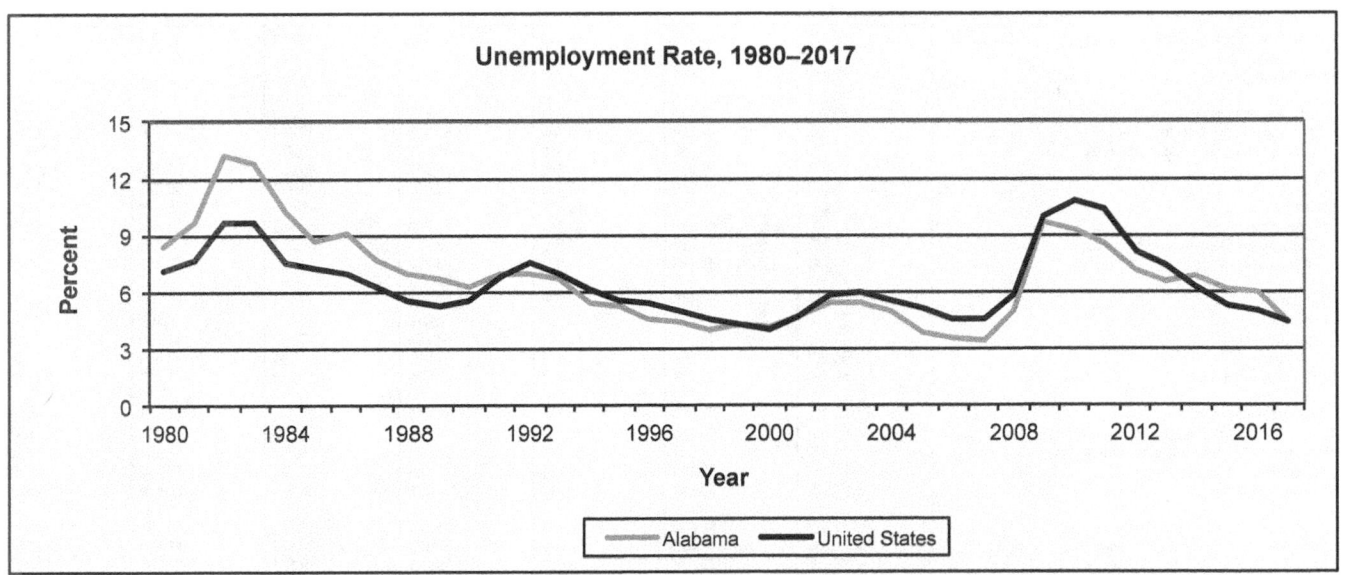

Table AL-8. Employment Status of the Civilian Noninstitutional Population Age 16 Years and Over

(Number, percent.)

Year	Civilian labor force	Civilian participation rate	Employed	Unemployed	Unemployment rate
2009..........................	2,162,999	59.7	1,924,747	238,252	11.0
2010..........................	2,196,042	59.5	1,964,559	231,483	10.5
2011..........................	2,202,670	59.1	1,990,413	212,257	9.6
2012..........................	2,176,337	58.1	2,003,290	173,047	8.0
2013..........................	2,174,000	57.8	2,017,043	156,957	7.2
2014..........................	2,161,618	57.2	2,015,087	146,531	6.8
2015..........................	2,157,376	56.8	2,025,949	131,427	6.1
2016..........................	2,173,175	57.0	2,045,624	127,551	5.9
2017..........................	2,168,444	56.6	2,073,106	95,338	4.4

Table AL-9. Employment and Average Wages by Industry

(Estimates through 2010 are based on the 2007 *North American Industry Classification System* [NAICS]. Estimates from 2011 onward are based on the 2012 NAICS.)

Industry	2010	2011	2012	2013	2014	2015	2016
	Number of Jobs						
Wage and Salary Employment by Industry........................	1,951,485	1,951,695	1,965,084	1,980,147	1,997,256	2,024,641	2,049,083
Farm Wage and Salary Employment...............................	7,826	8,188	7,348	7,724	5,317	7,452	7,213
Nonfarm Wage and Salary Employment...........................	1,943,659	1,943,507	1,957,736	1,972,423	1,991,939	2,017,189	2,041,870
Private wage and salary employment...............................	1,530,423	1,535,438	1,554,240	1,571,512	1,591,548	1,618,368	1,641,657
Forestry, fishing, and related activities............................	8,751	8,512	8,581	8,806	8,893	8,874	8,929
Mining..	7,765	8,287	8,593	7,990	7,548	6,836	5,351
Utilities..	14,089	14,262	14,246	14,382	14,293	14,438	14,173
Construction...	90,243	83,447	82,010	81,853	82,096	83,729	86,500
Manufacturing...	236,759	237,850	243,929	249,470	253,170	258,185	260,890
Durable goods manufacturing.................................	146,518	148,059	154,435	159,675	165,098	169,251	170,158
Nondurable goods manufacturing............................	90,241	89,791	89,494	89,795	88,072	88,934	90,732
Wholesale trade	72,084	72,331	72,915	73,383	73,221	73,925	74,056
Retail trade...	225,250	226,833	225,986	226,212	229,291	232,630	234,602
Transportation and warehousing.................................	52,615	53,889	55,519	57,164	58,978	59,631	60,035
Information	23,973	23,134	22,696	22,590	21,952	21,505	20,701
Finance and insurance	70,108	71,785	72,133	73,213	74,330	74,690	75,158
Real estate and rental and leasing...............................	22,294	21,624	21,751	22,268	22,195	22,364	22,884
Professional, scientific, and technical services.................	95,256	94,483	95,043	95,300	95,337	96,750	99,122
Management of companies and enterprises......................	15,503	15,986	16,882	15,935	15,132	15,425	16,461
Administrative and waste services...............................	99,964	104,326	107,967	109,121	113,746	117,814	119,900
Educational services	28,218	28,615	28,789	29,455	29,519	29,561	30,040
Health care and social assistance................................	197,726	198,675	201,010	204,147	205,388	209,653	214,546
Arts, entertainment, and recreation.............................	16,625	16,050	15,774	16,004	16,274	16,906	19,115
Accommodation and food services...............................	152,075	154,265	158,987	163,867	168,533	174,048	179,604
Other services, except public administration......................	101,125	101,084	101,429	100,352	101,652	101,404	99,590
Government and government enterprises........................	413,236	408,069	403,496	400,911	400,391	398,821	400,213
	Dollars						
Average Wages and Salaries by Industry	39,635	40,485	41,317	41,592	42,644	43,622	45,287
Average Farm Wages and Salaries	22,863	18,821	27,739	19,497	23,998	26,452	21,518
Average Nonfarm Wages and Salaries	39,703	40,577	41,368	41,678	42,694	43,686	45,371
Average private wages and salaries...............................	38,838	39,699	40,704	41,060	42,064	43,116	44,742
Forestry, fishing, and related activities............................	32,048	32,595	33,458	33,957	35,373	36,448	38,771
Mining..	74,445	77,634	76,348	78,022	80,858	80,462	84,213
Utilities..	78,776	85,829	88,196	88,367	88,433	95,521	98,193
Construction	43,392	43,501	45,271	45,536	47,815	48,737	51,776
Manufacturing...	48,307	49,091	50,345	50,898	52,863	53,485	55,010
Durable goods manufacturing.................................	51,067	51,712	52,908	53,255	55,079	55,710	57,131
Nondurable goods manufacturing............................	43,827	44,768	45,921	46,707	48,709	49,251	51,031
Wholesale trade	54,926	56,118	56,936	57,881	59,941	62,108	63,782
Retail trade...	24,509	24,732	25,299	25,618	25,876	26,493	27,198
Transportation and warehousing.................................	41,823	42,913	44,147	44,152	45,960	46,790	49,005
Information	48,351	50,865	51,279	51,608	53,961	55,865	57,048
Finance and insurance	58,221	62,067	64,327	65,035	67,920	71,712	72,698
Real estate and rental and leasing...............................	35,290	36,639	38,782	38,487	40,046	41,564	43,455
Professional, scientific, and technical services.................	66,031	68,145	69,703	70,637	71,513	73,288	78,143
Management of companies and enterprises......................	74,562	78,601	80,751	83,524	85,363	87,561	96,021
Administrative and waste services...............................	26,198	26,109	26,721	26,705	27,120	27,388	28,605
Educational services	24,088	24,538	25,214	25,225	26,045	26,516	26,349
Health care and social assistance................................	41,578	42,263	43,284	43,381	44,159	45,494	46,983
Arts, entertainment, and recreation.............................	18,832	18,850	19,878	20,329	20,478	21,418	20,922
Accommodation and food services...............................	15,206	15,578	16,051	16,281	16,587	17,201	18,323
Other services, except public administration......................	27,863	28,435	28,975	29,785	30,815	32,136	34,428
Government and government enterprises.............................	42,907	43,879	43,927	44,101	45,200	45,995	47,951

Table AL-10. Employment Characteristics by Family Type

(Number, percent.)

Family type and labor force status	2014		2015		2016	
	Total	Families with own children under 18 years	Total	Families with own children under 18 years	Total	Families with own children under 18 years
All Families...	1,229,579	485,990	1,213,540	486,977	1,208,362	473,593
FAMILY TYPE AND LABOR FORCE STATUS						
Married-Couple Families.............................	867,090	305,881	863,674	306,591	864,330	304,039
Both husband and wife in labor force..............	46.3	63.6	45.6	64.0	46.2	64.6
Husband in labor force, wife not in labor force..........	23.7	29.0	23.7	28.5	23.1	28.3
Wife in labor force, husband not in labor force..........	8.5	4.8	8.0	4.2	8.4	4.3
Both husband and wife not in labor force....................	21.5	2.5	22.2	3.0	21.7	2.7
Other Families	362,489	180,109	349,866	180,386	344,032	169,554
Female householder, no husband present........................	78.6	82.7	77.6	80.8	76.4	79.2
In labor force..	48.8	64.5	49.1	63.7	47.8	64.1
Not in labor force	29.8	18.2	28.5	17.1	28.6	15.1
Male householder, no wife present...................	21.4	17.3	22.4	19.2	23.6	20.8
In labor force..	14.4	14.7	15.5	16.3	15.6	17.9
Not in labor force	7.0	2.6	6.8	2.9	7.9	2.9

Table AL-11. School Enrollment and Educational Attainment, 2016

(Number, percent.)

Item	State	U.S.
Enrollment		
Total population 3 years and over, enrolled in school	1,186,076	81,572,277
Enrolled in nursery school or preschool (percent)	5.4	6.0
Enrolled in kindergarten (percent)...	5.4	5.0
Enrolled in elementary school, grades 1-8 (percent).....................................	41.4	40.3
Enrolled in high school, grades 9-12 (percent)..	21.7	21.0
Enrolled in college or graduate school (percent)..	26.1	27.7
Attainment		
Total population 25 years and over	3,300,713	218,475,480
Less than ninth grade (percent)	4.8	5.4
9th to 12th grade, no diploma (percent)	10.1	7.2
High school graduate, including equivalency (percent)...................................	30.6	27.2
Some college, no degree (percent)	21.5	20.6
Associate's degree (percent)	8.2	8.4
Bachelor's degree (percent)	15.4	19.3
Graduate or professional degree (percent)...	9.4	11.9
High school graduate or higher (percent)	85.1	87.5
Bachelor's degree or higher (percent)...	24.7	31.3

Table AL-12. Public School Characteristics and Educational Indicators

(Number, percent; data derived from National Center of Education Statistics.)

Item	State	U.S.
Public Schools, 2015–2016 (except where noted)		
Number of school districts..	180	18,328
Number of schools..	1,509	98,456
Number of students...	743,789	50,327,015
Number of teachers	40,766	3,151,497
Student-teacher ratio	18.2	16.0
Expenditures per student (dollars), 2014-2015..	9,146	11,445
Four-year adjusted cohort graduation rate (ACGR)[1,2]	87.1	84.1
Students eligible for free or reduced-price lunch (percent), 2014-2015...............	51.8	51.8
English language learners (percent), Fall 2015	2.7	9.5
Students age 3 to 21 served under IDEA, part B (percent)...............................	11.3	13.2

Public Schools by Type	Number	Percent of state public schools
Total number of schools..	1,509	100.0
Regular	1,326	87.9
Special education	34	2.3
Vocational education...	68	4.5
Alternative education..	81	5.4

NOTE: Every school is assigned only one school type based on its instructional emphasis.
[1] ACGR data represents a new method of calculating high-school completion rates and may not be comparable to previous years' data for Averaged Freshmen Graduation Rates (AFGR).
[2] The United States 4-year ACGRs were estimated using both the reported 4-year ACGR data from 49 states and the District of Columbia and using imputed data for Idaho. The estimate for American Indian/Alaska Native students also includes imputed data for Virginia.

Table AL-13. Reported Voting and Registration of the Voting-Age Population, November 2016

(Numbers in thousands, percent.)

Item	Total population	Total citizen population	Registered			Voted		
			Total registered	Percent registered (total population)	Percent registered (total citizen population)	Total voted	Percent voted (total population)	Percent voted (total citizen population)
U.S. Total	245,502	224,059	157,596	64.2	70.3	137,537	56.0	61.4
State Total..............................	3,717	3,651	2,526	68.0	69.2	2,095	56.4	57.4
Sex								
Male	1,761	1,718	1,155	65.6	67.2	944	53.6	54.9
Female	1,955	1,933	1,371	70.1	70.9	1,151	58.9	59.6
Race								
White alone..............................	2,633	2,604	1,772	67.3	68.0	1,465	55.6	56.2
White, non-Hispanic alone	2,532	2,526	1,742	68.8	69.0	1,441	56.9	57.0
Black alone..............................	962	953	694	72.2	72.8	579	60.2	60.8
Asian alone	27	10	3	(B)	(B)	3	(B)	(B)
Hispanic (of any race).....................	117	83	32	(B)	(B)	27	(B)	(B)
White alone or in combination	2,673	2,644	1,801	67.4	68.1	1,489	55.7	56.3
Black alone or in combination...........	985	976	704	71.5	72.1	587	59.6	60.2
Asian alone or in combination...........	36	19	6	(B)	(B)	6	(B)	(B)
Age								
18 to 24 years.............................	513	497	283	55.2	57.0	212	41.4	42.7
25 to 34 years.............................	583	568	393	67.5	69.2	310	53.1	54.5
35 to 44 years.............................	566	548	363	64.1	66.3	306	54.0	55.8
45 to 64 years.............................	1,293	1,280	881	68.1	68.8	761	58.8	59.4
65 years and over	761	758	606	79.5	79.9	507	66.5	66.9

- = Zero or rounds to zero.
B = Base is less than 75,000 and therefore too small to show the derived measure.

Table AL-14. Crime

(Number, rate per 100,000. Data are derived from the FBI Uniform Crime Reports.)

Item	State [1]			U.S. [1,2,3,4]		
	2015	2016	Percent change	2015	2016	Percent change
TOTAL POPULATION [5]	4,858,979	4,863,300	0.1	321,418,820	323,127,513	0.5
VIOLENT CRIME						
Number..............................	22,952	25,886	12.8	1,231,566	1,248,185	1.3
Rate..............................	472.4	532.3	12.7	383.2	386.3	0.8
Murder and Nonnegligent Manslaughter						
Number..............................	348	407	17.0	15,696	17,250	9.9
Rate..............................	7.2	8.4	16.7	4.9	5.3	8.2
Rape[6]						
Number..............................	2,039	1,916	-6.0	124,047	130,603	5.3
Rate..............................	42.0	39.4	-6.2	38.6	40.4	4.7
Robbery						
Number..............................	4,611	4,686	1.6	327,374	332,198	1.5
Rate..............................	94.9	96.4	1.6	101.9	102.8	0.9
Aggravated Assault						
Number..............................	15,954	18,877	18.3	764,449	803,007	5.0
Rate..............................	328.3	388.2	18.2	237.8	248.5	4.5
PROPERTY CRIME						
Number..............................	144,746	143,362	-1.0	7,993,631	7,919,035	-0.9
Rate..............................	2,978.9	2,947.8	-1.0	2,487.0	2,450.7	-1.5
Burglary						
Number..............................	35,255	34,065	-3.4	1,579,527	1,515,096	-4.1
Rate..............................	725.6	700.5	-3.5	491.4	468.9	-4.6
Larceny-Theft						
Number..............................	99,156	97,574	-1.6	5,706,346	5,638,455	-1.2
Rate..............................	2,040.7	2,006.3	-1.7	1,775.4	1,745.0	-1.7
Motor Vehicle Theft						
Number..............................	10,335	11,723	13.4	707,758	765,484	8.2
Rate..............................	212.7	241.1	13.4	220.2	236.9	7.6

NOTE: Although arson data are included in the trend and clearance tables, sufficient data are not available to estimate totals for this offense. Therefore, no arson data are published in this table.
X = Not applicable.
- = Zero or rounds to zero.
[1] Because of changes in the state's reporting practices, figures are not comparable to previous years' data.
[2] The crime figures have been adjusted.
[3] The data collection methodology for the offense of forcible rape used by the Minnesota state Uniform Crime Reporting (UCR) Program (with the exception of Minneapolis and St. Paul, Minnesota) does not comply with national UCR Program guidelines. Consequently, its figures for forcible rape and violent crime (of which forcible rape is a part) are not published in this table.
[4] Includes offenses reported by the Zoological Police and the Metro Transit Police.
[5] Populations are U.S. Census Bureau provisional estimates as of July 1 of each year.
[6] The figures shown for the 2013 offense of rape were estimated using the revised Uniform Crime Reporting (UCR) definition of rape. Figures are not comparable to data from previous years.

Table AL-15. State Government Finances, 2016

(Dollar amounts in thousands, percent distribution.)

Item	Dollars	Percent distribution
Total Revenue	30,502,706	100.0
General revenue	25,619,102	84.0
Intergovernmental revenue	9,746,605	32.0
Taxes	9,919,794	32.5
General sales	2,596,223	8.5
Selective sales	2,509,879	8.2
License taxes	507,479	1.7
Individual income tax	3,492,904	11.5
Corporate income tax	376,680	1.2
Other taxes	436,629	1.4
Current charges	4,849,827	15.9
Miscellaneous general revenue	1,102,876	3.6
Utility revenue	0	-
Liquor stores revenue	325,393	1.1
Insurance trust revenue [1]	4,558,211	14.9
Total Expenditure	30,434,595	100.0
Intergovernmental expenditure	6,741,304	22.2
Direct expenditure	23,693,291	77.8
Current operation	17,181,943	56.5
Capital outlay	1,857,949	6.1
Insurance benefits and repayments	3,541,484	11.6
Assistance and subsidies	773,560	2.5
Interest on debt	338,355	1.1
Exhibit: Salaries and wages	4,760,946	15.6
Total Expenditure	30,434,595	100.0
General expenditure	26,568,093	87.3
Intergovernmental expenditure	6,741,304	22.2
Direct expenditure	19,826,789	65.1
General expenditure, by function:		
Education	11,376,230	37.4
Public welfare	7,272,507	23.9
Hospitals	2,636,578	8.7
Health	517,728	1.7
Highways	1,653,128	5.4
Police protection	170,514	0.6
Correction	542,699	1.8
Natural resources	274,859	0.9
Parks and recreation	18,359	0.1
Governmental administration	592,730	1.9
Interest on general debt	338,355	1.1
Other and unallocable	1,174,406	3.9
Utility expenditure	75	-
Liquor stores expenditure	324,943	1.1
Insurance trust expenditure	3,541,484	11.6
Debt at End of Fiscal Year	8,667,105	X
Cash and Security Holdings	42,962,452	X

X = Not applicable.
- = Zero or rounds to zero.
[1] Within insurance trust revenue, net earnings of state retirement systems is a calculated statistic (the item code in the data file is X08), and thus can be positive or negative. Net earnings is the sum of earnings on investments plus gains on investments minus losses on investments. The change made in 2002 for asset valuation from book to market value in accordance with Statement 34 of the Governmental Accounting Standards Board is reflected in the calculated statistics.

Table AL-16. State Government Tax Collections, 2017

(Dollars in thousands, percent.)

Item	Dollars	Percent distribution
Total Taxes	10,418,152	100.0
Property taxes	395,930	3.8
Sales and gross receipts	5,247,294	50.4
General sales and gross receipts	2,654,883	25.5
Selective sales and gross receipts	2,592,411	24.9
Alcoholic beverages	217,790	2.1
Amusements	0	-
Insurance premiums	339,719	3.3
Motor fuels	588,992	5.7
Pari-mutuels	1,226	-
Public utilities	688,756	6.6
Tobacco products	188,783	1.8
Other selective sales	567,145	5.4
Licenses	529,607	5.1
Alcoholic beverages	4,086	-
Amusements	X	-
Corporations in general	173,265	1.7
Hunting and fishing	24,024	0.2
Motor vehicle	219,393	2.1
Motor vehicle operators	33,730	0.3
Public utilities	14,346	0.1
Occupation and business, NEC	60,763	0.6
Other licenses	0	-
Income taxes	4,144,656	39.8
Individual income	3,624,543	34.8
Corporation net income	520,113	5.0
Other taxes	100,665	1.0
Death and gift	X	-
Documentary and stock transfer	46,150	0.4
Severance	54,515	0.5
Taxes, NEC	0	-

- = Zero or rounds to zero.
X = Not applicable.

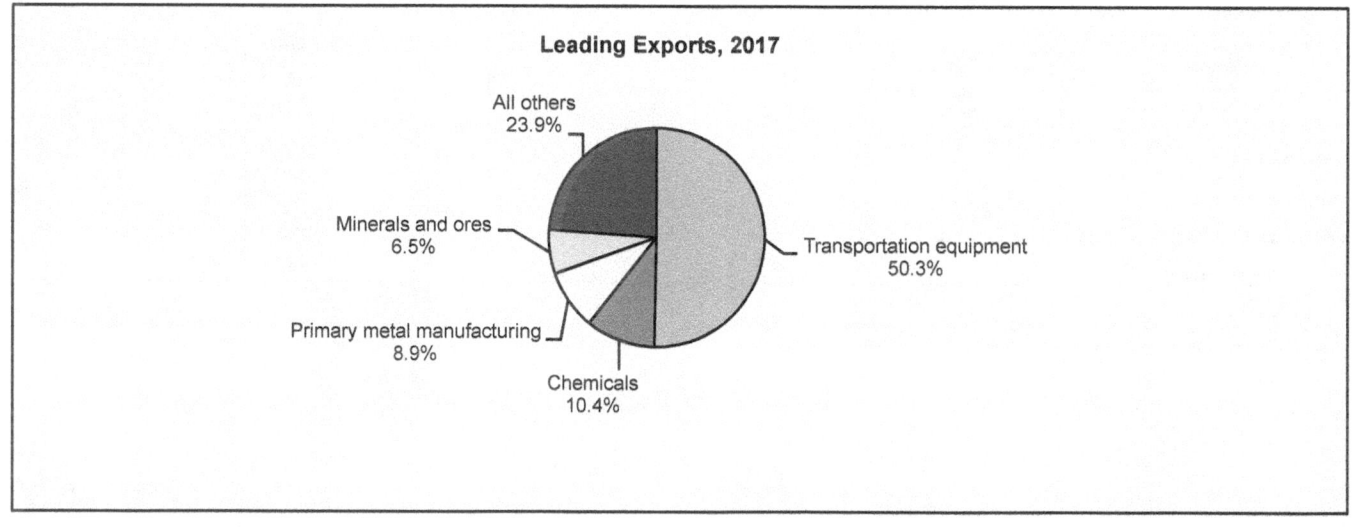

Leading Exports, 2017

All others 23.9%

Minerals and ores 6.5%

Primary metal manufacturing 8.9%

Chemicals 10.4%

Transportation equipment 50.3%

ALASKA

Facts and Figures

Location: Northwestern North America; bordered on the N by the Arctic Ocean, on the E by Canada, on the S by the Pacific Ocean and the Gulf of Alaska, and on the W by the Bering Sea

Area: 665,384 sq. mi. (1,717,854 sq. sq. km.); rank—1st

Population: 739,795 (2017 est.); rank—48th

Principal Cities: capital—Juneau; largest—Anchorage

Statehood: January 3, 1959; 49th state

U.S. Congress: 2 senators, 1 representative

State Motto: North to the Future

State Song: "Alaska's Flag"

State Nicknames: The Last Frontier; The Land of the Midnight Sun

Abbreviations: AK

State Symbols: flower—forget-me-not; tree—Sitka spruce; bird—willow ptarmigan

At a Glance

- With an increase in population of 3.6 percent, Alaska ranked 27th among the states for growth from 2010 to 2017.

- Alaska's 2016 violent crime rate ranked 2nd in the nation at 804.2 per 100,000 population, and the property crime rate (3,353.0 per 100,000 population) ranked 4th.

- Alaska was the state with the 2nd highest birth rate in 2016, at 15.1 births per 1,000 population.

- In 2016, 9.9 percent of Alaskans lived below the poverty level, the 6th lowest percent in the nation.

- Of all the states, Alaska had the 4th highest percentage of residents under 18 years old (25.0 percent) and the second lowest percentage of residents age 65 and over (11.2 percent) in 2017.

Table AK-1. Population by Age, Sex, Race, and Hispanic Origin

(Number, percent, except where noted.)

Sex, age, race, and Hispanic origin	2000	2010	2017 [1]	Average annual percent change, 2010–2017
Total Population...	626,932	710,231	739,795	4.2
Percent of total U.S. population	0.2	0.2	0.2	X
Sex				
Male..	324,112	369,628	386,792	4.6
Female	302,820	340,603	353,003	3.6
Age				
Under 5 years...	47,591	53,996	54,083	0.2
5 to 19 years...	160,526	153,844	148,337	-3.6
20 to 64 years...	383,116	447,453	454,795	1.6
65 years and over	35,699	54,938	82,580	50.3
Median age (years)	32.4	33.8	34.3	1.5
Race and Hispanic Origin				
One race				
White	434,534	483,873	486,724	0.6
Black...	21,787	24,441	27,595	12.9
American Indian and Alaska Native	98,043	106,268	112,994	6.3
Asian..	25,116	38,882	47,754	22.8
Native Hawaiian or Other Pacific Islander	3,309	7,622	10,084	32.3
Two or more races	34,146	49,105	54,644	11.3
Hispanic (of any race).....................................	25,852	44,490	52,250	17.4

X = Not applicable.
[1] Population figures for 2017 are July 1 estimates. The 2010 estimates are taken from the 2010 Census.
- = Zero or rounds to zero.

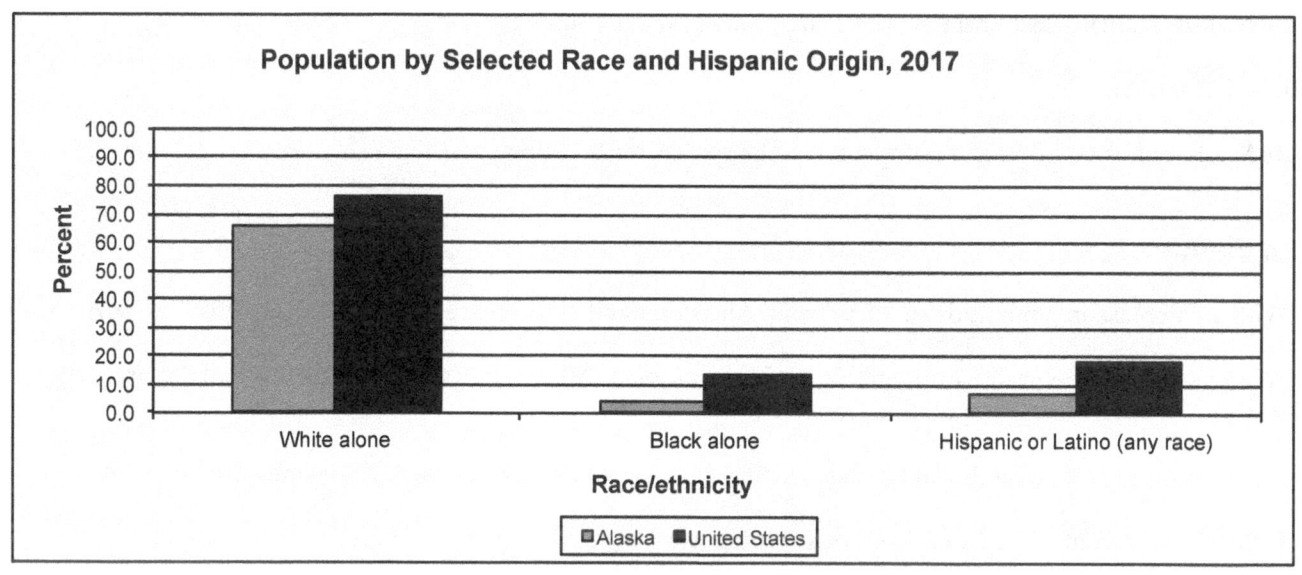

Population by Selected Race and Hispanic Origin, 2017

Table AK-2. Marital Status

(Number, percent distribution.)

Sex, age, and marital status	2000	2010	2016
Males, 15 Years and Over	243,024	290,598	307,284
Never married	32.5	35.5	40.7
Now married, except separated..	53.6	49.7	46.1
Separated...	1.7	1.7	1.7
Widowed..	1.4	1.8	1.8
Divorced..	10.8	11.4	9.7
Females, 15 Years and Over	225,837	267,563	277,386
Never married	24.1	27.3	30.9
Now married, except separated..	55.6	50.2	48.9
Separated...	2.3	2.6	1.9
Widowed..	5.6	6.1	5.4
Divorced..	12.5	13.7	12.8

Table AK-3. Households and Housing Characteristics

(Number, percent, dollars.)

Item	2000	2010	2016	Average annual percent change, 2010–2016
Total Households....	221,600	254,610	248,468	-0.4
Family households	152,337	170,859	164,102	-0.7
Married-couple family	116,318	127,969	122,168	-0.8
Other family	36,019	42,890	41,934	-0.4
Male householder, no wife present.....	12,082	14,211	14,394	0.2
Female householder, no husband present.....	23,937	28,679	27,540	-0.7
Nonfamily households	69,263	83,751	84,366	0.1
Householder living alone.....	52,060	63,698	62,482	-0.3
Householder not living alone.....	17,203	20,053	21,884	1.5
Housing Characteristics				
Total housing units.....	260,978	307,065	310,672	0.2
Occupied housing units	221,600	254,610	248,468	-0.4
Owner occupied	138,509	162,785	160,215	-0.3
Renter occupied.....	83,091	91,825	88,253	-0.6
Average household size.....	2.74	2.70	2.87	1.0
Financial Characteristics				
Median gross rent of renter-occupied housing	720	981	1,208	3.9
Median monthly owner costs for housing units with a mortgage	1,315	1,772	1,851	0.7
Median value of owner-occupied housing units.....	144,200	241,400	267,800	1.8

Table AK-4. Migration, Origin, and Language

(Number, percent.)

Characteristic	State 2015	State 2016	State Percent change	U.S. 2015	U.S. 2016	U.S. Percent change
Residence 1 Year Ago						
Population 1 year and over	727,862	731,760	0.5	317,635,720	319,361,956	0.5
Same house	80.1	81.2	X	85.3	85.4	X
Different house in the U.S.	19.3	17.9	X	14.1	13.9	X
Same county	11.9	10.8	X	8.5	8.3	X
Different county	7.4	7.2	X	5.6	5.6	X
Same state	2.7	2.9	X	3.2	3.2	X
Different state	4.8	4.3	X	2.4	2.4	X
Abroad	0.6	0.9	X	0.7	0.7	X
Place of Birth						
Native born	679,888	684,530	0.7	278,128,449	279,388,170	0.5
Male	53.3	53	X	49.3	49.3	X
Female	46.7	47	X	50.7	50.7	X
Foreign born	58,544	57,364	-2.0	43,290,372	43,739,345	1.0
Male	44.8	48.1	X	48.6	48.5	X
Female	55.2	51.9	X	51.4	51.5	X
Foreign born; naturalized U.S. citizen.....	32,367	32,772	1.3	20,697,103	21,238,372	2.6
Male	45.7	49.8	X	45.9	45.9	X
Female	54.3	50.2	X	54.1	54.1	X
Foreign born; not a U.S. citizen.....	26,177	24,592	-6.1	22,593,269	22,500,973	-0.4
Male	43.6	45.9	X	51.1	51	X
Female	56.4	54.1	X	48.9	49	X
Entered 2010 or later	17.8	24.1	X	15.6	18.6	X
Entered 2000 to 2009	29.6	24.8	X	27.9	26.7	X
Entered before 2000.....	52.7	51.1	X	56.5	54.7	X
World Region of Birth, Foreign						
Foreign-born population, excluding population born at sea	58,544	57,364	-2.0	43,289,646	43,738,901	1.0
Europe	15.4	13.4	X	11.1	10.9	X
Asia.....	55.9	57.8	X	30.6	30.8	X
Africa	4.3	2.6	X	4.8	4.9	X
Oceania	1.9	2.3	X	0.6	0.6	X
Latin America	18.0	19.8	X	51.1	51	X
North America	4.4	4	X	1.9	1.8	X
Language Spoken at Home and Ability to Speak English						
Population 5 years and over.....	683,671	689,399	0.8	301,625,014	303,328,961	0.6
English only	83.8	83.5	X	78.5	78.4	X
Language other than English.....	16.2	16.5	X	21.5	21.6	X
Speaks English less than "very well".....	5.1	5.3	X	8.6	8.6	X

NA = Not available.
X = Not applicable.
- = Zero or rounds to zero.

Table AK-5. Median Income and Poverty Status, 2016

(Number, percent, except as noted.)

Characteristic	State		U.S.	
	Number	Percent	Number	Percent
Median Income				
Households (dollars)	76,440	X	57,617	X
Families (dollars)	88,604	X	71,062	X
Below Poverty Level (All People)	71,566	9.9	44,268,996	14.0
Sex				
Male	34,994	9.3	19,760,056	12.8
Female	36,572	10.6	24,508,940	15.2
Age				
Under 18 years	25,938	14.1	14,115,713	19.5
Related children under 18 years	25,169	13.8	13,805,435	19.1
18 to 64 years	42,505	9.1	25,723,818	13.2
65 years and over	3,123	4.2	4,429,465	9.2

X = Not applicable.

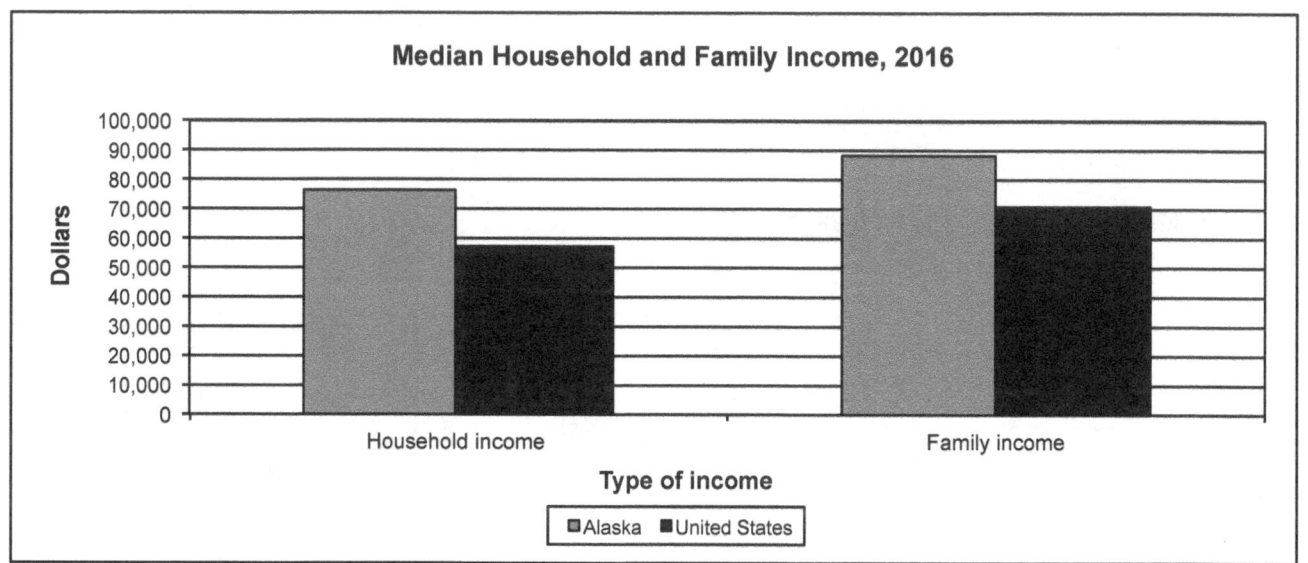

Table AK-6. Health Insurance Coverage Status for the Civilian Noninstitutionalized Population and Children Under 18 Years of Age

(Number; percent.)

Item	2008	2009	2010	2011	2012	2013	2014	2015	2016
Civilian Noninstitutionalized Population	659084	678081	689249	699272	708946	712,248	711,541	713,082	718,419
Covered by Private or Public Insurance									
Number	526,934	535,078	552,409	558,612	563,658	580,262	589,105	607,116	617,791
Percent	79.9	78.9	80.1	79.9	79.5	81.5	82.8	85.1	86.0
Not Covered									
Number	132,150	143,003	136,840	140,660	145,288	131,986	122,436	105,966	100,628
Percent	20.1	21.1	19.9	20.1	20.5	18.5	17.2	14.9	14.0
Percent in the U.S. not covered	15.1	15.1	15.5	15.1	14.8	14.5	11.7	9.4	8.6
Children Under 18 Years of Age	180431	183,261	187,984	187,708	187,072	187,885	186,245	185,917	186,839
Covered by Private or Public Insurance									
Number	157,232	158,268	165,141	165,599	161,115	166,043	164,993	166,252	168,245
Percent	87.1	86.4	87.8	88.2	86.1	88.4	88.6	89.4	90.0
Not Covered									
Number	23,199	24,993	22,843	22,109	25,957	21,842	21,252	19,665	18,594
Percent	12.9	13.6	12.2	11.8	13.9	11.6	11.4	10.6	10.0
Percent in the U.S. not covered	9.9	8.6	8.0	7.5	7.2	7.1	6.0	4.8	4.5

Table AK-7. Employment Status by Demographic Group, 2017

(Numbers in thousands, percent.)

Characteristic	Civilian noninstitutional population	Civilian labor force		Employed		Unemployed	
		Number	Percent of population	Number	Percent of population	Number	Percent of population
Total...	547	366	67.0	338	61.8	28	7.7
Sex							
Male..	279	194	69.6	176	63.2	18	9.1
Female	268	172	64.3	162	60.3	11	6.2
Race, Sex, and Hispanic Origin							
White	358	244	68.1	232	64.7	12	5.0
Male..	185	131	71.1	124	67.0	7	5.7
Female	173	112	65.0	108	62.2	5	4.2
Black or African American..........................	18	12	68.1	11	59.2	2	12.9
Male..	NA	NA	NA	NA	NA	NA	NA
Female	NA	NA	NA	NA	NA	NA	NA
Hispanic or Latino ethnicity[1]	29	21	72.1	20	69.6	1	3.5
Male..	15	12	75.2	11	71.9	1	4.3
Female	NA	NA	NA	NA	NA	NA	NA
Age							
16 to 19 years...	39	13	34.3	10	25.4	3	26.1
20 to 24 years...	53	39	73.5	35	65.5	4	10.8
25 to 34 years...	109	89	81.6	81	74.4	8	8.9
35 to 44 years...	83	70	84.6	65	78.2	5	7.5
45 to 54 years...	90	72	80.3	68	75.4	5	6.2
55 to 64 years...	90	59	65.7	57	63.1	2	3.9
65 years and over	83	23	28.0	23	27.2	1	3.0

NOTE: Data in Table 7 are from the Current Population Survey (CPS) and do not match the estimates in Table 8. See notes and definitions for further information.
[1] May be of any race.
NA = Not available.

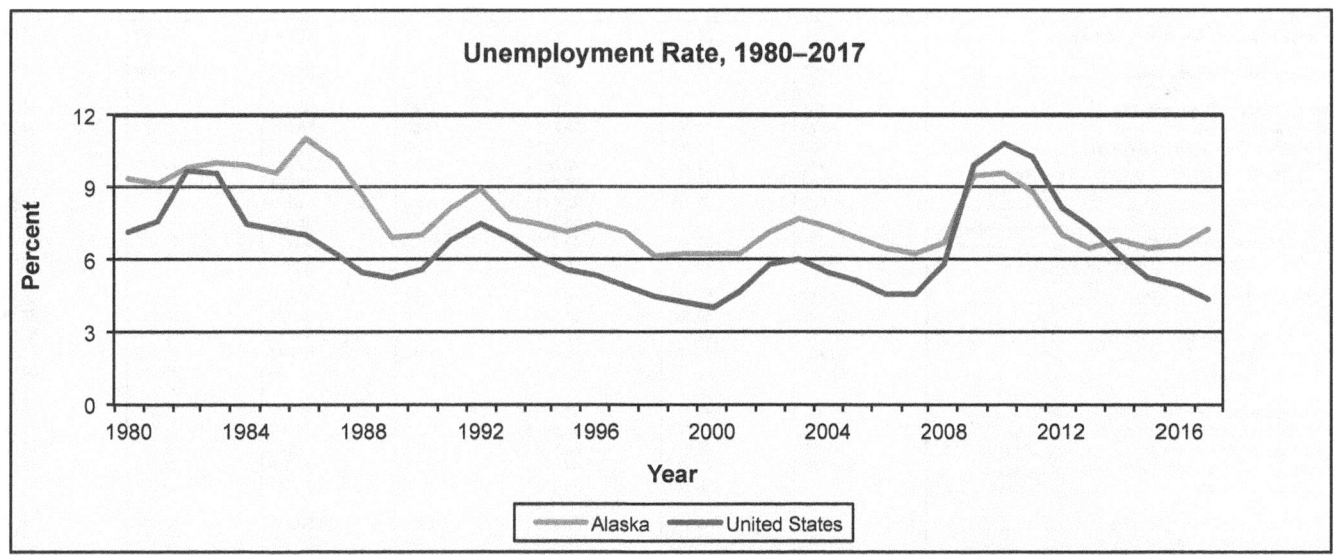

Unemployment Rate, 1980–2017

Table AK-8. Employment Status of the Civilian Noninstitutional Population Age 16 Years and Over

(Number, percent.)

Year	Civilian labor force	Civilian participation rate	Employed	Unemployed	Unemployment rate
2009..	359,647	70.3	331,792	27,855	7.7
2010..	361,913	69.8	333,416	28,497	7.9
2011..	365,913	69.2	338,161	27,752	7.6
2012..	365,519	68.3	339,474	26,045	7.1
2013..	365,292	67.9	339,801	25,491	7.0
2014..	365,704	67.7	340,585	25,119	6.9
2015..	363,872	67.0	340,132	23,740	6.5
2016..	363,047	66.4	337,947	25,100	6.9
2017..	362,783	66.4	336,806	25,977	7.2

Table AK-9. Employment and Average Wages by Industry

(Estimates through 2010 are based on the 2007 *North American Industry Classification System* [NAICS]. Estimates from 2011 onward are based on the 2012 NAICS.)

Industry	2010	2011	2012	2013	2014	2015	2016
	Number of Jobs						
Wage and Salary Employment by Industry.........................	352,718	358,857	365,191	365,944	366,208	367,355	361,183
Farm Wage and Salary Employment..............................	522	602	421	427	510	465	435
Nonfarm Wage and Salary Employment..........................	352,196	358,255	364,770	365,517	365,698	366,890	360,748
Private wage and salary employment.............................	244,008	249,399	255,836	258,465	260,634	262,320	257,238
Forestry, fishing, and related activities............................	657	896	656	660	693	702	650
Mining...	15,020	15,592	16,611	16,997	17,586	17,062	14,185
Utilities..	2,141	2,106	2,117	2,135	2,112	2,139	2,123
Construction...	16,607	16,324	16,721	16,882	17,597	18,137	16,726
Manufacturing...	12,758	13,705	14,109	14,462	14,436	14,067	13,620
Durable goods manufacturing................................	1,888	1,862	2,203	2,253	2,073	2,143	2,012
Nondurable goods manufacturing...........................	10,870	11,843	11,906	12,209	12,363	11,924	11,608
Wholesale trade..	6,310	6,354	6,309	6,647	6,541	6,572	6,463
Retail trade..	35,845	36,123	36,195	36,201	37,094	37,727	37,371
Transportation and warehousing................................	18,995	19,383	19,900	19,633	19,536	19,786	19,960
Information..	6,449	6,327	6,210	6,156	6,248	6,303	6,289
Finance and insurance...	7,303	7,386	7,393	7,412	7,325	7,354	7,398
Real estate and rental and leasing.............................	5,129	5,039	4,956	4,966	4,961	4,926	4,839
Professional, scientific, and technical services...............	13,980	14,560	15,010	15,214	14,919	14,766	13,633
Management of companies and enterprises....................	2,724	2,773	3,008	3,058	3,003	3,140	2,914
Administrative and waste services.............................	11,389	11,614	12,123	12,166	12,298	12,300	12,142
Educational services..	3,143	3,212	3,207	3,295	3,298	3,385	3,347
Health care and social assistance..............................	40,538	41,911	43,874	44,652	44,256	44,681	46,076
Arts, entertainment, and recreation............................	4,472	4,801	4,902	4,912	4,861	4,845	5,036
Accommodation and food services.............................	27,226	27,921	28,593	29,015	29,544	30,337	30,551
Other services, except public administration..................	13,322	13,372	13,942	14,002	14,326	14,091	13,915
Government and government enterprises.......................	108,188	108,856	108,934	107,052	105,064	104,570	103,510
	Dollars						
Average Wages and Salaries by Industry	51,070	52,365	53,658	54,545	56,348	57,740	55,917
Average Farm Wages and Salaries	29,933	24,882	39,606	39,466	33,643	38,966	42,591
Average Nonfarm Wages and Salaries	51,101	52,411	53,674	54,563	56,380	57,764	55,933
Average private wages and salaries.............................	49,575	50,861	52,290	53,460	55,541	57,093	54,139
Forestry, fishing, and related activities........................	48,457	51,664	58,331	63,388	61,359	60,128	57,163
Mining...	121,745	124,558	128,007	130,797	137,532	141,148	122,071
Utilities..	75,420	81,402	85,969	88,148	88,473	93,159	90,958
Construction	72,663	72,537	74,449	77,220	81,759	83,914	71,559
Manufacturing...	41,145	41,325	43,338	45,126	45,425	50,817	50,671
Durable goods manufacturing................................	51,287	51,402	55,714	58,459	59,753	63,015	54,807
Nondurable goods manufacturing...........................	39,383	39,740	41,048	42,666	43,023	48,624	49,954
Wholesale trade..	54,317	55,474	56,158	56,190	57,655	60,027	58,301
Retail trade..	30,026	30,580	31,394	31,630	32,448	32,951	32,588
Transportation and warehousing................................	60,853	62,591	63,158	64,324	66,085	66,515	67,555
Information..	57,703	61,579	62,060	63,544	65,843	68,255	61,524
Finance and insurance...	58,382	60,060	62,606	63,364	65,800	68,410	68,584
Real estate and rental and leasing.............................	40,481	40,715	41,833	42,492	44,021	45,352	45,854
Professional, scientific, and technical services...............	67,780	70,873	72,401	74,276	77,030	77,656	71,622
Management of companies and enterprises....................	83,852	85,027	84,446	81,416	87,302	87,662	88,219
Administrative and waste services.............................	43,681	43,607	44,461	44,421	46,346	47,820	46,614
Educational services	28,712	28,378	29,406	29,646	29,049	29,069	31,384
Health care and social assistance..............................	44,870	46,811	47,687	48,882	50,398	52,897	55,565
Arts, entertainment, and recreation............................	20,823	21,858	22,490	23,463	24,326	25,102	26,589
Accommodation and food services.............................	23,129	23,934	24,694	25,312	26,739	27,742	28,326
Other services, except public administration..................	34,280	34,795	35,092	36,093	37,282	38,645	39,855
Government and government enterprises.......................	54,542	55,962	56,923	57,225	58,460	59,445	60,389

Table AK-10. Employment Characteristics by Family Type

(Number, percent.)

Family type and labor force status	2014		2015		2016	
	Total	Families with own children under 18 years	Total	Families with own children under 18 years	Total	Families with own children under 18 years
All Families..	164,518	81,338	163,800	77,964	164,102	76,055
FAMILY TYPE AND LABOR FORCE STATUS						
Married-Couple Families...	123,531	56,246	120,348	50,683	122,168	52,831
Both husband and wife in labor force...............................	55.9	61.4	56.4	64.3	55.9	66.6
Husband in labor force, wife not in labor force	23.2	30.0	24.2	30.4	21.5	24.8
Wife in labor force, husband not in labor force........................	8.2	5.3	6.5	3.5	9.0	6.5
Both husband and wife not in labor force.............................	12.8	3.3	12.4	1.5	12.7	2.0
Other Families	40,987	25,092	43,452	27,281	41,934	23,224
Female householder, no husband present............................	64.2	65.7	65.2	66.7	65.7	65.7
In labor force	47.6	54.1	50	58.8	48.5	55.5
Not in labor force	16.6	11.5	15.2	7.9	17.1	10.2
Male householder, no wife present.................................	35.8	34.3	34.8	33.3	34.3	34.3
In labor force...	28.5	30.5	27.9	28.4	27.3	30.7
Not in labor force	7.3	3.9	6.9	4.9	7.1	3.6

Table AK-11. School Enrollment and Educational Attainment, 2016

(Number, percent.)

Item	State	U.S.
Enrollment		
Total population 3 years and over, enrolled in school	187,359	81,572,277
Enrolled in nursery school or preschool (percent)..............................	5.4	6.0
Enrolled in kindergarten (percent)..	4.5	5.0
Enrolled in elementary school, grades 1-8 (percent)...........................	44.7	40.3
Enrolled in high school, grades 9-12 (percent)................................	22.2	21.0
Enrolled in college or graduate school (percent)..............................	23.2	27.7
Attainment		
Total population 25 years and over	478,951	218,475,480
Less than ninth grade (percent)	2.2	5.4
9th to 12th grade, no diploma (percent)..	4.7	7.2
High school graduate, including equivalency (percent)........................	28.0	27.2
Some college, no degree (percent)	27.1	20.6
Associate's degree (percent)...	8.5	8.4
Bachelor's degree (percent)..	19.0	19.3
Graduate or professional degree (percent)......................................	10.6	11.9
High school graduate or higher (percent)	93.1	87.5
Bachelor's degree or higher (percent)...	29.6	31.3

Table AK-12. Public School Characteristics and Educational Indicators

(Number, percent; data derived from National Center of Education Statistics.)

Item	State	U.S.
Public Schools, 2015–2016 (except where noted)		
Number of school districts..	54	18,328
Number of schools..	508	98,456
Number of students...	132,477	50,327,015
Number of teachers...	7,832	3,151,497
Student-teacher ratio	16.9	16.0
Expenditures per student (dollars), 2014-2015.................................	20,191	11,445
Four-year adjusted cohort graduation rate (ACGR)[1,2]	76.1	84.1
Students eligible for free or reduced-price lunch (percent), 2014-2015........	43.1	51.8
English language learners (percent), Fall 2015	11.5	9.5
Students age 3 to 21 served under IDEA, part B (percent).....................	13.9	13.2

Public Schools by Type	Number	Percent of state public schools
Total number of schools...	508	100.0
Regular	478	94.1
Special education..	3	0.6
Vocational education...	3	0.6
Alternative education..	24	4.7

NOTE: Every school is assigned only one school type based on its instructional emphasis.

[1] ACGR data represents a new method of calculating high-school completion rates and may not be comparable to previous years' data for Averaged Freshmen Graduation Rates (AFGR).

[2] The United States 4-year ACGRs were estimated using both the reported 4-year ACGR data from 49 states and the District of Columbia and using imputed data for Idaho. The estimate for American Indian/Alaska Native students also includes imputed data for Virginia.

Table AK-13. Reported Voting and Registration of the Voting-Age Population, November 2016

(Numbers in thousands, percent.)

Item	Total population	Total citizen population	Registered			Voted		
			Total registered	Percent registered (total population)	Percent registered (total citizen population)	Total voted	Percent voted (total population)	Percent voted (total citizen population)
U.S. Total	245,502	224,059	157,596	64.2	70.3	137,537	56.0	61.4
State Total................................	518	502	358	69.1	71.3	308	59.4	61.3
Sex								
Male	267	258	181	67.9	70.1	152	57.0	58.8
Female	251	243	177	70.3	72.6	156	62.0	64.0
Race								
White alone...............................	346	340	261	75.5	76.8	234	67.7	68.9
White, non-Hispanic alone............	334	329	252	75.5	76.7	226	67.7	68.7
Black alone...............................	17	17	10	(B)	(B)	8	(B)	(B)
Asian alone...............................	27	19	9	(B)	(B)	8	(B)	(B)
Hispanic (of any race)...................	24	23	17	(B)	(B)	17	(B)	(B)
White alone or in combination	369	363	279	75.8	77.0	250	67.9	69.0
Black alone or in combination...........	26	26	14	(B)	(B)	12	(B)	(B)
Asian alone or in combination...........	32	24	13	(B)	(B)	12	(B)	(B)
Age								
18 to 24 years..........................	65	65	32	(B)	(B)	26	(B)	(B)
25 to 34 years..........................	113	109	71	62.6	64.8	58	51.0	52.7
35 to 44 years..........................	83	79	58	(B)	(B)	48	(B)	(B)
45 to 64 years..........................	180	174	138	77.0	79.6	122	67.9	70.2
65 years and over	77	75	59	(B)	(B)	54	(B)	(B)

B = Base is less than 75,000 and therefore too small to show the derived measure.

Table AK-14. Crime

(Number, rate per 100,000. Data are derived from the FBI Uniform Crime Reports.)

Item	State			U.S. [1,2,3,4]		
	2015	2016	Percent change	2015	2016	Percent change
TOTAL POPULATION [5]	738,432	741,894	0.5	321,418,820	323,127,513	0.5
VIOLENT CRIME						
Number......................................	5,392	5,966	10.6	1,231,566	1,248,185	1.3
Rate	730.2	804.2	10.1	383.2	386.3	0.8
Murder and Nonnegligent Manslaughter						
Number......................................	59	52	-11.9	15,696	17,250	9.9
Rate	8.0	7.0	-12.5	4.9	5.3	8.2
Rape[6]						
Number[6]...................................	901	1,053	16.9	124,047	130,603	5.3
Rate	122.0	141.9	16.3	38.6	40.4	4.7
Robbery						
Number......................................	761	850	11.7	327,374	332,198	1.5
Rate	103.1	114.6	11.2	101.9	102.8	0.9
Aggravated Assault						
Number......................................	3,671	4,011	9.3	764,449	803,007	5.0
Rate	497.1	540.6	8.8	237.8	248.5	4.5
PROPERTY CRIME						
Number......................................	20,806	24,876	19.6	7,993,631	7,919,035	-0.9
Rate	2,817.6	3,353.0	19.0	2,487.0	2,450.7	-1.5
Burglary						
Number......................................	3,511	4,053	15.4	1,579,527	1,515,096	-4.1
Rate	475.5	546.3	14.9	491.4	468.9	-4.6
Larceny-Theft						
Number......................................	15,249	17,766	16.5	5,706,346	5,638,455	-1.2
Rate	2,065.1	2,394.7	16.0	1,775.4	1,745.0	-1.7
Motor Vehicle Theft						
Number......................................	2,046	3,057	49.4	707,758	765,484	8.2
Rate	277.1	412.1	48.7	220.2	236.9	7.6

NOTE: Although arson data are included in the trend and clearance tables, sufficient data are not available to estimate totals for this offense. Therefore, no arson data are published in this table.
X = Not applicable.
- = Zero or rounds to zero.
[1] Because of changes in the state's reporting practices, figures are not comparable to previous years' data.
[2] The crime figures have been adjusted.
[3] The data collection methodology for the offense of forcible rape used by the Minnesota state Uniform Crime Reporting (UCR) Program (with the exception of Minneapolis and St. Paul, Minnesota) does not comply with national UCR Program guidelines. Consequently, its figures for forcible rape and violent crime (of which forcible rape is a part) are not published in this table.
[4] Includes offenses reported by the Zoological Police and the Metro Transit Police.
[5] Populations are U.S. Census Bureau provisional estimates as of July 1 of each year.
[6] The figures shown for the offense of rape were estimated using the revised Uniform Crime Reporting (UCR) definition of rape.

Table AK-15. State Government Finances, 2016

(Dollar amounts in thousands, percent distribution.)

Item	Dollars	Percent distribution
Total Revenue	8,071,737	100.0
General revenue	7,628,656	94.5
Intergovernmental revenue	2,853,202	35.3
Taxes	1,042,164	12.9
General sales	0	-
Selective sales	260,846	3.2
License taxes	120,529	1.5
Individual income tax	0	-
Corporate income tax	212,252	2.6
Other taxes	448,537	5.6
Current charges	700,790	8.7
Miscellaneous general revenue	3,032,500	37.6
Utility revenue	18,640	0.2
Liquor stores revenue	0	-
Insurance trust revenue [1]	424,441	5.3
Total Expenditure	12,452,033	100.0
Intergovernmental expenditure	2,038,078	16.4
Direct expenditure	10,413,955	83.6
Current operation	7,223,114	58.0
Capital outlay	1,520,889	12.2
Insurance benefits and repayments	1,329,941	10.7
Assistance and subsidies	155,125	1.2
Interest on debt	184,886	1.5
Exhibit: Salaries and wages	1,718,737	13.8
Total Expenditure	12,452,033	100.0
General expenditure	10,889,343	87.5
Intergovernmental expenditure	2,038,078	16.4
Direct expenditure	8,851,265	71.1
General expenditure, by function:		
Education	2,864,158	23.0
Public welfare	2,372,655	19.1
Hospitals	28,295	0.2
Health	252,016	2.0
Highways	1,290,503	10.4
Police protection	140,154	1.1
Correction	344,067	2.8
Natural resources	479,717	3.9
Parks and recreation	16,121	0.1
Governmental administration	701,168	5.6
Interest on general debt	181,709	1.5
Other and unallocable	2,218,780	17.8
Utility expenditure	232,749	2.9
Liquor stores expenditure	0	-
Insurance trust expenditure	1,329,941	10.7
Debt at End of Fiscal Year	5,953,933	X
Cash and Security Holdings	74,144,627	X

X = Not applicable.
- = Zero or rounds to zero.
[1] Within insurance trust revenue, net earnings of state retirement systems is a calculated statistic (the item code in the data file is X08), and thus can be positive or negative. Net earnings is the sum of earnings on investments plus gains on investments minus losses on investments. The change made in 2002 for asset valuation from book to market value in accordance with Statement 34 of the Governmental Accounting Standards Board is reflected in the calculated statistics.

Table AK-16. State Government Tax Collections, 2017

(Dollars in thousands, percent.)

Item	Dollars	Percent distribution
Total Taxes	1,189,786	100.0
Property taxes	120,805	10.2
Sales and gross receipts	263,120	22.1
General sales and gross receipts	X	-
Selective sales and gross receipts	263,120	22.1
Alcoholic beverages	40,097	3.4
Amusements	10,668	0.9
Insurance premiums	62,500	5.3
Motor fuels	45,944	3.9
Pari-mutuels	X	-
Public utilities	4,370	0.4
Tobacco products	67,555	5.7
Other selective sales	31,986	2.7
Licenses	134,928	11.3
Alcoholic beverages	1,996	0.2
Amusements	0	-
Corporations in general	X	-
Hunting and fishing	32,900	2.8
Motor vehicle	38,900	3.3
Motor vehicle operators	X	-
Public utilities	9,316	0.8
Occupation and business, NEC	49,272	4.1
Other licenses	2,544	0.2
Income taxes	87,775	7.4
Individual income	X	-
Corporation net income	87,775	7.4
Other taxes	583,158	49.0
Death and gift	X	-
Documentary and stock transfer	X	-
Severance	583,158	49.0
Taxes, NEC	0	-

X = Not applicable.
- = Zero or rounds to zero.

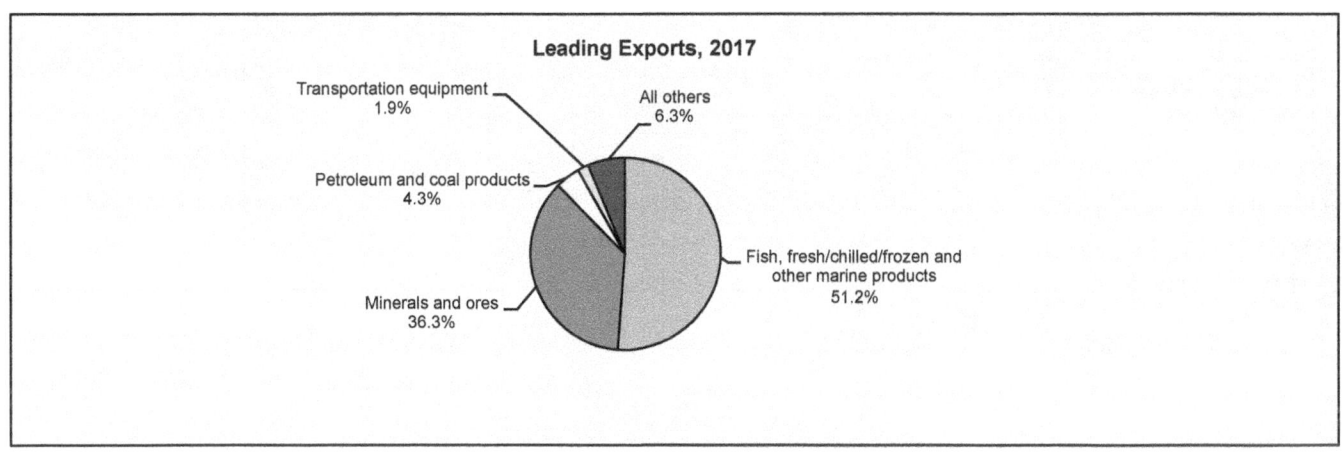

Leading Exports, 2017

Transportation equipment 1.9%

All others 6.3%

Petroleum and coal products 4.3%

Fish, fresh/chilled/frozen and other marine products 51.2%

Minerals and ores 36.3%

ARIZONA

Facts and Figures

Location: Southwestern United States; bordered on the North by Utah, on the East by New Mexico, on the South by Mexico, and on the West by Nevada and California; Arizona is one of the Four Corner states—at its NE corner it touches Colorado, New Mexico, and Utah

Area: 113,990 sq, mi. (295,254 sq. km.); rank—6th

Population: 7,016,270 (2017 est.); rank—14th

Principal Cities: capital—Phoenix; largest—Phoenix

Statehood: February 14, 1912; 48th state

U.S. Congress: 2 senators, 9 representatives

State Motto: *Ditat Deus* ("God enriches")

State Song: "Arizona"

State Nickname: The Grand Canyon State

Abbreviations: AZ; Ariz.

State Symbols: flower—saguaro cactus blossom; tree—paloverde; bird—cactus wren

At a Glance

- With an increase in population of 9.5 percent, Arizona ranked 9th among the states in growth from 2010 to 2017.

- In 2017, 17.1 percent of Arizonans were age 65 and older, the 11th highest percent in the nation.

- Arizona's median household income in 2016 was $53,558, compared to the national median household income of $57,617.

- In 2016, 16.4 percent of Arizonans lived below the poverty level, a percentage that ranked 9th in the country.

- Arizona's violent crime rate in 2016 was 470.1 per 100,000 population, ranking 13th in the nation.

Table AZ-1. Population by Age, Sex, Race, and Hispanic Origin

(Number, percent, except where noted.)

Sex, age, race, and Hispanic origin	2000	2010	2017 [1]	Average annual percent change, 2010–2017
Total Population.........................	5,130,632	6,392,017	7,016,270	9.8
Percent of total U.S. population	1.8	2.1	2.2	X
Sex				
Male..........	2,561,057	3,175,823	3,488,301	9.8
Female	2,569,575	3,216,814	3,527,969	9.7
Age				
Under 5 years..........	382,386	455,715	437,262	-4.0
5 to 19 years	1,135,802	1,363,926	1,384,369	1.5
20 to 64 years	2,944,605	3,690,545	3,992,893	8.2
65 years and over	667,839	881,831	1,201,746	36.3
Median age (years)	34.2	35.9	37.7	5.0
Race and Hispanic Origin				
One race				
White..........	3,873,611	5,418,483	5,827,866	7.6
Black..........	158,873	280,905	349,944	24.6
American Indian and Alaska Native	255,879	335,278	373,532	11.4
Asian..........	92,236	188,456	247,790	31.5
Native Hawaiian or Other Pacific Islander	6,733	16,112	19,091	18.5
Two or more races..........	146,526	152,783	198,047	29.6
Hispanic (of any race)..........	1,295,617	1,943,466	2,202,172	13.3

X = Not applicable.
[1] Population figures for 2017 are July 1 estimates. The 2010 estimates are taken from the 2010 Census.

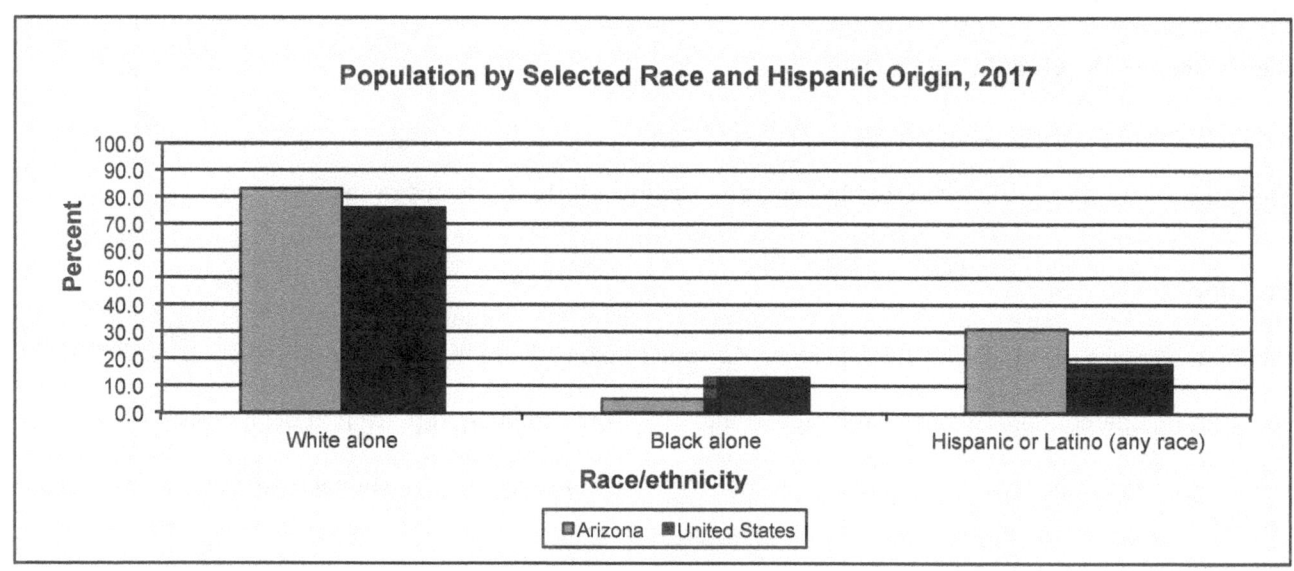

Population by Selected Race and Hispanic Origin, 2017

Table AZ-2. Marital Status

(Number, percent distribution.)

Sex, age, and marital status	2000	2010	2016
Males, 15 Years and Over..........	1,966,032	2,492,590	2,754,161
Never married	29.6	35.3	37.1
Now married, except separated..........	56.4	50.1	48.0
Separated..........	1.6	1.4	1.4
Widowed..........	2.6	2.5	2.8
Divorced..........	9.8	10.7	10.8
Females, 15 Years and Over..........	2,013,304	2,559,409	2,825,145
Never married	22.5	28.0	29.7
Now married, except separated..........	53.6	48.0	45.8
Separated..........	2.1	2.2	2.0
Widowed..........	9.4	8.3	8.5
Divorced..........	12.3	13.5	14.1

Table AZ-3. Households and Housing Characteristics

(Number, percent, dollars.)

Item	2000	2010	2016	Average annual percent change, 2010–2016
Total Households..	1,901,327	2,334,050	2,519,052	1.3
Family households..	1,287,367	1,548,428	1,648,739	1.1
Married-couple family	986,303	1,134,229	1,194,185	0.9
Other family	310,064	414,199	454,554	1.6
Male householder, no wife present.............................	90,283	123,772	137,509	1.8
Female householder, no husband present....................	210,781	290,427	317,045	1.5
Nonfamily households	613,960	785,622	870,313	1.8
Householder living alone..	472,006	621,291	687,147	1.8
Householder not living alone.....................................	141,954	164,331	183,166	1.9
Housing Characteristics				
Total housing units	2,189,189	2,846,738	2,961,136	0.7
Occupied housing units	1,901,327	2,334,050	2,519,052	1.3
Owner occupied	1,293,556	1,522,938	1,593,014	0.8
Renter occupied..	607,771	811,112	926,038	2.4
Average household size...	2.64	2.69	2.69	-
Financial Characteristics				
Median gross rent of renter-occupied housing	619	844	976	2.6
Median monthly owner costs for housing units with a mortgage	1,039	1,442	1,328	-1.3
Median value of owner-occupied housing units.................	121,300	168,800	205,900	3.7

- = Zero or rounds to zero.

Table AZ-4. Migration, Origin, and Language

(Number, percent.)

Characteristic	State			U.S.		
	2015	2016	Percent change	2015	2016	Percent change
Residence 1 Year Ago						
Population 1 year and over	6,747,595	6,851,836	1.5	317,635,720	319,361,956	0.5
Same house	82.0	81.5	X	85.3	85.4	X
Different house in the U.S.	17.3	17.7	X	14.1	13.9	X
Same county..	11.8	11.8	X	8.5	8.3	X
Different county	5.4	5.8	X	5.6	5.6	X
Same state..	1.7	1.8	X	3.2	3.2	X
Different state..	3.8	4	X	2.4	2.4	X
Abroad	0.7	0.8	X	0.7	0.7	X
Place of Birth						
Native born	5,913,665	5,996,188	1.4	278,128,449	279,388,170	0.5
Male	49.9	49.9	X	49.3	49.3	X
Female	50.1	50.1	X	50.7	50.7	X
Foreign born	914,400	934,883	2.2	43,290,372	43,739,345	1.0
Male	47.7	48.7	X	48.6	48.5	X
Female	52.3	51.3	X	51.4	51.5	X
Foreign born; naturalized U.S. citizen.........................	380,187	399,036	5.0	20,697,103	21,238,372	2.6
Male	45	45.5	X	45.9	45.9	X
Female	55	54.5	X	54.1	54.1	X
Foreign born; not a U.S. citizen................................	534,213	535,847	0.3	22,593,269	22,500,973	-0.4
Male	49.6	51.1	X	51.1	51	X
Female	50.4	48.9	X	48.9	49	X
Entered 2010 or later	14.6	16.5	X	15.6	18.6	X
Entered 2000 to 2009	25.1	24.7	X	27.9	26.7	X
Entered before 2000...	60.3	58.8	X	56.5	54.7	X
World Region of Birth, Foreign						
Foreign-born population, excluding population born at sea	914,400	934,770	2.2	43,289,646	43,738,901	1.0
Europe	9.0	9.2	X	11.1	10.9	X
Asia..	20.2	20.5	X	30.6	30.8	X
Africa	3.0	3.3	X	4.8	4.9	X
Oceania	0.5	0.6	X	0.6	0.6	X
Latin America...	62.9	61.6	X	51.1	51	X
North America..	4.3	4.8	X	1.9	1.8	X
Language Spoken at Home and Ability to Speak English						
Population 5 years and over..	6,398,205	6,494,749	1.5	301,625,014	303,328,961	0.6
English only	72.9	72.9	X	78.5	78.4	X
Language other than English.....................................	27.1	27.1	X	21.5	21.6	X
Speaks English less than "very well"...........................	8.9	8.8	X	8.6	8.6	X

NA = Not available.
X = Not applicable.
- = Zero or rounds to zero.

Table AZ-5. Median Income and Poverty Status, 2016

(Number, percent, except as noted.)

Characteristic	State		U.S.	
	Number	Percent	Number	Percent
Median Income				
Households (dollars)...	53,558	X	57,617	X
Families (dollars)	63,877	X	71,062	X
Below Poverty Level (All People)	1,107,464	16.4	44,268,996	14.0
Sex				
Male	516,500	15.5	19,760,056	12.8
Female	590,964	17.2	24,508,940	15.2
Age				
Under 18 years...	378,800	23.6	14,115,713	19.5
Related children under 18 years...	372,144	23.3	13,805,435	19.1
18 to 64 years..	624,605	15.6	25,723,818	13.2
65 years and over	104,059	9.0	4,429,465	9.2

X = Not applicable.

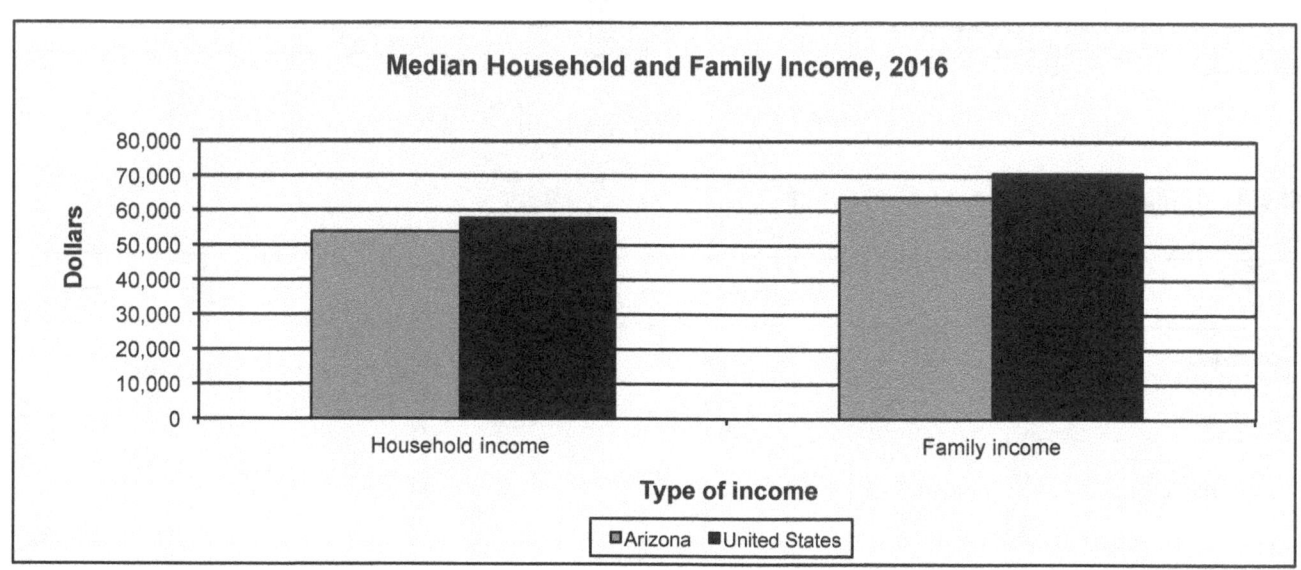

Table AZ-6. Health Insurance Coverage Status for the Civilian Noninstitutionalized Population and Children Under 18 Years of Age

(Number, percent.)

Item	2008	2009	2010	2011	2012	2013	2014	2015	2016
Civilian Noninstitutionalized Population	6,402,786	6,501,531	6,310,174	6,378,280	6,443,654	6,521,226	6,623,074	6,719,354	6,824,645
Covered by Private or Public Insurance									
Number...	5,206,519	5,375,026	5,245,042	5,283,270	5,312,695	5,403,040	5,719,746	5,991,378	6,143,407
Percent..	81.3	82.7	83.1	82.8	82.4	82.9	86.4	89.2	90.0
Not Covered									
Number...	1,196,267	1,126,505	1,065,132	1,095,010	1,130,959	1,118,186	903,328	727,976	681,238
Percent..	18.7	17.3	16.9	17.2	17.6	17.1	13.6	10.8	10.0
Percent in the U.S. not covered...	15.1	15.1	15.5	15.1	14.8	14.5	11.7	9.4	8.6
Children Under 18 Years of Age	1,705,841	1,729,814	1,629,931	1,621,830	1,617,380	1,613,505	1,620,576	1,619,393	1,629,040
Covered by Private or Public Insurance									
Number...	1,429,668	1,521,961	1,421,964	1,413,411	1,403,418	1,421,745	1,458,722	1,485,146	1,509,594
Percent..	83.8	88.0	87.2	87.1	86.8	88.1	90.0	91.7	92.7
Not Covered									
Number...	276,173	207,853	207,967	208,419	213,962	191,760	161,854	134,247	119,446
Percent..	16.2	12.0	12.8	12.9	13.2	11.9	10.0	8.3	7.3
Percent in the U.S. not covered...	9.9	8.6	8.0	7.5	7.2	7.1	6.0	4.8	4.5

Table AZ-7. Employment Status by Demographic Group, 2017

(Numbers in thousands, percent.)

Characteristic	Civilian noninstitutional population	Civilian labor force		Employed		Unemployed	
		Number	Percent of population	Number	Percent of population	Number	Percent of population
Total...	5,469	3,298	60.3	3,142	57.5	156	4.7
Sex							
Male....................................	2,662	1,773	66.6	1,700	63.8	73	4.1
Female..................................	2,807	1,525	54.3	1,443	51.4	82	5.4
Race, Sex, and Hispanic Origin							
White.....................................	4,759	2,838	59.6	2,716	57.1	121	4.3
Male..................................	2,311	1,531	66.2	1,474	63.8	57	3.7
Female..............................	2,448	1,307	53.4	1,242	50.8	64	4.9
Black or African American..................	261	181	69.5	165	63.3	16	9.0
Male..................................	131	95	72.3	88	67.2	7	7.0
Female..............................	129	86	66.7	77	59.2	10	11.2
Hispanic or Latino ethnicity[1]...............	1,687	1,078	63.9	1,015	60.2	63	5.9
Male..................................	849	615	72.5	584	68.8	31	5.1
Female..............................	838	463	55.2	431	51.4	32	6.9
Age							
16 to 19 years...........................	400	141	35.3	119	29.8	22	15.5
20 to 24 years...........................	476	352	74.0	330	69.3	22	6.3
25 to 34 years...........................	882	706	80.1	673	76.3	33	4.7
35 to 44 years...........................	830	674	81.2	658	79.2	16	2.4
45 to 54 years...........................	926	738	79.8	703	76.0	35	4.8
55 to 64 years...........................	833	505	60.7	489	58.7	16	3.2
65 years and over........................	1,123	181	16.1	171	15.2	10	5.6

NOTE: Data in Table 7 are from the Current Population Survey (CPS) and do not match the estimates in Table 8. See notes and definitions for further information.
[1] May be of any race.
NA = Not available.

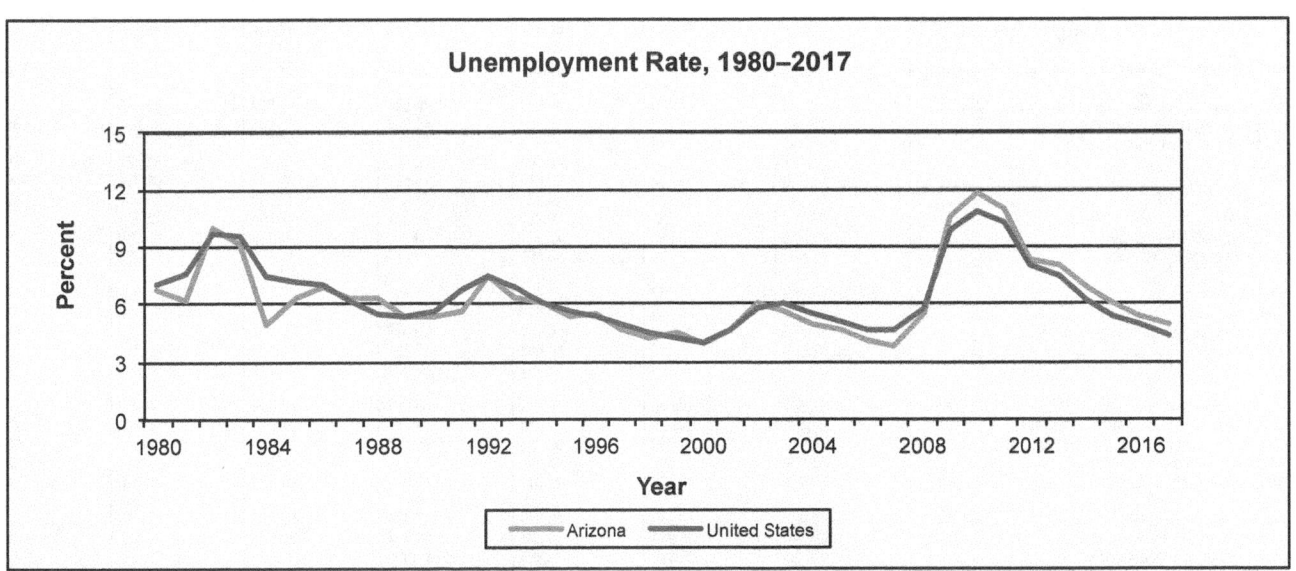

Table AZ-8. Employment Status of the Civilian Noninstitutional Population Age 16 Years and Over

(Number, percent.)

Year	Civilian labor force	Civilian participation rate	Employed	Unemployed	Unemployment rate
2009....................	3,128,110	63.2	2,817,577	310,533	9.9
2010....................	3,089,705	63.1	2,769,454	320,251	10.4
2011....................	3,037,017	61.7	2,748,470	288,547	9.5
2012....................	3,028,878	60.6	2,776,349	252,529	8.3
2013....................	3,029,425	59.7	2,794,697	234,728	7.7
2014....................	3,087,942	59.9	2,878,611	209,331	6.8
2015....................	3,153,040	60.0	2,962,245	190,795	6.1
2016....................	3,225,703	60.2	3,052,788	172,915	5.4
2017....................	3,312,720	60.6	3,151,405	161,315	4.9

Table AZ-9. Employment and Average Wages by Industry

(Estimates through 2010 are based on the 2007 *North American Industry Classification System* [NAICS]. Estimates from 2011 onward are based on the 2012 NAICS.)

Industry	2010	2011	2012	2013	2014	2015	2016
	Number of Jobs						
Wage and Salary Employment by Industry	2,476,001	2,503,192	2,560,624	2,619,199	2,671,930	2,743,361	2,818,420
Farm Wage and Salary Employment	11,417	11,523	12,626	13,966	12,360	13,584	15,203
Nonfarm Wage and Salary Employment	2,464,584	2,491,669	2,547,998	2,605,233	2,659,570	2,729,777	2,803,217
Private wage and salary employment	2,015,596	2,049,819	2,104,857	2,160,867	2,214,415	2,285,701	2,357,221
Forestry, fishing, and related activities	12,364	12,464	12,114	12,000	12,143	12,166	12,898
Mining	10,285	10,918	11,925	12,615	12,303	11,740	11,306
Utilities	12,076	11,971	12,290	11,934	11,952	12,089	12,371
Construction	115,305	114,556	119,652	127,236	128,519	130,904	138,862
Manufacturing	146,607	148,223	153,571	153,973	155,052	156,565	158,543
Durable goods manufacturing	116,467	117,570	121,639	121,323	121,562	121,133	121,258
Nondurable goods manufacturing	30,140	30,653	31,932	32,650	33,490	35,432	37,285
Wholesale trade	98,420	98,233	98,901	99,415	95,697	95,547	96,458
Retail trade	295,500	297,748	300,258	301,971	315,447	324,639	331,080
Transportation and warehousing	66,901	70,603	72,849	73,490	75,765	79,866	83,507
Information	36,660	36,764	38,239	41,815	43,400	45,142	45,393
Finance and insurance	121,252	124,943	129,249	135,852	140,639	149,790	157,107
Real estate and rental and leasing	46,260	45,935	47,027	48,170	48,850	49,215	50,774
Professional, scientific, and technical services	122,700	125,139	124,986	128,549	131,778	134,606	142,394
Management of companies and enterprises	25,435	25,216	26,607	28,756	29,704	31,362	31,735
Administrative and waste services	196,580	200,401	208,356	220,794	226,119	235,043	242,512
Educational services	52,022	54,240	57,053	55,988	57,492	59,002	59,443
Health care and social assistance	296,149	303,221	312,356	319,633	326,240	340,732	355,055
Arts, entertainment, and recreation	33,480	33,345	34,905	35,690	38,215	40,176	41,551
Accommodation and food services	221,955	227,441	233,464	241,618	249,775	260,758	269,960
Other services, except public administration	105,645	108,458	111,055	111,368	115,325	116,359	116,272
Government and government enterprises	448,988	441,850	443,141	444,366	445,155	444,076	445,996
	Dollars						
Average Wages and Salaries by Industry	44,140	45,407	46,489	46,839	47,842	48,854	51,770
Average Farm Wages and Salaries	34,082	34,114	35,557	36,287	39,505	34,127	33,948
Average Nonfarm Wages and Salaries	44,186	45,459	46,543	46,896	47,881	48,928	51,866
Average private wages and salaries	43,931	45,282	46,536	46,906	47,953	48,960	51,998
Forestry, fishing, and related activities	22,508	23,244	23,708	24,088	25,945	27,459	27,625
Mining	71,527	78,684	80,883	79,002	79,256	81,527	79,235
Utilities	92,220	95,406	95,578	97,520	102,471	101,084	106,056
Construction	45,048	45,979	47,923	48,410	49,558	50,250	57,068
Manufacturing	66,962	70,152	70,717	70,917	72,604	73,931	76,252
Durable goods manufacturing	73,536	77,288	77,914	78,209	80,159	82,036	84,533
Nondurable goods manufacturing	41,560	42,782	43,300	43,821	45,183	46,220	49,319
Wholesale trade	64,449	67,052	71,450	68,757	72,257	74,860	77,985
Retail trade	29,359	30,909	30,879	30,350	31,171	31,946	33,379
Transportation and warehousing	48,736	49,680	50,441	50,619	51,002	52,726	56,928
Information	57,968	59,857	61,681	63,189	66,702	67,836	70,587
Finance and insurance	61,074	63,794	67,151	69,575	70,991	73,041	78,527
Real estate and rental and leasing	42,689	44,645	46,793	46,633	48,599	50,255	52,981
Professional, scientific, and technical services	67,432	69,939	73,473	74,383	74,824	76,593	79,649
Management of companies and enterprises	74,633	77,280	82,733	85,738	92,231	89,840	93,850
Administrative and waste services	33,338	33,594	33,997	34,832	35,957	37,113	38,899
Educational services	39,255	39,910	40,687	40,912	41,221	40,846	42,507
Health care and social assistance	48,035	48,735	49,210	49,488	50,264	51,173	54,533
Arts, entertainment, and recreation	36,740	36,934	38,221	38,427	39,536	39,062	45,338
Accommodation and food services	19,903	20,337	20,993	21,309	21,959	22,802	24,930
Other services, except public administration	28,230	28,689	29,575	30,718	31,984	32,819	35,934
Government and government enterprises	45,332	46,283	46,579	46,849	47,520	48,761	51,170

Table AZ-10. Employment Characteristics by Family Type

(Number, percent.)

Family type and labor force status	2014 Total	2014 Families with own children under 18 years	2015 Total	2015 Families with own children under 18 years	2016 Total	2016 Families with own children under 18 years
All Families..	1,573,546	657,330	1,598,414	665,587	1,648,739	671,482
FAMILY TYPE AND LABOR FORCE STATUS						
Married-Couple Families..............................	1,135,360	428,399	1,153,542	426,411	1,194,185	440,131
Both husband and wife in labor force................	43.9	58.9	42.7	59.1	42.7	59.4
Husband in labor force, wife not in labor force	23.9	34.4	23.4	34.2	23.9	34.4
Wife in labor force, husband not in labor force	7.7	3.9	8.0	4.5	7.6	3.9
Both husband and wife not in labor force............	24.5	2.7	25.2	2.0	24.9	1.8
Other Families	438,186	228,931	444,872	239,176	454,554	231,351
Female householder, no husband present................	69.4	71.8	69.2	71.5	69.7	73.3
In labor force..	48.3	58.0	48.5	59.3	49.3	60.3
Not in labor force	21.1	13.8	20.6	12.3	20.4	13.0
Male householder, no wife present......................	30.6	28.2	30.8	28.5	30.3	26.7
In labor force..	24.3	25.6	24.5	25.4	23.8	23.9
Not in labor force	6.3	2.6	6.4	3.1	6.5	2.8

Table AZ-11. School Enrollment and Educational Attainment, 2016

(Number, percent.)

Item	State	U.S.
Enrollment		
Total population 3 years and over, enrolled in school	1,761,534	81,572,277
Enrolled in nursery school or preschool (percent)..	4.9	6.0
Enrolled in kindergarten (percent)..	5.1	5.0
Enrolled in elementary school, grades 1-8 (percent)...	41.7	40.3
Enrolled in high school, grades 9-12 (percent)...	21.6	21.0
Enrolled in college or graduate school (percent)..	26.8	27.7
Attainment		
Total population 25 years and over	4,626,409	218,475,480
Less than ninth grade (percent)..	5.7	5.4
9th to 12th grade, no diploma (percent)..	7.5	7.2
High school graduate, including equivalency (percent)..	23.9	27.2
Some college, no degree (percent)..	25.5	20.6
Associate's degree (percent)..	8.4	8.4
Bachelor's degree (percent)...	18.1	19.3
Graduate or professional degree (percent)..	10.8	11.9
High school graduate or higher (percent)...	86.7	87.5
Bachelor's degree or higher (percent)..	28.9	31.3

Table AZ-12. Public School Characteristics and Educational Indicators

(Number, percent; data derived from National Center of Education Statistics.)

Item	State	U.S.
Public Schools, 2015–2016 (except where noted)		
Number of school districts..	692	18,328
Number of schools..	2,284	98,456
Number of students	1,109,040	50,327,015
Number of teachers	47,944	3,151,497
Student-teacher ratio	23.1	16.0
Expenditures per student (dollars), 2014-2015..	7,590	11,445
Four-year adjusted cohort graduation rate (ACGR)[1,2]	79.5	84.1
Students eligible for free or reduced-price lunch (percent), 2014-2015............................	43.0	51.8
English language learners (percent), Fall 2015..	6.1	9.5
Students age 3 to 21 served under IDEA, part B (percent)...	12.0	13.2

Public Schools by Type	Number	Percent of state public schools
Total number of schools...	2,284	100.0
Regular	1,963	85.9
Special education..	20	0.9
Vocational education...	242	10.6
Alternative education..	59	2.6

NOTE: Every school is assigned only one school type based on its instructional emphasis.
[1] ACGR data represents a new method of calculating high-school completion rates and may not be comparable to previous years' data for Averaged Freshmen Graduation Rates (AFGR).
[2] The United States 4-year ACGRs were estimated using both the reported 4-year ACGR data from 49 states and the District of Columbia and using imputed data for Idaho. The estimate for American Indian/Alaska Native students also includes imputed data for Virginia.

Table AZ-13. Reported Voting and Registration of the Voting-Age Population, November 2016

(Numbers in thousands, percent.)

Item	Total population	Total citizen population	Registered			Voted		
			Total registered	Percent registered (total population)	Percent registered (total citizen population)	Total voted	Percent voted (total population)	Percent voted (total citizen population)
U.S. Total	245,502	224,059	157,596	64.2	70.3	137,537	56.0	61.4
State Total..............................	5,196	4,585	3,145	60.5	68.6	2,769	53.3	60.4
Sex								
Male	2,525	2,256	1,485	58.8	65.8	1,273	50.4	56.5
Female	2,671	2,329	1,660	62.2	71.3	1,496	56.0	64.2
Race								
White alone.....................	4,471	3,950	2,773	62.0	70.2	2,480	55.5	62.8
White, non-Hispanic alone	2,940	2,875	2,145	73.0	74.6	1,963	66.8	68.3
Black alone.................................	252	237	165	65.6	69.8	121	47.9	50.9
Asian alone..........................	169	108	69	40.6	63.3	56	33.1	51.6
Hispanic (of any race)......................	1,613	1,145	654	40.5	57.1	543	33.7	47.4
White alone or in combination	4,571	4,048	2,815	61.6	69.5	2,518	55.1	62.2
Black alone or in combination...........	296	281	183	61.7	65.0	138	46.6	49.1
Asian alone or in combination...........	180	117	78	43.0	66.1	56	31.0	47.7
Age								
18 to 24 years........................	735	654	346	47.1	52.8	263	35.8	40.2
25 to 34 years........................	854	729	460	53.9	63.1	377	44.1	51.7
35 to 44 years........................	776	663	423	54.5	63.7	349	45.0	52.6
45 to 64 years........................	1,736	1,510	1,143	65.9	75.7	1,038	59.8	68.7
65 years and over	1,096	1,028	774	70.6	75.3	743	67.8	72.2

Table AZ-14. Crime

(Number, rate per 100,000. Data are derived from the FBI Uniform Crime Reports.)

Item	State			U.S. [1,2,3,4]		
	2015	2016	Percent change	2015	2016	Percent change
TOTAL POPULATION [5]	6,828,065	6,931,071	1.5	321,418,820	323,127,513	0.5
VIOLENT CRIME						
Number...	28,012	32,583	16.3	1,231,566	1,248,185	1.3
Rate...	410.2	470.1	14.6	383.2	386.3	0.8
Murder and Nonnegligent Manslaughter						
Number...	309	380	23.0	15,696	17,250	9.9
Rate...	4.5	5.5	22.2	4.9	5.3	8.2
Rape [6]						
Number...	3,108	3,290	5.9	124,047	130,603	5.3
Rate...	45.5	47.5	4.4	38.6	40.4	4.7
Robbery						
Number...	6,360	7,055	10.9	327,374	332,198	1.5
Rate...	93.1	101.8	9.3	101.9	102.8	0.9
Aggravated Assault						
Number...	18,235	21,858	19.9	764,449	803,007	5.0
Rate...	267.1	315.4	18.1	237.8	248.5	4.5
PROPERTY CRIME						
Number...	207,107	206,432	-0.3	7,993,631	7,919,035	-0.9
Rate...	3,033.2	2,978.4	-1.8	2,487.0	2,450.7	-1.5
Burglary						
Number...	37,957	37,736	-0.6	1,579,527	1,515,096	-4.1
Rate...	555.9	544.4	-2.1	491.4	468.9	-4.6
Larceny-Theft						
Number...	152,365	150,275	-1.4	5,706,346	5,638,455	-1.2
Rate...	2,231.5	2,168.1	-2.8	1,775.4	1,745.0	-1.7
Motor Vehicle Theft						
Number...	16,785	18,421	9.7	707,758	765,484	8.2
Rate...	245.8	265.8	8.1	220.2	236.9	7.6

NOTE: Although arson data are included in the trend and clearance tables, sufficient data are not available to estimate totals for this offense. Therefore, no arson data are published in this table.

X = Not applicable.

- = Zero or rounds to zero.

[1] Because of changes in the state's reporting practices, figures are not comparable to previous years' data.

[2] The data collection methodology for the offense of forcible rape used by the Minnesota state Uniform Crime Reporting (UCR) Program (with the exception of Minneapolis and St. Paul, Minnesota) does not comply with national UCR Program guidelines. Consequently, its figures for forcible rape and violent crime (of which forcible rape is a part) are not published in this table.

[3] Includes offenses reported by the Zoological Police and the Metro Transit Police.

[4] The crime figures have been adjusted.

[5] Populations are U.S. Census Bureau provisional estimates as of July 1 of each year.

[6] The figures shown for the offense of rape were estimated using the revised Uniform Crime Reporting (UCR) definition of rape.

Table AZ-15. State Government Finances, 2016

(Dollar amounts in thousands, percent distribution.)

Item	Dollars	Percent distribution
Total Revenue	38,338,699	100.0
General revenue	34,689,284	90.5
Intergovernmental revenue	14,629,239	38.2
Taxes	14,693,921	38.3
General sales	6,660,817	17.4
Selective sales	2,019,192	5.3
License taxes	499,908	1.3
Individual income tax	3,967,924	10.3
Corporate income tax	570,548	1.5
Other taxes	975,532	2.5
Current charges	2,880,476	7.5
Miscellaneous general revenue	2,485,648	6.5
Utility revenue	29,095	0.1
Liquor stores revenue	0	-
Insurance trust revenue [1]	3,620,320	9.4
Total Expenditure	42,204,155	100.0
Intergovernmental expenditure	10,905,314	25.8
Direct expenditure	31,298,841	74.2
Current operation	24,140,918	57.2
Capital outlay	1,597,391	3.8
Insurance benefits and repayments	4,266,980	10.1
Assistance and subsidies	654,100	1.5
Interest on debt	639,452	1.5
Exhibit: Salaries and wages	3,973,399	9.4
Total Expenditure	42,204,155	100.0
General expenditure	37,907,557	89.8
Intergovernmental expenditure	10,905,314	25.8
Direct expenditure	27,002,243	64.0
General expenditure, by function:		
Education	12,806,598	30.3
Public welfare	14,300,784	33.9
Hospitals	53,321	0.1
Health	2,640,144	6.3
Highways	2,194,035	5.2
Police protection	247,392	0.6
Correction	1,074,044	2.5
Natural resources	287,964	0.7
Parks and recreation	80,650	0.2
Governmental administration	777,015	1.8
Interest on general debt	637,325	1.5
Other and unallocable	2,808,285	6.7
Utility expenditure	29,618	0.1
Liquor stores expenditure	0	-
Insurance trust expenditure	4,266,980	10.1
Debt at End of Fiscal Year	14,400,191	X
Cash and Security Holdings	58,120,830	X

X = Not applicable.
- = Zero or rounds to zero.
[1] Within insurance trust revenue, net earnings of state retirement systems is a calculated statistic (the item code in the data file is X08), and thus can be positive or negative. Net earnings is the sum of earnings on investments plus gains on investments minus losses on investments. The change made in 2002 for asset valuation from book to market value in accordance with Statement 34 of the Governmental Accounting Standards Board is reflected in the calculated statistics.

Table AZ-16. State Government Tax Collections, 2017

(Dollars in thousands, percent.)

Item	Dollars	Percent distribution
Total Taxes	13,888,611	100.0
Property taxes	993,615	7.2
Sales and gross receipts	8,539,726	61.5
General sales and gross receipts	6,566,503	47.3
Selective sales and gross receipts	1,973,223	14.2
Alcoholic beverages	74,126	0.5
Amusements	X	-
Insurance premiums	536,820	3.9
Motor fuels	856,495	6.2
Pari-mutuels	129	-
Public utilities	22,325	0.2
Tobacco products	310,706	2.2
Other selective sales	172,622	1.2
Licenses	505,494	3.6
Alcoholic beverages	8,921	0.1
Amusements	X	-
Corporations in general	41,357	0.3
Hunting and fishing	35,849	0.3
Motor vehicle	215,991	1.6
Motor vehicle operators	31,074	0.2
Public utilities	X	-
Occupation and business, NEC	170,700	1.2
Other licenses	1,602	-
Income taxes	3,813,786	27.5
Individual income	3,445,650	24.8
Corporation net income	368,136	2.7
Other taxes	35,990	0.3
Death and gift	X	-
Documentary and stock transfer	17,613	0.1
Severance	18,377	0.1
Taxes, NEC	0	-

- = Zero or rounds to zero.
X = Not applicable.

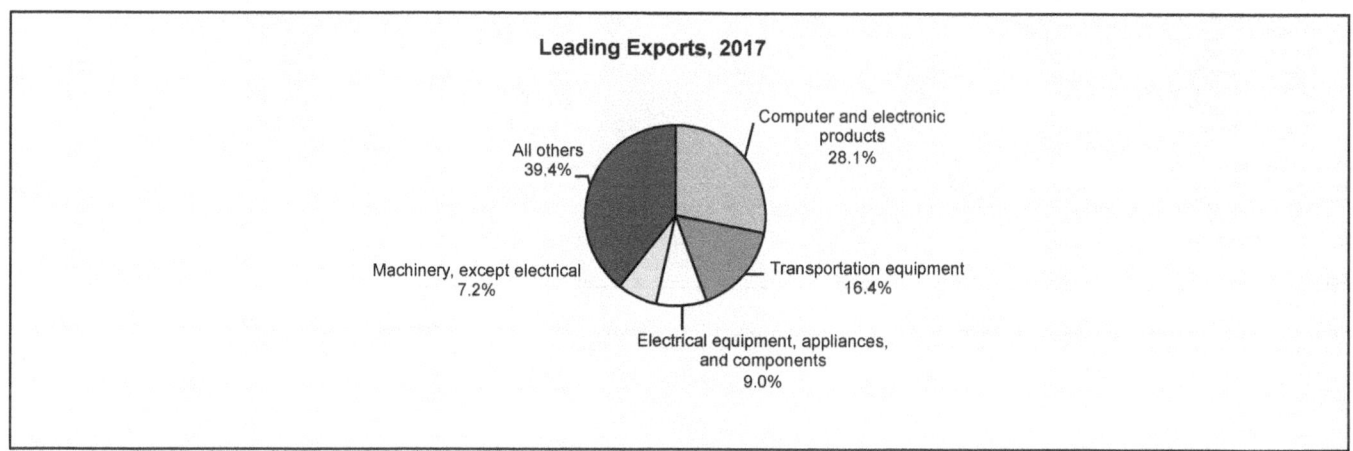

Leading Exports, 2017

Computer and electronic products 28.1%

All others 39.4%

Transportation equipment 16.4%

Machinery, except electrical 7.2%

Electrical equipment, appliances, and components 9.0%

ARKANSAS

Facts and Figures

Location: South central United States; bordered on the N by Missouri, on the E by Tennessee and Mississippi, on the S by Louisiana, and on the W by Oklahoma and Texas

Area: 53,178 sq. mi. (137,733 sq. km.); rank—29th

Population: 3,004,279 (2017 est.); rank—32nd

Principal Cities: capital—Little Rock; largest—Little Rock

Statehood: June 15, 1836; 25th state

U.S. Congress: 2 senators, 4 representatives

State Motto: *Regnat populus* ("The people rule")

State Song: "Arkansas"

State Nicknames: The Natural State; The Land of Opportunity

Abbreviations: AR; Ark.

State Symbols: flower—apple blossom; tree—pine; bird—mockingbird

At a Glance

- With an increase in population of 2.8 percent, Arkansas ranked 30th among the states in growth from 2010 to 2017.

- In 2016, 22.4 percent of Arkansas residents had a bachelor's degree or higher, the 3rd lowest percent in the nation.

- Arkansas's median household income in 2016 was $44,334, and 17.2 percent of the population lived below the poverty level.

- In 2016, 7.9 percent of Arkansans did not have health insurance, which was down from 9.5 percent the previous year.

- Arkansas' property crime rate in 2016 was 3,268.6 per 100,000 population, which ranked 6th in the nation.

Table AR-1. Population by Age, Sex, Race, and Hispanic Origin

(Number, percent, except where noted.)

Sex, age, race, and Hispanic origin	2000	2010	2017 [1]	Average annual percent change, 2010–2017
Total Population...	2,673,400	2,915,918	3,004,279	3.0
Percent of total U.S. population	0.9	0.9	0.9	X
Sex				
Male..	1,304,693	1,431,637	1,476,064	3.1
Female	1,368,707	1,484,281	1,528,215	3.0
Age				
Under 5 years...	181,585	197,689	191,435	-3.2
5 to 19 years..	578,924	598,241	592,628	-0.9
20 to 64 years..	1,538,872	1,700,007	1,721,072	1.2
65 years and over	374,019	419,981	499,144	18.8
Median age (years)......................................	36.0	37.4	38.1	1.9
Race and Hispanic Origin				
One race				
White	2,138,598	2,342,403	2,381,662	1.7
Black..	418,950	454,021	471,145	3.8
American Indian and Alaska Native	17,808	26,134	29,722	13.7
Asian..	20,220	37,537	49,292	31.3
Native Hawaiian or Other Pacific Islander	1,668	6,685	9,653	44.4
Two or more races	35,744	49,138	62,805	27.8
Hispanic (of any race)......................................	86,866	191,535	227,673	18.9

X = Not applicable.
[1] Population figures for 2017 are July 1 estimates. The 2010 estimates are taken from the 2010 Census.

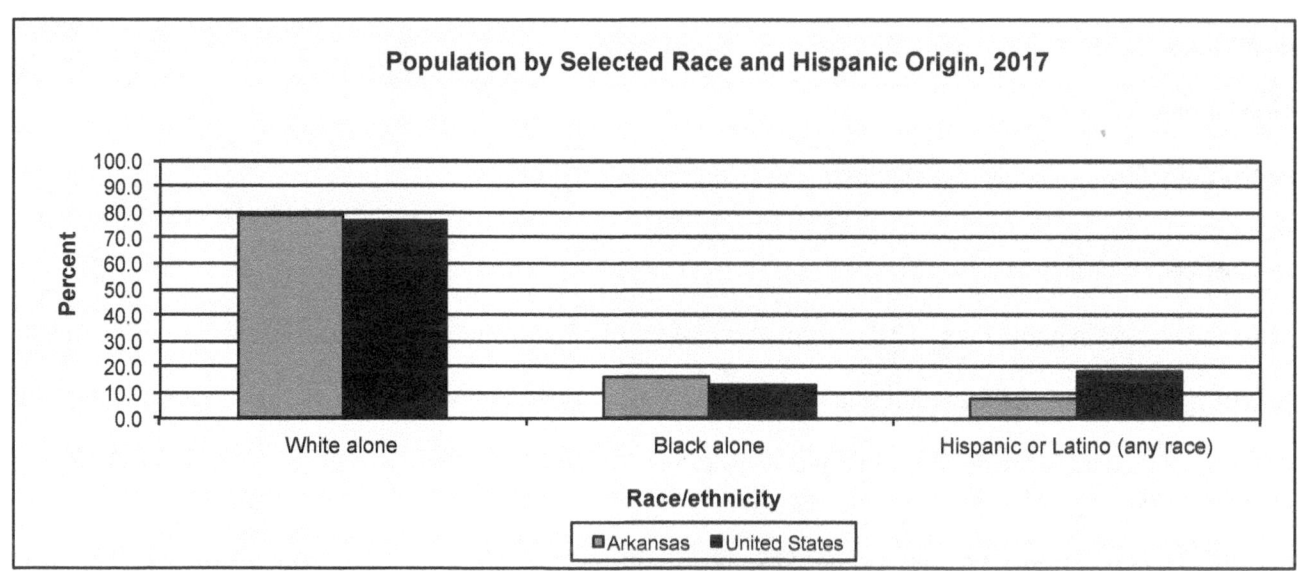

Population by Selected Race and Hispanic Origin, 2017

□ Arkansas ■ United States

Table AR-2. Marital Status

(Number, percent distribution.)

Sex, age, and marital status	2000	2010	2016
Males, 15 Years and Over	1,015,594	1,128,804	1,164,988
Never married	24.2	29.5	31.4
Now married, except separated...................................	61.0	53.3	50.8
Separated..	1.6	2.2	2.2
Widowed...	2.7	3.1	3.2
Divorced...	10.4	12.0	12.4
Females, 15 Years and Over	1,096,069	1,200,974	1,235,920
Never married	18.4	23.5	25.0
Now married, except separated...................................	55.7	48.8	47.2
Separated..	2.2	2.9	3.0
Widowed...	12.2	11.2	10.3
Divorced...	11.6	13.6	14.5

Table AR-3. Households and Housing Characteristics

(Number, percent, dollars.)

Item	2000	2010	2016	Average annual percent change, 2010–2016
Total Households	1,042,696	1,114,902	1,142,718	0.4
Family households	732,261	761,361	747,917	-0.3
Married-couple family	566,401	554,946	549,997	-0.1
Other family	165,860	206,415	197,920	-0.7
Male householder, no wife present	39,299	51,620	47,221	-1.4
Female householder, no husband present	126,561	154,795	150,699	-0.4
Nonfamily households	310,435	353,541	394,801	1.9
Householder living alone	266,585	302,127	334,369	1.8
Householder not living alone	43,850	51,414	60,432	2.9
Housing Characteristics				
Total housing units	1,173,043	1,317,818	1,354,801	0.5
Occupied housing units	1,042,696	1,114,902	1,142,718	0.4
Owner occupied	723,535	751,568	737,632	-0.3
Renter occupied	319,161	363,334	405,086	1.9
Average household size	2.49	2.55	2.54	-0.1
Financial Characteristics				
Median gross rent of renter-occupied housing	453	638	701	1.6
Median monthly owner costs for housing units with a mortgage	737	987	1017	0.5
Median value of owner-occupied housing units	72,800	106,300	123,300	2.7

Table AR-4. Migration, Origin, and Language

(Number, percent.)

Characteristic	State			U.S.		
	2015	2016	Percent change	2015	2016	Percent change
Residence 1 Year Ago						
Population 1 year and over	2,938,341	2,949,650	0.4	317,635,720	319,361,956	0.5
Same house	83.1	84.2	X	85.3	85.4	X
Different house in the U.S.	16.6	15.5	X	14.1	13.9	X
Same county	9.9	9.4	X	8.5	8.3	X
Different county	6.7	6.1	X	5.6	5.6	X
Same state	3.9	3.7	X	3.2	3.2	X
Different state	2.8	2.4	X	2.4	2.4	X
Abroad	0.3	0.3	X	0.7	0.7	X
Place of Birth						
Native born	2835363	2,849,656	0.5	278,128,449	279,388,170	0.5
Male	49.0	49.1	X	49.3	49.3	X
Female	51.0	50.9	X	50.7	50.7	X
Foreign born	142841	138,592	-3.0	43,290,372	43,739,345	1.0
Male	51.2	49.4	X	48.6	48.5	X
Female	48.8	50.6	X	51.4	51.5	X
Foreign born; naturalized U.S. citizen	47232	44,284	-6.2	20,697,103	21,238,372	2.6
Male	47.5	50.6	X	45.9	45.9	X
Female	52.5	49.4	X	54.1	54.1	X
Foreign born; not a U.S. citizen	95609	94,308	-1.4	22,593,269	22,500,973	-0.4
Male	53.1	48.8	X	51.1	51	X
Female	46.9	51.2	X	48.9	49	X
Entered 2010 or later	16.3	22	X	15.6	18.6	X
Entered 2000 to 2009	37.4	28.6	X	27.9	26.7	X
Entered before 2000	46.2	49.4	X	56.5	54.7	X
World Region of Birth, Foreign						
Foreign-born population, excluding population born at sea	142841	138,592	-3.0	43,289,646	43,738,901	1.0
Europe	6.9	7.9	X	11.1	10.9	X
Asia	24.3	23.7	X	30.6	30.8	X
Africa	2.4	3.7	X	4.8	4.9	X
Oceania	3.2	4.5	X	0.6	0.6	X
Latin America	61.3	58.9	X	51.1	51	X
North America	1.9	1.3	X	1.9	1.8	X
Language Spoken at Home and Ability to Speak English						
Population 5 years and over	2789500	2,799,532	0.4	301,625,014	303,328,961	0.6
English only	92.7	92.7	X	78.5	78.4	X
Language other than English	7.3	7.3	X	21.5	21.6	X
Speaks English less than "very well"	3.3	3.1	X	8.6	8.6	X

NA = Not available.
X = Not applicable.
- = Zero or rounds to zero.

Table AR-5. Median Income and Poverty Status, 2016

(Number, percent, except as noted.)

Characteristic	State		U.S.	
	Number	Percent	Number	Percent
Median Income				
Households (dollars)..	44,334	X	57,617	X
Families (dollars)	55,484	X	71,062	X
Below Poverty Level (All People)...................................	499,225	17.2	44,268,996	14.0
Sex				
Male..	223,750	15.8	19,760,056	12.8
Female	275,475	18.6	24,508,940	15.2
Age				
Under 18 years...	165,100	23.8	14,115,713	19.5
Related children under 18 years.....................................	161,993	23.5	13,805,435	19.1
18 to 64 years..	284,551	16.4	25,723,818	13.2
65 years and over	49,574	10.5	4,429,465	9.2

X = Not applicable.

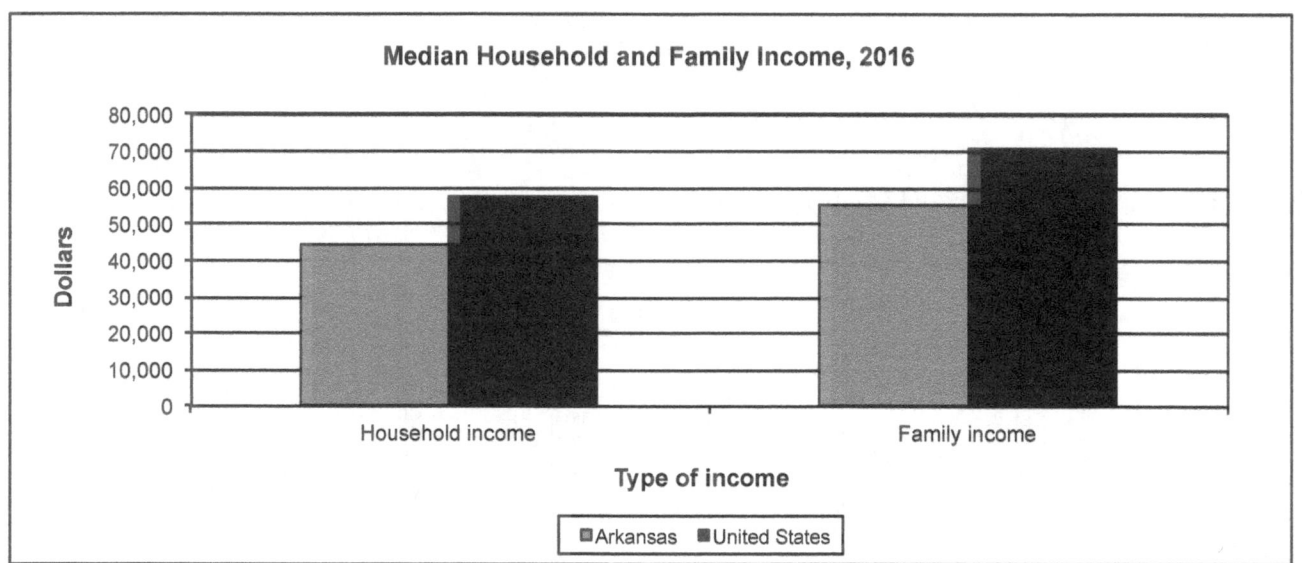

Median Household and Family Income, 2016

Table AR-6. Health Insurance Coverage Status for the Civilian Noninstitutionalized Population and Children Under 18 Years of Age

(Number, percent.)

Item	2008	2009	2010	2011	2012	2013	2014	2015	2016
Civilian Noninstitutionalized Population	2,801,628	2,833,391	2,867,611	2,885,212	2,896,297	2,907,014	2,914,376	2,924,307	2,934,272
Covered by Private or Public Insurance									
Number..	2,296,493	2,350,818	2,366,998	2,392,902	2,419,987	2,442,064	2,571,205	2,646,760	2,702,497
Percent...	82.0	83.0	82.5	82.9	83.6	84.0	88.2	90.5	92.1
Not Covered									
Number..	505,135	482,573	500,613	492,310	476,310	464,950	343,171	277,547	231,775
Percent...	18.0	17.0	17.5	17.1	16.4	16.0	11.8	9.5	7.9
Percent in the U.S. not covered....................................	15.1	15.1	15.5	15.1	14.8	14.5	11.7	9.4	8.6
Children Under 18 Years of Age	701,489	706,684	709,374	708,888	709,407	709,125	703,811	703,701	705,155
Covered by Private or Public Insurance									
Number..	640,134	662,623	662,879	668,938	667,257	669,866	669,732	669,147	679,612
Percent...	91.3	93.8	93.4	94.4	94.1	94.5	95.2	95.1	96.4
Not Covered									
Number..	61,355	44,061	46,495	39,950	42,150	39,259	34,079	34,554	25,543
Percent...	8.7	6.2	6.6	5.6	5.9	5.5	4.8	4.9	3.6
Percent in the U.S. not covered....................................	9.9	8.6	8.0	7.5	7.2	7.1	6.0	4.8	4.5

Table AR-7. Employment Status by Demographic Group, 2017

(Numbers in thousands, percent.)

Characteristic	Civilian noninstitutional population	Civilian labor force		Employed		Unemployed	
		Number	Percent of population	Number	Percent of population	Number	Percent of population
Total..	2,327	1,362	58.5	1,312	56.4	50	3.7
Sex							
Male........................	1,119	702	62.8	674	60.3	28	4.0
Female......................	1,208	660	54.6	638	52.8	22	3.3
Race, Sex, and Hispanic Origin							
White........................	1,868	1,084	58.0	1,048	56.1	36	3.3
Male........................	906	568	62.6	548	60.4	20	3.5
Female......................	961	516	53.7	500	52.0	16	3.0
Black or African American...........	341	208	61.1	197	57.8	11	5.3
Male........................	153	93	61.1	87	57.0	6	6.7
Female......................	188	115	61.1	110	58.5	5	4.2
Hispanic or Latino ethnicity[1].......	148	104	70.4	102	69.0	2	2.0
Male........................	75	63	83.4	62	82.0	1	1.5
Female......................	73	41	57.0	40	55.4	1	2.7
Age							
16 to 19 years.................	156	49	31.1	44	28.5	4	8.6
20 to 24 years.................	209	156	74.6	147	70.2	9	6.0
25 to 34 years.................	397	322	81.2	309	77.9	13	4.1
35 to 44 years.................	333	263	79.0	253	76.1	10	3.7
45 to 54 years.................	369	286	77.6	280	75.8	7	2.3
55 to 64 years.................	368	203	55.2	198	53.8	5	2.6
65 years and over..............	495	82	16.6	81	16.3	2	1.8

NOTE: Data in Table 7 are from the Current Population Survey (CPS) and do not match the estimates in Table 8. See notes and definitions for further information.
[1] May be of any race.

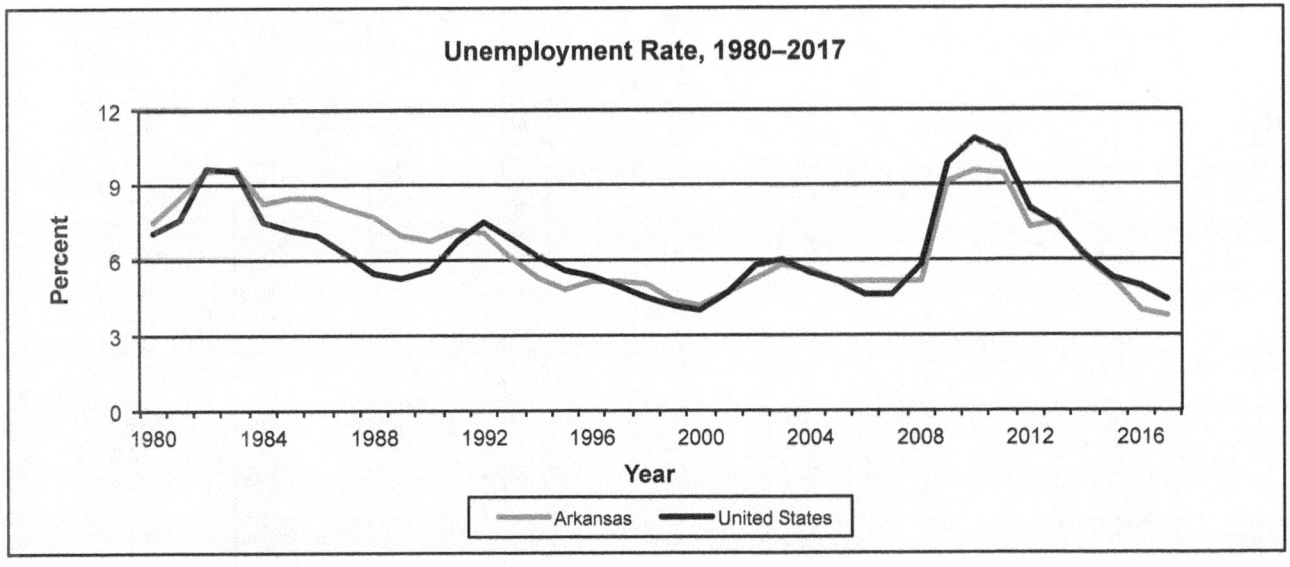

Table AR-8. Employment Status of the Civilian Noninstitutional Population Age 16 Years and Over

(Number, percent.)

Year	Civilian labor force	Civilian participation rate	Employed	Unemployed	Unemployment rate
2009..................................	1,358,911	61.7	1,252,399	106,512	7.8
2010..................................	1,353,338	60.6	1,242,496	110,842	8.2
2011..................................	1,362,682	60.5	1,249,514	113,168	8.3
2012..................................	1,342,753	59.3	1,241,127	101,626	7.6
2013..................................	1,322,576	58.2	1,226,859	95,717	7.2
2014..................................	1,316,595	57.6	1,237,316	79,279	6.0
2015..................................	1,332,255	58.0	1,265,166	67,089	5.0
2016..................................	1,342,561	58.1	1,289,549	53,012	3.9
2017..................................	1,354,265	58.2	1,304,434	49,831	3.7

Table AR-9. Employment and Average Wages by Industry

(Estimates through 2010 are based on the 2007 *North American Industry Classification System* [NAICS]. Estimates from 2011 onward are based on the 2012 NAICS.)

Industry	2010	2011	2012	2013	2014	2015	2016
	Number of Jobs						
Wage and Salary Employment by Industry	1,221,252	1,225,681	1,230,546	1,232,187	1,244,466	1,264,657	1,280,755
Farm Wage and Salary Employment	12,869	12,021	9,006	11,182	11,319	12,578	15,486
Nonfarm Wage and Salary Employment	1,208,383	1,213,660	1,221,540	1,221,005	1,233,147	1,252,079	1,265,269
Private wage and salary employment	971,515	979,016	985,988	987,105	1,000,809	1,021,901	1,036,313
Forestry, fishing, and related activities	8,258	7,967	8,101	8,115	8,157	8,046	8,194
Mining	8,523	8,985	8,657	7,530	6,708	5,873	4,137
Utilities	7,313	7,169	7,705	8,089	7,903	7,951	7,710
Construction	50,544	48,838	48,847	46,791	47,407	50,485	51,712
Manufacturing	158,433	157,440	154,607	152,129	153,251	155,058	154,996
Durable goods manufacturing	77,131	77,746	76,820	75,356	76,252	75,989	74,309
Nondurable goods manufacturing	81,302	79,694	77,787	76,773	76,999	79,069	80,687
Wholesale trade	46,626	46,850	47,441	46,495	46,754	47,426	46,444
Retail trade	130,519	132,451	133,585	134,090	137,217	141,488	143,254
Transportation and warehousing	52,146	53,934	54,596	54,171	55,061	56,828	57,140
Information	16,515	16,108	15,592	15,365	14,843	13,319	13,247
Finance and insurance	36,372	37,239	36,780	37,092	37,069	37,430	38,489
Real estate and rental and leasing	13,789	13,547	13,510	13,460	13,227	13,360	13,550
Professional, scientific, and technical services	38,900	39,528	39,151	40,225	40,964	41,677	42,904
Management of companies and enterprises	26,738	26,907	30,913	31,441	32,437	33,438	35,077
Administrative and waste services	53,009	55,576	54,558	57,999	61,233	64,365	65,280
Educational services	15,129	15,655	15,678	16,390	16,584	16,870	16,529
Health care and social assistance	156,054	156,453	159,899	160,153	160,680	163,557	169,166
Arts, entertainment, and recreation	9,883	9,731	9,788	10,121	10,572	10,772	11,294
Accommodation and food services	89,699	91,063	93,593	95,424	97,765	101,566	104,827
Other services, except public administration	53,065	53,575	52,987	52,025	52,977	52,392	52,363
Government and government enterprises	236,868	234,644	235,552	233,900	232,338	230,178	228,956
	Dollars						
Average Wages and Salaries by Industry	36,691	37,817	38,937	39,629	40,543	41,486	43,224
Average Farm Wages and Salaries	18,934	17,819	29,729	26,322	22,053	25,880	21,878
Average Nonfarm Wages and Salaries	36,880	38,015	39,005	39,751	40,712	41,642	43,486
Average private wages and salaries	36,679	37,880	39,082	39,854	40,899	41,839	43,739
Forestry, fishing, and related activities	30,742	31,572	32,519	33,099	34,505	36,005	38,652
Mining	64,511	67,673	67,717	69,194	71,794	70,910	59,791
Utilities	71,615	74,945	76,779	79,103	82,609	83,802	87,159
Construction	40,231	40,819	42,242	41,654	43,215	44,960	48,148
Manufacturing	40,887	42,273	43,532	44,371	45,840	46,351	48,975
Durable goods manufacturing	42,775	44,395	45,634	46,752	48,169	48,428	51,374
Nondurable goods manufacturing	39,095	40,202	41,456	42,034	43,534	44,355	46,765
Wholesale trade	56,406	58,129	59,853	62,363	63,910	66,669	69,671
Retail trade	23,930	24,346	24,925	25,296	25,762	26,274	27,401
Transportation and warehousing	41,535	44,119	45,360	46,259	47,697	48,217	47,900
Information	48,326	50,153	49,648	51,185	53,445	55,801	55,015
Finance and insurance	52,581	54,870	57,766	57,838	59,827	61,952	64,167
Real estate and rental and leasing	31,484	32,897	34,298	34,671	35,918	37,125	39,082
Professional, scientific, and technical services	53,109	56,451	55,002	57,066	58,223	59,886	63,104
Management of companies and enterprises	88,420	89,560	95,986	103,321	105,614	107,717	110,392
Administrative and waste services	25,905	26,984	27,163	26,922	27,590	28,080	30,076
Educational services	26,038	26,731	26,725	27,338	27,793	27,842	28,999
Health care and social assistance	36,313	37,536	38,496	39,139	40,283	41,617	44,320
Arts, entertainment, and recreation	19,233	20,402	20,771	21,039	21,418	22,336	23,652
Accommodation and food services	14,573	15,048	15,616	15,831	16,287	16,931	18,193
Other services, except public administration	25,831	26,395	27,368	28,254	29,334	30,670	32,286
Government and government enterprises	37,705	38,582	38,680	39,318	39,909	40,769	42,339

Table AR-10. Employment Characteristics by Family Type

(Number, percent.)

Family type and labor force status	2014		2015		2016	
	Total	Families with own children under 18 years	Total	Families with own children under 18 years	Total	Families with own children under 18 years
All Families...	749,751	310,218	761,494	311,436	747,917	305,770
FAMILY TYPE AND LABOR FORCE STATUS						
Married-Couple Families.............................	544,067	197,290	561,297	205,898	549,997	199,797
Both husband and wife in labor force............	46.9	64.9	47.0	62.4	46.4	64.7
Husband in labor force, wife not in labor force	22.5	27.5	21.7	29.2	21.9	26.9
Wife in labor force, husband not in labor force	9.1	5.0	9.0	5.0	10.1	6.1
Both husband and wife not in labor force.........	21.5	2.6	21.8	3.1	21.2	2.2
Other Families	205,684	112,928	200,197	105,538	197,920	105,973
Female householder, no husband present............	74	75.6	75.0	74.9	76.1	77.7
In labor force.......................................	48.3	59.8	48.0	59.3	50.3	62.6
Not in labor force..................................	25.6	15.8	26.9	15.5	25.9	15.2
Male householder, no wife present.................	26.0	24.4	25.0	25.1	23.9	22.3
In labor force.......................................	19.5	21.5	18.3	21.5	17.4	19.7
Not in labor force..................................	6.6	3.0	6.8	3.6	6.5	2.5

Table AR-11. School Enrollment and Educational Attainment, 2016

(Number, percent.)

Item	State	U.S.
Enrollment		
Total population 3 years and over, enrolled in school	739,490	81,572,277
Enrolled in nursery school or preschool (percent)...................	6.4	6.0
Enrolled in kindergarten (percent)...................	5.8	5.0
Enrolled in elementary school, grades 1-8 (percent)...................	42.1	40.3
Enrolled in high school, grades 9-12 (percent)	21.7	21.0
Enrolled in college or graduate school (percent)...................	24.0	27.7
Attainment		
Total population 25 years and over	1,990,448	218,475,480
Less than ninth grade (percent)	5.0	5.4
9th to 12th grade, no diploma (percent)	9.0	7.2
High school graduate, including equivalency (percent)...................	34.3	27.2
Some college, no degree (percent)...................	22.6	20.6
Associate's degree (percent)...................	6.7	8.4
Bachelor's degree (percent)...................	14.2	19.3
Graduate or professional degree (percent)...................	8.2	11.9
High school graduate or higher (percent)...................	86.0	87.5
Bachelor's degree or higher (percent)...................	22.4	31.3

Table AR-12. Public School Characteristics and Educational Indicators

(Number, percent; data derived from National Center of Education Statistics.)

Item	State	U.S.
Public Schools, 2014–2015 (except where noted)		
Number of school districts...................	289	18,328
Number of schools...................	1,088	98,456
Number of students...................	492,132	50,327,015
Number of teachers	35,804	3,151,497
Student-teacher ratio...................	13.7	16.0
Expenditures per student (dollars), FY 2014	9,805	11,445
Four-year adjusted cohort graduation rate (ACGR)[1,2]	87.0	84.1
Students eligible for free or reduced-price lunch (percent)...................	62.3	51.8
English language learners (percent)...................	7.8	9.5
Students age 3 to 21 served under IDEA, part B (percent)...................	13.9	13.2

Public Schools by Type	Number	Percent of state public schools
Total number of schools...................	1,088	100.0
Regular	1,052	96.7
Special education...................	4	0.4
Vocational education...................	26	2.4
Alternative education...................	6	0.6

NOTE: Every school is assigned only one school type based on its instructional emphasis.
[1] ACGR data represents a new method of calculating high-school completion rates and may not be comparable to previous years' data for Averaged Freshmen Graduation Rates (AFGR).
[2] The United States 4-year ACGRs were estimated using both the reported 4-year ACGR data from 49 states and the District of Columbia and using imputed data for Idaho. The estimate for American Indian/Alaska Native students also includes imputed data for Virginia.

Table AR-13. Reported Voting and Registration of the Voting-Age Population, November 2016

(Numbers in thousands, percent.)

Item	Total population	Total citizen population	Registered			Voted		
			Total registered	Percent registered (total population)	Percent registered (total citizen population)	Total voted	Percent voted (total population)	Percent voted (total citizen population)
U.S. Total	245,502	224,059	157,596	64.2	70.3	137,537	56.0	61.4
State Total..............................	2,216	2,116	1,456	65.7	68.8	1,241	56.0	58.7
Sex								
Male	1,055	1,001	679	64.4	67.8	574	54.4	57.4
Female	1,161	1,115	777	66.9	69.7	667	57.4	59.8
Race								
White alone..............................	1,822	1,749	1,196	65.6	68.4	1,032	56.7	59.0
White, non-Hispanic alone	1,689	1,674	1,166	69.1	69.7	1,008	59.7	60.2
Black alone................................	321	316	231	71.9	73.0	186	57.9	58.8
Asian alone	36	16	6	(B)	(B)	6	(B)	(B)
Hispanic (of any race)................	135	77	29	(B)	(B)	24	(B)	(B)
White alone or in combination	1,848	1,775	1,213	65.6	68.3	1,043	56.5	58.8
Black alone or in combination	325	320	235	72.2	73.3	190	58.4	59.3
Asian alone or in combination	36	16	6	(B)	(B)	6	(B)	(B)
Age								
18 to 24 years............................	187	180	92	49.1	51.2	62	33.1	34.5
25 to 34 years............................	409	367	224	54.8	61.1	173	42.3	47.1
35 to 44 years............................	387	362	244	63.1	67.5	211	54.5	58.3
45 to 64 years............................	716	697	503	70.2	72.2	452	63.1	64.8
65 years and over	516	510	392	76.0	76.9	343	66.6	67.3

B = Base is less than 75,000 and therefore too small to show the derived measure.

Table AR-14. Crime

(Number, rate per 100,000. Data are derived from the FBI Uniform Crime Reports.)

Item	State			U.S. [1,2,3,4]		
	2015	2016	Percent change	2015	2016	Percent change
TOTAL POPULATION [5]	2,978,204	2,988,248	0.3	321,418,820	323,127,513	0.5
VIOLENT CRIME						
Number...	15,526	16,461	6.0	1,231,566	1,248,185	1.3
Rate	521.3	550.9	5.7	383.2	386.3	0.8
Murder and Nonnegligent Manslaughter						
Number...	181	216	19.3	15,696	17,250	9.9
Rate	6.1	7.2	18.0	4.9	5.3	8.2
Rape[6]						
Number...	1,931	2,143	11.0	124,047	130,603	5.3
Rate	64.8	71.7	10.6	38.6	40.4	4.7
Robbery						
Number...	2,098	2,120	1.0	327,374	332,198	1.5
Rate	70.4	70.9	0.7	101.9	102.8	0.9
Aggravated Assault						
Number...	11,316	11,982	5.9	764,449	803,007	5.0
Rate	380.0	401.0	5.5	237.8	248.5	4.5
PROPERTY CRIME						
Number...	96,836	97,673	0.9	7,993,631	7,919,035	-0.9
Rate	3,251.5	3,268.6	0.5	2,487.0	2,450.7	-1.5
Burglary						
Number...	22,640	23,771	5.0	1,579,527	1,515,096	-4.1
Rate	760.2	795.5	4.6	491.4	468.9	-4.6
Larceny-Theft						
Number...	68,424	66,747	-2.5	5,706,346	5,638,455	-1.2
Rate	2,297.5	2,233.6	-2.8	1,775.4	1,745.0	-1.7
Motor Vehicle Theft						
Number...	5,772	7,155	24.0	707,758	765,484	8.2
Rate	193.8	239.4	23.5	220.2	236.9	7.6

NOTE: Although arson data are included in the trend and clearance tables, sufficient data are not available to estimate totals for this offense. Therefore, no arson data are published in this table.
X = Not applicable.
- = Zero or rounds to zero.
[1] The crime figures have been adjusted.
[2] The data collection methodology for the offense of forcible rape used by the Minnesota state Uniform Crime Reporting (UCR) Program (with the exception of Minneapolis and St. Paul, Minnesota) does not comply with national UCR Program guidelines. Consequently, its figures for forcible rape and violent crime (of which forcible rape is a part) are not published in this table.
[3] Includes offenses reported by the Zoological Police and the Metro Transit Police.
[4] Because of changes in the state's reporting practices, figures are not comparable to previous years' data.
[5] Populations are U.S. Census Bureau provisional estimates as of July 1 of each year.
[6] The figures shown for the offense of rape were estimated using the revised Uniform Crime Reporting (UCR) definition of rape.

Table AR-15. State Government Finances, 2016

(Dollar amounts in thousands, percent distribution.)

Item	Dollars	Percent distribution
Total Revenue	21,439,227	100.0
General revenue	20,346,096	94.9
Intergovernmental revenue	7,431,541	34.7
Taxes	9,452,883	44.1
General sales	3,314,363	15.5
Selective sales	1,275,709	6.0
License taxes	396,891	1.9
Individual income tax	2,781,458	13.0
Corporate income tax	450,159	2.1
Other taxes	1,234,303	5.8
Current charges	2,454,868	11.5
Miscellaneous general revenue	1,006,804	4.7
Utility revenue	0	-
Liquor stores revenue	0	-
Insurance trust revenue [1]	1,093,131	5.1
Total Expenditure	22,910,901	100.0
Intergovernmental expenditure	5,882,840	25.7
Direct expenditure	17,028,061	74.3
Current operation	13,374,375	58.4
Capital outlay	1,101,042	4.8
Insurance benefits and repayments	1,936,105	8.5
Assistance and subsidies	485,634	2.1
Interest on debt	130,905	0.6
Exhibit: Salaries and wages	3,006,878	13.1
Total Expenditure	22,910,901	100.0
General expenditure	20,974,796	91.5
Intergovernmental expenditure	5,882,840	25.7
Direct expenditure	15,091,956	65.9
General expenditure, by function:		
Education	8,449,234	36.9
Public welfare	6,979,738	30.5
Hospitals	1,021,700	4.5
Health	296,508	1.3
Highways	1,443,384	6.3
Police protection	119,889	0.5
Correction	429,314	1.9
Natural resources	324,202	1.4
Parks and recreation	71,110	0.3
Governmental administration	658,278	2.9
Interest on general debt	130,905	0.6
Other and unallocable	1,050,534	4.6
Utility expenditure	0	-
Liquor stores expenditure	0	-
Insurance trust expenditure	1,936,105	8.5
Debt at End of Fiscal Year	4,828,756	X
Cash and Security Holdings	32,770,092	X

X = Not applicable.
- = Zero or rounds to zero.
[1] Within insurance trust revenue, net earnings of state retirement systems is a calculated statistic (the item code in the data file is X08), and thus can be positive or negative. Net earnings is the sum of earnings on investments plus gains on investments minus losses on investments. The change made in 2002 for asset valuation from book to market value in accordance with Statement 34 of the Governmental Accounting Standards Board is reflected in the calculated statistics.

Table AR-16. State Government Tax Collections, 2017

(Dollars in thousands, percent.)

Item	Dollars	Percent distribution
Total Taxes	9,516,281	100.0
Property taxes	1,137,886	12.0
Sales and gross receipts	4,701,868	49.4
General sales and gross receipts	3,384,394	35.6
Selective sales and gross receipts	1,317,474	13.8
Alcoholic beverages	55,831	0.6
Amusements	60,380	0.6
Insurance premiums	213,212	2.2
Motor fuels	487,517	5.1
Pari-mutuels	2,497	-
Public utilities	X	-
Tobacco products	228,540	2.4
Other selective sales	269,497	2.8
Licenses	384,559	4.0
Alcoholic beverages	4,787	0.1
Amusements	462	-
Corporations in general	28,106	0.3
Hunting and fishing	26,912	0.3
Motor vehicle	158,446	1.7
Motor vehicle operators	25,521	0.3
Public utilities	9,157	0.1
Occupation and business, NEC	129,289	1.4
Other licenses	1,879	-
Income taxes	3,164,756	33.3
Individual income	2,767,767	29.1
Corporation net income	396,989	4.2
Other taxes	127,212	1.3
Death and gift	198	-
Documentary and stock transfer	43,255	0.5
Severance	55,815	0.6
Taxes, NEC	27,944	0.3

- = Zero or rounds to zero.
X = Not applicable.

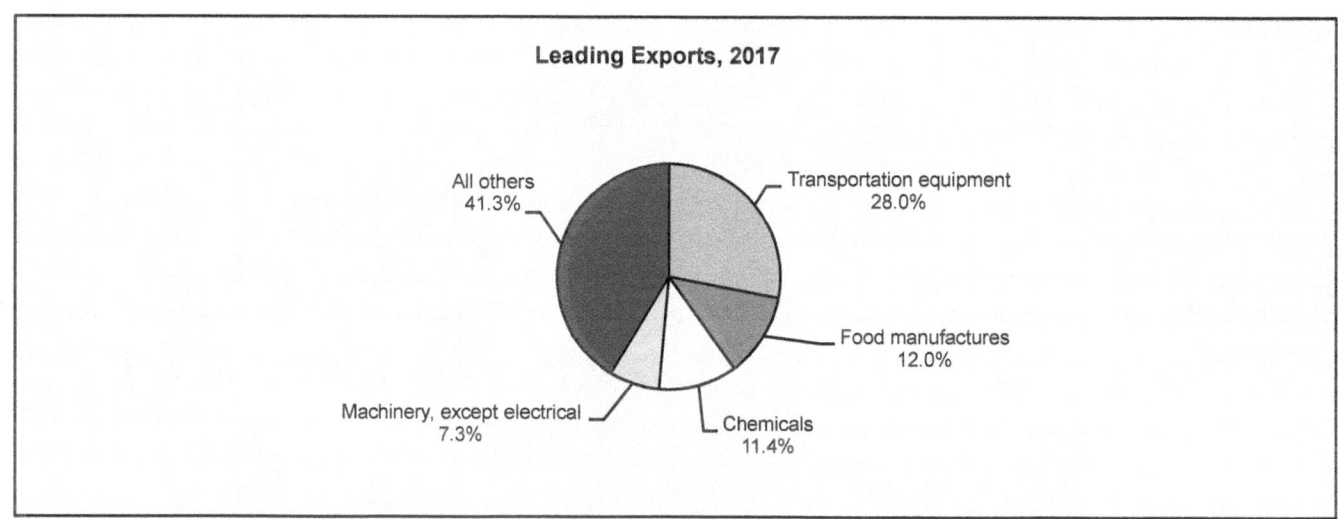

Leading Exports, 2017

All others 41.3%
Transportation equipment 28.0%
Food manufactures 12.0%
Chemicals 11.4%
Machinery, except electrical 7.3%

CALIFORNIA

Facts and Figures

Location: Western United States; bordered on the N by Oregon, on the E by Nevada and Arizona, on the S by Mexico, and on the W by the Pacific Ocean

Area: 163,694 sq. mi. (423,970 sq. km.); rank—3rd

Population: 39,536,653 (2017 est.); rank—1st

Principal Cities: capital—Sacramento; largest—Los Angeles

Statehood: September 9, 1850; 31st state

U.S. Congress: 2 senators, 53 representatives

State Motto: *Eureka* ("I have found it")

State Song: "I Love You, California"

State Nickname: The Golden State

Abbreviations: CA; Calif.

State Symbols: flower—California poppy; tree—redwood; bird—California valley quail

At a Glance

- With an increase in population of 5.9 percent, California ranked 18th among the states in growth from 2010 to 2017.

- In 2016, California's median household income was $67,739, and 14.3 percent of the population lived below the poverty level.

- California's violent crime rate in 2016 was 445.3 per 100,000 population, compared to 386.3 for the entire nation.

- In 2017, California's unemployment rate of 4.8 percent ranked 13th in the nation.

- Approximately 15.2 percent of Californians self-identified their race as "Asian Alone" in 2017, which was the 2nd highest percent in the country.

Table CA-1. Population by Age, Sex, Race, and Hispanic Origin

(Number, percent, except where noted.)

Sex, age, race, and Hispanic origin	2000	2010	2017 [1]	Average annual percent change, 2010–2017
Total population..	33,871,648	37,253,956	39,536,653	6.1
Percent of total U.S. population	12.0	12.1	12.1	X
Sex				
Male..	16,874,892	18,517,830	19,647,553	6.1
Female	16,996,756	18,736,126	19,889,100	6.2
Age				
Under 5 years...	2,486,981	2,531,333	2,471,513	-2.4
5 to 19 years	7,747,590	7,920,709	7,619,800	-3.8
20 to 64 years	20,041,419	22,555,400	23,939,982	6.1
65 years and over	3,595,658	4,246,514	5,505,358	29.6
Median age (years)	33.3	35.2	36.6	4.0
Race and Hispanic origin				
One race				
White	20,170,059	27,636,403	28,611,160	3.5
Black	2,263,882	2,486,549	2,553,498	2.7
American Indian and Alaska Native	333,346	622,107	650,250	4.5
Asian	3,697,513	5,038,123	5,993,089	19.0
Native Hawaiian or Other Pacific Islander	116,961	181,431	199,449	9.9
Two or more races	1,607,646	1,289,343	1,529,207	18.6
Hispanic (of any race)	10,966,556	14,440,187	15,477,304	7.2

X = Not applicable.

[1] Population figures for 2017 are July 1 estimates. The 2010 estimates are taken from the 2010 Census.

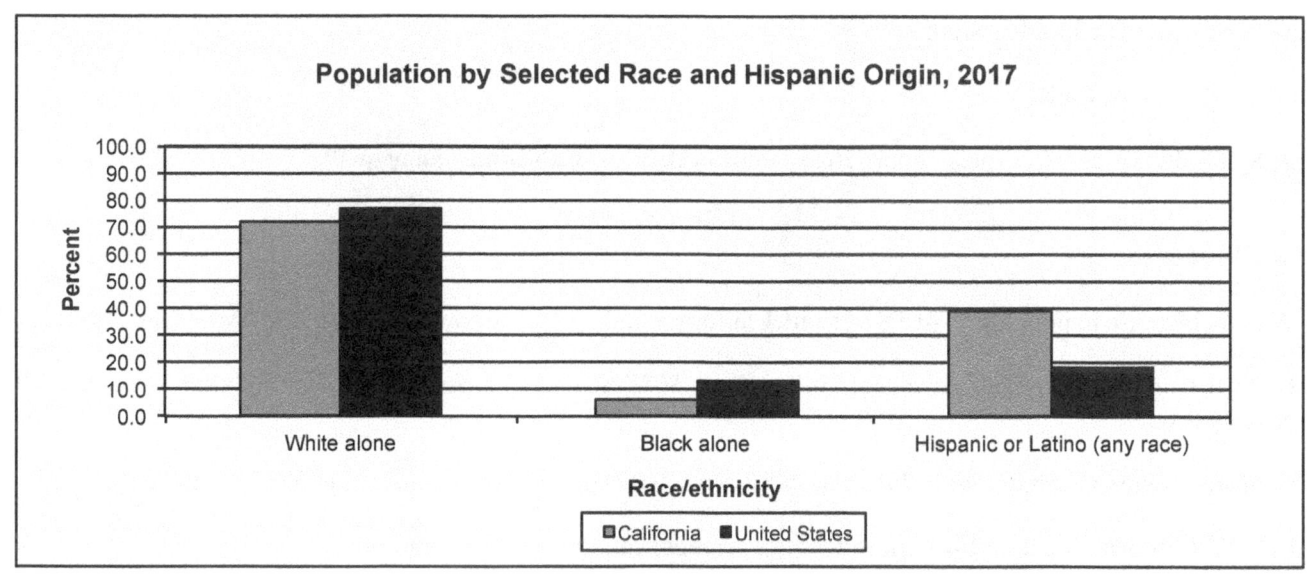

Population by Selected Race and Hispanic Origin, 2017

Table CA-2. Marital Status

(Number, percent distribution.)

Sex, age, and marital status	2000	2010	2016
Males, 15 Years and Over	12,844,669	14,662,335	15,633,439
Never married	33.8	39.8	40.6
Now married, except separated..................................	54.1	48.2	47.8
Separated...	2.0	1.9	1.7
Widowed...	2.2	2.1	2.2
Divorced...	7.9	8.0	7.7
Females, 15 Years and Over	13,231,494	15,043,190	16,063,076
Never married	26.5	32.3	33.6
Now married, except separated..................................	50.7	45.7	45.3
Separated...	2.9	2.7	2.4
Widowed...	8.9	8.1	7.8
Divorced...	11.0	11.2	10.9

Table CA-3. Households and Housing Characteristics

(Number, percent, dollars.)

Item	2000	2010	2016	Average annual percent change, 2010–2016
Total Households..	11,502,870	12,406,475	12,944,178	0.7
Family households	7,920,049	8,507,856	8,887,761	0.7
Married-couple family	5,877,084	6,082,566	6,406,893	0.9
Other family	2,042,965	2,425,290	2,480,868	0.4
Male householder, no wife present.....................................	594,455	736,626	777,253	0.9
Female householder, no husband present............................	1,448,510	1,688,664	1,703,615	0.1
Nonfamily households	3,582,821	3,898,619	4,056,417	0.7
Householder living alone...	2,708,308	3,001,307	3,092,067	0.5
Householder not living alone..	874,513	897,312	964,350	1.2
Housing Characteristics				
Total housing units...	12,214,549	13,682,976	14,061,375	0.5
Occupied housing units	11,502,870	12,406,475	12,944,178	0.7
Owner occupied	6,546,334	6,903,175	6,943,428	0.1
Renter occupied	4,956,536	5,503,300	6,000,750	1.5
Average household size..	2.87	2.94	2.97	0.2
Financial Characteristics				
Median gross rent of renter-occupied housing	747	1,163	1,375	3.0
Median monthly owner costs for housing units with a mortgage	1,478	2,242	2,188	-0.4
Median value of owner-occupied housing units.......................	211,500	370,900	477,500	4.8

Table CA-4. Migration, Origin, and Language

(Number, percent.)

Characteristic	State 2015	State 2016	State Percent change	U.S. 2015	U.S. 2016	U.S. Percent change
Residence 1 Year Ago						
Population 1 year and over	38,675,135	38,783,436	0.3	317,635,720	319,361,956	0.5
Same house	86.5	86.6	X	85.3	85.4	X
Different house in the U.S.	12.6	12.5	X	14.1	13.9	X
Same county	8.6	8.4	X	8.5	8.3	X
Different county	4.1	4.1	X	5.6	5.6	X
Same state	2.8	2.8	X	3.2	3.2	X
Different state	1.3	1.3	X	2.4	2.4	X
Abroad	0.9	0.9	X	0.7	0.7	X
Place of Birth						
Native born	28,456,482	28,572,354	0.4	278,128,449	279,388,170	0.5
Male	50.2	50.2	X	49.3	49.3	X
Female	49.8	49.8	X	50.7	50.7	X
Foreign born	10,688,336	10,677,663	-0.1	43,290,372	43,739,345	1.0
Male	48.2	48.3	X	48.6	48.5	X
Female	51.8	51.7	X	51.4	51.5	X
Foreign born; naturalized U.S. citizen...................................	5,314,136	5,369,508	1.0	20,697,103	21,238,372	2.6
Male	45.9	45.8	X	45.9	45.9	X
Female...	54.1	54.2	X	54.1	54.1	X
Foreign born; not a U.S. citizen..	5,374,200	5,308,155	-1.2	22,593,269	22,500,973	-0.4
Male	50.5	50.8	X	51.1	51	X
Female...	49.5	49.2	X	48.9	49	X
Entered 2010 or later	11.2	13.6	X	15.6	18.6	X
Entered 2000 to 2009	23.7	23	X	27.9	26.7	X
Entered before 2000...	65	63.4	X	56.5	54.7	X
World Region of Birth, Foreign						
Foreign-born population, excluding population born at sea	10,688,122	10,677,502	-0.1	43,289,646	43,738,901	1.0
Europe	6.4	6.3	X	11.1	10.9	X
Asia	38.6	38.9	X	30.6	30.8	X
Africa	1.8	1.8	X	4.8	4.9	X
Oceania	0.7	0.8	X	0.6	0.6	X
Latin America	51.2	51.1	X	51.1	51	X
North America...	1.3	1.1	X	1.9	1.8	X
Language Spoken at Home and Ability to Speak English						
Population 5 years and over..	36,637,169	36,767,595	0.4	301,625,014	303,328,961	0.6
English only	55.4	55.4	X	78.5	78.4	X
Language other than English...	44.6	44.6	X	21.5	21.6	X
Speaks English less than "very well"..................................	18.6	18.6	X	8.6	8.6	X

NA = Not available.
X = Not applicable.
- = Zero or rounds to zero.

Table CA-5. Median Income and Poverty Status, 2016

(Number, percent, except as noted.)

Characteristic	State		U.S.	
	Number	Percent	Number	Percent
Median Income				
Households (dollars)..	67,739	X	57,617	X
Families (dollars)..	77,359	X	71,062	X
Below Poverty Level (All People)	5,525,524	14.3	44,268,996	14.0
Sex				
Male	2,522,564	13.3	19,760,056	12.8
Female	3,002,960	15.4	24,508,940	15.2
Age				
Under 18 years..	1,785,347	19.9	14,115,713	19.5
Related children under 18 years......................................	1,747,994	19.6	13,805,435	19.1
18 to 64 years...	3,198,774	13.2	25,723,818	13.2
65 years and over	541,403	10.3	4,429,465	9.2

X = Not applicable.

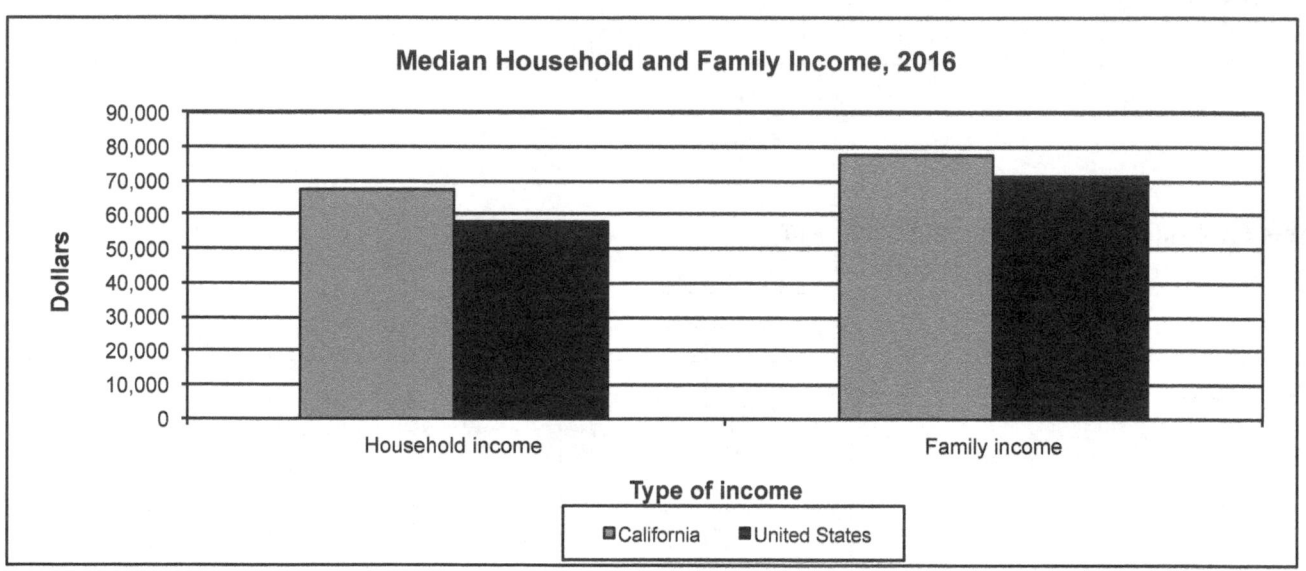

Table CA-6. Health Insurance Coverage Status for the Civilian Noninstitutionalized Population and Children Under 18 Years of Age

(Number, percent.)

Item	2008	2009	2010	2011	2012	2013	2014	2015	2016
Civilian Noninstitutionalized Population	36,160,600	36,376,938	36,815,569	37,161,789	37,524,274	37,831,553	38,297,457	38,649,621	38,763,815
Covered by Private or Public Insurance									
Number..	29,730,114	29,817,590	29,990,656	30,436,185	30,814,688	31,331,374	33,530,746	35,332,356	35,919,912
Percent..	82.2	82.0	81.5	81.9	82.1	82.8	87.6	91.4	92.7
Not Covered									
Number..	6,430,486	6,559,348	6,824,913	6,725,604	6,709,586	6,500,179	4,766,711	3,317,265	2,843,903
Percent..	17.8	18.0	18.5	18.1	17.9	17.2	12.4	8.6	7.3
Percent in the U.S. not covered	15.1	15.1	15.5	15.1	14.8	14.5	11.7	9.4	8.6
Children Under 18 Years of Age	9,347,714	9,422,686	9,288,691	9,252,466	9,223,488	9,157,955	9,135,133	9,103,139	9,079,778
Covered by Private or Public Insurance									
Number..	8,337,162	8,531,688	8,455,939	8,507,669	8,493,396	8,484,747	8,638,043	8,800,771	8,811,963
Percent..	89.2	90.5	91.0	92.0	92.1	92.6	94.6	96.7	97.1
Not Covered									
Number..	1,010,552	890,998	832,752	744,797	730,092	673,208	497,090	302,368	267,815
Percent..	10.8	9.5	9.0	8.0	7.9	7.4	5.4	3.3	2.9
Percent in the U.S. not covered	9.9	8.6	8.0	7.5	7.2	7.1	6.0	4.8	4.5

Table CA-7. Employment Status by Demographic Group, 2017

(Numbers in thousands, percent.)

Characteristic	Civilian noninstitutional population	Civilian labor force		Employed		Unemployed	
		Number	Percent of population	Number	Percent of population	Number	Percent of population
Total...	30,931	19,224	62.2	18,305	59.2	919	4.8
Sex							
Male..	15,105	10,476	69.4	10,000	66.2	476	4.5
Female...	15,826	8,748	55.3	8,305	52.5	443	5.1
Race, Sex, and Hispanic Origin							
White..	22,355	13,926	62.3	13,266	59.3	660	4.7
Male...	11,031	7,745	70.2	7,400	67.1	345	4.5
Female...	11,324	6,181	54.6	5,866	51.8	315	5.1
Black or African American.....................	1,944	1,186	61.0	1,105	56.8	81	6.8
Male...	924	568	61.5	527	57.0	41	7.2
Female...	1,020	618	60.6	578	56.7	40	6.5
Hispanic or Latino ethnicity[1]...............	10,883	7,103	65.3	6,705	61.6	399	5.6
Male...	5,381	4,028	74.8	3,832	71.2	196	4.9
Female...	5,502	3,076	55.9	2,873	52.2	203	6.6
Age							
16 to 19 years....................................	2,035	560	27.5	461	22.7	99	17.7
20 to 24 years....................................	2,768	1,820	65.8	1,679	60.7	141	7.8
25 to 34 years....................................	5,657	4,550	80.4	4,325	76.5	224	4.9
35 to 44 years....................................	5,213	4,187	80.3	4,034	77.4	153	3.6
45 to 54 years....................................	5,114	4,036	78.9	3,900	76.3	136	3.4
55 to 64 years....................................	4,767	3,020	63.3	2,900	60.8	120	4.0
65 years and over...............................	5,378	1,051	19.5	1,006	18.7	46	4.3

NOTE: Data in Table 7 are from the Current Population Survey (CPS) and do not match the estimates in Table 8. See notes and definitions for further information.
[1] May be of any race.

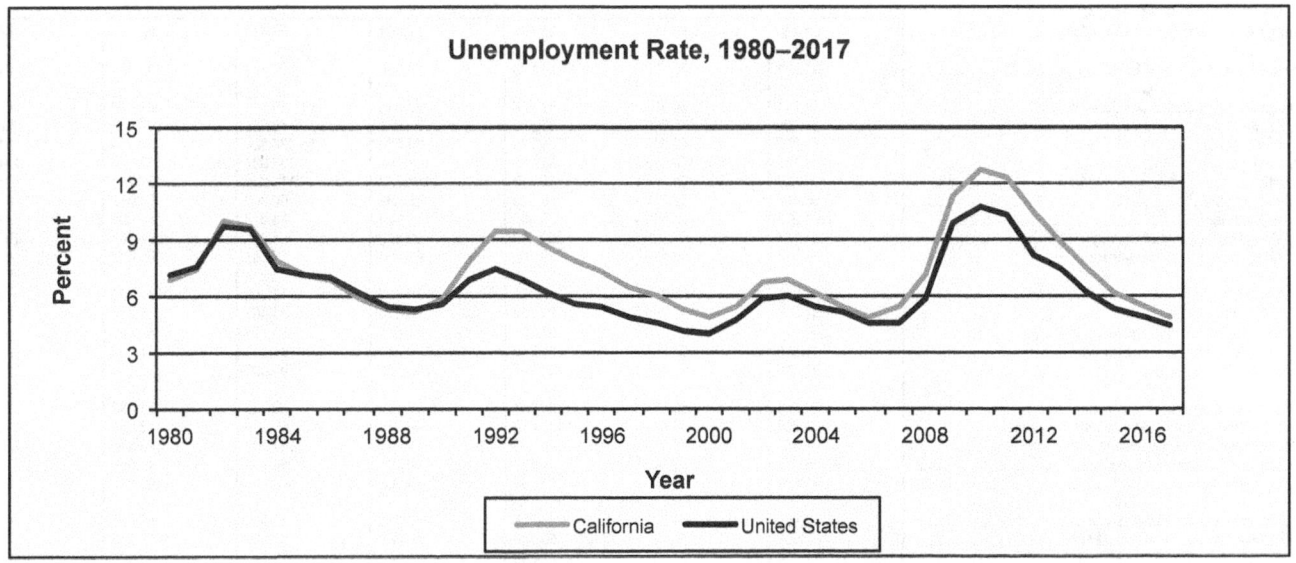

Unemployment Rate, 1980–2017

Table CA-8. Employment Status of the Civilian Noninstitutional Population Age 16 Years and Over

(Number, percent.)

Year	Civilian labor force	Civilian participation rate	Employed	Unemployed	Unemployment rate
2009..	18,215,140	65.2	16,182,572	2,032,568	11.2
2010..	18,336,271	64.2	16,091,945	2,244,326	12.2
2011..	18,415,100	63.5	16,258,133	2,156,967	11.7
2012..	18,523,793	63.1	16,602,672	1,921,121	10.4
2013..	18,624,992	62.7	16,958,403	1,666,589	8.9
2014..	18,758,399	62.4	17,351,318	1,407,081	7.5
2015..	18,896,477	62.1	17,724,799	1,171,678	6.2
2016..	19,093,658	62.2	18,048,827	1,044,831	5.5
2017..	19,311,958	62.3	18,393,077	918,881	4.8

Table CA-9. Employment and Average Wages by Industry

(Estimates through 2010 are based on the 2007 *North American Industry Classification System* [NAICS]. Estimates from 2011 onward are based on the 2012 NAICS.)

Industry	2010	2011	2012	2013	2014	2015	2016
	Number of Jobs						
Wage and Salary Employment by Industry.........................	14,958,113	15,109,943	15,726,659	16,221,907	16,696,981	17,173,162	17,614,572
Farm Wage and Salary Employment..............................	167,173	163,477	158,790	165,882	180,222	179,440	176,653
Nonfarm Wage and Salary Employment..........................	14,790,940	14,946,466	15,567,869	16,056,025	16,516,759	16,993,722	17,437,919
Private wage and salary employment.............................	12,112,855	12,330,255	12,976,597	13,454,561	13,885,352	14,308,482	14,686,648
Forestry, fishing, and related activities........................	191,774	195,126	202,791	212,849	216,452	220,780	228,201
Mining..	24,372	26,290	28,048	27,858	28,597	26,219	22,022
Utilities..	57,109	58,292	59,386	58,934	57,872	57,600	58,639
Construction...	578,257	578,864	607,023	655,178	691,325	749,035	796,342
Manufacturing..	1,240,714	1,246,393	1,252,300	1,252,619	1,271,594	1,294,660	1,305,059
Durable goods manufacturing.................................	769,935	777,645	781,131	779,730	793,601	811,711	817,899
Nondurable goods manufacturing...........................	470,779	468,748	471,169	472,889	477,993	482,949	487,160
Wholesale trade	647,748	662,000	678,929	701,382	715,544	722,462	724,251
Retail trade..	1,526,808	1,550,561	1,582,568	1,613,810	1,643,658	1,675,045	1,692,914
Transportation and warehousing................................	410,597	418,153	428,470	445,635	465,738	499,315	533,369
Information..	426,557	430,873	434,346	446,949	460,760	487,002	523,496
Finance and insurance	532,879	541,683	553,120	552,516	550,475	560,606	581,074
Real estate and rental and leasing............................	256,416	255,635	258,234	265,707	271,321	277,541	283,640
Professional, scientific, and technical services	1,032,268	1,068,397	1,116,103	1,152,308	1,184,378	1,215,406	1,230,512
Management of companies and enterprises.................	193,199	199,316	203,755	219,138	227,024	231,705	227,555
Administrative and waste services	863,137	888,260	940,979	989,531	1,035,046	1,065,505	1,094,537
Educational services	337,717	347,355	361,713	367,579	380,982	385,342	392,449
Health care and social assistance..............................	1,501,079	1,522,010	1,843,849	1,983,750	2,046,843	2,131,469	2,216,696
Arts, entertainment, and recreation...........................	250,182	251,465	260,263	271,543	281,750	292,154	306,375
Accommodation and food services.............................	1,263,900	1,293,501	1,346,219	1,413,031	1,486,165	1,545,742	1,605,332
Other services, except public administration..............	778,142	796,081	818,501	824,244	869,828	870,894	864,185
Government and government enterprises.....................	2,678,085	2,616,211	2,591,272	2,601,464	2,631,407	2,685,240	2,751,271
	Dollars						
Average Wages and Salaries by Industry	54,450	56,155	57,462	57,601	59,414	62,104	66,401
Average Farm Wages and Salaries	31,331	26,753	31,575	34,006	29,170	33,109	31,803
Average Nonfarm Wages and Salaries	54,711	56,476	57,726	57,845	59,744	62,410	66,752
Average private wages and salaries.............................	54,405	56,266	57,589	57,651	59,584	62,402	66,842
Forestry, fishing, and related activities.......................	22,899	23,615	24,724	25,728	26,624	28,434	31,769
Mining..	131,186	129,586	135,288	135,964	138,907	138,023	104,627
Utilities..	103,320	108,064	110,932	117,337	118,310	127,705	128,068
Construction	55,858	57,232	58,949	59,059	60,300	63,062	69,849
Manufacturing..	74,238	76,505	79,002	79,512	83,047	85,564	92,056
Durable goods manufacturing.................................	85,624	88,798	90,609	90,378	95,056	97,407	107,021
Nondurable goods manufacturing...........................	55,617	56,112	59,760	61,597	63,107	65,657	66,929
Wholesale trade	65,910	68,396	70,038	70,527	73,458	77,368	79,435
Retail trade..	31,932	32,566	33,622	33,514	34,302	35,753	36,902
Transportation and warehousing................................	48,576	49,776	51,257	51,831	52,754	53,966	62,167
Information..	101,596	107,897	114,760	134,269	138,163	147,550	165,518
Finance and insurance	94,010	97,188	102,697	103,202	109,400	114,130	121,071
Real estate and rental and leasing............................	50,156	53,094	55,977	57,120	60,439	63,882	68,696
Professional, scientific, and technical services	91,109	94,876	103,618	98,971	105,266	113,000	118,135
Management of companies and enterprises.................	97,161	103,629	108,365	113,055	121,702	126,552	129,258
Administrative and waste services	38,027	39,140	40,627	40,037	40,759	42,656	46,061
Educational services	41,201	42,326	43,197	43,968	45,428	46,017	47,826
Health care and social assistance..............................	53,459	54,825	49,337	47,352	47,939	49,666	53,294
Arts, entertainment, and recreation...........................	52,699	55,199	56,786	55,960	57,597	58,575	61,198
Accommodation and food services.............................	21,328	21,962	22,649	22,888	23,717	25,135	27,889
Other services, except public administration..............	30,171	30,720	31,213	31,864	32,513	34,035	38,865
Government and government enterprises.....................	56,093	57,469	58,410	58,849	60,588	62,451	66,272

Table CA-10. Employment Characteristics by Family Type

(Number, percent.)

Family type and labor force status	2014		2015		2016	
	Total	Families with own children under 18 years	Total	Families with own children under 18 years	Total	Families with own children under 18 years
All Families...	8,708,774	3,976,389	8,835,906	3,973,103	8,887,761	3,938,382
FAMILY TYPE AND LABOR FORCE STATUS						
Married-Couple Families...................................	6,185,858	2,754,933	6,342,293	2,783,907	6,406,893	2,779,534
Both husband and wife in labor force...........................	50.0	59.9	49.0	59.7	49.2	60.0
Husband in labor force, wife not in labor force..........................	26.5	34.0	26.2	33.9	25.7	33.7
Wife in labor force, husband not in labor force.......................	7.6	4.1	7.5	3.9	7.5	4.0
Both husband and wife not in labor force....................	15.9	2.0	16.2	2.0	16.4	1.9
Other Families	2,522,916	1,221,456	2,493,613	1,189,196	2,480,868	1,158,848
Female householder, no husband present...........................	69.4	71.9	68.9	71.3	68.7	70.7
In labor force..................................	48.0	56.9	47.0	56.0	46.9	56.4
Not in labor force................................	21.4	15.0	21.8	15.2	21.7	14.2
Male householder, no wife present...........................	30.6	28.1	31.1	28.7	31.3	29.3
In labor force..................................	24.8	25.6	25.0	26.3	25.1	27.0
Not in labor force................................	5.8	2.5	6.1	2.5	6.2	2.4

Table CA-11. School Enrollment and Educational Attainment, 2016

(Number, percent.)

Item	State	U.S.
Enrollment		
Total population 3 years and over, enrolled in school	10,490,279	81,572,277
Enrolled in nursery school or preschool (percent)	5.8	6.0
Enrolled in kindergarten (percent).....................	5.1	5.0
Enrolled in elementary school, grades 1-8 (percent).....................	37.8	40.3
Enrolled in high school, grades 9-12 (percent).....................	20.5	21.0
Enrolled in college or graduate school (percent).....................	30.8	27.7
Attainment		
Total population 25 years and over	26,304,241	218,475,480
Less than ninth grade (percent).....................	9.7	5.4
9th to 12th grade, no diploma (percent)	7.8	7.2
High school graduate, including equivalency (percent).....................	20.5	27.2
Some college, no degree (percent).....................	21.3	20.6
Associate's degree (percent).....................	7.7	8.4
Bachelor's degree (percent)	20.6	19.3
Graduate or professional degree (percent).....................	12.3	11.9
High school graduate or higher (percent).....................	82.4	87.5
Bachelor's degree or higher (percent).....................	32.9	31.3

Table CA-12. Public School Characteristics and Educational Indicators

(Number, percent; data derived from National Center of Education Statistics.)

Item	State	U.S.
Public Schools, 2015–2016 (except where noted)		
Number of school districts....................	1,163	18,328
Number of schools....................	10,303	98,456
Number of students	6,312,161	50,327,015
Number of teachers	267,685	3,151,497
Student-teacher ratio	23.6	16.0
Expenditures per student (dollars), 2014-2015....................	9,671	11,445
Four-year adjusted cohort graduation rate (ACGR)[1,2]	82.0	84.1
Students eligible for free or reduced-price lunch (percent), 2014-2015....................	58.7	51.8
English language learners (percent), Fall 2015	22.4	9.5
Students age 3 to 21 served under IDEA, part B (percent)....................	11.3	13.2

Public Schools by Type	Number	Percent of state public schools
Total number of schools....................	10,303	100.0
Regular	8,936	86.7
Special education....................	151	1.5
Vocational education....................	74	0.7
Alternative education....................	1,142	11.1

NOTE: Every school is assigned only one school type based on its instructional emphasis.
[1] ACGR data represents a new method of calculating high-school completion rates and may not be comparable to previous years' data for Averaged Freshmen Graduation Rates (AFGR).
[2] The United States 4-year ACGRs were estimated using both the reported 4-year ACGR data from 49 states and the District of Columbia and using imputed data for Idaho. The estimate for American Indian/Alaska Native students also includes imputed data for Virginia.

Table CA-13. Reported Voting and Registration of the Voting-Age Population, November 2016

(Numbers in thousands, percent.)

Item	Total population	Total citizen population	Registered			Voted		
			Total registered	Percent registered (total population)	Percent registered (total citizen population)	Total voted	Percent voted (total population)	Percent voted (total citizen population)
U.S. Total	245,502	224,059	157,596	64.2	70.3	137,537	56.0	61.4
State Total.................................	29,894	24,890	16,096	53.8	64.7	14,416	48.2	57.9
Sex								
Male	14,604	12,131	7,663	52.5	63.2	6,833	46.8	56.3
Female	15,289	12,759	8,433	55.2	66.1	7,583	49.6	59.4
Race								
White alone..............................	21,592	18,104	12,084	56.0	66.7	10,908	50.5	60.3
White, non-Hispanic alone	12,480	11,954	8,732	70.0	73.0	8,020	64.3	67.1
Black alone..............................	1,849	1,768	1,018	55.0	57.6	856	46.3	48.4
Asian alone..............................	4,838	3,585	2,080	43.0	58.0	1,859	38.4	51.9
Hispanic (of any race)......................	10,221	7,092	3,882	38.0	54.7	3,345	32.7	47.2
White alone or in combination	22,327	18,781	12,589	56.4	67.0	11,363	50.9	60.5
Black alone or in combination...........	2,111	2,007	1,161	55.0	57.9	990	46.9	49.3
Asian alone or in combination...........	5,066	3,798	2,243	44.3	59.0	2,007	39.6	52.8
Age								
18 to 24 years..............................	3,760	3,308	1,656	44.0	50.1	1,411	37.5	42.7
25 to 34 years..............................	5,742	4,579	2,795	48.7	61.0	2,379	41.4	51.9
35 to 44 years..............................	5,145	3,797	2,412	46.9	63.5	2,074	40.3	54.6
45 to 64 years..............................	9,835	8,252	5,581	56.8	67.6	5,124	52.1	62.1
65 years and over	5,412	4,955	3,651	67.5	73.7	3,429	63.4	69.2

Table CA-14. Crime

(Number, rate per 100,000. Data are derived from the FBI Uniform Crime Reports.)

Item	State			U.S. [1,2,3,4]		
	2015	2016	Percent change	2015	2016	Percent change
TOTAL POPULATION [5]	39,144,818	39,250,017	0.3	321,418,820	323,127,513	0.5
VIOLENT CRIME						
Number..	166,883	174,796	4.7	1,231,566	1,248,185	1.3
Rate	426.3	445.3	4.5	383.2	386.3	0.8
Murder and Nonnegligent Manslaughter						
Number..	1,861	1,930	3.7	15,696	17,250	9.9
Rate	4.8	4.9	2.1	4.9	5.3	8.2
Rape [6]						
Number..	12,811	13,702	7.0	124,047	130,603	5.3
Rate	32.7	34.9	6.7	38.6	40.4	4.7
Robbery						
Number..	52,862	54,789	3.6	327,374	332,198	1.5
Rate	135.0	139.6	3.4	101.9	102.8	0.9
Aggravated Assault						
Number..	99,349	104,375	5.1	764,449	803,007	5.0
Rate	253.8	265.9	4.8	237.8	248.5	4.5
PROPERTY CRIME						
Number..	1,024,914	1,002,070	-2.2	7,993,631	7,919,035	-0.9
Rate	2,618.3	2,553.0	-2.5	2,487.0	2,450.7	-1.5
Burglary						
Number..	197,404	188,304	-4.6	1,579,527	1,515,096	-4.1
Rate	504.3	479.8	-4.9	491.4	468.9	-4.6
Larceny-Theft						
Number..	656,517	637,010	-3.0	5,706,346	5,638,455	-1.2
Rate	1,677.1	1,623.0	-3.2	1,775.4	1,745.0	-1.7
Motor Vehicle Theft						
Number..	170,993	176,756	3.4	707,758	765,484	8.2
Rate	436.8	450.3	3.1	220.2	236.9	7.6

NOTE: Although arson data are included in the trend and clearance tables, sufficient data are not available to estimate totals for this offense. Therefore, no arson data are published in this table.
X = Not applicable.
- = Zero or rounds to zero.
[1] The crime figures have been adjusted.
[2] The data collection methodology for the offense of forcible rape used by the Minnesota state Uniform Crime Reporting (UCR) Program (with the exception of Minneapolis and St. Paul, Minnesota) does not comply with national UCR Program guidelines. Consequently, its figures for forcible rape and violent crime (of which forcible rape is a part) are not published in this table.
[3] Includes offenses reported by the Zoological Police and the Metro Transit Police.
[4] Because of changes in the state's reporting practices, figures are not comparable to previous years' data.
[5] Populations are U.S. Census Bureau provisional estimates as of July 1 of each year.
[6] The figures shown for the offense of rape were estimated using the revised Uniform Crime Reporting (UCR) definition of rape.

Table CA-15. State Government Finances, 2016

(Dollar amounts in thousands, percent distribution.)

Item	Dollars	Percent distribution
Total Revenue	322,332,341	100.0
General revenue	282,907,926	87.8
Intergovernmental revenue	94,336,283	29.3
Taxes	155,231,252	48.2
General sales	39,189,007	12.2
Selective sales	14,176,746	4.4
License taxes	8,551,427	2.7
Individual income tax	80,753,345	25.1
Corporate income tax	9,902,185	3.1
Other taxes	2,658,542	0.8
Current charges	23,164,164	7.2
Miscellaneous general revenue	10,176,227	3.2
Utility revenue	775,236	0.2
Liquor stores revenue	0	-
Insurance trust revenue [1]	38,649,179	12.0
Total Expenditure	326,837,836	100.0
Intergovernmental expenditure	103,512,395	31.7
Direct expenditure	223,325,441	68.3
Current operation	151,325,034	46.3
Capital outlay	10,333,559	3.2
Insurance benefits and repayments	49,297,544	15.1
Assistance and subsidies	5,182,384	1.6
Interest on debt	7,186,920	2.2
Exhibit: Salaries and wages	33,914,171	10.4
Total Expenditure	326,837,836	100.0
General expenditure	276,187,498	84.5
Intergovernmental expenditure	103,512,395	31.7
Direct expenditure	172,675,103	52.8
General expenditure, by function:		
Education	93,606,370	28.6
Public welfare	107,043,559	32.8
Hospitals	10,968,673	3.4
Health	9,053,782	2.8
Highways	10,923,189	3.3
Police protection	1,920,894	0.6
Correction	9,528,475	2.9
Natural resources	6,898,403	2.1
Parks and recreation	632,840	0.2
Governmental administration	8,043,094	2.5
Interest on general debt	6,993,920	2.1
Other and unallocable	10,574,299	3.2
Utility expenditure	1,352,794	0.4
Liquor stores expenditure	0	-
Insurance trust expenditure	49,297,544	15.1
Debt at End of Fiscal Year	151,307,658	X
Cash and Security Holdings	634,296,643	X

X = Not applicable.
- = Zero or rounds to zero.
[1] Within insurance trust revenue, net earnings of state retirement systems is a calculated statistic (the item code in the data file is X08), and thus can be positive or negative. Net earnings is the sum of earnings on investments plus gains on investments minus losses on investments. The change made in 2002 for asset valuation from book to market value in accordance with Statement 34 of the Governmental Accounting Standards Board is reflected in the calculated statistics.

Table CA-16. State Government Tax Collections, 2017

(Dollars in thousands, percent.)

Item	Dollars	Percent distribution
Total Taxes	155,632,088	100.0
Property taxes	2,681,872	1.7
Sales and gross receipts	47,940,362	30.8
General sales and gross receipts	35,357,699	22.7
Selective sales and gross receipts	12,582,663	8.1
Alcoholic beverages	370,714	0.2
Amusements	X	-
Insurance premiums	2,422,105	1.6
Motor fuels	4,842,749	3.1
Pari-mutuels	14,743	-
Public utilities	728,045	0.5
Tobacco products	852,894	0.5
Other selective sales	3,351,413	2.2
Licenses	10,525,972	6.8
Alcoholic beverages	58,202	-
Amusements	22,212	-
Corporations in general	74,365	-
Hunting and fishing	104,176	0.1
Motor vehicle	4,261,054	2.7
Motor vehicle operators	222,241	0.1
Public utilities	779,990	0.5
Occupation and business, NEC	4,999,288	3.2
Other licenses	4,444	-
Income taxes	94,309,271	60.6
Individual income	84,196,751	54.1
Corporation net income	10,112,520	6.5
Other taxes	174,611	0.1
Death and gift	1,360	-
Documentary and stock transfer	X	-
Severance	93,928	0.1
Taxes, NEC	79,323	0.1

- = Zero or rounds to zero.
X = Not applicable.

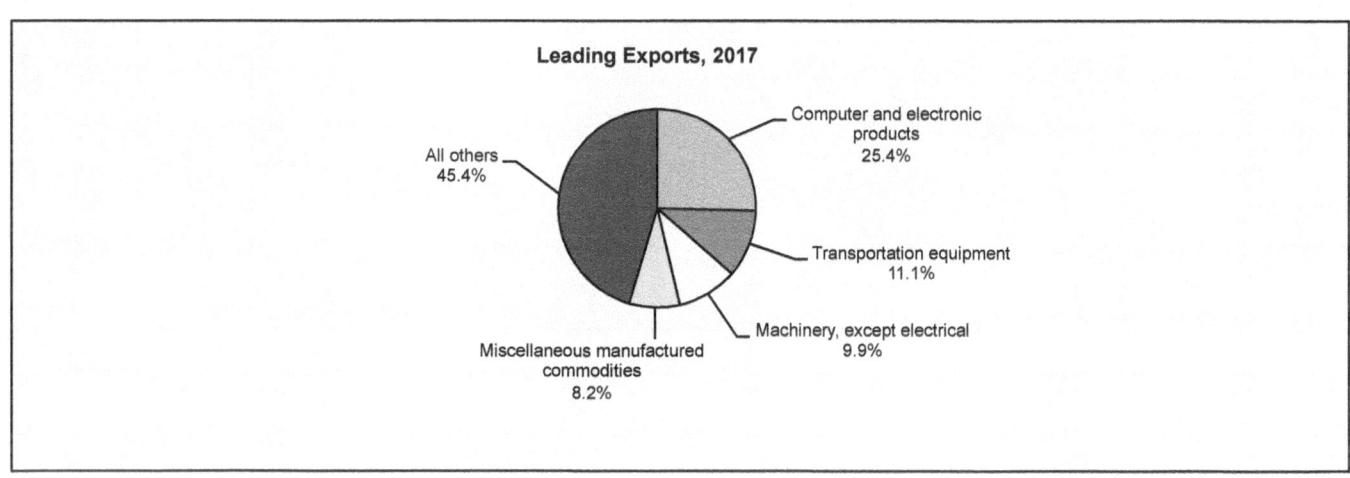

Leading Exports, 2017

Computer and electronic products 25.4%

Transportation equipment 11.1%

Machinery, except electrical 9.9%

Miscellaneous manufactured commodities 8.2%

All others 45.4%

COLORADO

Facts and Figures

Location: Western United States; bordered on the N by Wyoming and Nebraska, on the E by Nebraska and Kansas, on the S by Oklahoma and New Mexico, and on the W by Utah; Colorado is one of the Four Corner states—at its SW corner it touches Arizona, New Mexico, and Utah

Area: 104,093 sq. mi. (269,601 sq. km.); rank—8th

Population: 5,607,154 (2017 est.); rank—21st

Principal Cities: capital—Denver; largest—Denver

Statehood: August 1, 1876; 38th state

U.S. Congress: 2 senators, 7 representatives

State Motto: *Nil sine numine* ("Nothing without providence")

State Songs: "Where the Columbines Grow"; "Rocky Mountain High"

State Nicknames: The Centennial State; Colorful Colorado

Abbreviations: CO; Colo.

State Symbols: flower—Rocky Mountain columbine; tree—Colorado blue spruce; bird—lark bunting

At a Glance

- With an increase in population of 11.1 percent, Colorado ranked 6th among the states in growth from 2010 to 2017.

- In 2016, 7.5 percent of Coloradans did not have health insurance, compared to 8.6 percent of the total U.S. population.

- At a rate of 16.6 per 100,000 residents, the 2016 drug overdose death rate in Colorado was lower than the national average of 19.8 deaths per 100,000 population.

- In Colorado, 11.0 percent of the total population and 13.4 percent of persons under 18 years old lived below the poverty level in 2016, compared to nationwide poverty levels of 14.0 percent and 19.5 percent, respectively.

Table CO-1. Population by Age, Sex, Race, and Hispanic Origin

(Number, percent, except where noted.)

Sex, age, race, and Hispanic origin	2000	2010	2017 [1]	Average annual percent change, 2010–2017
Total Population...	4,301,261	5,029,196	5,607,154	11.5
Percent of total U.S. population	1.5	1.6	1.7	X
Sex				
Male...	2,165,983	2,520,662	2,822,333	12.0
Female...	2,135,278	2,508,534	2,784,821	11.0
Age				
Under 5 years..	297,505	343,960	336,207	-2.3
5 to 19 years..	927,163	1,020,732	1,069,489	4.8
20 to 64 years...	2,660,520	3,114,879	3,429,416	10.1
65 years and over	416,073	549,625	772,042	40.5
Median age (years)	34.3	36.1	36.8	1.9
Race and Hispanic Origin				
One race				
White	3,560,005	4,450,623	4,894,372	10.0
Black..	165,063	214,919	253,666	18.0
American Indian and Alaska Native	44,241	78,144	89,116	14.0
Asian..	95,213	144,819	188,635	30.3
Native Hawaiian or Other Pacific Islander	4,621	8,420	10,546	25.2
Two or more races..	122,187	132,271	170,819	29.1
Hispanic (of any race)...	735,601	1,078,225	1,206,724	11.9

X = Not applicable.
[1] Population figures for 2017 are July 1 estimates. The 2010 estimates are taken from the 2010 Census.

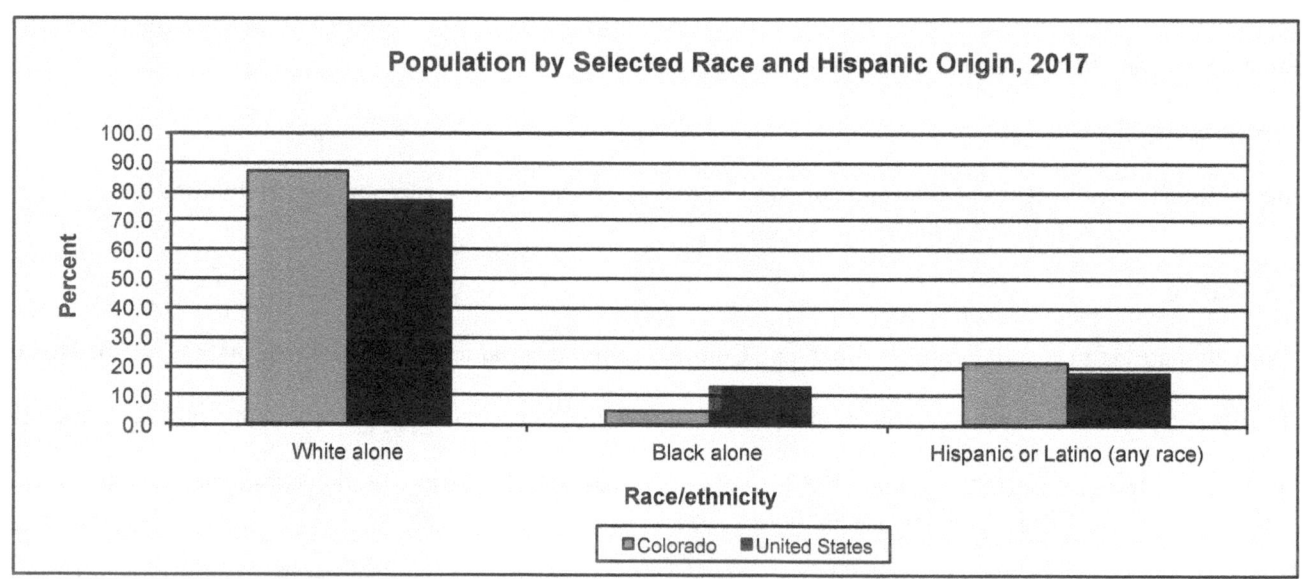

Population by Selected Race and Hispanic Origin, 2017

Table CO-2. Marital Status

(Number, percent distribution.)

Sex, age, and marital status	2000	2010	2016
Males, 15 Years and Over	1,694,635	2,004,303	2,251,218
Never married	30.5	34.4	35.7
Now married, except separated....................................	56.6	51.7	50.5
Separated..	1.4	1.6	1.2
Widowed..	1.9	2.0	2.1
Divorced...	9.6	10.3	10.6
Females, 15 Years and Over	1,690,734	2,017,425	2,239,356
Never married	23.4	26.9	28.3
Now married, except separated....................................	54.7	50.8	50.3
Separated..	1.8	2.0	1.7
Widowed..	7.6	7.0	6.7
Divorced...	12.5	13.3	13.0

Table CO-3. Households and Housing Characteristics

(Number, percent, dollars.)

Item	2000	2010	2016	Average annual percent change, 2010–2016
Total Households...................................	1,658,238	1,960,585	2,108,992	1.3
Family households	1,084,461	1,258,885	1,347,936	1.2
Married-couple family	858,671	959,624	1,051,388	1.6
Other family	225,790	299,261	296,548	-0.2
Male householder, no wife present.............	66,811	90,518	98,819	1.5
Female householder, no husband present...........	158,979	208,743	197,729	-0.9
Nonfamily households	573,777	701,700	761,056	1.4
Householder living alone............................	435,778	555,080	574,809	0.6
Householder not living alone........................	137,999	146,620	186,247	4.5
Housing Characteristics				
Total housing units...................................	1,808,037	2,214,262	2,339,140	0.9
Occupied housing units	1,658,238	1,960,585	2,108,992	1.3
Owner occupied	1,116,173	1,292,792	1,365,832	0.9
Renter occupied	542,101	667,793	743,160	1.9
Average household size..............................	2.53	2.52	2.57	0.3
Financial Characteristics				
Median gross rent of renter-occupied housing	671	863	1171	5.9
Median monthly owner costs for housing units with a mortgage	1,197	1,590	1,597	0.1
Median value of owner-occupied housing units...................	166,600	236,600	314,200	5.5

Table CO-4. Migration, Origin, and Language

(Number, percent.)

Characteristic	State			U.S.		
	2015	2016	Percent change	2015	2016	Percent change
Residence 1 Year Ago						
Population 1 year and over	5,393,067	5,476,928	1.6	317,635,720	319,361,956	0.5
Same house	81.7	81.5	X	85.3	85.4	X
Different house in the U.S.	17.7	17.9	X	14.1	13.9	X
Same county	8.6	8.7	X	8.5	8.3	X
Different county	9.1	9.1	X	5.6	5.6	X
Same state	4.9	5	X	3.2	3.2	X
Different state	4.2	4.1	X	2.4	2.4	X
Abroad	0.6	0.6	X	0.7	0.7	X
Place of Birth						
Native born	4,919,508	4,995,812	1.6	278,128,449	279,388,170	0.5
Male	50.3	50.6	X	49.3	49.3	X
Female	49.7	49.4	X	50.7	50.7	X
Foreign born	537,066	544,733	1.4	43,290,372	43,739,345	1.0
Male	49.6	48.3	X	48.6	48.5	X
Female	50.4	51.7	X	51.4	51.5	X
Foreign born; naturalized U.S. citizen.........	207,694	215,995	4.0	20,697,103	21,238,372	2.6
Male	44.2	44.6	X	45.9	45.9	X
Female	55.8	55.4	X	54.1	54.1	X
Foreign born; not a U.S. citizen.........	329,372	328,738	-0.2	22,593,269	22,500,973	-0.4
Male	52.9	50.7	X	51.1	51	X
Female	47.1	49.3	X	48.9	49	X
Entered 2010 or later	15.2	19	X	15.6	18.6	X
Entered 2000 to 2009	32.1	29	X	27.9	26.7	X
Entered before 2000.....................	52.8	51.9	X	56.5	54.7	X
World Region of Birth, Foreign						
Foreign-born population, excluding population born at sea	537,066	544,733	1.4	43,289,646	43,738,901	1.0
Europe	13.4	13.1	X	11.1	10.9	X
Asia.................................	23.2	24.7	X	30.6	30.8	X
Africa	5.8	5.8	X	4.8	4.9	X
Oceania	0.7	1.4	X	0.6	0.6	X
Latin America	54.4	52.3	X	51.1	51	X
North America	2.5	2.7	X	1.9	1.8	X
Language Spoken at Home and Ability to Speak English						
Population 5 years and over..................	5,123,035	5,205,474	1.6	301,625,014	303,328,961	0.6
English only	82.8	82.9	X	78.5	78.4	X
Language other than English.................	17.2	17.1	X	21.5	21.6	X
Speaks English less than "very well".............	6.2	6.1	X	8.6	8.6	X

NA = Not available.
X = Not applicable.
- = Zero or rounds to zero.

Table CO-5. Median Income and Poverty Status, 2016

(Number, percent, except as noted.)

Characteristic	State		U.S.	
	Number	Percent	Number	Percent
Median Income				
Households (dollars)..	65,685	X	57,617	X
Families (dollars)	80,761	X	71,062	X
Below Poverty Level (All People)	598,736	11.0	44,268,996	14.0
Sex				
Male	273,088	10.1	19,760,056	12.8
Female	325,648	12.0	24,508,940	15.2
Age				
Under 18 years..	166,204	13.4	14,115,713	19.5
Related children under 18 years...	161,845	13.1	13,805,435	19.1
18 to 64 years...	377,172	10.9	25,723,818	13.2
65 years and over	55,360	7.6	4,429,465	9.2

X = Not applicable.

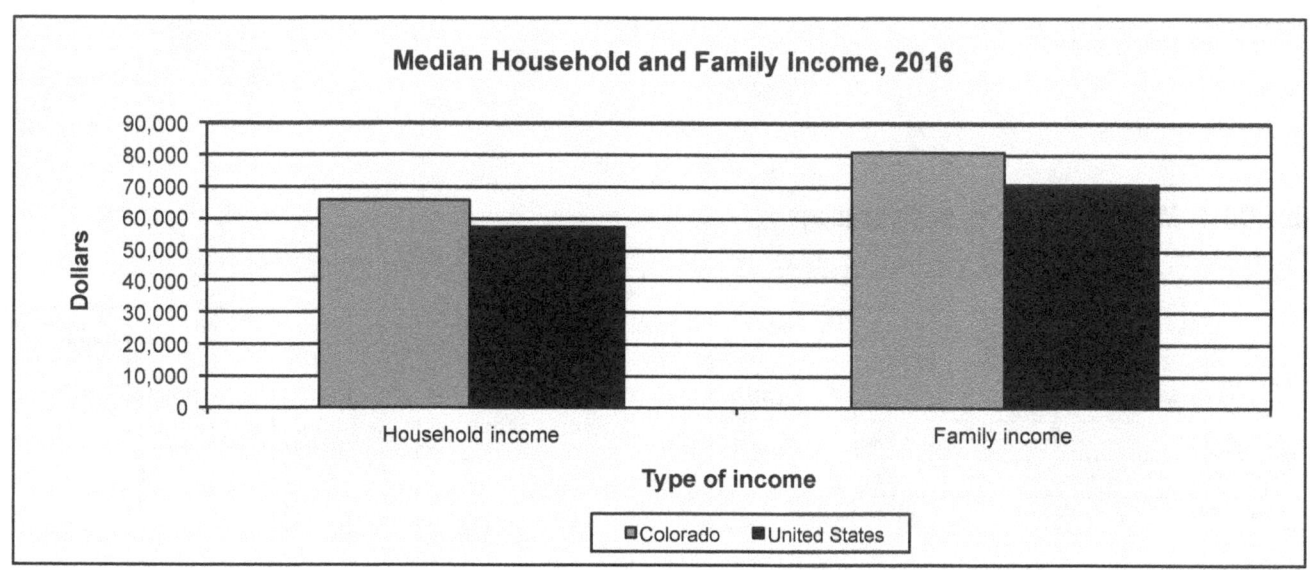

Table CO-6. Health Insurance Coverage Status for the Civilian Noninstitutionalized Population and Children Under 18 Years of Age

(Number, percent.)

Item	2008	2009	2010	2011	2012	2013	2014	2015	2016
Civilian Noninstitutionalized Population	4,853,404	4,930,142	4,956,873	5,024,885	5,094,766	5,173,272	5,266,022	5,367,335	5,447,760
Covered by Private or Public Insurance									
Number..	4,019,540	4,152,348	4,167,764	4,265,266	4,343,522	4,444,084	4,723,411	4,934,713	5,038,017
Percent..	82.8	84.2	84.1	84.9	85.3	85.9	89.7	91.9	92.5
Not Covered									
Number..	833,864	777,794	789,109	759,619	751,244	729,188	542,611	432,622	409,743
Percent..	17.2	15.8	15.9	15.1	14.7	14.1	10.3	8.1	7.5
Percent in the U.S. not covered......................	15.1	15.1	15.5	15.1	14.8	14.5	11.7	9.4	8.6
Children Under 18 Years of Age	1,203,936	1,225,211	1,226,208	1,226,828	1,229,008	1,239,191	1,245,432	1,254,800	1,258,167
Covered by Private or Public Insurance									
Number..	1,030,982	1,100,845	1,102,080	1,111,102	1,120,313	1,137,042	1,175,348	1,202,377	1,207,518
Percent..	85.6	89.8	89.9	90.6	91.2	91.8	94.4	95.8	96.0
Not Covered									
Number..	172,954	124,366	124,128	115,726	108,695	102,149	70,084	52,423	50,649
Percent..	14.4	10.2	10.1	9.4	8.8	8.2	5.6	4.2	4.0
Percent in the U.S. not covered......................	9.9	8.6	8.0	7.5	7.2	7.1	6.0	4.8	4.5

Table CO-7. Employment Status by Demographic Group, 2017

(Numbers in thousands, percent.)

Characteristic	Civilian noninstitutional population	Civilian labor force		Employed		Unemployed	
		Number	Percent of population	Number	Percent of population	Number	Percent of population
Total............	4,403	3,017	68.5	2,929	66.5	88	2.9
Sex							
Male..............	2,181	1,645	75.4	1,593	73.0	52	3.1
Female	2,221	1,372	61.8	1,336	60.2	36	2.6
Race, Sex, and Hispanic Origin							
White.............	3,919	2,669	68.1	2,599	66.3	71	2.6
Male..........	1,944	1,454	74.8	1,412	72.6	42	2.9
Female........	1,975	1,215	61.5	1,187	60.1	28	2.3
Black or African American.........	184	134	73.0	128	69.4	7	4.8
Male..........	NA	NA	NA	NA	NA	NA	NA
Female........	NA	NA	NA	NA	NA	NA	NA
Hispanic or Latino ethnicity[1]	879	588	66.9	568	64.7	20	3.4
Male..........	432	327	75.9	316	73.2	12	3.5
Female........	447	260	58.2	252	56.4	8	3.2
Age							
16 to 19 years........	NA	NA	NA	NA	NA	NA	NA
20 to 24 years........	376	301	80.1	284	75.5	17	5.7
25 to 34 years........	879	771	87.7	750	85.3	21	2.7
35 to 44 years........	740	635	85.8	619	83.6	16	2.5
45 to 54 years........	692	579	83.7	568	82.1	11	1.9
55 to 64 years........	695	460	66.1	450	64.8	10	2.1
65 years and over	779	180	23.2	176	22.6	4	2.4

NOTE: Data in Table 7 are from the Current Population Survey (CPS) and do not match the estimates in Table 8. See notes and definitions for further information.
[1] May be of any race.
NA = Not available.

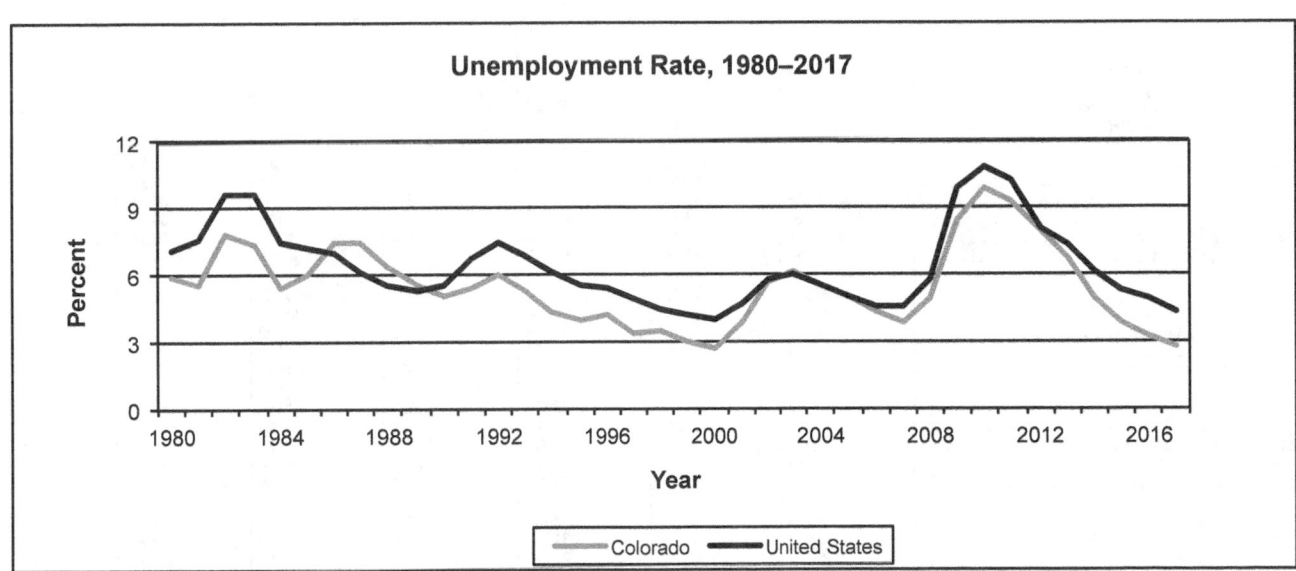

Table CO-8. Employment Status of the Civilian Noninstitutional Population Age 16 Years and Over

(Number, percent.)

Year	Civilian labor force	Civilian participation rate	Employed	Unemployed	Unemployment rate
2009........	2,722,982	70.9	2,524,443	198,539	7.3
2010........	2,724,417	70.4	2,486,404	238,013	8.7
2011........	2,736,079	69.7	2,507,265	228,814	8.4
2012........	2,757,222	69.1	2,539,941	217,281	7.9
2013........	2,767,153	68.2	2,577,556	189,597	6.9
2014........	2,799,491	67.7	2,659,474	140,017	5.0
2015........	2,824,759	66.8	2,715,059	109,700	3.9
2016........	2,893,268	67.0	2,798,928	94,340	3.3
2017........	2,992,307	68.1	2,907,468	84,839	2.8

Table CO-9. Employment and Average Wages by Industry

(Estimates through 2010 are based on the 2007 *North American Industry Classification System* [NAICS]. Estimates from 2011 onward are based on the 2012 NAICS.)

Industry	2010	2011	2012	2013	2014	2015	2016
	Number of Jobs						
Wage and Salary Employment by Industry.......................	2,349,153	2,387,218	2,438,809	2,508,945	2,595,372	2,669,849	2,729,045
Farm Wage and Salary Employment.................................	12,592	11,877	11,957	12,763	11,975	11,633	12,285
Nonfarm Wage and Salary Employment...........................	2,336,561	2,375,341	2,426,852	2,496,182	2,583,397	2,658,216	2,716,760
Private wage and salary employment...............................	1,881,939	1,919,927	1,970,009	2,030,850	2,112,518	2,179,526	2,230,493
Forestry, fishing, and related activities	5,720	5,845	6,123	6,405	6,424	6,424	6,560
Mining..	24,046	27,602	30,067	30,282	33,680	30,419	23,468
Utilities..	8,179	8,138	8,045	7,842	8,148	8,210	8,237
Construction..	119,224	115,869	119,294	131,491	146,265	152,528	159,572
Manufacturing...	125,597	129,321	132,160	132,867	136,528	141,078	142,606
Durable goods manufacturing...	81,212	84,036	86,437	86,028	88,175	90,297	90,065
Nondurable goods manufacturing...................................	44,385	45,285	45,723	46,839	48,353	50,781	52,541
Wholesale trade	91,240	92,201	94,601	97,135	100,420	103,748	105,416
Retail trade...	238,843	242,221	245,887	251,368	257,326	265,301	271,252
Transportation and warehousing.....................................	60,733	61,863	63,946	66,496	69,434	71,561	72,331
Information	71,749	72,474	69,954	69,965	70,179	70,597	71,832
Finance and insurance	101,650	102,496	104,569	107,617	108,848	111,434	114,378
Real estate and rental and leasing	42,460	42,382	42,885	43,968	45,516	47,912	49,751
Professional, scientific, and technical services	169,405	173,677	179,917	190,520	198,317	206,122	211,832
Management of companies and enterprises.....................	28,834	29,920	31,811	34,657	35,489	36,525	36,838
Administrative and waste services..................................	134,717	138,793	146,734	150,022	155,419	158,590	159,801
Educational services...	41,102	42,210	44,094	45,250	47,802	48,805	50,536
Health care and social assistance..................................	236,918	243,186	250,481	254,375	265,199	278,923	291,187
Arts, entertainment, and recreation................................	45,525	46,188	47,374	47,922	49,702	51,312	53,790
Accommodation and food services.................................	219,411	227,117	234,160	243,440	252,637	263,107	272,135
Other services, except public administration...................	116,586	118,424	117,907	119,228	125,185	126,930	128,971
Government and government enterprises.........................	454,622	455,414	456,843	465,332	470,879	478,690	486,267
	Dollars						
Average Wages and Salaries by Industry	48,437	49,664	51,260	51,654	53,442	54,900	58,306
Average Farm Wages and Salaries	31,724	33,979	38,509	40,726	41,821	40,872	43,090
Average Nonfarm Wages and Salaries	48,527	49,742	51,323	51,710	53,496	54,961	58,375
Average private wages and salaries................................	48,818	50,192	52,033	52,340	54,244	55,745	59,246
Forestry, fishing, and related activities	24,122	24,717	25,275	26,128	27,557	29,381	35,267
Mining..	100,276	105,864	104,927	109,964	113,847	115,803	126,480
Utilities..	87,151	91,745	100,647	90,933	93,545	96,924	100,736
Construction..	48,815	49,856	51,118	51,966	54,567	56,221	62,388
Manufacturing...	61,761	63,371	64,040	64,245	67,023	68,360	72,180
Durable goods manufacturing...	67,851	69,995	70,900	71,194	73,717	76,012	81,726
Nondurable goods manufacturing...................................	50,616	51,081	51,073	51,481	54,818	54,754	55,817
Wholesale trade	69,688	72,904	75,091	75,691	78,933	80,972	85,600
Retail trade...	27,852	28,110	28,930	29,322	30,264	31,249	32,708
Transportation and warehousing.....................................	46,330	47,504	49,648	52,102	54,520	55,661	62,959
Information	83,611	85,856	90,251	92,109	97,855	96,236	99,071
Finance and insurance	73,432	76,342	79,736	81,358	84,896	89,899	94,609
Real estate and rental and leasing.................................	43,188	45,195	48,328	50,529	51,969	54,437	59,688
Professional, scientific, and technical services	81,097	82,811	85,508	86,369	88,620	90,355	96,344
Management of companies and enterprises.....................	127,324	133,543	155,549	127,658	136,933	145,515	157,067
Administrative and waste services..................................	35,348	36,061	36,857	35,890	37,175	38,919	41,852
Educational services...	33,932	34,476	35,060	35,653	35,459	35,325	36,348
Health care and social assistance..................................	45,390	46,167	47,118	47,360	48,241	49,699	52,548
Arts, entertainment, and recreation................................	33,516	34,359	34,755	35,796	37,060	39,548	41,789
Accommodation and food services.................................	19,774	20,449	21,119	21,662	22,491	23,591	25,865
Other services, except public administration...................	31,973	32,522	34,166	35,166	35,854	37,378	40,361
Government and government enterprises............................	47,324	47,846	48,262	48,962	50,136	51,390	54,380

Table CO-10. Employment Characteristics by Family Type

(Number, percent.)

Family type and labor force status	2014		2015		2016	
	Total	Families with own children under 18 years	Total	Families with own children under 18 years	Total	Families with own children under 18 years
All Families..	1,309,702	599,088	1,331,861	597,501	1,347,936	595,865
FAMILY TYPE AND LABOR FORCE STATUS						
Married-Couple Families...	1,000,145	421,101	1,038,040	435,028	1,051,388	437,459
Both husband and wife in labor force...............................	54.0	64.4	54.3	65.4	53.9	65.9
Husband in labor force, wife not in labor force	23.3	30.5	22.0	28.5	22.5	29.0
Wife in labor force, husband not in labor force	6.8	3.6	7.2	3.9	7.3	3.4
Both husband and wife not in labor force.............................	15.8	1.5	15.5	1.7	15.4	1.1
Other Families	309,557	177,987	293,821	162,473	296,548	158,406
Female householder, no husband present..............................	68.0	69.1	68.3	69.9	66.7	71.9
In labor force..	51.2	58.6	50.1	57.9	50.6	61.8
Not in labor force	16.8	10.5	18.2	11.9	16.1	10.1
Male householder, no wife present....................................	32.0	30.9	31.7	30.1	33.3	28.1
In labor force..	26.9	29.0	26.4	28.6	27.4	26.4
Not in labor force	5.1	1.9	5.3	1.5	5.9	1.7

Table CO-11. School Enrollment and Educational Attainment, 2016

(Number, percent.)

Item	State	U.S.
Enrollment		
Total population 3 years and over, enrolled in school	1,382,107	81,572,277
Enrolled in nursery school or preschool (percent)	5.9	6.0
Enrolled in kindergarten (percent)..	5.0	5.0
Enrolled in elementary school, grades 1-8 (percent)...	41.6	40.3
Enrolled in high school, grades 9-12 (percent)...	20.4	21.0
Enrolled in college or graduate school (percent)...	27.1	27.7
Attainment		
Total population 25 years and over	3,745,506	218,475,480
Less than ninth grade (percent)	3.4	5.4
9th to 12th grade, no diploma (percent)	5.1	7.2
High school graduate, including equivalency (percent)...	22.0	27.2
Some college, no degree (percent)	21.0	20.6
Associate's degree (percent)	8.6	8.4
Bachelor's degree (percent)	24.9	19.3
Graduate or professional degree (percent)	14.9	11.9
High school graduate or higher (percent)..	91.4	87.5
Bachelor's degree or higher (percent)...	39.9	31.3

Table CO-12. Public School Characteristics and Educational Indicators

(Number, percent; data derived from National Center of Education Statistics.)

Item	State	U.S.
Public Schools, 2015–2016 (except where noted)		
Number of school districts...	265	18,328
Number of schools...	1,862	98,456
Number of students..	899,112	50,327,015
Number of teachers..	51,798	3,151,497
Student-teacher ratio	17.4	16.0
Expenditures per student (dollars), 2014-2015..	9,292	11,445
Four-year adjusted cohort graduation rate (ACGR)[1,2]	78.9	84.1
Students eligible for free or reduced-price lunch (percent), 2014-2015................................	41.6	51.8
English language learners (percent), Fall 2015	11.6	9.5
Students age 3 to 21 served under IDEA, part B (percent)..	10.6	13.2

Public Schools by Type	Number	Percent of state public schools
Total number of schools..	1,862	100.0
Regular	1,756	94.3
Special education	6	0.3
Vocational education	6	0.3
Alternative education..	94	5.0

NOTE: Every school is assigned only one school type based on its instructional emphasis.
[1] ACGR data represents a new method of calculating high-school completion rates and may not be comparable to previous years' data for Averaged Freshmen Graduation Rates (AFGR).
[2] The United States 4-year ACGRs were estimated using both the reported 4-year ACGR data from 49 states and the District of Columbia and using imputed data for Idaho. The estimate for American Indian/Alaska Native students also includes imputed data for Virginia.

Table CO-13. Reported Voting and Registration of the Voting-Age Population, November 2016

(Numbers in thousands, percent.)

Item	Total population	Total citizen population	Registered			Voted		
			Total registered	Percent registered (total population)	Percent registered (total citizen population)	Total voted	Percent voted (total population)	Percent voted (total citizen population)
U.S. Total	245,502	224,059	157,596	64.2	70.3	137,537	56.0	61.4
State Total..............................	4,242	3,895	2,893	68.2	74.3	2,707	63.8	69.5
Sex								
Male	2,102	1,902	1,401	66.7	73.7	1,297	61.7	68.2
Female	2,140	1,994	1,492	69.7	74.8	1,410	65.9	70.7
Race								
White alone..............................	3,743	3,517	2,663	71.2	75.7	2,494	66.6	70.9
White, non-Hispanic alone...........	3,181	3,125	2,421	76.1	77.5	2,281	71.7	73.0
Black alone..............................	185	167	124	67.0	74.1	124	67.0	74.1
Asian alone.............................	170	104	39	22.7	37.0	35	20.5	33.4
Hispanic (of any race).................	633	426	272	42.9	63.8	237	37.4	55.6
White alone or in combination	3,857	3,595	2,711	70.3	75.4	2,538	65.8	70.6
Black alone or in combination	188	170	127	67.6	74.6	127	67.6	74.6
Asian alone or in combination.......	188	122	52	27.5	42.2	44	23.5	36.1
Age								
18 to 24 years..........................	410	361	210	51.2	58.2	177	43.1	49.0
25 to 34 years..........................	922	851	596	64.7	70.1	535	58.0	62.9
35 to 44 years..........................	774	683	535	69.1	78.2	514	66.5	75.3
45 to 64 years..........................	1,342	1,243	914	68.1	73.6	867	64.6	69.7
65 years and over	794	757	638	80.4	84.3	614	77.3	81.1

B = Base is less than 75,000 and therefore too small to show the derived measure.

Table CO-14. Crime

(Number, rate per 100,000. Data are derived from the FBI Uniform Crime Reports.)

Item	State			U.S. [1,2,3,4]		
	2015	2016	Percent change	2015	2016	Percent change
TOTAL POPULATION [5]	5,456,574	5,540,545	1.5	321,418,820	323,127,513	0.5
VIOLENT CRIME						
Number..	17,515	18,983	8.4	1,231,566	1,248,185	1.3
Rate	321.0	342.6	6.7	383.2	386.3	0.8
Murder and Nonnegligent Manslaughter						
Number..	176	204	15.9	15,696	17,250	9.9
Rate	3.2	3.7	15.6	4.9	5.3	8.2
Rape [6]						
Number..	3,257	3,555	9.1	124,047	130,603	5.3
Rate	59.7	64.2	7.5	38.6	40.4	4.7
Robbery						
Number..	3,323	3,528	6.2	327,374	332,198	1.5
Rate	60.9	63.7	4.6	101.9	102.8	0.9
Aggravated Assault						
Number..	10,759	11,696	8.7	764,449	803,007	5.0
Rate	197.2	211.1	7.0	237.8	248.5	4.5
PROPERTY CRIME						
Number..	144,136	151,850	5.4	7,993,631	7,919,035	-0.9
Rate	2,641.5	2,740.7	3.8	2,487.0	2,450.7	-1.5
Burglary						
Number..	23,454	23,903	1.9	1,579,527	1,515,096	-4.1
Rate	429.8	431.4	0.4	491.4	468.9	-4.6
Larceny-Theft						
Number..	104,682	108,336	3.5	5,706,346	5,638,455	-1.2
Rate	1,918.5	1,955.3	1.9	1,775.4	1,745.0	-1.7
Motor Vehicle Theft						
Number..	16,000	19,611	22.6	707,758	765,484	8.2
Rate	293.2	354.0	20.7	220.2	236.9	7.6

NOTE: Although arson data are included in the trend and clearance tables, sufficient data are not available to estimate totals for this offense. Therefore, no arson data are published in this table.
X = Not applicable.
- = Zero or rounds to zero.
[1] The crime figures have been adjusted.
[2] The data collection methodology for the offense of forcible rape used by the Minnesota state Uniform Crime Reporting (UCR) Program (with the exception of Minneapolis and St. Paul, Minnesota) does not comply with national UCR Program guidelines. Consequently, its figures for forcible rape and violent crime (of which forcible rape is a part) are not published in this table.
[3] Includes offenses reported by the Zoological Police and the Metro Transit Police.
[4] Because of changes in the state's reporting practices, figures are not comparable to previous years' data.
[5] Populations are U.S. Census Bureau provisional estimates as of July 1 of each year.
[6] The figures shown for the offense of rape were estimated using the revised Uniform Crime Reporting (UCR) definition of rape.

Table CO-15. State Government Finances, 2016

(Dollar amounts in thousands, percent distribution.)

Item	Dollars	Percent distribution
Total Revenue	31,399,864	100.0
General revenue	27,529,600	87.7
Intergovernmental revenue	8,703,745	27.7
Taxes	12,795,318	40.7
General sales	2,840,173	9.0
Selective sales	2,056,856	6.6
License taxes	702,499	2.2
Individual income tax	6,485,602	20.7
Corporate income tax	626,109	2.0
Other taxes	84,079	0.3
Current charges	3,861,835	12.3
Miscellaneous general revenue	2,168,702	6.9
Utility revenue	0	-
Liquor stores revenue	0	-
Insurance trust revenue [1]	3,870,264	12.3
Total Expenditure	34,596,327	100.0
Intergovernmental expenditure	7,310,747	21.1
Direct expenditure	27,285,580	78.9
Current operation	18,649,419	53.9
Capital outlay	1,814,511	5.2
Insurance benefits and repayments	5,483,219	15.8
Assistance and subsidies	478,980	1.4
Interest on debt	859,451	2.5
Exhibit: Salaries and wages	5,242,693	15.2
Total Expenditure	34,596,327	100.0
General expenditure	29,099,805	84.1
Intergovernmental expenditure	7,310,747	21.1
Direct expenditure	21,789,058	63.0
General expenditure, by function:		
Education	11,792,772	34.1
Public welfare	8,639,905	25.0
Hospitals	914,126	2.6
Health	620,427	1.8
Highways	1,863,367	5.4
Police protection	239,939	0.7
Correction	1,079,854	3.1
Natural resources	338,162	1.0
Parks and recreation	105,737	0.3
Governmental administration	955,678	2.8
Interest on general debt	847,767	2.5
Other and unallocable	1,702,071	4.9
Utility expenditure	13,303	-
Liquor stores expenditure	0	-
Insurance trust expenditure	5,483,219	15.8
Debt at End of Fiscal Year	16,686,588	X
Cash and Security Holdings	72,096,139	X

X = Not applicable.
- = Zero or rounds to zero.
[1] Within insurance trust revenue, net earnings of state retirement systems is a calculated statistic (the item code in the data file is X08), and thus can be positive or negative. Net earnings is the sum of earnings on investments plus gains on investments minus losses on investments. The change made in 2002 for asset valuation from book to market value in accordance with Statement 34 of the Governmental Accounting Standards Board is reflected in the calculated statistics.

Table CO-16. State Government Tax Collections, 2017

(Dollars in thousands, percent.)

Item	Dollars	Percent distribution
Total Taxes	13,197,606	100.0
Property taxes	X	-
Sales and gross receipts	5,128,852	38.9
General sales and gross receipts	2,978,382	22.6
Selective sales and gross receipts	2,150,470	16.3
Alcoholic beverages	44,866	0.3
Amusements	97,630	0.7
Insurance premiums	256,212	1.9
Motor fuels	653,790	5.0
Pari-mutuels	625	-
Public utilities	X	-
Tobacco products	199,989	1.5
Other selective sales	897,358	6.8
Licenses	748,284	5.7
Alcoholic beverages	7,840	0.1
Amusements	723	-
Corporations in general	17,638	0.1
Hunting and fishing	75,573	0.6
Motor vehicle	536,975	4.1
Motor vehicle operators	41,502	0.3
Public utilities	13,245	0.1
Occupation and business, NEC	54,671	0.4
Other licenses	117	-
Income taxes	7,320,470	55.5
Individual income	6,791,929	51.5
Corporation net income	528,541	4.0
Other taxes	0	-
Death and gift	X	-
Documentary and stock transfer	X	-
Severance	0	-
Taxes, NEC	0	-

X = Not applicable.
- = Zero or rounds to zero.

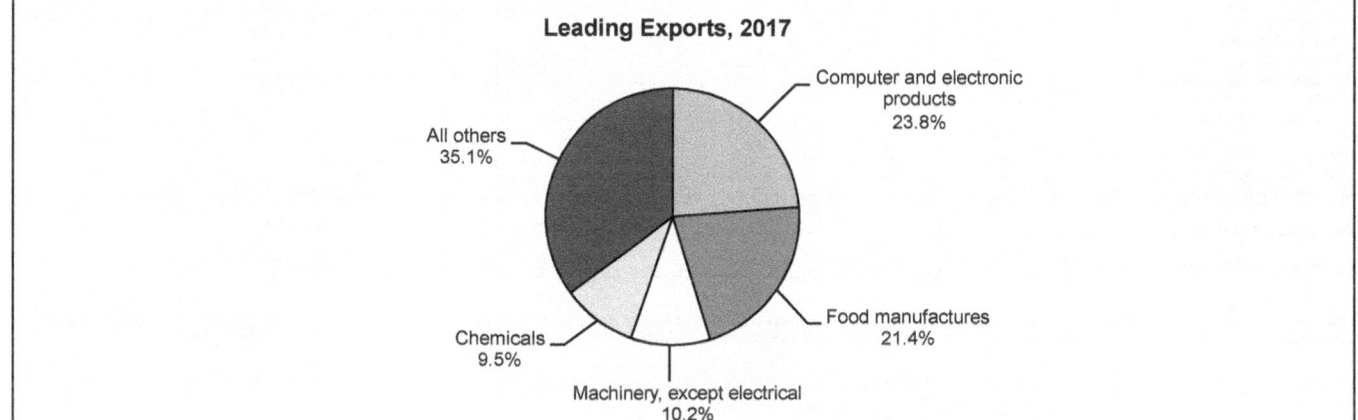

Leading Exports, 2017

Computer and electronic products 23.8%

All others 35.1%

Chemicals 9.5%

Machinery, except electrical 10.2%

Food manufactures 21.4%

CONNECTICUT

Facts and Figures

Location: Northeastern United States; bordered on the N by Massachusetts, on the E by Rhode Island, on the S by Long Island Sound, and on the W by New York

Area: 5,543 sq. mi. (14,357); rank—48th

Population: 3,588,184 (2017 est.); rank—29th

Principal Cities: capital—Hartford; largest—Bridgeport

Statehood: January 9, 1788; 5th state

U.S. Congress: 2 senators, 5 representatives

State Motto: *Qui transtulit sustinet* ("He who transplanted still sustains")

State Song: "Yankee Doodle"

State Nicknames: The Constitution State; The Nutmeg State

Abbreviations: CT; Conn.

State Symbols: flower—mountain laurel; tree—white oak; bird—American robin

At a Glance

- With an increase in population of just 0.2 percent, Connecticut experienced the smallest population growth among the states between 2010 and 2017.

- Connecticut's median household income in 2016 was $73,433, compared to the national median household income of $57,617.

- In 2016, 38.6 percent of Connecticut residents age 25 and older had a bachelor's degree or higher, which was the 5th highest percent in the country.

- Connecticut's per capita personal income in 2017 was $70,121, ranking 2nd in the nation.

- The violent and property crime rates in Connecticut in 2016 were below the national average, at 227.1 and 1,808.0 incidents per 100,000 population respectively.

Table CT-1. Population by Age, Sex, Race, and Hispanic Origin

(Number, percent, except where noted.)

Sex, age, race, and Hispanic origin	2000	2010	2017 [1]	Average annual percent change, 2010–2017
Total Population..	3,405,565	3,574,097	3,588,184	0.4
Percent of total U.S. population	1.2	1.2	1.1	X
Sex				
Male...	1,649,319	1,739,614	1,751,800	0.7
Female	1,756,246	1,834,483	1,836,384	0.1
Age				
Under 5 years...	233,344	202,106	183,321	-9.3
5 to 19 years...	702,358	713,670	664,554	-6.9
20 to 64 years...	2,009,680	2,151,762	2,137,899	-0.6
65 years and over	470,183	506,559	602,410	18.9
Median age (years)	37.4	40.0	40.9	2.2
Race and Hispanic Origin				
One race				
White..	2,780,355	2,950,820	2,879,759	-2.4
Black..	309,843	392,131	426,851	8.9
American Indian and Alaska Native	9,639	16,734	19,480	16.4
Asian..	82,313	140,516	173,633	23.6
Native Hawaiian or Other Pacific Islander	1,366	3,491	3,845	10.1
Two or more races	74,848	70,405	84,616	20.2
Hispanic (of any race).......................................	320,323	498,638	578,833	16.1

X = Not applicable.
[1] Population figures for 2017 are July 1 estimates. The 2010 estimates are taken from the 2010 Census.
- = Zero or rounds to zero.

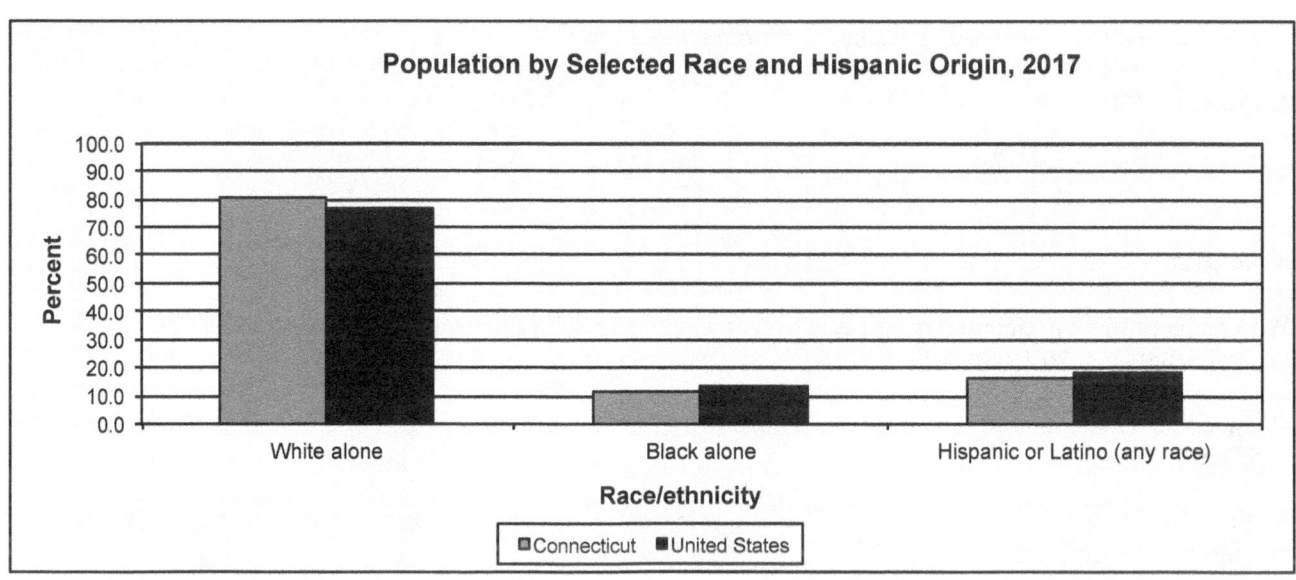

Table CT-2. Marital Status

(Number, percent distribution.)

Sex, age, and marital status	2000	2010	2016
Males, 15 Years and Over	1,284,881	1,399,329	1,433,885
Never married	30.0	36.3	38.7
Now married, except separated..	58.0	50.6	48.6
Separated..	1.3	1.1	1.1
Widowed..	2.7	2.7	2.7
Divorced..	7.9	9.3	8.9
Females, 15 Years and Over	1,411,369	1,512,492	1,532,640
Never married	24.5	29.9	32.0
Now married, except separated..	52.3	46.5	45.3
Separated..	1.8	1.8	1.4
Widowed..	10.8	9.3	8.7
Divorced..	10.5	12.5	12.6

Table CT-3. Households and Housing Characteristics

(Number, percent, dollars.)

Item	2000	2010	2016	Average annual percent change, 2010–2016
Total Households	1,301,670	1,358,809	1,357,269	-
Family households	881,170	890,770	880,600	-0.2
Married-couple family	676,467	656,629	648,449	-0.2
Other family	204,703	234,141	232,151	-0.1
Male householder, no wife present	47,292	58,325	59,511	0.3
Female householder, no husband present	157,411	175,816	172,640	-0.3
Nonfamily households	420,500	468,039	476,669	0.3
Householder living alone	334,224	384,382	389,271	0.2
Householder not living alone	76,276	83,657	87,398	0.7
Housing Characteristics				
Total housing units	1,385,975	1,488,215	1,499,145	0.1
Occupied housing units	1,301,670	1,358,809	1,357,269	-
Owner occupied	869,729	923,617	879,073	-0.8
Renter occupied	431,941	435,192	478,196	1.6
Average household size	2.53	2.55	2.55	-
Financial Characteristics				
Median gross rent of renter-occupied housing	681	992	1,115	2.1
Median monthly owner costs for housing units with a mortgage	1,426	2,068	1,997	-0.6
Median value of owner-occupied housing units	166,900	288,800	274,600	-0.8

- = Zero or rounds to zero

Table CT-4. Migration, Origin, and Language

(Number, percent.)

Characteristic	State			U.S.		
	2015	2016	Percent change	2015	2016	Percent change
Residence 1 Year Ago						
Population 1 year and over	3,554,844	3,541,758	-0.4	317,635,720	319,361,956	0.5
Same house	87.5	88.0	X	85.3	85.4	X
Different house in the U.S.	11.7	11.3	X	14.1	13.9	X
Same county	7.4	7.2	X	8.5	8.3	X
Different county	4.4	4	X	5.6	5.6	X
Same state	2.2	1.9	X	3.2	3.2	X
Different state	2.2	2.1	X	2.4	2.4	X
Abroad	0.8	0.7	X	0.7	0.7	X
Place of Birth						
Native born	3071238	3,062,402	-0.3	278,128,449	279,388,170	0.5
Male	48.8	49.1	X	49.3	49.3	X
Female	51.2	50.9	X	50.7	50.7	X
Foreign born	519648	514,050	-1.1	43,290,372	43,739,345	1.0
Male	48.9	47.1	X	48.6	48.5	X
Female	51.1	52.9	X	51.4	51.5	X
Foreign born; naturalized U.S. citizen	253505	270,273	6.6	20,697,103	21,238,372	2.6
Male	45	43.9	X	45.9	45.9	X
Female	55	56.1	X	54.1	54.1	X
Foreign born; not a U.S. citizen	266143	243,777	-8.4	22,593,269	22,500,973	-0.4
Male	52.6	50.8	X	51.1	51	X
Female	47.4	49.2	X	48.9	49	X
Entered 2010 or later	17	19.2	X	15.6	18.6	X
Entered 2000 to 2009	28.6	26	X	27.9	26.7	X
Entered before 2000	54.3	54.8	X	56.5	54.7	X
World Region of Birth, Foreign						
Foreign-born population, excluding population born at sea	519648	514,050	-1.1	43,289,646	43,738,901	1.0
Europe	25.6	24.2	X	11.1	10.9	X
Asia	24.3	25.1	X	30.6	30.8	X
Africa	3.9	5	X	4.8	4.9	X
Oceania	0.4	0.4	X	0.6	0.6	X
Latin America	42.9	42.7	X	51.1	51	X
North America	2.9	2.6	X	1.9	1.8	X
Language Spoken at Home and Ability to Speak English						
Population 5 years and over	3404358	3,391,423	-0.4	301,625,014	303,328,961	0.6
English only	77.6	77.3	X	78.5	78.4	X
Language other than English	22.4	22.7	X	21.5	21.6	X
Speaks English less than "very well"	8.2	7.9	X	8.6	8.6	X

NA = Not available.
X = Not applicable.
- = Zero or rounds to zero.

Table CT-5. Median Income and Poverty Status, 2016

(Number, percent, except as noted.)

Characteristic	State		U.S.	
	Number	Percent	Number	Percent
Median Income				
Households (dollars)	73,433	X	57,617	X
Families (dollars)	94,449	X	71,062	X
Below Poverty Level (All People)	339,128	9.8	44,268,996	14.0
Sex				
Male	150,954	8.9	19,760,056	12.8
Female	188,174	10.6	24,508,940	15.2
Age				
Under 18 years	95,597	12.9	14,115,713	19.5
Related children under 18 years	93,289	12.6	13,805,435	19.1
18 to 64 years	207,443	9.6	25,723,818	13.2
65 years and over	36,088	6.5	4,429,465	9.2

X = Not applicable.

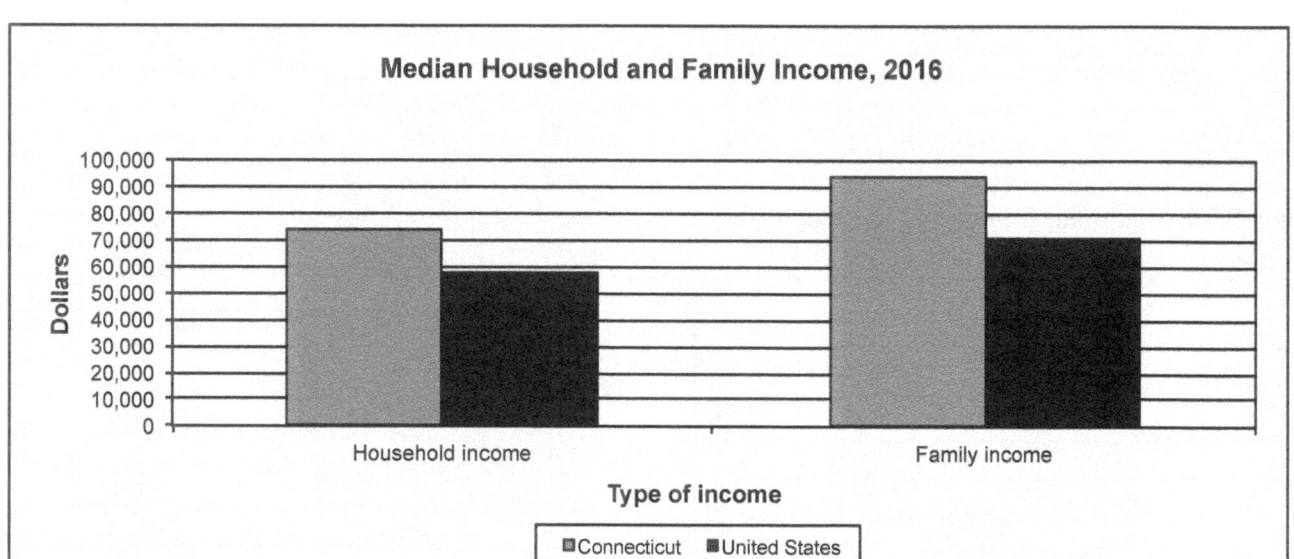

Table CT-6. Health Insurance Coverage Status for the Civilian Noninstitutionalized Population and Children Under 18 Years of Age

(Number, percent.)

Item	2008	2009	2010	2011	2012	2013	2014	2015	2016
Civilian Noninstitutionalized Population	3,440,844	3,456,856	3,519,913	3,522,709	3,534,619	3,541,409	3,541,282	3,537,983	3,525,154
Covered by Private or Public Insurance									
Number	3,130,247	3,151,646	3,199,780	3,213,764	3,212,647	3,208,906	3,295,883	3,327,461	3,352,940
Percent	91.0	91.2	90.9	91.2	90.9	90.6	93.1	94.0	95.1
Not Covered									
Number	310,597	305,210	320,133	308,945	321,972	332,503	245,399	210,522	172,214
Percent	9.0	8.8	9.1	8.8	9.1	9.4	6.9	6.0	4.9
Percent in the U.S. not covered	15.1	15.1	15.5	15.1	14.8	14.5	11.7	9.4	8.6
Children Under 18 Years of Age	809,967	806,799	815,010	802,350	791,825	784,159	774,021	761,921	751,459
Covered by Private or Public Insurance									
Number	770,389	776,366	790,896	778,973	761,897	750,504	745,151	736,821	730,592
Percent	95.1	96.2	97.0	97.1	96.2	95.7	96.3	96.7	97.2
Not Covered									
Number	39,578	30,433	24,114	23,377	29,928	33,655	28,870	25,100	20,867
Percent	4.9	3.8	3.0	2.9	3.8	4.3	3.7	3.3	2.8
Percent in the U.S. not covered	9.9	8.6	8.0	7.5	7.2	7.1	6.0	4.8	4.5

Table CT-7. Employment Status by Demographic Group, 2017

(Numbers in thousands, percent.)

Characteristic	Civilian noninstitutional population	Civilian labor force		Employed		Unemployed	
		Number	Percent of population	Number	Percent of population	Number	Percent of population
Total...	2,877	1,915	66.6	1,822	63.3	93	4.9
Sex							
Male...	1,384	992	71.7	941	68.0	51	5.2
Female..	1,493	923	61.9	881	59.0	42	4.6
Race, Sex, and Hispanic Origin							
White..	2,401	1,607	67.0	1,530	63.7	78	4.8
Male...	1,169	840	71.8	795	68.0	45	5.3
Female..	1,231	768	62.4	735	59.7	33	4.3
Black or African American................	316	205	64.7	192	60.8	12	6.0
Male...	146	99	67.9	93	63.9	6	5.8
Female..	171	106	61.9	99	58.1	7	6.2
Hispanic or Latino ethnicity[1]............	425	285	67.1	260	61.2	25	8.7
Male...	202	148	73.1	135	66.7	13	8.8
Female..	223	137	61.6	125	56.3	12	8.6
Age							
16 to 19 years.................................	182	64	35.3	55	30.3	9	14.4
20 to 24 years.................................	222	150	67.7	138	62.2	12	8.0
25 to 34 years.................................	483	408	84.5	388	80.3	20	4.9
35 to 44 years.................................	403	347	86.2	336	83.6	11	3.1
45 to 54 years.................................	489	407	83.2	387	79.1	20	4.9
55 to 64 years.................................	531	398	74.9	383	72.0	16	3.9
65 years and over............................	566	141	24.8	135	23.8	6	4.1

NOTE: Data in Table 7 are from the Current Population Survey (CPS) and do not match the estimates in Table 8. See notes and definitions for further information.
[1] May be of any race.

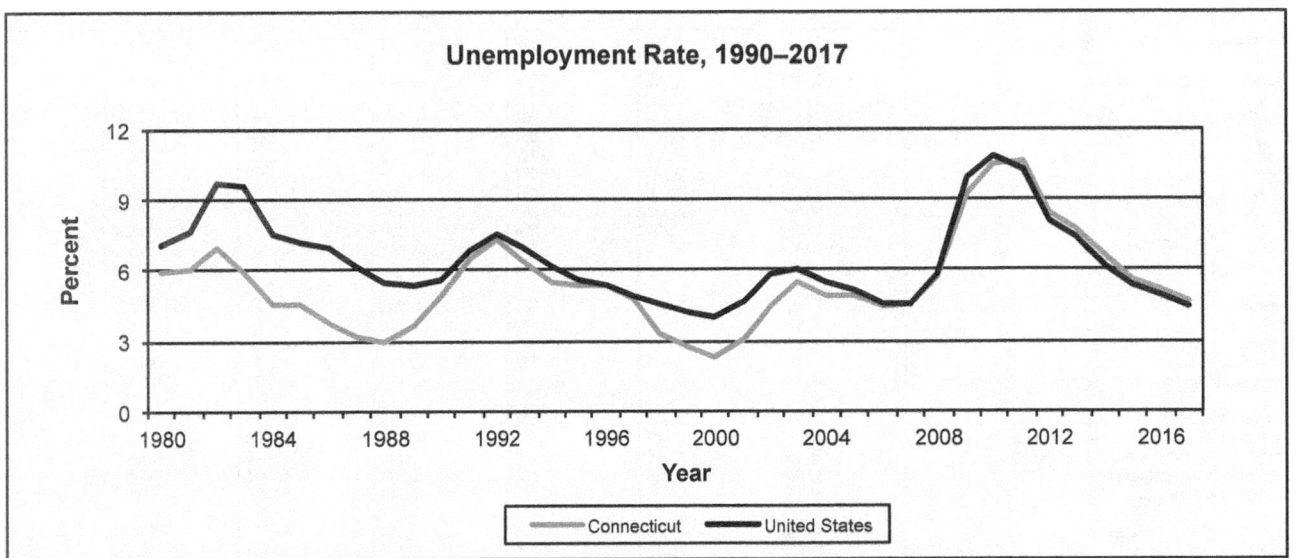

Table CT-8. Employment Status of the Civilian Noninstitutional Population Age 16 Years and Over

(Number, percent.)

Year	Civilian labor force	Civilian participation rate	Employed	Unemployed	Unemployment rate
2009...	1,891,077	68.8	1,740,971	150,106	7.9
2010...	1,911,712	68.3	1,737,449	174,263	9.1
2011...	1,914,775	67.6	1,745,967	168,808	8.8
2012...	1,887,419	66.3	1,729,838	157,581	8.3
2013...	1,863,337	65.1	1,717,764	145,573	7.8
2014...	1,892,451	65.9	1,767,282	125,169	6.6
2015...	1,895,832	65.9	1,787,434	108,398	5.7
2016...	1,904,556	66.1	1,806,575	97,981	5.1
2017...	1,918,576	66.4	1,828,858	89,718	4.7

Table CT-9. Employment and Average Wages by Industry

(Estimates through 2010 are based on the 2007 *North American Industry Classification System* [NAICS]. Estimates from 2011 onward are based on the 2012 NAICS.)

Industry	2010	2011	2012	2013	2014	2015	2016
	Number of Jobs						
Wage and Salary Employment by Industry..........................	1,673,114	1,688,186	1,706,144	1,718,152	1,731,804	1,740,112	1,742,685
Farm Wage and Salary Employment................................	4,395	4,806	4,775	5,463	5,478	5,458	5,094
Nonfarm Wage and Salary Employment............................	1,668,719	1,683,380	1,701,369	1,712,689	1,726,326	1,734,654	1,737,591
Private wage and salary employment...................................	1,403,233	1,422,376	1,439,674	1,451,008	1,465,127	1,474,937	1,482,065
Forestry, fishing, and related activities............................	697	688	661	680	707	692	663
Mining..	571	542	554	543	547	553	556
Utilities...	6,308	6,172	5,935	6,042	5,943	5,609	5,624
Construction...	51,686	53,150	53,136	55,195	57,414	59,386	60,712
Manufacturing..	165,769	166,429	165,402	164,021	159,793	159,163	156,601
Durable goods manufacturing.................................	127,381	128,567	128,740	127,608	124,402	123,778	122,931
Nondurable goods manufacturing............................	38,388	37,862	36,662	36,413	35,391	35,385	33,670
Wholesale trade	62,988	63,707	63,505	63,421	63,381	62,807	62,827
Retail trade...	179,971	182,004	183,882	185,197	186,544	186,288	186,196
Transportation and warehousing...............................	39,809	41,081	41,819	42,551	43,717	45,286	46,217
Information...	31,760	31,502	31,332	32,093	32,058	32,414	32,456
Finance and insurance	118,200	118,013	116,438	114,287	111,613	112,060	111,893
Real estate and rental and leasing............................	19,498	19,438	19,411	19,508	19,708	20,317	20,435
Professional, scientific, and technical services	86,845	88,750	90,300	91,094	96,019	96,416	97,771
Management of companies and enterprises.....................	27,837	28,621	30,608	30,693	31,899	32,934	32,961
Administrative and waste services.............................	78,348	81,570	84,698	85,669	86,366	88,499	89,070
Educational services	65,116	65,999	67,063	67,206	69,023	69,441	70,606
Health care and social assistance.............................	251,518	254,353	258,265	261,820	264,250	266,256	268,538
Arts, entertainment, and recreation............................	23,920	24,300	25,160	26,181	26,674	27,063	27,942
Accommodation and food services............................	110,791	114,006	118,413	122,133	124,696	125,134	127,240
Other services, except public administration..................	81,601	82,051	83,092	82,674	84,775	84,619	83,757
Government and government enterprises............................	265,486	261,004	261,695	261,681	261,199	259,717	255,526
	Dollars						
Average Wages and Salaries by Industry	58,483	60,182	61,119	61,396	62,963	64,551	64,976
Average Farm Wages and Salaries	26,135	20,919	31,008	27,945	29,499	27,182	32,107
Average Nonfarm Wages and Salaries	58,568	60,294	61,204	61,502	63,069	64,669	65,072
Average private wages and salaries................................	59,670	61,400	62,554	62,753	64,301	65,807	66,267
Forestry, fishing, and related activities........................	23,735	24,028	25,442	25,859	26,358	28,042	29,291
Mining..	68,023	68,865	64,532	64,803	70,311	71,403	70,849
Utilities...	103,567	111,556	109,731	110,984	111,305	116,904	113,945
Construction	58,580	58,332	59,267	59,406	61,085	64,258	66,039
Manufacturing..	73,394	77,201	78,926	81,590	81,398	80,502	83,096
Durable goods manufacturing.................................	72,978	76,322	78,603	81,647	82,106	80,816	84,521
Nondurable goods manufacturing............................	74,775	80,186	80,058	81,389	78,911	79,406	77,895
Wholesale trade	81,517	83,379	85,380	85,982	87,722	92,692	93,165
Retail trade...	30,861	31,173	31,509	31,560	32,099	33,010	33,197
Transportation and warehousing...............................	46,347	47,312	47,933	46,991	47,757	48,639	49,405
Information...	77,161	78,926	82,327	89,138	93,028	99,296	97,132
Finance and insurance	143,441	152,257	153,271	150,119	159,035	163,571	160,942
Real estate and rental and leasing............................	55,196	59,735	64,697	64,006	65,763	69,433	66,655
Professional, scientific, and technical services	88,279	89,660	91,718	92,646	95,859	98,993	101,133
Management of companies and enterprises.....................	135,100	139,184	156,139	161,131	163,440	162,453	146,641
Administrative and waste services.............................	40,008	40,829	41,269	40,827	43,017	44,101	46,140
Educational services	45,644	46,906	48,767	50,949	52,390	53,372	54,436
Health care and social assistance.............................	46,955	47,563	48,441	48,559	49,811	50,244	51,623
Arts, entertainment, and recreation............................	28,857	29,043	29,245	29,218	30,153	31,221	32,536
Accommodation and food services............................	20,298	20,614	21,234	21,364	22,055	23,303	24,723
Other services, except public administration..................	30,999	31,408	31,997	32,808	33,570	34,762	36,510
Government and government enterprises............................	52,743	54,268	53,779	54,567	56,161	58,209	58,138

Table CT-10. Employment Characteristics by Family Type

(Number, percent.)

Family type and labor force status	2014		2015		2016	
	Total	Families with own children under 18 years	Total	Families with own children under 18 years	Total	Families with own children under 18 years
All Families..	881,355	378,078	876,188	365,594	880,600	359,819
FAMILY TYPE AND LABOR FORCE STATUS						
Married-Couple Families..............................	644,765	256,409	647,589	248,839	648,449	246,535
Both husband and wife in labor force...........................	57.2	70.7	57.3	71.1	56.8	71.4
Husband in labor force, wife not in labor force	20.1	25.0	19.8	24.3	19.3	23.5
Wife in labor force, husband not in labor force....................	7.8	3.1	7.4	2.9	7.5	3.4
Both husband and wife not in labor force........................	14.9	1.2	14.6	1.2	15.7	1.1
Other Families	236,590	121,669	228,599	116,755	232,151	113,284
Female householder, no husband present........................	72.6	76.5	74.6	78.9	74.4	79.3
In labor force..	55.5	65.7	55.3	69.0	54.4	68.0
Not in labor force	17.1	10.8	19.4	9.8	19.9	11.3
Male householder, no wife present...........................	27.4	23.5	25.4	21.1	25.6	20.7
In labor force..	22.6	21.7	20.9	19.8	20.2	19.1
Not in labor force	4.8	1.8	4.5	1.4	5.4	1.6

Table CT-11. School Enrollment and Educational Attainment, 2016

(Number, percent.)

Item	State	U.S.
Enrollment		
Total population 3 years and over, enrolled in school	914,755	81,572,277
Enrolled in nursery school or preschool (percent)	6.3	6.0
Enrolled in kindergarten (percent)..	4.5	5.0
Enrolled in elementary school, grades 1-8 (percent)..............................	37.6	40.3
Enrolled in high school, grades 9-12 (percent)	21.4	21.0
Enrolled in college or graduate school (percent)................................	30.2	27.7
Attainment		
Total population 25 years and over	2,467,737	218,475,480
Less than ninth grade (percent)	4.1	5.4
9th to 12th grade, no diploma (percent)	5.4	7.2
High school graduate, including equivalency (percent)...........................	27.5	27.2
Some college, no degree (percent)	16.8	20.6
Associate's degree (percent)...	7.5	8.4
Bachelor's degree (percent)..	21.9	19.3
Graduate or professional degree (percent).................................	16.7	11.9
High school graduate or higher (percent)	90.5	87.5
Bachelor's degree or higher (percent)..	38.6	31.3

Table CT-12. Public School Characteristics and Educational Indicators

(Number, percent; data derived from National Center of Education Statistics.)

Item	State	U.S.
Public Schools, 2015–2016 (except where noted)		
Number of school districts..	205	18,328
Number of schools..	1,369	98,456
Number of students	537,933	50,327,015
Number of teachers	43,772	3,151,497
Student-teacher ratio	12.3	16.0
Expenditures per student (dollars), 2014-2015..............................	19,020	11,445
Four-year adjusted cohort graduation rate (ACGR)[1,2]	87.4	84.1
Students eligible for free or reduced-price lunch (percent), 2014-2015............	37.7	51.8
English language learners (percent), Fall 2015	6.5	9.5
Students age 3 to 21 served under IDEA, part B (percent).......................	13.9	13.2

Public Schools by Type	Number	Percent of state public schools
Total number of schools...	1,369	100.0
Regular	1,062	77.6
Special education	168	12.3
Vocational education	17	1.2
Alternative education..	122	8.9

NOTE: Every school is assigned only one school type based on its instructional emphasis.
[1] ACGR data represents a new method of calculating high-school completion rates and may not be comparable to previous years' data for Averaged Freshmen Graduation Rates (AFGR).
[2] The United States 4-year ACGRs were estimated using both the reported 4-year ACGR data from 49 states and the District of Columbia and using imputed data for Idaho. The estimate for American Indian/Alaska Native students also includes imputed data for Virginia.

Table CT-13. Reported Voting and Registration of the Voting-Age Population, November 2016

(Numbers in thousands, percent.)

Item	Total population	Total citizen population	Registered			Voted		
			Total registered	Percent registered (total population)	Percent registered (total citizen population)	Total voted	Percent voted (total population)	Percent voted (total citizen population)
U.S. Total	245,502	224,059	157,596	64.2	70.3	137,537	56.0	61.4
State Total.............................	2,759	2,483	1,763	63.9	71.0	1,586	57.5	63.9
Sex								
Male	1,321	1,182	798	60.4	67.5	718	54.4	60.7
Female	1,438	1,301	965	67.1	74.2	868	60.4	66.7
Race								
White alone............................	2,258	2,090	1,538	68.1	73.6	1,378	61.0	65.9
White, non-Hispanic alone	1,959	1,897	1,427	72.8	75.2	1,287	65.7	67.8
Black alone............................	297	266	157	53.0	59.2	142	47.9	53.5
Asian alone	143	83	31	(B)	(B)	29	(B)	(B)
Hispanic (of any race)...............	417	278	151	36.3	54.4	131	31.5	47.2
White alone or in combination	2,281	2,113	1,561	68.4	73.9	1,401	61.4	66.3
Black alone or in combination...........	324	293	185	57.0	63.0	170	52.3	57.9
Asian alone or in combination...........	148	88	36	(B)	(B)	34	(B)	(B)
Age								
18 to 24 years........................	263	225	123	46.6	54.6	97	37.0	43.3
25 to 34 years........................	505	425	279	55.2	65.5	244	48.4	57.5
35 to 44 years........................	397	347	236	59.5	68.1	208	52.5	60.1
45 to 64 years........................	1,034	943	700	67.7	74.3	636	61.5	67.4
65 years and over	560	544	425	75.9	78.2	400	71.4	73.6

B = Base is less than 75,000 and therefore too small to show the derived measure.

Table CT-14. Crime

(Number, rate per 100,000. Data are derived from the FBI Uniform Crime Reports.)

Item	State			U.S. [1,2,3,4]		
	2015	2016	Percent change	2015	2016	Percent change
TOTAL POPULATION [5]	3,590,886	3,576,452	-0.4	321,418,820	323,127,513	0.5
VIOLENT CRIME						
Number....................................	7,845	8,123	3.5	1,231,566	1,248,185	1.3
Rate..	218.5	227.1	3.9	383.2	386.3	0.8
Murder and Nonnegligent Manslaughter						
Number....................................	117	78	-33.3	15,696	17,250	9.9
Rate	3.3	2.2	-33.3	4.9	5.3	8.2
Rape [6]						
Number....................................	773	763	-1.3	124,047	130,603	5.3
Rate	21.5	21.3	-0.9	38.6	40.4	4.7
Robbery						
Number....................................	2,892	2,703	-6.5	327,374	332,198	1.5
Rate	80.5	75.6	-6.1	101.9	102.8	0.9
Aggravated Assault						
Number....................................	4,063	4,579	12.7	764,449	803,007	5.0
Rate	113.1	128.0	13.2	237.8	248.5	4.5
PROPERTY CRIME						
Number....................................	65,066	64,664	-0.6	7,993,631	7,919,035	-0.9
Rate	1,812.0	1,808.0	-0.2	2,487.0	2,450.7	-1.5
Burglary						
Number....................................	10,053	10,045	-0.1	1,579,527	1,515,096	-4.1
Rate	280.0	280.9	0.3	491.4	468.9	-4.6
Larceny-Theft						
Number....................................	48,675	47,512	-2.4	5,706,346	5,638,455	-1.2
Rate	1,355.5	1,328.5	-2.0	1,775.4	1,745.0	-1.7
Motor Vehicle Theft						
Number....................................	6,338	7,107	12.1	707,758	765,484	8.2
Rate	176.5	198.7	12.6	220.2	236.9	7.6

NOTE: Although arson data are included in the trend and clearance tables, sufficient data are not available to estimate totals for this offense. Therefore, no arson data are published in this table.
X = Not applicable.
- = Zero or rounds to zero.
[1] The crime figures have been adjusted.
[2] The data collection methodology for the offense of forcible rape used by the Minnesota state Uniform Crime Reporting (UCR) Program (with the exception of Minneapolis and St. Paul, Minnesota) does not comply with national UCR Program guidelines. Consequently, its figures for forcible rape and violent crime (of which forcible rape is a part) are not published in this table.
[3] Includes offenses reported by the Zoological Police and the Metro Transit Police.
[4] Because of changes in the state's reporting practices, figures are not comparable to previous years' data.
[5] Populations are U.S. Census Bureau provisional estimates as of July 1 of each year.
[6] The figures shown for the offense of rape were estimated using the revised Uniform Crime Reporting (UCR) definition of rape.

Table CT-15. State Government Finances, 2016

(Dollar amounts in thousands, percent distribution.)

Item	Dollars	Percent distribution
Total Revenue	28,139,072	100.0
General revenue	26,171,704	93.0
Intergovernmental revenue	7,320,793	26.0
Taxes	15,244,947	54.2
General sales	3,752,793	13.3
Selective sales	2,396,989	8.5
License taxes	455,454	1.6
Individual income tax	7,557,153	26.9
Corporate income tax	719,467	2.6
Other taxes	363,091	1.3
Current charges	2,038,995	7.2
Miscellaneous general revenue	1,566,969	5.6
Utility revenue	34,650	0.1
Liquor stores revenue	0	-
Insurance trust revenue [1]	1,932,718	6.9
Total Expenditure	32,202,351	100.0
Intergovernmental expenditure	5,438,230	16.9
Direct expenditure	26,764,121	83.1
Current operation	17,888,919	55.6
Capital outlay	2,305,066	7.2
Insurance benefits and repayments	4,514,111	14.0
Assistance and subsidies	563,907	1.8
Interest on debt	1,492,118	4.6
Exhibit: Salaries and wages	4,576,230	14.2
Total Expenditure	32,202,351	100.0
General expenditure	26,929,325	83.6
Intergovernmental expenditure	5,438,230	16.9
Direct expenditure	21,491,095	66.7
General expenditure, by function:		
Education	8,528,978	26.5
Public welfare	7,726,922	24.0
Hospitals	1,416,094	4.4
Health	1,085,064	3.4
Highways	1,413,880	4.4
Police protection	241,020	0.7
Correction	693,520	2.2
Natural resources	234,803	0.7
Parks and recreation	68,926	0.2
Governmental administration	1,518,277	4.7
Interest on general debt	1,492,118	4.6
Other and unallocable	2,509,723	7.8
Utility expenditure	758,915	2.7
Liquor stores expenditure	0	-
Insurance trust expenditure	4,514,111	14.0
Debt at End of Fiscal Year	37,024,731	X
Cash and Security Holdings	46,766,950	X

X = Not applicable.
- = Zero or rounds to zero.
[1] Within insurance trust revenue, net earnings of state retirement systems is a calculated statistic (the item code in the data file is X08), and thus can be positive or negative. Net earnings is the sum of earnings on investments plus gains on investments minus losses on investments. The change made in 2002 for asset valuation from book to market value in accordance with Statement 34 of the Governmental Accounting Standards Board is reflected in the calculated statistics.

Table CT-16. State Government Tax Collections, 2017

(Dollars in thousands, percent.)

Item	Dollars	Percent distribution
Total Taxes	16,345,525	100.0
Property taxes	X	-
Sales and gross receipts	6,649,708	40.7
General sales and gross receipts	4,236,619	25.9
Selective sales and gross receipts	2,413,089	14.8
Alcoholic beverages	63,155	0.4
Amusements	297,003	1.8
Insurance premiums	199,497	1.2
Motor fuels	484,479	3.0
Pari-mutuels	5,792	-
Public utilities	283,433	1.7
Tobacco products	381,778	2.3
Other selective sales	697,952	4.3
Licenses	442,290	2.7
Alcoholic beverages	9,204	0.1
Amusements	231	-
Corporations in general	29,791	0.2
Hunting and fishing	5,603	-
Motor vehicle	235,105	1.4
Motor vehicle operators	46,805	0.3
Public utilities	738	-
Occupation and business, NEC	111,366	0.7
Other licenses	3,447	-
Income taxes	8,856,739	54.2
Individual income	7,959,492	48.7
Corporation net income	897,247	5.5
Other taxes	396,788	2.4
Death and gift	218,789	1.3
Documentary and stock transfer	177,725	1.1
Severance	X	-
Taxes, NEC	274	-

- = Zero or rounds to zero.
X = Not applicable.

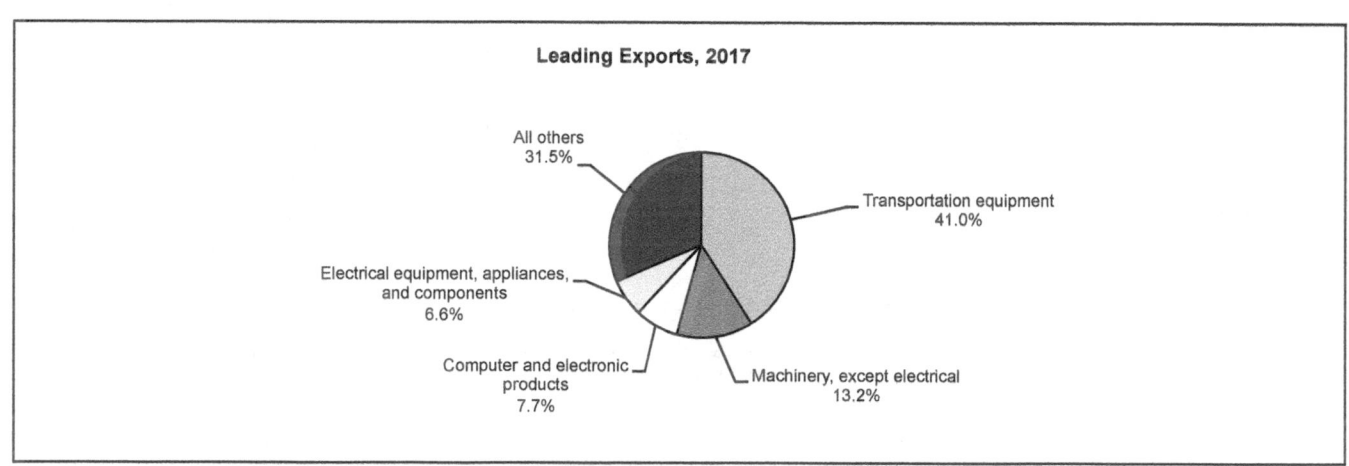

Leading Exports, 2017

- Transportation equipment 41.0%
- Machinery, except electrical 13.2%
- Computer and electronic products 7.7%
- Electrical equipment, appliances, and components 6.6%
- All others 31.5%

DELAWARE

Facts and Figures

Location: Northeastern United States; bordered on the N by Pennsylvania, on the E by New Jersey, and on the S and W by Maryland

Area: 2,488 sq. mi. (6,447 sq. km.); rank—49th

Population: 961,939 (2017 est.); rank—45th

Principal Cities: capital—Dover; largest—Wilmington

Statehood: December 7, 1787; 1st state

U.S. Congress: 2 senators, 1 representative

State Motto: Liberty and Independence

State Song: "Our Delaware"

State Nickname: The First State

Abbreviations: DE; Del.

State Symbols: flower—peach blossom; tree—American holly; bird—blue hen chicken

At a Glance

- With an increase in population of 6.9 percent, Delaware ranked 15th among the states in growth from 2010 to 2017.

- In 2016, 5.7 percent of Delawareans did not have health insurance, compared to 8.6 percent of the total U.S. population.

- Delaware's violent crime rate in 2016 was 508.8 per 100,000 population, compared to 386.3 for the entire nation.

- Delaware's homeownership rate ranked 2nd in the nation in 2017, with 70.0 percent of the population owning homes.

- In 2016, 11.7 percent of Delawareans lived below the poverty level, compared to 14.0 percent of the total U.S. population.

Table DE-1. Population by Age, Sex, Race, and Hispanic Origin

(Number, percent, except where noted.)

Sex, age, race, and Hispanic origin	2000	2010	2017 [1]	Average annual percent change, 2010–2017
Total Population..	783,600	897,934	961,939	7.1
Percent of total U.S. population	0.3	0.3	0.3	X
Sex				
Male...	380,541	434,939	465,514	7.0
Female..	403,059	462,995	496,425	7.2
Age				
Under 5 years..	51,531	55,886	54,992	-1.6
5 to 19 years...	166,719	177,917	174,816	-1.7
20 to 64 years...	463,624	648,387	558,003	-13.9
65 years and over	101,726	129,277	174,128	34.7
Median age (years)...	36.0	38.8	40.4	4.1
Race and Hispanic Origin				
One race				
White...	584,773	645,770	670,512	3.8
Black..	150,666	196,281	219,310	11.7
American Indian and Alaska Native	2,731	5,929	6,228	5.0
Asian..	16,259	29,342	39,768	35.5
Native Hawaiian or Other Pacific Islander	283	690	878	27.2
Two or more races..	13,033	19,922	25,243	26.7
Hispanic (of any race)..	37,277	76,137	89,539	17.6

X = Not applicable.
[1] Population figures for 2017 are July 1 estimates. The 2010 estimates are taken from the 2010 Census.
- = Zero or rounds to zero.

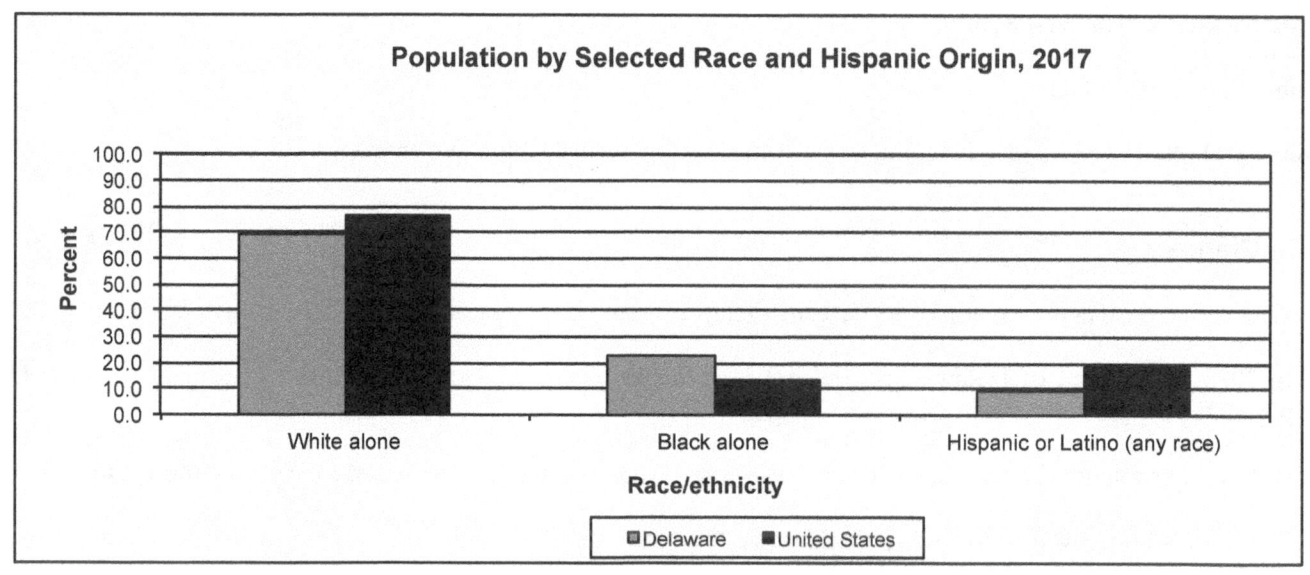

Population by Selected Race and Hispanic Origin, 2017

Table DE-2. Marital Status

(Number, percent distribution.)

Sex, age, and marital status	2000	2010	2016
Males, 15 Years and Over	296,619	350,025	374,374
Never married	29.4	35.3	37.4
Now married, except separated..	57.4	50.4	49.2
Separated..	1.8	1.9	1.3
Widowed..	2.8	2.9	2.9
Divorced..	8.7	9.4	9.3
Females, 15 Years and Over..	324,042	380,618	408,459
Never married	25.3	30.8	31.6
Now married, except separated..	50.9	45.3	44.2
Separated..	2.2	2.0	2.2
Widowed..	10.7	9.8	9.0
Divorced..	10.9	12.1	13.0

Table DE-3. Households and Housing Characteristics

(Number, percent, dollars.)

Item	2000	2010	2016	Average annual percent change, 2010–2016
Total Households...	298,736	328,765	351,085	1.1
Family households	204,590	221,233	232,433	0.8
Married-couple family	153,136	161,575	167,306	0.6
Other family	51,454	59,658	65,127	1.5
Male householder, no wife present..............	12,468	14,124	13,930	-0.2
Female householder, no husband present......	38,986	45,534	51,197	2.1
Nonfamily households	94,146	107,532	118,652	1.7
Householder living alone................................	74,639	86,990	96,794	1.9
Householder not living alone..........................	19,507	20,542	21,858	1.1
Housing Characteristics				
Total housing units...	343,072	406,489	426,154	0.8
Occupied housing units	298,736	328,765	351,085	1.1
Owner occupied	216,038	239,884	245,005	0.4
Renter occupied	86,698	88,881	106,080	3.2
Average household size.....................................	2.54	2.66	2.64	-0.1
Financial Characteristics				
Median gross rent of renter-occupied housing	639	952	1048	1.7
Median monthly owner costs for housing units with a mortgage	1,101	1,569	1,463	-1.1
Median value of owner-occupied housing units	130,400	243,600	243,400	-

- = Zero or rounds to zero.

Table DE-4. Migration, Origin, and Language

(Number, percent.)

Characteristic	State			U.S.		
	2015	2016	Percent change	2015	2016	Percent change
Residence 1 Year Ago						
Population 1 year and over	935,813	942,073	0.7	317,635,720	319,361,956	0.5
Same house	85.6	86.8	X	85.3	85.4	X
Different house in the U.S.	13.9	12.6	X	14.1	13.9	X
Same county	7.9	8.1	X	8.5	8.3	X
Different county	6.1	4.4	X	5.6	5.6	X
Same state	1.3	0.9	X	3.2	3.2	X
Different state	4.8	3.5	X	2.4	2.4	X
Abroad	0.5	0.6	X	0.7	0.7	X
Place of Birth						
Native born	858,425	862,674	0.5	278,128,449	279,388,170	0.5
Male	48.4	48.2	X	49.3	49.3	X
Female	51.6	51.8	X	50.7	50.7	X
Foreign born	87,509	89,391	2.2	43,290,372	43,739,345	1.0
Male	48.4	50.0	X	48.6	48.5	X
Female	51.6	50.0	X	51.4	51.5	X
Foreign born; naturalized U.S. citizen	39,523	44,083	11.5	20,697,103	21,238,372	2.6
Male	44.0	47.9	X	45.9	45.9	X
Female	56.0	52.1	X	54.1	54.1	X
Foreign born; not a U.S. citizen	47,986	45,308	-5.6	22,593,269	22,500,973	-0.4
Male	52.1	51.9	X	51.1	51	X
Female	47.9	48.1	X	48.9	49	X
Entered 2010 or later	19.1	22.3	X	15.6	18.6	X
Entered 2000 to 2009	33.0	31.8	X	27.9	26.7	X
Entered before 2000..................................	47.9	46	X	56.5	54.7	X
World Region of Birth, Foreign						
Foreign-born population, excluding population born at sea	87,509	89,391	2.2	43,289,646	43,738,901	1.0
Europe	9.6	11	X	11.1	10.9	X
Asia...	35.7	33.0	X	30.6	30.8	X
Africa	12.2	11.6	X	4.8	4.9	X
Oceania	-	0.2	X	0.6	0.6	X
Latin America	41.3	43.0	X	51.1	51	X
North America..	1.2	1.3	X	1.9	1.8	X
Language Spoken at Home and Ability to Speak English						
Population 5 years and over...........................	890,489	896,824	0.7	301,625,014	303,328,961	0.6
English only	86.9	87.1	X	78.5	78.4	X
Language other than English......................	13.1	12.9	X	21.5	21.6	X
Speaks English less than "very well"............	4.4	4.6	X	8.6	8.6	X

NA = Not available.
X = Not applicable.
- = Zero or rounds to zero.

Table DE-5. Median Income and Poverty Status, 2016

(Number, percent, except as noted.)

Characteristic	State		U.S.	
	Number	Percent	Number	Percent
Median Income				
Households (dollars)..	61,757	X	57,617	X
Families (dollars)	74,251	X	71,062	X
Below Poverty Level (All People)	108,211	11.7	44,268,996	14.0
Sex				
Male	46,076	10.3	19,760,056	12.8
Female	62,135	12.9	24,508,940	15.2
Age				
Under 18 years..	35,002	17.4	14,115,713	19.5
Related children under 18 years....................................	33,934	17.0	13,805,435	19.1
18 to 64 years...	62,008	11.0	25,723,818	13.2
65 years and over	11,201	6.9	4,429,465	9.2

X = Not applicable.

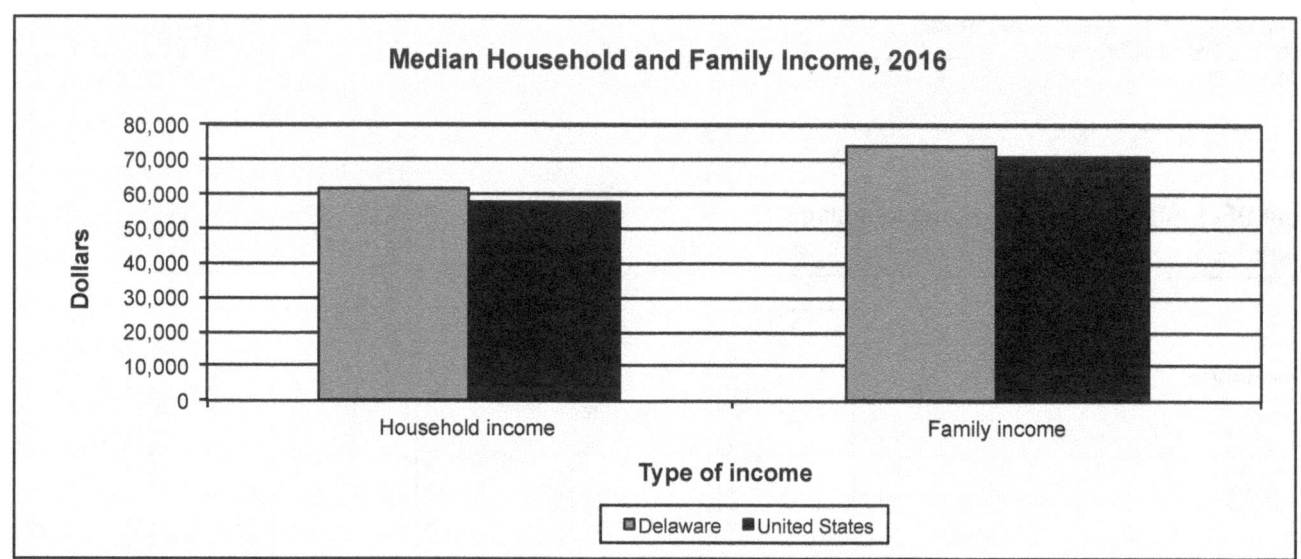

Table DE-6. Health Insurance Coverage Status for the Civilian Noninstitutionalized Population and Children Under 18 Years of Age

(Number, percent.)

Item	2008	2009	2010	2011	2012	2013	2014	2015	2016
Civilian Noninstitutionalized Population	856,131	869,483	885,232	892132	902,915	911,502	920,930	931,203	937,935
Covered by Private or Public Insurance									
Number...	768,202	780,384	799,431	808,137	823,021	828,218	849,333	876,705	884,796
Percent...	89.7	89.8	90.3	90.6	91.2	90.9	92.2	94.1	94.3
Not Covered									
Number...	87,929	89,099	85,801	83,995	79,894	83,284	71,597	54,498	53,139
Percent...	10.3	10.2	9.7	9.4	8.8	9.1	7.8	5.9	5.7
Percent in the U.S. not covered.......................................	15.1	15.1	15.5	15.1	14.8	14.5	11.7	9.4	8.6
Children Under 18 Years of Age	206,043	206,764	206,046	204,295	204,494	203,339	203,414	203,771	203,704
Covered by Private or Public Insurance									
Number...	190,057	195,454	195,034	194,916	197,329	194,251	191,762	197,686	197,461
Percent...	92.2	94.5	94.7	95.4	96.5	95.5	94.3	97.0	96.9
Not Covered									
Number...	15,986	11,310	11,012	9,379	7,165	9,088	11,652	6,085	6,243
Percent...	7.8	5.5	5.3	4.6	3.5	4.5	5.7	3.0	3.1
Percent in the U.S. not covered.......................................	9.9	8.6	8.0	7.5	7.2	7.1	6.0	4.8	4.5

Table DE-7. Employment Status by Demographic Group, 2017

(Numbers in thousands, percent.)

Characteristic	Civilian noninstitutional population	Civilian labor force		Employed		Unemployed	
		Number	Percent of population	Number	Percent of population	Number	Percent of population
Total..	763	477	62.6	454	59.5	23	4.8
Sex							
Male..	361	245	67.7	233	64.4	12	4.8
Female..	402	233	57.9	221	55.1	11	4.9
Race, Sex, and Hispanic Origin							
White...	551	335	60.9	323	58.6	12	3.7
Male...	265	178	67.0	171	64.4	7	3.9
Female..	285	157	55.1	152	53.2	6	3.5
Black or African American............................	161	109	67.4	100	61.8	9	8.3
Male...	73	49	67.7	45	61.9	4	8.5
Female..	89	60	67.1	55	61.7	5	8.1
Hispanic or Latino ethnicity[1]	71	49	69.6	48	67.4	2	3.1
Male...	33	26	77.5	25	75.4	1	2.7
Female..	38	24	62.6	23	60.3	1	3.5
Age							
16 to 19 years..	49	21	43	18	37	3	13
20 to 24 years..	64	48	74.5	45	69.5	3	6.7
25 to 34 years..	122	105	85.9	98	80.6	7	6.2
35 to 44 years..	103	88	85.8	85	83.1	3	3.3
45 to 54 years..	119	96	80.6	93	77.9	3	3.4
55 to 64 years..	138	89	64.4	85	62.0	4	3.9
65 years and over......................................	169	31	18.2	30	17.5	1	3.3

NOTE: Data in Table 7 are from the Current Population Survey (CPS) and do not match the estimates in Table 8. See notes and definitions for further information.
[1] May be of any race.
NA = Not Available

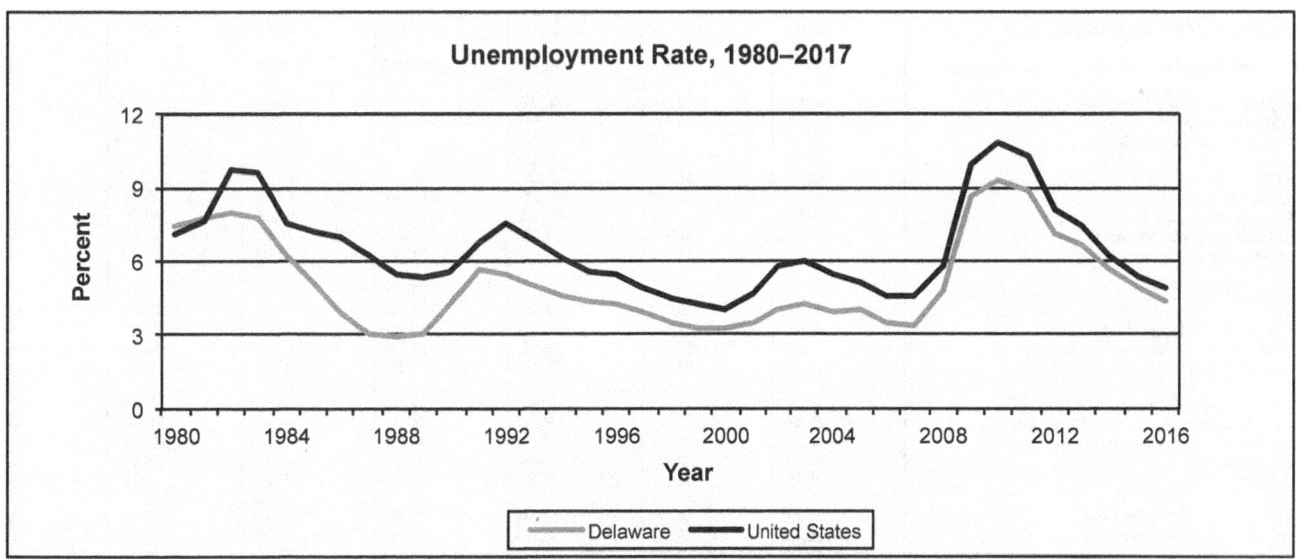

Table DE-8. Employment Status of the Civilian Noninstitutional Population Age 16 Years and Over

(Number, percent.)

Year	Civilian labor force	Civilian participation rate	Employed	Unemployed	Unemployment rate
2009..	437,500	63.8	401,312	36,188	8.3
2010..	434,419	62.0	397,869	36,550	8.4
2011..	443,346	62.3	410,086	33,260	7.5
2012..	445,572	61.9	413,457	32,115	7.2
2013..	442,728	60.8	413,119	29,609	6.7
2014..	453,312	61.4	427,386	25,926	5.7
2015..	467,110	62.5	444,404	22,706	4.9
2016..	473,881	62.6	452,434	21,447	4.5
2017..	477,349	62.3	455,427	21,922	4.6

Table DE-9. Employment and Average Wages by Industry

(Estimates through 2010 are based on the 2007 *North American Industry Classification System* [NAICS]. Estimates from 2011 onward are based on the 2012 NAICS.)

Industry	2010	2011	2012	2013	2014	2015	2016
	Number of Jobs						
Wage and Salary Employment by Industry	426,675	430,161	433,583	441,611	450,941	460,699	464,301
Farm Wage and Salary Employment	1,145	1,144	1,813	1,674	1,796	1,740	2,099
Nonfarm Wage and Salary Employment	425,530	429,017	431,770	439,937	449,145	458,959	462,202
Private wage and salary employment	352,593	356,226	357,982	365,798	375,026	384,392	388,518
Forestry, fishing, and related activities	(D)	(D)	(D)	(D)	(D)	(D)	(D)
Mining	(D)	(D)	(D)	(D)	(D)	(D)	(D)
Utilities	2,089	1,961	2,017	2,086	2,148	2,159	2,156
Construction	20,022	19,905	19,091	20,152	20,954	21,265	21,511
Manufacturing	26,163	25,694	25,783	25,378	25,708	27,073	25,771
Durable goods manufacturing	9,734	9,694	9,640	9,427	9,196	9,372	9,323
Nondurable goods manufacturing	16,429	16,000	16,143	15,951	16,512	17,701	16,448
Wholesale trade	12,552	12,548	12,527	12,257	12,040	11,854	11,963
Retail trade	50,338	51,057	51,111	51,886	52,837	53,345	54,033
Transportation and warehousing	9,977	10,182	10,513	11,758	12,948	14,432	14,684
Information	5,976	5,664	5,457	5,259	4,896	4,719	4,615
Finance and insurance	37,657	37,750	37,991	39,227	40,634	42,023	42,426
Real estate and rental and leasing	5,758	5,663	5,556	5,630	5,402	5,458	5,591
Professional, scientific, and technical services	24,038	26,160	27,434	28,716	29,134	28,648	25,864
Management of companies and enterprises	9,412	8,050	7,539	5,968	5,499	4,892	8,655
Administrative and waste services	21,310	22,071	22,024	23,900	25,499	26,812	27,174
Educational services	6,744	6,724	6,690	6,721	6,936	6,948	6,759
Health care and social assistance	57,303	58,554	59,885	61,973	64,172	66,887	68,621
Arts, entertainment, and recreation	8,842	9,115	8,883	9,736	10,055	10,209	10,069
Accommodation and food services	33,832	34,546	35,312	36,348	37,288	38,766	39,768
Other services, except public administration	20,122	20,001	19,573	18,135	18,207	18,212	18,173
Government and government enterprises	72,937	72,791	73,788	74,139	74,119	74,567	73,684
	Dollars						
Average Wages and Salaries by Industry	47,916	49,644	50,847	51,194	52,392	53,175	55,084
Average Farm Wages and Salaries	25,874	22,667	23,206	25,913	25,566	24,228	22,143
Average Nonfarm Wages and Salaries	47,976	49,716	50,963	51,290	52,499	53,285	55,234
Average private wages and salaries	48,407	50,301	51,627	51,913	53,216	53,994	55,559
Forestry, fishing, and related activities	(D)	(D)	(D)	(D)	(D)	(D)	(D)
Mining	(D)	(D)	(D)	(D)	(D)	(D)	(D)
Utilities	94,438	96,254	95,652	98,749	104,330	106,585	113,147
Construction	49,029	52,477	51,049	53,046	53,831	55,125	59,630
Manufacturing	56,998	56,139	57,102	57,909	59,581	64,065	61,187
Durable goods manufacturing	65,806	67,995	67,290	68,282	70,867	71,352	69,241
Nondurable goods manufacturing	51,780	48,955	51,018	51,779	53,296	60,207	56,622
Wholesale trade	76,846	82,546	81,336	79,124	83,265	79,870	65,353
Retail trade	25,789	25,994	26,182	26,439	27,184	28,287	28,503
Transportation and warehousing	42,993	43,843	46,018	45,476	46,313	45,956	46,483
Information	56,453	57,330	59,151	61,118	62,439	63,748	62,282
Finance and insurance	79,128	84,255	86,402	89,502	90,992	91,826	97,980
Real estate and rental and leasing	40,763	41,525	42,021	42,687	44,532	46,158	49,083
Professional, scientific, and technical services	85,445	89,452	97,514	94,592	100,173	107,041	102,997
Management of companies and enterprises	105,341	127,282	129,251	143,251	143,761	115,399	140,073
Administrative and waste services	32,400	32,720	33,686	33,751	35,345	36,520	39,743
Educational services	35,942	36,262	38,479	39,082	41,208	40,178	39,682
Health care and social assistance	47,286	48,729	49,744	49,855	50,972	52,000	54,558
Arts, entertainment, and recreation	28,400	30,712	30,178	27,713	27,120	27,189	28,077
Accommodation and food services	18,655	18,469	18,731	18,901	19,481	20,406	21,216
Other services, except public administration	28,477	28,825	30,106	32,565	33,262	34,575	35,451
Government and government enterprises	45,889	46,850	47,739	48,215	48,871	49,631	53,518

D = Not shown to avoid disclosure of confidential information, but the estimates for this item are included in the total.
L = Less than 10 jobs, but the estimates for this item are included in the total.

Table DE-10. Employment Characteristics by Family Type

(Number, percent.)

Family type and labor force status	2014		2015		2016	
	Total	Families with own children under 18 years	Total	Families with own children under 18 years	Total	Families with own children under 18 years
All Families..	230,988	89,297	235,385	90,959	232,433	86,100
FAMILY TYPE AND LABOR FORCE STATUS						
Married-Couple Families..........................	163,350	55,964	170,416	57,755	167,306	54,769
Both husband and wife in labor force......................	51.8	73.2	50.1	69.4	49.9	73.0
Husband in labor force, wife not in labor force	16.9	21.3	18.9	24.8	18.9	23.0
Wife in labor force, husband not in labor force	8.9	3.2	8.6	4.8	8.0	2.5
Both husband and wife not in labor force...................	22.4	2.3	21.1	0.5	21.9	1.3
Other Families	67,638	33,333	64,969	33,204	65,127	31,331
Female householder, no husband present...................	73.2	77.5	75.1	77.9	78.6	80.9
In labor force..	53.6	64.5	54.9	66.7	57.5	72.3
Not in labor force......................................	19.6	13.0	20.2	11.2	21.1	8.6
Male householder, no wife present........................	26.8	22.5	24.9	22.1	21.4	19.1
In labor force...	20.9	21.6	19.1	19.2	15.9	17.8
Not in labor force.......................................	5.9	0.9	5.8	2.9	5.5	1.3

Table DE-11. School Enrollment and Educational Attainment, 2016

(Number, percent.)

Item	State	U.S.
Enrollment		
Total population 3 years and over, enrolled in school	227,224	81,572,277
Enrolled in nursery school or preschool (percent)..............................	6.3	6.0
Enrolled in kindergarten (percent)...	5.3	5.0
Enrolled in elementary school, grades 1-8 (percent)............................	39.8	40.3
Enrolled in high school, grades 9-12 (percent)................................	21.0	21.0
Enrolled in college or graduate school (percent)...............................	27.6	27.7
Attainment		
Total population 25 years and over	662,547	218,475,480
Less than ninth grade (percent)..	3.4	5.4
9th to 12th grade, no diploma (percent)	7.3	7.2
High school graduate, including equivalency (percent).........................	32.1	27.2
Some college, no degree (percent)	18.4	20.6
Associate's degree (percent)..	7.9	8.4
Bachelor's degree (percent)	18.4	19.3
Graduate or professional degree (percent).....................................	12.6	11.9
High school graduate or higher (percent).......................................	89.3	87.5
Bachelor's degree or higher (percent)...	31.0	31.3

Table DE-12. Public School Characteristics and Educational Indicators

(Number, percent; data derived from National Center of Education Statistics.)

Item	State	U.S.
Public Schools, 2015–2016 (except where noted)		
Number of school districts..	50	18,328
Number of schools...	223	98,456
Number of students..	134,847	50,327,015
Number of teachers..	8,962	3,151,497
Student-teacher ratio	15.0	16.0
Expenditures per student (dollars), 2014-2015................................	13,882	11,445
Four-year adjusted cohort graduation rate (ACGR)[1,2]	85.5	84.1
Students eligible for free or reduced-price lunch (percent), 2014-2015.........	37.1	51.8
English language learners (percent), Fall 2015................................	7.2	9.5
Students age 3 to 21 served under IDEA, part B (percent)......................	15.4	13.2

Public Schools by Type	Number	Percent of state public schools
Total number of schools..	223	100.0
Regular	198	88.8
Special education..	13	5.8
Vocational education...	6	2.7
Alternative education..	6	2.7

NOTE: Every school is assigned only one school type based on its instructional emphasis.

[1] ACGR data represents a new method of calculating high-school completion rates and may not be comparable to previous years' data for Averaged Freshmen Graduation Rates (AFGR).

[2] The United States 4-year ACGRs were estimated using both the reported 4-year ACGR data from 49 states and the District of Columbia and using imputed data for Idaho. The estimate for American Indian/Alaska Native students also includes imputed data for Virginia.

Table DE-13. Reported Voting and Registration of the Voting-Age Population, November 2016

(Numbers in thousands, percent.)

Item	Total population	Total citizen population	Registered			Voted		
			Total registered	Percent registered (total population)	Percent registered (total citizen population)	Total voted	Percent voted (total population)	Percent voted (total citizen population)
U.S. Total	245,502	224,059	157,596	64.2	70.3	137,537	56.0	61.4
State Total................................	729	669	487	66.8	72.8	417	57.2	62.3
Sex								
Male	342	306	216	63.0	70.4	183	53.5	59.7
Female	387	362	271	70.1	74.8	234	60.4	64.5
Race								
White alone	527	494	372	70.6	75.4	319	60.6	64.7
White, non-Hispanic alone	472	464	360	76.3	77.6	308	65.2	66.3
Black alone.............................	148	144	96	64.9	66.5	82	55.1	56.5
Asian alone	44	22	12	(B)	(B)	11	(B)	(B)
Hispanic (of any race).................	66	39	19	(B)	(B)	14	(B)	(B)
White alone or in combination	535	501	378	70.7	75.5	323	60.3	64.4
Black alone or in combination..........	154	150	100	65.2	66.8	83	54.2	55.5
Asian alone or in combination..........	45	22	12	(B)	(B)	12	(B)	(B)
Age								
18 to 24 years.........................	82	69	44	(B)	(B)	29	(B)	(B)
25 to 34 years.........................	110	91	62	(B)	(B)	48	(B)	(B)
35 to 44 years.........................	115	102	77	66.4	75.0	62	54.0	61.1
45 to 64 years.........................	253	242	177	70.1	73.2	162	64.1	66.8
65 years and over	169	164	127	75.3	77.2	116	68.7	70.5

B = Base is less than 75,000 and therefore too small to show the derived measure.

Table DE-14. Crime

(Number, rate per 100,000. Data are derived from the FBI Uniform Crime Reports.)

Item	State			U.S. [1,2,3,4]		
	2015	2016	Percent change	2015	2016	Percent change
TOTAL POPULATION [5]	945,934	952,065	0.6	321,418,820	323,127,513	0.5
VIOLENT CRIME						
Number..................................	4,720	4,844	2.6	1,231,566	1,248,185	1.3
Rate	499.0	508.8	2.0	383.2	386.3	0.8
Murder and Nonnegligent Manslaughter						
Number..................................	63	56	-11.1	15,696	17,250	9.9
Rate	6.7	5.9	-11.9	4.9	5.3	8.2
Rape [6]						
Number..................................	341	308	-9.7	124,047	130,603	5.3
Rate	36.0	32.4	-10.0	38.6	40.4	4.7
Robbery						
Number..................................	1,235	1,359	10.0	327,374	332,198	1.5
Rate	130.6	142.7	9.3	101.9	102.8	0.9
Aggravated Assault						
Number..................................	3,081	3,121	1.3	764,449	803,007	5.0
Rate	325.7	327.8	0.6	237.8	248.5	4.5
PROPERTY CRIME						
Number..................................	25,455	26,334	3.5	7,993,631	7,919,035	-0.9
Rate	2,691.0	2,766.0	2.8	2,487.0	2,450.7	-1.5
Burglary						
Number..................................	4,773	5,023	5.2	1,579,527	1,515,096	-4.1
Rate	504.6	527.6	4.6	491.4	468.9	-4.6
Larceny-Theft						
Number..................................	19,501	19,791	1.5	5,706,346	5,638,455	-1.2
Rate	2,061.6	2,078.7	0.8	1,775.4	1,745.0	-1.7
Motor Vehicle Theft						
Number..................................	1,181	1,520	28.7	707,758	765,484	8.2
Rate	124.9	159.7	27.9	220.2	236.9	7.6

NOTE: Although arson data are included in the trend and clearance tables, sufficient data are not available to estimate totals for this offense. Therefore, no arson data are published in this table.
X = Not applicable.
- = Zero or rounds to zero.
[1] The crime figures have been adjusted.
[2] The data collection methodology for the offense of forcible rape used by the Minnesota state Uniform Crime Reporting (UCR) Program (with the exception of Minneapolis and St. Paul, Minnesota) does not comply with national UCR Program guidelines. Consequently, its figures for forcible rape and violent crime (of which forcible rape is a part) are not published in this table.
[3] Includes offenses reported by the Zoological Police and the Metro Transit Police.
[4] Because of changes in the state's reporting practices, figures are not comparable to previous years' data.
[5] Populations are U.S. Census Bureau provisional estimates as of July 1 of each year.
[6] The figures shown for the offense of rape were estimated using the revised Uniform Crime Reporting (UCR) definition of rape.

Table DE-15. State Government Finances, 2016

(Dollar amounts in thousands, percent distribution.)

Item	Dollars	Percent distribution
Total Revenue	8,083,659	100.0
General revenue	7,962,885	98.5
Intergovernmental revenue	2,231,253	27.6
Taxes	3,522,301	43.6
General sales	0	-
Selective sales	539,193	6.7
License taxes	1,452,596	18.0
Individual income tax	1,112,368	13.8
Corporate income tax	318,152	3.9
Other taxes	99,992	1.2
Current charges	1,200,655	14.9
Miscellaneous general revenue	1,008,676	12.5
Utility revenue	20,827	0.3
Liquor stores revenue	0	-
Insurance trust revenue [1]	99,947	1.2
Total Expenditure	9,378,888	100.0
Intergovernmental expenditure	1,511,805	16.1
Direct expenditure	7,867,083	83.9
Current operation	5,970,535	63.7
Capital outlay	692,113	7.4
Insurance benefits and repayments	678,409	7.2
Assistance and subsidies	327,965	3.5
Interest on debt	198,061	2.1
Exhibit: Salaries and wages	1,405,778	15.0
Total Expenditure	9,378,888	100.0
General expenditure	8,563,491	91.3
Intergovernmental expenditure	1,511,805	16.1
Direct expenditure	7,051,686	75.2
General expenditure, by function:		
Education	3,082,061	32.9
Public welfare	2,454,630	26.2
Hospitals	45,578	0.5
Health	456,558	4.9
Highways	603,206	6.4
Police protection	132,830	1.4
Correction	308,341	3.3
Natural resources	88,379	0.9
Parks and recreation	55,288	0.6
Governmental administration	519,097	5.5
Interest on general debt	198,061	2.1
Other and unallocable	619,462	6.6
Utility expenditure	136,988	1.7
Liquor stores expenditure	0	-
Insurance trust expenditure	678,409	7.2
Debt at End of Fiscal Year	5,045,161	X
Cash and Security Holdings	12,004,076	X

X = Not applicable.
- = Zero or rounds to zero.
[1] Within insurance trust revenue, net earnings of state retirement systems is a calculated statistic (the item code in the data file is X08), and thus can be positive or negative. Net earnings is the sum of earnings on investments plus gains on investments minus losses on investments. The change made in 2002 for asset valuation from book to market value in accordance with Statement 34 of the Governmental Accounting Standards Board is reflected in the calculated statistics.

Table DE-16. State Government Tax Collections, 2017

(Dollars in thousands, percent.)

Item	Dollars	Percent distribution
Total Taxes	3,588,905	100.0
Property taxes	X	-
Sales and gross receipts	556,490	15.5
General sales and gross receipts	X	-
Selective sales and gross receipts	556,490	15.5
Alcoholic beverages	20,577	0.6
Amusements	X	-
Insurance premiums	100,144	2.8
Motor fuels	129,487	3.6
Pari-mutuels	63	-
Public utilities	53,798	1.5
Tobacco products	112,349	3.1
Other selective sales	140,072	3.9
Licenses	1,503,083	41.9
Alcoholic beverages	2,034	0.1
Amusements	312	-
Corporations in general	1,304,919	36.4
Hunting and fishing	3,249	0.1
Motor vehicle	57,982	1.6
Motor vehicle operators	6,771	0.2
Public utilities	X	-
Occupation and business, NEC	120,843	3.4
Other licenses	6,973	0.2
Income taxes	1,427,150	39.8
Individual income	1,180,975	32.9
Corporation net income	246,175	6.9
Other taxes	102,182	2.8
Death and gift	2,156	0.1
Documentary and stock transfer	98,889	2.8
Severance	X	-
Taxes, NEC	1,137	-

X = Not applicable.
- = Zero or rounds to zero.

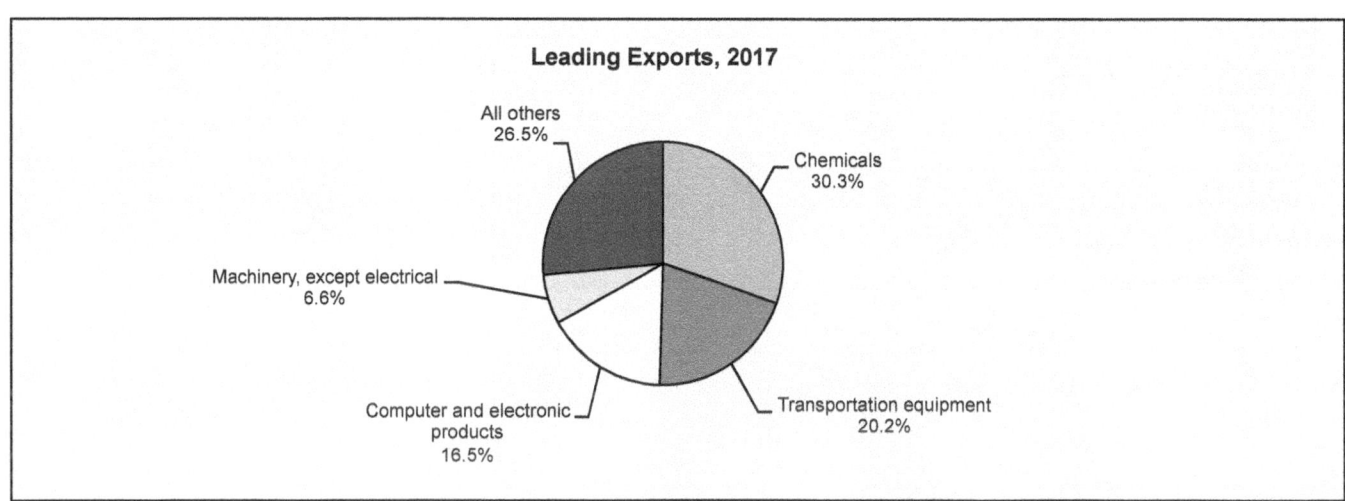

Leading Exports, 2017

- All others 26.5%
- Chemicals 30.3%
- Transportation equipment 20.2%
- Computer and electronic products 16.5%
- Machinery, except electrical 6.6%

DISTRICT OF COLUMBIA

Facts and Figures:

Location: South Atlantic United States; bordered on the SE, NE, and NW by Maryland and on the SW by Virginia

Area: 68 sq. mi.

Population: 693,972 (2017 est.); rank—49th

Official Motto: Justitia omnibus ("Justice for All")

U.S. Congress: 1 delegate

Abbreviation: D.C.

Symbols: flower—American beauty rose; tree—scarlet oak; bird—wood thrush

At a Glance

- From 2010 to 2017, the population of the District of Columbia rose 14.7 percent, the highest increase in the country.

- The violent crime rate in the District of Columbia was 1,205.9 per 100,000 population in 2016, more than triple the national rate of 386.3 per 100,000.

- In 2016, the District of Columbia's property crime rate was the highest in the country at 4,802.9 per 100,000 population.

- Compared to the 50 states, the District of Columbia had the lowest percentage of people under 18 years of age (17.9 percent), and the 3rd lowest percentage of people over age 65 (12.1 percent) in 2017.

- Despite having the highest median family income in the United States ($98,498) in 2016, the District of Columbia had the 4th highest percent of residents below the poverty level (18.6 percent) and the 4th highest percent of children under 18 years of age in poverty (25.8 percent).

Table DC-1. Population by Age, Sex, Race, and Hispanic Origin

(Number, percent, except where noted.)

Sex, age, race, and Hispanic origin	2000	2010	2017 [1]	Average annual percent change, 2010–2017
Total Population...	572,059	601,723	693,972	15.3
Percent of total U.S. population	0.2	0.2	0.2	X
Sex				
Male...	269,366	284,222	329,199	15.8
Female	302,693	317,501	364,773	14.9
Age				
Under 5 years..	32,536	32,613	45,035	38.1
5 to 19 years...	103,270	91,107	100,645	10.5
20 to 64 years...	366,355	409,194	464,558	13.5
65 years and over	69,898	68,809	83,734	21.7
Median age (years)	34.8	33.8	34.0	0.6
Race and Hispanic Origin				
One race				
White	176,101	251,265	313,234	24.7
Black..	343,312	310,379	326,807	5.3
American Indian and Alaska Native	1,713	3,264	4,139	26.8
Asian..	15,189	21,705	29,747	37.1
Native Hawaiian or Other Pacific Islander	348	770	976	26.8
Two or more races	13,446	14,340	19,069	33.0
Hispanic (of any race)...	44,953	57,833	76,526	32.3

X = Not applicable.
- = Zero or rounds to zero.
[1] Population figures for 2017 are July 1 estimates. The 2010 estimates are taken from the 2010 Census.

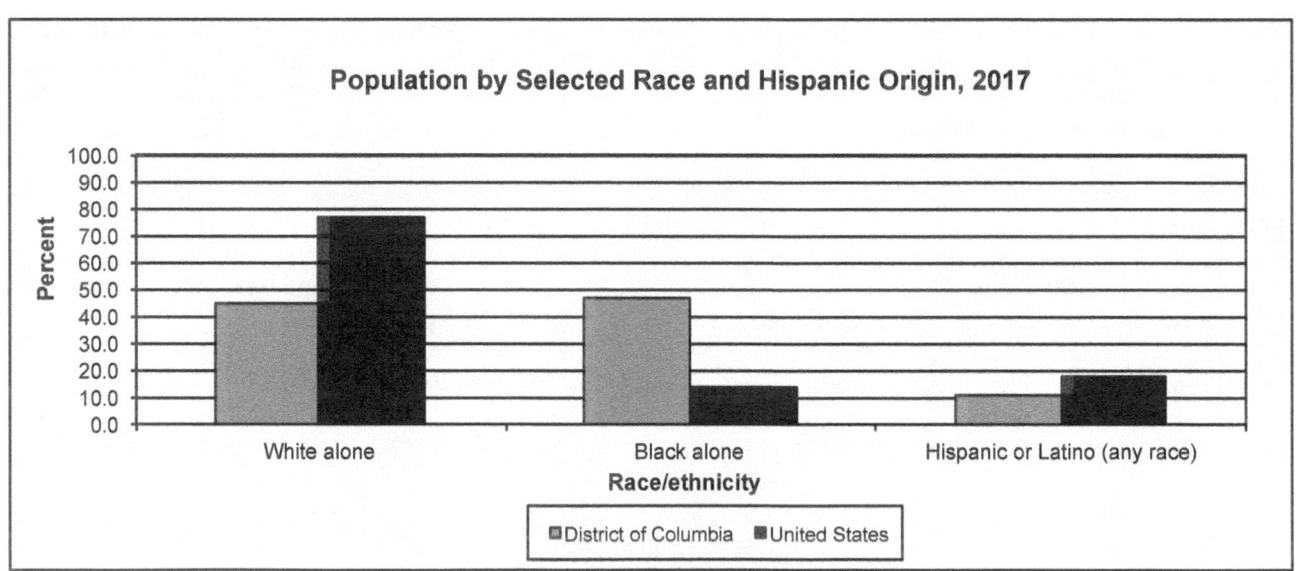

Table DC-2. Marital Status

(Number, percent distribution.)

Sex, age, and marital status	2000	2010	2016
Males, 15 Years and Over..	219,706	243,152	270,633
Never married	51.2	58.9	57.3
Now married, except separated...	32.8	28.2	31.2
Separated..	3.9	2.4	1.7
Widowed..	3.4	2.1	1.8
Divorced..	8.7	8.4	8.0
Females, 15 Years and Over...	254,711	277,203	305,407
Never married	46.0	55.8	56.0
Now married, except separated...	27.5	22.8	25.6
Separated..	4.4	3.1	2.1
Widowed..	11.6	7.5	6.5
Divorced..	10.6	10.8	9.7

Table DC-3. Households and Housing Characteristics

(Number, percent, dollars.)

Item	2000	2010	2016	Average annual percent change, 2010–2016
Total Households...	248,338	252,388	281,241	1.9
Family households	114,166	101,519	122,732	3.5
Married-couple family	56,631	57,275	71,204	4.1
Other family	57,535	44,244	51,528	2.7
Male householder, no wife present..................	10,503	8,740	9,235	0.9
Female householder, no husband present........	47,032	35,504	42,293	3.2
Nonfamily households	134,172	150,869	158,509	0.8
Householder living alone.................................	108,744	121,036	123,322	0.3
Householder not living alone...........................	25,428	29,833	35,187	3.0
Housing Characteristics				
Total housing units..	274,845	296,836	313,703	0.9
Occupied housing units	248,338	252,388	281,241	1.9
Owner occupied	101,214	107,193	110,376	0.5
Renter occupied	147,124	145,195	170,865	2.9
Average household size.......................................	2.16	2.24	2.28	0.3
Financial Characteristics				
Median gross rent of renter-occupied housing	618	1,198	1,376	2.5
Median monthly owner costs for housing units with a mortgage	1,291	2,297	2,422	0.9
Median value of owner-occupied housing units...........	157,200	426,900	576,100	5.8

Table DC-4. Migration, Origin, and Language

(Number, percent.)

Characteristic	State			U.S.		
	2015	2016	Percent change	2015	2016	Percent change
Residence 1 Year Ago						
Population 1 year and over	663,006	672,022	1.4	317,635,720	319,361,956	0.5
Same house...	79.2	80.1	X	85.3	85.4	X
Different house in the U.S..	19.2	18.2	X	14.1	13.9	X
Same county...	10.1	9.5	X	8.5	8.3	X
Different county	9.0	8.7	X	5.6	5.6	X
Same state	N/A	0.0	X	3.2	3.2	X
Different state	9.0	8.7	X	2.4	2.4	X
Abroad	1.6	1.7	X	0.7	0.7	X
Place of Birth						
Native born	577,111	590,539	2.3	278,128,449	279,388,170	0.5
Male	47.5	47.3	X	49.3	49.3	X
Female	52.5	52.7	X	50.7	50.7	X
Foreign born	95,117	90,631	-4.7	43,290,372	43,739,345	1.0
Male	48.0	48.7	X	48.6	48.5	X
Female	52.0	51.3	X	51.4	51.5	X
Foreign born; naturalized U.S. citizen.........................	41,645	40,003	-3.9	20,697,103	21,238,372	2.6
Male	45.4	45.1	X	45.9	45.9	X
Female	54.6	54.9	X	54.1	54.1	X
Foreign born; not a U.S. citizen..................................	53,472	50,628	-5.3	22,593,269	22,500,973	-0.4
Male	50.0	51.5	X	51.1	51.0	X
Female	50.0	48.5	X	48.9	49.0	X
Entered 2010 or later	26.3	25.6	X	15.6	18.6	X
Entered 2000 to 2009	27.4	31.5	X	27.9	26.7	X
Entered before 2000...	46.3	43	X	56.5	54.7	X
World Region of Birth, Foreign						
Foreign-born population, excluding population born at sea	95,117	90,631	-4.7	43,289,646	43,738,901	1.0
Europe	18.1	17.1	X	11.1	10.9	X
Asia..	23.1	19.3	X	30.6	30.8	X
Africa	14.6	15.4	X	4.8	4.9	X
Oceania	1.3	0.8	X	0.6	0.6	X
Latin America	40.3	45.1	X	51.1	51.0	X
North America...	2.7	2.3	X	1.9	1.8	X
Language Spoken at Home and Ability to Speak English						
Population 5 years and over..	628,998	637,624	1.4	301,625,014	303,328,961	0.6
English only	82.6	82.9	X	78.5	78.4	X
Language other than English..	17.4	17.1	X	21.5	21.6	X
Speaks English less than "very well"........................	5.4	6.1	X	8.6	8.6	X

NA = Not available.
X = Not applicable.
- = Zero or rounds to zero.

Table DC-5. Median Income and Poverty Status, 2016

(Number, percent, except as noted.)

Characteristic	State		U.S.	
	Number	Percent	Number	Percent
Median Income				
Households (dollars)...	75,506	X	57,617	X
Families (dollars)	98,498	X	71,062	X
Below Poverty Level (All People)	120,308	18.6	44,268,996	14.0
Sex				
Male	53,059	17.3	19,760,056	12.8
Female	67,249	19.7	24,508,940	15.2
Age				
Under 18 years...	30,551	25.8	14,115,713	19.5
Related children under 18 years..	30,108	25.5	13,805,435	19.1
18 to 64 years..	79,453	17.6	25,723,818	13.2
65 years and over	10,304	13.4	4,429,465	9.2

X = Not applicable.

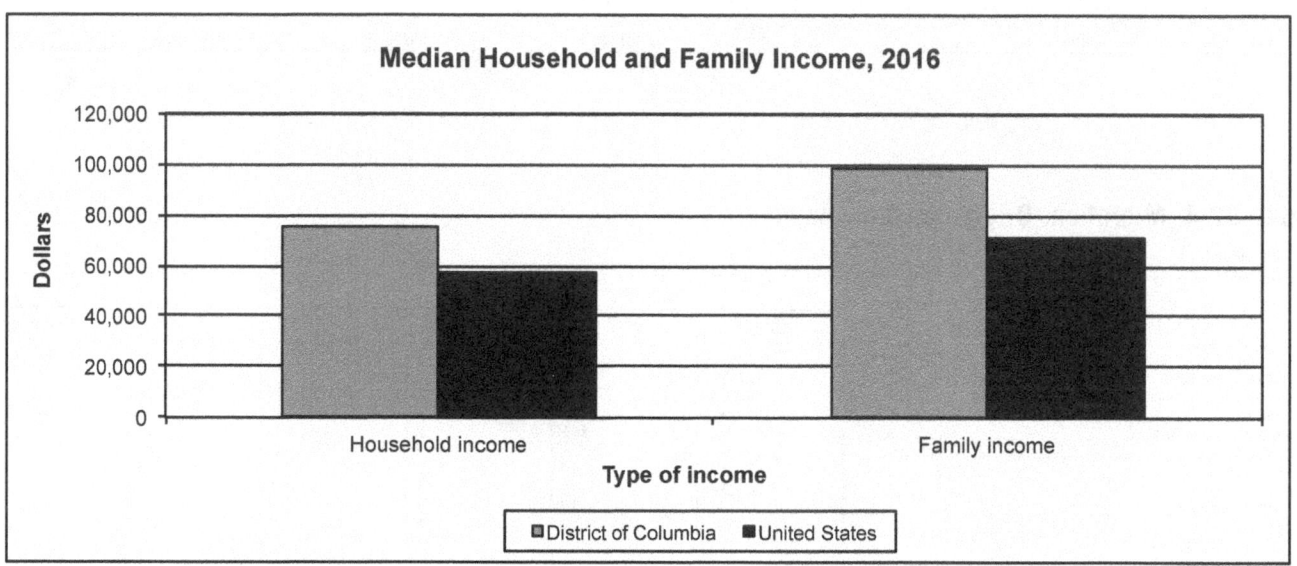

Table DC-6. Health Insurance Coverage Status for the Civilian Noninstitutionalized Population and Children Under 18 Years of Age

(Number, percent.)

Item	2008	2009	2010	2011	2012	2013	2014	2015	2016
Civilian Noninstitutionalized Population	580,464	589,408	594,282	608,165	621,380	635,833	647,966	660,682	670,985
Covered by Private or Public Insurance									
Number..	533,755	548,016	549,118	566,158	584,526	593,538	613,778	635,702	644,639
Percent..	92.0	93.0	92.4	93.1	94.1	93.3	94.7	96.2	96.1
Not Covered									
Number..	46,709	41,392	45,164	42,007	36,854	42,295	34,188	24,980	26,346
Percent..	8.0	7.0	7.6	6.9	5.9	6.7	5.3	3.8	3.9
Percent in the U.S. not covered................................	15.1	15.1	15.5	15.1	14.8	14.5	11.7	9.4	8.6
Children Under 18 Years of Age	111,263	113,710	100,990	105,312	109,182	111,287	114,834	117,415	120,313
Covered by Private or Public Insurance									
Number..	106,506	110,512	98,681	101,179	107,312	108,657	112,449	115,609	116,572
Percent..	95.7	97.2	97.7	96.1	98.3	97.6	97.9	98.5	96.9
Not Covered									
Number..	4,757	3,198	2,309	4,133	1,870	2,630	2,385	1,806	3,741
Percent..	4.3	2.8	2.3	3.9	1.7	2.4	2.1	1.5	3.1
Percent in the U.S. not covered................................	9.9	8.6	8.0	7.5	7.2	7.1	6.0	4.8	4.5

Table DC-7. Employment Status by Demographic Group, 2017

(Numbers in thousands, percent.)

Characteristic	Civilian noninstitutional population	Civilian labor force		Employed		Unemployed	
		Number	Percent of population	Number	Percent of population	Number	Percent of population
Total..	569	401	70.5	376	66.1	25	6.2
Sex							
Male..	264	196	74.2	184	69.5	12	6.3
Female...	304	205	67.3	192	63.1	13	6.2
Race, Sex, and Hispanic Origin							
White...	264	218	82.7	214	81.0	5	2.0
Male..	131	112	85.8	110	84.0	2	2.1
Female...	133	106	79.7	104	78.1	2	2.0
Black or African American............................	258	148	57.3	129	49.9	19	12.9
Male..	113	69	60.5	59	52.3	9	13.4
Female...	145	80	54.8	70	48.0	10	12.5
Hispanic or Latino ethnicity[1]	53	40	74.7	38	71.9	2	3.7
Male..	25	20	79.2	19	76.6	1	3.1
Female...	28	20	70.7	19	67.7	1	4.3
Age							
16 to 19 years...	NA	NA	NA	NA	NA	NA	NA
20 to 24 years...	55	40	72.5	35	63.4	5	12.5
25 to 34 years...	169	149	88.2	141	83.4	8	5.6
35 to 44 years...	98	87	88.2	83	84.0	4	4.8
45 to 54 years...	73	58	79.9	55	75.3	3	5.7
55 to 64 years...	63	40	63.2	38	60.2	2	4.8
65 years and over	89	22	25.1	21	24.2	1	3.2

NOTE: Data in Table 7 are from the Current Population Survey (CPS) and do not match the estimates in Table 8. See notes and definitions for further information.
[1] May be of any race.
NA = Not available.

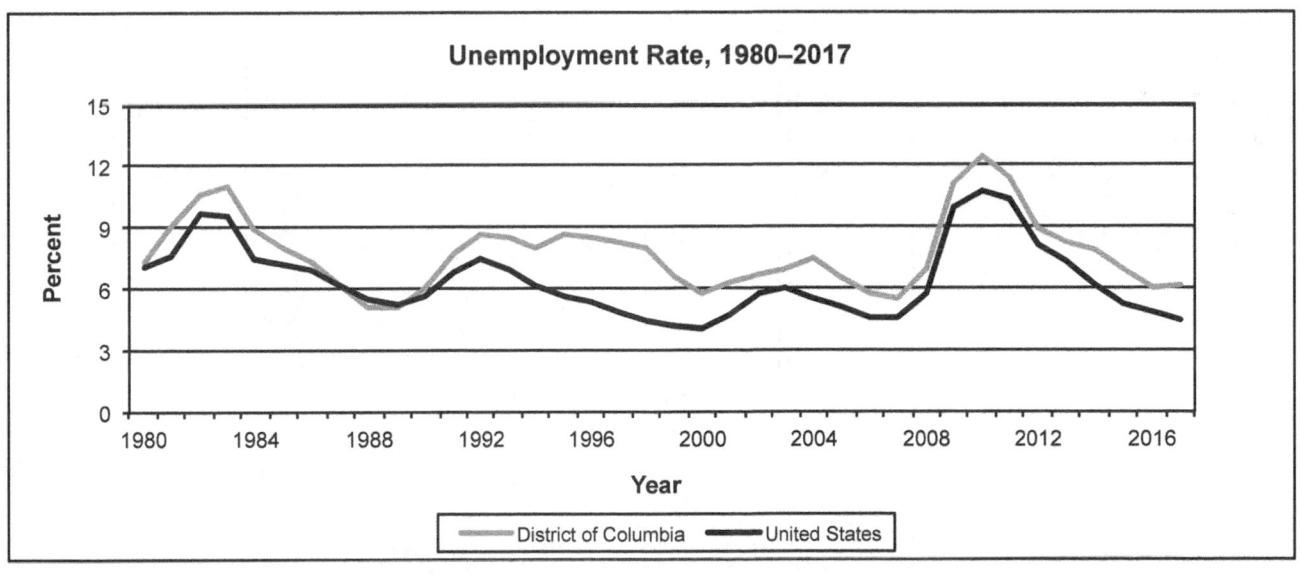

Unemployment Rate, 1980–2017

Table DC-8. Employment Status of the Civilian Noninstitutional Population Age 16 Years and Over

(Number, percent.)

Year	Civilian labor force	Civilian participation rate	Employed	Unemployed	Unemployment rate
2009..	335,672	69.1	304,500	31,172	9.3
2010..	346,065	68.8	313,508	32,557	9.4
2011..	350,778	67.9	315,171	35,607	10.2
2012..	364,989	69.1	331,984	33,005	9.0
2013..	374,126	69.6	342,351	31,775	8.5
2014..	378,380	69.3	348,981	29,399	7.8
2015..	388,057	70.0	361,324	26,733	6.9
2016..	394,586	70.1	370,521	24,065	6.1
2017..	400,894	70.4	376,633	24,261	6.1

Table DC-9. Employment and Average Wages by Industry

(Estimates through 2010 are based on the 2007 *North American Industry Classification System* [NAICS]. Estimates from 2011 onward are based on the 2012 NAICS.)

Industry	2010	2011	2012	2013	2014	2015	2016
	Number of Jobs						
Wage and Salary Employment by Industry	732,179	744,088	749,686	759,102	767,860	776,441	789,137
Farm Wage and Salary Employment	0	0	0	0	0	0	0
Nonfarm Wage and Salary Employment	732,179	744,088	749,686	759,102	767,860	776,441	789,137
Private wage and salary employment	469,820	482,804	493,273	506,154	516,038	527,814	538,108
Forestry, fishing, and related activities	0	0	0	0	0	0	0
Mining	0	0	0	0	0	0	0
Utilities	1,832	1,830	1,850	1,891	1,920	2,005	1,998
Construction	11,108	12,546	14,047	14,484	14,723	14,981	15,827
Manufacturing	1,275	1,043	973	1,008	1,032	1,103	1,218
Durable goods manufacturing	475	424	423	441	418	456	542
Nondurable goods manufacturing	800	619	550	567	614	647	676
Wholesale trade	4,801	4,647	4,974	4,870	4,939	4,872	5,034
Retail trade	18,828	18,898	19,186	20,232	21,509	22,708	23,108
Transportation and warehousing	4,119	4,120	4,070	4,031	4,157	4,598	4,619
Information	18,715	18,713	17,524	17,059	17,223	17,167	17,070
Finance and insurance	14,976	14,925	14,942	14,820	15,140	15,146	14,992
Real estate and rental and leasing	10,196	10,501	11,054	11,084	12,107	12,277	12,635
Professional, scientific, and technical services	101,714	103,664	107,412	108,715	109,588	112,981	115,820
Management of companies and enterprises	2,020	2,018	2,012	2,046	2,157	2,141	2,433
Administrative and waste services	42,528	45,457	45,929	46,428	46,991	47,947	48,094
Educational services	49,162	50,566	50,229	55,716	56,583	57,232	57,854
Health care and social assistance	59,897	61,598	62,734	64,596	65,183	66,155	68,177
Arts, entertainment, and recreation	7,167	7,037	7,119	7,013	7,394	7,752	8,419
Accommodation and food services	53,483	55,857	58,643	61,279	63,051	65,667	66,645
Other services, except public administration	67,999	69,384	70,575	70,882	72,341	73,082	74,165
Government and government enterprises	262,359	261,284	256,413	252,948	251,822	248,627	251,029
	Dollars						
Average Wages and Salaries by Industry	79,114	80,464	81,626	81,992	84,272	87,008	91,809
Average Farm Wages and Salaries	0	0	0	0	0	0	0
Average Nonfarm Wages and Salaries	79,114	80,464	81,626	81,992	84,272	87,008	91,809
Average private wages and salaries	72,268	73,868	75,594	76,143	78,327	80,742	85,057
Forestry, fishing, and related activities	0	0	0	0	0	0	0
Mining	0	0	0	0	0	0	0
Utilities	85,298	91,295	91,640	98,335	98,391	103,181	113,960
Construction	61,069	63,403	63,613	62,920	65,119	63,621	69,202
Manufacturing	84,315	104,685	107,628	109,951	95,328	95,840	90,570
Durable goods manufacturing	78,133	83,344	83,163	83,789	82,533	91,156	91,701
Nondurable goods manufacturing	87,986	119,302	126,444	130,300	104,039	99,142	89,663
Wholesale trade	100,871	107,664	114,085	116,518	120,436	121,038	117,545
Retail trade	30,641	32,259	34,289	33,267	33,264	33,867	35,934
Transportation and warehousing	66,051	70,447	73,459	73,247	75,991	74,031	77,864
Information	103,207	106,859	112,008	122,437	120,802	121,608	135,783
Finance and insurance	128,488	137,690	142,834	148,742	156,429	167,316	177,381
Real estate and rental and leasing	70,642	74,977	77,652	80,019	94,279	94,315	112,490
Professional, scientific, and technical services	117,447	120,097	122,664	122,655	126,658	128,775	136,959
Management of companies and enterprises	218,151	201,889	235,179	219,006	232,865	297,394	253,160
Administrative and waste services	43,778	45,886	46,986	48,384	49,076	51,190	51,464
Educational services	45,211	45,669	47,289	47,199	47,698	51,015	49,916
Health care and social assistance	56,769	57,529	58,171	57,753	60,384	62,701	64,175
Arts, entertainment, and recreation	63,600	55,132	50,295	54,650	57,413	60,360	73,368
Accommodation and food services	31,699	32,330	32,516	33,507	34,441	35,847	37,545
Other services, except public administration	74,691	77,255	78,567	81,692	83,461	86,781	91,956
Government and government enterprises	91,375	92,652	93,231	93,696	96,453	100,312	106,281

Table DC-10. Employment Characteristics by Family Type

(Number, percent.)

Family type and labor force status	2014		2015		2016	
	Total	Families with own children under 18 years	Total	Families with own children under 18 years	Total	Families with own children under 18 years
All Families..	115,477	48,881	125,178	54,494	122,732	52,056
FAMILY TYPE AND LABOR FORCE STATUS						
Married-Couple Families................................	63,857	24,341	71,857	27,840	71,204	27,175
Both husband and wife in labor force...................	62.0	71.6	65.0	76.8	62.5	76.3
Husband in labor force, wife not in labor force........	17.2	22.8	14.1	18.8	15.1	19.6
Wife in labor force, husband not in labor force........	7.5	4.3	5.2	0.8	7.4	2.7
Both husband and wife not in labor force..............	13.2	1.3	12.2	2.5	9.7	0.3
Other Families..	51,620	24,540	53,321	26,654	51,528	24,881
Female householder, no husband present...............	81.6	85.3	79.7	82.6	82.1	86.0
In labor force.......................................	55.8	69.3	52.3	65.1	54.0	69.5
Not in labor force...................................	25.8	16.0	27.4	17.5	28.1	16.5
Male householder, no wife present.....................	18.4	14.7	20.3	17.4	17.9	14.0
In labor force.......................................	13.6	13.7	15.6	16.2	14.2	12.8
Not in labor force...................................	4.8	1.0	4.7	1.2	3.8	1.2

Table DC-11. School Enrollment and Educational Attainment, 2016

(Number, percent.)

Item	District	U.S.
Enrollment		
Total population 3 years and over, enrolled in school..................................	168,430	81,572,277
Enrolled in nursery school or preschool (percent).................................	8.8	6.0
Enrolled in kindergarten (percent)...	4.6	5.0
Enrolled in elementary school, grades 1-8 (percent)..............................	28.3	40.3
Enrolled in high school, grades 9-12 (percent)..................................	14.3	21.0
Enrolled in college or graduate school (percent).................................	44.0	27.7
Attainment		
Total population 25 years and over..	480,158	218,475,480
Less than ninth grade (percent)...	3.6	5.4
9th to 12th grade, no diploma (percent)...	6.0	7.2
High school graduate, including equivalency (percent)............................	17.8	27.2
Some college, no degree (percent)..	13.0	20.6
Associate's degree (percent)...	2.9	8.4
Bachelor's degree (percent)..	24.0	19.3
Graduate or professional degree (percent).......................................	32.9	11.9
High school graduate or higher (percent)..	90.5	87.5
Bachelor's degree or higher (percent)...	56.8	31.3

Table DC-12. Public School Characteristics and Educational Indicators

(Number, percent; data derived from National Center of Education Statistics.)

Item	District	U.S.
Public Schools, 2015–2016 (except where noted)		
Number of school districts...	64	18,328
Number of schools..	228	98,456
Number of students...	84,024	50,327,015
Number of teachers...	6,789	3,151,497
Student-teacher ratio...	12.4	16.0
Expenditures per student (dollars), 2014-2015....................................	20,610	11,445
Four-year adjusted cohort graduation rate (ACGR)[1,2]............................	69.2	84.1
Students eligible for free or reduced-price lunch (percent), 2014-2015............	92.4	51.8
English language learners (percent), Fall 2015...................................	7.4	9.5
Students age 3 to 21 served under IDEA, part B (percent)..........................	14.6	13.2

Public Schools by Type	Number	Percent of D.C. public schools
Total number of schools...	228	100.0
Regular..	216	94.7
Special education...	3	1.3
Vocational education..	0	-
Alternative education...	9	3.9

NOTE: Every school is assigned only one school type based on its instructional emphasis.

[1] ACGR data represents a new method of calculating high-school completion rates and may not be comparable to previous years' data for Averaged Freshmen Graduation Rates (AFGR).

[2] The United States 4-year ACGRs were estimated using both the reported 4-year ACGR data from 49 states and the District of Columbia and using imputed data for Idaho. The estimate for American Indian/Alaska Native students also includes imputed data for Virginia.

Table DC-13. Reported Voting and Registration of the Voting-Age Population, November 2016

(Numbers in thousands, percent.)

Item	Total population	Total citizen population	Registered			Voted		
			Total registered	Percent registered (total population)	Percent registered (total citizen population)	Total voted	Percent voted (total population)	Percent voted (total citizen population)
U.S. Total	245,502	224,059	157,596	64.2	70.3	137,537	56.0	61.4
State Total.............................	553	512	420	75.9	82.1	380	68.7	74.3
Sex								
Male	255	237	190	74.8	80.4	168	66.1	71.0
Female	299	275	229	76.8	83.5	212	71.0	77.2
Race								
White alone................................	264	243	209	79.5	86.3	194	73.7	80.0
White, non-Hispanic alone............	231	222	195	84.6	88.2	181	78.6	81.9
Black alone.................................	250	238	184	73.9	77.5	162	64.8	68.0
Asian alone	27	18	14	(B)	(B)	13	(B)	(B)
Hispanic (of any race)......................	42	28	20	(B)	(B)	18	(B)	(B)
White alone or in combination	274	253	219	80.0	86.6	203	74.3	80.5
Black alone or in combination...........	259	247	192	74.2	77.7	169	65.4	68.4
Asian alone or in combination...........	29	20	16	(B)	(B)	15	(B)	(B)
Age								
18 to 24 years.............................	59	55	40	(B)	(B)	34	(B)	(B)
25 to 34 years.............................	179	164	130	72.9	79.6	120	67.1	73.3
35 to 44 years.............................	91	80	70	(B)	(B)	64	(B)	(B)
45 to 64 years.............................	139	131	110	79.5	84.2	99	71.4	75.7
65 years and over	86	82	70	(B)	(B)	63	(B)	(B)

B = Base is less than 75,000 and therefore too small to show the derived measure.

Table DC-14. Crime

(Number, rate per 100,000. Data are derived from the FBI Uniform Crime Reports.)

Item	District [1]			U.S. [1,2,3,4]		
	2015	2016	Percent change	2015	2016	Percent change
TOTAL POPULATION [5]	672,228	681,170	1.3	321,418,820	323,127,513	0.5
VIOLENT CRIME						
Number..	8,531	8,214	-3.7	1,231,566	1,248,185	1.3
Rate	1,269.1	1,205.9	-5.0	383.2	386.3	0.8
Murder and Nonnegligent Manslaughter						
Number..	162	139	-14.2	15,696	17,250	9.9
Rate	24.1	20.4	-15.4	4.9	5.3	8.2
Rape [6]						
Number..	494	532	7.7	124,047	130,603	5.3
Rate	73.5	78.1	6.3	38.6	40.4	4.7
Robbery						
Number..	3,742	3,480	-7.0	327,374	332,198	1.5
Rate	556.7	510.9	-8.2	101.9	102.8	0.9
Aggravated Assault						
Number..	4,133	4,063	-1.7	764,449	803,007	5.0
Rate	614.8	596.5	-3.0	237.8	248.5	4.5
PROPERTY CRIME						
Number..	31,435	32,716	4.1	7,993,631	7,919,035	-0.9
Rate	4,676.2	4,802.9	2.7	2,487.0	2,450.7	-1.5
Burglary						
Number..	2,971	2,361	-20.5	1,579,527	1,515,096	-4.1
Rate	442.0	346.6	-21.6	491.4	468.9	-4.6
Larceny-Theft						
Number..	25,200	27,382	8.7	5,706,346	5,638,455	-1.2
Rate	3,748.7	4,019.8	7.2	1,775.4	1,745.0	-1.7
Motor Vehicle Theft						
Number..	3,264	2,973	-8.9	707,758	765,484	8.2
Rate	485.5	436.5	-10.1	220.2	236.9	7.6

NOTE: Although arson data are included in the trend and clearance tables, sufficient data are not available to estimate totals for this offense. Therefore, no arson data are published in this table.
X = Not applicable.
- = Zero or rounds to zero.
[1] Includes offenses reported by the Zoological Police and the Metro Transit Police.
[2] The crime figures have been adjusted.
[3] The data collection methodology for the offense of forcible rape used by the Minnesota state Uniform Crime Reporting (UCR) Program (with the exception of Minneapolis and St. Paul, Minnesota) does not comply with national UCR Program guidelines. Consequently, its figures for forcible rape and violent crime (of which forcible rape is a part) are not published in this table.
[4] Because of changes in the state's reporting practices, figures are not comparable to previous years' data.
[5] Populations are U.S. Census Bureau provisional estimates as of July 1 of each year.
[6] The figures shown for the offense of rape were estimated using the revised Uniform Crime Reporting (UCR) definition of rape.

Table DC-15. Local Government Finances, 2015

(Dollar amounts in thousands, percent distribution.)

Item	Dollars	Percent distribution
Total Revenue	15,137,352	100.0
General revenue	13,216,040	87.3
Intergovernmental revenue	4,302,223	28.4
Taxes	7,109,236	47.0
Property	2,251,724	14.9
Sales and gross receipts	1,751,874	11.6
Individual income tax	1,868,468	12.3
Corporate income tax	448,259	3.0
Motor vehicle license	37,649	0.2
Other taxes	751,262	5.0
Current charges	791,740	5.2
Miscellaneous general revenue	1,012,841	6.7
Utility revenue	1,067,057	7.0
Liquor stores revenue	0	-
Insurance trust revenue [1]	854,255	5.6
Total Expenditure	15,742,002	100.0
Intergovernmental expenditure	0	-
Direct expenditure	15,742,002	100.0
Current operation	12,084,460	76.8
Capital outlay	2,487,744	15.8
Insurance benefits and repayments	482,572	3.1
Assistance and subsidies	149,327	0.9
Interest on debt	537,899	3.4
Exhibit: Salaries and wages	3,751,793	23.8
Direct Expenditure	15,742,002	100.0
Direct expenditure by function:		
Direct general expenditure	12,424,661	78.9
Education	2,762,245	17.5
Public welfare	3,563,573	22.6
Hospitals	277,154	1.8
Health	472,754	3.0
Highways	469,871	3.0
Police protection	584,667	3.7
Correction	142,372	0.9
Natural resources	60,291	0.4
Parks and recreation	220,494	1.4
Governmental administration	641,819	4.1
Interest on general debt	521,577	3.3
Other and unallocable	901,080	5.7
Utility expenditure	2,834,769	18.0
Liquor stores expenditure	0	-
Insurance trust expenditure	482,572	3.1
Debt at End of Fiscal Year	13,924,244	X
Cash and Security Holdings	15,567,836	X

Note: At the time of publication, the Census Bureau had not yet released 2015 finance data for the District of Columbia.
X = Not applicable.
- = Zero or rounds to zero.
[1] Within insurance trust revenue, net earnings of state retirement systems is a calculated statistic (the item code in the data file is X08), and thus can be positive or negative. Net earnings is the sum of earnings on investments plus gains on investments minus losses on investments. The change made in 2002 for asset valuation from book to market value in accordance with Statement 34 of the Governmental Accounting Standards Board is reflected in the calculated statistics.

Table DC-16. District Government Tax Collections, 2017

(Dollars in thousands, percent.)

Item	Dollars	Percent distribution
Total Taxes	7,653,053	100.0
Property taxes	2,536,634	33.1
Sales and gross receipts	1,860,804	24.3
General sales and gross receipts	1,418,935	18.5
Selective sales and gross receipts	441,869	5.8
Alcoholic beverages	6,641	0.1
Amusements	X	-
Insurance premiums	110,392	1.4
Motor fuels	26,098	0.3
Pari-mutuels	X	-
Public utilities	187,667	2.5
Tobacco products	29,530	0.4
Other selective sales	81,541	1.1
Licenses	185,529	2.4
Alcoholic beverages	5,724	0.1
Amusements	X	-
Corporations in general	31,107	0.4
Hunting and fishing	97	-
Motor vehicle	38,935	0.5
Motor vehicle operators	6,207	0.1
Public utilities	X	-
Occupation and business, NEC	57,656	0.8
Other licenses	45,803	0.6
Income taxes	2,512,522	32.8
Individual income	1,958,277	25.6
Corporation net income	554,245	7.2
Other taxes	557,564	7.3
Death and gift	41,215	0.5
Documentary and stock transfer	460,901	6.0
Severance	X	-
Taxes, NEC	55,448	0.7

X = Not applicable.
- = Zero or rounds to zero.

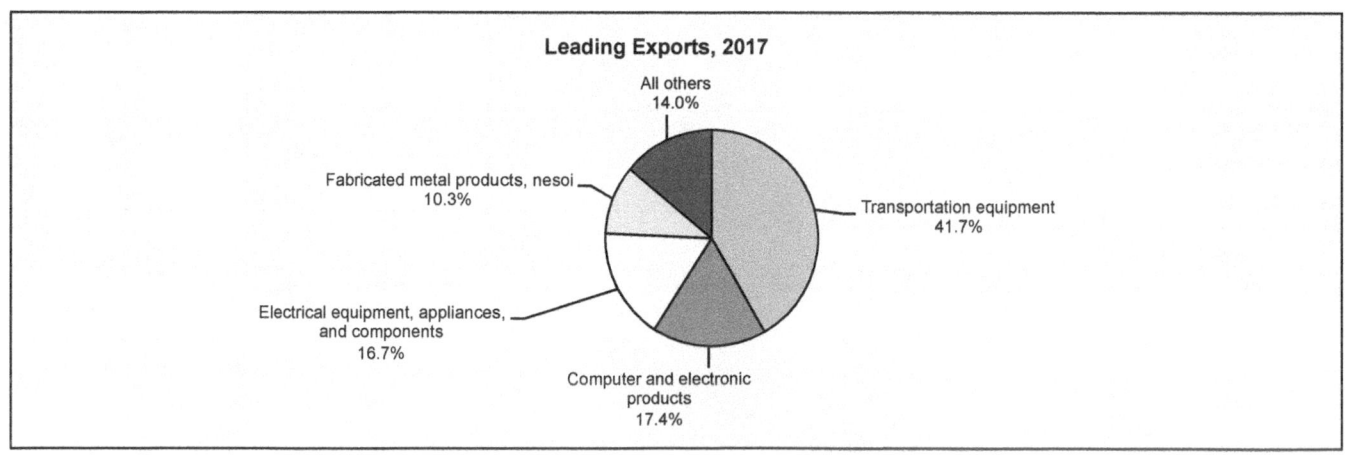

Leading Exports, 2017

All others 14.0%

Fabricated metal products, nesoi 10.3%

Transportation equipment 41.7%

Electrical equipment, appliances, and components 16.7%

Computer and electronic products 17.4%

FLORIDA

Facts and Figures

Location: Southeastern United States; bordered on the N by Georgia and Alabama, on the E by the Atlantic Ocean, on the S by the Straits of Florida, and on the W by Alabama and the Gulf of Mexico

Area: 65,757 sq. mi. (170,304 sq. km.); rank—22nd

Population: 20,984,400 (2017 est.); rank—3rd

Principal Cities: capital—Tallahassee; largest—Jacksonville

Statehood: March 3, 1845; 27th state

U.S. Congress: 2 senators, 27 representatives

State Motto: In God We Trust

State Song: "The Swanee River (Old Folks at Home)"

State Nickname: The Sunshine State

Abbreviations: FL; Fla.

State Symbols: flower—orange blossom; tree—Sabal palm (cabbage palm); bird—mockingbird

At a Glance

- With an increase in population of 11.3 percent, Florida ranked 5th among the states in growth from 2010 to 2017.

- Florida's violent crime rate in 2016 was 430.3 incidents per 100,000 population, compared to 386.3 for the entire nation.

- In 2017, Florida was once again the state with the largest percentage of its population in the 65 and older age group (20.1 percent).

- Florida ranked 6th among the states for the highest percent of Hispanic or Latino residents (25.6 percent) in 2017. Hispanic or Latino residents may be of any race.

- In 2016, 12.5 percent of all Florida residents were uninsured, compared to the national average of 8.6 percent.

Table FL-1. Population by Age, Sex, Race, and Hispanic Origin

(Number, percent, except where noted.)

Sex, age, race, and Hispanic origin	2000	2010	2017 [1]	Average annual percent change, 2010–2017
Total Population...........	15,982,378	18,801,310	20,984,400	11.6
Percent of total U.S. population	5.7	6.1	6.4	X
Sex				
Male........	7,797,715	9,189,355	10,256,819	11.6
Female	8,184,663	9,611,955	10,727,581	11.6
Age				
Under 5 years........	945,823	1,073,506	1,138,095	6.0
5 to 19 years........	3,102,809	3,439,484	3,536,508	2.8
20 to 64 years........	9,126,149	11,034,718	12,095,162	9.6
65 years and over	2,807,597	3,259,602	4,214,635	29.3
Median age (years)........	38.7	40.7	42.1	3.4
Race and Hispanic Origin				
One race				
White	12,465,029	14,808,867	16,247,613	9.7
Black........	2,335,505	3,078,067	3,547,464	15.2
American Indian and Alaska Native	53,541	89,119	104,511	17.3
Asian........	266,256	474,199	613,880	29.5
Native Hawaiian or Other Pacific Islander	8,625	18,790	23,660	25.9
Two or more races	376,315	332,268	447,272	34.6
Hispanic (of any race)........	2,682,715	4,301,853	5,371,385	24.9

X = Not applicable.
[1] Population figures for 2017 are July 1 estimates. The 2010 estimates are taken from the 2010 Census.

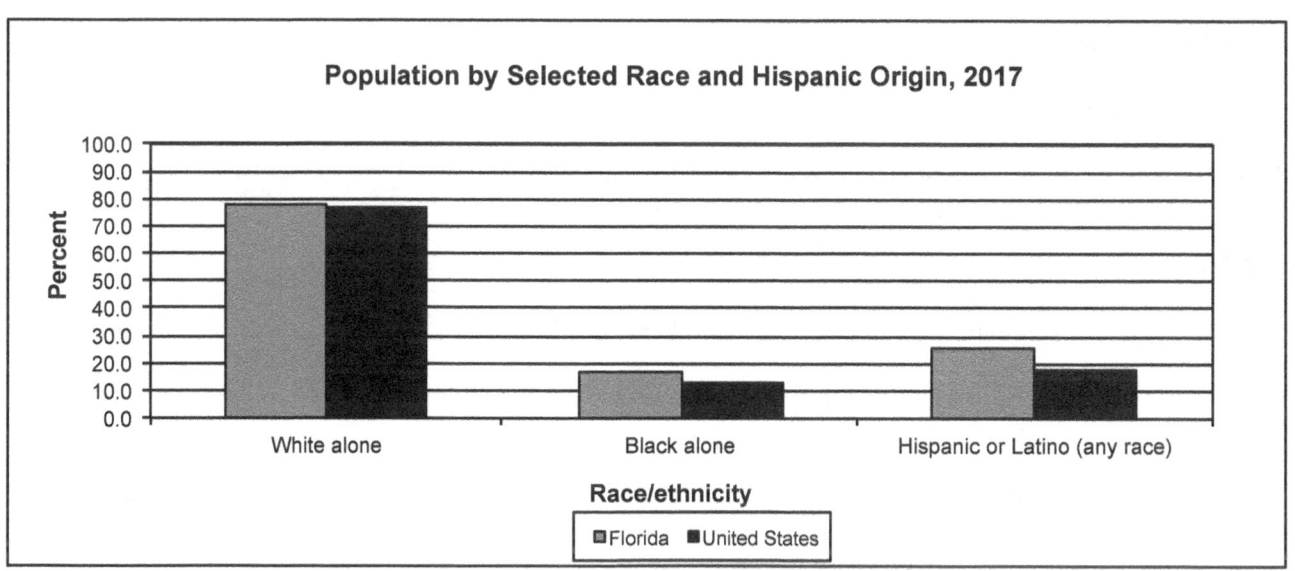

Table FL-2. Marital Status

(Number, percent distribution.)

Sex, age, and marital status	2000	2010	2016
Males, 15 Years and Over	6,232,987	7,534,535	8,325,278
Never married	27.3	33.9	35.2
Now married, except separated........	56.9	49.3	48.0
Separated........	2.1	2.2	2.0
Widowed........	3.2	3.2	3.3
Divorced........	10.5	11.5	11.6
Females, 15 Years and Over	6,714,003	8,021,290	8,869,962
Never married	20.5	26.6	28.7
Now married, except separated........	51.9	45.1	43.7
Separated........	2.7	3.0	2.7
Widowed........	12.3	10.8	10.3
Divorced........	12.7	14.5	14.6

Table FL-3. Households and Housing Characteristics

(Number, percent, dollars.)

Item	2000	2010	2016	Average annual percent change, 2010–2016
Total Households..	6,337,929	7,035,068	7,573,456	1.3
Family households..	4,210,760	4,556,930	4,864,461	1.1
Married-couple family....................................	3,192,266	3,307,884	3,513,794	1.0
Other family...	1,018,494	1,249,046	1,350,667	1.4
Male householder, no wife present..............	259,924	313,305	364,873	2.7
Female householder, no husband present.....	759,000	935,741	985,794	0.9
Nonfamily households..	2,127,169	2,478,138	2,708,995	1.6
Householder living alone................................	1,687,303	2,013,028	2,184,465	1.4
Householder not living alone.........................	439,886	465,110	524,530	2.1
Housing Characteristics				
Total housing units...	7,302,947	8,994,091	9,302,140	0.6
Occupied housing units.....................................	6,337,929	7,035,068	7,573,456	1.3
Owner occupied..	4,441,799	4,794,130	4,857,125	0.2
Renter occupied...	1,896,130	2,240,938	2,716,331	3.5
Average household size......................................	2.46	2.62	2.66	0.3
Financial Characteristics				
Median gross rent of renter-occupied housing	641	947	1086	2.4
Median monthly owner costs for housing units with a mortgage	1,004	1,505	1,410	-1.1
Median value of owner-occupied housing units.........	105,500	164,200	197,700	3.4

Table FL-4. Migration, Origin, and Language

(Number, percent.)

Characteristic	State			U.S.		
	2015	2016	Percent change	2015	2016	Percent change
Residence 1 Year Ago						
Population 1 year and over......................................	20,068,392	20,401,575	1.7	317,635,720	319,361,956	0.5
Same house..	83.9	84.2	X	85.3	85.4	X
Different house in the U.S..................................	15.1	14.7	X	14.1	13.9	X
Same county..	9.0	8.7	X	8.5	8.3	X
Different county...	6.1	6.0	X	5.6	5.6	X
Same state...	3.1	3.0	X	3.2	3.2	X
Different state...	2.9	3.0	X	2.4	2.4	X
Abroad..	1.1	1.1	X	0.7	0.7	X
Place of Birth						
Native born..	16,185,032	16,375,928	1.2	278,128,449	279,388,170	0.5
Male..	49.2	49.4	X	49.3	49.3	X
Female...	50.8	50.6	X	50.7	50.7	X
Foreign born...	4,086,240	4,236,511	3.7	43,290,372	43,739,345	1.0
Male..	47.4	46.9	X	48.6	48.5	X
Female...	52.6	53.1	X	51.4	51.5	X
Foreign born; naturalized U.S. citizen.................	2,195,000	2,334,825	6.4	20,697,103	21,238,372	2.6
Male...	44.4	43.9	X	45.9	45.9	X
Female..	55.6	56.1	X	54.1	54.1	X
Foreign born; not a U.S. citizen.........................	1,891,240	1,901,686	0.6	22,593,269	22,500,973	-0.4
Male...	50.8	50.6	X	51.1	51.0	X
Female..	49.2	49.4	X	48.9	49.0	X
Entered 2010 or later..	16.9	20.7	X	15.6	18.6	X
Entered 2000 to 2009..	28.3	26.5	X	27.9	26.7	X
Entered before 2000..	54.8	52.8	X	56.5	54.7	X
World Region of Birth, Foreign						
Foreign-born population, excluding population born at sea.......	4,086,240	4,236,511	3.7	43,289,646	43,738,901	1.0
Europe..	9.3	9.7	X	11.1	10.9	X
Asia..	10.9	10.8	X	30.6	30.8	X
Africa...	1.8	1.8	X	4.8	4.9	X
Oceania..	0.2	0.2	X	0.6	0.6	X
Latin America..	75.1	74.9	X	51.1	51.0	X
North America...	2.8	2.6	X	1.9	1.8	X
Language Spoken at Home and Ability to Speak English						
Population 5 years and over..................................	19,172,999	19,494,972	1.7	301,625,014	303,328,961	0.6
English only..	71.0	71.2	X	78.5	78.4	X
Language other than English..............................	29.0	28.8	X	21.5	21.6	X
Speaks English less than "very well"................	11.8	12.0	X	8.6	8.6	X

NA = Not available.
X = Not applicable.
- = Zero or rounds to zero.

Table FL-5. Median Income and Poverty Status, 2016

(Number, percent, except as noted.)

Characteristic	State		U.S.	
	Number	Percent	Number	Percent
Median Income				
Households (dollars)........................	50,860	X	57,617	X
Families (dollars)	61,289	X	71,062	X
Below Poverty Level (All People)	2,973,512	14.7	44,268,996	14.0
Sex				
Male	1,329,354	13.6	19,760,056	12.8
Female	1,644,158	15.8	24,508,940	15.2
Age				
Under 18 years...........................	858,711	21.0	14,115,713	19.5
Related children under 18 years............	842,396	20.7	13,805,435	19.1
18 to 64 years............................	1,696,425	14.0	25,723,818	13.2
65 years and over	418,376	10.4	4,429,465	9.2

X = Not applicable.

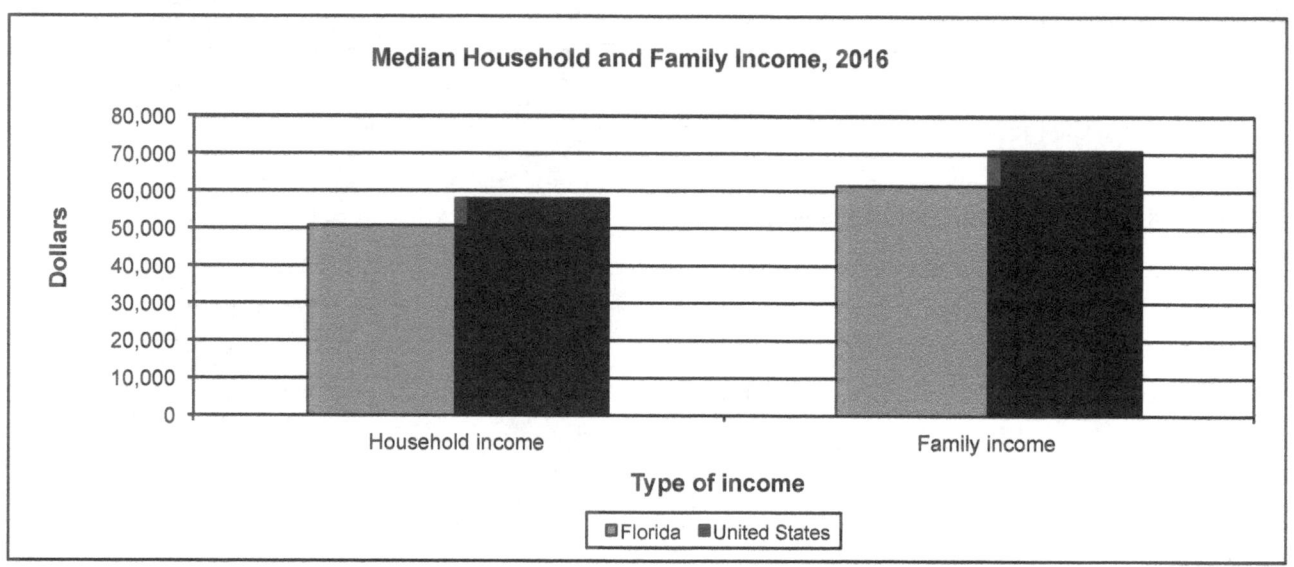

Table FL-6. Health Insurance Coverage Status for the Civilian Noninstitutionalized Population and Children Under 18 Years of Age

(Number, percent.)

Item	2008	2009	2010	2011	2012	2013	2014	2015	2016
Civilian Noninstitutionalized Population	17,995,843	18,192,784	18,534,081	18,752,294	19,011,070	19,245,127	19,583,357	19,960,169	20,294,479
Covered by Private or Public Insurance									
Number........................	14,246,667	14,397,455	14,593,021	14,840,913	15,195,230	15,392,164	16,338,196	17,298,620	17,750,232
Percent........................	79.2	79.1	78.7	79.1	79.9	80.0	83.4	86.7	87.5
Not Covered									
Number........................	3,749,176	3,795,329	3,941,060	3,911,381	3,815,840	3,852,963	3,245,161	2,661,549	2,544,247
Percent........................	20.8	20.9	21.3	20.9	20.1	20.0	16.6	13.3	12.5
Percent in the U.S. not covered..............	15.1	15.1	15.5	15.1	14.8	14.5	11.7	9.4	8.6
Children Under 18 Years of Age	3,996,332	4,050,661	3,990,247	3,986,946	3,991,143	4,019,835	4,046,150	4,093,401	4,136,345
Covered by Private or Public Insurance									
Number........................	3,295,275	3,450,124	3,483,313	3,511,834	3,554,977	3,574,800	3,668,163	3,809,595	3,879,598
Percent........................	82.5	85.2	87.3	88.1	89.1	88.9	90.7	93.1	93.8
Not Covered									
Number........................	701,057	600,537	506,934	475,112	436,166	445,035	377,987	283,806	256,747
Percent........................	17.5	14.8	12.7	11.9	10.9	11.1	9.3	6.9	6.2
Percent in the U.S. not covered..............	9.9	8.6	8.0	7.5	7.2	7.1	6.0	4.8	4.5

Table FL-7. Employment Status by Demographic Group, 2017

(Numbers in thousands, percent.)

Characteristic	Civilian noninstitutional population	Civilian labor force		Employed		Unemployed	
		Number	Percent of population	Number	Percent of population	Number	Percent of population
Total...	16,926	10,113	59.7	9,699	57.3	414	4.1
Sex							
Male....................................	8,105	5,303	65.4	5,104	63.0	199	3.7
Female................................	8,821	4,810	54.5	4,595	52.1	215	4.5
Race, Sex, and Hispanic Origin							
White...................................	13,516	7,912	58.5	7,632	56.5	280	3.5
Male..............................	6,535	4,236	64.8	4,094	62.7	142	3.3
Female..........................	6,981	3,676	52.7	3,538	50.7	138	3.8
Black or African American............	2,621	1,678	64.0	1,564	59.7	115	6.8
Male..............................	1,203	787	65.4	741	61.6	47	5.9
Female..........................	1,418	891	62.8	823	58.1	68	7.6
Hispanic or Latino ethnicity[1]...........	4,247	2,729	64.2	2,612	61.5	117	4.3
Male..............................	2,068	1,519	73.5	1,461	70.7	58	3.8
Female..........................	2,180	1,210	55.5	1,151	52.8	59	4.9
Age							
16 to 19 years........................	986	300	30.4	251	25.5	49	16.3
20 to 24 years........................	1,225	870	71.0	815	66.5	55	6.4
25 to 34 years........................	2,659	2,162	81.3	2,074	78.0	88	4.1
35 to 44 years........................	2,393	1,962	82.0	1,903	79.5	59	3.0
45 to 54 years........................	2,969	2,359	79.4	2,282	76.9	76	3.2
55 to 64 years........................	2,766	1,741	62.9	1,682	60.8	59	3.4
65 years and over	3,927	719	18.3	691	17.6	28	3.9

NOTE: Data in Table 7 are from the Current Population Survey (CPS) and do not match the estimates in Table 8. See notes and definitions for further information.
[1] May be of any race.

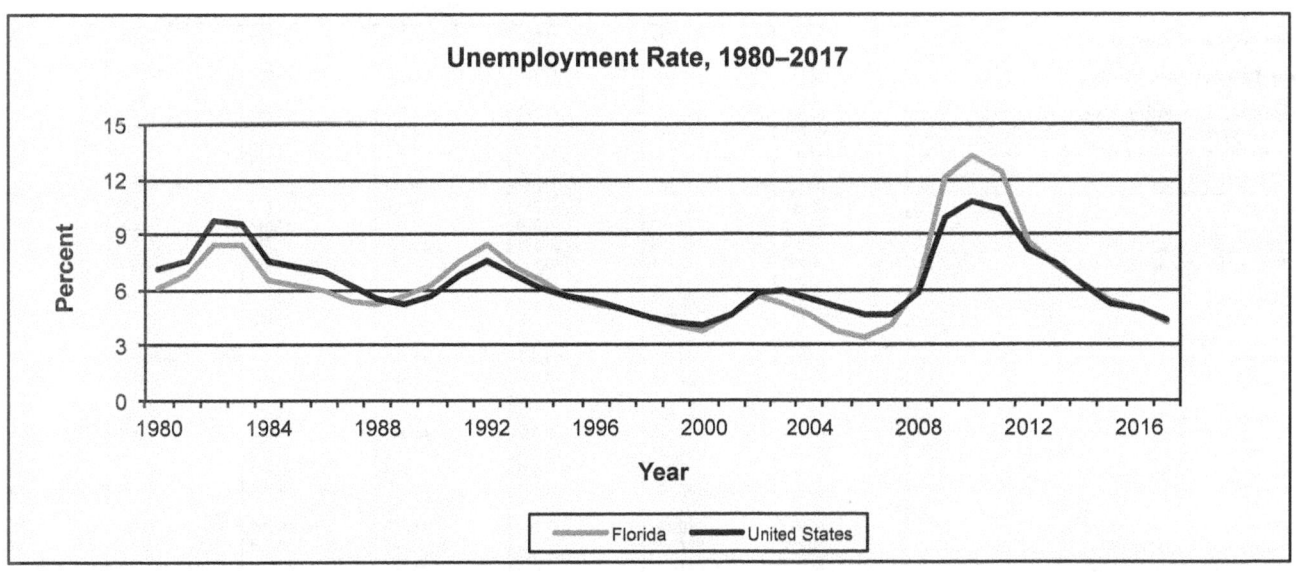

Unemployment Rate, 1980–2017

Table FL-8. Employment Status of the Civilian Noninstitutional Population Age 16 Years and Over

(Number, percent.)

Year	Civilian labor force	Civilian participation rate	Employed	Unemployed	Unemployment rate
2009...	9,094,825	62.3	8,148,123	946,702	10.4
2010...	9,212,066	61.6	8,193,659	1,018,407	11.1
2011...	9,300,542	61.0	8,371,638	928,904	10.0
2012...	9,382,993	60.6	8,588,669	794,324	8.5
2013...	9,453,747	60.2	8,770,084	683,663	7.2
2014...	9,581,083	59.9	8,979,399	601,684	6.3
2015...	9,629,632	59.0	9,104,357	525,275	5.5
2016...	9,846,000	59.1	9,373,059	472,941	4.8
2017...	10,100,266	59.6	9,680,820	419,446	4.2

Table FL-9. Employment and Average Wages by Industry

(Estimates through 2010 are based on the 2007 *North American Industry Classification System* [NAICS]. Estimates from 2011 onward are based on the 2012 NAICS.)

Industry	2010	2011	2012	2013	2014	2015	2016
	Number of Jobs						
Wage and Salary Employment by Industry	7,528,307	7,612,793	7,767,188	7,939,949	8,196,734	8,470,602	8,739,974
Farm Wage and Salary Employment	43,191	44,307	47,948	44,695	48,772	42,091	40,153
Nonfarm Wage and Salary Employment	7,485,116	7,568,486	7,719,240	7,895,254	8,147,962	8,428,511	8,699,821
Private wage and salary employment	6,282,399	6,387,586	6,554,478	6,731,919	6,989,620	7,262,925	7,523,205
Forestry, fishing, and related activities	44,455	43,233	42,293	44,472	45,272	44,757	44,385
Mining	3,622	3,872	3,950	3,957	4,100	4,089	4,214
Utilities	22,529	22,433	22,656	22,301	21,994	22,479	22,875
Construction	359,371	345,080	352,818	376,584	408,079	442,562	487,590
Manufacturing	307,721	311,671	317,199	322,333	331,711	343,213	355,457
Durable goods manufacturing	202,755	205,662	209,481	214,915	222,834	233,380	240,746
Nondurable goods manufacturing	104,966	106,009	107,718	107,418	108,877	109,833	114,711
Wholesale trade	309,861	309,674	318,618	323,333	329,555	336,432	341,488
Retail trade	936,659	964,924	988,999	1,013,165	1,050,988	1,090,860	1,111,274
Transportation and warehousing	204,504	213,508	220,516	227,674	236,048	247,135	259,183
Information	135,784	134,653	134,183	134,306	137,011	136,311	136,897
Finance and insurance	330,180	339,871	350,784	355,323	362,838	373,492	384,103
Real estate and rental and leasing	154,982	156,010	164,934	169,995	175,098	181,581	184,913
Professional, scientific, and technical services	438,983	449,101	455,591	472,608	490,454	511,693	534,351
Management of companies and enterprises	78,208	81,039	83,695	91,063	94,224	97,003	100,366
Administrative and waste services	537,734	533,392	545,876	563,070	590,262	623,004	660,279
Educational services	145,405	150,009	149,731	150,580	156,964	159,678	162,125
Health care and social assistance	936,182	951,342	972,164	989,676	1,013,948	1,051,455	1,088,395
Arts, entertainment, and recreation	186,688	191,629	197,725	199,810	210,555	218,730	227,813
Accommodation and food services	741,125	769,748	807,265	843,687	881,002	921,046	956,000
Other services, except public administration	408,406	416,397	425,481	427,982	449,517	457,405	461,497
Government and government enterprises	1,202,717	1,180,900	1,164,762	1,163,335	1,158,342	1,165,586	1,176,616
	Dollars						
Average Wages and Salaries by Industry	42,895	43,672	44,580	45,138	46,202	47,686	50,307
Average Farm Wages and Salaries	28,152	23,921	21,475	28,280	23,692	26,771	31,493
Average Nonfarm Wages and Salaries	42,980	43,788	44,723	45,233	46,337	47,790	50,393
Average private wages and salaries	42,058	42,978	44,087	44,615	45,736	47,268	49,915
Forestry, fishing, and related activities	22,306	23,079	24,274	24,558	25,040	26,966	30,815
Mining	59,880	60,928	68,082	64,267	66,343	67,514	71,016
Utilities	80,205	84,360	86,092	88,025	92,431	95,384	100,144
Construction	42,226	42,070	42,634	43,176	44,706	46,762	52,217
Manufacturing	53,912	54,492	55,379	56,261	57,647	59,504	61,807
Durable goods manufacturing	56,851	57,533	58,598	59,420	60,747	62,115	65,195
Nondurable goods manufacturing	48,235	48,591	49,119	49,941	51,301	53,956	54,697
Wholesale trade	62,486	65,036	67,178	68,375	70,201	72,758	75,671
Retail trade	28,114	28,292	28,778	29,157	29,793	30,731	31,788
Transportation and warehousing	47,030	48,059	49,229	50,605	52,093	53,919	57,172
Information	63,375	66,555	68,867	70,734	72,991	76,062	80,889
Finance and insurance	68,266	71,159	73,603	75,464	79,037	81,736	87,599
Real estate and rental and leasing	40,442	41,850	43,126	44,265	46,630	48,657	51,100
Professional, scientific, and technical services	65,421	66,992	69,483	69,650	71,503	73,615	79,078
Management of companies and enterprises	91,269	95,597	106,264	101,673	104,288	106,910	111,671
Administrative and waste services	33,461	34,065	34,699	34,654	35,361	36,561	38,592
Educational services	36,271	37,706	37,587	37,882	38,601	38,781	39,141
Health care and social assistance	45,937	46,896	47,757	48,216	49,206	50,984	53,256
Arts, entertainment, and recreation	36,617	37,261	38,368	38,148	38,980	40,846	43,977
Accommodation and food services	21,079	21,684	22,382	22,967	23,595	24,454	25,400
Other services, except public administration	29,707	29,821	30,600	31,585	32,415	33,729	35,584
Government and government enterprises	47,792	48,167	48,302	48,813	49,966	51,044	53,455

Table FL-10. Employment Characteristics by Family Type

(Number, percent.)

Family type and labor force status	2014		2015		2016	
	Total	Families with own children under 18 years	Total	Families with own children under 18 years	Total	Families with own children under 18 years
All Families...	4,675,046	1,744,542	4,806,611	1,781,366	4,864,461	1,787,004
FAMILY TYPE AND LABOR FORCE STATUS						
Married-Couple Families..................................	3,361,738	1,094,773	3,444,776	1,117,422	3,513,794	1,133,704
Both husband and wife in labor force.................	44.7	64.3	44.3	64.9	43.8	65.0
Husband in labor force, wife not in labor force..........	20.9	28.9	20.2	27.7	20.1	27.4
Wife in labor force, husband not in labor force..........	8.4	4.7	8.4	4.9	8.3	4.7
Both husband and wife not in labor force...............	26.0	2.2	26.3	2.2	26.7	2.4
Other Families	1,313,308	649,769	1,361,835	663,944	1,350,667	653,300
Female householder, no husband present..............	73.1	76.1	73.6	75.7	73.0	75.9
In labor force...	51.7	63.4	51.4	63.3	51.0	64.2
Not in labor force	21.4	12.7	22.2	12.4	22.0	11.6
Male householder, no wife present......................	26.9	23.9	26.4	24.3	27.0	24.1
In labor force...	20.8	21.9	20.3	22.3	20.5	22.2
Not in labor force	6.1	2.1	6.1	2.0	6.5	2.0

Table FL-11. School Enrollment and Educational Attainment, 2016

(Number, percent.)

Item	State	U.S.
Enrollment		
Total population 3 years and over, enrolled in school	4,718,808	81,572,277
Enrolled in nursery school or preschool (percent).........................	6.0	6.0
Enrolled in kindergarten (percent).......................................	4.9	5.0
Enrolled in elementary school, grades 1-8 (percent)......................	39.0	40.3
Enrolled in high school, grades 9-12 (percent)..........................	21.0	21.0
Enrolled in college or graduate school (percent)........................	28.9	27.7
Attainment		
Total population 25 years and over	14,703,671	218,475,480
Less than ninth grade (percent)...	5.2	5.4
9th to 12th grade, no diploma (percent).................................	7.4	7.2
High school graduate, including equivalency (percent)...................	28.9	27.2
Some college, no degree (percent)	20.1	20.6
Associate's degree (percent)..	9.7	8.4
Bachelor's degree (percent)	18.2	19.3
Graduate or professional degree (percent)...............................	10.4	11.9
High school graduate or higher (percent)................................	87.4	87.5
Bachelor's degree or higher (percent)...................................	28.6	31.3

Table FL-12. Public School Characteristics and Educational Indicators

(Number, percent; data derived from National Center of Education Statistics.)

Item	State	U.S.
Public Schools, 2015–2016 (except where noted)		
Number of school districts...	76	18,328
Number of schools..	4,322	98,456
Number of students...	2,792,234	50,327,015
Number of teachers...	182,586	3,151,497
Student-teacher ratio...	15.3	16.0
Expenditures per student (dollars), 2014-2015...........................	9,113	11,445
Four-year adjusted cohort graduation rate (ACGR)[1,2]	80.7	84.1
Students eligible for free or reduced-price lunch (percent), 2014-2015....	58.4	51.8
English language learners (percent), Fall 2015	9.6	9.5
Students age 3 to 21 served under IDEA, part B (percent).................	13.3	13.2

Public Schools by Type	Number	Percent of state public schools
Total number of schools...	4,322	100.0
Regular	3,716	86.0
Special education...	174	4.0
Vocational education..	53	1.2
Alternative education...	379	8.8

NOTE: Every school is assigned only one school type based on its instructional emphasis.
[1] ACGR data represents a new method of calculating high-school completion rates and may not be comparable to previous years' data for Averaged Freshmen Graduation Rates (AFGR).
[2] The United States 4-year ACGRs were estimated using both the reported 4-year ACGR data from 49 states and the District of Columbia and using imputed data for Idaho. The estimate for American Indian/Alaska Native students also includes imputed data for Virginia.

Table FL-13. Reported Voting and Registration of the Voting-Age Population, November 2016

(Numbers in thousands, percent.)

Item	Total population	Total citizen population	Registered			Voted		
			Total registered	Percent registered (total population)	Percent registered (total citizen population)	Total voted	Percent voted (total population)	Percent voted (total citizen population)
U.S. Total	245,502	224,059	157,596	64.2	70.3	137,537	56.0	61.4
State Total..............................	16,202	14,428	9,604	59.3	66.6	8,578	52.9	59.5
Sex								
Male	7,736	6,868	4,377	56.6	63.7	3,920	50.7	57.1
Female	8,466	7,560	5,226	61.7	69.1	4,658	55.0	61.6
Race								
White alone..............................	13,097	11,793	8,141	62.2	69.0	7,277	55.6	61.7
White, non-Hispanic alone	9,307	9,066	6,432	69.1	70.9	5,781	62.1	63.8
Black alone................................	2,434	2,083	1,149	47.2	55.2	1,051	43.2	50.5
Asian alone	483	381	192	39.7	50.3	154	31.9	40.4
Hispanic (of any race)......................	4,010	2,871	1,779	44.4	62.0	1,552	38.7	54.1
White alone or in combination	13,217	11,899	8,212	62.1	69.0	7,336	55.5	61.7
Black alone or in combination...........	2,496	2,135	1,184	47.4	55.4	1,077	43.2	50.4
Asian alone or in combination...........	525	424	212	40.4	50.1	170	32.3	40.0
Age								
18 to 24 years..............................	1,589	1,413	728	45.8	51.5	527	33.1	37.3
25 to 34 years..............................	2,582	2,245	1,357	52.5	60.5	1,157	44.8	51.6
35 to 44 years..............................	2,505	1,985	1,315	52.5	66.3	1,144	45.7	57.6
45 to 64 years..............................	5,661	5,091	3,446	60.9	67.7	3,171	56.0	62.3
65 years and over	3,865	3,694	2,758	71.4	74.7	2,578	66.7	69.8

Table FL-14. Crime

(Number, rate per 100,000. Data are derived from the FBI Uniform Crime Reports.)

Item	State			U.S. [1,2,3,4]		
	2015	2016	Percent change	2015	2016	Percent change
TOTAL POPULATION [5]	20,271,272	20,612,439	1.7	321,418,820	323,127,513	0.5
VIOLENT CRIME						
Number...	93,626	88,700	-5.3	1,231,566	1,248,185	1.3
Rate	461.9	430.3	-6.8	383.2	386.3	0.8
Murder and Nonnegligent Manslaughter						
Number...	1,041	1,111	6.7	15,696	17,250	9.9
Rate	5.1	5.4	5.9	4.9	5.3	8.2
Rape[6]						
Number...	7,553	7,598	0.6	124,047	130,603	5.3
Rate	37.3	36.9	-1.1	38.6	40.4	4.7
Robbery						
Number...	21,137	20,175	-4.6	327,374	332,198	1.5
Rate	104.3	97.9	-6.1	101.9	102.8	0.9
Aggravated Assault						
Number...	63,895	59,816	-6.4	764,449	803,007	5.0
Rate	315.2	290.2	-7.9	237.8	248.5	4.5
PROPERTY CRIME						
Number...	570,270	553,812	-2.9	7,993,631	7,919,035	-0.9
Rate	2,813.2	2,686.8	-4.5	2,487.0	2,450.7	-1.5
Burglary						
Number...	109,268	100,325	-8.2	1,579,527	1,515,096	-4.1
Rate	539.0	486.7	-9.7	491.4	468.9	-4.6
Larceny-Theft						
Number...	420,341	410,352	-2.4	5,706,346	5,638,455	-1.2
Rate	2,073.6	1,990.8	-4.0	1,775.4	1,745.0	-1.7
Motor Vehicle Theft						
Number...	40,661	43,135	6.1	707,758	765,484	8.2
Rate	200.6	209.3	4.3	220.2	236.9	7.6

NOTE: Although arson data are included in the trend and clearance tables, sufficient data are not available to estimate totals for this offense. Therefore, no arson data are published in this table.

X = Not applicable.

- = Zero or rounds to zero.

[1] The crime figures have been adjusted.

[2] The data collection methodology for the offense of forcible rape used by the Minnesota state Uniform Crime Reporting (UCR) Program (with the exception of Minneapolis and St. Paul, Minnesota) does not comply with national UCR Program guidelines. Consequently, its figures for forcible rape and violent crime (of which forcible rape is a part) are not published in this table.

[3] Includes offenses reported by the Zoological Police and the Metro Transit Police.

[4] Because of changes in the state's reporting practices, figures are not comparable to previous years' data.

[5] Populations are U.S. Census Bureau provisional estimates as of July 1 of each year.

[6] The figures shown for the offense of rape were estimated using the revised Uniform Crime Reporting (UCR) definition of rape.

Table FL-15. State Government Finances, 2016

(Dollar amounts in thousands, percent distribution.)

Item	Dollars	Percent distribution
Total Revenue	85,575,636	100.0
General revenue	80,261,324	93.8
Intergovernmental revenue	27,390,107	32.0
Taxes	37,640,420	44.0
General sales	22,291,157	26.0
Selective sales	8,138,145	9.5
License taxes	2,241,468	2.6
Individual income tax	0	-
Corporate income tax	2,272,230	2.7
Other taxes	2,697,420	3.2
Current charges	8,234,288	9.6
Miscellaneous general revenue	6,996,509	8.2
Utility revenue	24,757	-
Liquor stores revenue	0	-
Insurance trust revenue [1]	5,289,555	6.2
Total Expenditure	88,220,438	100.0
Intergovernmental expenditure	20,407,866	23.1
Direct expenditure	67,812,572	76.9
Current operation	49,464,098	56.1
Capital outlay	6,473,452	7.3
Insurance benefits and repayments	8,892,649	10.1
Assistance and subsidies	1,987,559	2.3
Interest on debt	994,814	1.1
Exhibit: Salaries and wages	9,126,839	10.3
Total Expenditure	88,220,438	100.0
General expenditure	79,065,870	89.6
Intergovernmental expenditure	20,407,866	23.1
Direct expenditure	58,658,004	66.5
General expenditure, by function:		
Education	26,633,264	30.2
Public welfare	25,597,070	29.0
Hospitals	957,317	1.1
Health	3,612,735	4.1
Highways	8,007,319	9.1
Police protection	566,008	0.6
Correction	2,308,698	2.6
Natural resources	1,120,806	1.3
Parks and recreation	147,043	0.2
Governmental administration	2,445,200	2.8
Interest on general debt	994,814	1.1
Other and unallocable	6,675,596	7.6
Utility expenditure	261,919	0.3
Liquor stores expenditure	0	-
Insurance trust expenditure	8,892,649	10.1
Debt at End of Fiscal Year	33,469,117	X
Cash and Security Holdings	193,258,838	X

X = Not applicable.
- = Zero or rounds to zero.
[1] Within insurance trust revenue, net earnings of state retirement systems is a calculated statistic (the item code in the data file is X08), and thus can be positive or negative. Net earnings is the sum of earnings on investments plus gains on investments minus losses on investments. The change made in 2002 for asset valuation from book to market value in accordance with Statement 34 of the Governmental Accounting Standards Board is reflected in the calculated statistics.

Table FL-16. State Government Tax Collections, 2017

(Dollars in thousands, percent.)

Item	Dollars	Percent distribution
Total Taxes	40,218,365	100.0
Property taxes	X	-
Sales and gross receipts	33,339,556	82.9
General sales and gross receipts	25,346,166	63.0
Selective sales and gross receipts	7,993,390	19.9
Alcoholic beverages	323,393	0.8
Amusements	207,144	0.5
Insurance premiums	959,339	2.4
Motor fuels	2,727,802	6.8
Pari-mutuels	7,800	-
Public utilities	1,972,968	4.9
Tobacco products	1,197,666	3.0
Other selective sales	597,278	1.5
Licenses	2,032,331	5.1
Alcoholic beverages	7,005	-
Amusements	19,181	-
Corporations in general	238,350	0.6
Hunting and fishing	15,166	-
Motor vehicle	1,374,140	3.4
Motor vehicle operators	164,813	0.4
Public utilities	24,526	0.1
Occupation and business, NEC	180,240	0.4
Other licenses	8,910	-
Income taxes	2,383,783	5.9
Individual income	X	-
Corporation net income	2,383,783	5.9
Other taxes	2,462,695	6.1
Death and gift	644	-
Documentary and stock transfer	2,427,903	6.0
Severance	34,148	0.1
Taxes, NEC	0	-

X = Not applicable.
- = Zero or rounds to zero.

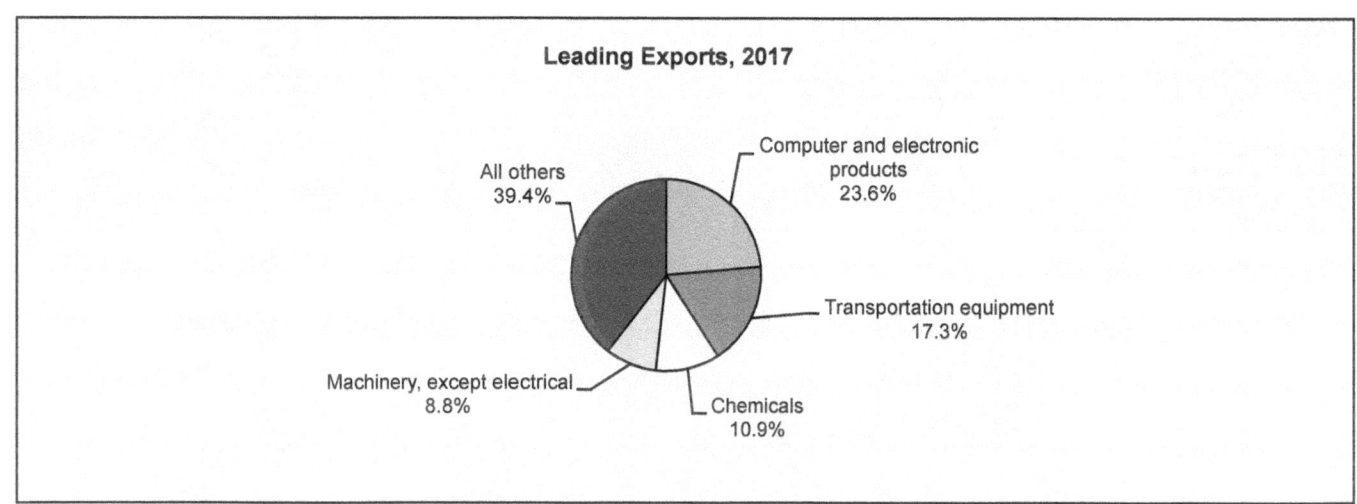

Leading Exports, 2017

All others 39.4%

Computer and electronic products 23.6%

Transportation equipment 17.3%

Chemicals 10.9%

Machinery, except electrical 8.8%

GEORGIA

Facts and Figures

Location: Southeastern United States; bordered on the N by Tennessee and North Carolina, on the E by South Carolina and the Atlantic Ocean, on the S by Florida, and on the W by Florida and Alabama

Area: 59,425 sq. mi. (153,909 sq. km.); rank—21st

Population: 10,429,379 (2017 est.); rank—8th

Principal Cities: capital—Atlanta; largest—Atlanta

Statehood: January 2, 1788; 4th state

U.S. Congress: 2 senators, 14 representatives

State Motto: Wisdom, Justice, and Moderation

State Song: "Georgia on My Mind"

State Nicknames: The Empire State of the South; The Peach State

Abbreviations: GA; Ga.

State Symbols: flower—Cherokee rose; tree—live oak; bird—brown thrasher

At a Glance

- With an increase in population of 7.4 percent, Georgia ranked 13th among the states in growth from 2010 to 2017.

- Georgia's median household income in 2016 was $53,559, and 16.0 percent of the state's population lived below the poverty level.

- In 2016, 12.9 percent of Georgians did not have health insurance, which was the 4th highest percent among the states.

- Georgia's violent crime rate was 397.6 per 100,000 population, compared to 386.3 for the U.S. as a whole in 2016.

- The property crime rate in Georgia in 2016 was 3,004.5 per 100,000 population, a rate that ranked 8th among the states.

Table GA-1. Population by Age, Sex, Race, and Hispanic Origin

(Number, percent, except where noted.)

Sex, age, race, and Hispanic origin	2000	2010	2017 [1]	Average annual percent change, 2010–2017
Total Population..................................	8,186,453	9,687,653	10,429,379	7.7
Percent of total U.S. population	2.9	3.1	3.2	X
Sex				
Male...................................	4,027,113	4,729,171	5,075,507	7.3
Female	4,159,340	4,958,482	5,353,872	8.0
Age				
Under 5 years........................	595,150	686,785	660,313	-3.9
5 to 19 years.........................	1,819,620	2,094,844	2,139,468	2.1
20 to 64 years........................	4,986,408	5,873,989	6,221,788	5.9
65 years and over	785,275	1,032,035	1,407,810	36.4
Median age (years)	33.4	35.3	36.7	4.0
Race and Hispanic Origin				
One race				
White	5,327,281	6,144,931	6,341,768	3.2
Black	2,349,542	2,993,927	3,361,924	12.3
American Indian and Alaska Native	21,737	48,599	53,646	10.4
Asian	173,170	323,459	440,104	36.1
Native Hawaiian or Other Pacific Islander	4,246	10,454	12,198	16.7
Two or more races	114,188	166,283	219,739	32.1
Hispanic (of any race)	435,227	911,863	1,005,959	10.3

X = Not applicable.

[1] Population figures for 2017 are July 1 estimates. The 2010 estimates are taken from the 2010 Census.

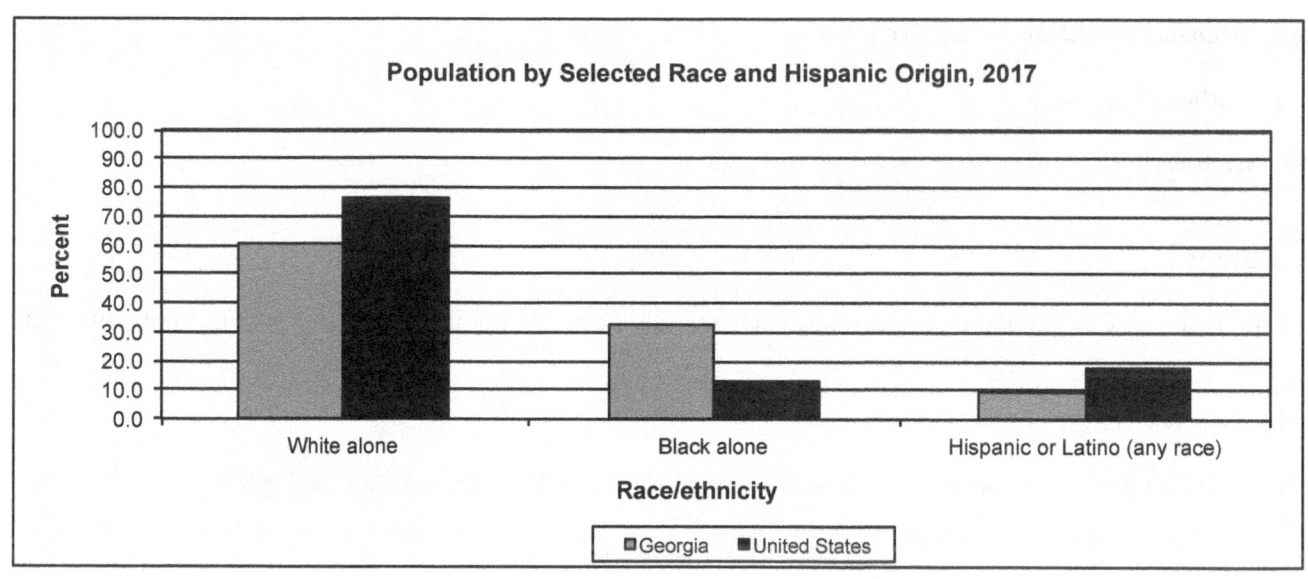

Population by Selected Race and Hispanic Origin, 2017

Table GA-2. Marital Status

(Number, percent distribution.)

Sex, age, and marital status	2000	2010	2016
Males, 15 Years and Over	3,092,736	3,683,258	3,957,018
Never married	30.4	35.4	36.9
Now married, except separated..........	56.5	50.5	48.9
Separated	2.0	2.1	1.8
Widowed	2.1	2.2	2.5
Divorced	9.0	9.9	10.0
Females, 15 Years and Over	3,273,889	3,954,542	4,275,043
Never married	24.4	29.7	31.5
Now married, except separated..........	51.5	46.1	44.5
Separated	2.7	2.9	2.7
Widowed	9.8	8.6	8.4
Divorced	11.6	12.7	13.0

Table GA-3. Households and Housing Characteristics

(Number, percent, dollars.)

Item	2000	2010	2016	Average annual percent change, 2010–2016
Total Households................................	3,006,369	3,482,420	3,686,135	1.0
Family households	2,111,647	2,385,969	2,479,003	0.6
Married-couple family	1,548,800	1,688,896	1,748,096	0.6
Other family	562,847	697,073	730,907	0.8
Male householder, no wife present................	127,437	161,001	174,962	1.4
Female householder, no husband present............	435,410	536,072	555,945	0.6
Nonfamily households	894,722	1,096,451	1,207,132	1.7
Householder living alone................................	710,523	921,005	1,002,425	1.5
Householder not living alone............................	184,199	175,446	204,707	2.8
Housing Characteristics				
Total housing units................................	3,281,737	4,091,482	4,219,103	0.5
Occupied housing units	3,006,369	3,482,420	3,686,135	1.0
Owner occupied	2,029,154	2,304,165	2,268,606	-0.3
Renter occupied	977,215	1,178,255	1,417,529	3.4
Average household size................................	2.65	2.72	2.73	0.1
Financial Characteristics				
Median gross rent of renter-occupied housing	613	819	933	2.3
Median monthly owner costs for housing units with a mortgage	1,039	1,390	1,336	-0.6
Median value of owner-occupied housing units............	111,200	156,200	166,800	1.1

Table GA-4. Migration, Origin, and Language

(Number, percent.)

Characteristic	State			U.S.		
	2015	2016	Percent change	2015	2016	Percent change
Residence 1 Year Ago						
Population 1 year and over	10,088,525	10,179,860	0.9	317,635,720	319,361,956	0.5
Same house	84.2	83.6	X	85.9	86.1	X
Different house in the U.S.	15.3	15.7	X	14.1	13.9	X
Same county	7.8	7.8	X	8.5	8.3	X
Different county	7.5	7.9	X	5.6	5.6	X
Same state	4.7	4.9	X	3.2	3.2	X
Different state	2.8	3	X	2.4	2.4	X
Abroad	0.6	0.7	X	0.7	0.7	X
Place of Birth						
Native born	9,191,143	9,272,059	0.9	278,128,449	279,388,170	0.5
Male	48.5	48.5	X	49.3	49.3	X
Female	51.5	51.5	X	50.7	50.7	X
Foreign born	1,023,717	1,038,312	1.4	43,290,372	43,739,345	1.0
Male	50.4	50.1	X	48.6	48.5	X
Female	49.6	49.9	X	51.4	51.5	X
Foreign born; naturalized U.S. citizen................	428,570	427,092	-0.3	20,697,103	21,238,372	2.6
Male	47.6	47	X	45.9	45.9	X
Female	52.4	53	X	54.1	54.1	X
Foreign born; not a U.S. citizen................	595,147	611,220	2.7	22,593,269	22,500,973	-0.4
Male	52.5	52.3	X	51.1	51.0	X
Female	47.5	47.7	X	48.9	49.0	X
Entered 2010 or later	16.4	20.8	X	15.6	18.6	X
Entered 2000 to 2009	34.2	32.4	X	27.9	26.7	X
Entered before 2000................................	49.4	46.8	X	56.5	54.7	X
World Region of Birth, Foreign						
Foreign-born population, excluding population born at sea	1,023,717	1,038,312	1.4	43,289,646	43,738,901	1.0
Europe	8.9	8.7	X	11.1	10.9	X
Asia................................	28.6	30.1	X	30.6	30.8	X
Africa................................	10.1	10.2	X	4.8	4.9	X
Oceania	0.4	0.3	X	0.6	0.6	X
Latin America................................	50.1	49.1	X	51.1	51.0	X
North America................................	2.0	1.6	X	1.9	1.8	X
Language Spoken at Home and Ability to Speak English						
Population 5 years and over................	9,565,500	9,655,493	0.9	301,625,014	303,328,961	0.6
English only	86	86	X	78.5	78.4	X
Language other than English................	14	14	X	21.5	21.6	X
Speaks English less than "very well"................	5.8	5.7	X	8.6	8.6	X

NA = Not available.
X = Not applicable.
- = Zero or rounds to zero.

Table GA-5. Median Income and Poverty Status, 2016

(Number, percent, except as noted.)

Characteristic	State		U.S.	
	Number	Percent	Number	Percent
Median Income				
Households (dollars)	53,559	X	57,617	X
Families (dollars)	65,018	X	71,062	X
Below Poverty Level (All People)	1,603,013	16.0	44,268,996	14.0
Sex				
Male	698,527	14.4	19,760,056	12.8
Female	904,486	17.4	24,508,940	15.2
Age				
Under 18 years	566,005	22.9	14,115,713	19.5
Related children under 18 years	556,759	22.6	13,805,435	19.1
18 to 64 years	903,267	14.5	25,723,818	13.2
65 years and over	133,741	10.1	4,429,465	9.2

X = Not applicable.

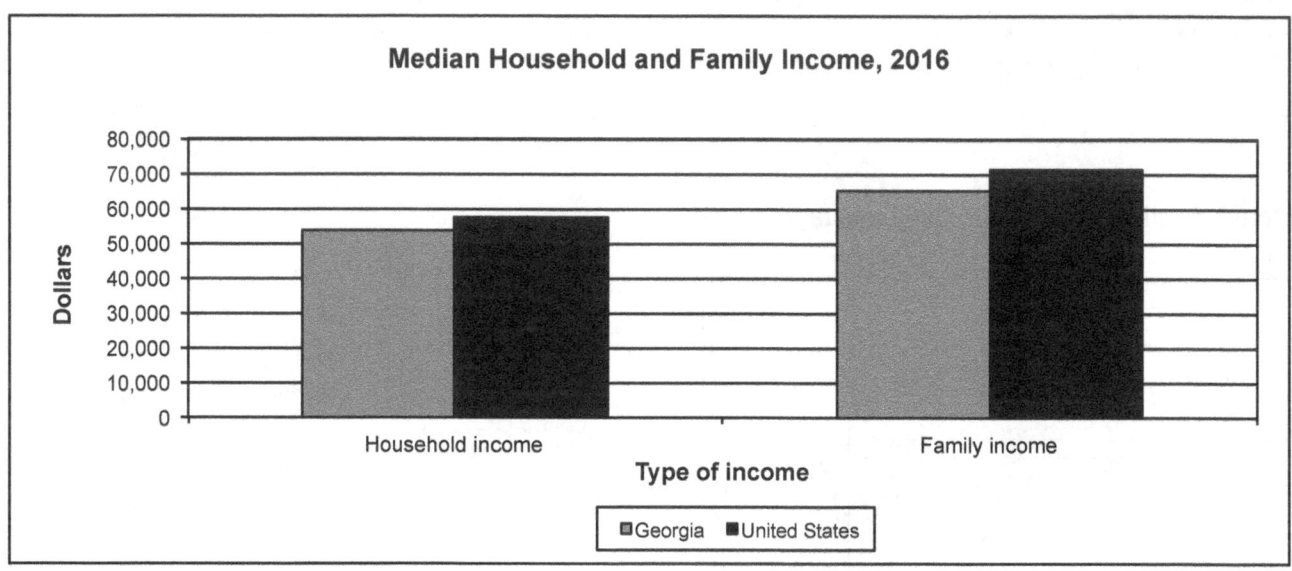

Table GA-6. Health Insurance Coverage Status for the Civilian Noninstitutionalized Population and Children Under 18 Years of Age

(Number, percent.)

Item	2008	2009	2010	2011	2012	2013	2014	2015	2016
Civilian Noninstitutionalized Population	9,473,441	9,594,277	9,519,836	9,619,740	9,719,411	9,800,887	9,906,878	10,024,056	10,120,788
Covered by Private or Public Insurance									
Number	7,693,669	7,757,931	7,644,270	7,736,982	7,927,092	7,954,582	8,338,497	8,635,656	8,811,215
Percent	81.2	80.9	80.3	80.4	81.6	81.2	84.2	86.1	87.1
Not Covered									
Number	1,779,772	1,836,346	1,875,566	1,882,758	1,792,319	1,846,305	1,568,381	1,388,400	1,309,573
Percent	18.8	19.1	19.7	19.6	18.4	18.8	15.8	13.9	12.9
Percent in the U.S. not covered	15.1	15.1	15.5	15.1	14.8	14.5	11.7	9.4	8.6
Children Under 18 Years of Age	2,536,058	2,575,689	2,492,281	2,484,715	2,492,161	2,487,079	2,488,247	2,499,334	2,506,326
Covered by Private or Public Insurance									
Number	2,245,226	2,294,545	2,248,277	2,248,147	2,272,200	2,249,028	2,299,212	2,333,101	2,343,554
Percent	88.5	89.1	90.2	90.5	91.2	90.4	92.4	93.3	93.5
Not Covered									
Number	290,832	281,144	244,004	236,568	219,961	238,051	189,035	166,233	162,772
Percent	11.5	10.9	9.8	9.5	8.8	9.6	7.6	6.7	6.5
Percent in the U.S. not covered	9.9	8.6	8.0	7.5	7.2	7.1	6.0	4.8	4.5

Table GA-7. Employment Status by Demographic Group, 2017

(Numbers in thousands, percent.)

Characteristic	Civilian noninstitutional population	Civilian labor force		Employed		Unemployed	
		Number	Percent of population	Number	Percent of population	Number	Percent of population
Total..	7,989	5,061	63.3	4,825	60.4	235	4.7
Sex							
Male..	3,778	2,633	69.7	2,510	66.4	123	4.7
Female...	4,212	2,428	57.6	2,315	55.0	112	4.6
Race, Sex, and Hispanic Origin							
White..	4,988	3,106	62.3	3,004	60.2	102	3.3
Male..	2,427	1,708	70.4	1,654	68.1	54	3.2
Female...	2,561	1,398	54.6	1,350	52.7	48	3.4
Black or African American........................	2,498	1,617	64.7	1,494	59.8	123	7.6
Male..	1,108	747	67.4	683	61.6	65	8.6
Female...	1,389	870	62.6	811	58.4	58	6.7
Hispanic or Latino ethnicity[1]	646	443	68.6	427	66.1	16	3.6
Male..	322	261	81.2	253	78.6	9	3.2
Female...	324	182	56.0	174	53.7	7	4.1
Age							
16 to 19 years..	541	168	31.1	132	24.4	36	21.3
20 to 24 years..	696	487	70.0	451	64.9	36	7.3
25 to 34 years..	1,418	1,146	80.8	1,087	76.7	59	5.1
35 to 44 years..	1,317	1,073	81.5	1,036	78.7	37	3.4
45 to 54 years..	1,431	1,146	80.1	1,108	77.5	38	3.3
55 to 64 years..	1,250	774	62.0	754	60.3	21	2.7
65 years and over	1,338	267	19.9	257	19.2	10	3.6

NOTE: Data in Table 7 are from the Current Population Survey (CPS) and do not match the estimates in Table 8. See notes and definitions for further information.
[1] May be of any race.

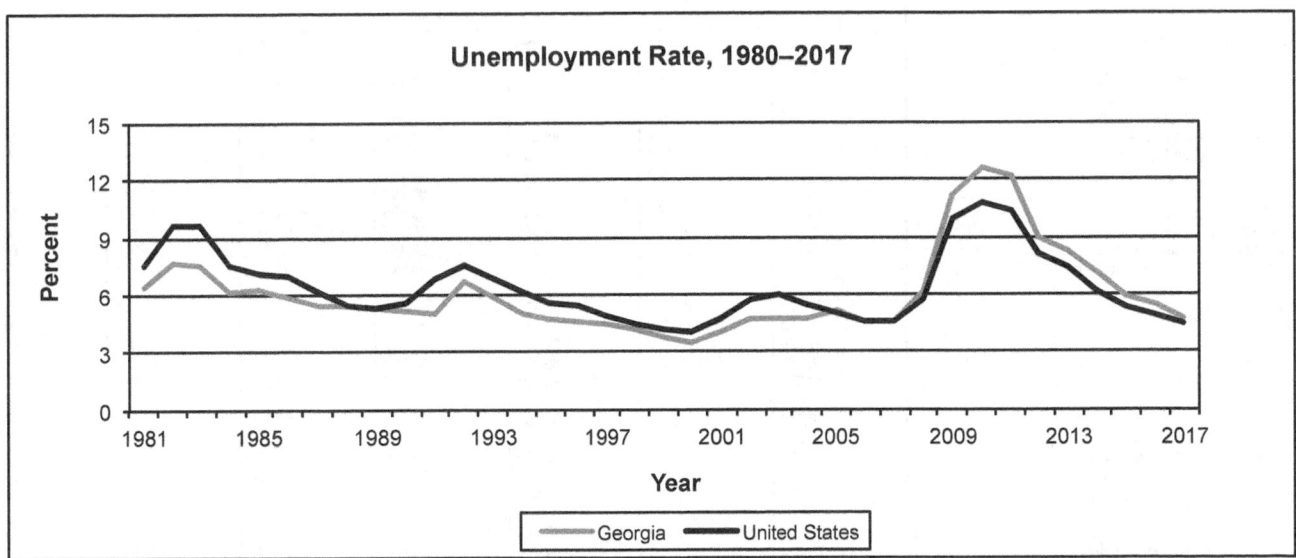

Unemployment Rate, 1980–2017

Table GA-8. Employment Status of the Civilian Noninstitutional Population Age 16 Years and Over

(Number, percent.)

Year	Civilian labor force	Civilian participation rate	Employed	Unemployed	Unemployment rate
2009..	4,787,749	65.6	4,311,854	475,895	9.9
2010..	4,696,676	64.1	4,202,052	494,624	10.5
2011..	4,748,754	64.3	4,263,305	485,449	10.2
2012..	4,787,367	64.0	4,348,083	439,284	9.2
2013..	4,756,157	62.9	4,366,374	389,783	8.2
2014..	4,752,639	62.0	4,416,145	336,494	7.1
2015..	4,788,858	61.6	4,503,150	285,708	6.0
2016..	4,926,945	62.4	4,662,849	264,096	5.4
2017..	5,061,399	63.2	4,821,622	239,777	4.7

Table GA-9. Employment and Average Wages by Industry

(Estimates through 2010 are based on the 2007 *North American Industry Classification System* [NAICS]. Estimates from 2011 onward are based on the 2012 NAICS.)

Industry	2010	2011	2012	2013	2014	2015	2016
	\multicolumn{7}{c}{Number of Jobs}						
Wage and Salary Employment by Industry	4,032,763	4,072,502	4,126,774	4,203,063	4,323,003	4,440,645	4,553,324
Farm Wage and Salary Employment	13,636	14,838	16,206	15,271	16,194	15,830	19,164
Nonfarm Wage and Salary Employment	4,019,127	4,057,664	4,110,568	4,187,792	4,306,809	4,424,815	4,534,160
Private wage and salary employment	3,222,181	3,274,156	3,332,693	3,417,125	3,542,001	3,658,838	3,765,706
Forestry, fishing, and related activities	14,805	14,690	14,653	15,125	15,368	15,829	16,080
Mining	4,942	4,806	4,669	4,727	4,850	4,841	5,066
Utilities	19,732	19,997	19,852	19,862	19,784	20,084	20,123
Construction	155,028	150,622	145,738	150,324	161,142	170,210	181,604
Manufacturing	346,225	351,357	354,831	357,742	367,306	378,283	388,604
Durable goods manufacturing	155,689	161,622	166,766	171,269	176,714	182,851	187,857
Nondurable goods manufacturing	190,536	189,735	188,065	186,473	190,592	195,432	200,747
Wholesale trade	197,322	198,615	202,702	206,198	211,734	218,692	221,074
Retail trade	438,668	445,976	448,769	457,129	471,250	488,894	496,279
Transportation and warehousing	160,849	165,961	169,258	170,483	177,512	185,659	196,250
Information	97,769	98,741	99,994	102,998	107,130	106,299	111,449
Finance and insurance	156,045	158,936	163,271	166,299	171,948	174,972	179,103
Real estate and rental and leasing	57,446	57,580	57,577	58,538	60,818	63,894	65,445
Professional, scientific, and technical services	219,742	225,991	234,029	240,480	253,940	262,618	263,715
Management of companies and enterprises	52,900	54,025	57,404	59,654	62,521	66,043	68,221
Administrative and waste services	258,039	268,355	275,207	291,043	306,634	315,094	326,220
Educational services	78,967	80,394	80,906	81,913	82,913	83,642	84,090
Health care and social assistance	402,244	407,869	417,568	430,252	438,167	454,449	472,175
Arts, entertainment, and recreation	39,863	40,548	41,634	43,048	44,446	47,051	50,391
Accommodation and food services	337,507	343,853	354,939	370,940	387,223	403,086	419,695
Other services, except public administration	184,088	185,840	189,692	190,370	197,315	199,198	200,122
Government and government enterprises	796,946	783,508	777,875	770,667	764,808	765,977	768,454
	\multicolumn{7}{c}{Dollars}						
Average Wages and Salaries by Industry	44,924	46,117	47,359	47,783	49,086	50,519	53,375
Average Farm Wages and Salaries	23,010	18,899	26,483	21,153	24,200	26,412	21,294
Average Nonfarm Wages and Salaries	44,998	46,217	47,441	47,880	49,179	50,606	53,510
Average private wages and salaries	45,356	46,712	48,202	48,767	50,065	51,497	54,494
Forestry, fishing, and related activities	31,431	31,569	32,753	33,480	34,166	35,122	36,326
Mining	55,502	57,380	59,289	61,211	63,301	66,111	72,436
Utilities	76,817	84,508	84,895	85,499	87,020	93,119	95,645
Construction	46,572	47,166	48,783	49,805	51,763	53,901	59,806
Manufacturing	51,832	53,727	54,856	55,927	56,948	57,851	60,395
Durable goods manufacturing	54,799	57,080	57,108	58,464	59,786	60,842	62,721
Nondurable goods manufacturing	49,407	50,870	52,858	53,597	54,317	55,054	58,217
Wholesale trade	67,625	69,932	71,417	72,526	74,059	76,205	79,030
Retail trade	27,125	27,366	27,822	28,274	28,842	30,277	31,552
Transportation and warehousing	51,026	52,737	54,234	56,346	58,858	59,500	66,121
Information	76,781	79,930	85,038	85,834	89,014	88,703	95,973
Finance and insurance	72,875	76,786	79,967	81,698	84,082	88,010	92,311
Real estate and rental and leasing	46,344	49,001	51,107	51,894	53,703	55,171	59,861
Professional, scientific, and technical services	72,390	74,446	77,915	77,428	79,274	82,243	88,232
Management of companies and enterprises	88,926	94,492	100,262	99,235	106,110	110,236	110,917
Administrative and waste services	34,546	34,975	35,600	35,733	36,386	37,840	39,977
Educational services	40,402	41,383	42,642	43,240	44,399	44,775	46,930
Health care and social assistance	44,689	45,725	47,027	47,596	48,422	50,097	52,741
Arts, entertainment, and recreation	35,020	35,701	34,980	35,613	36,748	37,014	39,083
Accommodation and food services	18,374	18,877	19,514	19,665	20,203	20,077	21,424
Other services, except public administration	29,578	29,795	30,194	31,089	31,734	33,124	35,299
Government and government enterprises	43,552	44,148	44,181	43,946	45,076	46,348	48,688

Table GA-10. Employment Characteristics by Family Type

(Number, percent.)

Family type and labor force status	2014		2015		2016	
	Total	Families with own children under 18 years	Total	Families with own children under 18 years	Total	Families with own children under 18 years
All Families..	2,419,167	1,103,236	2,466,415	1,097,585	2,479,003	1,103,858
FAMILY TYPE AND LABOR FORCE STATUS						
Married-Couple Families...............................	1,684,808	702,051	1,750,409	714,312	1,748,096	716,617
Both husband and wife in labor force............................	50.7	63.8	50.3	63.8	50.8	65.6
Husband in labor force, wife not in labor force................	24.3	30.0	24.0	30.3	23.6	28.6
Wife in labor force, husband not in labor force...............	8.2	4.3	7.9	3.9	7.9	4.0
Both husband and wife not in labor force........................	16.8	1.9	17.3	1.7	17.0	1.4
Other Families	734,359	401,185	716,006	383,273	730,907	387,241
Female householder, no husband present........................	76.5	78.5	76.6	78.6	76.1	78.8
In labor force..	54.1	65.2	53.6	65.7	53.8	66.8
Not in labor force..	22.4	13.3	23.0	12.8	22.3	12.0
Male householder, no wife present.............................	23.5	21.5	23.4	21.4	23.9	21.2
In labor force..	18.2	19.4	17.7	18.8	18.0	19.2
Not in labor force..	5.2	2.0	5.7	2.6	6.0	2.0

Table GA-11. School Enrollment and Educational Attainment, 2016

(Number, percent.)

Item	State	U.S.
Enrollment		
Total population 3 years and over, enrolled in school	2,747,236	81,572,277
Enrolled in nursery school or preschool (percent)...	6.1	6.0
Enrolled in kindergarten (percent)...	5.1	5.0
Enrolled in elementary school, grades 1-8 (percent)......................................	41.8	40.3
Enrolled in high school, grades 9-12 (percent)..	21.4	21.0
Enrolled in college or graduate school (percent)..	25.6	27.7
Attainment		
Total population 25 years and over	6,785,395	218,475,480
Less than ninth grade (percent)...	4.9	5.4
9th to 12th grade, no diploma (percent)	8.7	7.2
High school graduate, including equivalency (percent)......................................	27.8	27.2
Some college, no degree (percent)..	20.5	20.6
Associate's degree (percent)..	7.6	8.4
Bachelor's degree (percent)..	18.7	19.3
Graduate or professional degree (percent)...	11.7	11.9
High school graduate or higher (percent)	86.4	87.5
Bachelor's degree or higher (percent)..	30.5	31.3

Table GA-12. Public School Characteristics and Educational Indicators

(Number, percent; data derived from National Center of Education Statistics.)

Item	State	U.S.
Public Schools, 2015–2016 (except where noted)		
Number of school districts..	223	18,328
Number of schools..	2,297	98,456
Number of students..	1,757,237	50,327,015
Number of teachers..	113,031	3,151,497
Student-teacher ratio	15.5	16.0
Expenditures per student (dollars), 2014-2015..	9,476	11,445
Four-year adjusted cohort graduation rate (ACGR)[1,2]	79.4	84.1
Students eligible for free or reduced-price lunch (percent), 2014-2015.......................	62.4	51.8
English language learners (percent), Fall 2015..	6.4	9.5
Students age 3 to 21 served under IDEA, part B (percent)...................................	11.5	13.2

Public Schools by Type	Number	Percent of state public schools
Total number of schools...	2,297	100.0
Regular	2,237	97.4
Special education	19	0.8
Vocational education	0	-
Alternative education...	41	1.8

NOTE: Every school is assigned only one school type based on its instructional emphasis.
[1] ACGR data represents a new method of calculating high-school completion rates and may not be comparable to previous years' data for Averaged Freshmen Graduation Rates (AFGR).
[2] The United States 4-year ACGRs were estimated using both the reported 4-year ACGR data from 49 states and the District of Columbia and using imputed data for Idaho. The estimate for American Indian/Alaska Native students also includes imputed data for Virginia.

Table GA-13. Reported Voting and Registration of the Voting-Age Population, November 2016

(Numbers in thousands, percent.)

Item	Total population	Total citizen population	Registered			Voted		
			Total registered	Percent registered (total population)	Percent registered (total citizen population)	Total voted	Percent voted (total population)	Percent voted (total citizen population)
U.S. Total	245,502	224,059	157,596	64.2	70.3	137,537	56.0	61.4
State Total..............................	7,626	7,048	4,892	64.1	69.4	4,246	55.7	60.2
Sex								
Male	3,623	3,317	2,237	61.7	67.4	1,908	52.7	57.5
Female	4,003	3,731	2,655	66.3	71.2	2,338	58.4	62.7
Race								
White alone............................	4,798	4,453	3,179	66.2	71.4	2,786	58.1	62.6
White, non-Hispanic alone............	4,184	4,142	3,028	72.4	73.1	2,643	63.2	63.8
Black alone.............................	2,325	2,255	1,552	66.8	68.8	1,346	57.9	59.7
Asian alone............................	365	225	101	27.7	44.9	71	19.3	31.3
Hispanic (of any race)................	680	335	168	24.8	50.2	161	23.6	47.9
White alone or in combination	4,872	4,526	3,224	66.2	71.2	2,815	57.8	62.2
Black alone or in combination...........	2,364	2,294	1,578	66.8	68.8	1,360	57.5	59.3
Asian alone or in combination...........	375	235	106	28.3	45.1	71	18.8	30.0
Age								
18 to 24 years.........................	991	923	511	51.6	55.4	401	40.5	43.5
25 to 34 years.........................	1,316	1,119	712	54.1	63.6	609	46.3	54.4
35 to 44 years.........................	1,352	1,211	790	58.4	65.3	672	49.7	55.5
45 to 64 years.........................	2,599	2,456	1,801	69.3	73.3	1,593	61.3	64.9
65 years and over	1,368	1,340	1,078	78.8	80.4	971	71.0	72.4

Table GA-14. Crime

(Number, rate per 100,000. Data are derived from the FBI Uniform Crime Reports.)

Item	State			U.S. [1,2,3,4]		
	2015	2016	Percent change	2015	2016	Percent change
TOTAL POPULATION [5]	10,214,860	10,310,371	0.9	321,418,820	323,127,513	0.5
VIOLENT CRIME						
Number..	38,643	40,990	6.1	1,231,566	1,248,185	1.3
Rate...	378.3	397.6	5.1	383.2	386.3	0.8
Murder and Nonnegligent Manslaughter						
Number..	615	681	10.7	15,696	17,250	9.9
Rate...	6.0	6.6	10.0	4.9	5.3	8.2
Rape[6]						
Number..	3,224	3,509	8.8	124,047	130,603	5.3
Rate...	31.6	34.0	7.6	38.6	40.4	4.7
Robbery						
Number..	12,247	12,205	-0.3	327,374	332,198	1.5
Rate...	119.9	118.4	-1.3	101.9	102.8	0.9
Aggravated Assault						
Number..	22,557	24,595	9.0	764,449	803,007	5.0
Rate...	220.8	238.5	8.0	237.8	248.5	4.5
PROPERTY CRIME						
Number..	308,723	309,770	0.3	7,993,631	7,919,035	-0.9
Rate...	3,022.3	3,004.5	-0.6	2,487.0	2,450.7	-1.5
Burglary						
Number..	66,374	63,344	-4.6	1,579,527	1,515,096	-4.1
Rate...	649.8	614.4	-5.4	491.4	468.9	-4.6
Larceny-Theft						
Number..	215,867	219,625	1.7	5,706,346	5,638,455	-1.2
Rate...	2,113.3	2,130.1	0.8	1,775.4	1,745.0	-1.7
Motor Vehicle Theft						
Number..	26,482	26,801	1.2	707,758	765,484	8.2
Rate...	259.2	259.9	0.3	220.2	236.9	7.6

NOTE: Although arson data are included in the trend and clearance tables, sufficient data are not available to estimate totals for this offense. Therefore, no arson data are published in this table.
X = Not applicable.
- = Zero or rounds to zero.
[1] The crime figures have been adjusted.
[2] The data collection methodology for the offense of forcible rape used by the Minnesota state Uniform Crime Reporting (UCR) Program (with the exception of Minneapolis and St. Paul, Minnesota) does not comply with national UCR Program guidelines. Consequently, its figures for forcible rape and violent crime (of which forcible rape is a part) are not published in this table.
[3] Includes offenses reported by the Zoological Police and the Metro Transit Police.
[4] Because of changes in the state's reporting practices, figures are not comparable to previous years' data.
[5] Populations are U.S. Census Bureau provisional estimates as of July 1 of each year.
[6] The figures shown for the offense of rape were estimated using the revised Uniform Crime Reporting (UCR) definition of rape.

Table GA-15. State Government Finances, 2016

(Dollar amounts in thousands, percent distribution.)

Item	Dollars	Percent distribution
Total Revenue	45,859,181	100.0
General revenue	42,278,966	92.2
Intergovernmental revenue	14,571,741	31.8
Taxes	21,454,446	46.8
General sales	5,480,196	12.0
Selective sales	2,928,260	6.4
License taxes	663,946	1.4
Individual income tax	10,439,534	22.8
Corporate income tax	981,002	2.1
Other taxes	961,508	2.1
Current charges	3,679,950	8.0
Miscellaneous general revenue	2,572,829	5.6
Utility revenue	5,699	-
Liquor stores revenue	0	-
Insurance trust revenue [1]	3,574,516	7.8
Total Expenditure	47,867,768	100.0
Intergovernmental expenditure	11,836,729	24.7
Direct expenditure	36,031,039	75.3
Current operation	24,706,272	51.6
Capital outlay	3,131,267	6.5
Insurance benefits and repayments	6,372,959	13.3
Assistance and subsidies	1,185,669	2.5
Interest on debt	634,872	1.3
Exhibit: Salaries and wages	6,354,544	13.3
Total Expenditure	47,867,768	100.0
General expenditure	41,408,938	86.5
Intergovernmental expenditure	11,836,729	24.7
Direct expenditure	29,572,209	61.8
General expenditure, by function:		
Education	18,583,348	38.8
Public welfare	12,006,325	25.1
Hospitals	1,290,511	2.7
Health	1,451,470	3.0
Highways	2,772,343	5.8
Police protection	436,293	0.9
Correction	1,230,802	2.6
Natural resources	475,851	1.0
Parks and recreation	226,249	0.5
Governmental administration	919,536	1.9
Interest on general debt	634,872	1.3
Other and unallocable	1,381,338	2.9
Utility expenditure	85,871	0.2
Liquor stores expenditure	0	-
Insurance trust expenditure	6,372,959	13.3
Debt at End of Fiscal Year	13,130,551	X
Cash and Security Holdings	94,038,910	X

X = Not applicable.
- = Zero or rounds to zero.
[1] Within insurance trust revenue, net earnings of state retirement systems is a calculated statistic (the item code in the data file is X08), and thus can be positive or negative. Net earnings is the sum of earnings on investments plus gains on investments minus losses on investments. The change made in 2002 for asset valuation from book to market value in accordance with Statement 34 of the Governmental Accounting Standards Board is reflected in the calculated statistics.

Table GA-16. State Government Tax Collections, 2017

(Dollars in thousands, percent.)

Item	Dollars	Percent distribution
Total Taxes	22,419,440	100.0
Property taxes	989,001	4.4
Sales and gross receipts	8,807,950	39.3
General sales and gross receipts	5,729,916	25.6
Selective sales and gross receipts	3,078,034	13.7
Alcoholic beverages	193,438	0.9
Amusements	X	-
Insurance premiums	480,154	2.1
Motor fuels	1,741,092	7.8
Pari-mutuels	X	-
Public utilities	X	-
Tobacco products	220,774	1.0
Other selective sales	442,576	2.0
Licenses	672,897	3.0
Alcoholic beverages	3,975	-
Amusements	X	-
Corporations in general	56,999	0.3
Hunting and fishing	27,000	0.1
Motor vehicle	364,255	1.6
Motor vehicle operators	112,419	0.5
Public utilities	X	-
Occupation and business, NEC	81,354	0.4
Other licenses	26,895	0.1
Income taxes	11,949,591	53.3
Individual income	10,977,693	49.0
Corporation net income	971,898	4.3
Other taxes	1	-
Death and gift	0	-
Documentary and stock transfer	1	-
Severance	X	-
Taxes, NEC	0	-

X = Not applicable.
- = Zero or rounds to zero.

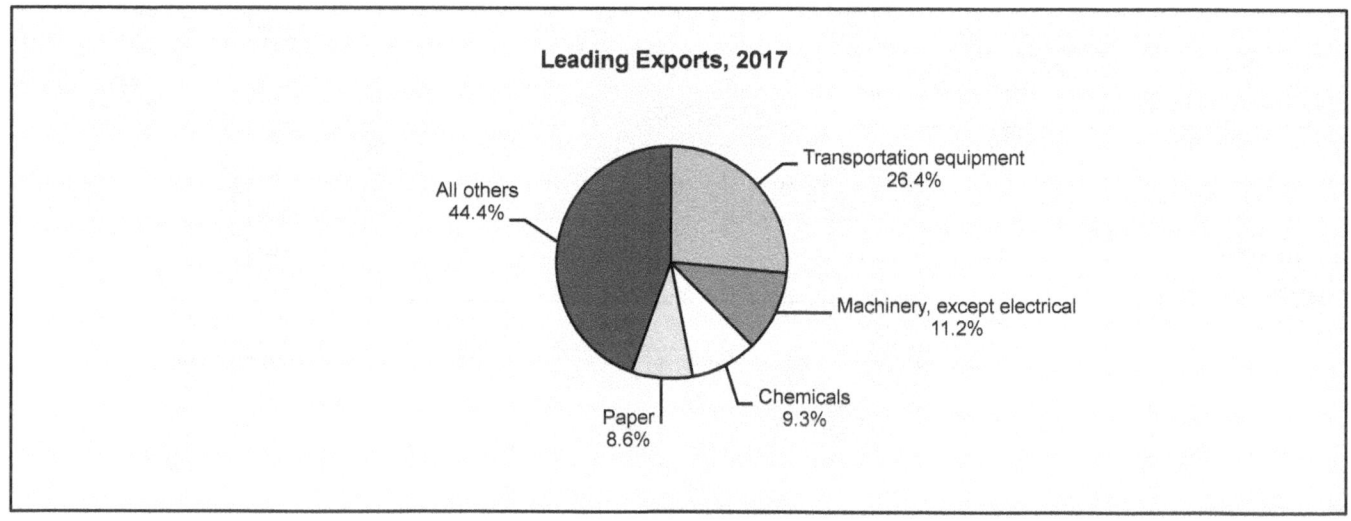

Leading Exports, 2017

- Transportation equipment 26.4%
- Machinery, except electrical 11.2%
- Chemicals 9.3%
- Paper 8.6%
- All others 44.4%

HAWAII

Location: North Pacific Ocean

Area: 10,931 sq. mi. (28,311 sq. km.); rank—43rd

Population: 1,427,538 (2017 est.); rank—40th

Principal Cities: capital—Honolulu; largest—Honolulu

Statehood: August 21, 1959; 50th state

U.S. Congress: 2 senators, 2 representatives

State Motto: *Ua mau ke ea o ka'ina i ka pono* ("The life of the land is perpetuated in righteousness")

State Song: "Hawai'i Pono' (Hawaii's Own)"

State Nickname: The Aloha State

Abbreviations: HI

State Symbols: flower—native yellow hibiscus; tree—kukui (candlenut tree); bird—nene (Hawaiian goose)

At a Glance

- With an increase in population of 4.7 percent, Hawaii ranked 23rd among the states in growth from 2010 to 2017.

- In 2016, 3.5 percent of Hawaiians did not have health insurance, compared to 8.6 percent of the total U.S. population, a rate that was the 2nd lowest in the country.

- Hawaii had the 9th highest property crime rate in the country in 2016, with 2,992.7 incidents per 100,000 population.

- Hawaii had the highest proportion of state government employees to total residents in 2016, with 41.2 state employees per 1,000 residents, compared to the national average of 13.4 employees per 1,000 residents.

- Hawaii had the largest percent of Asian Alone residents in 2017, with 37.8 percent of its residents self-identifying as Asian.

Table HI-1. Population by Age, Sex, Race, and Hispanic Origin

(Number, percent, except where noted.)

Sex, age, race, and Hispanic origin	2000	2010	2017 [1]	Average annual percent change, 2010–2017
Total Population.....................................	1,211,537	1,360,301	1,427,538	4.9
Percent of total U.S. population	0.4	0.4	0.4	X
Sex				
Male..	563,891	681,243	716,087	5.1
Female	544,338	679,058	711,451	4.8
Age				
Under 5 years..	78,163	87,407	90,109	3.1
5 to 19 years..	249,088	250,894	245,821	-2.0
20 to 64 years..	723,685	826,868	838,048	1.4
65 years and over	160,601	195,138	253,560	29.9
Median age (years)	36.2	38.6	39.0	1.0
Race and Hispanic Origin				
One race				
White	294,102	349,051	366,546	5.0
Black..	22,003	22,473	31,147	38.6
American Indian and Alaska Native	3,535	4,960	5,574	12.4
Asian..	503,868	531,633	539,280	1.4
Native Hawaiian or Other Pacific Islander	113,539	138,292	145,554	5.3
Two or more races..	259,343	313,892	339,437	8.1
Hispanic (of any race)...................................	87,699	133,342	150,125	12.6

X = Not applicable.

[1] Population figures for 2017 are July 1 estimates. The 2010 estimates are taken from the 2010 Census.

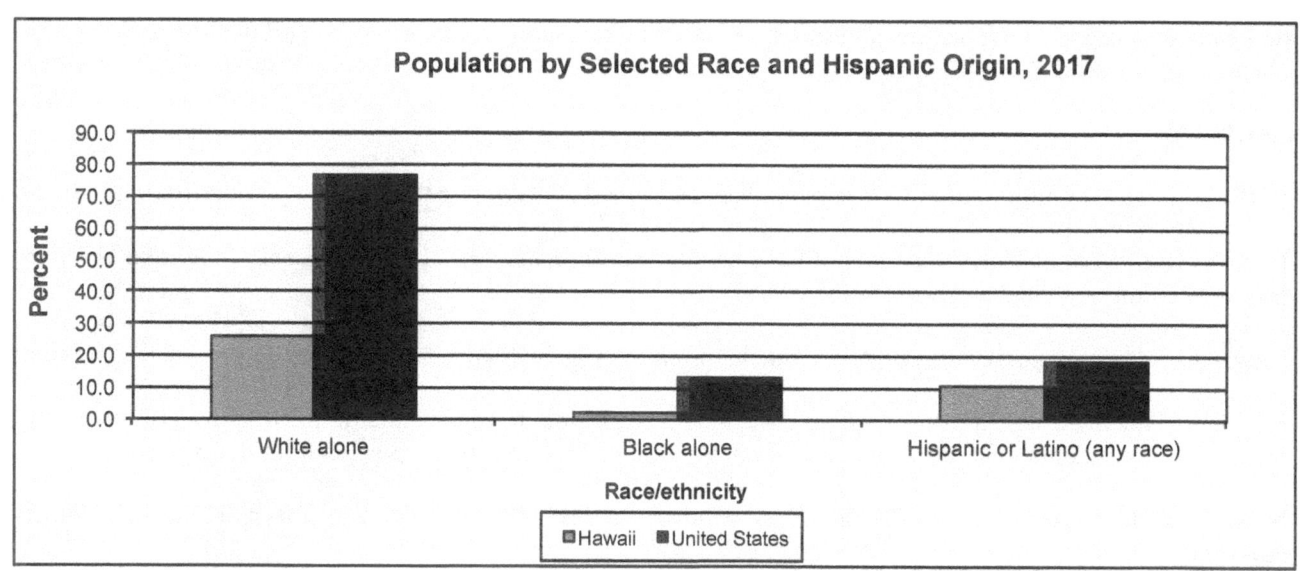

Table HI-2. Marital Status

(Number, percent distribution.)

Sex, age, and marital status	2000	2010	2016
Males, 15 Years and Over..	481,768	554,154	583,715
Never married	34.6	37.8	38.3
Now married, except separated...	53.7	49.1	49.5
Separated...	1.4	1.2	1.2
Widowed...	2.2	2.7	2.7
Divorced...	8.1	9.2	8.2
Females, 15 Years and Over..	484,107	556,915	584,318
Never married	25.9	28.7	29.2
Now married, except separated...	52.5	48.5	49.1
Separated...	1.7	1.8	1.5
Widowed...	9.8	10.1	10.2
Divorced...	10.0	11.0	9.9

Table HI-3. Households and Housing Characteristics

(Number, percent, dollars.)

Item	2000	2010	2016	Average annual percent change, 2010–2016
Total Households..........	403,240	445,812	455,868	0.4
Family households	287,068	303,075	315,505	0.7
Married-couple family	216,077	224,402	236,236	0.9
Other family	70,991	78,673	79,269	0.1
Male householder, no wife present........	21,068	24,247	26,017	1.2
Female householder, no husband present........	49,923	54,426	53,252	-0.4
Nonfamily households	116,172	142,737	140,363	-0.3
Householder living alone........	88,153	108,872	111,861	0.5
Householder not living alone........	28,019	33,865	28,502	-2.6
Housing Characteristics				
Total housing units........	460,542	519,992	537,170	0.6
Occupied housing units	403,240	445,812	455,868	0.4
Owner occupied	227,888	258,533	260,626	0.1
Renter occupied	175,352	187,279	195,242	0.7
Average household size........	2.92	2.96	3.04	0.5
Financial Characteristics				
Median gross rent of renter-occupied housing	779	1,291	1,483	2.5
Median monthly owner costs for housing units with a mortgage	1,636	2,240	2,239	-0.0
Median value of owner-occupied housing units	272,700	525,400	592,000	2.1

Table HI-4. Migration, Origin, and Language

(Number, percent.)

Characteristic	State			U.S.		
	2015	2016	Percent change	2015	2016	Percent change
Residence 1 Year Ago						
Population 1 year and over	1,414,355	1,410,258	-0.3	317,635,720	319,361,956	0.5
Same house	85.3	86.3	X	85.3	85.4	X
Different house in the U.S.	13.5	12.4	X	14.1	13.9	X
Same county	9.1	7.8	X	8.5	8.3	X
Different county	4.4	4.6	X	5.6	5.6	X
Same state	0.6	0.6	X	3.2	3.2	X
Different state	3.8	4.1	X	2.4	2.4	X
Abroad	1.3	1.2	X	0.7	0.7	X
Place of Birth						
Native born	1,178,189	1,166,072	-1.0	278,128,449	279,388,170	0.5
Male	52.4	52.3	X	49.3	49.3	X
Female	47.6	47.7	X	50.7	50.7	X
Foreign born	253,414	262,485	3.6	43,290,372	43,739,345	1.0
Male	42.2	41.4	X	48.6	48.5	X
Female	57.8	58.6	X	51.4	51.5	X
Foreign born; naturalized U.S. citizen	146,485	149,397	2.0	20,697,103	21,238,372	2.6
Male	42.4	41.8	X	45.9	45.9	X
Female	57.6	58.2	X	54.1	54.1	X
Foreign born; not a U.S. citizen	106,929	113,088	5.8	22,593,269	22,500,973	-0.4
Male	42.0	40.9	X	51.1	51.0	X
Female	58.0	59.1	X	48.9	49.0	X
Entered 2010 or later	15.3	18.6	X	15.6	18.6	X
Entered 2000 to 2009	22.9	22.9	X	27.9	26.7	X
Entered before 2000........	61.8	58.5	X	56.5	54.7	X
World Region of Birth, Foreign						
Foreign-born population, excluding population born at sea	253,414	262,485	3.6	43,289,646	43,738,901	1.0
Europe	4.9	3.7	X	11.1	10.9	X
Asia........	80	78.8	X	30.6	30.8	X
Africa	0.8	0.4	X	4.8	4.9	X
Oceania	7.4	10.9	X	0.6	0.6	X
Latin America........	5.7	4.6	X	51.1	51.0	X
North America	1.2	1.7	X	1.9	1.8	X
Language Spoken at Home and Ability to Speak English						
Population 5 years and over........	1,339,510	1,337,835	-0.1	301,625,014	303,328,961	0.6
English only	73.9	73.5	X	78.5	78.4	X
Language other than English........	26.1	26.5	X	21.5	21.6	X
Speaks English less than "very well"........	12.4	12.2	X	8.6	8.6	X

NA = Not available.
X = Not applicable.
- = Zero or rounds to zero.

Table HI-5. Median Income and Poverty Status, 2016

(Number, percent, except as noted.)

Characteristic	State		U.S.	
	Number	Percent	Number	Percent
Median Income				
Households (dollars)..	74,511	X	57,617	X
Families (dollars)	86,768	X	71,062	X
Below Poverty Level (All People)	129,569	9.3	44,268,996	14.0
Sex				
Male	57,530	8.3	19,760,056	12.8
Female	72,039	10.3	24,508,940	15.2
Age				
Under 18 years...	30,507	10.1	14,115,713	19.5
Related children under 18 years.............................	28,909	9.7	13,805,435	19.1
18 to 64 years..	77,713	9.1	25,723,818	13.2
65 years and over	21,349	8.9	4,429,465	9.2

X = Not applicable.

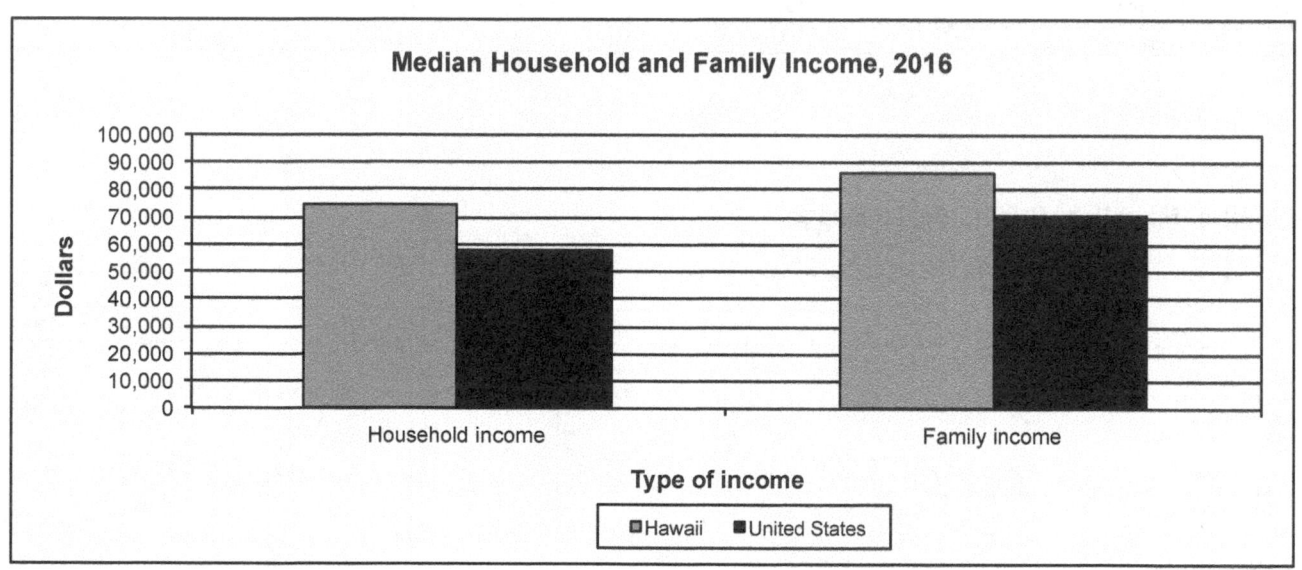

Table HI-6. Health Insurance Coverage Status for the Civilian Noninstitutionalized Population and Children Under 18 Years of Age

(Number, percent.)

Item	2008	2009	2010	2011	2012	2013	2014	2015	2016
Civilian Noninstitutionalized Population	1,236,665	1,231,549	1,315,677	1,326,065	1,341,708	1,345,168	1,367,770	1,375,062	1,378,730
Covered by Private or Public Insurance									
Number..	1,153,554	1,145,658	1,211,913	1,231,666	1,249,370	1,254,413	1,295,659	1,320,531	1,330,057
Percent...	93.3	93.0	92.1	92.9	93.1	93.3	94.7	96.0	96.5
Not Covered									
Number..	83,111	85,891	103,764	94,399	92,338	90,755	72,111	54,531	48,673
Percent...	6.7	7.0	7.9	7.1	6.9	6.7	5.3	4.0	3.5
Percent in the U.S. not covered..............................	15.1	15.1	15.5	15.1	14.8	14.5	11.7	9.4	8.6
Children Under 18 Years of Age	284,493	287,944	303,661	304,077	302,565	306,848	308,018	310,995	307,561
Covered by Private or Public Insurance									
Number..	274,161	280,878	292,545	293,097	292,102	297,513	298,466	305,950	300,664
Percent...	96.4	97.5	96.3	96.4	96.5	97.0	96.9	98.4	97.8
Not Covered									
Number..	10,332	7,066	11,116	10,980	10,463	9,335	9,552	5,045	6,897
Percent...	3.6	2.5	3.7	3.6	3.5	3.0	3.1	1.6	2.2
Percent in the U.S. not covered..............................	9.9	8.6	8.0	7.5	7.2	7.1	6.0	4.8	4.5

Table HI-7. Employment Status by Demographic Group, 2017

(Numbers in thousands, percent.)

Characteristic	Civilian noninstitutional population	Civilian labor force		Employed		Unemployed	
		Number	Percent of population	Number	Percent of population	Number	Percent of population
Total...	1,097	685	62.4	668	60.9	17	2.4
Sex							
Male..	530	357	67.4	348	65.6	9	2.6
Female..	566	328	57.8	320	56.6	7	2.2
Race, Sex, and Hispanic Origin							
White..	249	149	60.1	146	58.8	3	2.0
Male..	122	81	66.7	80	65.7	1	1.4
Female..	127	68	53.7	66	52.3	2	2.7
Black or African American..................	NA	NA	NA	NA	NA	NA	NA
Male..	NA	NA	NA	NA	NA	NA	NA
Female..	NA	NA	NA	NA	NA	NA	NA
Hispanic or Latino ethnicity[1]............	100	65	64.9	63	62.9	2	3.1
Male..	NA	NA	NA	NA	NA	NA	NA
Female..	NA	NA	NA	NA	NA	NA	NA
Age							
16 to 19 years...................................	NA	NA	NA	NA	NA	NA	NA
20 to 24 years...................................	89	70	77.7	66	73.9	4	5.0
25 to 34 years...................................	175	139	79.3	135	77.1	4	2.8
35 to 44 years...................................	167	137	81.8	134	80.0	3	2.2
45 to 54 years...................................	174	145	83.4	143	82.0	2	1.7
55 to 64 years...................................	188	124	65.9	122	65.0	2	1.4
65 years and over..............................	240	50	21.0	50	20.8	...	0.8

NOTE: Data in Table 7 are from the Current Population Survey (CPS) and do not match the estimates in Table 8. See notes and definitions for further information.
[1] May be of any race.
NA = Not available.
... = Fewer than 500 people.

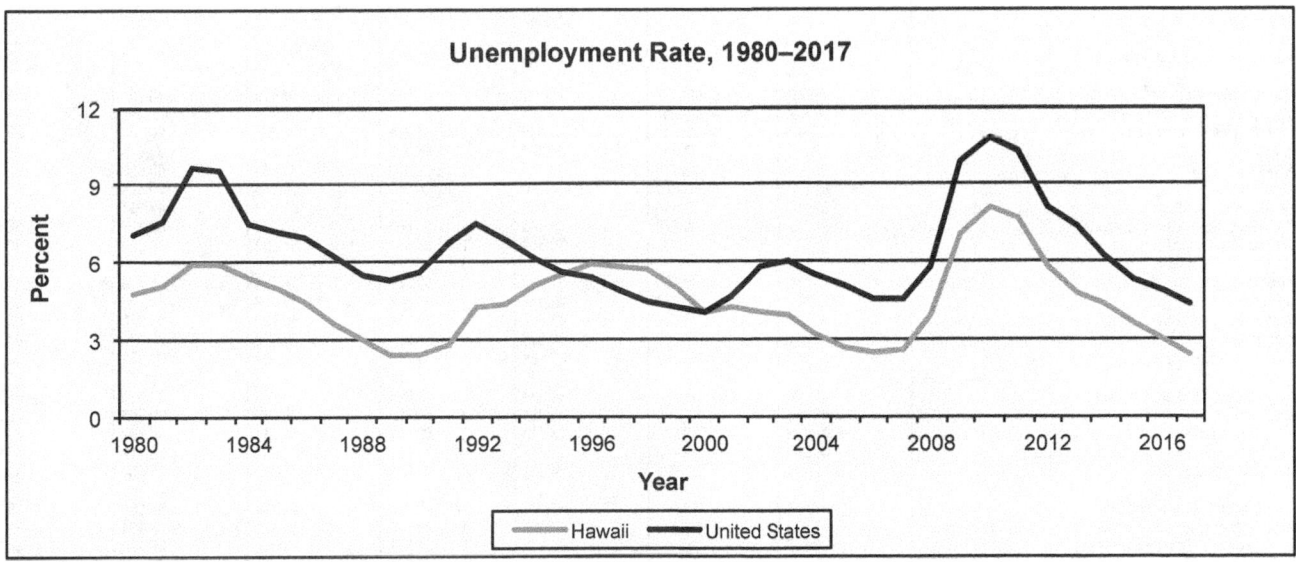

Table HI-8. Employment Status of the Civilian Noninstitutional Population Age 16 Years and Over

(Number, percent.)

Year	Civilian labor force	Civilian participation rate	Employed	Unemployed	Unemployment rate
2009...	631,690	64.3	586,522	45,168	7.2
2010...	647,249	62.8	602,282	44,967	6.9
2011...	660,253	62.6	615,319	44,934	6.8
2012...	647,185	60.8	608,302	38,883	6.0
2013...	651,557	60.7	619,691	31,866	4.9
2014...	666,674	61.6	637,661	29,013	4.4
2015...	675,506	62.0	651,459	24,047	3.6
2016...	684,167	62.5	664,032	20,135	2.9
2017...	685,418	62.6	669,241	16,177	2.4

Table HI-9. Employment and Average Wages by Industry

(Estimates through 2010 are based on the 2007 *North American Industry Classification System* [NAICS]. Estimates from 2011 onward are based on the 2012 NAICS.)

Industry	2010	2011	2012	2013	2014	2015	2016
	Number of Jobs						
Wage and Salary Employment by Industry.......................	661,830	669,911	681,247	693,899	703,401	714,856	723,454
Farm Wage and Salary Employment................................	5,662	6,528	6,099	6,176	7,375	6,734	6,295
Nonfarm Wage and Salary Employment..........................	656,168	663,383	675,148	687,723	696,026	708,122	717,159
Private wage and salary employment...............................	474,096	481,281	492,070	504,956	512,970	522,758	533,681
Forestry, fishing, and related activities..........................	1,311	1,425	1,473	1,521	1,543	1,565	1,528
Mining..	338	332	298	255	252	279	232
Utilities..	3,214	3,328	3,567	3,771	3,808	3,827	3,772
Construction..	29,561	29,303	30,066	31,643	32,689	35,508	38,668
Manufacturing...	12,937	13,185	13,348	13,586	13,933	14,076	14,140
Durable goods manufacturing......................................	3,789	3,884	3,619	3,630	3,595	3,699	3,733
Nondurable goods manufacturing................................	9,148	9,301	9,729	9,956	10,338	10,377	10,407
Wholesale trade...	17,774	17,535	17,745	17,824	17,798	18,085	17,906
Retail trade...	66,612	67,774	69,456	70,245	70,458	71,355	71,190
Transportation and warehousing...................................	23,311	23,979	25,107	25,981	26,568	27,347	28,233
Information..	9,913	8,535	8,459	8,792	8,481	8,697	8,819
Finance and insurance..	16,096	15,987	16,035	15,765	15,677	15,931	16,178
Real estate and rental and leasing................................	11,649	11,643	11,794	12,052	12,280	12,221	12,550
Professional, scientific, and technical services	24,414	24,519	24,603	24,599	24,561	24,701	24,644
Management of companies and enterprises....................	6,652	6,925	7,512	8,255	8,379	8,508	8,720
Administrative and waste services................................	41,102	44,353	45,545	47,641	49,855	50,791	50,801
Educational services...	15,833	15,852	16,284	16,067	15,772	15,738	16,810
Health care and social assistance.................................	61,978	62,194	62,827	64,986	65,795	67,890	69,228
Arts, entertainment, and recreation...............................	10,575	10,713	11,451	12,112	12,179	11,860	12,284
Accommodation and food services................................	90,463	93,079	96,479	99,678	101,763	103,168	106,694
Other services, except public administration..................	30,363	30,620	30,021	30,183	31,179	31,211	31,284
Government and government enterprises......................	182,072	182,102	183,078	182,767	183,056	185,364	183,478
	Dollars						
Average Wages and Salaries by Industry	43,253	44,020	45,042	45,452	46,687	48,371	50,985
Average Farm Wages and Salaries	29,919	24,880	39,574	39,499	33,674	38,951	42,596
Average Nonfarm Wages and Salaries	43,368	44,208	45,092	45,505	46,825	48,461	51,058
Average private wages and salaries................................	39,954	40,553	41,663	42,371	43,483	45,347	48,077
Forestry, fishing, and related activities..........................	21,963	22,354	23,050	24,218	24,553	26,868	29,799
Mining..	73,544	77,340	82,822	88,329	93,786	96,975	88,375
Utilities..	83,871	88,478	90,384	92,309	94,493	99,635	98,665
Construction...	62,559	63,593	64,746	65,060	66,498	70,624	69,235
Manufacturing...	39,256	40,344	40,055	40,701	41,269	42,901	45,001
Durable goods manufacturing......................................	48,285	50,970	49,978	50,886	53,290	55,125	58,552
Nondurable goods manufacturing................................	35,516	35,907	36,364	36,988	37,089	38,544	40,141
Wholesale trade...	48,192	49,750	51,348	52,585	54,236	55,799	59,028
Retail trade...	28,174	28,181	28,370	28,806	29,672	30,298	32,318
Transportation and warehousing...................................	42,035	43,518	44,751	46,384	48,220	50,676	58,867
Information..	55,598	57,609	58,690	58,683	62,012	63,690	61,547
Finance and insurance	58,163	60,297	63,154	64,473	65,680	69,152	72,824
Real estate and rental and leasing................................	41,295	42,536	44,034	46,226	46,975	49,916	55,747
Professional, scientific, and technical services	63,147	63,535	65,854	66,763	68,329	69,868	72,957
Management of companies and enterprises....................	76,773	79,844	83,712	82,657	84,337	86,732	88,793
Administrative and waste services................................	30,277	29,706	30,841	31,051	31,587	32,912	33,905
Educational services...	32,971	33,631	34,032	34,599	34,871	35,221	33,826
Health care and social assistance.................................	45,564	46,663	47,926	48,290	49,734	51,501	55,325
Arts, entertainment, and recreation...............................	27,936	27,177	27,529	28,600	30,024	30,154	32,551
Accommodation and food services................................	29,403	30,461	31,808	32,581	33,742	35,376	38,865
Other services, except public administration..................	32,341	32,763	33,387	34,101	34,784	36,139	39,187
Government and government enterprises...........................	52,257	53,868	54,306	54,164	56,191	57,241	59,731

Table HI-10. Employment Characteristics by Family Type

(Number, percent.)

Family type and labor force status	2014		2015		2016	
	Total	Families with own children under 18 years	Total	Families with own children under 18 years	Total	Families with own children under 18 years
All Families...	312,380	122,610	309,386	115,039	315,505	115,996
FAMILY TYPE AND LABOR FORCE STATUS						
Married-Couple Families..............................	230,278	89,744	232,451	87,488	236,236	85,855
Both husband and wife in labor force.................	51.1	64.3	51.2	64.8	52.4	65.3
Husband in labor force, wife not in labor force	21.9	28.9	22.0	29.6	19.3	27.0
Wife in labor force, husband not in labor force	9.7	4.5	8.3	4.1	10.3	5.5
Both husband and wife not in labor force................	17.3	2.3	17.6	1.3	16.9	1.9
Other Families	82,102	32,866	76,935	27,551	79,269	30,141
Female householder, no husband present....................	68.1	70.9	67.7	68.8	67.2	66.7
In labor force	44.4	58.4	41.6	56.8	40.9	54.5
Not in labor force	23.7	12.5	26.1	12.0	26.3	12.2
Male householder, no wife present........................	31.9	29.1	32.3	31.2	32.8	33.3
In labor force	22.1	25.9	23.1	27.7	24.6	30.7
Not in labor force	9.8	3.2	9.2	3.5	8.2	2.6

Table HI-11. School Enrollment and Educational Attainment, 2016

(Number, percent.)

Item	State	U.S.
Enrollment		
Total population 3 years and over, enrolled in school	331,540	81,572,277
Enrolled in nursery school or preschool (percent)....................................	7.1	6.0
Enrolled in kindergarten (percent)..	4.9	5.0
Enrolled in elementary school, grades 1-8 (percent)........................	38.8	40.3
Enrolled in high school, grades 9-12 (percent).............................	19.0	21.0
Enrolled in college or graduate school (percent)...........................	30.2	27.7
Attainment		
Total population 25 years and over	990,937	218,475,480
Less than ninth grade (percent)	3.6	5.4
9th to 12th grade, no diploma (percent)	4.4	7.2
High school graduate, including equivalency (percent).....................	28.0	27.2
Some college, no degree (percent)	21.5	20.6
Associate's degree (percent)..	10.5	8.4
Bachelor's degree (percent)...	21.4	19.3
Graduate or professional degree (percent)................................	10.6	11.9
High school graduate or higher (percent)..................................	92.0	87.5
Bachelor's degree or higher (percent).....................................	31.9	31.3

Table HI-12. Public School Characteristics and Educational Indicators

(Number, percent; data derived from National Center of Education Statistics.)

Item	State	U.S.
Public Schools, 2015–2016 (except where noted)		
Number of school districts..	1	18,328
Number of schools...	290	98,456
Number of students..	181,995	50,327,015
Number of teachers..	11,747	3,151,497
Student-teacher ratio..	15.5	16.0
Expenditures per student (dollars), 2014-2015.............................	12,855	11,445
Four-year adjusted cohort graduation rate (ACGR)[1][2]	82.7	84.1
Students eligible for free or reduced-price lunch (percent), 2014-2015......	50.1	51.8
English language learners (percent), Fall 2015.............................	7.5	9.5
Students age 3 to 21 served under IDEA, part B (percent)...................	10.6	13.2

Public Schools by Type	Number	Percent of state public schools
Total number of schools..	290	100.0
Regular	288	99.3
Special education..	1	0.3
Vocational education...	0	-
Alternative education..	1	0.3

NOTE: Every school is assigned only one school type based on its instructional emphasis.
[1] ACGR data represents a new method of calculating high-school completion rates and may not be comparable to previous years' data for Averaged Freshmen Graduation Rates (AFGR).
[2] The United States 4-year ACGRs were estimated using both the reported 4-year ACGR data from 49 states and the District of Columbia and using imputed data for Idaho. The estimate for American Indian/Alaska Native students also includes imputed data for Virginia.

Table HI-13. Reported Voting and Registration of the Voting-Age Population, November 2016

(Numbers in thousands, percent.)

Item	Total population	Total citizen population	Registered			Voted		
			Total registered	Percent registered (total population)	Percent registered (total citizen population)	Total voted	Percent voted (total population)	Percent voted (total citizen population)
U.S. Total	245,502	224,059	157,596	64.2	70.3	137,537	56.0	61.4
State Total..............................	1,064	974	530	49.8	54.4	460	43.3	47.3
Sex								
Male	519	476	249	48.0	52.3	215	41.5	45.2
Female	545	498	281	51.6	56.5	245	45.0	49.3
Race								
White alone..................................	225	220	144	63.9	65.4	129	57.4	58.7
White, non-Hispanic alone	209	205	138	66.3	67.5	126	60.2	61.3
Black alone..................................	24	24	16	(B)	(B)	15	(B)	(B)
Asian alone	492	417	206	41.8	49.3	182	37.0	43.6
Hispanic (of any race)......................	78	74	43	(B)	(B)	36	(B)	(B)
White alone or in combination	368	361	229	62.2	63.2	197	53.6	54.6
Black alone or in combination...........	31	30	19	(B)	(B)	17	(B)	(B)
Asian alone or in combination...........	624	548	281	45.0	51.2	246	39.4	44.8
Age								
18 to 24 years.............................	115	108	38	33.4	35.6	23	20.4	21.7
25 to 34 years.............................	198	178	76	38.5	42.8	61	30.8	34.3
35 to 44 years.............................	161	148	79	49.3	53.6	69	42.8	46.6
45 to 64 years.............................	366	333	200	54.6	60.1	182	49.7	54.6
65 years and over	224	207	136	60.8	65.7	125	55.8	60.3

B = Base is less than 75,000 and therefore too small to show the derived measure.

Table HI-14. Crime

(Number, rate per 100,000. Data are derived from the FBI Uniform Crime Reports.)

Item	State			U.S. [1,2,3,4]		
	2015	2016	Percent change	2015	2016	Percent change
TOTAL POPULATION [5]	1,431,603	1,428,557	-0.2	321,418,820	323,127,513	0.5
VIOLENT CRIME						
Number..	4,201	4,417	5.1	1,231,566	1,248,185	1.3
Rate..	293.4	309.2	5.4	383.2	386.3	0.8
Murder and Nonnegligent Manslaughter						
Number..	19	35	84.2	15,696	17,250	9.9
Rate..	1.3	2.5	92.3	4.9	5.3	8.2
Rape [6]						
Number [6]..	561	619	10.3	124,047	130,603	5.3
Rate..	39.2	43.3	10.5	38.6	40.4	4.7
Robbery						
Number..	1,203	994	-17.4	327,374	332,198	1.5
Rate..	84.0	69.6	-17.1	101.9	102.8	0.9
Aggravated Assault						
Number..	2,418	2,769	14.5	764,449	803,007	5.0
Rate..	168.9	193.8	14.7	237.8	248.5	4.5
PROPERTY CRIME						
Number..	54,346	42,753	-21.3	7,993,631	7,919,035	-0.9
Rate..	3,796.2	2,992.7	-21.2	2,487.0	2,450.7	-1.5
Burglary						
Number..	6,557	6,017	-8.2	1,579,527	1,515,096	-4.1
Rate..	458.0	421.2	-8.0	491.4	468.9	-4.6
Larceny-Theft						
Number..	42,010	31,082	-26.0	5,706,346	5,638,455	-1.2
Rate..	2,934.5	2,175.8	-25.9	1,775.4	1,745.0	-1.7
Motor Vehicle Theft						
Number..	5,779	5,654	-2.2	707,758	765,484	8.2
Rate..	403.7	395.8	-2.0	220.2	236.9	7.6

NOTE: Although arson data are included in the trend and clearance tables, sufficient data are not available to estimate totals for this offense. Therefore, no arson data are published in this table.
X = Not applicable.
- = Zero or rounds to zero.
[1] The crime figures have been adjusted.
[2] The data collection methodology for the offense of forcible rape used by the Minnesota state Uniform Crime Reporting (UCR) Program (with the exception of Minneapolis and St. Paul, Minnesota) does not comply with national UCR Program guidelines. Consequently, its figures for forcible rape and violent crime (of which forcible rape is a part) are not published in this table.
[3] Includes offenses reported by the Zoological Police and the Metro Transit Police.
[4] Because of changes in the state's reporting practices, figures are not comparable to previous years' data.
[5] Populations are U.S. Census Bureau provisional estimates as of July 1 of each year.
[6] The figures shown for the offense of rape were estimated using the revised Uniform Crime Reporting (UCR) definition of rape.

Table HI-15. State Government Finances, 2016

(Dollar amounts in thousands, percent distribution.)

Item	Dollars	Percent distribution
Total Revenue	13,417,610	100.0
General revenue	12,919,339	96.3
Intergovernmental revenue	2,943,377	21.9
Taxes	6,919,035	51.6
General sales	3,206,154	23.9
Selective sales	1,109,748	8.3
License taxes	263,130	2.0
Individual income tax	2,116,130	15.8
Corporate income tax	108,169	0.8
Other taxes	115,704	0.9
Current charges	1,799,125	13.4
Miscellaneous general revenue	1,257,802	9.4
Utility revenue	0	-
Liquor stores revenue	95	-
Insurance trust revenue [1]	498,176	3.7
Total Expenditure	12,425,875	100.0
Intergovernmental expenditure	147,934	1.2
Direct expenditure	12,277,941	98.8
Current operation	9,467,400	76.2
Capital outlay	1,166,420	9.4
Insurance benefits and repayments	1,385,193	11.1
Assistance and subsidies	138,178	1.1
Interest on debt	120,750	1.0
Exhibit: Salaries and wages	3,233,075	26.0
Total Expenditure	12,425,875	100.0
General expenditure	11,033,159	88.8
Intergovernmental expenditure	147,934	1.2
Direct expenditure	10,885,225	87.6
General expenditure, by function:		
Education	3,386,370	27.3
Public welfare	2,758,485	22.2
Hospitals	627,076	5.0
Health	515,683	4.2
Highways	456,996	3.7
Police protection	39,097	0.3
Correction	266,716	2.1
Natural resources	200,612	1.6
Parks and recreation	71,879	0.6
Governmental administration	563,903	4.5
Interest on general debt	120,750	1.0
Other and unallocable	2,025,592	16.3
Utility expenditure	7,523	0.1
Liquor stores expenditure	0	-
Insurance trust expenditure	1,385,193	11.1
Debt at End of Fiscal Year	9,216,583	X
Cash and Security Holdings	22,382,636	X

X = Not applicable.
- = Zero or rounds to zero.
[1] Within insurance trust revenue, net earnings of state retirement systems is a calculated statistic (the item code in the data file is X08), and thus can be positive or negative. Net earnings is the sum of earnings on investments plus gains on investments minus losses on investments. The change made in 2002 for asset valuation from book to market value in accordance with Statement 34 of the Governmental Accounting Standards Board is reflected in the calculated statistics.

Table HI-16. State Government Tax Collections, 2017

(Dollars in thousands, percent.)

Item	Dollars	Percent distribution
Total Taxes..	7,029,026	100.0
Property taxes..	X	-
Sales and gross receipts	4,365,856	62.1
General sales and gross receipts	3,239,225	46.1
Selective sales and gross receipts	1,126,631	16.0
Alcoholic beverages	51,167	0.7
Amusements..	X	-
Insurance premiums..	170,118	2.4
Motor fuels	87,026	1.2
Pari-mutuels	X	-
Public utilities	122,159	1.7
Tobacco products..	124,160	1.8
Other selective sales	572,001	8.1
Licenses...	269,224	3.8
Alcoholic beverages	X	-
Amusements..	X	-
Corporations in general..	1,723	-
Hunting and fishing..	567	-
Motor vehicle	187,986	2.7
Motor vehicle operators	316	-
Public utilities	17,352	0.2
Occupation and business, NEC	48,633	0.7
Other licenses	12,647	0.2
Income taxes..	2,280,441	32.4
Individual income...	2,095,601	29.8
Corporation net income	184,840	2.6
Other taxes..	113,505	1.6
Death and gift..	18,968	0.3
Documentary and stock transfer..	94,537	1.3
Severance	X	-
Taxes, NEC..	0	-

X = Not applicable.
- = Zero or rounds to zero.

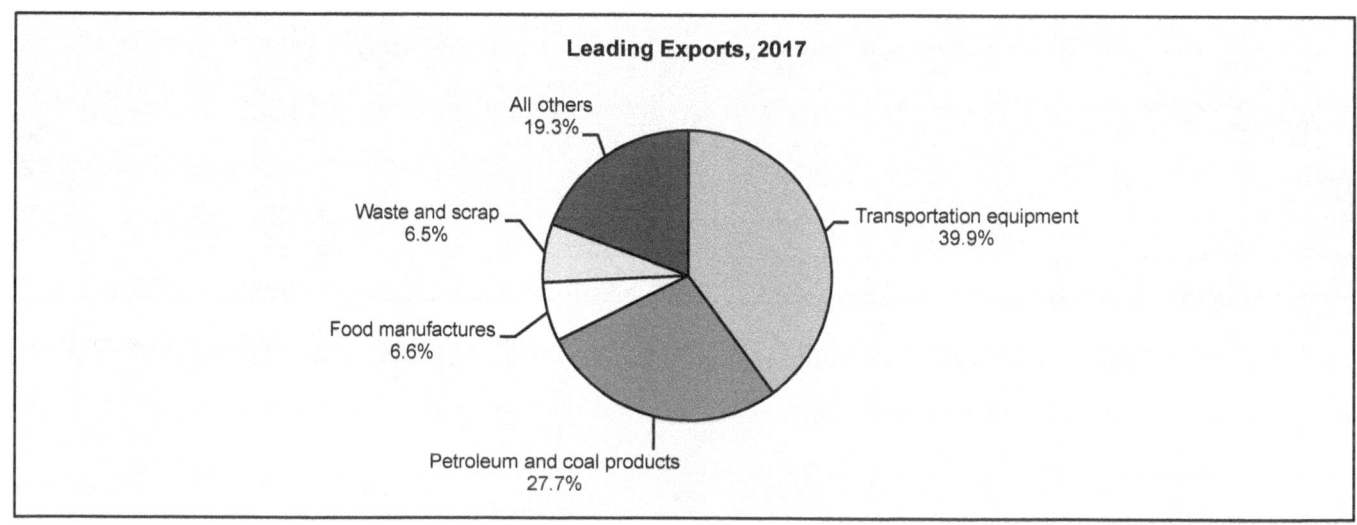

Leading Exports, 2017

- All others 19.3%
- Waste and scrap 6.5%
- Food manufactures 6.6%
- Petroleum and coal products 27.7%
- Transportation equipment 39.9%

Facts and Figures

Location: Northwestern United States; bordered on the N by Canada, on the E by Montana and Wyoming, on the S by Nevada and Utah, and on the W by Washington and Oregon

Area: 83,568 sq. mi. (216,446 sq. km.); rank—14th

Population: 1,716,943 (2017 est.); rank—39th

Principal Cities: capital—Boise; largest—Boise

Statehood: July 3, 1890; 43rd state

U.S. Congress: 2 senators, 2 representatives

State Motto: *Esto perpetua* ("Let it be perpetual")

State Song: "Here We Have Idaho"

State Nickname: The Gem State

Abbreviations: ID

State Symbols: flower—syringa (mock orange); tree—Western white pine; bird—mountain bluebird

At a Glance

- With an increase in population of 9.3 percent, Idaho ranked 10th among the states in growth from 2010 to 2017.

- With 1,744.2 incidents per 100,000 population, Idaho had the 8th lowest property crime rate in the country in 2016.

- Idaho's violent crime rate in 2016 was 230.3 per 100,000 population, compared to 386.3 for the entire nation.

- With 25.8 percent of its population under age 18, Idaho ranked 3rd among the states for the highest percent children in 2017.

- Idaho's unemployment rate ranked 43rd in the nation in 2016, with 3.2 percent of the population unemployed, compared to 4.4 of the entire country.

Table ID-1. Population by Age, Sex, Race, and Hispanic Origin

(Number, percent, except where noted.)

Sex, age, race, and Hispanic origin	2000	2010	2017 [1]	Average annual percent change, 2010–2017
Total Population	1,293,953	1,567,582	1,716,943	9.5
Percent of total U.S. population	0.5	0.5	0.5	X
Sex				
Male	648,660	785,324	860,458	9.6
Female	645,293	782,258	856,485	9.5
Age				
Under 5 years	97,643	121,772	117,037	-3.9
5 to 19 years	316,222	353,509	372,812	5.5
20 to 64 years	734,172	897,633	962,193	7.2
65 years and over	145,916	194,668	264,901	36.1
Median age (years)	33.2	34.6	36.3	4.9
Race and Hispanic Origin				
One race				
White	1,177,304	1,476,097	1,599,814	8.4
Black	5,456	10,950	15,052	37.5
American Indian and Alaska Native	17,645	25,782	29,973	16.3
Asian	11,889	20,034	26,359	31.6
Native Hawaiian or Other Pacific Islander	1,308	2,786	3,700	32.8
Two or more races	25,609	31,933	42,045	31.7
Hispanic (of any race)	101,690	182,424	215,392	18.1

X = Not applicable.
[1] Population figures for 2017 are July 1 estimates. The 2010 estimates are taken from the 2010 Census.

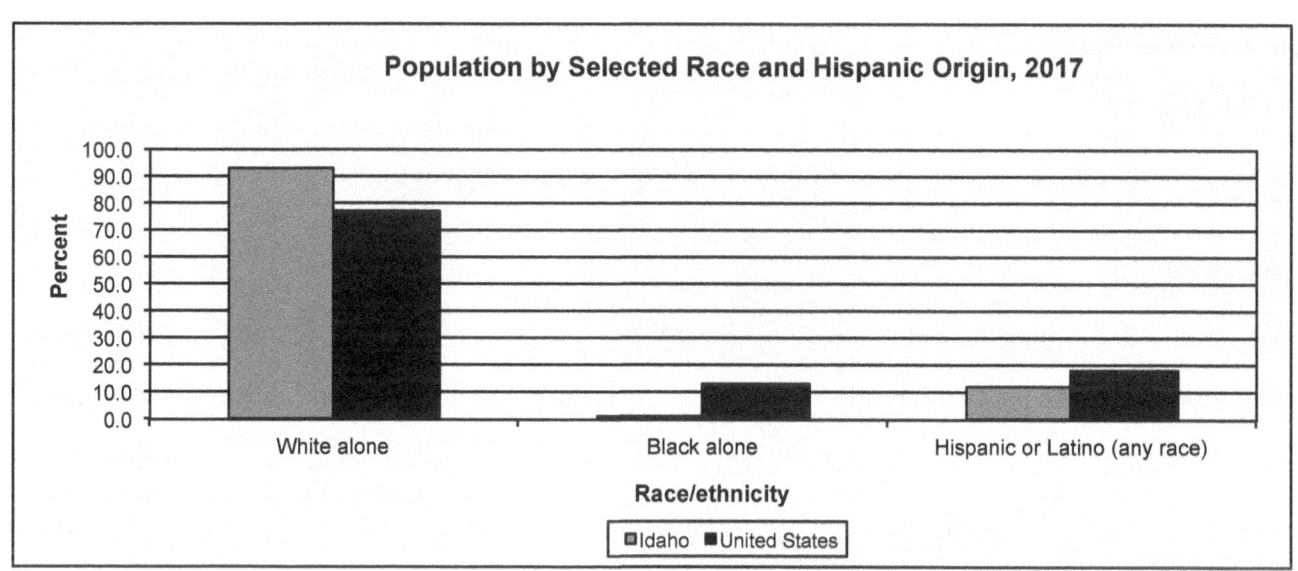

Table ID-2. Marital Status

(Number, percent distribution.)

Sex, age, and marital status	2000	2010	2016
Males, 15 Years and Over	493,045	602,308	655,592
Never married	26.1	28.3	30.8
Now married, except separated	61.0	57.0	54.4
Separated	1.0	1.4	1.1
Widowed	2.1	2.4	2.5
Divorced	9.9	10.9	11.2
Females, 15 Years and Over	498,579	608,900	665,205
Never married	19.6	22.4	24.4
Now married, except separated	59.0	55.3	53.4
Separated	1.3	1.6	1.3
Widowed	8.6	7.6	7.2
Divorced	11.4	13.1	13.7

Table ID-3. Households and Housing Characteristics

(Number, percent, dollars.)

Item	2000	2010	2016	Average annual percent change, 2010–2016
Total Households..	469,645	576,709	610,872	1.0
Family households	333,588	401,806	411,617	0.4
Married-couple family	276,511	322,129	328,906	0.4
Other family	59,077	79,677	82,711	0.6
Male householder, no wife present................................	18,228	23,583	27,394	2.7
Female householder, no husband present.........................	40,849	56,094	55,317	-0.2
Nonfamily households	134,057	174,903	199,255	2.3
Householder living alone...	105,175	139,909	162,256	2.7
Householder not living alone...	28,882	34,994	36,999	1.0
Housing Characteristics				
Total housing units..	527,824	668,634	700,829	0.8
Occupied housing units	469,645	576,709	610,872	1.0
Owner occupied	339,960	401,532	418,217	0.7
Renter occupied	129,685	175,177	192,655	1.7
Average household size..	2.69	2.67	2.71	0.2
Financial Characteristics				
Median gross rent of renter-occupied housing	515	683	790	2.6
Median monthly owner costs for housing units with a mortgage	887	1,187	1,168	-0.3
Median value of owner-occupied housing units...................	106,300	165,100	189,400	2.5

- = Zero or rounds to zero.

Table ID-4. Migration, Origin, and Language

(Number, percent.)

	State			U.S.		
Characteristic	2015	2016	Percent change	2015	2016	Percent change
Residence 1 Year Ago						
Population 1 year and over	1,635,366	1,663,756	1.7	317,635,720	319,361,956	0.5
Same house	81.6	82.3	X	85.3	85.4	X
Different house in the U.S..	17.9	17.2	X	14.1	13.9	X
Same county	10.3	9.4	X	8.5	8.3	X
Different county	7.6	7.8	X	5.6	5.6	X
Same state	3.1	3.5	X	3.2	3.2	X
Different state	4.5	4.3	X	2.4	2.4	X
Abroad	0.6	0.5	X	0.7	0.7	X
Place of Birth						
Native born	1,560,566	1,585,187	1.6	278,128,449	279,388,170	0.5
Male	50.1	50.1	X	49.3	49.3	X
Female	49.9	49.9	X	50.7	50.7	X
Foreign born	94,364	97,953	3.8	43,290,372	43,739,345	1.0
Male	48.3	48.4	X	48.6	48.5	X
Female	51.7	51.6	X	51.4	51.5	X
Foreign born; naturalized U.S. citizen...........................	35,909	37,899	5.5	20,697,103	21,238,372	2.6
Male	43.3	46.4	X	45.9	45.9	X
Female	56.7	53.6	X	54.1	54.1	X
Foreign born; not a U.S. citizen...................................	58,455	60,054	2.7	22,593,269	22,500,973	-0.4
Male	51.5	49.6	X	51.1	51.0	X
Female	48.5	50.4	X	48.9	49.0	X
Entered 2010 or later	18.7	19.4	X	15.6	18.6	X
Entered 2000 to 2009	24.8	29.9	X	27.9	26.7	X
Entered before 2000...	56.5	50.8	X	56.5	54.7	X
World Region of Birth, Foreign						
Foreign-born population, excluding population born at sea	94,364	97,953	3.8	43,289,646	43,738,901	1.0
Europe	15.6	13.9	X	11.1	10.9	X
Asia...	19.9	21.1	X	30.6	30.8	X
Africa	2.8	1.9	X	4.8	4.9	X
Oceania	1.2	0.9	X	0.6	0.6	X
Latin America	55.8	58.1	X	51.1	51.0	X
North America	4.7	4.0	X	1.9	1.8	X
Language Spoken at Home and Ability to Speak English						
Population 5 years and over..	1,543,083	1,568,997	1.7	301,625,014	303,328,961	0.6
English only	89.8	89.2	X	78.5	78.4	X
Language other than English.......................................	10.2	10.8	X	21.5	21.6	X
Speaks English less than "very well"............................	3.7	4.2	X	8.6	8.6	X

NA = Not available.
X = Not applicable.
- = Zero or rounds to zero.

Table ID-5. Median Income and Poverty Status, 2016

(Number, percent, except as noted.)

Characteristic	State		U.S.	
	Number	Percent	Number	Percent
Median Income				
Households (dollars)..	51,807	X	57,617	X
Families (dollars)	63,182	X	71,062	X
Below Poverty Level (All People)	237,445	14.4	44,268,996	14.0
Sex				
Male	111,162	13.5	19,760,056	12.8
Female	126,283	15.2	24,508,940	15.2
Age				
Under 18 years...	76,266	17.7	14,115,713	19.5
Related children under 18 years..........................	73,761	17.2	13,805,435	19.1
18 to 64 years...	135,876	14.0	25,723,818	13.2
65 years and over	25,303	10.0	4,429,465	9.2

X = Not applicable.

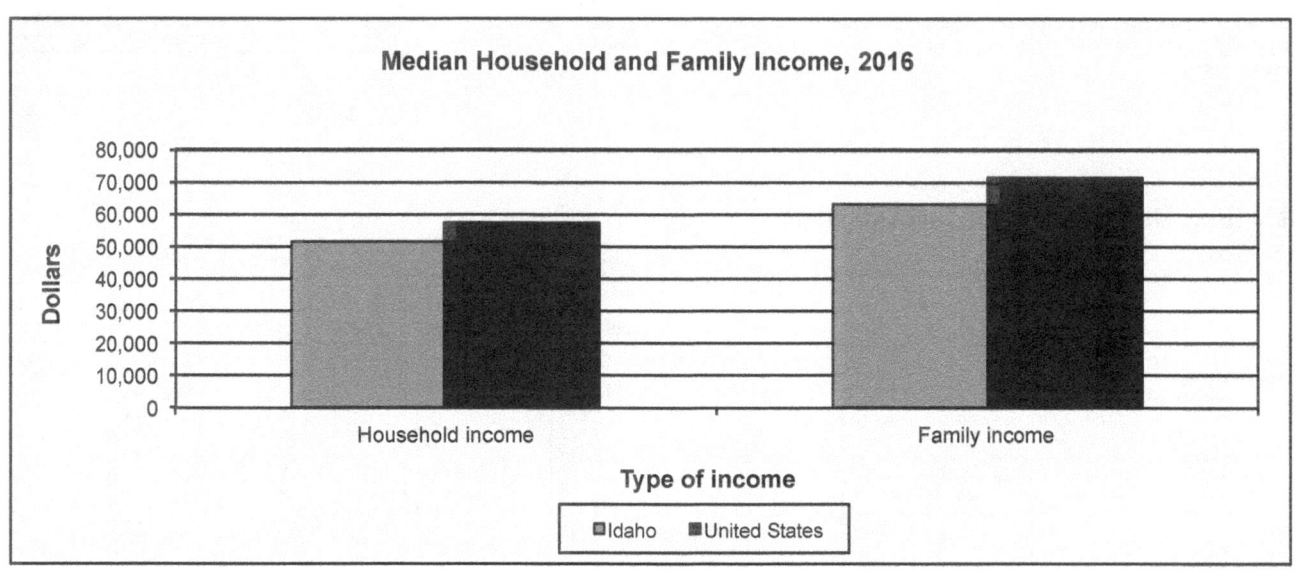

Median Household and Family Income, 2016

Table ID-6. Health Insurance Coverage Status for the Civilian Noninstitutionalized Population and Children Under 18 Years of Age

(Number, percent.)

Item	2008	2009	2010	2011	2012	2013	2014	2015	2016
Civilian Noninstitutionalized Population	1,498,787	1,520,563	1,551,635	1,565,645	1,575,682	1,592,172	1,612,889	1,632,247	1,662,867
Covered by Private or Public Insurance									
Number...	1,232,175	1,256,279	1,276,231	1,306,551	1,320,939	1,334,697	1,394,182	1,451,902	1,494,757
Percent...	82.2	82.6	82.3	83.5	83.8	83.8	86.4	89.0	89.9
Not Covered									
Number...	266,612	264,284	275,404	259,094	254,743	257,475	218,707	180,345	168,110
Percent...	17.8	17.4	17.7	16.5	16.2	16.2	13.6	11.0	10.1
Percent in the U.S. not covered...............................	15.1	15.1	15.5	15.1	14.8	14.5	11.7	9.4	8.6
Children Under 18 Years of Age	412,970	418,172	428,296	427,064	423,926	425,948	430,662	431,339	435,630
Covered by Private or Public Insurance									
Number...	356,521	371,201	383,292	388,096	387,897	387,931	396,885	406,497	415,147
Percent...	86.3	88.8	89.5	90.9	91.5	91.1	92.2	94.2	95.3
Not Covered									
Number...	56,449	46,971	45,004	38,968	36,029	38,017	33,777	24,842	20,483
Percent...	13.7	11.2	10.5	9.1	8.5	8.9	7.8	5.8	4.7
Percent in the U.S. not covered...............................	9.9	8.6	8.0	7.5	7.2	7.1	6.0	4.8	4.5

Table ID-7. Employment Status by Demographic Group, 2017

(Numbers in thousands, percent.)

Characteristic	Civilian noninstitutional population	Civilian labor force		Employed		Unemployed	
		Number	Percent of population	Number	Percent of population	Number	Percent of population
Total..	1,297	831	64.1	805	62.0	27	3.2
Sex							
Male..	642	453	70.5	430	68.3	14	3.1
Female..	655	379	57.8	366	55.9	13	3.3
Race, Sex, and Hispanic Origin							
White...	1,228	785	63.9	760	61.9	25	3.2
Male...	607	426	70.1	412	67.9	14	3.2
Female.....................................	621	359	57.8	348	55.9	12	3.2
Black or African American............	NA	NA	NA	NA	NA	NA	NA
Male...	NA	NA	NA	NA	NA	NA	NA
Female.....................................	NA	NA	NA	NA	NA	NA	NA
Hispanic or Latino ethnicity[1].......	143	103	72.1	98	68.5	5	4.9
Male...	76	60	78.8	57	75.7	2	4.0
Female.....................................	67	43	64.4	41	60.6	3	6.2
Age							
16 to 19 years.............................	87	36	41.2	32	37.0	4	10.2
20 to 24 years.............................	118	92	77.4	87	73.1	5	5.6
25 to 34 years.............................	220	181	81.9	174	78.9	7	3.7
35 to 44 years.............................	207	175	84.7	172	83.0	3	1.9
45 to 54 years.............................	204	173	84.7	168	82.5	4	2.5
55 to 64 years.............................	209	137	65.4	134	64.3	2	1.8
65 years and over........................	251	39	15.4	37	14.9	1	2.8

NOTE: Data in Table 7 are from the Current Population Survey (CPS) and do not match the estimates in Table 8. See notes and definitions for further information.
[1] May be of any race.
NA = Not available.

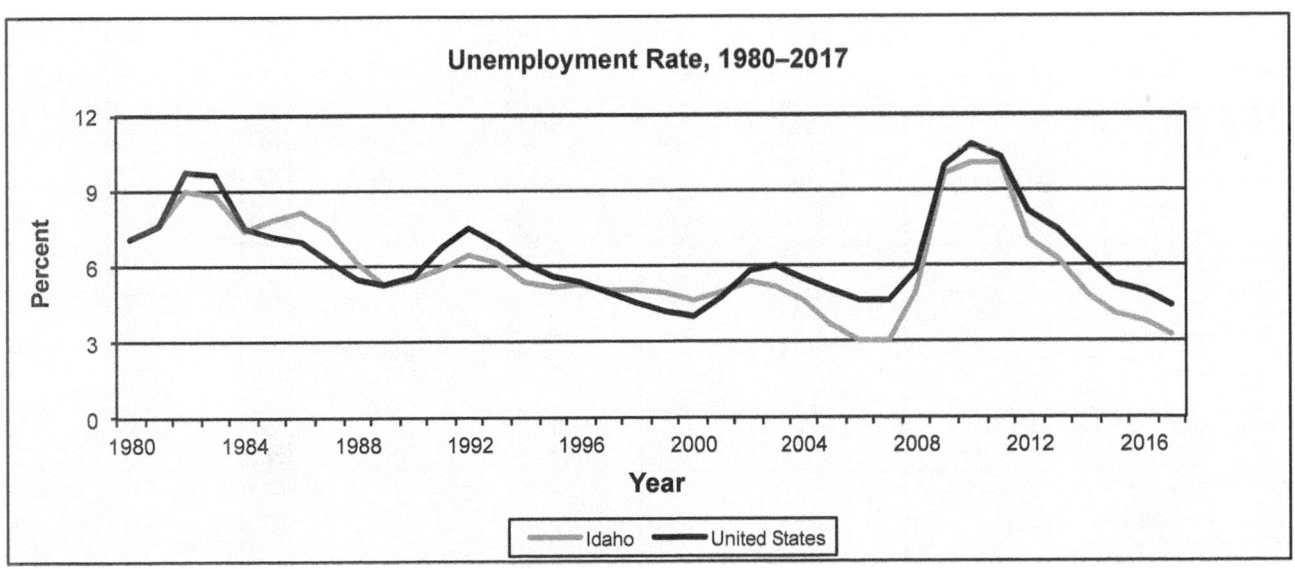

Table ID-8. Employment Status of the Civilian Noninstitutional Population Age 16 Years and Over

(Number, percent.)

Year	Civilian labor force	Civilian participation rate	Employed	Unemployed	Unemployment rate
2009...	757,131	65.8	690,722	66,409	8.8
2010...	761,056	65.3	692,826	68,230	9.0
2011...	765,178	64.9	701,466	63,712	8.3
2012...	769,256	64.5	713,704	55,552	7.2
2013...	770,833	63.8	723,636	47,197	6.1
2014...	779,631	63.6	741,525	38,106	4.9
2015...	794,675	63.9	761,009	33,666	4.2
2016...	812,856	64.0	782,279	30,577	3.8
2017...	833,462	64.0	807,163	26,299	3.2

Table ID-9. Employment and Average Wages by Industry

(Estimates through 2010 are based on the 2007 *North American Industry Classification System* [NAICS]. Estimates from 2011 onward are based on the 2012 NAICS.)

Industry	2010	2011	2012	2013	2014	2015	2016
	Number of Jobs						
Wage and Salary Employment by Industry.........................	643,274	647,201	652,559	668,126	685,655	702,372	726,927
Farm Wage and Salary Employment.............................	14,489	16,704	16,505	16,402	17,624	17,001	17,215
Nonfarm Wage and Salary Employment.........................	628,785	630,497	636,054	651,724	668,031	685,371	709,712
Private wage and salary employment..	500,211	503,690	509,535	525,045	540,591	557,077	578,422
Forestry, fishing, and related activities...............................	7,821	7,758	7,854	8,202	8,405	8,589	8,500
Mining..	2,273	2,566	2,673	2,547	2,417	2,323	2,365
Utilities...	2,729	2,797	2,826	2,806	2,912	3,013	3,010
Construction	32,295	30,459	30,438	32,688	34,783	37,075	40,554
Manufacturing...	53,345	54,590	56,596	59,235	59,923	61,570	63,884
Durable goods manufacturing..	29,941	31,293	32,654	34,026	34,473	35,626	36,863
Nondurable goods manufacturing..................................	23,404	23,297	23,942	25,209	25,450	25,944	27,021
Wholesale trade	25,846	26,302	26,994	28,278	28,751	28,731	28,460
Retail trade..	75,641	75,663	77,087	78,600	80,368	83,463	85,148
Transportation and warehousing......................................	18,127	18,374	18,648	18,726	19,437	20,378	20,602
Information	9,684	9,435	9,301	9,236	9,218	9,175	9,009
Finance and insurance	20,916	21,329	21,346	21,751	22,253	22,778	23,790
Real estate and rental and leasing..................................	7,013	6,836	6,698	6,843	6,978	7,309	7,403
Professional, scientific, and technical services	32,585	32,559	31,651	31,261	32,740	34,392	35,477
Management of companies and enterprises........................	5,865	5,874	5,918	5,435	5,480	5,642	5,301
Administrative and waste services	36,351	36,923	37,332	39,831	40,307	40,067	44,540
Educational services	10,375	10,723	11,059	11,166	11,447	11,848	12,100
Health care and social assistance....................................	76,047	77,176	77,871	80,873	83,581	86,183	89,098
Arts, entertainment, and recreation..................................	8,642	8,558	9,056	9,342	9,790	9,690	10,429
Accommodation and food services..................................	49,731	50,872	52,020	53,679	56,108	58,545	61,905
Other services, except public administration........................	24,925	24,896	24,167	24,546	25,693	26,306	26,847
Government and government enterprises................................	128,574	126,807	126,519	126,679	127,440	128,294	131,290
	Dollars						
Average Wages and Salaries by Industry	35,714	36,303	37,027	37,828	38,866	39,633	42,607
Average Farm Wages and Salaries	35,256	30,894	35,052	39,817	37,879	35,139	38,635
Average Nonfarm Wages and Salaries	35,724	36,446	37,079	37,778	38,892	39,744	42,703
Average private wages and salaries....................................	35,655	36,525	37,109	37,960	39,200	39,941	43,124
Forestry, fishing, and related activities...............................	27,083	28,315	27,887	29,046	30,466	31,764	35,836
Mining..	67,840	69,004	71,415	76,038	76,522	71,355	66,693
Utilities...	73,492	74,966	76,801	78,930	81,007	82,894	85,363
Construction	38,972	39,360	39,975	39,813	40,034	40,758	46,018
Manufacturing...	50,800	51,716	52,014	54,780	59,982	56,947	62,048
Durable goods manufacturing..	58,643	58,199	57,967	62,228	69,794	63,609	69,501
Nondurable goods manufacturing..................................	40,766	43,009	43,895	44,728	46,690	47,799	51,879
Wholesale trade	47,305	48,824	49,681	50,896	53,225	56,767	59,761
Retail trade..	25,738	26,163	26,862	27,645	28,730	29,715	31,793
Transportation and warehousing......................................	37,514	38,660	40,392	41,012	42,096	42,659	45,944
Information	42,458	44,329	46,949	46,886	48,156	48,791	51,106
Finance and insurance	48,496	49,418	52,464	53,872	55,643	57,892	62,974
Real estate and rental and leasing..................................	28,383	28,681	30,188	31,969	33,946	34,536	37,404
Professional, scientific, and technical services	56,415	58,029	57,115	59,096	59,286	61,372	65,422
Management of companies and enterprises........................	80,751	86,647	89,636	87,249	78,853	78,188	94,659
Administrative and waste services	26,577	26,985	27,048	27,075	27,818	29,579	35,099
Educational services	26,116	26,739	26,861	27,155	27,318	27,763	28,066
Health care and social assistance....................................	36,264	37,434	37,576	38,612	39,595	40,796	42,776
Arts, entertainment, and recreation..................................	19,340	18,916	18,812	19,475	19,903	20,646	22,741
Accommodation and food services..................................	14,960	15,284	15,873	16,013	16,613	17,305	19,073
Other services, except public administration........................	24,398	24,761	26,061	26,891	27,537	28,529	31,660
Government and government enterprises................................	35,992	36,132	36,957	37,025	37,587	38,890	40,849

Table ID-10. Employment Characteristics by Family Type

(Number, percent.)

Family type and labor force status	2014		2015		2016	
	Total	Families with own children under 18 years	Total	Families with own children under 18 years	Total	Families with own children under 18 years
All Families..	406,767	180,018	400,347	175,338	411,617	176,108
FAMILY TYPE AND LABOR FORCE STATUS						
Married-Couple Families.............................	323,887	131,393	320,853	126,719	328,906	128,484
Both husband and wife in labor force......................	48.7	61.0	48.4	62.7	47.4	59.3
Husband in labor force, wife not in labor force	23.9	33.6	23.1	31.9	25.2	35.2
Wife in labor force, husband not in labor force	6.8	3.0	7.2	3.2	7.0	3.6
Both husband and wife not in labor force..................	20.6	2.5	20.9	2.1	19.9	1.7
Other Families	82,880	48,625	79,494	48,619	82,711	47,624
Female householder, no husband present..................	66.7	67.9	70.7	70.7	66.9	68.5
In labor force...	47.8	53.1	49.7	57.6	46.1	54.6
Not in labor force	18.9	14.8	21.0	13.1	20.8	13.9
Male householder, no wife present	33.3	32.1	29.3	29.3	33.1	31.5
In labor force...	26.3	29.2	23.7	26.6	25.6	28.0
Not in labor force.......................................	7.0	2.9	5.7	2.7	7.6	3.4

Table ID-11. School Enrollment and Educational Attainment, 2016

(Number, percent.)

Item	State	U.S.
Enrollment		
Total population 3 years and over, enrolled in school	454,191	81,572,277
Enrolled in nursery school or preschool (percent)..	5.0	6.0
Enrolled in kindergarten (percent)...	5.0	5.0
Enrolled in elementary school, grades 1-8 (percent)..	43.6	40.3
Enrolled in high school, grades 9-12 (percent)	21.7	21.0
Enrolled in college or graduate school (percent)...	24.8	27.7
Attainment		
Total population 25 years and over	1,087,265	218,475,480
Less than ninth grade (percent)	3.2	5.4
9th to 12th grade, no diploma (percent)	6.4	7.2
High school graduate, including equivalency (percent).......................................	27.9	27.2
Some college, no degree (percent)...	25.3	20.6
Associate's degree (percent)...	9.6	8.4
Bachelor's degree (percent)...	18.7	19.3
Graduate or professional degree (percent)...	8.9	11.9
High school graduate or higher (percent)..	90.4	87.5
Bachelor's degree or higher (percent)...	27.6	31.3

Table ID-12. Public School Characteristics and Educational Indicators

(Number, percent; data derived from National Center of Education Statistics.)

Item	State	U.S.
Public Schools, 2015–2016 (except where noted)		
Number of school districts...	159	18,328
Number of schools..	744	98,456
Number of students	292,277	50,327,015
Number of teachers	15,656	3,151,497
Student-teacher ratio	18.7	16.0
Expenditures per student (dollars), 2014-2015..	6,929	11,445
Four-year adjusted cohort graduation rate (ACGR)[1,2]	79.7	84.1
Students eligible for free or reduced-price lunch (percent), 2014-2015........................	48.5	51.8
English language learners (percent), Fall 2015	4.6	9.5
Students age 3 to 21 served under IDEA, part B (percent)....................................	10.2	13.2

Public Schools by Type	Number	Percent of state public schools
Total number of schools..	744	100.0
Regular	635	85.3
Special education...	18	2.4
Vocational education..	14	1.9
Alternative education...	77	10.3

NOTE: Every school is assigned only one school type based on its instructional emphasis.
[1] ACGR data represents a new method of calculating high-school completion rates and may not be comparable to previous years' data for Averaged Freshmen Graduation Rates (AFGR).
[2] The United States 4-year ACGRs were estimated using both the reported 4-year ACGR data from 49 states and the District of Columbia and using imputed data for Idaho. The estimate for American Indian/Alaska Native students also includes imputed data for Virginia.
NA = Not available.

Table ID-13. Reported Voting and Registration of the Voting-Age Population, November 2016

(Numbers in thousands, percent.)

Item	Total population	Total citizen population	Registered			Voted		
			Total registered	Percent registered (total population)	Percent registered (total citizen population)	Total voted	Percent voted (total population)	Percent voted (total citizen population)
U.S. Total	245,502	224,059	157,596	64.2	70.3	137,537	56.0	61.4
State Total..............................	1,224	1,150	790	64.5	68.7	714	58.3	62.1
Sex								
Male	607	571	386	63.5	67.5	346	57.0	60.6
Female	618	579	404	65.4	69.8	368	59.5	63.5
Race								
White alone................................	1,151	1,095	757	65.8	69.1	687	59.7	62.8
White, non-Hispanic alone	1,002	994	711	70.9	71.5	647	64.6	65.1
Black alone.................................	6	5	3	(B)	(B)	2	(B)	(B)
Asian alone	27	12	7	(B)	(B)	6	(B)	(B)
Hispanic (of any race).....................	163	114	55	33.5	48.0	49	29.9	42.9
White alone or in combination	1,175	1,118	770	65.5	68.9	698	59.3	62.4
Black alone or in combination............	8	7	3	(B)	(B)	2	(B)	(B)
Asian alone or in combination............	31	14	9	(B)	(B)	8	(B)	(B)
Age								
18 to 24 years.............................	166	153	79	47.4	51.7	68	40.7	44.3
25 to 34 years.............................	217	198	116	53.5	58.8	102	46.8	51.4
35 to 44 years.............................	187	172	109	58.3	63.6	96	51.1	55.7
45 to 64 years.............................	381	357	265	69.5	74.1	247	64.8	69.1
65 years and over	272	270	220	80.9	81.5	202	74.1	74.7

- = Zero or rounds to zero.
B = Base is less than 75,000 and therefore too small to show the derived measure.

Table ID-14. Crime

(Number, rate per 100,000. Data are derived from the FBI Uniform Crime Reports.)

Item	State			U.S. [1,2,3,4]		
	2015	2016	Percent change	2015	2016	Percent change
TOTAL POPULATION [5]	1,654,930	1,683,140	1.7	321,418,820	323,127,513	0.5
VIOLENT CRIME						
Number..	3,568	3,876	8.6	1,231,566	1,248,185	1.3
Rate...	215.6	230.3	6.8	383.2	386.3	0.8
Murder and Nonnegligent Manslaughter						
Number..	32	49	53.1	15,696	17,250	9.9
Rate	1.9	2.9	52.6	4.9	5.3	8.2
Rape [6]						
Number..	694	719	3.6	124,047	130,603	5.3
Rate	41.9	42.7	1.9	38.6	40.4	4.7
Robbery						
Number..	192	213	10.9	327,374	332,198	1.5
Rate	11.6	12.7	9.5	101.9	102.8	0.9
Aggravated Assault						
Number..	2,650	2,895	9.2	764,449	803,007	5.0
Rate	160.1	172.0	7.4	237.8	248.5	4.5
PROPERTY CRIME						
Number..	28,858	29,357	1.7	7,993,631	7,919,035	-0.9
Rate	1,743.8	1,744.2	-	2,487.0	2,450.7	-1.5
Burglary						
Number..	6,124	6,318	3.2	1,579,527	1,515,096	-4.1
Rate	370.0	375.4	1.5	491.4	468.9	-4.6
Larceny-Theft						
Number..	20,863	20,962	0.5	5,706,346	5,638,455	-1.2
Rate	1,260.7	1,245.4	-1.2	1,775.4	1,745.0	-1.7
Motor Vehicle Theft						
Number..	1,871	2,077	11.0	707,758	765,484	8.2
Rate	113.1	123.4	9.1	220.2	236.9	7.6

NOTE: Although arson data are included in the trend and clearance tables, sufficient data are not available to estimate totals for this offense. Therefore, no arson data are published in this table.
X = Not applicable.
- = Zero or rounds to zero.
[1] The crime figures have been adjusted.
[2] The data collection methodology for the offense of forcible rape used by the Minnesota state Uniform Crime Reporting (UCR) Program (with the exception of Minneapolis and St. Paul, Minnesota) does not comply with national UCR Program guidelines. Consequently, its figures for forcible rape and violent crime (of which forcible rape is a part) are not published in this table.
[3] Includes offenses reported by the Zoological Police and the Metro Transit Police.
[4] Because of changes in the state's reporting practices, figures are not comparable to previous years' data.
[5] Populations are U.S. Census Bureau provisional estimates as of July 1 of each year.
[6] The figures shown for the offense of rape were estimated using the revised Uniform Crime Reporting (UCR) definition of rape.

Table ID-15. State Government Finances, 2016

(Dollar amounts in thousands, percent distribution.)

Item	Dollars	Percent distribution
Total Revenue	9,405,581	100.0
General revenue	8,154,365	86.7
Intergovernmental revenue	2,721,813	28.9
Taxes	4,209,359	44.8
General sales	1,559,332	16.6
Selective sales	561,607	6.0
License taxes	372,883	4.0
Individual income tax	1,521,238	16.2
Corporate income tax	188,996	2.0
Other taxes	5,303	0.1
Current charges	771,231	8.2
Miscellaneous general revenue	451,962	4.8
Utility revenue	0	-
Liquor stores revenue	155,416	1.7
Insurance trust revenue [1]	1,095,800	11.7
Total Expenditure	9,377,948	100.0
Intergovernmental expenditure	2,278,174	24.3
Direct expenditure	7,099,774	75.7
Current operation	5,167,498	55.1
Capital outlay	486,367	5.2
Insurance benefits and repayments	1,113,302	11.9
Assistance and subsidies	177,837	1.9
Interest on debt	154,770	1.7
Exhibit: Salaries and wages	1,422,187	15.2
Total Expenditure	9,377,948	100.0
General expenditure	8,144,579	86.8
Intergovernmental expenditure	2,278,174	24.3
Direct expenditure	5,866,405	62.6
General expenditure, by function:		
Education	3,042,233	32.4
Public welfare	2,461,021	26.2
Hospitals	47,715	0.5
Health	152,781	1.6
Highways	682,385	7.3
Police protection	64,660	0.7
Correction	266,752	2.8
Natural resources	237,985	2.5
Parks and recreation	35,297	0.4
Governmental administration	309,364	4.2
Interest on general debt	154,770	1.7
Other and unallocable	609,616	6.5
Utility expenditure	0	-
Liquor stores expenditure	120,067	1.3
Insurance trust expenditure	1,113,302	11.9
Debt at End of Fiscal Year	3,542,856	X
Cash and Security Holdings	23,793,309	X

X = Not applicable.
- = Zero or rounds to zero.
[1] Within insurance trust revenue, net earnings of state retirement systems is a calculated statistic (the item code in the data file is X08), and thus can be positive or negative. Net earnings is the sum of earnings on investments plus gains on investments minus losses on investments. The change made in 2002 for asset valuation from book to market value in accordance with Statement 34 of the Governmental Accounting Standards Board is reflected in the calculated statistics.

Table ID-16. State Government Tax Collections, 2017

(Dollars in thousands, percent.)

Item	Dollars	Percent distribution
Total Taxes	4,511,208	100.0
Property taxes	X	-
Sales and gross receipts	2,245,356	49.8
General sales and gross receipts	1,650,498	36.6
Selective sales and gross receipts	594,858	13.2
Alcoholic beverages	9,468	0.2
Amusements	X	-
Insurance premiums	91,985	2.0
Motor fuels	353,548	7.8
Pari-mutuels	637	-
Public utilities	15,752	0.3
Tobacco products	50,883	1.1
Other selective sales	72,585	1.6
Licenses	383,702	8.5
Alcoholic beverages	1,878	-
Amusements	260	-
Corporations in general	2,693	0.1
Hunting and fishing	42,886	1.0
Motor vehicle	187,156	4.1
Motor vehicle operators	11,460	0.3
Public utilities	54,947	1.2
Occupation and business, NEC	78,716	1.7
Other licenses	3,706	0.1
Income taxes	1,876,889	41.6
Individual income	1,660,248	36.8
Corporation net income	216,641	4.8
Other taxes	5,261	0.1
Death and gift	X	-
Documentary and stock transfer	X	-
Severance	5,261	0.1
Taxes, NEC	0	-

X = Not applicable.
- = Zero or rounds to zero.

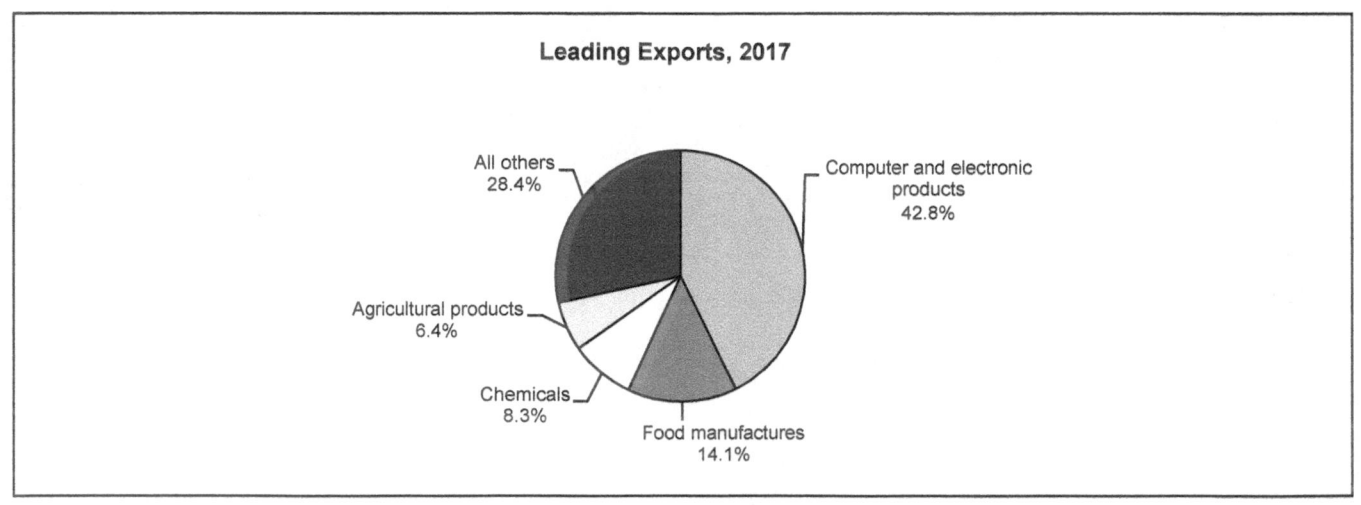

Leading Exports, 2017

All others 28.4%
Computer and electronic products 42.8%
Agricultural products 6.4%
Chemicals 8.3%
Food manufactures 14.1%

Facts and Figures

Location: North central United States; bordered on the N by Wisconsin, on the E by Lake Michigan and Indiana, on the S by Kentucky, and on the W by Iowa and Missouri

Area: 57,913 sq. mi. (149,998 sq. km.); rank—25th

Population: 12,802,023 (2017 est.); rank—6th

Principal Cities: capital—Springfield; largest—Chicago

Statehood: December 3, 1818; 21st state

U.S. Congress: 2 senators, 18 representatives

State Motto: State Sovereignty, National Union

State Song: "Illinois"

State Nicknames: The Prairie State; The Land of Lincoln

Abbreviations: IL; Ill.

State Symbols: flower—native violet; tree—white oak; bird—cardinal

At a Glance

- Illinois was one of three states that experienced a population decline between 2010 and 2017, with a decrease in population of 0.3 percent.

- In 2016, Illinois employed 9.7 state government employees per 1,000 residents, which was the 4th lowest ratio in the country.

- The violent crime rate in Illinois rose to 436.3 per 100,000 residents in 2016, compared to the 2015 rate of 383.8 per 100,000 population.

- Illinois ranked 17th for median household income in 2016, with an income of $60,960.

- In 2016, 6.5 percent of Illinois residents did not have health insurance, compared to 8.6 percent of the entire U.S. population.

Table IL-1. Population by Age, Sex, Race, and Hispanic Origin

(Number, percent, except where noted.)

Sex, age, race, and Hispanic origin	2000	2010	2017 [1]	Average annual percent change, 2010–2017
Total Population...	12,419,293	12,830,632	12,802,023	-0.2
Percent of total U.S. population	4.4	4.2	3.9	X
Sex				
Male..	6,080,336	6,292,276	6,292,478	0.0
Female	6,338,957	6,538,356	6,509,545	-0.4
Age				
Under 5 years..	876,549	835,557	773,049	-7.5
5 to 19 years...	2,728,957	2,660,945	2,452,880	-7.8
20 to 64 years...	7,313,762	7,724,917	7,630,696	-1.2
65 years and over	1,500,025	1,609,213	1,945,398	20.9
Median age (years)	34.7	36.6	38.1	4.1
Race and Hispanic Origin				
One race				
White	9,125,471	10,030,587	9,864,942	-1.7
Black..	1,878,875	1,903,458	1,872,275	-1.6
American Indian and Alaska Native	31,006	73,486	75,867	3.2
Asian..	423,603	604,399	729,694	20.7
Native Hawaiian or Other Pacific Islander	4,610	7,436	8,374	12.6
Two or more races	235,016	210,906	250,871	18.9
Hispanic (of any race)...	1,530,262	2,073,054	2,209,337	6.6

X = Not applicable.
[1] Population figures for 2017 are July 1 estimates. The 2010 estimates are taken from the 2010 Census.
- = Zero or rounds to zero.

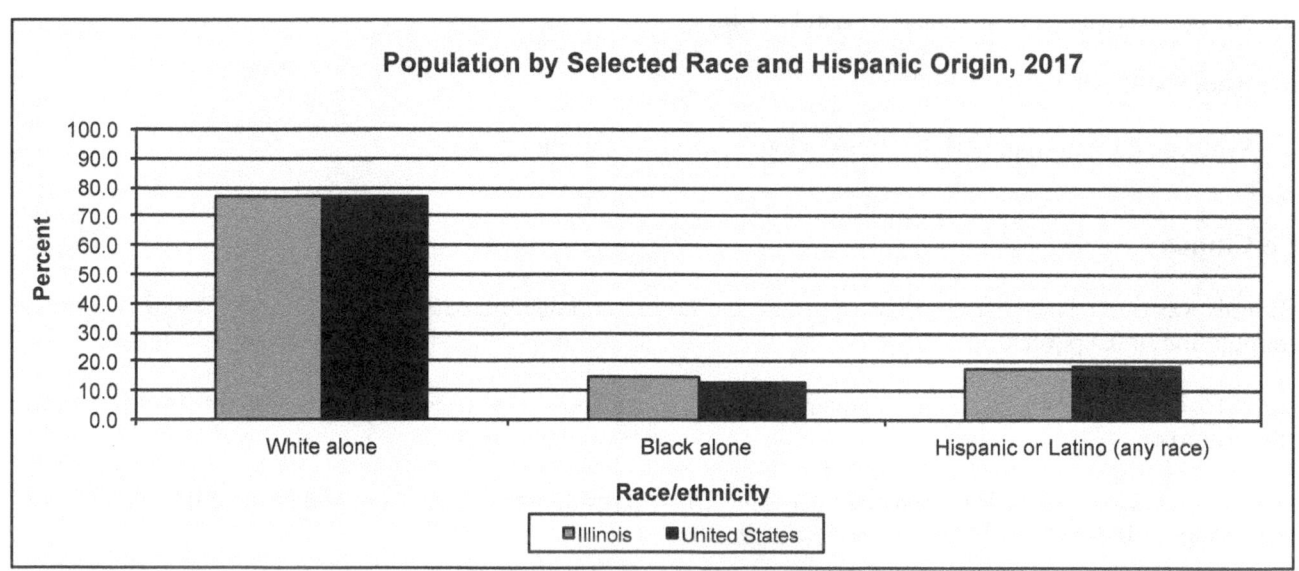

Population by Selected Race and Hispanic Origin, 2017

Table IL-2. Marital Status

(Number, percent distribution.)

Sex, age, and marital status	2000	2010	2016
Males, 15 Years and Over	4,685,982	4,977,964	5,056,969
Never married	31.9	37.2	38.4
Now married, except separated......................................	56.1	50.0	48.9
Separated..	1.6	1.4	1.4
Widowed..	2.5	2.6	2.7
Divorced..	7.9	8.8	8.7
Females, 15 Years and Over	5,021,855	5,289,803	5,337,098
Never married	26.1	31.1	32.7
Now married, except separated......................................	51.3	46.3	45.3
Separated..	2.0	2.1	1.9
Widowed..	10.7	9.5	8.9
Divorced..	9.9	11.0	11.2

Table IL-3. Households and Housing Characteristics

(Number, percent, dollars.)

Item	2000	2010	2016	Average annual percent change, 2010–2016
Total Households	4,591,779	4,752,857	4,822,046	0.2
Family households	3,105,513	3,133,813	3,100,613	-0.2
Married-couple family	2,353,892	2,301,009	2,266,786	-0.2
Other family	751,621	832,804	833,827	-
Male householder, no wife present	187,903	220,197	224,158	0.3
Female householder, no husband present	563,718	612,607	609,669	-0.1
Nonfamily households	1,486,266	1,619,044	1,721,433	1.1
Householder living alone	1,229,807	1,340,394	1,425,675	1.1
Householder not living alone	256,459	278,650	295,758	1.0
Housing Characteristics				
Total housing units	4,885,615	5,297,077	5,327,165	0.1
Occupied housing units	4,591,779	4,752,857	4,822,046	0.2
Owner occupied	3,088,884	3,219,338	3,146,858	-0.4
Renter occupied	1,502,895	1,533,519	1,675,188	1.5
Average household size	2.63	2.64	2.59	-0.3
Financial Characteristics				
Median gross rent of renter-occupied housing	605	848	950	2.0
Median monthly owner costs for housing units with a mortgage	1,198	1,655	1,588	-0.7
Median value of owner-occupied housing units	130,800	191,800	186,500	-0.5

- = Zero or rounds to zero.

Table IL-4. Migration, Origin, and Language

(Number, percent.)

Characteristic	State			U.S.		
	2015	2016	Percent change	2015	2016	Percent change
Residence 1 Year Ago						
Population 1 year and over	12,706,393	12,654,142	-0.4	317,635,720	319,361,956	0.5
Same house	86.8	86.9	X	85.3	85.4	X
Different house in the U.S.	12.7	12.6	X	14.1	13.9	X
Same county	8.4	8.3	X	8.5	8.3	X
Different county	4.2	4.2	X	5.6	5.6	X
Same state	2.6	2.6	X	3.2	3.2	X
Different state	1.7	1.6	X	2.4	2.4	X
Abroad	0.5	0.5	X	0.7	0.7	X
Place of Birth						
Native born	11,033,839	11,018,065	-0.1	278,128,449	279,388,170	0.5
Male	49.0	49.0	X	49.3	49.3	X
Female	51.0	51.0	X	50.7	50.7	X
Foreign born	1,826,156	1,783,474	-2.3	43,290,372	43,739,345	1.0
Male	49.8	50.1	X	48.6	48.5	X
Female	50.2	49.9	X	51.4	51.5	X
Foreign born; naturalized U.S. citizen	880,242	883,621	0.4	20,697,103	21,238,372	2.6
Male	47.6	47.6	X	45.9	45.9	X
Female	52.4	52.4	X	54.1	54.1	X
Foreign born; not a U.S. citizen	945,914	899,853	-4.9	22,593,269	22,500,973	-0.4
Male	51.8	52.5	X	51.1	51.0	X
Female	48.2	47.5	X	48.9	49.0	X
Entered 2010 or later	13.0	15.4	X	15.6	18.6	X
Entered 2000 to 2009	27.4	25.7	X	27.9	26.7	X
Entered before 2000	59.6	58.9	X	56.5	54.7	X
World Region of Birth, Foreign						
Foreign-born population, excluding population born at sea	1,826,156	1,783,474	-2.3	43,289,646	43,738,901	1.0
Europe	20.0	20.7	X	11.1	10.9	X
Asia	29.2	30.0	X	30.6	30.8	X
Africa	4.0	3.5	X	4.8	4.9	X
Oceania	0.2	0.3	X	0.6	0.6	X
Latin America	45.7	44.6	X	51.1	51.0	X
North America	1.0	0.9	X	1.9	1.8	X
Language Spoken at Home and Ability to Speak English						
Population 5 years and over	12,080,329	12,032,049	-0.4	301,625,014	303,328,961	0.6
English only	77.0	77.1	X	78.5	78.4	X
Language other than English	23.0	22.9	X	21.5	21.6	X
Speaks English less than "very well"	9.0	8.7	X	8.6	8.6	X

NA = Not available.
X = Not applicable.
- = Zero or rounds to zero.

Table IL-5. Median Income and Poverty Status, 2016

(Number, percent, except as noted.)

Characteristic	State		U.S.	
	Number	Percent	Number	Percent
Median Income				
Households (dollars)...	60,960	X	57,617	X
Families (dollars)	76,950	X	71,062	X
Below Poverty Level (All People)	1,621,508	13.0	44,268,996	14.0
Sex				
Male	711,436	11.6	19,760,056	12.8
Female	910,072	14.2	24,508,940	15.2
Age				
Under 18 years...	511,679	17.7	14,115,713	19.5
Related children under 18 years	501,827	17.5	13,805,435	19.1
18 to 64 years...	943,685	12.1	25,723,818	13.2
65 years and over	166,144	9.2	4,429,465	9.2

X = Not applicable.

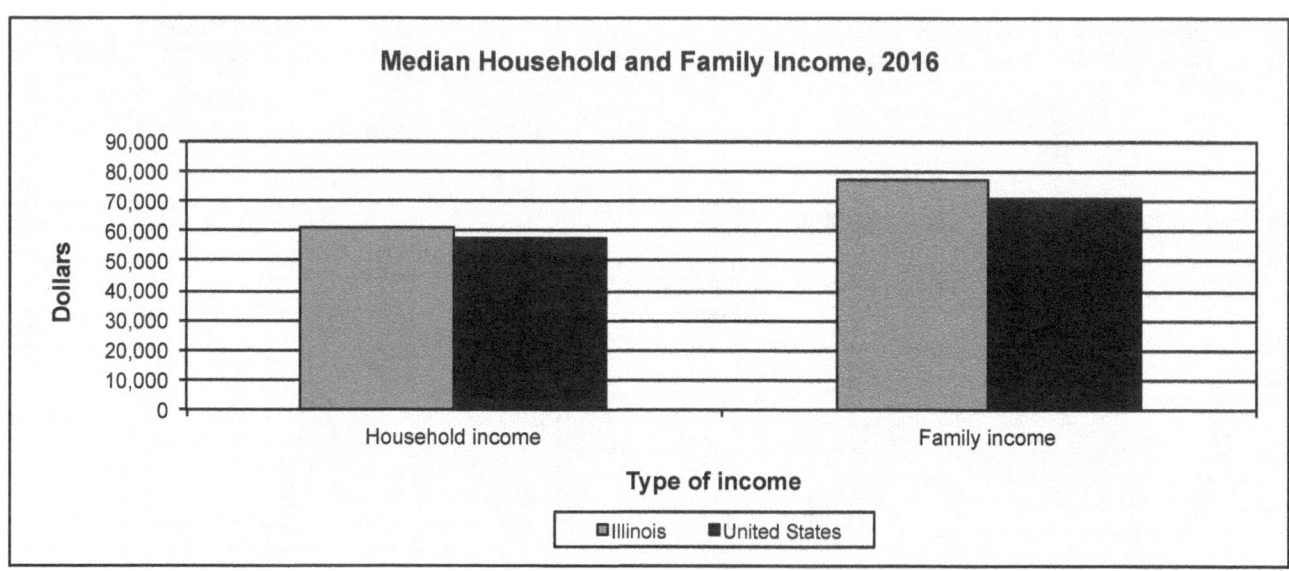

Table IL-6. Health Insurance Coverage Status for the Civilian Noninstitutionalized Population and Children Under 18 Years of Age

(Number, percent.)

Item	2008	2009	2010	2011	2012	2013	2014	2015	2016
Civilian Noninstitutionalized Population	12,709,312	12,719,575	12,673,245	12,688,006	12,698,371	12,704,616	12,702,393	12,679,860	12,620,388
Covered by Private or Public Insurance									
Number..	11,085,984	11,025,183	10,927,689	11,028,731	11,075,906	11,086,412	11,464,467	11,779,571	11,803,786
Percent...	87.2	86.7	86.2	86.9	87.2	87.3	90.3	92.9	93.5
Not Covered									
Number..	1,623,328	1,694,392	1,745,556	1,659,275	1,622,465	1,618,204	1,237,926	900,289	816,602
Percent...	12.8	13.3	13.8	13.1	12.8	12.7	9.7	7.1	6.5
Percent in the U.S. not covered..	15.1	15.1	15.5	15.1	14.8	14.5	11.7	9.4	8.6
Children Under 18 Years of Age	3,175,518	3,168,258	3,121,719	3,091,887	3,059,055	3,017,960	2,980,902	2,956,262	2,919,863
Covered by Private or Public Insurance									
Number..	2,996,660	3,025,989	2,981,614	2,978,576	2,957,589	2,892,609	2,881,400	2,880,990	2,848,544
Percent...	94.4	95.5	95.5	96.3	96.7	95.8	96.7	97.5	97.6
Not Covered									
Number..	178,858	142,269	140,105	113,311	101,466	125,351	99,502	75,272	71,319
Percent...	5.6	4.5	4.5	3.7	3.3	4.2	3.3	2.5	2.4
Percent in the U.S. not covered..	9.9	8.6	8.0	7.5	7.2	7.1	6.0	4.8	4.5

Table IL-7. Employment Status by Demographic Group, 2017

(Numbers in thousands, percent.)

Characteristic	Civilian noninstitutional population	Civilian labor force		Employed		Unemployed	
		Number	Percent of population	Number	Percent of population	Number	Percent of population
Total...	10,036	6,455	64.3	6,142	61.2	313	4.9
Sex							
Male...	4,850	3,398	70.1	3,229	66.6	169	5.0
Female...	5,187	3,057	58.9	2,913	56.2	144	4.7
Race, Sex, and Hispanic Origin							
White...	7,834	5,144	65.7	4,924	62.9	220	4.3
Male..	3,858	2,776	72.0	2,656	68.8	120	4.3
Female...	3,976	2,368	59.6	2,268	57.0	100	4.2
Black or African American.........................	1,407	799	56.8	728	51.7	71	8.9
Male..	629	365	58.0	325	51.7	40	10.9
Female...	778	434	55.7	403	51.7	31	7.2
Hispanic or Latino ethnicity[1]	1,495	1,055	70.5	1,003	67.1	52	4.9
Male..	753	595	79.0	568	75.4	27	4.6
Female...	742	459	61.9	435	58.6	25	5.4
Age							
16 to 19 years..	664	240	36.1	203	30.6	37	15.5
20 to 24 years..	866	614	70.9	562	64.9	52	8.5
25 to 34 years..	1,723	1,434	83.2	1,371	79.5	64	4.4
35 to 44 years..	1,592	1,313	82.5	1,254	78.8	59	4.5
45 to 54 years..	1,673	1,374	82.1	1,320	78.9	54	3.9
55 to 64 years..	1,664	1,103	66.3	1,067	64.1	36	3.3
65 years and over	1,854	377	20.3	366	19.7	12	3.1

NOTE: Data in Table 7 are from the Current Population Survey (CPS) and do not match the estimates in Table 8. See notes and definitions for further information.
[1] May be of any race.

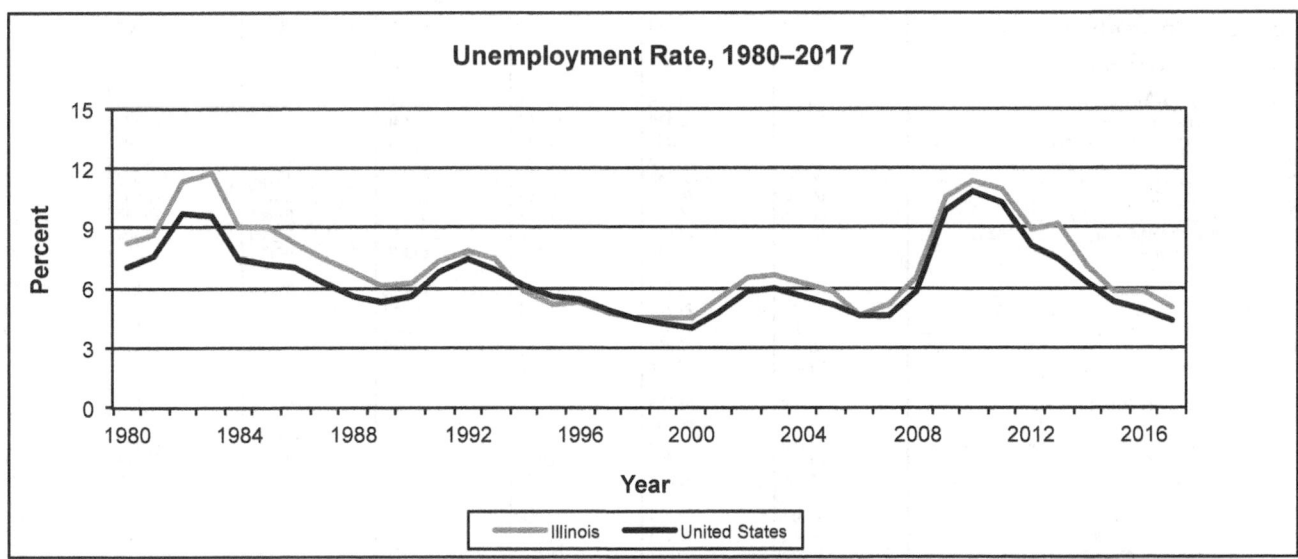

Unemployment Rate, 1980–2017

Table IL-8. Employment Status of the Civilian Noninstitutional Population Age 16 Years and Over

(Number, percent.)

Year	Civilian labor force	Civilian participation rate	Employed	Unemployed	Unemployment rate
2009..	6,618,658	67.0	5,943,229	675,429	10.2
2010..	6,625,321	66.9	5,937,047	688,274	10.4
2011..	6,586,893	66.2	5,948,366	638,527	9.7
2012..	6,581,867	65.9	5,990,644	591,223	9.0
2013..	6,549,473	65.3	5,956,749	592,724	9.0
2014..	6,508,356	64.8	6,047,243	461,113	7.1
2015..	6,507,228	64.7	6,119,271	387,957	6.0
2016..	6,549,991	65.1	6,169,560	380,431	5.8
2017..	6,492,578	64.5	6,170,676	321,902	5.0

Table IL-9. Employment and Average Wages by Industry

(Estimates through 2010 are based on the 2007 *North American Industry Classification System* [NAICS]. Estimates from 2011 onward are based on the 2012 NAICS.)

Industry	2010	2011	2012	2013	2014	2015	2016
	Number of Jobs						
Wage and Salary Employment by Industry	5,795,826	5,858,922	5,926,484	5,968,301	6,047,821	6,139,938	6,178,249
Farm Wage and Salary Employment	17,706	16,970	15,801	12,669	11,709	14,742	14,215
Nonfarm Wage and Salary Employment	5,778,120	5,841,952	5,910,683	5,955,632	6,036,112	6,125,196	6,164,034
Private wage and salary employment	4,870,773	4,950,824	5,029,034	5,078,294	5,160,976	5,249,182	5,294,581
Forestry, fishing, and related activities	4,187	4,305	4,637	4,828	5,940	5,460	5,509
Mining	9,047	9,498	10,089	9,648	9,860	9,285	7,947
Utilities	23,182	23,524	23,858	23,795	24,016	24,180	24,337
Construction	205,752	202,070	194,794	196,931	207,330	218,857	224,570
Manufacturing	561,451	574,733	583,781	580,229	580,253	582,140	575,262
Durable goods manufacturing	329,581	343,627	354,546	350,849	349,854	348,495	338,331
Nondurable goods manufacturing	231,870	231,106	229,235	229,380	230,399	233,645	236,931
Wholesale trade	287,678	290,917	295,669	300,143	301,559	303,215	303,592
Retail trade	593,731	601,359	602,374	603,976	610,071	619,647	623,510
Transportation and warehousing	229,360	238,197	243,762	244,833	250,554	259,682	263,874
Information	101,711	100,348	100,489	98,983	99,399	101,054	99,831
Finance and insurance	292,989	291,710	294,508	293,630	292,479	300,759	301,305
Real estate and rental and leasing	74,360	73,522	73,672	75,540	76,839	78,947	81,184
Professional, scientific, and technical services	348,798	358,053	367,039	379,480	390,983	405,554	413,416
Management of companies and enterprises	96,403	98,255	102,790	103,688	103,297	94,759	94,772
Administrative and waste services	364,158	382,452	401,441	412,508	428,650	428,916	431,422
Educational services	158,223	162,030	165,375	166,547	167,059	168,528	171,491
Health care and social assistance	699,865	708,915	720,569	730,867	740,058	757,812	766,324
Arts, entertainment, and recreation	77,506	77,620	79,972	80,931	82,972	85,267	89,637
Accommodation and food services	441,380	448,443	459,908	469,331	477,937	495,503	511,541
Other services, except public administration	300,992	304,873	304,307	302,406	311,720	309,617	305,057
Government and government enterprises	907,347	891,128	881,649	877,338	875,136	876,014	869,453
	Dollars						
Average Wages and Salaries by Industry	50,214	51,719	53,124	53,651	55,136	57,037	58,804
Average Farm Wages and Salaries	23,773	31,982	27,940	31,522	36,652	36,745	37,041
Average Nonfarm Wages and Salaries	50,295	51,776	53,191	53,698	55,172	57,086	58,854
Average private wages and salaries	50,613	52,178	53,603	54,040	55,695	57,774	59,664
Forestry, fishing, and related activities	27,859	28,307	28,371	27,438	30,260	32,698	37,909
Mining	68,107	66,405	67,927	70,891	74,215	75,831	74,399
Utilities	98,277	104,545	107,866	106,962	113,082	115,572	121,111
Construction	59,898	60,772	61,298	62,924	65,725	68,697	70,415
Manufacturing	60,955	62,988	64,772	65,369	67,861	70,347	71,501
Durable goods manufacturing	61,536	64,508	65,749	65,710	67,120	68,409	70,418
Nondurable goods manufacturing	60,129	60,728	63,260	64,848	68,985	73,237	73,047
Wholesale trade	69,330	73,174	75,592	75,662	78,004	80,377	83,088
Retail trade	27,210	27,773	28,484	28,859	29,263	30,409	31,100
Transportation and warehousing	48,839	50,422	51,983	52,851	54,580	55,882	58,889
Information	68,659	72,819	74,851	77,546	79,787	82,938	81,670
Finance and insurance	91,325	97,207	101,064	99,776	105,519	110,710	115,115
Real estate and rental and leasing	51,686	53,536	56,404	58,405	61,017	65,003	68,484
Professional, scientific, and technical services	84,155	86,163	88,889	89,192	91,922	95,756	98,876
Management of companies and enterprises	114,260	117,316	121,284	123,511	124,622	129,847	129,771
Administrative and waste services	34,729	34,896	35,554	35,255	36,705	38,879	41,218
Educational services	41,109	42,572	43,244	44,132	45,336	46,182	46,268
Health care and social assistance	44,581	45,333	45,952	46,436	47,402	48,576	51,165
Arts, entertainment, and recreation	34,647	35,643	37,029	36,957	36,451	38,791	40,666
Accommodation and food services	19,335	20,021	20,802	21,150	21,632	22,786	24,109
Other services, except public administration	33,681	34,527	34,999	35,986	37,579	38,943	41,204
Government and government enterprises	48,593	49,544	50,844	51,720	52,088	52,967	53,922

Table IL-10. Employment Characteristics by Family Type

(Number, percent.)

Family type and labor force status	2014		2015		2016	
	Total	Families with own children under 18 years	Total	Families with own children under 18 years	Total	Families with own children under 18 years
All Families..	3,086,335	1,350,738	3,099,463	1,348,476	3,100,613	1,342,579
FAMILY TYPE AND LABOR FORCE STATUS						
Married-Couple Families..............................	2,256,449	926,959	2,285,540	929,523	2,266,786	911,333
Both husband and wife in labor force...........................	54.3	67.1	53.3	66.4	54.1	68.5
Husband in labor force, wife not in labor force	22.1	28.1	22.2	28.6	20.9	26.3
Wife in labor force, husband not in labor force	7.7	3.6	7.6	3.3	7.6	3.7
Both husband and wife not in labor force................	15.9	1.3	16.2	1.4	16.6	1.1
Other Families	829,886	423,779	813,923	418,953	833,827	431,246
Female householder, no husband present........................	72.6	76.4	73.7	77.0	73.1	75.5
In labor force..	51.9	64.0	53.1	65.5	53.0	64.5
Not in labor force....................................	20.6	12.5	20.6	11.5	20.2	11.0
Male householder, no wife present........................	27.4	23.6	26.3	23.0	26.9	24.5
In labor force..	21.6	21.7	20.8	21.5	21.4	22.6
Not in labor force....................................	5.9	1.9	5.5	1.4	5.5	2.0

Table IL-11. School Enrollment and Educational Attainment, 2016

(Number, percent.)

Item	State	U.S.
Enrollment		
Total population 3 years and over, enrolled in school	3,286,606	81,572,277
Enrolled in nursery school or preschool (percent)........................	6.8	6.0
Enrolled in kindergarten (percent)........................	4.9	5.0
Enrolled in elementary school, grades 1-8 (percent)........................	39.9	40.3
Enrolled in high school, grades 9-12 (percent)	21.1	21.0
Enrolled in college or graduate school (percent)........................	27.3	27.7
Attainment		
Total population 25 years and over	8,665,219	218,475,480
Less than ninth grade (percent)	5.0	5.4
9th to 12th grade, no diploma (percent)	6.2	7.2
High school graduate, including equivalency (percent)........................	26.0	27.2
Some college, no degree (percent)	21.0	20.6
Associate's degree (percent)........................	7.9	8.4
Bachelor's degree (percent)........................	20.9	19.3
Graduate or professional degree (percent)........................	13.0	11.9
High school graduate or higher (percent)	88.8	87.5
Bachelor's degree or higher (percent)........................	34.0	31.3

Table IL-12. Public School Characteristics and Educational Indicators

(Number, percent; data derived from National Center of Education Statistics.)

Item	State	U.S.
Public Schools, 2015–2016 (except where noted)		
Number of school districts....................	1,052	18,328
Number of schools....................	4,175	98,456
Number of students....................	2,041,779	50,327,015
Number of teachers....................	129,948	3,151,497
Student-teacher ratio....................	15.7	16.0
Expenditures per student (dollars), 2014-2015....................	13,935	11,445
Four-year adjusted cohort graduation rate (ACGR)[1,2]	85.5	84.1
Students eligible for free or reduced-price lunch (percent), 2014-2015....................	54.1	51.8
English language learners (percent), Fall 2015	9.5	9.5
Students age 3 to 21 served under IDEA, part B (percent)....................	14.5	13.2

Public Schools by Type	Number	Percent of state public schools
Total number of schools....................	4,175	100.0
Regular	3,929	94.1
Special education....................	108	2.6
Vocational education....................	0	-
Alternative education....................	138	3.3

NOTE: Every school is assigned only one school type based on its instructional emphasis.
[1] ACGR data represents a new method of calculating high-school completion rates and may not be comparable to previous years' data for Averaged Freshmen Graduation Rates (AFGR).
[2] The United States 4-year ACGRs were estimated using both the reported 4-year ACGR data from 49 states and the District of Columbia and using imputed data for Idaho. The estimate for American Indian/Alaska Native students also includes imputed data for Virginia.

Table IL-13. Reported Voting and Registration of the Voting-Age Population, November 2016

(Numbers in thousands, percent.)

Item	Total population	Total citizen population	Registered			Voted		
			Total registered	Percent registered (total population)	Percent registered (total citizen population)	Total voted	Percent voted (total population)	Percent voted (total citizen population)
U.S. Total	245,502	224,059	157,596	64.2	70.3	137,537	56.0	61.4
State Total.............................	9,723	8,970	6,665	68.5	74.3	5,719	58.8	63.8
Sex								
Male	4,692	4,307	3,174	67.7	73.7	2,673	57.0	62.1
Female	5,031	4,663	3,490	69.4	74.9	3,046	60.6	65.3
Race								
White alone...........................	7,647	7,100	5,391	70.5	75.9	4,636	60.6	65.3
White, non-Hispanic alone	6,297	6,153	4,839	76.8	78.6	4,174	66.3	67.8
Black alone...........................	1,358	1,321	932	68.6	70.6	776	57.1	58.7
Asian alone...........................	542	391	231	42.5	58.9	200	37.0	51.3
Hispanic (of any race).................	1,490	1,073	634	42.5	59.1	527	35.4	49.2
White alone or in combination	7,711	7,165	5,438	70.5	75.9	4,679	60.7	65.3
Black alone or in combination	1,390	1,353	963	69.3	71.2	807	58.1	59.7
Asian alone or in combination...........	563	408	244	43.3	59.7	214	37.9	52.4
Age								
18 to 24 years......................	1,330	1,287	802	60.3	62.3	603	45.3	46.8
25 to 34 years......................	1,664	1,460	975	58.6	66.8	795	47.8	54.5
35 to 44 years......................	1,527	1,331	996	65.3	74.8	811	53.1	60.9
45 to 64 years......................	3,456	3,202	2,539	73.5	79.3	2,272	65.8	71.0
65 years and over	1,746	1,690	1,352	77.4	80.0	1,237	70.9	73.2

Table IL-14. Crime

(Number, rate per 100,000. Data are derived from the FBI Uniform Crime Reports.)

Item	State			U.S. [1,2,3,4]		
	2015	2016	Percent change	2015	2016	Percent change
TOTAL POPULATION [5]	12,859,995	12,801,539	-0.5	321,418,820	323,127,513	0.5
VIOLENT CRIME						
Number...	49,354	55,854	13.2	1,231,566	1,248,185	1.3
Rate...	383.8	436.3	13.7	383.2	386.3	0.8
Murder and Nonnegligent Manslaughter						
Number...	744	1,054	41.7	15,696	17,250	9.9
Rate...	5.8	8.2	41.4	4.9	5.3	8.2
Rape [6]						
Number...	4,821	4,908	1.8	124,047	130,603	5.3
Rate...	37.5	38.3	2.1	38.6	40.4	4.7
Robbery						
Number...	14,910	17,827	19.6	327,374	332,198	1.5
Rate...	115.9	139.3	20.2	101.9	102.8	0.9
Aggravated Assault						
Number...	28,879	32,065	11.0	764,449	803,007	5.0
Rate...	224.6	250.5	11.5	237.8	248.5	4.5
PROPERTY CRIME						
Number...	255,729	262,306	2.6	7,993,631	7,919,035	-0.9
Rate...	1,988.6	2,049.0	3.0	2,487.0	2,450.7	-1.5
Burglary						
Number...	46,443	47,989	3.3	1,579,527	1,515,096	-4.1
Rate...	361.1	374.9	3.8	491.4	468.9	-4.6
Larceny-Theft						
Number...	191,634	194,407	1.4	5,706,346	5,638,455	-1.2
Rate...	1,490.2	1,518.6	1.9	1,775.4	1,745.0	-1.7
Motor Vehicle Theft						
Number...	17,652	19,910	12.8	707,758	765,484	8.2
Rate...	137.3	155.5	13.3	220.2	236.9	7.6

NOTE: Although arson data are included in the trend and clearance tables, sufficient data are not available to estimate totals for this offense. Therefore, no arson data are published in this table.

X = Not applicable.

- = Zero or rounds to zero.

[1] The crime figures have been adjusted.

[2] The data collection methodology for the offense of forcible rape used by the Minnesota state Uniform Crime Reporting (UCR) Program (with the exception of Minneapolis and St. Paul, Minnesota) does not comply with national UCR Program guidelines. Consequently, its figures for forcible rape and violent crime (of which forcible rape is a part) are not published in this table.

[3] Includes offenses reported by the Zoological Police and the Metro Transit Police.

[4] Because of changes in the state's reporting practices, figures are not comparable to previous years' data.

[5] Populations are U.S. Census Bureau provisional estimates as of July 1 of each year.

[6] The figures shown for the offense of rape were estimated using the revised Uniform Crime Reporting (UCR) definition of rape.

Table IL-15. State Government Finances, 2016

(Dollar amounts in thousands, percent distribution.)

Item	Dollars	Percent distribution
Total Revenue	75,492,133	100.0
General revenue	68,847,197	91.2
Intergovernmental revenue	20,264,895	26.8
Taxes	38,907,220	51.5
General sales	11,344,480	15.0
Selective sales	7,179,785	9.5
License taxes	2,745,949	3.6
Individual income tax	13,806,525	18.3
Corporate income tax	3,367,461	4.5
Other taxes	463,020	0.6
Current charges	5,233,549	6.9
Miscellaneous general revenue	4,441,533	5.9
Utility revenue	0	-
Liquor stores revenue	0	-
Insurance trust revenue [1]	6,644,936	8.8
Total Expenditure	78,334,318	100.0
Intergovernmental expenditure	18,109,138	23.1
Direct expenditure	60,225,180	76.9
Current operation	35,802,788	45.7
Capital outlay	5,632,820	7.2
Insurance benefits and repayments	14,375,834	18.4
Assistance and subsidies	1,178,148	1.5
Interest on debt	3,235,590	4.1
Exhibit: Salaries and wages	8,200,310	10.5
Total Expenditure	78,334,318	100.0
General expenditure	63,958,484	81.6
Intergovernmental expenditure	18,109,138	23.1
Direct expenditure	45,849,346	58.5
General expenditure, by function:		
Education	17,795,169	22.7
Public welfare	21,878,017	27.9
Hospitals	1,525,969	1.9
Health	1,803,293	2.3
Highways	6,745,686	8.6
Police protection	396,860	0.5
Correction	1,056,155	1.3
Natural resources	172,708	0.2
Parks and recreation	261,054	0.3
Governmental administration	1,298,447	1.7
Interest on general debt	3,235,590	4.1
Other and unallocable	7,789,536	9.9
Utility expenditure	0	-
Liquor stores expenditure	0	-
Insurance trust expenditure	14,375,834	18.4
Debt at End of Fiscal Year	65,791,900	X
Cash and Security Holdings	148,349,302	X

X = Not applicable.
- = Zero or rounds to zero.
[1] Within insurance trust revenue, net earnings of state retirement systems is a calculated statistic (the item code in the data file is X08), and thus can be positive or negative. Net earnings is the sum of earnings on investments plus gains on investments minus losses on investments. The change made in 2002 for asset valuation from book to market value in accordance with Statement 34 of the Governmental Accounting Standards Board is reflected in the calculated statistics.

Table IL-16. State Government Tax Collections, 2017

(Dollars in thousands, percent.)

Item	Dollars	Percent distribution
Total Taxes	37,978,923	100.0
Property taxes	63,283	0.2
Sales and gross receipts	18,629,894	49.1
General sales and gross receipts	11,363,366	29.9
Selective sales and gross receipts	7,266,528	19.1
Alcoholic beverages	294,304	0.8
Amusements	835,445	2.2
Insurance premiums	418,582	1.1
Motor fuels	1,348,414	3.6
Pari-mutuels	6,131	-
Public utilities	1,527,274	4.0
Tobacco products	781,528	2.1
Other selective sales	2,054,850	5.4
Licenses	2,793,983	7.4
Alcoholic beverages	17,021	-
Amusements	15,491	-
Corporations in general	364,482	1.0
Hunting and fishing	40,808	0.1
Motor vehicle	1,728,151	4.6
Motor vehicle operators	114,629	0.3
Public utilities	18,025	-
Occupation and business, NEC	465,109	1.2
Other licenses	30,267	0.1
Income taxes	16,134,268	42.5
Individual income	13,256,769	34.9
Corporation net income	2,877,499	7.6
Other taxes	357,495	0.9
Death and gift	280,940	0.7
Documentary and stock transfer	76,555	0.2
Severance	X	-
Taxes, NEC	0	-

X = Not applicable.
- = Zero or rounds to zero.

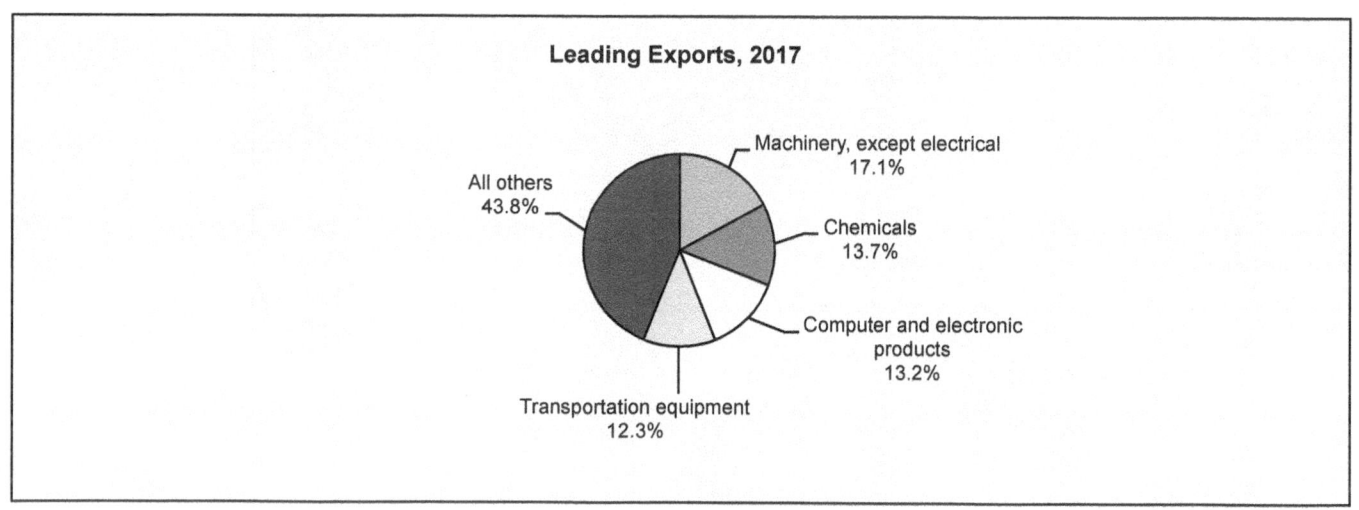

Leading Exports, 2017

Machinery, except electrical 17.1%
Chemicals 13.7%
Computer and electronic products 13.2%
Transportation equipment 12.3%
All others 43.8%

INDIANA

Facts and Figures

Location: East north central United States; bordered on the N by Michigan and Lake Michigan, on the E by Ohio, on the S by Kentucky, and on the W by Illinois

Area: 36,418 sq. mi. (94,321 sq. km.); rank—38th

Population: 6,666,818 (2017 est.); rank—17th

Principal Cities: capital—Indianapolis; largest—Indianapolis

Statehood: December 11, 1816; 19th state

U.S. Congress: 2 senators, 9 representatives

State Motto: The Crossroads of America

State Song: "On the Banks of the Wabash, Far Away"

State Nickname: The Hoosier State

Abbreviations: IN; Ind.

State Symbols: flower—peony; tree—tulip tree; bird—cardinal

At a Glance

- With an increase in population of 2.7 percent, Indiana ranked 31st among the states in growth from 2010 to 2017.

- Indiana's violent crime rate in 2016 was 404.7 per 100,000 population, compared to 386.3 for the entire nation.

- The property crime rate in Indiana in 2016 was 2,589.4 per 100,000 population, ranking 25th in the nation.

- The median household income in Indiana in 2016 was $52,314, compared to the nationwide median of $57,617.

- Approximately 14.1 percent of all Indianans and 19.5 percent of children under 18 years of age in Indiana lived in poverty in 2016.

Table IN-1. Population by Age, Sex, Race, and Hispanic Origin

(Number, percent, except where noted.)

Sex, age, race, and Hispanic origin	2000	2010	2017 [1]	Average annual percent change, 2010–2017
Total Population..	6,080,485	6,483,802	6,666,818	2.8
Percent of total U.S. population	2.2	2.1	2.0	X
Sex				
Male..	2,982,474	3,189,737	3,287,095	3.1
Female..	3,098,011	3,294,065	3,379,723	2.6
Age				
Under 5 years..	423,215	434,075	421,176	-3.0
5 to 19 years..	1,340,171	1,372,507	1,335,502	-2.7
20 to 64 years...	3,564,268	3,836,112	3,885,250	1.3
65 years and over..	752,831	841,108	1,024,890	21.8
Median age (years)...	35.2	37.0	37.7	1.9
Race and Hispanic Origin				
One race				
White...	5,320,022	5,638,833	5,690,929	0.9
Black...	510,034	603,797	649,813	7.6
American Indian and Alaska Native.......................................	15,815	24,487	27,274	11.4
Asian...	59,126	105,535	157,668	49.4
Native Hawaiian or Other Pacific Islander...............................	2,005	3,532	4,439	25.7
Two or more races..	75,672	107,618	136,695	27.0
Hispanic (of any race)...	214,536	403,234	466,453	15.7

X = Not applicable.
[1] Population figures for 2017 are July 1 estimates. The 2010 estimates are taken from the 2010 Census.

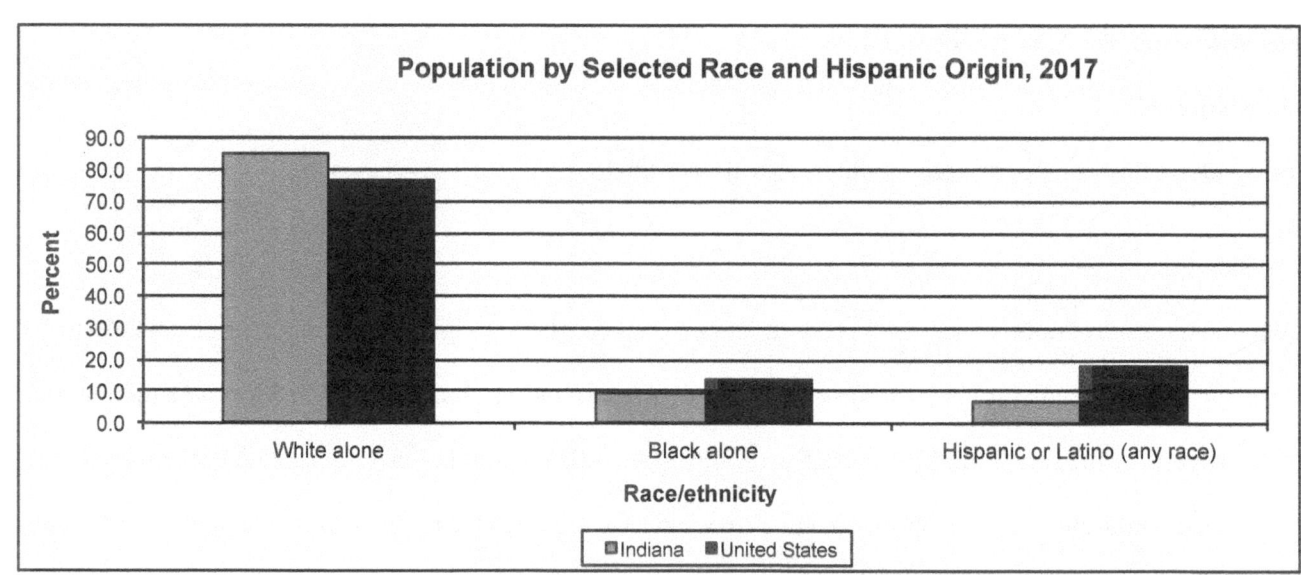

Table IN-2. Marital Status

(Number, percent distribution.)

Sex, age, and marital status	2000	2010	2016
Males, 15 Years and Over..	2,308,917	2,513,953	2,600,798
Never married	27.9	32.6	34.7
Now married, except separated...	58.5	52.3	49.9
Separated..	1.3	1.1	1.2
Widowed..	2.4	2.5	2.7
Divorced...	10.0	11.4	11.5
Females, 15 Years and Over..	2,462,123	2,644,068	2,730,273
Never married	22.0	26.7	28.5
Now married, except separated...	54.3	49.1	47.3
Separated..	1.5	1.8	1.6
Widowed..	10.6	9.2	8.9
Divorced...	11.6	13.2	13.6

Table IN-3. Households and Housing Characteristics

(Number, percent, dollars.)

Item	2000	2010	2016	Average annual percent change, 2010–2016
Total Households...	2,336,306	2,470,905	2,533,270	0.4
Family households	1,602,501	1,656,386	1,645,758	-0.1
Married-couple family	1,251,458	1,236,518	1,225,255	-0.2
Other family	351,043	419,868	420,503	-
Male householder, no wife present............	91,671	110,663	121,367	1.6
Female householder, no husband present......	259,372	309,205	299,136	-0.5
Nonfamily households	733,805	814,519	887,512	1.5
Householder living alone...........................	605,428	678,460	724,036	1.1
Householder not living alone......................	128,377	136,059	163,476	3.4
Housing Characteristics				
Total housing units	2,532,319	2,797,172	2,854,595	0.3
Occupied housing units	2,336,306	2,470,905	2,533,270	0.4
Owner occupied	1,669,192	1,736,751	1,731,421	-0.1
Renter occupied	667,144	734,154	801,849	1.5
Average household size...............................	2.53	2.55	2.54	-0.1
Financial Characteristics				
Median gross rent of renter-occupied housing	521	683	768	2.1
Median monthly owner costs for housing units with a mortgage	869	1,090	1,070	-0.3
Median value of owner-occupied housing units	94,300	123,300	134,800	1.6

Table IN-4. Migration, Origin, and Language

(Number, percent.)

Characteristic	State			U.S.		
	2015	2016	Percent change	2015	2016	Percent change
Residence 1 Year Ago						
Population 1 year and over	6,540,691	6,554,084	0.2	317,635,720	319,361,956	0.5
Same house	84.5	85.1	X	85.3	85.4	X
Different house in the U.S.	15.1	14.5	X	14.1	13.0	X
Same county	9.2	8.5	X	8.5	8.3	X
Different county	5.9	6.0	X	5.6	5.6	X
Same state	3.6	3.7	X	3.2	3.2	X
Different state	2.3	2.2	X	2.4	2.4	X
Abroad	0.3	0.4	X	0.7	0.7	X
Place of Birth						
Native born	6,298,372	6,283,884	-0.2	278,128,449	279,388,170	0.5
Male	49.1	49.2	X	49.3	49.3	X
Female	50.9	50.8	X	50.7	50.7	X
Foreign born	321,308	349,169	8.7	43,290,372	43,739,345	1.0
Male	50.8	51.0	X	48.6	48.5	X
Female	49.2	49.0	X	51.4	51.5	X
Foreign born; naturalized U.S. citizen...........	123,109	139,428	13.3	20,697,103	21,238,372	2.6
Male	47.0	46.6	X	45.9	45.9	X
Female	53.0	53.4	X	54.1	54.1	X
Foreign born; not a U.S. citizen..................	198,199	209,741	5.8	22,593,269	22,500,973	-0.4
Male	53.1	53.9	X	51.1	51.0	X
Female	46.9	46.1	X	48.9	49.0	X
Entered 2010 or later	21.6	27.6	X	15.6	18.6	X
Entered 2000 to 2009	34.3	29.9	X	27.9	26.7	X
Entered before 2000..................................	44.0	42.4	X	56.5	54.7	X
World Region of Birth, Foreign						
Foreign-born population, excluding population born at sea	321,308	349,169	8.7	43,289,646	43,738,901	1.0
Europe	11.9	12.4	X	11.1	10.9	X
Asia	33.7	35.8	X	30.6	30.8	X
Africa	6.3	7.0	X	4.8	4.9	X
Oceania	0.5	0.6	X	0.6	0.6	X
Latin America	45.4	42.5	X	51.1	51.0	X
North America	2.2	1.8	X	1.9	1.8	X
Language Spoken at Home and Ability to Speak English						
Population 5 years and over	6,200,471	6,212,686	0.2	301,625,014	303,328,961	0.6
English only	91.6	91.3	X	78.5	78.4	X
Language other than English......................	8.4	8.7	X	21.5	21.6	X
Speaks English less than "very well"...........	3.3	3.3	X	8.6	8.6	X

NA = Not available.
X = Not applicable.
- = Zero or rounds to zero.

Table IN-5. Median Income and Poverty Status, 2016

(Number, percent, except as noted.)

Characteristic	State		U.S.	
	Number	Percent	Number	Percent
Median Income				
Households (dollars)..	52,314	X	57,617	X
Families (dollars)	66,032	X	71,062	X
Below Poverty Level (All People)	906,077	14.1	44,268,996	14.0
Sex				
Male...	400,731	12.7	19,760,056	12.8
Female	505,346	15.4	24,508,940	15.2
Age				
Under 18 years..	301,156	19.5	14,115,713	19.5
Related children under 18 years.......................	293,333	19.1	13,805,435	19.1
18 to 64 years..	531,325	13.5	25,723,818	13.2
65 years and over	73,596	7.7	4,429,465	9.2

X = Not applicable.

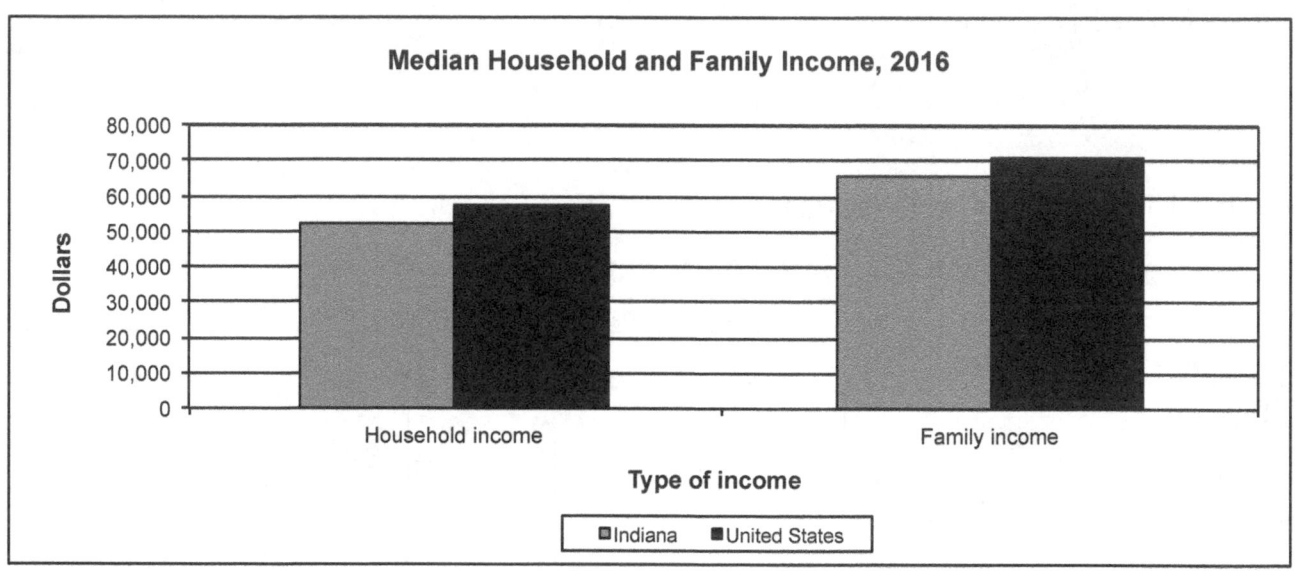

Table IN-6. Health Insurance Coverage Status for the Civilian Noninstitutionalized Population and Children Under 18 Years of Age

(Number, percent.)

Item	2008	2009	2010	2011	2012	2013	2014	2015	2016
Civilian Noninstitutionalized Population	6,271,184	6,316,260	6,391,470	6,417,644	6,437,142	6,471,551	6,498,029	6,520,267	6,534,914
Covered by Private or Public Insurance									
Number..	5,399,907	5,415,098	5,443,550	5,486,815	5,517,276	5,568,640	5,722,145	5,892,506	6,004,551
Percent...	86.1	85.7	85.2	85.5	85.7	86.0	88.1	90.4	91.9
Not Covered									
Number..	871,277	901,162	947,920	930,829	919,866	902,911	775,884	627,761	530,363
Percent...	13.9	14.3	14.8	14.5	14.3	14.0	11.9	9.6	8.1
Percent in the U.S. not covered.........................	15.1	15.1	15.5	15.1	14.8	14.5	11.7	9.4	8.6
Children Under 18 Years of Age	1,579,871	1,582,770	1,602,320	1,593,636	1,585,435	1,584,015	1,579,992	1,576,006	1,573,925
Covered by Private or Public Insurance									
Number..	1,419,511	1,442,759	1,459,648	1,464,911	1,451,515	1,454,011	1,466,497	1,469,681	1,481,775
Percent...	89.8	91.2	91.1	91.9	91.6	91.8	92.8	93.3	94.1
Not Covered									
Number..	160,360	140,011	142,672	128,725	133,920	130,004	113,495	106,325	92,150
Percent...	10.2	8.8	8.9	8.1	8.4	8.2	7.2	6.7	5.9
Percent in the U.S. not covered.........................	9.9	8.6	8.0	7.5	7.2	7.1	6.0	4.8	4.5

Table IN-7. Employment Status by Demographic Group, 2017

(Numbers in thousands, percent.)

Characteristic	Civilian noninstitutional population	Civilian labor force		Employed		Unemployed	
		Number	Percent of population	Number	Percent of population	Number	Percent of population
Total................................	5,175	3,314	64.0	3,195	61.7	119	3.6
Sex							
Male..................................	2,516	1,753	69.7	1,686	67.0	67	3.8
Female	2,659	1,561	58.7	1,509	56.8	51	3.3
Race, Sex, and Hispanic Origin							
White.................................	4,494	2,889	64.3	2,796	62.2	92	3.2
Male..............................	2,204	1,546	70.1	1,494	67.8	52	3.4
Female...........................	2,291	1,343	58.6	1,302	56.9	41	3.0
Black or African American........	481	292	60.8	269	56.0	23	7.9
Male..............................	217	134	61.6	120	55.4	13	10.0
Female...........................	264	159	60.1	149	56.5	10	6.0
Hispanic or Latino ethnicity[1].....	303	213	70.3	204	67.3	9	4.4
Male..............................	161	125	77.7	120	74.6	5	4.0
Female...........................	143	89	62.0	84	59.0	4	4.9
Age							
16 to 19 years.....................	420	180	42.8	158	37.7	22	12.0
20 to 24 years.....................	470	367	78.0	346	73.7	21	5.6
25 to 34 years.....................	798	676	84.7	649	81.3	28	4.1
35 to 44 years.....................	798	664	83.3	647	81.1	17	2.6
45 to 54 years.....................	823	667	81.0	649	78.9	18	2.7
55 to 64 years.....................	912	610	66.9	598	65.6	11	1.8
65 years and over	954	150	15.7	147	15.4	3	2.0

NOTE: Data in Table 7 are from the Current Population Survey (CPS) and do not match the estimates in Table 8. See notes and definitions for further information.
[1] May be of any race.

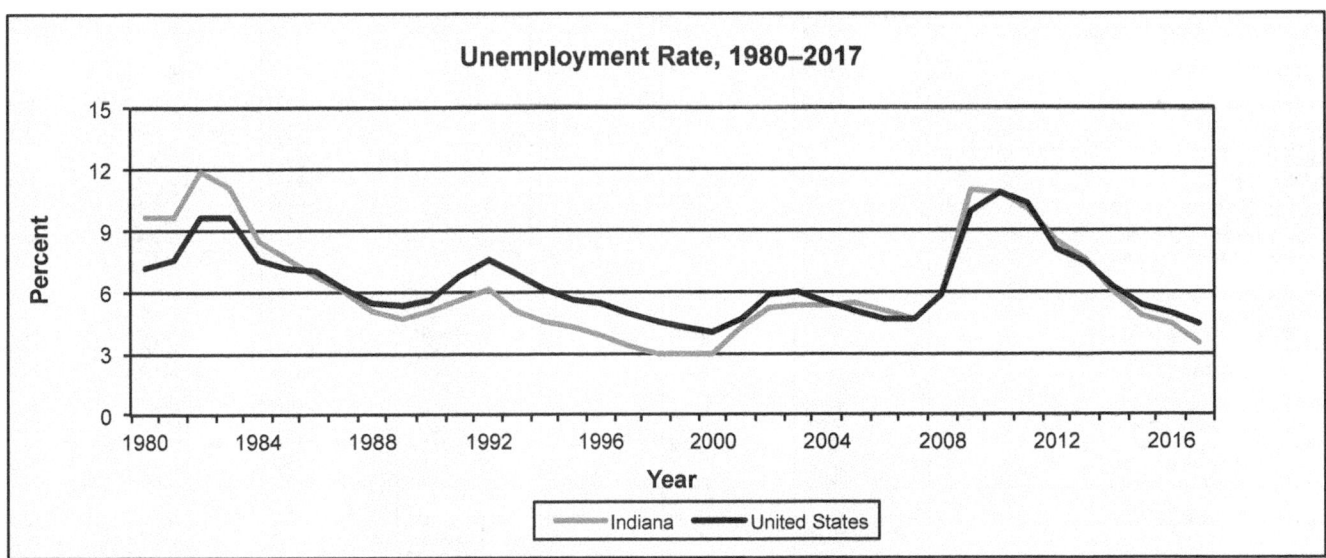

Unemployment Rate, 1980–2017

Table IN-8. Employment Status of the Civilian Noninstitutional Population Age 16 Years and Over

(Number, percent.)

Year	Civilian labor force	Civilian participation rate	Employed	Unemployed	Unemployment rate
2009................................	3,193,989	65.1	2,864,985	329,004	10.3
2010................................	3,175,192	64.0	2,845,608	329,584	10.4
2011................................	3,181,991	63.6	2,891,945	290,046	9.1
2012................................	3,169,835	63.0	2,905,549	264,286	8.3
2013................................	3,188,406	63.0	2,944,275	244,131	7.7
2014................................	3,224,871	63.3	3,032,693	192,178	6.0
2015................................	3,267,121	63.8	3,109,362	157,759	4.8
2016................................	3,327,139	64.6	3,180,104	147,035	4.4
2017................................	3,320,409	64.1	3,203,351	117,058	3.5

Table IN-9. Employment and Average Wages by Industry

(Estimates through 2010 are based on the 2007 *North American Industry Classification System* [NAICS]. Estimates from 2011 onward are based on the 2012 NAICS.)

Industry	2010	2011	2012	2013	2014	2015	2016
	Number of jobs						
Wage and Salary Employment by Industry	2,877,455	2,920,175	2,978,283	3,011,101	3,055,554	3,105,074	3,150,848
Farm Wage and Salary Employment	13,906	10,519	13,757	12,390	11,533	10,443	10,556
Nonfarm Wage and Salary Employment	2,863,549	2,909,656	2,964,526	2,998,711	3,044,021	3,094,631	3,140,292
Private wage and salary employment	2,405,359	2,458,273	2,517,691	2,555,724	2,600,626	2,651,516	2,696,149
Forestry, fishing, and related activities	3,278	3,208	3,329	3,475	4,124	3,961	4,121
Mining	6,267	6,575	6,738	6,685	6,876	6,519	5,904
Utilities	14,947	14,726	14,349	14,176	14,131	13,981	13,783
Construction	119,771	123,954	128,784	126,941	126,449	130,297	135,360
Manufacturing	448,663	464,482	482,763	492,411	507,753	519,478	523,290
Durable goods manufacturing	314,365	330,539	346,500	352,165	363,453	373,484	375,758
Nondurable goods manufacturing	134,298	133,943	136,263	140,246	144,300	145,994	147,532
Wholesale trade	114,422	115,567	116,553	117,516	118,289	119,809	118,692
Retail trade	307,231	310,875	315,024	318,730	321,552	327,318	334,949
Transportation and warehousing	110,682	114,531	117,706	120,792	124,243	125,377	129,013
Information	35,749	34,348	35,761	35,780	35,602	33,628	32,741
Finance and insurance	97,329	97,963	98,102	97,796	99,278	101,074	103,070
Real estate and rental and leasing	32,591	32,846	33,065	33,293	33,569	34,029	35,198
Professional, scientific, and technical services	96,961	99,262	100,807	102,805	106,024	110,293	113,600
Management of companies and enterprises	27,006	28,093	29,166	31,072	32,154	33,392	34,648
Administrative and waste services	152,708	163,966	171,602	176,038	185,187	188,555	187,754
Educational services	62,629	64,515	65,162	65,910	66,345	67,758	68,537
Health care and social assistance	355,818	359,494	366,767	374,802	375,247	384,278	397,182
Arts, entertainment, and recreation	42,464	41,427	41,459	41,663	41,159	41,141	42,255
Accommodation and food services	233,085	238,406	245,661	250,595	254,487	261,686	266,762
Other services, except public administration	143,758	144,035	144,893	145,244	148,157	148,942	149,290
Government and government enterprises	458,190	451,383	446,835	442,987	443,395	443,115	444,143
	Dollars						
Average Wages and Salaries by Industry	39,774	40,837	41,862	42,366	43,262	44,634	46,855
Average Farm Wages and Salaries	24,289	30,764	27,411	32,031	36,281	36,912	36,275
Average Nonfarm Wages and Salaries	39,850	40,873	41,929	42,408	43,288	44,660	46,890
Average private wages and salaries	40,217	41,357	42,485	42,967	43,925	45,360	47,689
Forestry, fishing, and related activities	22,556	22,949	23,871	24,382	29,069	30,762	32,777
Mining	62,637	65,061	65,172	68,323	70,396	69,902	68,254
Utilities	79,435	82,402	84,760	88,380	90,446	94,704	94,622
Construction	50,359	52,407	54,951	54,397	53,349	54,567	59,568
Manufacturing	55,999	57,054	57,976	58,055	59,427	60,851	63,442
Durable goods manufacturing	55,347	56,700	57,944	57,401	58,713	60,334	62,972
Nondurable goods manufacturing	57,524	57,929	58,058	59,696	61,226	62,172	64,640
Wholesale trade	54,970	56,951	58,557	59,610	61,966	64,300	67,427
Retail trade	24,430	24,776	25,317	25,501	26,172	27,152	28,320
Transportation and warehousing	41,665	42,656	43,604	43,941	45,421	46,844	48,356
Information	50,410	52,148	54,123	55,515	56,550	57,977	56,993
Finance and insurance	56,339	59,236	62,095	63,149	65,585	68,413	70,384
Real estate and rental and leasing	35,242	36,677	38,009	39,001	41,571	42,883	45,242
Professional, scientific, and technical services	56,098	58,558	60,139	62,985	62,568	64,842	70,507
Management of companies and enterprises	79,027	84,392	86,302	88,130	90,644	94,290	95,602
Administrative and waste services	27,898	28,418	28,731	29,165	29,568	30,344	32,803
Educational services	29,782	30,404	31,155	31,412	32,087	32,644	32,737
Health care and social assistance	40,874	42,032	43,398	43,889	44,857	46,581	50,037
Arts, entertainment, and recreation	32,644	32,800	33,021	33,369	33,809	35,032	36,819
Accommodation and food services	14,987	15,414	15,988	16,185	16,534	17,365	18,323
Other services, except public administration	27,572	28,044	28,939	29,668	30,629	31,856	33,419
Government and government enterprises	37,920	38,236	38,795	39,189	39,552	40,468	42,043

Table IN-10. Employment Characteristics by Family Type

(Number, percent.)

Family type and labor force status	2014 Total	2014 Families with own children under 18 years	2015 Total	2015 Families with own children under 18 years	2016 Total	2016 Families with own children under 18 years
All Families..	1,651,536	707,467	1,633,695	702,854	1,645,758	700,451
FAMILY TYPE AND LABOR FORCE STATUS						
Married-Couple Families..	1,213,708	459,653	1,213,558	465,663	1,225,255	463,721
Both husband and wife in labor force...................................	53.6	69.8	52.1	68.4	52.4	67.7
Husband in labor force, wife not in labor force.........................	21.0	25.1	21.4	26.0	21.2	26.4
Wife in labor force, husband not in labor force.........................	7.8	3.3	7.7	3.7	7.8	3.9
Both husband and wife not in labor force..............................	17.6	1.8	18.1	1.5	17.9	1.6
Other Families	437,828	247,814	420,137	237,191	420,503	236,730
Female householder, no husband present...............................	72.5	74.3	71.8	73.2	71.1	73.0
In labor force..	52.3	62.3	50.9	60.9	50.9	62.0
Not in labor force	20.1	12.1	20.9	12.3	20.3	11.0
Male householder, no wife present.......................................	27.5	25.7	28.2	26.8	28.9	27.0
In labor force..	21.8	23.7	22.4	24.2	22.5	24.4
Not in labor force	5.8	2.0	5.8	2.5	6.3	2.7

Table IN-11. School Enrollment and Educational Attainment, 2016

(Number, percent.)

Item	State	U.S.
Enrollment		
Total population 3 years and over, enrolled in school	1,684,219	81,572,277
Enrolled in nursery school or preschool (percent)...	6.1	6.0
Enrolled in kindergarten (percent)..	5.3	5.0
Enrolled in elementary school, grades 1-8 (percent)..	42.0	40.3
Enrolled in high school, grades 9-12 (percent)	21.5	21.0
Enrolled in college or graduate school (percent)...	25.2	27.7
Attainment		
Total population 25 years and over	4,392,576	218,475,480
Less than ninth grade (percent)..	3.8	5.4
9th to 12th grade, no diploma (percent)	7.9	7.2
High school graduate, including equivalency (percent)...	33.7	27.2
Some college, no degree (percent)	20.5	20.6
Associate's degree (percent)	8.5	8.4
Bachelor's degree (percent)	16.3	19.3
Graduate or professional degree (percent)..	9.3	11.9
High school graduate or higher (percent)	88.4	87.5
Bachelor's degree or higher (percent)...	25.6	31.3

Table IN-12. Public School Characteristics and Educational Indicators

(Number, percent; data derived from National Center of Education Statistics.)

Item	State	U.S.
Public Schools, 2015–2016 (except where noted)		
Number of school districts...	418	18,328
Number of schools...	1,921	98,456
Number of students..	1,046,757	50,327,015
Number of teachers..	57,675	3,151,497
Student-teacher ratio	18.1	16.0
Expenditures per student (dollars), 2014-2015...	9,529	11,445
Four-year adjusted cohort graduation rate (ACGR)[1,2]	86.8	84.1
Students eligible for free or reduced-price lunch (percent), 2014-2015........................	49.2	51.8
English language learners (percent), Fall 2015	4.8	9.5
Students age 3 to 21 served under IDEA, part B (percent)....................................	16.4	13.2

Public Schools by Type	Number	Percent of state public schools
Total number of schools..	1,921	100.0
Regular	1,863	97.0
Special education	22	1.1
Vocational education	28	1.5
Alternative education...	8	0.4

NOTE: Every school is assigned only one school type based on its instructional emphasis.

[1] ACGR data represents a new method of calculating high-school completion rates and may not be comparable to previous years' data for Averaged Freshmen Graduation Rates (AFGR).

[2] The United States 4-year ACGRs were estimated using both the reported 4-year ACGR data from 49 states and the District of Columbia and using imputed data for Idaho. The estimate for American Indian/Alaska Native students also includes imputed data for Virginia.

Table IN-13. Reported Voting and Registration of the Voting-Age Population, November 2016

(Numbers in thousands, percent.)

Item	Total population	Total citizen population	Registered			Voted		
			Total registered	Percent registered (total population)	Percent registered (total citizen population)	Total voted	Percent voted (total population)	Percent voted (total citizen population)
U.S. Total	245,502	224,059	157,596	64.2	70.3	137,537	56.0	61.4
State Total...............................	4,988	4,795	3,298	66.1	68.8	2,795	56.0	58.3
Sex								
Male	2,426	2,306	1,595	65.7	69.2	1,343	55.4	58.3
Female	2,562	2,490	1,704	66.5	68.4	1,452	56.6	58.3
Race								
White alone..............................	4,309	4,191	2,895	67.2	69.1	2,467	57.2	58.9
White, non-Hispanic alone	4,102	4,059	2,832	69.0	69.8	2,409	58.7	59.4
Black alone...............................	473	442	284	59.9	64.2	228	48.2	51.6
Asian alone..............................	109	77	55	(B)	(B)	48	(B)	(B)
Hispanic (of any race).................	224	138	69	30.9	50.1	63	28.3	46.0
White alone or in combination	4,378	4,260	2,949	67.4	69.2	2,513	57.4	59.0
Black alone or in combination..........	491	460	298	60.8	64.9	238	48.5	51.8
Asian alone or in combination..........	130	97	72	(B)	(B)	65	(B)	(B)
Age								
18 to 24 years..........................	618	587	338	54.7	57.6	252	40.8	43.0
25 to 34 years..........................	917	881	550	60.0	62.5	442	48.2	50.2
35 to 44 years..........................	758	713	492	65.0	69.0	426	56.2	59.7
45 to 64 years..........................	1,742	1,682	1,192	68.4	70.9	1,043	59.9	62.0
65 years and over	953	933	725	76.1	77.8	632	66.3	67.7

B = Base is less than 75,000 and therefore too small to show the derived measure.

Table IN-14. Crime

(Number, rate per 100,000. Data are derived from the FBI Uniform Crime Reports.)

Item	State			U.S. [1,2,3,4]		
	2015	2016	Percent change	2015	2016	Percent change
TOTAL POPULATION [5]	6,619,680	6,633,053	0.2	321,418,820	323,127,513	0.5
VIOLENT CRIME						
Number..	25,653	26,845	4.6	1,231,566	1,248,185	1.3
Rate..	387.5	404.7	4.4	383.2	386.3	0.8
Murder and Nonnegligent Manslaughter						
Number..	373	439	17.7	15,696	17,250	9.9
Rate..	5.6	6.6	17.9	4.9	5.3	8.2
Rape[6]						
Number..	2,404	2,501	4.0	124,047	130,603	5.3
Rate..	36.3	37.7	3.9	38.6	40.4	4.7
Robbery						
Number..	7,111	7,330	3.1	327,374	332,198	1.5
Rate..	107.4	110.5	2.9	101.9	102.8	0.9
Aggravated Assault						
Number..	15,765	16,575	5.1	764,449	803,007	5.0
Rate..	238.2	249.9	4.9	237.8	248.5	4.5
PROPERTY CRIME						
Number..	171,847	171,759	-0.1	7,993,631	7,919,035	-0.9
Rate..	2,596.0	2,589.4	-0.3	2,487.0	2,450.7	-1.5
Burglary						
Number..	34,410	34,097	-0.9	1,579,527	1,515,096	-4.1
Rate..	519.8	514.0	-1.1	491.4	468.9	-4.6
Larceny-Theft						
Number..	123,918	122,931	-0.8	5,706,346	5,638,455	-1.2
Rate..	1,872.0	1,853.3	-1.0	1,775.4	1,745.0	-1.7
Motor Vehicle Theft						
Number..	13,519	14,731	9.0	707,758	765,484	8.2
Rate..	204.2	222.1	8.8	220.2	236.9	7.6

NOTE: Although arson data are included in the trend and clearance tables, sufficient data are not available to estimate totals for this offense. Therefore, no arson data are published in this table.

X = Not applicable.

- = Zero or rounds to zero.

[1] The crime figures have been adjusted.

[2] The data collection methodology for the offense of forcible rape used by the Minnesota state Uniform Crime Reporting (UCR) Program (with the exception of Minneapolis and St. Paul, Minnesota) does not comply with national UCR Program guidelines. Consequently, its figures for forcible rape and violent crime (of which forcible rape is a part) are not published in this table.

[3] Includes offenses reported by the Zoological Police and the Metro Transit Police.

[4] Because of changes in the state's reporting practices, figures are not comparable to previous years' data.

[5] Populations are U.S. Census Bureau provisional estimates as of July 1 of each year.

[6] The figures shown for the offense of rape were estimated using the revised Uniform Crime Reporting (UCR) definition of rape.

Table IN-15. State Government Finances, 2016

(Dollar amounts in thousands, percent distribution.)

Item	Dollars	Percent distribution
Total Revenue	38,687,720	100.0
General revenue	36,259,733	93.7
Intergovernmental revenue	13,041,760	33.7
Taxes	17,587,958	45.5
General sales	7,306,331	18.9
Selective sales	3,301,876	8.5
License taxes	714,634	1.8
Individual income tax	5,218,166	13.5
Corporate income tax	1,034,367	2.7
Other taxes	12,584	0.0
Current charges	3,617,636	9.4
Miscellaneous general revenue	2,012,379	5.2
Utility revenue	0	-
Liquor stores revenue	0	-
Insurance trust revenue [1]	2,427,987	6.3
Total Expenditure	39,557,565	100.0
Intergovernmental expenditure	9,711,681	24.6
Direct expenditure	29,845,884	75.4
Current operation	22,403,006	56.6
Capital outlay	2,224,190	5.6
Insurance benefits and repayments	2,881,905	7.3
Assistance and subsidies	1,357,840	3.4
Interest on debt	978,943	2.5
Exhibit: Salaries and wages	4,425,938	11.2
Total Expenditure	39,557,565	100.0
General expenditure	36,675,286	92.7
Intergovernmental expenditure	9,711,681	24.6
Direct expenditure	26,963,605	68.2
General expenditure, by function:		
Education	15,894,974	40.2
Public welfare	12,709,202	32.1
Hospitals	154,233	0.4
Health	568,635	1.4
Highways	2,543,104	6.4
Police protection	234,088	0.6
Correction	731,005	1.8
Natural resources	366,545	0.9
Parks and recreation	91,639	0.2
Governmental administration	731,025	1.8
Interest on general debt	978,943	2.5
Other and unallocable	1,671,893	4.2
Utility expenditure	374	-
Liquor stores expenditure	0	-
Insurance trust expenditure	2,881,905	7.3
Debt at End of Fiscal Year	22,470,543	X
Cash and Security Holdings	57,672,184	X

X = Not applicable.
- = Zero or rounds to zero.
[1] Within insurance trust revenue, net earnings of state retirement systems is a calculated statistic (the item code in the data file is X08), and thus can be positive or negative. Net earnings is the sum of earnings on investments plus gains on investments minus losses on investments. The change made in 2002 for asset valuation from book to market value in accordance with Statement 34 of the Governmental Accounting Standards Board is reflected in the calculated statistics.

Table IN-16. State Government Tax Collections, 2017

(Dollars in thousands, percent.)

Item	Dollars	Percent distribution
Total Taxes	18,051,598	100.0
Property taxes	12,251	0.1
Sales and gross receipts	10,894,428	60.4
General sales and gross receipts	7,556,326	41.9
Selective sales and gross receipts	3,338,102	18.5
Alcoholic beverages	49,403	0.3
Amusements	477,977	2.6
Insurance premiums	235,171	1.3
Motor fuels	854,529	4.7
Pari-mutuels	1,866	-
Public utilities	193,613	1.1
Tobacco products	434,351	2.4
Other selective sales	1,091,192	6.0
Licenses	681,547	3.8
Alcoholic beverages	12,582	0.1
Amusements	5,782	-
Corporations in general	9,488	0.1
Hunting and fishing	18,902	0.1
Motor vehicle	284,202	1.6
Motor vehicle operators	229,689	1.3
Public utilities	X	-
Occupation and business, NEC	36,207	0.2
Other licenses	84,695	0.5
Income taxes	6,460,790	35.8
Individual income	5,435,292	30.1
Corporation net income	1,025,498	5.7
Other taxes	2,582	-
Death and gift	1,571	-
Documentary and stock transfer	X	-
Severance	1,011	-
Taxes, NEC	0	-

- = Zero or rounds to zero.
X = Not applicable.

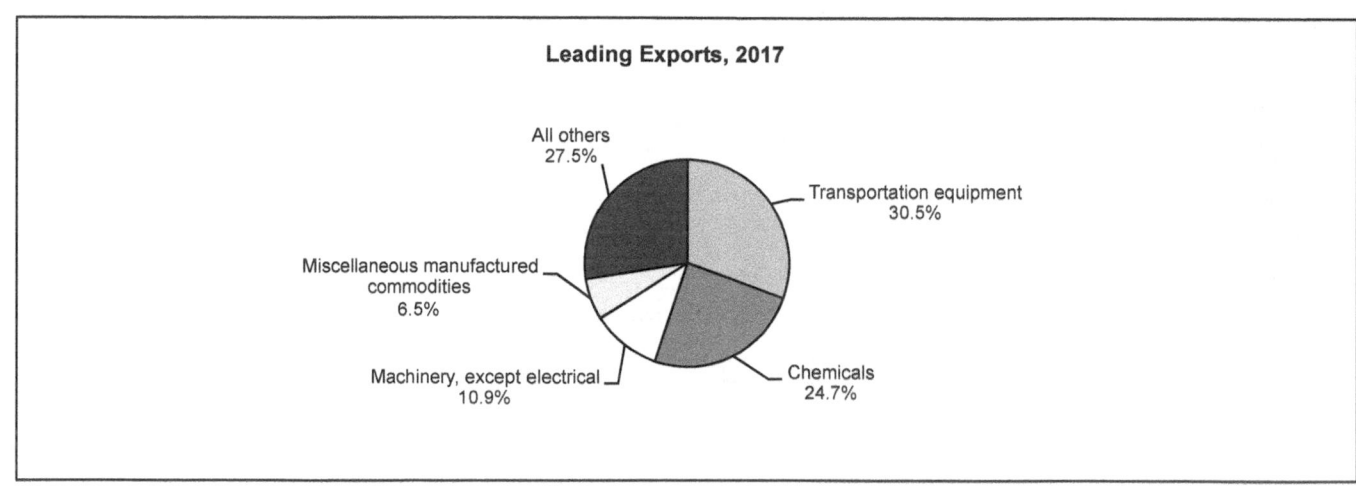

Leading Exports, 2017

All others 27.5%
Transportation equipment 30.5%
Miscellaneous manufactured commodities 6.5%
Machinery, except electrical 10.9%
Chemicals 24.7%

IOWA

Facts and Figures

Location: North central United States; bordered on the N by Minnesota, on the E by Wisconsin and Illinois, on the S by Missouri, and on the W by Nebraska and South Dakota

Area: 56,272 sq. mi. (145,743 sq. km.); rank—26th

Population: 3,145,711 (2017 est.); rank—30th

Principal Cities: capital—Des Moines; largest—Des Moines

Statehood: December 28, 1846; 29th state

U.S. Congress: 2 senators, 4 representatives

State Motto: Our Liberties We Prize and Our Rights We Will Maintain

State Song: "The Song of Iowa"

State Nickname: The Hawkeye State

Abbreviations: IA; Ia.

State Symbols: flower—wild prairie rose; tree—oak; bird—Eastern goldfinch

At a Glance

- With an increase in population of 3.1 percent, Iowa ranked 28th among the states in growth from 2010 to 2017.

- In 2016, Iowa's median household income was $56,247, and 11.8 percent of the population lived below the poverty level.

- Compared to 8.6 percent of the total U.S. population, 4.3 percent of Iowans did not have health insurance in 2016.

- Iowa's violent crime rate in 2016 was 290.6 per 100,000 population, compared to the rate of 386.3 for the United States as a whole.

- Iowa had the 2nd highest percent of single-family homes in 2016, with 78.8 percent of housing units being one-unit attached or detached homes.

Table IA-1. Population by Age, Sex, Race, and Hispanic Origin

(Number, percent, except where noted.)

Sex, age, race, and Hispanic origin	2000	2010	2017 [1]	Average annual percent change, 2010–2017
Total Population..	2,926,324	3,046,355	3,145,711	3.3
Percent of total U.S. population	1.0	1.0	1.0	X
Sex				
Male...	1,435,515	1,508,319	1,564,733	3.7
Female	1,490,809	1,538,036	1,580,978	2.8
Age				
Under 5 years...................................	188,413	202,123	198,996	-1.5
5 to 19 years....................................	639,570	618,387	624,147	0.9
20 to 64 years..................................	1,662,128	1,772,957	1,796,511	1.3
65 years and over	436,213	452,888	526,057	16.2
Median age (years)...........................	36.6	38.1	38.1	-
Race and Hispanic Origin				
One race				
White	2,748,640	2,839,615	2,864,664	0.9
Black	61,853	91,695	120,218	31.1
American Indian and Alaska Native	8,989	13,563	16,222	19.6
Asian..	36,635	54,232	82,346	51.8
Native Hawaiian or Other Pacific Islander	1,009	2,419	3,712	53.5
Two or more races............................	31,778	44,831	58,549	30.6
Hispanic (of any race)........................	82,473	156,932	189,818	21.0

X = Not applicable.
- = Zero or rounds to zero.
[1] Population figures for 2017 are July 1 estimates. The 2010 estimates are taken from the 2010 Census.

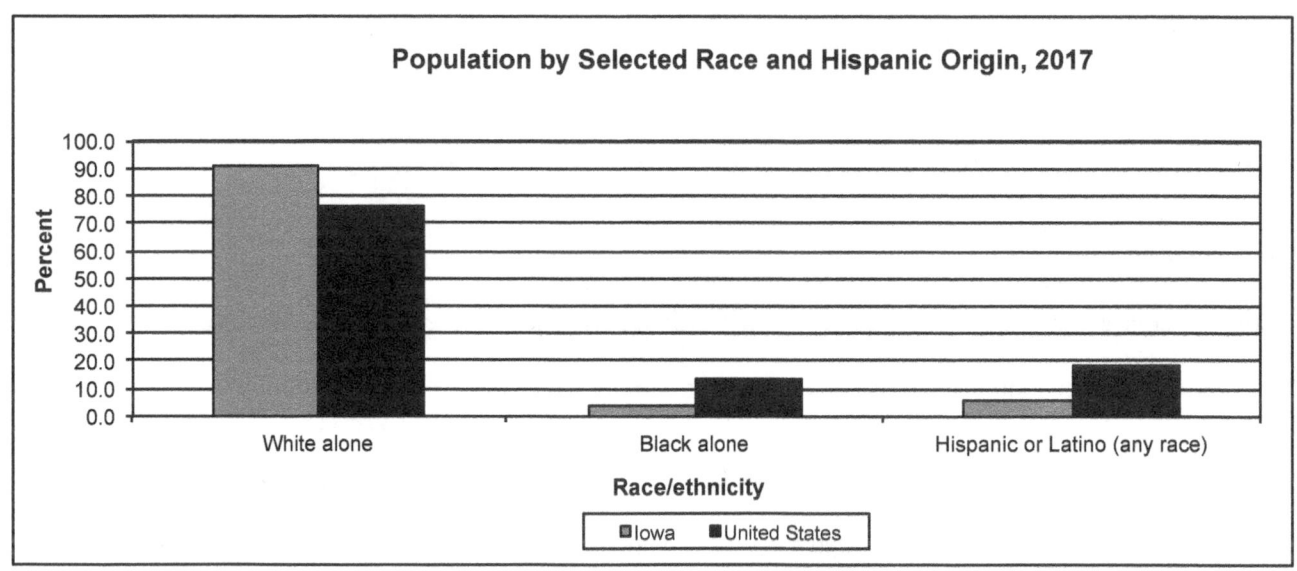

Population by Selected Race and Hispanic Origin, 2017

Legend: Iowa, United States
Race/ethnicity categories: White alone, Black alone, Hispanic or Latino (any race)

Table IA-2. Marital Status

(Number, percent distribution.)

Sex, age, and marital status	2000	2010	2016
Males, 15 Years and Over	1,126,566	1,199,509	1,245,027
Never married	28.2	31.3	33.4
Now married, except separated............................	59.8	55.2	53.1
Separated...	0.9	1.1	0.9
Widowed..	2.5	2.6	2.6
Divorced..	8.5	9.7	9.9
Females, 15 Years and Over	1,198,297	1,250,612	1,284,420
Never married	21.8	24.7	26.3
Now married, except separated............................	55.8	52.4	51.3
Separated...	1.1	1.5	1.3
Widowed..	11.6	10.2	9.4
Divorced..	9.6	11.2	11.6

Table IA-3. Households and Housing Characteristics

(Number, percent, dollars.)

Item	2000	2010	2016	Average annual percent change, 2010–2016
Total Households..	1,149,276	1,223,439	1,247,932	0.3
Family households..	769,684	793,768	795,043	-
Married-couple family..	633,254	633,602	630,993	-0.1
Other family..	136,430	160,166	164,050	0.4
Male householder, no wife present............................	38,160	46,829	50,267	1.2
Female householder, no husband present....................	98,270	113,337	113,783	0.1
Nonfamily households..	379,592	429,671	452,889	0.9
Householder living alone..	313,083	349,736	367,051	0.8
Householder not living alone....................................	66,509	79,935	85,838	1.2
Housing Characteristics				
Total housing units..	1,232,511	1,337,563	1,380,087	0.5
Occupied housing units..	1,149,276	1,223,439	1,247,932	0.3
Owner occupied..	831,419	885,284	881,435	-0.1
Renter occupied..	317,857	338,155	366,497	1.4
Average household size..	2.46	2.41	2.43	0.1
Financial Characteristics				
Median gross rent of renter-occupied housing..............	470	629	741	3.0
Median monthly owner costs for housing units with a mortgage	829	1,140	1,186	0.7
Median value of owner-occupied housing units.............	82,500	123,400	142,300	2.6

- = Zero or rounds to zero.

Table IA-4. Migration, Origin, and Language

(Number, percent.)

Characteristic	State			U.S.		
	2015	2016	Percent change	2015	2016	Percent change
Residence 1 Year Ago						
Population 1 year and over	3,081,446	3,097,283	0.5	317,635,720	319,361,956	0.5
Same house	84.3	84.7	X	85.3	85.4	X
Different house in the U.S.	15.3	14.9	X	14.1	13.9	X
Same county..	8.7	8.7	X	8.5	8.3	X
Different county	6.7	6.2	X	5.6	5.6	X
Same state	3.9	3.7	X	3.2	3.2	X
Different state	2.8	2.5	X	2.4	2.4	X
Abroad	0.3	0.4	X	0.7	0.7	X
Place of Birth						
Native born	2,975,178	2,974,504	-0.0	278,128,449	279,388,170	0.5
Male	49.5	49.6	X	49.3	49.3	X
Female	50.5	50.4	X	50.7	50.7	X
Foreign born	148,721	160,189	7.7	43,290,372	43,739,345	1.0
Male	50.7	51.5	X	48.6	48.5	X
Female	49.3	48.5	X	51.4	51.5	X
Foreign born; naturalized U.S. citizen	55,685	62,016	11.4	20,697,103	21,238,372	2.6
Male	47.2	48.3	X	45.9	45.9	X
Female	52.8	51.7	X	54.1	54.1	X
Foreign born; not a U.S. citizen	93,036	98,173	5.5	22,593,269	22,500,973	-0.4
Male	52.8	53.4	X	51.1	51.0	X
Female	47.2	46.6	X	48.9	49.0	X
Entered 2010 or later	25.4	30.2	X	15.6	18.6	X
Entered 2000 to 2009	30.6	29.8	X	27.9	26.7	X
Entered before 2000...	44.0	40.0	X	56.5	54.7	X
World Region of Birth, Foreign						
Foreign-born population, excluding population born at sea ...	148,721	160,189	7.7	43,289,646	43,738,901	1.0
Europe	12.9	12.4	X	11.1	10.9	X
Asia	35.8	36.2	X	30.6	30.8	X
Africa	9.6	10.4	X	4.8	4.9	X
Oceania	0.9	1.0	X	0.6	0.6	X
Latin America	39.3	38.2	X	51.1	51.0	X
North America	1.5	1.9	X	1.9	1.8	X
Language Spoken at Home and Ability to Speak English						
Population 5 years and over......................................	2,928,815	2,937,206	0.3	301,625,014	303,328,961	0.6
English only	92.3	92.3	X	78.5	78.4	X
Language other than English.....................................	7.7	7.7	X	21.5	21.6	X
Speaks English less than "very well"...........................	3.3	3.4	X	8.6	8.6	X

NA = Not available.
X = Not applicable.
- = Zero or rounds to zero.

Table IA-5. Median Income and Poverty Status, 2016

(Number, percent, except as noted.)

Characteristic	State		U.S.	
	Number	Percent	Number	Percent
Median Income				
Households (dollars)..	56,247	X	57,617	X
Families (dollars)	72,351	X	71,062	X
Below Poverty Level (All People)	356,378	11.8	44,268,996	14.0
Sex				
Male	156,197	10.4	19,760,056	12.8
Female	200,181	13.1	24,508,940	15.2
Age				
Under 18 years..	105,032	14.8	14,115,713	19.5
Related children under 18 years.....................	102,194	14.4	13,805,435	19.1
18 to 64 years...	217,533	11.9	25,723,818	13.2
65 years and over	33,813	6.9	4,429,465	9.2

X = Not applicable.

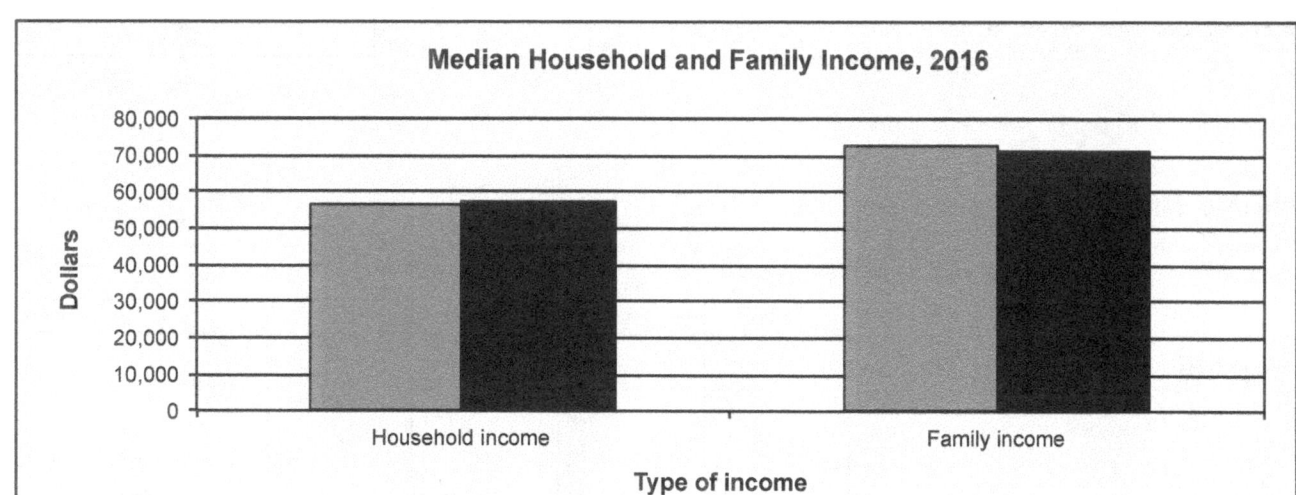

Median Household and Family Income, 2016

Table IA-6. Health Insurance Coverage Status for the Civilian Noninstitutionalized Population and Children Under 18 Years of Age

(Number, percent.)

Item	2008	2009	2010	2011	2012	2013	2014	2015	2016
Civilian Noninstitutionalized Population	2,951,468	2,956,722	3,004,885	3,017,465	3,028,864	3,045,284	3,062,900	3,080,411	3,091,437
Covered by Private or Public Insurance									
Number...	2,683,056	2,701,821	2,725,074	2,747,975	2,774,589	2,797,567	2,874,015	2,925,441	2,959,825
Percent..	90.9	91.4	90.7	91.1	91.6	91.9	93.8	95.0	95.7
Not Covered									
Number...	268,412	254,901	279,811	269,490	254,275	247,717	188,885	154,970	131,612
Percent..	9.1	8.6	9.3	8.9	8.4	8.1	6.2	5.0	4.3
Percent in the U.S. not covered.......................	15.1	15.1	15.5	15.1	14.8	14.5	11.7	9.4	8.6
Children Under 18 Years of Age	708,251	706,873	721,762	721,561	720,427	721,264	723,351	726,495	724,997
Covered by Private or Public Insurance									
Number...	668,594	674,561	692,716	689,820	691,735	691,509	700,117	700,899	706,555
Percent..	94.4	95.4	96.0	95.6	96.0	95.9	96.8	96.5	97.5
Not Covered									
Number...	39,657	32,312	29,046	31,741	28,692	29,755	23,234	25,596	18,442
Percent..	5.6	4.6	4.0	4.4	4.0	4.1	3.2	3.5	2.5
Percent in the U.S. not covered.......................	9.9	8.6	8.0	7.5	7.2	7.1	6.0	4.8	4.5

Table IA-7. Employment Status by Demographic Group, 2017

(Numbers in thousands, percent.)

Characteristic	Civilian noninstitutional population	Civilian labor force		Employed		Unemployed	
		Number	Percent of population	Number	Percent of population	Number	Percent of population
Total..................................	2,460	1,679	68.3	1,625	66.1	54	3.2
Sex							
Male	1,214	895	73.8	864	71.1	32	3.5
Female	1,246	784	62.9	762	61.1	22	2.8
Race, Sex, and Hispanic Origin							
White	2,292	1,565	68.3	1,518	66.2	46	3.0
Male	1,130	836	74.0	809	71.6	27	3.3
Female	1,162	729	62.7	710	61.1	19	2.6
Black or African American................	NA	NA	NA	NA	NA	NA	NA
Male	NA	NA	NA	NA	NA	NA	NA
Female	NA	NA	NA	NA	NA	NA	NA
Hispanic or Latino ethnicity[1]	139	107	77.5	100	71.8	8	7.3
Male	NA	NA	NA	NA	NA	NA	NA
Female	NA	NA	NA	NA	NA	NA	NA
Age							
16 to 19 years.......................	159	81	51.2	74	46.8	7	8.6
20 to 24 years.......................	216	177	81.6	169	78.0	8	4.4
25 to 34 years.......................	430	377	87.7	366	85.2	11	2.9
35 to 44 years.......................	355	316	89.1	306	86.4	9	3.0
45 to 54 years.......................	360	314	87.1	306	85.0	8	2.4
55 to 64 years.......................	417	302	72.3	294	70.6	7	2.5
65 years and over	524	113	21.7	110	20.9	4	3.4

NOTE: Data in Table 7 are from the Current Population Survey (CPS) and do not match the estimates in Table 8. See notes and definitions for further information.
[1] May be of any race.
NA = Not available

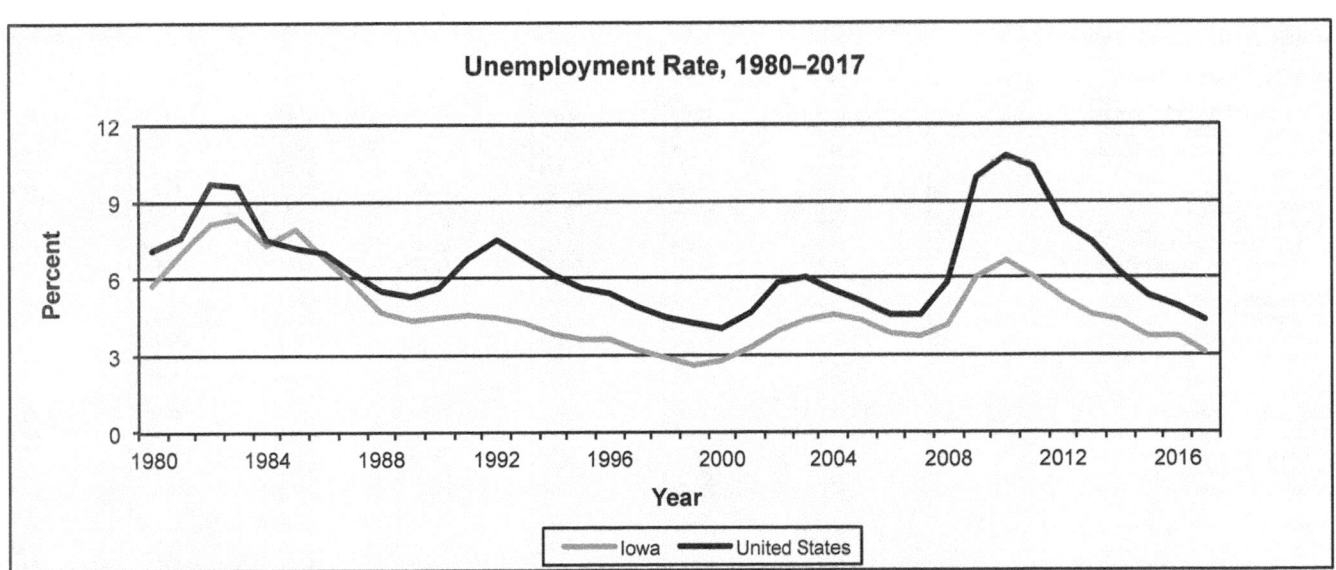

Table IA-8. Employment Status of the Civilian Noninstitutional Population Age 16 Years and Over

(Number, percent.)

Year	Civilian labor force	Civilian participation rate	Employed	Unemployed	Unemployment rate
2009..................................	1,687,411	72.3	1,579,248	108,163	6.4
2010..................................	1,678,281	71.2	1,577,447	100,834	6.0
2011..................................	1,662,376	70.0	1,570,177	92,199	5.5
2012..................................	1,653,141	69.2	1,569,879	83,262	5.0
2013..................................	1,674,190	69.7	1,594,891	79,299	4.7
2014..................................	1,700,756	70.4	1,628,505	72,251	4.2
2015..................................	1,701,317	70.1	1,637,118	64,199	3.8
2016..................................	1,696,113	69.5	1,634,964	61,149	3.6
2017..................................	1,678,549	68.4	1,626,036	52,513	3.1

Table IA-9. Employment and Average Wages by Industry

(Estimates through 2010 are based on the 2007 *North American Industry Classification System* [NAICS]. Estimates from 2011 onward are based on the 2012 NAICS.)

Industry	2010	2011	2012	2013	2014	2015	2016
	Number of jobs						
Wage and Salary Employment by Industry	1,537,132	1,553,036	1,571,483	1,593,351	1,608,122	1,625,722	1,635,851
Farm Wage and Salary Employment	18,657	18,154	15,984	19,258	14,834	19,160	18,686
Nonfarm Wage and Salary Employment	1,518,475	1,534,882	1,555,499	1,574,093	1,593,288	1,606,562	1,617,165
Private wage and salary employment	1,249,767	1,266,721	1,288,057	1,306,874	1,325,609	1,339,472	1,347,394
Forestry, fishing, and related activities	7,158	7,147	7,852	8,555	7,636	7,430	7,537
Mining	2,132	2,173	2,198	2,228	2,165	2,234	2,119
Utilities	6,783	6,606	6,499	6,456	6,483	6,577	6,468
Construction	63,735	64,427	66,519	69,761	76,323	80,216	83,053
Manufacturing	201,225	206,405	211,033	214,693	217,215	216,574	214,159
Durable goods manufacturing	116,692	122,278	126,649	128,861	130,922	129,102	124,808
Nondurable goods manufacturing	84,533	84,127	84,384	85,832	86,293	87,472	89,351
Wholesale trade	66,311	67,206	68,957	69,616	69,377	68,004	67,077
Retail trade	174,321	175,949	177,344	177,477	178,344	181,755	183,991
Transportation and warehousing	54,648	56,493	57,341	59,388	59,963	60,980	60,556
Information	28,722	28,236	27,019	26,152	25,721	24,970	22,690
Finance and insurance	91,642	92,112	92,997	94,052	94,438	95,606	98,344
Real estate and rental and leasing	13,798	13,403	13,364	13,781	14,290	14,539	14,656
Professional, scientific, and technical services	43,025	43,670	45,168	46,975	48,737	49,729	52,200
Management of companies and enterprises	13,212	14,851	16,076	16,590	18,218	19,226	19,055
Administrative and waste services	66,152	68,002	69,740	69,556	70,418	70,362	68,237
Educational services	39,090	39,998	40,429	40,596	40,499	41,028	42,366
Health care and social assistance	179,188	179,901	182,737	185,940	187,741	189,940	192,297
Arts, entertainment, and recreation	19,971	20,442	19,793	18,702	18,801	19,025	21,054
Accommodation and food services	110,772	112,115	115,218	118,639	119,825	121,579	122,566
Other services, except public administration	67,882	67,585	67,773	67,717	69,415	69,698	68,969
Government and government enterprises	268,708	268,161	267,442	267,219	267,679	267,090	269,771
	Dollars						
Average Wages and Salaries by Industry	37,250	38,273	39,578	40,182	41,762	43,134	44,403
Average Farm Wages and Salaries	28,145	28,096	42,613	30,874	47,537	34,423	33,758
Average Nonfarm Wages and Salaries	37,362	38,393	39,547	40,296	41,708	43,238	44,526
Average private wages and salaries	37,111	38,256	39,501	40,222	41,717	43,277	44,454
Forestry, fishing, and related activities	24,648	25,413	26,997	26,857	29,712	30,781	34,078
Mining	43,583	45,470	45,574	46,949	51,842	53,932	62,667
Utilities	76,425	79,992	82,981	80,942	86,371	86,931	86,321
Construction	43,735	45,119	47,138	48,521	51,971	54,947	50,717
Manufacturing	49,757	51,113	52,107	52,891	54,394	55,892	58,384
Durable goods manufacturing	52,486	54,504	55,164	55,990	57,394	58,766	60,342
Nondurable goods manufacturing	45,989	46,184	47,520	48,239	49,842	51,651	55,650
Wholesale trade	51,523	53,942	55,882	57,045	58,791	60,295	62,264
Retail trade	22,635	23,210	23,781	23,903	24,598	25,204	26,247
Transportation and warehousing	40,272	40,893	42,204	42,127	44,448	45,759	47,239
Information	45,224	46,721	47,045	49,011	50,825	52,979	52,577
Finance and insurance	58,991	61,202	63,338	65,913	68,242	71,503	73,611
Real estate and rental and leasing	37,438	39,333	41,090	41,116	42,777	44,767	45,661
Professional, scientific, and technical services	51,691	53,930	57,646	58,910	60,412	62,942	67,463
Management of companies and enterprises	70,049	71,652	76,962	75,656	77,913	81,838	80,838
Administrative and waste services	26,356	26,249	27,279	27,732	28,544	29,624	31,350
Educational services	23,570	23,607	23,920	24,077	24,680	24,907	25,384
Health care and social assistance	36,348	37,394	38,157	38,393	39,417	41,322	42,568
Arts, entertainment, and recreation	20,588	20,606	20,197	18,920	19,683	20,255	19,288
Accommodation and food services	13,774	14,321	15,119	15,619	16,173	16,883	18,186
Other services, except public administration	25,679	26,453	27,591	28,515	29,456	30,953	31,437
Government and government enterprises	38,528	39,042	39,766	40,659	41,660	43,039	44,885

Table IA-10. Employment Characteristics by Family Type

(Number, percent.)

Family type and labor force status	2014		2015		2016	
	Total	Families with own children under 18 years	Total	Families with own children under 18 years	Total	Families with own children under 18 years
All Families..	796,909	348,223	796,799	340,225	795,043	350,304
FAMILY TYPE AND LABOR FORCE STATUS						
Married-Couple Families.................................	632,094	245,038	628,004	235,322	630,993	243,407
Both husband and wife in labor force..................	59.6	78.2	58.4	77.5	58.0	76.6
Husband in labor force, wife not in labor force.........	16.6	17.9	16.8	18.4	17.6	19.3
Wife in labor force, husband not in labor force........	7.2	2.8	7.1	2.6	7.1	2.7
Both husband and wife not in labor force............	16.6	1.2	17.1	1.2	16.6	1.0
Other Families	164,815	103,185	168,795	104,903	164,050	106,897
Female householder, no husband present...............	67.0	67.5	68.3	68.9	69.4	71.5
In labor force..	51.4	58.6	53.0	61.1	53.4	61.3
Not in labor force	15.6	8.9	15.3	7.8	16.0	10.2
Male householder, no wife present...................	33.0	32.5	31.7	31.1	30.6	28.5
In labor force..	27.1	30.2	26.6	28.7	25.7	26.1
Not in labor force	5.9	2.3	5.1	2.5	4.9	2.4

Table IA-11. School Enrollment and Educational Attainment, 2016

(Number, percent.)

Item	State	U.S.
Enrollment		
Total population 3 years and over, enrolled in school	804,741	81,572,277
Enrolled in nursery school or preschool (percent)	6.9	6.0
Enrolled in kindergarten (percent)................................	5.2	5.0
Enrolled in elementary school, grades 1-8 (percent)................................	40.0	40.3
Enrolled in high school, grades 9-12 (percent)................................	20.0	21.0
Enrolled in college or graduate school (percent)................................	27.9	27.7
Attainment		
Total population 25 years and over	2,087,020	218,475,480
Less than ninth grade (percent)................................	3.2	5.4
9th to 12th grade, no diploma (percent)	5.1	7.2
High school graduate, including equivalency (percent)................................	31.1	27.2
Some college, no degree (percent)	21.0	20.6
Associate's degree (percent)................................	11.2	8.4
Bachelor's degree (percent)................................	19.1	19.3
Graduate or professional degree (percent)................................	9.3	11.9
High school graduate or higher (percent)................................	91.8	87.5
Bachelor's degree or higher (percent)................................	28.4	31.3

Table IA-12. Public School Characteristics and Educational Indicators

(Number, percent; data derived from National Center of Education Statistics.)

Item	State	U.S.
Public Schools, 2015–2016 (except where noted)		
Number of school districts................................	345	18,328
Number of schools................................	1,349	98,456
Number of students................................	508,014	50,327,015
Number of teachers	35,687	3,151,497
Student-teacher ratio	14.2	16.0
Expenditures per student (dollars), 2014-2015................................	10,938	11,445
Four-year adjusted cohort graduation rate (ACGR)[1,2]	91.3	84.1
Students eligible for free or reduced-price lunch (percent), 2014-2015................................	40.7	51.8
English language learners (percent), Fall 2015	5.4	9.5
Students age 3 to 21 served under IDEA, part B (percent)................................	12.6	13.2

Public Schools by Type	Number	Percent of state public schools
Total number of schools................................	1,349	100.0
Regular	1,324	98.1
Special education................................	3	0.2
Vocational education................................	0	-
Alternative education................................	22	1.6

NOTE: Every school is assigned only one school type based on its instructional emphasis.
[1] ACGR data represents a new method of calculating high-school completion rates and may not be comparable to previous years' data for Averaged Freshmen Graduation Rates (AFGR).
[2] The United States 4-year ACGRs were estimated using both the reported 4-year ACGR data from 49 states and the District of Columbia and using imputed data for Idaho. The estimate for American Indian/Alaska Native students also includes imputed data for Virginia.
- = Zero or rounds to zero.

Table IA-13. Reported Voting and Registration of the Voting-Age Population, November 2016

(Numbers in thousands, percent.)

Item	Total population	Total citizen population	Registered			Voted		
			Total registered	Percent registered (total population)	Percent registered (total citizen population)	Total voted	Percent voted (total population)	Percent voted (total citizen population)
U.S. Total	245,502	224,059	157,596	64.2	70.3	137,537	56.0	61.4
State Total................................	2,394	2,292	1,657	69.2	72.3	1,454	60.7	63.4
Sex								
Male	1,172	1,111	780	66.5	70.2	673	57.4	60.6
Female	1,221	1,181	877	71.8	74.2	781	63.9	66.1
Race								
White alone...............................	2,201	2,159	1,587	72.1	73.5	1,393	63.3	64.5
White, non-Hispanic alone	2,126	2,114	1,558	73.3	73.7	1,370	64.4	64.8
Black alone................................	73	65	39	(B)	(B)	34	(B)	(B)
Asian alone	66	30	15	(B)	(B)	13	(B)	(B)
Hispanic (of any race).....................	97	51	29	(B)	(B)	23	(B)	(B)
White alone or in combination	2,226	2,184	1,599	71.8	73.2	1,403	63.0	64.2
Black alone or in combination............	84	76	39	(B)	(B)	34	(B)	(B)
Asian alone or in combination...........	68	32	17	(B)	(B)	13	(B)	(B)
Age								
18 to 24 years............................	295	278	142	48.3	51.2	105	35.5	37.6
25 to 34 years............................	450	405	305	67.8	75.2	241	53.6	59.5
35 to 44 years............................	343	325	228	66.4	70.1	196	57.1	60.2
45 to 64 years............................	768	754	545	71.0	72.3	499	65.0	66.2
65 years and over	538	529	436	81.2	82.4	413	76.8	78.0

B = Base is less than 75,000 and therefore too small to show the derived measure.

Table IA-14. Crime

(Number, rate per 100,000. Data are derived from the FBI Uniform Crime Reports.)

Item	State			U.S. [1,2,3,4]		
	2015	2016	Percent change	2015	2016	Percent change
TOTAL POPULATION [5]	3,123,899	3,134,693	0.3	321,418,820	323,127,513	0.5
VIOLENT CRIME						
Number..	8,936	9,110	1.9	1,231,566	1,248,185	1.3
Rate	286.1	290.6	1.6	383.2	386.3	0.8
Murder and Nonnegligent Manslaughter						
Number..	72	71	-1.4	15,696	17,250	9.9
Rate	2.3	2.3	-	4.9	5.3	8.2
Rape [6]						
Number..	1,156	1,247	7.9	124,047	130,603	5.3
Rate	37.0	39.8	7.6	38.6	40.4	4.7
Robbery						
Number..	1,047	1,148	9.6	327,374	332,198	1.5
Rate	33.5	36.6	9.3	101.9	102.8	0.9
Aggravated Assault						
Number..	6,661	6,644	-0.3	764,449	803,007	5.0
Rate	213.2	212.0	-0.6	237.8	248.5	4.5
PROPERTY CRIME						
Number..	63,957	65,391	2.2	7,993,631	7,919,035	-0.9
Rate	2,047.3	2,086.0	1.9	2,487.0	2,450.7	-1.5
Burglary						
Number..	14,892	15,030	0.9	1,579,527	1,515,096	-4.1
Rate	476.7	479.5	0.6	491.4	468.9	-4.6
Larceny-Theft						
Number..	44,723	45,378	1.5	5,706,346	5,638,455	-1.2
Rate	1,431.6	1,447.6	1.1	1,775.4	1,745.0	-1.7
Motor Vehicle Theft						
Number..	4,342	4,983	14.8	707,758	765,484	8.2
Rate	139.0	159.0	14.4	220.2	236.9	7.6

NOTE: Although arson data are included in the trend and clearance tables, sufficient data are not available to estimate totals for this offense. Therefore, no arson data are published in this table.
- = Zero or rounds to zero.
X = Not applicable.
[1] The crime figures have been adjusted.
[2] The data collection methodology for the offense of forcible rape used by the Minnesota state Uniform Crime Reporting (UCR) Program (with the exception of Minneapolis and St. Paul, Minnesota) does not comply with national UCR Program guidelines. Consequently, its figures for forcible rape and violent crime (of which forcible rape is a part) are not published in this table.
[3] Includes offenses reported by the Zoological Police and the Metro Transit Police.
[4] Because of changes in the state's reporting practices, figures are not comparable to previous years' data.
[5] Populations are U.S. Census Bureau provisional estimates as of July 1 of each year.
[6] The figures shown for the offense of rape were estimated using the revised Uniform Crime Reporting (UCR) definition of rape.

Table IA-15. State Government Finances, 2016

(Dollar amounts in thousands, percent distribution.)

Item	Dollars	Percent distribution
Total Revenue	23,715,865	100.0
General revenue	21,074,247	88.9
Intergovernmental revenue	6,645,648	28.0
Taxes	9,559,058	40.3
General sales	3,162,854	13.3
Selective sales	1,430,472	6.0
License taxes	925,958	3.9
Individual income tax	3,553,325	15.0
Corporate income tax	376,865	1.6
Other taxes	109,584	0.5
Current charges	3,502,827	14.8
Miscellaneous general revenue	1,366,714	5.8
Utility revenue	0	-
Liquor stores revenue	290,651	1.2
Insurance trust revenue [1]	2,350,967	9.9
Total Expenditure	23,731,772	100.0
Intergovernmental expenditure	5,470,729	23.1
Direct expenditure	18,261,043	76.9
Current operation	12,881,622	54.3
Capital outlay	2,058,930	8.7
Insurance benefits and repayments	2,520,429	10.6
Assistance and subsidies	593,571	2.5
Interest on debt	206,491	0.9
Exhibit: Salaries and wages	3,425,661	14.4
Total Expenditure	23,731,772	100.0
General expenditure	21,010,971	88.5
Intergovernmental expenditure	5,470,729	23.1
Direct expenditure	15,540,242	65.5
General expenditure, by function:		
Education	7,524,562	31.7
Public welfare	6,500,571	27.4
Hospitals	1,784,719	7.5
Health	264,957	1.1
Highways	2,178,645	9.2
Police protection	102,930	0.4
Correction	294,576	1.2
Natural resources	295,745	1.2
Parks and recreation	33,352	0.1
Governmental administration	578,370	2.4
Interest on general debt	206,491	0.9
Other and unallocable	1,246,053	5.3
Utility expenditure	0	-
Liquor stores expenditure	200,372	0.8
Insurance trust expenditure	2,520,429	10.6
Debt at End of Fiscal Year	5,956,424	X
Cash and Security Holdings	42,462,384	X

X = Not applicable.
- = Zero or rounds to zero.
[1] Within insurance trust revenue, net earnings of state retirement systems is a calculated statistic (the item code in the data file is X08), and thus can be positive or negative. Net earnings is the sum of earnings on investments plus gains on investments minus losses on investments. The change made in 2002 for asset valuation from book to market value in accordance with Statement 34 of the Governmental Accounting Standards Board is reflected in the calculated statistics.

Table IA-16. State Government Tax Collections, 2017

(Dollars in thousands, percent.)

Item	Dollars	Percent distribution
Total Taxes	9,755,430	100.0
Property taxes	1,840	-
Sales and gross receipts	4,613,085	47.3
General sales and gross receipts	3,205,997	32.9
Selective sales and gross receipts	1,407,088	14.4
Alcoholic beverages	22,535	0.2
Amusements	300,172	3.1
Insurance premiums	113,469	1.2
Motor fuels	674,603	6.9
Pari-mutuels	3,484	-
Public utilities	31,386	0.3
Tobacco products	220,938	2.3
Other selective sales	40,501	0.4
Licenses	947,549	9.7
Alcoholic beverages	15,442	0.2
Amusements	31,770	0.3
Corporations in general	45,765	0.5
Hunting and fishing	28,832	0.3
Motor vehicle	637,933	6.5
Motor vehicle operators	14,444	0.1
Public utilities	12,292	0.1
Occupation and business, NEC	158,098	1.6
Other licenses	2,973	-
Income taxes	4,087,482	41.9
Individual income	3,655,462	37.5
Corporation net income	432,020	4.4
Other taxes	105,474	1.1
Death and gift	84,649	0.9
Documentary and stock transfer	20,825	0.2
Severance	X	-
Taxes, NEC	0	-

X = Not applicable.
- = Zero or rounds to zero.

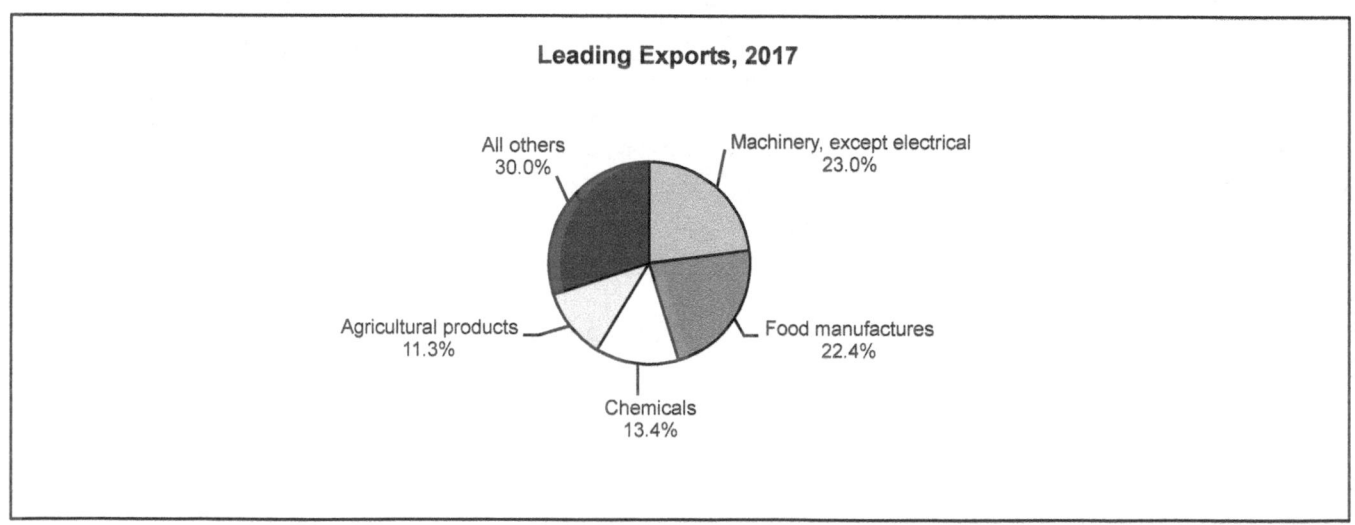

Leading Exports, 2017

All others 30.0%
Machinery, except electrical 23.0%
Agricultural products 11.3%
Chemicals 13.4%
Food manufactures 22.4%

KANSAS

Facts and Figures

Location: Central United States; bordered on the N by Nebraska, on the E by Missouri, on the S by Oklahoma, and on the W by Colorado

Area: 82,277 sq. mi. (213,096 sq. km.); rank—15th

Population: 2,913,123 (2017 est.); rank—35th

Principal Cities: capital—Topeka; largest—Wichita

Statehood: January 29, 1861; 34th state

U.S. Congress: 2 senators, 4 representatives

State Motto: *Ad astra per aspera* ("To the stars through difficulties")

State Song: "Home on the Range"

State Nicknames: The Sunflower State; The Jayhawk State

Abbreviations: KS; Kan.; Kans.

State Symbols: flower—wild native sunflower; tree—cottonwood; bird—Western meadowlark

At a Glance

- With an increase in population of 1.9 percent, Kansas ranked 38th among the states in growth from 2010 to 2017.

- In 2016, 8.7 percent of Kansans did not have health insurance, compared to 8.6 percent of the total U.S. population.

- Approximately 24.5 percent of Kansans were under 18 years old in 2017, the 7th highest percentage in the United States.

- Kansas's unemployment rate was 3.6 percent in 2017, compared to the national rate of 4.4 percent.

- In Kansas, 12.1 percent of the total population and 14.1 percent of children under age 18 lived in poverty in 2016, compared to that national averages of 14.0 percent and 19.5 percent respectively.

Table KS-1. Population by Age, Sex, Race, and Hispanic Origin

(Number, percent, except where noted.)

Sex, age, race, and Hispanic origin	2000	2010	2017 [1]	Average annual percent change, 2010–2017
Total Population....................................	2,688,418	2,853,118	2,913,123	2.1
Percent of total U.S. population	1.0	0.9	0.9	X
Sex				
Male....................................	1,328,474	1,415,408	1,451,956	2.6
Female	1,359,944	1,437,710	1,461,167	1.6
Age				
Under 5 years....................................	188,708	205,492	193,139	-6.0
5 to 19 years....................................	609,710	605,152	600,366	-0.8
20 to 64 years....................................	1,533,771	1,666,358	1,670,055	0.2
65 years and over	356,229	376,116	449,563	19.5
Median age (years)	35.2	36.0	36.6	1.7
Race and Hispanic Origin				
One race				
White....................................	2,313,944	2,501,057	2,519,176	0.7
Black....................................	154,198	173,298	179,569	3.6
American Indian and Alaska Native	24,936	33,044	34,664	4.9
Asian....................................	46,806	69,628	89,908	29.1
Native Hawaiian or Other Pacific Islander	1,313	2,864	3,430	19.8
Two or more races	56,496	73,227	86,376	18.0
Hispanic (of any race)....................................	188,252	311,460	347,459	11.6

X = Not applicable.
- = Zero or rounds to zero.
[1] Population figures for 2017 are July 1 estimates. The 2010 estimates are taken from the 2010 Census.

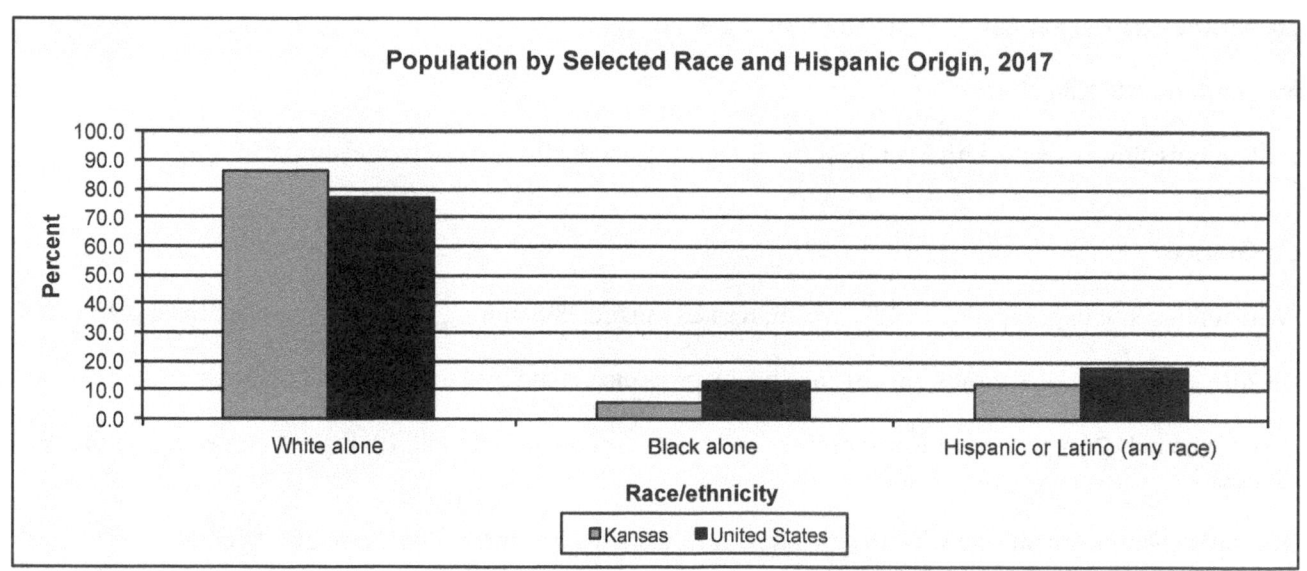

Population by Selected Race and Hispanic Origin, 2017

Kansas ■ United States

Table KS-2. Marital Status

(Number, percent distribution.)

Sex, age, and marital status	2000	2010	2016
Males, 15 Years and Over	1,025,114	1,106,102	1,142,169
Never married	27.4	31.6	33.8
Now married, except separated....................................	59.9	53.9	51.7
Separated....................................	1.1	1.4	1.0
Widowed....................................	2.3	2.6	2.8
Divorced....................................	9.2	10.5	10.6
Females, 15 Years and Over	1,075,542	1,145,453	1,168,135
Never married	20.8	25.1	26.4
Now married, except separated....................................	56.4	51.4	50.3
Separated....................................	1.3	1.7	1.6
Widowed....................................	10.6	9.2	9.2
Divorced....................................	10.9	12.6	12.5

Table KS-3. Households and Housing Characteristics

(Number, percent, dollars.)

Item	2000	2010	2016	Average annual percent change, 2010–2016
Total Households..	1,037,891	1,101,658	1,110,407	0.1
Family households	701,547	721,592	716,005	-0.1
Married-couple family	567,924	559,199	555,970	-0.1
Other family	133,623	162,393	160,035	-0.2
Male householder, no wife present.................................	36,962	46,692	49,460	1.0
Female householder, no husband present........................	96,661	115,701	110,575	-0.7
Nonfamily households	336,344	380,066	394,402	0.6
Householder living alone...	280,387	313,390	328,183	0.8
Householder not living alone..	55,957	66,676	66,219	-0.1
Housing Characteristics				
Total housing units..	1,131,200	1,234,037	1,259,870	0.3
Occupied housing units	1,037,891	1,101,658	1,110,407	0.1
Owner occupied	718,703	749,907	729,392	-0.5
Renter occupied	319,188	351,751	381,015	1.4
Average household size..	2.51	2.52	2.55	0.2
Financial Characteristics				
Median gross rent of renter-occupied housing	498	682	789	2.6
Median monthly owner costs for housing units with a mortgage	888	1,239	1,264	0.3
Median value of owner-occupied housing units	83,500	127,300	144,900	2.3

Table KS-4. Migration, Origin, and Language

(Number, percent.)

Characteristic	State			U.S.		
	2015	2016	Percent change	2015	2016	Percent change
Residence 1 Year Ago						
Population 1 year and over	2,875,640	2,870,529	-0.2	317,635,720	319,361,956	0.5
Same house	83.7	83.4	X	85.3	85.4	X
Different house in the U.S.	15.7	16.0	X	14.1	13.9	X
Same county	9.1	9.4	X	8.5	8.3	X
Different county	6.6	6.6	X	5.6	5.6	X
Same state	3.4	3.5	X	3.2	3.2	X
Different state	3.2	3.1	X	2.4	2.4	X
Abroad	0.6	0.6	X	0.7	0.7	X
Place of Birth						
Native born	2,705,921	2,701,767	-0.2	278,128,449	279,388,170	0.5
Male	49.7	49.9	X	49.3	49.3	X
Female	50.3	50.1	X	50.7	50.7	X
Foreign born	205,720	205,522	-0.1	43,290,372	43,739,345	1.0
Male	51.3	49.5	X	48.6	48.5	X
Female	48.7	50.5	X	51.4	51.5	X
Foreign born; naturalized U.S. citizen................................	77,110	81,256	5.4	20,697,103	21,238,372	2.6
Male	48.0	45.6	X	45.9	45.9	X
Female	52.0	54.4	X	54.1	54.1	X
Foreign born; not a U.S. citizen..	128,610	124,266	-3.4	22,593,269	22,500,973	-0.4
Male	53.3	52.0	X	51.1	51.0	X
Female	46.7	48.0	X	48.9	49.0	X
Entered 2010 or later	21.0	20.6	X	15.6	18.6	X
Entered 2000 to 2009	32.2	32.9	X	27.9	26.7	X
Entered before 2000..	46.8	46.5	X	56.5	54.7	X
World Region of Birth, Foreign						
Foreign-born population, excluding population born at sea	205,720	205,522	-0.1	43,289,646	43,738,901	1.0
Europe	7.8	7.0	X	11.1	10.9	X
Asia...	31.1	32.2	X	30.6	30.8	X
Africa	7.4	3.7	X	4.8	4.9	X
Oceania	0.2	0.5	X	0.6	0.6	X
Latin America..	51.7	55.0	X	51.1	51.0	X
North America...	1.9	1.6	X	1.9	1.8	X
Language Spoken at Home and Ability to Speak English						
Population 5 years and over...	2,714,575	2,709,883	-0.2	301,625,014	303,328,961	0.6
English only	88.2	88.3	X	78.5	78.4	X
Language other than English..	11.8	11.7	X	21.5	21.6	X
Speaks English less than "very well".............................	4.6	4.6	X	8.6	8.6	X

NA = Not available.
X = Not applicable.
- = Zero or rounds to zero.

Table KS-5. Median Income and Poverty Status, 2016

(Number, percent, except as noted.)

Characteristic	State		U.S.	
	Number	Percent	Number	Percent
Median Income				
Households (dollars)..	54,935	X	57,617	X
Families (dollars)	70,792	X	71,062	X
Below Poverty Level (All People)	342,544	12.1	44,268,996	14.0
Sex				
Male	154,310	11.0	19,760,056	12.8
Female	188,234	13.2	24,508,940	15.2
Age				
Under 18 years...	99,323	14.1	14,115,713	19.5
Related children under 18 years...	96,576	13.8	13,805,435	19.1
18 to 64 years..	209,698	12.3	25,723,818	13.2
65 years and over	33,523	8.0	4,429,465	9.2

X = Not applicable.

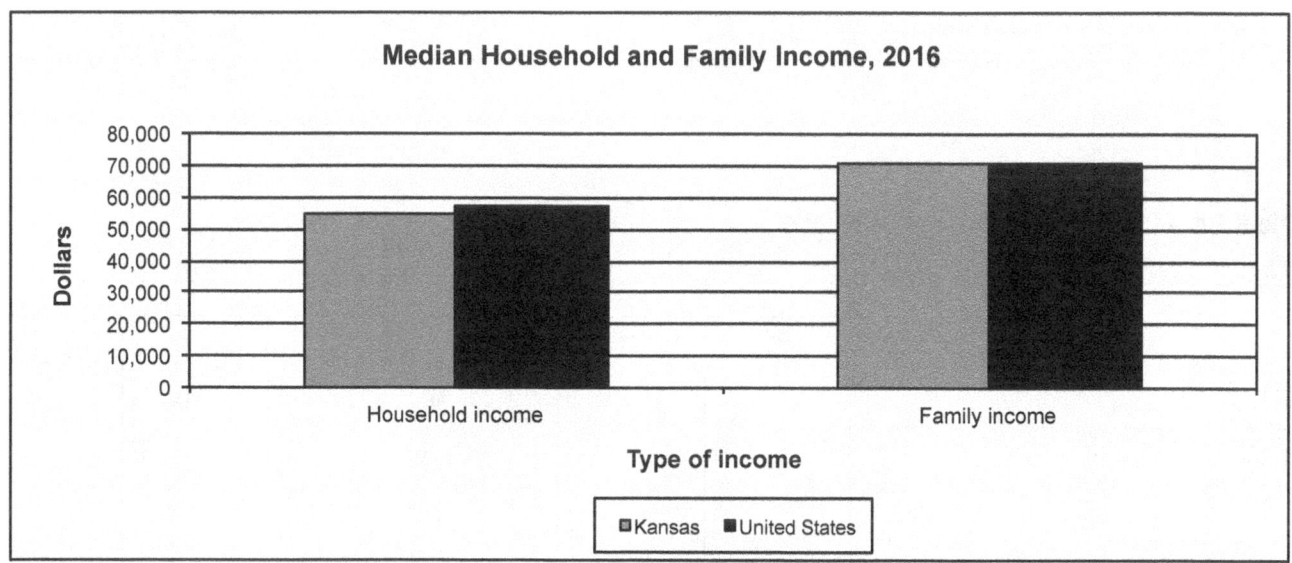

Table KS-6. Health Insurance Coverage Status for the Civilian Noninstitutionalized Population and Children Under 18 Years of Age

(Number, percent.)

Item	2008	2009	2010	2011	2012	2013	2014	2015	2016
Civilian Noninstitutionalized Population	2,738,746	2,756,827	2,804,461	2,813,530	2,825,416	2,836,733	2,845,414	2,850,159	2,850,862
Covered by Private or Public Insurance									
Number....................	2,405,417	2,394,276	2,415,015	2,458,900	2,469,852	2,488,636	2,553,940	2,589,651	2,601,888
Percent....................	87.8	86.8	86.1	87.4	87.4	87.7	89.8	90.9	91.3
Not Covered									
Number....................	333,329	362,551	389,446	354,630	355,564	348,097	291,474	260,508	248,974
Percent....................	12.2	13.2	13.9	12.6	12.6	12.3	10.2	9.1	8.7
Percent in the U.S. not covered..	15.1	15.1	15.5	15.1	14.8	14.5	11.7	9.4	8.6
Children Under 18 Years of Age	698,223	700,794	725,437	721,211	719,917	718,934	720,908	718,994	713,102
Covered by Private or Public Insurance									
Number....................	640,513	643,077	665,654	674,866	672,059	674,804	681,497	682,459	682,190
Percent....................	91.7	91.8	91.8	93.6	93.4	93.9	94.5	94.9	95.7
Not Covered									
Number....................	57,710	57,717	59,783	46,345	47,858	44,130	39,411	36,535	30,912
Percent....................	8.3	8.2	8.2	6.4	6.6	6.1	5.5	5.1	4.3
Percent in the U.S. not covered..	9.9	8.6	8.0	7.5	7.2	7.1	6.0	4.8	4.5

Table KS-7. Employment Status by Demographic Group, 2017

(Numbers in thousands, percent.)

Characteristic	Civilian noninstitutional population	Civilian labor force		Employed		Unemployed	
		Number	Percent of population	Number	Percent of population	Number	Percent of population
Total...	2,218	1,480	66.7	1,427	64.3	53	3.6
Sex							
Male...	1,085	785	72.3	753	69.4	32	4.1
Female...	1,133	695	61.3	674	59.5	21	3.0
Race, Sex, and Hispanic Origin							
White...	1,947	1,295	66.5	1,257	64.6	38	2.9
Male...	951	687	72.3	663	69.7	24	3.5
Female...	996	608	61.1	595	59.7	14	2.3
Black or African American...........................	124	78	63.4	69	56.0	9	11.7
Male...	NA	NA	NA	NA	NA	NA	NA
Female...	NA	NA	NA	NA	NA	NA	NA
Hispanic or Latino ethnicity[1]	251	187	74.5	180	71.6	7	3.9
Male...	129	107	82.9	102	79.4	5	4.2
Female...	122	80	65.7	77	63.3	3	3.6
Age							
16 to 19 years..	154	63	41.2	58	37.4	6	9.2
20 to 24 years..	193	155	80.2	147	76.3	7	4.7
25 to 34 years..	373	320	85.9	307	82.3	13	4.2
35 to 44 years..	355	301	85.0	290	81.9	11	3.6
45 to 54 years..	336	277	82.6	270	80.3	8	2.8
55 to 64 years..	386	263	68.2	257	66.6	6	2.3
65 years and over......................................	422	100	23.6	99	23.4	1	1.2

NOTE: Data in Table 7 are from the Current Population Survey (CPS) and do not match the estimates in Table 8. See notes and definitions for further information.
[1] May be of any race.

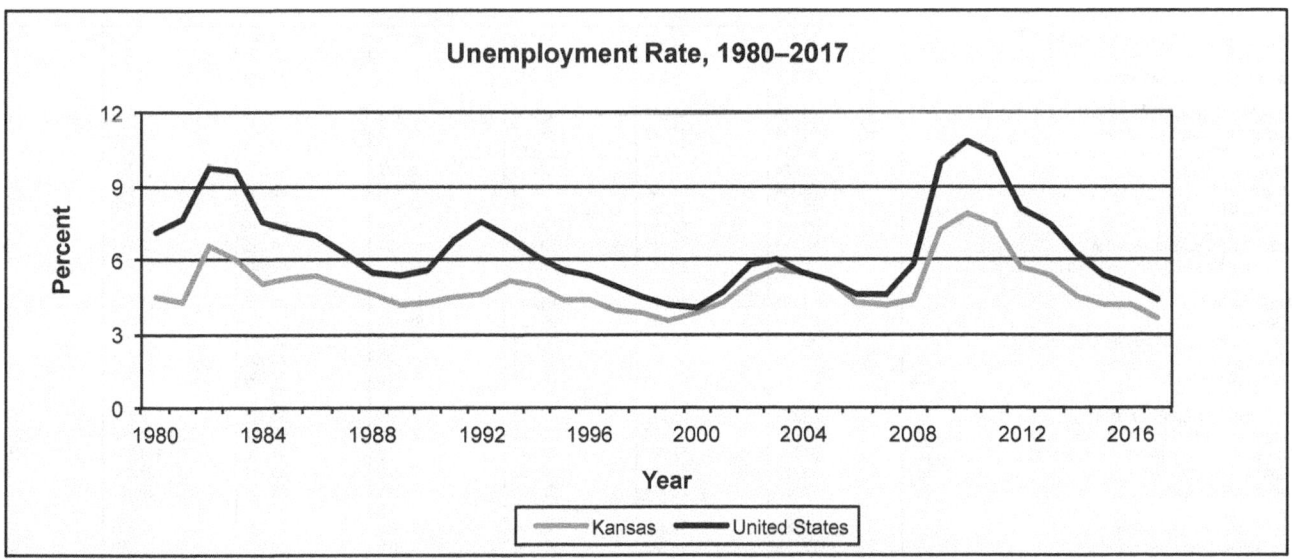

Unemployment Rate, 1980–2017

Table KS-8. Employment Status of the Civilian Noninstitutional Population Age 16 Years and Over

(Number, percent.)

Year	Civilian labor force	Civilian participation rate	Employed	Unemployed	Unemployment rate
2009..	1,518,207	71.3	1,413,873	104,334	6.9
2010..	1,500,764	69.8	1,394,958	105,806	7.1
2011..	1,491,087	69.0	1,394,082	97,005	6.5
2012..	1,485,220	68.3	1,400,122	85,098	5.7
2013..	1,485,917	68.1	1,407,217	78,700	5.3
2014..	1,491,710	68.0	1,424,016	67,694	4.5
2015..	1,489,829	67.7	1,427,731	62,098	4.2
2016..	1,485,336	67.2	1,425,413	59,923	4.0
2017..	1,478,783	66.6	1,425,216	53,567	3.6

Table KS-9. Employment and Average Wages by Industry

(Estimates through 2010 are based on the 2007 *North American Industry Classification System* [NAICS]. Estimates from 2011 onward are based on the 2012 NAICS.)

Industry	2010	2011	2012	2013	2014	2015	2016
	Number of jobs						
Wage and Salary Employment by Industry	1,408,765	1,418,264	1,433,367	1,448,151	1,471,837	1,481,514	1,482,415
Farm Wage and Salary Employment	10,025	12,101	10,890	9,340	11,907	12,622	13,056
Nonfarm Wage and Salary Employment	1,398,740	1,406,163	1,422,477	1,438,811	1,459,930	1,468,892	1,469,359
Private wage and salary employment	1,094,999	1,106,362	1,124,558	1,141,223	1,163,349	1,173,674	1,177,250
Forestry, fishing, and related activities	4,109	4,252	4,516	4,773	4,882	4,908	4,956
Mining	8,508	9,042	9,915	10,386	10,388	8,459	6,804
Utilities	7,806	8,047	7,978	7,752	7,779	6,752	6,678
Construction	56,276	54,590	56,641	58,496	61,430	62,549	63,032
Manufacturing	160,410	161,271	163,133	163,197	162,463	161,361	160,479
Durable goods manufacturing	97,506	98,053	100,110	100,574	98,710	98,025	95,879
Nondurable goods manufacturing	62,904	63,218	63,023	62,623	63,753	63,336	64,600
Wholesale trade	59,761	59,691	59,135	60,126	61,672	60,487	60,054
Retail trade	142,049	143,131	143,886	145,398	147,663	149,785	151,381
Transportation and warehousing	44,125	46,250	48,046	48,361	49,489	50,267	52,369
Information	29,364	27,984	27,818	27,560	27,818	20,978	20,625
Finance and insurance	58,166	60,146	60,950	61,406	62,483	63,861	63,388
Real estate and rental and leasing	14,719	14,965	14,103	14,261	14,821	15,437	15,678
Professional, scientific, and technical services	61,056	61,049	63,213	66,756	67,924	70,334	73,613
Management of companies and enterprises	15,189	13,982	13,640	15,197	18,630	27,602	24,445
Administrative and waste services	70,609	75,173	78,067	81,371	84,063	82,124	81,451
Educational services	19,402	19,667	20,270	20,438	20,955	21,267	21,002
Health care and social assistance	164,960	167,438	169,645	170,837	172,378	177,636	180,014
Arts, entertainment, and recreation	13,360	13,859	15,628	16,049	16,307	16,445	17,108
Accommodation and food services	100,761	101,917	104,571	106,034	107,265	110,086	111,263
Other services, except public administration	64,369	63,908	63,403	62,825	64,939	63,336	62,910
Government and government enterprises	303,741	299,801	297,919	297,588	296,581	295,218	292,109
	Dollars						
Average Wages and Salaries by Industry	39,824	40,981	42,272	42,725	43,781	44,998	45,831
Average Farm Wages and Salaries	35,036	35,637	43,617	41,780	41,678	40,193	43,425
Average Nonfarm Wages and Salaries	39,858	41,026	42,261	42,731	43,798	45,040	45,852
Average private wages and salaries	40,334	41,577	43,025	43,547	44,693	46,001	46,795
Forestry, fishing, and related activities	23,914	23,865	24,595	25,014	25,876	27,631	28,481
Mining	51,084	54,844	57,493	56,407	59,914	56,488	54,529
Utilities	79,234	88,106	85,025	88,173	89,280	90,885	94,092
Construction	45,615	46,003	48,169	48,736	50,524	51,720	51,862
Manufacturing	52,096	53,520	53,791	54,589	55,249	56,821	58,763
Durable goods manufacturing	56,443	58,219	58,488	58,734	59,345	60,743	60,098
Nondurable goods manufacturing	45,358	46,231	46,331	47,931	48,907	50,753	56,782
Wholesale trade	59,193	60,022	63,446	63,104	65,326	66,364	68,916
Retail trade	24,143	24,815	25,530	25,643	26,058	26,931	27,115
Transportation and warehousing	43,747	45,808	47,494	47,951	49,467	50,060	52,538
Information	64,098	64,601	67,214	69,742	73,196	62,631	58,207
Finance and insurance	57,763	61,308	66,244	66,715	69,560	71,802	74,210
Real estate and rental and leasing	33,854	35,347	36,215	36,989	38,421	40,610	41,538
Professional, scientific, and technical services	57,321	59,698	62,261	63,649	65,767	68,682	70,085
Management of companies and enterprises	81,016	87,709	95,045	93,023	94,580	104,901	105,637
Administrative and waste services	33,622	35,552	36,769	37,320	36,742	36,886	36,956
Educational services	27,352	28,318	28,761	29,146	29,658	30,189	29,821
Health care and social assistance	38,680	39,476	40,901	40,839	41,501	42,703	43,301
Arts, entertainment, and recreation	17,779	18,343	20,532	20,972	20,908	21,563	21,836
Accommodation and food services	14,645	15,078	15,697	16,070	16,695	17,420	18,405
Other services, except public administration	26,783	27,722	28,545	29,416	30,325	31,788	33,464
Government and government enterprises	38,143	38,996	39,378	39,604	40,287	41,219	42,053

Table KS-10. Employment Characteristics by Family Type

(Number, percent.)

Family type and labor force status	2014		2015		2016	
	Total	Families with own children under 18 years	Total	Families with own children under 18 years	Total	Families with own children under 18 years
All Families..	726,061	325,507	720,780	324,072	716,005	315,508
FAMILY TYPE AND LABOR FORCE STATUS						
Married-Couple Families..................................	562,330	226,937	560,633	228,023	555,970	219,403
Both husband and wife in labor force..........................	55.7	69.0	55.5	69.3	55.7	69.3
Husband in labor force, wife not in labor force	21.3	26.5	21.2	25.3	20.7	26.2
Wife in labor force, husband not in labor force	7.2	3.0	7.1	3.6	7.1	3.2
Both husband and wife not in labor force....................	15.9	1.4	15.6	1.3	15.9	1.0
Other Families	163,731	98,570	160,147	96,049	160,035	96,105
Female householder, no husband present......................	68.8	70.1	68.5	70.9	69.1	70.7
In labor force	50.4	59.2	51.2	59.8	53.4	62.7
Not in labor force	18.4	10.9	17.3	11.2	15.7	8.0
Male householder, no wife present...........................	31.2	29.9	31.5	29.1	30.9	29.3
In labor force...	26.5	28.1	25.5	26.4	25.9	26.7
Not in labor force	4.7	1.8	5.9	2.7	5.0	2.7

Table KS-11. School Enrollment and Educational Attainment, 2016

(Number, percent.)

Item	State	U.S.
Enrollment		
Total population 3 years and over, enrolled in school	774,902	81,572,277
Enrolled in nursery school or preschool (percent)..	6.5	6.0
Enrolled in kindergarten (percent)..	5.1	5.0
Enrolled in elementary school, grades 1-8 (percent).....................................	41.1	40.3
Enrolled in high school, grades 9-12 (percent)..	20.5	21.0
Enrolled in college or graduate school (percent)..	26.9	27.7
Attainment		
Total population 25 years and over	1,891,936	218,475,480
Less than ninth grade (percent)..	3.6	5.4
9th to 12th grade, no diploma (percent)	5.8	7.2
High school graduate, including equivalency (percent)...................................	26.2	27.2
Some college, no degree (percent)..	23.2	20.6
Associate's degree (percent)	8.3	8.4
Bachelor's degree (percent)..	20.7	19.3
Graduate or professional degree (percent)..	12.2	11.9
High school graduate or higher (percent)...	90.5	87.5
Bachelor's degree or higher (percent)..	32.8	31.3

Table KS-12. Public School Characteristics and Educational Indicators

(Number, percent; data derived from National Center of Education Statistics.)

Item	State	U.S.
Public Schools, 2015–2016 (except where noted)		
Number of school districts..	317	18,328
Number of schools..	1,320	98,456
Number of students...	495,884	50,327,015
Number of teachers...	40,035	3,151,497
Student-teacher ratio	12.4	16.0
Expenditures per student (dollars), 2014-2015..	10,329	11,445
Four-year adjusted cohort graduation rate (ACGR)[1,2]	85.7	84.1
Students eligible for free or reduced-price lunch (percent), 2014-2015..................	49.9	51.8
English language learners (percent), Fall 2015..	10.6	9.5
Students age 3 to 21 served under IDEA, part B (percent)................................	14.3	13.2

Public Schools by Type	Number	Percent of state public schools
Total number of schools...	1,320	100.0
Regular	1,315	99.6
Special education	4	0.3
Vocational education	0	-
Alternative education..	1	0.1

NOTE: Every school is assigned only one school type based on its instructional emphasis.
[1] ACGR data represents a new method of calculating high-school completion rates and may not be comparable to previous years' data for Averaged Freshmen Graduation Rates (AFGR).
[2] The United States 4-year ACGRs were estimated using both the reported 4-year ACGR data from 49 states and the District of Columbia and using imputed data for Idaho. The estimate for American Indian/Alaska Native students also includes imputed data for Virginia.

Table KS-13. Reported Voting and Registration of the Voting-Age Population, November 2016

(Numbers in thousands, percent.)

Item	Total population	Total citizen population	Registered			Voted		
			Total registered	Percent registered (total population)	Percent registered (total citizen population)	Total voted	Percent voted (total population)	Percent voted (total citizen population)
U.S. Total	245,502	224,059	157,596	64.2	70.3	137,537	56.0	61.4
State Total............................	2,142	2,029	1,438	67.1	70.9	1,243	58.0	61.3
Sex								
Male	1,048	992	671	64.0	67.6	570	54.4	57.5
Female	1,094	1,036	767	70.1	74.0	673	61.5	64.9
Race								
White alone...........................	1,883	1,798	1,307	69.4	72.7	1,149	61.0	63.9
White, non-Hispanic alone...........	1,678	1,672	1,244	74.1	74.4	1,091	65.0	65.3
Black alone.............................	121	121	75	61.8	61.8	54	44.5	44.5
Asian alone	59	31	15	(B)	(B)	7	(B)	(B)
Hispanic (of any race).................	217	138	76	34.9	54.7	68	31.2	48.9
White alone or in combination	1,923	1,838	1,335	69.4	72.6	1,170	60.8	63.6
Black alone or in combination...........	136	136	82	60.4	60.4	56	41.2	41.2
Asian alone or in combination...........	64	36	19	(B)	(B)	11	(B)	(B)
Age								
18 to 24 years.........................	269	254	126	46.7	49.5	91	33.8	35.8
25 to 34 years.........................	402	362	219	54.5	60.5	184	45.9	50.8
35 to 44 years.........................	328	314	240	73.2	76.4	210	63.9	66.7
45 to 64 years.........................	719	682	502	69.9	73.7	445	61.8	65.2
65 years and over	424	417	350	82.6	84.1	314	73.9	75.2

B = Base is less than 75,000 and therefore too small to show the derived measure.

Table KS-14. Crime

(Number, rate per 100,000. Data are derived from the FBI Uniform Crime Reports.)

Item	State			U.S. [1,2,3,4]		
	2015	2016	Percent change	2015	2016	Percent change
TOTAL POPULATION [5]	2,911,641	2,907,289	-0.1	321,418,820	323,127,513	0.5
VIOLENT CRIME						
Number........................	11,353	11,060	-2.6	1,231,566	1,248,185	1.3
Rate............................	389.9	380.4	-2.4	383.2	386.3	0.8
Murder and Nonnegligent Manslaughter						
Number........................	128	111	-13.3	15,696	17,250	9.9
Rate............................	4.4	3.8	-13.6	4.9	5.3	8.2
Rape [6]						
Number........................	1,615	1,312	-18.8	124,047	130,603	5.3
Rate............................	55.5	45.1	-18.7	38.6	40.4	4.7
Robbery						
Number........................	1,818	1,671	-8.1	327,374	332,198	1.5
Rate............................	62.4	57.5	-7.9	101.9	102.8	0.9
Aggravated Assault						
Number........................	7,792	7,966	2.2	764,449	803,007	5.0
Rate............................	267.6	274.0	2.4	237.8	248.5	4.5
PROPERTY CRIME						
Number........................	79,199	78,367	-1.1	7,993,631	7,919,035	-0.9
Rate............................	2,720.1	2,695.5	-0.9	2,487.0	2,450.7	-1.5
Burglary						
Number........................	15,362	14,364	-6.5	1,579,527	1,515,096	-4.1
Rate............................	527.6	494.1	-6.3	491.4	468.9	-4.6
Larceny-Theft						
Number........................	56,880	57,066	0.3	5,706,346	5,638,455	-1.2
Rate............................	1,953.5	1,962.9	0.5	1,775.4	1,745.0	-1.7
Motor Vehicle Theft						
Number........................	6,957	6,937	-0.3	707,758	765,484	8.2
Rate............................	238.9	238.6	-0.1	220.2	236.9	7.6

NOTE: Although arson data are included in the trend and clearance tables, sufficient data are not available to estimate totals for this offense. Therefore, no arson data are published in this table.
X = Not applicable.
- = Zero or rounds to zero.
[1] The crime figures have been adjusted.
[2] The data collection methodology for the offense of forcible rape used by the Minnesota state Uniform Crime Reporting (UCR) Program (with the exception of Minneapolis and St. Paul, Minnesota) does not comply with national UCR Program guidelines. Consequently, its figures for forcible rape and violent crime (of which forcible rape is a part) are not published in this table.
[3] Includes offenses reported by the Zoological Police and the Metro Transit Police.
[4] Because of changes in the state's reporting practices, figures are not comparable to previous years' data.
[5] Populations are U.S. Census Bureau provisional estimates as of July 1 of each year.
[6] The figures shown for the offense of rape were estimated using the revised Uniform Crime Reporting (UCR) definition of rape.

Table KS-15. State Government Finances, 2016

(Dollar amounts in thousands, percent distribution.)

Item	Dollars	Percent distribution
Total Revenue	17,609,012	100.0
General revenue	16,459,697	93.5
Intergovernmental revenue	3,828,203	21.7
Taxes	8,058,949	45.8
General sales	3,240,354	18.4
Selective sales	1,084,599	6.2
License taxes	396,648	2.3
Individual income tax	2,231,902	12.7
Corporate income tax	391,877	2.2
Other taxes	713,569	4.1
Current charges	3,452,928	19.6
Miscellaneous general revenue	1,119,617	6.4
Utility revenue	0	-
Liquor stores revenue	0	-
Insurance trust revenue [1]	1,149,315	6.5
Total Expenditure	18,748,723	100.0
Intergovernmental expenditure	4,799,630	25.6
Direct expenditure	13,949,093	74.4
Current operation	10,222,601	54.5
Capital outlay	1,411,421	7.5
Insurance benefits and repayments	1,892,459	10.1
Assistance and subsidies	248,499	1.3
Interest on debt	174,113	0.9
Exhibit: Salaries and wages	2,849,650	15.2
Total Expenditure	18,748,723	100.0
General expenditure	16,856,264	89.9
Intergovernmental expenditure	4,799,630	25.6
Direct expenditure	12,056,634	64.3
General expenditure, by function:		
Education	7,246,839	38.7
Public welfare	4,150,491	22.1
Hospitals	2,018,521	10.8
Health	201,042	1.1
Highways	1,336,182	7.1
Police protection	100,614	0.5
Correction	355,523	1.9
Natural resources	239,692	1.3
Parks and recreation	39,714	0.2
Governmental administration	438,922	2.3
Interest on general debt	174,113	0.9
Other and unallocable	554,611	3.0
Utility expenditure	0	-
Liquor stores expenditure	0	-
Insurance trust expenditure	1,892,459	10.1
Debt at End of Fiscal Year	9,537,833	X
Cash and Security Holdings	23,300,641	X

X = Not applicable.
- = Zero or rounds to zero.
[1] Within insurance trust revenue, net earnings of state retirement systems is a calculated statistic (the item code in the data file is X08), and thus can be positive or negative. Net earnings is the sum of earnings on investments plus gains on investments minus losses on investments. The change made in 2002 for asset valuation from book to market value in accordance with Statement 34 of the Governmental Accounting Standards Board is reflected in the calculated statistics.

Table KS-16. State Government Tax Collections, 2017

(Dollars in thousands, percent.)

Item	Dollars	Percent distribution
Total Taxes	8,173,821	100.0
Property taxes	683,827	8.4
Sales and gross receipts	4,301,565	52.6
General sales and gross receipts	3,209,506	39.3
Selective sales and gross receipts	1,092,059	13.4
Alcoholic beverages	137,801	1.7
Amusements	313	-
Insurance premiums	310,420	3.8
Motor fuels	458,008	5.6
Pari-mutuels	X	-
Public utilities	378	-
Tobacco products	138,504	1.7
Other selective sales	46,635	0.6
Licenses	421,080	5.2
Alcoholic beverages	2,668	-
Amusements	7,950	0.1
Corporations in general	19,732	0.2
Hunting and fishing	30,961	0.4
Motor vehicle	224,198	2.7
Motor vehicle operators	32,757	0.4
Public utilities	4,972	0.1
Occupation and business, NEC	95,358	1.2
Other licenses	2,484	-
Income taxes	2,714,618	33.2
Individual income	2,327,652	28.5
Corporation net income	386,966	4.7
Other taxes	52,731	0.6
Death and gift	0	-
Documentary and stock transfer	X	-
Severance	52,731	0.6
Taxes, NEC	0	-

- = Zero or rounds to zero.

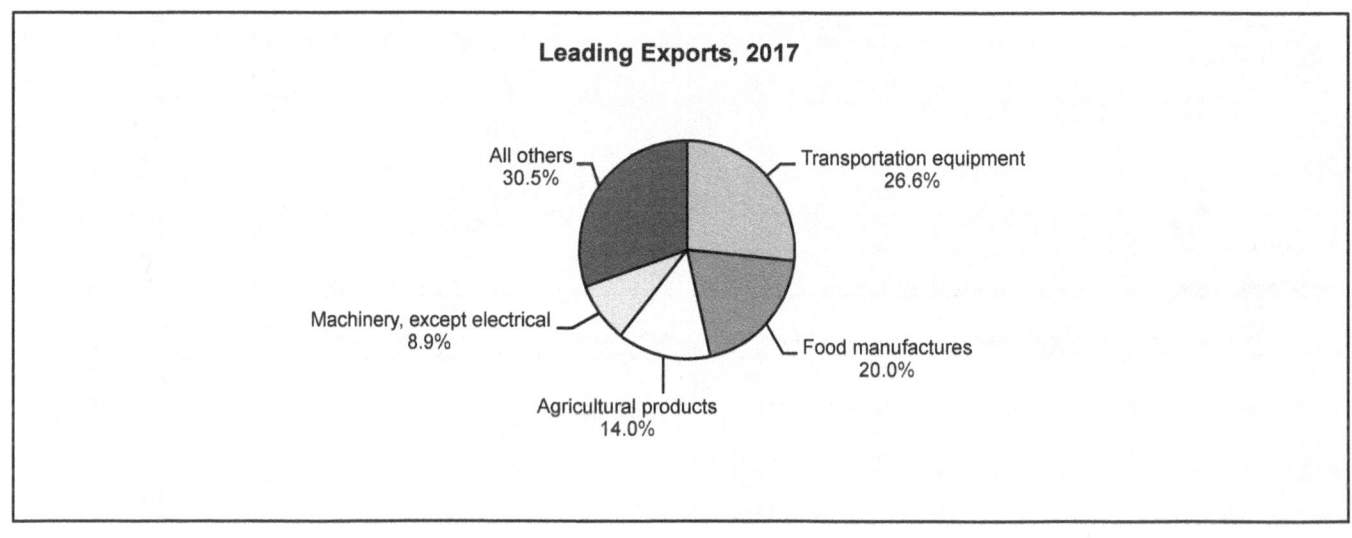

Leading Exports, 2017

All others 30.5%
Transportation equipment 26.6%
Food manufactures 20.0%
Agricultural products 14.0%
Machinery, except electrical 8.9%

KENTUCKY

Facts and Figures

Location: East central United States; bordered on the N by Illinois, Indiana, and Ohio, on the E by West Virginia and Virginia, on the S by Tennessee, and on the W by Missouri and Illinois

Area: 40,409 sq. mi. (104,659 sq. km.); rank—37th

Population: 4,454,189 (2017 est.); rank—26th

Principal Cities: capital—Frankfort; largest—Lexington

Statehood: June 1, 1792; 15th state

U.S. Congress: 2 senators, 6 representatives

State Motto: United We Stand, Divided We Fall

State Song: "My Old Kentucky Home"

State Nickname: The Bluegrass State

Abbreviations: KY; Ky.

State Symbols: flower—goldenrod; tree—tulip poplar; bird—cardinal

At a Glance

- With an increase in population of 2.4 percent, Kentucky ranked 33rd among the states in growth from 2010 to 2017.

- Kentucky ranked 6th in the nation for the highest rate of drug overdose deaths in 2016, with 33.5 deaths per 100,000 population.

- In 2016, Kentucky's median household income was $46,659, the 6th lowest in the country, and 18.5 percent of the population lived below the poverty level.

- The property crime rate in Kentucky in 2016 was 2,189.7 per 100,000 population, compared to the U.S. rate of 2,450.7 per 100,000 population.

- In 2016, 5.1 percent of Kentucky residents did not have health insurance, compared to 8.6 percent of all U.S. residents.

Table KY-1. Population by Age, Sex, Race, and Hispanic Origin

(Number, percent, except where noted.)

Sex, age, race, and Hispanic origin	2000	2010	2017 [1]	Average annual percent change, 2010–2017
Total Population..	4,041,769	4,339,367	4,454,189	2.6
Percent of total U.S. population	1.4	1.4	1.4	X
Sex				
Male..	1,975,368	2,134,952	2,194,318	2.8
Female	2,066,401	2,204,425	2,259,871	2.5
Age				
Under 5 years..	265,901	282,367	276,883	-1.9
5 to 19 years...	847,743	863,837	848,880	-1.7
20 to 64 years...	2,423,332	2,614,936	2,617,077	0.1
65 years and over	504,793	578,227	711,349	23.0
Median age (years)	35.9	38.1	38.8	1.8
Race and Hispanic Origin				
One race				
White	3,640,889	3,864,193	3,908,964	1.2
Black	295,994	342,804	372,839	8.8
American Indian and Alaska Native	8,616	12,105	13,263	9.6
Asian	29,744	50,177	69,734	39.0
Native Hawaiian or Other Pacific Islander	1,460	3,199	3,848	20.3
Two or more races	42,443	66,889	85,541	27.9
Hispanic (of any race)...	59,939	138,618	163,489	17.9

X = Not applicable.
[1] Population figures for 2017 are July 1 estimates. The 2010 estimates are taken from the 2010 Census.
- = Zero or rounds to zero.

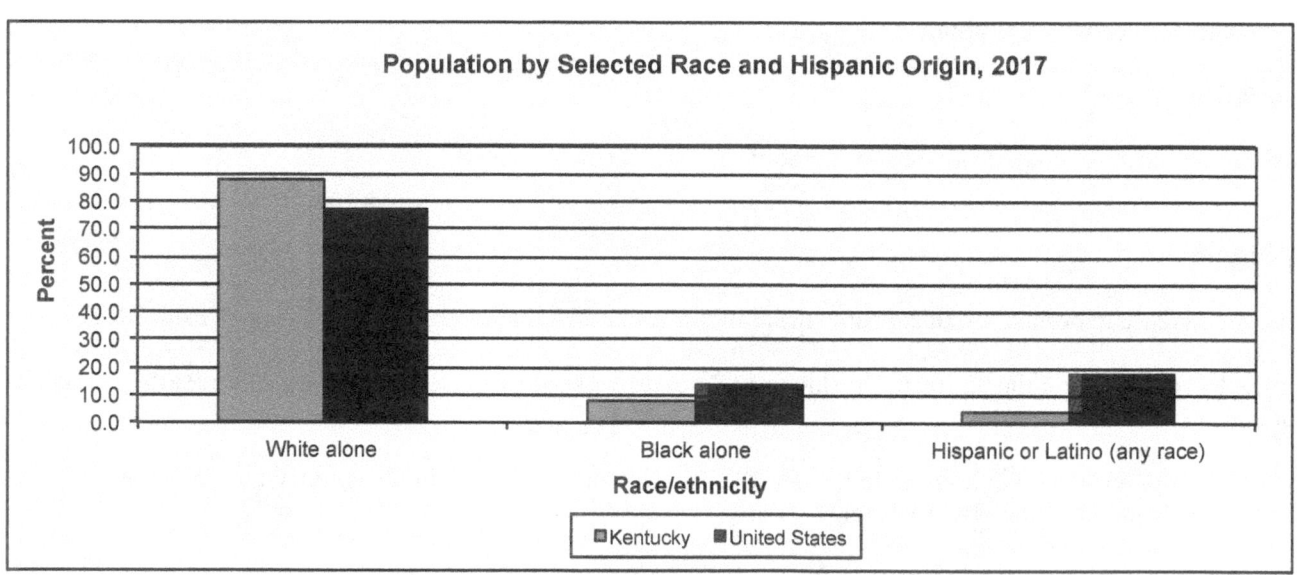

Population by Selected Race and Hispanic Origin, 2017

Table KY-2. Marital Status

(Number, percent distribution.)

Sex, age, and marital status	2000	2010	2016
Males, 15 Years and Over	1,551,174	1,702,020	1,752,576
Never married	25.9	30.8	33.1
Now married, except separated...	59.9	52.0	49.8
Separated..	1.5	2.1	1.8
Widowed..	2.6	2.8	3.2
Divorced..	10.2	12.3	12.2
Females, 15 Years and Over	1,665,993	1,794,164	1,848,114
Never married	19.7	24.2	26.5
Now married, except separated...	55.0	48.9	46.6
Separated..	2.1	2.6	2.6
Widowed..	11.5	10.6	10.0
Divorced..	11.8	13.7	14.3

Table KY-3. Households and Housing Characteristics

(Number, percent, dollars.)

Item	2000	2010	2016	Average annual percent change, 2010–2016
Total Households...............	1,590,647	1,684,348	1,717,706	0.3
Family households........................	1,104,398	1,126,685	1,121,404	-0.1
Married-couple family...................	857,944	833,872	812,069	-0.4
Other family............................	246,454	292,813	309,335	0.9
Male householder, no wife present.....	58,497	76,832	83,429	1.4
Female householder, no husband present...	187,957	215,981	225,906	0.8
Nonfamily households.....................	486,249	557,663	596,302	1.2
Householder living alone...............	414,095	470,103	494,731	0.9
Householder not living alone...........	72,154	87,560	101,571	2.7
Housing Characteristics				
Total housing units......................	1,750,927	1,928,617	1,965,577	0.3
Occupied housing units...................	1,590,647	1,684,348	1,717,706	0.3
Owner occupied........................	1,125,397	1,156,292	1,148,175	-0.1
Renter occupied.......................	465,250	528,056	569,531	1.3
Average household size....................	2.47	2.51	2.51	-
Financial Characteristics				
Median gross rent of renter-occupied housing.......	445	613	707	2.6
Median monthly owner costs for housing units with a mortgage..........	816	1,072	1,111	0.6
Median value of owner-occupied housing units...........	86,700	121,600	135,600	1.9

- = Zero or rounds to zero.

Table KY-4. Migration, Origin, and Language

(Number, percent.)

Characteristic	State			U.S.		
	2015	2016	Percent change	2015	2016	Percent change
Residence 1 Year Ago						
Population 1 year and over................	4,373,403	4,385,213	0.3	317,635,720	319,361,956	0.5
Same house................	84.8	84.3	X	85.3	85.4	X
Different house in the U.S..................	14.9	15.2	X	14.1	13.9	X
Same county..................	8.3	8.9	X	8.5	8.3	X
Different county..................	6.5	6.3	X	5.6	5.6	X
Same state..................	4.1	3.7	X	3.2	3.2	X
Different state..................	2.4	2.6	X	2.4	2.4	X
Abroad..................	0.4	0.4	X	0.7	0.7	X
Place of Birth						
Native born..................	4,267,756	4,281,010	0.3	278,128,449	279,388,170	0.5
Male..................	49.1	49.0	X	49.3	49.3	X
Female..................	50.9	51.0	X	50.7	50.7	X
Foreign born..................	157,336	155,964	-0.9	43,290,372	43,739,345	1.0
Male..................	50.2	52.1	X	48.6	48.5	X
Female..................	49.8	47.9	X	51.4	51.5	X
Foreign born; naturalized U.S. citizen..................	58,196	60,913	4.7	20,697,103	21,238,372	2.6
Male..................	44.4	47.7	X	45.9	45.9	X
Female..................	55.6	52.3	X	54.1	54.1	X
Foreign born; not a U.S. citizen..................	99,140	95,051	-4.1	22,593,269	22,500,973	-0.4
Male..................	53.6	54.9	X	51.1	51.0	X
Female..................	46.4	45.1	X	48.9	49.0	X
Entered 2010 or later..................	28.3	29.8	X	15.6	18.6	X
Entered 2000 to 2009..................	34.5	35.3	X	27.9	26.7	X
Entered before 2000..................	37.2	34.9	X	56.5	54.7	X
World Region of Birth, Foreign						
Foreign-born population, excluding population born at sea......	157,336	155,964	-0.9	43,289,646	43,738,901	1.0
Europe..................	15.1	12.8	X	11.1	10.9	X
Asia..................	35.6	36.7	X	30.6	30.8	X
Africa..................	8.1	11.2	X	4.8	4.9	X
Oceania..................	0.7	0.8	X	0.6	0.6	X
Latin America..................	37.7	36.2	X	51.1	51.0	X
North America..................	2.8	2.2	X	1.9	1.8	X
Language Spoken at Home and Ability to Speak English						
Population 5 years and over..................	4,151,726	4,164,025	0.3	301,625,014	303,328,961	0.6
English only..................	94.7	94.8	X	78.5	78.4	X
Language other than English..................	5.3	5.2	X	21.5	21.6	X
Speaks English less than "very well"..................	2.1	2.1	X	8.6	8.6	X

NA = Not available.
X = Not applicable.
- = Zero or rounds to zero.

Table KY-5. Median Income and Poverty Status, 2016

(Number, percent, except as noted.)

Characteristic	State		U.S.	
	Number	Percent	Number	Percent
Median Income				
Households (dollars)...	46,659	X	57,617	X
Families (dollars)	59,023	X	71,062	X
Below Poverty Level (All People)	794,060	18.5	44,268,996	14.0
Sex				
Male	343,504	16.4	19,760,056	12.8
Female	450,556	20.5	24,508,940	15.2
Age				
Under 18 years..	247,780	25.0	14,115,713	19.5
Related children under 18 years............................	240,988	24.5	13,805,435	19.1
18 to 64 years...	472,126	17.9	25,723,818	13.2
65 years and over	74,154	11.1	4,429,465	9.2

X = Not applicable.

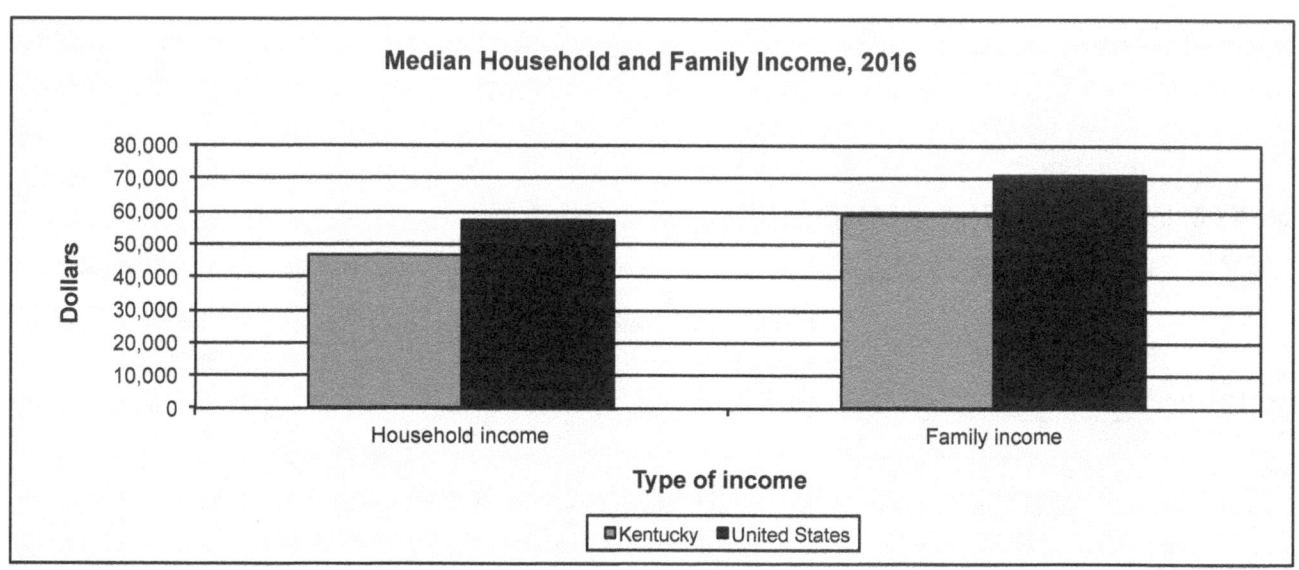

Median Household and Family Income, 2016

Kentucky United States

Table KY-6. Health Insurance Coverage Status for the Civilian Noninstitutionalized Population and Children Under 18 Years of Age

(Number, percent.)

Item	2008	2009	2010	2011	2012	2013	2014	2015	2016
Civilian Noninstitutionalized Population	4,187,839	4,225,355	4,242,714	4,284,357	4,292,718	4,312,100	4,328,524	4,342,711	4,354,380
Covered by Private or Public Insurance									
Number..	3,597,707	3,612,074	3,595,673	3,665,899	3,697,258	3,695,652	3,962,462	4,081,243	4,131,030
Percent..	85.9	85.5	84.7	85.6	86.1	85.7	91.5	94.0	94.9
Not Covered									
Number..	590,132	613,281	647,041	618,458	595,460	616,448	366,062	261,468	223,350
Percent..	14.1	14.5	15.3	14.4	13.9	14.3	8.5	6.0	5.1
Percent in the U.S. not covered..........................	15.1	15.1	15.5	15.1	14.8	14.5	11.7	9.4	8.6
Children Under 18 Years of Age	1,004,446	1,014,997	1,018,375	1,022,948	1,016,026	1,012,120	1,012,771	1,008,187	1,009,986
Covered by Private or Public Insurance									
Number..	934,473	950,590	957,195	960,504	959,668	952,590	969,473	965,380	977,991
Percent..	93.0	93.7	94.0	93.9	94.5	94.1	95.7	95.8	96.8
Not Covered									
Number..	69,973	64,407	61,180	62,444	56,358	59,530	43,298	42,807	31,995
Percent..	7.0	6.3	6.0	6.1	5.5	5.9	4.3	4.2	3.2
Percent in the U.S. not covered..........................	9.9	8.6	8.0	7.5	7.2	7.1	6.0	4.8	4.5

Table KY-7. Employment Status by Demographic Group, 2017

(Numbers in thousands, percent.)

Characteristic	Civilian noninstitutional population	Civilian labor force		Employed		Unemployed	
		Number	Percent of population	Number	Percent of population	Number	Percent of population
Total...................................	3,476	2,073	59.7	1,966	56.6	107	5.2
Sex							
Male....................................	1,683	1,102	65.5	1,042	61.9	61	5.5
Female.................................	1,793	971	54.2	925	51.6	47	4.8
Race, Sex, and Hispanic Origin							
White...................................	3,121	1,845	59.1	1,756	56.3	89	4.8
Male.................................	1,508	980	65.0	929	61.6	51	5.2
Female..............................	1,613	865	53.6	827	51.3	38	4.4
Black or African American.........	275	175	63.6	161	58.3	15	8.3
Male.................................	134	93	69.1	85	63.1	8	8.7
Female..............................	141	82	58.3	76	53.6	7	8.0
Hispanic or Latino ethnicity[1].....	110	66	60.5	63	57.1	4	5.6
Male.................................	NA	NA	NA	NA	NA	NA	NA
Female..............................	NA	NA	NA	NA	NA	NA	NA
Age							
16 to 19 years.......................	251	99	39.3	87	34.8	12	11.6
20 to 24 years.......................	264	205	77.7	187	70.9	18	8.7
25 to 34 years.......................	560	455	81.2	425	75.8	30	6.6
35 to 44 years.......................	544	427	78.5	406	74.6	21	4.9
45 to 54 years.......................	569	431	75.8	418	73.6	13	2.9
55 to 64 years.......................	580	344	59.3	334	57.6	10	2.8
65 years and over...................	708	113	16.0	108	15.3	5	4.5

NOTE: Data in Table 7 are from the Current Population Survey (CPS) and do not match the estimates in Table 8. See notes and definitions for further information.
[1] May be of any race.
NA = Not available.

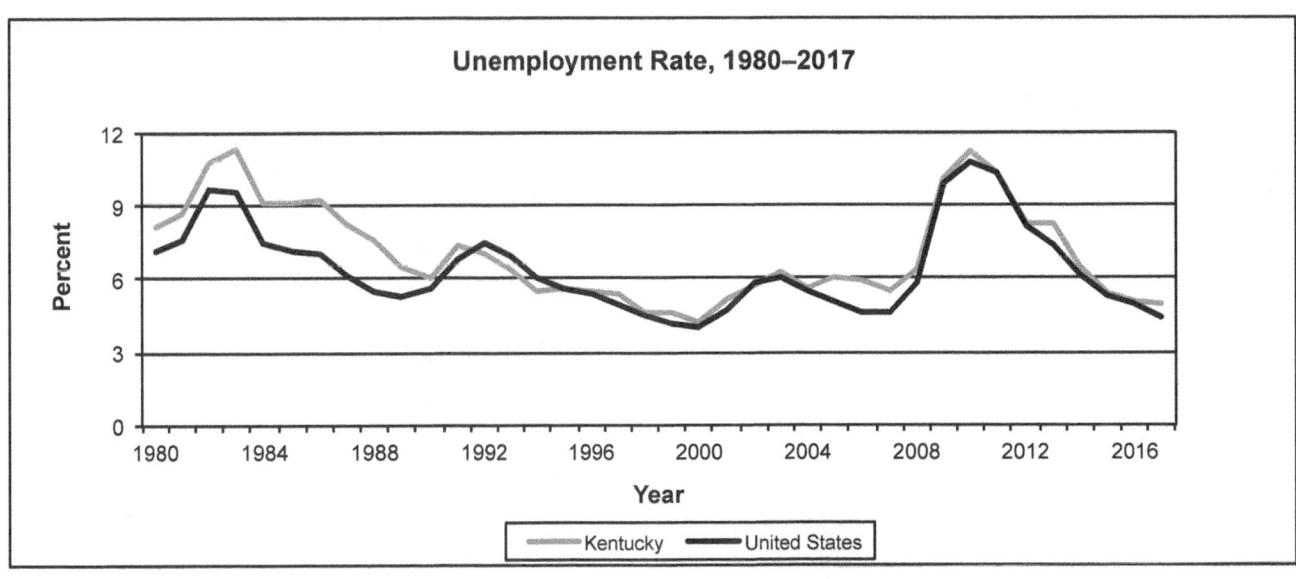

Unemployment Rate, 1980–2017

Table KY-8. Employment Status of the Civilian Noninstitutional Population Age 16 Years and Over

(Number, percent.)

Year	Civilian labor force	Civilian participation rate	Employed	Unemployed	Unemployment rate
2009..........	2,060,162	61.9	1,847,126	213,036	10.3
2010..........	2,054,375	61.3	1,844,650	209,725	10.2
2011..........	2,056,410	61.0	1,862,928	193,482	9.4
2012..........	2,059,127	60.8	1,891,162	167,965	8.2
2013..........	2,055,442	60.4	1,890,879	164,563	8.0
2014..........	2,003,842	58.6	1,874,516	129,326	6.5
2015..........	1,976,967	57.5	1,872,326	104,641	5.3
2016..........	2,012,279	58.2	1,909,158	103,121	5.1
2017..........	2,052,368	59.0	1,952,066	100,302	4.9

Table KY-9. Employment and Average Wages by Industry

(Estimates through 2010 are based on the 2007 *North American Industry Classification System* [NAICS]. Estimates from 2011 onward are based on the 2012 NAICS.)

Industry	2010	2011	2012	2013	2014	2015	2016
	Number of jobs						
Wage and Salary Employment by Industry	1,866,856	1,887,646	1,910,516	1,923,908	1,949,783	1,979,661	1,997,289
Farm Wage and Salary Employment	12,662	14,003	14,781	13,660	14,615	16,632	13,700
Nonfarm Wage and Salary Employment	1,854,194	1,873,643	1,895,735	1,910,248	1,935,168	1,963,029	1,983,589
Private wage and salary employment	1,470,901	1,492,161	1,523,431	1,542,651	1,572,666	1,605,288	1,631,713
Forestry, fishing, and related activities	7,575	7,328	7,276	7,434	7,511	7,559	7,659
Mining	21,800	22,623	20,295	17,189	16,235	13,698	10,255
Utilities	6,422	6,514	6,566	6,512	6,624	6,569	6,618
Construction	70,257	69,768	69,366	70,046	74,852	77,622	79,016
Manufacturing	209,255	212,914	223,357	229,626	235,074	241,640	247,954
Durable goods manufacturing	124,981	128,840	138,706	143,808	149,164	155,651	161,314
Nondurable goods manufacturing	84,274	84,074	84,651	85,818	85,910	85,989	86,640
Wholesale trade	72,113	72,561	73,086	74,323	74,764	75,124	76,084
Retail trade	202,117	202,920	204,597	204,821	206,669	211,304	216,012
Transportation and warehousing	82,554	85,723	87,256	86,636	90,901	95,877	101,057
Information	26,221	26,881	26,593	26,325	26,360	25,340	22,784
Finance and insurance	69,631	70,162	72,204	73,802	74,992	76,764	77,719
Real estate and rental and leasing	18,605	18,260	18,249	18,641	18,604	18,911	19,567
Professional, scientific, and technical services	70,037	69,782	68,299	69,960	72,168	73,840	75,292
Management of companies and enterprises	19,462	20,013	20,526	20,570	20,677	19,972	20,868
Administrative and waste services	91,904	98,934	105,185	111,676	119,153	122,832	122,335
Educational services	30,996	31,683	32,052	32,006	32,600	32,723	32,383
Health care and social assistance	222,785	225,810	232,734	233,373	231,634	236,822	241,945
Arts, entertainment, and recreation	18,924	18,557	19,842	20,265	20,291	21,271	22,271
Accommodation and food services	149,848	152,074	156,258	160,290	163,004	167,696	172,810
Other services, except public administration	80,395	79,654	79,690	79,156	80,553	79,724	79,084
Government and government enterprises	383,293	381,482	372,304	367,597	362,502	357,741	351,876
	Dollars						
Average Wages and Salaries by Industry	38,549	39,545	40,370	40,707	41,797	43,108	44,747
Average Farm Wages and Salaries	20,674	16,363	21,340	23,808	22,787	19,003	25,432
Average Nonfarm Wages and Salaries	38,671	39,719	40,519	40,828	41,941	43,312	44,880
Average private wages and salaries	38,087	39,106	40,116	40,477	41,699	43,109	44,729
Forestry, fishing, and related activities	26,307	26,425	26,931	27,634	28,278	29,556	32,571
Mining	67,353	69,617	66,776	68,397	68,696	68,485	66,832
Utilities	70,649	72,240	74,123	76,425	79,776	82,320	84,438
Construction	43,590	44,005	45,923	47,382	49,900	51,603	52,718
Manufacturing	49,656	51,280	52,617	53,294	55,081	56,704	57,792
Durable goods manufacturing	51,094	53,230	54,322	54,829	56,382	58,308	58,909
Nondurable goods manufacturing	47,524	48,293	49,822	50,722	52,823	53,800	55,711
Wholesale trade	51,758	53,664	54,842	55,085	57,408	60,110	62,256
Retail trade	23,731	24,113	24,672	24,817	25,143	25,998	27,106
Transportation and warehousing	47,845	47,677	48,895	49,391	50,533	51,763	55,180
Information	43,486	44,472	45,933	46,393	49,046	48,951	52,252
Finance and insurance	56,615	58,925	60,333	60,938	63,893	66,590	69,419
Real estate and rental and leasing	33,492	35,399	36,421	35,430	37,188	38,381	40,963
Professional, scientific, and technical services	51,062	52,835	55,096	56,280	57,915	60,413	62,005
Management of companies and enterprises	86,258	91,249	95,273	91,138	91,831	96,922	95,857
Administrative and waste services	25,398	25,657	26,533	26,774	27,252	28,308	30,260
Educational services	23,885	24,247	24,718	25,027	24,750	24,969	26,012
Health care and social assistance	40,782	41,992	42,903	43,448	44,561	46,576	48,539
Arts, entertainment, and recreation	21,464	21,847	22,091	22,462	23,906	23,521	23,809
Accommodation and food services	15,143	15,498	16,063	16,167	16,841	17,566	18,884
Other services, except public administration	27,030	27,746	29,351	30,095	30,989	32,298	34,016
Government and government enterprises	40,914	42,116	42,164	42,302	42,990	44,224	45,582

Table KY-10. Employment Characteristics by Family Type

(Number, percent.)

Family type and labor force status	2014		2015		2016	
	Total	Families with own children under 18 years	Total	Families with own children under 18 years	Total	Families with own children under 18 years
All Families...	1,121,747	464,494	1,131,839	455,703	1,121,404	463,090
FAMILY TYPE AND LABOR FORCE STATUS						
Married-Couple Families..........................	826,087	307,360	828,120	300,055	812,069	298,129
Both husband and wife in labor force...................	48.5	65.6	46.7	65.2	48.1	67.2
Husband in labor force, wife not in labor force	20.8	25.9	21.1	25.3	20.0	24.3
Wife in labor force, husband not in labor force	9.0	4.5	9.5	5.5	9.3	5.0
Both husband and wife not in labor force................	21.7	4.0	22.1	3.6	22.0	3.0
Other Families	295,660	157,134	303,719	155,648	309,335	164,961
Female householder, no husband present................	73.2	74.9	71.8	73.8	73.0	74.9
In labor force..	45.2	57.4	43.6	56.6	46.5	59.3
Not in labor force	28.0	17.4	28.1	17.2	26.5	15.6
Male householder, no wife present....................	26.8	25.1	28.2	26.2	27.0	25.1
In labor force..	18.1	20.3	19.4	21.1	18.2	20.8
Not in labor force	8.7	4.8	8.8	5.1	8.8	4.3

Table KY-11. School Enrollment and Educational Attainment, 2016

(Number, percent.)

Item	State	U.S.
Enrollment		
Total population 3 years and over, enrolled in school	1,085,033	81,572,277
Enrolled in nursery school or preschool (percent)...................	5.7	6.0
Enrolled in kindergarten (percent)................................	4.8	5.0
Enrolled in elementary school, grades 1-8 (percent)................	42.3	40.3
Enrolled in high school, grades 9-12 (percent)....................	21.6	21.0
Enrolled in college or graduate school (percent)..................	25.5	27.7
Attainment		
Total population 25 years and over	2,995,509	218,475,480
Less than ninth grade (percent)	5.7	5.4
9th to 12th grade, no diploma (percent)	8.6	7.2
High school graduate, including equivalency (percent).............	32.3	27.2
Some college, no degree (percent)	21.4	20.6
Associate's degree (percent)....................................	8.6	8.4
Bachelor's degree (percent)	14.0	19.3
Graduate or professional degree (percent)........................	9.5	11.9
High school graduate or higher (percent)	85.7	87.5
Bachelor's degree or higher (percent)............................	23.4	31.3

Table KY-12. Public School Characteristics and Educational Indicators

(Number, percent; data derived from National Center of Education Statistics.)

Item	State	U.S.
Public Schools, 2015–2016 (except where noted)		
Number of school districts..	186	18,328
Number of schools..	1,541	98,456
Number of students	686,598	50,327,015
Number of teachers	41,902	3,151,497
Student-teacher ratio	16.4	16.0
Expenditures per student (dollars), 2014-2015.....................	9,560	11,445
Four-year adjusted cohort graduation rate (ACGR)[1,2]	88.6	84.1
Students eligible for free or reduced-price lunch (percent), 2014-2015...	56.9	51.8
English language learners (percent), Fall 2015	3.2	9.5
Students age 3 to 21 served under IDEA, part B (percent)...........	14.5	13.2

Public Schools by Type	Number	Percent of state public schools
Total number of schools..	1,541	100.0
Regular	1,230	79.8
Special education..	8	0.5
Vocational education...	121	7.9
Alternative education..	182	11.8

NOTE: Every school is assigned only one school type based on its instructional emphasis.
[1] ACGR data represents a new method of calculating high-school completion rates and may not be comparable to previous years' data for Averaged Freshmen Graduation Rates (AFGR).
[2] The United States 4-year ACGRs were estimated using both the reported 4-year ACGR data from 49 states and the District of Columbia and using imputed data for Idaho. The estimate for American Indian/Alaska Native students also includes imputed data for Virginia.

Table KY-13. Reported Voting and Registration of the Voting-Age Population, November 2016

(Numbers in thousands, percent.)

Item	Total population	Total citizen population	Registered			Voted		
			Total registered	Percent registered (total population)	Percent registered (total citizen population)	Total voted	Percent voted (total population)	Percent voted (total citizen population)
U.S. Total	245,502	224,059	157,596	64.2	70.3	137,537	56.0	61.4
State Total..............................	3,348	3,246	2,253	67.3	69.4	1,850	55.3	57.0
Sex								
Male	1,614	1,550	1,035	64.1	66.8	861	53.3	55.5
Female	1,734	1,697	1,218	70.3	71.8	989	57.0	58.3
Race								
White alone	3,014	2,953	2,038	67.6	69.0	1,669	55.4	56.5
White, non-Hispanic alone	2,892	2,881	1,998	69.1	69.3	1,634	56.5	56.7
Black alone	250	231	187	74.9	81.2	159	63.7	69.1
Asian alone	28	14	3	(B)	(B)	3	(B)	(B)
Hispanic (of any race)	138	79	44	(B)	(B)	38	(B)	(B)
White alone or in combination	3,052	2,991	2,055	67.3	68.7	1,680	55.0	56.1
Black alone or in combination	281	262	210	74.5	80.0	175	62.3	66.9
Asian alone or in combination	36	23	8	(B)	(B)	8	(B)	(B)
Age								
18 to 24 years	406	384	249	61.5	64.9	207	51.1	53.9
25 to 34 years	530	496	336	63.3	67.7	273	51.5	55.1
35 to 44 years	553	529	360	65.1	68.1	300	54.2	56.7
45 to 64 years	1,244	1,229	853	68.6	69.4	703	56.6	57.2
65 years and over	615	609	455	73.9	74.7	366	59.5	60.2

B = Base is less than 75,000 and therefore too small to show the derived measure.

Table KY-14. Crime

(Number, rate per 100,000. Data are derived from the FBI Uniform Crime Reports.)

Item	State			U.S. [1,2,3,4]		
	2015	2016	Percent change	2015	2016	Percent change
TOTAL POPULATION [5]	4,425,092	4,436,974	0.3	321,418,820	323,127,513	0.5
VIOLENT CRIME						
Number	9,676	10,308	6.5	1,231,566	1,248,185	1.3
Rate	218.7	232.3	6.2	383.2	386.3	0.8
Murder and Nonnegligent Manslaughter						
Number	209	260	24.4	15,696	17,250	9.9
Rate	4.7	5.9	25.5	4.9	5.3	8.2
Rape [6]						
Number [6]	1,492	1,641	10.0	124,047	130,603	5.3
Rate	33.7	37.0	9.8	38.6	40.4	4.7
Robbery						
Number	3,307	3,369	1.9	327,374	332,198	1.5
Rate	74.7	75.9	1.6	101.9	102.8	0.9
Aggravated Assault						
Number	4,668	5,038	7.9	764,449	803,007	5.0
Rate	105.5	113.5	7.6	237.8	248.5	4.5
PROPERTY CRIME						
Number	96,362	97,158	0.8	7,993,631	7,919,035	-0.9
Rate	2,177.6	2,189.7	0.6	2,487.0	2,450.7	-1.5
Burglary						
Number	22,260	20,834	-6.4	1,579,527	1,515,096	-4.1
Rate	503.0	469.6	-6.6	491.4	468.9	-4.6
Larceny-Theft						
Number	66,320	66,438	0.2	5,706,346	5,638,455	-1.2
Rate	1,498.7	1,497.4	-0.1	1,775.4	1,745.0	-1.7
Motor Vehicle Theft						
Number	7,782	9,886	27.0	707,758	765,484	8.2
Rate	175.9	222.8	26.7	220.2	236.9	7.6

NOTE: Although arson data are included in the trend and clearance tables, sufficient data are not available to estimate totals for this offense. Therefore, no arson data are published in this table.

X = Not applicable.

- = Zero or rounds to zero.

[1] The crime figures have been adjusted.

[2] The data collection methodology for the offense of forcible rape used by the Minnesota state Uniform Crime Reporting (UCR) Program (with the exception of Minneapolis and St. Paul, Minnesota) does not comply with national UCR Program guidelines. Consequently, its figures for forcible rape and violent crime (of which forcible rape is a part) are not published in this table.

[3] Includes offenses reported by the Zoological Police and the Metro Transit Police.

[4] Because of changes in the state's reporting practices, figures are not comparable to previous years' data.

[5] Populations are U.S. Census Bureau provisional estimates as of July 1 of each year.

[6] The figures shown for the offense of rape were estimated using the revised Uniform Crime Reporting (UCR) definition of rape.

Table KY-15. State Government Finances, 2016

(Dollar amounts in thousands, percent distribution.)

Item	Dollars	Percent distribution
Total Revenue	29,941,369	100.0
General revenue	28,222,220	94.3
Intergovernmental revenue	11,579,669	38.7
Taxes	11,778,866	39.3
General sales	3,462,704	11.6
Selective sales	2,140,416	7.1
License taxes	505,377	1.7
Individual income tax	4,282,080	14.3
Corporate income tax	606,840	2.0
Other taxes	781,449	2.6
Current charges	3,684,666	12.3
Miscellaneous general revenue	1,179,019	3.9
Utility revenue	0	-
Liquor stores revenue	0	-
Insurance trust revenue [1]	1,719,149	5.7
Total Expenditure	35,347,118	100.0
Intergovernmental expenditure	4,785,754	13.5
Direct expenditure	30,561,364	86.5
Current operation	21,995,960	62.2
Capital outlay	2,431,274	6.9
Insurance benefits and repayments	4,396,382	12.4
Assistance and subsidies	1,083,914	3.1
Interest on debt	653,834	1.8
Exhibit: Salaries and wages	4,323,891	12.2
Total Expenditure	35,347,118	100.0
General expenditure	30,919,288	87.5
Intergovernmental expenditure	4,785,754	13.5
Direct expenditure	26,133,534	73.9
General expenditure, by function:		
Education	10,371,844	29.3
Public welfare	11,265,798	31.9
Hospitals	1,865,675	5.3
Health	481,814	1.4
Highways	2,414,369	6.8
Police protection	248,820	0.7
Correction	631,663	1.8
Natural resources	438,325	1.2
Parks and recreation	126,847	0.4
Governmental administration	1,144,131	3.2
Interest on general debt	653,834	1.8
Other and unallocable	1,276,168	3.6
Utility expenditure	25,738	0.1
Liquor stores expenditure	5710	-
Insurance trust expenditure	4,396,382	12.4
Debt at End of Fiscal Year	14,453,423	X
Cash and Security Holdings	39,481,499	X

X = Not applicable.
- = Zero or rounds to zero.
[1] Within insurance trust revenue, net earnings of state retirement systems is a calculated statistic (the item code in the data file is X08), and thus can be positive or negative. Net earnings is the sum of earnings on investments plus gains on investments minus losses on investments. The change made in 2002 for asset valuation from book to market value in accordance with Statement 34 of the Governmental Accounting Standards Board is reflected in the calculated statistics.

Table KY-16. State Government Tax Collections, 2017

(Dollars in thousands, percent.)

Item	Dollars	Percent distribution
Total Taxes	11,907,759	100.0
Property taxes	709,772	6.0
Sales and gross receipts	5,649,708	47.4
General sales and gross receipts	3,490,639	29.3
Selective sales and gross receipts	2,159,069	18.1
Alcoholic beverages	146,227	1.2
Amusements	174	-
Insurance premiums	153,728	1.3
Motor fuels	701,440	5.9
Pari-mutuels	6,643	0.1
Public utilities	58,298	0.5
Tobacco products	243,096	2.0
Other selective sales	849,463	7.1
Licenses	500,447	4.2
Alcoholic beverages	6,638	0.1
Amusements	277	-
Corporations in general	110,072	0.9
Hunting and fishing	28,532	0.2
Motor vehicle	208,389	1.8
Motor vehicle operators	16,827	0.1
Public utilities	X	-
Occupation and business, NEC	125,994	1.1
Other licenses	3,718	-
Income taxes	4,852,835	40.8
Individual income	4,394,185	36.9
Corporation net income	458,650	3.9
Other taxes	194,997	1.6
Death and gift	46,345	0.4
Documentary and stock transfer	3,530	-
Severance	145,122	1.2
Taxes, NEC	0	-

- = Zero or rounds to zero.
X = Not applicable.

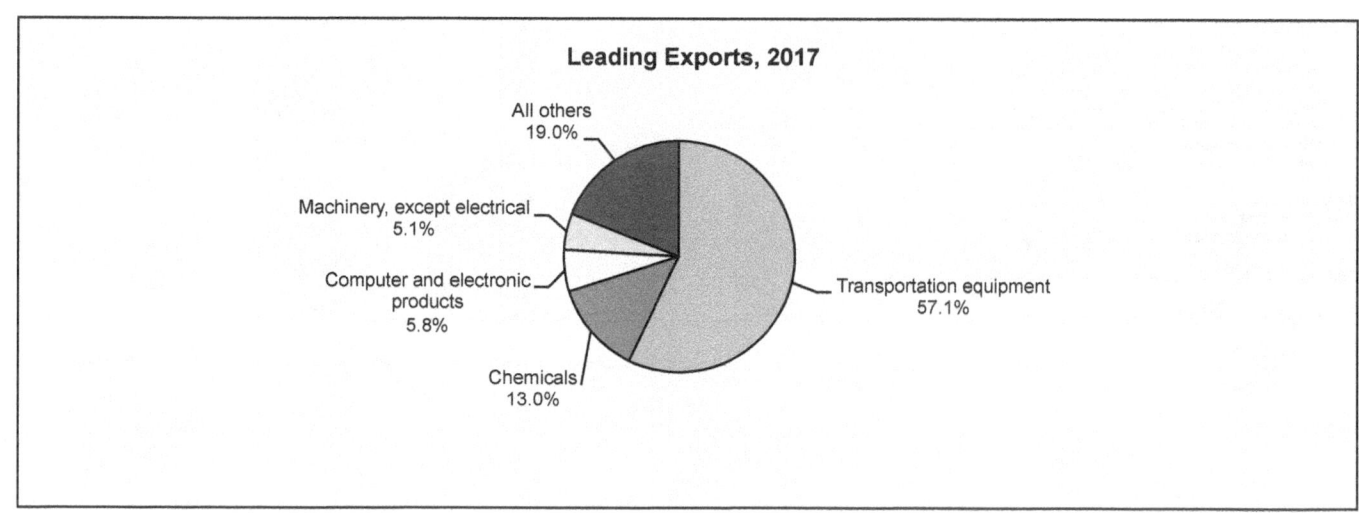

Leading Exports, 2017

All others 19.0%

Machinery, except electrical 5.1%

Computer and electronic products 5.8%

Chemicals 13.0%

Transportation equipment 57.1%

LOUISIANA

Location: South central United States; bordered on the N by Arkansas, on the E by Mississippi, on the S by the Gulf of Mexico, and on the W by Texas

Area: 51,840 sq. mi. (134,264 sq. km.); rank—31st

Population: 4,684,333 (2017 est.); rank—25th

Principal Cities: capital—Baton Rouge; largest—New Orleans

Statehood: April 30, 1812; 18th state

U.S. Congress: 2 senators, 6 representatives

State Motto: Union, Justice, Confidence

State Song: "Give Me Louisiana"

State Nicknames: The Pelican State; The Bayou State

Abbreviations: LA; La.

State Symbols: flower—magnolia; tree—bald cypress; bird—Eastern brown pelican

At a Glance

- With an increase in population of 3.1 percent, Louisiana ranked 28th in population growth from 2010 to 2017.

- Louisiana's median household income in 2016 was $45,146, the 4th lowest in the country, and 20.2 percent of the population lived below the poverty level, which was the 2nd highest poverty rate among the states.

- In 2017, Louisiana had the 3rd highest percent of residents who self-identified as "Black or African-American Alone," with 32.6 percent of residents in this category.

- In 2016, 10.3 percent of Louisiana's population did not have health insurance, compared to 8.6 percent of the entire U.S. population.

- Louisiana consumed the most energy per capita in 2016, using 897.4 million Btu per person, compared to the U.S. average of 300.9 million Btu per capita.

Table LA-1. Population by Age, Sex, Race, and Hispanic Origin

(Number, percent, except where noted.)

Sex, age, race, and Hispanic origin	2000	2010	2017 [1]	Average annual percent change, 2010–2017
Total Population....................................	4,468,976	4,533,372	4,684,333	3.3
Percent of total U.S. population	1.6	1.5	1.4	X
Sex				
Male..	2,162,903	2,219,292	2,289,446	3.2
Female	2,306,073	2,314,080	2,394,887	3.5
Age				
Under 5 years....................................	317,392	314,260	312,038	-0.7
5 to 19 years	1,050,637	939,977	911,830	-3.0
20 to 64 years	2,584,018	2,721,278	2,763,082	1.5
65 years and over	516,929	557,857	697,383	25.0
Median age (years)	34.0	35.8	36.8	2.8
Race and Hispanic Origin				
One race				
White	2,856,161	2,902,875	2,951,003	1.7
Black	1,451,944	1,462,969	1,528,167	4.5
American Indian and Alaska Native	25,477	33,037	36,526	10.6
Asian...	54,758	71,829	87,305	21.5
Native Hawaiian or Other Pacific Islander	1,240	2,588	2,937	13.5
Two or more races	48,265	60,074	78,395	30.5
Hispanic (of any race).......................	107,738	200,653	245,135	22.2

X = Not applicable.

[1] Population figures for 2017 are July 1 estimates. The 2010 estimates are taken from the 2010 Census.

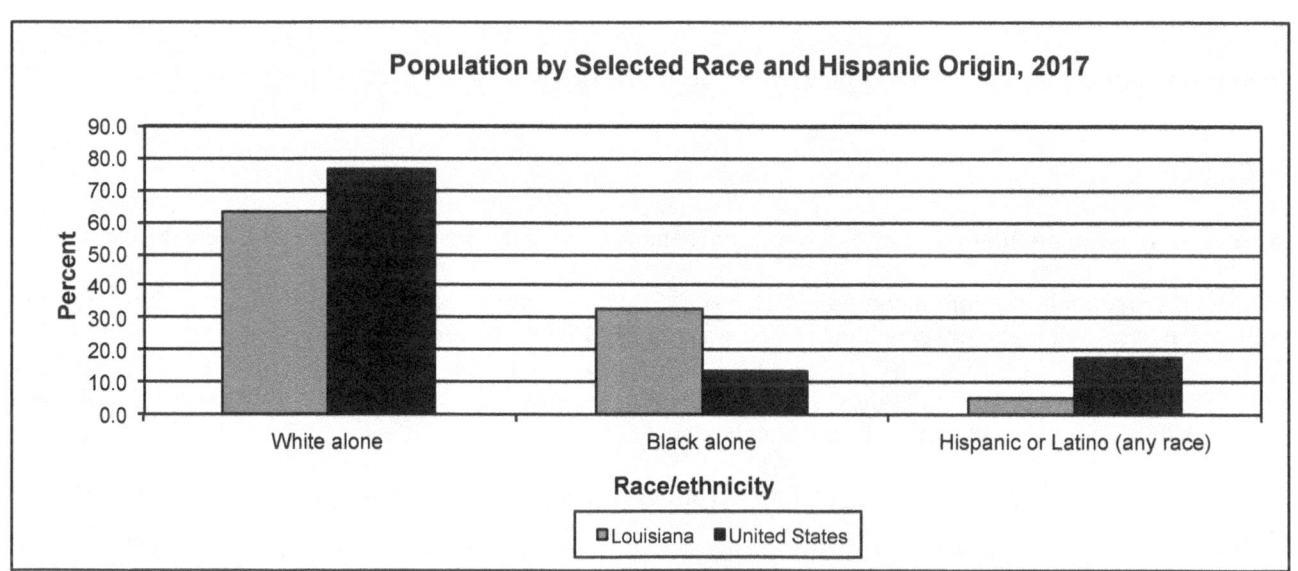

Population by Selected Race and Hispanic Origin, 2017

Table LA-2. Marital Status

(Number, percent distribution.)

Sex, age, and marital status	2000	2010	2016
Males, 15 Years and Over	1,648,133	1,751,556	1,815,491
Never married	31.2	37.0	40.0
Now married, except separated................................	54.5	47.2	44.4
Separated...	2.2	2.2	2.2
Widowed...	2.8	2.8	2.7
Divorced...	9.2	10.8	10.8
Females, 15 Years and Over	1,828,247	1,861,490	1,936,224
Never married	26.3	30.8	33.1
Now married, except separated................................	48.2	42.6	40.8
Separated...	2.9	3.2	3.0
Widowed...	11.5	10.1	9.4
Divorced...	11.1	13.3	13.7

Table LA-3. Households and Housing Characteristics

(Number, percent, dollars.)

Item	2000	2010	2016	Average annual percent change, 2010–2016
Total Households........	1,656,053	1,689,822	1,720,801	0.3
Family households........	1,156,438	1,129,117	1,097,712	-0.5
Married-couple family........	809,498	753,423	735,458	-0.4
Other family........	346,940	375,694	362,254	-0.6
Male householder, no wife present........	71,865	79,560	86,597	1.5
Female householder, no husband present........	275,075	296,134	275,657	-1.2
Nonfamily households........	499,615	560,705	623,089	1.9
Householder living alone........	419,200	468,853	520,404	1.8
Householder not living alone........	80,415	91,852	102,685	2.0
Housing Characteristics				
Total housing units........	1,847,181	1,967,947	2,037,067	0.6
Occupied housing units........	1,656,053	1,689,822	1,720,801	0.3
Owner occupied........	1,125,135	1,141,504	1,105,710	-0.5
Renter occupied........	530,918	548,318	615,091	2.0
Average household size........	2.62	2.61	2.65	0.3
Financial Characteristics				
Median gross rent of renter-occupied housing........	466	736	808	1.6
Median monthly owner costs for housing units with a mortgage........	816	1,163	1,214	0.7
Median value of owner-occupied housing units........	85,000	137,500	158,000	2.5

Table LA-4. Migration, Origin, and Language

(Number, percent.)

Characteristic	State			U.S.		
	2015	2016	Percent change	2015	2016	Percent change
Residence 1 Year Ago						
Population 1 year and over........	4,612,024	4,622,042	0.2	317,635,720	319,361,956	0.5
Same house........	86.9	86.4	X	85.3	85.4	X
Different house in the U.S........	12.8	13.2	X	14.1	13.9	X
Same county........	7.7	8.1	X	8.5	8.3	X
Different county........	5.1	5.1	X	5.6	5.6	X
Same state........	3.1	3.2	X	3.2	3.2	X
Different state........	2.0	1.8	X	2.4	2.4	X
Abroad........	0.3	0.3	X	0.7	0.7	X
Place of Birth						
Native born........	4,484,355	4,491,745	0.2	278,128,449	279,388,170	0.5
Male........	48.9	48.8	X	49.3	49.3	X
Female........	51.1	51.2	X	50.7	50.7	X
Foreign born........	186,369	189,921	1.9	43,290,372	43,739,345	1.0
Male........	49.9	52.0	X	48.6	48.5	X
Female........	50.1	48.0	X	51.4	51.5	X
Foreign born; naturalized U.S. citizen........	76,294	79,688	4.4	20,697,103	21,238,372	2.6
Male........	44.8	48.0	X	45.9	45.9	X
Female........	55.2	52.0	X	54.1	54.1	X
Foreign born; not a U.S. citizen........	110,075	110,233	0.1	22,593,269	22,500,973	-0.4
Male........	53.5	55.0	X	51.1	51.0	X
Female........	46.5	45.0	X	48.9	49.0	X
Entered 2010 or later........	21.9	26.8	X	15.6	18.6	X
Entered 2000 to 2009........	30.9	29.1	X	27.9	26.7	X
Entered before 2000........	47.2	44.1	X	56.5	54.7	X
World Region of Birth, Foreign						
Foreign-born population, excluding population born at sea........	186,369	189,921	1.9	43,289,646	43,738,901	1.0
Europe........	9.7	8.5	X	11.1	10.9	X
Asia........	32.4	31.2	X	30.6	30.8	X
Africa........	3.1	4.2	X	4.8	4.9	X
Oceania........	0.3	0.4	X	0.6	0.6	X
Latin America........	52.7	54.5	X	51.1	51.0	X
North America........	1.8	1.2	X	1.9	1.8	X
Language Spoken at Home and Ability to Speak English						
Population 5 years and over........	4,365,879	4,374,703	0.2	301,625,014	303,328,961	0.6
English only........	91.8	91.9	X	78.5	78.4	X
Language other than English........	8.2	8.1	X	21.5	21.6	X
Speaks English less than "very well"........	2.8	2.8	X	8.6	8.6	X

NA = Not available.
X = Not applicable.
- = Zero or rounds to zero.

Table LA-5. Median Income and Poverty Status, 2016

(Number, percent, except as noted.)

Characteristic	State		U.S.	
	Number	Percent	Number	Percent
Median Income				
Households (dollars)	45,146	X	57,617	X
Families (dollars)	57,490	X	71,062	X
Below Poverty Level (All People)	918,187	20.2	44,268,996	14.0
Sex				
Male	398,738	18.1	19,760,056	12.8
Female	519,449	22.1	24,508,940	15.2
Age				
Under 18 years	313,926	28.6	14,115,713	19.5
Related children under 18 years	309,676	28.4	13,805,435	19.1
18 to 64 years	519,463	18.6	25,723,818	13.2
65 years and over	84,798	13.0	4,429,465	9.2

X = Not applicable.

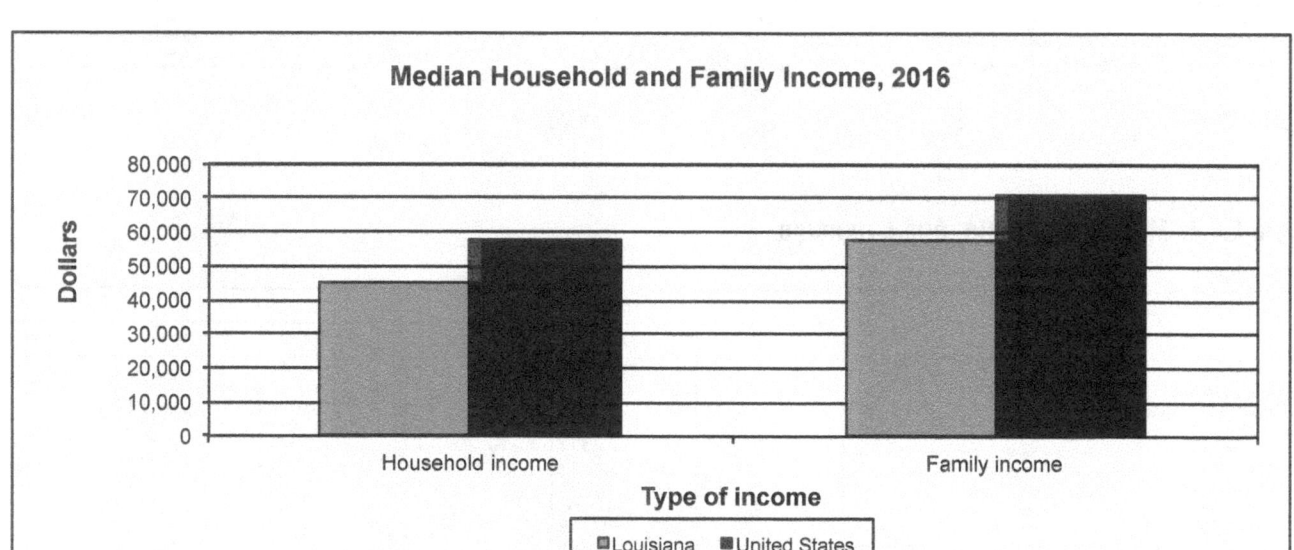

Table LA-6. Health Insurance Coverage Status for the Civilian Noninstitutionalized Population and Children Under 18 Years of Age

(Number, percent.)

Item	2008	2009	2010	2011	2012	2013	2014	2015	2016
Civilian Noninstitutionalized Population	4,312,891	4,391,561	4,440,314	4,473,068	4,498,884	4,522,910	4,547,572	4,567,431	4,577,182
Covered by Private or Public Insurance									
Number	3,545,757	3,629,320	3,649,327	3,689,053	3,739,257	3,771,587	3,875,819	4,021,800	4,107,350
Percent	82.2	82.6	82.2	82.5	83.1	83.4	85.2	88.1	89.7
Not Covered									
Number	767,134	762,241	790,987	784,015	759,627	751,323	671,753	545,631	469,832
Percent	17.8	17.4	17.8	17.5	16.9	16.6	14.8	11.9	10.3
Percent in the U.S. not covered	15.1	15.1	15.5	15.1	14.8	14.5	11.7	9.4	8.6
Children Under 18 Years of Age	1,105,606	1,120,435	1,113,329	1,117,293	1,117,427	1,110,977	1,112,618	1,114,678	1,115,457
Covered by Private or Public Insurance									
Number	1,020,019	1,047,677	1,051,611	1,052,658	1,058,356	1,047,665	1,055,087	1,074,755	1,081,831
Percent	92.3	93.5	94.5	94.2	94.7	94.3	94.8	96.4	97.0
Not Covered									
Number	85,587	72,758	61,718	64,635	59,071	63,312	57,531	39,923	33,626
Percent	7.7	6.5	5.5	5.8	5.3	5.7	5.2	3.6	3.0
Percent in the U.S. not covered	9.9	8.6	8.0	7.5	7.2	7.1	6.0	4.8	4.5

Table LA-7. Employment Status by Demographic Group, 2017

(Numbers in thousands, percent.)

Characteristic	Civilian noninstitutional population	Civilian labor force		Employed		Unemployed	
		Number	Percent of population	Number	Percent of population	Number	Percent of population
Total..	3,602	2,114	58.7	2,005	55.7	109	5.1
Sex							
Male..	1,707	1,111	65.1	1,046	61.3	66	5.9
Female..	1,895	1,003	52.9	960	50.6	43	4.3
Race, Sex, and Hispanic Origin							
White..	2,331	1,391	59.7	1,344	57.7	47	3.4
Male..	1,131	770	68.1	742	65.6	28	3.7
Female..	1,200	621	51.8	603	50.2	19	3.0
Black or African American..........................	1,117	627	56.2	571	51.1	56	8.9
Male..	500	286	57.2	252	50.5	33	11.7
Female..	618	342	55.4	319	51.7	23	6.7
Hispanic or Latino ethnicity[1]	183	127	69.2	122	66.8	4	3.4
Male..	102	84	82.1	81	79.3	3	3.4
Female..	82	43	53.1	42	51.2	2	3.5
Age							
16 to 19 years...	236	68	29.0	55	23.3	14	19.8
20 to 24 years...	303	195	64.4	176	58.2	19	9.8
25 to 34 years...	644	505	78.4	478	74.2	27	5.3
35 to 44 years...	572	463	81.0	441	77.1	22	4.8
45 to 54 years...	551	420	76.2	408	73.9	13	3.0
55 to 64 years...	597	329	55.1	318	53.2	11	3.3
65 years and over	699	134	19.1	130	18.6	4	2.9

NOTE: Data in Table 7 are from the Current Population Survey (CPS) and do not match the estimates in Table 8. See notes and definitions for further information.
[1] May be of any race.

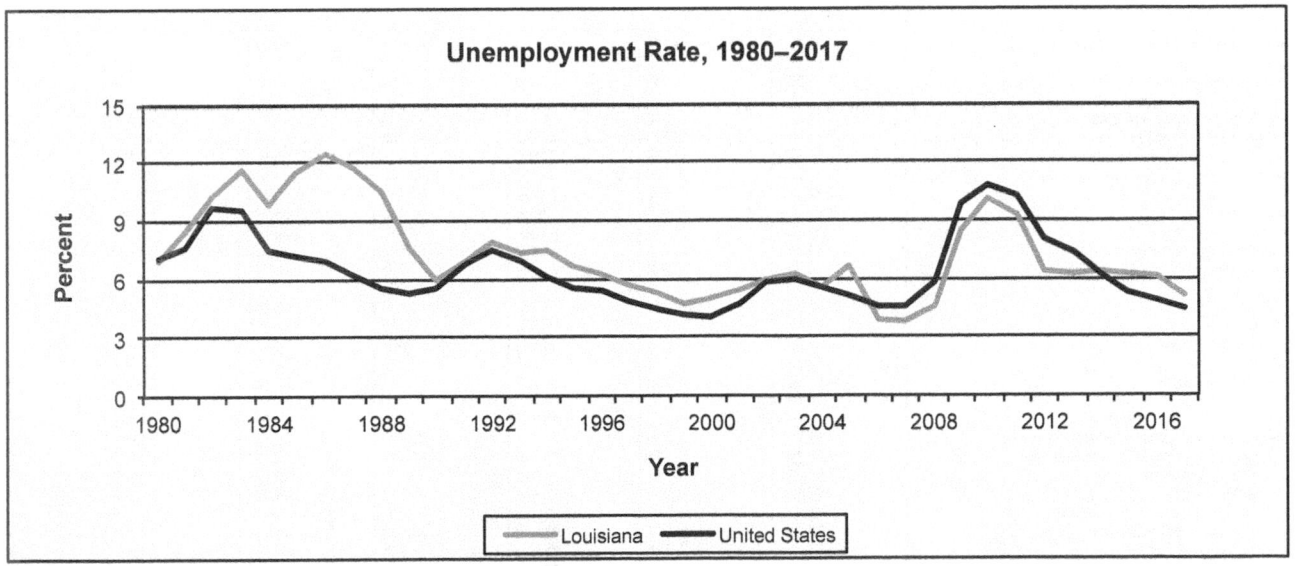

Table LA-8. Employment Status of the Civilian Noninstitutional Population Age 16 Years and Over

(Number, percent.)

Year	Civilian labor force	Civilian participation rate	Employed	Unemployed	Unemployment rate
2009..	2,064,768	60.9	1,923,884	140,884	6.8
2010..	2,086,076	60.7	1,919,852	166,224	8.0
2011..	2,073,217	59.6	1,911,021	162,196	7.8
2012..	2,080,280	59.4	1,933,137	147,143	7.1
2013..	2,101,416	59.6	1,960,539	140,877	6.7
2014..	2,153,613	60.7	2,016,083	137,530	6.4
2015..	2,162,410	60.5	2,025,661	136,749	6.3
2016..	2,125,934	59.2	1,997,358	128,576	6.0
2017..	2,112,320	58.8	2,004,003	108,317	5.1

Table LA-9. Employment and Average Wages by Industry

(Estimates through 2010 are based on the 2007 *North American Industry Classification System* [NAICS]. Estimates from 2011 onward are based on the 2012 NAICS.)

Industry	2010	2011	2012	2013	2014	2015	2016
	Number of jobs						
Wage and Salary Employment by Industry........................	1,984,467	1,998,993	2,018,389	2,039,085	2,067,420	2,075,222	2,050,046
Farm Wage and Salary Employment...............................	8,911	8,286	7,181	6,553	6,186	8,839	7,889
Nonfarm Wage and Salary Employment...........................	1,975,556	1,990,707	2,011,208	2,032,532	2,061,234	2,066,383	2,042,157
Private wage and salary employment..............................	1,566,457	1,593,091	1,623,566	1,654,461	1,695,054	1,703,512	1,681,356
Forestry, fishing, and related activities.............................	7,304	7,051	7,097	7,186	7,363	7,279	7,366
Mining..	48,602	50,306	51,725	51,174	50,866	44,917	35,590
Utilities...	9,479	9,340	9,152	9,155	8,838	8,608	8,436
Construction	125,118	125,873	130,242	135,129	143,188	144,319	143,759
Manufacturing..	137,555	139,640	141,997	144,067	147,272	143,889	136,044
Durable goods manufacturing....................................	69,642	71,160	73,105	74,637	77,226	73,116	65,202
Nondurable goods manufacturing.................................	67,913	68,480	68,892	69,430	70,046	70,773	70,842
Wholesale trade	70,772	72,504	72,881	73,634	73,845	72,745	70,796
Retail trade...	219,709	222,854	224,417	225,924	228,990	234,878	236,729
Transportation and warehousing.................................	69,222	72,204	74,670	77,220	80,509	79,935	74,872
Information	24,578	23,757	24,909	26,672	26,104	26,741	23,667
Finance and insurance	60,308	61,953	60,800	60,708	61,167	60,810	61,097
Real estate and rental and leasing...............................	30,904	31,743	32,294	33,418	32,636	31,905	30,784
Professional, scientific, and technical services	80,366	81,879	85,490	87,197	89,182	89,744	87,452
Management of companies and enterprises........................	23,872	24,369	25,122	25,286	25,225	23,707	23,374
Administrative and waste services................................	90,885	92,147	94,732	96,732	100,118	101,403	100,832
Educational services	38,979	39,227	40,441	42,662	43,174	43,713	44,091
Health care and social assistance................................	236,509	239,744	243,450	248,703	256,755	261,816	266,920
Arts, entertainment, and recreation..............................	28,572	28,086	28,778	29,871	30,622	30,582	29,949
Accommodation and food services...............................	167,498	174,173	179,508	184,721	191,898	198,958	203,274
Other services, except public administration......................	96,225	96,241	95,861	95,002	97,302	97,563	96,324
Government and government enterprises............................	409,099	397,616	387,642	378,071	366,180	362,871	360,801
	Dollars						
Average Wages and Salaries by Industry	42,163	43,107	44,118	44,851	46,172	46,784	47,003
Average Farm Wages and Salaries	18,508	17,143	29,539	25,584	21,314	24,827	21,904
Average Nonfarm Wages and Salaries	42,270	43,216	44,170	44,913	46,246	46,878	47,100
Average private wages and salaries...............................	42,248	43,295	44,383	45,287	46,779	47,381	47,373
Forestry, fishing, and related activities.............................	32,850	33,119	34,550	35,468	35,976	35,879	37,343
Mining..	82,246	85,176	88,509	90,813	95,805	95,878	83,487
Utilities...	72,441	76,686	78,373	80,350	84,586	87,718	90,625
Construction	51,294	51,890	52,386	53,495	56,608	58,586	64,957
Manufacturing..	61,611	63,890	65,566	66,510	69,341	71,287	73,444
Durable goods manufacturing....................................	54,357	56,757	57,752	58,515	60,834	60,722	60,649
Nondurable goods manufacturing.................................	69,049	71,303	73,857	75,105	78,721	82,203	85,221
Wholesale trade	55,873	57,321	59,786	61,114	63,208	64,083	64,099
Retail trade...	25,548	25,905	26,650	27,072	27,375	27,900	28,164
Transportation and warehousing.................................	57,262	57,674	60,154	61,997	64,733	63,495	58,790
Information	49,796	51,441	51,791	49,794	52,508	53,261	52,996
Finance and insurance	55,181	58,956	60,180	61,992	65,782	66,065	68,352
Real estate and rental and leasing...............................	45,940	48,219	48,317	49,085	50,064	49,324	47,443
Professional, scientific, and technical services	61,113	62,878	64,427	66,837	68,169	69,900	69,317
Management of companies and enterprises........................	67,220	70,947	73,255	79,415	78,434	80,885	83,009
Administrative and waste services................................	34,894	34,348	35,022	35,431	36,812	38,388	37,368
Educational services	33,063	34,316	34,579	34,644	34,824	34,272	34,784
Health care and social assistance................................	38,125	38,914	39,433	39,873	41,164	42,887	43,940
Arts, entertainment, and recreation..............................	34,921	35,014	34,529	34,705	34,689	36,197	37,795
Accommodation and food services...............................	18,791	18,987	19,510	19,852	20,380	21,119	21,507
Other services, except public administration......................	28,287	28,871	30,106	31,372	32,107	33,353	34,020
Government and government enterprises............................	42,355	42,896	43,275	43,275	43,780	44,517	45,824

Table LA-10. Employment Characteristics by Family Type

(Number, percent.)

Family type and labor force status	2014		2015		2016	
	Total	Families with own children under 18 years	Total	Families with own children under 18 years	Total	Families with own children under 18 years
All Families..	1,109,475	468,474	1,108,586	471,898	1,097,712	463,602
FAMILY TYPE AND LABOR FORCE STATUS						
Married-Couple Families...............................	738,715	270,836	746,504	278,801	735,458	271,349
Both husband and wife in labor force.................	47.4	63.4	48.0	65.2	47.4	67.4
Husband in labor force, wife not in labor force	24.9	30.0	24.8	28.3	23.8	26.2
Wife in labor force, husband not in labor force	8.8	4.4	8.2	4.5	8.4	3.9
Both husband and wife not in labor force....................	18.9	2.2	18.4	1.7	19.8	2.3
Other Families	370,760	197,638	362,082	193,097	362,254	192,253
Female householder, no husband present.....................	75.0	78.8	76.3	78.7	76.1	78.1
In labor force..	49.1	62.1	50.8	64.2	50.3	63.0
Not in labor force	26.0	16.6	25.4	14.6	25.8	15.1
Male householder, no wife present.........................	25.0	21.2	23.7	21.3	23.9	21.9
In labor force..	18.6	18.7	17.4	19.4	16.4	18.3
Not in labor force	6.4	2.6	6.4	1.8	7.5	3.6

Table LA-11. School Enrollment and Educational Attainment, 2016

(Number, percent.)

Item	State	U.S.
Enrollment		
Total population 3 years and over, enrolled in school	1,172,916	81,572,277
Enrolled in nursery school or preschool (percent)................	6.5	6.0
Enrolled in kindergarten (percent)............................	5.0	5.0
Enrolled in elementary school, grades 1-8 (percent).............	43.3	40.3
Enrolled in high school, grades 9-12 (percent).................	21.5	21.0
Enrolled in college or graduate school (percent)	23.7	27.7
Attainment		
Total population 25 years and over	3,115,020	218,475,480
Less than ninth grade (percent)	5.2	5.4
9th to 12th grade, no diploma (percent)	10.4	7.2
High school graduate, including equivalency (percent)...........	34.0	27.2
Some college, no degree (percent)	21.0	20.6
Associate's degree (percent)...................................	6.0	8.4
Bachelor's degree (percent)....................................	15.2	19.3
Graduate or professional degree (percent)......................	8.2	11.9
High school graduate or higher (percent)	84.4	87.5
Bachelor's degree or higher (percent)..........................	23.4	31.3

Table LA-12. Public School Characteristics and Educational Indicators

(Number, percent; data derived from National Center of Education Statistics.)

Item	State	U.S.
Public Schools, 2015–2016 (except where noted)		
Number of school districts..	179	18,328
Number of schools..	1,390	98,456
Number of students	718,711	50,327,015
Number of teachers	58,469	3,151,497
Student-teacher ratio	12.3	16.0
Expenditures per student (dollars), 2014-2015....................	11,106	11,445
Four-year adjusted cohort graduation rate (ACGR)[1,2]	78.6	84.1
Students eligible for free or reduced-price lunch (percent), 2014-2015	63.6	51.8
English language learners (percent), Fall 2015	3.3	9.5
Students age 3 to 21 served under IDEA, part B (percent).........	11.7	13.2

Public Schools by Type	Number	Percent of state public schools
Total number of schools..	1,390	100.0
Regular	1,341	96.5
Special education..	32	2.3
Vocational education...	12	0.9
Alternative education..	5	0.4

NOTE: Every school is assigned only one school type based on its instructional emphasis.
[1] ACGR data represents a new method of calculating high-school completion rates and may not be comparable to previous years' data for Averaged Freshmen Graduation Rates (AFGR).
[2] The United States 4-year ACGRs were estimated using both the reported 4-year ACGR data from 49 states and the District of Columbia and using imputed data for Idaho. The estimate for American Indian/Alaska Native students also includes imputed data for Virginia.

Table LA-13. Reported Voting and Registration of the Voting-Age Population, November 2016

(Numbers in thousands, percent.)

Item	Total population	Total citizen population	Registered			Voted		
			Total registered	Percent registered (total population)	Percent registered (total citizen population)	Total voted	Percent voted (total population)	Percent voted (total citizen population)
U.S. Total	245,502	224,059	157,596	64.2	70.3	137,537	56.0	61.4
State Total................................	3,463	3,353	2,446	70.6	73.0	2,067	59.7	61.6
Sex								
Male	1,650	1,580	1,119	67.8	70.8	925	56.1	58.5
Female	1,813	1,773	1,327	73.2	74.8	1,142	63.0	64.4
Race								
White alone.............................	2,251	2,193	1,631	72.4	74.4	1,368	60.8	62.4
White, non-Hispanic alone	2,112	2,100	1,557	73.7	74.2	1,311	62.1	62.5
Black alone..............................	1,062	1,054	755	71.1	71.6	646	60.9	61.3
Asian alone..............................	101	65	26	(B)	(B)	23	(B)	(B)
Hispanic (of any race)...................	174	121	99	56.7	81.5	82	47.2	67.9
White alone or in combination	2,275	2,216	1,652	72.6	74.6	1,386	60.9	62.5
Black alone or in combination...........	1,078	1,070	771	71.5	72.0	661	61.3	61.8
Asian alone or in combination...........	103	67	26	(B)	(B)	23	(B)	(B)
Age								
18 to 24 years...........................	458	453	283	61.7	62.5	225	49.2	49.8
25 to 34 years...........................	628	602	425	67.6	70.5	318	50.7	52.8
35 to 44 years...........................	536	510	348	64.9	68.2	308	57.4	60.4
45 to 64 years...........................	1,233	1,197	913	74.1	76.3	801	64.9	66.9
65 years and over	608	592	478	78.5	80.7	415	68.3	70.2

B = Base is less than 75,000 and therefore too small to show the derived measure.

Table LA-14. Crime

(Number, rate per 100,000. Data are derived from the FBI Uniform Crime Reports.)

Item	State			U.S. [1,2,3,4]		
	2015	2016	Percent change	2015	2016	Percent change
TOTAL POPULATION [5]	4,670,724	4,681,666	0.2	321,418,820	323,127,513	0.5
VIOLENT CRIME						
Number...............................	25,208	26,502	5.1	1,231,566	1,248,185	1.3
Rate....................................	539.7	566.1	4.9	383.2	386.3	0.8
Murder and Nonnegligent Manslaughter						
Number...............................	481	554	15.2	15,696	17,250	9.9
Rate....................................	10.3	11.8	14.6	4.9	5.3	8.2
Rape [6]						
Number...............................	1,723	1,816	5.4	124,047	130,603	5.3
Rate....................................	36.9	38.8	5.1	38.6	40.4	4.7
Robbery						
Number...............................	5,550	5,576	0.5	327,374	332,198	1.5
Rate....................................	118.8	119.1	0.3	101.9	102.8	0.9
Aggravated Assault						
Number...............................	17,454	18,556	6.3	764,449	803,007	5.0
Rate....................................	373.7	396.4	6.1	237.8	248.5	4.5
PROPERTY CRIME						
Number...............................	156,629	154,386	-1.4	7,993,631	7,919,035	-0.9
Rate....................................	3,353.4	3,297.7	-1.7	2,487.0	2,450.7	-1.5
Burglary						
Number...............................	35,453	34,667	-2.2	1,579,527	1,515,096	-4.1
Rate....................................	759.0	740.5	-2.4	491.4	468.9	-4.6
Larceny-Theft						
Number...............................	111,435	109,380	-1.8	5,706,346	5,638,455	-1.2
Rate....................................	2,385.8	2,336.3	-2.1	1,775.4	1,745.0	-1.7
Motor Vehicle Theft						
Number...............................	9,741	10,339	6.1	707,758	765,484	8.2
Rate....................................	208.6	220.8	5.8	220.2	236.9	7.6

NOTE: Although arson data are included in the trend and clearance tables, sufficient data are not available to estimate totals for this offense. Therefore, no arson data are published in this table.
X = Not applicable.
- = Zero or rounds to zero.
[1] The crime figures have been adjusted.
[2] The data collection methodology for the offense of forcible rape used by the Minnesota state Uniform Crime Reporting (UCR) Program (with the exception of Minneapolis and St. Paul, Minnesota) does not comply with national UCR Program guidelines. Consequently, its figures for forcible rape and violent crime (of which forcible rape is a part) are not published in this table.
[3] Includes offenses reported by the Zoological Police and the Metro Transit Police.
[4] Because of changes in the state's reporting practices, figures are not comparable to previous years' data.
[5] Populations are U.S. Census Bureau provisional estimates as of July 1 of each year.
[6] The figures shown for the offense of rape were estimated using the revised Uniform Crime Reporting (UCR) definition of rape.

Table LA-15. State Government Finances, 2016

(Dollar amounts in thousands, percent distribution.)

Item	Dollars	Percent distribution
Total Revenue	26,842,105	100.0
General revenue	24,110,397	89.8
Intergovernmental revenue	10,361,925	38.6
Taxes	9,309,673	34.7
General sales	3,186,614	11.9
Selective sales	2,166,293	8.1
License taxes	400,191	1.5
Individual income tax	2,866,456	10.7
Corporate income tax	171,579	0.6
Other taxes	518,540	1.9
Current charges	1,950,249	7.3
Miscellaneous general revenue	2,488,550	9.3
Utility revenue	12,706	-
Liquor stores revenue	0	-
Insurance trust revenue [1]	2,719,002	10.1
Total Expenditure	31,444,186	100.0
Intergovernmental expenditure	5,766,006	18.3
Direct expenditure	25,678,180	81.7
Current operation	16,915,220	53.8
Capital outlay	2,423,944	7.7
Insurance benefits and repayments	4,480,757	14.2
Assistance and subsidies	978,447	3.1
Interest on debt	879,812	2.8
Exhibit: Salaries and wages	4,021,668	12.8
Total Expenditure	31,444,186	100.0
General expenditure	26,954,119	85.7
Intergovernmental expenditure	5,766,006	18.3
Direct expenditure	21,188,113	67.4
General expenditure, by function:		
Education	9,563,548	30.4
Public welfare	8,805,375	28.0
Hospitals	461,054	1.5
Health	492,242	1.6
Highways	1,612,860	5.1
Police protection	330,826	1.1
Correction	661,918	2.1
Natural resources	795,725	2.5
Parks and recreation	340,558	1.1
Governmental administration	988,794	3.1
Interest on general debt	879,812	2.8
Other and unallocable	2,021,407	6.4
Utility expenditure	9,310	-
Liquor stores expenditure	0	-
Insurance trust expenditure	4,480,757	14.2
Debt at End of Fiscal Year	17,913,229	X
Cash and Security Holdings	58,561,185	X

X = Not applicable.
- = Zero or rounds to zero.
[1] Within insurance trust revenue, net earnings of state retirement systems is a calculated statistic (the item code in the data file is X08), and thus can be positive or negative. Net earnings is the sum of earnings on investments plus gains on investments minus losses on investments. The change made in 2002 for asset valuation from book to market value in accordance with Statement 34 of the Governmental Accounting Standards Board is reflected in the calculated statistics.

Table LA-16. State Government Tax Collections, 2017

(Dollars in thousands, percent.)

Item	Dollars	Percent distribution
Total Taxes	11,104,720	100.0
Property taxes	70,366	0.6
Sales and gross receipts	7,014,497	63.2
General sales and gross receipts	4,215,378	38.0
Selective sales and gross receipts	2,799,119	25.2
Alcoholic beverages	77,107	0.7
Amusements	698,306	6.3
Insurance premiums	813,975	7.3
Motor fuels	634,883	5.7
Pari-mutuels	4,659	-
Public utilities	9,110	0.1
Tobacco products	174,001	1.6
Other selective sales	387,078	3.5
Licenses	368,318	3.3
Alcoholic beverages	X	-
Amusements	X	-
Corporations in general	125,998	1.1
Hunting and fishing	30,684	0.3
Motor vehicle	83,002	0.7
Motor vehicle operators	13,987	0.1
Public utilities	6,182	0.1
Occupation and business, NEC	104,207	0.9
Other licenses	4,258	-
Income taxes	3,241,260	29.2
Individual income	2,949,939	26.6
Corporation net income	291,321	2.6
Other taxes	410,279	3.7
Death and gift	X	-
Documentary and stock transfer	X	-
Severance	410,279	3.7
Taxes, NEC	0	-

- = Zero or rounds to zero.
X = Not applicable.

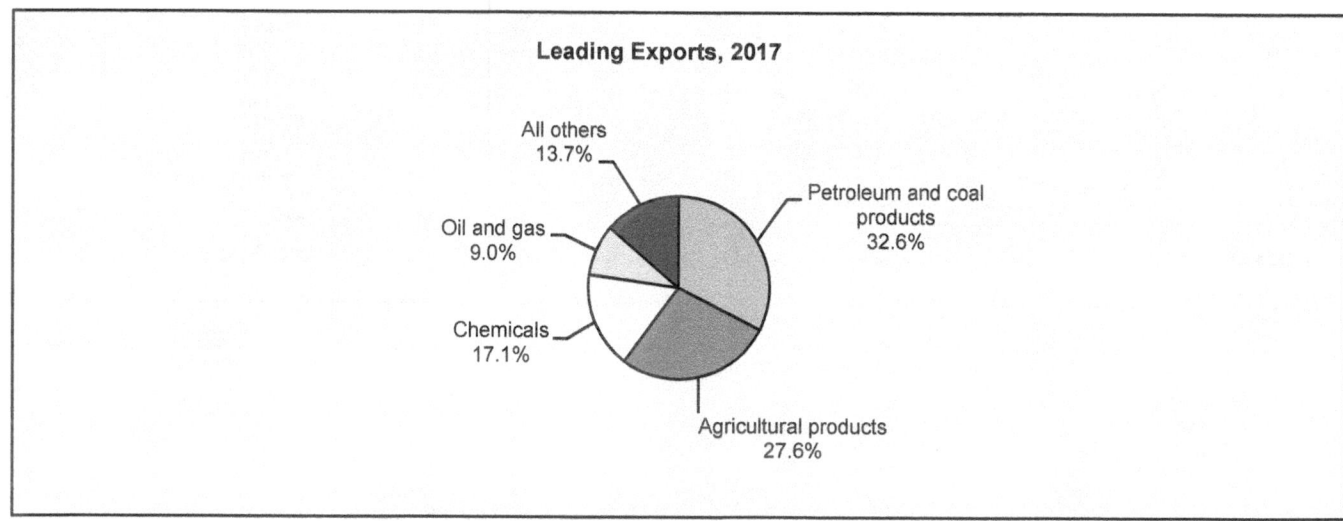

Leading Exports, 2017

All others 13.7%

Oil and gas 9.0%

Chemicals 17.1%

Agricultural products 27.6%

Petroleum and coal products 32.6%

MAINE

Facts and Figures

Location: Northeast corner of the United States; bordered on the N and E by New Brunswick, Canada; on the S by the Atlantic Ocean; on the W by New Hampshire; and on the NW by Quebec, Canada

Area: 35,385 sq. mi. (91,646 sq. km.); rank—39th

Population: 1,335,907 (2017 est.); rank—42nd

Principal Cities: capital—Augusta; largest—Portland

Statehood: March 15, 1820; 23rd state

U.S. Congress: 2 senators, 2 representatives

State Motto: *Dirigo* ("I lead")

State Song: "State of Maine Song"

State Nickname: The Pine Tree State

Abbreviations: ME; Me.

State Symbols: flower—white pinecone and tassel; tree—Eastern white pine; bird—chickadee

At a Glance

- With a population that grew 0.6 percent, Maine ranked 45th among the states in growth from 2010 to 2017.

- Maine had the highest percent of residents who identified as "White alone" in 2017, with 94.7 percent of its residents in this category.

- Of all states, Maine had the 2nd lowest percent of its population who identified as "Hispanic or Latino" in 2017, with just 1.6 percent of residents in this category.

- With 19.9 percent of its population in the 65 and older age group, Maine ranked 2nd in this category in 2017.

- Maine's birth rate of 9.5 per 1,000 population was the 3rd lowest in the country in 2016.

Table ME-1. Population by Age, Sex, Race, and Hispanic Origin

(Number, percent, except where noted.)

Sex, age, race, and Hispanic origin	2000	2010	2017 [1]	Average annual percent change, 2010–2017
Total Population...	1,274,923	1,328,361	1,335,907	0.6
Percent of total U.S. population	0.5	0.4	0.4	X
Sex				
Male...	620,309	650,056	654,520	0.7
Female	654,614	678,305	681,387	0.5
Age				
Under 5 years..	70,726	69,520	64,502	-7.2
5 to 19 years..	264,729	241,439	221,304	-8.3
20 to 64 years...	756,036	806,322	783,887	-2.8
65 years and over...	183,402	211,080	266,214	26.1
Median age (years)	38.6	42.7	44.7	4.7
Race and Hispanic Origin				
One race				
White	1,236,014	1,269,764	1,264,744	-0.4
Black	6,760	16,269	21,093	29.7
American Indian and Alaska Native	7,098	8,771	9,511	8.4
Asian	9,111	13,783	16,643	20.8
Native Hawaiian or Other Pacific Islander	382	377	474	25.7
Two or more races...	12,647	19,397	23,442	20.9
Hispanic (of any race)...	9,360	18,261	22,042	20.7

X = Not applicable.
- = Zero or rounds to zero.
[1] Population figures for 2017 are July 1 estimates. The 2010 estimates are taken from the 2010 Census.

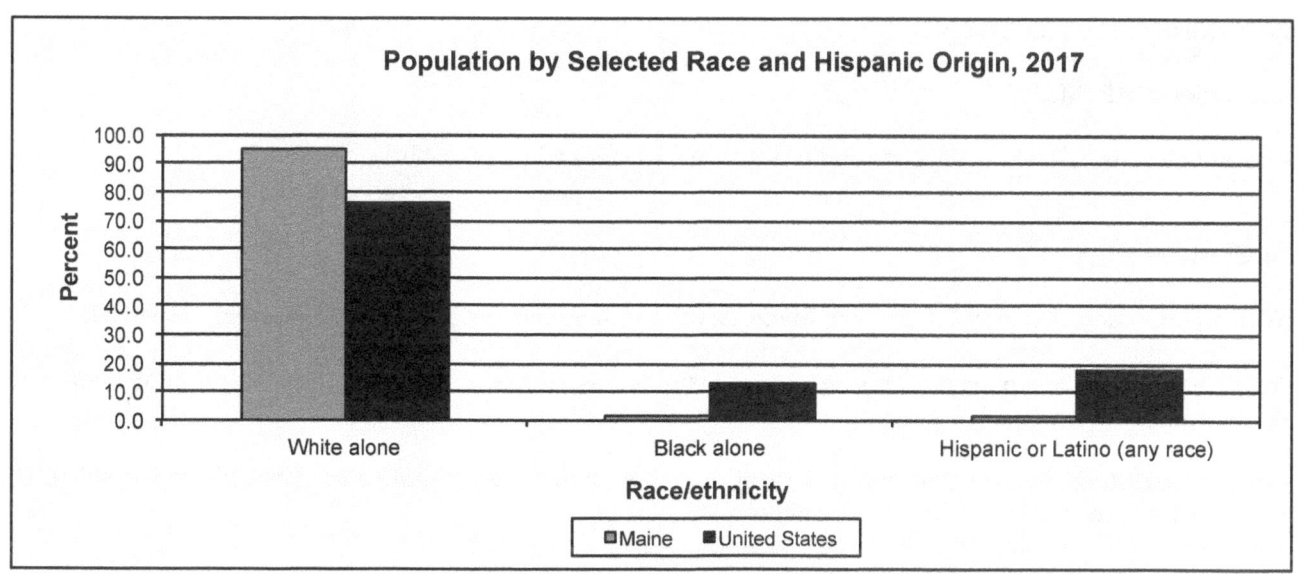

Table ME-2. Marital Status

(Number, percent distribution.)

Sex, age, and marital status	2000	2010	2016
Males, 15 Years and Over	494,217	534,474	544,729
Never married	26.8	31.0	32.6
Now married, except separated..	58.8	52.5	49.6
Separated..	1.1	1.2	1.0
Widowed..	2.8	2.9	3.0
Divorced..	10.5	12.5	13.8
Females, 15 Years and Over	534,606	570,281	578,999
Never married	21.2	24.2	25.9
Now married, except separated..	54.1	49.3	47.9
Separated..	1.3	1.6	1.2
Widowed..	11.0	9.9	9.7
Divorced..	12.4	15.0	15.3

Table ME-3. Households and Housing Characteristics

(Number, percent, dollars.)

Item	2000	2010	2016	Average annual percent change, 2010–2016
Total Households...	518,200	545,417	531,660	-0.4
Family households	340,685	345,328	329,554	-0.8
Married-couple family	272,152	266,670	256,503	-0.6
Other family	68,533	78,658	73,051	-1.2
Male householder, no wife present............................	19,511	23,620	24,410	0.6
Female householder, no husband present...................	49,022	55,038	48,641	-1.9
Nonfamily households	177,515	200,089	202,106	0.2
Householder living alone..	139,969	155,623	159,326	0.4
Householder not living alone....................................	37,546	44,466	42,780	-0.6
Housing Characteristics				
Total housing units	651,901	722,217	730,786	0.2
Occupied housing units	518,200	545,417	531,660	-0.4
Owner occupied	370,905	396,395	382,116	-0.6
Renter occupied	147,295	149,022	149,544	0.1
Average household size...	2.39	2.37	2.44	0.5
Financial Characteristics				
Median gross rent of renter-occupied housing	497	707	797	2.1
Median monthly owner costs for housing units with a mortgage	923	1,289	1,328	0.5
Median value of owner-occupied housing units.............	98,700	179,100	184,700	0.5

Table ME-4. Migration, Origin, and Language

(Number, percent.)

Characteristic	State			U.S.		
	2015	2016	Percent change	2015	2016	Percent change
Residence 1 Year Ago						
Population 1 year and over	1,317,444	1,319,292	0.1	317,635,720	319,361,956	0.5
Same house	85.6	86.9	X	85.3	85.4	X
Different house in the U.S.	14.1	12.8	X	14.1	13.9	X
Same county	8.7	7.1	X	8.5	8.3	X
Different county	5.4	5.7	X	5.6	5.6	X
Same state	3.2	2.8	X	3.2	3.2	X
Different state	2.3	2.9	X	2.4	2.4	X
Abroad	0.3	0.3	X	0.7	0.7	X
Place of Birth						
Native born	1,284,634	1,280,711	-0.3	278,128,449	279,388,170	0.5
Male	49.3	49.1	X	49.3	49.3	X
Female	50.7	50.9	X	50.7	50.7	X
Foreign born	44,694	50,768	13.6	43,290,372	43,739,345	1.0
Male	40.6	42.2	X	48.6	48.5	X
Female	59.4	57.8	X	51.4	51.5	X
Foreign born; naturalized U.S. citizen..................	25,556	28,046	9.7	20,697,103	21,238,372	2.6
Male	39.7	42.7	X	45.9	45.9	X
Female	60.3	57.3	X	54.1	54.1	X
Foreign born; not a U.S. citizen.........................	19,138	22,722	18.7	22,593,269	22,500,973	-0.4
Male	41.7	41.5	X	51.1	51.0	X
Female	58.3	58.5	X	48.9	49.0	X
Entered 2010 or later	19.3	23.6	X	15.6	18.6	X
Entered 2000 to 2009	22.3	21.9	X	27.9	26.7	X
Entered before 2000..	58.4	54.5	X	56.5	54.7	X
World Region of Birth, Foreign						
Foreign-born population, excluding population born at sea	44,694	50,768	13.6	43,289,646	43,738,901	1.0
Europe	24.0	20.5	X	11.1	10.9	X
Asia...	30.0	30.8	X	30.6	30.8	X
Africa	13.0	16.2	X	4.8	4.9	X
Oceania	0.9	1.1	X	0.6	0.6	X
Latin America	10.2	9.7	X	51.1	51.0	X
North America	21.8	21.7	X	1.9	1.8	X
Language Spoken at Home and Ability to Speak English						
Population 5 years and over.................................	1,265,476	1,267,538	0.2	301,625,014	303,328,961	0.6
English only	93.9	93.8	X	78.5	78.4	X
Language other than English................................	6.1	6.2	X	21.5	21.6	X
Speaks English less than "very well"...................	1.6	1.7	X	8.6	8.6	X

NA = Not available.
X = Not applicable.
- = Zero or rounds to zero.

Table ME-5. Median Income and Poverty Status, 2016

(Number, percent, except as noted.)

Characteristic	State		U.S.	
	Number	Percent	Number	Percent
Median Income				
Households (dollars)............................	53,079	X	57,617	X
Families (dollars)	68,277	X	71,062	X
Below Poverty Level (All People)	161,749	12.5	44,268,996	14.0
Sex				
Male	71,563	11.3	19,760,056	12.8
Female	90,186	13.6	24,508,940	15.2
Age				
Under 18 years..................................	42,753	17.2	14,115,713	19.5
Related children under 18 years................	41,067	16.6	13,805,435	19.1
18 to 64 years	96,374	12.1	25,723,818	13.2
65 years and over	22,622	9.1	4,429,465	9.2

X = Not applicable.

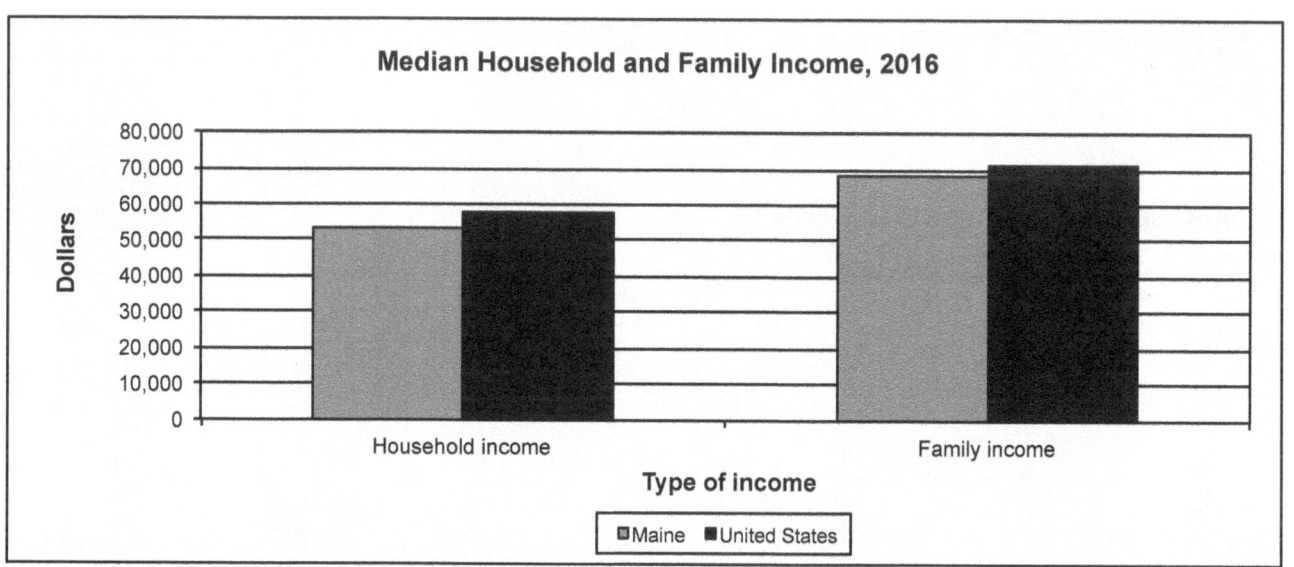

Table ME-6. Health Insurance Coverage Status for the Civilian Noninstitutionalized Population and Children Under 18 Years of Age

(Number, percent.)

Item	2008	2009	2010	2011	2012	2013	2014	2015	2016
Civilian Noninstitutionalized Population	1,299,288	1,300,904	1,313,037	1,314,121	1,315,703	1,314,191	1,315,996	1,314,849	1,317,148
Covered by Private or Public Insurance									
Number...	1,157,155	1,163,900	1,179,972	1,173,956	1,180,994	1,167,176	1,182,465	1,204,341	1,211,175
Percent...	89.1	89.5	89.9	89.3	89.8	88.8	89.9	91.6	92.0
Not Covered									
Number...	142,133	137,004	133,065	140,165	134,709	147,015	133,531	110,508	105,973
Percent...	10.9	10.5	10.1	10.7	10.2	11.2	10.1	8.4	8.0
Percent in the U.S. not covered..........................	15.1	15.1	15.5	15.1	14.8	14.5	11.7	9.4	8.6
Children Under 18 Years of Age	274,570	270,440	273,098	269,901	265,495	259,827	257,390	255,319	254,723
Covered by Private or Public Insurance									
Number...	254,314	255,246	262,163	255,736	253,255	244,441	241,098	240,871	243,104
Percent...	92.6	94.4	96.0	94.8	95.4	94.1	93.7	94.3	95.4
Not Covered									
Number...	20,256	15,194	10,935	14,165	12,240	15,386	16,292	14,448	11,619
Percent...	7.4	5.6	4.0	5.2	4.6	5.9	6.3	5.7	4.6
Percent in the U.S. not covered..........................	9.9	8.6	8.0	7.5	7.2	7.1	6.0	4.8	4.5

Table ME-7. Employment Status by Demographic Group, 2017

(Numbers in thousands, percent.)

Characteristic	Civilian noninstitutional population	Civilian labor force		Employed		Unemployed	
		Number	Percent of population	Number	Percent of population	Number	Percent of population
Total..	1,099	702	63.9	679	61.8	23	3.3
Sex							
Male...	534	374	70.0	361	67.6	13	3.4
Female...	565	328	58.1	318	56.4	10	3.1
Race, Sex, and Hispanic Origin							
White..	1,044	668	64.0	647	62.0	21	3.1
Male...	507	354	69.8	343	67.5	12	3.3
Female...	537	314	58.5	305	56.7	9	3.0
Black or African American...................	NA	NA	NA	NA	NA	NA	NA
Male...	NA	NA	NA	NA	NA	NA	NA
Female...	NA	NA	NA	NA	NA	NA	NA
Hispanic or Latino ethnicity[1]..............	NA	NA	NA	NA	NA	NA	NA
Male...	NA	NA	NA	NA	NA	NA	NA
Female...	NA	NA	NA	NA	NA	NA	NA
Age							
16 to 19 years.......................................	NA	NA	NA	NA	NA	NA	NA
20 to 24 years.......................................	75	56	74.1	52	69.5	4	6.3
25 to 34 years.......................................	154	129	84.1	125	81.3	4	3.3
35 to 44 years.......................................	151	127	83.8	123	81.6	3	2.6
45 to 54 years.......................................	197	160	80.9	157	79.6	3	1.6
55 to 64 years.......................................	206	151	73.2	148	72.0	2	1.5
65 years and over..................................	249	49	19.5	47	18.8	2	3.5

NOTE: Data in Table 7 are from the Current Population Survey (CPS) and do not match the estimates in Table 8. See notes and definitions for further information.
[1] May be of any race.
NA = Not available.

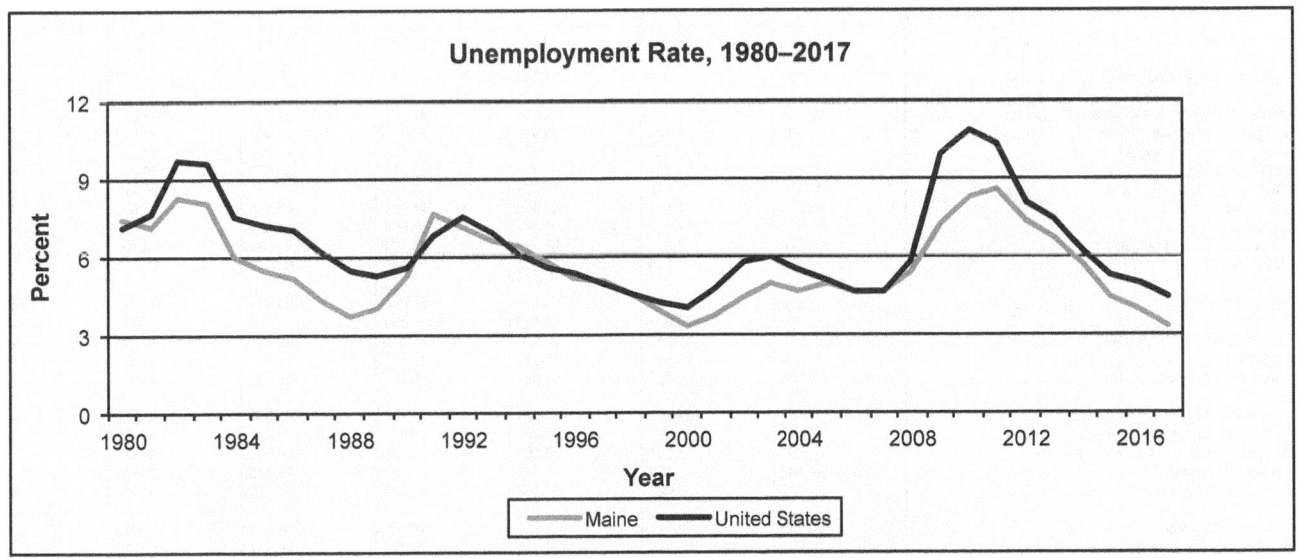

Table ME-8. Employment Status of the Civilian Noninstitutional Population Age 16 Years and Over

(Number, percent.)

Year	Civilian labor force	Civilian participation rate	Employed	Unemployed	Unemployment rate
2009..	696,219	65.4	639,954	56,265	8.1
2010..	695,182	64.8	638,630	56,552	8.1
2011..	699,281	64.8	644,085	55,196	7.9
2012..	702,636	64.9	650,117	52,519	7.5
2013..	705,417	65.0	658,522	46,895	6.6
2014..	696,298	64.0	657,066	39,232	5.6
2015..	683,369	62.7	653,330	30,039	4.4
2016..	692,154	63.3	665,911	26,243	3.8
2017..	700,099	63.6	677,141	22,958	3.3

Table ME-9. Employment and Average Wages by Industry

(Estimates through 2010 are based on the 2007 *North American Industry Classification System* [NAICS]. Estimates from 2011 onward are based on the 2012 NAICS.)

Industry	2010	2011	2012	2013	2014	2015	2016
	Number of jobs						
Wage and Salary Employment by Industry........................	608,555	609,684	612,168	615,536	619,810	625,249	631,914
Farm Wage and Salary Employment................................	2,808	3,071	3,632	4,155	4,167	4,152	3,875
Nonfarm Wage and Salary Employment...........................	605,747	606,613	608,536	611,381	615,643	621,097	628,039
Private wage and salary employment................................	494,913	497,882	500,408	504,402	508,895	514,908	521,356
Forestry, fishing, and related activities.............................	4,130	4,051	(D)	4,102	4,199	4,285	4,078
Mining..	179	203	(D)	187	190	191	211
Utilities..	1,816	1,609	1,629	1,619	1,551	1,630	1,647
Construction	25,180	26,037	26,351	26,287	26,699	27,287	28,120
Manufacturing..	50,678	50,825	50,771	50,421	50,254	50,700	50,785
Durable goods manufacturing..	26,959	27,179	27,108	27,253	27,770	28,159	28,509
Nondurable goods manufacturing...................................	23,719	23,646	23,663	23,168	22,484	22,541	22,276
Wholesale trade	19,099	19,136	19,524	19,672	19,825	20,125	20,028
Retail trade..	82,019	81,957	82,014	81,972	82,289	82,298	82,653
Transportation and warehousing....................................	15,522	15,760	15,643	16,033	16,580	16,589	17,011
Information...	9,136	8,304	7,913	7,641	7,453	7,594	7,726
Finance and insurance	24,704	25,242	24,960	24,998	23,688	23,988	24,082
Real estate and rental and leasing.................................	6,613	6,442	6,487	6,613	6,562	6,522	6,729
Professional, scientific, and technical services	23,671	23,703	23,967	24,831	25,026	25,357	25,494
Management of companies and enterprises......................	6,993	7,141	7,567	7,428	9,091	9,124	9,958
Administrative and waste services	25,640	27,088	27,131	28,318	29,682	30,511	30,793
Educational services	14,180	14,356	14,709	14,997	15,283	15,688	16,263
Health care and social assistance..................................	101,150	100,942	101,972	102,320	102,268	103,799	104,701
Arts, entertainment, and recreation................................	8,200	8,152	8,821	8,886	8,600	8,750	9,262
Accommodation and food services.................................	52,001	52,439	53,218	54,205	55,046	55,747	56,953
Other services, except public administration....................	24,002	24,495	23,406	23,872	24,609	24,723	24,862
Government and government enterprises..........................	110,834	108,731	108,128	106,979	106,748	106,189	106,683
	Dollars						
Average Wages and Salaries by Industry	38,378	39,067	39,752	40,461	41,610	42,930	43,843
Average Farm Wages and Salaries	26,137	20,919	31,010	27,948	29,499	24,803	30,976
Average Nonfarm Wages and Salaries	38,434	39,159	39,805	40,546	41,692	43,051	43,922
Average private wages and salaries................................	37,830	38,710	39,490	40,256	41,462	42,828	43,680
Forestry, fishing, and related activities.............................	38,725	40,189	(D)	40,576	41,973	43,757	44,756
Mining..	53,531	53,207	(D)	55,818	58,853	59,602	59,019
Utilities..	71,186	75,646	77,637	79,957	87,727	82,712	83,616
Construction	41,294	42,551	43,410	44,584	45,888	46,666	47,493
Manufacturing..	51,620	52,158	52,292	53,354	54,622	55,918	56,001
Durable goods manufacturing..	51,670	52,604	52,274	53,409	54,581	56,103	56,287
Nondurable goods manufacturing...................................	51,564	51,645	52,313	53,289	54,673	55,687	55,635
Wholesale trade	53,036	54,761	55,855	57,000	59,643	62,757	63,629
Retail trade..	25,094	25,279	25,519	25,895	26,689	27,567	28,106
Transportation and warehousing....................................	38,898	38,545	39,496	40,574	41,957	43,182	43,317
Information...	46,859	45,595	45,971	47,611	47,969	49,892	53,181
Finance and insurance	58,696	61,924	63,961	66,307	68,726	70,504	71,558
Real estate and rental and leasing.................................	33,885	35,568	37,015	37,686	39,046	40,840	42,056
Professional, scientific, and technical services	56,271	58,023	60,007	60,996	63,718	66,493	68,314
Management of companies and enterprises......................	68,090	71,594	75,166	75,335	74,508	76,332	79,840
Administrative and waste services	32,482	32,736	33,079	33,483	34,429	35,870	36,928
Educational services	32,809	34,003	34,667	35,278	36,019	36,889	37,143
Health care and social assistance..................................	40,757	42,021	42,751	43,358	44,533	45,900	46,754
Arts, entertainment, and recreation................................	24,601	25,012	24,900	26,333	26,824	27,149	28,301
Accommodation and food services.................................	17,936	18,349	18,990	19,647	20,641	21,741	22,659
Other services, except public administration....................	26,151	26,591	27,860	28,689	29,443	30,590	31,530
Government and government enterprises..........................	41,132	41,215	41,260	41,914	42,791	44,131	45,104

D = Not shown to avoid disclosure of confidential information, but the estimates for this item are included in the total.

Table ME-10. Employment Characteristics by Family Type

(Number, percent.)

Family type and labor force status	2014		2015		2016	
	Total	Families with own children under 18 years	Total	Families with own children under 18 years	Total	Families with own children under 18 years
All Families...	342,108	128,896	342,926	126,257	329,554	118,579
FAMILY TYPE AND LABOR FORCE STATUS						
Married-Couple Families................................	261,227	81,849	264,442	79,988	256,503	78,442
Both husband and wife in labor force....................	53.6	72.7	51.3	71.0	52.4	75.5
Husband in labor force, wife not in labor force.........	17.3	21.5	17.4	21.2	16.0	16.6
Wife in labor force, husband not in labor force.........	9.0	4.0	9.4	4.8	9.4	5.2
Both husband and wife not in labor force................	20.1	1.8	20.7	2.2	21.3	2.4
Other Families	80,881	47,047	78,484	46,269	73,051	40,137
Female householder, no husband present..............	67.9	68.4	68.3	68.3	66.6	65.4
In labor force..................................	46.9	54.0	47.8	53.0	46.9	53.4
Not in labor force.............................	21.0	14.4	20.5	15.3	19.6	12.0
Male householder, no wife present......................	32.1	31.6	31.7	31.7	33.4	34.6
In labor force..................................	24.7	27.5	24.4	28.0	25.2	30.0
Not in labor force.............................	7.5	4.2	7.3	3.7	8.3	4.6

Table ME-11. School Enrollment and Educational Attainment, 2016

(Number, percent.)

Item	State	U.S.
Enrollment		
Total population 3 years and over, enrolled in school	293,857	81,572,277
Enrolled in nursery school or preschool (percent)	6.2	6.0
Enrolled in kindergarten (percent)................................	5.3	5.0
Enrolled in elementary school, grades 1-8 (percent)................................	38.1	40.3
Enrolled in high school, grades 9-12 (percent)................................	21.7	21.0
Enrolled in college or graduate school (percent)................................	28.8	27.7
Attainment		
Total population 25 years and over	966,569	218,475,480
Less than ninth grade (percent)................................	2.7	5.4
9th to 12th grade, no diploma (percent)	5.0	7.2
High school graduate, including equivalency (percent)................................	32.9	27.2
Some college, no degree (percent)	19.4	20.6
Associate's degree (percent)................................	9.8	8.4
Bachelor's degree (percent)................................	18.8	19.3
Graduate or professional degree (percent)................................	11.3	11.0
High school graduate or higher (percent)	92.3	87.5
Bachelor's degree or higher (percent)................................	30.1	31.3

Table ME-12. Public School Characteristics and Educational Indicators

(Number, percent; data derived from National Center of Education Statistics.)

Item	State	U.S.
Public Schools, 2015–2016 (except where noted)		
Number of school districts................................	267	18,328
Number of schools................................	611	98,456
Number of students................................	181,613	50,327,015
Number of teachers................................	14,857	3,151,497
Student-teacher ratio	12.2	16.0
Expenditures per student (dollars), 2014-2015................................	13,976	11,445
Four-year adjusted cohort graduation rate (ACGR)[1,2]	87.0	84.1
Students eligible for free or reduced-price lunch (percent), 2014-2015................................	47.1	51.8
English language learners (percent), Fall 2015................................	2.8	9.5
Students age 3 to 21 served under IDEA, part B (percent)................................	17.9	13.2

Public Schools by Type	Number	Percent of state public schools
Total number of schools................................	611	100.0
Regular	582	95.3
Special education................................	2	0.3
Vocational education................................	27	4.4
Alternative education................................	0	-

NOTE: Every school is assigned only one school type based on its instructional emphasis.
[1] ACGR data represents a new method of calculating high-school completion rates and may not be comparable to previous years' data for Averaged Freshmen Graduation Rates (AFGR).
[2] The United States 4-year ACGRs were estimated using both the reported 4-year ACGR data from 49 states and the District of Columbia and using imputed data for Idaho. The estimate for American Indian/Alaska Native students also includes imputed data for Virginia.
- = Zero or rounds to zero.

Table ME-13. Reported Voting and Registration of the Voting-Age Population, November 2016

(Numbers in thousands, percent.)

Item	Total population	Total citizen population	Registered			Voted		
			Total registered	Percent registered (total population)	Percent registered (total citizen population)	Total voted	Percent voted (total population)	Percent voted (total citizen population)
U.S. Total	245,502	224,059	157,596	64.2	70.3	137,537	56.0	61.4
State Total................................	1,058	1,038	830	78.5	80.0	754	71.3	72.7
Sex								
Male	510	500	388	76.1	77.5	347	68.1	69.3
Female	548	537	442	80.7	82.3	408	74.3	75.8
Race								
White alone..............................	1,001	988	793	79.2	80.3	720	71.9	72.9
White, non-Hispanic alone	982	972	786	80.1	80.9	713	72.6	73.3
Black alone................................	13	10	9	(B)	(B)	7	(B)	(B)
Asian alone...............................	11	8	6	(B)	(B)	5	(B)	(B)
Hispanic (of any race).................	20	16	7	(B)	(B)	7	(B)	(B)
White alone or in combination	1,026	1,013	811	79.0	80.0	738	71.9	72.8
Black alone or in combination...........	17	14	9	(B)	(B)	7	(B)	(B)
Asian alone or in combination...........	13	9	7	(B)	(B)	6	(B)	(B)
Age								
18 to 24 years...........................	101	100	63	61.7	62.4	49	48.8	49.4
25 to 34 years...........................	157	154	109	69.2	70.8	95	60.4	61.8
35 to 44 years...........................	146	139	107	73.3	76.9	97	66.4	69.6
45 to 64 years...........................	421	418	354	83.9	84.6	327	77.5	78.2
65 years and over	232	227	198	85.4	87.3	186	80.3	82.0

B = Base is less than 75,000 and therefore too small to show the derived measure.

Table ME-14. Crime

(Number, rate per 100,000. Data are derived from the FBI Uniform Crime Reports.)

Item	State			U.S. [1,2,3,4]		
	2015	2016	Percent change	2015	2016	Percent change
TOTAL POPULATION [5]	1,329,328	1,331,479	0.2	321,418,820	323,127,513	0.5
VIOLENT CRIME						
Number...	1,729	1,648	-4.7	1,231,566	1,248,185	1.3
Rate..	130.1	123.8	-4.8	383.2	386.3	0.8
Murder and Nonnegligent Manslaughter						
Number...	23	20	-13.0	15,696	17,250	9.9
Rate..	1.7	1.5	-11.8	4.9	5.3	8.2
Rape[6]						
Number[6]...	474	412	-13.1	124,047	130,603	5.3
Rate..	35.7	30.9	-13.4	38.6	40.4	4.7
Robbery						
Number...	311	266	-14.5	327,374	332,198	1.5
Rate..	23.4	20.0	-14.5	101.9	102.8	0.9
Aggravated Assault						
Number...	921	950	3.1	764,449	803,007	5.0
Rate..	69.3	71.3	2.9	237.8	248.5	4.5
PROPERTY CRIME						
Number...	24,327	21,912	-9.9	7,993,631	7,919,035	-0.9
Rate..	1,830.0	1,645.7	-10.1	2,487.0	2,450.7	-1.5
Burglary						
Number...	4,684	4,003	-14.5	1,579,527	1,515,096	-4.1
Rate..	352.4	300.6	-14.7	491.4	468.9	-4.6
Larceny-Theft						
Number...	18,829	17,134	-9.0	5,706,346	5,638,455	-1.2
Rate..	1,416.4	1,286.8	-9.1	1,775.4	1,745.0	-1.7
Motor Vehicle Theft						
Number...	814	775	-4.8	707,758	765,484	8.2
Rate..	61.2	58.2	-4.9	220.2	236.9	7.6

NOTE: Although arson data are included in the trend and clearance tables, sufficient data are not available to estimate totals for this offense. Therefore, no arson data are published in this table.
X = Not applicable.
- = Zero or rounds to zero.
[1] The crime figures have been adjusted.
[2] The data collection methodology for the offense of forcible rape used by the Minnesota state Uniform Crime Reporting (UCR) Program (with the exception of Minneapolis and St. Paul, Minnesota) does not comply with national UCR Program guidelines. Consequently, its figures for forcible rape and violent crime (of which forcible rape is a part) are not published in this table.
[3] Includes offenses reported by the Zoological Police and the Metro Transit Police.
[4] Because of changes in the state's reporting practices, figures are not comparable to previous years' data.
[5] Populations are U.S. Census Bureau provisional estimates as of July 1 of each year.
[6] The figures shown for the offense of rape were estimated using the revised Uniform Crime Reporting (UCR) definition of rape.

Table ME-15. State Government Finances, 2016

(Dollar amounts in thousands, percent distribution.)

Item	Dollars	Percent distribution
Total Revenue	9,003,011	100.0
General revenue	8,326,381	92.5
Intergovernmental revenue	2,893,679	32.1
Taxes	4,130,242	45.9
General sales	1,359,190	15.1
Selective sales	718,723	8.0
License taxes	272,253	3.0
Individual income tax	1,551,637	17.2
Corporate income tax	137,492	1.5
Other taxes	90,947	1.0
Current charges	839,240	9.3
Miscellaneous general revenue	463,220	5.1
Utility revenue	9,148	0.1
Liquor stores revenue	165399	1.8
Insurance trust revenue [1]	502,083	5.6
Total Expenditure	9,403,020	100.0
Intergovernmental expenditure	1,312,041	14.0
Direct expenditure	8,090,979	86.0
Current operation	6,251,632	66.5
Capital outlay	490,050	5.2
Insurance benefits and repayments	997,403	10.6
Assistance and subsidies	169,246	1.8
Interest on debt	182,648	1.9
Exhibit: Salaries and wages	1,055,553	11.2
Total Expenditure	9,403,020	100.0
General expenditure	8,382,046	89.1
Intergovernmental expenditure	1,312,041	14.0
Direct expenditure	7,070,005	75.2
General expenditure, by function:		
Education	2,211,255	23.5
Public welfare	3,355,616	35.7
Hospitals	78,846	0.8
Health	221,889	2.4
Highways	721,109	7.7
Police protection	96,243	1.0
Correction	191,160	2.0
Natural resources	198,999	2.1
Parks and recreation	8,239	0.1
Governmental administration	431,579	4.6
Interest on general debt	182,648	1.9
Other and unallocable	684,463	7.3
Utility expenditure	23,564	0.3
Liquor stores expenditure	7	-
Insurance trust expenditure	997,403	10.6
Debt at End of Fiscal Year	4,845,408	X
Cash and Security Holdings	18,311,224	X

X = Not applicable.
- = Zero or rounds to zero.
[1] Within insurance trust revenue, net earnings of state retirement systems is a calculated statistic (the item code in the data file is X08), and thus can be positive or negative. Net earnings is the sum of earnings on investments plus gains on investments minus losses on investments. The change made in 2002 for asset valuation from book to market value in accordance with Statement 34 of the Governmental Accounting Standards Board is reflected in the calculated statistics.

Table ME-16. State Government Tax Collections, 2017

(Dollars in thousands, percent.)

Item	Dollars	Percent distribution
Total Taxes	4,232,556	100.0
Property taxes	38,643	0.9
Sales and gross receipts	2,165,142	51.2
General sales and gross receipts	1,441,867	34.1
Selective sales and gross receipts	723,275	17.1
Alcoholic beverages	19,266	0.5
Amusements	54,400	1.3
Insurance premiums	95,943	2.3
Motor fuels	252,870	6.0
Pari-mutuels	1,479	-
Public utilities	21,944	0.5
Tobacco products	144,243	3.4
Other selective sales	133,130	3.1
Licenses	274,760	6.5
Alcoholic beverages	6,698	0.2
Amusements	586	-
Corporations in general	10,577	0.2
Hunting and fishing	16,579	0.4
Motor vehicle	109,723	2.6
Motor vehicle operators	11,025	0.3
Public utilities	X	-
Occupation and business, NEC	109,737	2.6
Other licenses	9,835	0.2
Income taxes	1,710,105	40.4
Individual income	1,534,866	36.3
Corporation net income	175,239	4.1
Other taxes	43,906	1.0
Death and gift	11,718	0.3
Documentary and stock transfer	32,188	0.8
Severance	X	-
Taxes, NEC	0	-

X = Not applicable.
- = Zero or rounds to zero.

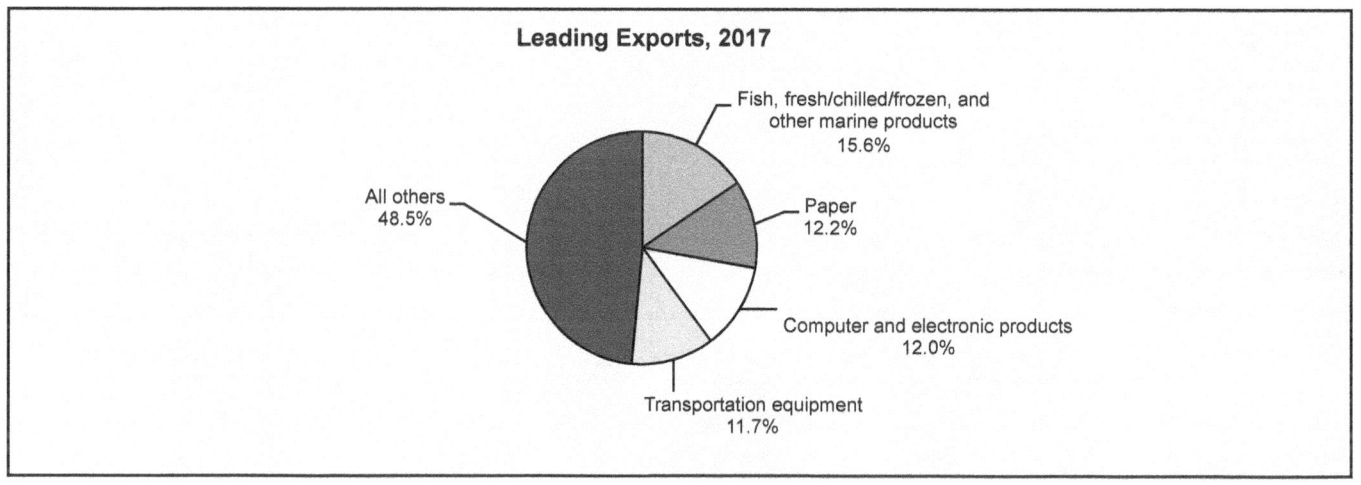

Leading Exports, 2017

Fish, fresh/chilled/frozen, and other marine products 15.6%
Paper 12.2%
Computer and electronic products 12.0%
Transportation equipment 11.7%
All others 48.5%

MARYLAND

Facts and Figures

Location: Eastern United States; bordered on the N by Pennsylvania, on the E by Delaware and the Atlantic Ocean, and on the S and W by Virginia and West Virginia

Area: 12,407 sq. mi. (32,133 sq. km.); rank—42nd

Population: 6,052,177 (2017 est.); rank—19th

Principal Cities: capital—Annapolis; largest—Baltimore

Statehood: April 28, 1788; 7th state

U.S. Congress: 2 senators, 8 representatives

State Motto: *Fatti maschii parole femine* ("Manly deeds, womanly words")

State Song: "Maryland, My Maryland"

State Nicknames: The Old Line State; The Free State

Abbreviations: MD; Md.

State Symbols: flower—black-eyed susan; tree—white oak; bird—Baltimore oriole

At a Glance

- With an increase in population of 4.6 percent, Maryland ranked 24th among the states in growth from 2010 to 2017.

- Maryland's 2016 median household income of $78,945 was the highest in the country, and its poverty rate of 9.7 percent was the 3rd lowest among the states.

- Maryland's violent crime rate in 2016 was 472.0 per 100,000 population, compared to 386.3 for the entire nation.

- In 2016, 6.1 percent of all Marylanders were uninsured, compared to the national average of 8.6 percent.

- Approximately 30.8 percent of Marylanders self-identified their race as "Black or African American alone" in 2017, the 5th highest percentage in the country.

Table MD-1. Population by Age, Sex, Race, and Hispanic Origin

(Number, percent, except where noted.)

Sex, age, race, and Hispanic origin	2000	2010	2017 [1]	Average annual percent change, 2010–2017
Total Population.........	5,296,486	5,773,552	6,052,177	4.8
Percent of total U.S. population	1.9	1.9	1.9	X
Sex				
Male.........	2,557,794	2,791,762	2,934,154	5.1
Female	2,738,692	2,981,790	3,118,023	4.6
Age				
Under 5 years.........	353,393	364,488	366,385	0.5
5 to 19 years.........	1,139,572	1,152,138	1,135,387	-1.5
20 to 64 years.........	3,204,214	3,549,284	3,645,734	2.7
65 years and over	599,307	707,642	904,671	27.8
Median age (years)	36.0	38.0	38.7	1.8
Race and Hispanic Origin				
One race				
White.........	3,391,308	3,542,379	3,568,679	0.7
Black.........	1,477,411	1,731,513	1,862,566	7.6
American Indian and Alaska Native	15,423	30,885	35,386	14.6
Asian.........	210,929	326,655	407,369	24.7
Native Hawaiian or Other Pacific Islander	2,303	5,391	6,581	22.1
Two or more races.........	103,587	137,729	171,596	24.6
Hispanic (of any race).........	227,916	493,811	614,248	24.4

X = Not applicable.
[1] Population figures for 2017 are July 1 estimates. The 2010 estimates are taken from the 2010 Census.

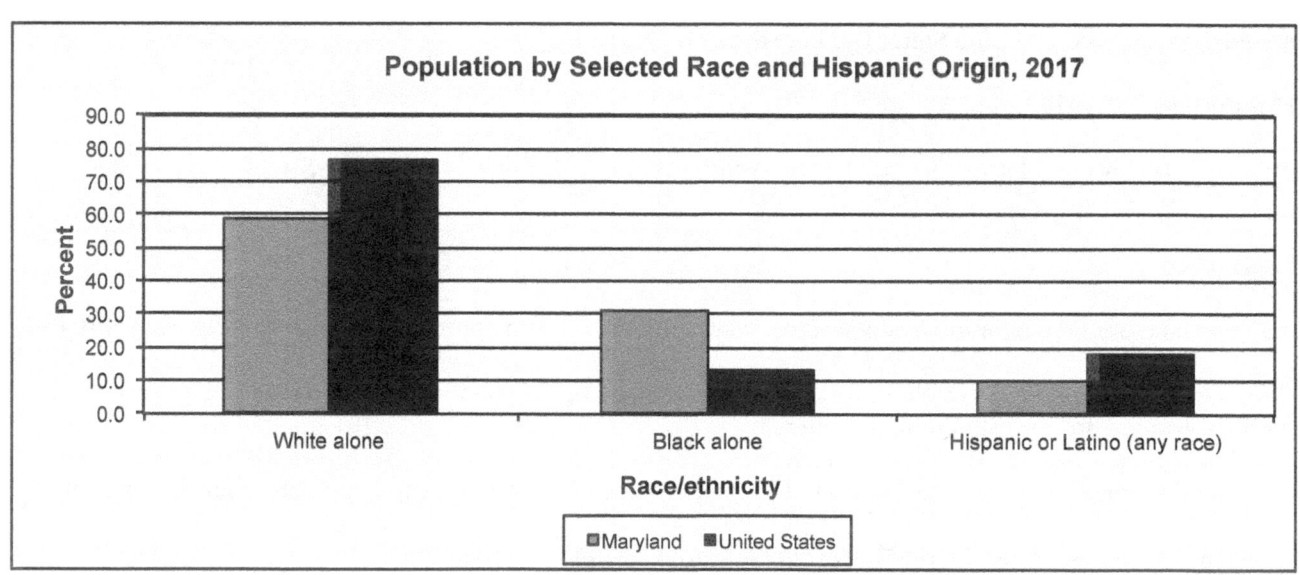

Population by Selected Race and Hispanic Origin, 2017

Table MD-2. Marital Status

(Number, percent distribution.)

Sex, age, and marital status	2000	2010	2016
Males, 15 Years and Over	1,972,921	2,232,162	2,346,134
Never married	31.0	36.8	38.5
Now married, except separated.........	56.3	50.2	48.6
Separated.........	2.8	2.3	2.2
Widowed.........	2.5	2.7	2.3
Divorced.........	7.4	8.0	8.4
Females, 15 Years and Over	2,186,715	2,442,021	2,556,180
Never married	26.8	32.2	33.3
Now married, except separated.........	49.7	45.3	44.3
Separated.........	3.4	2.9	2.3
Widowed.........	10.1	9.0	8.5
Divorced.........	10.1	10.7	11.6

Table MD-3. Households and Housing Characteristics

(Number, percent, dollars.)

Item	2000	2010	2016	Average annual percent change, 2010–2016
Total Households..	1,980,859	2,127,439	2,194,657	0.5
Family households..	1,359,318	1,431,958	1,458,953	0.3
Married-couple family...	994,549	1,022,613	1,039,902	0.3
Other family...	364,789	409,345	419,051	0.4
Male householder, no wife present...........................	84,893	104,112	111,361	1.2
Female householder, no husband present....................	279,876	305,233	307,690	0.1
Nonfamily households	621,541	695,481	735,704	1.0
Householder living alone.......................................	495,459	570,388	598,228	0.8
Householder not living alone.................................	126,082	125,093	137,476	1.6
Housing Characteristics				
Total housing units...	2,145,283	2,380,605	2,447,211	0.5
Occupied housing units	1,980,859	2,127,439	2,194,657	0.5
Owner occupied	1,341,751	1,426,267	1,445,953	0.2
Renter occupied	639,108	701,172	748,704	1.1
Average household size..	2.61	2.65	2.68	0.2
Financial Characteristics				
Median gross rent of renter-occupied housing	689	1,131	1,314	2.7
Median monthly owner costs for housing units with a mortgage ...	1,296	2,016	1,918	-0.8
Median value of owner-occupied housing units	146,000	301,400	306,900	0.3

Table MD-4. Migration, Origin, and Language

(Number, percent.)

Characteristic	State			U.S.		
	2015	2016	Percent change	2015	2016	Percent change
Residence 1 Year Ago						
Population 1 year and over	5,934,005	5,949,566	0.3	317,635,720	319,361,956	0.5
Same house..	85.6	86.4	X	85.3	85.4	X
Different house in the U.S.	13.6	12.9	X	14.1	13.9	X
Same county.......................................	7.8	7.3	X	8.5	8.3	X
Different county	5.8	5.6	X	5.6	5.6	X
Same state	3.0	2.9	X	3.2	3.2	X
Different state	2.8	2.7	X	2.4	2.4	X
Abroad	0.8	0.7	X	0.7	0.7	X
Place of Birth						
Native born	5,094,819	5,094,577	-0.0	278,128,449	279,388,170	0.5
Male	48.5	48.4	X	49.3	49.3	X
Female	51.5	51.6	X	50.7	50.7	X
Foreign born	911,582	921,870	1.1	43,290,372	43,739,345	1.0
Male	48.7	49.0	X	48.6	48.5	X
Female	51.3	51.0	X	51.4	51.5	X
Foreign born; naturalized U.S. citizen.....................	447,550	467,964	3.4	20,697,103	21,238,372	2.6
Male	46.2	46.8	X	45.9	45.9	X
Female	53.8	53.2	X	54.1	54.1	X
Foreign born; not a U.S. citizen	464,032	453,906	-2.2	22,593,269	22,500,973	-0.4
Male	51.1	51.2	X	51.1	51.0	X
Female	48.9	48.8	X	48.9	49.0	X
Entered 2010 or later	17.5	19.9	X	15.6	18.6	X
Entered 2000 to 2009	33.9	32.7	X	27.9	26.7	X
Entered before 2000.................................	48.6	47.4	X	56.5	54.7	X
World Region of Birth, Foreign						
Foreign-born population, excluding population born at sea	911,582	921,870	1.1	43,289,646	43,738,901	1.0
Europe	9.3	9.3	X	11.1	10.9	X
Asia...	33.4	32.8	X	30.6	30.8	X
Africa...	16.6	17.3	X	4.8	4.9	X
Oceania	0.3	0.2	X	0.6	0.6	X
Latin America......................................	39.3	39.5	X	51.1	51.0	X
North America	1.1	0.7	X	1.9	1.8	X
Language Spoken at Home and Ability to Speak English						
Population 5 years and over...........................	5,639,774	5,653,552	0.2	301,625,014	303,328,961	0.6
English only	81.5	81.1	X	78.5	78.4	X
Language other than English...........................	18.5	18.9	X	21.5	21.6	X
Speaks English less than "very well".................	6.9	7.0	X	8.6	8.6	X

NA = Not available.
X = Not applicable.
- = Zero or rounds to zero.

Table MD-5. Median Income and Poverty Status, 2016

(Number, percent, except as noted.)

Characteristic	State		U.S.	
	Number	Percent	Number	Percent
Median Income				
Households (dollars)	78,945	X	57,617	X
Families (dollars)	95,336	X	71,062	X
Below Poverty Level (All People)	567,715	9.7	44,268,996	14.0
Sex				
Male	251,438	8.9	19,760,056	12.8
Female	316,277	10.4	24,508,940	15.2
Age				
Under 18 years	168,811	12.7	14,115,713	19.5
Related children under 18 years	163,634	12.4	13,805,435	19.1
18 to 64 years	329,042	8.9	25,723,818	13.2
65 years and over	69,862	8.2	4,429,465	9.2

X = Not applicable.

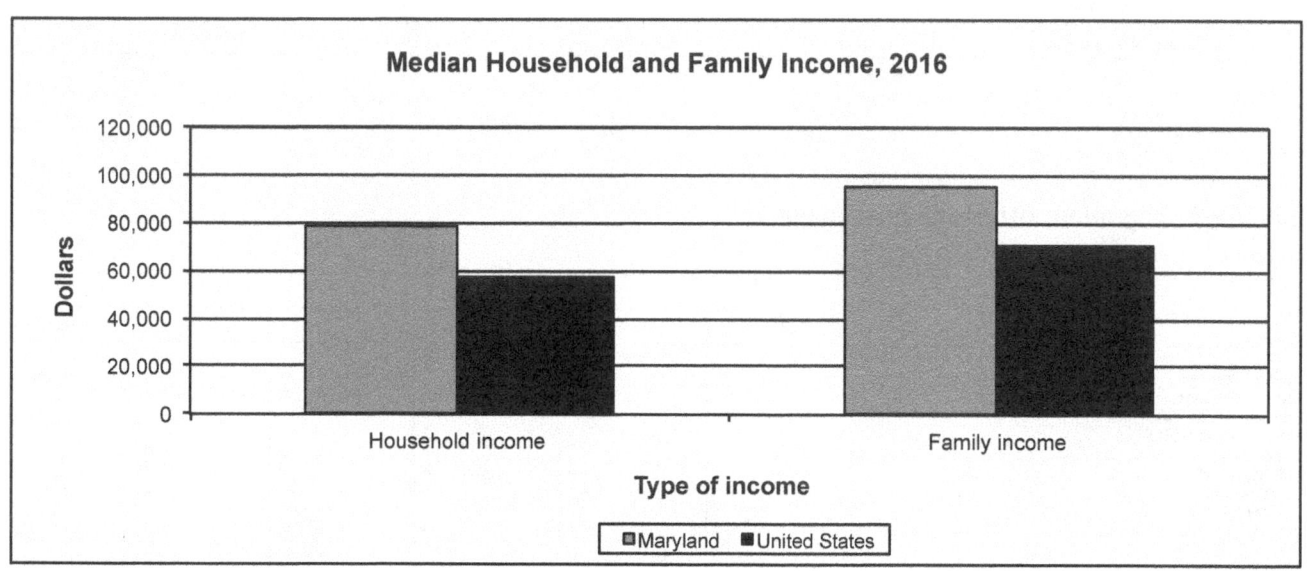

Table MD-6. Health Insurance Coverage Status for the Civilian Noninstitutionalized Population and Children Under 18 Years of Age

(Number, percent.)

Item	2008	2009	2010	2011	2012	2013	2014	2015	2016
Civilian Noninstitutionalized Population	5,530,013	5,589,768	5,687,998	5,736,588	5,788,196	5,834,039	5,885,847	5,908,522	5,918,535
Covered by Private or Public Insurance									
Number	4,918,880	4,968,978	5,047,137	5,138,144	5,190,642	5,240,861	5,422,579	5,519,323	5,555,356
Percent	88.9	88.9	88.7	89.6	89.7	89.8	92.1	93.4	93.9
Not Covered									
Number	611,133	620,790	640,861	598,444	597,554	593,178	463,268	389,199	363,179
Percent	11.1	11.1	11.3	10.4	10.3	10.2	7.9	6.6	6.1
Percent in the U.S. not covered	15.1	15.1	15.5	15.1	14.8	14.5	11.7	9.4	8.6
Children Under 18 Years of Age	1,338,996	1,348,039	1,350,011	1,344,498	1,341,118	1,343,118	1,349,767	1,346,154	1,344,588
Covered by Private or Public Insurance									
Number	1,268,644	1,283,491	1,285,713	1,283,012	1,289,667	1,283,833	1,307,172	1,293,887	1,299,633
Percent	94.7	95.2	95.2	95.4	96.2	95.6	96.8	96.1	96.7
Not Covered									
Number	70,352	64,548	64,298	61,486	51,451	59,285	42,595	52,267	44,955
Percent	5.3	4.8	4.8	4.6	3.8	4.4	3.2	3.9	3.3
Percent in the U.S. not covered	9.9	8.6	8.0	7.5	7.2	7.1	6.0	4.8	4.5

Table MD-7. Employment Status by Demographic Group, 2017

(Numbers in thousands, percent.)

Characteristic	Civilian noninstitutional population	Civilian labor force		Employed		Unemployed	
		Number	Percent of population	Number	Percent of population	Number	Percent of population
Total...	4,748	3,213	67.7	3,078	64.8	136	4.2
Sex							
Male...	2,246	1,652	73.6	1,584	70.6	68	4.1
Female	2,502	1,561	62.4	1,493	59.7	68	4.4
Race, Sex, and Hispanic Origin							
White	2,815	1,880	66.8	1,820	64.7	60	3.2
Male..	1,367	1,000	73.1	968	70.8	32	3.1
Female	1,448	880	60.8	852	58.8	28	3.2
Black or African American.....................	1,428	994	69.6	933	65.3	60	6.1
Male..	637	464	72.8	436	68.4	28	6.0
Female	791	530	66.9	497	62.8	33	6.1
Hispanic or Latino ethnicity[1]	447	348	77.9	333	74.3	16	4.5
Male..	222	199	89.7	194	87.2	6	2.8
Female	225	149	66.2	139	61.7	10	6.9
Age							
16 to 19 years................................	NA	NA	NA	NA	NA	NA	NA
20 to 24 years................................	386	296	76.6	269	69.6	27	9.1
25 to 34 years................................	826	692	83.8	663	80.3	29	4.2
35 to 44 years................................	746	644	86.3	620	83.2	23	3.6
45 to 54 years................................	862	730	84.7	711	82.5	19	2.6
55 to 64 years................................	792	541	68.3	523	66.0	18	3.3
65 years and over	857	211	24.6	204	23.9	6	3.0

NOTE: Data in Table 7 are from the Current Population Survey (CPS) and do not match the estimates in Table 8. See notes and definitions for further information.
[1] May be of any race.

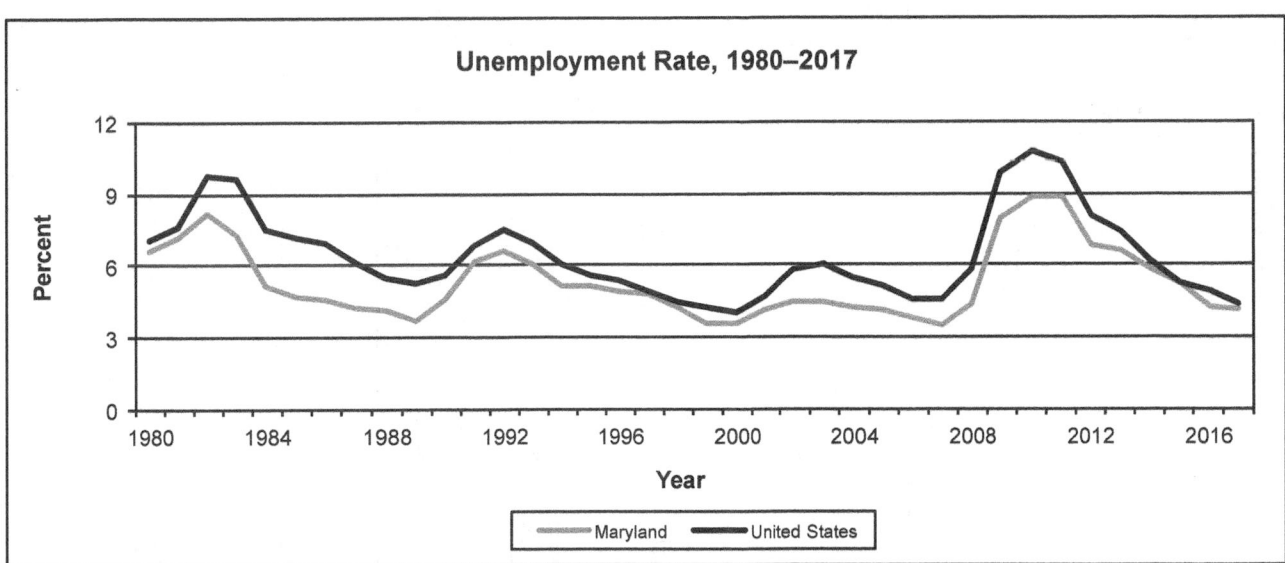

Unemployment Rate, 1980–2017

Table MD-8. Employment Status of the Civilian Noninstitutional Population Age 16 Years and Over

(Number, percent.)

Year	Civilian labor force	Civilian participation rate	Employed	Unemployed	Unemployment rate
2009..	3,032,700	69.0	2,820,245	212,455	7.0
2010..	3,073,826	68.5	2,838,492	235,334	7.7
2011..	3,096,561	68.0	2,872,084	224,477	7.2
2012..	3,119,647	67.8	2,902,307	217,340	7.0
2013..	3,129,352	67.4	2,923,498	205,854	6.6
2014..	3,129,933	66.9	2,947,943	181,990	5.8
2015..	3,151,142	66.9	2,990,942	160,200	5.1
2016..	3,178,646	67.1	3,037,763	140,883	4.4
2017..	3,219,455	67.6	3,086,246	133,209	4.1

Table MD-9. Employment and Average Wages by Industry

(Estimates through 2010 are based on the 2007 *North American Industry Classification System* [NAICS]. Estimates from 2011 onward are based on the 2012 NAICS.)

Industry	2010	2011	2012	2013	2014	2015	2016
	Number of jobs						
Wage and Salary Employment by Industry........................	2,625,019	2,650,584	2,685,280	2,702,959	2,728,522	2,767,317	2,805,670
Farm Wage and Salary Employment..............................	4,748	4,744	6,475	5,980	6,416	6,214	7,499
Nonfarm Wage and Salary Employment...........................	2,620,271	2,645,840	2,678,805	2,696,979	2,722,106	2,761,103	2,798,171
Private wage and salary employment................................	2,056,337	2,078,218	2,109,420	2,128,533	2,155,027	2,193,577	2,229,728
Forestry, fishing, and related activities.............................	2,209	2,019	1,977	2,022	2,060	2,124	2,180
Mining..	1,468	1,433	1,524	1,339	1,259	1,297	1,165
Utilities..	9,716	10,069	10,103	9,781	9,738	9,579	9,836
Construction..	147,757	147,885	147,456	150,364	153,666	158,226	165,473
Manufacturing..	114,958	112,919	108,831	106,370	103,376	103,643	103,403
Durable goods manufacturing..................................	61,488	60,189	57,860	56,302	53,714	54,436	53,956
Nondurable goods manufacturing.............................	53,470	52,730	50,971	50,068	49,662	49,207	49,447
Wholesale trade..	85,818	86,534	86,448	86,188	85,303	86,284	86,227
Retail trade...	279,657	283,148	286,405	286,608	289,186	291,677	292,939
Transportation and warehousing..................................	65,333	66,187	67,456	68,719	71,133	76,562	78,384
Information..	43,868	41,081	39,909	39,537	38,972	38,349	38,440
Finance and insurance...	98,987	98,692	98,986	99,383	98,476	99,379	100,249
Real estate and rental and leasing................................	43,326	43,129	43,686	44,125	44,589	45,548	45,892
Professional, scientific, and technical services...................	226,313	231,104	235,966	237,301	241,056	243,456	248,514
Management of companies and enterprises........................	19,569	22,267	24,725	25,906	25,574	25,202	26,284
Administrative and waste services................................	144,151	147,539	152,558	156,700	159,818	164,484	171,079
Educational services...	70,211	71,489	72,585	71,682	73,696	75,067	76,040
Health care and social assistance................................	329,856	334,550	342,513	346,073	350,187	359,235	365,839
Arts, entertainment, and recreation..............................	36,331	36,622	38,209	42,311	44,530	45,950	46,467
Accommodation and food services................................	195,521	198,661	207,332	213,536	217,437	223,161	228,017
Other services, except public administration......................	141,288	142,890	142,751	140,588	144,971	144,354	143,300
Government and government enterprises...........................	563,934	567,622	569,385	568,446	567,079	567,526	568,443
	Dollars						
Average Wages and Salaries by Industry........................	53,083	54,489	55,444	55,547	56,854	58,639	61,084
Average Farm Wages and Salaries...............................	25,881	22,673	23,208	25,910	25,563	24,232	22,135
Average Nonfarm Wages and Salaries...........................	53,132	54,546	55,522	55,612	56,927	58,717	61,188
Average private wages and salaries................................	50,539	51,822	53,079	53,208	54,420	56,119	58,455
Forestry, fishing, and related activities.............................	27,067	27,692	28,068	28,721	29,215	30,750	34,263
Mining..	56,032	61,075	61,333	60,153	62,712	61,488	68,426
Utilities..	107,343	110,167	118,943	115,073	114,520	122,096	119,774
Construction..	55,076	56,025	56,907	57,117	59,179	61,012	64,998
Manufacturing..	67,998	68,822	70,363	70,981	72,306	75,281	80,750
Durable goods manufacturing..................................	76,107	76,131	77,458	78,375	78,035	80,109	85,067
Nondurable goods manufacturing.............................	58,674	60,478	62,309	62,665	66,109	69,940	76,039
Wholesale trade..	70,739	72,939	74,437	75,214	77,445	79,659	80,630
Retail trade...	28,931	29,018	29,414	29,503	30,102	31,475	32,272
Transportation and warehousing..................................	48,006	49,931	50,370	50,288	52,829	53,975	56,227
Information..	74,193	78,548	80,343	83,120	85,281	86,354	83,689
Finance and insurance...	82,529	85,537	93,568	93,248	96,557	100,331	102,130
Real estate and rental and leasing................................	55,401	56,579	57,971	58,007	60,631	62,824	68,811
Professional, scientific, and technical services...................	85,388	88,541	91,159	90,290	92,592	94,237	97,675
Management of companies and enterprises........................	107,421	106,413	105,241	107,488	111,088	116,214	118,491
Administrative and waste services................................	38,265	38,796	39,142	39,510	40,212	41,977	43,445
Educational services...	43,382	45,531	47,145	47,629	49,007	49,851	52,233
Health care and social assistance................................	47,756	48,968	49,641	49,973	50,958	52,918	54,811
Arts, entertainment, and recreation..............................	30,963	31,493	32,542	32,629	33,217	34,680	37,612
Accommodation and food services................................	19,965	20,481	20,951	21,265	21,871	22,844	25,370
Other services, except public administration......................	34,636	35,206	36,512	37,790	38,423	40,048	42,552
Government and government enterprises...........................	62,587	64,521	64,574	64,616	66,456	68,757	71,908

Table MD-10. Employment Characteristics by Family Type

(Number, percent.)

Family type and labor force status	2014		2015		2016	
	Total	Families with own children under 18 years	Total	Families with own children under 18 years	Total	Families with own children under 18 years
All Families..	1,437,457	625,063	1,454,839	629,970	1,458,953	624,358
FAMILY TYPE AND LABOR FORCE STATUS						
Married-Couple Families...............................	1,013,543	415,627	1,042,467	429,625	1,039,902	419,478
Both husband and wife in labor force......................	58.4	72.9	57.5	71.5	57.8	73.3
Husband in labor force, wife not in labor force	19.9	22.6	19.9	23.6	19.0	21.6
Wife in labor force, husband not in labor force	7.4	3.3	7.4	3.3	7.7	3.4
Both husband and wife not in labor force....................	14.4	1.1	14.2	1.0	14.4	1.1
Other Families	423,914	209,436	412,372	200,345	419,051	204,880
Female householder, no husband present.....................	75.0	76.2	73.7	75.4	73.4	74.2
In labor force...	56.6	66.0	55.2	65.5	54.8	65.2
Not in labor force	18.4	10.2	18.6	9.9	18.6	9.0
Male householder, no wife present.......................	25.0	23.8	26.3	24.6	26.6	25.8
In labor force...	20.1	22.5	21.0	22.5	22.3	24.5
Not in labor force	4.9	1.3	5.3	2.2	4.3	1.4

Table MD-11. School Enrollment and Educational Attainment, 2016

(Number, percent.)

Item	State	U.S.
Enrollment		
Total population 3 years and over, enrolled in school	1,540,625	81,572,277
Enrolled in nursery school or preschool (percent)	6.1	6.0
Enrolled in kindergarten (percent)	4.6	5.0
Enrolled in elementary school, grades 1-8 (percent)............................	39.0	40.3
Enrolled in high school, grades 9-12 (percent)	20.0	21.0
Enrolled in college or graduate school (percent)	30.4	27.7
Attainment		
Total population 25 years and over	4,122,508	218,475,480
Less than ninth grade (percent)	4.0	5.4
9th to 12th grade, no diploma (percent)	5.8	7.2
High school graduate, including equivalency (percent).........................	25.4	27.2
Some college, no degree (percent)...	18.9	20.6
Associate's degree (percent)	6.5	8.4
Bachelor's degree (percent)	20.9	19.3
Graduate or professional degree (percent)....................................	18.5	11.9
High school graduate or higher (percent)	90.1	87.5
Bachelor's degree or higher (percent)..	39.3	31.3

Table MD-12. Public School Characteristics and Educational Indicators

(Number, percent; data derived from National Center of Education Statistics.)

Item	State	U.S.
Public Schools, 2015–2016 (except where noted)		
Number of school districts...	25	18,328
Number of schools...	1,437	98,456
Number of students	879,601	50,327,015
Number of teachers	59,414	3,151,497
Student-teacher ratio	14.8	16.0
Expenditures per student (dollars), 2014-2015................................	14,431	11,445
Four-year adjusted cohort graduation rate (ACGR)[1,2]	87.6	84.1
Students eligible for free or reduced-price lunch (percent), 2014-2015..........	45.0	51.8
English language learners (percent), Fall 2015	7.2	9.5
Students age 3 to 21 served under IDEA, part B (percent)......................	12.0	13.2

Public Schools by Type	Number	Percent of state public schools
Total number of schools..	1,437	100.0
Regular	1,329	92.5
Special education	37	2.6
Vocational education	27	1.9
Alternative education..	44	3.1

NOTE: Every school is assigned only one school type based on its instructional emphasis.
[1] ACGR data represents a new method of calculating high-school completion rates and may not be comparable to previous years' data for Averaged Freshmen Graduation Rates (AFGR).
[2] The United States 4-year ACGRs were estimated using both the reported 4-year ACGR data from 49 states and the District of Columbia and using imputed data for Idaho. The estimate for American Indian/Alaska Native students also includes imputed data for Virginia.

Table MD-13. Reported Voting and Registration of the Voting-Age Population, November 2016

(Numbers in thousands, percent.)

Item	Total population	Total citizen population	Registered			Voted		
			Total registered	Percent registered (total population)	Percent registered (total citizen population)	Total voted	Percent voted (total population)	Percent voted (total citizen population)
U.S. Total	245,502	224,059	157,596	64.2	70.3	137,537	56.0	61.4
State Total...............................	4,623	4,158	3,114	67.3	74.9	2,737	59.2	65.8
Sex								
Male	2,203	1,963	1,454	66.0	74.1	1,253	56.9	63.8
Female	2,420	2,194	1,659	68.6	75.6	1,484	61.3	67.6
Race								
White alone..............................	2,784	2,593	1,975	70.9	76.2	1,727	62.0	66.6
White, non-Hispanic alone	2,434	2,392	1,829	75.2	76.5	1,605	65.9	67.1
Black alone...............................	1,386	1,289	954	68.9	74.0	858	61.9	66.6
Asian alone..............................	349	213	147	42.0	69.1	117	33.4	54.9
Hispanic (of any race)......................	450	250	170	37.9	68.2	148	32.8	59.1
White alone or in combination	2,820	2,629	2,002	71.0	76.2	1,752	62.1	66.6
Black alone or in combination...........	1,421	1,324	984	69.2	74.3	884	62.2	66.8
Asian alone or in combination...........	349	213	147	42.0	69.1	117	33.4	54.9
Age								
18 to 24 years..........................	468	414	279	59.7	67.4	225	48.0	54.3
25 to 34 years..........................	819	711	505	61.7	71.1	424	51.8	59.7
35 to 44 years..........................	833	668	490	58.8	73.3	424	50.9	63.6
45 to 64 years..........................	1,702	1,586	1,243	73.0	78.4	1,133	66.6	71.4
65 years and over	801	778	596	74.4	76.6	530	66.2	68.1

Table MD-14. Crime

(Number, rate per 100,000. Data are derived from the FBI Uniform Crime Reports.)

Item	State			U.S. [1,2,3,4]		
	2015	2016	Percent change	2015	2016	Percent change
TOTAL POPULATION [5]	6,006,401	6,016,447	0.2	321,418,820	323,127,513	0.5
VIOLENT CRIME						
Number..	27,462	28,400	3.4	1,231,566	1,248,185	1.3
Rate..	457.2	472.0	3.2	383.2	386.3	0.8
Murder and Nonnegligent Manslaughter						
Number..	516	481	-6.8	15,696	17,250	9.9
Rate..	8.6	8.0	-7.0	4.9	5.3	8.2
Rape [6]						
Number [6]..	1,666	1,756	5.4	124,047	130,603	5.3
Rate..	27.7	29.2	5.4	38.6	40.4	4.7
Robbery						
Number..	9,863	10,289	4.3	327,374	332,198	1.5
Rate..	164.2	171.0	4.1	101.9	102.8	0.9
Aggravated Assault						
Number..	15,417	15,874	3.0	764,449	803,007	5.0
Rate..	256.7	263.8	2.8	237.8	248.5	4.5
PROPERTY CRIME						
Number..	139,048	137,445	-1.2	7,993,631	7,919,035	-0.9
Rate..	2,315.0	2,284.5	-1.3	2,487.0	2,450.7	-1.5
Burglary						
Number..	25,678	24,692	-3.8	1,579,527	1,515,096	-4.1
Rate..	427.5	410.4	-4.0	491.4	468.9	-4.6
Larceny-Theft						
Number..	100,219	100,919	0.7	5,706,346	5,638,455	-1.2
Rate..	1,668.5	1,677.4	0.5	1,775.4	1,745.0	-1.7
Motor Vehicle Theft						
Number..	13,151	11,834	-10.0	707,758	765,484	8.2
Rate..	218.9	196.7	-10.1	220.2	236.9	7.6

NOTE: Although arson data are included in the trend and clearance tables, sufficient data are not available to estimate totals for this offense. Therefore, no arson data are published in this table.
X = Not applicable.
- = Zero or rounds to zero.
[1] The crime figures have been adjusted.
[2] The data collection methodology for the offense of forcible rape used by the Minnesota state Uniform Crime Reporting (UCR) Program (with the exception of Minneapolis and St. Paul, Minnesota) does not comply with national UCR Program guidelines. Consequently, its figures for forcible rape and violent crime (of which forcible rape is a part) are not published in this table.
[3] Includes offenses reported by the Zoological Police and the Metro Transit Police.
[4] Because of changes in the state's reporting practices, figures are not comparable to previous years' data.
[5] Populations are U.S. Census Bureau provisional estimates as of July 1 of each year.
[6] The figures shown for the offense of rape were estimated using the revised Uniform Crime Reporting (UCR) definition of rape.

Table MD-15. State Government Finances, 2016

(Dollar amounts in thousands, percent distribution.)

Item	Dollars	Percent distribution
Total Revenue	42,037,052	100.0
General revenue	39,159,671	93.2
Intergovernmental revenue	12,290,258	29.2
Taxes	20,894,199	49.7
General sales	4,504,242	10.7
Selective sales	4,435,188	10.6
License taxes	884,363	2.1
Individual income tax	8,517,529	20.3
Corporate income tax	1,129,008	2.7
Other taxes	1,423,869	3.4
Current charges	3,665,456	8.7
Miscellaneous general revenue	2,309,758	5.5
Utility revenue	156,390	0.4
Liquor stores revenue	0	-
Insurance trust revenue [1]	2,720,991	6.5
Total Expenditure	44,089,713	100.0
Intergovernmental expenditure	9,398,276	21.3
Direct expenditure	34,691,437	78.7
Current operation	24,191,917	54.9
Capital outlay	3,147,303	7.1
Insurance benefits and repayments	4,344,038	9.9
Assistance and subsidies	1,861,189	4.2
Interest on debt	1,146,990	2.6
Exhibit: Salaries and wages	5,346,953	12.1
Total Expenditure	44,089,713	100.0
General expenditure	38,755,911	87.9
Intergovernmental expenditure	9,398,276	21.3
Direct expenditure	29,357,635	66.6
General expenditure, by function:		
Education	12,923,522	29.3
Public welfare	11,933,432	27.1
Hospitals	551,398	1.3
Health	2,284,125	5.2
Highways	2,556,540	5.8
Police protection	615,231	1.4
Correction	1,476,235	3.3
Natural resources	524,554	1.2
Parks and recreation	122,170	0.3
Governmental administration	1,509,345	3.4
Interest on general debt	1,146,990	2.6
Other and unallocable	3,112,369	7.1
Utility expenditure	989,764	2.4
Liquor stores expenditure	0	-
Insurance trust expenditure	4,344,038	9.9
Debt at End of Fiscal Year	27,871,287	X
Cash and Security Holdings	50,279,725	X

X = Not applicable.
- = Zero or rounds to zero.
[1] Within insurance trust revenue, net earnings of state retirement systems is a calculated statistic (the item code in the data file is X08), and thus can be positive or negative. Net earnings is the sum of earnings on investments plus gains on investments minus losses on investments. The change made in 2002 for asset valuation from book to market value in accordance with Statement 34 of the Governmental Accounting Standards Board is reflected in the calculated statistics.

Table MD-16. State Government Tax Collections, 2017

(Dollars in thousands, percent.)

Item	Dollars	Percent distribution
Total Taxes	21,599,795	100.0
Property taxes	777,064	3.6
Sales and gross receipts	9,242,760	42.8
General sales and gross receipts	4,609,538	21.3
Selective sales and gross receipts	4,633,222	21.5
Alcoholic beverages	32,151	0.1
Amusements	847,455	3.9
Insurance premiums	516,533	2.4
Motor fuels	1,078,313	5.0
Pari-mutuels	1,182	-
Public utilities	138,251	0.6
Tobacco products	386,965	1.8
Other selective sales	1,632,372	7.6
Licenses	866,391	4.0
Alcoholic beverages	1,486	-
Amusements	2,780	-
Corporations in general	109,767	0.5
Hunting and fishing	18,043	0.1
Motor vehicle	501,360	2.3
Motor vehicle operators	37,616	0.2
Public utilities	X	-
Occupation and business, NEC	193,485	0.9
Other licenses	1,854	-
Income taxes	10,068,643	46.6
Individual income	9,066,709	42.0
Corporation net income	1,001,934	4.6
Other taxes	644,937	3.0
Death and gift	227,940	1.1
Documentary and stock transfer	214,581	1.0
Severance	X	-
Taxes, NEC	202,416	0.9

X = Not applicable.
- = Zero or rounds to zero.

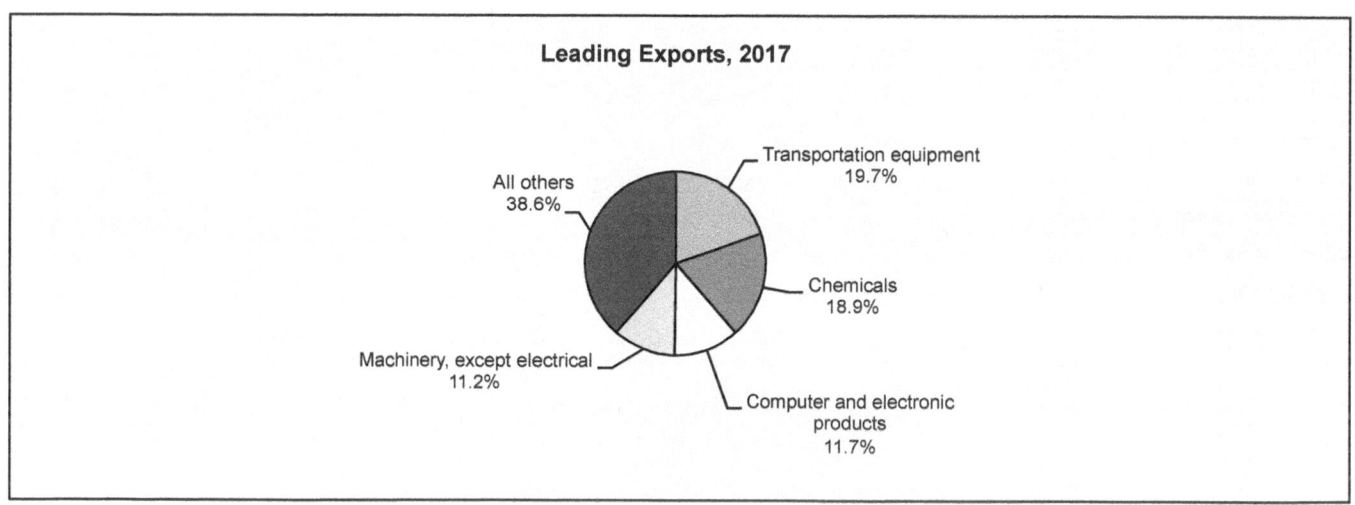

Leading Exports, 2017

Transportation equipment 19.7%
Chemicals 18.9%
Computer and electronic products 11.7%
Machinery, except electrical 11.2%
All others 38.6%

MASSACHUSETTS

Facts and Figures

Location: Northeastern United States; bordered on the N by Vermont and New Hampshire, on the E by the Atlantic Ocean, on the S by Connecticut and Rhode Island, and on the W by New York

Area: 10,555 sq. mi. (27,336 sq. km.); rank—44th

Population: 6,859,819 (2017 est.); rank—15th

Principal Cities: capital—Boston; largest—Boston

Statehood: February 6, 1788; 6th state

U.S. Congress: 2 senators, 9 representatives

State Motto: *Ense petit placidam sub libertate quietem* ("By the sword we seek peace, but peace only under liberty")

State Song: "All Hail to Massachusetts"

State Nickname: The Bay State

Abbreviations: MA; Mass.

State Symbols: flower—mayflower; tree—American elm; bird—chickadee

At a Glance

- With an increase in population of 4.5 percent, Massachusetts ranked 26th among the states in growth from 2010 to 2017.

- Massachusetts's median household income in 2016 was $75,297, the 5th highest in the country.

- Approximately 10.4 percent of Massachusetts' population lived below the poverty level in 2016, compared to 14.0 percent of the entire U.S. population.

- Massachusetts's violent crime rate in 2016 was 376.9 per 100,000 population, compared to 386.3 for the entire nation.

- Massachusetts's drug overdose death rate ranked 8th in the nation, with 33.0 deaths per 100,000 population.

Table MA-1. Population by Age, Sex, Race, and Hispanic Origin

(Number, percent, except where noted.)

Sex, age, race, and Hispanic origin	2000	2010	2017 [1]	Average annual percent change, 2010–2017
Total Population...	6,349,097	6,547,629	6,859,819	4.8
Percent of total U.S. population	2.3	2.1	2.1	X
Sex				
Male..	3,058,816	3,166,628	3,330,365	5.2
Female..	3,290,281	3,381,001	3,529,454	4.4
Age				
Under 5 years..	397,268	367,087	360,588	-1.8
5 to 19 years...	1,277,845	1,254,056	1,215,606	-3.1
20 to 64 years...	3,813,822	4,023,762	4,175,016	3.8
65 years and over..	860,162	902,724	1,108,609	22.8
Median age (years)..	36.5	39.1	39.5	1.0
Race and Hispanic Origin				
One race				
White..	5,367,286	5,524,937	5,576,725	0.9
Black..	343,454	504,365	603,433	19.6
American Indian and Alaska Native	15,015	29,944	33,341	11.3
Asian..	238,124	359,673	473,001	31.5
Native Hawaiian or Other Pacific Islander	2,489	5,971	7,065	18.3
Two or more races..	146,005	122,739	166,254	35.5
Hispanic (of any race)..	428,729	656,888	813,359	23.8

X = Not applicable.
[1] Population figures for 2017 are July 1 estimates. The 2010 estimates are taken from the 2010 Census.
- = Zero or rounds to zero.

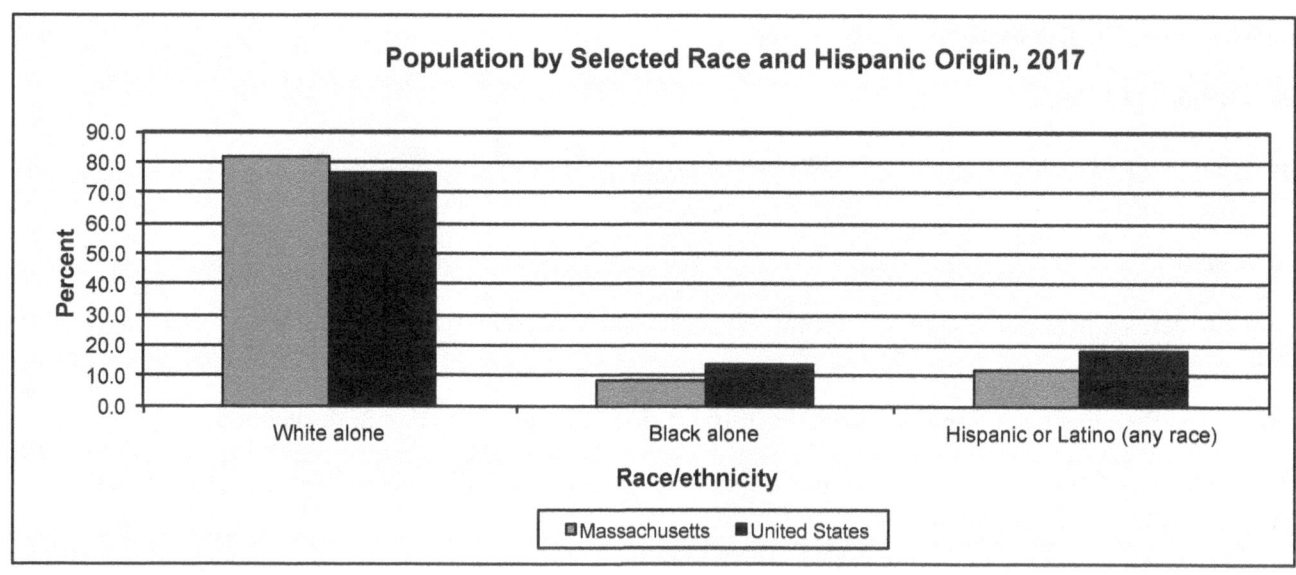

Population by Selected Race and Hispanic Origin, 2017

Legend: ▣ Massachusetts ■ United States

X-axis: White alone, Black alone, Hispanic or Latino (any race) — Race/ethnicity
Y-axis: Percent

Table MA-2. Marital Status

(Number, percent distribution.)

Sex, age, and marital status	2000	2010	2016
Males, 15 Years and Over	2,412,349	2,579,221	2,728,402
Never married	33.9	38.7	40.3
Now married, except separated.............................	54.7	49.1	47.8
Separated...	1.6	1.6	1.3
Widowed...	2.7	2.7	2.5
Divorced...	7.0	8.0	8.1
Females, 15 Years and Over	2,679,020	2,819,768	2,954,831
Never married	28.5	33.2	34.8
Now married, except separated.............................	48.9	44.1	44.0
Separated...	2.3	2.4	2.1
Widowed...	10.8	9.1	8.2
Divorced...	9.5	11.1	10.9

Table MA-3. Households and Housing Characteristics

(Number, percent, dollars.)

Item	2000	2010	2016	Average annual percent change, 2010–2016
Total Households..	2,443,580	2,520,419	2,579,398	0.4
Family households..	1,576,696	1,590,257	1,633,661	0.5
Married-couple family...	1,197,917	1,166,204	1,194,726	0.4
Other family..	378,779	424,053	438,935	0.6
Male householder, no wife present.....................	88,835	100,400	115,736	2.5
Female householder, no husband present............	289,944	323,653	323,199	-
Nonfamily households	866,884	930,162	945,737	0.3
Householder living alone.......................................	684,345	736,320	746,219	0.2
Householder not living alone.................................	182,539	193,842	199,518	0.5
Housing Characteristics				
Total housing units...	2,621,989	2,808,727	2,858,087	0.3
Occupied housing units...	2,443,580	2,520,419	2,579,398	0.4
Owner occupied...	1,508,052	1,568,382	1,598,930	0.3
Renter occupied...	935,528	952,037	980,468	0.5
Average household size..	2.51	2.51	2.54	0.2
Financial Characteristics				
Median gross rent of renter-occupied housing	684	1,009	1,179	2.8
Median monthly owner costs for housing units with a mortgage	1,353	2,036	2,069	0.3
Median value of owner-occupied housing units	185,700	334,100	366,900	1.6

- = Zero or rounds to zero.

Table MA-4. Migration, Origin, and Language

(Number, percent.)

Characteristic	State			U.S.		
	2015	2016	Percent change	2015	2016	Percent change
Residence 1 Year Ago						
Population 1 year and over	6,725,678	6,745,441	0.3	317,635,720	319,361,956	0.5
Same house..	87.6	87.0	X	85.3	85.4	X
Different house in the U.S.....................................	11.4	12.0	X	14.1	13.9	X
Same county	6.6	7.1	X	8.5	8.3	X
Different county	4.8	4.8	X	5.6	5.6	X
Same state	2.8	2.6	X	3.2	3.2	X
Different state	2.0	2.2	X	2.4	2.4	X
Abroad	1.0	1.1	X	0.7	0.7	X
Place of Birth						
Native born	5,698,469	5,687,897	-0.2	278,128,449	279,388,170	0.5
Male	48.6	48.6	X	49.3	49.3	X
Female	51.4	51.4	X	50.7	50.7	X
Foreign born	1,095,953	1,123,882	2.5	43,290,372	43,739,345	1.0
Male	48.2	47.9	X	48.6	48.5	X
Female	51.8	52.1	X	51.4	51.5	X
Foreign born; naturalized U.S. citizen...................	572,765	592,761	3.5	20,697,103	21,238,372	2.6
Male	46.2	45.4	X	45.9	45.9	X
Female	53.8	54.6	X	54.1	54.1	X
Foreign born; not a U.S. citizen............................	523,188	531,121	1.5	22,593,269	22,500,973	-0.4
Male	50.3	50.8	X	51.1	51.0	X
Female	49.7	49.2	X	48.9	49.0	X
Entered 2010 or later	19.7	23.9	X	15.6	18.6	X
Entered 2000 to 2009	28.2	26.1	X	27.9	26.7	X
Entered before 2000...	52.1	50.0	X	56.5	54.7	X
World Region of Birth, Foreign						
Foreign-born population, excluding population born at sea	1,095,953	1,123,882	2.5	43,289,646	43,738,901	1.0
Europe	21.2	20.5	X	11.1	10.9	X
Asia..	30.3	30.3	X	30.6	30.8	X
Africa	9.1	9.3	X	4.8	4.9	X
Oceania	0.3	0.4	X	0.6	0.6	X
Latin America..	35.8	37.0	X	51.1	51.0	X
North America..	3.2	2.5	X	1.9	1.8	X
Language Spoken at Home and Ability to Speak English						
Population 5 years and over....................................	6,429,039	6,452,005	0.4	301,625,014	303,328,961	0.6
English only	77.0	76.3	X	78.5	78.4	X
Language other than English..................................	23.0	23.7	X	21.5	21.6	X
Speaks English less than "very well"	9.0	9.2	X	8.6	8.6	X

NA = Not available.
X = Not applicable.
- = Zero or rounds to zero.

Table MA-5. Median Income and Poverty Status, 2016

(Number, percent, except as noted.)

Characteristic	State		U.S.	
	Number	Percent	Number	Percent
Median Income				
Households (dollars)	75,297	X	57,617	X
Families (dollars)	95,207	X	71,062	X
Below Poverty Level (All People)	686,597	10.4	44,268,996	14.0
Sex				
Male	296,508	9.3	19,760,056	12.8
Female	390,089	11.5	24,508,940	15.2
Age				
Under 18 years	184,743	13.6	14,115,713	19.5
Related children under 18 years	179,022	13.3	13,805,435	19.1
18 to 64 years	413,841	9.9	25,723,818	13.2
65 years and over	88,013	8.5	4,429,465	9.2

X = Not applicable.

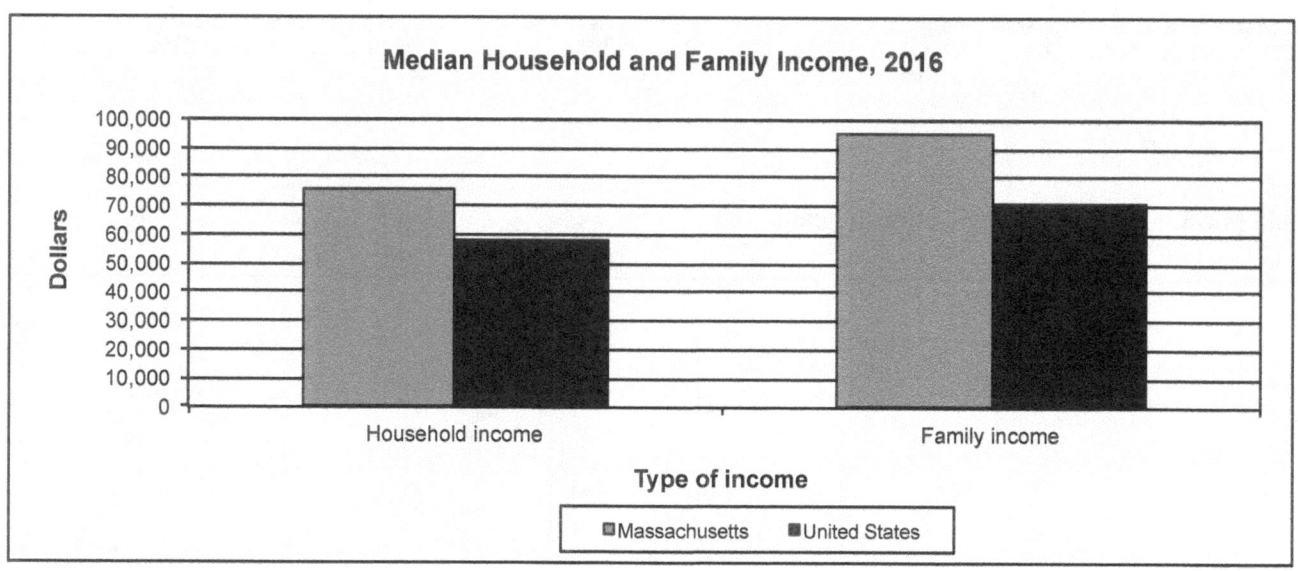

Table MA-6. Health Insurance Coverage Status for the Civilian Noninstitutionalized Population and Children Under 18 Years of Age

(Number, percent.)

Item	2008	2009	2010	2011	2012	2013	2014	2015	2016
Civilian Noninstitutionalized Population	6,398,787	6,495,905	6,478,067	6,507,596	6,566,851	6,613,654	6,668,348	6,718,090	6,736,017
Covered by Private or Public Insurance									
Number	6,135,273	6,224,815	6,192,350	6,230,656	6,312,556	6,366,988	6,449,626	6,528,817	6,564,958
Percent	95.9	95.8	95.6	95.7	96.1	96.3	96.7	97.2	97.5
Not Covered									
Number	263,514	271,090	285,717	276,940	254,295	246,666	218,722	189,273	171,059
Percent	4.1	4.2	4.4	4.3	3.9	3.7	3.3	2.8	2.5
Percent in the U.S. not covered	15.1	15.1	15.5	15.1	14.8	14.5	11.7	9.4	8.6
Children Under 18 Years of Age	1,426,668	1,430,695	1,414,746	1,401,873	1,397,972	1,389,165	1,387,398	1,383,924	1,375,244
Covered by Private or Public Insurance									
Number	1,396,888	1,410,879	1,393,064	1,377,774	1,377,766	1,368,086	1,366,087	1,368,039	1,362,535
Percent	97.9	98.6	98.5	98.3	98.6	98.5	98.5	98.9	99.1
Not Covered									
Number	29,780	19,816	21,682	24,099	20,206	21,079	21,311	15,885	12,709
Percent	2.1	1.4	1.5	1.7	1.4	1.5	1.5	1.1	0.9
Percent in the U.S. not covered	9.9	8.6	8.0	7.5	7.2	7.1	6.0	4.8	4.5

Table MA-7. Employment Status by Demographic Group, 2017

(Numbers in thousands, percent.)

Characteristic	Civilian noninstitutional population	Civilian labor force		Employed		Unemployed	
		Number	Percent of population	Number	Percent of population	Number	Percent of population
Total...	5,566	3,666	65.9	3,523	63.3	142	3.9
Sex							
Male..	2,666	1,890	70.9	1,811	67.9	79	4.2
Female.......................................	2,900	1,776	61.2	1,712	59.1	64	3.6
Race, Sex, and Hispanic Origin							
White..	4,574	3,010	65.8	2,904	63.5	107	3.5
Male......................................	2,193	1,555	70.9	1,495	68.2	60	3.8
Female....................................	2,381	1,456	61.1	1,409	59.2	47	3.2
Black or African American...........	451	312	69.1	288	63.7	24	7.8
Male......................................	212	151	70.9	138	64.7	13	8.6
Female....................................	239	161	67.6	150	62.9	11	7.0
Hispanic or Latino ethnicity[1].........	544	354	65.1	329	60.5	25	7.2
Male......................................	256	185	72.2	171	66.8	14	7.5
Female....................................	288	169	58.8	158	54.8	12	6.8
Age							
16 to 19 years............................	339	118	34.7	103	30.3	15	12.9
20 to 24 years............................	481	328	68.2	309	64.3	19	5.7
25 to 34 years............................	986	829	84.0	800	81.1	29	3.4
35 to 44 years............................	828	705	85.2	682	82.4	23	3.2
45 to 54 years............................	939	790	84.1	764	81.4	25	3.2
55 to 64 years............................	906	649	71.6	627	69.2	22	3.4
65 years and over	1,086	248	22.8	238	21.9	10	3.8

NOTE: Data in Table 7 are from the Current Population Survey (CPS) and do not match the estimates in Table 8. See notes and definitions for further information.
[1] May be of any race.

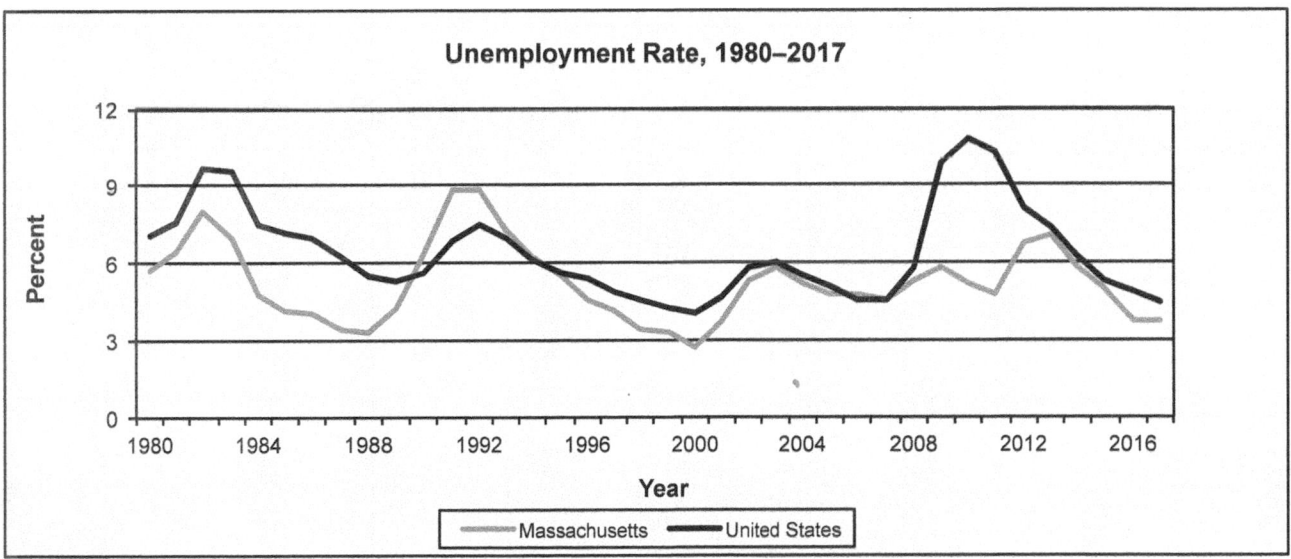

Table MA-8. Employment Status of the Civilian Noninstitutional Population Age 16 Years and Over

(Number, percent.)

Year	Civilian labor force	Civilian participation rate	Employed	Unemployed	Unemployment rate
2009..	3,470,382	66.3	3,189,010	281,372	8.1
2010..	3,480,083	66.3	3,190,818	289,265	8.3
2011..	3,469,308	65.5	3,217,754	251,554	7.3
2012..	3,485,161	65.2	3,252,531	232,630	6.7
2013..	3,512,827	65.0	3,276,792	236,035	6.7
2014..	3,566,237	65.3	3,361,811	204,426	5.7
2015..	3,588,241	65.2	3,415,874	172,367	4.8
2016..	3,611,418	65.2	3,471,112	140,306	3.9
2017..	3,657,173	65.5	3,521,482	135,691	3.7

Table MA-9. Employment and Average Wages by Industry

(Estimates through 2010 are based on the 2007 *North American Industry Classification System* [NAICS]. Estimates from 2011 onward are based on the 2012 NAICS.)

Industry	2010	2011	2012	2013	2014	2015	2016
	Number of jobs						
Wage and Salary Employment by Industry	3,304,140	3,343,033	3,423,005	3,476,147	3,543,338	3,608,821	3,674,116
Farm Wage and Salary Employment	3,676	4,019	4,433	5,071	5,085	5,067	4,729
Nonfarm Wage and Salary Employment	3,300,464	3,339,014	3,418,572	3,471,076	3,538,253	3,603,754	3,669,387
Private wage and salary employment	2,845,946	2,888,245	2,965,379	3,015,357	3,076,773	3,141,864	3,206,495
Forestry, fishing, and related activities	5,115	4,210	4,085	3,800	3,985	4,253	4,272
Mining	1,048	1,002	866	886	930	986	995
Utilities	10,429	10,451	10,267	10,056	10,683	10,438	10,749
Construction	110,854	114,269	119,023	126,048	132,444	142,190	150,256
Manufacturing	254,666	254,221	252,184	250,865	250,653	249,631	246,016
Durable goods manufacturing	166,126	167,191	165,409	163,547	162,433	161,273	158,764
Nondurable goods manufacturing	88,540	87,030	86,775	87,318	88,220	88,358	87,252
Wholesale trade	123,456	123,874	122,217	123,976	124,587	124,257	125,846
Retail trade	342,360	346,545	348,785	350,169	352,720	355,972	358,199
Transportation and warehousing	73,000	74,226	75,517	77,531	80,565	83,468	85,871
Information	85,234	84,621	87,110	86,170	86,253	88,237	89,363
Finance and insurance	172,816	173,349	171,567	170,718	171,548	173,303	176,074
Real estate and rental and leasing	40,898	41,297	42,070	43,062	44,033	44,887	46,307
Professional, scientific, and technical services	250,884	258,899	268,035	276,265	285,437	295,829	306,796
Management of companies and enterprises	57,464	58,632	63,352	64,315	63,563	65,227	65,604
Administrative and waste services	157,738	163,349	165,133	169,389	173,213	177,294	181,221
Educational services	182,605	186,522	189,831	193,479	195,388	199,113	201,623
Health care and social assistance	510,540	516,969	557,896	571,075	587,863	607,133	625,107
Arts, entertainment, and recreation	49,664	49,970	51,282	52,834	55,094	57,303	60,370
Accommodation and food services	260,069	267,253	276,731	284,008	289,926	295,025	304,203
Other services, except public administration	157,106	158,586	159,428	160,711	167,888	167,318	167,623
Government and government enterprises	454,518	450,769	453,193	455,719	461,480	461,890	462,892
	Dollars						
Average Wages and Salaries by Industry	56,761	58,578	59,533	60,405	62,646	65,196	68,546
Average Farm Wages and Salaries	26,132	20,922	31,008	27,949	29,503	27,183	32,107
Average Nonfarm Wages and Salaries	56,795	58,623	59,570	60,452	62,694	65,250	68,593
Average private wages and salaries	57,635	59,496	60,407	61,204	63,531	66,109	69,646
Forestry, fishing, and related activities	52,543	53,152	55,342	54,144	49,341	49,237	55,430
Mining	56,178	57,113	57,639	58,372	62,129	65,043	66,426
Utilities	104,090	109,951	107,859	107,738	110,024	111,819	130,710
Construction	62,129	63,257	65,175	66,430	68,662	71,160	76,377
Manufacturing	75,209	77,549	79,518	79,825	83,378	86,043	85,790
Durable goods manufacturing	83,890	86,718	89,043	88,688	91,996	92,864	95,356
Nondurable goods manufacturing	58,920	59,933	61,361	63,223	67,512	73,591	68,384
Wholesale trade	79,230	82,166	82,365	84,458	88,321	91,558	96,310
Retail trade	27,797	27,912	28,323	28,923	30,077	31,364	33,383
Transportation and warehousing	44,006	45,351	46,412	46,569	48,158	49,648	53,174
Information	92,042	95,864	97,039	97,452	103,372	108,059	112,451
Finance and insurance	114,551	119,326	124,434	126,301	136,232	144,150	150,787
Real estate and rental and leasing	60,242	63,222	66,495	69,829	72,789	73,189	78,058
Professional, scientific, and technical services	101,060	103,898	108,211	110,277	113,996	118,860	131,569
Management of companies and enterprises	104,229	123,029	115,667	118,769	126,628	140,175	132,447
Administrative and waste services	38,530	39,805	41,054	41,125	42,264	44,320	47,364
Educational services	44,367	45,576	46,344	47,144	48,485	49,388	51,726
Health care and social assistance	51,307	52,154	51,232	51,634	52,521	53,509	55,771
Arts, entertainment, and recreation	36,909	37,818	38,243	38,515	38,673	39,942	42,291
Accommodation and food services	21,248	21,807	22,441	23,115	23,969	25,348	27,733
Other services, except public administration	31,067	31,816	32,767	33,341	34,113	35,444	37,303
Government and government enterprises	51,533	53,029	54,095	55,479	57,111	59,404	61,297

Table MA-10. Employment Characteristics by Family Type

(Number, percent.)

Family type and labor force status	2014		2015		2016	
	Total	Families with own children under 18 years	Total	Families with own children under 18 years	Total	Families with own children under 18 years
All Families..	1,596,764	693,261	1,613,404	684,676	1,633,661	683,699
FAMILY TYPE AND LABOR FORCE STATUS						
Married-Couple Families.................................	1,169,707	475,565	1,188,714	474,202	1,194,726	471,078
Both husband and wife in labor force..................	59.2	73.1	57.7	72.5	58.6	74.9
Husband in labor force, wife not in labor force.........	18.4	22.5	18.1	22.0	17.3	20.1
Wife in labor force, husband not in labor force.........	7.5	3.3	7.7	3.4	7.7	3.3
Both husband and wife not in labor force..............	15.0	1.1	15.1	1.2	14.9	1.0
Other Families	427,057	217,696	424,690	210,474	438,935	212,621
Female householder, no husband present...............	74.8	80.3	75.2	80.4	73.6	76.5
In labor force..	54.1	66.5	53.7	66.2	52.1	62.2
Not in labor force	20.7	13.8	21.5	14.3	21.6	14.3
Male householder, no wife present......................	25.2	19.7	24.8	19.6	26.4	23.5
In labor force..	20.3	18.0	19.3	18.0	21.0	21.9
Not in labor force	4.9	1.7	5.5	1.6	5.3	1.6

Table MA-11. School Enrollment and Educational Attainment, 2016

(Number, percent.)

Item	State	U.S.
Enrollment		
Total population 3 years and over, enrolled in school	1,737,713	81,572,277
Enrolled in nursery school or preschool (percent)................................	6.3	6.0
Enrolled in kindergarten (percent)................................	4.5	5.0
Enrolled in elementary school, grades 1-8 (percent)................................	35.4	40.3
Enrolled in high school, grades 9-12 (percent)................................	20.1	21.0
Enrolled in college or graduate school (percent)................................	33.7	27.7
Attainment		
Total population 25 years and over	4,727,515	218,475,480
Less than ninth grade (percent)................................	4.5	5.4
9th to 12th grade, no diploma (percent)................................	5.1	7.2
High school graduate, including equivalency (percent)................................	24.5	27.2
Some college, no degree (percent)................................	15.5	20.6
Associate's degree (percent)................................	7.7	8.4
Bachelor's degree (percent)................................	23.8	19.3
Graduate or professional degree (percent)................................	19.0	11.9
High school graduate or higher (percent)................................	90.4	87.5
Bachelor's degree or higher (percent)................................	42.7	31.3

Table MA-12. Public School Characteristics and Educational Indicators

(Number, percent; data derived from National Center of Education Statistics.)

Item	State	U.S.
Public Schools, 2015–2016 (except where noted)		
Number of school districts................................	408	18,328
Number of schools................................	1,862	98,456
Number of students................................	964,026	50,327,015
Number of teachers................................	71,969	3,151,497
Student-teacher ratio	13.4	16.0
Expenditures per student (dollars), 2014-2015................................	16,450	11,445
Four-year adjusted cohort graduation rate (ACGR)[1,2]	87.5	84.1
Students eligible for free or reduced-price lunch (percent), 2014-2015................................	39.9	51.8
English language learners (percent), Fall 2015................................	8.6	9.5
Students age 3 to 21 served under IDEA, part B (percent)................................	17.4	13.2

Public Schools by Type	Number	Percent of state public schools
Total number of schools................................	1,862	100.0
Regular	1,796	96.5
Special education	7	0.4
Vocational education................................	38	2.0
Alternative education................................	21	1.1

NOTE: Every school is assigned only one school type based on its instructional emphasis.
[1] ACGR data represents a new method of calculating high-school completion rates and may not be comparable to previous years' data for Averaged Freshmen Graduation Rates (AFGR).
[2] The United States 4-year ACGRs were estimated using both the reported 4-year ACGR data from 49 states and the District of Columbia and using imputed data for Idaho. The estimate for American Indian/Alaska Native students also includes imputed data for Virginia.

Table MA-13. Reported Voting and Registration of the Voting-Age Population, November 2016

(Numbers in thousands, percent.)

Item	Total population	Total citizen population	Registered			Voted		
			Total registered	Percent registered (total population)	Percent registered (total citizen population)	Total voted	Percent voted (total population)	Percent voted (total citizen population)
U.S. Total	245,502	224,059	157,596	64.2	70.3	137,537	56.0	61.4
State Total................................	5,374	4,967	3,660	68.1	73.7	3,315	61.7	66.7
Sex								
Male	2,585	2,382	1,767	68.3	74.2	1,599	61.9	67.1
Female	2,788	2,585	1,893	67.9	73.2	1,715	61.5	66.4
Race								
White alone................................	4,464	4,260	3,229	72.3	75.8	2,919	65.4	68.5
White, non-Hispanic alone	4,083	3,969	3,078	75.4	77.5	2,789	68.3	70.3
Black alone	438	368	266	60.8	72.4	242	55.3	65.8
Asian alone	353	238	128	36.3	53.8	121	34.2	50.8
Hispanic (of any race)......................	500	397	199	39.8	50.1	177	35.4	44.6
White alone or in combination	4,573	4,357	3,263	71.4	74.9	2,950	64.5	67.7
Black alone or in combination............	513	431	284	55.4	65.9	260	50.7	60.3
Asian alone or in combination............	369	254	133	36.0	52.4	126	34.1	49.5
Age								
18 to 24 years................................	596	555	298	50.0	53.6	238	39.9	42.8
25 to 34 years................................	1,035	919	615	59.5	67.0	555	53.6	60.4
35 to 44 years................................	811	696	506	62.4	72.6	475	58.6	68.3
45 to 64 years................................	1,850	1,743	1,383	74.8	79.3	1,263	68.3	72.5
65 years and over	1,082	1,054	858	79.3	81.4	784	72.4	74.3

Table MA-14. Crime

(Number, rate per 100,000. Data are derived from the FBI Uniform Crime Reports.)

Item	State			U.S. [1,2,3,4]		
	2015	2016	Percent change	2015	2016	Percent change
TOTAL POPULATION [5]	6,794,422	6,811,779	0.3	321,418,820	323,127,513	0.5
VIOLENT CRIME						
Number..	26,562	25,677	-3.3	1,231,566	1,248,185	1.3
Rate..	390.9	376.9	-3.6	383.2	386.3	0.8
Murder and Nonnegligent Manslaughter						
Number..	128	134	4.7	15,696	17,250	9.9
Rate	1.9	2.0	5.3	4.9	5.3	8.2
Rape [6]						
Number..	2,075	2,128	2.6	124,047	130,603	5.3
Rate	30.5	31.2	2.3	38.6	40.4	4.7
Robbery						
Number..	5,288	5,365	1.5	327,374	332,198	1.5
Rate	77.8	78.8	1.3	101.9	102.8	0.9
Aggravated Assault						
Number..	19,071	18,050	-5.4	764,449	803,007	5.0
Rate	280.7	265.0	-5.6	237.8	248.5	4.5
PROPERTY CRIME						
Number..	114,871	106,339	-7.4	7,993,631	7,919,035	-0.9
Rate	1,690.7	1,561.1	-7.7	2,487.0	2,450.7	-1.5
Burglary						
Number..	21,890	19,193	-12.3	1,579,527	1,515,096	-4.1
Rate	322.2	281.8	-12.5	491.4	468.9	-4.6
Larceny-Theft						
Number..	84,912	79,088	-6.9	5,706,346	5,638,455	-1.2
Rate	1,249.7	1,161.0	-7.1	1,775.4	1,745.0	-1.7
Motor Vehicle Theft						
Number..	8,069	8,058	-0.1	707,758	765,484	8.2
Rate	118.8	118.3	-0.4	220.2	236.9	7.6

NOTE: Although arson data are included in the trend and clearance tables, sufficient data are not available to estimate totals for this offense. Therefore, no arson data are published in this table.
X = Not applicable.
- = Zero or rounds to zero.
[1] The crime figures have been adjusted.
[2] The data collection methodology for the offense of forcible rape used by the Minnesota state Uniform Crime Reporting (UCR) Program (with the exception of Minneapolis and St. Paul, Minnesota) does not comply with national UCR Program guidelines. Consequently, its figures for forcible rape and violent crime (of which forcible rape is a part) are not published in this table.
[3] Includes offenses reported by the Zoological Police and the Metro Transit Police.
[4] Because of changes in the state's reporting practices, figures are not comparable to previous years' data.
[5] Populations are U.S. Census Bureau provisional estimates as of July 1 of each year.
[6] The figures shown for the offense of rape were estimated using the revised Uniform Crime Reporting (UCR) definition of rape.

Table MA-15. State Government Finances, 2016

(Dollar amounts in thousands, percent distribution.)

Item	Dollars	Percent distribution
Total Revenue	60,312,959	100.0
General revenue	54,702,779	90.7
Intergovernmental revenue	16,401,221	27.2
Taxes	27,277,284	45.2
General sales	6,089,860	10.1
Selective sales	2,594,006	4.3
License taxes	1,122,219	1.9
Individual income tax	14,430,331	23.9
Corporate income tax	2,333,892	3.9
Other taxes	706,976	1.2
Current charges	5,338,364	8.9
Miscellaneous general revenue	5,685,910	9.4
Utility revenue	878,435	1.5
Liquor stores revenue	0	-
Insurance trust revenue [1]	4,731,745	7.8
Total Expenditure	63,562,063	100.0
Intergovernmental expenditure	9,080,507	14.3
Direct expenditure	54,481,556	85.7
Current operation	38,749,533	61.0
Capital outlay	4,562,236	7.2
Insurance benefits and repayments	6,665,039	10.5
Assistance and subsidies	1,278,165	2.0
Interest on debt	3,226,583	5.1
Exhibit: Salaries and wages	6,890,768	10.8
Total Expenditure	63,562,063	100.0
General expenditure	53,641,097	84.4
Intergovernmental expenditure	9,080,507	14.3
Direct expenditure	44,560,590	70.1
General expenditure, by function:		
Education	13,604,676	21.4
Public welfare	20,186,031	31.8
Hospitals	550,799	0.9
Health	1,881,864	3.0
Highways	3,005,878	4.7
Police protection	905,695	1.4
Correction	1,121,625	1.8
Natural resources	386,644	0.6
Parks and recreation	263,787	0.4
Governmental administration	1,877,709	3.0
Interest on general debt	2,885,213	4.5
Other and unallocable	6,971,176	11.0
Utility expenditure	3,255,927	5.4
Liquor stores expenditure	0	-
Insurance trust expenditure	6,665,039	10.5
Debt at End of Fiscal Year	76,861,071	X
Cash and Security Holdings	84,501,273	X

X = Not applicable.
- = Zero or rounds to zero.
[1] Within insurance trust revenue, net earnings of state retirement systems is a calculated statistic (the item code in the data file is X08), and thus can be positive or negative. Net earnings is the sum of earnings on investments plus gains on investments minus losses on investments. The change made in 2002 for asset valuation from book to market value in accordance with Statement 34 of the Governmental Accounting Standards Board is reflected in the calculated statistics.

Table MA-16. State Government Tax Collections, 2017

(Dollars in thousands, percent.)

Item	Dollars	Percent distribution
Total Taxes	27,518,360	100.0
Property taxes	6,598	-
Sales and gross receipts	8,818,347	32.0
General sales and gross receipts	6,240,822	22.7
Selective sales and gross receipts	2,577,525	9.4
Alcoholic beverages	85,397	0.3
Amusements	65,744	0.2
Insurance premiums	397,519	1.4
Motor fuels	769,442	2.8
Pari-mutuels	902	-
Public utilities	26,727	0.1
Tobacco products	619,437	2.3
Other selective sales	612,357	2.2
Licenses	1,112,162	4.0
Alcoholic beverages	3,634	-
Amusements	14,825	0.1
Corporations in general	26,645	0.1
Hunting and fishing	5,482	-
Motor vehicle	438,855	1.6
Motor vehicle operators	96,905	0.4
Public utilities	X	-
Occupation and business, NEC	290,524	1.1
Other licenses	235,292	0.9
Income taxes	16,920,751	61.5
Individual income	14,724,277	53.5
Corporation net income	2,196,474	8.0
Other taxes	660,502	2.4
Death and gift	336,633	1.2
Documentary and stock transfer	323,869	1.2
Severance	X	-
Taxes, NEC	0	-

X = Not applicable.
- = Zero or rounds to zero.

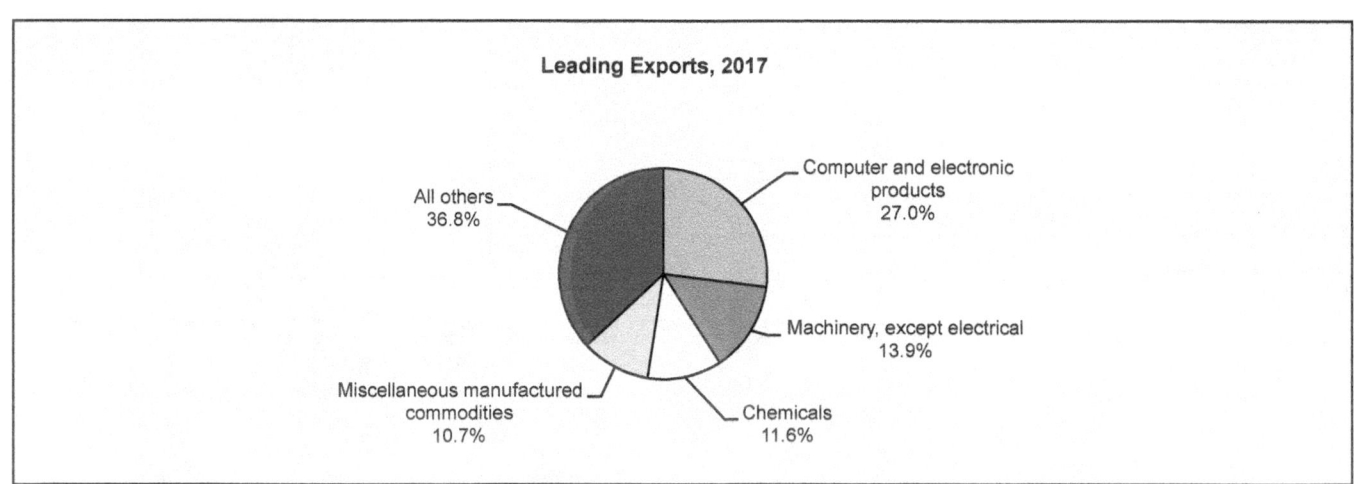

Leading Exports, 2017

All others 36.8%

Computer and electronic products 27.0%

Machinery, except electrical 13.9%

Chemicals 11.6%

Miscellaneous manufactured commodities 10.7%

MICHIGAN

Facts and Figures

Location: East north central United States; bordered on the N by Lake Superior, on the E by Ontario, Canada, and Lakes Huron and Erie, on the S by Indiana and Ohio, and on the W by Wisconsin and Lake Michigan

Area: 96,716 sq. mi. (250,494 sq. km.); rank—11th

Population: 9,962,311 (2017 est.); rank—10th

Principal Cities: capital—Lansing; largest—Detroit

Statehood: January 26, 1837; 26th state

U.S. Congress: 2 senators, 14 representatives

State Motto: *Si quaeris peninsulam amoenam, circumspice* ("If you seek a pleasant peninsula, look about you")

State Song: "Michigan, My Michigan"

State Nicknames: The Wolverine State; The Great Lakes State

Abbreviations: MI; Mich.

State Symbols: flower—apple blossom; tree—Eastern white pine; bird—robin

At a Glance

- With an increase in population of 0.9 percent, Michigan ranked 43rd among the states in growth from 2010 to 2017.

- In 2016, 5.4 percent of Michiganders did not have health insurance, compared to 8.6 percent of the total U.S. population.

- Michigan's violent crime rate in 2016 was 459.0 per 100,000 population, compared to the U.S. rate of 386.3 per 100,000 population.

- Approximately 15.0 percent of Michigan residents lived below the poverty level in 2016, compared to the national poverty rate of 14.0 percent.

- Michigan's unemployment rate of 4.6 percent ranked 18th in the nation in 2016.

Table MI-1. Population by Age, Sex, Race, and Hispanic Origin

(Number, percent, except where noted.)

Sex, age, race, and Hispanic origin	2000	2010	2017 [1]	Average annual percent change, 2010–2017
Total Population..	9,938,444	9,883,640	9,962,311	0.8
Percent of total U.S. population	3.5	3.2	3.1	X
Sex				
Male...	4,873,095	4,848,114	4,903,752	1.1
Female	5,065,349	5,035,526	5,058,559	0.5
Age				
Under 5 years..	672,005	596,286	573,282	-3.9
5 to 19 years..	2,212,060	2,052,599	1,871,502	-8.8
20 to 64 years...	5,835,361	5,873,225	5,850,331	-0.4
65 years and over	1,219,018	1,361,530	1,667,196	22.5
Median age (years)	35.5	38.9	39.8	2.3
Race and Hispanic Origin				
One race				
White..	7,966,053	7,949,497	7,914,418	-0.4
Black..	1,412,742	1,416,067	1,408,605	-0.5
American Indian and Alaska Native	58,479	68,396	73,124	6.9
Asian..	176,510	243,062	319,772	31.6
Native Hawaiian or Other Pacific Islander	2,692	3,442	4,087	18.7
Two or more races	192,416	203,176	242,305	19.3
Hispanic (of any race)...	323,877	459,751	504,857	9.8

X = Not applicable.
- = Zero or rounds to zero.
[1] Population figures for 2017 are July 1 estimates. The 2010 estimates are taken from the 2010 Census.

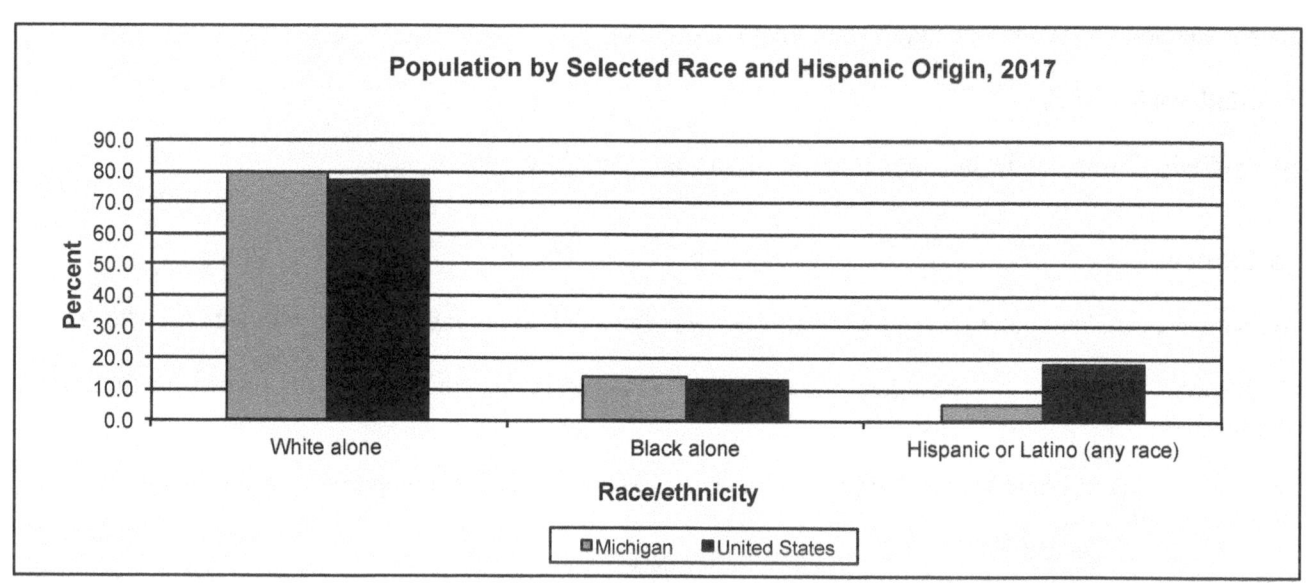

Population by Selected Race and Hispanic Origin, 2017

Table MI-2. Marital Status

(Number, percent distribution.)

Sex, age, and marital status	2000	2010	2016
Males, 15 Years and Over	3,761,881	3,875,107	3,967,891
Never married	30.8	34.9	36.5
Now married, except separated..	56.1	50.5	48.6
Separated...	1.3	1.3	1.2
Widowed...	2.5	2.7	2.9
Divorced..	9.3	10.6	10.8
Females, 15 Years and Over	4,013,722	4,099,384	4,170,573
Never married	25.0	29.0	30.4
Now married, except separated..	51.8	47.2	46.4
Separated...	1.6	1.6	1.3
Widowed...	10.4	9.7	9.0
Divorced..	11.2	12.5	12.8

Table MI-3. Households and Housing Characteristics

(Number, percent, dollars.)

Item	2000	2010	2016	Average annual percent change, 2010–2016
Total Households..	3,785,661	3,806,621	3,884,153	0.3
Family households	2,575,699	2,508,780	2,476,595	-0.2
Married-couple family	1,947,610	1,845,094	1,819,434	-0.2
Other family	627,989	663,686	657,161	-0.2
Male householder, no wife present.................	154,187	168,337	179,962	1.2
Female householder, no husband present............	473,802	495,349	477,199	-0.6
Nonfamily households	1,209,962	1,297,841	1,407,558	1.4
Householder living alone.............................	993,607	1,090,126	1,155,068	1.0
Householder not living alone........................	216,335	207,715	252,490	3.6
Housing Characteristics				
Total housing units.......................................	4,234,279	4,531,231	4,560,164	0.1
Occupied housing units	3,785,661	3,806,621	3,884,153	0.3
Owner occupied	2,793,124	2,769,474	2,731,283	-0.2
Renter occupied	992,537	1,037,147	1,152,870	1.9
Average household size................................	2.56	2.53	2.5	-0.2
Financial Characteristics				
Median gross rent of renter-occupied housing	546	730	818	2.0
Median monthly owner costs for housing units with a mortgage	972	1,288	1,215	-0.9
Median value of owner-occupied housing units..............	115,600	123,300	147,100	3.2

Table MI-4. Migration, Origin, and Language

(Number, percent.)

Characteristic	State			U.S.		
	2015	2016	Percent change	2015	2016	Percent change
Residence 1 Year Ago						
Population 1 year and over	9,811,416	9,813,772	-	317,635,720	319,361,956	0.5
Same house	85.6	85.2	X	85.3	85.4	X
Different house in the U.S.................................	14.0	14.2	X	14.1	13.9	X
Same county	9.0	8.8	X	8.5	8.3	X
Different county	5.0	5.4	X	5.6	5.6	X
Same state	3.6	3.8	X	3.2	3.2	X
Different state	1.5	1.6	X	2.4	2.4	X
Abroad	0.5	0.6	X	0.7	0.7	X
Place of Birth						
Native born	9,270,486	9,266,021	-	278,128,449	279,388,170	0.5
Male	49.2	49.1	X	49.3	49.3	X
Female	50.8	50.9	X	50.7	50.7	X
Foreign born	652,090	662,279	1.6	43,290,372	43,739,345	1.0
Male	49.1	50.1	X	48.6	48.5	X
Female	50.9	49.9	X	51.4	51.5	X
Foreign born; naturalized U.S. citizen...................	342,465	342,999	0.2	20,697,103	21,238,372	2.6
Male	47.2	48.5	X	45.9	45.9	X
Female	52.8	51.5	X	54.1	54.1	X
Foreign born; not a U.S. citizen........................	309,625	319,280	3.1	22,593,269	22,500,973	-0.4
Male	51.1	51.8	X	51.1	51.0	X
Female	48.9	48.2	X	48.9	49.0	X
Entered 2010 or later	20.8	26.0	X	15.6	18.6	X
Entered 2000 to 2009	26.4	25.0	X	27.9	26.7	X
Entered before 2000......................................	52.8	49.0	X	56.5	54.7	X
World Region of Birth, Foreign						
Foreign-born population, excluding population born at sea	652,090	662,202	1.6	43,289,646	43,738,901	1.0
Europe	20.6	20.2	X	11.1	10.9	X
Asia..	50.7	51.0	X	30.6	30.8	X
Africa	4.3	4.1	X	4.8	4.9	X
Oceania	0.5	0.3	X	0.6	0.6	X
Latin America	18.6	19.1	X	51.1	51.0	X
North America	5.3	5.3	X	1.9	1.8	X
Language Spoken at Home and Ability to Speak English						
Population 5 years and over...............................	9,351,921	9,356,637	0.1	301,625,014	303,328,961	0.6
English only	90.5	90.5	X	78.5	78.4	X
Language other than English.............................	9.5	9.5	X	21.5	21.6	X
Speaks English less than "very well"...................	3.4	3.5	X	8.6	8.6	X

NA = Not available.
X = Not applicable.
- = Zero or rounds to zero.

Table MI-5. Median Income and Poverty Status, 2016

(Number, percent, except as noted.)

Characteristic	State		U.S.	
	Number	Percent	Number	Percent
Median Income				
Households (dollars)..	52,492	X	57,617	X
Families (dollars)	67,330	X	71,062	X
Below Poverty Level (All People)	1,451,936	15.0	44,268,996	14.0
Sex				
Male	661,185	13.9	19,760,056	12.8
Female	790,751	16.0	24,508,940	15.2
Age				
Under 18 years...	445,803	20.7	14,115,713	19.5
Related children under 18 years	432,405	20.2	13,805,435	19.1
18 to 64 years..	878,685	14.7	25,723,818	13.2
65 years and over	127,448	8.1	4,429,465	9.2

X = Not applicable.

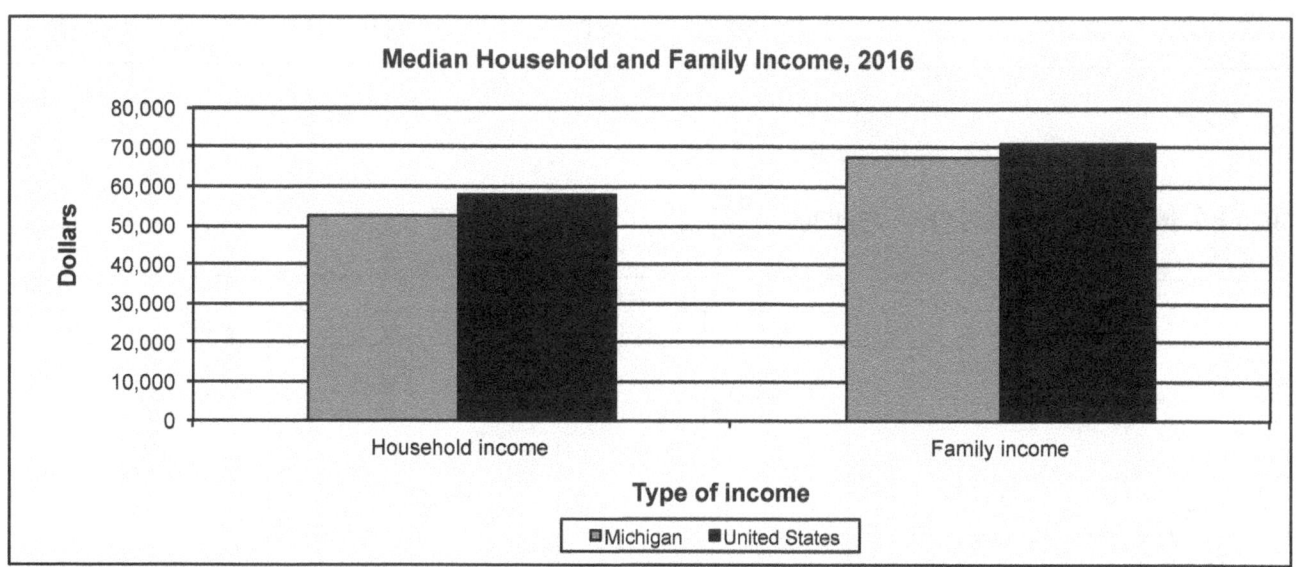

Median Household and Family Income, 2016

Table MI-6. Health Insurance Coverage Status for the Civilian Noninstitutionalized Population and Children Under 18 Years of Age

(Number, percent.)

Item	2008	2009	2010	2011	2012	2013	2014	2015	2016
Civilian Noninstitutionalized Population	9,866,139	9,834,865	9,763,683	9,762,306	9,772,550	9,784,451	9,798,621	9,810,800	9,818,099
Covered by Private or Public Insurance									
Number...	8,734,157	8,632,028	8,556,299	8,612,395	8,658,229	8,712,930	8,961,893	9,214,158	9,291,109
Percent..	88.5	87.8	87.6	88.2	88.6	89.0	91.5	93.9	94.6
Not Covered									
Number...	1,131,982	1,202,837	1,207,384	1,149,911	1,114,321	1,071,521	836,728	596,642	526,990
Percent..	11.5	12.2	12.4	11.8	11.4	11.0	8.5	6.1	5.4
Percent in the U.S. not covered..............................	15.1	15.1	15.5	15.1	14.8	14.5	11.7	9.4	8.6
Children Under 18 Years of Age	2,388,510	2,342,793	2,331,475	2,289,531	2,263,671	2,240,003	2,219,940	2,204,443	2,187,554
Covered by Private or Public Insurance									
Number...	2,264,404	2,235,984	2,236,372	2,195,721	2,173,626	2,150,062	2,136,686	2,136,367	2,124,318
Percent..	94.8	95.4	95.9	95.9	96.0	96.0	96.2	96.9	97.1
Not Covered									
Number...	124,106	106,809	95,103	93,810	90,045	89,941	83,254	68,076	63,236
Percent..	5.2	4.6	4.1	4.1	4.0	4.0	3.8	3.1	2.9
Percent in the U.S. not covered..............................	9.9	8.6	8.0	7.5	7.2	7.1	6.0	4.8	4.5

Table MI-7. Employment Status by Demographic Group, 2017

(Numbers in thousands, percent.)

Characteristic	Civilian noninstitutional population	Civilian labor force		Employed		Unemployed	
		Number	Percent of population	Number	Percent of population	Number	Percent of population
Total..	7,927	4,868	61.4	4,641	58.5	227	4.7
Sex							
Male	3,842	2,595	67.5	2,479	64.5	116	4.5
Female	4,084	2,273	55.7	2,162	52.9	112	4.9
Race, Sex, and Hispanic Origin							
White	6,492	4,017	61.9	3,858	59.4	159	4.0
Male...	3,176	2,164	68.1	2,080	65.5	84	3.9
Female	3,316	1,853	55.9	1,778	53.6	75	4.1
Black or African American..............	1,057	596	56.3	539	51.0	57	9.5
Male...	477	285	59.8	259	54.3	26	9.1
Female	580	311	53.5	280	48.2	31	9.9
Hispanic or Latino ethnicity[1]	338	223	65.8	208	61.3	15	6.8
Male...	191	144	75.5	135	70.8	9	6.2
Female	NA	NA	NA	NA	NA	NA	NA
Age							
16 to 19 years..............................	494	203	41.0	175	35.4	28	13.7
20 to 24 years..............................	626	480	76.6	434	69.3	46	9.6
25 to 34 years..............................	1,324	1,093	82.6	1,044	78.8	49	4.5
35 to 44 years..............................	1,156	929	80.4	897	77.5	33	3.5
45 to 54 years..............................	1,363	1,078	79.1	1,040	76.3	38	3.5
55 to 64 years..............................	1,353	824	60.9	800	59.2	23	2.8
65 years and over	1,611	261	16.2	251	15.6	10	3.9

NOTE: Data in Table 7 are from the Current Population Survey (CPS) and do not match the estimates in Table 8. See notes and definitions for further information.
[1] May be of any race.

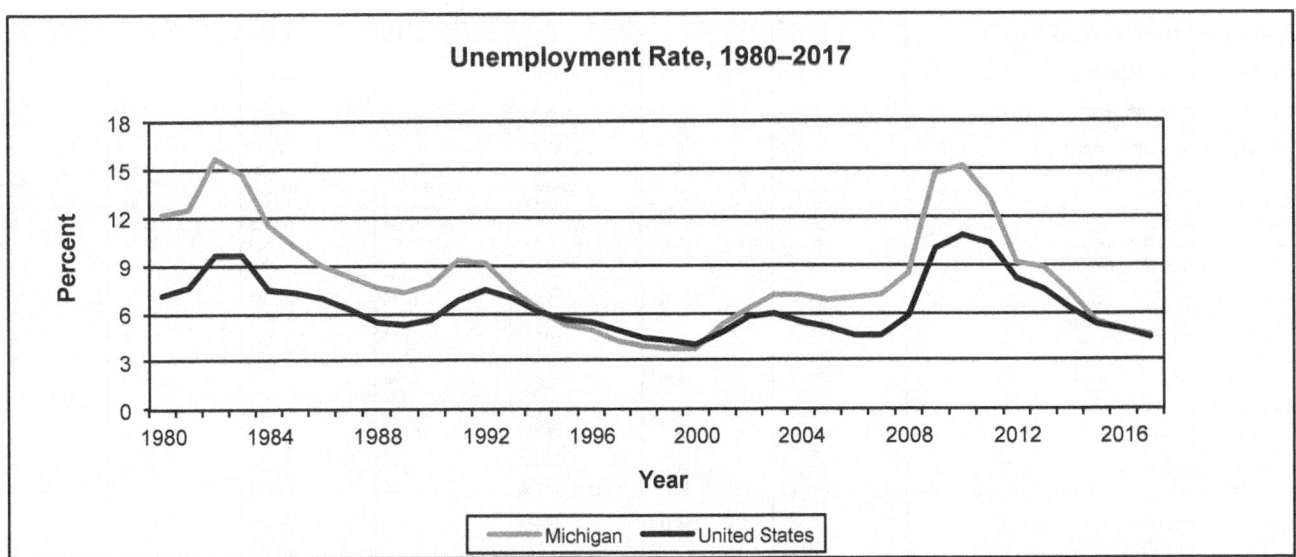

Table MI-8. Employment Status of the Civilian Noninstitutional Population Age 16 Years and Over

(Number, percent.)

Year	Civilian labor force	Civilian participation rate	Employed	Unemployed	Unemployment rate
2009..	4,903,544	63.1	4,233,803	669,741	13.7
2010..	4,798,954	62.0	4,194,041	604,913	12.6
2011..	4,685,164	60.5	4,198,349	486,815	10.4
2012..	4,672,695	60.0	4,246,658	426,037	9.1
2013..	4,723,945	60.4	4,308,030	415,915	8.8
2014..	4,753,626	60.6	4,409,394	344,232	7.2
2015..	4,751,234	60.4	4,493,447	257,787	5.4
2016..	4,840,281	61.2	4,599,266	241,015	5.0
2017..	4,883,815	61.5	4,657,272	226,543	4.6

Table MI-9. Employment and Average Wages by Industry

(Estimates through 2010 are based on the 2007 *North American Industry Classification System* [NAICS]. Estimates from 2011 onward are based on the 2012 NAICS.)

Industry	2010	2011	2012	2013	2014	2015	2016
	Number of jobs						
Wage and Salary Employment by Industry	3,940,724	4,031,623	4,104,082	4,181,596	4,257,161	4,329,598	4,407,823
Farm Wage and Salary Employment	16,371	23,531	20,286	21,935	22,981	25,200	23,887
Nonfarm Wage and Salary Employment	3,924,353	4,008,092	4,083,796	4,159,661	4,234,180	4,304,398	4,383,936
Private wage and salary employment	3,272,883	3,376,805	3,464,062	3,548,796	3,627,974	3,700,242	3,774,020
Forestry, fishing, and related activities	7,481	7,618	7,898	8,045	8,875	8,661	8,835
Mining	5,612	5,913	6,302	6,484	6,643	6,005	5,446
Utilities	19,474	19,333	19,213	19,365	19,771	19,895	20,090
Construction	124,543	128,953	132,074	137,367	145,615	151,862	159,397
Manufacturing	479,048	513,120	538,454	547,834	569,120	587,498	601,840
Durable goods manufacturing	353,580	382,995	406,032	412,375	429,747	444,462	453,352
Nondurable goods manufacturing	125,468	130,125	132,422	135,459	139,373	143,036	148,488
Wholesale trade	150,997	155,751	159,920	164,529	168,419	170,466	172,763
Retail trade	449,725	452,316	453,205	458,709	464,369	470,398	476,164
Transportation and warehousing	94,170	99,776	103,280	106,776	111,769	116,906	119,510
Information	57,190	55,954	56,177	57,915	60,543	59,312	59,727
Finance and insurance	136,741	139,290	143,765	147,373	148,061	149,698	154,023
Real estate and rental and leasing	50,395	51,548	49,278	50,668	51,816	52,295	53,700
Professional, scientific, and technical services	224,981	237,367	249,951	270,882	278,962	289,641	298,386
Management of companies and enterprises	48,151	50,856	52,135	54,692	55,232	56,437	58,832
Administrative and waste services	246,018	270,075	280,453	289,151	290,633	294,086	292,682
Educational services	76,014	76,787	76,794	78,788	79,985	81,195	79,136
Health care and social assistance	540,677	546,514	557,232	562,136	565,135	575,905	589,999
Arts, entertainment, and recreation	51,945	48,367	47,539	48,681	49,679	50,921	52,731
Accommodation and food services	326,207	332,798	343,848	352,007	359,088	365,385	375,417
Other services, except public administration	183,514	184,469	186,544	187,394	194,259	193,676	195,342
Government and government enterprises	651,470	631,287	619,734	610,865	606,206	604,156	609,916
	Dollars						
Average Wages and Salaries by Industry	43,857	45,179	46,222	46,643	47,997	49,590	52,029
Average Farm Wages and Salaries	27,814	24,677	36,899	31,996	35,884	36,622	42,354
Average Nonfarm Wages and Salaries	43,923	45,299	46,268	46,720	48,063	49,666	52,082
Average private wages and salaries	43,551	45,207	46,201	46,685	48,093	49,809	52,353
Forestry, fishing, and related activities	24,720	25,082	25,834	27,185	27,651	29,620	34,887
Mining	73,773	74,828	73,509	73,413	77,204	75,759	73,804
Utilities	93,779	98,214	102,212	104,109	109,032	112,232	112,682
Construction	50,539	52,002	53,193	53,624	55,592	57,323	63,215
Manufacturing	59,733	62,190	62,793	62,524	63,563	65,081	66,865
Durable goods manufacturing	62,237	65,296	65,336	64,900	65,884	67,415	69,176
Nondurable goods manufacturing	52,677	53,049	54,995	55,291	56,405	57,827	59,807
Wholesale trade	64,302	66,990	67,788	67,338	69,912	71,170	74,041
Retail trade	25,629	26,030	26,398	26,510	27,356	28,492	29,959
Transportation and warehousing	47,438	48,943	50,327	50,611	52,080	53,132	57,352
Information	58,572	62,024	62,081	64,334	65,488	67,984	65,339
Finance and insurance	62,045	63,941	66,378	68,195	70,849	74,008	78,684
Real estate and rental and leasing	34,134	36,010	37,631	38,254	39,684	42,283	46,307
Professional, scientific, and technical services	70,759	73,177	74,389	75,939	77,812	80,486	84,922
Management of companies and enterprises	103,207	113,271	116,160	110,684	119,925	122,505	137,746
Administrative and waste services	30,854	30,999	31,734	31,715	32,444	33,936	35,229
Educational services	28,493	28,356	29,869	29,911	30,783	31,092	32,420
Health care and social assistance	43,317	44,410	44,944	45,522	46,432	48,135	49,683
Arts, entertainment, and recreation	30,502	30,263	31,950	32,597	33,120	33,898	37,098
Accommodation and food services	15,652	16,409	16,834	17,059	17,577	18,728	20,367
Other services, except public administration	28,290	28,770	29,444	30,186	31,227	32,692	33,961
Government and government enterprises	45,793	45,795	46,645	46,923	47,887	48,788	50,404

Table MI-10. Employment Characteristics by Family Type

(Number, percent.)

Family type and labor force status	2014		2015		2016	
	Total	Families with own children under 18 years	Total	Families with own children under 18 years	Total	Families with own children under 18 years
All Families..	2,478,645	1,026,180	2,479,724	1,004,689	2,476,595	992,441
FAMILY TYPE AND LABOR FORCE STATUS						
Married-Couple Families...............................	1,808,447	670,411	1,821,803	658,920	1,819,434	652,348
Both husband and wife in labor force..............	48.9	67.2	48.4	67.0	48.7	66.7
Husband in labor force, wife not in labor force......	20.2	26.2	20.7	26.3	20.6	26.5
Wife in labor force, husband not in labor force......	8.8	4.3	8.5	4.5	8.6	4.6
Both husband and wife not in labor force..........	22.1	2.3	22.1	2.0	21.6	1.9
Other Families	670,198	355,769	657,921	345,769	657,161	340,093
Female householder, no husband present.................	72.8	74.0	72.3	74.4	72.6	75.0
In labor force..	49.5	60.6	48.6	60.6	49.3	61.6
Not in labor force	23.3	13.4	23.7	13.8	23.3	13.4
Male householder, no wife present.....................	27.2	26.0	27.7	25.6	27.4	25.0
In labor force..	20.0	22.7	20.5	22.7	20.3	22.4
Not in labor force	7.2	3.3	7.2	2.9	7.1	2.7

Table MI-11. School Enrollment and Educational Attainment, 2016

(Number, percent.)

Item	State	U.S.
Enrollment		
Total population 3 years and over, enrolled in school	2,488,397	81,572,277
Enrolled in nursery school or preschool (percent)...............................	5.8	6.0
Enrolled in kindergarten (percent)..	4.9	5.0
Enrolled in elementary school, grades 1-8 (percent)............................	39.1	40.3
Enrolled in high school, grades 9-12 (percent)...................................	21.5	21.0
Enrolled in college or graduate school (percent)................................	28.8	27.7
Attainment		
Total population 25 years and over	6,760,402	218,475,480
Less than ninth grade (percent)	3.0	5.4
9th to 12th grade, no diploma (percent)	6.6	7.2
High school graduate, including equivalency (percent)........................	29.3	27.2
Some college, no degree (percent)...	23.6	20.6
Associate's degree (percent)..	9.3	8.4
Bachelor's degree (percent)	17.2	19.3
Graduate or professional degree (percent).......................................	11.1	11.9
High school graduate or higher (percent)...	90.4	87.5
Bachelor's degree or higher (percent)...	28.3	31.3

Table MI-12. Public School Characteristics and Educational Indicators

(Number, percent; data derived from National Center of Education Statistics.)

Item	State	U.S.
Public Schools, 2015–2016 (except where noted)		
Number of school districts..	902	18,328
Number of schools...	3,468	98,456
Number of students	1,536,231	50,327,015
Number of teachers	84,181	3,151,497
Student-teacher ratio	18.2	16.0
Expenditures per student (dollars), 2014-2015.................................	10,956	11,445
Four-year adjusted cohort graduation rate (ACGR)[1,2]	79.7	84.1
Students eligible for free or reduced-price lunch (percent), 2014-2015.........	46.6	51.8
English language learners (percent), Fall 2015..................................	5.8	9.5
Students age 3 to 21 served under IDEA, part B (percent).....................	12.8	13.2

Public Schools by Type	Number	Percent of state public schools
Total number of schools..	3,468	100.0
Regular	2,962	85.4
Special education	187	5.4
Vocational education	4	0.1
Alternative education...	315	9.1

NOTE: Every school is assigned only one school type based on its instructional emphasis.
[1] ACGR data represents a new method of calculating high-school completion rates and may not be comparable to previous years' data for Averaged Freshmen Graduation Rates (AFGR).
[2] The United States 4-year ACGRs were estimated using both the reported 4-year ACGR data from 49 states and the District of Columbia and using imputed data for Idaho. The estimate for American Indian/Alaska Native students also includes imputed data for Virginia.

Table MI-13. Reported Voting and Registration of the Voting-Age Population, November 2016

(Numbers in thousands, percent.)

Item	Total population	Total citizen population	Registered			Voted		
			Total registered	Percent registered (total population)	Percent registered (total citizen population)	Total voted	Percent voted (total population)	Percent voted (total citizen population)
U.S. Total	245,502	224,059	157,596	64.2	70.3	137,537	56.0	61.4
State Total.................................	7,624	7,332	5,434	71.3	74.1	4,713	61.8	64.3
Sex								
Male	3,650	3,473	2,540	69.6	73.1	2,150	58.9	61.9
Female	3,974	3,859	2,893	72.8	75.0	2,563	64.5	66.4
Race								
White alone...............................	6,264	6,071	4,579	73.1	75.4	3,984	63.6	65.6
White, non-Hispanic alone	6,006	5,890	4,498	74.9	76.4	3,914	65.2	66.5
Black alone................................	1,039	1,020	708	68.1	69.4	623	59.9	61.0
Asian alone................................	182	108	63	34.5	58.3	58	32.0	54.2
Hispanic (of any race).................	288	206	101	35.0	49.0	74	25.7	36.0
White alone or in combination	6,365	6,167	4,648	73.0	75.4	4,021	63.2	65.2
Black alone or in combination...........	1,100	1,080	752	68.4	69.6	642	58.4	59.4
Asian alone or in combination...........	192	113	63	32.7	55.6	58	30.4	51.7
Age								
18 to 24 years..........................	853	813	453	53.1	55.7	308	36.1	37.8
25 to 34 years..........................	1,397	1,305	911	65.2	69.8	706	50.6	54.1
35 to 44 years..........................	1,047	1,012	750	71.7	74.1	650	62.1	64.2
45 to 64 years..........................	2,848	2,740	2,158	75.8	78.7	1,962	68.9	71.6
65 years and over......................	1,480	1,462	1,162	78.5	79.5	1,088	73.5	74.4

Table MI-14. Crime

(Number, rate per 100,000. Data are derived from the FBI Uniform Crime Reports.)

Item	State			U.S. [1,2,3,4]		
	2015	2016	Percent change	2015	2016	Percent change
TOTAL POPULATION [5]	9,922,576	9,928,300	0.1	321,418,820	323,127,513	0.5
VIOLENT CRIME						
Number..........................	41,231	45,572	10.5	1,231,566	1,248,185	1.3
Rate	415.5	459.0	10.5	383.2	386.3	0.8
Murder and Nonnegligent Manslaughter						
Number..........................	571	598	4.7	15,696	17,250	9.9
Rate	5.8	6.0	3.4	4.9	5.3	8.2
Rape[6]						
Number..........................	6,450	7,125	10.5	124,047	130,603	5.3
Rate	65.0	71.8	10.5	38.6	40.4	4.7
Robbery						
Number..........................	7,796	7,120	-8.7	327,374	332,198	1.5
Rate	78.6	71.7	-8.8	101.9	102.8	0.9
Aggravated Assault						
Number..........................	26,414	30,729	16.3	764,449	803,007	5.0
Rate	266.2	309.5	16.3	237.8	248.5	4.5
PROPERTY CRIME						
Number..........................	187,101	189,620	1.3	7,993,631	7,919,035	-0.9
Rate	1,885.6	1,909.9	1.3	2,487.0	2,450.7	-1.5
Burglary						
Number..........................	40,041	39,568	-1.2	1,579,527	1,515,096	-4.1
Rate	403.5	398.5	-1.2	491.4	468.9	-4.6
Larceny-Theft						
Number..........................	131,296	129,876	-1.1	5,706,346	5,638,455	-1.2
Rate	1,323.2	1,308.1	-1.1	1,775.4	1,745.0	-1.7
Motor Vehicle Theft						
Number..........................	15,764	20,176	28.0	707,758	765,484	8.2
Rate	158.9	203.2	27.9	220.2	236.9	7.6

NOTE: Although arson data are included in the trend and clearance tables, sufficient data are not available to estimate totals for this offense. Therefore, no arson data are published in this table.

X = Not applicable.

- = Zero or rounds to zero.

[1] The crime figures have been adjusted.

[2] The data collection methodology for the offense of forcible rape used by the Minnesota state Uniform Crime Reporting (UCR) Program (with the exception of Minneapolis and St. Paul, Minnesota) does not comply with national UCR Program guidelines. Consequently, its figures for forcible rape and violent crime (of which forcible rape is a part) are not published in this table.

[3] Includes offenses reported by the Zoological Police and the Metro Transit Police.

[4] Because of changes in the state's reporting practices, figures are not comparable to previous years' data.

[5] Populations are U.S. Census Bureau provisional estimates as of July 1 of each year.

[6] The figures shown for the offense of rape were estimated using the revised Uniform Crime Reporting (UCR) definition of rape.

Table MI-15. State Government Finances, 2016

(Dollar amounts in thousands, percent distribution.)

Item	Dollars	Percent distribution
Total Revenue	71,188,554	100.0
General revenue	61,246,103	86.0
Intergovernmental revenue	20,908,261	29.4
Taxes	27,436,607	38.5
General sales	9,163,542	12.9
Selective sales	4,075,591	5.7
License taxes	1,660,663	2.3
Individual income tax	9,303,847	13.1
Corporate income tax	898,213	1.3
Other taxes	2,334,751	3.3
Current charges	8,688,398	12.2
Miscellaneous general revenue	4,212,837	5.9
Utility revenue	0	-
Liquor stores revenue	1,021,890	1.4
Insurance trust revenue [1]	8,920,561	12.5
Total Expenditure	70,811,041	100.0
Intergovernmental expenditure	20,788,310	29.4
Direct expenditure	50,022,731	70.6
Current operation	36,926,542	52.1
Capital outlay	2,287,310	3.2
Insurance benefits and repayments	7,769,172	11.0
Assistance and subsidies	1,372,717	1.9
Interest on debt	1,666,990	2.4
Exhibit: Salaries and wages	9,534,602	13.5
Total Expenditure	70,811,041	100.0
General expenditure	62,216,940	87.9
Intergovernmental expenditure	20,788,310	29.4
Direct expenditure	41,428,630	58.5
General expenditure, by function:		
Education	25,725,807	36.3
Public welfare	18,707,348	26.4
Hospitals	3,789,047	5.4
Health	1,591,379	2.2
Highways	2,743,085	3.9
Police protection	487,890	0.7
Correction	1,900,994	2.7
Natural resources	349,307	0.5
Parks and recreation	142,474	0.2
Governmental administration	1,226,724	1.7
Interest on general debt	1,666,990	2.4
Other and unallocable	3,885,895	5.5
Utility expenditure	0	-
Liquor stores expenditure	824,929	1.2
Insurance trust expenditure	7,769,172	11.0
Debt at End of Fiscal Year	33,744,508	X
Cash and Security Holdings	85,112,135	X

X = Not applicable.
- = Zero or rounds to zero.
[1] Within insurance trust revenue, net earnings of state retirement systems is a calculated statistic (the item code in the data file is X08), and thus can be positive or negative. Net earnings is the sum of earnings on investments plus gains on investments minus losses on investments. The change made in 2002 for asset valuation from book to market value in accordance with Statement 34 of the Governmental Accounting Standards Board is reflected in the calculated statistics.

Table MI-16. State Government Tax Collections, 2017

(Dollars in thousands, percent.)

Item	Dollars	Percent distribution
Total Taxes	28,628,517	100.0
Property taxes	2,124,075	7.4
Sales and gross receipts	13,696,741	47.8
General sales and gross receipts	9,223,737	32.2
Selective sales and gross receipts	4,473,004	15.6
Alcoholic beverages	159,378	0.6
Amusements	113,048	0.4
Insurance premiums	337,254	1.2
Motor fuels	1,210,628	4.2
Pari-mutuels	3,487	-
Public utilities	28,381	0.1
Tobacco products	1,038,594	3.6
Other selective sales	1,582,234	5.5
Licenses	1,787,867	6.2
Alcoholic beverages	19,204	0.1
Amusements	X	-
Corporations in general	24,509	0.1
Hunting and fishing	63,756	0.2
Motor vehicle	1,191,927	4.2
Motor vehicle operators	58,838	0.2
Public utilities	33,180	0.1
Occupation and business, NEC	167,908	0.6
Other licenses	228,545	0.8
Income taxes	10,680,724	37.3
Individual income	9,485,325	33.1
Corporation net income	1,195,399	4.2
Other taxes	339,110	1.2
Death and gift	26	-
Documentary and stock transfer	310,149	1.1
Severance	28,935	0.1
Taxes, NEC	0	-

- = Zero or rounds to zero.
X = Not applicable.

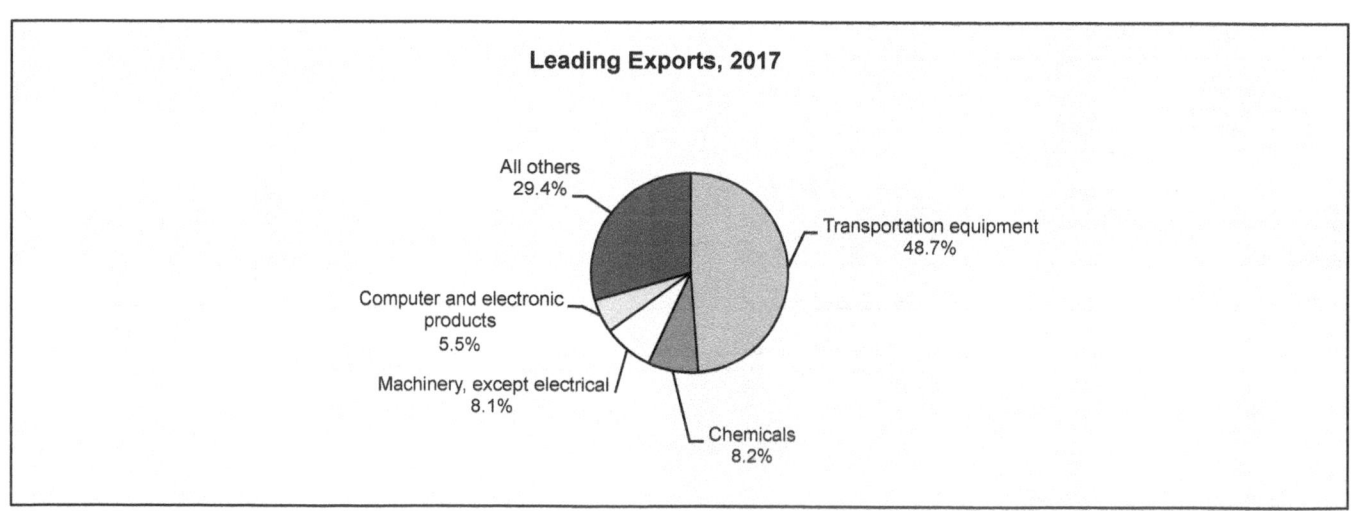

Leading Exports, 2017

All others 29.4%

Transportation equipment 48.7%

Computer and electronic products 5.5%

Machinery, except electrical 8.1%

Chemicals 8.2%

MINNESOTA

Facts and Figures

Location: North central United States; bordered on the N by Canada (Manitoba and Ontario), on the E by Lake Superior and Wisconsin, on the S by Iowa, and on the W by North Dakota and South Dakota

Area: 86,939 sq. mi. (225,171 sq. km.); rank—12th

Population: 5,576,606 (2017 est.); rank—22nd

Principal Cities: capital—St. Paul; largest—Minneapolis

Statehood: May 11, 1858; 32nd state

U.S. Congress: 2 senators, 8 representatives

State Motto: *L'Etoile du Nord* ("The Star of the North")

State Song: "Hail! Minnesota"

State Nicknames: The North Star State; The Land of 10,000 Lakes; The Gopher State

Abbreviations: MN; Minn.

State Symbols: flower—showy (pink and white) lady's slipper; tree—red (Norway) pine; bird—loon

At a Glance

- With an increase in population of 5.0 percent, Minnesota ranked 21st among the states in growth from 2010 to 2017.

- Minnesota's violent crime rate in 2016 was 242.6 per 100,000 population, compared to 386.3 for the entire nation.

- With a property crime rate of 2,133.3 per 100,000 population in 2016, Minnesota ranked 33rd in the nation.

- Minnesota's median household income was $65,599 in 2016, which ranked 14th among the states.

- In 2016, 9.9 percent of all Minnesotans and 12.7 percent of children in Minnesota lived below the poverty level, compared to 14.0 percent of the entire U.S. population and 19.5 percent of all U.S. children.

Table MN-1. Population by Age, Sex, Race, and Hispanic Origin

(Number, percent, except where noted.)

Sex, age, race, and Hispanic origin	2000	2010	2017 [1]	Average annual percent change, 2010–2017
Total Population...	4,919,479	5,303,925	5,576,606	5.1
Percent of total U.S. population	1.7	1.7	1.7	X
Sex				
Male...	2,435,631	2,632,132	2,776,846	5.5
Female...	2,483,848	2,671,793	2,799,760	4.8
Age				
Under 5 years..	329,594	355,504	355,231	-0.1
5 to 19 years...	1,105,251	1,075,707	1,084,416	0.8
20 to 64 years...	2,890,368	3,189,593	3,276,750	2.7
65 years and over	594,266	683,121	860,209	25.9
Median age (years)...	35.4	37.4	37.9	1.3
Race and Hispanic Origin				
One race				
White	4,400,282	4,623,461	4,708,215	1.8
Black..	171,731	280,949	365,225	30.0
American Indian and Alaska Native	54,967	67,325	75,402	12.0
Asian..	141,968	217,792	284,643	30.7
Native Hawaiian or Other Pacific Islander	1,979	2,958	3,970	34.2
Two or more races...	82,742	111,440	139,151	24.9
Hispanic (of any race)..	143,382	264,432	301,407	14.0

X = Not applicable.
- = Zero or rounds to zero.
[1] Population figures for 2017 are July 1 estimates. The 2010 estimates are taken from the 2010 Census.

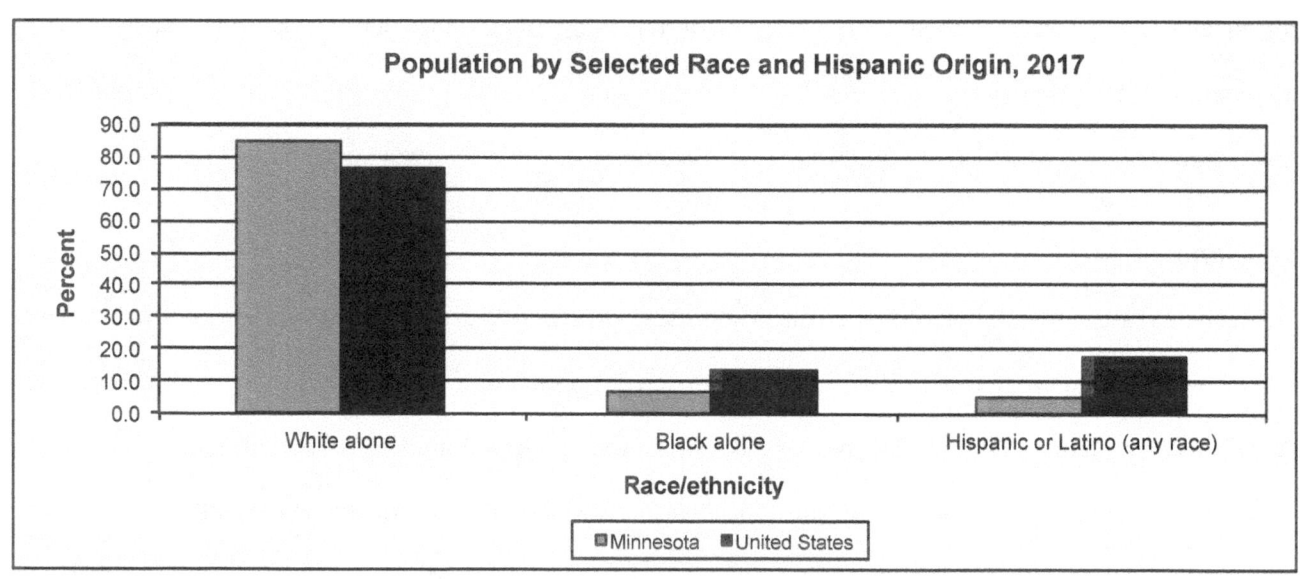

Table MN-2. Marital Status

(Number, percent distribution.)

Sex, age, and marital status	2000	2010	2016
Males, 15 Years and Over	1,889,936	2,090,940	2,197,537
Never married	31.3	34.6	35.7
Now married, except separated..	57.7	53.5	51.7
Separated...	0.9	0.9	0.9
Widowed...	2.1	2.2	2.3
Divorced...	8.0	8.7	9.5
Females, 15 Years and Over	1,967,819	2,155,042	2,249,169
Never married	25.0	28.2	28.8
Now married, except separated..	55.0	51.5	50.9
Separated...	1.2	1.2	1.1
Widowed...	9.4	8.4	8.0
Divorced...	9.5	10.7	11.2

Table MN-3. Households and Housing Characteristics

(Number, percent, dollars.)

Item	2000	2010	2016	Average annual percent change, 2010–2016
Total Households.................................	1,895,127	2,091,548	2,148,725	0.5
Family households	1,255,141	1,353,758	1,367,104	0.2
Married-couple family	1,018,245	1,069,000	1,081,567	0.2
Other family	236,986	284,758	285,537	0.0
Male householder, no wife present............	68,114	87,757	94,441	1.3
Female householder, no husband present.......	168,782	197,001	191,096	-0.5
Nonfamily households	639,986	737,790	781,621	1.0
Householder living alone.........................	509,468	591,124	628,368	1.1
Householder not living alone.....................	130,518	146,666	153,253	0.7
Housing Characteristics				
Total housing units	2,065,946	2,348,242	2,409,701	0.4
Occupied housing units	1,895,127	2,091,548	2,148,725	0.5
Owner occupied	1,412,865	1,527,328	1,532,031	0.1
Renter occupied....................................	482,262	564,220	616,694	1.6
Average household size..............................	2.52	2.47	2.51	0.3
Financial Characteristics				
Median gross rent of renter-occupied housing	566	764	912	3.2
Median monthly owner costs for housing units with a mortgage	1,044	1,503	1,472	-0.3
Median value of owner-occupied housing units	122,400	194,300	211,800	1.5

Table MN-4. Migration, Origin, and Language

(Number, percent.)

Characteristic	State			U.S.		
	2015	2016	Percent change	2015	2016	Percent change
Residence 1 Year Ago						
Population 1 year and over	5,419,822	5,455,904	0.6	317,635,720	319,361,956	0.5
Same house	85.2	85.6	X	85.3	85.4	X
Different house in the U.S.	14.2	13.9	X	14.1	13.9	X
Same county..	7.6	7.1	X	8.5	8.3	X
Different county	6.6	6.7	X	5.6	5.6	X
Same state	4.6	4.7	X	3.2	3.2	X
Different state	2.0	2.0	X	2.4	2.4	X
Abroad	0.6	0.6	X	0.7	0.7	X
Place of Birth						
Native born	5,032,409	5,067,516	0.2	278,128,449	279,388,170	0.5
Male	49.8	49.8	X	49.3	49.3	X
Female	50.2	50.2	X	50.7	50.7	X
Foreign born	457,185	452,436	6.1	43,290,372	43,739,345	1.0
Male	48.8	49.8	X	48.6	48.5	X
Female	51.2	50.2	X	51.4	51.5	X
Foreign born; naturalized U.S. citizen.................	224,718	229,473	3.5	20,697,103	21,238,372	2.6
Male	45.7	47.9	X	45.9	45.9	X
Female	54.3	52.1	X	54.1	54.1	X
Foreign born; not a U.S. citizen......................	232,467	222,963	8.9	22,593,269	22,500,973	-0.4
Male	51.8	51.8	X	51.1	51.0	X
Female	48.2	48.2	X	48.9	49.0	X
Entered 2010 or later	23.5	24.6	X	15.6	18.6	X
Entered 2000 to 2009	33.8	31.6	X	27.9	26.7	X
Entered before 2000................................	42.7	43.7	X	56.5	54.7	X
World Region of Birth, Foreign						
Foreign-born population, excluding population born at sea	457,185	452,436	6.1	43,289,646	43,738,901	1.0
Europe	10.5	10.1	X	11.1	10.9	X
Asia..	38.8	37.4	X	30.6	30.8	X
Africa..	22.0	23.8	X	4.8	4.9	X
Oceania	0.6	0.4	X	0.6	0.6	X
Latin America	25.1	25.8	X	51.1	51.0	X
North America	3.1	2.4	X	1.9	1.8	X
Language Spoken at Home and Ability to Speak English						
Population 5 years and over..........................	5,138,667	5,168,872	0.7	301,625,014	303,328,961	0.6
English only	88.5	88.4	X	78.5	78.4	X
Language other than English.........................	11.5	11.6	X	21.5	21.6	X
Speaks English less than "very well"...............	4.8	4.6	X	8.6	8.6	X

NA = Not available.
X = Not applicable.
- = Zero or rounds to zero.

Table MN-5. Median Income and Poverty Status, 2016

(Number, percent, except as noted.)

Characteristic	State		U.S.	
	Number	Percent	Number	Percent
Median Income				
Households (dollars)........................	65,599	X	57,617	X
Families (dollars).............................	83,344	X	71,062	X
Below Poverty Level (All People)..................	533,276	9.9	44,268,996	14.0
Sex				
Male......................................	241,562	9.0	19,760,056	12.8
Female...................................	291,714	10.8	24,508,940	15.2
Age				
Under 18 years............................	160,626	12.7	14,115,713	19.5
Related children under 18 years...........	154,580	12.3	13,805,435	19.1
18 to 64 years............................	314,769	9.5	25,723,818	13.2
65 years and over.........................	57,881	7.2	4,429,465	9.2

X = Not applicable.

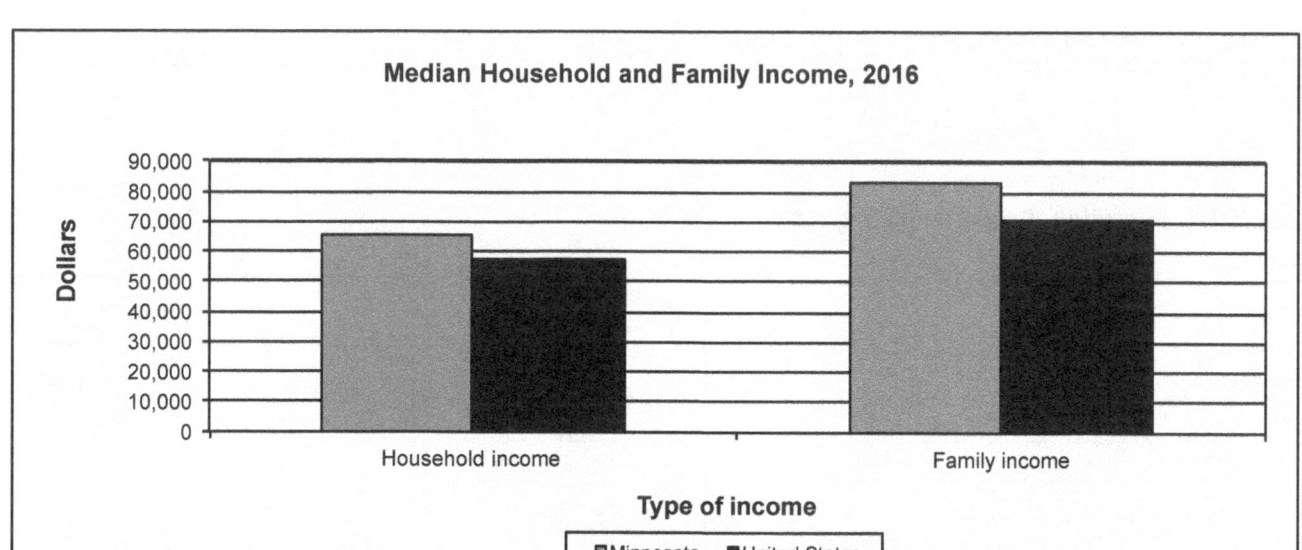

Median Household and Family Income, 2016

Legend: ▦ Minnesota ■ United States

Table MN-6. Health Insurance Coverage Status for the Civilian Noninstitutionalized Population and Children Under 18 Years of Age

(Number, percent.)

Item	2008	2009	2010	2011	2012	2013	2014	2015	2016
Civilian Noninstitutionalized Population	5,150,617	5,196,720	5,252,092	5,286,728	5,319,783	5,362,681	5,398,211	5,431,894	5,462,438
Covered by Private or Public Insurance									
Number............................	4,703,895	4,723,891	4,775,833	4,819,295	4,895,121	4,922,902	5,080,954	5,186,786	5,237,492
Percent............................	91.3	90.9	90.9	91.2	92.0	91.8	94.1	95.5	95.9
Not Covered									
Number............................	446,722	472,829	476,259	467,433	424,662	439,779	317,257	245,108	224,946
Percent............................	8.7	9.1	9.1	8.8	8.0	8.2	5.9	4.5	4.1
Percent in the U.S. not covered...........	15.1	15.1	15.5	15.1	14.8	14.5	11.7	9.4	8.6
Children Under 18 Years of Age	1,248,041	1,255,596	1,281,022	1,276,035	1,275,509	1,280,236	1,280,791	1,280,978	1,286,323
Covered by Private or Public Insurance									
Number............................	1,169,412	1,172,539	1,196,857	1,196,211	1,207,024	1,208,254	1,231,774	1,241,570	1,243,038
Percent............................	93.7	93.4	93.4	93.7	94.6	94.4	96.2	96.9	96.6
Not Covered									
Number............................	78,629	83,057	84,165	79,824	68,485	71,982	49,017	39,408	43,285
Percent............................	6.3	6.6	6.6	6.3	5.4	5.6	3.8	3.1	3.4
Percent in the U.S. not covered...........	9.9	8.6	8.0	7.5	7.2	7.1	6.0	4.8	4.5

Table MN-7. Employment Status by Demographic Group, 2017

(Numbers in thousands, percent.)

Characteristic	Civilian noninstitutional population	Civilian labor force		Employed		Unemployed	
		Number	Percent of population	Number	Percent of population	Number	Percent of population
Total..	4,350	3,099	71.2	2,993	68.8	106	3.4
Sex							
Male...............................	2,151	1,627	75.6	1,560	72.5	67	4.1
Female.............................	2,199	1,473	67.0	1,434	65.2	39	2.6
Race, Sex, and Hispanic Origin							
White...............................	3,801	2,714	71.4	2,634	69.3	80	2.9
Male...............................	1,901	1,444	76.0	1,391	73.2	53	3.7
Female............................	1,900	1,270	66.8	1,243	65.4	27	2.1
Black or African American............	234	166	71.0	154	65.7	12	7.5
Male...............................	NA	NA	NA	NA	NA	NA	NA
Female............................	NA	NA	NA	NA	NA	NA	NA
Hispanic or Latino ethnicity[1].........	198	162	81.7	153	77.6	8	5.0
Male...............................	NA	NA	NA	NA	NA	NA	NA
Female............................	NA	NA	NA	NA	NA	NA	NA
Age							
16 to 19 years......................	289	151	52.3	136	47.1	15	9.8
20 to 24 years......................	308	247	80.2	233	75.7	14	5.5
25 to 34 years......................	751	671	89.5	652	86.8	20	2.9
35 to 44 years......................	727	648	89.2	628	86.4	21	3.2
45 to 54 years......................	708	629	88.9	611	86.4	18	2.8
55 to 64 years......................	755	564	74.6	549	72.7	15	2.6
65 years and over..................	813	188	23.2	184	22.6	5	2.6

NOTE: Data in Table 7 are from the Current Population Survey (CPS) and do not match the estimates in Table 8. See notes and definitions for further information.
[1] May be of any race.
NA = Not available.

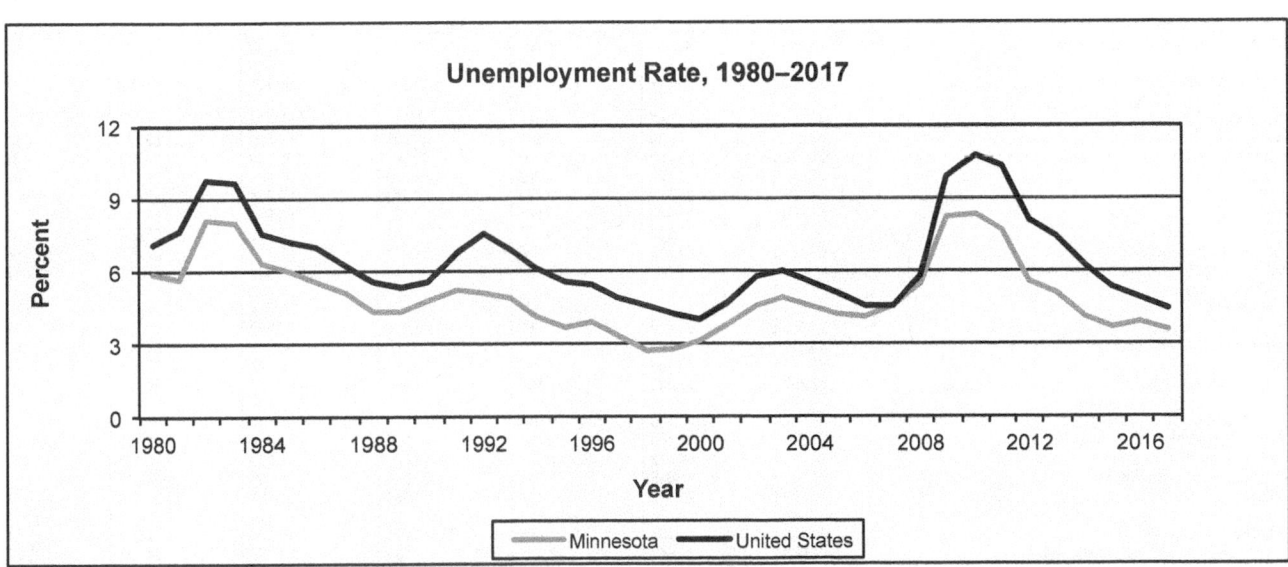

Table MN-8. Employment Status of the Civilian Noninstitutional Population Age 16 Years and Over

(Number, percent.)

Year	Civilian labor force	Civilian participation rate	Employed	Unemployed	Unemployment rate
2009..........................	2,941,976	72.0	2,713,426	228,550	7.8
2010..........................	2,938,795	71.4	2,721,194	217,601	7.4
2011..........................	2,946,279	71.0	2,755,264	191,015	6.5
2012..........................	2,946,356	70.4	2,781,141	165,215	5.6
2013..........................	2,958,596	70.1	2,811,762	146,834	5.0
2014..........................	2,973,073	69.9	2,849,017	124,056	4.2
2015..........................	2,998,352	70.0	2,887,683	110,669	3.7
2016..........................	3,036,278	70.3	2,919,097	117,181	3.9
2017..........................	3,063,604	70.2	2,957,838	105,766	3.5

Table MN-9. Employment and Average Wages by Industry

(Estimates through 2010 are based on the 2007 *North American Industry Classification System* [NAICS]. Estimates from 2011 onward are based on the 2012 NAICS.)

Industry	2010	2011	2012	2013	2014	2015	2016
	Number of jobs						
Wage and Salary Employment by Industry	2,710,413	2,751,062	2,791,399	2,834,955	2,875,681	2,923,079	2,961,350
Farm Wage and Salary Employment	19,300	16,872	17,591	15,802	14,250	17,516	15,630
Nonfarm Wage and Salary Employment	2,691,113	2,734,190	2,773,808	2,819,153	2,861,431	2,905,563	2,945,720
Private wage and salary employment	2,270,160	2,319,008	2,357,002	2,401,595	2,441,903	2,483,959	2,520,091
Forestry, fishing, and related activities	5,641	5,690	5,798	5,955	6,048	6,306	6,313
Mining	5,220	5,810	6,247	6,219	6,370	6,166	5,361
Utilities	12,687	12,804	12,707	13,012	12,863	12,788	12,504
Construction	90,671	94,676	97,751	103,549	110,611	118,007	119,225
Manufacturing	292,370	301,283	305,864	307,543	312,309	317,539	317,991
Durable goods manufacturing	183,344	190,230	194,502	195,236	198,700	202,729	201,767
Nondurable goods manufacturing	109,026	111,053	111,362	112,307	113,609	114,810	116,224
Wholesale trade	124,076	126,500	129,085	131,037	132,561	133,465	132,353
Retail trade	279,971	282,854	285,208	288,710	290,862	295,411	300,268
Transportation and warehousing	77,029	79,920	80,009	81,238	84,094	86,628	89,880
Information	54,209	53,837	53,788	53,354	52,704	51,731	50,498
Finance and insurance	138,165	141,385	141,764	144,280	142,070	145,016	144,473
Real estate and rental and leasing	36,727	36,722	39,859	40,629	40,155	40,115	35,254
Professional, scientific, and technical services	124,504	129,110	131,609	136,965	142,126	146,632	159,652
Management of companies and enterprises	70,684	72,685	74,841	77,025	78,767	78,192	78,548
Administrative and waste services	122,093	130,351	132,790	133,969	134,784	134,934	137,533
Educational services	69,338	70,428	70,303	71,140	71,567	72,598	74,208
Health care and social assistance	395,140	398,404	408,369	421,266	429,338	438,478	450,604
Arts, entertainment, and recreation	37,778	38,199	39,228	39,869	40,746	42,185	43,808
Accommodation and food services	199,613	203,511	207,865	211,963	215,318	218,910	223,184
Other services, except public administration	134,244	134,839	133,917	133,872	138,610	138,858	138,434
Government and government enterprises	420,953	415,182	416,806	417,558	419,528	421,604	425,629
	Dollars						
Average Wages and Salaries by Industry	45,845	46,935	48,502	49,254	50,753	52,632	55,098
Average Farm Wages and Salaries	28,320	25,319	39,306	32,721	36,717	37,003	43,985
Average Nonfarm Wages and Salaries	45,970	47,068	48,560	49,347	50,823	52,726	55,157
Average private wages and salaries	46,448	47,650	49,342	50,096	51,589	53,589	56,033
Forestry, fishing, and related activities	25,876	26,890	28,609	28,962	29,359	30,671	34,601
Mining	73,542	81,400	82,203	84,172	85,524	79,699	88,609
Utilities	86,368	90,398	92,774	97,249	99,321	102,117	104,330
Construction	51,868	53,460	55,587	57,333	58,954	61,512	66,122
Manufacturing	56,323	57,524	58,737	59,561	61,095	63,202	64,614
Durable goods manufacturing	60,747	61,812	63,090	64,227	65,819	67,825	68,729
Nondurable goods manufacturing	48,883	50,180	51,133	51,450	52,835	55,039	57,472
Wholesale trade	69,521	71,757	74,404	76,006	76,975	79,135	82,916
Retail trade	24,455	24,875	25,382	25,971	27,220	28,235	29,284
Transportation and warehousing	44,513	45,971	47,922	48,279	50,159	51,166	55,900
Information	62,140	66,104	65,018	66,777	69,527	72,258	70,976
Finance and insurance	77,753	82,032	89,504	88,625	92,771	96,827	99,821
Real estate and rental and leasing	44,982	46,890	51,848	53,610	55,039	58,234	52,288
Professional, scientific, and technical services	74,546	76,168	79,009	81,014	83,864	85,915	90,542
Management of companies and enterprises	110,411	109,612	112,101	112,835	115,280	120,493	120,403
Administrative and waste services	31,341	31,646	32,349	32,276	33,899	36,013	40,237
Educational services	28,883	29,377	30,198	30,084	30,664	30,675	31,327
Health care and social assistance	43,185	43,483	44,686	44,933	45,825	47,982	51,252
Arts, entertainment, and recreation	31,639	31,662	31,457	32,290	32,537	34,023	37,538
Accommodation and food services	15,909	16,547	17,102	17,478	18,233	19,570	21,543
Other services, except public administration	27,073	27,910	28,884	29,985	30,956	32,257	34,829
Government and government enterprises	43,395	43,818	44,139	45,041	46,362	47,641	49,969

Table MN-10. Employment Characteristics by Family Type

(Number, percent.)

Family type and labor force status	2014		2015		2016	
	Total	Families with own children under 18 years	Total	Families with own children under 18 years	Total	Families with own children under 18 years
All Families.........	1,362,032	603,414	1,383,950	613,580	1,367,104	608,671
FAMILY TYPE AND LABOR FORCE STATUS						
Married-Couple Families............	1,068,394	428,952	1,091,358	433,140	1,081,567	435,650
Both husband and wife in labor force..............	60.6	77.1	60.1	77.3	60.6	77.8
Husband in labor force, wife not in labor force	15.7	18.5	15.9	18.2	15.1	17.3
Wife in labor force, husband not in labor force	7.5	3.6	7.2	3.2	6.9	3.3
Both husband and wife not in labor force.............	16.3	0.8	16.1	0.9	16.6	1.2
Other Families	293,638	174,462	292,592	180,440	285,537	173,021
Female householder, no husband present..........	69.4	71.5	67.4	69.8	66.9	69.2
In labor force.......	52.5	60.0	52.4	60.4	51.4	59.5
Not in labor force	16.9	11.5	15.1	9.4	15.5	9.7
Male householder, no wife present..........	30.6	28.5	32.6	30.2	33.1	30.8
In labor force.......	25.4	26.3	27.8	28.1	28.5	29.3
Not in labor force	5.2	2.2	4.7	2.1	4.6	1.5

Table MN-11. School Enrollment and Educational Attainment, 2016

(Number, percent.)

Item	State	U.S.
Enrollment		
Total population 3 years and over, enrolled in school	1,392,956	81,572,277
Enrolled in nursery school or preschool (percent).........	6.7	6.0
Enrolled in kindergarten (percent).........	5.1	5.0
Enrolled in elementary school, grades 1-8 (percent).........	41.1	40.3
Enrolled in high school, grades 9-12 (percent).........	21.0	21.0
Enrolled in college or graduate school (percent).........	26.0	27.7
Attainment		
Total population 25 years and over	3,725,283	218,475,480
Less than ninth grade (percent).........	3.0	5.4
9th to 12th grade, no diploma (percent).........	4.1	7.2
High school graduate, including equivalency (percent).........	25.2	27.2
Some college, no degree (percent).........	21.4	20.6
Associate's degree (percent).........	11.5	8.4
Bachelor's degree (percent).........	23.1	19.3
Graduate or professional degree (percent).........	11.7	11.9
High school graduate or higher (percent).........	92.9	87.5
Bachelor's degree or higher (percent).........	34.8	31.3

Table MN-12. Public School Characteristics and Educational Indicators

(Number, percent; data derived from National Center of Education Statistics.)

Item	State	U.S.
Public Schools, 2015–2016 (except where noted)		
Number of school districts.........	564	18,328
Number of schools.........	2,478	98,456
Number of students.........	864,384	50,327,015
Number of teachers.........	55,985	3,151,497
Student-teacher ratio.........	15.4	16.0
Expenditures per student (dollars), 2014-2015.........	11,924	11,445
Four-year adjusted cohort graduation rate (ACGR)[1,2]	82.2	84.1
Students eligible for free or reduced-price lunch (percent), 2014-2015.........	38.3	51.8
English language learners (percent), Fall 2015	8.2	9.5
Students age 3 to 21 served under IDEA, part B (percent).........	14.8	13.2

Public Schools by Type	Number	Percent of state public schools
Total number of schools.........	2,478	100.0
Regular	1,686	68.0
Special education.........	292	11.8
Vocational education.........	9	0.4
Alternative education.........	491	19.8

NOTE: Every school is assigned only one school type based on its instructional emphasis.
[1] ACGR data represents a new method of calculating high-school completion rates and may not be comparable to previous years' data for Averaged Freshmen Graduation Rates (AFGR).
[2] The United States 4-year ACGRs were estimated using both the reported 4-year ACGR data from 49 states and the District of Columbia and using imputed data for Idaho. The estimate for American Indian/Alaska Native students also includes imputed data for Virginia.

Table MN-13. Reported Voting and Registration of the Voting-Age Population, November 2016

(Numbers in thousands, percent.)

Item	Total population	Total citizen population	Registered			Voted		
			Total registered	Percent registered (total population)	Percent registered (total citizen population)	Total voted	Percent voted (total population)	Percent voted (total citizen population)
U.S. Total	245,502	224,059	157,596	64.2	70.3	137,537	56.0	61.4
State Total................................	4,190	3,985	3,055	72.9	76.7	2,738	65.3	68.7
Sex								
Male	2,063	1,952	1,457	70.6	74.6	1,312	63.6	67.2
Female	2,127	2,033	1,598	75.1	78.6	1,426	67.1	70.2
Race								
White alone..............................	3,614	3,506	2,723	75.4	77.7	2,457	68.0	70.1
White, non-Hispanic alone	3,425	3,405	2,680	78.2	78.7	2,417	70.6	71.0
Black alone................................	193	169	126	65.3	74.7	112	58.0	66.3
Asian alone...............................	172	124	79	46.1	63.7	64	37.4	51.6
Hispanic (of any race)...................	255	136	54	21.0	39.6	50	19.4	36.6
White alone or in combination	3,671	3,563	2,756	75.1	77.4	2,489	67.8	69.9
Black alone or in combination...........	201	176	134	66.6	75.8	120	59.6	67.7
Asian alone or in combination...........	196	148	97	49.8	65.7	82	42.1	55.6
Age								
18 to 24 years............................	524	476	297	56.7	62.4	260	49.6	54.7
25 to 34 years............................	708	674	491	69.3	72.8	435	61.4	64.5
35 to 44 years............................	684	625	476	69.7	76.2	438	64.1	70.1
45 to 64 years............................	1,503	1,441	1,158	77.1	80.3	1,047	69.7	72.6
65 years and over	772	769	633	82.0	82.3	558	72.3	72.6

Table MN-14. Crime

(Number, rate per 100,000. Data are derived from the FBI Uniform Crime Reports.)

Item	State [1]			U.S. [1,2,3,4]		
	2015	2016	Percent change	2015	2016	Percent change
TOTAL POPULATION [5]	5,489,594	5,519,952	0.6	321,418,820	323,127,513	0.5
VIOLENT CRIME						
Number...	13,319	13,394	0.6	1,231,566	1,248,185	1.3
Rate	242.6	242.6	-	383.2	386.3	0.8
Murder and Nonnegligent Manslaughter						
Number...	133	101	-24.1	15,696	17,250	9.9
Rate	2.4	1.8	-25.0	4.9	5.3	8.2
Rape [6]						
Number...	2,321	2,348	1.2	124,047	130,603	5.3
Rate	42.3	42.5	0.5	38.6	40.4	4.7
Robbery						
Number...	3,771	3,728	-1.1	327,374	332,198	1.5
Rate	68.7	67.5	-1.7	101.9	102.8	0.9
Aggravated Assault						
Number...	7,094	7,217	1.7	764,449	803,007	5.0
Rate	129.2	130.7	1.2	237.8	248.5	4.5
PROPERTY CRIME						
Number...	121,984	117,756	-3.5	7,993,631	7,919,035	-0.9
Rate	2,222.1	2,133.3	-4.0	2,487.0	2,450.7	-1.5
Burglary						
Number...	19,299	18,606	-3.6	1,579,527	1,515,096	-4.1
Rate	351.6	337.1	-4.1	491.4	468.9	-4.6
Larceny-Theft						
Number...	94,704	90,422	-4.5	5,706,346	5,638,455	-1.2
Rate	1,725.2	1,638.1	-5.0	1,775.4	1,745.0	-1.7
Motor Vehicle Theft						
Number...	7,981	8,728	9.4	707,758	765,484	8.2
Rate	145.4	158.1	8.7	220.2	236.9	7.6

NOTE: Although arson data are included in the trend and clearance tables, sufficient data are not available to estimate totals for this offense. Therefore, no arson data are published in this table.

X = Not applicable.

- = Zero or rounds to zero.

[1] The data collection methodology for the offense of forcible rape used by the Minnesota state Uniform Crime Reporting (UCR) Program (with the exception of Minneapolis and St. Paul, Minnesota) does not comply with national UCR Program guidelines. Consequently, its figures for forcible rape and violent crime (of which forcible rape is a part) are not published in this table.

[2] The crime figures have been adjusted.

[3] Includes offenses reported by the Zoological Police and the Metro Transit Police.

[4] Because of changes in the state's reporting practices, figures are not comparable to previous years' data.

[5] Populations are U.S. Census Bureau provisional estimates as of July 1 of each year.

[6] The figures shown for the offense of rape were estimated using the revised Uniform Crime Reporting (UCR) definition of rape.

Table MN-15. State Government Finances, 2016

(Dollar amounts in thousands, percent distribution.)

Item	Dollars	Percent distribution
Total Revenue	44,247,753	100.0
General revenue	41,213,212	93.1
Intergovernmental revenue	11,321,336	25.6
Taxes	25,189,128	56.9
General sales	5,583,910	12.6
Selective sales	4,536,737	10.3
License taxes	1,426,235	3.2
Individual income tax	10,732,570	24.3
Corporate income tax	1,515,697	3.4
Other taxes	1,393,979	3.2
Current charges	2,636,013	6.0
Miscellaneous general revenue	2,066,735	4.7
Utility revenue	104,120	0.2
Liquor stores revenue	0	-
Insurance trust revenue [1]	2,930,421	6.6
Total Expenditure	46,694,801	100.0
Intergovernmental expenditure	13,143,647	28.1
Direct expenditure	33,551,154	71.9
Current operation	24,177,528	51.8
Capital outlay	2,279,139	4.9
Insurance benefits and repayments	5,353,191	11.5
Assistance and subsidies	1,149,595	2.5
Interest on debt	591,701	1.3
Exhibit: Salaries and wages	5,439,188	11.6
Total Expenditure	46,694,801	100.0
General expenditure	40,870,370	87.5
Intergovernmental expenditure	13,143,647	28.1
Direct expenditure	27,726,723	59.4
General expenditure, by function:		
Education	15,131,545	32.4
Public welfare	14,873,839	31.9
Hospitals	303,151	0.6
Health	529,725	1.1
Highways	3,195,546	6.8
Police protection	446,435	1.0
Correction	620,117	1.3
Natural resources	674,515	1.4
Parks and recreation	296,279	0.6
Governmental administration	1,139,234	2.4
Interest on general debt	591,658	1.3
Other and unallocable	3,068,326	6.6
Utility expenditure	471,240	1.1
Liquor stores expenditure	0	-
Insurance trust expenditure	5,353,191	11.5
Debt at End of Fiscal Year	16,213,046	X
Cash and Security Holdings	76,448,020	X

X = Not applicable.
- = Zero or rounds to zero.
[1] Within insurance trust revenue, net earnings of state retirement systems is a calculated statistic (the item code in the data file is X08), and thus can be positive or negative. Net earnings is the sum of earnings on investments plus gains on investments minus losses on investments. The change made in 2002 for asset valuation from book to market value in accordance with Statement 34 of the Governmental Accounting Standards Board is reflected in the calculated statistics.

Table MN-16. State Government Tax Collections, 2017

(Dollars in thousands, percent.)

Item	Dollars	Percent distribution
Total Taxes	25,594,522	100.0
Property taxes	854,945	3.3
Sales and gross receipts	10,607,635	41.4
General sales and gross receipts	5,888,795	23.0
Selective sales and gross receipts	4,718,840	18.4
Alcoholic beverages	88,222	0.3
Amusements	63,870	0.2
Insurance premiums	486,403	1.9
Motor fuels	912,644	3.6
Pari-mutuels	863	-
Public utilities	54	-
Tobacco products	681,018	2.7
Other selective sales	2,485,766	9.7
Licenses	1,477,319	5.8
Alcoholic beverages	2,611	-
Amusements	1,195	-
Corporations in general	8,551	-
Hunting and fishing	63,665	0.2
Motor vehicle	790,116	3.1
Motor vehicle operators	46,489	0.2
Public utilities	681	-
Occupation and business, NEC	500,603	2.0
Other licenses	63,408	0.2
Income taxes	12,183,233	47.6
Individual income	10,956,205	42.8
Corporation net income	1,227,028	4.8
Other taxes	471,390	1.8
Death and gift	129,657	0.5
Documentary and stock transfer	245,089	1.0
Severance	46,593	0.2
Taxes, NEC	50,051	0.2

- = Zero or rounds to zero.

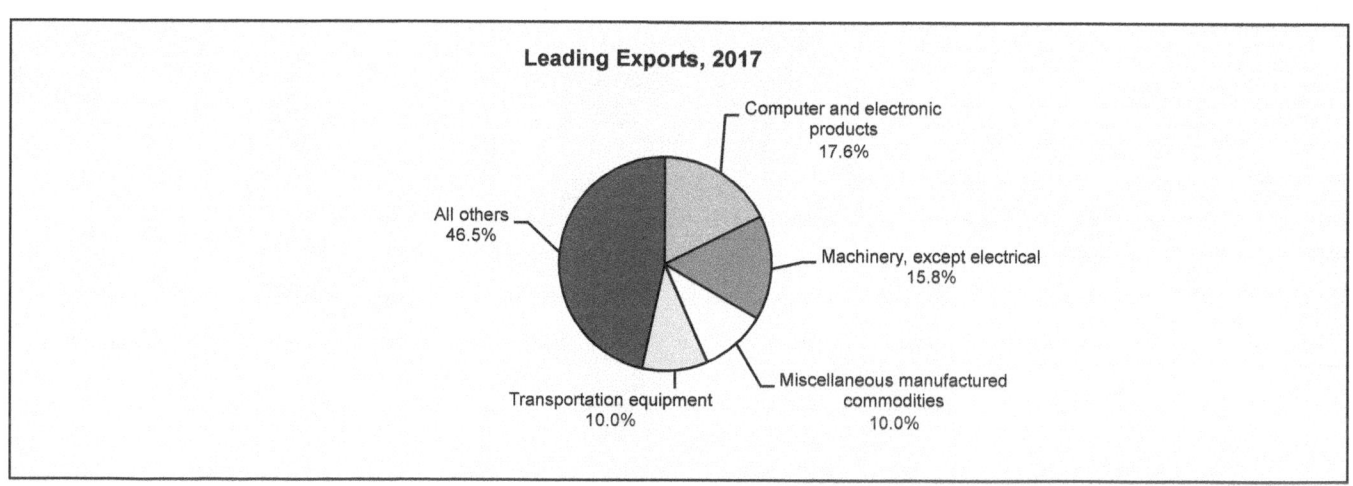

Leading Exports, 2017

- Computer and electronic products 17.6%
- Machinery, except electrical 15.8%
- Miscellaneous manufactured commodities 10.0%
- Transportation equipment 10.0%
- All others 46.5%

MISSISSIPPI

Facts and Figures

Location: South central United States; bordered on the N by Tennessee, on the E by Alabama, on the S by Louisiana and the Gulf of Mexico, and on the W by Arkansas and Louisiana

Area: 48,430 sq. mi. (125,434 sq. km.); rank—32nd

Population: 2,984,100 (2017 est.); rank—34th

Principal Cities: capital—Jackson; largest—Jackson

Statehood: December 10, 1817; 20th state

U.S. Congress: 2 senators, 4 representatives

State Motto: *Virtute et armis* ("By valor and arms")

State Song: "Go, Mississippi"

State Nicknames: The Magnolia State; The Hospitality State

Abbreviations: MS; Miss.

State Symbols: flower—magnolia blossom; tree—Southern magnolia; bird—mockingbird

At a Glance

- With an increase in population of 0.5 percent, Mississippi ranked 47th among the states in growth from 2010 to 2017.

- In 2015, Mississippi had the lowest median household income in the country ($41,754) and the highest percent of population living the below the poverty level (20.8 percent).

- In 2016, 11.8 percent of Mississippians did not have health insurance, compared to 8.6 percent of the total U.S. population.

- Mississippi had the 4th highest traffic fatality rate in 2016, with 1.63 deaths per 100 million vehicle miles.

- In 2016, 21.8 percent of Mississippians had a bachelor's degree or higher, which was the 2nd lowest percentage among states.

Table MS-1. Population by Age, Sex, Race, and Hispanic Origin

(Number, percent, except where noted.)

Sex, age, race, and Hispanic origin	2000	2010	2017 [1]	Average annual percent change, 2010–2017
Total Population.....................................	2,844,658	2,967,297	2,984,100	0.6
Percent of total U.S. population	1.0	1.0	0.9	X
Sex				
Male..	1,373,554	1,441,240	1,445,878	0.3
Female...	1,471,104	1,526,057	1,538,222	0.8
Age				
Under 5 years...	204,364	210,956	187,177	-11.3
5 to 19 years..	668,850	638,539	609,380	-4.6
20 to 64 years...	1,627,921	1,737,395	1,726,024	-0.7
65 years and over....................................	343,523	380,407	461,519	21.3
Median age (years)...................................	33.8	36.0	37.4	3.9
Race and Hispanic Origin				
One race				
White	1,746,099	1,789,391	1,766,950	-1.3
Black...	1,033,809	1,103,101	1,126,498	2.1
American Indian and Alaska Native	11,652	16,837	18,179	8.0
Asian...	18,626	26,477	32,515	22.8
Native Hawaiian or Other Pacific Islander	667	1,700	1,787	5.1
Two or more races.......................................	20,021	29,791	38,171	28.1
Hispanic (of any race)...................................	39,569	85,107	94,385	10.9

X = Not applicable.
- = Zero or rounds to zero.
[1] Population figures for 2017 are July 1 estimates. The 2010 estimates are taken from the 2010 Census.

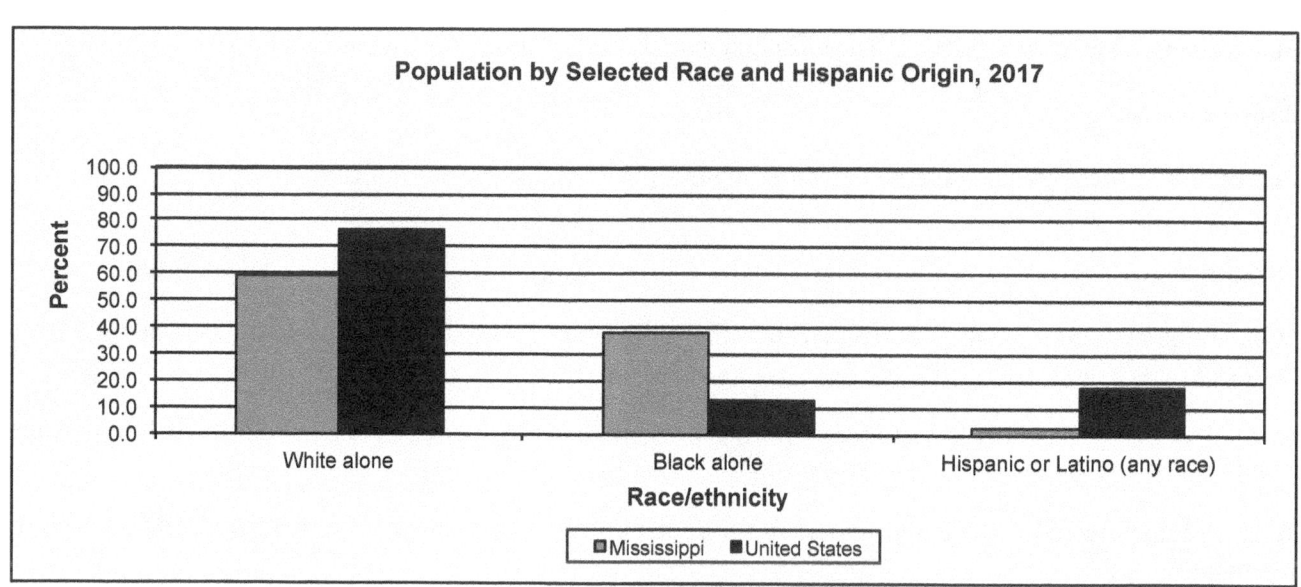

Population by Selected Race and Hispanic Origin, 2017

Table MS-2. Marital Status

(Number, percent distribution.)

Sex, age, and marital status	2000	2010	2016
Males, 15 Years and Over	1,046,252	1,121,265	1,137,123
Never married	30.6	34.9	36.9
Now married, except separated...........................	54.6	48.3	46.7
Separated...	2.4	2.5	2.6
Widowed..	2.9	2.7	3.1
Divorced..	9.5	11.7	10.7
Females, 15 Years and Over	1,157,363	1,224,423	1,251,035
Never married	25.1	29.8	31.7
Now married, except separated...........................	48.6	43.8	42.0
Separated...	3.2	3.4	3.3
Widowed..	12.5	10.8	10.8
Divorced..	10.6	12.3	12.1

Table MS-3. Households and Housing Characteristics

(Number, percent, dollars.)

Item	2000	2010	2016	Average annual percent change, 2010–2016
Total Households..	1,046,434	1,079,999	1,091,245	0.2
Family households..	747,159	746,115	730,719	-0.3
Married-couple family.................................	520,884	501,571	489,734	-0.4
Other family...	226,315	244,544	240,985	-0.2
Male householder, no wife present............	45,610	51,400	47,385	-1.3
Female householder, no husband present....	180,705	193,144	193,600	-
Nonfamily households	299,275	333,884	360,526	1.3
Householder living alone............................	257,708	293,185	314,455	1.2
Householder not living alone.......................	41,567	40,699	46,071	2.2
Housing Characteristics				
Total housing units..	1,161,953	1,276,441	1,307,492	0.4
Occupied housing units	1,046,434	1,079,999	1,091,245	0.2
Owner occupied	756,967	753,374	734,114	-0.4
Renter occupied	289,467	326,625	357,131	1.6
Average household size..................................	2.63	2.66	2.65	-0.1
Financial Characteristics				
Median gross rent of renter-occupied housing	439	672	728	1.4
Median monthly owner costs for housing units with a mortgage	762	1,043	1,087	0.7
Median value of owner-occupied housing units........	71,400	100,100	113,900	2.3

- = Zero or rounds to zero.

Table MS-4. Migration, Origin, and Language

(Number, percent.)

Characteristic	State			U.S.		
	2015	2016	Percent change	2015	2016	Percent change
Residence 1 Year Ago						
Population 1 year and over	2,959,289	2,951,081	-0.3	317,635,720	319,361,956	0.5
Same house..	86.3	86.6	X	85.3	85.4	X
Different house in the U.S.	13.4	13.2	X	14.1	13.9	X
Same county..	7.6	7.6	X	8.5	8.3	X
Different county	5.8	5.6	X	5.6	5.6	X
Same state	3.5	3.4	X	3.2	3.2	X
Different state	2.3	2.2	X	2.4	2.4	X
Abroad..	0.3	0.2	X	0.7	0.7	X
Place of Birth						
Native born	2,920,075	2,929,960	0.3	278,128,449	279,388,170	0.5
Male	48.3	48.2	X	49.3	49.3	X
Female	51.7	51.8	X	50.7	50.7	X
Foreign born	72,258	58,766	-18.7	43,290,372	43,739,345	1.0
Male	53.7	49.0	X	48.6	48.5	X
Female	46.3	51.0	X	51.4	51.5	X
Foreign born; naturalized U.S. citizen.............	24,140	23,466	-2.8	20,697,103	21,238,372	2.6
Male	46.7	45.1	X	45.9	45.9	X
Female	53.3	54.9	X	54.1	54.1	X
Foreign born; not a U.S. citizen.....................	48,118	35,300	-26.6	22,593,269	22,500,973	-0.4
Male	57.3	51.6	X	51.1	51.0	X
Female	42.7	48.4	X	48.9	49.0	X
Entered 2010 or later	21.8	22.4	X	15.6	18.6	X
Entered 2000 to 2009	37.9	30.4	X	27.9	26.7	X
Entered before 2000..................................	40.3	47.2	X	56.5	54.7	X
World Region of Birth, Foreign						
Foreign-born population, excluding population born at sea	72,258	58,766	-18.7	43,289,646	43,738,901	1.0
Europe	11.0	8.9	X	11.1	10.9	X
Asia...	28.7	34.2	X	30.6	30.8	X
Africa	6.0	5.4	X	4.8	4.9	X
Oceania	0.7	0.5	X	0.6	0.6	X
Latin America	51.5	47.9	X	51.1	51.0	X
North America	2.2	3.1	X	1.9	1.8	X
Language Spoken at Home and Ability to Speak English						
Population 5 years and over............................	2,803,484	2,801,896	-0.1	301,625,014	303,328,961	0.6
English only	96.1	96.2	X	78.5	78.4	X
Language other than English.........................	3.9	3.8	X	21.5	21.6	X
Speaks English less than "very well"...........	1.7	1.4	X	8.6	8.6	X

NA = Not available.
X = Not applicable.
- = Zero or rounds to zero.

Table MS-5. Median Income and Poverty Status, 2016

(Number, percent, except as noted.)

Characteristic	State		U.S.	
	Number	Percent	Number	Percent
Median Income				
Households (dollars)	41,754	X	57,617	X
Families (dollars)	52,672	X	71,062	X
Below Poverty Level (All People)	602,768	20.8	44,268,996	14.0
Sex				
Male	257,714	18.7	19,760,056	12.8
Female	345,054	22.8	24,508,940	15.2
Age				
Under 18 years	211,466	29.7	14,115,713	19.5
Related children under 18 years	208,699	29.4	13,805,435	19.1
18 to 64 years	337,697	19.4	25,723,818	13.2
65 years and over	53,605	12.3	4,429,465	9.2

X = Not applicable.

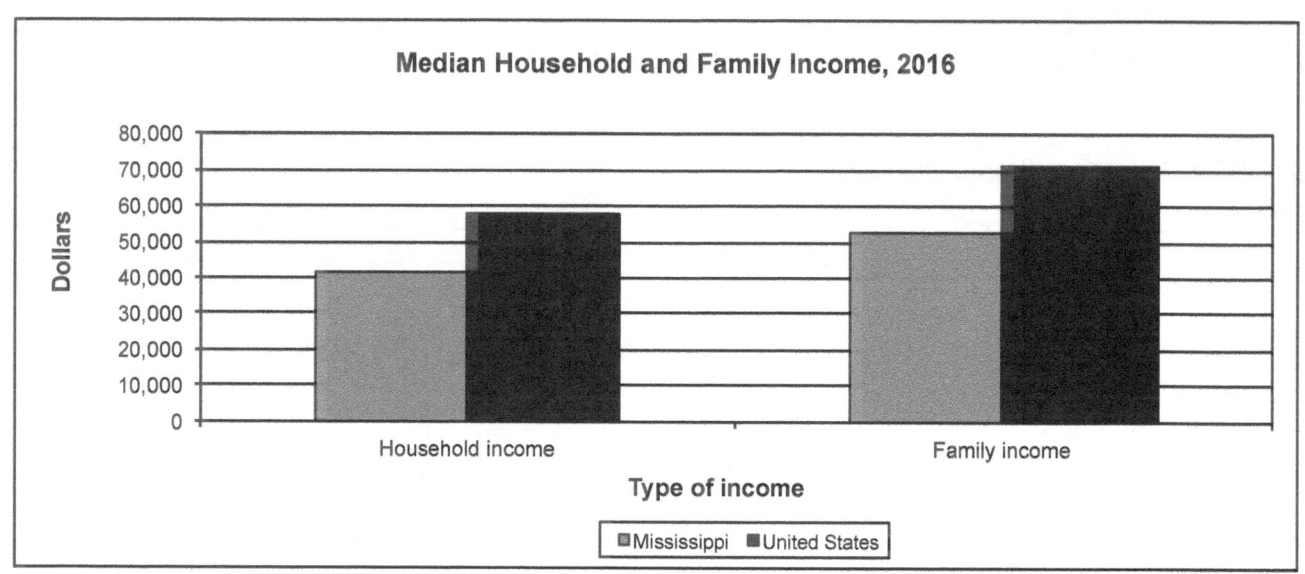

Median Household and Family Income, 2016

Table MS-6. Health Insurance Coverage Status for the Civilian Noninstitutionalized Population and Children Under 18 Years of Age

(Number, percent.)

Item	2008	2009	2010	2011	2012	2013	2014	2015	2016
Civilian Noninstitutionalized Population	2,867,519	2,879,805	2,902,907	2,911,811	2,918,405	2,925,211	2,927,088	2,927,568	2,924,168
Covered by Private or Public Insurance									
Number	2,355,256	2,365,681	2,374,812	2,395,398	2,420,895	2,425,362	2,502,958	2,555,983	2,577,987
Percent	82.1	82.1	81.8	82.3	83.0	82.9	85.5	87.3	88.2
Not Covered									
Number	512,263	514,124	528,095	516,413	497,510	499,849	424,130	371,585	346,181
Percent	17.9	17.9	18.2	17.7	17.0	17.1	14.5	12.7	11.8
Percent in the U.S. not covered	15.1	15.1	15.5	15.1	14.8	14.5	11.7	9.4	8.6
Children Under 18 Years of Age	762,887	764,182	751,985	749,572	745,603	734,075	729,802	725,664	721,108
Covered by Private or Public Insurance									
Number	666,219	685,673	688,483	688,589	690,862	677,926	690,970	696,297	688,518
Percent	87.3	89.7	91.6	91.9	92.7	92.4	94.7	96.0	95.5
Not Covered									
Number	96,668	78,509	63,502	60,983	54,741	56,149	38,832	29,367	32,590
Percent	12.7	10.3	8.4	8.1	7.3	7.6	5.3	4.0	4.5
Percent in the U.S. not covered	9.9	8.6	8.0	7.5	7.2	7.1	6.0	4.8	4.5

Table MS-7. Employment Status by Demographic Group, 2017

(Numbers in thousands, percent.)

Characteristic	Civilian noninstitutional population	Civilian labor force		Employed		Unemployed	
		Number	Percent of population	Number	Percent of population	Number	Percent of population
Total....................................	2,293	1,281	55.9	1,215	53.0	66	5.1
Sex							
Male....................................	1,078	658	61.0	624	57.9	34	5.1
Female.................................	1,215	623	51.3	591	48.6	32	5.1
Race, Sex, and Hispanic Origin							
White....................................	1,401	778	55.5	749	53.5	29	3.7
Male....................................	678	428	63.1	412	60.7	16	3.8
Female.................................	723	350	48.4	338	46.7	13	3.6
Black or African American...............	831	469	56.5	435	52.3	34	7.3
Male....................................	371	212	57.3	196	52.8	17	7.8
Female.................................	460	257	55.8	239	51.9	18	6.9
Hispanic or Latino ethnicity[1].........	53	34	64.7	33	61.9	1	4.2
Male....................................	NA	NA	NA	NA	NA	NA	NA
Female.................................	NA	NA	NA	NA	NA	NA	NA
Age							
16 to 19 years..........................	173	44	25.6	34	19.6	10	23.3
20 to 24 years..........................	183	123	67.1	111	60.8	11	9.2
25 to 34 years..........................	364	283	77.7	265	72.8	18	6.3
35 to 44 years..........................	375	302	80.4	290	77.4	11	3.7
45 to 54 years..........................	358	262	73.2	253	70.6	10	3.6
55 to 64 years..........................	391	210	53.8	207	52.9	4	1.9
65 years and over.......................	449	57	12.7	55	12.3	2	2.6

NOTE: Data in Table 7 are from the Current Population Survey (CPS) and do not match the estimates in Table 8. See notes and definitions for further information.
[1] May be of any race.
NA = Not available.

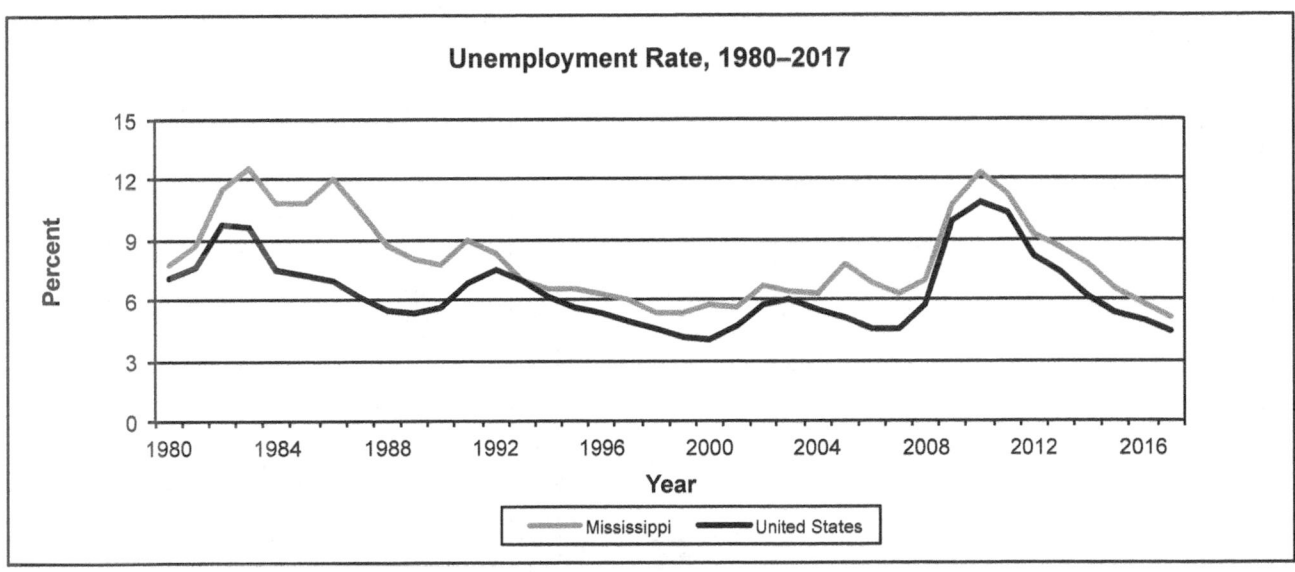

Unemployment Rate, 1980–2017

Table MS-8. Employment Status of the Civilian Noninstitutional Population Age 16 Years and Over

(Number, percent.)

Year	Civilian labor force	Civilian participation rate	Employed	Unemployed	Unemployment rate
2009....................................	1,269,219	57.7	1,148,930	120,289	9.5
2010....................................	1,306,608	58.6	1,170,879	135,729	10.4
2011....................................	1,342,808	59.8	1,208,747	134,061	10.0
2012....................................	1,316,536	58.4	1,198,196	118,340	9.0
2013....................................	1,272,477	56.2	1,163,752	108,725	8.5
2014....................................	1,248,014	55.0	1,154,058	93,956	7.5
2015....................................	1,263,925	55.5	1,182,779	81,146	6.4
2016....................................	1,278,960	56.0	1,204,481	74,479	5.8
2017....................................	1,280,071	55.9	1,215,115	64,956	5.1

Table MS-9. Employment and Average Wages by Industry

(Estimates through 2010 are based on the 2007 *North American Industry Classification System* [NAICS]. Estimates from 2011 onward are based on the 2012 NAICS.)

Industry	2010	2011	2012	2013	2014	2015	2016
	Number of jobs						
Wage and Salary Employment by Industry	1,167,548	1,167,750	1,175,222	1,179,604	1,194,267	1,202,838	1,211,218
Farm Wage and Salary Employment	9,928	9,232	8,188	6,950	12,119	9,375	8,367
Nonfarm Wage and Salary Employment	1,157,620	1,158,518	1,167,034	1,172,654	1,182,148	1,193,463	1,202,851
Private wage and salary employment	875,525	879,098	887,597	895,874	906,773	918,974	928,837
Forestry, fishing, and related activities	7,876	7,713	7,678	7,846	7,902	7,897	8,127
Mining	5,694	6,131	6,316	6,174	6,248	5,038	3,839
Utilities	7,731	7,732	7,727	7,870	7,826	7,876	7,946
Construction	51,418	50,376	49,784	52,723	50,467	47,269	45,701
Manufacturing	136,124	135,464	137,136	136,974	139,687	141,823	143,298
Durable goods manufacturing	87,349	88,072	90,805	90,645	93,613	94,674	94,976
Nondurable goods manufacturing	48,775	47,392	46,331	46,329	46,074	47,149	48,322
Wholesale trade	34,389	34,455	34,377	34,284	34,235	34,672	34,468
Retail trade	133,467	134,290	134,635	134,549	136,797	139,188	141,754
Transportation and warehousing	39,098	39,862	40,163	41,039	42,657	44,770	46,982
Information	12,296	11,901	12,586	12,806	13,247	13,620	12,188
Finance and insurance	33,883	34,062	34,154	33,497	33,171	33,203	33,421
Real estate and rental and leasing	11,678	11,650	11,703	11,754	11,756	11,775	11,802
Professional, scientific, and technical services	31,911	31,934	31,488	30,883	31,240	31,043	31,005
Management of companies and enterprises	9,752	10,141	10,222	10,777	10,660	10,616	11,056
Administrative and waste services	51,166	52,650	55,598	57,935	60,441	63,845	66,586
Educational services	19,703	19,407	19,893	19,830	19,613	19,963	19,323
Health care and social assistance	120,803	121,991	122,856	123,697	124,974	127,627	129,765
Arts, entertainment, and recreation	12,119	10,897	11,271	11,593	11,325	11,422	11,619
Accommodation and food services	106,890	109,049	111,098	113,104	115,255	118,389	122,168
Other services, except public administration	49,527	49,393	48,912	48,539	49,272	48,938	47,789
Government and government enterprises	282,095	279,420	279,437	276,780	275,375	274,489	274,014
	Dollars						
Average Wages and Salaries by Industry	35,263	35,917	36,920	37,469	38,005	38,603	39,511
Average Farm Wages and Salaries	18,508	17,142	29,392	25,584	21,320	24,826	21,904
Average Nonfarm Wages and Salaries	35,407	36,067	36,973	37,540	38,176	38,711	39,633
Average private wages and salaries	34,729	35,553	36,667	37,287	37,946	38,410	39,218
Forestry, fishing, and related activities	29,873	30,641	31,621	32,620	33,845	35,499	35,839
Mining	65,836	69,826	75,055	75,775	78,680	79,157	80,020
Utilities	67,401	68,280	71,131	71,800	73,995	77,878	80,862
Construction	41,481	42,488	44,732	46,679	47,282	47,217	47,402
Manufacturing	42,258	43,689	45,037	45,853	47,600	48,300	49,703
Durable goods manufacturing	43,860	45,283	46,421	47,294	49,031	49,457	51,154
Nondurable goods manufacturing	39,390	40,728	42,323	43,033	44,691	45,978	46,850
Wholesale trade	48,932	50,419	52,042	53,074	54,613	56,276	59,160
Retail trade	23,700	24,019	24,676	25,035	25,351	25,871	26,190
Transportation and warehousing	40,811	41,670	43,359	43,708	44,504	45,553	46,739
Information	42,223	44,087	44,872	46,409	47,721	46,125	46,095
Finance and insurance	48,982	50,212	52,499	54,720	55,841	57,558	59,462
Real estate and rental and leasing	30,787	31,879	33,464	33,496	34,834	35,646	36,633
Professional, scientific, and technical services	52,189	53,082	54,815	55,788	55,949	57,897	59,768
Management of companies and enterprises	73,202	77,953	81,444	80,302	82,949	84,821	84,294
Administrative and waste services	25,805	25,556	26,400	27,643	27,764	27,900	27,082
Educational services	24,899	26,663	27,719	28,519	28,832	27,554	29,087
Health care and social assistance	38,852	39,724	40,719	40,626	40,999	41,683	43,355
Arts, entertainment, and recreation	24,653	24,216	23,884	23,866	23,609	24,253	18,564
Accommodation and food services	18,042	18,409	18,615	18,774	18,926	19,016	20,067
Other services, except public administration	26,222	26,465	27,730	28,645	29,568	30,558	31,900
Government and government enterprises	37,512	37,683	37,943	38,358	38,933	39,720	41,043

Table MS-10. Employment Characteristics by Family Type

(Number, percent.)

Family type and labor force status	2014		2015		2016	
	Total	Families with own children under 18 years	Total	Families with own children under 18 years	Total	Families with own children under 18 years
All Families..	736,864	305,343	743,154	308,522	730,719	297,034
FAMILY TYPE AND LABOR FORCE STATUS						
Married-Couple Families.............................	480,622	173,656	485,198	175,460	489,734	175,322
Both husband and wife in labor force.................	48.6	67.6	47.3	67.5	48.2	67.9
Husband in labor force, wife not in labor force...........	21.8	24.9	21.4	24.0	22.1	25.0
Wife in labor force, husband not in labor force...........	9.1	4.4	9.4	5.4	8.8	4.7
Both husband and wife not in labor force...............	20.5	3.1	21.6	3.0	20.5	2.2
Other Families	256,242	131,687	257,956	133,062	240,985	121,712
Female householder, no husband present............	78.3	79.4	78.1	80.1	80.3	83.1
In labor force......................................	49.7	63.7	50.3	63.9	51.1	68.3
Not in labor force	28.6	15.7	27.8	16.2	29.2	14.8
Male householder, no wife present...................	21.7	20.6	21.9	19.9	19.7	16.9
In labor force......................................	16.0	18.3	15.7	17.8	13.8	14.6
Not in labor force	5.7	2.3	6.2	2.1	5.8	2.3

Table MS-11. School Enrollment and Educational Attainment, 2016

(Number, percent.)

Item	State	U.S.
Enrollment		
Total population 3 years and over, enrolled in school	781,666	81,572,277
Enrolled in nursery school or preschool (percent)	5.8	6.0
Enrolled in kindergarten (percent)	5.6	5.0
Enrolled in elementary school, grades 1-8 (percent)...	42.8	40.3
Enrolled in high school, grades 9-12 (percent)...	21.3	21.0
Enrolled in college or graduate school (percent)...	24.5	27.7
Attainment		
Total population 25 years and over	1,957,022	218,475,480
Less than ninth grade (percent)	4.8	5.4
9th to 12th grade, no diploma (percent)	11.0	7.2
High school graduate, including equivalency (percent)..	30.8	27.2
Some college, no degree (percent)	22.4	20.6
Associate's degree (percent)..	9.1	8.4
Bachelor's degree (percent)..	13.5	19.3
Graduate or professional degree (percent)...	8.2	11.9
High school graduate or higher (percent)	84.1	87.5
Bachelor's degree or higher (percent)...	21.8	31.3

Table MS-12. Public School Characteristics and Educational Indicators

(Number, percent; data derived from National Center of Education Statistics.)

Item	State	U.S.
Public Schools, 2015–2016 (except where noted)		
Number of school districts...	157	18,328
Number of schools..	1,076	98,456
Number of students...	487,200	50,327,015
Number of teachers	32,175	3,151,497
Student-teacher ratio	15.1	16.0
Expenditures per student (dollars), 2014-2015...	8,445	11,445
Four-year adjusted cohort graduation rate (ACGR)[1,2]	82.3	84.1
Students eligible for free or reduced-price lunch (percent), 2014-2015..........................	73.7	51.8
English language learners (percent), Fall 2015	2.0	9.5
Students age 3 to 21 served under IDEA, part B (percent).......................................	13.7	13.2

Public Schools by Type	Number	Percent of state public schools
Total number of schools..	1,076	100.0
Regular	915	85.0
Special education	2	0.2
Vocational education	91	8.5
Alternative education...	68	6.3

NOTE: Every school is assigned only one school type based on its instructional emphasis.
[1] ACGR data represents a new method of calculating high-school completion rates and may not be comparable to previous years' data for Averaged Freshmen Graduation Rates (AFGR).
[2] The United States 4-year ACGRs were estimated using both the reported 4-year ACGR data from 49 states and the District of Columbia and using imputed data for Idaho. The estimate for American Indian/Alaska Native students also includes imputed data for Virginia.

Table MS-13. Reported Voting and Registration of the Voting-Age Population, November 2016

(Numbers in thousands, percent.)

Item	Total population	Total citizen population	Registered			Voted		
			Total registered	Percent registered (total population)	Percent registered (total citizen population)	Total voted	Percent voted (total population)	Percent voted (total citizen population)
U.S. Total	245,502	224,059	157,596	64.2	70.3	137,537	56.0	61.4
State Total.............................	2,203	2,170	1,725	78.3	. 79.5	1,470	66.7	67.7
Sex								
Male	1,026	1,010	780	76.0	77.2	657	64.0	65.0
Female	1,177	1,160	945	80.3	81.5	813	69.1	70.1
Race								
White alone..............................	1,377	1,355	1,070	77.7	79.0	918	66.7	67.8
White, non-Hispanic alone	1,345	1,339	1,056	78.5	78.8	907	67.4	67.7
Black alone	782	777	632	80.9	81.4	537	68.7	69.1
Asian alone	18	13	8	(B)	(B)	6	(B)	(B)
Hispanic (of any race)...................	41	23	18	(B)	(B)	15	(B)	(B)
White alone or in combination	1,394	1,371	1,081	77.6	78.9	923	66.2	67.3
Black alone or in combination............	791	786	639	80.8	81.3	544	68.8	69.2
Asian alone or in combination...........	22	18	10	(B)	(B)	6	(B)	(B)
Age								
18 to 24 years..........................	283	279	170	60.0	60.9	130	46.1	46.7
25 to 34 years..........................	356	345	262	73.7	76.1	203	57.0	58.9
35 to 44 years..........................	368	358	278	75.4	77.6	245	66.5	68.4
45 to 64 years..........................	763	758	635	83.1	83.8	557	72.9	73.5
65 years and over	433	431	380	87.9	88.4	335	77.3	77.7

B = Base is less than 75,000 and therefore too small to show the derived measure.

Table MS-14. Crime

(Number, rate per 100,000. Data are derived from the FBI Uniform Crime Reports.)

Item	State			U.S. [1,2,3,4]		
	2015	2016	Percent change	2015	2016	Percent change
TOTAL POPULATION [5]	2,992,333	2,988,726	-0.1	321,418,820	323,127,513	0.5
VIOLENT CRIME						
Number..	8,254	8,383	1.6	1,231,566	1,248,185	1.3
Rate..	275.8	280.5	1.7	383.2	386.3	0.8
Murder and Nonnegligent Manslaughter						
Number..	259	238	-8.1	15,696	17,250	9.9
Rate..	8.7	8.0	-8.0	4.9	5.3	8.2
Rape[6]						
Number..	1,203	1,277	6.2	124,047	130,603	5.3
Rate..	40.2	42.7	6.2	38.6	40.4	4.7
Robbery						
Number..	2,294	2,397	4.5	327,374	332,198	1.5
Rate..	76.7	80.2	4.6	101.9	102.8	0.9
Aggravated Assault						
Number..	4,498	4,471	-0.6	764,449	803,007	5.0
Rate..	150.3	149.6	-0.5	237.8	248.5	4.5
PROPERTY CRIME						
Number..	84,790	82,732	-2.4	7,993,631	7,919,035	-0.9
Rate..	2,833.6	2,768.1	-2.3	2,487.0	2,450.7	-1.5
Burglary						
Number..	24,799	23,354	-5.8	1,579,527	1,515,096	-4.1
Rate..	828.8	781.4	-5.7	491.4	468.9	-4.6
Larceny-Theft						
Number..	55,748	55,054	-1.2	5,706,346	5,638,455	-1.2
Rate..	1,863.0	1,842.1	-1.1	1,775.4	1,745.0	-1.7
Motor Vehicle Theft						
Number..	4,243	4,324	1.9	707,758	765,484	8.2
Rate..	141.8	144.7	2.0	220.2	236.9	7.6

NOTE: Although arson data are included in the trend and clearance tables, sufficient data are not available to estimate totals for this offense. Therefore, no arson data are published in this table.
X = Not applicable.
- = Zero or rounds to zero.
[1] The crime figures have been adjusted.
[2] The data collection methodology for the offense of forcible rape used by the Minnesota state Uniform Crime Reporting (UCR) Program (with the exception of Minneapolis and St. Paul, Minnesota) does not comply with national UCR Program guidelines. Consequently, its figures for forcible rape and violent crime (of which forcible rape is a part) are not published in this table.
[3] Includes offenses reported by the Zoological Police and the Metro Transit Police.
[4] Because of changes in the state's reporting practices, figures are not comparable to previous years' data.
[5] Populations are U.S. Census Bureau provisional estimates as of July 1 of each year.
[6] The figures shown for the offense of rape were estimated using the revised Uniform Crime Reporting (UCR) definition of rape.

Table MS-15. State Government Finances, 2016

(Dollar amounts in thousands, percent distribution.)

Item	Dollars	Percent distribution
Total Revenue	20,880,790	100.0
General revenue	18,953,934	90.8
Intergovernmental revenue	8,299,349	39.7
Taxes	7,660,391	36.7
General sales	3,297,760	15.8
Selective sales	1,480,034	7.1
License taxes	553,510	2.7
Individual income tax	1,800,053	8.6
Corporate income tax	463,111	2.2
Other taxes	65,923	0.3
Current charges	2,296,501	11.0
Miscellaneous general revenue	697,693	3.3
Utility revenue	0	-
Liquor stores revenue	337,971	1.6
Insurance trust revenue [1]	1,588,885	7.6
Total Expenditure	22,247,200	100.0
Intergovernmental expenditure	5,251,972	23.6
Direct expenditure	16,995,228	76.4
Current operation	12,553,665	56.4
Capital outlay	1,170,296	5.3
Insurance benefits and repayments	2,645,918	11.9
Assistance and subsidies	362,632	1.6
Interest on debt	262,717	1.2
Exhibit: Salaries and wages	2,599,943	11.7
Total Expenditure	22,247,200	100.0
General expenditure	19,322,070	86.9
Intergovernmental expenditure	5,251,972	23.6
Direct expenditure	14,070,098	63.2
General expenditure, by function:		
Education	6,515,704	29.3
Public welfare	6,633,077	29.8
Hospitals	1,469,107	6.6
Health	422,536	1.9
Highways	1,336,544	6.0
Police protection	138,506	0.6
Correction	336,391	1.5
Natural resources	258,672	1.2
Parks and recreation	46,045	0.2
Governmental administration	388,402	1.7
Interest on general debt	262,717	1.2
Other and unallocable	1,514,369	6.8
Utility expenditure	0	-
Liquor stores expenditure	279,212	1.3
Insurance trust expenditure	2,645,918	11.9
Debt at End of Fiscal Year	7,283,371	X
Cash and Security Holdings	32,634,787	X

X = Not applicable.
 = Zero or rounds to zero.
[1] Within insurance trust revenue, net earnings of state retirement systems is a calculated statistic (the item code in the data file is X08), and thus can be positive or negative. Net earnings is the sum of earnings on investments plus gains on investments minus losses on investments. The change made in 2002 for asset valuation from book to market value in accordance with Statement 34 of the Governmental Accounting Standards Board is reflected in the calculated statistics.

Table MS-16. State Government Tax Collections, 2017

(Dollars in thousands, percent.)

Item	Dollars	Percent distribution
Total Taxes	7,783,031	100.0
Property taxes	28,589	0.4
Sales and gross receipts	4,988,338	64.1
General sales and gross receipts	3,526,913	45.3
Selective sales and gross receipts	1,461,425	18.8
Alcoholic beverages	41,835	0.5
Amusements	132,778	1.7
Insurance premiums	327,778	4.2
Motor fuels	443,522	5.7
Pari-mutuels	X	-
Public utilities	1,490	-
Tobacco products	145,059	1.9
Other selective sales	368,963	4.7
Licenses	480,741	6.2
Alcoholic beverages	1,243	-
Amusements	26,664	0.3
Corporations in general	127,445	1.6
Hunting and fishing	2,562	-
Motor vehicle	157,290	2.0
Motor vehicle operators	13,267	0.2
Public utilities	6,549	0.1
Occupation and business, NEC	76,882	1.0
Other licenses	68,839	0.9
Income taxes	2,242,601	28.8
Individual income	1,834,688	23.6
Corporation net income	407,913	5.2
Other taxes	42,762	0.5
Death and gift	4	-
Documentary and stock transfer	X	-
Severance	42,758	0.5
Taxes, NEC	0	-

- = Zero or rounds to zero.
X = Not applicable.

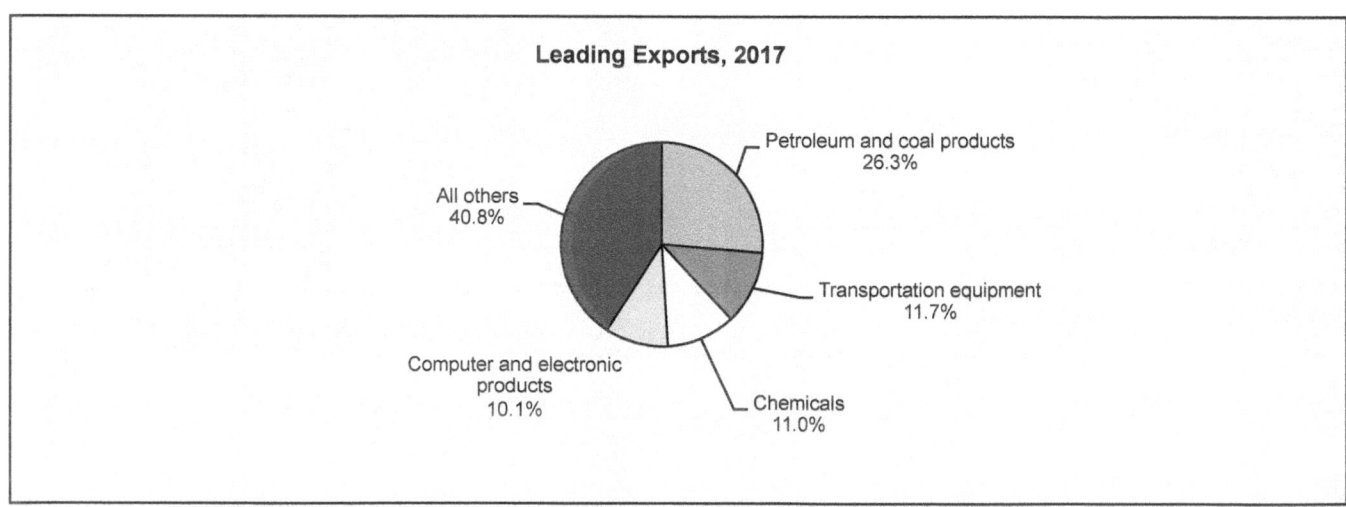

Leading Exports, 2017

Petroleum and coal products 26.3%

Transportation equipment 11.7%

Chemicals 11.0%

Computer and electronic products 10.1%

All others 40.8%

Facts and Figures

Location: Central United States; bordered on the N by Iowa, on the E by Illinois, Kentucky, and Tennessee, on the S by Arkansas, and on the W by Oklahoma, Kansas, and Nebraska

Area: 69,704 sq. mi. (180,533 sq. km.); rank—21st

Population: 6,113,532 (2017 est.); rank—18th

Principal Cities: capital—Jefferson City; largest—Kansas City

Statehood: August 10, 1821; 24th state

U.S. Congress: 2 senators, 8 representatives

State Motto: *Salus populi suprema lex esto* ("The welfare of the people shall be the supreme law")

State Song: "Missouri Waltz"

State Nickname: The Show Me State

Abbreviations: MO; Mo

State Symbols: flower—hawthorn; tree—flowering dogwood; bird—Eastern bluebird

At a Glance

- With an increase in population of 2.0 percent, Missouri ranked 36th among the states in growth from 2010 to 2017.

- In 2016, 8.9 percent of Missourians did not have health insurance, which was slightly above the national average of 8.6 percent.

- Missouri's violent crime rate was 519.4 per 100,000 population in 2016, compared to the U.S. rate of 386.3 per 100,000 population.

- Missouri's median household income of $51,746 ranked 38th in the country in 2016.

- In Missouri in 2016, 14.0 percent of residents lived below the poverty level, which was the same as the national average; 19.2 percent of Missouri children lived in poverty, which was slightly lower than the national average of 19.5 percent.

Table MO-1. Population by Age, Sex, Race, and Hispanic Origin

(Number, percent, except where noted.)

Sex, age, race, and Hispanic origin	2000	2010	2017 [1]	Average annual percent change, 2010–2017
Total Population...	5,595,211	5,988,927	6,113,532	2.1
Percent of total U.S. population	2.0	1.9	1.9	X
Sex				
Male...	2,720,177	2,933,477	3,002,236	2.3
Female...	2,875,034	3,055,450	3,111,296	1.8
Age				
Under 5 years...	269,898	390,237	374,479	-4.0
5 to 19 years...	1,224,274	1,211,174	1,165,027	-3.8
20 to 64 years...	3,245,660	3,549,222	3,566,993	0.5
65 years and over...	755,379	838,294	1,007,033	20.1
Median age (years)...	36.1	37.9	38.6	1.8
Race and Hispanic Origin				
One race				
White...	4,748,083	5,038,407	5,080,444	0.8
Black...	629,391	700,178	723,029	3.3
American Indian and Alaska Native	25,076	30,595	34,635	13.2
Asian...	61,595	100,213	126,443	26.2
Native Hawaiian or Other Pacific Islander	3,178	7,178	9,122	27.1
Two or more races...	82,061	112,356	139,859	24.5
Hispanic (of any race)...	118,592	223,421	259,154	16.0

X = Not applicable.
[1] Population figures for 2017 are July 1 estimates. The 2010 estimates are taken from the 2010 Census.
- = Zero or rounds to zero.

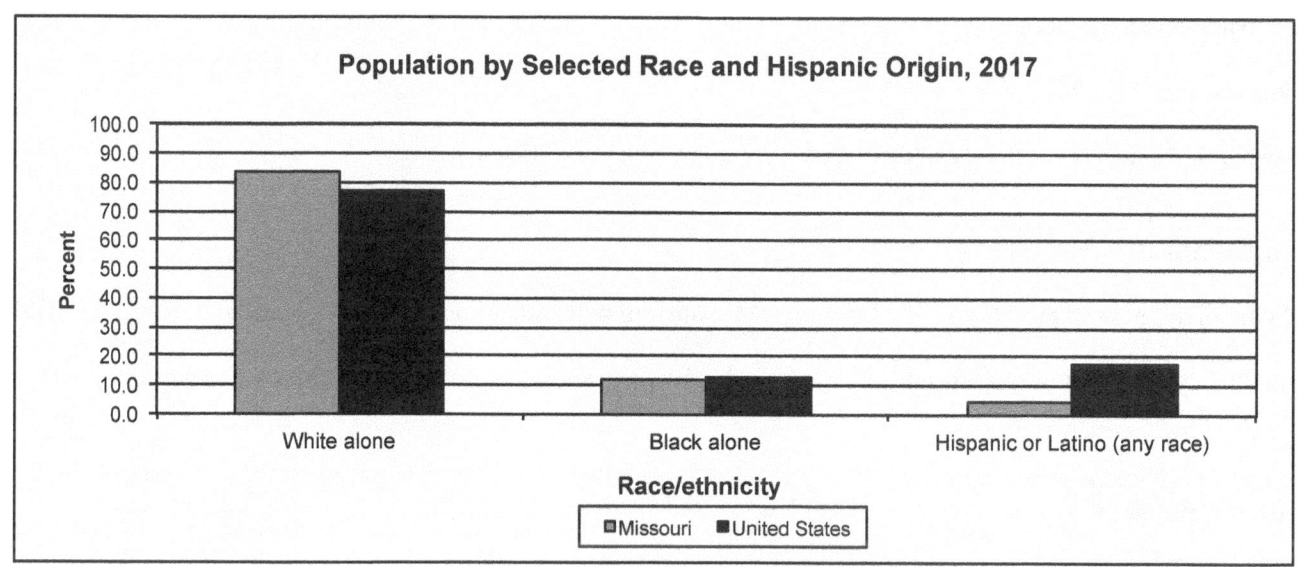

Table MO-2. Marital Status

(Number, percent distribution.)

Sex, age, and marital status	2000	2010	2016
Males, 15 Years and Over	2,114,280	2,332,888	2,402,847
Never married	27.8	32.1	34.1
Now married, except separated...	58.0	52.5	50.1
Separated...	1.6	1.7	1.6
Widowed...	2.6	2.6	3.1
Divorced...	10.0	11.0	11.1
Females, 15 Years and Over	2,300,111	2,492,198	2,540,876
Never married	22.1	26.8	27.7
Now married, except separated...	53.1	48.2	47.5
Separated...	2.0	2.2	2.0
Widowed...	11.3	10.0	9.7
Divorced...	11.5	12.8	13.1

Table MO-3. Households and Housing Characteristics

(Number, percent, dollars.)

Item	2000	2010	2016	Average annual percent change, 2010–2016
Total Households.........................	2,194,594	2,350,628	2,372,190	0.2
Family households	1,476,516	1,524,078	1,527,349	-
Married-couple family	1,140,866	1,146,501	1,139,135	-0.1
Other family	335,650	377,577	388,214	0.5
Male householder, no wife present.........	81,890	99,807	108,738	1.5
Female householder, no husband present......	253,760	277,770	279,476	0.1
Nonfamily households	718,078	826,550	844,841	0.4
Householder living alone..................	599,808	689,361	691,914	0.1
Householder not living alone..............	118,270	137,189	152,927	1.9
Housing Characteristics				
Total housing units.......................	2,442,017	2,714,017	2,760,226	0.3
Occupied housing units	2,194,594	2,350,628	2,372,190	0.2
Owner occupied	1,542,149	1,621,371	1,567,597	-0.6
Renter occupied	652,445	729,257	804,593	1.7
Average household size....................	2.48	2.48	2.49	0.1
Financial Characteristics				
Median gross rent of renter-occupied housing	484	682	771	2.2
Median monthly owner costs for housing units with a mortgage	861	1,182	1,210	0.4
Median value of owner-occupied housing units........	89,900	139,000	151,400	1.5

- = Zero or rounds to zero

Table MO-4. Migration, Origin, and Language

(Number, percent.)

Characteristic	State			U.S.		
	2015	2016	Percent change	2015	2016	Percent change
Residence 1 Year Ago						
Population 1 year and over	6,015,580	6,022,165	0.1	317,635,720	319,361,956	0.5
Same house............................	84.1	84.3	X	85.3	85.4	X
Different house in the U.S..............	15.6	15.3	X	14.1	13.9	X
Same county	8.6	8.5	X	8.5	8.3	X
Different county	7.0	6.8	X	5.6	5.6	X
Same state	4.3	4.1	X	3.2	3.2	X
Different state	2.6	2.7	X	2.4	2.4	X
Abroad................................	0.4	0.4	X	0.7	0.7	X
Place of Birth						
Native born	5,840,911	5,843,798	-	278,128,449	279,388,170	0.5
Male	49.0	49.2	X	49.3	49.3	X
Female	51.0	50.8	X	50.7	50.7	X
Foreign born	242,761	249,202	2.7	43,290,372	43,739,345	1.0
Male	49.6	49.0	X	48.6	48.5	X
Female	50.4	51.0	X	51.4	51.5	X
Foreign born; naturalized U.S. citizen....	107,781	118,808	10.2	20,697,103	21,238,372	2.6
Male	47.0	46.6	X	45.9	45.9	X
Female	53.0	53.4	X	54.1	54.1	X
Foreign born; not a U.S. citizen..........	134,980	130,394	-3.4	22,593,269	22,500,973	-0.4
Male	51.6	51.1	X	51.1	51.0	X
Female	48.4	48.9	X	48.9	49.0	X
Entered 2010 or later	23.5	23.9	X	15.6	18.6	X
Entered 2000 to 2009	31.9	30.3	X	27.9	26.7	X
Entered before 2000....................	44.6	45.7	X	56.5	54.7	X
World Region of Birth, Foreign						
Foreign-born population, excluding population born at sea	242,761	249,202	2.7	43,289,646	43,738,901	1.0
Europe	16.2	18.5	X	11.1	10.9	X
Asia...............................	39.5	39.5	X	30.6	30.8	X
Africa.............................	10.0	8.4	X	4.8	4.9	X
Oceania	0.9	1.5	X	0.6	0.6	X
Latin America......................	31.1	29.6	X	51.1	51.0	X
North America......................	2.3	2.5	X	1.9	1.8	X
Language Spoken at Home and Ability to Speak English						
Population 5 years and over.............	5,709,302	5,721,468	0.2	301,625,014	303,328,961	0.6
English only	94.0	93.7	X	78.5	78.4	X
Language other than English............	6.0	6.3	X	21.5	21.6	X
Speaks English less than "very well"......	2.1	2.2	X	8.6	8.6	X

NA = Not available.
X = Not applicable.
- = Zero or rounds to zero.

Table MO-5. Median Income and Poverty Status, 2016

(Number, percent, except as noted.)

Characteristic	State		U.S.	
	Number	Percent	Number	Percent
Median Income				
Households (dollars)..	51,746	X	57,617	X
Families (dollars)	65,058	X	71,062	X
Below Poverty Level (All People)	826,954	14.0	44,268,996	14.0
Sex				
Male	371,592	12.8	19,760,056	12.8
Female	455,362	15.1	24,508,940	15.2
Age				
Under 18 years...	261,353	19.2	14,115,713	19.5
Related children under 18 years......................................	251,783	18.6	13,805,435	19.1
18 to 64 years	488,350	13.5	25,723,818	13.2
65 years and over	77,251	8.2	4,429,465	9.2

X = Not applicable.

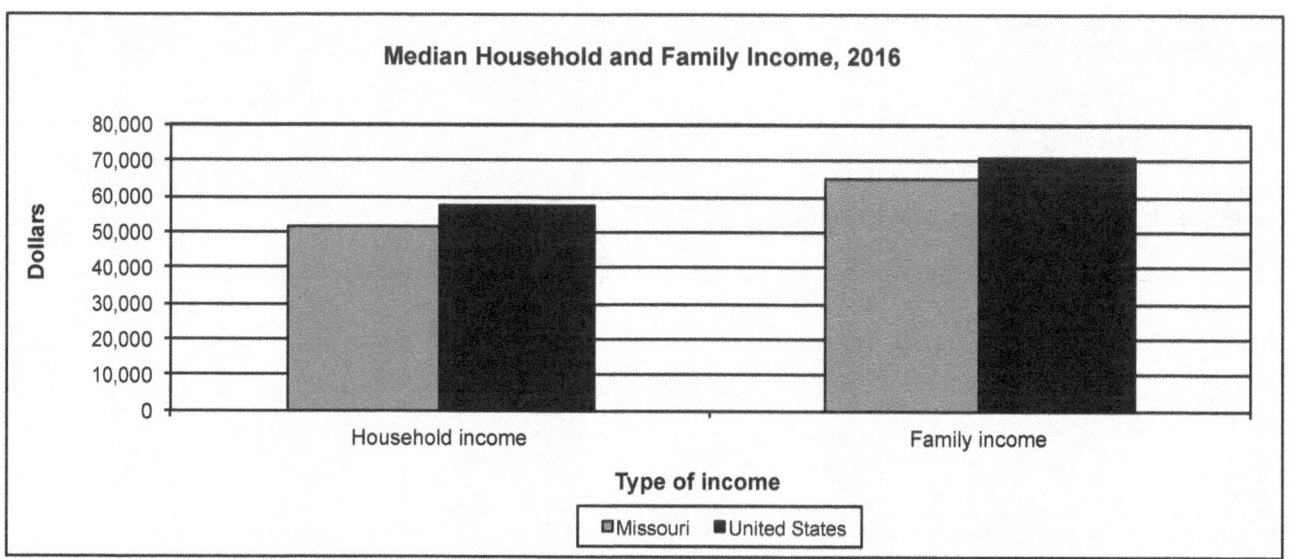

Table MO-6. Health Insurance Coverage Status for the Civilian Noninstitutionalized Population and Children Under 18 Years of Age

(Number, percent.)

Item	2008	2009	2010	2011	2012	2013	2014	2015	2016
Civilian Noninstitutionalized Population	5,795,164	5,871,474	5,879,864	5,898,968	5,908,769	5,930,677	5,950,606	5,969,392	5,977,199
Covered by Private or Public Insurance									
Number..	5,039,596	5,097,861	5,105,970	5,091,554	5,107,389	5,157,844	5,256,728	5,386,284	5,445,276
Percent..	87.0	86.8	86.8	86.3	86.4	87.0	88.3	90.2	91.1
Not Covered									
Number..	755,568	773,613	773,894	807,414	801,380	772,833	693,878	583,108	531,923
Percent..	13.0	13.2	13.2	13.7	13.6	13.0	11.7	9.8	8.9
Percent in the U.S. not covered..	15.1	15.1	15.5	15.1	14.8	14.5	11.7	9.4	8.6
Children Under 18 Years of Age	1,418,342	1,426,899	1,413,730	1,409,255	1,399,674	1,394,588	1,387,561	1,387,714	1,386,471
Covered by Private or Public Insurance									
Number..	1,317,076	1,328,434	1,325,585	1,314,321	1,301,641	1,297,042	1,287,589	1,308,016	1,324,598
Percent..	92.9	93.1	93.8	93.3	93.0	93.0	92.8	94.3	95.5
Not Covered									
Number..	101,266	98,465	88,145	94,934	98,033	97,546	99,972	79,698	61,873
Percent..	7.1	6.9	6.2	6.7	7.0	7.0	7.2	5.7	4.5
Percent in the U.S. not covered..	9.9	8.6	8.0	7.5	7.2	7.1	6.0	4.8	4.5

Table MO-7. Employment Status by Demographic Group, 2017

(Numbers in thousands, percent.)

Characteristic	Civilian noninstitutional population	Civilian labor force		Employed		Unemployed	
		Number	Percent of population	Number	Percent of population	Number	Percent of population
Total..	4,784	3,010	62.9	2,895	60.5	114	3.8
Sex							
Male..	2,309	1,557	67.4	1,489	64.5	68	4.3
Female......................................	2,475	1,453	58.7	1,406	56.8	47	3.2
Race, Sex, and Hispanic Origin							
White..	4,019	2,526	62.8	2,440	60.7	86	3.4
Male......................................	1,965	1,331	67.7	1,282	65.2	49	3.7
Female...................................	2,054	1,195	58.2	1,158	56.4	37	3.1
Black or African American...............	525	346	66.0	325	61.9	22	6.3
Male......................................	237	160	67.7	147	61.9	14	8.6
Female...................................	288	186	64.6	178	61.8	8	4.3
Hispanic or Latino ethnicity[1]...........	186	130	70.0	124	67.0	6	4.3
Male......................................	NA	NA	NA	NA	NA	NA	NA
Female...................................	NA	NA	NA	NA	NA	NA	NA
Age							
16 to 19 years............................	327	130	39.7	118	36.1	12	8.9
20 to 24 years............................	370	276	74.8	259	70.2	17	6.2
25 to 34 years............................	749	632	84.4	600	80.2	32	5.0
35 to 44 years............................	789	669	84.8	649	82.2	20	3.0
45 to 54 years............................	763	625	81.8	610	80.0	15	2.3
55 to 64 years............................	770	483	62.7	468	60.8	15	3.1
65 years and over	1,017	195	19.2	191	18.8	4	2.3

NOTE: Data in Table 7 are from the Current Population Survey (CPS) and do not match the estimates in Table 8. See notes and definitions for further information.
[1] May be of any race.

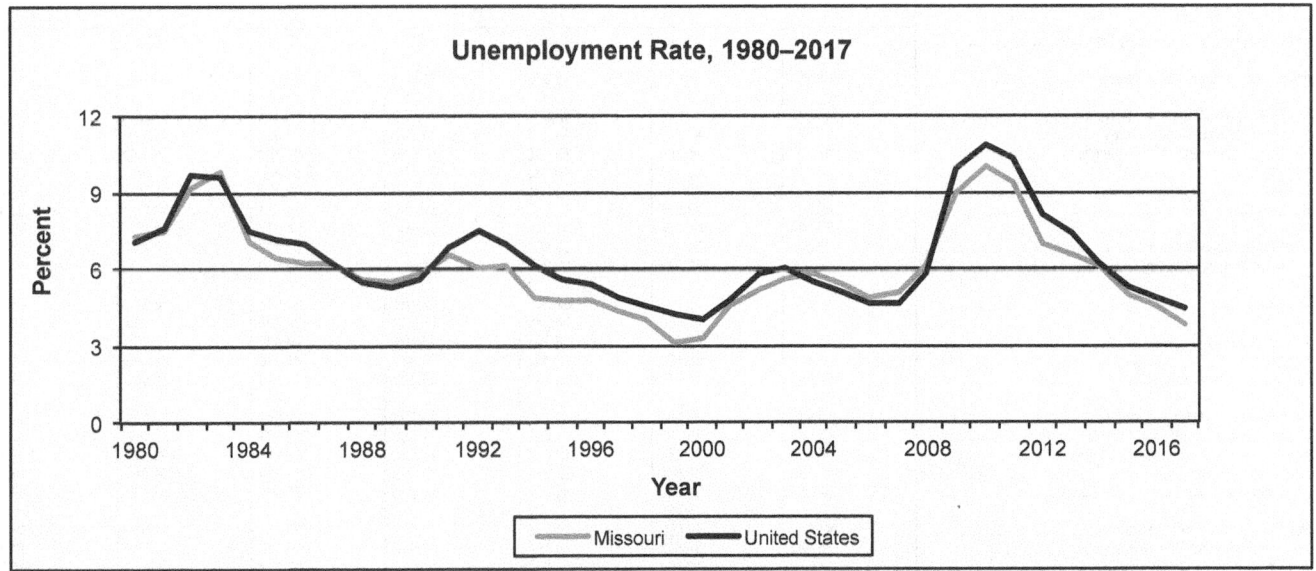

Table MO-8. Employment Status of the Civilian Noninstitutional Population Age 16 Years and Over

(Number, percent.)

Year	Civilian labor force	Civilian participation rate	Employed	Unemployed	Unemployment rate
2009..	3,049,563	66.1	2,766,711	282,852	9.3
2010..	3,056,484	66.0	2,763,535	292,949	9.6
2011..	3,047,786	65.6	2,789,224	258,562	8.5
2012..	3,025,309	64.8	2,815,275	210,034	6.9
2013..	3,020,202	64.4	2,817,435	202,767	6.7
2014..	3,048,576	64.7	2,861,721	186,855	6.1
2015..	3,077,535	65.0	2,923,107	154,428	5.0
2016..	3,079,559	64.8	2,939,309	140,250	4.6
2017..	3,050,713	63.8	2,936,126	114,587	3.8

Table MO-9. Employment and Average Wages by Industry

(Estimates through 2010 are based on the 2007 *North American Industry Classification System* [NAICS]. Estimates from 2011 onward are based on the 2012 NAICS.)

Industry	2010	2011	2012	2013	2014	2015	2016
				Number of jobs			
Wage and Salary Employment by Industry	2,740,634	2,746,857	2,780,514	2,810,852	2,837,229	2,887,885	2,928,414
Farm Wage and Salary Employment	8,829	8,837	9,093	8,677	7,131	9,971	10,251
Nonfarm Wage and Salary Employment	2,731,805	2,738,020	2,771,421	2,802,175	2,830,098	2,877,914	2,918,163
Private wage and salary employment	2,240,686	2,256,882	2,295,033	2,326,343	2,357,466	2,406,875	2,446,746
Forestry, fishing, and related activities	4,981	5,193	5,345	5,445	5,527	5,505	5,544
Mining	4,092	4,017	3,977	3,947	3,896	3,927	3,876
Utilities	12,598	12,342	12,178	12,119	11,960	11,874	11,696
Construction	109,953	106,573	107,737	111,078	113,175	117,334	123,964
Manufacturing	243,578	246,598	248,802	252,913	256,196	261,615	263,646
Durable goods manufacturing	140,283	143,252	144,099	147,841	152,324	157,291	158,301
Nondurable goods manufacturing	103,295	103,346	104,703	105,072	103,872	104,324	105,345
Wholesale trade	116,870	116,686	117,932	119,052	121,458	120,921	120,952
Retail trade	301,596	303,962	305,050	304,313	307,717	314,263	318,247
Transportation and warehousing	86,674	87,879	89,822	92,360	94,359	97,963	98,910
Information	56,220	53,691	52,910	52,592	52,340	50,188	49,463
Finance and insurance	123,768	124,921	128,691	127,917	127,984	128,456	130,229
Real estate and rental and leasing	37,059	35,893	35,570	35,129	35,697	36,540	37,370
Professional, scientific, and technical services	122,549	125,025	131,529	133,752	137,293	147,048	154,362
Management of companies and enterprises	61,608	63,490	60,618	63,607	66,125	65,537	65,161
Administrative and waste services	140,834	147,222	147,489	151,886	155,409	159,635	161,316
Educational services	62,344	63,677	66,101	66,258	66,460	66,803	67,026
Health care and social assistance	348,759	353,844	374,109	381,468	382,617	393,057	401,065
Arts, entertainment, and recreation	43,270	41,831	42,200	43,383	43,836	41,814	43,118
Accommodation and food services	230,869	230,909	234,248	239,127	244,000	252,497	258,462
Other services, except public administration	133,064	133,129	130,725	129,997	131,417	131,898	132,339
Government and government enterprises	491,119	481,138	476,388	475,832	472,632	471,039	471,417
				Dollars			
Average Wages and Salaries by Industry	41,606	42,468	43,689	44,070	45,318	46,582	48,380
Average Farm Wages and Salaries	28,913	29,635	43,328	31,234	49,283	33,201	34,046
Average Nonfarm Wages and Salaries	41,647	42,509	43,690	44,109	45,308	46,628	48,430
Average private wages and salaries	42,027	42,969	44,313	44,707	45,976	47,326	49,209
Forestry, fishing, and related activities	27,100	25,296	26,109	26,629	27,229	28,229	33,192
Mining	59,740	69,748	70,236	68,208	69,630	69,565	70,862
Utilities	79,462	82,736	83,300	85,828	89,328	91,066	96,771
Construction	49,284	49,632	51,253	51,650	53,421	55,282	58,443
Manufacturing	51,024	52,096	54,027	54,666	56,871	58,207	59,110
Durable goods manufacturing	52,567	54,371	55,507	57,337	59,846	60,443	61,136
Nondurable goods manufacturing	48,929	48,942	51,991	50,908	52,510	54,835	56,065
Wholesale trade	58,982	60,352	62,205	62,181	64,513	66,297	68,919
Retail trade	25,401	25,560	26,246	26,417	26,897	27,822	28,706
Transportation and warehousing	44,020	44,841	46,161	47,194	48,447	49,061	51,371
Information	65,216	68,196	72,441	70,527	71,270	74,798	71,523
Finance and insurance	62,040	65,040	69,142	69,348	71,673	74,985	79,942
Real estate and rental and leasing	35,498	36,568	38,759	39,107	40,577	42,917	44,612
Professional, scientific, and technical services	67,988	68,786	71,289	71,063	72,643	76,092	80,562
Management of companies and enterprises	89,358	90,863	96,026	97,530	102,871	100,885	103,104
Administrative and waste services	31,376	31,852	32,331	32,893	33,924	34,378	36,160
Educational services	32,086	32,843	34,077	34,968	35,938	36,199	36,527
Health care and social assistance	41,652	42,603	42,519	42,699	43,057	44,546	46,740
Arts, entertainment, and recreation	35,694	37,875	38,164	40,048	40,120	42,370	40,415
Accommodation and food services	16,560	16,887	17,261	17,540	18,112	19,103	20,614
Other services, except public administration	28,259	28,907	30,025	30,695	31,623	33,000	34,469
Government and government enterprises	39,913	40,351	40,688	41,189	41,976	43,060	44,388

Table MO-10. Employment Characteristics by Family Type

(Number, percent.)

Family type and labor force status	2014		2015		2016	
	Total	Families with own children under 18 years	Total	Families with own children under 18 years	Total	Families with own children under 18 years
All Families..	1,503,886	629,862	1,519,299	633,503	1,527,349	633,173
FAMILY TYPE AND LABOR FORCE STATUS						
Married-Couple Families..	1,119,785	417,923	1,137,014	423,324	1,139,135	422,248
Both husband and wife in labor force........................	52.1	70.2	52.6	70.9	52.2	71.9
Husband in labor force, wife not in labor force..............	19.2	23.5	19.1	23.4	19.2	22.6
Wife in labor force, husband not in labor force..............	8.9	4.2	8.6	3.9	8.2	3.3
Both husband and wife not in labor force....................	19.8	2.1	19.2	1.5	19.8	1.7
Other Families	384,101	211,939	382,285	210,179	388,214	210,925
Female householder, no husband present...................	73.1	72.8	73.3	74.8	72.0	73.5
In labor force..	50.4	59.4	51.8	62.4	51.4	62.2
Not in labor force	22.7	13.4	21.5	12.4	20.6	11.3
Male householder, no wife present.........................	26.9	27.2	26.7	25.2	28.0	26.5
In labor force...	21.2	24.2	20.3	22.6	21.3	24.1
Not in labor force	5.7	3.0	6.4	2.7	6.7	2.5

Table MO-11. School Enrollment and Educational Attainment, 2016

(Number, percent.)

Item	State	U.S.
Enrollment		
Total population 3 years and over, enrolled in school	1,507,305	81,572,277
Enrolled in nursery school or preschool (percent).....................	6.3	6.0
Enrolled in kindergarten (percent)...................................	5.1	5.0
Enrolled in elementary school, grades 1-8 (percent).................	41.0	40.3
Enrolled in high school, grades 9-12 (percent)......................	21.4	21.0
Enrolled in college or graduate school (percent)....................	26.2	27.7
Attainment		
Total population 25 years and over	4,121,014	218,475,480
Less than ninth grade (percent).....................................	3.3	5.4
9th to 12th grade, no diploma (percent)..............................	7.1	7.2
High school graduate, including equivalency (percent)...............	30.7	27.2
Some college, no degree (percent)..................................	22.5	20.6
Associate's degree (percent)..	7.9	8.4
Bachelor's degree (percent)...	17.7	19.3
Graduate or professional degree (percent)...........................	10.8	11.9
High school graduate or higher (percent)............................	89.6	87.5
Bachelor's degree or higher (percent)...............................	28.5	31.3

Table MO-12. Public School Characteristics and Educational Indicators

(Number, percent; data derived from National Center of Education Statistics.)

Item	State	U.S.
Public Schools, 2015–2016 (except where noted)		
Number of school districts...	567	18,328
Number of schools..	2,424	98,456
Number of students...	919,234	50,327,015
Number of teachers...	67,635	3,151,497
Student-teacher ratio...	13.6	16.0
Expenditures per student (dollars), 2014-2015......................	10,231	11,445
Four-year adjusted cohort graduation rate (ACGR)[1,2]	89.0	84.1
Students eligible for free or reduced-price lunch (percent), 2014-2015...	51.3	51.8
English language learners (percent), Fall 2015......................	3.2	9.5
Students age 3 to 21 served under IDEA, part B (percent)............	13.7	13.2

Public Schools by Type	Number	Percent of state public schools
Total number of schools...	2,424	100.0
Regular	2,247	92.7
Special education	53	2.2
Vocational education..	63	2.6
Alternative education...	61	2.5

NOTE: Every school is assigned only one school type based on its instructional emphasis.
[1] ACGR data represents a new method of calculating high-school completion rates and may not be comparable to previous years' data for Averaged Freshmen Graduation Rates (AFGR).
[2] The United States 4-year ACGRs were estimated using both the reported 4-year ACGR data from 49 states and the District of Columbia and using imputed data for Idaho. The estimate for American Indian/Alaska Native students also includes imputed data for Virginia.

Table MO-13. Reported Voting and Registration of the Voting-Age Population, November 2016

(Numbers in thousands, percent.)

Item	Total population	Total citizen population	Registered			Voted		
			Total registered	Percent registered (total population)	Percent registered (total citizen population)	Total voted	Percent voted (total population)	Percent voted (total citizen population)
U.S. Total	245,502	224,059	157,596	64.2	70.3	137,537	56.0	61.4
State Total	4,626	4,486	3,333	72.1	74.3	2,906	62.8	64.8
Sex								
Male	2,231	2,159	1,534	68.8	71.1	1,328	59.5	61.5
Female	2,395	2,328	1,799	75.1	77.3	1,577	65.9	67.8
Race								
White alone	3,957	3,860	2,886	72.9	74.8	2,529	63.9	65.5
White, non-Hispanic alone	3,808	3,779	2,832	74.4	75.0	2,485	65.2	65.8
Black alone	491	491	385	78.4	78.4	325	66.2	66.2
Asian alone	77	34	21	(B)	(B)	21	(B)	(B)
Hispanic (of any race)	160	93	59	(B)	(B)	50	(B)	(B)
White alone or in combination	4,015	3,919	2,898	72.2	73.9	2,538	63.2	64.8
Black alone or in combination	532	532	414	77.9	77.9	348	65.5	65.5
Asian alone or in combination	81	38	25	(B)	(B)	25	(B)	(B)
Age								
18 to 24 years	565	540	326	57.7	60.4	259	45.9	48.0
25 to 34 years	757	734	497	65.6	67.7	404	53.4	55.1
35 to 44 years	753	692	473	62.9	68.4	418	55.5	60.4
45 to 64 years	1,537	1,519	1,184	77.0	77.9	1,065	69.3	70.1
65 years and over	1,013	1,002	854	84.2	85.2	759	74.9	75.8

B = Base is less than 75,000 and therefore too small to show the derived measure.

Table MO-14. Crime

(Number, rate per 100,000. Data are derived from the FBI Uniform Crime Reports.)

Item	State			U.S. [1,2,3,4]		
	2015	2016	Percent change	2015	2016	Percent change
TOTAL POPULATION [5]	6,083,672	6,093,000	0.2	321,418,820	323,127,513	0.5
VIOLENT CRIME						
Number	30,261	31,644	4.6	1,231,566	1,248,185	1.3
Rate	497.4	519.4	4.4	383.2	386.3	0.8
Murder and Nonnegligent Manslaughter						
Number	502	537	7.0	15,696	17,250	9.9
Rate	8.3	8.8	6.0	4.9	5.3	8.2
Rape [6]						
Number	2,553	2,554	-	124,047	130,603	5.3
Rate	42.0	41.9	-0.2	38.6	40.4	4.7
Robbery						
Number	6,376	6,570	3.0	327,374	332,198	1.5
Rate	104.8	107.8	2.9	101.9	102.8	0.9
Aggravated Assault						
Number	20,830	21,983	5.5	764,449	803,007	5.0
Rate	342.4	360.8	5.4	237.8	248.5	4.5
PROPERTY CRIME						
Number	173,642	170,549	-1.8	7,993,631	7,919,035	-0.9
Rate	2,854.2	2,799.1	-1.9	2,487.0	2,450.7	-1.5
Burglary						
Number	34,006	31,710	-6.8	1,579,527	1,515,096	-4.1
Rate	559.0	520.4	-6.9	491.4	468.9	-4.6
Larceny-Theft						
Number	122,637	120,544	-1.7	5,706,346	5,638,455	-1.2
Rate	2,015.8	1,978.4	-1.9	1,775.4	1,745.0	-1.7
Motor Vehicle Theft						
Number	16,999	18,295	7.6	707,758	765,484	8.2
Rate	279.4	300.3	7.5	220.2	236.9	7.6

NOTE: Although arson data are included in the trend and clearance tables, sufficient data are not available to estimate totals for this offense. Therefore, no arson data are published in this table.
X = Not applicable.
- = Zero or rounds to zero.
[1] The crime figures have been adjusted.
[2] The data collection methodology for the offense of forcible rape used by the Minnesota state Uniform Crime Reporting (UCR) Program (with the exception of Minneapolis and St. Paul, Minnesota) does not comply with national UCR Program guidelines. Consequently, its figures for forcible rape and violent crime (of which forcible rape is a part) are not published in this table.
[3] Includes offenses reported by the Zoological Police and the Metro Transit Police.
[4] Because of changes in the state's reporting practices, figures are not comparable to previous years' data.
[5] Populations are U.S. Census Bureau provisional estimates as of July 1 of each year.
[6] The figures shown for the offense of rape were estimated using the revised Uniform Crime Reporting (UCR) definition of rape.

Table MO-15. State Government Finances, 2016

(Dollar amounts in thousands, percent distribution.)

Item	Dollars	Percent distribution
Total Revenue	33,039,255	100.0
General revenue	28,850,421	87.3
Intergovernmental revenue	10,987,857	33.3
Taxes	12,245,169	37.1
General sales	3,536,396	10.7
Selective sales	1,765,868	5.3
License taxes	547,326	1.7
Individual income tax	6,023,701	18.2
Corporate income tax	328,736	1.0
Other taxes	43,142	0.1
Current charges	3,045,528	9.2
Miscellaneous general revenue	2,571,867	7.8
Utility revenue	0	-
Liquor stores revenue	0	-
Insurance trust revenue [1]	4,188,834	12.7
Total Expenditure	32,778,347	100.0
Intergovernmental expenditure	6,172,736	18.8
Direct expenditure	26,605,611	81.2
Current operation	19,489,455	59.5
Capital outlay	1,277,634	3.9
Insurance benefits and repayments	4,537,344	13.8
Assistance and subsidies	531,621	1.6
Interest on debt	769,557	2.3
Exhibit: Salaries and wages	3,926,595	12.0
Total Expenditure	32,778,347	100.0
General expenditure	28,241,003	86.2
Intergovernmental expenditure	6,172,736	18.8
Direct expenditure	22,068,267	67.3
General expenditure, by function:		
Education	10,023,638	30.6
Public welfare	8,666,452	26.4
Hospitals	1,991,846	6.1
Health	1,838,161	5.6
Highways	1,375,206	4.2
Police protection	230,785	0.7
Correction	814,328	2.5
Natural resources	306,015	0.9
Parks and recreation	82,539	0.3
Governmental administration	557,284	1.7
Interest on general debt	769,557	2.3
Other and unallocable	1,585,192	4.8
Utility expenditure	0	-
Liquor stores expenditure	0	-
Insurance trust expenditure	4,537,344	13.8
Debt at End of Fiscal Year	19,103,212	X
Cash and Security Holdings	70,627,828	X

X = Not applicable.
- = Zero or rounds to zero.
[1] Within insurance trust revenue, net earnings of state retirement systems is a calculated statistic (the item code in the data file is X08), and thus can be positive or negative. Net earnings is the sum of earnings on investments plus gains on investments minus losses on investments. The change made in 2002 for asset valuation from book to market value in accordance with Statement 34 of the Governmental Accounting Standards Board is reflected in the calculated statistics.

Table MO-16. State Government Tax Collections, 2017

(Dollars in thousands, percent.)

Item	Dollars	Percent distribution
Total Taxes	12,495,505	100.0
Property taxes	31,643	0.3
Sales and gross receipts	5,403,936	43.2
General sales and gross receipts	3,604,570	28.8
Selective sales and gross receipts	1,799,366	14.4
Alcoholic beverages	37,863	0.3
Amusements	366,839	2.9
Insurance premiums	432,560	3.5
Motor fuels	720,849	5.8
Pari-mutuels	X	-
Public utilities	X	-
Tobacco products	100,391	0.8
Other selective sales	140,864	1.1
Licenses	590,747	4.7
Alcoholic beverages	5,304	-
Amusements	2,178	-
Corporations in general	2,678	-
Hunting and fishing	33,083	0.3
Motor vehicle	288,210	2.3
Motor vehicle operators	15,888	0.1
Public utilities	19,937	0.2
Occupation and business, NEC	147,569	1.2
Other licenses	75,900	0.6
Income taxes	6,456,911	51.7
Individual income	6,149,468	49.2
Corporation net income	307,443	2.5
Other taxes	12,268	0.1
Death and gift	0	-
Documentary and stock transfer	12,191	0.1
Severance	18	-
Taxes, NEC	59	-

- = Zero or rounds to zero.
X = Not applicable.

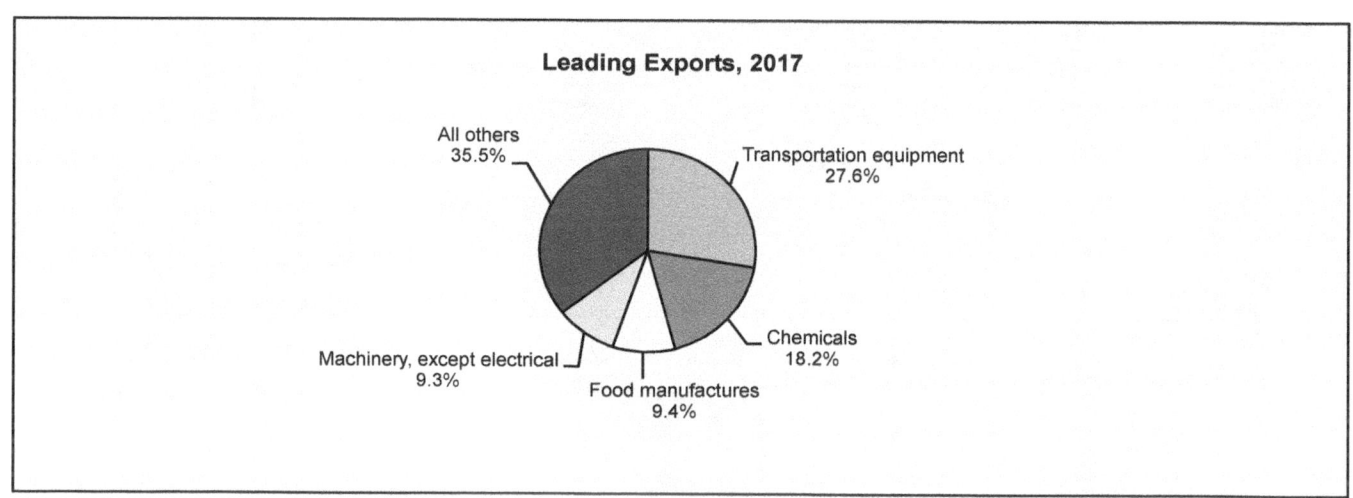

Leading Exports, 2017

All others 35.5%
Transportation equipment 27.6%
Chemicals 18.2%
Food manufactures 9.4%
Machinery, except electrical 9.3%

MONTANA

Facts and Figures

Location: Northwestern United States; bordered on the N by Canada (British Columbia, Alberta, and Saskatchewan), on the E by North Dakota and South Dakota, on the S by Idaho and Wyoming, and on the W by Idaho

Area: 147,042 sq. mi. (380,838 sq. km.); rank—4th

Population: 1,050,493 (2017 est.); rank—44th

Principal Cities: capital—Helena; largest—Billings

Statehood: November 8, 1889; 41st state

U.S. Congress: 2 senators, 1 representative

State Motto: *Oro y plata* ("Gold and silver")

State Song: "Montana"

State Nicknames: The Treasure State; Big Sky Country

Abbreviations: MT; Mont.

State Symbols: flower—bitterroot; tree—ponderosa pine; bird—Western meadowlark

At a Glance

- With an increase in population of 6.1 percent, Montana ranked 17th among the states in growth from 2010 to 2017.

- The median household income in Montana in 2016 was $50,027 compared to the national median household income of $57,617.

- In 2017, 18.1 percent of Montana residents were in the 65 and older age group, a percentage that ranked 5th in the country.

- Approximately 0.6 percent of Montana residents self-identified as "Black or African-American alone" in 2017, which was the lowest percentage among all the states.

Table MT-1. Population by Age, Sex, Race, and Hispanic Origin

(Number, percent, except where noted.)

Sex, age, race, and Hispanic origin	2000	2010	2017 [1]	Average annual percent change, 2010–2017
Total Population..	902,195	989,415	1,050,493	6.2
Percent of total U.S. population	0.3	0.3	0.3	X
Sex				
Male..	449,480	496,667	528,956	6.5
Female	452,715	492,748	521,537	5.8
Age				
Under 5 years...	54,869	62,423	63,291	1.4
5 to 19 years..	202,571	188,613	191,221	1.4
20 to 64 years..	523,806	591,637	605,458	2.3
65 years and over	120,949	146,742	190,523	29.8
Median age (years)	37.5	39.8	39.8	-
Race and Hispanic Origin				
One race				
White	817,229	891,529	935,792	5.0
Black	2,692	4,215	6,114	45.1
American Indian and Alaska Native	56,068	63,495	69,913	10.1
Asian..	4,691	6,379	8,842	38.6
Native Hawaiian or Other Pacific Islander	470	734	910	24.0
Two or more races.....................................	15,730	23,063	28,922	25.4
Hispanic (of any race).................................	18,081	31,018	39,633	27.8

X = Not applicable.

[1] Population figures for 2017 are July 1 estimates. The 2010 estimates are taken from the 2010 Census.

- = Zero or rounds to zero.

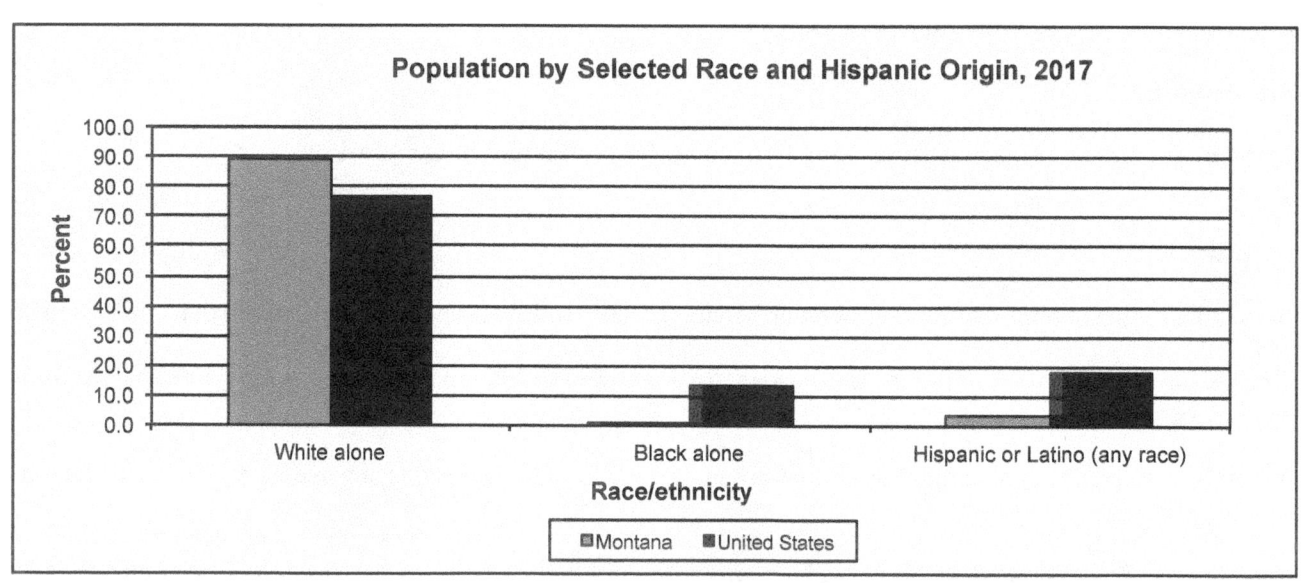

Population by Selected Race and Hispanic Origin, 2017

Table MT-2. Marital Status

(Number, percent distribution.)

Sex, age, and marital status	2000	2010	2016
Males, 15 Years and Over...	353,801	404,179	427,876
Never married	27.7	30.5	33.3
Now married, except separated.....................................	58.3	53.4	51.5
Separated..	1.2	1.5	0.9
Widowed..	2.6	2.3	2.8
Divorced..	10.2	12.4	11.5
Females, 15 Years and Over.......................................	362,114	403,766	424,417
Never married	20.4	23.5	25.1
Now married, except separated.....................................	56.3	52.9	51.8
Separated..	1.3	1.6	1.3
Widowed..	10.4	9.7	8.5
Divorced..	11.6	12.3	13.3

Table MT-3. Households and Housing Characteristics

(Number, percent, dollars.)

Item	2000	2010	2016	Average annual percent change, 2010–2016
Total Households..	358,667	402,747	416,125	0.6
Family households	237,407	255,199	257,449	0.1
Married-couple family	192,067	203,500	207,675	0.3
Other family	45,340	51,699	49,774	-0.6
Male householder, no wife present.....................	13,324	16,926	16,755	-0.2
Female householder, no husband present............	32,016	34,773	33,019	-0.8
Nonfamily households	121,260	147,548	158,676	1.3
Householder living alone...................................	98,422	119,762	127,832	1.1
Householder not living alone..............................	22,838	27,786	30,844	1.8
Housing Characteristics				
Total housing units...	412,633	483,006	497,749	0.5
Occupied housing units	358,667	402,747	416,125	0.6
Owner occupied	247,723	280,633	282,995	0.1
Renter occupied	110,944	122,114	133,130	1.5
Average household size......................................	2.45	2.39	2.44	0.3
Financial Characteristics				
Median gross rent of renter-occupied housing	447	642	741	2.6
Median monthly owner costs for housing units with a mortgage	863	1,217	1,327	1.5
Median value of owner-occupied housing units	99,500	181,200	217,200	3.3

Table MT-4. Migration, Origin, and Language

(Number, percent.)

Characteristic	State			U.S.		
	2015	2016	Percent change	2015	2016	Percent change
Residence 1 Year Ago						
Population 1 year and over	1,019,646	1,032,794	1.3	317,635,720	319,361,956	0.5
Same house	83.9	83.6	X	85.3	85.4	X
Different house in the U.S.	15.8	16.1	X	14.1	13.9	X
Same county	8.3	8.9	X	8.5	8.3	X
Different county	7.5	7.2	X	5.6	5.6	X
Same state	3.3	3.5	X	3.2	3.2	X
Different state	4.2	3.7	X	2.4	2.4	X
Abroad	0.3	0.3	X	0.7	0.7	X
Place of Birth						
Native born	1,011,593	1,020,627	0.9	278,128,449	279,388,170	0.5
Male	50.4	50.7	X	49.3	49.3	X
Female	49.6	49.3	X	50.7	50.7	X
Foreign born	21,356	21,893	2.5	43,290,372	43,739,345	1.0
Male	44.8	39.1	X	48.6	48.5	X
Female	55.2	60.9	X	51.4	51.5	X
Foreign born; naturalized U.S. citizen...................	11,373	11,585	1.9	20,697,103	21,238,372	2.6
Male	40.7	28.8	X	45.9	45.9	X
Female	59.3	71.2	X	54.1	54.1	X
Foreign born; not a U.S. citizen...........................	9,983	10,308	3.3	22,593,269	22,500,973	-0.4
Male	49.5	50.8	X	51.1	51.0	X
Female	50.5	49.2	X	48.9	49.0	X
Entered 2010 or later	21.1	24.1	X	15.6	18.6	X
Entered 2000 to 2009	19.1	16.7	X	27.9	26.7	X
Entered before 2000..	59.8	59.2	X	56.5	54.7	X
World Region of Birth, Foreign						
Foreign-born population, excluding population born at sea	21,356	21,893	2.5	43,289,646	43,738,901	1.0
Europe	22.8	33.9	X	11.1	10.9	X
Asia...	25.9	34.0	X	30.6	30.8	X
Africa..	4.4	2.9	X	4.8	4.9	X
Oceania	2.3	0.7	X	0.6	0.6	X
Latin America	21.7	10.3	X	51.1	51.0	X
North America	22.9	18.2	X	1.9	1.8	X
Language Spoken at Home and Ability to Speak English						
Population 5 years and over................................	972,529	981,377	0.9	301,625,014	303,328,961	0.6
English only	95.8	96.3	X	78.5	78.4	X
Language other than English.............................	4.2	3.7	X	21.5	21.6	X
Speaks English less than "very well"...................	0.9	0.7	X	8.6	8.6	X

NA = Not available.
X = Not applicable.
- = Zero or rounds to zero.

Table MT-5. Median Income and Poverty Status, 2016

(Number, percent, except as noted.)

Characteristic	State		U.S.	
	Number	Percent	Number	Percent
Median Income				
Households (dollars)..	50,027	X	57,617	X
Families (dollars)	66,288	X	71,062	X
Below Poverty Level (All People)	135,638	13.3	44,268,996	14.0
Sex				
Male	65,978	12.9	19,760,056	12.8
Female	69,660	13.8	24,508,940	15.2
Age				
Under 18 years..	33,818	15.1	14,115,713	19.5
Related children under 18 years...	32,956	14.8	13,805,435	19.1
18 to 64 years..	85,825	14.0	25,723,818	13.2
65 years and over	15,995	8.9	4,429,465	9.2

X = Not applicable.

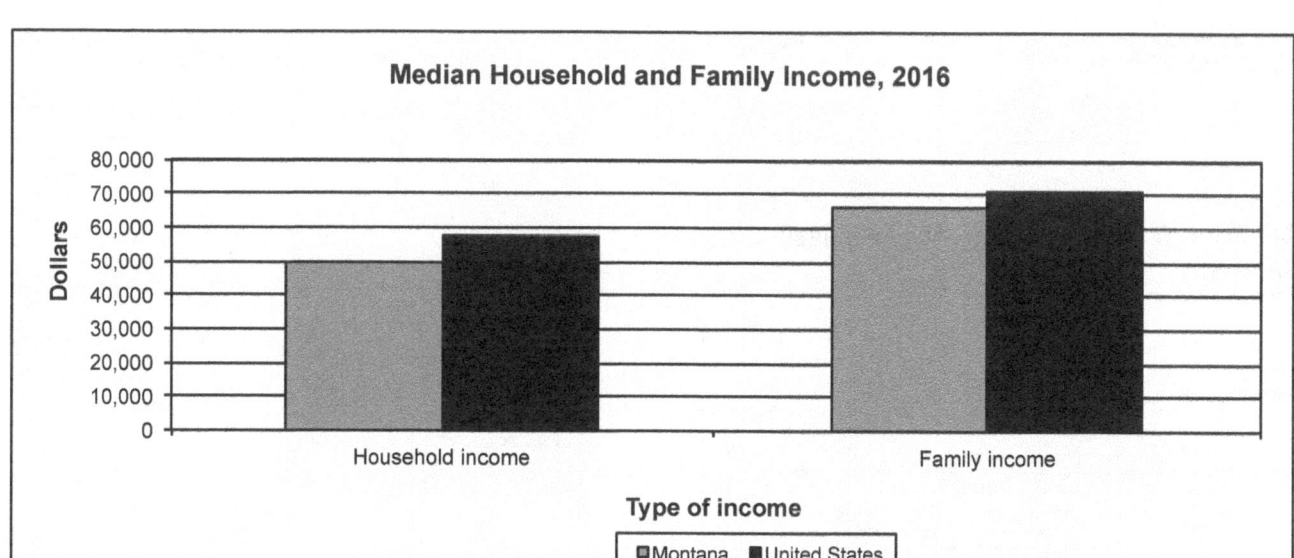

Table MT-6. Health Insurance Coverage Status for the Civilian Noninstitutionalized Population and Children Under 18 Years of Age

(Number, percent.)

Item	2008	2009	2010	2011	2012	2013	2014	2015	2016
Civilian Noninstitutionalized Population	950,414	957,586	975,562	983,214	989,823	999,390	1,008,116	1,017,458	1,027,510
Covered by Private or Public Insurance									
Number..	774,793	783,294	806,581	803,639	811,411	834,842	864,795	898,949	944,094
Percent..	81.5	81.8	82.7	81.7	82.0	83.5	85.8	88.4	91.9
Not Covered									
Number..	175,621	174,292	168,981	179,575	178,412	164,548	143,321	118,509	83,416
Percent..	18.5	18.2	17.3	18.3	18.0	16.5	14.2	11.6	8.1
Percent in the U.S. not covered..	15.1	15.1	15.5	15.1	14.8	14.5	11.7	9.4	8.6
Children Under 18 Years of Age	221,829	220,411	221,455	222,102	219,198	223,043	224,051	225,169	227,631
Covered by Private or Public Insurance									
Number..	189,720	191,941	193,897	196,540	194,796	200,548	205,630	208,050	217,003
Percent..	85.5	87.1	87.6	88.5	88.9	89.9	91.8	92.4	95.3
Not Covered									
Number..	32,109	28,470	27,558	25,562	24,402	22,495	18,421	17,119	10,628
Percent..	14.5	12.9	12.4	11.5	11.1	10.1	8.2	7.6	4.7
Percent in the U.S. not covered..	9.9	8.6	8.0	7.5	7.2	7.1	6.0	4.8	4.5

Table MT-7. Employment Status by Demographic Group, 2017

(Numbers in thousands, percent.)

Characteristic	Civilian noninstitutional population	Civilian labor force		Employed		Unemployed	
		Number	Percent of population	Number	Percent of population	Number	Percent of population
Total...	832	522	62.7	500	60.1	21	4.0
Sex							
Male...	415	280	67.5	268	64.6	12	4.3
Female..	418	242	57.8	232	55.7	9	3.8
Race, Sex, and Hispanic Origin							
White..	775	486	62.7	469	60.5	17	3.4
Male..	387	261	67.4	251	65.0	9	3.6
Female.......................................	389	225	57.9	218	56.1	7	3.2
Black or African American..................	NA	NA	NA	NA	NA	NA	NA
Male..	NA	NA	NA	NA	NA	NA	NA
Female.......................................	NA	NA	NA	NA	NA	NA	NA
Hispanic or Latino ethnicity[1]	26	19	73.4	18	67.7	1	7.5
Male..	NA	NA	NA	NA	NA	NA	NA
Female.......................................	NA	NA	NA	NA	NA	NA	NA
Age							
16 to 19 years...............................	48	21	44.3	19	39.3	2	11.4
20 to 24 years...............................	63	49	77.7	46	73.0	3	6.1
25 to 34 years...............................	137	117	85.4	110	80.7	6	5.4
35 to 44 years...............................	124	104	83.9	102	81.7	3	2.6
45 to 54 years...............................	116	91	78.2	88	75.9	3	3.0
55 to 64 years...............................	151	102	67.7	99	65.9	3	2.8
65 years and over...........................	194	38	19.4	37	18.9	1	2.4

NOTE: Data in Table 7 are from the Current Population Survey (CPS) and do not match the estimates in Table 8. See notes and definitions for further information.
[1] May be of any race.
NA = Not available.

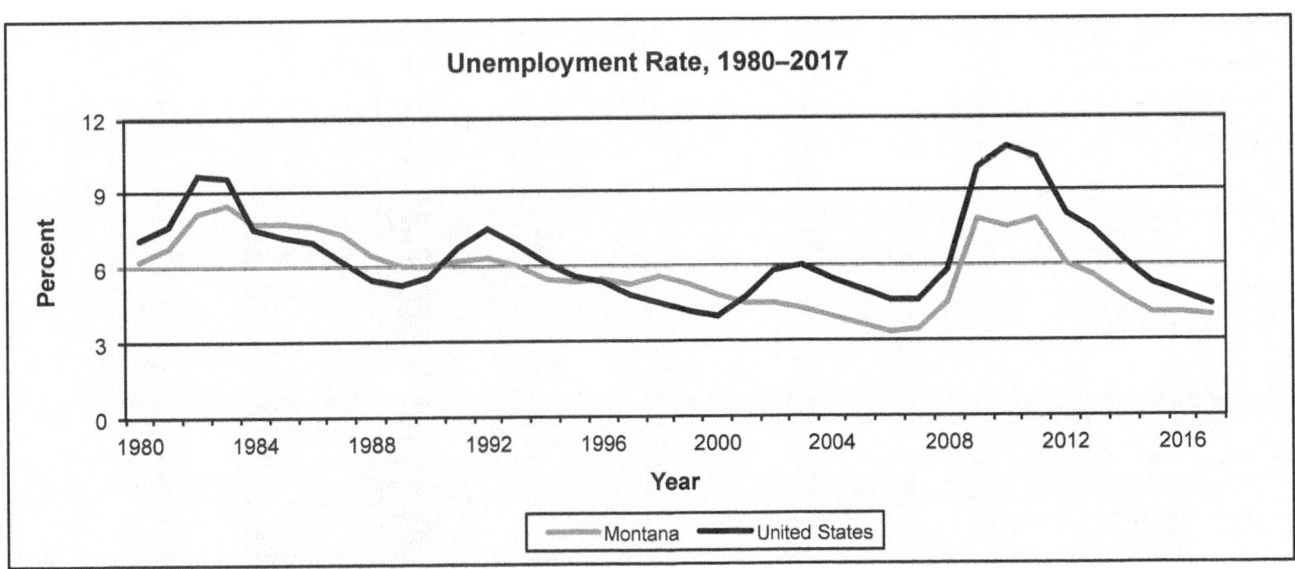

Table MT-8. Employment Status of the Civilian Noninstitutional Population Age 16 Years and Over

(Number, percent.)

Year	Civilian labor force	Civilian participation rate	Employed	Unemployed	Unemployment rate
2009..	501,014	65.3	466,713	34,301	6.8
2010..	500,525	64.4	463,998	36,527	7.3
2011..	501,225	63.9	466,403	34,822	6.9
2012..	506,485	64.1	476,174	30,311	6.0
2013..	510,781	64.0	483,071	27,710	5.4
2014..	511,501	63.5	487,629	23,872	4.7
2015..	516,845	63.6	495,298	21,547	4.2
2016..	521,628	63.5	499,990	21,638	4.1
2017..	525,453	63.2	504,279	21,174	4.0

Table MT-9. Employment and Average Wages by Industry

(Estimates through 2010 are based on the 2007 *North American Industry Classification System* [NAICS]. Estimates from 2011 onward are based on the 2012 NAICS.)

Industry	2010	2011	2012	2013	2014	2015	2016
	Number of jobs						
Wage and Salary Employment by Industry	447,718	451,920	460,613	467,095	470,632	479,586	484,911
Farm Wage and Salary Employment	4,761	5,488	6,667	6,626	6,407	6,868	6,954
Nonfarm Wage and Salary Employment	442,957	446,432	453,946	460,469	464,225	472,718	477,957
Private wage and salary employment	345,850	350,399	358,791	365,367	368,908	376,992	381,575
Forestry, fishing, and related activities	3,047	3,198	3,469	3,582	3,667	3,781	3,843
Mining	6,831	7,558	8,719	8,828	8,522	7,564	6,380
Utilities	3,046	3,116	3,197	3,179	3,157	3,080	3,029
Construction	23,500	23,437	23,752	24,790	25,661	27,153	27,818
Manufacturing	16,331	16,849	17,576	18,353	18,902	19,139	19,494
Durable goods manufacturing	9,394	9,743	10,621	11,113	11,557	11,718	11,790
Nondurable goods manufacturing	6,937	7,106	6,955	7,240	7,345	7,421	7,704
Wholesale trade	15,727	15,713	16,330	17,131	17,017	17,627	17,386
Retail trade	55,155	55,267	55,772	56,437	57,768	59,179	59,782
Transportation and warehousing	13,202	13,824	14,584	15,145	15,472	15,551	15,263
Information	7,397	7,227	6,942	6,907	6,417	6,365	6,337
Finance and insurance	16,201	16,263	15,701	15,947	16,064	16,180	16,230
Real estate and rental and leasing	5,304	5,234	5,250	5,399	5,413	5,706	5,695
Professional, scientific, and technical services	18,824	19,207	19,693	20,215	20,303	20,981	21,799
Management of companies and enterprises	1,695	2,009	2,057	1,973	1,962	2,067	2,074
Administrative and waste services	18,347	19,241	19,695	17,743	17,324	17,539	16,948
Educational services	5,363	5,540	5,687	5,920	6,049	6,234	6,219
Health care and social assistance	59,951	59,953	62,082	63,385	64,032	65,183	67,359
Arts, entertainment, and recreation	10,924	10,837	10,860	11,286	11,300	11,606	11,933
Accommodation and food services	45,094	45,957	47,431	49,028	49,372	51,388	52,939
Other services, except public administration	19,911	19,969	19,994	20,119	20,506	20,669	21,047
Government and government enterprises	97,107	96,033	95,155	95,102	95,317	95,726	96,382
	Dollars						
Average Wages and Salaries by Industry	34,673	35,824	37,172	37,741	39,059	40,182	42,236
Average Farm Wages and Salaries	35,252	30,896	35,054	39,815	39,672	35,137	38,636
Average Nonfarm Wages and Salaries	34,667	35,884	37,203	37,711	39,051	40,255	42,289
Average private wages and salaries	33,638	35,005	36,507	37,092	38,547	39,767	41,652
Forestry, fishing, and related activities	26,362	27,187	28,548	29,435	31,059	33,315	38,579
Mining	74,685	80,433	81,978	83,471	88,364	87,606	85,112
Utilities	74,989	78,160	76,655	78,669	81,119	87,494	84,448
Construction	40,857	42,736	43,855	44,789	46,109	47,823	50,132
Manufacturing	42,591	42,598	43,491	43,699	45,753	47,227	48,997
Durable goods manufacturing	39,384	39,952	41,802	42,915	44,100	45,708	47,170
Nondurable goods manufacturing	46,934	46,225	46,072	44,903	48,355	49,624	51,793
Wholesale trade	45,199	47,891	49,855	50,793	53,231	54,829	55,774
Retail trade	24,210	24,685	25,341	25,851	26,870	27,684	28,864
Transportation and warehousing	43,784	46,810	48,339	49,394	51,574	51,354	52,729
Information	41,648	41,895	43,036	44,059	45,714	48,494	50,356
Finance and insurance	48,890	49,814	53,656	55,558	57,617	60,156	64,292
Real estate and rental and leasing	26,575	28,437	30,579	30,460	32,234	34,490	37,917
Professional, scientific, and technical services	49,657	51,753	57,585	54,414	57,885	59,337	62,041
Management of companies and enterprises	58,056	59,506	68,618	73,094	71,992	75,757	74,709
Administrative and waste services	27,095	27,847	29,310	28,769	30,154	32,092	34,101
Educational services	20,497	22,009	21,708	22,014	22,702	22,924	24,418
Health care and social assistance	37,705	39,153	39,963	41,055	42,111	44,362	48,254
Arts, entertainment, and recreation	19,450	20,234	20,298	21,066	22,690	23,290	24,858
Accommodation and food services	15,304	16,043	16,788	17,288	18,170	18,985	20,341
Other services, except public administration	24,646	25,399	26,287	26,992	27,969	29,237	31,222
Government and government enterprises	38,329	39,093	39,827	40,090	41,003	42,177	44,808

Table MT-10. Employment Characteristics by Family Type

(Number, percent.)

Family type and labor force status	2014		2015		2016	
	Total	Families with own children under 18 years	Total	Families with own children under 18 years	Total	Families with own children under 18 years
All Families..	250,636	99,341	253,101	99,864	257,449	101,061
FAMILY TYPE AND LABOR FORCE STATUS						
Married-Couple Families...............................	198,955	69,152	202,848	70,742	207,675	74,795
Both husband and wife in labor force........................	52.5	69.9	51.2	68.1	53.0	71.6
Husband in labor force, wife not in labor force	19.2	24.9	19.5	25.3	17.3	22.0
Wife in labor force, husband not in labor force	8.0	3.1	8.8	3.8	8.1	3.6
Both husband and wife not in labor force...................	20.3	2.1	20.2	2.6	21.1	2.6
Other Families	51,681	30,189	50,253	29,122	49,774	26,266
Female householder, no husband present...................	65.5	63.2	69.0	68.5	66.3	67.2
In labor force..	46.0	50.2	46.4	53.0	46.0	57.3
Not in labor force	19.6	13.0	22.5	15.5	20.3	9.9
Male householder, no wife present...........................	34.5	36.8	31.0	31.5	33.7	32.8
In labor force..	29.0	34.8	23.6	27.6	25.3	31.0
Not in labor force	5.5	2.0	7.4	3.9	8.3	1.9

Table MT-11. School Enrollment and Educational Attainment, 2016

(Number, percent.)

Item	State	U.S.
Enrollment		
Total population 3 years and over, enrolled in school	242,914	81,572,277
Enrolled in nursery school or preschool (percent).................................	6.1	6.0
Enrolled in kindergarten (percent)..	5.5	5.0
Enrolled in elementary school, grades 1-8 (percent).............................	42.3	40.3
Enrolled in high school, grades 9-12 (percent)	21.0	21.0
Enrolled in college or graduate school (percent).................................	25.3	27.7
Attainment		
Total population 25 years and over	712,616	218,475,400
Less than ninth grade (percent)..	1.9	5.4
9th to 12th grade, no diploma (percent)	5.3	7.2
High school graduate, including equivalency (percent)...........................	29.0	27.2
Some college, no degree (percent)	23.6	20.6
Associate's degree (percent)	9.3	8.4
Bachelor's degree (percent)	20.9	19.3
Graduate or professional degree (percent).......................................	10.1	11.9
High school graduate or higher (percent)	92.8	87.5
Bachelor's degree or higher (percent)..	31.0	31.3

Table MT-12. Public School Characteristics and Educational Indicators

(Number, percent; data derived from National Center of Education Statistics.)

Item	State	U.S.
Public Schools, 2015–2016 (except where noted)		
Number of school districts..	490	18,328
Number of schools..	823	98,456
Number of students...	145,319	50,327,015
Number of teachers...	10,412	3,151,497
Student-teacher ratio	14.0	16.0
Expenditures per student (dollars), 2014-2015...................................	11,078	11,445
Four-year adjusted cohort graduation rate (ACGR)[1,2]	85.6	84.1
Students eligible for free or reduced-price lunch (percent), 2014-2015..........	43.6	51.8
English language learners (percent), Fall 2015	2.2	9.5
Students age 3 to 21 served under IDEA, part B (percent)........................	12.0	13.2

Public Schools by Type	Number	Percent of state public schools
Total number of schools...	823	100.0
Regular	817	99.3
Special education	2	0.2
Vocational education	0	-
Alternative education..	4	0.5

NOTE: Every school is assigned only one school type based on its instructional emphasis.
[1] ACGR data represents a new method of calculating high-school completion rates and may not be comparable to previous years' data for Averaged Freshmen Graduation Rates (AFGR).
[2] The United States 4-year ACGRs were estimated using both the reported 4-year ACGR data from 49 states and the District of Columbia and using imputed data for Idaho. The estimate for American Indian/Alaska Native students also includes imputed data for Virginia.
- =Zero or rounds to zero.

Table MT-13. Reported Voting and Registration of the Voting-Age Population, November 2016

(Numbers in thousands, percent.)

Item	Total population	Total citizen population	Registered			Voted		
			Total registered	Percent registered (total population)	Percent registered (total citizen population)	Total voted	Percent voted (total population)	Percent voted (total citizen population)
U.S. Total	245,502	224,059	157,596	64.2	70.3	137,537	56.0	61.4
State Total...............................	798	790	581	72.8	73.5	521	65.2	65.9
Sex								
Male	399	396	287	71.9	72.5	256	64.0	64.6
Female	399	395	294	73.7	74.4	265	66.5	67.2
Race								
White alone............................	738	735	542	73.4	73.8	492	66.7	67.0
White, non-Hispanic alone	721	718	532	73.8	74.1	483	67.0	67.3
Black alone.............................	5	3	2	(B)	(B)	2	(B)	(B)
Asian alone.............................	7	5	3	(B)	(B)	2	(B)	(B)
Hispanic (of any race)	20	19	12	(B)	(B)	11	(B)	(B)
White alone or in combination	754	751	554	73.4	73.7	504	66.7	67.1
Black alone or in combination...........	8	5	4	(B)	(B)	4	(B)	(B)
Asian alone or in combination...........	8	7	3	(B)	(B)	3	(B)	(B)
Age								
18 to 24 years........................	97	95	51	(B)	(B)	38	(B)	(B)
25 to 34 years........................	131	129	83	63.2	64.4	65	49.8	50.7
35 to 44 years........................	114	113	84	73.6	74.3	77	67.2	67.8
45 to 64 years........................	274	272	212	77.4	77.9	199	72.5	73.0
65 years and over	182	182	151	82.9	82.9	142	78.1	78.1

- = Zero or rounds to zero.
B = Base is less than 75,000 and therefore too small to show the derived measure.

Table MT-14. Crime

(Number, rate per 100,000. Data are derived from the FBI Uniform Crime Reports.)

Item	State			U.S. [1,2,3,4]		
	2015	2016	Percent change	2015	2016	Percent change
TOTAL POPULATION [5]	1,032,949	1,042,520	0.9	321,418,820	323,127,513	0.5
VIOLENT CRIME						
Number................................	3,611	3,840	6.3	1,231,566	1,248,185	1.3
Rate..................................	349.6	368.3	5.3	383.2	386.3	0.8
Murder and Nonnegligent Manslaughter						
Number................................	36	36	-	15,696	17,250	9.9
Rate	3.5	3.5	-	4.9	5.3	8.2
Rape[6]						
Number................................	547	578	5.7	124,047	130,603	5.3
Rate	53.0	55.4	4.5	38.6	40.4	4.7
Robbery						
Number................................	210	266	26.7	327,374	332,198	1.5
Rate	20.3	25.5	25.6	101.9	102.8	0.9
Aggravated Assault						
Number................................	2,818	2,960	5.0	764,449	803,007	5.0
Rate	272.8	283.9	4.1	237.8	248.5	4.5
PROPERTY CRIME						
Number................................	27,100	27,976	3.2	7,993,631	7,919,035	-0.9
Rate	2,623.6	2,683.5	2.3	2,487.0	2,450.7	-1.5
Burglary						
Number................................	3,838	3,934	2.5	1,579,527	1,515,096	-4.1
Rate	371.6	377.4	1.6	491.4	468.9	-4.6
Larceny-Theft						
Number................................	20,844	21,299	2.2	5,706,346	5,638,455	-1.2
Rate	2,017.9	2,043.0	1.2	1,775.4	1,745.0	-1.7
Motor Vehicle Theft						
Number................................	2,418	2,743	13.4	707,758	765,484	8.2
Rate	234.1	263.1	12.4	220.2	236.9	7.6

NOTE: Although arson data are included in the trend and clearance tables, sufficient data are not available to estimate totals for this offense. Therefore, no arson data are published in this table.
X = Not applicable.
- = Zero or rounds to zero.
[1] Because of changes in the state's reporting practices, figures are not comparable to previous years' data.
[2] The crime figures have been adjusted.
[3] The data collection methodology for the offense of forcible rape used by the Minnesota state Uniform Crime Reporting (UCR) Program (with the exception of Minneapolis and St. Paul, Minnesota) does not comply with national UCR Program guidelines. Consequently, its figures for forcible rape and violent crime (of which forcible rape is a part) are not published in this table.
[4] Includes offenses reported by the Zoological Police and the Metro Transit Police.
[5] Populations are U.S. Census Bureau provisional estimates as of July 1 of each year.
[6] The figures shown for the offense of rape were estimated using the revised Uniform Crime Reporting (UCR) definition of rape.

Table MT-15. State Government Finances, 2016

(Dollar amounts in thousands, percent distribution.)

Item	Dollars	Percent distribution
Total Revenue	6,878,900	100.0
General revenue	6,027,319	87.6
Intergovernmental revenue	2,455,420	35.7
Taxes	2,627,943	38.2
General sales	0	-
Selective sales	562,474	8.2
License taxes	319,020	4.6
Individual income tax	1,181,042	17.2
Corporate income tax	118,969	1.7
Other taxes	446,438	6.5
Current charges	496,582	7.2
Miscellaneous general revenue	447,374	6.5
Utility revenue	0	-
Liquor stores revenue	93,996	1.4
Insurance trust revenue [1]	757,585	11.0
Total Expenditure	7,316,671	100.0
Intergovernmental expenditure	1,182,607	16.2
Direct expenditure	6,134,064	83.8
Current operation	4,573,620	62.5
Capital outlay	396,673	5.4
Insurance benefits and repayments	944,515	12.9
Assistance and subsidies	108,254	1.5
Interest on debt	111,002	1.5
Exhibit: Salaries and wages	1,081,620	14.8
Total Expenditure	7,316,671	100.0
General expenditure	6,272,823	85.7
Intergovernmental expenditure	1,182,607	16.2
Direct expenditure	5,090,216	69.6
General expenditure, by function:		
Education	1,917,939	26.2
Public welfare	1,769,351	24.2
Hospitals	70,542	1.0
Health	222,479	3.0
Highways	645,768	8.8
Police protection	38,824	0.5
Correction	215,757	2.9
Natural resources	271,989	3.7
Parks and recreation	23,056	0.3
Governmental administration	459,371	6.3
Interest on general debt	111,002	1.5
Other and unallocable	526,745	7.2
Utility expenditure	17,794	0.3
Liquor stores expenditure	81,539	1.1
Insurance trust expenditure	944,515	12.9
Debt at End of Fiscal Year	3,052,423	X
Cash and Security Holdings	18,742,883	X

X = Not applicable.
- = Zero or rounds to zero.
[1] Within insurance trust revenue, net earnings of state retirement systems is a calculated statistic (the item code in the data file is X08), and thus can be positive or negative. Net earnings is the sum of earnings on investments plus gains on investments minus losses on investments. The change made in 2002 for asset valuation from book to market value in accordance with Statement 34 of the Governmental Accounting Standards Board is reflected in the calculated statistics.

Table MT-16. State Government Tax Collections, 2017

(Dollars in thousands, percent.)

Item	Dollars	Percent distribution
Total Taxes	2,654,444	100.0
Property taxes	274,431	10.3
Sales and gross receipts	576,214	21.7
General sales and gross receipts	X	-
Selective sales and gross receipts	576,214	21.7
Alcoholic beverages	32,926	1.2
Amusements	59,819	2.3
Insurance premiums	108,383	4.1
Motor fuels	189,561	7.1
Pari-mutuels	46	-
Public utilities	43,505	1.6
Tobacco products	83,606	3.1
Other selective sales	58,368	2.2
Licenses	329,874	12.4
Alcoholic beverages	3,484	0.1
Amusements	7,348	0.3
Corporations in general	4,594	0.2
Hunting and fishing	39,240	1.5
Motor vehicle	143,624	5.4
Motor vehicle operators	9,007	0.3
Public utilities	12	-
Occupation and business, NEC	111,462	4.2
Other licenses	11,103	0.4
Income taxes	1,302,961	49.1
Individual income	1,177,958	44.4
Corporation net income	125,003	4.7
Other taxes	170,964	6.4
Death and gift	X	-
Documentary and stock transfer	X	-
Severance	167,484	6.3
Taxes, NEC	3,480	0.1

X = Not applicable.
- = Zero or rounds to zero.

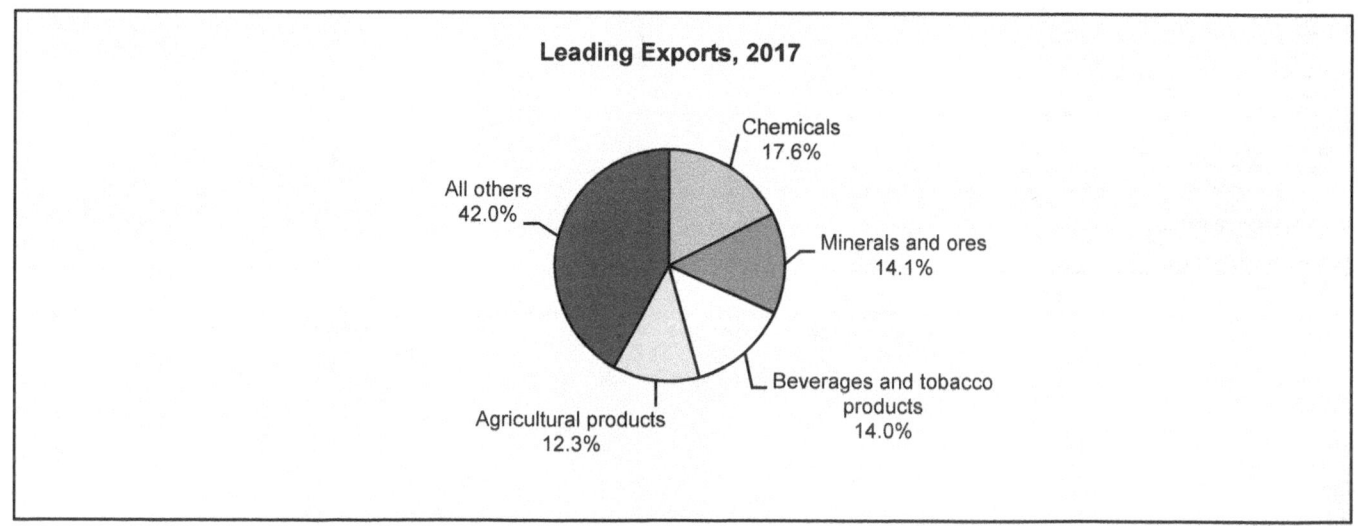

Leading Exports, 2017

Chemicals 17.6%
Minerals and ores 14.1%
Beverages and tobacco products 14.0%
Agricultural products 12.3%
All others 42.0%

NEBRASKA

Facts and Figures

Location: Central United States; bordered on the N by South Dakota, on the E by Iowa and Missouri, on the S by Kansas and Colorado, and on the W by Wyoming

Area: 77,354 sq. mi. (200,345 sq. km.); rank—16th

Population: 1,920,076 (2017 est.); rank—37th

Principal Cities: capital—Lincoln; largest—Omaha

Statehood: March 1, 1867; 37th state

U.S. Congress: 2 senators, 3 representatives

State Motto: Equality Before the Law

State Song: "Beautiful Nebraska"

State Nickname: The Cornhusker State

Abbreviations: NE; Nebr.; Neb.

State Symbols: flower—goldenrod; tree—cottonwood; bird—Western meadowlark

At a Glance

- With an increase in population of 4.9 percent, Nebraska ranked 22nd among the states in growth from 2010 to 2017.

- In 2016, 8.6 percent of Nebraskans did not have health insurance, a percent that matched the national average.

- The birth rate in Nebraska in 2016 was 13.9 births per 1,000 population, compared to the national average of 12.2 births per 1,000 population.

- Nebraska had the lowest rate of drug overdose deaths among the states in 2016, with 6.4 deaths per 100,000 population.

- The state's violent crime rate in 2016 was 291.0 per 100,000 population, compared to the national rate of 386.3 per 100,000 population.

Table NE-1. Population by Age, Sex, Race, and Hispanic Origin

(Number, percent, except where noted.)

Sex, age, race, and Hispanic origin	2000	2010	2017 [1]	Average annual percent change, 2010–2017
Total Population...	1,711,263	1,826,341	1,920,076	5.1
Percent of total U.S. population	0.6	0.6	0.6	X
Sex				
Male..	843,351	906,296	958,131	5.7
Female	867,912	920,045	961,945	4.6
Age				
Under 5 years..	117,048	131,908	133,061	0.9
5 to 19 years...	387,288	380,564	395,799	4.0
20 to 64 years...	974,732	1,067,192	1,095,843	2.7
65 years and over	232,195	246,677	295,373	19.7
Median age (years)	35.3	36.2	36.4	0.6
Race and Hispanic Origin				
One race				
White	1,533,261	1,649,264	1,700,881	3.1
Black..	68,541	85,971	97,078	12.9
American Indian and Alaska Native	14,896	23,418	27,965	19.4
Asian..	21,931	33,322	49,912	49.8
Native Hawaiian or Other Pacific Islander	836	2,061	2,313	12.2
Two or more races	23,953	32,305	41,927	29.8
Hispanic (of any race)..	94,425	173,058	210,911	21.9

X = Not applicable.
- = Zero or rounds to zero.
[1] Population figures for 2017 are July 1 estimates. The 2010 estimates are taken from the 2010 Census.

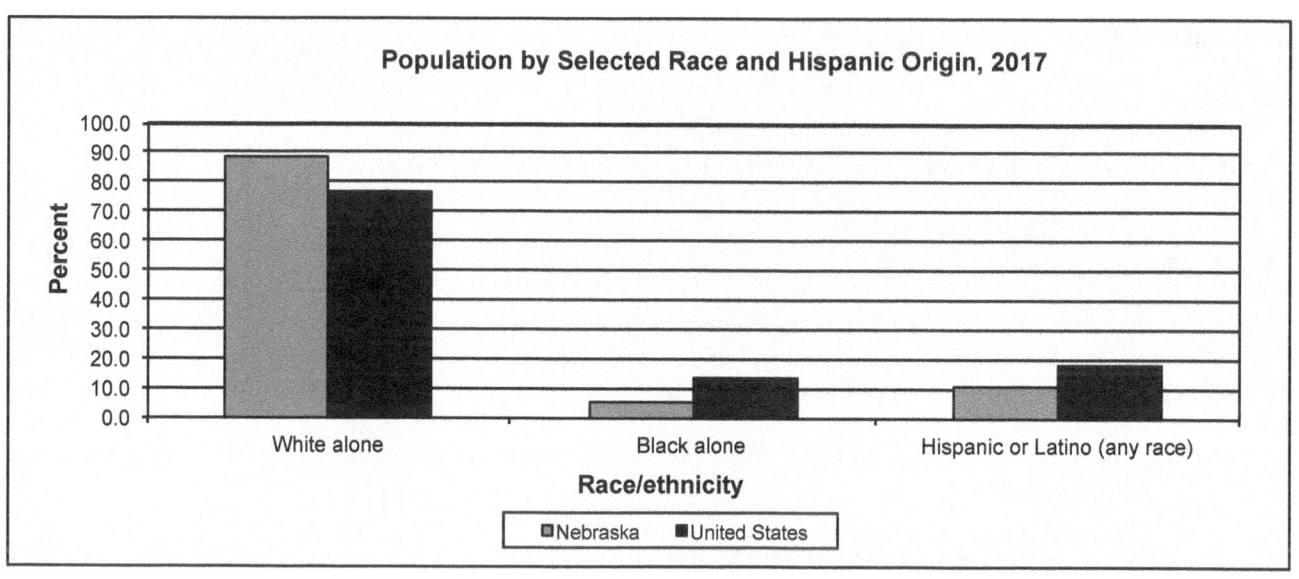

Table NE-2. Marital Status

(Number, percent distribution.)

Sex, age, and marital status	2000	2010	2016
Males, 15 Years and Over	654,559	708,783	747,768
Never married	29.2	32.4	33.9
Now married, except separated...	59.1	54.0	52.9
Separated..	1.0	1.4	1.0
Widowed..	2.4	2.3	2.7
Divorced..	8.3	9.9	9.5
Females, 15 Years and Over	687,863	735,744	761,670
Never married	22.5	25.3	27.1
Now married, except separated...	55.7	52.7	50.5
Separated..	1.3	1.5	1.2
Widowed..	10.8	9.5	9.4
Divorced..	9.7	10.9	11.8

Table NE-3. Households and Housing Characteristics

(Number, percent, dollars.)

Item	2000	2010	2016	Average annual percent change, 2010–2016
Total Households...	666,184	719,304	747,562	0.7
Family households	443,411	468,407	476,436	0.3
Married-couple family	360,996	368,023	369,253	0.1
Other family	82,415	100,384	107,183	1.1
Male householder, no wife present........................	22,072	31,177	29,238	-1.0
Female householder, no husband present..............	60,343	69,207	77,945	2.1
Nonfamily households	222,773	250,897	271,126	1.3
Householder living alone...	183,550	205,263	223,822	1.5
Householder not living alone...................................	39,223	45,634	47,304	0.6
Housing Characteristics				
Total housing units	722,668	797,677	827,191	0.6
Occupied housing units	666,184	719,304	747,562	0.7
Owner occupied	449,317	484,649	488,339	0.1
Renter occupied	216,867	234,655	259,223	1.7
Average household size..	2.49	2.47	2.48	0.1
Financial Characteristics				
Median gross rent of renter-occupied housing	491	669	769	2.5
Median monthly owner costs for housing units with a mortgage	895	1,218	1,290	1.0
Median value of owner-occupied housing units	88,000	127,600	148,100	2.7

Table NE-4. Migration, Origin, and Language

(Number, percent.)

Characteristic	State			U.S.		
	2015	2016	Percent change	2015	2016	Percent change
Residence 1 Year Ago						
Population 1 year and over	1,869,217	1,882,987	0.7	317,635,720	319,361,956	0.5
Same house..	84.0	83.5	X	85.3	85.4	X
Different house in the U.S.	15.5	15.9	X	14.1	13.9	X
Same county	9.0	9.4	X	8.5	8.3	X
Different county	6.4	6.5	X	5.6	5.6	X
Same state	3.6	3.7	X	3.2	3.2	X
Different state	2.8	2.7	X	2.4	2.4	X
Abroad	0.5	0.5	X	0.7	0.7	X
Place of Birth						
Native born	1,767,800	1,772,979	0.3	278,128,449	279,388,170	0.5
Male	49.6	49.7	X	49.3	49.3	X
Female	50.4	50.3	X	50.7	50.7	X
Foreign born	128,390	134,137	4.5	43,290,372	43,739,345	1.0
Male	50.8	51.3	X	48.6	48.5	X
Female	49.2	48.7	X	51.4	51.5	X
Foreign born; naturalized U.S. citizen......................	48,394	44,976	-7.1	20,697,103	21,238,372	2.6
Male	48.9	44.4	X	45.9	45.9	X
Female	51.1	55.6	X	54.1	54.1	X
Foreign born; not a U.S. citizen	79,996	89,161	11.5	22,593,269	22,500,973	-0.4
Male	52.0	54.9	X	51.1	51.0	X
Female	48.0	45.1	X	48.9	49.0	X
Entered 2010 or later	23.9	29.8	X	15.6	18.6	X
Entered 2000 to 2009	30.8	33.1	X	27.9	26.7	X
Entered before 2000...	45.3	37.2	X	56.5	54.7	X
World Region of Birth, Foreign						
Foreign-born population, excluding population born at sea	128,390	134,137	4.5	43,289,646	43,738,901	1.0
Europe	6.5	6.3	X	11.1	10.9	X
Asia...	28.0	29.7	X	30.6	30.8	X
Africa	9.3	8.4	X	4.8	4.9	X
Oceania	0.1	0.3	X	0.6	0.6	X
Latin America..	55.0	54.6	X	51.1	51.0	X
North America	1.0	0.8	X	1.9	1.8	X
Language Spoken at Home and Ability to Speak English						
Population 5 years and over..	1,765,526	1,774,959	0.5	301,625,014	303,328,961	0.6
English only	88.9	88.5	X	78.5	78.4	X
Language other than English....................................	11.1	11.5	X	21.5	21.6	X
Speaks English less than "very well"....................	4.8	5.4	X	8.6	8.6	X

NA = Not available.
X = Not applicable.
- = Zero or rounds to zero.

Table NE-5. Median Income and Poverty Status, 2016

(Number, percent, except as noted.)

Characteristic	State		U.S.	
	Number	Percent	Number	Percent
Median Income				
Households (dollars)...	56,927	X	57,617	X
Families (dollars)	73,488	X	71,062	X
Below Poverty Level (All People)	211,453	11.4	44,268,996	14.0
Sex				
Male	94,539	10.3	19,760,056	12.8
Female	116,914	12.6	24,508,940	15.2
Age				
Under 18 years...	65,847	14.2	14,115,713	19.5
Related children under 18 years...	64,005	13.9	13,805,435	19.1
18 to 64 years..	124,204	11.1	25,723,818	13.2
65 years and over	21,402	7.8	4,429,465	9.2

X = Not applicable.

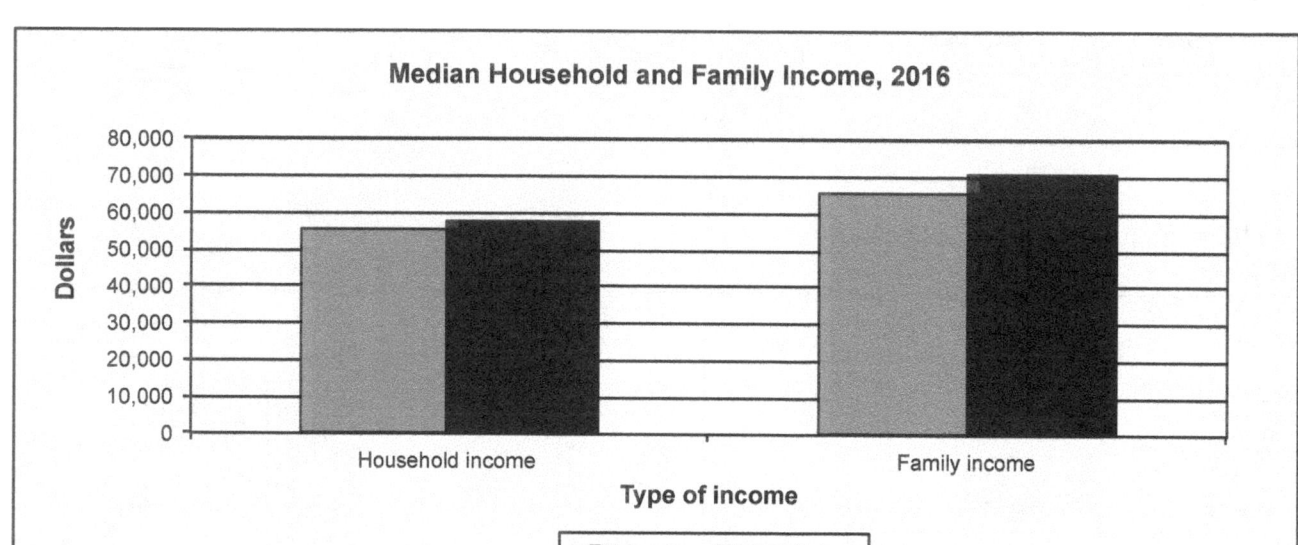

Median Household and Family Income, 2016

Table NE-6. Health Insurance Coverage Status for the Civilian Noninstitutionalized Population and Children Under 18 Years of Age

(Number, percent.)

Item	2008	2009	2010	2011	2012	2013	2014	2015	2016
Civilian Noninstitutionalized Population	1,749,849	1,762,977	1,802,049	1,814,388	1,826,832	1,840,659	1,853,684	1,866,488	1,877,654
Covered by Private or Public Insurance									
Number...	1,555,439	1,552,712	1,594,396	1,607,294	1,621,225	1,632,081	1,674,478	1,712,699	1,717,091
Percent..	88.9	88.1	88.5	88.6	88.7	88.7	90.3	91.8	91.4
Not Covered									
Number...	194,410	210,265	207,653	207,094	205,607	208,578	179,206	153,789	160,563
Percent..	11.1	11.9	11.5	11.4	11.3	11.3	9.7	8.2	8.6
Percent in the U.S. not covered..	15.1	15.1	15.5	15.1	14.8	14.5	11.7	9.4	8.6
Children Under 18 Years of Age	444,803	444,973	458,869	459,191	461,309	462,637	466,590	469,243	472,689
Covered by Private or Public Insurance									
Number...	414,233	416,973	433,135	432,299	433,503	437,258	441,795	444,513	448,982
Percent..	93.1	93.7	94.4	94.1	94.0	94.5	94.7	94.7	95.0
Not Covered									
Number...	30,570	28,000	25,734	26,892	27,806	25,379	24,795	24,730	23,707
Percent..	6.9	6.3	5.6	5.9	6.0	5.5	5.3	5.3	5.0
Percent in the U.S. not covered..	9.9	8.6	8.0	7.5	7.2	7.1	6.0	4.8	4.5

Table NE-7. Employment Status by Demographic Group, 2017

(Numbers in thousands, percent.)

Characteristic	Civilian noninstitutional population	Civilian labor force		Employed		Unemployed	
		Number	Percent of population	Number	Percent of population	Number	Percent of population
Total..	1,466	1,005	68.6	977	66.6	29	2.8
Sex							
Male..	721	534	74.0	517	71.6	17	3.2
Female...	745	471	63.3	460	61.7	11	2.4
Race, Sex, and Hispanic Origin							
White...	1,339	924	69.0	900	67.2	24	2.6
Male...	665	493	74.2	479	72.0	14	2.9
Female..	674	431	63.9	421	62.5	10	2.2
Black or African American....................	NA	NA	NA	NA	NA	NA	NA
Male...	NA	NA	NA	NA	NA	NA	NA
Female..	NA	NA	NA	NA	NA	NA	NA
Hispanic or Latino ethnicity[1]	143	108	75.2	102	71.0	6	5.7
Male...	72	60	84.0	57	79.2	4	5.8
Female..	72	48	66.4	45	62.8	3	5.5
Age							
16 to 19 years.................................	100	50	49.5	46	46.2	3	6.7
20 to 24 years.................................	134	108	80.2	102	76.0	6	5.3
25 to 34 years.................................	239	209	87.4	204	85.5	5	2.2
35 to 44 years.................................	243	212	87.6	207	85.4	5	2.4
45 to 54 years.................................	222	195	87.6	191	85.8	4	2.1
55 to 64 years.................................	225	165	73.5	162	72.1	3	1.9
65 years and over	303	67	22.0	64	21.2	3	3.7

NOTE: Data in Table 7 are from the Current Population Survey (CPS) and do not match the estimates in Table 8. See notes and definitions for further information.
[1] May be of any race.
NA = Not available.

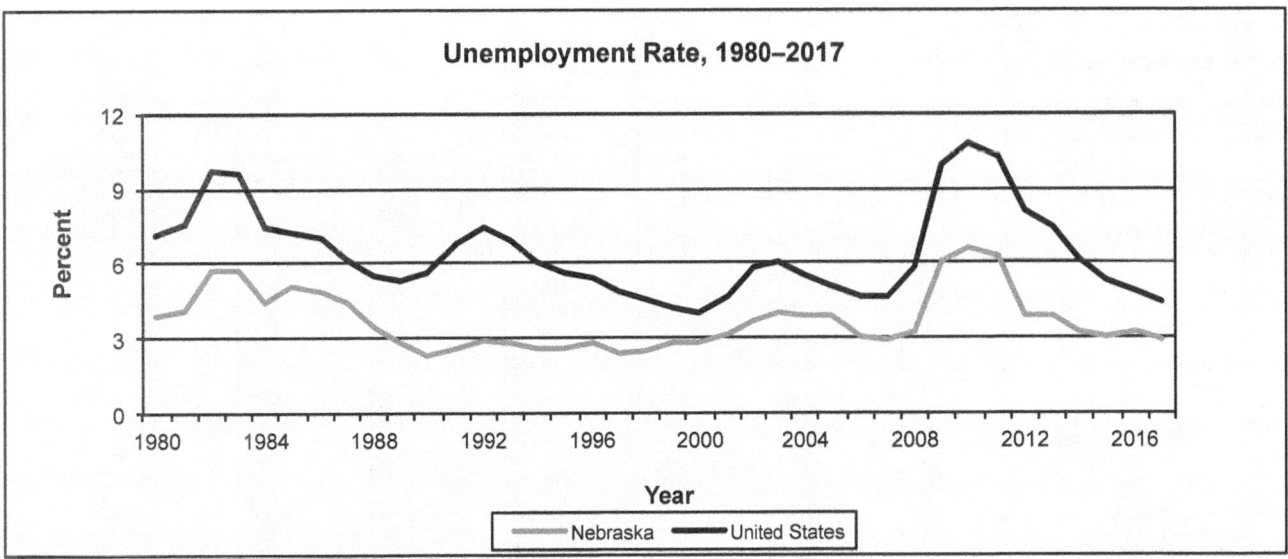

Unemployment Rate, 1980–2017

Table NE-8. Employment Status of the Civilian Noninstitutional Population Age 16 Years and Over

(Number, percent.)

Year	Civilian labor force	Civilian participation rate	Employed	Unemployed	Unemployment rate
2009..	991,583	72.7	945,648	45,935	4.6
2010..	993,398	71.6	947,360	46,038	4.6
2011..	1,003,256	71.6	959,059	44,197	4.4
2012..	1,014,980	71.9	974,428	40,552	4.0
2013..	1,018,294	71.6	979,937	38,357	3.8
2014..	1,011,564	70.6	978,377	33,187	3.3
2015..	1,007,585	69.9	977,279	30,306	3.0
2016..	1,008,715	69.4	977,622	31,093	3.1
2017..	1,007,011	68.7	977,444	29,567	2.9

Table NE-9. Employment and Average Wages by Industry

(Estimates through 2010 are based on the 2007 *North American Industry Classification System* [NAICS]. Estimates from 2011 onward are based on the 2012 NAICS.)

Industry	2010	2011	2012	2013	2014	2015	2016
	Number of jobs						
Wage and Salary Employment by Industry	967,772	972,146	989,737	1,001,155	1,014,518	1,030,578	1,038,471
Farm Wage and Salary Employment	12,992	13,694	12,116	12,293	12,168	16,088	14,485
Nonfarm Wage and Salary Employment	954,780	958,452	977,621	988,862	1,002,350	1,014,490	1,023,986
Private wage and salary employment	777,635	783,995	804,150	815,559	828,358	840,035	847,832
Forestry, fishing, and related activities	5,124	5,339	5,698	6,119	6,023	5,573	5,927
Mining	940	1,024	1,126	1,042	1,133	1,066	982
Utilities	1,655	1,627	1,605	1,290	1,264	1,081	1,072
Construction	43,128	41,742	43,439	45,497	47,473	50,109	51,991
Manufacturing	91,682	93,694	95,092	96,556	97,532	97,423	97,024
Durable goods manufacturing	41,422	42,759	44,008	44,995	45,886	45,430	44,083
Nondurable goods manufacturing	50,260	50,935	51,084	51,561	51,646	51,993	52,941
Wholesale trade	40,670	41,035	41,536	42,139	43,131	42,500	42,056
Retail trade	105,311	105,670	106,436	107,249	108,945	110,736	111,312
Transportation and warehousing	50,377	51,583	52,338	52,583	53,073	54,103	51,959
Information	16,932	17,199	17,199	17,220	17,071	17,566	18,547
Finance and insurance	55,094	55,146	55,506	55,728	56,647	57,108	58,389
Real estate and rental and leasing	9,199	9,189	9,053	9,226	9,344	9,614	9,921
Professional, scientific, and technical services	43,225	43,595	45,127	44,397	44,378	44,883	44,371
Management of companies and enterprises	17,157	16,670	16,742	19,340	20,413	22,119	21,453
Administrative and waste services	41,710	43,145	45,378	46,714	48,966	50,490	52,265
Educational services	18,596	18,526	18,554	18,137	18,338	18,795	18,849
Health care and social assistance	111,890	113,063	120,611	122,136	123,124	124,024	127,146
Arts, entertainment, and recreation	12,425	12,436	13,018	13,392	13,740	14,287	14,425
Accommodation and food services	69,035	69,962	71,714	72,950	73,821	74,660	76,612
Other services, except public administration	43,485	43,350	43,978	43,844	43,942	43,898	43,531
Government and government enterprises	177,145	174,457	173,471	173,303	173,992	174,455	176,154
	Dollars						
Average Wages and Salaries by Industry	38,771	39,719	40,899	41,499	42,812	44,385	46,190
Average Farm Wages and Salaries	34,064	35,259	41,844	40,724	42,548	40,103	41,915
Average Nonfarm Wages and Salaries	38,835	39,783	40,887	41,509	42,815	44,453	46,251
Average private wages and salaries	38,340	39,231	40,431	41,032	42,408	44,117	45,927
Forestry, fishing, and related activities	21,153	23,345	24,031	25,331	26,628	28,662	30,687
Mining	45,847	47,741	51,673	52,363	53,194	54,452	56,808
Utilities	88,526	90,719	91,398	86,072	111,397	108,795	98,446
Construction	41,777	41,998	43,497	44,167	46,626	48,227	49,919
Manufacturing	43,738	44,471	45,111	45,688	47,348	48,454	51,322
Durable goods manufacturing	46,189	47,894	48,084	48,854	50,450	51,038	52,817
Nondurable goods manufacturing	41,719	41,597	42,550	42,926	44,592	46,196	50,078
Wholesale trade	51,344	52,700	55,196	56,271	58,699	60,453	61,469
Retail trade	23,890	23,919	24,791	25,152	25,638	26,431	27,883
Transportation and warehousing	48,322	50,049	52,908	51,926	54,814	55,994	58,498
Information	51,264	53,889	54,772	56,498	57,608	59,958	60,806
Finance and insurance	54,886	57,209	59,309	61,257	62,732	65,493	69,592
Real estate and rental and leasing	32,872	34,036	35,804	37,365	39,107	40,496	42,531
Professional, scientific, and technical services	58,580	59,560	62,018	60,869	61,965	64,644	68,985
Management of companies and enterprises	78,355	80,415	90,199	92,161	95,401	99,896	95,657
Administrative and waste services	29,106	29,927	31,167	32,394	34,200	36,032	37,664
Educational services	29,887	30,422	31,009	30,517	29,575	29,997	30,802
Health care and social assistance	40,076	41,043	40,532	40,954	41,547	44,076	46,145
Arts, entertainment, and recreation	17,602	18,019	18,358	18,855	19,254	19,438	21,402
Accommodation and food services	14,034	14,436	15,150	15,493	16,164	17,211	18,602
Other services, except public administration	26,537	27,307	27,764	28,635	29,853	30,892	32,527
Government and government enterprises	41,010	42,261	42,998	43,753	44,756	46,071	47,807

Table NE-10. Employment Characteristics by Family Type

(Number, percent.)

Family type and labor force status	2014		2015		2016	
	Total	Families with own children under 18 years	Total	Families with own children under 18 years	Total	Families with own children under 18 years
All Families...	479,357	217,321	469,797	214,069	476,436	216,690
FAMILY TYPE AND LABOR FORCE STATUS						
Married-Couple Families............................	370,736	150,724	369,426	153,745	369,253	153,651
Both husband and wife in labor force........................	61.9	76.1	59.9	74.5	61.4	75.4
Husband in labor force, wife not in labor force..............	16.9	20.4	18.7	21.5	17.3	20.3
Wife in labor force, husband not in labor force.............	6.4	2.8	6.4	3.0	6.5	3.3
Both husband and wife not in labor force...................	14.8	0.8	14.5	0.8	14.3	0.8
Other Families	108,621	66,597	100,371	60,324	107,183	63,039
Female householder, no husband present......................	71.8	74.6	70.7	73.2	72.7	76.5
In labor force..	57.3	66.1	54.5	65.1	56.6	68.3
Not in labor force	14.5	8.6	16.2	8.1	16.1	8.2
Male householder, no wife present...........................	28.2	25.4	29.3	26.8	27.3	23.5
In labor force..	24.4	23.8	24.5	25.0	22.5	22.0
Not in labor force	3.7	1.5	4.8	1.8	4.8	1.5

Table NE-11. School Enrollment and Educational Attainment, 2016

(Number, percent.)

Item	State	U.S.
Enrollment		
Total population 3 years and over, enrolled in school	505,491	81,572,277
Enrolled in nursery school or preschool (percent).............................	6.4	6.0
Enrolled in kindergarten (percent)..	5.2	5.0
Enrolled in elementary school, grades 1-8 (percent)...........................	41.4	40.3
Enrolled in high school, grades 9-12 (percent)	20.2	21.0
Enrolled in college or graduate school (percent).............................	26.9	27.7
Attainment		
Total population 25 years and over	1,243,820	218,475,480
Less than ninth grade (percent)	4.1	5.4
9th to 12th grade, no diploma (percent)......................................	5.0	7.2
High school graduate, including equivalency (percent)........................	26.4	27.2
Some college, no degree (percent)	22.6	20.6
Associate's degree (percent)...	10.4	8.4
Bachelor's degree (percent)...	21.1	19.3
Graduate or professional degree (percent)....................................	10.4	11.9
High school graduate or higher (percent)....................................	90.9	87.5
Bachelor's degree or higher (percent)..	31.4	31.3

Table NE-12. Public School Characteristics and Educational Indicators

(Number, percent; data derived from National Center of Education Statistics.)

Item	State	U.S.
Public Schools, 2015–2016 (except where noted)		
Number of school districts...	284	18,328
Number of schools...	1,085	98,456
Number of students..	316,014	50,327,015
Number of teachers	23,308	3,151,497
Student-teacher ratio...	13.6	16.0
Expenditures per student (dollars), 2014-2015................................	12,174	11,445
Four-year adjusted cohort graduation rate (ACGR)[1,2]	89.3	84.1
Students eligible for free or reduced-price lunch (percent), 2014-2015........	44.3	51.8
English language learners (percent), Fall 2015	6.6	9.5
Students age 3 to 21 served under IDEA, part B (percent)......................	15.1	13.2

Public Schools by Type	Number	Percent of state public schools
Total number of schools..	1,085	100.0
Regular	1,009	93.0
Special education..	25	2.3
Vocational education...	0	-
Alternative education..	51	4.7

NOTE: Every school is assigned only one school type based on its instructional emphasis.
[1] ACGR data represents a new method of calculating high-school completion rates and may not be comparable to previous years' data for Averaged Freshmen Graduation Rates (AFGR).
[2] The United States 4-year ACGRs were estimated using both the reported 4-year ACGR data from 49 states and the District of Columbia and using imputed data for Idaho. The estimate for American Indian/Alaska Native students also includes imputed data for Virginia.
- =Zero or rounds to zero.

Table NE-13. Reported Voting and Registration of the Voting-Age Population, November 2016

(Numbers in thousands, percent.)

Item	Total population	Total citizen population	Registered			Voted		
			Total registered	Percent registered (total population)	Percent registered (total citizen population)	Total voted	Percent voted (total population)	Percent voted (total citizen population)
U.S. Total	245,502	224,059	157,596	64.2	70.3	137,537	56.0	61.4
State Total...............................	1,407	1,336	1,008	71.7	75.5	893	63.4	66.8
Sex								
Male	696	661	480	68.9	72.6	419	60.2	63.4
Female	711	676	529	74.3	78.2	474	66.6	70.1
Race								
White alone..............................	1,253	1,202	927	74.0	77.1	837	66.8	69.6
White, non-Hispanic alone	1,150	1,138	882	76.7	77.5	800	69.6	70.3
Black alone...............................	56	52	41	(B)	(B)	30	(B)	(B)
Asian alone	35	23	12	(B)	(B)	7	(B)	(B)
Hispanic (of any race)......................	109	65	47	(B)	(B)	37	(B)	(B)
White alone or in combination	1,280	1,228	938	73.2	76.3	844	65.9	68.7
Black alone or in combination...........	63	58	42	(B)	(B)	31	(B)	(B)
Asian alone or in combination...........	35	23	12	(B)	(B)	7	(B)	(B)
Age								
18 to 24 years	190	180	115	60.5	63.8	95	50.1	52.9
25 to 34 years	258	238	162	62.5	68.0	130	50.4	54.8
35 to 44 years	212	191	146	69.1	76.5	131	62.0	68.7
45 to 64 years	454	438	341	75.1	77.9	306	67.3	69.8
65 years and over	293	290	245	83.5	84.4	230	78.6	79.5

B = Base is less than 75,000 and therefore too small to show the derived measure.
- = Zero or rounds to zero.

Table NE-14. Crime

(Number, rate per 100,000. Data are derived from the FBI Uniform Crime Reports.)

Item	State			U.S. [1,2,3,4]		
	2015	2016	Percent change	2015	2016	Percent change
TOTAL POPULATION [5]	1,896,190	1,907,116	0.6	321,418,820	323,127,513	0.5
VIOLENT CRIME						
Number..	5,212	5,550	6.5	1,231,566	1,248,185	1.3
Rate...	274.9	291.0	5.9	383.2	386.3	0.8
Murder and Nonnegligent Manslaughter						
Number..	62	49	-21.0	15,696	17,250	9.9
Rate...	3.3	2.6	-21.2	4.9	5.3	8.2
Rape[6]						
Number..	873	994	13.9	124,047	130,603	5.3
Rate...	46.0	52.1	13.3	38.6	40.4	4.7
Robbery						
Number..	994	946	-4.8	327,374	332,198	1.5
Rate...	52.4	49.6	-5.3	101.9	102.8	0.9
Aggravated Assault						
Number..	3,283	3,561	8.5	764,449	803,007	5.0
Rate...	173.1	186.7	7.9	237.8	248.5	4.5
PROPERTY CRIME						
Number..	42,495	43,163	1.6	7,993,631	7,919,035	-0.9
Rate...	2,241.1	2,263.3	1.0	2,487.0	2,450.7	-1.5
Burglary						
Number..	6,422	6,444	0.3	1,579,527	1,515,096	-4.1
Rate...	338.7	337.9	-0.2	491.4	468.9	-4.6
Larceny-Theft						
Number..	32,072	31,994	-0.2	5,706,346	5,638,455	-1.2
Rate...	1,691.4	1,677.6	-0.8	1,775.4	1,745.0	-1.7
Motor Vehicle Theft						
Number..	4,001	4,725	18.1	707,758	765,484	8.2
Rate...	211.0	247.8	17.4	220.2	236.9	7.6

NOTE: Although arson data are included in the trend and clearance tables, sufficient data are not available to estimate totals for this offense. Therefore, no arson data are published in this table.
X = Not applicable.
- = Zero or rounds to zero.
[1] The crime figures have been adjusted.
[2] The data collection methodology for the offense of forcible rape used by the Minnesota state Uniform Crime Reporting (UCR) Program (with the exception of Minneapolis and St. Paul, Minnesota) does not comply with national UCR Program guidelines. Consequently, its figures for forcible rape and violent crime (of which forcible rape is a part) are not published in this table.
[3] Includes offenses reported by the Zoological Police and the Metro Transit Police.
[4] Because of changes in the state's reporting practices, figures are not comparable to previous years' data.
[5] Populations are U.S. Census Bureau provisional estimates as of July 1 of each year.
[6] The figures shown for the offense of rape were estimated using the revised Uniform Crime Reporting (UCR) definition of rape.

Table NE-15. State Government Finances, 2016

(Dollar amounts in thousands, percent distribution.)

Item	Dollars	Percent distribution
Total Revenue	10,881,575	100.0
General revenue	10,129,757	93.1
Intergovernmental revenue	3,162,157	29.1
Taxes	5,117,133	47.0
General sales	1,783,498	16.4
Selective sales	579,220	5.3
License taxes	185,082	1.7
Individual income tax	2,244,719	20.6
Corporate income tax	307,672	2.8
Other taxes	16,942	0.2
Current charges	1,174,744	10.8
Miscellaneous general revenue	675,723	6.2
Utility revenue	0	-
Liquor stores revenue	0	-
Insurance trust revenue [1]	751,818	6.9
Total Expenditure	11,026,935	100.0
Intergovernmental expenditure	2,417,506	21.9
Direct expenditure	8,609,429	78.1
Current operation	6,583,818	59.7
Capital outlay	1,044,511	9.5
Insurance benefits and repayments	740,452	6.7
Assistance and subsidies	180,754	1.6
Interest on debt	59,894	0.5
Exhibit: Salaries and wages	1,538,887	14.0
Total Expenditure	11,026,935	100.0
General expenditure	10,286,483	93.3
Intergovernmental expenditure	2,417,506	21.9
Direct expenditure	7,868,977	71.4
General expenditure, by function:		
Education	3,993,210	36.2
Public welfare	2,638,151	23.9
Hospitals	178,769	1.6
Health	552,677	5.0
Highways	905,694	8.2
Police protection	94,821	0.9
Correction	362,811	3.3
Natural resources	222,222	2.0
Parks and recreation	51,746	0.5
Governmental administration	233,511	2.1
Interest on general debt	59,894	0.5
Other and unallocable	992,977	9.0
Utility expenditure	0	-
Liquor stores expenditure	0	-
Insurance trust expenditure	740,452	6.7
Debt at End of Fiscal Year	1,950,506	X
Cash and Security Holdings	19,804,076	X

X = Not applicable.
- = Zero or rounds to zero.
[1] Within insurance trust revenue, net earnings of state retirement systems is a calculated statistic (the item code in the data file is X08), and thus can be positive or negative. Net earnings is the sum of earnings on investments plus gains on investments minus losses on investments. The change made in 2002 for asset valuation from book to market value in accordance with Statement 34 of the Governmental Accounting Standards Board is reflected in the calculated statistics.

Table NE-16. State Government Tax Collections, 2017

(Dollars in thousands, percent.)

Item	Dollars	Percent distribution
Total Taxes	5,103,105	100.0
Property taxes	123	-
Sales and gross receipts	2,407,514	47.2
General sales and gross receipts	1,835,037	36.0
Selective sales and gross receipts	572,477	11.2
Alcoholic beverages	30,911	0.6
Amusements	5,780	0.1
Insurance premiums	54,350	1.1
Motor fuels	354,234	6.9
Pari-mutuels	154	-
Public utilities	44,297	0.9
Tobacco products	56,954	1.1
Other selective sales	25,797	0.5
Licenses	182,791	3.6
Alcoholic beverages	715	-
Amusements	534	-
Corporations in general	6,260	0.1
Hunting and fishing	15,861	0.3
Motor vehicle	110,538	2.2
Motor vehicle operators	10,975	0.2
Public utilities	X	-
Occupation and business, NEC	36,916	0.7
Other licenses	992	-
Income taxes	2,492,926	48.9
Individual income	2,228,486	43.7
Corporation net income	264,440	5.2
Other taxes	19,751	0.4
Death and gift	X	-
Documentary and stock transfer	16,462	0.3
Severance	3,289	0.1
Taxes, NEC	0	-

- = Zero or rounds to zero.
X = Not applicable.

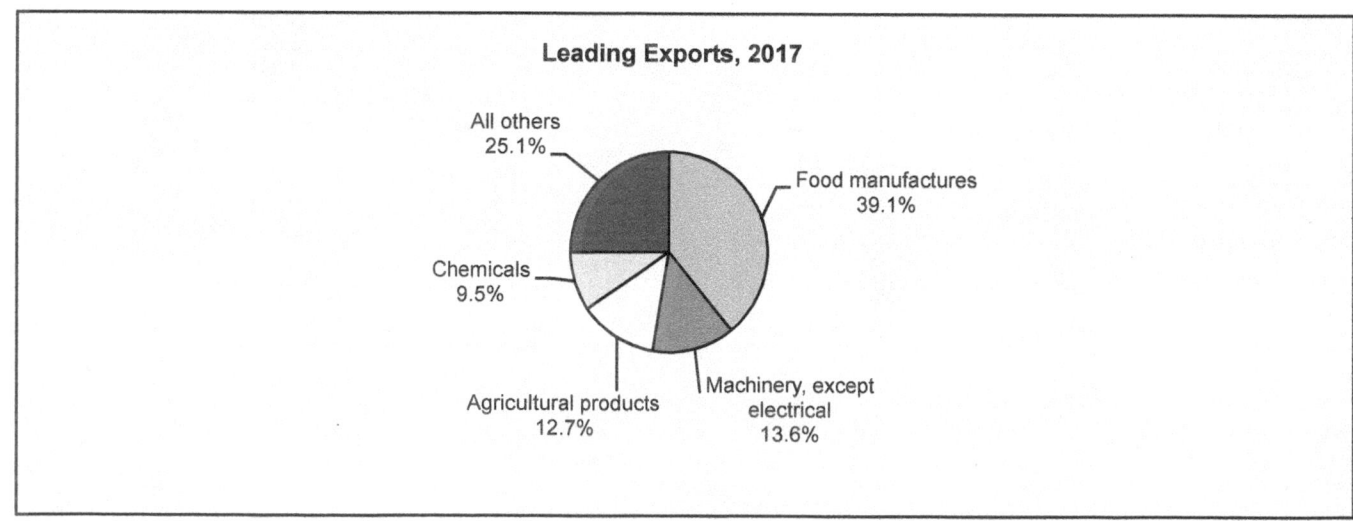

Leading Exports, 2017

All others 25.1%
Food manufactures 39.1%
Chemicals 9.5%
Agricultural products 12.7%
Machinery, except electrical 13.6%

NEVADA

Location: Western United States; bordered on the N by Oregon and Idaho, on the E by Utah and Arizona, on the S by Arizona and California, and on the W by California

Area: 110,561 sq. mi. (286,351 sq. km.); rank—7th

Population: 2,998,039 (2017 est.); rank—33rd

Principal Cities: capital—Carson City; largest—Las Vegas

Statehood: October 31, 1864; 36th state

U.S. Congress: 2 senators, 4 representatives

State Motto: All for Our Country

State Song: "Home Means Nevada"

State Nicknames: The Silver State; The Sagebrush State

Abbreviations: NV; Nev.

State Symbols: flower—sagebrush; tree—single-leaf piñon and bristlecone pine; bird—mountain bluebird

At a Glance

- With an increase in population of 10.9 percent, Nevada ranked 7th among the states in growth from 2010 to 2017.

- In 2016, 5.0 percent of Nevadans were unemployed, compared to 4.4 percent of the total U.S. population.

- Nevada's violent crime rate in 2016 was 678.1 per 100,000 population, which ranked 4th among the states. The national violent crime rate was 386.3 per 100,000 population.

- Approximately 28.8 percent of Nevadans self-identified their ethnicity as "Hispanic or Latino" in 2017, the 5th highest percentage in the country.

Table NV-1. Population by Age, Sex, Race, and Hispanic Origin

(Number, percent, except where noted.)

Sex, age, race, and Hispanic origin	2000	2010	2017 [1]	Average annual percent change, 2010–2017
Total Population..	1,998,257	2,700,551	2,998,039	11.0
Percent of total U.S. population	0.7	0.9	0.9	X
Sex				
Male..	1,018,051	1,363,616	1,503,749	10.3
Female	980,206	1,336,935	1,494,290	11.8
Age				
Under 5 years...	145,817	187,478	185,837	-0.9
5 to 19 years..	415,684	548,850	565,347	3.0
20 to 64 years..	1,217,827	1,639,864	1,787,796	9.0
65 years and over	218,929	324,359	459,059	41.5
Median age (years)	35.0	36.3	37.9	4.4
Race and Hispanic Origin				
One race				
White..	1,501,886	2,106,494	2,235,657	6.1
Black..	135,477	231,224	294,676	27.4
American Indian and Alaska Native	26,420	42,965	49,722	15.7
Asian..	90,266	203,478	264,533	30.0
Native Hawaiian or Other Pacific Islander	8,426	19,307	23,301	20.7
Two or more races	76,428	97,083	130,150	34.1
Hispanic (of any race)..	393,970	741,200	864,665	16.7

X = Not applicable.
[1] Population figures for 2017 are July 1 estimates. The 2010 estimates are taken from the 2010 Census.

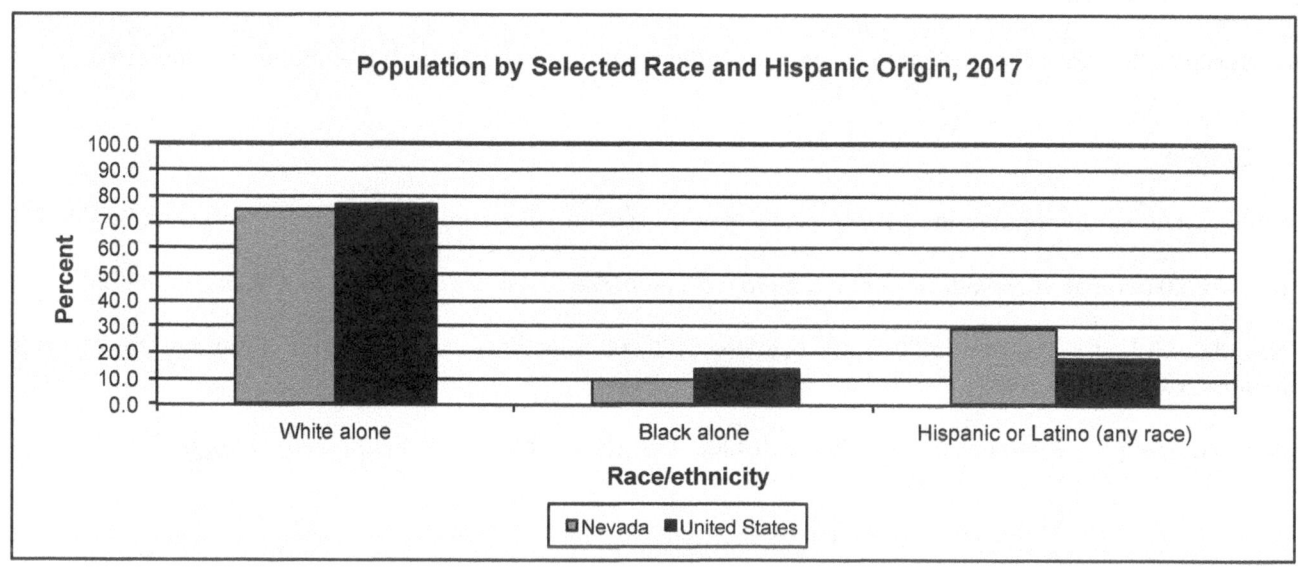

Population by Selected Race and Hispanic Origin, 2017

Table NV-2. Marital Status

(Number, percent distribution.)

Sex, age, and marital status	2000	2010	2016
Males, 15 Years and Over	792,317	1,081,514	1,185,734
Never married	28.8	35.0	38.0
Now married, except separated...	53.8	47.6	44.3
Separated..	2.0	2.0	2.0
Widowed..	2.5	2.9	2.4
Divorced..	12.9	12.5	13.3
Females, 15 Years and Over	771,263	1,069,123	1,190,516
Never married	20.9	27.2	29.9
Now married, except separated...	53.1	47.2	44.2
Separated..	2.7	2.8	2.7
Widowed..	8.6	8.0	8.2
Divorced..	14.7	14.8	15.1

Table NV-3. Households and Housing Characteristics

(Number, percent, dollars.)

Item	2000	2010	2016	Average annual percent change, 2010–2016
Total Households..	751,165	989,811	1,055,158	1.1
Family households	498,333	639,686	670,968	0.8
Married-couple family	373,201	452,361	469,014	0.6
Other family	125,132	187,325	201,954	1.3
Male householder, no wife present............................	41,650	63,327	64,875	0.4
Female householder, no husband present....................	83,482	123,998	137,079	1.8
Nonfamily households	252,832	350,125	384,190	1.6
Householder living alone...	186,745	266,232	301,597	2.2
Householder not living alone......................................	66,087	83,893	82,593	-0.3
Housing Characteristics				
Total housing units...	827,457	1,175,070	1,221,759	0.7
Occupied housing units	751,165	989,811	1,055,158	1.1
Owner occupied	457,247	565,869	578,762	0.4
Renter occupied	293,918	423,942	476,396	2.1
Average household size..	2.62	2.70	2.75	0.3
Financial Characteristics				
Median gross rent of renter-occupied housing	699	952	1003	0.9
Median monthly owner costs for housing units with a mortgage	1,190	1,638	1,401	-2.4
Median value of owner-occupied housing units	142,000	174,800	239,500	6.2

Table NV-4. Migration, Origin, and Language

(Number, percent.)

Characteristic	State			U.S.		
	2015	2016	Percent change	2015	2016	Percent change
Residence 1 Year Ago						
Population 1 year and over	2,859,489	2,907,243	1.7	317,635,720	319,361,956	0.5
Same house	80.1	82.6	X	85.3	85.4	X
Different house in the U.S.	19.2	16.9	X	14.1	13.9	X
Same county	13.6	12.0	X	8.5	8.3	X
Different county	5.6	4.9	X	5.6	5.6	X
Same state	0.9	0.9	X	3.2	3.2	X
Different state	4.8	4.1	X	2.4	2.4	X
Abroad	0.6	0.5	X	0.7	0.7	X
Place of Birth						
Native born	2,332,675	2,353,259	0.9	278,128,449	279,388,170	0.5
Male	50.7	51.0	X	49.3	49.3	X
Female	49.3	49.0	X	50.7	50.7	X
Foreign born	558,170	586,799	5.1	43,290,372	43,739,345	1.0
Male	47.2	46.7	X	48.6	48.5	X
Female	52.8	53.3	X	51.4	51.5	X
Foreign born; naturalized U.S. citizen...........................	261,316	278,711	6.7	20,697,103	21,238,372	2.6
Male	45.6	45.2	X	45.9	45.9	X
Female	54.4	54.8	X	54.1	54.1	X
Foreign born; not a U.S. citizen....................................	296,854	308,088	3.8	22,593,269	22,500,973	-0.4
Male	48.7	48.1	X	51.1	51.0	X
Female	51.3	51.9	X	48.9	49.0	X
Entered 2010 or later	11.7	13.8	X	15.6	18.6	X
Entered 2000 to 2009	26.6	28.0	X	27.9	26.7	X
Entered before 2000...	61.7	58.2	X	56.5	54.7	X
World Region of Birth, Foreign						
Foreign-born population, excluding population born at sea	558,170	586,741	5.1	43,289,646	43,738,901	1.0
Europe	7.9	7.2	X	11.1	10.9	X
Asia..	30.1	30.6	X	30.6	30.8	X
Africa	3.8	3.1	X	4.8	4.9	X
Oceania	0.4	0.7	X	0.6	0.6	X
Latin America	56.2	56.3	X	51.1	51.0	X
North America	1.6	2.1	X	1.9	1.8	X
Language Spoken at Home and Ability to Speak English						
Population 5 years and over..	2,713,912	2,756,697	1.6	301,625,014	303,328,961	0.6
English only	69.8	69.3	X	78.5	78.4	X
Language other than English..	30.2	30.7	X	21.5	21.6	X
Speaks English less than "very well"..........................	12.2	11.8	X	8.6	8.6	X

NA = Not available.
X = Not applicable.
- = Zero or rounds to zero.

Table NV-5. Median Income and Poverty Status, 2016

(Number, percent, except as noted.)

Characteristic	State		U.S.	
	Number	Percent	Number	Percent
Median Income				
Households (dollars)...	55,180	X	57,617	X
Families (dollars)	65,384	X	71,062	X
Below Poverty Level (All People)	399,420	13.8	44,268,996	14.0
Sex				
Male	182,898	12.7	19,760,056	12.8
Female	216,522	14.9	24,508,940	15.2
Age				
Under 18 years...	126,874	19.1	14,115,713	19.5
Related children under 18 years...........................	123,307	18.6	13,805,435	19.1
18 to 64 years	234,408	13.1	25,723,818	13.2
65 years and over	38,138	8.7	4,429,465	9.2

X = Not applicable.

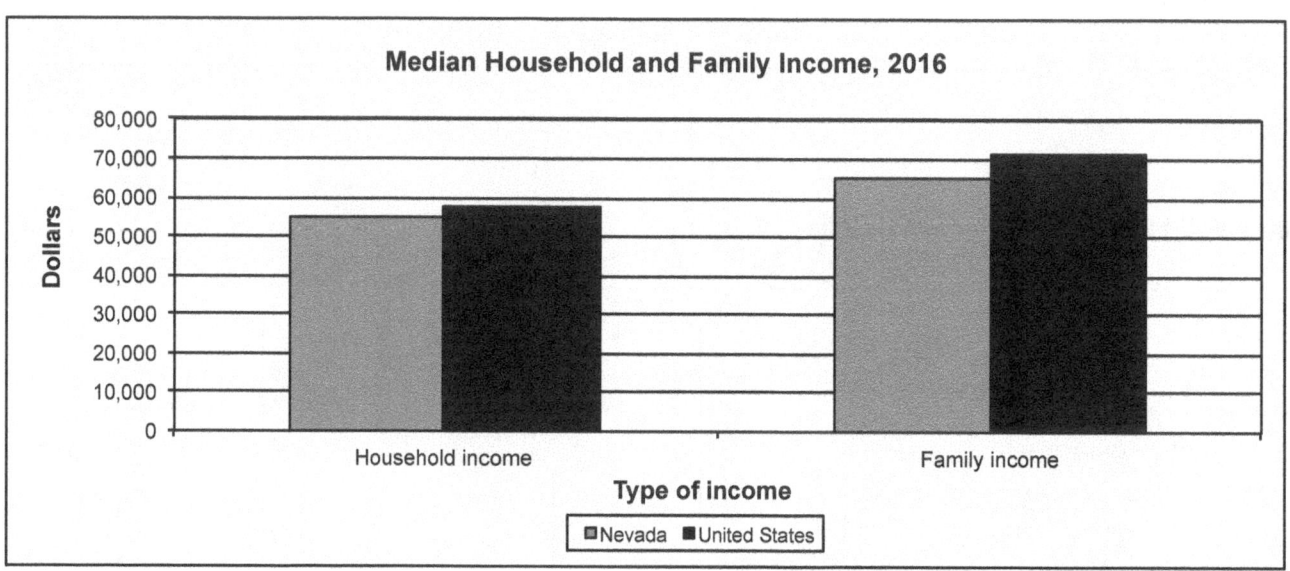

Table NV-6. Health Insurance Coverage Status for the Civilian Noninstitutionalized Population and Children Under 18 Years of Age

(Number, percent.)

Item	2008	2009	2010	2011	2012	2013	2014	2015	2016
Civilian Noninstitutionalized Population	2,568,111	2,610,041	2,668,966	2,686,989	2,723,965	2,757,207	2,805,532	2,855,974	2,905,767
Covered by Private or Public Insurance									
Number..	2,020,412	2,038,426	2,065,266	2,098,195	2,120,540	2,187,128	2,378,879	2,505,290	2,575,349
Percent..	78.7	78.1	77.4	78.1	77.8	79.3	84.8	87.7	88.6
Not Covered									
Number..	547,699	571,615	603,700	588,794	603,425	570,079	426,653	350,684	330,418
Percent..	21.3	21.9	22.6	21.9	22.2	20.7	15.2	12.3	11.4
Percent in the U.S. not covered..................................	15.1	15.1	15.5	15.1	14.8	14.5	11.7	9.4	8.6
Children Under 18 Years of Age	666,937	681,911	663,742	662,359	663,481	661,097	661,634	667,602	676,435
Covered by Private or Public Insurance									
Number..	531,968	560,525	548,403	554,955	553,334	562,588	597,902	617,152	630,576
Percent..	79.8	82.2	82.6	83.8	83.4	85.1	90.4	92.4	93.2
Not Covered									
Number..	134,969	121,386	115,339	107,404	110,147	98,509	63,732	50,450	45,859
Percent..	20.2	17.8	17.4	16.2	16.6	14.9	9.6	7.6	6.8
Percent in the U.S. not covered..................................	9.9	8.6	8.0	7.5	7.2	7.1	6.0	4.8	4.5

Table NV-7. Employment Status by Demographic Group, 2017

(Numbers in thousands, percent.)

Characteristic	Civilian noninstitutional population	Civilian labor force		Employed		Unemployed	
		Number	Percent of population	Number	Percent of population	Number	Percent of population
Total..	2,340	1,454	62.1	1,381	59.0	73	5.0
Sex							
Male...	1,154	801	69.4	757	65.6	44	5.5
Female..	1,186	654	55.1	624	52.6	29	4.5
Race, Sex, and Hispanic Origin							
White..	1,769	1,081	61.1	1,031	58.3	50	4.6
Male..	885	602	68.0	571	64.5	31	5.1
Female...	884	479	54.2	460	52.1	19	4.0
Black or African American.........................	217	145	66.8	133	61.3	12	8.2
Male..	103	79	76.8	73	70.7	6	8.0
Female...	114	66	57.7	60	52.9	6	8.4
Hispanic or Latino ethnicity[1]	618	433	70.0	410	66.4	23	5.2
Male..	309	243	78.8	230	74.5	13	5.4
Female...	309	189	61.3	180	58.2	10	5.0
Age							
16 to 19 years...	144	53	36.5	45	31.2	8	14.6
20 to 24 years...	195	152	77.8	139	71.1	13	8.7
25 to 34 years...	413	331	80.1	316	76.4	16	4.7
35 to 44 years...	377	311	82.5	301	79.8	10	3.2
45 to 54 years...	378	298	78.9	286	75.7	12	4.1
55 to 64 years...	368	220	60.0	211	57.4	9	4.2
65 years and over....................................	465	89	19.1	84	18.0	5	5.5

NOTE: Data in Table 7 are from the Current Population Survey (CPS) and do not match the estimates in Table 8. See notes and definitions for further information.
[1] May be of any race.

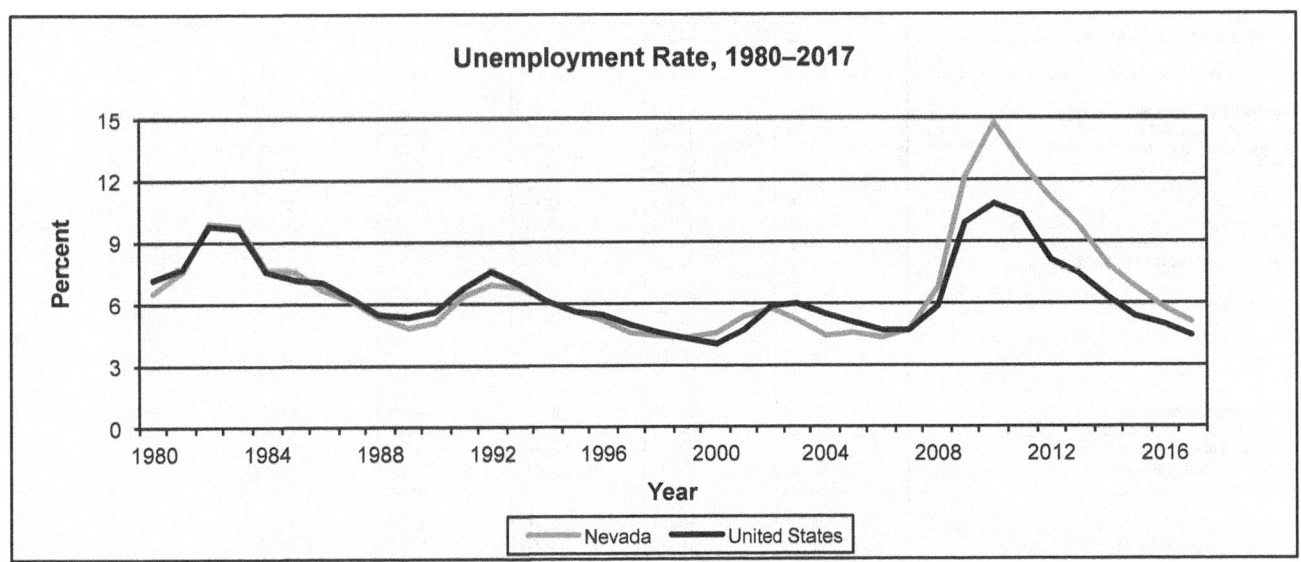

Table NV-8. Employment Status of the Civilian Noninstitutional Population Age 16 Years and Over

(Number, percent.)

Year	Civilian labor force	Civilian participation rate	Employed	Unemployed	Unemployment rate
2009..	1,349,299	67.5	1,196,758	152,541	11.3
2010..	1,358,578	65.9	1,174,774	183,804	13.5
2011..	1,373,115	65.5	1,194,264	178,851	13.0
2012..	1,376,381	64.6	1,222,710	153,671	11.2
2013..	1,381,157	63.8	1,248,122	133,035	9.6
2014..	1,394,758	63.3	1,284,292	110,466	7.9
2015..	1,413,739	62.9	1,318,024	95,715	6.8
2016..	1,430,344	62.3	1,348,265	82,079	5.7
2017..	1,462,955	62.3	1,389,372	73,583	5.0

Table NV-9. Employment and Average Wages by Industry

(Estimates through 2010 are based on the 2007 *North American Industry Classification System* [NAICS]. Estimates from 2011 onward are based on the 2012 NAICS.)

Industry	2010	2011	2012	2013	2014	2015	2016
	Number of jobs						
Wage and Salary Employment by Industry........................	1,155,166	1,162,730	1,180,454	1,208,421	1,251,977	1,292,689	1,332,225
Farm Wage and Salary Employment.............................	2,100	1,980	2,106	2,248	2,109	2,049	2,164
Nonfarm Wage and Salary Employment.........................	1,153,066	1,160,750	1,178,348	1,206,173	1,249,868	1,290,640	1,330,061
Private wage and salary employment............................	983,971	994,212	1,013,040	1,039,518	1,081,824	1,121,203	1,158,158
Forestry, fishing, and related activities..........................	633	656	687	701	712	712	699
Mining..	12,200	13,885	15,423	15,311	14,380	14,182	13,686
Utilities..	4,324	4,187	4,037	3,967	3,884	3,964	4,069
Construction	61,360	53,781	53,427	58,533	64,939	71,965	77,912
Manufacturing..	37,950	38,244	39,283	40,611	41,537	42,180	43,612
Durable goods manufacturing.................................	24,789	24,680	25,119	25,646	25,769	26,126	26,861
Nondurable goods manufacturing............................	13,161	13,564	14,164	14,965	15,768	16,054	16,751
Wholesale trade	33,165	32,918	32,789	33,094	34,136	34,586	34,754
Retail trade..	128,354	130,114	133,470	136,348	141,049	144,445	145,289
Transportation and warehousing................................	46,168	47,716	49,750	50,627	53,625	57,610	60,483
Information	12,523	12,599	12,826	12,834	13,731	13,882	14,390
Finance and insurance	31,948	31,446	31,930	33,053	33,430	34,558	36,065
Real estate and rental and leasing.............................	22,126	22,266	22,313	23,241	24,127	25,714	26,471
Professional, scientific, and technical services	47,801	47,566	48,174	49,455	50,812	52,647	54,935
Management of companies and enterprises...................	18,313	18,130	19,628	20,230	20,913	22,632	24,027
Administrative and waste services.............................	71,486	75,627	78,589	81,371	85,474	92,671	98,508
Educational services	9,571	9,799	9,763	9,956	10,479	10,580	10,961
Health care and social assistance.............................	93,980	95,731	97,905	100,474	104,461	109,773	115,705
Arts, entertainment, and recreation............................	25,809	27,028	27,094	27,451	28,369	28,997	30,781
Accommodation and food services............................	284,803	290,324	291,564	297,957	309,218	313,361	317,039
Other services, except public administration..................	41,457	42,195	44,388	44,304	46,548	46,744	48,772
Government and government enterprises......................	169,095	166,538	165,308	166,655	168,044	169,437	171,903
	Dollars						
Average Wages and Salaries by Industry	43,635	44,355	44,962	45,467	46,071	47,091	50,402
Average Farm Wages and Salaries	31,719	33,985	38,506	40,722	41,821	40,868	43,085
Average Nonfarm Wages and Salaries	43,657	44,372	44,973	45,476	46,078	47,101	50,414
Average private wages and salaries............................	42,327	43,216	43,983	44,578	45,163	46,200	49,333
Forestry, fishing, and related activities........................	32,673	33,582	34,585	34,926	35,801	34,966	38,159
Mining..	82,981	84,462	83,070	87,127	88,633	92,088	94,983
Utilities..	89,927	94,646	96,341	107,063	103,124	106,040	105,116
Construction	55,451	53,114	52,103	51,427	52,627	53,304	62,466
Manufacturing..	50,384	51,740	53,003	53,738	54,803	55,589	60,980
Durable goods manufacturing.................................	54,941	56,740	58,721	60,413	61,846	62,242	69,551
Nondurable goods manufacturing............................	41,800	42,642	42,862	42,298	43,294	44,762	47,236
Wholesale trade	60,639	62,929	65,876	65,565	67,754	70,528	77,145
Retail trade..	27,688	28,202	28,741	29,160	29,579	29,953	31,542
Transportation and warehousing................................	47,401	50,135	50,683	51,383	51,404	52,730	54,251
Information	55,551	56,797	58,223	58,543	59,490	61,606	65,007
Finance and insurance	57,413	59,714	62,568	65,330	66,999	71,609	75,770
Real estate and rental and leasing.............................	39,265	40,178	40,841	42,069	43,612	46,763	49,280
Professional, scientific, and technical services	66,437	68,327	69,894	70,301	71,385	72,212	76,573
Management of companies and enterprises...................	102,353	110,897	116,678	121,209	120,679	114,153	126,731
Administrative and waste services.............................	29,636	29,949	29,762	29,660	30,274	31,343	33,278
Educational services	35,854	35,502	36,063	37,400	37,451	37,807	41,339
Health care and social assistance.............................	48,538	49,422	50,244	50,545	51,232	52,491	56,130
Arts, entertainment, and recreation............................	32,555	34,456	34,235	34,272	36,079	36,912	36,844
Accommodation and food services............................	33,593	34,602	35,136	35,489	35,887	36,488	37,705
Other services, except public administration..................	30,846	31,665	31,172	32,048	32,445	33,703	36,333
Government and government enterprises......................	51,396	51,278	51,046	51,081	51,969	53,063	57,696

Table NV-10. Employment Characteristics by Family Type

(Number, percent.)

Family type and labor force status	2014		2015		2016	
	Total	Families with own children under 18 years	Total	Families with own children under 18 years	Total	Families with own children under 18 years
All Families..	640,193	278,290	659,355	282,664	670,968	282,717
FAMILY TYPE AND LABOR FORCE STATUS						
Married-Couple Families............................	444,894	175,570	456,740	176,363	469,014	179,823
Both husband and wife in labor force............................	47.7	62.8	47.5	62.4	48.0	63.6
Husband in labor force, wife not in labor force	23.3	30.1	22.7	31.8	23.2	30.4
Wife in labor force, husband not in labor force	8.8	5.5	8.3	3.3	8.3	3.9
Both husband and wife not in labor force...........	20.1	1.7	20.6	2.1	19.3	1.4
Other Families	195,299	102,720	202,615	106,301	201,954	102,894
Female householder, no husband present...........................	65.5	67.9	68.7	70.8	67.9	70.2
In labor force...........................	49.8	57.0	50.1	59.0	50.0	59.3
Not in labor force	15.7	11.0	18.6	11.8	17.9	11.0
Male householder, no wife present...........................	34.5	32.1	31.3	29.2	32.1	29.8
In labor force...........................	28.9	30.5	25.8	27.6	25.9	27.4
Not in labor force	5.6	1.6	5.5	1.6	6.2	2.4

Table NV-11. School Enrollment and Educational Attainment, 2016

(Number, percent.)

Item	State	U.S.
Enrollment		
Total population 3 years and over, enrolled in school	700,680	81,572,277
Enrolled in nursery school or preschool (percent).....................	5.2	6.0
Enrolled in kindergarten (percent).....................	5.1	5.0
Enrolled in elementary school, grades 1-8 (percent).....................	43.0	40.3
Enrolled in high school, grades 9-12 (percent).....................	22.6	21.0
Enrolled in college or graduate school (percent).....................	24.1	27.7
Attainment		
Total population 25 years and over	2,010,610	218,475,480
Less than ninth grade (percent).....................	6.1	5.4
9th to 12th grade, no diploma (percent).....................	7.8	7.2
High school graduate, including equivalency (percent).....................	29.1	27.2
Some college, no degree (percent).....................	25.7	20.6
Associate's degree (percent).....................	7.8	8.4
Bachelor's degree (percent).....................	15.3	19.3
Graduate or professional degree (percent).....................	8.1	11.9
High school graduate or higher (percent).....................	86.0	87.5
Bachelor's degree or higher (percent).....................	23.5	31.3

Table NV-12. Public School Characteristics and Educational Indicators

(Number, percent; data derived from National Center of Education Statistics.)

Item	State	U.S.
Public Schools, 2015–2016 (except where noted)		
Number of school districts...................	19	18,328
Number of schools...................	662	98,456
Number of students...................	467,527	50,327,015
Number of teachers...................	22,702	3,151,497
Student-teacher ratio...................	20.6	16.0
Expenditures per student (dollars), 2014-2015...................	8,451	11,445
Four-year adjusted cohort graduation rate (ACGR)[1,2]	73.6	84.1
Students eligible for free or reduced-price lunch (percent), 2014-2015...................	52.3	51.8
English language learners (percent), Fall 2015...................	16.8	9.5
Students age 3 to 21 served under IDEA, part B (percent)...................	11.9	13.2

Public Schools by Type	Number	Percent of state public schools
Total number of schools...................	662	100.0
Regular	610	92.1
Special education...................	14	2.1
Vocational education...................	0	-
Alternative education...................	38	5.7

NOTE: Every school is assigned only one school type based on its instructional emphasis.
[1] ACGR data represents a new method of calculating high-school completion rates and may not be comparable to previous years' data for Averaged Freshmen Graduation Rates (AFGR).
[2] The United States 4-year ACGRs were estimated using both the reported 4-year ACGR data from 49 states and the District of Columbia and using imputed data for Idaho. The estimate for American Indian/Alaska Native students also includes imputed data for Virginia.

Table NV-13. Reported Voting and Registration of the Voting-Age Population, November 2016

(Numbers in thousands, percent.)

Item	Total population	Total citizen population	Registered			Voted		
			Total registered	Percent registered (total population)	Percent registered (total citizen population)	Total voted	Percent voted (total population)	Percent voted (total citizen population)
U.S. Total	245,502	224,059	157,596	64.2	70.3	137,537	56.0	61.4
State Total..............................	2,234	1,975	1,371	61.4	69.4	1,195	53.5	60.5
Sex								
Male	1,098	974	663	60.4	68.0	570	51.9	58.5
Female	1,136	1,001	708	62.4	70.8	625	55.0	62.4
Race								
White alone............................	1,730	1,537	1,076	62.2	70.0	948	54.8	61.7
White, non-Hispanic alone............	1,275	1,236	879	69.0	71.1	781	61.3	63.2
Black alone.............................	182	169	122	67.3	72.3	110	60.7	65.1
Asian alone.............................	198	163	91	46.0	56.0	72	36.5	44.4
Hispanic (of any race).......................	517	346	234	45.3	67.7	196	37.9	56.6
White alone or in combination	1,775	1,581	1,109	62.5	70.2	977	55.1	61.8
Black alone or in combination...........	204	191	143	70.2	74.7	128	62.9	67.1
Asian alone or in combination...........	214	178	99	46.2	55.3	78	36.4	43.6
Age								
18 to 24 years........................	261	229	124	47.3	53.9	98	37.6	42.9
25 to 34 years........................	415	361	222	53.3	61.4	183	43.9	50.6
35 to 44 years........................	365	305	220	60.3	72.1	186	50.9	60.9
45 to 64 years........................	774	678	480	62.0	70.8	431	55.6	63.5
65 years and over	418	402	326	78.1	81.1	297	71.2	74.0

Table NV-14. Crime

(Number, rate per 100,000. Data are derived from the FBI Uniform Crime Reports.)

Item	State			U.S. [1,2,3,4]		
	2015	2016	Percent change	2015	2016	Percent change
TOTAL POPULATION [5]	2,890,845	2,940,058	1.7	321,418,820	323,127,513	0.5
VIOLENT CRIME						
Number..................	20,118	19,936	-0.9	1,231,566	1,248,185	1.3
Rate	695.9	678.1	-2.6	383.2	386.3	0.8
Murder and Nonnegligent Manslaughter						
Number..................	178	224	25.8	15,696	17,250	9.9
Rate	6.2	7.6	22.6	4.9	5.3	8.2
Rape[6]						
Number..................	1,688	1,733	2.7	124,047	130,603	5.3
Rate	58.4	58.9	0.9	38.6	40.4	4.7
Robbery						
Number..................	6,287	6,340	0.8	327,374	332,198	1.5
Rate	217.5	215.6	-0.9	101.9	102.8	0.9
Aggravated Assault						
Number..................	11,965	11,639	-2.7	764,449	803,007	5.0
Rate	413.9	395.9	-4.3	237.8	248.5	4.5
PROPERTY CRIME						
Number..................	77,137	76,047	-1.4	7,993,631	7,919,035	-0.9
Rate	2,668.3	2,586.6	-3.1	2,487.0	2,450.7	-1.5
Burglary						
Number..................	22,360	18,850	-15.7	1,579,527	1,515,096	-4.1
Rate	773.5	641.1	-17.1	491.4	468.9	-4.6
Larceny-Theft						
Number..................	43,426	44,017	1.4	5,706,346	5,638,455	-1.2
Rate	1,502.2	1,497.1	-0.3	1,775.4	1,745.0	-1.7
Motor Vehicle Theft						
Number..................	11,351	13,180	16.1	707,758	765,484	8.2
Rate	392.7	448.3	14.2	220.2	236.9	7.6

NOTE: Although arson data are included in the trend and clearance tables, sufficient data are not available to estimate totals for this offense. Therefore, no arson data are published in this table.

X = Not applicable.

- = Zero or rounds to zero.

[1] The crime figures have been adjusted.

[2] The data collection methodology for the offense of forcible rape used by the Minnesota state Uniform Crime Reporting (UCR) Program (with the exception of Minneapolis and St. Paul, Minnesota) does not comply with national UCR Program guidelines. Consequently, its figures for forcible rape and violent crime (of which forcible rape is a part) are not published in this table.

[3] Includes offenses reported by the Zoological Police and the Metro Transit Police.

[4] Because of changes in the state's reporting practices, figures are not comparable to previous years' data.

[5] Populations are U.S. Census Bureau provisional estimates as of July 1 of each year.

[6] The figures shown for the offense of rape were estimated using the revised Uniform Crime Reporting (UCR) definition of rape.

Table NV-15. State Government Finances, 2016

(Dollar amounts in thousands, percent distribution.)

Item	Dollars	Percent distribution
Total Revenue	16,808,682	100.0
General revenue	13,904,474	82.7
Intergovernmental revenue	4,558,408	27.1
Taxes	8,025,043	47.7
General sales	4,266,267	25.4
Selective sales	2,081,507	12.4
License taxes	651,067	3.9
Individual income tax	0	-
Corporate income tax	0	-
Other taxes	1,026,202	6.1
Current charges	775,386	4.6
Miscellaneous general revenue	545,637	3.2
Utility revenue	48,742	0.3
Liquor stores revenue	0	-
Insurance trust revenue [1]	2,855,466	17.0
Total Expenditure	15,315,276	100.0
Intergovernmental expenditure	4,429,481	28.9
Direct expenditure	10,885,795	71.1
Current operation	7,127,353	46.5
Capital outlay	626,461	4.1
Insurance benefits and repayments	2,578,586	16.8
Assistance and subsidies	426,281	2.8
Interest on debt	127,114	0.8
Exhibit: Salaries and wages	1,637,787	10.7
Total Expenditure	15,315,276	100.0
General expenditure	12,686,171	82.8
Intergovernmental expenditure	4,429,481	28.9
Direct expenditure	8,256,690	53.9
General expenditure, by function:		
Education	4,885,614	31.9
Public welfare	4,034,671	26.3
Hospitals	247,890	1.6
Health	244,929	1.6
Highways	717,606	4.7
Police protection	84,059	0.5
Correction	283,158	1.8
Natural resources	114,354	0.7
Parks and recreation	18,490	0.1
Governmental administration	307,430	2.0
Interest on general debt	127,114	0.8
Other and unallocable	1,620,856	10.6
Utility expenditure	50,519	0.3
Liquor stores expenditure	0	-
Insurance trust expenditure	2,578,586	16.8
Debt at End of Fiscal Year	3,222,367	X
Cash and Security Holdings	38,262,037	X

X = Not applicable.
- = Zero or rounds to zero.
[1] Within insurance trust revenue, net earnings of state retirement systems is a calculated statistic (the item code in the data file is X08), and thus can be positive or negative. Net earnings is the sum of earnings on investments plus gains on investments minus losses on investments. The change made in 2002 for asset valuation from book to market value in accordance with Statement 34 of the Governmental Accounting Standards Board is reflected in the calculated statistics.

Table NV-16. State Government Tax Collections, 2017

(Dollars in thousands, percent.)

Item	Dollars	Percent distribution
Total Taxes	8,624,618	100.0
Property taxes	300,490	3.5
Sales and gross receipts	6,923,284	80.3
General sales and gross receipts	4,756,243	55.1
Selective sales and gross receipts	2,167,041	25.1
Alcoholic beverages	45,011	0.5
Amusements	919,642	10.7
Insurance premiums	359,741	4.2
Motor fuels	326,425	3.8
Pari-mutuels	3	-
Public utilities	24,676	0.3
Tobacco products	195,371	2.3
Other selective sales	296,172	3.4
Licenses	666,527	7.7
Alcoholic beverages	X	-
Amusements	85,047	1.0
Corporations in general	77,101	0.9
Hunting and fishing	13,447	0.2
Motor vehicle	213,455	2.5
Motor vehicle operators	30,521	0.4
Public utilities	X	-
Occupation and business, NEC	242,142	2.8
Other licenses	4,814	0.1
Income taxes	X	-
Individual income	X	-
Corporation net income	X	-
Other taxes	734,317	8.5
Death and gift	X	-
Documentary and stock transfer	90,479	1.0
Severance	68,605	0.8
Taxes, NEC	575,233	6.7

X = Not applicable.
- = Zero or rounds to zero.

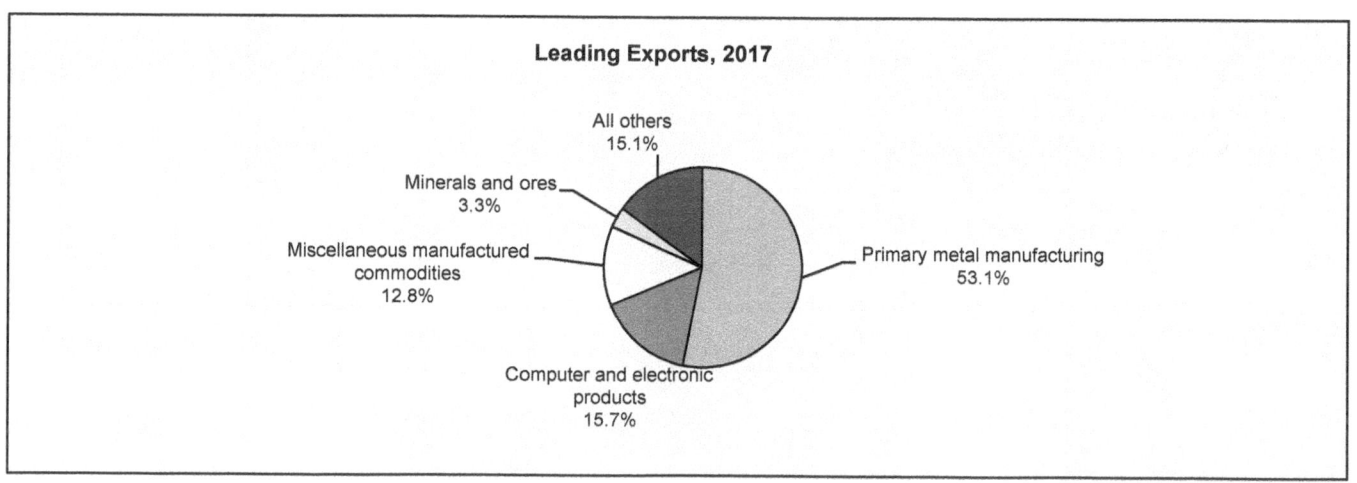

Leading Exports, 2017

All others 15.1%

Minerals and ores 3.3%

Miscellaneous manufactured commodities 12.8%

Primary metal manufacturing 53.1%

Computer and electronic products 15.7%

NEW HAMPSHIRE

Facts and Figures

Location: Northeastern United States; bordered on the N by Canada (Quebec), on the E by Maine, on the SE by the Atlantic Ocean, on the S by Massachusetts, and on the W by Vermont

Area: 9,350 sq. mi. (24,216 sq. km.); rank—46th

Population: 1,342,795 (2017 est.); rank—41st

Principal Cities: capital—Concord; largest—Manchester

Statehood: June 21, 1788; 9th state

U.S. Congress: 2 senators, 2 representatives

State Motto: Live Free or Die

State Song: "Old New Hampshire"

State Nickname: The Granite State

Abbreviations: NH; N.H.

State Symbols: flower—purple lilac; tree—white birch; bird—purple finch

At a Glance

- With an increase in population of 2.0 percent, New Hampshire ranked 36th among the states in growth from 2010 to 2017.

- New Hampshire's violent crime rate in 2016 was 197.6 per 100,000 population, the third lowest in the country, compared to a rate of 386.3 for the entire nation.

- The state's property crime rate, 1,512.9 per 100,000 population, was the lowest in the country in 2016.

- New Hampshire had the third highest rate of drug overdose deaths in 2016, with 39.0 deaths per 100,000 population.

- New Hampshire tied with Vermont for the lowest birth rate in the country in 2016, with 9.2 births per 1,000 population.

Table NH-1. Population by Age, Sex, Race, and Hispanic Origin

(Number, percent, except where noted.)

Sex, age, race, and Hispanic origin	2000	2010	2017 [1]	Average annual percent change, 2010–2017
Total Population..	1,235,786	1,316,470	1,342,795	2.0
Percent of total U.S. population	0.4	0.4	0.4	X
Sex				
Male..	607,687	649,394	665,009	2.4
Female	628,099	667,076	677,786	1.6
Age				
Under 5 years..	75,685	69,806	64,481	-7.6
5 to 19 years..	268,480	255,996	230,907	-9.8
20 to 64 years...	743,651	812,400	811,250	-0.1
65 years and over	147,970	178,268	236,157	32.5
Median age (years)..	37.1	41.1	43.1	4.9
Race and Hispanic Origin				
One race				
White	1,186,851	1,248,321	1,256,807	0.7
Black...	9,035	16,365	21,239	29.8
American Indian and Alaska Native	2,964	3,530	3,978	12.7
Asian...	15,931	28,933	37,202	28.6
Native Hawaiian or Other Pacific Islander	371	532	615	15.6
Two or more races..	13,214	18,789	22,954	22.2
Hispanic (of any race)...	20,489	38,688	49,567	28.1

X = Not applicable.
- = Zero or rounds to zero.
[1] Population figures for 2017 are July 1 estimates. The 2010 estimates are taken from the 2010 Census.

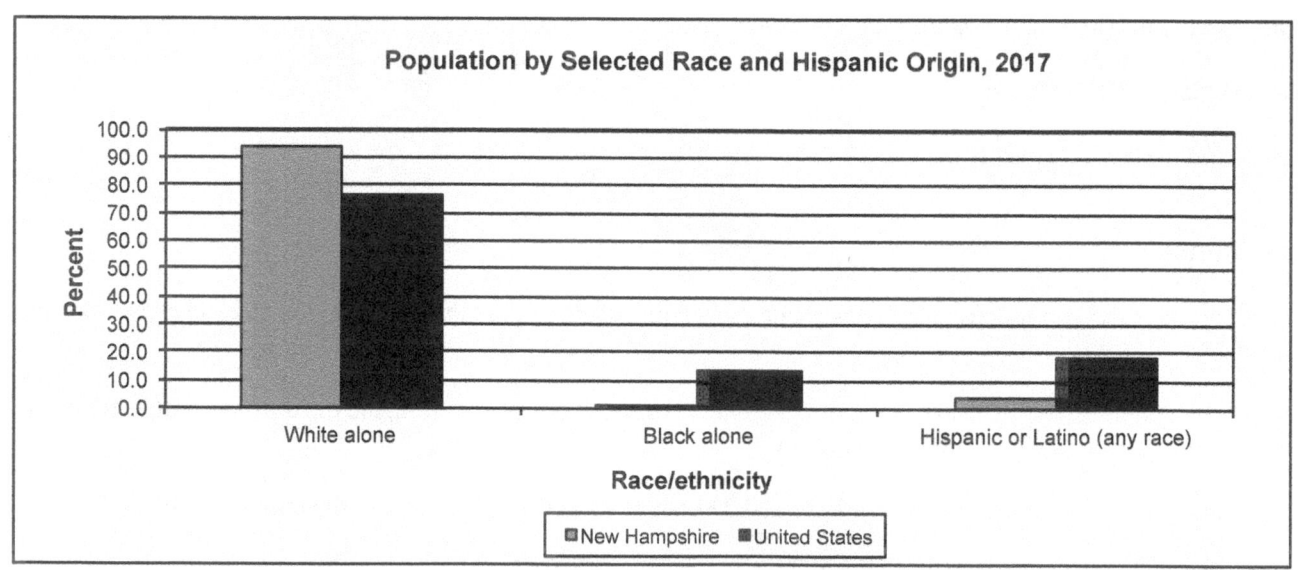

Table NH-2. Marital Status

(Number, percent distribution.)

Sex, age, and marital status	2000	2010	2016
Males, 15 Years and Over...	476,409	529,439	555,109
Never married	27.7	30.5	33.0
Now married, except separated...	59.1	54.7	52.2
Separated..	1.2	1.3	1.1
Widowed..	2.4	2.6	2.8
Divorced..	9.6	10.9	10.9
Females, 15 Years and Over..	502,232	555,698	568,597
Never married	22.3	25.4	26.7
Now married, except separated...	55.7	51.4	50.3
Separated..	1.5	1.3	1.2
Widowed..	9.2	8.6	8.6
Divorced..	11.3	13.4	13.2

Table NH-3. Households and Housing Characteristics

(Number, percent, dollars.)

Item	2000	2010	2016	Average annual percent change, 2010–2016
Total Households..	474,606	515,431	520,643	0.2
Family households	323,651	344,057	342,912	-0.1
Married-couple family	262,438	274,195	271,458	-0.2
Other family	61,213	69,862	71,454	0.4
Male householder, no wife present........................	18,261	22,205	23,146	0.7
Female householder, no husband present...............	42,952	47,657	48,308	0.2
Nonfamily households	150,955	171,374	177,731	0.6
Householder living alone.....................................	116,014	130,327	137,192	0.9
Householder not living alone................................	34,941	41,047	40,539	-0.2
Housing Characteristics				
Total housing units...	547,024	614,996	625,337	0.3
Occupied housing units	474,606	515,431	520,643	0.2
Owner occupied	330,700	369,448	365,021	-0.2
Renter occupied	143,906	145,983	155,622	1.1
Average household size...	2.53	2.48	2.48	-
Financial Characteristics				
Median gross rent of renter-occupied housing	646	951	1026	1.3
Median monthly owner costs for housing units with a mortgage	1,226	1,853	1,821	-0.3
Median value of owner-occupied housing units...........	133,300	243,000	251,100	0.6

- = Zero or rounds to zero.

Table NH-4. Migration, Origin, and Language

(Number, percent.)

Characteristic	State			U.S.		
	2015	2016	Percent change	2015	2016	Percent change
Residence 1 Year Ago						
Population 1 year and over	1,318,121	1,322,101	0.3	317,635,720	319,361,956	0.5
Same house	86.1	84.9	X	85.3	85.4	X
Different house in the U.S.	13.3	14.6	X	14.1	13.9	X
Same county	7.3	8.0	X	8.5	8.3	X
Different county	6.0	6.6	X	5.6	5.6	X
Same state	2.0	2.6	X	3.2	3.2	X
Different state	4.1	4.0	X	2.4	2.4	X
Abroad	0.6	0.5	X	0.7	0.7	X
Place of Birth						
Native born	1,250,649	1,258,486	0.6	278,128,449	279,388,170	0.5
Male	49.5	49.8	X	49.3	49.3	X
Female	50.5	50.2	X	50.7	50.7	X
Foreign born	79,959	76,309	-4.6	43,290,372	43,739,345	1.0
Male	48.3	49.8	X	48.6	48.5	X
Female	51.7	50.2	X	51.4	51.5	X
Foreign born; naturalized U.S. citizen...................	45,461	40,403	-11.1	20,697,103	21,238,372	2.6
Male	43.3	45.7	X	45.9	45.9	X
Female	56.7	54.3	X	54.1	54.1	X
Foreign born; not a U.S. citizen.........................	34,498	35,906	4.1	22,593,269	22,500,973	-0.4
Male	54.8	54.3	X	51.1	51.0	X
Female	45.2	45.7	X	48.9	49.0	X
Entered 2010 or later	17.6	26.0	X	15.6	18.6	X
Entered 2000 to 2009	28.0	22.6	X	27.9	26.7	X
Entered before 2000..	54.4	51.4	X	56.5	54.7	X
World Region of Birth, Foreign						
Foreign-born population, excluding population born at sea	79,959	76,309	-4.6	43,289,646	43,738,901	1.0
Europe..	25.4	22.7	X	11.1	10.9	X
Asia..	34.5	37.9	X	30.6	30.8	X
Africa..	6.4	8.2	X	4.8	4.9	X
Oceania...	0.2	1.2	X	0.6	0.6	X
Latin America	20.9	19.5	X	51.1	51.0	X
North America...	12.6	10.5	X	1.9	1.8	X
Language Spoken at Home and Ability to Speak English						
Population 5 years and over................................	1,267,099	1,270,317	0.3	301,625,014	303,328,961	0.6
English only	92.2	92.3	X	78.5	78.4	X
Language other than English.............................	7.8	7.7	X	21.5	21.6	X
Speaks English less than "very well"...................	2.2	2.5	X	8.6	8.6	X

NA = Not available.
X = Not applicable.
- = Zero or rounds to zero.

Table NH-5. Median Income and Poverty Status, 2016

(Number, percent, except as noted.)

Characteristic	State		U.S.	
	Number	Percent	Number	Percent
Median Income				
Households (dollars)...	70,936	X	57,617	X
Families (dollars)...	86,696	X	71,062	X
Below Poverty Level (All People)	94,289	7.3	44,268,996	14.0
Sex				
Male	41,869	6.5	19,760,056	12.8
Female	52,420	8.1	24,508,940	15.2
Age				
Under 18 years...	20,141	7.9	14,115,713	19.5
Related children under 18 years.......................................	18,896	7.4	13,805,435	19.1
18 to 64 years..	64,145	7.8	25,723,818	13.2
65 years and over..	10,003	4.6	4,429,465	9.2

X = Not applicable.

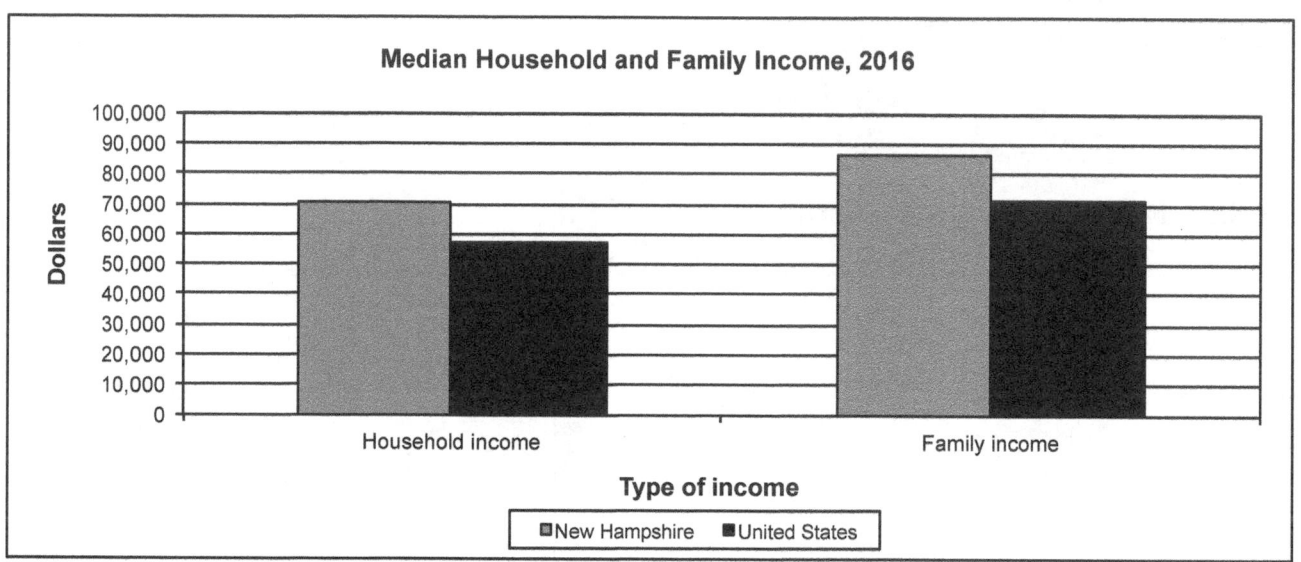

Median Household and Family Income, 2016

Table NH-6. Health Insurance Coverage Status for the Civilian Noninstitutionalized Population and Children Under 18 Years of Age

(Number, percent.)

Item	2008	2009	2010	2011	2012	2013	2014	2015	2016
Civilian Noninstitutionalized Population	1,299,356	1,308,729	1,302,639	1,303,868	1,306,026	1,308,658	1,311,921	1,314,249	1,316,467
Covered by Private or Public Insurance									
Number...	1,159,047	1,174,696	1,157,626	1,166,946	1,167,184	1,168,406	1,191,465	1,230,861	1,238,790
Percent..	89.2	89.8	88.9	89.5	89.4	89.3	90.8	93.7	94.1
Not Covered									
Number...	140,309	134,033	145,013	136,922	138,842	140,252	120,456	83,388	77,677
Percent..	10.8	10.2	11.1	10.5	10.6	10.7	9.2	6.3	5.9
Percent in the U.S. not covered......................................	15.1	15.1	15.5	15.1	14.8	14.5	11.7	9.4	8.6
Children Under 18 Years of Age	292,592	288,780	285,730	279,210	274,563	270,642	266,833	262,932	259,410
Covered by Private or Public Insurance									
Number...	277,639	275,304	272,051	269,018	263,665	260,381	255,132	255,940	252,563
Percent..	94.9	95.3	95.2	96.3	96.0	96.2	95.6	97.3	97.4
Not Covered									
Number...	14,953	13,476	13,679	10,192	10,898	10,261	11,701	6,992	6,847
Percent..	5.1	4.7	4.8	3.7	4.0	3.8	4.4	2.7	2.6
Percent in the U.S. not covered......................................	9.9	8.6	8.0	7.5	7.2	7.1	6.0	4.8	4.5

Table NH-7. Employment Status by Demographic Group, 2017

(Numbers in thousands, percent.)

Characteristic	Civilian noninstitutional population	Civilian labor force		Employed		Unemployed	
		Number	Percent of population	Number	Percent of population	Number	Percent of population
Total..........................	1,096	741	67.6	721	65.8	20	2.8
Sex							
Male.........................	538	388	72.1	377	70.2	10	2.7
Female......................	558	354	63.4	343	61.6	10	2.9
Race, Sex, and Hispanic Origin							
White........................	1,036	700	67.5	682	65.8	18	2.5
Male.........................	506	366	72.3	357	70.5	9	2.5
Female......................	530	334	63.0	325	61.3	9	2.6
Black or African American........	NA	NA	NA	NA	NA	NA	NA
Male.........................	NA	NA	NA	NA	NA	NA	NA
Female......................	NA	NA	NA	NA	NA	NA	NA
Hispanic or Latino ethnicity[1] ...	NA	NA	NA	NA	NA	NA	NA
Male.........................	NA	NA	NA	NA	NA	NA	NA
Female......................	NA	NA	NA	NA	NA	NA	NA
Age							
16 to 19 years...............	71	32	45.2	29	40.3	4	10.9
20 to 24 years...............	87	69	79.2	65	75.0	4	5.4
25 to 34 years...............	166	145	87.5	141	85.4	4	2.4
35 to 44 years...............	144	125	86.8	122	84.8	3	2.2
45 to 54 years...............	176	155	88.2	153	86.9	2	1.5
55 to 64 years...............	217	160	73.8	157	72.5	3	1.9
65 years and over	235	55	23.3	53	22.6	2	2.9

NOTE: Data in Table 7 are from the Current Population Survey (CPS) and do not match the estimates in Table 8. See notes and definitions for further information.
[1] May be of any race.
NA = Not available.

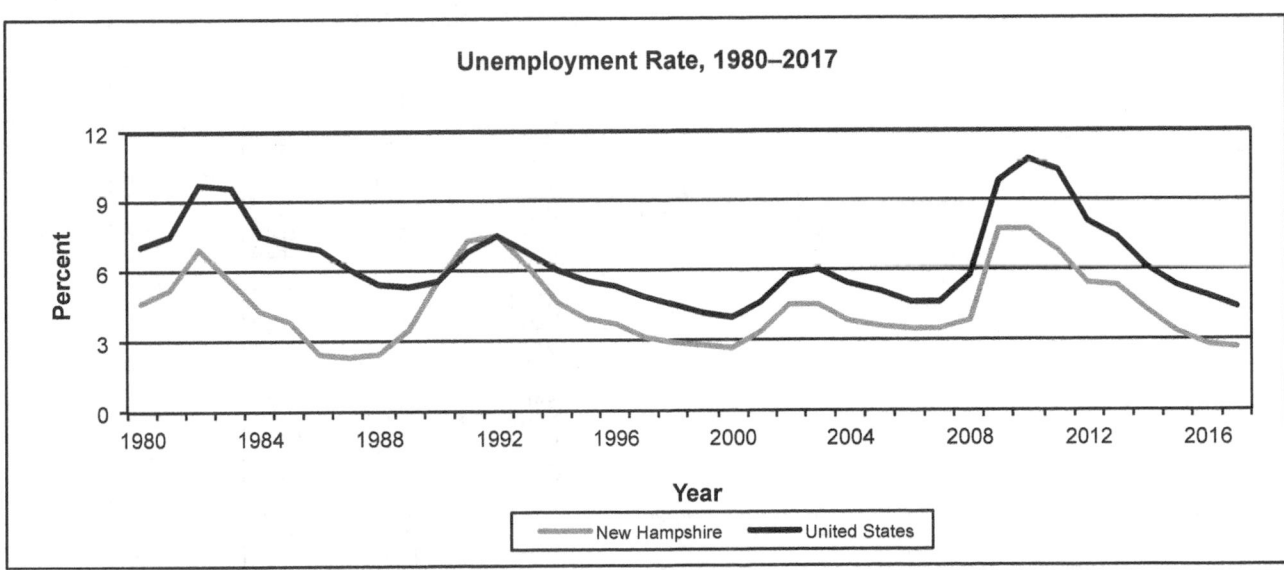

Table NH-8. Employment Status of the Civilian Noninstitutional Population Age 16 Years and Over

(Number, percent.)

Year	Civilian labor force	Civilian participation rate	Employed	Unemployed	Unemployment rate
2009..........................	744,227	70.4	697,802	46,425	6.2
2010..........................	738,257	69.9	695,135	43,122	5.8
2011..........................	736,302	69.6	696,532	39,770	5.4
2012..........................	741,097	69.5	700,371	40,726	5.5
2013..........................	741,285	69.2	703,534	37,751	5.1
2014..........................	740,667	68.7	708,977	31,690	4.3
2015..........................	741,937	68.5	716,874	25,063	3.4
2016..........................	746,452	68.4	725,154	21,298	2.9
2017..........................	746,549	67.9	726,607	19,942	2.7

Table NH-9. Employment and Average Wages by Industry

(Estimates through 2010 are based on the 2007 *North American Industry Classification System* [NAICS]. Estimates from 2011 onward are based on the 2012 NAICS.)

Industry	2010	2011	2012	2013	2014	2015	2016
	Number of jobs						
Wage and Salary Employment by Industry	630,596	634,658	640,890	647,438	655,973	665,995	677,409
Farm Wage and Salary Employment	1,125	1,230	1,451	1,660	1,664	1,658	1,547
Nonfarm Wage and Salary Employment	629,471	633,428	639,439	645,778	654,309	664,337	675,862
Private wage and salary employment	531,746	538,117	544,521	551,094	559,252	569,899	580,743
Forestry, fishing, and related activities	765	737	751	788	826	816	803
Mining	490	494	500	531	532	526	556
Utilities	2,513	2,472	2,454	2,481	2,320	2,185	2,136
Construction	22,170	22,857	22,835	23,197	23,857	24,853	26,205
Manufacturing	65,784	66,686	66,059	66,074	66,578	67,306	68,238
Durable goods manufacturing	50,303	51,179	50,205	49,884	49,938	50,169	50,827
Nondurable goods manufacturing	15,481	15,507	15,854	16,190	16,640	17,137	17,411
Wholesale trade	26,010	26,324	26,733	26,875	27,241	27,677	27,911
Retail trade	93,256	93,975	95,244	95,563	95,260	95,740	96,793
Transportation and warehousing	12,198	12,432	12,569	12,623	13,035	13,502	14,377
Information	11,202	11,177	12,093	11,927	12,044	12,274	12,547
Finance and insurance	27,378	28,065	28,777	29,181	29,430	30,109	30,967
Real estate and rental and leasing	6,903	6,978	6,727	6,934	6,984	6,818	7,033
Professional, scientific, and technical services	29,523	30,174	30,706	32,006	32,696	33,680	34,207
Management of companies and enterprises	8,016	8,096	8,155	8,187	8,193	8,634	8,905
Administrative and waste services	27,515	28,836	29,985	30,708	33,229	34,800	35,162
Educational services	21,959	21,909	22,255	22,803	23,294	24,289	24,755
Health care and social assistance	85,344	85,456	85,964	86,774	87,527	89,220	91,066
Arts, entertainment, and recreation	11,225	11,342	11,342	11,391	11,163	11,456	11,852
Accommodation and food services	51,733	52,394	53,589	55,240	56,273	57,469	58,486
Other services, except public administration	27,762	27,713	27,783	27,811	28,770	28,545	28,744
Government and government enterprises	97,725	95,311	94,918	94,684	95,057	94,438	95,119
	Dollars						
Average Wages and Salaries by Industry	45,182	46,476	47,575	48,251	50,380	51,752	54,539
Average Farm Wages and Salaries	26,130	20,918	30,999	27,939	29,502	27,184	32,120
Average Nonfarm Wages and Salaries	45,216	46,526	47,612	48,303	50,434	51,814	54,591
Average private wages and salaries	45,946	47,269	48,526	49,219	51,544	52,883	55,854
Forestry, fishing, and related activities	36,197	37,312	44,023	40,786	45,105	47,180	47,090
Mining	55,894	55,326	56,796	53,343	54,195	57,797	57,908
Utilities	87,825	96,454	94,513	94,655	102,359	103,123	108,182
Construction	49,367	50,143	51,516	52,969	54,211	57,279	62,217
Manufacturing	61,916	63,203	63,505	64,635	66,258	66,891	70,598
Durable goods manufacturing	65,468	66,679	66,784	67,993	69,839	70,090	73,763
Nondurable goods manufacturing	50,375	51,731	53,122	54,291	55,513	57,524	61,358
Wholesale trade	74,712	77,816	80,552	82,165	84,833	90,564	91,058
Retail trade	26,731	27,391	27,940	28,485	29,674	30,755	31,249
Transportation and warehousing	37,347	38,523	39,431	40,250	41,135	43,197	45,181
Information	75,234	74,492	75,495	78,953	91,556	82,763	85,710
Finance and insurance	78,077	81,359	84,488	85,898	94,501	94,668	94,616
Real estate and rental and leasing	41,118	47,289	45,040	46,133	47,655	50,861	54,660
Professional, scientific, and technical services	74,394	76,934	79,372	80,194	84,853	86,952	105,021
Management of companies and enterprises	80,800	82,358	97,866	89,768	106,426	106,638	109,525
Administrative and waste services	39,997	40,286	42,705	42,391	43,552	45,234	47,198
Educational services	40,004	40,808	41,711	42,730	43,902	44,666	44,433
Health care and social assistance	46,483	47,859	48,526	49,097	50,346	51,819	55,527
Arts, entertainment, and recreation	21,120	21,485	22,034	23,150	24,414	24,533	25,457
Accommodation and food services	18,737	19,192	19,719	20,118	20,888	21,957	23,636
Other services, except public administration	30,106	30,744	31,644	32,725	33,254	34,902	35,284
Government and government enterprises	41,243	42,327	42,368	42,968	43,898	45,361	46,879

Table NH-10. Employment Characteristics by Family Type

(Number, percent.)

Family type and labor force status	2014		2015		2016	
	Total	Families with own children under 18 years	Total	Families with own children under 18 years	Total	Families with own children under 18 years
All Families...	343,363	137,776	341,473	128,997	342,912	130,641
FAMILY TYPE AND LABOR FORCE STATUS						
Married-Couple Families..............................	268,440	94,424	268,944	91,828	271,458	92,165
Both husband and wife in labor force............................	57.3	70.9	57.5	74.1	55.9	73.4
Husband in labor force, wife not in labor force................	19.4	25.1	17.3	21.3	18.2	21.0
Wife in labor force, husband not in labor force..............	8.0	2.9	7.3	3.1	8.2	4.0
Both husband and wife not in labor force......................	15.3	1.1	16.8	1.1	16.4	1.3
Other Families	74,923	43,352	72,529	37,169	71,454	38,476
Female householder, no husband present.......................	67.7	69.3	71.1	74.3	67.6	66.9
In labor force..	52.2	60.2	50.7	59.5	50.0	55.4
Not in labor force	15.5	9.1	20.4	14.8	17.6	11.5
Male householder, no wife present...............................	32.3	30.7	28.9	25.7	32.4	33.1
In labor force..	27.7	29.3	22.4	23.9	27.8	30.7
Not in labor force	4.6	1.4	6.4	1.8	4.6	2.5

Table NH-11. School Enrollment and Educational Attainment, 2016

(Number, percent.)

Item	State	U.S.
Enrollment		
Total population 3 years and over, enrolled in school	307,848	81,572,277
Enrolled in nursery school or preschool (percent)..	5.3	6.0
Enrolled in kindergarten (percent)...	4.8	5.0
Enrolled in elementary school, grades 1-8 (percent).....................................	38.5	40.3
Enrolled in high school, grades 9-12 (percent)..	21.1	21.0
Enrolled in college or graduate school (percent)...	30.3	27.7
Attainment		
Total population 25 years and over	947,586	218,475,480
Less than ninth grade (percent)..	2.2	5.4
9th to 12th grade, no diploma (percent)	5.0	7.2
High school graduate, including equivalency (percent)...................................	27.0	27.2
Some college, no degree (percent)..	18.9	20.6
Associate's degree (percent)...	10.3	8.4
Bachelor's degree (percent)..	22.5	19.3
Graduate or professional degree (percent)...	14.1	11.9
High school graduate or higher (percent)	92.8	87.5
Bachelor's degree or higher (percent)..	36.6	31.3

Table NH-12. Public School Characteristics and Educational Indicators

(Number, percent; data derived from National Center of Education Statistics.)

Item	State	U.S.
Public Schools, 2015–2016 (except where noted)		
Number of school districts...	299	18,328
Number of schools...	490	98,456
Number of students..	182,425	50,327,015
Number of teachers..	14,770	3,151,497
Student-teacher ratio..	12.4	16.0
Expenditures per student (dollars), 2014-2015..	14,969	11,445
Four-year adjusted cohort graduation rate (ACGR)[1,2]	88.2	84.1
Students eligible for free or reduced-price lunch (percent), 2014-2015............	29.0	51.8
English language learners (percent), Fall 2015..	2.3	9.5
Students age 3 to 21 served under IDEA, part B (percent).............................	15.8	13.2

Public Schools by Type	Number	Percent of state public schools
Total number of schools..	490	100.0
Regular	490	100.0
Special education...	0	-
Vocational education...	0	-
Alternative education...	0	-

NOTE: Every school is assigned only one school type based on its instructional emphasis.
[1] ACGR data represents a new method of calculating high-school completion rates and may not be comparable to previous years' data for Averaged Freshmen Graduation Rates (AFGR).
[2] The United States 4-year ACGRs were estimated using both the reported 4-year ACGR data from 49 states and the District of Columbia and using imputed data for Idaho. The estimate for American Indian/Alaska Native students also includes imputed data for Virginia.
- = Zero or rounds to zero.

Table NH-13. Reported Voting and Registration of the Voting-Age Population, November 2016

(Numbers in thousands, percent.)

Item	Total population	Total citizen population	Registered			Voted		
			Total registered	Percent registered (total population)	Percent registered (total citizen population)	Total voted	Percent voted (total population)	Percent voted (total citizen population)
U.S. Total	245,502	224,059	157,596	64.2	70.3	137,537	56.0	61.4
State Total	1,044	1,012	763	73.1	75.4	698	66.9	69.0
Sex								
Male	509	494	359	70.6	72.7	327	64.3	66.2
Female	535	518	404	75.4	77.9	371	69.3	71.6
Race								
White alone................................	990	973	740	74.7	76.0	677	68.4	69.6
White, non-Hispanic alone	976	964	733	75.2	76.1	672	68.9	69.7
Black alone................................	11	9	5	(B)	(B)	5	(B)	(B)
Asian alone	27	16	9	(B)	(B)	9	(B)	(B)
Hispanic (of any race)	19	11	9	(B)	(B)	7	(B)	(B)
White alone or in combination	1,002	984	746	74.5	75.9	681	68.0	69.3
Black alone or in combination............	16	13	8	(B)	(B)	5	(B)	(B)
Asian alone or in combination............	28	17	11	(B)	(B)	11	(B)	(B)
Age								
18 to 24 years.............................	98	96	66	(B)	(B)	55	(B)	(B)
25 to 34 years.............................	157	149	103	65.4	68.8	89	56.9	59.8
35 to 44 years.............................	164	154	109	66.3	70.4	102	62.5	66.3
45 to 64 years.............................	396	386	310	78.1	80.1	287	72.3	74.2
65 years and over	228	225	175	76.9	77.8	165	72.3	73.2

B = Base is less than 75,000 and therefore too small to show the derived measure.

Table NH-14. Crime

(Number, rate per 100,000. Data are derived from the FBI Uniform Crime Reports.)

Item	State			U.S. [1,2,3,4]		
	2015	2016	Percent change	2015	2016	Percent change
TOTAL POPULATION [5]	1,330,608	1,334,795	0.3	321,418,820	323,127,513	0.5
VIOLENT CRIME						
Number...................	2,652	2,637	-0.6	1,231,566	1,248,185	1.3
Rate........................	199.3	197.6	-0.9	383.2	386.3	0.8
Murder and Nonnegligent Manslaughter						
Number...................	14	17	21.4	15,696	17,250	9.9
Rate........................	1.1	1.3	18.2	4.9	5.3	8.2
Rape [6]						
Number...................	627	582	-7.2	124,047	130,603	5.3
Rate........................	47.1	43.6	-7.4	38.6	40.4	4.7
Robbery						
Number...................	468	427	-8.8	327,374	332,198	1.5
Rate........................	35.2	32.0	-9.1	101.9	102.8	0.9
Aggravated Assault						
Number...................	1,543	1,611	4.4	764,449	803,007	5.0
Rate........................	116.0	120.7	4.1	237.8	248.5	4.5
PROPERTY CRIME						
Number...................	23,229	20,194	-13.1	7,993,631	7,919,035	-0.9
Rate........................	1,745.7	1,512.9	-13.3	2,487.0	2,450.7	-1.5
Burglary						
Number...................	3,467	2,963	-14.5	1,579,527	1,515,096	-4.1
Rate........................	260.6	222.0	-14.8	491.4	468.9	-4.6
Larceny-Theft						
Number...................	18,871	16,360	-13.3	5,706,346	5,638,455	-1.2
Rate........................	1,418.2	1,225.7	-13.6	1,775.4	1,745.0	-1.7
Motor Vehicle Theft						
Number...................	891	871	-2.2	707,758	765,484	8.2
Rate........................	67.0	65.3	-2.5	220.2	236.9	7.6

NOTE: Although arson data are included in the trend and clearance tables, sufficient data are not available to estimate totals for this offense. Therefore, no arson data are published in this table.
X = Not applicable.
- = Zero or rounds to zero.
[1] The crime figures have been adjusted.
[2] The data collection methodology for the offense of forcible rape used by the Minnesota state Uniform Crime Reporting (UCR) Program (with the exception of Minneapolis and St. Paul, Minnesota) does not comply with national UCR Program guidelines. Consequently, its figures for forcible rape and violent crime (of which forcible rape is a part) are not published in this table.
[3] Includes offenses reported by the Zoological Police and the Metro Transit Police.
[4] Because of changes in the state's reporting practices, figures are not comparable to previous years' data.
[5] Populations are U.S. Census Bureau provisional estimates as of July 1 of each year.
[6] The figures shown for the offense of rape were estimated using the revised Uniform Crime Reporting (UCR) definition of rape.

Table NH-15. State Government Finances, 2016

(Dollar amounts in thousands, percent distribution.)

Item	Dollars	Percent distribution
Total Revenue	8,343,685	100.0
General revenue	6,996,686	83.9
Intergovernmental revenue	2,609,075	31.3
Taxes	2,641,946	31.7
General sales	0	-
Selective sales	982,832	11.8
License taxes	329,549	3.9
Individual income tax	87,973	1.1
Corporate income tax	700,237	8.4
Other taxes	541,355	6.5
Current charges	923,320	11.1
Miscellaneous general revenue	822,345	9.9
Utility revenue	0	-
Liquor stores revenue	671,035	8.0
Insurance trust revenue [1]	675,964	8.1
Total Expenditure	7,687,843	100.0
Intergovernmental expenditure	460,600	6.0
Direct expenditure	7,227,243	94.0
Current operation	5,490,969	71.4
Capital outlay	450,651	5.9
Insurance benefits and repayments	762,071	9.9
Assistance and subsidies	194,596	2.5
Interest on debt	328,956	4.3
Exhibit: Salaries and wages	1,113,709	14.5
Total Expenditure	7,687,843	100.0
General expenditure	6,390,364	83.1
Intergovernmental expenditure	460,600	6.0
Direct expenditure	5,929,764	77.1
General expenditure, by function:		
Education	1,535,811	20.0
Public welfare	2,389,176	31.1
Hospitals	54,828	0.7
Health	152,301	2.0
Highways	477,474	6.2
Police protection	62,254	0.8
Correction	122,052	1.6
Natural resources	65,956	0.9
Parks and recreation	24,943	0.3
Governmental administration	275,287	3.6
Interest on general debt	328,956	4.3
Other and unallocable	901,326	11.7
Utility expenditure	6,780	0.1
Liquor stores expenditure	528,628	6.9
Insurance trust expenditure	762,071	9.9
Debt at End of Fiscal Year	7,869,122	X
Cash and Security Holdings	13,973,384	X

X = Not applicable.
- = Zero or rounds to zero.
[1] Within insurance trust revenue, net earnings of state retirement systems is a calculated statistic (the item code in the data file is X08), and thus can be positive or negative. Net earnings is the sum of earnings on investments plus gains on investments minus losses on investments. The change made in 2002 for asset valuation from book to market value in accordance with Statement 34 of the Governmental Accounting Standards Board is reflected in the calculated statistics.

Table NH-16. State Government Tax Collections, 2017

(Dollars in thousands, percent.)

Item	Dollars	Percent distribution
Total Taxes	2,496,719	100.0
Property taxes	405,186	16.2
Sales and gross receipts	959,384	38.4
General sales and gross receipts	X	-
Selective sales and gross receipts	959,384	38.4
Alcoholic beverages	12,678	0.5
Amusements	538	-
Insurance premiums	108,013	4.3
Motor fuels	152,086	6.1
Pari-mutuels	633	-
Public utilities	53,427	2.1
Tobacco products	203,102	8.1
Other selective sales	428,907	17.2
Licenses	329,719	13.2
Alcoholic beverages	17,263	0.7
Amusements	322	-
Corporations in general	63,123	2.5
Hunting and fishing	11,233	0.4
Motor vehicle	102,438	4.1
Motor vehicle operators	8,305	0.3
Public utilities	21,540	0.9
Occupation and business, NEC	104,531	4.2
Other licenses	964	-
Income taxes	639,120	25.6
Individual income	65,467	2.6
Corporation net income	573,653	23.0
Other taxes	163,310	6.5
Death and gift	X	-
Documentary and stock transfer	163,310	6.5
Severance	X	-
Taxes, NEC	0	-

X = Not applicable.
- = Zero or rounds to zero.

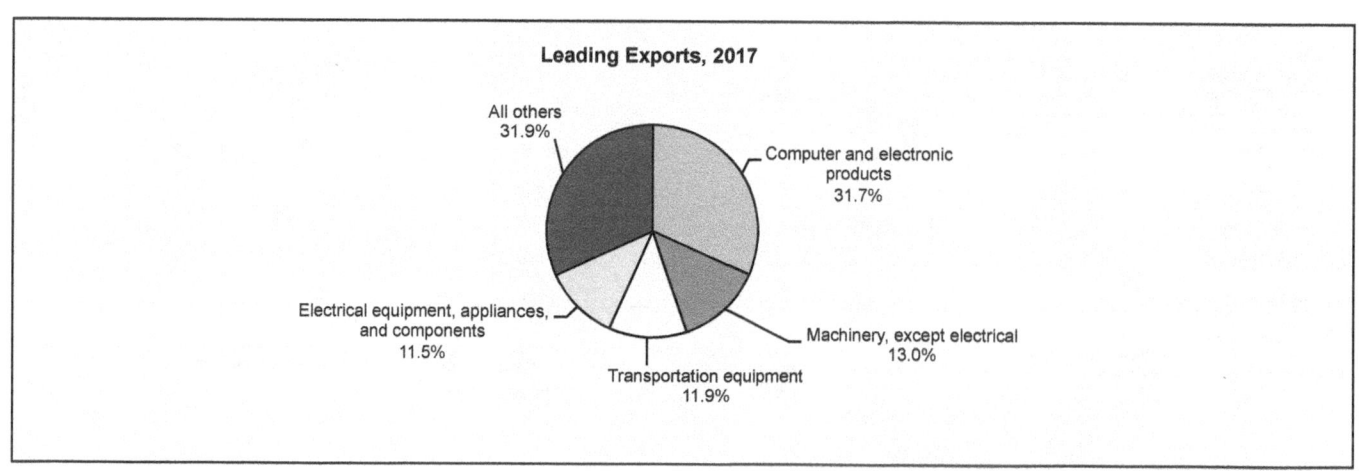

Leading Exports, 2017

All others 31.9%

Computer and electronic products 31.7%

Electrical equipment, appliances, and components 11.5%

Transportation equipment 11.9%

Machinery, except electrical 13.0%

NEW JERSEY

Facts and Figures

Location: Middle Atlantic region of the United States; bordered on the N and NE by New York, on the E by the Atlantic Ocean, on the S by Delaware Bay, and on the W by Delaware and Pennsylvania

Area: 8,721 sq. mi. (22,588 sq. km.); rank—47th

Population: 8,005,644 (2017 est.); rank—11th

Principal Cities: capital—Trenton; largest—Newark

Statehood: December 18, 1787; 3rd state

U.S. Congress: 2 senators, 12 representatives

State Motto: Liberty and Prosperity

State Song: None

State Nickname: The Garden State

Abbreviations: NJ; N.J.

State Symbols: flower—common meadow violet; tree—red oak; bird—Eastern goldfinch

At a Glance

- With an increase in population of 2.3 percent, New Jersey ranked 34th among the states in growth from 2010 to 2017.

- New Jersey's median household income was $76,126 in 2016, the 3rd highest in the country.

- In 2016, 10.4 percent of the New Jersey's population lived below the poverty level, compared to 14.0 percent of the entire U.S. population.

- New Jersey's property crime rate of 1,544.6 incidents per 100,000 population, was the 2nd lowest rate in the country in 2016.

- Approximately 38.6 percent of New Jersey residents had a bachelor's degree or more in 2016, the 5th highest percentage in the country.

Table NJ-1. Population by Age, Sex, Race, and Hispanic Origin

(Number, percent, except where noted.)

Sex, age, race, and Hispanic origin	2000	2010	2017 [1]	Average annual percent change, 2010–2017
Total Population...	8,414,350	8,791,894	9,005,644	2.4
Percent of total U.S. population	3.0	2.8	2.8	X
Sex				
Male..	4,082,813	4,279,600	4,396,574	2.7
Female	4,331,357	4,512,294	4,609,070	2.1
Age				
Under 5 years..	563,785	541,020	521,718	-3.6
5 to 19 years...	1,720,332	1,750,184	1,674,173	-4.3
20 to 64 years..	5,017,107	5,314,697	5,391,150	1.4
65 years and over	1,113,136	1,185,993	1,418,603	19.6
Median age (years)	36.7	39.0	39.8	2.1
Race and Hispanic Origin				
One race				
White	6,104,705	6,546,498	6,489,409	-0.9
Black	1,141,821	1,282,005	1,346,893	5.1
American Indian and Alaska Native	19,492	49,907	54,683	9.6
Asian	480,276	746,212	906,671	21.5
Native Hawaiian or Other Pacific Islander	3,329	7,731	9,658	24.9
Two or more races	13,755	159,541	198,330	24.3
Hispanic (of any race)	1,117,191	1,606,006	1,840,433	14.6

X = Not applicable.
[1] Population figures for 2017 are July 1 estimates. The 2010 estimates are taken from the 2010 Census.
- = Zero or rounds to zero.

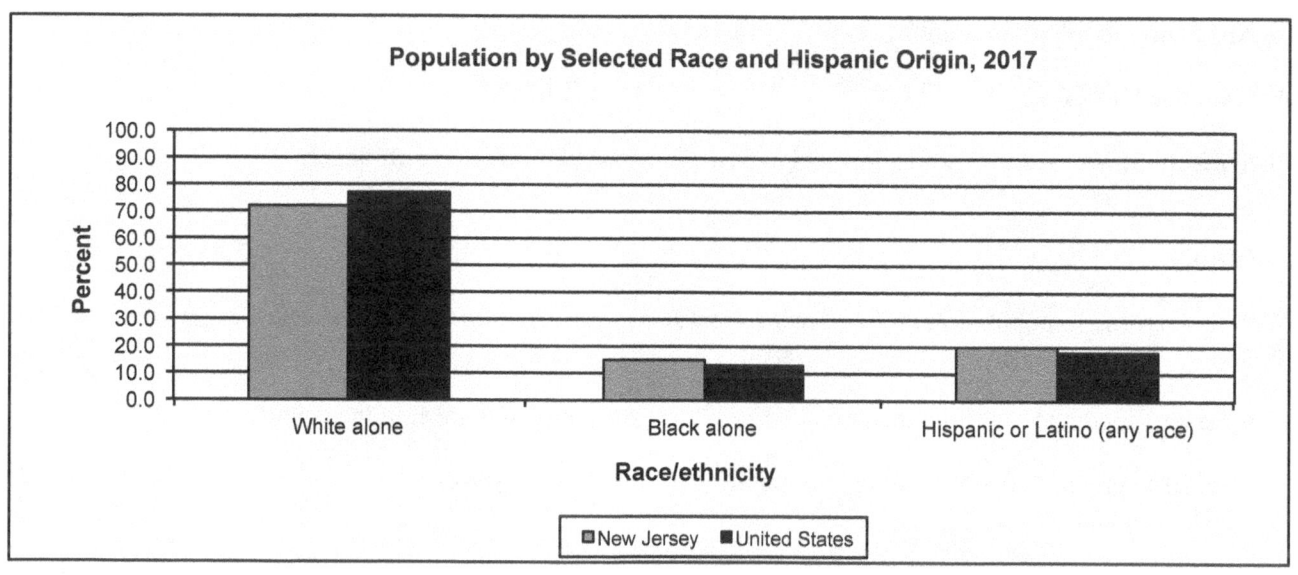

Table NJ-2. Marital Status

(Number, percent distribution.)

Sex, age, and marital status	2000	2010	2016
Males, 15 Years and Over	3,176,413	3,419,050	3,537,022
Never married	31.1	36.4	38.0
Now married, except separated..	57.7	52.1	51.0
Separated..	2.0	1.8	1.7
Widowed..	2.9	2.6	2.4
Divorced..	6.2	7.1	6.9
Females, 15 Years and Over	3,478,920	3,690,673	3,776,587
Never married	25.3	30.2	32.0
Now married, except separated..	51.8	47.6	46.4
Separated..	2.7	2.2	2.2
Widowed..	11.5	10.2	9.2
Divorced..	8.7	9.8	10.2

Table NJ-3. Households and Housing Characteristics

(Number, percent, dollars.)

Item	2000	2010	2016	Average annual percent change, 2010–2016
Total Households..	3,064,645	3,172,421	3,194,519	0.1
Family households	2,154,539	2,185,732	2,197,150	0.1
Married-couple family	1,638,322	1,614,230	1,623,674	0.1
Other family	516,217	571,502	573,476	0.1
Male householder, no wife present................	129,205	154,036	154,433	-
Female householder, no husband present........	387,012	417,466	419,043	0.1
Nonfamily households	910,106	986,689	997,369	0.2
Householder living alone..................................	751,287	827,294	841,329	0.3
Householder not living alone...........................	158,819	159,395	156,040	-0.4
Housing Characteristics				
Total housing units	3,310,275	3,554,909	3,604,688	0.2
Occupied housing units	3,064,645	3,172,421	3,194,519	0.1
Owner occupied	2,012,473	2,106,728	2,019,927	-0.7
Renter occupied	1,053,172	1,065,693	1,174,592	1.7
Average household size.....................................	2.68	2.72	2.74	0.1
Financial Characteristics				
Median gross rent of renter-occupied housing	751	1,114	1,244	1.9
Median monthly owner costs for housing units with a mortgage	1,560	2,370	2,343	-0.2
Median value of owner-occupied housing units............	170,800	339,200	328,200	-0.5

- = Zero or rounds to zero

Table NJ-4. Migration, Origin, and Language

(Number, percent.)

Characteristic	State			U.S.		
	2015	2016	Percent change	2015	2016	Percent change
Residence 1 Year Ago						
Population 1 year and over	8,854,363	8,852,286	-	317,635,720	319,361,956	0.5
Same house..	90.2	89.6	X	85.3	85.4	X
Different house in the U.S.	9.0	9.6	X	14.1	13.9	X
Same county..	5.2	5.5	X	8.5	8.3	X
Different county	3.8	4.0	X	5.6	5.6	X
Same state	2.2	2.4	X	3.2	3.2	X
Different state	1.6	1.6	X	2.4	2.4	X
Abroad	0.7	0.8	X	0.7	0.7	X
Place of Birth						
Native born	6,980,688	6,928,384	-0.7	278,128,449	279,388,170	0.5
Male	48.8	49.1	X	49.3	49.3	X
Female	51.2	50.9	X	50.7	50.7	X
Foreign born	1,977,325	2,016,085	2.0	43,290,372	43,739,345	1.0
Male	48.8	48.1	X	48.6	48.5	X
Female	51.2	51.9	X	51.4	51.5	X
Foreign born; naturalized U.S. citizen...............	1,091,687	1,103,588	1.1	20,697,103	21,238,372	2.6
Male	47.1	46.8	X	45.9	45.9	X
Female	52.9	53.2	X	54.1	54.1	X
Foreign born; not a U.S. citizen......................	885,638	912,497	3.0	22,593,269	22,500,973	-0.4
Male	50.9	49.6	X	51.1	51.0	X
Female	49.1	50.4	X	48.9	49.0	X
Entered 2010 or later	14.8	18.5	X	15.6	18.6	X
Entered 2000 to 2009	28.5	27.3	X	27.9	26.7	X
Entered before 2000..	56.7	54.2	X	56.5	54.7	X
World Region of Birth, Foreign						
Foreign-born population, excluding population born at sea	1,977,257	2,016,085	2.0	43,289,646	43,738,901	1.0
Europe	15.4	15.1	X	11.1	10.9	X
Asia...	33.4	33.2	X	30.6	30.8	X
Africa	5.3	4.9	X	4.8	4.9	X
Oceania	0.2	0.1	X	0.6	0.6	X
Latin America...	44.8	45.9	X	51.1	51.0	X
North America...	0.8	0.8	X	1.9	1.8	X
Language Spoken at Home and Ability to Speak English						
Population 5 years and over...........................	8,428,759	8,424,299	-0.1	301,625,014	303,328,961	0.6
English only	69.2	68.3	X	78.5	78.4	X
Language other than English...........................	30.8	31.7	X	21.5	21.6	X
Speaks English less than "very well"...............	12.1	12.6	X	8.6	8.6	X

NA = Not available.
X = Not applicable.
- = Zero or rounds to zero.

Table NJ-5. Median Income and Poverty Status, 2016

(Number, percent, except as noted.)

Characteristic	State		U.S.	
	Number	Percent	Number	Percent
Median Income				
Households (dollars)	76,126	X	57,617	X
Families (dollars)	94,546	X	71,062	X
Below Poverty Level (All People)	915,913	10.4	44,268,996	14.0
Sex				
Male	400,523	9.4	19,760,056	12.8
Female	515,390	11.4	24,508,940	15.2
Age				
Under 18 years	285,479	14.6	14,115,713	19.5
Related children under 18 years	280,542	14.3	13,805,435	19.1
18 to 64 years	519,305	9.5	25,723,818	13.2
65 years and over	111,129	8.3	4,429,465	9.2

X = Not applicable.

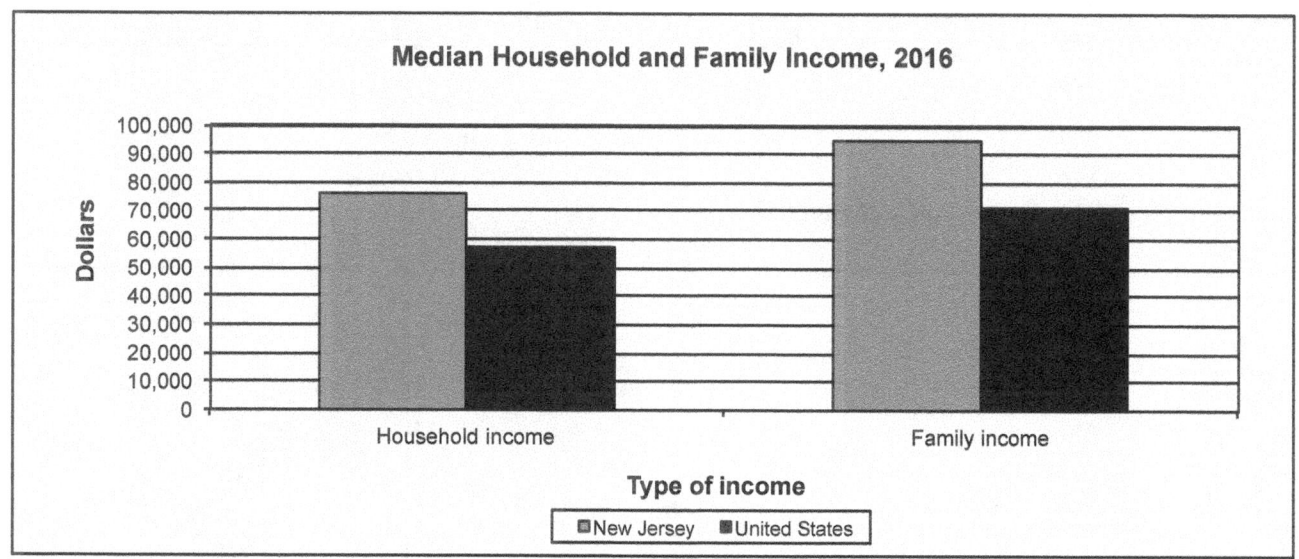

Table NJ-6. Health Insurance Coverage Status for the Civilian Noninstitutionalized Population and Children Under 18 Years of Age

(Number, percent.)

Item	2008	2009	2010	2011	2012	2013	2014	2015	2016
Civilian Noninstitutionalized Population	8,557,279	8,582,670	8,693,541	8,712,982	8,756,542	8,791,652	8,830,969	8,850,415	8,837,578
Covered by Private or Public Insurance									
Number	7,498,665	7,498,582	7,542,383	7,573,878	7,643,733	7,631,358	7,865,558	8,079,219	8,132,608
Percent	87.6	87.4	86.8	86.9	87.3	86.8	89.1	91.3	92.0
Not Covered									
Number	1,058,614	1,084,088	1,151,158	1,139,104	1,112,809	1,160,294	965,411	771,196	704,970
Percent	12.4	12.6	13.2	13.1	12.7	13.2	10.9	8.7	8.0
Percent in the U.S. not covered	15.1	15.1	15.5	15.1	14.8	14.5	11.7	9.4	8.6
Children Under 18 Years of Age	2,045,334	2,044,419	2,057,455	2,038,167	2,024,150	2,017,712	2,007,362	1,993,774	1,979,948
Covered by Private or Public Insurance									
Number	1,897,614	1,914,584	1,933,999	1,933,002	1,921,334	1,905,595	1,915,520	1,919,180	1,909,909
Percent	92.8	93.6	94.0	94.8	94.9	94.4	95.4	96.3	96.5
Not Covered									
Number	147,720	129,835	123,456	105,165	102,816	112,117	91,842	74,594	70,039
Percent	7.2	6.4	6.0	5.2	5.1	5.6	4.6	3.7	3.5
Percent in the U.S. not covered	9.9	8.6	8.0	7.5	7.2	7.1	6.0	4.8	4.5

Table NJ-7. Employment Status by Demographic Group, 2017

(Numbers in thousands, percent.)

Characteristic	Civilian noninstitutional population	Civilian labor force		Employed		Unemployed	
		Number	Percent of population	Number	Percent of population	Number	Percent of population
Total...	7,124	4,491	63.0	4,284	60.1	207	4.6
Sex							
Male..	3,429	2,363	68.9	2,258	65.8	105	4.4
Female.......................................	3,695	2,128	57.6	2,026	54.8	102	4.8
Race, Sex, and Hispanic Origin							
White...	5,347	3,323	62.2	3,197	59.8	126	3.8
Male..	2,598	1,776	68.4	1,710	65.8	66	3.7
Female.......................................	2,749	1,547	56.3	1,487	54.1	60	3.9
Black or African American...............	1,018	656	64.4	604	59.3	52	7.9
Male..	463	301	65.0	274	59.2	27	9.0
Female.......................................	555	355	63.9	330	59.4	25	7.0
Hispanic or Latino ethnicity[1]	1,161	779	67.1	739	63.6	40	5.1
Male..	557	422	75.7	403	72.3	19	4.5
Female.......................................	604	357	59.1	336	55.6	21	5.8
Age							
16 to 19 years...............................	449	113	25.0	97	21.6	15	13.6
20 to 24 years...............................	582	365	62.6	330	56.7	34	9.4
25 to 34 years...............................	1,135	960	84.5	915	80.6	45	4.7
35 to 44 years...............................	1,124	959	85.3	932	82.9	27	2.8
45 to 54 years...............................	1,213	981	80.9	943	77.7	39	3.9
55 to 64 years...............................	1,213	812	66.9	778	64.1	34	4.1
65 years and over	1,408	303	21.5	289	20.5	14	4.6

NOTE: Data in Table 7 are from the Current Population Survey (CPS) and do not match the estimates in Table 8. See notes and definitions for further information.
[1] May be of any race.

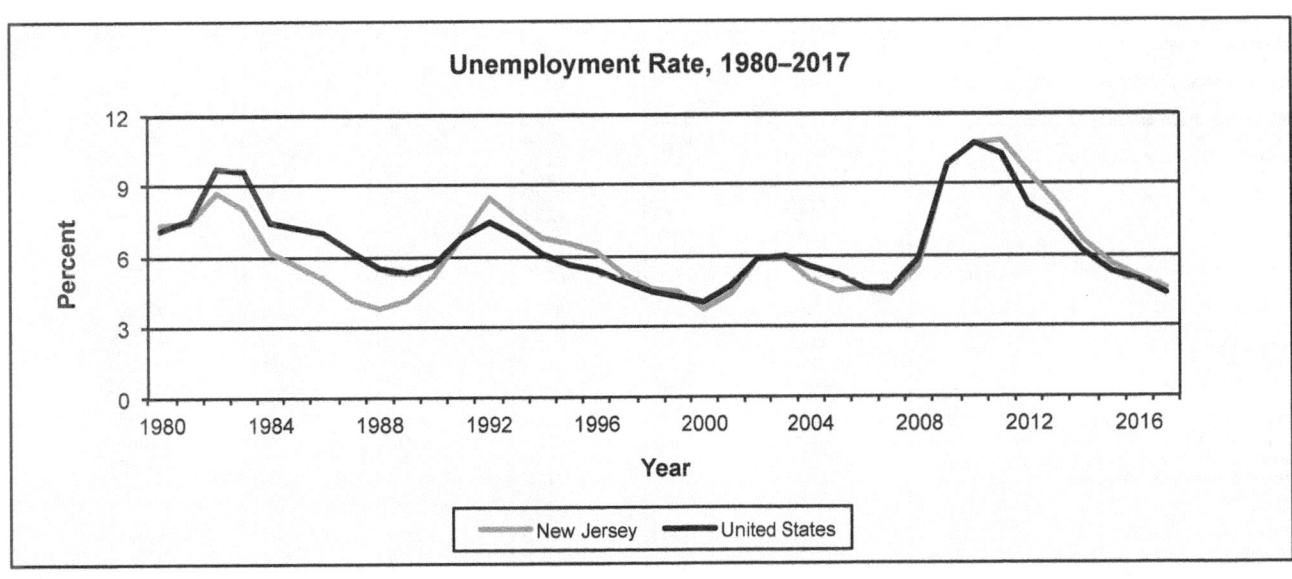

Table NJ-8. Employment Status of the Civilian Noninstitutional Population Age 16 Years and Over

(Number, percent.)

Year	Civilian labor force	Civilian participation rate	Employed	Unemployed	Unemployment rate
2009..	4,550,645	67.3	4,138,570	412,075	9.1
2010..	4,555,330	66.4	4,121,455	433,875	9.5
2011..	4,565,272	65.9	4,138,464	426,808	9.3
2012..	4,588,033	65.7	4,159,986	428,047	9.3
2013..	4,548,560	64.8	4,173,828	374,732	8.2
2014..	4,527,181	64.1	4,221,267	305,914	6.8
2015..	4,537,232	64.0	4,274,695	262,537	5.8
2016..	4,530,784	63.6	4,305,516	225,268	5.0
2017..	4,518,832	63.1	4,309,706	209,126	4.6

Table NJ-9. Employment and Average Wages by Industry

(Estimates through 2010 are based on the 2007 *North American Industry Classification System* [NAICS]. Estimates from 2011 onward are based on the 2012 NAICS.)

Industry	2010	2011	2012	2013	2014	2015	2016
	Number of jobs						
Wage and Salary Employment by Industry	3,911,956	3,908,751	3,940,169	3,980,038	4,012,486	4,061,802	4,121,989
Farm Wage and Salary Employment	7,462	7,456	9,641	8,903	9,552	9,252	11,165
Nonfarm Wage and Salary Employment	3,904,494	3,901,295	3,930,528	3,971,135	4,002,934	4,052,550	4,110,824
Private wage and salary employment	3,256,067	3,276,766	3,312,574	3,352,598	3,385,928	3,440,722	3,503,026
Forestry, fishing, and related activities	3,464	3,315	3,439	2,910	3,550	3,735	4,248
Mining	1,371	1,307	1,250	1,317	1,412	1,388	1,326
Utilities	14,341	13,592	13,806	13,671	13,659	14,210	14,176
Construction	134,391	133,854	134,271	141,669	145,329	151,835	157,504
Manufacturing	257,437	253,053	245,442	242,951	242,342	238,259	242,409
Durable goods manufacturing	114,263	114,388	112,052	110,854	108,829	109,400	110,026
Nondurable goods manufacturing	143,174	138,665	133,390	132,097	133,513	128,859	132,383
Wholesale trade	211,326	210,659	213,668	213,896	215,239	217,602	217,308
Retail trade	441,175	445,246	447,763	451,981	458,307	464,982	465,721
Transportation and warehousing	149,608	151,521	151,199	150,894	153,225	160,481	172,523
Information	79,350	75,926	77,872	75,223	75,525	74,694	73,311
Finance and insurance	192,387	192,237	191,491	191,177	184,657	189,375	191,463
Real estate and rental and leasing	55,748	54,517	54,159	55,627	55,923	56,994	58,602
Professional, scientific, and technical services	275,112	279,503	281,123	285,363	289,811	297,173	303,516
Management of companies and enterprises	72,815	77,388	79,566	83,332	79,016	80,000	80,752
Administrative and waste services	240,344	250,387	260,990	262,583	269,004	274,445	281,399
Educational services	92,390	93,366	94,770	96,630	97,501	99,360	101,516
Health care and social assistance	504,981	507,701	518,324	532,277	540,882	552,633	563,376
Arts, entertainment, and recreation	53,751	54,121	56,565	57,916	60,062	62,779	65,776
Accommodation and food services	283,552	283,824	291,381	297,260	299,105	299,347	306,941
Other services, except public administration	192,524	195,249	195,495	195,921	201,379	201,430	201,159
Government and government enterprises	648,427	624,529	617,954	618,537	617,006	611,828	607,798
	Dollars						
Average Wages and Salaries by Industry	55,537	56,716	57,893	58,804	59,960	61,765	63,547
Average Farm Wages and Salaries	25,882	22,672	23,208	25,912	25,565	24,232	22,137
Average Nonfarm Wages and Salaries	55,594	56,781	57,978	58,878	60,042	61,851	63,659
Average private wages and salaries	55,176	56,359	57,649	58,647	59,809	61,704	63,826
Forestry, fishing, and related activities	24,154	24,570	24,839	27,722	27,317	28,003	31,806
Mining	67,226	66,803	70,301	72,159	71,365	77,484	78,567
Utilities	99,495	106,157	108,454	107,128	113,039	116,162	118,251
Construction	60,652	61,692	62,322	63,794	64,995	67,618	70,583
Manufacturing	74,032	74,960	75,933	77,277	79,949	77,029	78,108
Durable goods manufacturing	65,848	67,957	68,934	69,701	72,152	73,698	76,199
Nondurable goods manufacturing	80,564	80,737	81,813	83,634	86,304	79,856	79,694
Wholesale trade	76,702	79,448	81,054	82,364	85,229	87,490	87,409
Retail trade	29,979	30,382	30,587	30,966	31,712	32,879	33,914
Transportation and warehousing	48,334	49,237	50,274	51,604	52,512	54,148	58,229
Information	86,149	89,556	92,818	96,261	98,999	102,634	101,191
Finance and insurance	104,134	106,878	108,745	110,970	115,923	120,798	129,708
Real estate and rental and leasing	54,137	54,173	58,976	58,604	60,340	63,656	64,341
Professional, scientific, and technical services	88,215	91,003	95,591	97,666	100,179	106,520	108,614
Management of companies and enterprises	132,531	136,935	146,319	150,460	151,791	159,388	167,981
Administrative and waste services	37,216	38,164	38,590	39,172	39,742	40,818	43,890
Educational services	37,368	38,256	38,906	40,009	41,221	41,511	41,566
Health care and social assistance	46,790	47,488	48,303	48,529	49,493	50,951	53,264
Arts, entertainment, and recreation	36,272	35,535	36,857	37,095	36,440	37,023	38,244
Accommodation and food services	22,449	22,668	23,097	23,715	24,506	24,801	25,692
Other services, except public administration	31,331	31,680	32,249	32,980	33,471	34,745	36,040
Government and government enterprises	57,692	58,999	59,740	60,131	61,322	62,679	62,698

Table NJ-10. Employment Characteristics by Family Type

(Number, percent.)

Family type and labor force status	2014		2015		2016	
	Total	Families with own children under 18 years	Total	Families with own children under 18 years	Total	Families with own children under 18 years
All Families..	2,194,075	971,317	2,205,886	966,402	2,197,150	947,058
FAMILY TYPE AND LABOR FORCE STATUS						
Married-Couple Families....................................	1,598,280	689,184	1,632,061	695,182	1,623,674	682,813
Both husband and wife in labor force.........................	55.7	67.6	54.8	66.6	54.6	67.3
Husband in labor force, wife not in labor force	22.5	27.9	22.4	27.9	22.3	27.6
Wife in labor force, husband not in labor force........................	7.5	3.4	7.4	3.7	7.6	3.6
Both husband and wife not in labor force..........................	14.3	1.0	14.6	1.4	14.7	1.1
Other Families	595,795	282,133	573,825	271,220	573,476	264,245
Female householder, no husband present..........................	74.1	77.7	72.8	77.0	73.1	76.2
In labor force...	54.2	65.8	52.9	65.1	52.3	64.6
Not in labor force	19.9	11.9	19.9	12.0	20.7	11.6
Male householder, no wife present...........................	25.9	22.3	27.2	23.0	26.9	23.8
In labor force...	20.9	21.0	21.8	20.8	21.6	22.0
Not in labor force	5.0	1.3	5.4	2.2	5.4	1.8

Table NJ-11. School Enrollment and Educational Attainment, 2016

(Number, percent.)

Item	State	U.S.
Enrollment		
Total population 3 years and over, enrolled in school	2,239,783	81,572,277
Enrolled in nursery school or preschool (percent)........................	7.5	6.0
Enrolled in kindergarten (percent)..	5.1	5.0
Enrolled in elementary school, grades 1-8 (percent)......................	39.5	40.3
Enrolled in high school, grades 9-12 (percent)...........................	21.2	21.0
Enrolled in college or graduate school (percent).........................	26.7	27.7
Attainment		
Total population 25 years and over	6,171,172	218,475,480
Less than ninth grade (percent)..	5.1	5.4
9th to 12th grade, no diploma (percent).................................	5.6	7.2
High school graduate, including equivalency (percent)....................	27.6	27.2
Some college, no degree (percent).....................................	16.6	20.6
Associate's degree (percent)...	6.5	8.4
Bachelor's degree (percent)..	23.7	19.3
Graduate or professional degree (percent)..............................	14.9	11.9
High school graduate or higher (percent)...............................	89.3	87.5
Bachelor's degree or higher (percent)..................................	38.6	31.3

Table NJ-12. Public School Characteristics and Educational Indicators

(Number, percent; data derived from National Center of Education Statistics.)

Item	State	U.S.
Public Schools, 2015–2016 (except where noted)		
Number of school districts...	694	18,328
Number of schools...	2,588	98,456
Number of students..	1,408,845	50,327,015
Number of teachers	114,969	3,151,497
Student-teacher ratio	12.3	16.0
Expenditures per student (dollars), 2014-2015..........................	18,559	11,445
Four-year adjusted cohort graduation rate (ACGR)[1,2]	90.1	84.1
Students eligible for free or reduced-price lunch (percent), 2014-2015....	36.8	51.8
English language learners (percent), Fall 2015	4.9	9.5
Students age 3 to 21 served under IDEA, part B (percent)................	16.5	13.2

Public Schools by Type	Number	Percent of state public schools
Total number of schools..	2,588	100.0
Regular	2,384	92.1
Special education..	64	2.5
Vocational education...	56	2.2
Alternative education..	84	3.2

NOTE: Every school is assigned only one school type based on its instructional emphasis.
[1] ACGR data represents a new method of calculating high-school completion rates and may not be comparable to previous years' data for Averaged Freshmen Graduation Rates (AFGR).
[2] The United States 4-year ACGRs were estimated using both the reported 4-year ACGR data from 49 states and the District of Columbia and using imputed data for Idaho. The estimate for American Indian/Alaska Native students also includes imputed data for Virginia.

Table NJ-13. Reported Voting and Registration of the Voting-Age Population, November 2016

(Numbers in thousands, percent.)

Item	Total population	Total citizen population	Registered			Voted		
			Total registered	Percent registered (total population)	Percent registered (total citizen population)	Total voted	Percent voted (total population)	Percent voted (total citizen population)
U.S. Total	245,502	224,059	157,596	64.2	70.3	137,537	56.0	61.4
State Total.............................	6,862	5,958	4,165	60.7	69.9	3,665	53.4	61.5
Sex								
Male	3,282	2,825	1,911	58.2	67.6	1,668	50.8	59.1
Female	3,580	3,132	2,255	63.0	72.0	1,997	55.8	63.7
Race								
White alone............................	5,237	4,669	3,349	64.0	71.7	2,961	56.6	63.4
White, non-Hispanic alone	4,048	3,891	2,933	72.5	75.4	2,604	64.3	66.9
Black alone............................	964	814	550	57.0	67.5	469	48.7	57.6
Asian alone	579	399	220	38.0	55.2	211	36.4	52.9
Hispanic (of any race)......................	1,379	913	486	35.2	53.2	395	28.6	43.2
White alone or in combination	5,274	4,702	3,374	64.0	71.7	2,982	56.5	63.4
Black alone or in combination...........	977	824	553	56.7	67.2	469	48.0	56.9
Asian alone or in combination...........	602	422	238	39.6	56.4	229	38.0	54.2
Age								
18 to 24 years........................	849	750	419	49.4	55.9	305	35.9	40.7
25 to 34 years........................	1,046	814	507	48.5	62.3	426	40.7	52.3
35 to 44 years........................	1,110	881	631	56.8	71.6	566	51.0	64.3
45 to 64 years........................	2,474	2,196	1,615	65.3	73.5	1,472	59.5	67.0
65 years and over	1,383	1,317	994	71.8	75.4	896	64.8	68.0

Table NJ-14. Crime

(Number, rate per 100,000. Data are derived from the FBI Uniform Crime Reports.)

Item	State			U.S. [1,2,3,4]		
	2015	2016	Percent change	2015	2016	Percent change
TOTAL POPULATION [5]	8,958,013	8,944,469	-0.2	321,418,820	323,127,513	0.5
VIOLENT CRIME						
Number..............................	22,879	21,914	-4.2	1,231,566	1,248,185	1.3
Rate	255.4	245.0	-4.1	383.2	386.3	0.8
Murder and Nonnegligent Manslaughter						
Number..............................	363	372	2.5	15,696	17,250	9.9
Rate	4.1	4.2	2.4	4.9	5.3	8.2
Rape[6]						
Number..............................	1,373	1,453	5.8	124,047	130,603	5.3
Rate	15.3	16.2	5.9	38.6	40.4	4.7
Robbery						
Number..............................	9,729	8,984	-7.7	327,374	332,198	1.5
Rate	108.6	100.4	-7.6	101.9	102.8	0.9
Aggravated Assault						
Number..............................	11,414	11,105	-2.7	764,449	803,007	5.0
Rate	127.4	124.2	-2.5	237.8	248.5	4.5
PROPERTY CRIME						
Number..............................	145,701	138,152	-5.2	7,993,631	7,919,035	-0.9
Rate	1,626.5	1,544.6	-5.0	2,487.0	2,450.7	-1.5
Burglary						
Number..............................	27,960	25,284	-9.6	1,579,527	1,515,096	-4.1
Rate	312.1	282.7	-9.4	491.4	468.9	-4.6
Larceny-Theft						
Number..............................	105,963	101,540	-4.2	5,706,346	5,638,455	-1.2
Rate	1,182.9	1,135.2	-4.0	1,775.4	1,745.0	-1.7
Motor Vehicle Theft						
Number..............................	11,778	11,328	-3.8	707,758	765,484	8.2
Rate	131.5	126.6	-3.7	220.2	236.9	7.6

NOTE: Although arson data are included in the trend and clearance tables, sufficient data are not available to estimate totals for this offense. Therefore, no arson data are published in this table.
X = Not applicable.
- = Zero or rounds to zero.
[1] The crime figures have been adjusted.
[2] The data collection methodology for the offense of forcible rape used by the Minnesota state Uniform Crime Reporting (UCR) Program (with the exception of Minneapolis and St. Paul, Minnesota) does not comply with national UCR Program guidelines. Consequently, its figures for forcible rape and violent crime (of which forcible rape is a part) are not published in this table.
[3] Includes offenses reported by the Zoological Police and the Metro Transit Police.
[4] Because of changes in the state's reporting practices, figures are not comparable to previous years' data.
[5] Populations are U.S. Census Bureau provisional estimates as of July 1 of each year.
[6] The figures shown for the offense of rape were estimated using the revised Uniform Crime Reporting (UCR) definition of rape.

Table NJ-15. State Government Finances, 2016

(Dollar amounts in thousands, percent distribution.)

Item	Dollars	Percent distribution
Total Revenue	65,689,159	100.0
General revenue	60,952,881	92.8
Intergovernmental revenue	17,976,242	27.4
Taxes	31,546,720	48.0
General sales	9,267,703	14.1
Selective sales	3,905,629	5.9
License taxes	1,499,889	2.3
Individual income tax	13,355,992	20.3
Corporate income tax	2,229,487	3.4
Other taxes	1,288,020	2.0
Current charges	6,547,341	10.0
Miscellaneous general revenue	4,882,578	7.4
Utility revenue	1,118,942	1.7
Liquor stores revenue	0	-
Insurance trust revenue [1]	3,617,336	5.5
Total Expenditure	72,617,584	100.0
Intergovernmental expenditure	11,672,318	16.1
Direct expenditure	60,945,266	83.9
Current operation	39,342,903	54.2
Capital outlay	4,748,484	6.5
Insurance benefits and repayments	13,139,220	18.1
Assistance and subsidies	1,534,401	2.1
Interest on debt	2,180,258	3.0
Exhibit: Salaries and wages	10,081,203	13.9
Total Expenditure	72,617,584	100.0
General expenditure	56,486,798	77.8
Intergovernmental expenditure	11,672,318	16.1
Direct expenditure	44,814,480	61.7
General expenditure, by function:		
Education	18,627,835	25.7
Public welfare	18,456,912	25.4
Hospitals	2,259,610	3.1
Health	1,385,587	1.9
Highways	3,310,280	4.6
Police protection	706,311	1.0
Correction	1,392,916	1.9
Natural resources	453,378	0.6
Parks and recreation	230,638	0.3
Governmental administration	1,760,490	2.4
Interest on general debt	2,178,788	3.0
Other and unallocable	5,724,053	7.9
Utility expenditure	2,991,566	4.6
Liquor stores expenditure	0	-
Insurance trust expenditure	13,139,220	18.1
Debt at End of Fiscal Year	66,721,791	X
Cash and Security Holdings	112,484,312	X

X = Not applicable.

- = Zero or rounds to zero.

[1] Within insurance trust revenue, net earnings of state retirement systems is a calculated statistic (the item code in the data file is X08), and thus can be positive or negative. Net earnings is the sum of earnings on investments plus gains on investments minus losses on investments. The change made in 2002 for asset valuation from book to market value in accordance with Statement 34 of the Governmental Accounting Standards Board is reflected in the calculated statistics.

Table NJ-16. State Government Tax Collections, 2017

(Dollars in thousands, percent.)

Item	Dollars	Percent distribution
Total Taxes..	32,325,850	100.0
Property taxes..	4,761	-
Sales and gross receipts	13,388,614	41.4
General sales and gross receipts	9,591,881	29.7
Selective sales and gross receipts	3,796,733	11.7
Alcoholic beverages..	137,757	0.4
Amusements..	218,650	0.7
Insurance premiums...	579,642	1.8
Motor fuels..	532,878	1.6
Pari-mutuels..	X	-
Public utilities	984,612	3.0
Tobacco products...	697,577	2.2
Other selective sales	645,617	2.0
Licenses...	1,550,059	4.8
Alcoholic beverages..	4,199	-
Amusements..	47,211	0.1
Corporations in general..	234,436	0.7
Hunting and fishing...	13,720	-
Motor vehicle...	667,056	2.1
Motor vehicle operators..	58,005	0.2
Public utilities	7,360	-
Occupation and business, NEC...	516,093	1.6
Other licenses	1,979	-
Income taxes..	16,068,049	49.7
Individual income...	13,958,119	43.2
Corporation net income	2,109,930	6.5
Other taxes..	1,314,367	4.1
Death and gift..	748,630	2.3
Documentary and stock transfer..	565,736	1.8
Severance	X	-
Taxes, NEC..	1	-

X = Not applicable.
- = Zero or rounds to zero.

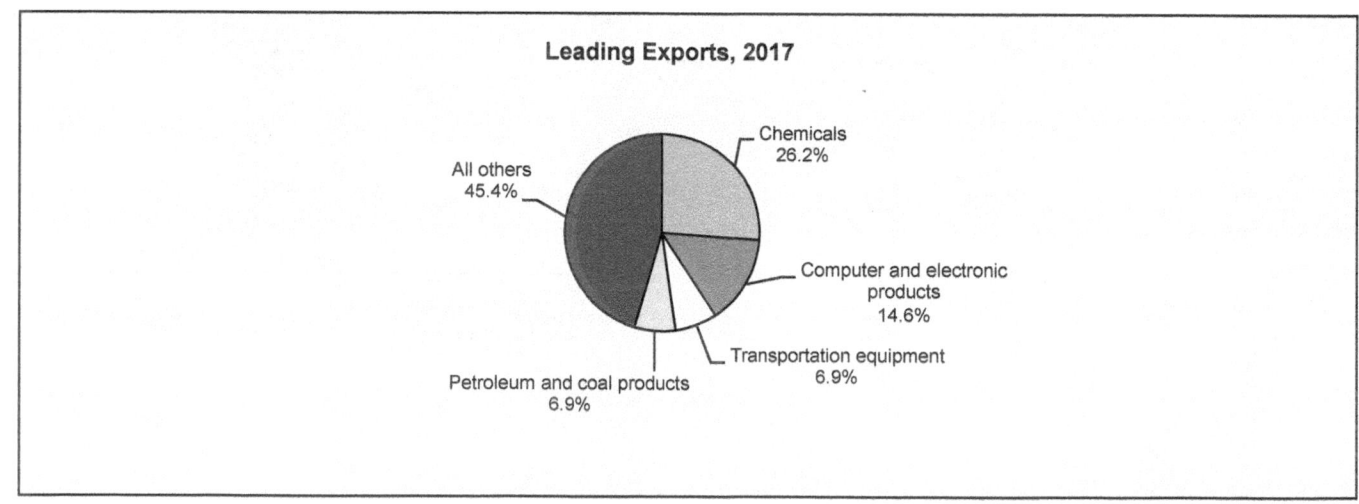

Leading Exports, 2017

Chemicals 26.2%
Computer and electronic products 14.6%
Transportation equipment 6.9%
Petroleum and coal products 6.9%
All others 45.4%

NEW MEXICO

Facts and Figures

Location: Southwestern United States; bordered on the N by Colorado, on the E by Oklahoma and Texas, on the S by Texas and Mexico, and on the W by Arizona; New Mexico is one of the Four Corner states—at its NW corner it touches Arizona, Colorado, and Utah

Area: 121,590 sq. mi. (314,915 sq. km.); rank—5th

Population: 2,088,070 (2017 est.); rank—36th

Principal Cities: capital—Santa Fe; largest—Albuquerque

Statehood: January 6, 1912; 47th state

U.S. Congress: 2 senators, 3 representatives

State Motto: *Crescit eundo* ("It grows as it goes")

State Song: "O, Fair New Mexico"

State Nickname: The Land of Enchantment

Abbreviations: NM; N. Mex.

State Symbols: flower—yucca; tree—piñon; bird—roadrunner

At a Glance

- With an increase in population of 1.1 percent, New Mexico ranked 41st among the states in growth from 2010 to 2017.

- In 2016, New Mexico's violent crime rate of 702.5 per 100,000 population was the 3rd highest rate in the country, and its property crime rate of 3,937.1 per 100,000 population, was the 2nd highest in the country.

- With approximately 48.8 percent of its residents self-identifying as "Hispanic or Latino," New Mexico was the state with the highest percentage of this population in 2017.

- New Mexico had the 3rd highest percentage of residents living below the poverty level in 2016 (19.8 percent).

- In 2017, New Mexico had the 2nd highest unemployment rate of all the states (6.2 percent). The U.S. unemployment rate was 4.4 percent.

Table NM-1. Population by Age, Sex, Race, and Hispanic Origin

(Number, percent, except where noted.)

Sex, age, race, and Hispanic origin	2000	2010	2017 [1]	Average annual percent change, 2010–2017
Total Population..	1,819,046	2,059,179	2,088,070	1.4
Percent of total U.S. population	0.6	0.7	0.6	X
Sex				
Male..	894,317	1,017,421	1,034,144	1.6
Female	924,729	1,041,758	1,053,926	1.2
Age				
Under 5 years..	130,628	144,981	128,145	-11.6
5 to 19 years...	434,231	434,860	415,289	-4.5
20 to 64 years...	1,041,962	1,207,083	1,192,035	-1.2
65 years and over..	212,225	272,255	352,601	29.5
Median age (years)..	34.6	36.7	37.8	3.0
Race and Hispanic origin				
One race				
White...	1,214,253	1,720,992	1,715,623	-0.3
Black..	34,343	49,006	52,622	7.4
American Indian and Alaska Native	173,483	208,890	227,132	8.7
Asian..	19,255	31,253	36,222	15.9
Native Hawaiian or Other Pacific Islander	1,503	3,132	3,372	7.7
Two or more races..	66,327	45,906	53,099	15.7
Hispanic (of any race).......................................	765,386	973,088	1,018,349	4.7

X = Not applicable.
- = Zero or rounds to zero.
[1] Population figures for 2017 are July 1 estimates. The 2010 estimates are taken from the 2010 Census.

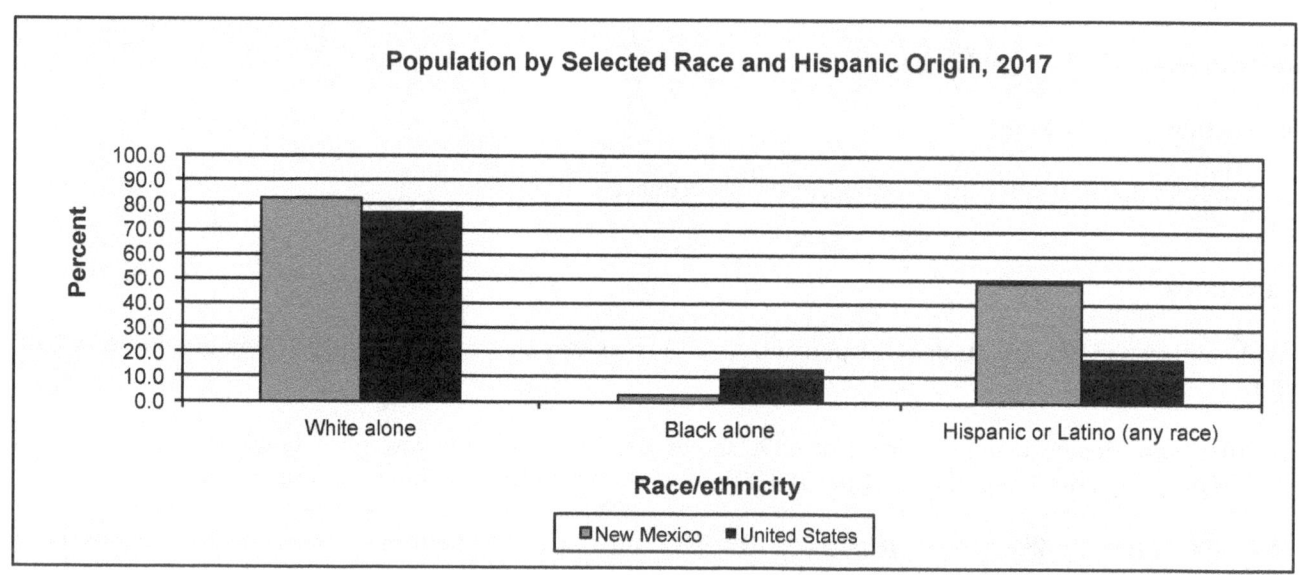

Table NM-2. Marital Status

(Number, percent distribution.)

Sex, age, and marital status	2000	2010	2016
Males, 15 Years and Over	677,967	801,901	824,879
Never married	30.5	35.4	38.0
Now married, except separated...	55.0	48.4	45.1
Separated...	1.6	1.6	1.6
Widowed...	2.6	2.6	3.0
Divorced...	10.4	11.9	12.3
Females, 15 Years and Over	720,529	833,357	851,780
Never married	24.7	29.9	31.6
Now married, except separated...	51.2	45.0	43.3
Separated...	2.0	2.6	1.9
Widowed...	9.4	8.5	9.0
Divorced...	12.8	14.1	14.2

Table NM-3. Households and Housing Characteristics

(Number, percent, dollars.)

Item	2000	2010	2016	Average annual percent change, 2010–2016
Total Households..	677,971	765,183	758,364	-0.1
Family households	466,515	501,092	481,127	-0.7
Married-couple family	341,818	349,344	334,266	-0.7
Other family	124,697	151,748	146,861	-0.5
Male householder, no wife present..............	35,075	49,041	41,051	-2.7
Female householder, no husband present.......	89,622	102,707	105,810	0.5
Nonfamily households	211,456	264,091	277,237	0.8
Householder living alone...............................	172,181	216,704	230,412	1.1
Householder not living alone..........................	39,275	47,387	46,825	-0.2
Housing Characteristics				
Total housing units..	780,579	902,242	917,641	0.3
Occupied housing units	677,971	765,183	758,364	-0.1
Owner occupied	474,445	519,864	511,099	-0.3
Renter occupied...	203,526	245,319	247,265	0.1
Average household size......................................	2.63	2.64	2.69	0.3
Financial Characteristics				
Median gross rent of renter-occupied housing	503	699	804	2.5
Median monthly owner costs for housing units with a mortgage	929	1,202	1,210	0.1
Median value of owner-occupied housing units................	108,100	161,200	167,500	0.7

Table NM-4. Migration, Origin, and Language

(Number, percent.)

Characteristic	State			U.S.		
	2015	2016	Percent change	2015	2016	Percent change
Residence 1 Year Ago						
Population 1 year and over	2,060,441	2,057,857	-0.1	317,635,720	319,361,956	0.5
Same house...	85.8	85.9	X	85.3	85.4	X
Different house in the U.S.	13.8	13.6	X	14.1	13.9	X
Same county..	8.8	8.3	X	8.5	8.3	X
Different county	5.0	5.3	X	5.6	5.6	X
Same state	2.3	2.1	X	3.2	3.2	X
Different state	2.7	3.1	X	2.4	2.4	X
Abroad...	0.4	0.5	X	0 7	0.7	X
Place of Birth						
Native born	1,888,154	1,882,609	-0.3	278,128,449	279,388,170	0.5
Male	49.6	49.6	X	49.3	49.3	X
Female	50.4	50.4	X	50.7	50.7	X
Foreign born	196,955	198,406	0.7	43,290,372	43,739,345	1.0
Male	49.8	48.5	X	48.6	48.5	X
Female	50.2	51.5	X	51.4	51.5	X
Foreign born; naturalized U.S. citizen.................	71,581	78,660	9.9	20,697,103	21,238,372	2.6
Male	47.8	44.5	X	45.9	45.9	X
Female	52.2	55.5	X	54.1	54.1	X
Foreign born; not a U.S. citizen..........................	125,374	119,746	-4.5	22,593,269	22,500,973	-0.4
Male	51.0	51.2	X	51.1	51.0	X
Female	49.0	48.8	X	48.9	49.0	X
Entered 2010 or later	13.7	14.1	X	15.6	18.6	X
Entered 2000 to 2009	27.2	24.7	X	27.9	26.7	X
Entered before 2000...	59.1	61.3	X	56.5	54.7	X
World Region of Birth, Foreign						
Foreign-born population, excluding population born at sea	196,955	198,406	0.7	43,289,646	43,738,901	1.0
Europe	7.5	8.6	X	11.1	10.9	X
Asia..	11.7	13.8	X	30.6	30.8	X
Africa	1.9	1.7	X	4.8	4.9	X
Oceania	0.3	0.2	X	0.6	0.6	X
Latin America...	76.9	74.5	X	51.1	51.0	X
North America...	1.7	1.3	X	1.9	1.8	X
Language Spoken at Home and Ability to Speak English						
Population 5 years and over................................	1,950,879	1,955,889	0.3	301,625,014	303,328,961	0.6
English only	65.7	65.5	X	78.5	78.4	X
Language other than English..............................	34.3	34.5	X	21.5	21.6	X
Speaks English less than "very well"	8.6	8.3	X	8.6	8.6	X

NA = Not available.
X = Not applicable.
- = Zero or rounds to zero.

Table NM-5. Median Income and Poverty Status, 2016

(Number, percent, except as noted.)

Characteristic	State		U.S.	
	Number	Percent	Number	Percent
Median Income				
Households (dollars)...	46,748	X	57,617	X
Families (dollars)	56,802	X	71,062	X
Below Poverty Level (All People)	404,463	19.8	44,268,996	14.0
Sex				
Male	182,798	18.3	19,760,056	12.8
Female	221,665	21.4	24,508,940	15.2
Age				
Under 18 years...	145,284	30.1	14,115,713	19.5
Related children under 18 years...	143,837	29.9	13,805,435	19.1
18 to 64 years..	220,568	18.1	25,723,818	13.2
65 years and over	38,611	11.5	4,429,465	9.2

X = Not applicable.

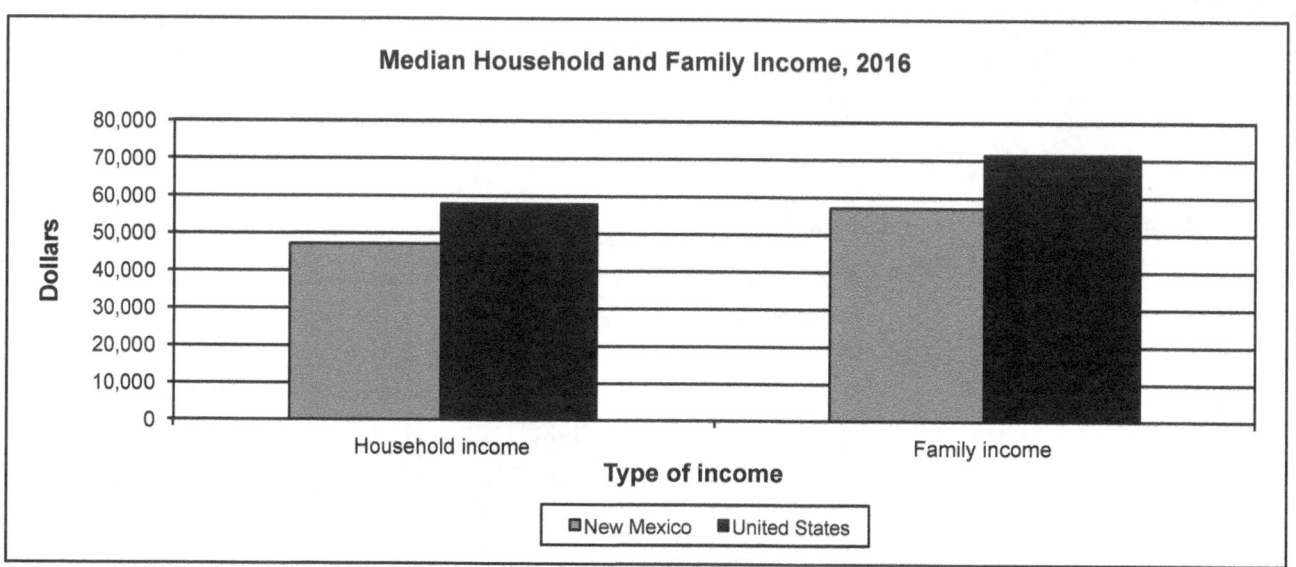

Table NM-6. Health Insurance Coverage Status for the Civilian Noninstitutionalized Population and Children Under 18 Years of Age

(Number, percent.)

Item	2008	2009	2010	2011	2012	2013	2014	2015	2016
Civilian Noninstitutionalized Population	1,951,866	1,975,830	2,032,699	2,047,242	2,051,805	2,051,900	2,050,369	2,050,178	2,046,001
Covered by Private or Public Insurance									
Number...	1,533,362	1,585,932	1,634,141	1,641,058	1,673,819	1,669,460	1,752,620	1,826,147	1,858,312
Percent..	78.6	80.3	80.4	80.2	81.6	81.4	85.5	89.1	90.8
Not Covered									
Number...	418,504	389,898	398,558	406,184	377,986	382,440	297,749	224,031	187,689
Percent..	21.4	19.7	19.6	19.8	18.4	18.6	14.5	10.9	9.2
Percent in the U.S. not covered............................	15.1	15.1	15.5	15.1	14.8	14.5	11.7	9.4	8.6
Children Under 18 Years of Age	500,994	514,098	517,658	516,787	515,341	506,951	498,680	498,415	488,598
Covered by Private or Public Insurance									
Number...	432,461	455,359	464,767	469,318	473,906	463,846	462,278	475,997	462,513
Percent..	86.3	88.6	89.8	90.8	92.0	91.5	92.7	95.5	94.7
Not Covered									
Number...	68,533	58,739	52,891	47,469	41,435	43,105	36,402	22,418	26,085
Percent..	13.7	11.4	10.2	9.2	8.0	8.5	7.3	4.5	5.3
Percent in the U.S. not covered............................	9.9	8.6	8.0	7.5	7.2	7.1	6.0	4.8	4.5

Table NM-7. Employment Status by Demographic Group, 2017

(Numbers in thousands, percent.)

Characteristic	Civilian noninstitutional population	Civilian labor force		Employed		Unemployed	
		Number	Percent of population	Number	Percent of population	Number	Percent of population
Total...	1,614	929	57.6	872	54.0	57	6.1
Sex							
Male.......................................	782	502	64.2	470	60.1	33	6.5
Female.....................................	832	427	51.3	403	48.4	24	5.6
Race, Sex, and Hispanic Origin							
White......................................	1,299	756	58.2	716	55.1	40	5.3
Male.......................................	625	411	65.7	389	62.2	22	5.4
Female.....................................	674	345	51.2	327	48.6	18	5.2
Black or African American.................	40	26	66.8	25	62.0	2	7.1
Male.......................................	NA	NA	NA	NA	NA	NA	NA
Female.....................................	NA	NA	NA	NA	NA	NA	NA
Hispanic or Latino ethnicity[1]	715	417	58.3	391	54.7	26	6.1
Male.......................................	353	233	65.9	218	61.7	15	6.3
Female.....................................	362	184	51.0	173	47.9	11	6.0
Age							
16 to 19 years............................	111	32	28.8	25	22.7	7	21.2
20 to 24 years............................	145	100	69.3	90	62.0	10	10.4
25 to 34 years............................	260	199	76.6	185	71.1	14	7.1
35 to 44 years............................	235	186	79.1	177	75.6	8	4.5
45 to 54 years............................	250	186	74.4	179	71.6	7	3.7
55 to 64 years............................	279	165	59.2	156	56.1	9	5.2
65 years and over	335	61	18.2	60	17.8	2	2.5

NOTE: Data in Table 7 are from the Current Population Survey (CPS) and do not match the estimates in Table 8. See notes and definitions for further information.
[1] May be of any race.
NA = Not available.

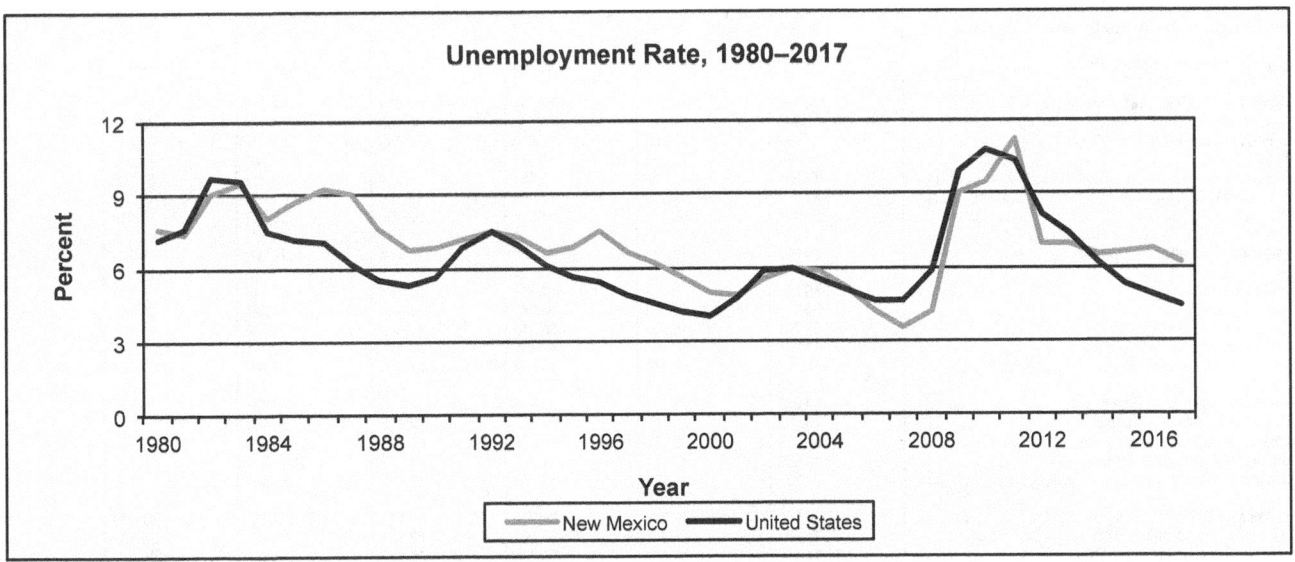

Unemployment Rate, 1980–2017

Table NM-8. Employment Status of the Civilian Noninstitutional Population Age 16 Years and Over

(Number, percent.)

Year	Civilian labor force	Civilian participation rate	Employed	Unemployed	Unemployment rate
2009..	940,352	62.0	869,491	70,861	7.5
2010..	936,088	60.0	860,154	75,934	8.1
2011..	930,356	58.8	860,305	70,051	7.5
2012..	927,795	58.4	861,617	66,178	7.1
2013..	923,899	57.9	859,804	64,095	6.9
2014..	927,142	58.0	865,229	61,913	6.7
2015..	927,999	57.8	867,387	60,612	6.5
2016..	928,732	57.6	866,704	62,028	6.7
2017..	929,567	57.4	872,382	57,185	6.2

Table NM-9. Employment and Average Wages by Industry

(Estimates through 2010 are based on the 2007 *North American Industry Classification System* [NAICS]. Estimates from 2011 onward are based on the 2012 NAICS.)

Industry	2010	2011	2012	2013	2014	2015	2016
	Number of jobs						
Wage and Salary Employment by Industry	837,320	837,281	839,789	846,896	852,861	859,738	862,115
Farm Wage and Salary Employment	6,547	6,608	6,934	7,671	6,789	7,461	8,350
Nonfarm Wage and Salary Employment	830,773	830,673	832,855	839,225	846,072	852,277	853,765
Private wage and salary employment	613,338	616,862	620,956	628,388	636,715	643,720	644,844
Forestry, fishing, and related activities	2,894	2,853	2,855	3,041	3,376	3,494	3,613
Mining	18,257	21,087	23,836	25,820	27,655	25,355	19,703
Utilities	4,373	4,367	4,386	4,446	4,418	4,384	4,441
Construction	45,408	43,593	42,366	43,493	43,967	44,542	44,450
Manufacturing	28,990	29,533	29,693	29,105	28,012	27,780	26,868
Durable goods manufacturing	19,036	19,336	19,077	18,289	17,283	16,859	15,632
Nondurable goods manufacturing	9,954	10,197	10,616	10,816	10,729	10,921	11,236
Wholesale trade	22,051	21,147	21,492	21,675	21,738	21,527	21,522
Retail trade	90,594	91,002	91,809	92,741	93,541	94,479	94,094
Transportation and warehousing	17,581	18,364	19,226	19,285	19,787	20,188	19,611
Information	14,307	13,520	13,584	13,085	12,565	12,693	13,042
Finance and insurance	22,228	22,097	22,071	22,281	22,876	23,126	23,510
Real estate and rental and leasing	9,966	9,900	9,880	10,129	10,229	10,275	10,236
Professional, scientific, and technical services	54,198	53,914	52,803	52,597	52,984	53,845	54,714
Management of companies and enterprises	4,956	5,075	4,990	5,081	5,056	5,178	5,313
Administrative and waste services	41,467	42,071	40,907	41,854	41,847	41,314	41,829
Educational services	10,371	10,383	10,383	10,284	10,233	10,373	10,244
Health care and social assistance	103,549	105,215	107,065	108,261	109,852	114,601	119,353
Arts, entertainment, and recreation	8,654	8,561	8,964	9,068	8,993	9,513	9,612
Accommodation and food services	75,659	76,412	77,770	79,886	82,437	84,255	86,490
Other services, except public administration	37,835	37,768	36,876	36,256	37,149	36,798	36,199
Government and government enterprises	217,435	213,811	211,899	210,837	209,357	208,557	208,921
	Dollars						
Average Wages and Salaries by Industry	40,055	40,860	41,684	41,823	42,958	43,553	44,469
Average Farm Wages and Salaries	34,082	34,113	35,560	36,285	39,502	34,126	33,949
Average Nonfarm Wages and Salaries	40,102	40,914	41,735	41,874	42,986	43,635	44,572
Average private wages and salaries	38,914	39,756	40,735	40,886	42,019	42,566	43,345
Forestry, fishing, and related activities	21,622	22,354	22,930	23,486	23,535	24,631	28,912
Mining	75,899	72,749	74,014	74,235	77,687	76,434	80,258
Utilities	72,955	74,065	75,489	76,911	79,614	81,304	80,143
Construction	41,436	41,900	42,460	42,266	43,446	44,212	48,579
Manufacturing	53,452	55,211	57,004	57,099	58,831	59,014	52,597
Durable goods manufacturing	59,463	61,839	64,066	64,161	66,171	65,421	56,918
Nondurable goods manufacturing	41,957	42,642	44,313	45,158	47,008	49,124	46,584
Wholesale trade	50,275	50,579	51,466	51,584	53,341	54,335	53,747
Retail trade	26,050	26,450	26,981	27,157	27,943	28,761	28,776
Transportation and warehousing	45,291	48,210	50,318	49,548	51,944	51,658	53,869
Information	43,098	45,756	47,461	47,524	49,765	52,565	48,894
Finance and insurance	52,571	55,061	57,334	58,650	59,669	61,905	63,520
Real estate and rental and leasing	34,003	36,124	36,285	36,780	37,887	38,627	38,789
Professional, scientific, and technical services	70,555	71,296	72,666	72,442	75,261	76,753	81,908
Management of companies and enterprises	62,044	63,404	67,568	66,511	69,876	70,195	68,181
Administrative and waste services	32,968	34,471	34,970	34,681	34,674	35,177	36,994
Educational services	31,220	31,507	32,189	32,649	32,881	32,895	33,618
Health care and social assistance	38,535	39,214	39,911	40,154	40,680	41,340	42,168
Arts, entertainment, and recreation	21,420	21,824	22,199	22,721	24,094	24,282	25,778
Accommodation and food services	17,113	17,425	17,920	18,306	18,898	19,426	20,068
Other services, except public administration	26,095	26,578	27,630	28,065	28,683	29,615	31,374
Government and government enterprises	43,455	44,254	44,666	44,817	45,927	46,936	48,361

Table NM-10. Employment Characteristics by Family Type

(Number, percent.)

Family type and labor force status	2014		2015		2016	
	Total	Families with own children under 18 years	Total	Families with own children under 18 years	Total	Families with own children under 18 years
All Families..	487,117	205,222	485,404	199,125	481,127	195,512
FAMILY TYPE AND LABOR FORCE STATUS						
Married-Couple Families.......................................	338,318	123,755	341,876	122,170	334,266	119,275
Both husband and wife in labor force.........................	44.3	58.8	43.6	58.6	43.7	60.3
Husband in labor force, wife not in labor force.............	23.7	34.4	24.3	32.6	23.1	31.8
Wife in labor force, husband not in labor force.............	9.8	4.9	9.3	4.9	9.6	4.8
Both husband and wife not in labor force....................	22.1	1.9	21.6	3.4	22.7	2.4
Other Families	148,799	81,467	143,528	76,955	146,861	76,237
Female householder, no husband present.....................	71.7	72.9	69.3	70.9	72.0	75.5
In labor force..	47.6	56.3	46.7	56.5	49.1	60.0
Not in labor force	24.1	16.6	22.6	14.4	23.0	15.4
Male householder, no wife present............................	28.3	27.1	30.7	29.1	28.0	24.5
In labor force..	21.8	24.1	23.3	26.7	20.3	20.4
Not in labor force	6.5	3.0	7.3	2.4	7.6	4.1

Table NM-11. School Enrollment and Educational Attainment, 2016

(Number, percent.)

Item	State	U.S.
Enrollment		
Total population 3 years and over, enrolled in school	539,773	81,572,277
Enrolled in nursery school or preschool (percent)...	5.1	6.0
Enrolled in kindergarten (percent)..	4.8	5.0
Enrolled in elementary school, grades 1-8 (percent)..	41.2	40.3
Enrolled in high school, grades 9-12 (percent)...	21.1	21.0
Enrolled in college or graduate school (percent)...	27.8	27.7
Attainment		
Total population 25 years and over	1,391,381	218,475,480
Less than ninth grade (percent)	6.1	5.4
9th to 12th grade, no diploma (percent)	8.5	7.2
High school graduate, including equivalency (percent).......................................	26.6	27.2
Some college, no degree (percent)	23.2	20.6
Associate's degree (percent)...	8.4	8.4
Bachelor's degree (percent)	15.5	19.3
Graduate or professional degree (percent)...	11.7	11.9
High school graduate or higher (percent)...	85.4	87.5
Bachelor's degree or higher (percent)...	27.2	31.3

Table NM-12. Public School Characteristics and Educational Indicators

(Number, percent; data derived from National Center of Education Statistics.)

Item	State	U.S.
Public Schools, 2015–2016 (except where noted)		
Number of school districts...	158	18,328
Number of schools..	884	98,456
Number of students	335,694	50,327,015
Number of teachers	21,722	3,151,497
Student-teacher ratio	15.5	16.0
Expenditures per student (dollars), 2014-2015...	9,724	11,445
Four-year adjusted cohort graduation rate (ACGR)[1,2]	71.0	84.1
Students eligible for free or reduced-price lunch (percent), 2014-2015.................	62.6	51.8
English language learners (percent), Fall 2015	15.7	9.5
Students age 3 to 21 served under IDEA, part B (percent).................................	14.8	13.2

Public Schools by Type	Number	Percent of state public schools
Total number of schools...	884	100.0
Regular	846	95.7
Special education..	6	0.7
Vocational education..	0	-
Alternative education...	32	3.6

NOTE: Every school is assigned only one school type based on its instructional emphasis.
[1] ACGR data represents a new method of calculating high-school completion rates and may not be comparable to previous years' data for Averaged Freshmen Graduation Rates (AFGR).
[2] The United States 4-year ACGRs were estimated using both the reported 4-year ACGR data from 49 states and the District of Columbia and using imputed data for Idaho. The estimate for American Indian/Alaska Native students also includes imputed data for Virginia.

Table NM-13. Reported Voting and Registration of the Voting-Age Population, November 2016

(Numbers in thousands, percent.)

Item	Total population	Total citizen population	Registered			Voted		
			Total registered	Percent registered (total population)	Percent registered (total citizen population)	Total voted	Percent voted (total population)	Percent voted (total citizen population)
U.S. Total	245,502	224,059	157,596	64.2	70.3	137,537	56.0	61.4
State Total................................	1,547	1,396	916	59.2	65.6	765	49.4	54.8
Sex								
Male	749	669	416	55.5	62.1	342	45.7	51.1
Female	798	727	500	62.7	68.8	423	53.0	58.2
Race								
White alone................................	1,183	1,053	722	61.1	68.6	620	52.4	58.8
White, non-Hispanic alone	554	543	420	75.8	77.3	376	67.8	69.2
Black alone................................	42	40	26	(B)	(B)	22	(B)	(B)
Asian alone................................	32	27	16	(B)	(B)	14	(B)	(B)
Hispanic (of any race).......................	705	571	340	48.3	59.6	276	39.1	48.2
White alone or in combination	1,211	1,074	738	61.0	68.7	635	52.4	59.1
Black alone or in combination...........	57	51	33	(B)	(B)	28	(B)	(B)
Asian alone or in combination...........	36	31	18	(B)	(B)	16	(B)	(B)
Age								
18 to 24 years................................	241	223	120	49.7	53.8	91	37.8	40.9
25 to 34 years................................	215	196	109	50.5	55.5	77	36.0	39.5
35 to 44 years................................	233	183	117	50.2	63.8	94	40.3	51.2
45 to 64 years................................	549	500	332	60.4	66.3	283	51.5	56.6
65 years and over	309	294	239	77.3	81.2	220	71.1	74.7

B = Base is less than 75,000 and therefore too small to show the derived measure.

Table NM-14. Crime

(Number, rate per 100,000. Data are derived from the FBI Uniform Crime Reports.)

Item	State			U.S. [1,2,3,4]		
	2015	2016	Percent change	2015	2016	Percent change
TOTAL POPULATION [5]	2,085,109	2,081,015	-0.2	321,418,820	323,127,513	0.5
VIOLENT CRIME						
Number................................	13,681	14,619	6.9	1,231,566	1,248,185	1.3
Rate	656.1	702.5	7.1	383.2	386.3	0.8
Murder and Nonnegligent Manslaughter						
Number................................	117	139	18.8	15,696	17,250	9.9
Rate	5.6	6.7	19.6	4.9	5.3	8.2
Rape [6]						
Number................................	1,672	1,526	-8.7	124,047	130,603	5.3
Rate	80.2	73.3	-8.6	38.6	40.4	4.7
Robbery						
Number................................	2,485	2,737	10.1	327,374	332,198	1.5
Rate	119.2	131.5	10.3	101.9	102.8	0.9
Aggravated Assault						
Number................................	9,407	10,217	8.6	764,449	803,007	5.0
Rate	451.2	491.0	8.8	237.8	248.5	4.5
PROPERTY CRIME						
Number................................	77,094	81,931	6.3	7,993,631	7,919,035	-0.9
Rate	3,697.4	3,937.1	6.5	2,487.0	2,450.7	-1.5
Burglary						
Number................................	17,085	17,281	1.1	1,579,527	1,515,096	-4.1
Rate	819.4	830.4	1.3	491.4	468.9	-4.6
Larceny-Theft						
Number................................	51,483	52,907	2.8	5,706,346	5,638,455	-1.2
Rate	2,469.1	2,542.4	3.0	1,775.4	1,745.0	-1.7
Motor Vehicle Theft						
Number................................	8,526	11,743	37.7	707,758	765,484	8.2
Rate	408.9	564.3	38.0	220.2	236.9	7.6

NOTE: Although arson data are included in the trend and clearance tables, sufficient data are not available to estimate totals for this offense. Therefore, no arson data are published in this table.
X = Not applicable.
- = Zero or rounds to zero.
[1] The crime figures have been adjusted.
[2] The data collection methodology for the offense of forcible rape used by the Minnesota state Uniform Crime Reporting (UCR) Program (with the exception of Minneapolis and St. Paul, Minnesota) does not comply with national UCR Program guidelines. Consequently, its figures for forcible rape and violent crime (of which forcible rape is a part) are not published in this table.
[3] Includes offenses reported by the Zoological Police and the Metro Transit Police.
[4] Because of changes in the state's reporting practices, figures are not comparable to previous years' data.
[5] Populations are U.S. Census Bureau provisional estimates as of July 1 of each year.
[6] The figures shown for the offense of rape were estimated using the revised Uniform Crime Reporting (UCR) definition of rape.

Table NM-15. State Government Finances, 2016

(Dollar amounts in thousands, percent distribution.)

Item	Dollars	Percent distribution
Total Revenue	18,602,071	100.0
General revenue	16,536,739	88.9
Intergovernmental revenue	7,030,082	37.8
Taxes	5,462,105	29.4
General sales	2,085,366	11.2
Selective sales	844,638	4.5
License taxes	342,527	1.8
Individual income tax	1,409,811	7.6
Corporate income tax	113,942	0.6
Other taxes	665,821	3.6
Current charges	1,628,297	8.8
Miscellaneous general revenue	2,416,255	13.0
Utility revenue	0	-
Liquor stores revenue	0	-
Insurance trust revenue [1]	2,065,332	11.1
Total Expenditure	20,158,082	100.0
Intergovernmental expenditure	4,986,006	24.7
Direct expenditure	15,172,076	75.3
Current operation	11,448,693	56.8
Capital outlay	860,818	4.3
Insurance benefits and repayments	2,309,050	11.5
Assistance and subsidies	255,283	1.3
Interest on debt	298,232	1.5
Exhibit: Salaries and wages	2,511,479	12.5
Total Expenditure	20,158,082	100.0
General expenditure	17,849,032	88.5
Intergovernmental expenditure	4,986,006	24.7
Direct expenditure	12,863,026	63.8
General expenditure, by function:		
Education	6,047,870	30.0
Public welfare	5,631,240	27.9
Hospitals	1,152,604	5.7
Health	485,089	2.4
Highways	715,713	3.6
Police protection	157,414	0.8
Correction	477,630	2.4
Natural resources	214,257	1.1
Parks and recreation	58,748	0.3
Governmental administration	605,342	3.0
Interest on general debt	298,232	1.5
Other and unallocable	2,004,893	9.9
Utility expenditure	0	-
Liquor stores expenditure	0	-
Insurance trust expenditure	2,309,050	11.5
Debt at End of Fiscal Year	6,951,535	X
Cash and Security Holdings	42,508,407	X

X = Not applicable.
- = Zero or rounds to zero.
[1] Within insurance trust revenue, net earnings of state retirement systems is a calculated statistic (the item code in the data file is X08), and thus can be positive or negative. Net earnings is the sum of earnings on investments plus gains on investments minus losses on investments. The change made in 2002 for asset valuation from book to market value in accordance with Statement 34 of the Governmental Accounting Standards Board is reflected in the calculated statistics.

Table NM-16. State Government Tax Collections, 2017

(Dollars in thousands, percent.)

Item	Dollars	Percent distribution
Total Taxes	5,776,271	100.0
Property taxes	81,694	1.4
Sales and gross receipts	3,069,641	53.1
General sales and gross receipts	2,258,767	39.1
Selective sales and gross receipts	810,874	14.0
Alcoholic beverages	44,916	0.8
Amusements	77,959	1.3
Insurance premiums	163,453	2.8
Motor fuels	242,627	4.2
Pari-mutuels	842	-
Public utilities	30,633	0.5
Tobacco products	89,703	1.6
Other selective sales	160,741	2.8
Licenses	307,671	5.3
Alcoholic beverages	0	-
Amusements	556	-
Corporations in general	30,013	0.5
Hunting and fishing	30,779	0.5
Motor vehicle	196,303	3.4
Motor vehicle operators	5,374	0.1
Public utilities	1,438	-
Occupation and business, NEC	43,208	0.7
Other licenses	0	-
Income taxes	1,430,644	24.8
Individual income	1,338,768	23.2
Corporation net income	91,876	1.6
Other taxes	886,621	15.3
Death and gift	1	-
Documentary and stock transfer	X	-
Severance	886,620	15.3
Taxes, NEC	0	-

- = Zero or rounds to zero.

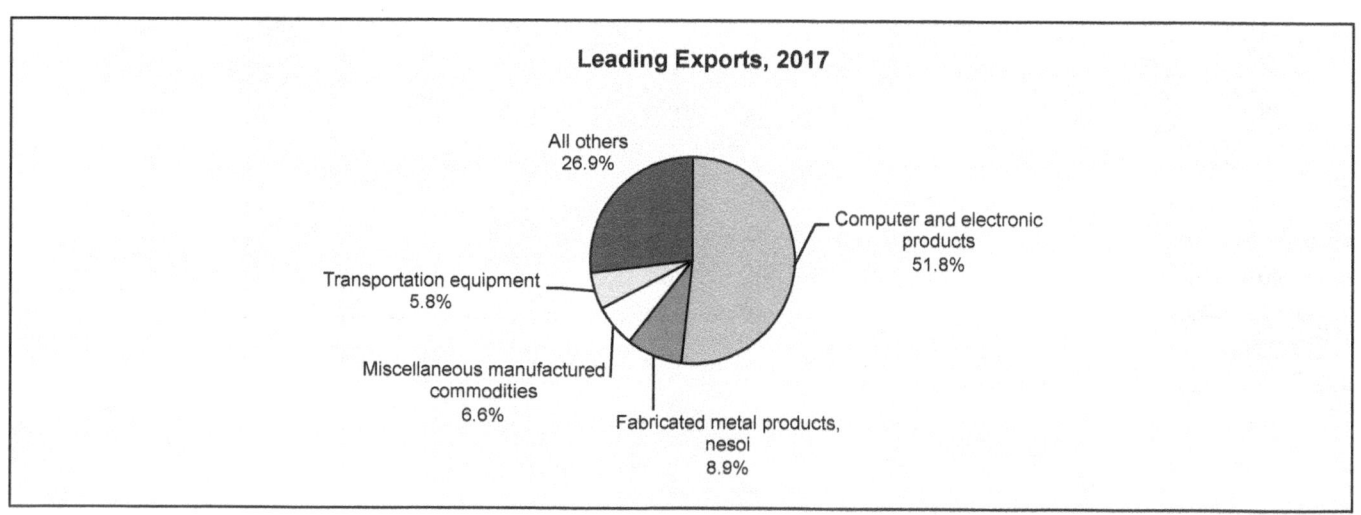

Leading Exports, 2017

All others 26.9%

Computer and electronic products 51.8%

Transportation equipment 5.8%

Miscellaneous manufactured commodities 6.6%

Fabricated metal products, nesoi 8.9%

NEW YORK

Facts and Figures

Location: Northeastern United States; bordered on the N by Canada (Ontario and Quebec) and Lake Ontario; on the E by Vermont, Massachusetts, and Connecticut; on the S by New Jersey and Pennsylvania; and on the W by Pennsylvania, Lake Erie, Canada (Ontario), and Lake Ontario

Area: 54,556 sq. mi. (141,299 sq. km.); rank—27th

Population: 19,849,399 (2017 est.); rank—4th

Principal Cities: capital—Albany; largest—New York City

Statehood: July 26, 1788; 11th state

U.S. Congress: 2 senators, 27 representatives

State Motto: *Excelsior* ("Ever upward")

State Song: "I Love New York"

State Nickname: The Empire State

Abbreviations: NY; N.Y.

State Symbols: flower—rose; tree—sugar maple; bird—bluebird

At a Glance

- With an increase in population of 2.3 percent, New York ranked 35th among the states in growth from 2010 to 2017.

- In 2016, 6.1 percent of New Yorkers did not have health insurance, compared to 8.6 percent of the total U.S. population.

- New York had the second lowest homeownership rate in 2017, with 51.1 percent of residents owning homes.

- New York had the 3rd lowest property crime rate in the country in 2016, at 1,545.6 incidents per 100,000 population.

- New York had the 3rd highest GDP of all states in 2017 ($1,294,571 million).

Table NY-1. Population by Age, Sex, Race, and Hispanic Origin

(Number, percent, except where noted.)

Sex, age, race, and Hispanic origin	2000	2010	2017 [1]	Average annual percent change, 2010–2017
Total Population..	18,976,457	19,378,102	19,849,399	2.4
Percent of total U.S. population	6.7	6.3	6.1	X
Sex				
Male..	9,146,748	9,377,147	9,637,462	2.8
Female	9,829,709	10,000,955	10,211,937	2.1
Age				
Under 5 years...	1,239,417	1,155,822	1,164,406	0.7
5 to 19 years..	3,971,834	3,741,689	3,498,321	-6.5
20 to 64 years..	11,316,854	11,862,648	12,024,479	1.4
65 years and over	2,448,352	2,617,943	3,162,193	20.8
Median age (years)...	35.9	38.0	38.7	1.8
Race and Hispanic Origin				
One race				
White..	12,893,689	13,901,661	13,807,127	-0.7
Black...	3,014,385	3,378,047	3,510,933	3.9
American Indian and Alaska Native	82,461	183,046	193,229	5.6
Asian..	1,044,976	1,481,555	1,806,646	21.9
Native Hawaiian or Other Pacific Islander	8,818	24,000	26,943	12.3
Two or more races...	590,182	409,793	504,521	23.1
Hispanic (of any race)...	2,867,583	3,564,228	3,811,945	7.0

X = Not applicable.
[1] Population figures for 2017 are July 1 estimates. The 2010 estimates are taken from the 2010 Census.
- = Zero or rounds to zero.

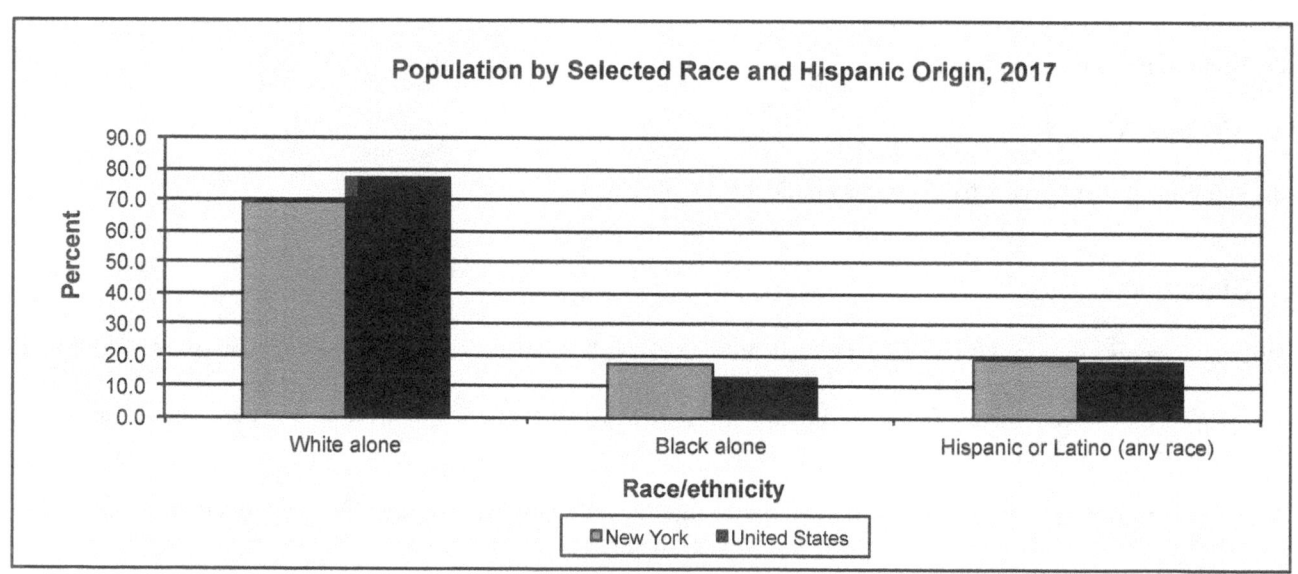

Table NY-2. Marital Status

(Number, percent distribution.)

Sex, age, and marital status	2000	2010	2016
Males, 15 Years and Over	7,125,715	7,586,733	7,816,473
Never married	34.7	40.5	41.4
Now married, except separated...	53.3	47.6	46.5
Separated..	2.7	2.2	2.1
Widowed..	2.8	2.6	2.6
Divorced..	6.5	7.2	7.4
Females, 15 Years and Over	7,932,161	8,283,542	8,470,991
Never married	29.0	34.8	36.4
Now married, except separated...	47.1	42.8	41.8
Separated..	3.7	3.1	2.9
Widowed..	11.2	9.6	8.9
Divorced..	8.9	9.7	10.1

Table NY-3. Households and Housing Characteristics

(Number, percent, dollars.)

Item	2000	2010	2016	Average annual percent change, 2010–2016
Total Households	7,056,860	7,196,427	7,209,054	-
Family households	4,639,387	4,632,676	4,541,583	-0.3
Married-couple family	3,289,514	3,210,895	3,159,748	-0.3
Other family	1,349,873	1,421,781	1,381,835	-0.5
Male householder, no wife present	311,697	355,236	364,163	0.4
Female householder, no husband present	1,038,176	1,066,545	1,017,672	-0.8
Nonfamily households	2,417,473	2,563,751	2,667,471	0.7
Householder living alone	1,982,742	2,089,816	2,158,740	0.5
Householder not living alone	434,731	473,935	508,731	1.2
Housing Characteristics				
Total housing units	7,679,301	8,108,211	8,232,039	0.3
Occupied housing units	7,056,860	7,196,427	7,209,054	-
Owner occupied	3,739,166	3,904,123	3,841,170	-0.3
Renter occupied	3,317,694	3,292,304	3,367,884	0.4
Average household size	2.61	2.61	2.66	0.3
Financial Characteristics				
Median gross rent of renter-occupied housing	627	1,020	1,194	2.8
Median monthly owner costs for housing units with a mortgage	1,357	1,963	2,020	0.5
Median value of owner-occupied housing units	148,700	296,500	302,400	0.3

- = Zero or rounds to zero.

Table NY-4. Migration, Origin, and Language

(Number, percent.)

Characteristic	State			U.S.		
	2015	2016	Percent change	2015	2016	Percent change
Residence 1 Year Ago						
Population 1 year and over	19,570,171	19,526,443	-0.2	317,635,720	319,361,956	0.5
Same house	89.5	89.4	X	85.3	85.4	X
Different house in the U.S.	9.8	9.7	X	14.1	13.9	X
Same county	6.0	5.9	X	8.5	8.3	X
Different county	3.8	3.8	X	5.6	5.6	X
Same state	2.5	2.5	X	3.2	3.2	X
Different state	1.3	1.3	X	2.4	2.4	X
Abroad	0.8	0.9	X	0.7	0.7	X
Place of Birth						
Native born	15,265,704	15,209,174	-0.4	278,128,449	279,388,170	0.5
Male	49.0	48.9	X	49.3	49.3	X
Female	51.0	51.1	X	50.7	50.7	X
Foreign born	4,530,087	4,536,115	0.1	43,290,372	43,739,345	1.0
Male	47.2	47.1	X	48.6	48.5	X
Female	52.8	52.9	X	51.4	51.5	X
Foreign born; naturalized U.S. citizen	2,502,783	2,513,779	0.4	20,697,103	21,238,372	2.6
Male	44.9	44.6	X	45.9	45.9	X
Female	55.1	55.4	X	54.1	54.1	X
Foreign born; not a U.S. citizen	2,027,304	2,022,336	-0.2	22,593,269	22,500,973	-0.4
Male	50.1	50.3	X	51.1	51.0	X
Female	49.9	49.7	X	48.9	49.0	X
Entered 2010 or later	14.9	17.9	X	15.6	18.6	X
Entered 2000 to 2009	25.7	25.2	X	27.9	26.7	X
Entered before 2000	59.4	56.9	X	56.5	54.7	X
World Region of Birth, Foreign						
Foreign-born population, excluding population born at sea	4,530,010	4,536,115	0.1	43,289,646	43,738,901	1.0
Europe	16.3	15.7	X	11.1	10.9	X
Asia	29.3	29.1	X	30.6	30.8	X
Africa	4.3	4.5	X	4.8	4.9	X
Oceania	0.3	0.3	X	0.6	0.6	X
Latin America	48.6	49.2	X	51.1	51.0	X
North America	1.2	1.2	X	1.9	1.8	X
Language Spoken at Home and Ability to Speak English						
Population 5 years and over	18,610,703	18,586,270	-0.1	301,625,014	303,328,961	0.6
English only	69.1	69.0	X	78.5	78.4	X
Language other than English	30.9	31.0	X	21.5	21.6	X
Speaks English less than "very well"	13.5	13.7	X	8.6	8.6	X

NA = Not available.
X = Not applicable.
- = Zero or rounds to zero.

Table NY-5. Median Income and Poverty Status, 2016

(Number, percent, except as noted.)

Characteristic	State		U.S.	
	Number	Percent	Number	Percent
Median Income				
Households (dollars)............................	62,909	X	57,617	X
Families (dollars)..............................	77,379	X	71,062	X
Below Poverty Level (All People)	2,832,824	14.7	44,268,996	14.0
Sex				
Male	1,237,361	13.3	19,760,056	12.8
Female	1,595,463	16.1	24,508,940	15.2
Age				
Under 18 years................................	847,288	20.7	14,115,713	19.5
Related children under 18 years..........	831,618	20.4	13,805,435	19.1
18 to 64 years................................	1,650,547	13.5	25,723,818	13.2
65 years and over	334,989	11.4	4,429,465	9.2

X = Not applicable.

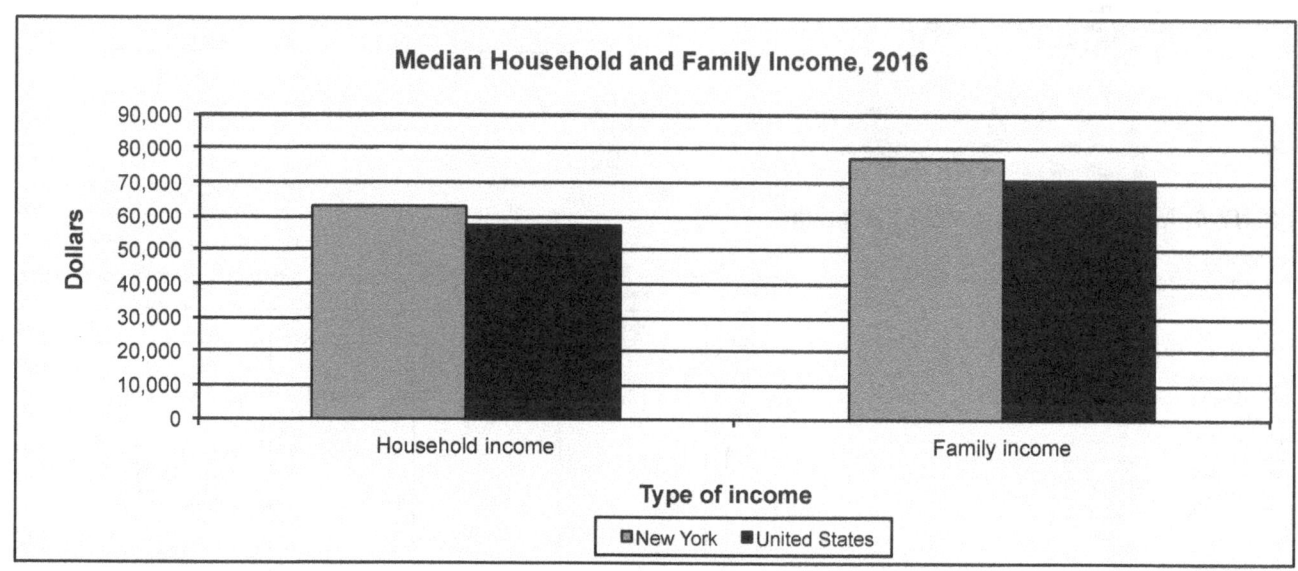

Table NY-6. Health Insurance Coverage Status for the Civilian Noninstitutionalized Population and Children Under 18 Years of Age

(Number, percent.)

Item	2008	2009	2010	2011	2012	2013	2014	2015	2016
Civilian Noninstitutionalized Population	19,207,057	19,264,374	19,134,281	19,208,419	19,316,728	19,400,069	19,499,548	19,556,452	19,505,596
Covered by Private or Public Insurance									
Number..	16,948,813	17,069,635	16,856,899	17,013,070	17,213,819	17,330,548	17,802,989	18,175,904	18,322,902
Percent...	88.2	88.6	88.1	88.6	89.1	89.3	91.3	92.9	93.9
Not Covered									
Number..	2,258,244	2,194,739	2,277,382	2,195,349	2,102,909	2,069,521	1,696,559	1,380,548	1,182,694
Percent...	11.8	11.4	11.9	11.4	10.9	10.7	8.7	7.1	6.1
Percent in the U.S. not covered...........................	15.1	15.1	15.5	15.1	14.8	14.5	11.7	9.4	8.6
Children Under 18 Years of Age	4,402,183	4,413,888	4,301,661	4,270,110	4,252,821	4,230,975	4,217,078	4,204,378	4,170,786
Covered by Private or Public Insurance									
Number..	4,147,027	4,208,891	4,093,200	4,089,276	4,085,154	4,060,192	4,079,553	4,100,735	4,069,720
Percent...	94.2	95.4	95.2	95.8	96.1	96.0	96.7	97.5	97.6
Not Covered									
Number..	255,156	204,997	208,461	180,834	167,667	170,783	137,525	103,643	101,066
Percent...	5.8	4.6	4.8	4.2	3.9	4.0	3.3	2.5	2.4
Percent in the U.S. not covered...........................	9.9	8.6	8.0	7.5	7.2	7.1	6.0	4.8	4.5

Table NY-7. Employment Status by Demographic Group, 2017

(Numbers in thousands, percent.)

Characteristic	Civilian noninstitutional population	Civilian labor force		Employed		Unemployed	
		Number	Percent of population	Number	Percent of population	Number	Percent of population
Total...	15,861	9,699	61.1	9,248	58.3	450	4.6
Sex							
Male	7,582	5,065	66.8	4,828	63.7	238	4.7
Female	8,279	4,633	56.0	4,421	53.4	213	4.6
Race, Sex, and Hispanic Origin							
White	11,321	6,939	61.3	6,660	58.8	280	4.0
Male	5,526	3,726	67.4	3,579	64.8	148	4.0
Female	5,795	3,213	55.4	3,081	53.2	132	4.1
Black or African American..................	2,691	1,588	59.0	1,467	54.5	121	7.6
Male	1,205	729	60.5	672	55.7	57	7.9
Female	1,486	859	57.8	796	53.5	63	7.4
Hispanic or Latino ethnicity[1]	2,651	1,663	62.7	1,572	59.3	91	5.4
Male	1,257	891	70.9	849	67.6	42	4.7
Female	1,395	772	55.3	723	51.9	48	6.3
Age							
16 to 19 years.................................	948	250	26.4	204	21.5	46	18.3
20 to 24 years.................................	1,346	832	61.8	750	55.7	82	9.8
25 to 34 years.................................	2,869	2,308	80.5	2,210	77.0	98	4.2
35 to 44 years.................................	2,475	2,011	81.3	1,943	78.5	68	3.4
45 to 54 years.................................	2,572	2,035	79.1	1,962	76.3	73	3.6
55 to 64 years.................................	2,517	1,641	65.2	1,586	63.0	55	3.4
65 years and over	3,135	621	19.8	593	18.9	28	4.6

NOTE: Data in Table 7 are from the Current Population Survey (CPS) and do not match the estimates in Table 8. See notes and definitions for further information.
[1] May be of any race.

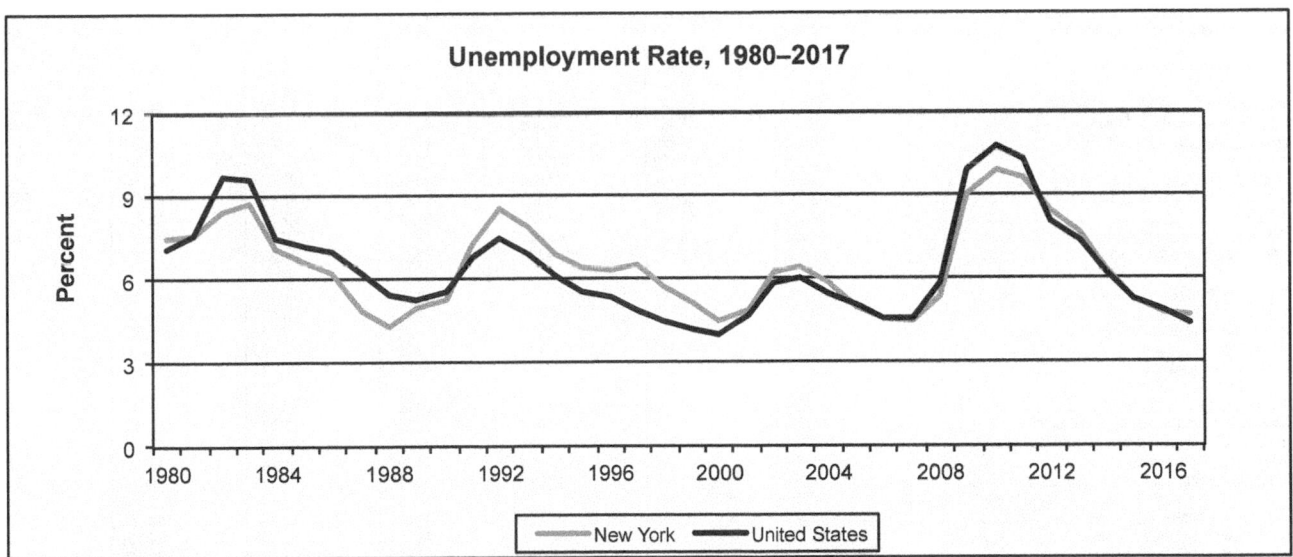

Unemployment Rate, 1980–2017

Table NY-8. Employment Status of the Civilian Noninstitutional Population Age 16 Years and Over

(Number, percent.)

Year	Civilian labor force	Civilian participation rate	Employed	Unemployed	Unemployment rate
2009..	9,647,485	62.8	8,844,486	802,999	8.3
2010..	9,595,362	62.4	8,769,723	825,639	8.6
2011..	9,517,361	61.4	8,728,057	789,304	8.3
2012..	9,612,232	61.6	8,793,385	818,847	8.5
2013..	9,659,170	61.5	8,913,788	745,382	7.7
2014..	9,591,309	60.7	8,984,074	607,235	6.3
2015..	9,644,615	60.8	9,136,151	508,464	5.3
2016..	9,668,687	60.8	9,200,266	468,421	4.8
2017..	9,704,695	60.9	9,249,225	455,470	4.7

Table NY-9. Employment and Average Wages by Industry

(Estimates through 2010 are based on the 2007 *North American Industry Classification System* [NAICS]. Estimates from 2011 onward are based on the 2012 NAICS.)

Industry	2010	2011	2012	2013	2014	2015	2016
	Number of jobs						
Wage and Salary Employment by Industry	8,718,528	8,821,283	8,939,979	9,055,889	9,226,937	9,388,514	9,506,287
Farm Wage and Salary Employment	18,129	19,822	19,706	22,545	22,607	22,525	21,022
Nonfarm Wage and Salary Employment	8,700,399	8,801,461	8,920,273	9,033,344	9,204,330	9,365,989	9,485,265
Private wage and salary employment	7,168,895	7,312,652	7,452,244	7,575,321	7,750,548	7,909,983	8,037,985
Forestry, fishing, and related activities	5,345	5,391	5,254	5,313	5,569	5,693	5,674
Mining	4,631	4,675	4,676	4,407	4,620	4,664	4,425
Utilities	38,315	37,267	36,035	36,174	37,698	38,319	37,698
Construction	317,506	318,184	323,895	336,773	352,480	370,305	387,077
Manufacturing	457,778	459,173	459,362	456,608	453,325	455,717	451,863
Durable goods manufacturing	268,331	271,184	269,505	266,736	265,124	266,317	262,900
Nondurable goods manufacturing	189,447	187,989	189,857	189,872	188,201	189,400	188,963
Wholesale trade	327,264	332,932	336,319	337,871	340,074	342,871	340,748
Retail trade	884,321	901,923	921,567	934,586	950,811	954,409	951,952
Transportation and warehousing	224,163	228,998	231,209	232,195	240,346	249,757	254,899
Information	252,642	257,252	261,262	261,361	265,671	267,104	267,950
Finance and insurance	502,625	517,633	516,586	511,664	520,874	528,109	531,593
Real estate and rental and leasing	182,465	183,427	184,305	187,418	190,881	195,637	199,570
Professional, scientific, and technical services	560,249	580,444	604,138	619,278	635,101	656,645	669,952
Management of companies and enterprises	132,173	133,394	134,793	138,822	142,442	143,389	143,090
Administrative and waste services	417,543	431,659	442,334	454,993	461,879	475,512	490,562
Educational services	358,551	365,620	375,994	380,425	388,861	403,092	409,498
Health care and social assistance	1,317,799	1,326,387	1,341,503	1,366,560	1,398,110	1,427,895	1,480,650
Arts, entertainment, and recreation	142,852	143,714	150,204	157,399	162,671	165,742	170,904
Accommodation and food services	599,088	629,802	659,089	687,788	714,887	737,244	754,520
Other services, except public administration	443,585	454,777	463,719	465,686	484,248	487,879	485,360
Government and government enterprises	1,531,504	1,488,809	1,468,029	1,458,023	1,453,782	1,456,006	1,447,280
	Dollars						
Average Wages and Salaries by Industry	59,462	61,011	61,957	62,408	65,155	66,774	69,151
Average Farm Wages and Salaries	26,133	20,920	31,009	27,617	29,501	27,183	32,109
Average Nonfarm Wages and Salaries	59,532	61,101	62,025	62,494	65,242	66,870	69,233
Average private wages and salaries	60,869	62,492	63,388	63,747	66,659	68,282	70,693
Forestry, fishing, and related activities	28,520	28,685	28,929	29,624	30,317	32,306	36,214
Mining	58,276	67,428	63,465	60,336	65,252	64,907	63,116
Utilities	97,923	102,987	108,836	106,107	107,822	110,560	117,376
Construction	60,250	61,465	62,359	63,428	65,252	67,520	71,343
Manufacturing	59,392	59,971	60,923	61,183	62,077	65,470	63,923
Durable goods manufacturing	62,753	64,380	66,008	66,343	66,891	70,319	68,451
Nondurable goods manufacturing	54,632	53,612	53,705	53,933	55,295	58,652	57,622
Wholesale trade	71,647	73,724	77,717	76,846	79,564	82,965	84,354
Retail trade	29,596	30,283	30,725	31,470	32,481	33,415	34,762
Transportation and warehousing	45,340	46,056	47,202	48,236	49,123	49,905	53,265
Information	90,828	95,824	100,138	102,527	110,429	114,644	115,581
Finance and insurance	191,634	198,005	197,182	197,252	216,945	214,004	218,777
Real estate and rental and leasing	54,724	56,793	59,690	60,054	63,838	66,701	72,376
Professional, scientific, and technical services	90,844	93,908	96,047	97,936	102,977	106,033	111,967
Management of companies and enterprises	143,384	145,794	144,086	142,751	143,605	148,958	143,949
Administrative and waste services	42,504	41,929	43,723	44,028	44,941	48,427	50,177
Educational services	41,226	42,461	43,671	44,761	46,102	49,200	51,089
Health care and social assistance	44,362	45,170	45,851	46,580	47,451	48,088	50,682
Arts, entertainment, and recreation	46,752	47,988	48,911	48,714	51,466	54,101	57,170
Accommodation and food services	24,420	25,311	26,222	26,605	27,714	28,475	31,847
Other services, except public administration	33,121	33,598	34,696	35,746	36,399	38,103	40,602
Government and government enterprises	53,272	54,272	55,109	55,984	57,692	59,195	61,124

Table NY-10. Employment Characteristics by Family Type

(Number, percent.)

Family type and labor force status	2014		2015		2016	
	Total	Families with own children under 18 years	Total	Families with own children under 18 years	Total	Families with own children under 18 years
All Families...	4,592,706	1,938,644	4,561,118	1,918,562	4,541,583	1,876,874
FAMILY TYPE AND LABOR FORCE STATUS						
Married-Couple Families...............................	3,147,131	1,269,381	3,156,019	1,261,456	3,159,748	1,257,707
Both husband and wife in labor force...........................	53.0	65.5	51.9	65.5	51.5	65.6
Husband in labor force, wife not in labor force	21.5	28.1	21.3	27.4	21.4	27.5
Wife in labor force, husband not in labor force	8.6	4.6	8.7	4.7	8.6	4.5
Both husband and wife not in labor force.......................	16.8	1.8	16.9	1.8	17.4	1.7
Other Families	1,445,575	669,263	1,405,099	657,106	1,381,835	619,167
Female householder, no husband present......................	74.6	77.9	74.4	77.1	73.6	77.4
In labor force..	49.9	61.6	50.4	61.2	49.4	61.4
Not in labor force	24.7	16.3	24.0	16.0	24.3	16.0
Male householder, no wife present.............................	25.4	22.1	25.6	22.9	26.4	22.6
In labor force..	19.3	19.6	19.6	20.2	19.9	19.9
Not in labor force	6.1	2.5	6.0	2.7	6.4	2.8

Table NY-11. School Enrollment and Educational Attainment, 2016

(Number, percent.)

Item	State	U.S.
Enrollment		
Total population 3 years and over, enrolled in school	4,843,659	81,572,277
Enrolled in nursery school or preschool (percent)...	6.1	6.0
Enrolled in kindergarten (percent)...	4.9	5.0
Enrolled in elementary school, grades 1-8 (percent)...	37.9	40.3
Enrolled in high school, grades 9-12 (percent)	20.4	21.0
Enrolled in college or graduate school (percent)	30.7	27.7
Attainment		
Total population 25 years and over	13,653,592	218,475,480
Less than ninth grade (percent)	6.3	5.4
9th to 12th grade, no diploma (percent)	7.3	7.2
High school graduate, including equivalency (percent)...	26.2	27.2
Some college, no degree (percent)	15.8	20.6
Associate's degree (percent)	8.7	8.4
Bachelor's degree (percent)	20.1	19.3
Graduate or professional degree (percent)	15.5	11.9
High school graduate or higher (percent)	86.3	87.5
Bachelor's degree or higher (percent)	35.7	31.3

Table NY-12. Public School Characteristics and Educational Indicators

(Number, percent; data derived from National Center of Education Statistics.)

Item	State	U.S.
Public Schools, 2015–2016 (except where noted)		
Number of school districts...	989	18,328
Number of schools..	4,824	98,456
Number of students...	2,711,626	50,327,015
Number of teachers...	206,086	3,151,497
Student-teacher ratio	13.2	16.0
Expenditures per student (dollars), 2014-2015...	20,744	11,445
Four-year adjusted cohort graduation rate (ACGR)[1,2]	80.4	84.1
Students eligible for free or reduced-price lunch (percent), 2014-2015...............................	50.9	51.8
English language learners (percent), Fall 2015..	8.0	9.5
Students age 3 to 21 served under IDEA, part B (percent)...	18.4	13.2

Public Schools by Type	Number	Percent of state public schools
Total number of schools..	4,824	100.0
Regular	4,618	95.7
Special education	131	2.7
Vocational education	21	0.4
Alternative education..	54	1.1

NOTE: Every school is assigned only one school type based on its instructional emphasis.
[1] ACGR data represents a new method of calculating high-school completion rates and may not be comparable to previous years' data for Averaged Freshmen Graduation Rates (AFGR).
[2] The United States 4-year ACGRs were estimated using both the reported 4-year ACGR data from 49 states and the District of Columbia and using imputed data for Idaho. The estimate for American Indian/Alaska Native students also includes imputed data for Virginia.

Table NY-13. Reported Voting and Registration of the Voting-Age Population, November 2016

(Numbers in thousands, percent.)

Item	Total population	Total citizen population	Registered			Voted		
			Total registered	Percent registered (total population)	Percent registered (total citizen population)	Total voted	Percent voted (total population)	Percent voted (total citizen population)
U.S. Total	245,502	224,059	157,596	64.2	70.3	137,537	56.0	61.4
State Total................................	15,506	13,751	9,142	59.0	66.5	7,869	50.7	57.2
Sex								
Male	7,389	6,513	4,225	57.2	64.9	3,592	48.6	55.2
Female	8,116	7,238	4,917	60.6	67.9	4,277	52.7	59.1
Race								
White alone...............................	11,101	10,159	6,997	63.0	68.9	6,049	54.5	59.5
White, non-Hispanic alone	9,270	8,870	6,264	67.6	70.6	5,418	58.4	61.1
Black alone................................	2,610	2,321	1,570	60.2	67.6	1,350	51.7	58.2
Asian alone...............................	1,547	1,059	430	27.8	40.6	365	23.6	34.5
Hispanic (of any race)...................	2,346	1,735	1,044	44.5	60.2	878	37.4	50.6
White alone or in combination	11,193	10,241	7,040	62.9	68.7	6,089	54.4	59.5
Black alone or in combination..........	2,692	2,387	1,607	59.7	67.3	1,374	51.0	57.6
Asian alone or in combination..........	1,561	1,073	443	28.4	41.3	379	24.3	35.4
Age								
18 to 24 years............................	1,756	1,590	832	47.4	52.3	607	34.6	38.2
25 to 34 years............................	2,952	2,503	1,510	51.1	60.3	1,276	43.2	51.0
35 to 44 years............................	2,528	2,092	1,363	53.9	65.1	1,153	45.6	55.1
45 to 64 years............................	5,070	4,531	3,234	63.8	71.4	2,875	56.7	63.4
65 years and over	3,201	3,035	2,204	68.8	72.6	1,957	61.1	64.5

Table NY-14. Crime

(Number, rate per 100,000. Data are derived from the FBI Uniform Crime Reports.)

Item	State			U.S. [1,2,3,4]		
	2015	2016	Percent change	2015	2016	Percent change
TOTAL POPULATION [5]	19,795,791	19,745,289	-0.3	321,418,820	323,127,513	0.5
VIOLENT CRIME						
Number..	75,165	74,285	-1.2	1,231,566	1,248,185	1.3
Rate...	379.7	376.2	-0.9	383.2	386.3	0.8
Murder and Nonnegligent Manslaughter						
Number..	609	630	3.4	15,696	17,250	9.9
Rate...	3.1	3.2	3.2	4.9	5.3	8.2
Rape[6]						
Number..	6,074	6,260	3.1	124,047	130,603	5.3
Rate...	30.7	31.7	3.3	38.6	40.4	4.7
Robbery						
Number..	23,936	22,316	-6.8	327,374	332,198	1.5
Rate...	120.9	113.0	-6.5	101.9	102.8	0.9
Aggravated Assault						
Number..	44,546	45,079	1.2	764,449	803,007	5.0
Rate...	225.0	228.3	1.5	237.8	248.5	4.5
PROPERTY CRIME						
Number..	317,529	305,181	-3.9	7,993,631	7,919,035	-0.9
Rate...	1,604.0	1,545.6	-3.6	2,487.0	2,450.7	-1.5
Burglary						
Number..	44,276	39,821	-10.1	1,579,527	1,515,096	-4.1
Rate...	223.7	201.7	-9.8	491.4	468.9	-4.6
Larceny-Theft						
Number..	257,940	250,968	-2.7	5,706,346	5,638,455	-1.2
Rate...	1,303.0	1,271.0	-2.5	1,775.4	1,745.0	-1.7
Motor Vehicle Theft						
Number..	15,313	14,392	-6.0	707,758	765,484	8.2
Rate...	77.4	72.9	-5.8	220.2	236.9	7.6

NOTE: Although arson data are included in the trend and clearance tables, sufficient data are not available to estimate totals for this offense. Therefore, no arson data are published in this table.

X = Not applicable.

- = Zero or rounds to zero.

[1] The crime figures have been adjusted.

[2] The data collection methodology for the offense of forcible rape used by the Minnesota state Uniform Crime Reporting (UCR) Program (with the exception of Minneapolis and St. Paul, Minnesota) does not comply with national UCR Program guidelines. Consequently, its figures for forcible rape and violent crime (of which forcible rape is a part) are not published in this table.

[3] Includes offenses reported by the Zoological Police and the Metro Transit Police.

[4] Because of changes in the state's reporting practices, figures are not comparable to previous years' data.

[5] Populations are U.S. Census Bureau provisional estimates as of July 1 of each year.

[6] The figures shown for the offense of rape were estimated using the revised Uniform Crime Reporting (UCR) definition of rape.

Table NY-15. State Government Finances, 2016

(Dollar amounts in thousands, percent distribution.)

Item	Dollars	Percent distribution
Total Revenue	185,619,993	100.0
General revenue	164,398,893	88.6
Intergovernmental revenue	56,822,852	30.6
Taxes	81,353,963	43.8
General sales	13,534,170	7.3
Selective sales	11,255,847	6.1
License taxes	1,794,987	1.0
Individual income tax	46,508,632	25.1
Corporate income tax	4,181,811	2.3
Other taxes	4,078,516	2.2
Current charges	9,800,144	5.3
Miscellaneous general revenue	16,421,934	8.8
Utility revenue	8,080,800	4.4
Liquor stores revenue	0	-
Insurance trust revenue [1]	13,140,300	7.1
Total Expenditure	195,571,229	100.0
Intergovernmental expenditure	61,639,619	31.5
Direct expenditure	133,931,610	68.5
Current operation	95,131,795	48.6
Capital outlay	9,541,591	4.9
Insurance benefits and repayments	21,598,629	11.0
Assistance and subsidies	2,011,000	1.0
Interest on debt	5,648,595	2.9
Exhibit: Salaries and wages	17,719,606	9.1
Total Expenditure	195,571,229	100.0
General expenditure	160,855,795	82.2
Intergovernmental expenditure	61,639,619	31.5
Direct expenditure	99,216,176	50.7
General expenditure, by function:		
Education	47,037,290	24.1
Public welfare	63,586,859	32.5
Hospitals	5,282,713	2.7
Health	8,506,029	4.3
Highways	5,270,887	2.7
Police protection	982,307	0.5
Correction	3,388,695	1.7
Natural resources	420,222	0.2
Parks and recreation	738,523	0.4
Governmental administration	5,522,322	2.8
Interest on general debt	4,069,002	2.1
Other and unallocable	16,050,946	8.2
Utility expenditure	13,116,805	7.1
Liquor stores expenditure	0	-
Insurance trust expenditure	21,598,629	11.0
Debt at End of Fiscal Year	137,479,990	X
Cash and Security Holdings	362,107,476	X

X = Not applicable.
- = Zero or rounds to zero.
[1] Within insurance trust revenue, net earnings of state retirement systems is a calculated statistic (the item code in the data file is X08), and thus can be positive or negative. Net earnings is the sum of earnings on investments plus gains on investments minus losses on investments. The change made in 2002 for asset valuation from book to market value in accordance with Statement 34 of the Governmental Accounting Standards Board is reflected in the calculated statistics.

Table NY-16. State Government Tax Collections, 2017

(Dollars in thousands, percent.)

Item	Dollars	Percent distribution
Total Taxes	79,678,037	100.0
Property taxes	X	-
Sales and gross receipts	25,362,583	31.8
General sales and gross receipts	14,132,141	17.7
Selective sales and gross receipts	11,230,442	14.1
Alcoholic beverages	257,690	0.3
Amusements	2,930	-
Insurance premiums	1,381,080	1.7
Motor fuels	1,647,240	2.1
Pari-mutuels	16,396	-
Public utilities	811,992	1.0
Tobacco products	1,265,699	1.6
Other selective sales	5,847,415	7.3
Licenses	1,814,065	2.3
Alcoholic beverages	62,334	0.1
Amusements	X	-
Corporations in general	26,241	-
Hunting and fishing	44,172	0.1
Motor vehicle	1,403,555	1.8
Motor vehicle operators	138,696	0.2
Public utilities	11,068	-
Occupation and business, NEC	126,505	0.2
Other licenses	1,494	-
Income taxes	48,658,122	61.1
Individual income	44,631,769	56.0
Corporation net income	4,026,353	5.1
Other taxes	3,843,267	4.8
Death and gift	1,190,881	1.5
Documentary and stock transfer	1,312,358	1.6
Severance	X	-
Taxes, NEC	1,340,028	1.7

X = Not applicable.
- = Zero or rounds to zero.

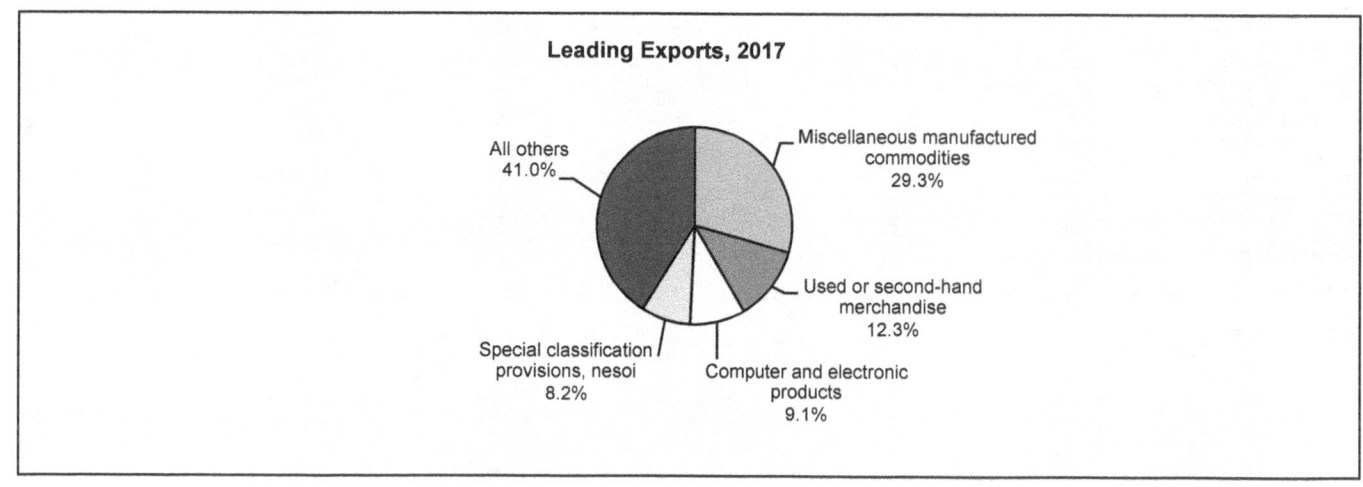

Leading Exports, 2017

All others 41.0%

Miscellaneous manufactured commodities 29.3%

Used or second-hand merchandise 12.3%

Special classification provisions, nesoi 8.2%

Computer and electronic products 9.1%

NORTH CAROLINA

Facts and Figures

Location: Southeastern United States; bordered on the N by Virginia, on the E by the Atlantic Ocean, on the S by South Carolina and Georgia, and on the W by Tennessee

Area: 53,819 sq. mi. (139,389 sq. km.); rank—28th

Population: 10,273,419 (2017 est.); rank—9th

Principal Cities: capital—Raleigh; largest—Charlotte

Statehood: November 21, 1789; 12th state

U.S. Congress: 2 senators, 13 representatives

State Motto: *Esse quam videri* ("To be rather than to seem")

State Song: "The Old North State"

State Nicknames: The Tar Heel State; The Old North State

Abbreviations: NC; N.C.

State Symbols: flower—flowering dogwood; tree—pine; bird—cardinal

At a Glance

- With an increase in population of 7.3 percent, North Carolina ranked 14th among the states in growth from 2010 to 2017.

- North Carolina's median household income in 2016 was $50,584, and 15.4 percent of the population lived below the poverty level.

- North Carolina's violent crime rate in 2016 was 372.2 per 100,000 population, compared to 386.3 for the entire nation.

- In 2016, 10.4 percent of North Carolinians did not have health insurance, compared to 8.6 percent of the entire U.S. population.

- North Carolina's unemployment rate of 4.6 percent ranked 18th in the nation in 2017.

Table NC-1. Population by Age, Sex, Race, and Hispanic Origin

(Number, percent, except where noted.)

Sex, age, race, and Hispanic origin	2000	2010	2017 [1]	Average annual percent change, 2010–2017
Total Population...........................	8,049,313	9,535,483	10,273,419	7.7
Percent of total U.S. population	2.9	3.1	3.2	X
Sex				
Male..	3,942,695	4,645,492	5,001,438	7.7
Female	4,106,618	4,889,991	5,271,981	7.8
Age				
Under 5 years..	539,509	632,040	609,713	-3.5
5 to 19 years..	1,653,851	1,926,640	1,968,156	2.2
20 to 64 years..	4,886,905	5,742,724	6,065,105	5.6
65 years and over..	969,048	1,234,079	1,630,445	32.1
Median age (years)..	35.3	37.4	38.7	3.5
Race and Hispanic Origin				
One race				
White	5,804,656	6,898,296	7,276,995	5.5
Black..	1,737,545	2,088,362	2,279,895	9.2
American Indian and Alaska Native.......................	99,551	147,566	160,909	9.0
Asian..	113,689	215,952	313,997	45.4
Native Hawaiian or Other Pacific Islander	3,983	10,309	12,752	23.7
Two or more races..	103,260	174,998	228,871	30.8
Hispanic (of any race)..	378,963	830,172	972,288	17.1

X = Not applicable.
[1] Population figures for 2017 are July 1 estimates. The 2010 estimates are taken from the 2010 Census.

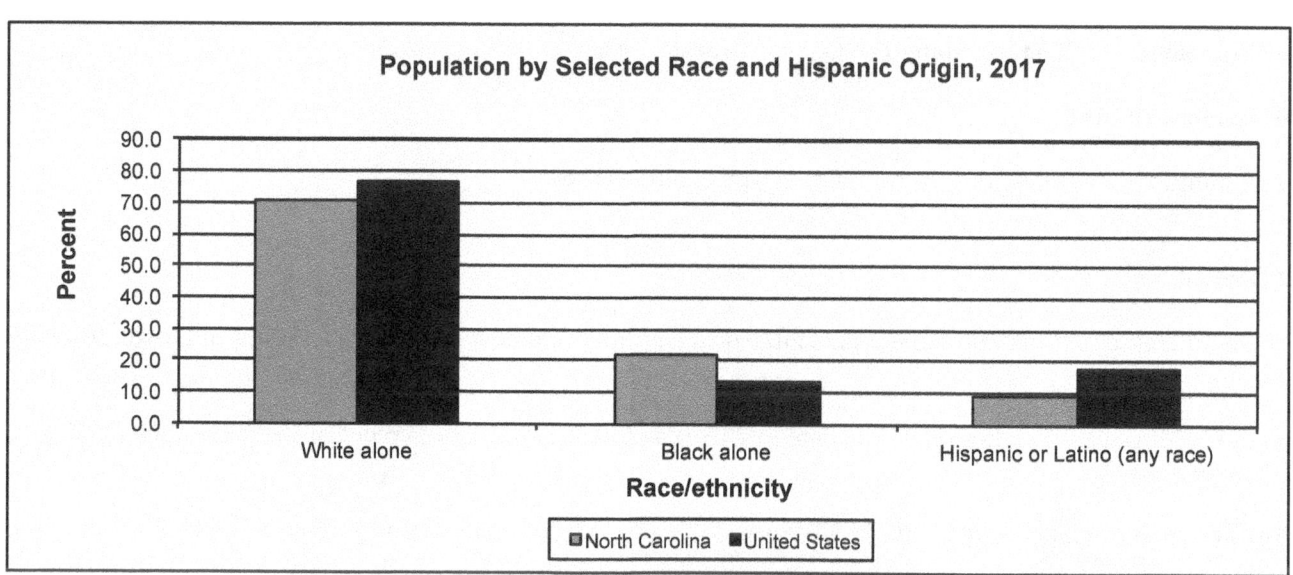

Table NC-2. Marital Status

(Number, percent distribution.)

Sex, age, and marital status	2000	2010	2016
Males, 15 Years and Over	3,092,380	3,678,950	3,961,788
Never married	28.2	33.3	34.8
Now married, except separated..	58.7	51.8	50.5
Separated...	2.7	2.9	2.5
Widowed...	2.4	2.5	2.7
Divorced...	8.1	9.6	9.4
Females, 15 Years and Over	3,301,327	3,975,748	4,288,628
Never married	22.0	27.3	29.3
Now married, except separated..	53.9	47.3	46.4
Separated...	3.3	3.5	2.9
Widowed...	10.9	9.8	9.3
Divorced...	9.9	12.1	12.2

Table NC-3. Households and Housing Characteristics

(Number, percent, dollars.)

Item	2000	2010	2016	Average annual percent change, 2010–2016
Total Households	3,132,012	3,670,859	3,882,423	1.0
Family households	2,158,869	2,441,916	2,542,663	0.7
Married-couple family	1,645,346	1,770,863	1,864,455	0.9
Other family	513,523	671,053	678,208	0.2
Male householder, no wife present	123,526	159,752	168,619	0.9
Female householder, no husband present	389,997	511,301	509,589	-0.1
Nonfamily households	973,144	1,228,943	1,339,760	1.5
Householder living alone	795,271	1,022,017	1,108,289	1.4
Householder not living alone	177,873	206,926	231,471	2.0
Housing Characteristics				
Total housing units	3,523,944	4,333,479	4,540,697	0.8
Occupied housing units	3,132,012	3,670,859	3,882,423	1.0
Owner occupied	2,172,355	2,465,551	2,493,388	0.2
Renter occupied	959,658	1,205,308	1,389,035	2.5
Average household size	2.49	2.53	2.55	0.1
Financial Characteristics				
Median gross rent of renter-occupied housing	548	731	839	2.5
Median monthly owner costs for housing units with a mortgage	985	1,250	1,225	-0.3
Median value of owner-occupied housing units	108,300	154,200	165,400	1.2

Table NC-4. Migration, Origin, and Language

(Number, percent.)

Characteristic	State			U.S.		
	2015	2016	Percent change	2015	2016	Percent change
Residence 1 Year Ago						
Population 1 year and over	9,927,547	10,032,407	1.1	317,635,720	319,361,956	0.5
Same house	84.4	84.3	X	85.3	85.4	X
Different house in the U.S.	15.2	15.2	X	14.1	13.9	X
Same county	8.4	8.0	X	8.5	8.3	X
Different county	6.7	7.1	X	5.6	5.6	X
Same state	3.6	3.8	X	3.2	3.2	X
Different state	3.1	3.3	X	2.4	2.4	X
Abroad	0.5	0.5	X	0.7	0.7	X
Place of Birth						
Native born	9,248,118	9,357,150	1.2	278,128,449	279,388,170	0.5
Male	48.5	48.4	X	49.3	49.3	X
Female	51.5	51.6	X	50.7	50.7	X
Foreign born	794,684	789,638	-0.6	43,290,372	43,739,345	1.0
Male	51.2	50.6	X	48.6	48.5	X
Female	48.8	49.4	X	51.4	51.5	X
Foreign born; naturalized U.S. citizen	297,427	313,140	5.3	20,697,103	21,238,372	2.6
Male	47.2	47.5	X	45.9	45.9	X
Female	52.8	52.5	X	54.1	54.1	X
Foreign born; not a U.S. citizen	497,257	476,498	-4.2	22,593,269	22,500,973	-0.4
Male	53.7	52.7	X	51.1	51.0	X
Female	46.3	47.3	X	48.9	49.0	X
Entered 2010 or later	17.0	20.7	X	15.6	18.6	X
Entered 2000 to 2009	36.6	31.8	X	27.9	26.7	X
Entered before 2000	46.3	47.6	X	56.5	54.7	X
World Region of Birth, Foreign						
Foreign-born population, excluding population born at sea	794,515	789,638	-0.6	43,289,646	43,738,901	1.0
Europe	11.1	10.1	X	11.1	10.9	X
Asia	26.4	27.9	X	30.6	30.8	X
Africa	6.0	6.8	X	4.8	4.9	X
Oceania	0.2	0.4	X	0.6	0.6	X
Latin America	53.6	52.5	X	51.1	51.0	X
North America	2.6	2.3	X	1.9	1.8	X
Language Spoken at Home and Ability to Speak English						
Population 5 years and over	9,443,944	9,552,195	1.1	301,625,014	303,328,961	0.6
English only	88.5	88.5	X	78.5	78.4	X
Language other than English	11.5	11.5	X	21.5	21.6	X
Speaks English less than "very well"	4.7	4.5	X	8.6	8.6	X

NA = Not available.
X = Not applicable.
- = Zero or rounds to zero.

Table NC-5. Median Income and Poverty Status, 2016

(Number, percent, except as noted.)

Characteristic	State		U.S.	
	Number	Percent	Number	Percent
Median Income				
Households (dollars)...	50,584	X	57,617	X
Families (dollars)...	62,289	X	71,062	X
Below Poverty Level (All People)	1,521,880	15.4	44,268,996	14.0
Sex				
Male	673,956	14.1	19,760,056	12.8
Female	847,924	16.6	24,508,940	15.2
Age				
Under 18 years..	489,553	21.7	14,115,713	19.5
Related children under 18 years..	478,586	21.3	13,805,435	19.1
18 to 64 years...	889,560	14.6	25,723,818	13.2
65 years and over	142,767	9.4	4,429,465	9.2

X = Not applicable.

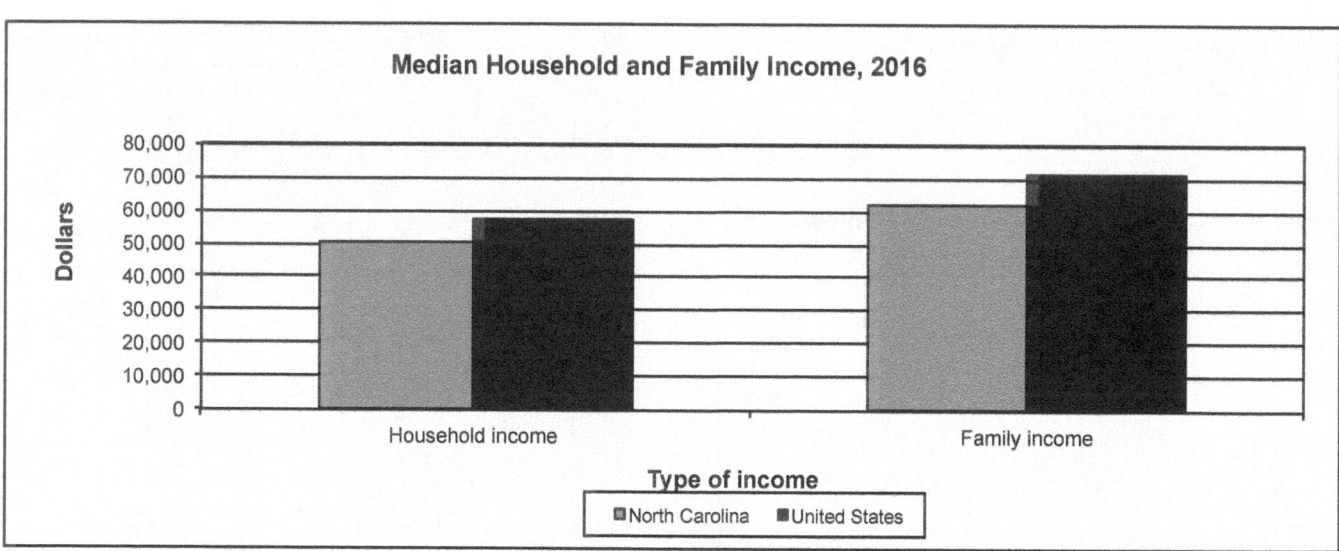

Table NC-6. Health Insurance Coverage Status for the Civilian Noninstitutionalized Population and Children Under 18 Years of Age

(Number, percent.)

Item	2008	2009	2010	2011	2012	2013	2014	2015	2016
Civilian Noninstitutionalized Population	9,004,442	9,149,289	9,360,661	9,461,018	9,552,529	9,645,320	9,752,148	9,855,612	9,957,830
Covered by Private or Public Insurance									
Number...	7,570,458	7,678,522	7,790,824	7,916,111	7,970,289	8,136,322	8,476,094	8,752,825	8,919,431
Percent..	84.1	83.9	83.2	83.7	83.4	84.4	86.9	88.8	89.6
Not Covered									
Number...	1,433,984	1,470,767	1,569,837	1,544,907	1,582,240	1,508,998	1,276,054	1,102,787	1,038,399
Percent..	15.9	16.1	16.8	16.3	16.6	15.6	13.1	11.2	10.4
Percent in the U.S. not covered..	15.1	15.1	15.5	15.1	14.8	14.5	11.7	9.4	8.6
Children Under 18 Years of Age	2,237,294	2,271,175	2,280,649	2,286,872	2,281,544	2,280,549	2,286,665	2,283,011	2,292,483
Covered by Private or Public Insurance									
Number...	2,017,899	2,085,273	2,103,949	2,112,300	2,108,583	2,136,355	2,167,587	2,183,693	2,190,251
Percent..	90.2	91.8	92.3	92.4	92.4	93.7	94.8	95.6	95.5
Not Covered									
Number...	219,395	185,902	176,700	174,572	172,961	144,194	119,078	99,318	102,232
Percent..	9.8	8.2	7.7	7.6	7.6	6.3	5.2	4.4	4.5
Percent in the U.S. not covered..	9.9	8.6	8.0	7.5	7.2	7.1	6.0	4.8	4.5

Table NC-7. Employment Status by Demographic Group, 2017

(Numbers in thousands, percent.)

Characteristic	Civilian noninstitutional population	Civilian labor force		Employed		Unemployed	
		Number	Percent of population	Number	Percent of population	Number	Percent of population
Total..	7,995	4,906	61.4	4,686	58.6	220	4.5
Sex							
Male...	3,782	2,543	67.2	2,429	64.2	114	4.5
Female.....................................	4,213	2,363	56.1	2,257	53.6	106	4.5
Race, Sex, and Hispanic Origin							
White..	5,717	3,534	61.8	3,402	59.5	131	3.7
Male......................................	2,758	1,887	68.4	1,816	65.8	71	3.7
Female..................................	2,958	1,647	55.7	1,586	53.6	61	3.7
Black or African American............	1,721	1,055	61.3	980	56.9	75	7.1
Male......................................	768	497	64.8	460	59.9	37	7.5
Female..................................	952	557	58.5	520	54.5	38	6.8
Hispanic or Latino ethnicity[1]	665	470	70.7	446	67.1	24	5.1
Male......................................	322	272	84.7	261	81.1	11	4.2
Female..................................	343	198	57.7	185	54.0	13	6.4
Age							
16 to 19 years..........................	493	160	32.4	134	27.2	26	16.1
20 to 24 years..........................	732	518	70.8	478	65.3	40	7.8
25 to 34 years..........................	1,313	1,048	79.8	989	75.4	59	5.6
35 to 44 years..........................	1,203	1,019	84.7	981	81.6	38	3.8
45 to 54 years..........................	1,386	1,067	77.0	1,040	75.0	27	2.5
55 to 64 years..........................	1,290	788	61.1	768	59.5	21	2.6
65 years and over	1,579	305	19.3	296	18.7	10	3.2

NOTE: Data in Table 7 are from the Current Population Survey (CPS) and do not match the estimates in Table 8. See notes and definitions for further information.
[1] May be of any race.

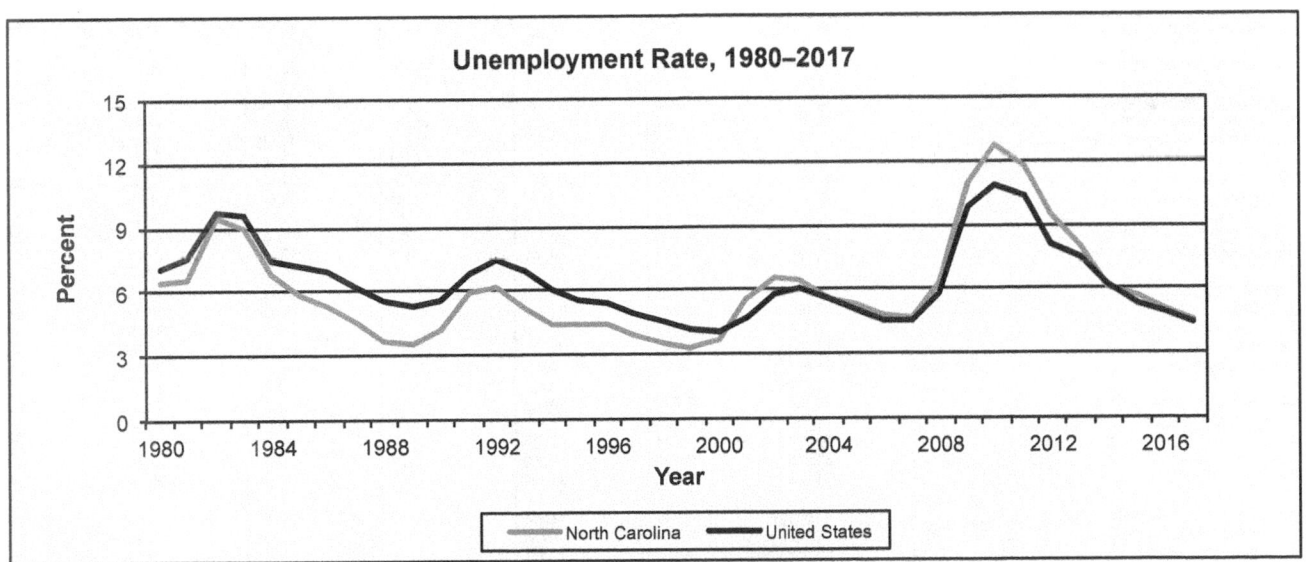

Table NC-8. Employment Status of the Civilian Noninstitutional Population Age 16 Years and Over

(Number, percent.)

Year	Civilian labor force	Civilian participation rate	Employed	Unemployed	Unemployment rate
2009..	4,570,789	64.2	4,087,105	483,684	10.6
2010..	4,616,691	63.3	4,115,629	501,062	10.9
2011..	4,633,072	62.4	4,157,543	475,529	10.3
2012..	4,680,057	62.3	4,245,675	434,382	9.3
2013..	4,692,940	61.8	4,318,114	374,826	8.0
2014..	4,699,058	61.1	4,402,450	296,608	6.3
2015..	4,768,806	61.2	4,495,190	273,616	5.7
2016..	4,854,828	61.4	4,608,229	246,599	5.1
2017..	4,941,701	61.5	4,716,832	224,869	4.6

Table NC-9. Employment and Average Wages by Industry

(Estimates through 2010 are based on the 2007 *North American Industry Classification System* [NAICS]. Estimates from 2011 onward are based on the 2012 NAICS.)

Industry	2010	2011	2012	2013	2014	2015	2016
	Number of jobs						
Wage and Salary Employment by Industry	4,128,548	4,181,050	4,244,301	4,308,542	4,392,125	4,492,941	4,594,888
Farm Wage and Salary Employment	20,057	22,797	20,095	22,656	24,334	27,259	27,288
Nonfarm Wage and Salary Employment	4,108,491	4,158,253	4,224,206	4,285,886	4,367,791	4,465,682	4,567,600
Private wage and salary employment	3,241,096	3,295,334	3,362,865	3,426,567	3,515,505	3,614,201	3,708,212
Forestry, fishing, and related activities	13,996	13,929	13,997	14,459	14,821	14,899	14,955
Mining	3,017	3,040	3,004	2,934	2,812	2,770	2,771
Utilities	12,313	12,304	12,273	12,460	13,645	14,045	13,942
Construction	182,297	178,488	176,853	178,644	184,005	194,067	206,032
Manufacturing	432,936	436,352	440,596	443,428	449,715	461,934	465,551
Durable goods manufacturing	222,477	226,917	234,532	236,280	240,318	248,678	251,323
Nondurable goods manufacturing	210,459	209,435	206,064	207,148	209,397	213,256	214,228
Wholesale trade	165,441	168,607	172,285	174,621	177,543	179,450	183,650
Retail trade	439,084	445,499	454,964	463,962	475,464	487,842	499,578
Transportation and warehousing	103,745	107,836	109,964	111,595	115,684	121,454	125,016
Information	68,256	68,842	69,257	69,843	72,592	75,993	78,905
Finance and insurance	151,743	154,029	155,067	156,943	161,089	166,138	171,744
Real estate and rental and leasing	48,559	48,604	49,257	51,222	53,443	55,848	57,985
Professional, scientific, and technical services	183,086	190,459	197,032	201,517	209,273	220,692	230,578
Management of companies and enterprises	72,749	76,800	80,636	77,928	80,509	81,986	83,992
Administrative and waste services	232,597	250,463	261,313	272,803	284,658	290,260	295,193
Educational services	87,415	88,363	90,080	92,049	94,282	96,191	98,890
Health care and social assistance	465,494	463,670	470,654	480,627	485,569	492,656	501,108
Arts, entertainment, and recreation	56,604	57,296	58,883	60,873	62,147	63,831	70,059
Accommodation and food services	338,374	345,164	359,131	372,524	384,135	398,054	413,775
Other services, except public administration	183,390	185,589	187,619	188,135	194,119	196,091	194,488
Government and government enterprises	867,395	862,919	861,341	859,319	852,286	851,481	859,388
	Dollars						
Average Wages and Salaries by Industry	42,065	43,087	44,099	44,769	45,933	47,465	50,002
Average Farm Wages and Salaries	18,324	20,243	28,172	25,966	23,309	23,054	27,269
Average Nonfarm Wages and Salaries	42,181	43,212	44,175	44,868	46,060	47,614	50,138
Average private wages and salaries	41,750	42,912	44,058	44,836	46,146	47,703	50,235
Forestry, fishing, and related activities	27,203	27,756	28,930	30,269	31,412	32,581	34,959
Mining	43,917	46,912	47,012	48,191	50,369	56,453	67,507
Utilities	81,537	82,987	86,362	93,359	91,112	92,587	95,149
Construction	41,111	42,251	43,795	44,765	46,449	48,564	53,925
Manufacturing	52,932	54,279	54,650	56,291	57,007	58,404	59,584
Durable goods manufacturing	56,561	58,246	59,132	61,205	61,041	62,275	63,852
Nondurable goods manufacturing	49,095	49,981	49,550	50,686	52,379	53,891	54,578
Wholesale trade	60,718	62,852	64,500	65,970	68,445	70,630	74,181
Retail trade	25,680	25,680	26,267	26,863	27,354	27,994	28,935
Transportation and warehousing	43,057	43,837	44,290	45,608	47,340	48,188	51,911
Information	63,163	66,053	69,327	72,327	76,148	78,758	79,349
Finance and insurance	74,017	77,123	79,376	82,811	86,691	90,867	96,728
Real estate and rental and leasing	38,116	39,811	42,612	43,605	45,213	47,223	50,714
Professional, scientific, and technical services	66,542	68,385	71,276	71,331	73,882	76,360	83,715
Management of companies and enterprises	88,244	92,044	95,034	97,331	102,846	108,652	107,517
Administrative and waste services	31,116	31,599	33,259	32,731	33,652	34,497	37,141
Educational services	34,773	36,045	36,333	37,172	37,950	38,148	36,232
Health care and social assistance	40,675	41,939	42,963	43,659	44,680	46,084	49,019
Arts, entertainment, and recreation	30,254	31,298	31,785	31,964	33,168	34,324	33,897
Accommodation and food services	16,515	16,852	17,441	17,612	18,078	18,783	20,238
Other services, except public administration	27,764	28,335	29,651	30,723	31,162	32,370	35,067
Government and government enterprises	43,792	44,359	44,631	44,997	45,703	47,233	49,717

Table NC-10. Employment Characteristics by Family Type

(Number, percent.)

Family type and labor force status	2014		2015		2016	
	Total	Families with own children under 18 years	Total	Families with own children under 18 years	Total	Families with own children under 18 years
All Families...	2,483,732	1,054,151	2,506,215	1,056,067	2,542,663	1,071,946
FAMILY TYPE AND LABOR FORCE STATUS						
Married-Couple Families.............................	1,795,558	683,564	1,829,450	698,000	1,864,455	704,965
Both husband and wife in labor force.................	49.9	65.1	49.4	64.4	49.2	65.4
Husband in labor force, wife not in labor force	22.4	28.9	22.7	29.4	22.0	28.2
Wife in labor force, husband not in labor force	8.5	4.4	8.1	4.2	8.6	4.4
Both husband and wife not in labor force.............	19.3	1.6	19.2	1.7	19.5	1.6
Other Families	688,174	370,587	676,765	358,067	678,208	366,981
Female householder, no husband present..................	75.1	76.4	75.0	76.3	75.1	77.3
In labor force..	52.5	63.8	51.5	63.5	52.4	64.9
Not in labor force	22.6	12.5	23.4	12.8	22.7	12.4
Male householder, no wife present.......................	24.9	23.6	25.0	23.7	24.9	22.7
In labor force..	18.7	20.9	18.8	21.5	18.8	20.7
Not in labor force	6.2	2.7	6.2	2.2	6.1	2.1

Table NC-11. School Enrollment and Educational Attainment, 2016

(Number, percent.)

Item	State	U.S.
Enrollment		
Total population 3 years and over, enrolled in school	2,523,926	81,572,277
Enrolled in nursery school or preschool (percent).............	5.3	6.0
Enrolled in kindergarten (percent)...........................	4.7	5.0
Enrolled in elementary school, grades 1-8 (percent)..........	41.2	40.3
Enrolled in high school, grades 9-12 (percent)...............	21.6	21.0
Enrolled in college or graduate school (percent)..............	27.2	27.7
Attainment		
Total population 25 years and over	6,877,185	218,475,480
Less than ninth grade (percent)	4.6	5.4
9th to 12th grade, no diploma (percent)	8.1	7.2
High school graduate, including equivalency (percent).........	25.8	27.2
Some college, no degree (percent)	21.6	20.6
Associate's degree (percent).................................	9.5	8.4
Bachelor's degree (percent).................................	19.6	19.3
Graduate or professional degree (percent)....................	10.8	11.9
High school graduate or higher (percent)	87.3	87.5
Bachelor's degree or higher (percent)........................	30.4	31.3

Table NC-12. Public School Characteristics and Educational Indicators

(Number, percent; data derived from National Center of Education Statistics.)

Item	State	U.S.
Public Schools, 2015–2016 (except where noted)		
Number of school districts...................................	297	18,328
Number of schools..	2,603	98,456
Number of students	1,544,934	50,327,015
Number of teachers	99,355	3,151,497
Student-teacher ratio	15.5	16.0
Expenditures per student (dollars), 2014-2015................	8,529	11,445
Four-year adjusted cohort graduation rate (ACGR)[1,2]	85.9	84.1
Students eligible for free or reduced-price lunch (percent), 2014-2015...	57.2	51.8
English language learners (percent), Fall 2015	6.6	9.5
Students age 3 to 21 served under IDEA, part B (percent).....	12.9	13.2

Public Schools by Type	Number	Percent of state public schools
Total number of schools.....................................	2,603	100.0
Regular	2,498	96.0
Special education	24	0.9
Vocational education	7	0.3
Alternative education..	74	2.8

NOTE: Every school is assigned only one school type based on its instructional emphasis.
[1] ACGR data represents a new method of calculating high-school completion rates and may not be comparable to previous years' data for Averaged Freshmen Graduation Rates (AFGR).
[2] The United States 4-year ACGRs were estimated using both the reported 4-year ACGR data from 49 states and the District of Columbia and using imputed data for Idaho. The estimate for American Indian/Alaska Native students also includes imputed data for Virginia.

Table NC-13. Reported Voting and Registration of the Voting-Age Population, November 2016

(Numbers in thousands, percent.)

Item	Total population	Total citizen population	Registered			Voted		
			Total registered	Percent registered (total population)	Percent registered (total citizen population)	Total voted	Percent voted (total population)	Percent voted (total citizen population)
U.S. Total	245,502	224,059	157,596	64.2	70.3	137,537	56.0	61.4
State Total.............................	7,631	6,960	5,194	68.1	74.6	4,700	61.6	67.5
Sex								
Male	3,596	3,243	2,414	67.1	74.4	2,181	60.6	67.2
Female	4,034	3,717	2,780	68.9	74.8	2,519	62.4	67.8
Race								
White alone..............................	5,480	4,997	3,776	68.9	75.6	3,412	62.3	68.3
White, non-Hispanic alone	4,740	4,679	3,595	75.8	76.8	3,253	68.6	69.5
Black alone..............................	1,625	1,582	1,191	73.3	75.3	1,094	67.3	69.1
Asian alone	312	211	151	48.4	71.5	124	39.6	58.5
Hispanic (of any race)......................	804	350	208	25.9	59.6	186	23.1	53.1
White alone or in combination	5,564	5,072	3,823	68.7	75.4	3,453	62.1	68.1
Black alone or in combination...........	1,685	1,633	1,223	72.6	74.9	1,126	66.8	69.0
Asian alone or in combination...........	318	217	156	49.3	72.2	124	38.9	57.0
Age								
18 to 24 years	924	817	505	54.7	61.8	414	44.8	50.7
25 to 34 years	1,319	1,111	784	59.5	70.6	666	50.5	60.0
35 to 44 years	1,180	1,037	754	63.9	72.8	676	57.3	65.2
45 to 64 years	2,712	2,520	1,979	73.0	78.5	1,841	67.9	73.1
65 years and over	1,496	1,476	1,172	78.4	79.4	1,102	73.7	74.7

B = Base is less than 75,000 and therefore too small to show the derived measure.

Table NC-14. Crime

(Number, rate per 100,000. Data are derived from the FBI Uniform Crime Reports.)

Item	State			U.S. [1,2,3,4]		
	2015	2016	Percent change	2015	2016	Percent change
TOTAL POPULATION [5]	10,042,802	10,146,788	1.0	321,418,820	323,127,513	0.5
VIOLENT CRIME						
Number...	34,852	37,769	8.4	1,231,566	1,248,185	1.3
Rate..	347.0	372.2	7.3	383.2	386.3	0.8
Murder and Nonnegligent Manslaughter						
Number...	517	678	31.1	15,696	17,250	9.9
Rate..	5.1	6.7	31.4	4.9	5.3	8.2
Rape[6]						
Number...	2,684	2,849	6.1	124,047	130,603	5.3
Rate..	26.7	28.1	5.2	38.6	40.4	4.7
Robbery						
Number...	8,825	9,336	5.8	327,374	332,198	1.5
Rate..	87.9	92.0	4.7	101.9	102.8	0.9
Aggravated Assault						
Number...	22,826	24,906	9.1	764,449	803,007	5.0
Rate..	227.3	245.5	8.0	237.8	248.5	4.5
PROPERTY CRIME						
Number...	276,183	277,765	0.6	7,993,631	7,919,035	-0.9
Rate..	2,750.1	2,737.5	-0.5	2,487.0	2,450.7	-1.5
Burglary						
Number...	74,841	72,082	-3.7	1,579,527	1,515,096	-4.1
Rate..	745.2	710.4	-4.7	491.4	468.9	-4.6
Larceny-Theft						
Number...	187,907	190,377	1.3	5,706,346	5,638,455	-1.2
Rate..	1,871.1	1,876.2	0.3	1,775.4	1,745.0	-1.7
Motor Vehicle Theft						
Number...	13,435	15,306	13.9	707,758	765,484	8.2
Rate..	133.8	150.8	12.7	220.2	236.9	7.6

NOTE: Although arson data are included in the trend and clearance tables, sufficient data are not available to estimate totals for this offense. Therefore, no arson data are published in this table.
X = Not applicable.
- = Zero or rounds to zero.
[1] The crime figures have been adjusted.
[2] The data collection methodology for the offense of forcible rape used by the Minnesota state Uniform Crime Reporting (UCR) Program (with the exception of Minneapolis and St. Paul, Minnesota) does not comply with national UCR Program guidelines. Consequently, its figures for forcible rape and violent crime (of which forcible rape is a part) are not published in this table.
[3] Includes offenses reported by the Zoological Police and the Metro Transit Police.
[4] Because of changes in the state's reporting practices, figures are not comparable to previous years' data.
[5] Populations are U.S. Census Bureau provisional estimates as of July 1 of each year.
[6] The figures shown for the offense of rape were estimated using the revised Uniform Crime Reporting (UCR) definition of rape.

Table NC-15. State Government Finances, 2016

(Dollar amounts in thousands, percent distribution.)

Item	Dollars	Percent distribution
Total Revenue	55,216,582	100.0
General revenue	51,110,192	92.6
Intergovernmental revenue	15,908,501	28.8
Taxes	26,201,576	47.5
General sales	7,187,844	13.0
Selective sales	3,961,266	7.2
License taxes	1,869,060	3.4
Individual income tax	12,042,957	21.8
Corporate income tax	1,066,511	1.9
Other taxes	73,938	0.1
Current charges	5,816,649	10.5
Miscellaneous general revenue	3,183,466	5.8
Utility revenue	13	-
Liquor stores revenue	0	-
Insurance trust revenue [1]	4,106,377	7.4
Total Expenditure	53,857,036	100.0
Intergovernmental expenditure	12,858,738	23.9
Direct expenditure	40,998,298	76.1
Current operation	29,519,434	54.8
Capital outlay	3,806,752	7.1
Insurance benefits and repayments	5,916,490	11.0
Assistance and subsidies	1,177,377	2.2
Interest on debt	578,245	1.1
Exhibit: Salaries and wages	7,601,593	14.1
Total Expenditure	53,857,036	100.0
General expenditure	47,759,083	88.7
Intergovernmental expenditure	12,858,738	23.9
Direct expenditure	34,900,345	64.8
General expenditure, by function:		
Education	20,826,728	38.7
Public welfare	12,938,720	24.0
Hospitals	2,132,768	4.0
Health	1,204,000	2.2
Highways	3,883,907	7.2
Police protection	725,037	1.3
Correction	1,256,922	2.3
Natural resources	527,158	1.0
Parks and recreation	201,158	0.4
Governmental administration	1,626,791	3.0
Interest on general debt	578,245	1.1
Other and unallocable	1,857,649	3.4
Utility expenditure	181,463	0.3
Liquor stores expenditure	0	-
Insurance trust expenditure	5,916,490	11.0
Debt at End of Fiscal Year	16,919,235	X
Cash and Security Holdings	116,224,191	X

X = Not applicable.
- = Zero or rounds to zero.
[1] Within insurance trust revenue, net earnings of state retirement systems is a calculated statistic (the item code in the data file is X08), and thus can be positive or negative. Net earnings is the sum of earnings on investments plus gains on investments minus losses on investments. The change made in 2002 for asset valuation from book to market value in accordance with Statement 34 of the Governmental Accounting Standards Board is reflected in the calculated statistics.

Table NC-16. State Government Tax Collections, 2017

(Dollars in thousands, percent.)

Item	Dollars	Percent distribution
Total Taxes	26,855,304	100.0
Property taxes	X	-
Sales and gross receipts	11,699,036	43.6
General sales and gross receipts	7,656,898	28.5
Selective sales and gross receipts	4,042,138	15.1
Alcoholic beverages	394,838	1.5
Amusements	7	-
Insurance premiums	517,095	1.9
Motor fuels	1,922,400	7.2
Pari-mutuels	X	-
Public utilities	259	-
Tobacco products	292,138	1.1
Other selective sales	915,401	3.4
Licenses	2,235,904	8.3
Alcoholic beverages	26,601	0.1
Amusements	184	-
Corporations in general	826,775	3.1
Hunting and fishing	33,799	0.1
Motor vehicle	831,878	3.1
Motor vehicle operators	129,086	0.5
Public utilities	19745	0.1
Occupation and business, NEC	341,503	1.3
Other licenses	26,333	0.1
Income taxes	12,843,373	47.8
Individual income	12,086,332	45.0
Corporation net income	757,041	2.8
Other taxes	76,991	0.3
Death and gift	713	-
Documentary and stock transfer	74,386	0.3
Severance	1,892	-
Taxes, NEC	0	-

X = Not applicable.
- = Zero or rounds to zero.

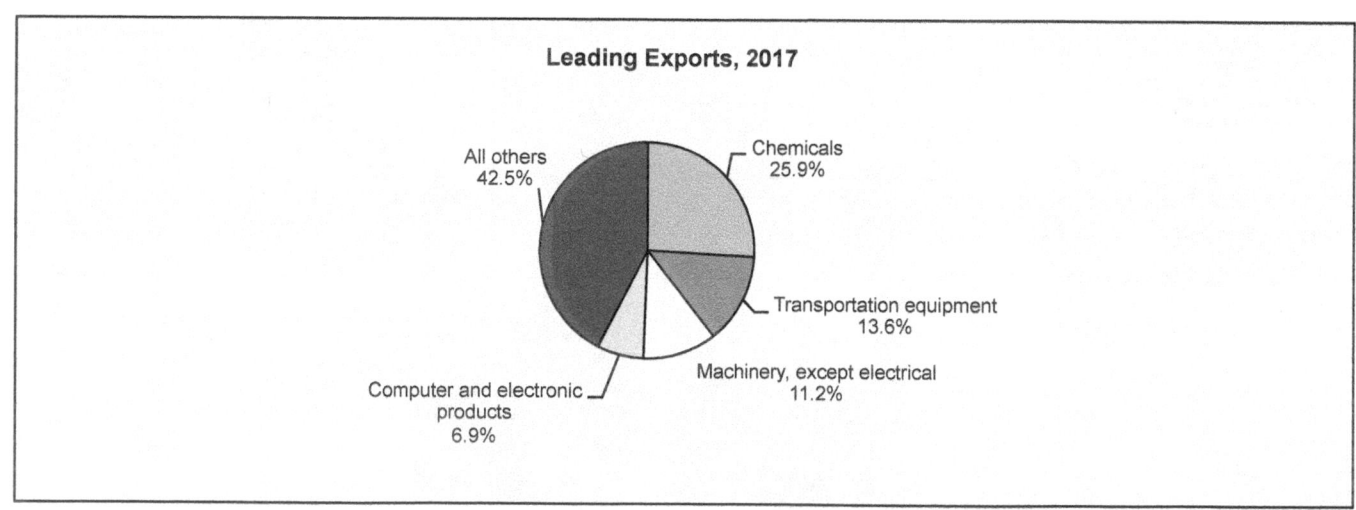

Leading Exports, 2017

- Chemicals 25.9%
- Transportation equipment 13.6%
- Machinery, except electrical 11.2%
- Computer and electronic products 6.9%
- All others 42.5%

NORTH DAKOTA

Facts and Figures

Location: North central United States; bordered on the N by Canada (Manitoba and Saskatchewan), on the E by Minnesota, on the S by South Dakota, and on the W by Montana

Area: 70,700 sq. mi. (183,112 sq. km.); rank—19th

Population: 755,393 (2017 est.); rank—47th

Principal Cities: capital—Bismarck; largest—Fargo

Statehood: November 2, 1889; 39th state

U.S. Congress: 2 senators, 1 representative

State Motto: Liberty and Union, Now and Forever, One and Inseparable

State Song: "North Dakota Hymn"

State Nicknames: The Peace Garden State; The Flickertail State; The Rough Rider State

Abbreviations: ND; N.D.; N. Dak.

State Symbols: flower—wild prairie rose; tree—American elm; bird—Western meadowlark

At a Glance

- With an increase in population of 12.0 percent, North Dakota ranked 3rd for population growth between 2010 and 2017.

- In 2016, 7.0 percent of North Dakotans did not have health insurance, compared to 8.6 percent of the total U.S. population.

- North Dakota had the 3rd highest birth rate in the country in 2016 (15.0 births per 1,000 population).

- In 2017, 2.6 percent of North Dakotans were unemployed, which was the 2nd lowest unemployment rate in the country.

- North Dakota had the 5th lowest childhood poverty rate in 2016, with 12.4 percent of children under 18 years old living in poverty. The national average was 19.5 percent.

Table ND-1. Population by Age, Sex, Race, and Hispanic Origin

(Number, percent, except where noted.)

Sex, age, race, and Hispanic origin	2000	2010	2017 [1]	Average annual percent change, 2010–2017
Total Population..	642,200	672,591	755,393	12.3
Percent of total U.S. population	0.2	0.2	0.2	X
Sex				
Male..	320,524	339,864	387,299	14.0
Female	321,676	332,727	368,094	10.6
Age				
Under 5 years...	39,400	44,595	54,043	21.2
5 to 19 years..	144,064	127,340	143,277	12.5
20 to 64 years	364,258	403,179	444,865	10.3
65 years and over	94,478	97,477	113,208	16.1
Median age (years)	36.2	37.0	35.1	-5.1
Race and Hispanic Origin				
One race				
White	593,181	609,136	661,217	8.5
Black...	3,916	8,248	23,533	185.3
American Indian and Alaska Native	31,329	36,948	41,588	12.6
Asian...	3,606	7,032	12,269	74.5
Native Hawaiian or Other Pacific Islander	230	334	522	56.3
Two or more races...	7,398	10,893	16,264	49.3
Hispanic (of any race)...	7,786	14,407	28,006	94.4

X = Not applicable.
[1] Population figures for 2017 are July 1 estimates. The 2010 estimates are taken from the 2010 Census.

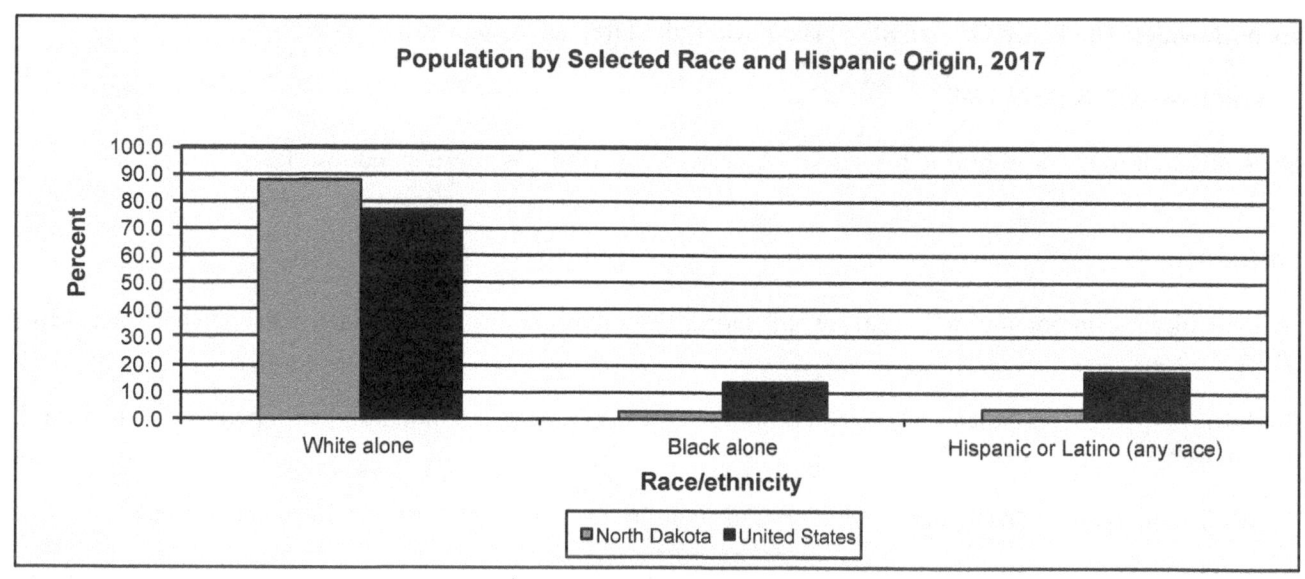

Table ND-2. Marital Status

(Number, percent distribution.)

Sex, age, and marital status	2000	2010	2016
Males, 15 Years and Over..	253,900	278,276	311,519
Never married	32.0	35.8	36.3
Now married, except separated..	57.5	53.1	50.9
Separated...	0.6	0.6	1.0
Widowed..	2.5	2.1	2.5
Divorced...	7.3	8.4	9.3
Females, 15 Years and Over..	258,381	271,462	296,993
Never married	23.2	26.6	27.2
Now married, except separated..	56.0	52.5	53.1
Separated...	0.8	0.7	0.9
Widowed..	11.7	10.1	8.7
Divorced...	8.2	10.2	10.2

Table ND-3. Households and Housing Characteristics

(Number, percent, dollars.)

Item	2000	2010	2016	Average annual percent change, 2010–2016
Total Households..	257,252	280,412	315,134	2.1
Family households..	166,150	171,945	184,904	1.3
Married-couple family	137,433	140,277	150,317	1.2
Other family	28,717	31,668	34,587	1.5
Male householder, no wife present..............	8,569	8,846	12,040	6.0
Female householder, no husband present......	20,148	22,822	22,547	-0.2
Nonfamily households	91,002	108,467	130,230	3.3
Householder living alone...............................	75,420	87,883	101,905	2.7
Householder not living alone..........................	15,582	20,584	28,325	6.3
Housing Characteristics				
Total housing units..	289,677	318,099	368,545	2.6
Occupied housing units	257,252	280,412	315,134	2.1
Owner occupied	171,299	187,673	199,208	1.0
Renter occupied	85,853	92,739	115,926	4.2
Average household size....................................	2.41	2.32	2.32	-
Financial Characteristics				
Median gross rent of renter-occupied housing	412	583	776	5.5
Median monthly owner costs for housing units with a mortgage	818	1,133	1,318	2.7
Median value of owner-occupied housing units	74,400	123,000	184,100	8.3

- = Zero or rounds to zero.

Table ND-4. Migration, Origin, and Language

(Number, percent.)

Characteristic	State			U.S.		
	2015	2016	Percent change	2015	2016	Percent change
Residence 1 Year Ago						
Population 1 year and over	745,291	746,271	0.1	317,635,720	319,361,956	0.5
Same house	81.6	83.2	X	85.3	85.4	X
Different house in the U.S.	17.9	16.2	X	14.1	13.0	X
Same county	8.9	9.0	X	8.5	8.3	X
Different county	9.0	7.2	X	5.6	5.6	X
Same state	3.3	3.2	X	3.2	3.2	X
Different state	5.7	4.0	X	2.4	2.4	X
Abroad	0.5	0.6	X	0.7	0.7	X
Place of Birth						
Native born	728,279	733,365	0.7	278,128,449	279,388,170	0.5
Male	51.3	51.5	X	49.3	49.3	X
Female	48.7	48.5	X	50.7	50.7	X
Foreign born	28,649	24,588	-14.2	43,290,372	43,739,345	1.0
Male	50.9	50.8	X	48.6	48.5	X
Female	49.1	49.2	X	51.4	51.5	X
Foreign born; naturalized U.S. citizen................	12,582	10,079	-19.9	20,697,103	21,238,372	2.6
Male	44.5	45.6	X	45.9	45.9	X
Female	55.5	54.4	X	54.1	54.1	X
Foreign born; not a U.S. citizen......................	16,067	14,509	-9.7	22,593,269	22,500,973	-0.4
Male	56.0	54.3	X	51.1	51.0	X
Female	44.0	45.7	X	48.9	49.0	X
Entered 2010 or later	40.5	38.8	X	15.6	18.6	X
Entered 2000 to 2009	25.5	30.0	X	27.9	26.7	X
Entered before 2000......................................	34.1	31.2	X	56.5	54.7	X
World Region of Birth, Foreign						
Foreign-born population, excluding population born at sea	28,649	24,588	-14.2	43,289,646	43,738,901	1.0
Europe	21.5	13.3	X	11.1	10.9	X
Asia..	33.2	35.8	X	30.6	30.8	X
Africa..	19.8	21.5	X	4.8	4.9	X
Oceania	0.2	0.5	X	0.6	0.6	X
Latin America	15.2	21.4	X	51.1	51.0	X
North America	10.1	7.5	X	1.9	1.8	X
Language Spoken at Home and Ability to Speak English						
Population 5 years and over.............................	704,756	703,055	-0.2	301,625,014	303,328,961	0.6
English only	94.1	94.8	X	78.5	78.4	X
Language other than English............................	5.9	5.2	X	21.5	21.6	X
Speaks English less than "very well".................	1.9	1.8	X	8.6	8.6	X

NA = Not available.
X = Not applicable.
- = Zero or rounds to zero.

Table ND-5. Median Income and Poverty Status, 2016

(Number, percent, except as noted.)

Characteristic	State		U.S.	
	Number	Percent	Number	Percent
Median Income				
Households (dollars)	60,656	X	57,617	X
Families (dollars)	79,530	X	71,062	X
Below Poverty Level (All People)	78,464	10.7	44,268,996	14.0
Sex				
Male	40,145	10.7	19,760,056	12.8
Female	38,319	10.8	24,508,940	15.2
Age				
Under 18 years	21,210	12.4	14,115,713	19.5
Related children under 18 years	20,353	12.0	13,805,435	19.1
18 to 64 years	49,012	10.7	25,723,818	13.2
65 years and over	8,242	7.9	4,429,465	9.2

X = Not applicable.

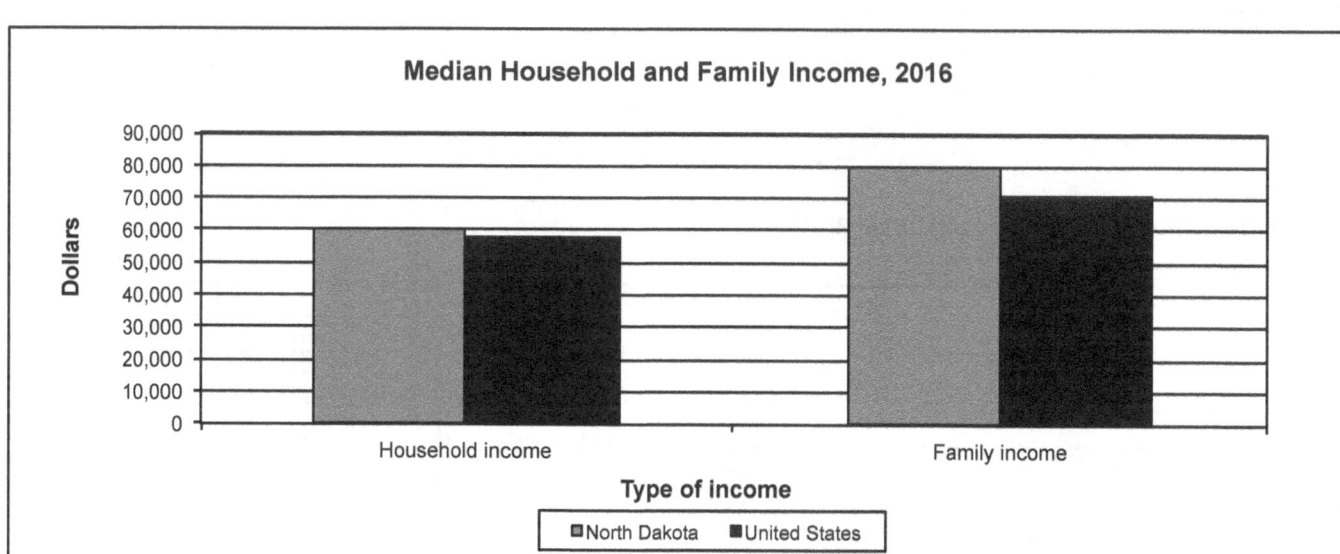

Table ND-6. Health Insurance Coverage Status for the Civilian Noninstitutionalized Population and Children Under 18 Years of Age

(Number, percent.)

Item	2008	2009	2010	2011	2012	2013	2014	2015	2016
Civilian Noninstitutionalized Population	623,970	630,082	660,611	669,425	684,776	708,181	724,451	740,547	741,486
Covered by Private or Public Insurance									
Number	558,309	569,250	596,076	603,977	616,252	634,882	667,553	683,096	689,348
Percent	89.5	90.3	90.2	90.2	90.0	89.6	92.1	92.2	93.0
Not Covered									
Number	65,661	60,832	64,535	65,448	68,524	73,299	56,898	57,451	52,138
Percent	10.5	9.7	9.8	9.8	10.0	10.4	7.9	7.8	7.0
Percent in the U.S. not covered	15.1	15.1	15.5	15.1	14.8	14.5	11.7	9.4	8.6
Children Under 18 Years of Age	140900	141231	150108	150853	153705	160,430	167,191	170,994	174,130
Covered by Private or Public Insurance									
Number	129,988	133,280	140,405	141,238	143,156	147,705	155,649	157,564	160,506
Percent	92.3	94.4	93.5	93.6	93.1	92.1	93.1	92.1	92.2
Not Covered									
Number	10,912	7,951	9,703	9,615	10,549	12,725	11,542	13,430	13,624
Percent	7.7	5.6	6.5	6.4	6.9	7.9	6.9	7.9	7.8
Percent in the U.S. not covered	9.9	8.6	8.0	7.5	7.2	7.1	6.0	4.8	4.5

Table ND-7. Employment Status by Demographic Group, 2017

(Numbers in thousands, percent.)

Characteristic	Civilian noninstitutional population	Civilian labor force		Employed		Unemployed	
		Number	Percent of population	Number	Percent of population	Number	Percent of population
Total...	582	416	71.5	406	69.7	11	2.6
Sex							
Male...	297	227	76.5	221	74.5	6	2.7
Female......................................	285	189	66.3	185	64.7	5	2.4
Race, Sex, and Hispanic Origin							
White..	518	375	72.3	367	70.8	8	2.1
Male......................................	266	205	77.0	200	75.4	5	2.2
Female....................................	253	170	67.3	167	66.1	3	1.8
Black or African American...............	NA	NA	NA	NA	NA	NA	NA
Male......................................	NA	NA	NA	NA	NA	NA	NA
Female....................................	NA	NA	NA	NA	NA	NA	NA
Hispanic or Latino ethnicity[1]...........	NA	NA	NA	NA	NA	NA	NA
Male......................................	NA	NA	NA	NA	NA	NA	NA
Female....................................	NA	NA	NA	NA	NA	NA	NA
Age							
16 to 19 years.............................	NA	NA	NA	NA	NA	NA	NA
20 to 24 years.............................	52	42	81.1	41	78.8	1	2.8
25 to 34 years.............................	118	103	86.8	100	84.0	4	3.4
35 to 44 years.............................	94	85	90.3	83	88.6	2	1.8
45 to 54 years.............................	84	73	86.8	71	84.8	2	2.2
55 to 64 years.............................	94	73	77.5	71	76.1	1	1.8
65 years and over.........................	106	26	24.4	25	23.9	1	1.9

NOTE: Data in Table 7 are from the Current Population Survey (CPS) and do not match the estimates in Table 8. See notes and definitions for further information.
[1] May be of any race.
NA = Not available.

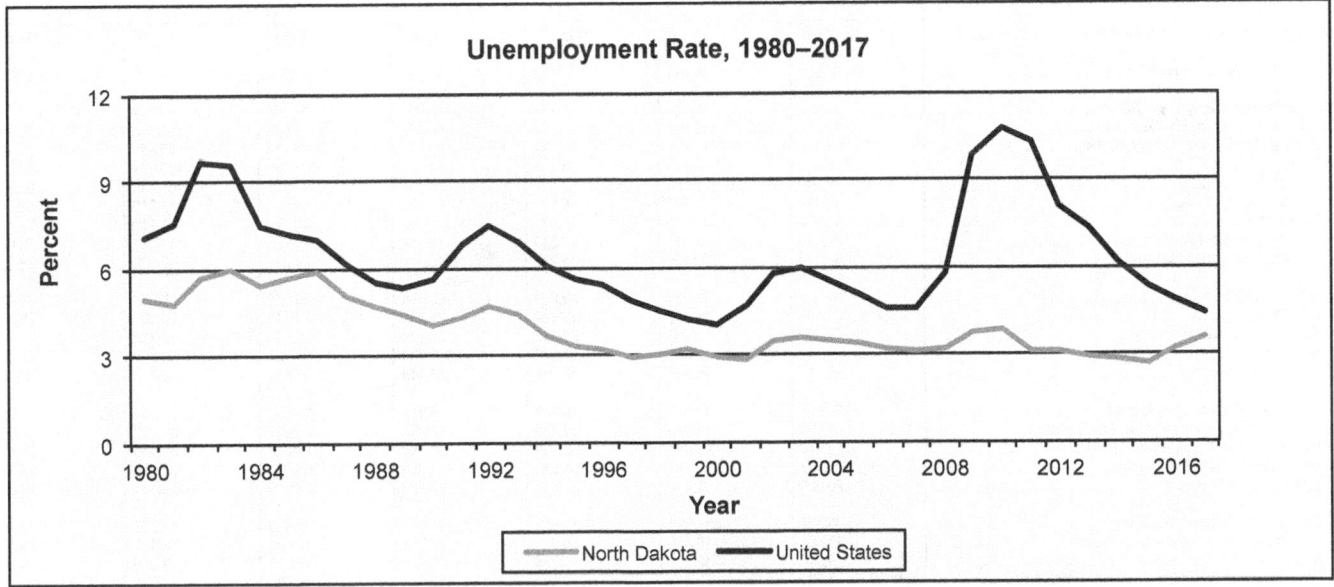

Unemployment Rate, 1980–2017

Table ND-8. Employment Status of the Civilian Noninstitutional Population Age 16 Years and Over

(Number, percent.)

Year	Civilian labor force	Civilian participation rate	Employed	Unemployed	Unemployment rate
2009......................................	368,665	73.2	353,455	15,210	4.1
2010......................................	378,342	72.6	364,053	14,289	3.8
2011......................................	388,634	73.0	375,153	13,481	3.5
2012......................................	397,867	73.1	385,674	12,193	3.1
2013......................................	406,193	72.7	394,392	11,801	2.9
2014......................................	414,413	72.6	403,362	11,051	2.7
2015......................................	414,210	71.4	402,667	11,543	2.8
2016......................................	414,431	71.3	401,671	12,760	3.1
2017......................................	414,399	71.5	403,610	10,789	2.6

Table ND-9. Employment and Average Wages by Industry

(Estimates through 2010 are based on the 2007 *North American Industry Classification System* [NAICS]. Estimates from 2011 onward are based on the 2012 NAICS.)

Industry	2010	2011	2012	2013	2014	2015	2016
	Number of jobs						
Wage and Salary Employment by Industry	392,470	413,535	447,582	463,457	480,912	470,976	451,059
Farm Wage and Salary Employment	4,729	5,316	6,260	6,607	7,292	5,149	4,849
Nonfarm Wage and Salary Employment	387,741	408,219	441,322	456,850	473,620	465,827	446,210
Private wage and salary employment	302,959	324,043	355,749	370,734	387,743	378,725	356,915
Forestry, fishing, and related activities	2,198	2,343	2,521	2,602	2,616	2,577	2,626
Mining	10,520	16,605	24,144	25,923	29,564	23,054	15,192
Utilities	3,417	3,418	3,506	3,593	3,702	3,831	3,843
Construction	21,995	25,050	30,299	33,288	35,720	34,930	31,966
Manufacturing	22,578	23,783	25,187	25,430	25,959	25,447	24,592
Durable goods manufacturing	14,626	15,842	16,955	17,233	17,642	17,086	16,206
Nondurable goods manufacturing	7,952	7,941	8,232	8,197	8,317	8,361	8,386
Wholesale trade	21,161	22,790	25,216	26,524	27,434	26,782	24,539
Retail trade	43,882	45,137	47,455	49,399	50,989	51,113	49,526
Transportation and warehousing	12,772	16,232	21,201	22,504	24,557	22,705	18,431
Information	7,307	7,135	6,960	6,820	6,839	6,613	6,644
Finance and insurance	17,011	17,373	17,446	17,928	18,527	18,870	18,906
Real estate and rental and leasing	3,660	4,116	4,728	5,210	5,852	5,737	5,202
Professional, scientific, and technical services	12,576	12,779	14,446	15,689	16,845	17,173	16,504
Management of companies and enterprises	4,330	4,470	4,765	5,133	5,292	5,338	5,259
Administrative and waste services	11,681	12,821	13,543	13,575	14,329	13,801	12,925
Educational services	3,969	3,953	4,027	4,174	4,119	4,212	4,434
Health care and social assistance	52,104	53,120	54,573	55,815	56,169	57,507	59,105
Arts, entertainment, and recreation	3,865	3,776	4,007	4,180	4,315	4,358	4,568
Accommodation and food services	30,674	31,887	34,279	35,241	36,399	36,288	34,996
Other services, except public administration	17,259	17,255	17,446	17,706	18,516	18,389	17,657
Government and government enterprises	84,782	84,176	85,573	86,116	85,877	87,102	89,295
	Dollars						
Average Wages and Salaries by Industry	37,612	41,103	45,121	46,841	49,910	49,795	48,669
Average Farm Wages and Salaries	37,200	36,634	45,112	39,939	40,952	38,826	42,589
Average Nonfarm Wages and Salaries	37,617	41,161	45,121	46,941	50,048	49,916	48,735
Average private wages and salaries	37,858	41,946	46,669	48,577	51,948	51,505	49,791
Forestry, fishing, and related activities	25,273	25,775	26,494	27,139	28,264	29,950	33,989
Mining	79,302	88,983	95,731	97,203	104,040	100,831	113,569
Utilities	78,500	81,955	82,096	86,456	90,560	95,230	95,883
Construction	46,472	51,147	56,417	60,155	64,861	64,919	53,887
Manufacturing	43,370	44,725	46,672	48,065	49,770	51,179	52,125
Durable goods manufacturing	44,130	45,391	47,343	48,611	49,985	50,766	50,670
Nondurable goods manufacturing	41,973	43,396	45,288	46,916	49,314	52,022	54,936
Wholesale trade	51,336	57,534	63,632	65,258	68,064	66,624	63,474
Retail trade	24,181	25,680	27,492	28,346	29,710	30,800	29,640
Transportation and warehousing	49,694	56,264	62,153	63,970	68,516	66,735	65,544
Information	49,062	50,886	54,447	55,754	58,394	59,859	60,944
Finance and insurance	46,713	49,871	52,930	54,118	56,331	59,317	61,514
Real estate and rental and leasing	34,617	44,213	50,412	53,413	59,654	56,584	51,794
Professional, scientific, and technical services	51,504	55,920	63,228	67,258	71,698	69,687	67,694
Management of companies and enterprises	63,706	65,947	69,339	69,949	76,648	81,419	79,619
Administrative and waste services	25,133	27,897	31,646	31,956	34,056	34,928	38,445
Educational services	20,986	21,706	22,538	22,472	23,659	23,335	24,383
Health care and social assistance	39,323	41,294	43,459	44,548	46,530	49,298	50,443
Arts, entertainment, and recreation	15,488	16,270	16,815	17,339	17,621	18,445	18,402
Accommodation and food services	14,010	15,305	17,313	18,464	19,555	19,918	19,562
Other services, except public administration	23,698	25,416	28,001	30,076	31,951	32,975	35,218
Government and government enterprises	36,758	38,139	38,682	39,896	41,472	43,007	44,514

Table ND-10. Employment Characteristics by Family Type

(Number, percent.)

Family type and labor force status	2014		2015		2016	
	Total	Families with own children under 18 years	Total	Families with own children under 18 years	Total	Families with own children under 18 years
All Families..	187,451	84,732	188,210	82,326	184,904	82,171
FAMILY TYPE AND LABOR FORCE STATUS						
Married-Couple Families................................	148,667	59,010	150,297	58,631	150,317	59,433
Both husband and wife in labor force.............................	60.8	74.6	60.5	76.5	60.0	76.3
Husband in labor force, wife not in labor force	17.7	21.0	17.1	19.6	17.2	18.8
Wife in labor force, husband not in labor force	6.7	2.9	6.6	2.3	7.3	3.1
Both husband and wife not in labor force.........................	14.9	1.5	15.3	0.9	14.9	1.6
Other Families	38,784	25,722	37,913	23,695	34,587	22,738
Female householder, no husband present.......................	63.6	68.5	64.1	66.0	65.2	65.0
In labor force..	47.1	55.7	49.8	56.1	51.2	55.1
Not in labor force	16.5	12.8	14.3	9.9	14.0	9.9
Male householder, no wife present.................................	36.4	31.5	35.9	34.0	34.8	35.0
In labor force..	31.1	27.9	30.2	31.1	30.6	33.2
Not in labor force	5.3	3.6	5.7	2.9	4.2	1.9

Table ND-11. School Enrollment and Educational Attainment, 2016

(Number, percent.)

Item	State	U.S.
Enrollment		
Total population 3 years and over, enrolled in school	181,543	81,572,277
Enrolled in nursery school or preschool (percent).................................	5.6	6.0
Enrolled in kindergarten (percent)...	5.4	5.0
Enrolled in elementary school, grades 1-8 (percent).............................	40.5	40.3
Enrolled in high school, grades 9-12 (percent).....................................	17.5	21.0
Enrolled in college or graduate school (percent)..................................	30.9	27.7
Attainment		
Total population 25 years and over	495,015	218,475,480
Less than ninth grade (percent)..	2.8	5.4
9th to 12th grade, no diploma (percent)...	4.8	7.2
High school graduate, including equivalency (percent).........................	27.1	27.2
Some college, no degree (percent)	22.1	20.6
Associate's degree (percent)..	13.6	8.4
Bachelor's degree (percent)...	21.7	19.3
Graduate or professional degree (percent)...	7.8	11.9
High school graduate or higher (percent)	92.4	87.5
Bachelor's degree or higher (percent)..	29.6	31.3

Table ND-12. Public School Characteristics and Educational Indicators

(Number, percent; data derived from National Center of Education Statistics.)

Item	State	U.S.
Public Schools, 2015–2016 (except where noted)		
Number of school districts...	222	18,328
Number of schools...	518	98,456
Number of students	108,644	50,327,015
Number of teachers	9,195	3,151,497
Student-teacher ratio	11.8	16.0
Expenditures per student (dollars), 2014-2015....................................	12,884	11,445
Four-year adjusted cohort graduation rate (ACGR)[1,2]	87.5	84.1
Students eligible for free or reduced-price lunch (percent), 2014-2015....	29.2	51.8
English language learners (percent), Fall 2015....................................	3.0	9.5
Students age 3 to 21 served under IDEA, part B (percent).....................	12.8	13.2

Public Schools by Type	Number	Percent of state public schools
Total number of schools..	518	100.0
Regular	474	91.5
Special education	31	6.0
Vocational education	13	2.5
Alternative education..	0	-

NOTE: Every school is assigned only one school type based on its instructional emphasis.
[1] ACGR data represents a new method of calculating high-school completion rates and may not be comparable to previous years' data for Averaged Freshmen Graduation Rates (AFGR).
[2] The United States 4-year ACGRs were estimated using both the reported 4-year ACGR data from 49 states and the District of Columbia and using imputed data for Idaho. The estimate for American Indian/Alaska Native students also includes imputed data for Virginia.
- = Zero or rounds to zero.

Table ND-13. Reported Voting and Registration of the Voting-Age Population, November 2016

(Numbers in thousands, percent.)

Item	Total population	Total citizen population	Registered			Voted		
			Total registered	Percent registered (total population)	Percent registered (total citizen population)	Total voted	Percent voted (total population)	Percent voted (total citizen population)
U.S. Total	245,502	224,059	157,596	64.2	70.3	137,537	56.0	61.4
State Total..............................	583	564	424	72.8	75.2	362	62.1	64.2
Sex								
Male	298	288	216	72.6	75.0	182	61.1	63.2
Female	285	276	208	73.1	75.4	180	63.2	65.2
Race								
White alone......................................	520	515	403	77.5	78.2	348	67.1	67.7
White, non-Hispanic alone	511	508	399	77.9	78.4	345	67.4	67.9
Black alone......................................	15	9	4	(B)	(B)	3	(B)	(B)
Asian alone	11	3	2	(B)	(B)	2	(B)	(B)
Hispanic (of any race)......................	9	7	5	(B)	(B)	4	(B)	(B)
White alone or in combination	528	523	406	77.0	77.7	351	66.5	67.1
Black alone or in combination...........	15	10	4	(B)	(B)	3	(B)	(B)
Asian alone or in combination...........	12	4	3	(B)	(B)	2	(B)	(B)
Age								
18 to 24 years.................................	79	78	47	(B)	(B)	37	(B)	(B)
25 to 34 years.................................	124	117	83	66.7	71.2	70	56.2	60.0
35 to 44 years.................................	90	87	65	(B)	(B)	56	(B)	(B)
45 to 64 years.................................	192	187	153	79.6	81.5	132	68.7	70.3
65 years and over	97	96	76	(B)	(B)	67	(B)	(B)

- = Zero or rounds to zero.
B = Base is less than 75,000 and therefore too small to show the derived measure.

Table ND-14. Crime

(Number, rate per 100,000. Data are derived from the FBI Uniform Crime Reports.)

Item	State			U.S. [1,2,3,4]		
	2015	2016	Percent change	2015	2016	Percent change
TOTAL POPULATION [5]	756,927	757,952	0.1	321,418,820	323,127,513	0.5
VIOLENT CRIME						
Number..	1,812	1,903	5.0	1,231,566	1,248,185	1.3
Rate	239.4	251.1	4.9	383.2	386.3	0.8
Murder and Nonnegligent Manslaughter						
Number..	21	15	-28.6	15,696	17,250	9.9
Rate	2.8	2.0	-28.6	4.9	5.3	8.2
Rape[6]						
Number..	345	342	-0.9	124,047	130,603	5.3
Rate	45.6	45.1	-1.1	38.6	40.4	4.7
Robbery						
Number..	148	181	22.3	327,374	332,198	1.5
Rate	19.6	23.9	21.9	101.9	102.8	0.9
Aggravated Assault						
Number..	1,298	1,365	5.2	764,449	803,007	5.0
Rate	171.5	180.1	5.0	237.8	248.5	4.5
PROPERTY CRIME						
Number..	16,020	17,402	8.6	7,993,631	7,919,035	-0.9
Rate	2,116.5	2,295.9	8.5	2,487.0	2,450.7	-1.5
Burglary						
Number..	2,997	3,243	8.2	1,579,527	1,515,096	-4.1
Rate	395.9	427.9	8.1	491.4	468.9	-4.6
Larceny-Theft						
Number..	11,440	12,195	6.6	5,706,346	5,638,455	-1.2
Rate	1,511.4	1,608.9	6.5	1,775.4	1,745.0	-1.7
Motor Vehicle Theft						
Number..	1,583	1,964	24.1	707,758	765,484	8.2
Rate	209.1	259.1	23.9	220.2	236.9	7.6

NOTE: Although arson data are included in the trend and clearance tables, sufficient data are not available to estimate totals for this offense. Therefore, no arson data are published in this table.
X = Not applicable.
- = Zero or rounds to zero.
[1] The crime figures have been adjusted.
[2] The data collection methodology for the offense of forcible rape used by the Minnesota state Uniform Crime Reporting (UCR) Program (with the exception of Minneapolis and St. Paul, Minnesota) does not comply with national UCR Program guidelines. Consequently, its figures for forcible rape and violent crime (of which forcible rape is a part) are not published in this table.
[3] Includes offenses reported by the Zoological Police and the Metro Transit Police.
[4] Because of changes in the state's reporting practices, figures are not comparable to previous years' data.
[5] Populations are U.S. Census Bureau provisional estimates as of July 1 of each year.
[6] The figures shown for the offense of rape were estimated using the revised Uniform Crime Reporting (UCR) definition of rape.

Table ND-15. State Government Finances, 2016

(Dollar amounts in thousands, percent distribution.)

Item	Dollars	Percent distribution
Total Revenue	7,330,392	100.0
General revenue	6,705,492	91.5
Intergovernmental revenue	1,647,517	22.5
Taxes	3,709,105	50.6
General sales	1,017,269	13.9
Selective sales	479,555	6.5
License taxes	204,055	2.8
Individual income tax	351,125	4.8
Corporate income tax	103,069	1.4
Other taxes	1,554,032	21.2
Current charges	825,463	11.3
Miscellaneous general revenue	523,407	7.1
Utility revenue	1	-
Liquor stores revenue	0	-
Insurance trust revenue [1]	624,899	8.5
Total Expenditure	8,287,006	100.0
Intergovernmental expenditure	2,126,704	25.7
Direct expenditure	6,160,302	74.3
Current operation	4,006,719	48.3
Capital outlay	1,073,009	12.9
Insurance benefits and repayments	747,049	9.0
Assistance and subsidies	254,917	3.1
Interest on debt	78,608	0.9
Exhibit: Salaries and wages	1,082,995	13.1
Total Expenditure	8,287,006	100.0
General expenditure	7,449,694	89.9
Intergovernmental expenditure	2,126,704	25.7
Direct expenditure	5,322,990	64.2
General expenditure, by function:		
Education	2,474,992	29.9
Public welfare	1,577,628	19.0
Hospitals	29,749	0.4
Health	271,893	3.3
Highways	1,316,191	15.9
Police protection	34,063	0.4
Correction	103,037	1.2
Natural resources	171,970	2.1
Parks and recreation	36,493	0.4
Governmental administration	217,569	2.6
Interest on general debt	78,608	0.9
Other and unallocable	1,137,501	13.7
Utility expenditure	90,263	1.2
Liquor stores expenditure	0	-
Insurance trust expenditure	747,049	9.0
Debt at End of Fiscal Year	2,355,700	X
Cash and Security Holdings	28,379,833	X

X = Not applicable.
- = Zero or rounds to zero.
[1] Within insurance trust revenue, net earnings of state retirement systems is a calculated statistic (the item code in the data file is X08), and thus can be positive or negative. Net earnings is the sum of earnings on investments plus gains on investments minus losses on investments. The change made in 2002 for asset valuation from book to market value in accordance with Statement 34 of the Governmental Accounting Standards Board is reflected in the calculated statistics.

Table ND-16. State Government Tax Collections, 2017

(Dollars in thousands, percent.)

Item	Dollars	Percent distribution
Total Taxes	3,465,326	100.0
Property taxes	4,401	0.1
Sales and gross receipts	1,349,428	38.9
General sales and gross receipts	872,176	25.2
Selective sales and gross receipts	477,252	13.8
Alcoholic beverages	8,872	0.3
Amusements	3,161	0.1
Insurance premiums	63,558	1.8
Motor fuels	189,718	5.5
Pari-mutuels	1,728	-
Public utilities	46,595	1.3
Tobacco products	28,977	0.8
Other selective sales	134,643	3.9
Licenses	213,985	6.2
Alcoholic beverages	381	-
Amusements	1123	-
Corporations in general	X	-
Hunting and fishing	18,370	0.5
Motor vehicle	119,853	3.5
Motor vehicle operators	4,101	0.1
Public utilities	5	-
Occupation and business, NEC	70,152	2.0
Other licenses	0	-
Income taxes	380,378	11.0
Individual income	319,507	9.2
Corporation net income	60,871	1.8
Other taxes	1,517,134	43.8
Death and gift	X	-
Documentary and stock transfer	X	-
Severance	1,517,134	43.8
Taxes, NEC	0	-

- = Zero or rounds to zero.
X = Not applicable.

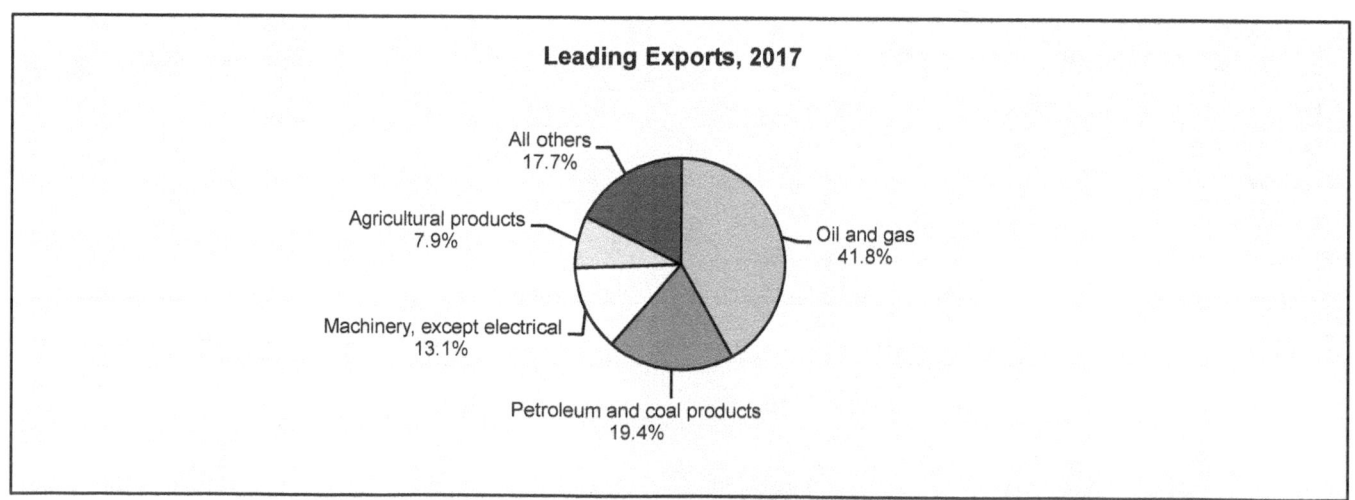

Leading Exports, 2017

- All others 17.7%
- Agricultural products 7.9%
- Machinery, except electrical 13.1%
- Petroleum and coal products 19.4%
- Oil and gas 41.8%

OHIO

Facts and Figures

Location: East north central United States; bordered on the N by Michigan and Lake Erie, on the E by Pennsylvania and West Virginia, on the S by West Virginia and Kentucky, and on the W by Indiana

Area: 44,825 sq. mi. (116,096 sq. km.); rank—34th

Population: 11,658,609 (2017 est.); rank—7th

Principal Cities: capital—Columbus; largest—Columbus

Statehood: March 1, 1803; 17th state

U.S. Congress: 2 senators, 16 representatives

State Motto: With God, All Things Are Possible

State Song: "Beautiful Ohio"

State Nickname: The Buckeye State

Abbreviations: OH

State Symbols: flower—scarlet carnation; tree—Ohio buckeye; bird—cardinal

At a Glance

- With an increase in population of 1.0 percent, Ohio ranked 42nd among the states in growth from 2010 to 2017.

- Ohio's violent crime rate in 2016 was 300.3 per 100,000 population, compared to 386.3 for the entire nation.

- In 2016, 5.6 percent of Ohioans did not have health insurance, compared to 8.6 percent of the entire U.S. population.

- Ohio had the 2nd highest drug overdose death rate in 2016, with 39.1 deaths per 100,000 population.

- Approximately 0.3 percent of Ohio's population identified as "American Indian or Alaska Native Alone" in 2017, which was the 2nd lowest percent among all states.

Table OH-1. Population by Age, Sex, Race, and Hispanic Origin

(Number, percent, except where noted.)

Sex, age, race, and Hispanic origin	2000	2010	2017 [1]	Average annual percent change, 2010–2017
Total Population..	11,353,140	11,536,504	11,658,609	1.1
Percent of total U.S. population	4.0	3.7	3.6	X
Sex				
Male..	5,512,262	5,632,156	5,713,100	1.4
Female	5,840,878	5,904,348	5,945,509	0.7
Age				
Under 5 years..	754,930	720,856	698,780	-3.1
5 to 19 years...	2,461,025	2,346,270	2,214,641	-5.6
20 to 64 years...	6,629,428	6,847,363	6,802,052	-0.7
65 years and over	1,507,757	1,622,015	1,943,136	19.8
Median age (years)	36.2	38.8	39.4	1.5
Race and Hispanic Origin				
One race				
White	9,645,453	9,664,524	9,579,207	-0.9
Black..	1,301,307	1,426,861	1,504,482	5.4
American Indian and Alaska Native	24,486	29,674	32,991	11.2
Asian..	132,633	196,693	271,531	38.0
Native Hawaiian or Other Pacific Islander	2,749	5,336	6,633	24.3
Two or more races..	157,885	213,416	263,765	23.6
Hispanic (of any race)...	217,123	375,004	440,886	17.6

X = Not applicable.
- = Zero or rounds to zero.
[1] Population figures for 2017 are July 1 estimates. The 2010 estimates are taken from the 2010 Census.

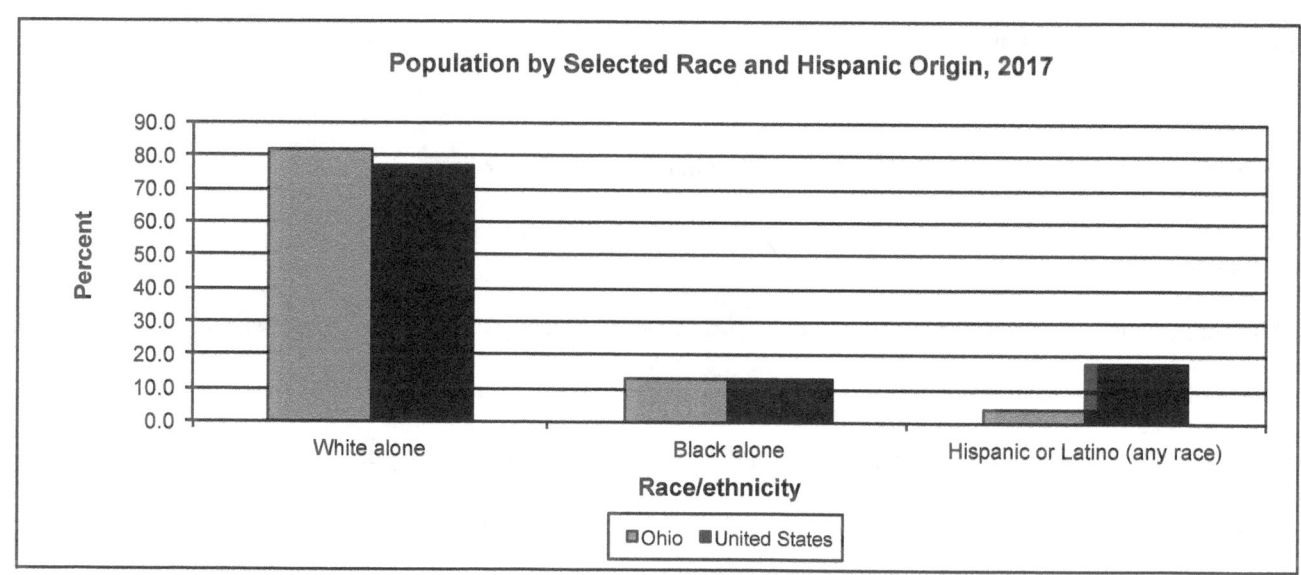

Table OH-2. Marital Status

(Number, percent distribution.)

Sex, age, and marital status	2000	2010	2016
Males, 15 Years and Over	4,281,736	4,487,900	4,597,677
Never married	29.2	33.5	35.7
Now married, except separated..................................	57.0	51.2	48.9
Separated...	1.4	1.7	1.5
Widowed...	2.7	2.9	2.9
Divorced...	9.7	10.8	11.0
Females, 15 Years and Over	4,670,985	4,809,613	4,871,843
Never married	23.5	27.9	29.5
Now married, except separated..................................	52.1	46.9	46.0
Separated...	1.7	2.1	1.8
Widowed...	11.1	10.1	9.5
Divorced...	11.5	12.9	13.2

Table OH-3. Households and Housing Characteristics

(Number, percent, dollars.)

Item	2000	2010	2016	Average annual percent change, 2010–2016
Total Households..	4,445,773	4,525,066	4,624,669	0.4
Family households	2,993,023	2,960,107	2,929,661	-0.2
Married-couple family	2,285,798	2,169,003	2,121,616	-0.4
Other family	707,225	791,104	808,045	0.4
Male householder, no wife present........................	170,347	196,130	221,513	2.2
Female householder, no husband present................	536,878	594,974	586,532	-0.2
Nonfamily households	1,452,750	1,564,959	1,695,008	1.4
Householder living alone......................................	1,215,614	1,315,321	1,402,427	1.1
Householder not living alone.................................	237,136	249,638	292,581	2.9
Housing Characteristics				
Total housing units..	4,783,051	5,128,113	5,164,400	0.1
Occupied housing units	4,445,773	4,525,066	4,624,669	0.4
Owner occupied	3,072,522	3,095,197	3,022,809	-0.4
Renter occupied	1,373,251	1,429,869	1,601,860	2.0
Average household size...	2.49	2.48	2.44	-0.3
Financial Characteristics				
Median gross rent of renter-occupied housing	515	685	759	1.8
Median monthly owner costs for housing units with a mortgage	983	1,246	1,211	-0.5
Median value of owner-occupied housing units..........	103,700	134,400	140,100	0.7

Table OH-4. Migration, Origin, and Language

(Number, percent.)

	State			U.S.		
Characteristic	2015	2016	Percent change	2015	2016	Percent change
Residence 1 Year Ago						
Population 1 year and over	11,482,142	11,481,752	-	317,635,720	319,361,956	0.5
Same house	84.7	85.0	X	85.3	85.4	X
Different house in the U.S.	14.9	14.6	X	14.1	13.9	X
Same county	9.7	9.4	X	8.5	8.3	X
Different county	5.3	5.2	X	5.6	5.6	X
Same state	3.5	3.5	X	3.2	3.2	X
Different state	1.8	1.7	X	2.4	2.4	X
Abroad	0.4	0.4	X	0.7	0.7	X
Place of Birth						
Native born	11,109,512	11,100,781	-0.1	278,128,449	279,388,170	0.5
Male	48.9	49.0	X	49.3	49.3	X
Female	51.1	51.0	X	50.7	50.7	X
Foreign born	503,911	513,592	1.9	43,290,372	43,739,345	1.0
Male	49.1	50.1	X	48.6	48.5	X
Female	50.9	49.9	X	51.4	51.5	X
Foreign born; naturalized U.S. citizen....................	255,342	270,314	5.9	20,697,103	21,238,372	2.6
Male	47.5	47.5	X	45.9	45.9	X
Female	52.5	52.5	X	54.1	54.1	X
Foreign born; not a U.S. citizen	248,569	243,278	-2.1	22,593,269	22,500,973	-0.4
Male	50.8	53.0	X	51.1	51.0	X
Female	49.2	47.0	X	48.9	49.0	X
Entered 2010 or later	25.8	26.9	X	15.6	18.6	X
Entered 2000 to 2009	29.2	29.7	X	27.9	26.7	X
Entered before 2000..	44.9	43.4	X	56.5	54.7	X
World Region of Birth, Foreign						
Foreign-born population, excluding population born at sea	503,911	513,592	1.9	43,289,646	43,738,901	1.0
Europe	22.3	21.7	X	11.1	10.9	X
Asia..	42.0	43.2	X	30.6	30.8	X
Africa	12.8	13.4	X	4.8	4.9	X
Oceania	0.5	0.5	X	0.6	0.6	X
Latin America	19.3	18.3	X	51.1	51.0	X
North America	3.0	2.9	X	1.9	1.8	X
Language Spoken at Home and Ability to Speak English						
Population 5 years and over.................................	10,924,135	10,921,628	-	301,625,014	303,328,961	0.6
English only	93.1	93.0	X	78.5	78.4	X
Language other than English..............................	6.9	7.0	X	21.5	21.6	X
Speaks English less than "very well".................	2.5	2.5	X	8.6	8.6	X

NA = Not available.
X = Not applicable.
- = Zero or rounds to zero.

Table OH-5. Median Income and Poverty Status, 2016

(Number, percent, except as noted.)

Characteristic	State		U.S.	
	Number	Percent	Number	Percent
Median Income				
Households (dollars)..	52,334	X	57,617	X
Families (dollars)	66,722	X	71,062	X
Below Poverty Level (All People)	1,645,382	14.6	44,268,996	14.0
Sex				
Male..	729,976	13.2	19,760,056	12.8
Female..	915,406	15.9	24,508,940	15.2
Age				
Under 18 years..	524,660	20.5	14,115,713	19.5
Related children under 18 years..	512,192	20.1	13,805,435	19.1
18 to 64 years...	973,638	14.1	25,723,818	13.2
65 years and over	147,084	8.1	4,429,465	9.2

X = Not applicable.

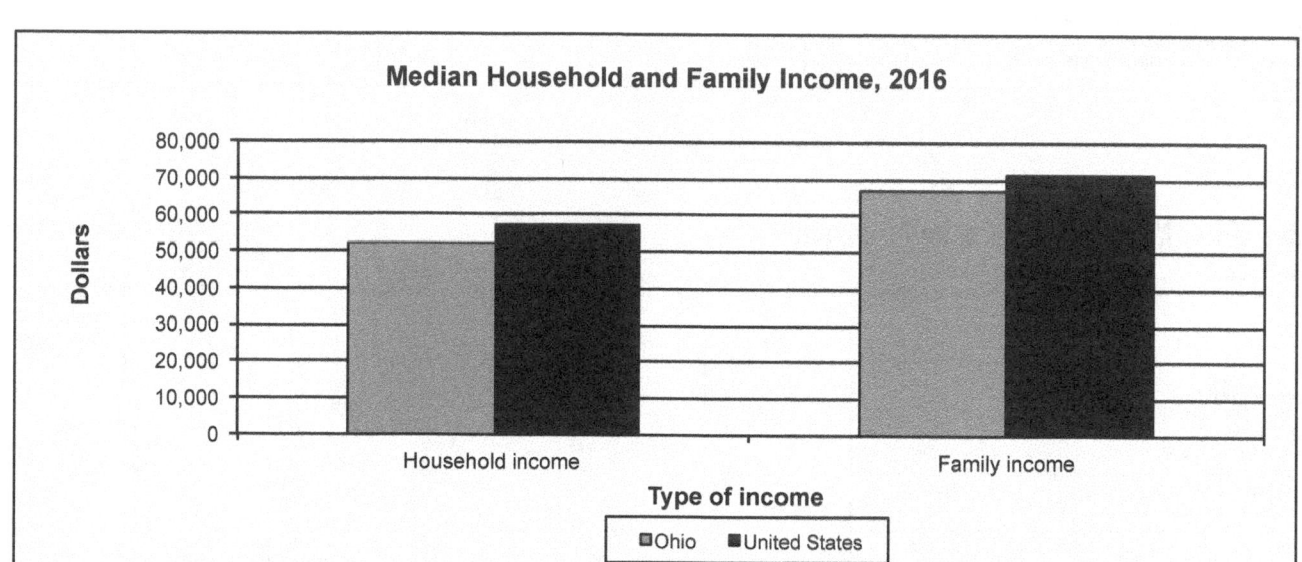

Table OH-6. Health Insurance Coverage Status for the Civilian Noninstitutionalized Population and Children Under 18 Years of Age

(Number, percent.)

Item	2008	2009	2010	2011	2012	2013	2014	2015	2016
Civilian Noninstitutionalized Population	11,296,200	11,351,905	11,358,640	11,369,102	11,371,766	11,398,298	11,420,809	11,442,029	11,439,848
Covered by Private or Public Insurance									
Number..	9,966,028	9,969,267	9,959,697	10,014,671	10,067,519	10,140,742	10,465,604	10,695,753	10,796,120
Percent..	88.2	87.8	87.7	88.1	88.5	89.0	91.6	93.5	94.4
Not Covered									
Number..	1,330,172	1,382,638	1,398,943	1,354,431	1,304,247	1,257,556	955,205	746,276	643,728
Percent..	11.8	12.2	12.3	11.9	11.5	11.0	8.4	6.5	5.6
Percent in the U.S. not covered..	15.1	15.1	15.5	15.1	14.8	14.5	11.7	9.4	8.6
Children Under 18 Years of Age	2,727,548	2,710,364	2,715,122	2,688,340	2,656,700	2,644,952	2,631,481	2,626,771	2,605,997
Covered by Private or Public Insurance									
Number..	2,530,448	2,538,017	2,553,168	2,531,138	2,516,034	2,503,584	2,505,342	2,511,790	2,511,444
Percent..	92.8	93.6	94.0	94.2	94.7	94.7	95.2	95.6	96.4
Not Covered									
Number..	197,100	172,347	161,954	157,202	140,666	141,368	126,139	114,981	94,553
Percent..	7.2	6.4	6.0	5.8	5.3	5.3	4.8	4.4	3.6
Percent in the U.S. not covered..	9.9	8.6	8.0	7.5	7.2	7.1	6.0	4.8	4.5

Table OH-7. Employment Status by Demographic Group, 2017

(Numbers in thousands, percent.)

Characteristic	Civilian noninstitutional population	Civilian labor force		Employed		Unemployed	
		Number	Percent of population	Number	Percent of population	Number	Percent of population
Total..	9,174	5,778	63.0	5,487	59.8	291	5.0
Sex							
Male..	4,426	3,037	68.6	2,877	65.0	161	5.3
Female.....................................	4,748	2,741	57.7	2,610	55.0	130	4.7
Race, Sex, and Hispanic Origin							
White..	7,711	4,872	63.2	4,660	60.4	212	4.4
Male..	3,752	2,585	68.9	2,469	65.8	116	4.5
Female.....................................	3,959	2,287	57.8	2,191	55.3	97	4.2
Black or African American..........	1,093	651	59.6	592	54.2	60	9.1
Male..	497	317	63.8	283	56.8	34	10.8
Female.....................................	596	335	56.1	309	51.9	25	7.5
Hispanic or Latino ethnicity[1]........	292	209	71.5	194	66.4	15	7.1
Male..	136	106	78.0	98	72.1	8	7.6
Female.....................................	157	103	65.9	96	61.5	7	6.7
Age							
16 to 19 years............................	617	288	46.6	246	39.9	42	14.5
20 to 24 years............................	779	604	77.6	548	70.4	56	9.3
25 to 34 years............................	1,539	1,280	83.2	1,213	78.8	67	5.3
35 to 44 years............................	1,260	1,079	85.6	1,037	82.2	43	4.0
45 to 54 years............................	1,537	1,200	78.1	1,161	75.6	39	3.2
55 to 64 years............................	1,513	974	64.4	947	62.6	28	2.8
65 years and over.......................	1,930	353	18.3	336	17.4	17	4.7

NOTE: Data in Table 7 are from the Current Population Survey (CPS) and do not match the estimates in Table 8. See notes and definitions for further information.
[1] May be of any race.

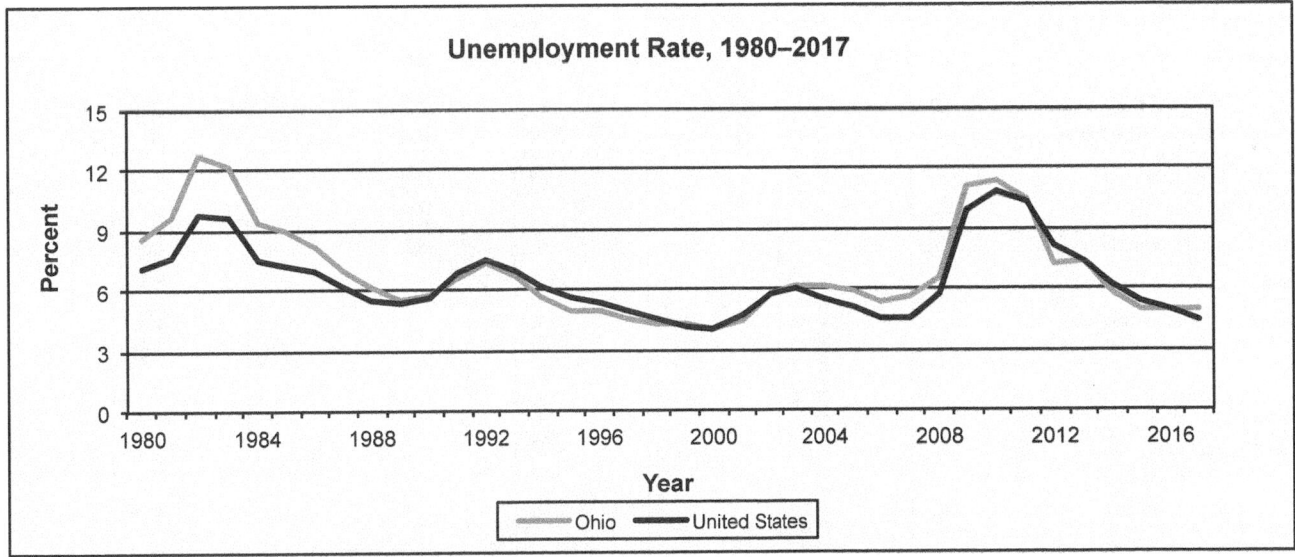

Unemployment Rate, 1980–2017

Table OH-8. Employment Status of the Civilian Noninstitutional Population Age 16 Years and Over

(Number, percent.)

Year	Civilian labor force	Civilian participation rate	Employed	Unemployed	Unemployment rate
2009..	5,906,768	66.0	5,297,098	609,670	10.3
2010..	5,846,886	65.2	5,247,050	599,836	10.3
2011..	5,771,469	64.2	5,261,238	510,231	8.8
2012..	5,705,591	63.3	5,284,001	421,590	7.4
2013..	5,716,730	63.2	5,290,609	426,121	7.5
2014..	5,701,477	62.7	5,370,560	330,917	5.8
2015..	5,694,303	62.5	5,414,872	279,431	4.9
2016..	5,739,296	62.7	5,451,315	287,981	5.0
2017..	5,780,021	62.9	5,491,174	288,847	5.0

Table OH-9. Employment and Average Wages by Industry

(Estimates through 2010 are based on the 2007 *North American Industry Classification System* [NAICS]. Estimates from 2011 onward are based on the 2012 NAICS.)

Industry	2010	2011	2012	2013	2014	2015	2016
	Number of jobs						
Wage and Salary Employment by Industry......................	5,168,965	5,228,768	5,319,551	5,371,183	5,444,825	5,525,739	5,589,230
Farm Wage and Salary Employment................................	13,347	13,254	19,593	16,081	12,576	18,013	20,093
Nonfarm Wage and Salary Employment...........................	5,155,618	5,215,514	5,299,958	5,355,102	5,432,249	5,507,726	5,569,137
Private wage and salary employment...............................	4,330,575	4,407,972	4,500,698	4,559,821	4,637,480	4,712,491	4,767,438
Forestry, fishing, and related activities...........................	4,603	4,600	4,885	5,111	5,250	5,357	5,417
Mining...	10,897	11,375	12,214	12,134	14,388	13,724	11,017
Utilities...	19,951	19,308	19,109	18,799	18,217	19,210	19,230
Construction...	174,975	181,890	186,456	191,406	201,029	205,353	211,615
Manufacturing...	621,524	638,976	657,622	663,376	675,125	686,892	686,061
Durable goods manufacturing..	412,151	429,033	444,884	449,296	459,786	467,773	463,060
Nondurable goods manufacturing..................................	209,373	209,943	212,738	214,080	215,339	219,119	223,001
Wholesale trade...	218,050	219,727	225,351	228,901	233,996	237,166	236,773
Retail trade..	557,113	560,667	564,908	567,546	571,007	575,637	579,821
Transportation and warehousing......................................	163,061	168,395	172,494	175,384	180,789	190,047	194,285
Information..	77,613	76,220	74,741	75,412	72,703	71,727	71,897
Finance and insurance...	215,060	217,368	219,562	220,341	220,352	224,423	230,782
Real estate and rental and leasing..................................	59,548	59,441	59,421	60,898	62,364	63,708	64,372
Professional, scientific, and technical services	241,100	247,909	244,260	246,524	250,425	252,677	259,337
Management of companies and enterprises.....................	107,329	112,862	127,247	132,404	137,549	138,940	138,064
Administrative and waste services...................................	280,657	295,144	306,110	313,943	324,918	328,030	330,729
Educational services..	114,771	116,887	115,630	113,283	114,186	117,380	117,945
Health care and social assistance...................................	741,552	747,221	759,706	770,270	776,822	790,708	805,811
Arts, entertainment, and recreation.................................	63,363	63,984	68,684	74,247	76,250	78,120	79,791
Accommodation and food services..................................	415,822	422,961	435,065	447,031	453,767	464,569	475,711
Other services, except public administration...................	243,586	243,037	247,233	242,811	248,343	248,823	248,780
Government and government enterprises.........................	825,043	807,542	799,260	795,281	794,769	795,235	801,699
	Dollars						
Average Wages and Salaries by Industry	42,314	43,685	44,984	45,520	46,837	48,007	49,984
Average Farm Wages and Salaries	23,163	29,747	27,100	30,897	35,465	36,272	35,647
Average Nonfarm Wages and Salaries	42,364	43,720	45,050	45,564	46,864	48,045	50,036
Average private wages and salaries.................................	42,004	43,424	44,830	45,404	46,810	47,973	49,862
Forestry, fishing, and related activities...........................	25,499	26,286	27,029	27,824	29,057	29,752	33,881
Mining...	66,799	71,353	73,284	65,255	71,207	69,537	71,770
Utilities...	84,183	86,823	88,802	90,586	93,316	96,921	97,645
Construction...	47,918	49,698	51,542	52,933	54,941	56,841	64,332
Manufacturing...	54,891	57,140	57,344	57,651	59,420	60,192	61,475
Durable goods manufacturing..	56,068	58,310	58,473	58,744	60,469	60,797	61,813
Nondurable goods manufacturing..................................	52,573	54,749	54,982	55,357	57,181	58,899	60,774
Wholesale trade...	60,057	62,471	64,079	64,677	66,491	68,500	70,786
Retail trade..	25,104	25,755	26,427	26,674	27,335	28,158	28,807
Transportation and warehousing......................................	44,996	46,229	47,534	47,773	49,203	50,163	52,513
Information..	58,350	60,318	61,957	63,636	64,870	67,016	67,122
Finance and insurance...	62,838	65,057	66,644	69,375	72,182	74,550	80,069
Real estate and rental and leasing..................................	37,738	39,534	41,312	42,397	44,414	46,020	47,922
Professional, scientific, and technical services	63,581	66,002	67,404	68,713	70,557	72,741	74,650
Management of companies and enterprises.....................	93,529	96,478	108,034	104,995	108,768	106,499	109,904
Administrative and waste services...................................	29,945	30,620	31,654	32,304	33,126	34,397	34,470
Educational services..	29,459	30,074	30,567	30,841	31,077	31,239	31,832
Health care and social assistance...................................	40,701	41,646	42,928	43,650	44,693	46,224	48,064
Arts, entertainment, and recreation.................................	31,069	30,619	32,105	32,083	34,225	35,107	38,638
Accommodation and food services..................................	15,198	15,701	16,370	16,712	17,290	18,076	19,053
Other services, except public administration...................	26,868	27,531	28,556	29,167	30,095	31,359	33,983
Government and government enterprises.........................	44,253	45,335	46,292	46,476	47,176	48,475	51,069

Table OH-10. Employment Characteristics by Family Type

(Number, percent.)

Family type and labor force status	2014		2015		2016	
	Total	Families with own children under 18 years	Total	Families with own children under 18 years	Total	Families with own children under 18 years
All Families......	2,914,550	1,218,710	2,922,095	1,218,342	2,929,661	1,212,345
FAMILY TYPE AND LABOR FORCE STATUS						
Married-Couple Families......	2,095,746	766,196	2,123,886	781,230	2,121,616	769,547
Both husband and wife in labor force......	52.6	69.9	52.0	69.8	51.9	69.8
Husband in labor force, wife not in labor force......	20.1	24.5	20.0	24.1	20.0	24.4
Wife in labor force, husband not in labor force......	8.3	4.1	8.6	4.0	8.2	3.9
Both husband and wife not in labor force......	19.0	1.5	19.0	1.8	19.3	1.5
Other Families......	818,804	452,514	798,209	437,112	808,045	442,798
Female householder, no husband present......	73.8	76.6	73.6	75.6	72.6	74.0
In labor force......	51.3	63.5	50.9	62.2	50.1	61.3
Not in labor force......	22.5	13.1	22.7	13.3	22.5	12.7
Male householder, no wife present......	26.2	23.4	26.4	24.4	27.4	26.0
In labor force......	20.0	21.0	20.2	21.7	21.1	23.3
Not in labor force......	6.2	2.4	6.2	2.7	6.4	2.7

Table OH-11. School Enrollment and Educational Attainment, 2016

(Number, percent.)

Item	State	U.S.
Enrollment		
Total population 3 years and over, enrolled in school......	2,830,005	81,572,277
Enrolled in nursery school or preschool (percent)......	5.8	6.0
Enrolled in kindergarten (percent)......	4.9	5.0
Enrolled in elementary school, grades 1-8 (percent)......	40.8	40.3
Enrolled in high school, grades 9-12 (percent)......	21.8	21.0
Enrolled in college or graduate school (percent)......	26.7	27.7
Attainment		
Total population 25 years and over......	7,922,061	218,475,480
Less than ninth grade (percent)......	2.8	5.4
9th to 12th grade, no diploma (percent)......	7.2	7.2
High school graduate, including equivalency (percent)......	33.3	27.2
Some college, no degree (percent)......	20.6	20.6
Associate's degree (percent)......	8.6	8.4
Bachelor's degree (percent)......	17.2	19.3
Graduate or professional degree (percent)......	10.3	11.9
High school graduate or higher (percent)......	90.0	87.5
Bachelor's degree or higher (percent)......	27.5	31.3

Table OH-12. Public School Characteristics and Educational Indicators

(Number, percent; data derived from National Center of Education Statistics.)

Item	State	U.S.
Public Schools, 2015–2016 (except where noted)		
Number of school districts......	1,103	18,328
Number of schools......	3,619	98,456
Number of students......	1,716,585	50,327,015
Number of teachers......	101,742	3,151,497
Student-teacher ratio......	16.9	16.0
Expenditures per student (dollars), 2014-2015......	11,730	11,445
Four-year adjusted cohort graduation rate (ACGR)[1,2]......	83.5	84.1
Students eligible for free or reduced-price lunch (percent), 2014-2015......	45.1	51.8
English language learners (percent), Fall 2015......	3.0	9.5
Students age 3 to 21 served under IDEA, part B (percent)......	14.8	13.2

Public Schools by Type	Number	Percent of state public schools
Total number of schools......	3,619	100.0
Regular......	3,495	96.6
Special education......	51	1.4
Vocational education......	73	2.0
Alternative education......	0	-

NOTE: Every school is assigned only one school type based on its instructional emphasis.
[1] ACGR data represents a new method of calculating high-school completion rates and may not be comparable to previous years' data for Averaged Freshmen Graduation Rates (AFGR).
[2] The United States 4-year ACGRs were estimated using both the reported 4-year ACGR data from 49 states and the District of Columbia and using imputed data for Idaho. The estimate for American Indian/Alaska Native students also includes imputed data for Virginia.

Table OH-13. Reported Voting and Registration of the Voting-Age Population, November 2016

(Numbers in thousands, percent.)

Item	Total population	Total citizen population	Registered			Voted		
			Total registered	Percent registered (total population)	Percent registered (total citizen population)	Total voted	Percent voted (total population)	Percent voted (total citizen population)
U.S. Total	245,502	224,059	157,596	64.2	70.3	137,537	56.0	61.4
State Total..............................	8,811	8,499	6,128	69.5	72.1	5,408	61.4	63.6
Sex								
Male	4,219	4,070	2,837	67.2	69.7	2,472	58.6	60.7
Female	4,593	4,429	3,291	71.7	74.3	2,936	63.9	66.3
Race								
White alone............................	7,340	7,226	5,235	71.3	72.4	4,642	63.2	64.2
White, non-Hispanic alone...........	7,108	7,058	5,121	72.0	72.6	4,547	64.0	64.4
Black alone.............................	1,031	977	722	70.0	73.9	637	61.8	65.2
Asian alone.............................	250	118	62	25.0	53.1	55	22.0	46.8
Hispanic (of any race)................	277	173	119	43.1	68.9	100	36.2	57.8
White alone or in combination	7,496	7,371	5,319	71.0	72.2	4,696	62.6	63.7
Black alone or in combination...........	1,127	1,072	769	68.3	71.8	662	58.8	61.8
Asian alone or in combination..........	262	129	68	25.9	52.5	60	23.1	46.8
Age								
18 to 24 years.........................	1,075	1,060	576	53.6	54.3	425	39.6	40.1
25 to 34 years.........................	1,425	1,276	859	60.2	67.3	718	50.4	56.3
35 to 44 years.........................	1,325	1,270	884	66.7	69.6	792	59.8	62.3
45 to 64 years.........................	3,061	2,997	2,271	74.2	75.8	2,072	67.7	69.1
65 years and over	1,925	1,895	1,537	79.8	81.1	1,402	72.8	74.0

B = Base is less than 75,000 and therefore too small to show the derived measure.

Table OH-14. Crime

(Number, rate per 100,000. Data are derived from the FBI Uniform Crime Reports.)

Item	State			U.S. [1,2,3,4]		
	2015	2016	Percent change	2015	2016	Percent change
TOTAL POPULATION [5]	11,613,423	11,614,373	-	321,418,820	323,127,513	0.5
VIOLENT CRIME						
Number..................	33,898	34,877	2.9	1,231,566	1,248,185	1.3
Rate	291.9	300.3	2.9	383.2	386.3	0.8
Murder and Nonnegligent Manslaughter						
Number..................	500	654	30.8	15,696	17,250	9.9
Rate	4.3	5.6	30.2	4.9	5.3	8.2
Rape [6]						
Number..................	5,149	5,589	8.5	124,047	130,603	5.3
Rate	44.3	48.1	8.6	38.6	40.4	4.7
Robbery						
Number..................	12,554	12,523	-0.2	327,374	332,198	1.5
Rate	108.1	107.8	-0.3	101.9	102.8	0.9
Aggravated Assault						
Number..................	15,695	16,111	2.7	764,449	803,007	5.0
Rate	135.1	138.7	2.7	237.8	248.5	4.5
PROPERTY CRIME						
Number..................	300,525	299,357	-0.4	7,993,631	7,919,035	-0.9
Rate	2,587.7	2,577.5	-0.4	2,487.0	2,450.7	-1.5
Burglary						
Number..................	69,303	66,883	-3.5	1,579,527	1,515,096	-4.1
Rate	596.7	575.9	-3.5	491.4	468.9	-4.6
Larceny-Theft						
Number..................	213,993	212,807	-0.6	5,706,346	5,638,455	-1.2
Rate	1,842.6	1,832.3	-0.6	1,775.4	1,745.0	-1.7
Motor Vehicle Theft						
Number..................	17,229	19,667	14.2	707,758	765,484	8.2
Rate	148.4	169.3	14.1	220.2	236.9	7.6

NOTE: Although arson data are included in the trend and clearance tables, sufficient data are not available to estimate totals for this offense. Therefore, no arson data are published in this table.

X = Not applicable.

- = Zero or rounds to zero.

[1] The crime figures have been adjusted.

[2] The data collection methodology for the offense of forcible rape used by the Minnesota state Uniform Crime Reporting (UCR) Program (with the exception of Minneapolis and St. Paul, Minnesota) does not comply with national UCR Program guidelines. Consequently, its figures for forcible rape and violent crime (of which forcible rape is a part) are not published in this table.

[3] Includes offenses reported by the Zoological Police and the Metro Transit Police.

[4] Because of changes in the state's reporting practices, figures are not comparable to previous years' data.

[5] Populations are U.S. Census Bureau provisional estimates as of July 1 of each year.

[6] The figures shown for the offense of rape were estimated using the revised Uniform Crime Reporting (UCR) definition of rape.

Table OH-15. State Government Finances, 2016

(Dollar amounts in thousands, percent distribution.)

Item	Dollars	Percent distribution
Total Revenue	78,331,623	100.0
General revenue	67,466,442	86.1
Intergovernmental revenue	24,257,560	31.0
Taxes	28,694,883	36.6
General sales	12,226,504	15.6
Selective sales	6,004,663	7.7
License taxes	2,223,747	2.8
Individual income tax	8,169,197	10.4
Corporate income tax	33,235	-
Other taxes	37,537	-
Current charges	9,075,474	11.6
Miscellaneous general revenue	5,438,525	6.9
Utility revenue	0	-
Liquor stores revenue	1,154,329	1.5
Insurance trust revenue [1]	9,710,852	12.4
Total Expenditure	87,016,871	100.0
Intergovernmental expenditure	18,552,156	21.3
Direct expenditure	68,464,715	78.7
Current operation	43,391,956	49.9
Capital outlay	4,912,026	5.6
Insurance benefits and repayments	17,200,064	19.8
Assistance and subsidies	1,678,516	1.9
Interest on debt	1,282,153	1.5
Exhibit: Salaries and wages	8,055,942	9.3
Total Expenditure	87,016,871	100.0
General expenditure	69,002,878	79.3
Intergovernmental expenditure	18,552,156	21.3
Direct expenditure	50,450,722	58.0
General expenditure, by function:		
Education	22,907,313	26.3
Public welfare	25,748,236	29.6
Hospitals	3,839,481	4.4
Health	2,422,922	2.8
Highways	4,076,963	4.7
Police protection	363,131	0.4
Correction	1,758,395	2.0
Natural resources	442,792	0.5
Parks and recreation	205,331	0.2
Governmental administration	2,066,464	2.4
Interest on general debt	1,282,153	1.5
Other and unallocable	3,889,697	4.5
Utility expenditure	0	-
Liquor stores expenditure	813,929	0.9
Insurance trust expenditure	17,200,064	19.8
Debt at End of Fiscal Year	33,164,507	X
Cash and Security Holdings	210,599,418	X

X = Not applicable.
- = Zero or rounds to zero.
[1] Within insurance trust revenue, net earnings of state retirement systems is a calculated statistic (the item code in the data file is X08), and thus can be positive or negative. Net earnings is the sum of earnings on investments plus gains on investments minus losses on investments. The change made in 2002 for asset valuation from book to market value in accordance with Statement 34 of the Governmental Accounting Standards Board is reflected in the calculated statistics.

Table OH-16. State Government Tax Collections, 2017

(Dollars in thousands, percent.)

Item	Dollars	Percent distribution
Total Taxes	30,306,468	100.0
Property taxes	X	-
Sales and gross receipts	19,573,408	64.6
General sales and gross receipts	13,343,149	44.0
Selective sales and gross receipts	6,230,259	20.6
Alcoholic beverages	107,060	0.4
Amusements	261,950	0.9
Insurance premiums	629,684	2.1
Motor fuels	1,984,392	6.5
Pari-mutuels	5,525	-
Public utilities	1,147,894	3.8
Tobacco products	1,109,777	3.7
Other selective sales	983,977	3.2
Licenses	2,300,778	7.6
Alcoholic beverages	42,978	0.1
Amusements	36,094	0.1
Corporations in general	263,294	0.9
Hunting and fishing	38,186	0.1
Motor vehicle	840,327	2.8
Motor vehicle operators	87,659	0.3
Public utilities	38,590	0.1
Occupation and business, NEC	901,294	3.0
Other licenses	52,356	0.2
Income taxes	8,386,283	27.7
Individual income	8,377,450	27.6
Corporation net income	8833	-
Other taxes	45,999	0.2
Death and gift	743	-
Documentary and stock transfer	X	-
Severance	45,256	0.1
Taxes, NEC	0	-

X = Not applicable.
- = Zero or rounds to zero.

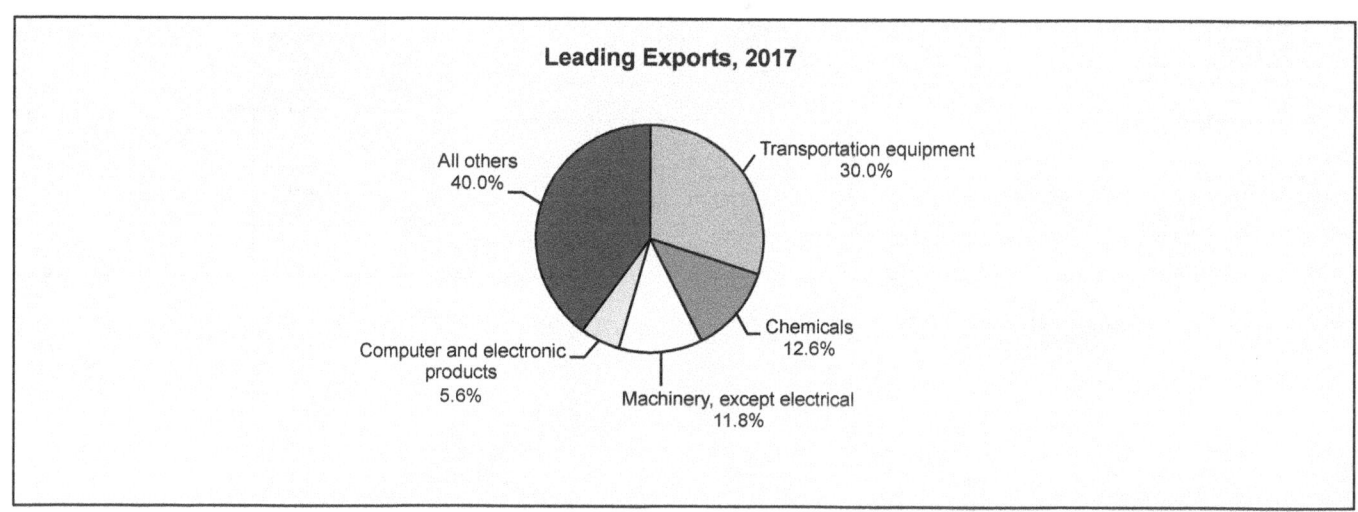

Leading Exports, 2017

All others 40.0%

Transportation equipment 30.0%

Chemicals 12.6%

Machinery, except electrical 11.8%

Computer and electronic products 5.6%

OKLAHOMA

Facts and Figures

Location: West south central United States; bordered on the N by Colorado and Kansas, on the E by Missouri and Arkansas, on the S by Texas, and on the W by Texas and New Mexico

Area: 69,898 sq. mi. (181,036 sq. km.); rank—20th

Population: 3,930,864 (2017 est.); rank—28th

Principal Cities: capital—Oklahoma City; largest—Oklahoma City

Statehood: November 16, 1907; 46th state

U.S. Congress: 2 senators, 5 representatives

State Motto: *Labor omnia vincit* ("Labor conquers all things")

State Song: "Oklahoma!"

State Nickname: The Sooner State

Abbreviations: OK; Okla.

State Symbols: flower—mistletoe; tree—redbud; bird—scissor-tailed flycatcher

At a Glance

- With an increase in population of 4.6 percent, Oklahoma ranked 24th among the states in growth from 2010 to 2017.

- Oklahoma's median household income in 2016 was $49,176, and 16.3 percent of the population lived below the poverty level.

- In 2016, 13.8 percent of Oklahomans did not have health insurance, making it the state with the 3rd highest percent of uninsured residents.

- Oklahoma's violent crime rate in 2016 was 449.8 per 100,000 population, compared to 386.3 for the entire nation.

- Its 2016 property crime rate of 2,982.9 incidents per 100,000 residents made Oklahoma as the state with the 10th highest property crime rate in the country.

Table OK-1. Population by Age, Sex, Race, and Hispanic Origin

(Number, percent, except where noted.)

Sex, age, race, and Hispanic origin	2000	2010	2017 [1]	Average annual percent change, 2010–2017
Total Population...	3,450,654	3,751,351	3,930,864	4.8
Percent of total U.S. population	1.2	1.2	1.2	X
Sex				
Male...	1,695,895	1,856,977	1,947,562	4.9
Female..	1,754,759	1,894,374	1,983,302	4.7
Age				
Under 5 years...	236,353	264,126	263,740	-0.1
5 to 19 years..	765,927	777,484	800,705	3.0
20 to 64 years..	1,992,424	2,203,027	2,263,596	2.7
65 years and over.......................................	455,950	506,714	602,823	19.0
Median age (years).....................................	35.5	36.2	36.5	0.8
Race and Hispanic Origin				
One race				
White..	2,628,434	2,851,510	2,921,390	2.5
Black..	260,968	284,332	306,089	7.7
American Indian and Alaska Native	273,230	335,664	363,551	8.3
Asian..	46,767	67,126	91,288	36.0
Native Hawaiian or Other Pacific Islander	2,372	5,354	7,423	38.6
Two or more races...	155,985	207,365	241,123	16.3
Hispanic (of any race)...................................	179,304	351,542	417,710	18.8

X = Not applicable.
- = Zero or rounds to zero.
[1] Population figures for 2017 are July 1 estimates. The 2010 estimates are taken from the 2010 Census.

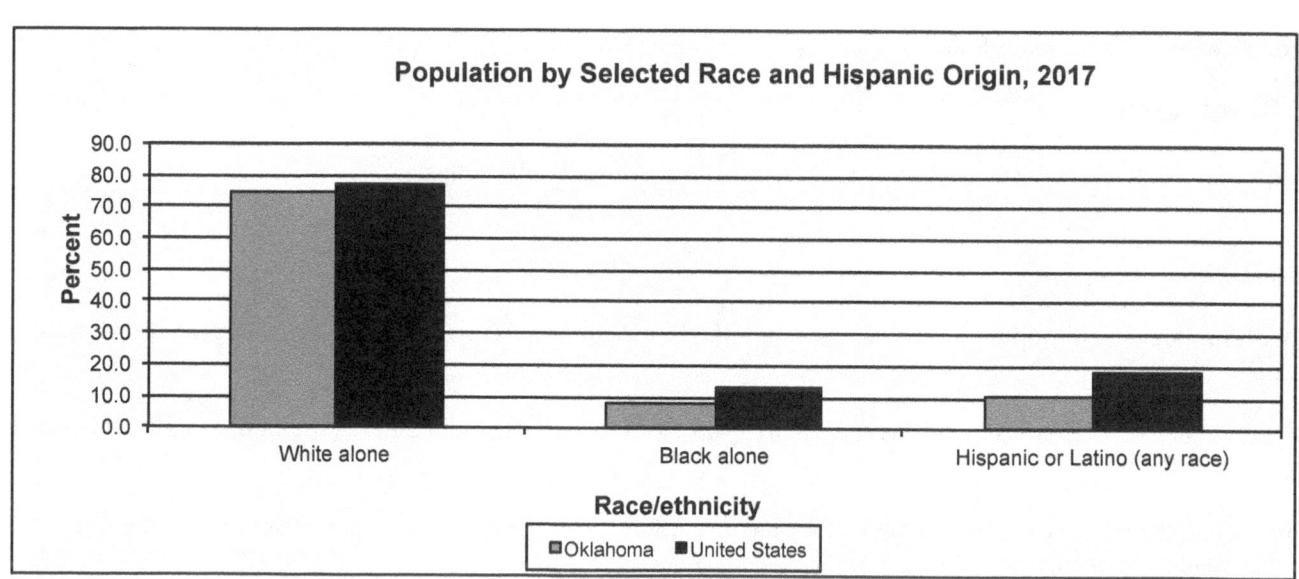

Population by Selected Race and Hispanic Origin, 2017

(Legend: Oklahoma, United States; x-axis: White alone, Black alone, Hispanic or Latino (any race); x-axis label: Race/ethnicity; y-axis label: Percent)

Table OK-2. Marital Status

(Number, percent distribution.)

Sex, age, and marital status	2000	2010	2016
Males, 15 Years and Over	1,318,729	1,457,860	1,528,795
Never married	25.8	30.7	32.8
Now married, except separated..	59.5	52.2	50.1
Separated..	1.6	1.8	1.9
Widowed..	2.5	3.0	3.1
Divorced..	10.6	12.3	12.1
Females, 15 Years and Over	1,398,823	1,521,546	1,588,487
Never married	19.1	23.8	25.7
Now married, except separated..	55.3	49.7	47.9
Separated..	1.9	2.7	2.4
Widowed..	11.1	10.1	9.6
Divorced..	12.5	13.7	14.4

Table OK-3. Households and Housing Characteristics

(Number, percent, dollars.)

Item	2000	2010	2016	Average annual percent change, 2010–2016
Total Households..	1,342,293	1,432,959	1,469,342	0.4
Family households..	921,750	954,622	961,731	0.1
Married-couple family...................................	717,611	709,256	710,097	-
Other family...	204,139	245,366	251,634	0.4
Male householder, no wife present...............	51,564	62,855	76,078	3.5
Female householder, no husband present........	152,575	182,511	175,556	-0.6
Nonfamily households	420,543	478,337	507,611	1.0
Householder living alone...............................	358,560	400,840	421,005	0.8
Householder not living alone..........................	61,983	77,497	86,606	2.0
Housing Characteristics				
Total housing units...	1,514,400	1,666,205	1,721,072	0.5
Occupied housing units	1,342,293	1,432,959	1,469,342	0.4
Owner occupied...	918,259	971,378	953,552	-0.3
Renter occupied..	424,034	461,581	515,790	2.0
Average household size.....................................	2.49	2.55	2.6	0.3
Financial Characteristics				
Median gross rent of renter-occupied housing	456	659	744	2.1
Median monthly owner costs for housing units with a mortgage	764	1,089	1,168	1.2
Median value of owner-occupied housing units........	70,700	111,400	132,200	3.1

- = Zero or rounds to zero.

Table OK-4. Migration, Origin, and Language

(Number, percent.)

Characteristic	State			U.S.		
	2015	2016	Percent change	2015	2016	Percent change
Residence 1 Year Ago						
Population 1 year and over	3,864,908	3,873,232	0.2	317,635,720	319,361,956	0.5
Same house..	82.9	83.3	X	85.3	85.4	X
Different house in the U.S................................	16.7	16.3	X	14.1	13.9	X
Same county	9.4	9.6	X	8.5	8.3	X
Different county	7.3	6.7	X	5.6	5.6	X
Same state..	4.4	4.1	X	3.2	3.2	X
Different state......................................	2.9	2.6	X	2.4	2.4	X
Abroad	0.5	0.4	X	0.7	0.7	X
Place of Birth						
Native born	3,675,988	3,695,147	0.5	278,128,449	279,388,170	0.5
Male...	49.4	49.4	X	49.3	49.3	X
Female...	50.6	50.6	X	50.7	50.7	X
Foreign born	235,350	228,414	-2.9	43,290,372	43,739,345	1.0
Male...	52.4	51.0	X	48.6	48.5	X
Female...	47.6	49.0	X	51.4	51.5	X
Foreign born; naturalized U.S. citizen.................	78,382	77,757	-0.8	20,697,103	21,238,372	2.6
Male...	47.8	47.1	X	45.9	45.9	X
Female...	52.2	52.9	X	54.1	54.1	X
Foreign born; not a U.S. citizen........................	156,968	150,657	-4.0	22,593,269	22,500,973	-0.4
Male...	54.7	53.1	X	51.1	51.0	X
Female...	45.3	46.9	X	48.9	49.0	X
Entered 2010 or later	19.7	21.8	X	15.6	18.6	X
Entered 2000 to 2009	33.0	34.1	X	27.9	26.7	X
Entered before 2000..	47.2	44.2	X	56.5	54.7	X
World Region of Birth, Foreign						
Foreign-born population, excluding population born at sea	235,350	228,414	-2.9	43,289,646	43,738,901	1.0
Europe	6.1	7.6	X	11.1	10.9	X
Asia...	27.1	27.7	X	30.6	30.8	X
Africa..	4.2	3.6	X	4.8	4.9	X
Oceania..	0.7	1.5	X	0.6	0.6	X
Latin America..	60.1	58.1	X	51.1	51.0	X
North America..	1.8	1.4	X	1.9	1.8	X
Language Spoken at Home and Ability to Speak English						
Population 5 years and over...............................	3,648,387	3,659,465	0.3	301,625,014	303,328,961	0.6
English only...	89.9	89.7	X	78.5	78.4	X
Language other than English.........................	10.1	10.3	X	21.5	21.6	X
Speaks English less than "very well"..........	4.1	4.0	X	8.6	8.6	X

NA = Not available.
X = Not applicable.
- = Zero or rounds to zero.

Table OK-5. Median Income and Poverty Status, 2016

(Number, percent, except as noted.)

Characteristic	State		U.S.	
	Number	Percent	Number	Percent
Median Income				
Households (dollars)...	49,176	X	57,617	X
Families (dollars)	61,633	X	71,062	X
Below Poverty Level (All People)	620,377	16.3	44,268,996	14.0
Sex				
Male	280,342	15.0	19,760,056	12.8
Female	340,035	17.6	24,508,940	15.2
Age				
Under 18 years..	216,713	22.9	14,115,713	19.5
Related children under 18 years.........................	212,165	22.6	13,805,435	19.1
18 to 64 years...	354,859	15.5	25,723,818	13.2
65 years and over..	48,805	8.6	4,429,465	9.2

X = Not applicable.

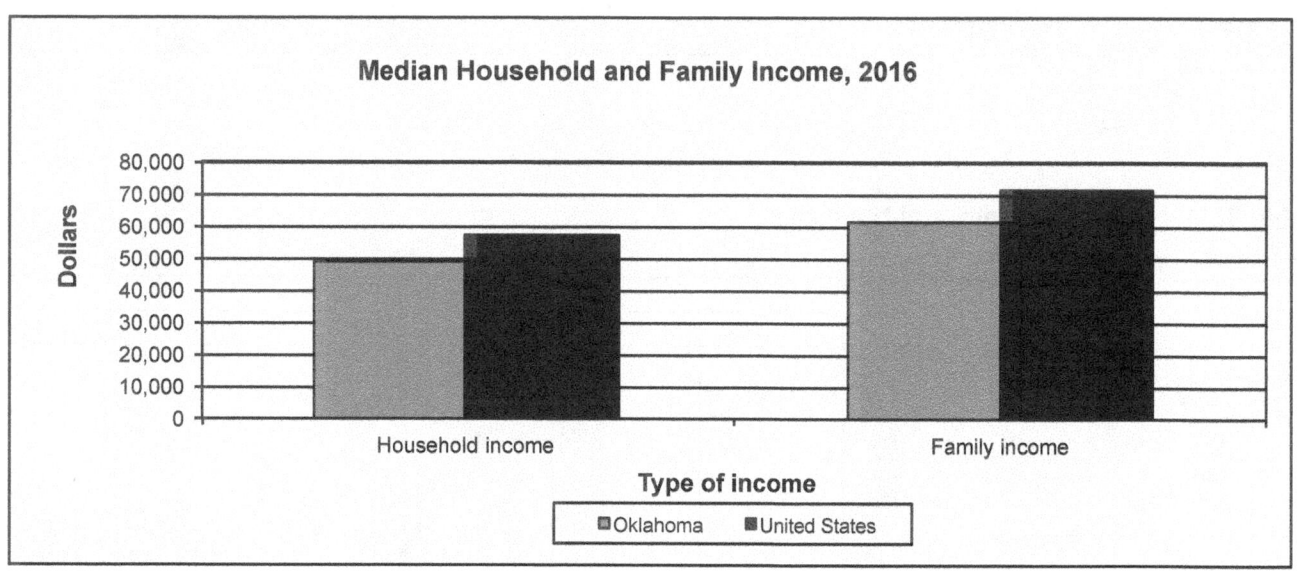

Table OK-6. Health Insurance Coverage Status for the Civilian Noninstitutionalized Population and Children Under 18 Years of Age

(Number, percent.)

Item	2008	2009	2010	2011	2012	2013	2014	2015	2016
Civilian Noninstitutionalized Population	3,550,098	3,590,307	3,677,206	3,710,368	3,733,058	3,770,254	3,797,966	3,830,329	3,845,697
Covered by Private or Public Insurance									
Number...	2,857,639	2,918,644	2,983,655	3,016,823	3,047,982	3,104,481	3,214,454	3,297,820	3,316,039
Percent..	80.5	81.3	81.1	81.3	81.6	82.3	84.6	86.1	86.2
Not Covered									
Number...	692,459	671,663	693,551	693,545	685,076	665,773	583,512	532,509	529,658
Percent..	19.5	18.7	18.9	18.7	18.4	17.7	15.4	13.9	13.8
Percent in the U.S. not covered.........................	15.1	15.1	15.5	15.1	14.8	14.5	11.7	9.4	8.6
Children Under 18 Years of Age	903,224	918,593	929,349	933,893	934,617	946,133	950,123	958,418	959,850
Covered by Private or Public Insurance									
Number...	786,513	815,915	836,828	834,509	840,408	851,091	867,872	887,310	889,761
Percent..	87.1	88.8	90.0	89.4	89.9	90.0	91.3	92.6	92.7
Not Covered									
Number...	116,711	102,678	92,521	99,384	94,209	95,042	82,251	71,108	70,089
Percent..	12.9	11.2	10.0	10.6	10.1	10.0	8.7	7.4	7.3
Percent in the U.S. not covered.........................	9.9	8.6	8.0	7.5	7.2	7.1	6.0	4.8	4.5

Table OK-7. Employment Status by Demographic Group, 2017

(Numbers in thousands, percent.)

Characteristic	Civilian noninstitutional population	Civilian labor force		Employed		Unemployed	
		Number	Percent of population	Number	Percent of population	Number	Percent of population
Total..	3,007	1,839	61.2	1,758	58.5	81	4.4
Sex							
Male..	1,455	1,006	69.1	965	66.3	41	4.1
Female.....................................	1,551	833	53.7	794	51.1	39	4.7
Race, Sex, and Hispanic Origin							
White.......................................	2,319	1,413	60.9	1,363	58.8	51	3.6
Male.....................................	1,137	791	69.6	764	67.2	27	3.4
Female...................................	1,181	622	52.6	598	50.6	24	3.8
Black or African American................	207	122	59.0	114	54.9	9	7.0
Male.....................................	97	63	65.5	61	62.8	3	4.1
Female...................................	110	59	53.4	53	48.0	6	10.1
Hispanic or Latino ethnicity[1]............	311	208	67.0	199	64.1	9	4.3
Male.....................................	166	133	80.1	127	76.9	5	4.0
Female...................................	145	76	52.0	72	49.5	4	4.9
Age							
16 to 19 years............................	211	76	35.8	61	29.0	14	19.0
20 to 24 years............................	229	166	72.5	157	68.3	10	5.8
25 to 34 years............................	554	443	80.0	419	75.7	24	5.4
35 to 44 years............................	471	379	80.4	365	77.4	14	3.8
45 to 54 years............................	454	345	76.1	336	74.0	9	2.7
55 to 64 years............................	485	311	64.2	305	62.8	7	2.2
65 years and over........................	602	119	19.7	116	19.3	2	1.9

NOTE: Data in Table 7 are from the Current Population Survey (CPS) and do not match the estimates in Table 8. See notes and definitions for further information.
[1] May be of any race.

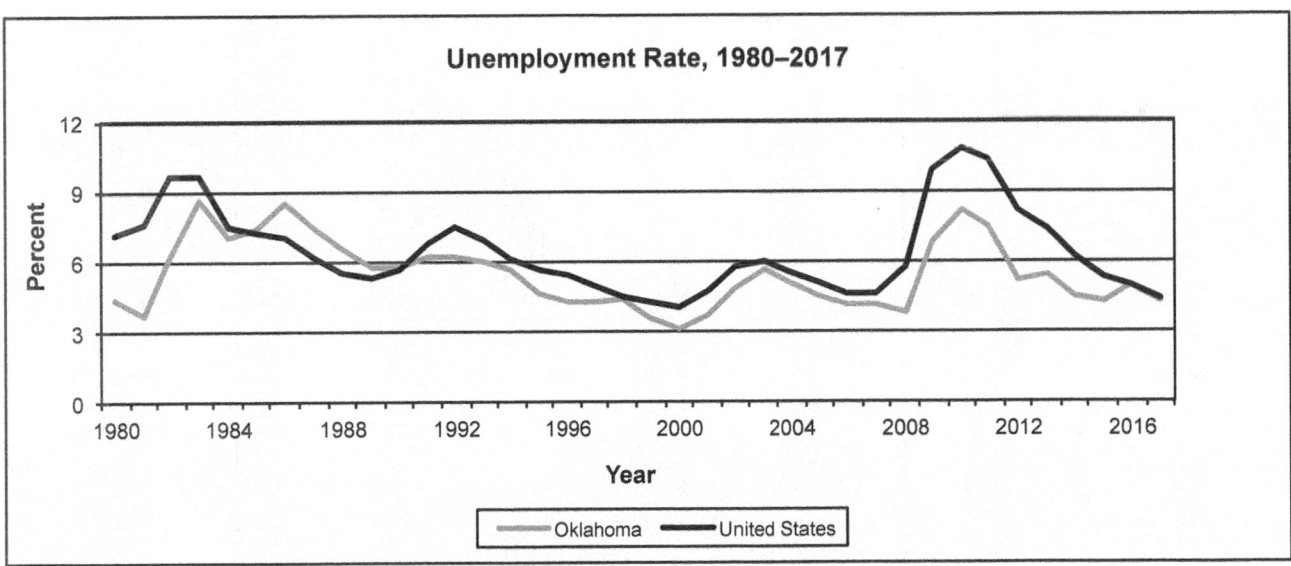

Table OK-8. Employment Status of the Civilian Noninstitutional Population Age 16 Years and Over

(Number, percent.)

Year	Civilian labor force	Civilian participation rate	Employed	Unemployed	Unemployment rate
2009..	1,764,432	63.6	1,652,023	112,409	6.4
2010..	1,768,284	62.4	1,648,138	120,146	6.8
2011..	1,772,666	61.9	1,668,418	104,248	5.9
2012..	1,803,863	62.4	1,709,258	94,605	5.2
2013..	1,802,073	61.8	1,706,861	95,212	5.3
2014..	1,796,183	61.0	1,715,600	80,583	4.5
2015..	1,830,358	61.7	1,749,626	80,732	4.4
2016..	1,829,413	61.3	1,741,277	88,136	4.8
2017..	1,834,312	61.2	1,755,604	78,708	4.3

Table OK-9. Employment and Average Wages by Industry

(Estimates through 2010 are based on the 2007 *North American Industry Classification System* [NAICS]. Estimates from 2011 onward are based on the 2012 NAICS.)

Industry	2010	2011	2012	2013	2014	2015	2016
	Number of jobs						
Wage and Salary Employment by Industry..........................	1,607,228	1,626,838	1,658,230	1,680,348	1,700,578	1,706,632	1,688,523
Farm Wage and Salary Employment...............................	9,486	8,747	10,449	11,413	9,772	5,799	7,400
Nonfarm Wage and Salary Employment..........................	1,597,742	1,618,091	1,647,781	1,668,935	1,690,806	1,700,833	1,681,123
Private wage and salary employment.............................	1,217,262	1,246,015	1,279,703	1,298,410	1,321,362	1,328,050	1,310,232
Forestry, fishing, and related activities........................	4,251	4,130	4,162	4,337	4,456	4,526	4,656
Mining...	43,111	50,919	57,807	59,588	61,330	53,599	43,888
Utilities...	11,230	11,189	11,729	11,722	12,021	12,095	11,495
Construction..	69,905	70,483	72,396	77,103	77,763	79,242	79,514
Manufacturing..	125,135	132,136	137,832	139,057	142,066	139,494	131,306
Durable goods manufacturing.............................	81,854	87,932	94,796	96,168	98,841	96,563	87,879
Nondurable goods manufacturing........................	43,281	44,204	43,036	42,889	43,225	42,931	43,427
Wholesale trade	55,821	58,496	60,705	62,269	63,687	60,479	58,601
Retail trade...	169,991	171,988	174,845	176,309	180,001	184,645	185,160
Transportation and warehousing............................	42,000	43,231	45,200	46,618	47,581	52,040	53,000
Information..	24,994	24,136	22,697	21,846	21,724	21,081	21,142
Finance and insurance...	57,750	57,873	59,163	58,807	59,792	60,195	60,151
Real estate and rental and leasing...........................	22,115	22,073	22,001	22,592	21,092	21,027	20,728
Professional, scientific, and technical services	63,383	65,317	66,561	67,573	68,303	69,801	69,782
Management of companies and enterprises................	15,166	14,927	16,060	16,599	18,681	18,688	18,104
Administrative and waste services..........................	93,387	94,939	96,612	96,290	98,630	98,200	94,314
Educational services	19,777	20,547	21,250	21,444	21,821	21,799	21,952
Health care and social assistance...........................	183,837	184,533	186,385	188,117	188,301	191,980	194,468
Arts, entertainment, and recreation.........................	13,970	14,136	14,464	14,773	15,058	16,171	17,323
Accommodation and food services..........................	125,460	129,416	133,551	137,576	141,583	146,001	148,649
Other services, except public administration..............	75,979	75,546	76,283	75,790	77,472	76,987	75,999
Government and government enterprises....................	380,480	372,076	368,078	370,525	369,444	372,783	370,891
	Dollars						
Average Wages and Salaries by Industry	38,833	40,713	42,320	43,044	44,403	45,045	45,620
Average Farm Wages and Salaries	27,828	33,019	33,722	25,527	33,064	38,063	31,741
Average Nonfarm Wages and Salaries	38,898	40,754	42,374	43,164	44,469	45,069	45,681
Average private wages and salaries...........................	38,759	40,931	42,728	43,653	45,041	45,577	46,055
Forestry, fishing, and related activities......................	22,833	23,246	23,891	24,698	26,261	27,538	34,301
Mining...	85,025	94,953	92,215	94,907	96,641	103,002	107,691
Utilities..	79,827	82,921	92,093	96,384	114,248	99,720	95,240
Construction	41,614	42,402	44,697	46,819	47,947	49,609	50,046
Manufacturing..	47,765	49,511	51,889	53,176	55,125	55,467	56,617
Durable goods manufacturing.............................	49,574	51,569	53,968	55,323	57,283	57,070	58,344
Nondurable goods manufacturing........................	44,345	45,415	47,310	48,361	50,190	51,862	53,124
Wholesale trade	50,360	52,455	54,912	55,682	57,950	59,105	60,332
Retail trade...	25,245	25,930	26,940	27,354	27,856	28,276	28,329
Transportation and warehousing............................	50,314	52,898	54,375	55,574	57,560	56,538	59,393
Information..	47,992	51,793	53,056	55,035	56,452	56,930	55,688
Finance and insurance...	50,313	52,455	55,152	56,767	59,913	60,454	62,977
Real estate and rental and leasing...........................	36,421	39,358	47,054	42,091	42,735	43,188	43,711
Professional, scientific, and technical services	54,206	55,769	59,349	60,962	62,058	62,908	64,766
Management of companies and enterprises................	75,002	96,091	88,111	88,731	81,844	88,672	86,692
Administrative and waste services..........................	30,992	31,745	33,134	33,411	34,596	35,868	37,401
Educational services	29,888	30,105	30,590	31,214	32,267	31,389	30,788
Health care and social assistance...........................	38,644	40,066	41,354	42,016	43,387	45,062	46,108
Arts, entertainment, and recreation.........................	27,834	28,697	31,205	31,308	33,802	35,175	32,545
Accommodation and food services..........................	15,544	15,977	16,707	16,974	17,524	18,021	18,755
Other services, except public administration..............	26,408	27,342	28,447	29,424	30,216	31,409	33,395
Government and government enterprises.....................	39,344	40,163	41,145	41,451	42,422	43,259	44,360

Table OK-10. Employment Characteristics by Family Type

(Number, percent.)

Family type and labor force status	2014		2015		2016	
	Total	Families with own children under 18 years	Total	Families with own children under 18 years	Total	Families with own children under 18 years
All Families...	963,008	418,186	969,588	417,301	961,731	412,764
FAMILY TYPE AND LABOR FORCE STATUS						
Married-Couple Families...	707,265	274,441	713,308	274,692	710,097	275,619
Both husband and wife in labor force.............................	48.7	62.3	48.5	62.7	48.5	63.1
Husband in labor force, wife not in labor force	24.6	30.9	23.9	30.2	24.0	29.6
Wife in labor force, husband not in labor force	8.3	4.5	8.2	4.2	8.0	4.5
Both husband and wife not in labor force.........................	18.4	2.3	18.7	2.3	18.8	2.5
Other Families	255,743	143,745	256,280	142,609	251,634	137,145
Female householder, no husband present........................	71.4	73.9	69.7	71.8	69.8	70.1
In labor force	48.2	58.2	47.6	57.5	46.5	56.2
Not in labor force	23.2	15.7	22.0	14.3	23.3	13.9
Male householder, no wife present................................	28.6	26.1	30.3	28.2	30.2	29.9
In labor force..	22.3	23.2	23.6	25.1	23.2	26.8
Not in labor force	6.3	2.9	6.7	3.1	7.0	3.1

Table OK-11. School Enrollment and Educational Attainment, 2016

(Number, percent.)

Item	State	U.S.
Enrollment		
Total population 3 years and over, enrolled in school	1,004,589	81,572,277
Enrolled in nursery school or preschool (percent)	6.4	6.0
Enrolled in kindergarten (percent)..	5.5	5.0
Enrolled in elementary school, grades 1-8 (percent)..	43.3	40.3
Enrolled in high school, grades 9-12 (percent)...	20.5	21.0
Enrolled in college or graduate school (percent)	24.2	27.7
Attainment		
Total population 25 years and over	2,571,636	218,475,480
Less than ninth grade (percent)...	4.0	5.4
9th to 12th grade, no diploma (percent)	8.2	7.2
High school graduate, including equivalency (percent)	31.2	27.2
Some college, no degree (percent)	23.5	20.6
Associate's degree (percent)...	7.9	8.4
Bachelor's degree (percent)...	16.8	19.3
Graduate or professional degree (percent)...	8.4	11.9
High school graduate or higher (percent)	87.8	87.5
Bachelor's degree or higher (percent)...	25.2	31.3

Table OK-12. Public School Characteristics and Educational Indicators

(Number, percent; data derived from National Center of Education Statistics.)

Item	State	U.S.
Public Schools, 2015–2016 (except where noted)		
Number of school districts...	605	18,328
Number of schools..	1,800	98,456
Number of students...	692,878	50,327,015
Number of teachers...	42,452	3,151,497
Student-teacher ratio	16.3	16.0
Expenditures per student (dollars), 2014-2015...	8,075	11,445
Four-year adjusted cohort graduation rate (ACGR)[1,2]...	81.6	84.1
Students eligible for free or reduced-price lunch (percent), 2014-2015....................................	60.9	51.8
English language learners (percent), Fall 2015..	6.8	9.5
Students age 3 to 21 served under IDEA, part B (percent)...	15.7	13.2

Public Schools by Type	Number	Percent of state public schools
Total number of schools...	1,800	100.0
Regular	1,791	99.5
Special education	4	0.2
Vocational education	0	-
Alternative education...	5	0.3

NOTE: Every school is assigned only one school type based on its instructional emphasis.
[1] ACGR data represents a new method of calculating high-school completion rates and may not be comparable to previous years' data for Averaged Freshmen Graduation Rates (AFGR).
[2] The United States 4-year ACGRs were estimated using both the reported 4-year ACGR data from 49 states and the District of Columbia and using imputed data for Idaho. The estimate for American Indian/Alaska Native students also includes imputed data for Virginia.
- = Zero or rounds to zero.

Table OK-13. Reported Voting and Registration of the Voting-Age Population, November 2016

(Numbers in thousands, percent.)

Item	Total population	Total citizen population	Registered			Voted		
			Total registered	Percent registered (total population)	Percent registered (total citizen population)	Total voted	Percent voted (total population)	Percent voted (total citizen population)
U.S. Total	245,502	224,059	157,596	64.2	70.3	137,537	56.0	61.4
State Total.............................	2,923	2,746	1,861	63.7	67.8	1,555	53.2	56.6
Sex								
Male	1,417	1,330	890	62.8	66.9	735	51.8	55.2
Female	1,507	1,416	971	64.5	68.6	820	54.4	57.9
Race								
White alone.............................	2,289	2,158	1,470	64.2	68.1	1,263	55.2	58.5
White, non-Hispanic alone	2,038	2,029	1,416	69.5	69.8	1,227	60.2	60.5
Black alone..............................	198	178	139	70.2	77.8	102	51.7	57.3
Asian alone	81	56	37	(B)	(B)	28	(B)	(B)
Hispanic (of any race)......................	280	150	68	24.2	45.2	50	17.9	33.4
White alone or in combination	2,380	2,250	1,520	63.9	67.6	1,300	54.6	57.8
Black alone or in combination...........	214	195	149	69.3	76.2	109	50.7	55.8
Asian alone or in combination...........	87	62	40	(B)	(B)	28	(B)	(B)
Age								
18 to 24 years............................	316	303	144	45.8	47.6	102	32.4	33.7
25 to 34 years............................	563	502	324	57.6	64.6	241	42.8	48.0
35 to 44 years............................	504	457	291	57.8	63.8	240	47.5	52.5
45 to 64 years............................	944	892	636	67.4	71.3	553	58.6	62.0
65 years and over	597	593	465	78.0	78.5	419	70.2	70.7

B = Base is less than 75,000 and therefore too small to show the derived measure.

Table OK-14. Crime

(Number, rate per 100,000. Data are derived from the FBI Uniform Crime Reports.)

Item	State			U.S. [1,2,3,4]		
	2015	2016	Percent change	2015	2016	Percent change
TOTAL POPULATION [5]	3,911,338	3,923,561	0.3	321,418,820	323,127,513	0.5
VIOLENT CRIME						
Number..	16,506	17,648	6.9	1,231,566	1,248,185	1.3
Rate..	422.0	449.8	6.6	383.2	386.3	0.8
Murder and Nonnegligent Manslaughter						
Number..	234	245	4.7	15,696	17,250	9.9
Rate	6.0	6.2	3.3	4.9	5.3	8.2
Rape[6]						
Number..	1,849	2,039	10.3	124,047	130,603	5.3
Rate	47.3	52.0	9.9	38.6	40.4	4.7
Robbery						
Number..	3,005	3,162	5.2	327,374	332,198	1.5
Rate	76.8	80.6	4.9	101.9	102.8	0.9
Aggravated Assault						
Number..	11,418	12,202	6.9	764,449	803,007	5.0
Rate	291.9	311.0	6.5	237.8	248.5	4.5
PROPERTY CRIME						
Number..	112,878	117,037	3.7	7,993,631	7,919,035	-0.9
Rate	2,885.9	2,982.9	3.4	2,487.0	2,450.7	-1.5
Burglary						
Number..	28,406	29,103	2.5	1,579,527	1,515,096	-4.1
Rate	726.2	741.7	2.1	491.4	468.9	-4.6
Larceny-Theft						
Number..	74,022	75,779	2.4	5,706,346	5,638,455	-1.2
Rate	1,892.5	1,931.4	2.1	1,775.4	1,745.0	-1.7
Motor Vehicle Theft						
Number..	10,450	12,155	16.3	707,758	765,484	8.2
Rate	267.2	309.8	15.9	220.2	236.9	7.6

NOTE: Although arson data are included in the trend and clearance tables, sufficient data are not available to estimate totals for this offense. Therefore, no arson data are published in this table.
X = Not applicable.
- = Zero or rounds to zero.
[1] The crime figures have been adjusted.
[2] The data collection methodology for the offense of forcible rape used by the Minnesota state Uniform Crime Reporting (UCR) Program (with the exception of Minneapolis and St. Paul, Minnesota) does not comply with national UCR Program guidelines. Consequently, its figures for forcible rape and violent crime (of which forcible rape is a part) are not published in this table.
[3] Includes offenses reported by the Zoological Police and the Metro Transit Police.
[4] Because of changes in the state's reporting practices, figures are not comparable to previous years' data.
[5] Populations are U.S. Census Bureau provisional estimates as of July 1 of each year.
[6] The figures shown for the offense of rape were estimated using the revised Uniform Crime Reporting (UCR) definition of rape.

Table OK-15. State Government Finances, 2016

(Dollar amounts in thousands, percent distribution.)

Item	Dollars	Percent distribution
Total Revenue	22,862,875	100.0
General revenue	20,920,581	91.5
Intergovernmental revenue	7,246,312	31.7
Taxes	8,491,187	37.1
General sales	2,471,242	10.8
Selective sales	1,307,157	5.7
License taxes	1,039,167	4.5
Individual income tax	2,996,870	13.1
Corporate income tax	327,783	1.4
Other taxes	348,968	1.5
Current charges	2,834,877	12.4
Miscellaneous general revenue	2,348,205	10.3
Utility revenue	614,914	2.7
Liquor stores revenue	0	-
Insurance trust revenue [1]	1,327,380	5.8
Total Expenditure	24,950,729	100.0
Intergovernmental expenditure	4,458,922	17.9
Direct expenditure	20,491,807	82.1
Current operation	14,401,509	57.7
Capital outlay	2,267,941	9.1
Insurance benefits and repayments	2,819,735	11.3
Assistance and subsidies	573,921	2.3
Interest on debt	428,701	1.7
Exhibit: Salaries and wages	3,356,066	13.5
Total Expenditure	24,950,729	100.0
General expenditure	21,227,857	85.1
Intergovernmental expenditure	4,458,922	17.9
Direct expenditure	16,768,935	67.2
General expenditure, by function:		
Education	8,488,724	34.0
Public welfare	6,572,413	26.3
Hospitals	208,434	0.8
Health	991,281	4.0
Highways	2,144,220	8.6
Police protection	232,745	0.9
Correction	571,005	2.3
Natural resources	165,643	0.7
Parks and recreation	86,044	0.3
Governmental administration	714,577	2.9
Interest on general debt	345,179	1.4
Other and unallocable	707,592	2.8
Utility expenditure	903,137	4.0
Liquor stores expenditure	0	-
Insurance trust expenditure	2,819,735	11.3
Debt at End of Fiscal Year	8,702,914	X
Cash and Security Holdings	43,180,928	X

X = Not applicable.
- = Zero or rounds to zero.
[1] Within insurance trust revenue, net earnings of state retirement systems is a calculated statistic (the item code in the data file is X08), and thus can be positive or negative. Net earnings is the sum of earnings on investments plus gains on investments minus losses on investments. The change made in 2002 for asset valuation from book to market value in accordance with Statement 34 of the Governmental Accounting Standards Board is reflected in the calculated statistics.

Table OK-16. State Government Tax Collections, 2017

(Dollars in thousands, percent.)

Item	Dollars	Percent distribution
Total Taxes	8,569,402	100.0
Property taxes	X	-
Sales and gross receipts	3,764,895	43.9
General sales and gross receipts	2,465,383	28.8
Selective sales and gross receipts	1,299,512	15.2
Alcoholic beverages	118,260	1.4
Amusements	20,807	0.2
Insurance premiums	304,448	3.6
Motor fuels	473,960	5.5
Pari-mutuels	1,064	-
Public utilities	42,267	0.5
Tobacco products	320,200	3.7
Other selective sales	18,506	0.2
Licenses	1,062,358	12.4
Alcoholic beverages	1,360	-
Amusements	158,766	1.9
Corporations in general	52,963	0.6
Hunting and fishing	20,344	0.2
Motor vehicle	753,639	8.8
Motor vehicle operators	27,304	0.3
Public utilities	4	-
Occupation and business, NEC	47,252	0.6
Other licenses	726	-
Income taxes	3,280,496	38.3
Individual income	3,122,602	36.4
Corporation net income	157,894	1.8
Other taxes	461,653	5.4
Death and gift	177	-
Documentary and stock transfer	19,505	0.2
Severance	441,971	5.2
Taxes, NEC	0	-

X = Not applicable.
- = Zero or rounds to zero.

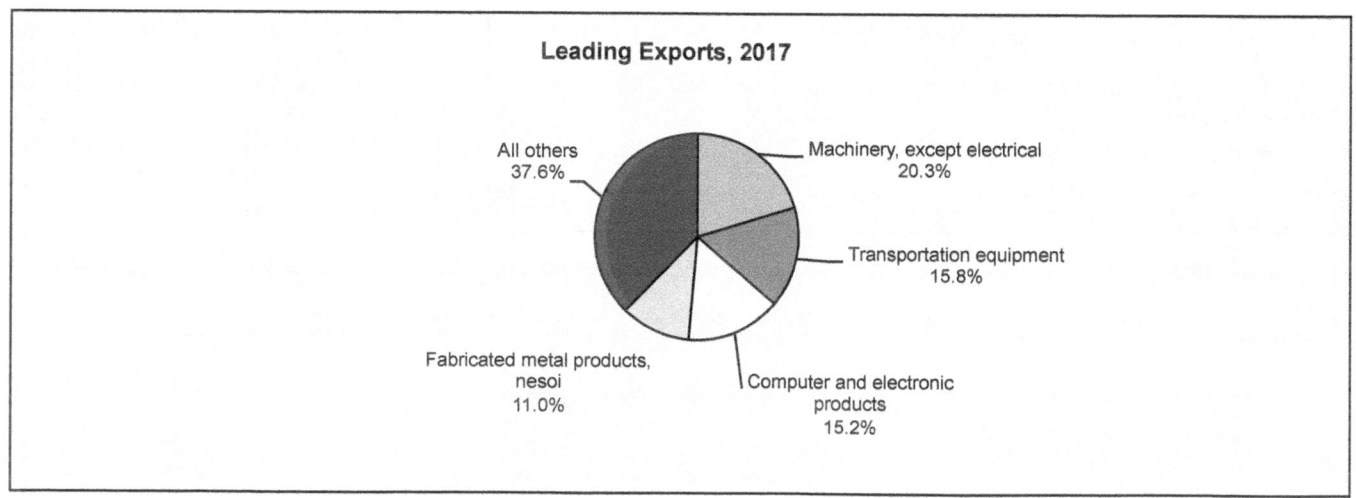

Leading Exports, 2017

All others 37.6%

Machinery, except electrical 20.3%

Transportation equipment 15.8%

Computer and electronic products 15.2%

Fabricated metal products, nesoi 11.0%

OREGON

Facts and Figures

Location: Northwestern United States; bordered on the N by Washington, on the E by Idaho, on the S by Nevada and California, and on the W by the Pacific Ocean

Area: 98,381 sq. mi. (254,805 sq. km.); rank—9th

Population: 4,142,776 (2017 est.); rank—27th

Principal Cities: capital—Salem; largest—Portland

Statehood: February 14, 1859; 33rd state

U.S. Congress: 2 senators, 5 representatives

State Motto: She Flies With Her Own Wings

State Song: "Oregon, My Oregon"

State Nickname: The Beaver State

Abbreviations: OR; Oreg.

State Symbols: flower—Oregon grape; tree—Douglas fir; bird—Western meadowlark

At a Glance

- With an increase in population of 8.0 percent, Oregon ranked 12th among the states in growth from 2010 to 2017.

- In 2016, 6.2 percent of Oregonians did not have health insurance, compared to 8.6 percent of the total U.S. population.

- Oregon's violent crime rate in 2016 was 264.6 per 100,000 population, compared to 386.3 for the entire nation.

- The homeownership rate in Oregon in 2017 was 61.8 percent, compared to the national homeownership rate of 63.9 percent.

- The median household income in Oregon was $57,532 in 2016, and the poverty rate was 13.3 percent.

Table OR-1. Population by Age, Sex, Race, and Hispanic Origin

(Number, percent, except where noted.)

Sex, age, race, and Hispanic origin	2000	2010	2017 [1]	Average annual percent change, 2010–2017
Total Population..	3,421,399	3,831,074	4,142,776	8.1
Percent of total U.S. population	1.2	1.2	1.3	X
Sex				
Male...	1,696,550	1,896,002	2,052,989	8.3
Female	1,724,849	1,935,072	2,089,787	8.0
Age				
Under 5 years...	223,005	237,556	235,968	-0.7
5 to 19 years..	720,999	734,627	736,026	0.2
20 to 64 years..	2,039,218	2,325,358	2,461,965	5.9
65 years and over	438,177	533,533	708,817	32.9
Median age (years)	36.3	38.4	39.3	2.3
Race and Hispanic Origin				
One race				
White..	2,961,623	3,403,252	3,607,515	6.0
Black...	55,662	74,414	90,128	21.1
American Indian and Alaska Native	45,211	66,784	74,655	11.8
Asian...	101,350	145,009	192,917	33.0
Native Hawaiian or Other Pacific Islander	7,976	14,649	18,336	25.2
Two or more races	104,745	126,966	159,225	25.4
Hispanic (of any race)...	275,314	467,030	540,923	15.8

X = Not applicable.
[1] Population figures for 2017 are July 1 estimates. The 2010 estimates are taken from the 2010 Census.

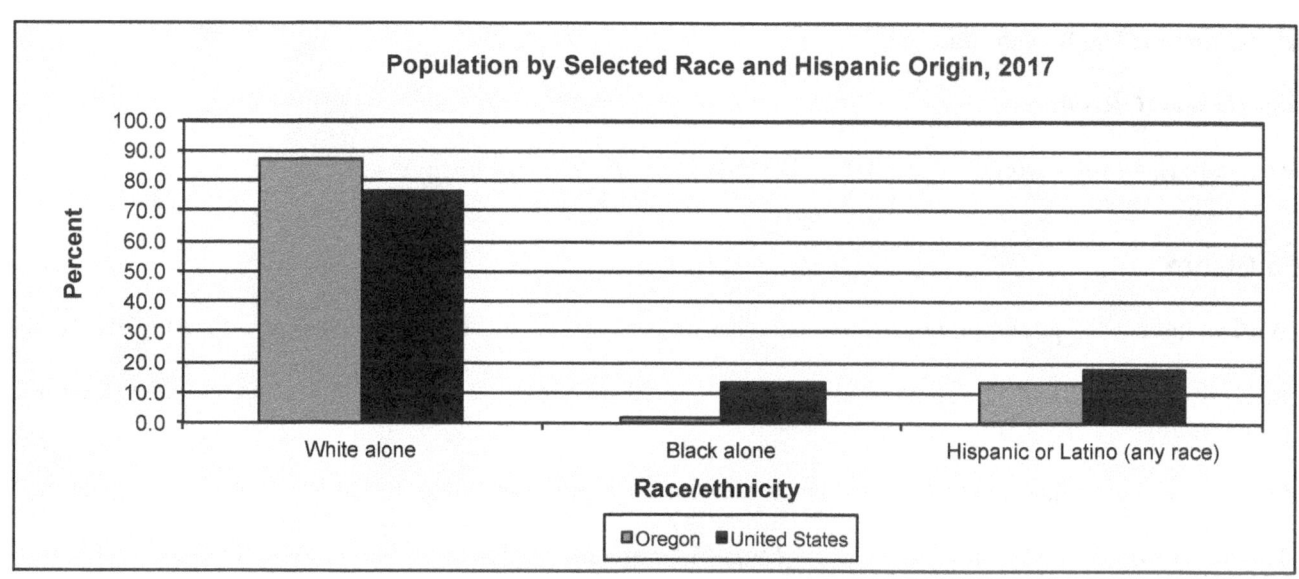

Population by Selected Race and Hispanic Origin, 2017

Table OR-2. Marital Status

(Number, percent distribution.)

Sex, age, and marital status	2000	2010	2016
Males, 15 Years and Over	1,336,805	1,533,177	1,657,986
Never married	28.5	32.6	34.2
Now married, except separated.......................................	57.1	51.4	50.3
Separated..	1.5	1.6	1.3
Widowed..	2.4	2.7	2.5
Divorced..	10.6	11.8	11.7
Females, 15 Years and Over	1,385,329	1,588,428	1,716,741
Never married	21.9	25.8	27.9
Now married, except separated.......................................	53.9	48.9	47.6
Separated..	1.9	1.9	1.8
Widowed..	9.6	8.5	8.3
Divorced..	12.7	14.9	14.4

Table OR-3. Households and Housing Characteristics

(Number, percent, dollars.)

Item	2000	2010	2016	Average annual percent change, 2010–2016
Total Households..	1,333,723	1,507,137	1,571,678	0.7
Family households	877,671	963,362	995,749	0.6
Married-couple family	692,532	733,095	766,154	0.8
Other family	185,139	230,267	229,595	-
Male householder, no wife present............................	54,357	65,972	70,175	1.1
Female householder, no husband present......................	130,782	164,295	159,420	-0.5
Nonfamily households	456,032	543,775	575,929	1.0
Householder living alone	347,624	416,500	430,988	0.6
Householder not living alone	108,428	127,275	144,941	2.3
Housing Characteristics				
Total housing units	1,452,709	1,676,476	1,732,887	0.6
Occupied housing units	1,333,723	1,507,137	1,571,678	0.7
Owner occupied	856,951	942,674	969,579	0.5
Renter occupied	476,772	564,463	602,099	1.1
Average household size...	2.51	2.49	2.55	0.4
Financial Characteristics				
Median gross rent of renter-occupied housing	620	816	1015	4.1
Median monthly owner costs for housing units with a mortgage	1,125	1,577	1,572	-0.1
Median value of owner-occupied housing units.................	152,100	244,500	287,100	2.9

- = Zero or rounds to zero.

Table OR-4. Migration, Origin, and Language

(Number, percent.)

Characteristic	State			U.S.		
	2015	2016	Percent change	2015	2016	Percent change
Residence 1 Year Ago						
Population 1 year and over	3,985,712	4,052,221	1.7	317,635,720	319,361,956	0.5
Same house...	82.2	81.6	X	85.3	85.4	X
Different house in the U.S.	17.2	17.7	X	14.1	13.9	X
Same county...	10.1	10.4	X	8.5	8.3	X
Different county	7.1	7.3	X	5.6	5.6	X
Same state	3.6	3.9	X	3.2	3.2	X
Different state	3.5	3.4	X	2.4	2.4	X
Abroad	0.6	0.7	X	0.7	0.7	X
Place of Birth						
Native born	3,631,684	3,699,248	1.9	278,128,449	279,388,170	0.5
Male	49.6	49.6	X	49.3	49.3	X
Female	50.4	50.4	X	50.7	50.7	X
Foreign born	397,293	394,217	-0.8	43,290,372	43,739,345	1.0
Male	48.3	48.6	X	48.6	48.5	X
Female	51.7	51.4	X	51.4	51.5	X
Foreign born; naturalized U.S. citizen......................	167,977	174,922	4.1	20,697,103	21,238,372	2.6
Male	45.4	45.3	X	45.9	45.9	X
Female	54.6	54.7	X	54.1	54.1	X
Foreign born; not a U.S. citizen............................	229,316	219,295	-4.4	22,593,269	22,500,973	-0.4
Male	50.5	51.2	X	51.1	51.0	X
Female	49.5	48.8	X	48.9	49.0	X
Entered 2010 or later	15.2	18.7	X	15.6	18.6	X
Entered 2000 to 2009.......................................	28.4	25.4	X	27.9	26.7	X
Entered before 2000...	56.4	55.9	X	56.5	54.7	X
World Region of Birth, Foreign						
Foreign-born population, excluding population born at sea	397,244	394,217	-0.8	43,289,646	43,738,901	1.0
Europe	13.8	16.1	X	11.1	10.9	X
Asia...	32.1	32.2	X	30.6	30.8	X
Africa	3.6	3.1	X	4.8	4.9	X
Oceania	2.3	1.8	X	0.6	0.6	X
Latin America...	44.8	42.9	X	51.1	51.0	X
North America...	3.5	4.0	X	1.9	1.8	X
Language Spoken at Home and Ability to Speak English						
Population 5 years and over.................................	3,799,838	3,858,883	1.6	301,625,014	303,328,961	0.6
English only	84.9	84.8	X	78.5	78.4	X
Language other than English.................................	15.1	15.2	X	21.5	21.6	X
Speaks English less than "very well"........................	6.0	5.9	X	8.6	8.6	X

NA = Not available.
X = Not applicable.
- = Zero or rounds to zero.

Table OR-5. Median Income and Poverty Status, 2016

(Number, percent, except as noted.)

Characteristic	State		U.S.	
	Number	Percent	Number	Percent
Median Income				
Households (dollars)..	57,532	X	57,617	X
Families (dollars)	70,929	X	71,062	X
Below Poverty Level (All People)	536,146	13.3	44,268,996	14.0
Sex				
Male	240,288	12.1	19,760,056	12.8
Female	295,858	14.5	24,508,940	15.2
Age				
Under 18 years..	144,361	17.0	14,115,713	19.5
Related children under 18 years.............................	136,951	16.2	13,805,435	19.1
18 to 64 years	340,889	13.7	25,723,818	13.2
65 years and over	50,896	7.5	4,429,465	9.2

X = Not applicable.

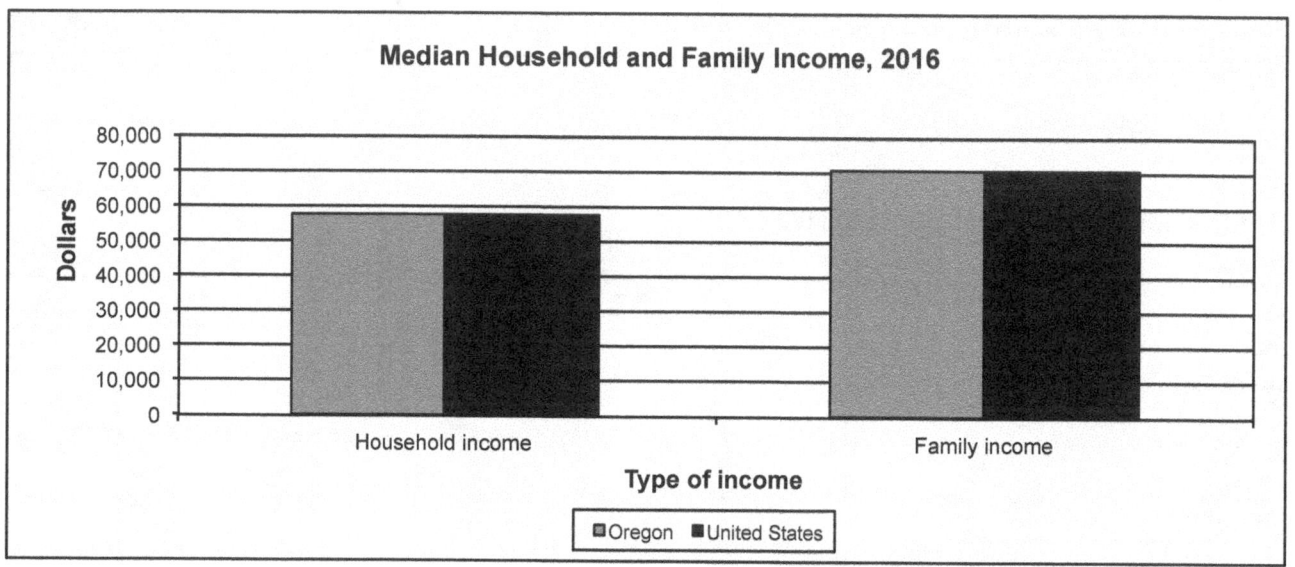

Table OR-6. Health Insurance Coverage Status for the Civilian Noninstitutionalized Population and Children Under 18 Years of Age

(Number, percent.)

Item	2008	2009	2010	2011	2012	2013	2014	2015	2016
Civilian Noninstitutionalized Population	3,746,320	3,779,860	3,799,107	3,832,640	3,860,452	3,893,092	3,931,306	3,991,133	4,054,353
Covered by Private or Public Insurance									
Number..	3,131,758	3,136,858	3,147,603	3,230,263	3,284,443	3,322,210	3,548,645	3,710,870	3,801,587
Percent..	83.6	83.0	82.9	84.3	85.1	85.3	90.3	93.0	93.8
Not Covered									
Number..	614,562	643,002	651,504	602,377	576,009	570,882	382,661	280,263	252,766
Percent..	16.4	17.0	17.1	15.7	14.9	14.7	9.7	7.0	6.2
Percent in the U.S. not covered..............................	15.1	15.1	15.5	15.1	14.8	14.5	11.7	9.4	8.6
Children Under 18 Years of Age	865,115	871,362	865,362	861,059	859,846	858,259	857,084	859,408	866,585
Covered by Private or Public Insurance									
Number..	754,694	780,835	789,611	798,172	805,216	808,087	818,051	828,340	837,985
Percent..	87.2	89.6	91.2	92.7	93.6	94.2	95.4	96.4	96.7
Not Covered									
Number..	110,421	90,527	75,751	62,887	54,630	50,172	39,033	31,068	28,600
Percent..	12.8	10.4	8.8	7.3	6.4	5.8	4.6	3.6	3.3
Percent in the U.S. not covered..............................	9.9	8.6	8.0	7.5	7.2	7.1	6.0	4.8	4.5

Table OR-7. Employment Status by Demographic Group, 2017

(Numbers in thousands, percent.)

Characteristic	Civilian noninstitutional population	Civilian labor force		Employed		Unemployed	
		Number	Percent of population	Number	Percent of population	Number	Percent of population
Total..	3,340	2,123	63.6	2,037	61.0	86	4.1
Sex							
Male..	1,632	1,124	68.8	1,076	65.9	48	4.3
Female...	1,708	999	58.5	961	56.3	38	3.8
Race, Sex, and Hispanic Origin							
White...	2,949	1,865	63.2	1,795	60.9	70	3.8
Male..	1,446	986	68.2	945	65.4	41	4.1
Female...	1,503	878	58.4	849	56.5	29	3.3
Black or African American....................	NA	NA	NA	NA	NA	NA	NA
Male..	NA	NA	NA	NA	NA	NA	NA
Female...	NA	NA	NA	NA	NA	NA	NA
Hispanic or Latino ethnicity[1]...............	386	283	73.3	269	69.9	13	4.7
Male..	201	167	82.7	157	77.9	10	5.8
Female...	184	116	63.0	112	61.0	4	3.2
Age							
16 to 19 years.................................	179	72	40.4	65	36.5	7	9.5
20 to 24 years.................................	262	195	74.4	180	68.8	15	7.6
25 to 34 years.................................	561	465	82.8	451	80.3	14	3.0
35 to 44 years.................................	576	480	83.3	462	80.2	18	3.8
45 to 54 years.................................	514	425	82.7	409	79.6	16	3.7
55 to 64 years.................................	551	357	64.9	347	63.0	10	2.9
65 years and over	698	129	18.5	123	17.7	6	4.7

NOTE: Data in Table 7 are from the Current Population Survey (CPS) and do not match the estimates in Table 8. See notes and definitions for further information.
[1] May be of any race.
NA = Not available.

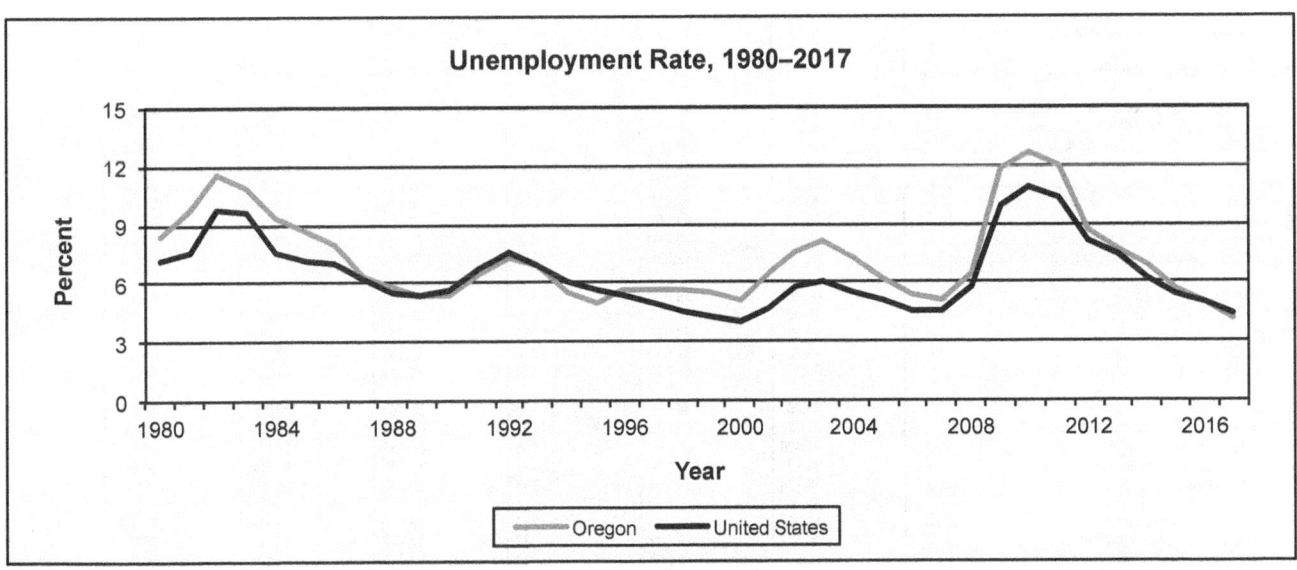

Table OR-8. Employment Status of the Civilian Noninstitutional Population Age 16 Years and Over

(Number, percent.)

Year	Civilian labor force	Civilian participation rate	Employed	Unemployed	Unemployment rate
2009..	1,976,638	65.7	1,753,682	222,956	11.3
2010..	1,984,039	65.4	1,773,076	210,963	10.6
2011..	1,993,889	65.1	1,804,320	189,569	9.5
2012..	1,953,439	63.1	1,780,790	172,649	8.8
2013..	1,910,702	61.2	1,760,302	150,400	7.9
2014..	1,935,884	61.2	1,804,417	131,467	6.8
2015..	1,978,226	61.6	1,867,407	110,819	5.6
2016..	2,049,480	62.6	1,951,218	98,262	4.8
2017..	2,104,078	63.2	2,017,292	86,786	4.1

Table OR-9. Employment and Average Wages by Industry

(Estimates through 2010 are based on the 2007 *North American Industry Classification System* [NAICS]. Estimates from 2011 onward are based on the 2012 NAICS.)

Industry	2010	2011	2012	2013	2014	2015	2016
	Number of Jobs						
Wage and Salary Employment by Industry	1,678,186	1,698,810	1,718,785	1,751,577	1,800,801	1,851,888	1,904,349
Farm Wage and Salary Employment	33,244	34,088	29,669	30,222	29,615	24,153	24,674
Nonfarm Wage and Salary Employment	1,644,942	1,664,722	1,689,116	1,721,355	1,771,186	1,827,735	1,879,675
Private wage and salary employment	1,356,999	1,381,021	1,409,712	1,445,880	1,493,610	1,545,553	1,591,612
Forestry, fishing, and related activities	20,169	20,326	21,221	22,330	22,500	22,772	22,291
Mining	1,575	1,599	1,593	1,527	1,546	1,699	1,749
Utilities	4,547	4,493	4,562	4,497	4,512	4,484	4,567
Construction	68,531	69,440	71,097	75,541	81,513	84,509	91,953
Manufacturing	163,410	167,925	171,659	174,829	179,219	185,647	187,911
Durable goods manufacturing	114,735	118,525	121,560	123,110	125,956	130,098	131,066
Nondurable goods manufacturing	48,675	49,400	50,099	51,719	53,263	55,549	56,845
Wholesale trade	73,300	74,302	75,498	71,665	72,657	73,999	75,658
Retail trade	184,201	185,899	188,350	192,672	197,498	203,587	206,540
Transportation and warehousing	48,087	49,465	50,159	50,989	53,066	55,137	56,813
Information	32,195	32,211	32,685	32,343	32,173	33,134	33,276
Finance and insurance	57,616	58,421	58,520	58,939	59,198	59,485	59,652
Real estate and rental and leasing	24,663	24,003	23,887	24,309	24,792	25,562	26,330
Professional, scientific, and technical services	70,660	74,108	77,335	80,546	84,657	87,934	92,613
Management of companies and enterprises	30,540	30,416	30,471	37,980	40,227	42,953	45,356
Administrative and waste services	81,422	83,914	88,489	91,299	95,420	98,590	101,566
Educational services	42,221	43,183	44,275	44,999	45,408	46,122	46,074
Health care and social assistance	212,055	215,042	218,341	223,046	230,142	240,980	250,674
Arts, entertainment, and recreation	21,848	22,117	21,927	22,651	23,540	24,058	26,094
Accommodation and food services	141,444	144,365	148,991	154,582	160,134	168,228	174,510
Other services, except public administration	78,515	79,792	80,652	81,136	85,408	86,673	87,985
Government and government enterprises	287,943	283,701	279,404	275,475	277,576	282,182	288,063
	Dollars						
Average Wages and Salaries by Industry	42,277	43,571	44,891	45,775	47,230	49,206	52,353
Average Farm Wages and Salaries	25,141	24,770	27,520	30,498	29,986	34,908	38,043
Average Nonfarm Wages and Salaries	42,623	43,956	45,196	46,043	47,519	49,395	52,541
Average private wages and salaries	42,020	43,434	44,770	45,535	47,016	48,966	52,112
Forestry, fishing, and related activities	30,138	31,864	33,363	34,444	36,231	38,353	39,948
Mining	45,495	48,465	48,140	50,623	51,238	53,625	59,419
Utilities	84,344	86,873	88,623	89,596	93,672	96,377	103,895
Construction	48,111	50,056	51,509	52,432	54,132	54,398	61,713
Manufacturing	59,174	61,887	63,860	63,526	65,669	67,414	68,528
Durable goods manufacturing	66,381	70,040	72,368	71,848	74,715	76,489	77,475
Nondurable goods manufacturing	42,186	42,325	43,216	43,716	44,275	46,161	47,898
Wholesale trade	66,361	69,521	71,480	63,131	65,046	67,544	72,185
Retail trade	26,954	27,250	27,842	28,276	29,027	29,881	32,083
Transportation and warehousing	43,339	43,976	44,938	45,252	46,928	47,749	51,873
Information	64,701	67,657	67,715	69,181	72,599	75,434	81,988
Finance and insurance	62,536	63,993	67,420	69,661	71,298	76,185	80,963
Real estate and rental and leasing	33,209	34,232	35,534	36,261	38,235	40,352	45,463
Professional, scientific, and technical services	61,322	63,515	66,357	67,693	70,496	73,742	80,778
Management of companies and enterprises	76,406	80,987	84,350	107,059	112,192	121,880	121,539
Administrative and waste services	30,231	30,706	31,637	32,057	33,338	34,848	36,676
Educational services	23,739	24,354	25,147	25,693	26,072	26,502	27,335
Health care and social assistance	42,884	44,251	45,234	45,945	46,992	49,192	52,142
Arts, entertainment, and recreation	26,152	25,383	28,092	27,225	27,583	28,890	32,060
Accommodation and food services	18,022	18,548	19,324	19,812	20,545	21,571	23,906
Other services, except public administration	28,390	28,815	29,892	30,680	31,273	32,732	34,947
Government and government enterprises	45,465	46,499	47,347	48,710	50,224	51,746	54,911

Table OR-10. Employment Characteristics by Family Type

(Number, percent.)

Family type and labor force status	2014		2015		2016	
	Total	Families with own children under 18 years	Total	Families with own children under 18 years	Total	Families with own children under 18 years
All Families..	960,100	398,763	978,396	396,731	995,749	402,585
FAMILY TYPE AND LABOR FORCE STATUS						
Married-Couple Families......................................	724,465	267,628	749,945	272,127	766,154	278,913
Both husband and wife in labor force...........................	49.1	66.0	48.8	65.6	48.1	64.3
Husband in labor force, wife not in labor force	21.0	27.9	20.0	27.0	21.4	29.0
Wife in labor force, husband not in labor force..............	8.5	4.3	8.2	4.9	8.3	4.6
Both husband and wife not in labor force.....................	21.4	1.8	21.8	1.8	21.2	1.6
Other Families	235,635	131,135	228,451	124,604	229,595	123,672
Female householder, no husband present.....................	69.7	72.0	70.2	73.2	69.4	69.2
In labor force...	48.5	57.8	49.7	61.0	49.7	58.3
Not in labor force..	21.2	14.2	20.5	12.1	19.7	10.9
Male householder, no wife present............................	30.3	28.0	29.8	26.8	30.6	30.8
In labor force...	24.1	25.1	23.5	24.5	25.1	28.2
Not in labor force..	6.3	2.9	6.2	2.4	5.5	2.6

Table OR-11. School Enrollment and Educational Attainment, 2016

(Number, percent.)

Item	State	U.S.
Enrollment		
Total population 3 years and over, enrolled in school	960,446	81,572,277
Enrolled in nursery school or preschool (percent).................................	6.2	6.0
Enrolled in kindergarten (percent)...	5.0	5.0
Enrolled in elementary school, grades 1-8 (percent).............................	39.9	40.3
Enrolled in high school, grades 9-12 (percent)...................................	20.5	21.0
Enrolled in college or graduate school (percent).................................	28.5	27.7
Attainment		
Total population 25 years and over	2,857,952	218,475,480
Less than ninth grade (percent)...	3.7	5.4
9th to 12th grade, no diploma (percent)...	6.0	7.2
High school graduate, including equivalency (percent).........................	22.9	27.2
Some college, no degree (percent)...	26.1	20.6
Associate's degree (percent)..	8.6	8.4
Bachelor's degree (percent)	20.0	19.3
Graduate or professional degree (percent)......................................	12.7	11.9
High school graduate or higher (percent)..	90.3	87.5
Bachelor's degree or higher (percent)..	32.7	31.3

Table OR-12. Public School Characteristics and Educational Indicators

(Number, percent; data derived from National Center of Education Statistics.)

Item	State	U.S.
Public Schools, 2015–2016 (except where noted)		
Number of school districts...	221	18,328
Number of schools..	1,242	98,456
Number of students...	576,407	50,327,015
Number of teachers...	29,086	3,151,497
Student-teacher ratio	19.8	16.0
Expenditures per student (dollars), 2014-2015..................................	10,457	11,445
Four-year adjusted cohort graduation rate (ACGR)[1,2]	74.8	84.1
Students eligible for free or reduced-price lunch (percent), 2014-2015........	52.9	51.8
English language learners (percent), Fall 2015...................................	9.2	9.5
Students age 3 to 21 served under IDEA, part B (percent).......................	13.9	13.2

Public Schools by Type	Number	Percent of state public schools
Total number of schools...	1,242	100.0
Regular	1,209	97.3
Special education...	1	0.1
Vocational education..	0	-
Alternative education..	32	2.6

NOTE: Every school is assigned only one school type based on its instructional emphasis.
[1] ACGR data represents a new method of calculating high-school completion rates and may not be comparable to previous years' data for Averaged Freshmen Graduation Rates (AFGR).
[2] The United States 4-year ACGRs were estimated using both the reported 4-year ACGR data from 49 states and the District of Columbia and using imputed data for Idaho. The estimate for American Indian/Alaska Native students also includes imputed data for Virginia.
- = Zero or rounds to zero.

Table OR-13. Reported Voting and Registration of the Voting-Age Population, November 2016

(Numbers in thousands, percent.)

			Registered			Voted		
Item	Total population	Total citizen population	Total registered	Percent registered (total population)	Percent registered (total citizen population)	Total voted	Percent voted (total population)	Percent voted (total citizen population)
U.S. Total	245,502	224,059	157,596	64.2	70.3	137,537	56.0	61.4
State Total................................	3,185	2,929	2,147	67.4	73.3	1,942	61.0	66.3
Sex								
Male	1,567	1,431	1,052	67.1	73.5	952	60.7	66.5
Female	1,618	1,497	1,095	67.7	73.2	990	61.2	66.1
Race								
White alone..............................	2,808	2,644	1,961	69.9	74.2	1,790	63.7	67.7
White, non-Hispanic alone............	2,466	2,448	1,836	74.4	75.0	1,684	68.3	68.8
Black alone..............................	57	41	28	(B)	(B)	23	(B)	(B)
Asian alone..............................	145	92	53	(B)	(B)	47	(B)	(B)
Hispanic (of any race).................	371	223	142	38.3	63.8	122	32.9	54.9
White alone or in combination	2,907	2,737	2,030	69.8	74.2	1,850	63.6	67.6
Black alone or in combination...........	82	65	44	(B)	(B)	37	(B)	(B)
Asian alone or in combination...........	172	116	77	44.8	66.4	66	38.3	56.7
Age								
18 to 24 years...........................	345	320	202	58.3	63.0	156	45.2	48.8
25 to 34 years...........................	577	504	341	59.1	67.8	275	47.6	54.6
35 to 44 years...........................	521	442	344	66.2	77.9	320	61.4	72.3
45 to 64 years...........................	1,044	977	724	69.3	74.0	679	65.1	69.5
65 years and over	698	685	536	76.9	78.2	512	73.4	74.7

B = Base is less than 75,000 and therefore too small to show the derived measure.

Table OR-14. Crime

(Number, rate per 100,000. Data are derived from the FBI Uniform Crime Reports.)

	State			U.S. [1,2,3,4]		
Item	2015	2016	Percent change	2015	2016	Percent change
TOTAL POPULATION [5]	4,028,977	4,093,465	1.6	321,418,820	323,127,513	0.5
VIOLENT CRIME						
Number...	10,468	10,830	3.5	1,231,566	1,248,185	1.3
Rate	259.8	264.6	1.8	383.2	386.3	0.8
Murder and Nonnegligent Manslaughter						
Number...	99	113	14.1	15,696	17,250	9.9
Rate	2.5	2.8	12.0	4.9	5.3	8.2
Rape[6]						
Number...	1,593	1,721	8.0	124,047	130,603	5.3
Rate	39.5	42.0	6.3	38.6	40.4	4.7
Robbery						
Number...	2,146	2,278	6.2	327,374	332,198	1.5
Rate	53.3	55.6	4.3	101.9	102.8	0.9
Aggravated Assault						
Number...	6,630	6,718	1.3	764,449	803,007	5.0
Rate	164.6	164.1	-0.3	237.8	248.5	4.5
PROPERTY CRIME						
Number...	118,719	121,345	2.2	7,993,631	7,919,035	-0.9
Rate	2,946.6	2,964.4	0.6	2,487.0	2,450.7	-1.5
Burglary						
Number...	18,336	16,866	-8.0	1,579,527	1,515,096	-4.1
Rate	455.1	412.0	-9.5	491.4	468.9	-4.6
Larceny-Theft						
Number...	89,836	91,286	1.6	5,706,346	5,638,455	-1.2
Rate	2,229.7	2,230.0	-	1,775.4	1,745.0	-1.7
Motor Vehicle Theft						
Number...	10,547	13,193	25.1	707,758	765,484	8.2
Rate	261.8	322.3	23.1	220.2	236.9	7.6

NOTE: Although arson data are included in the trend and clearance tables, sufficient data are not available to estimate totals for this offense. Therefore, no arson data are published in this table.
X = Not applicable.
- = Zero or rounds to zero.
[1] The crime figures have been adjusted.
[2] The data collection methodology for the offense of forcible rape used by the Minnesota state Uniform Crime Reporting (UCR) Program (with the exception of Minneapolis and St. Paul, Minnesota) does not comply with national UCR Program guidelines. Consequently, its figures for forcible rape and violent crime (of which forcible rape is a part) are not published in this table.
[3] Includes offenses reported by the Zoological Police and the Metro Transit Police.
[4] Because of changes in the state's reporting practices, figures are not comparable to previous years' data.
[5] Populations are U.S. Census Bureau provisional estimates as of July 1 of each year.
[6] The figures shown for the offense of rape were estimated using the revised Uniform Crime Reporting (UCR) definition of rape.

Table OR-15. State Government Finances, 2016

(Dollar amounts in thousands, percent distribution.)

Item	Dollars	Percent distribution
Total Revenue	32,781,473	100.0
General revenue	28,126,200	85.8
Intergovernmental revenue	10,044,740	30.6
Taxes	11,043,311	33.7
General sales	0	-
Selective sales	1,532,190	4.7
License taxes	1,048,709	3.2
Individual income tax	7,690,019	23.5
Corporate income tax	609,868	1.9
Other taxes	162,525	0.5
Current charges	4,643,902	14.2
Miscellaneous general revenue	2,394,247	7.3
Utility revenue	354	-
Liquor stores revenue	568,119	1.7
Insurance trust revenue [1]	4,086,800	12.5
Total Expenditure	34,331,929	100.0
Intergovernmental expenditure	5,561,470	16.2
Direct expenditure	28,770,459	83.8
Current operation	20,956,964	61.0
Capital outlay	1,408,726	4.1
Insurance benefits and repayments	5,392,924	15.7
Assistance and subsidies	550,349	1.6
Interest on debt	461,496	1.3
Exhibit: Salaries and wages	4,233,401	12.3
Total Expenditure	34,331,929	100.0
General expenditure	28,538,469	83.1
Intergovernmental expenditure	5,561,470	16.2
Direct expenditure	22,976,999	66.9
General expenditure, by function:		
Education	9,254,758	27.0
Public welfare	10,390,994	30.3
Hospitals	2,416,126	7.0
Health	626,975	1.8
Highways	1,170,688	3.4
Police protection	201,730	0.6
Correction	854,026	2.5
Natural resources	593,040	1.7
Parks and recreation	78,886	0.2
Governmental administration	1,486,033	4.3
Interest on general debt	461,496	1.3
Other and unallocable	1,003,717	2.9
Utility expenditure	31,676	0.1
Liquor stores expenditure	368,860	1.1
Insurance trust expenditure	5,392,924	15.7
Debt at End of Fiscal Year	13,355,878	X
Cash and Security Holdings	83,469,891	X

X = Not applicable.
- = Zero or rounds to zero.
[1] Within insurance trust revenue, net earnings of state retirement systems is a calculated statistic (the item code in the data file is X08), and thus can be positive or negative. Net earnings is the sum of earnings on investments plus gains on investments minus losses on investments. The change made in 2002 for asset valuation from book to market value in accordance with Statement 34 of the Governmental Accounting Standards Board is reflected in the calculated statistics.

Table OR-16. State Government Tax Collections, 2017

(Dollars in thousands, percent.)

Item	Dollars	Percent distribution
Total Taxes	11,914,567	100.0
Property taxes	20,065	0.2
Sales and gross receipts	1,598,677	13.4
General sales and gross receipts	X	-
Selective sales and gross receipts	1,598,677	13.4
Alcoholic beverages	18,796	0.2
Amusements	X	-
Insurance premiums	68,481	0.6
Motor fuels	529,658	4.4
Pari-mutuels	1,928	-
Public utilities	113,022	0.9
Tobacco products	247,406	2.1
Other selective sales	619,386	5.2
Licenses	1,067,836	9.0
Alcoholic beverages	4,706	-
Amusements	2,858	-
Corporations in general	37,421	0.3
Hunting and fishing	55,759	0.5
Motor vehicle	539,474	4.5
Motor vehicle operators	38,851	0.3
Public utilities	14,577	0.1
Occupation and business, NEC	367,539	3.1
Other licenses	6,651	0.1
Income taxes	9,012,271	75.6
Individual income	8,379,225	70.3
Corporation net income	633,046	5.3
Other taxes	215,718	1.8
Death and gift	198,363	1.7
Documentary and stock transfer	2,062	-
Severance	15,293	0.1
Taxes, NEC	0	-

X = Not applicable.
- = Zero or rounds to zero.

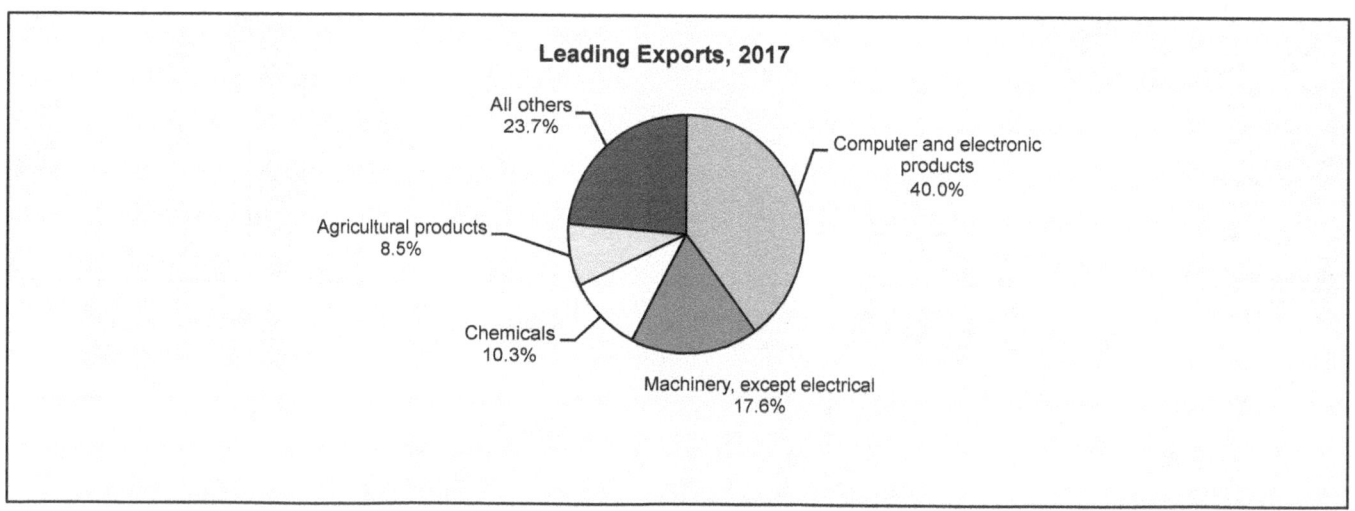

Leading Exports, 2017

All others 23.7%
Computer and electronic products 40.0%
Agricultural products 8.5%
Chemicals 10.3%
Machinery, except electrical 17.6%

PENNSYLVANIA

Facts and Figures

Location: Northeastern United States; bordered on the N by Lake Erie and New York, on the E by New York and New Jersey, on the S by Delaware, Maryland, and West Virginia, and on the W by West Virginia and Ohio

Area: 46,055 sq. mi. (119,283 sq. km.); rank—33rd

Population: 12,805,537 (2017 est.); rank—5th

Principal Cities: capital—Harrisburg; largest—Philadelphia

Statehood: December 12, 1787; 2nd state

U.S. Congress: 2 senators, 18 representatives

State Motto: Virtue, Liberty, and Independence

State Song: "Pennsylvania"

State Nicknames: The Keystone State; The Quaker State

Abbreviations: PA; Penn.

State Symbols: flower—mountain laurel; tree—Eastern hemlock; bird—ruffed grouse

At a Glance

- With an increase in population of 0.7 percent, Pennsylvania ranked 44th among the states in growth from 2010 to 2017.

- Pennsylvania's median household income in 2016 was $56,907, and 12.9 percent of the population lived below the poverty level.

- Approximately 5.6 percent of Pennsylvanians did not have health insurance in 2016, compared to the national rate of 8.6 percent.

- Pennsylvania's violent crime rate in 2016 was 316.4 per 100,000 population, compared to 386.3 for the entire nation.

- The unemployment rate in Pennsylvania was 4.9 percent in 2017, compared to the national unemployment rate of 4.4 percent.

Table PA-1. Population by Age, Sex, Race, and Hispanic Origin

(Number, percent, except where noted.)

Sex, age, race, and Hispanic origin	2000	2010	2017 [1]	Average annual percent change, 2010–2017
Total Population...	12,281,054	12,702,379	12,805,537	0.8
Percent of total U.S. population	4.4	4.1	3.9	X
Sex				
Male...	5,929,663	6,190,363	6,271,329	1.3
Female..	6,351,391	6,512,016	6,534,208	0.3
Age				
Under 5 years...	727,804	729,538	708,829	-2.8
5 to 19 years..	2,542,780	2,449,852	2,300,461	-6.1
20 to 64 years..	7,091,305	7,563,682	7,516,560	-0.6
65 years and over	1,919,165	1,959,307	2,279,687	16.4
Median age (years)	38.0	40.1	40.7	1.5
Race and Hispanic Origin				
One race				
White...	10,484,203	10,663,774	10,507,780	-1.5
Black...	1,224,612	1,431,826	1,520,035	6.2
American Indian and Alaska Native	18,348	39,735	47,983	20.8
Asian...	219,813	358,195	462,768	29.2
Native Hawaiian or Other Pacific Islander	3,417	7,115	9,606	35.0
Two or more races	142,224	201,734	257,365	27.6
Hispanic (of any race)...	394,088	758,058	940,635	24.1

X = Not applicable.
[1] Population figures for 2017 are July 1 estimates. The 2010 estimates are taken from the 2010 Census.
- = Zero or rounds to zero.

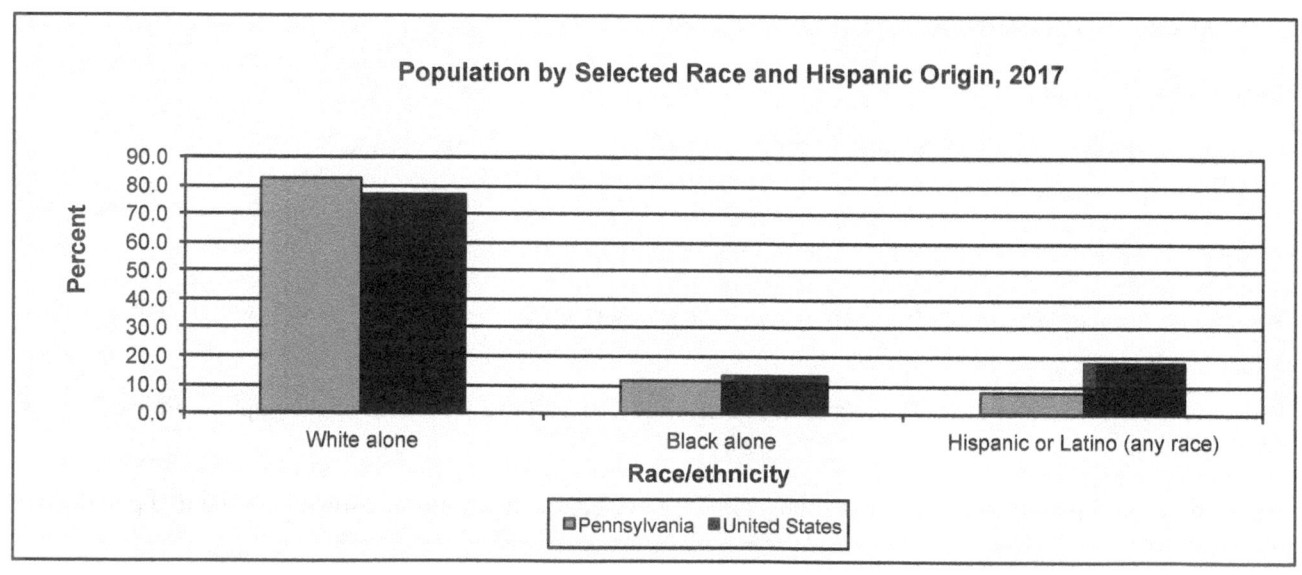

Population by Selected Race and Hispanic Origin, 2017

Table PA-2. Marital Status

(Number, percent distribution.)

Sex, age, and marital status	2000	2010	2016
Males, 15 Years and Over	4,686,277	5,031,761	5,138,564
Never married	30.1	35.9	37.3
Now married, except separated..	57.4	50.6	48.9
Separated..	1.9	2.0	1.8
Widowed..	3.3	3.1	3.1
Divorced..	7.3	8.5	8.9
Females, 15 Years and Over	5,175,436	5,406,494	5,447,040
Never married	24.6	29.8	31.3
Now married, except separated..	51.5	46.2	45.5
Separated..	2.4	2.7	2.3
Widowed..	12.7	11.2	10.2
Divorced..	8.8	10.2	10.8

Table PA-3. Households and Housing Characteristics

(Number, percent, dollars.)

Item	2000	2010	2016	Average annual percent change, 2010–2016
Total Households..	4,777,003	4,936,030	4,937,771	-
Family households	3,208,388	3,197,710	3,150,563	-0.2
Married-couple family	2,467,673	2,381,094	2,341,561	-0.3
Other family	740,715	816,616	809,002	-0.2
Male householder, no wife present..........	186,022	215,082	229,169	1.1
Female householder, no husband present....	554,693	601,534	579,833	-0.6
Nonfamily households	1,568,615	1,738,320	1,787,208	0.5
Householder living alone...........................	1,320,941	1,458,055	1,479,891	0.2
Householder not living alone.....................	247,674	280,265	307,317	1.6
Housing Characteristics				
Total housing units.....................................	5,249,750	5,568,820	5,611,995	0.1
Occupied housing units	4,777,003	4,936,030	4,937,771	-
Owner occupied	3,406,337	3,461,678	3,382,514	-0.4
Renter occupied	1,370,666	1,474,352	1,555,257	0.9
Average household size................................	2.48	2.49	2.50	0.1
Financial Characteristics				
Median gross rent of renter-occupied housing	531	763	881	2.6
Median monthly owner costs for housing units with a mortgage	1,010	1,390	1,416	0.3
Median value of owner-occupied housing units....	97,000	165,500	174,100	0.9

- = Zero or rounds to zero

Table PA-4. Migration, Origin, and Language

(Number, percent.)

Characteristic	State			U.S.		
	2015	2016	Percent change	2015	2016	Percent change
Residence 1 Year Ago						
Population 1 year and over	12,662,192	12,645,493	-0.1	317,635,720	319,361,956	0.5
Same house	87.7	87.1	X	85.3	85.4	X
Different house in the U.S.	11.8	12.3	X	14.1	13.9	X
Same county	7.3	7.6	X	8.5	8.3	X
Different county	4.5	4.8	X	5.6	5.6	X
Same state	2.6	2.8	X	3.2	3.2	X
Different state	1.8	2.0	X	2.4	2.4	X
Abroad	0.5	0.5	X	0.7	0.7	X
Place of Birth						
Native born	11,965,344	11,913,314	-0.4	278,128,449	279,388,170	0.5
Male	49.0	49.0	X	49.3	49.3	X
Female	51.0	51.0	X	50.7	50.7	X
Foreign born	837,159	870,913	4.0	43,290,372	43,739,345	1.0
Male	48.0	48.7	X	48.6	48.5	X
Female	52.0	51.3	X	51.4	51.5	X
Foreign born; naturalized U.S. citizen...........	440,198	454,730	3.3	20,697,103	21,238,372	2.6
Male	45.9	46.9	X	45.9	45.9	X
Female	54.1	53.1	X	54.1	54.1	X
Foreign born; not a U.S. citizen..................	396,961	416,183	4.8	22,593,269	22,500,973	-0.4
Male	50.4	50.8	X	51.1	51.0	X
Female	49.6	49.2	X	48.9	49.0	X
Entered 2010 or later	21.8	24.5	X	15.6	18.6	X
Entered 2000 to 2009	28.8	28.9	X	27.9	26.7	X
Entered before 2000....................................	49.4	46.6	X	56.5	54.7	X
World Region of Birth, Foreign						
Foreign-born population, excluding population born at sea	837,159	870,913	4.0	43,289,646	43,738,901	1.0
Europe	20.9	19.0	X	11.1	10.9	X
Asia..	40.2	38.7	X	30.6	30.8	X
Africa	7.9	9.3	X	4.8	4.9	X
Oceania	0.3	0.3	X	0.6	0.6	X
Latin America..	28.7	30.8	X	51.1	51.0	X
North America	1.9	2.0	X	1.9	1.8	X
Language Spoken at Home and Ability to Speak English						
Population 5 years and over..........................	12,087,611	12,074,484	-0.1	301,625,014	303,328,961	0.6
English only	89.1	88.7	X	78.5	78.4	X
Language other than English.......................	10.9	11.3	X	21.5	21.6	X
Speaks English less than "very well"...........	4.1	4.3	X	8.6	8.6	X

NA = Not available.
X = Not applicable.
- = Zero or rounds to zero.

Table PA-5. Median Income and Poverty Status, 2016

(Number, percent, except as noted.)

Characteristic	State Number	State Percent	U.S. Number	U.S. Percent
Median Income				
Households (dollars)...	56,907	X	57,617	X
Families (dollars)	72,313	X	71,062	X
Below Poverty Level (All People)	1,592,045	12.9	44,268,996	14.0
Sex				
Male	703,375	11.7	19,760,056	12.8
Female	888,670	14.0	24,508,940	15.2
Age				
Under 18 years...	486,029	18.5	14,115,713	19.5
Related children under 18 years.................................	473,068	18.1	13,805,435	19.1
18 to 64 years..	938,136	12.3	25,723,818	13.2
65 years and over	167,880	7.8	4,429,465	9.2

X = Not applicable.

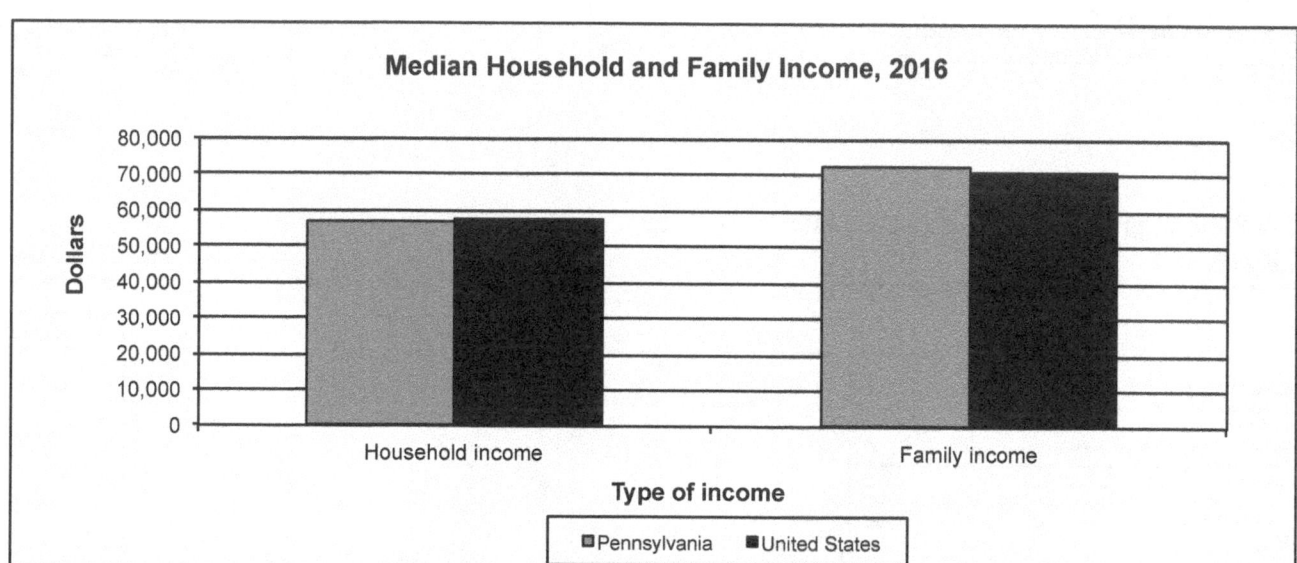

Table PA-6. Health Insurance Coverage Status for the Civilian Noninstitutionalized Population and Children Under 18 Years of Age

(Number, percent.)

Item	2008	2009	2010	2011	2012	2013	2014	2015	2016
Civilian Noninstitutionalized Population	12,209,227	12,365,826	12,506,000	12,539,757	12,559,315	12,569,375	12,582,815	12,599,417	12,579,422
Covered by Private or Public Insurance									
Number..	11,057,616	11,145,510	11,234,820	11,275,209	11,334,666	11,346,970	11,518,238	11,797,490	11,870,945
Percent...	90.6	90.1	89.8	89.9	90.2	90.3	91.5	93.6	94.4
Not Covered									
Number..	1,151,611	1,220,316	1,271,180	1,264,548	1,224,649	1,222,405	1,064,577	801,927	708,477
Percent...	9.4	9.9	10.2	10.1	9.8	9.7	8.5	6.4	5.6
Percent in the U.S. not covered..................................	15.1	15.1	15.5	15.1	14.8	14.5	11.7	9.4	8.6
Children Under 18 Years of Age	2,757,063	2,765,748	2,778,233	2,754,741	2,730,989	2,708,843	2,693,074	2,685,304	2,666,701
Covered by Private or Public Insurance									
Number..	2,588,412	2,618,320	2,634,049	2,605,514	2,592,035	2,561,540	2,553,957	2,573,940	2,550,327
Percent...	93.9	94.7	94.8	94.6	94.9	94.6	94.8	95.9	95.6
Not Covered									
Number..	168,651	147,428	144,184	149,227	138,954	147,303	139,117	111,364	116,374
Percent...	6.1	5.3	5.2	5.4	5.1	5.4	5.2	4.1	4.4
Percent in the U.S. not covered..................................	9.9	8.6	8.0	7.5	7.2	7.1	6.0	4.8	4.5

Table PA-7. Employment Status by Demographic Group, 2017

(Numbers in thousands, percent.)

Characteristic	Civilian noninstitutional population	Civilian labor force		Employed		Unemployed	
		Number	Percent of population	Number	Percent of population	Number	Percent of population
Total..	10,255	6,396	62.4	6,088	59.4	308	4.8
Sex							
Male...	4,937	3,359	68.0	3,184	64.5	175	5.2
Female..	5,318	3,037	57.1	2,905	54.6	133	4.4
Race, Sex, and Hispanic Origin							
White..	8,598	5,373	62.5	5,141	59.8	232	4.3
Male...	4,173	2,871	68.8	2,741	65.7	130	4.5
Female..	4,426	2,503	56.5	2,400	54.2	103	4.1
Black or African American...............	1,104	669	60.5	612	55.5	56	8.4
Male...	501	310	61.8	278	55.4	32	10.4
Female..	603	359	59.5	335	55.5	24	6.7
Hispanic or Latino ethnicity[1].........	647	404	62.4	375	58.1	28	7.0
Male...	330	231	70.0	216	65.3	15	6.6
Female..	316	173	54.6	160	50.5	13	7.6
Age							
16 to 19 years.................................	660	267	40.4	227	34.3	40	15.1
20 to 24 years.................................	783	588	75.2	551	70.4	38	6.4
25 to 34 years.................................	1,643	1,365	83.1	1,292	78.6	73	5.4
35 to 44 years.................................	1,472	1,214	82.5	1,169	79.4	46	3.8
45 to 54 years.................................	1,583	1,309	82.7	1,260	79.6	49	3.7
55 to 64 years.................................	1,862	1,218	65.4	1,176	63.1	42	3.4
65 years and over............................	2,252	434	19.3	414	18.4	20	4.6

NOTE: Data in Table 7 are from the Current Population Survey (CPS) and do not match the estimates in Table 8. See notes and definitions for further information.
[1] May be of any race.

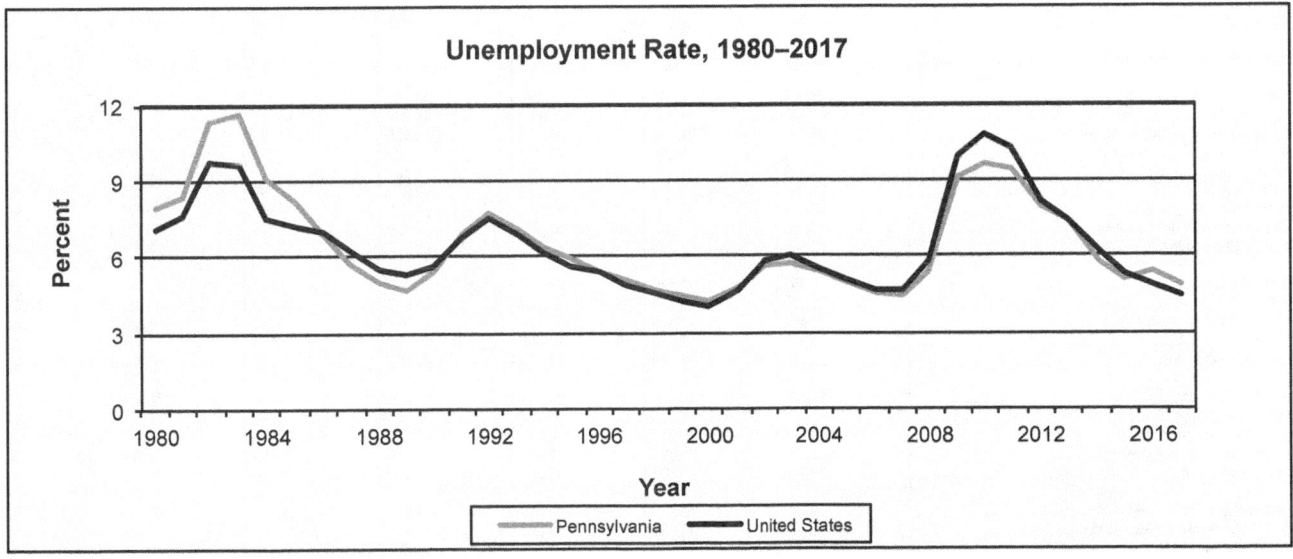

Table PA-8. Employment Status of the Civilian Noninstitutional Population Age 16 Years and Over

(Number, percent.)

Year	Civilian labor force	Civilian participation rate	Employed	Unemployed	Unemployment rate
2009..	6,400,263	64.4	5,885,351	514,912	8.0
2010..	6,380,949	63.5	5,840,887	540,062	8.5
2011..	6,395,506	63.2	5,888,745	506,761	7.9
2012..	6,462,939	63.6	5,957,314	505,625	7.8
2013..	6,442,411	63.3	5,967,811	474,600	7.4
2014..	6,396,041	62.7	6,021,005	375,036	5.9
2015..	6,420,702	62.8	6,080,219	340,483	5.3
2016..	6,452,812	63.0	6,105,223	347,589	5.4
2017..	6,427,370	62.6	6,111,633	315,737	4.9

Table PA-9. Employment and Average Wages by Industry

(Estimates through 2010 are based on the 2007 *North American Industry Classification System* [NAICS]. Estimates from 2011 onward are based on the 2012 NAICS.)

Industry	2010	2011	2012	2013	2014	2015	2016
	Number of jobs						
Wage and Salary Employment by Industry	5,800,496	5,861,034	5,912,279	5,937,016	5,991,194	6,038,056	6,088,293
Farm Wage and Salary Employment	18,550	18,537	24,201	22,349	21,096	23,224	28,026
Nonfarm Wage and Salary Employment	5,781,946	5,842,497	5,888,078	5,914,667	5,970,098	6,014,832	6,060,267
Private wage and salary employment	4,957,801	5,036,964	5,100,434	5,125,629	5,188,236	5,240,294	5,286,837
Forestry, fishing, and related activities	7,731	7,593	7,718	8,022	8,049	7,737	7,936
Mining	25,848	32,342	35,920	34,990	36,722	32,894	24,190
Utilities	21,783	22,294	22,301	22,007	21,466	24,202	23,957
Construction	223,895	229,814	232,554	232,295	237,517	241,267	245,656
Manufacturing	561,041	565,728	567,803	564,204	567,899	568,236	559,403
Durable goods manufacturing	334,786	342,332	347,894	346,367	346,525	346,274	335,866
Nondurable goods manufacturing	226,255	223,396	219,909	217,837	221,374	221,962	223,537
Wholesale trade	224,861	228,920	228,862	226,516	227,084	225,649	220,614
Retail trade	631,232	635,275	639,409	637,557	638,390	638,251	638,270
Transportation and warehousing	210,572	218,061	220,940	224,443	231,189	242,232	251,849
Information	93,215	91,430	90,627	88,568	85,317	85,049	84,569
Finance and insurance	260,349	260,840	262,121	263,489	266,878	266,132	265,380
Real estate and rental and leasing	60,369	59,870	59,878	60,325	62,196	63,397	64,056
Professional, scientific, and technical services	305,774	311,117	319,572	327,022	331,404	338,124	351,136
Management of companies and enterprises	117,434	123,139	129,662	133,362	132,894	132,422	135,013
Administrative and waste services	270,583	286,042	288,106	294,257	301,232	311,407	313,616
Educational services	239,701	243,178	244,157	245,178	248,859	251,020	255,487
Health care and social assistance	907,448	916,185	930,944	937,060	953,348	965,556	986,981
Arts, entertainment, and recreation	90,711	93,278	94,475	93,138	92,680	93,657	96,880
Accommodation and food services	414,217	420,749	432,263	442,671	448,410	455,095	464,939
Other services, except public administration	291,037	291,109	293,122	290,525	296,702	297,967	296,905
Government and government enterprises	824,145	805,533	787,644	789,038	781,862	774,538	773,430
	Dollars						
Average Wages and Salaries by Industry	44,793	46,072	47,382	48,057	49,486	51,044	52,695
Average Farm Wages and Salaries	25,883	22,671	23,208	25,613	27,360	24,232	22,137
Average Nonfarm Wages and Salaries	44,854	46,147	47,481	48,142	49,565	51,148	52,837
Average private wages and salaries	44,787	46,161	47,650	48,301	49,777	51,313	53,046
Forestry, fishing, and related activities	25,568	26,147	27,188	28,128	29,170	30,613	32,874
Mining	68,015	72,605	75,476	77,784	83,030	81,285	87,385
Utilities	94,538	100,369	101,831	103,329	109,284	109,586	111,060
Construction	53,064	54,644	56,072	56,824	58,769	60,146	65,822
Manufacturing	53,641	55,206	56,368	56,679	58,555	59,552	60,868
Durable goods manufacturing	54,110	56,157	56,861	57,304	59,341	60,112	61,443
Nondurable goods manufacturing	52,947	53,748	55,588	55,685	57,324	58,679	60,004
Wholesale trade	65,507	68,674	70,815	72,479	76,274	77,307	78,637
Retail trade	25,000	25,322	25,693	25,799	26,246	27,315	27,807
Transportation and warehousing	40,491	41,478	42,324	42,923	44,451	45,687	48,244
Information	63,458	65,693	67,456	69,093	70,688	73,620	75,471
Finance and insurance	72,026	74,969	78,979	80,538	84,367	87,442	91,924
Real estate and rental and leasing	46,475	48,629	51,142	51,226	54,085	56,570	58,255
Professional, scientific, and technical services	77,461	78,975	82,317	82,785	84,898	87,704	91,921
Management of companies and enterprises	101,107	106,940	114,448	115,056	120,850	130,132	124,388
Administrative and waste services	31,121	31,323	31,967	32,329	32,856	33,723	35,017
Educational services	39,346	40,162	41,265	42,140	42,716	43,537	44,757
Health care and social assistance	42,242	43,221	44,213	44,912	45,826	47,476	49,731
Arts, entertainment, and recreation	30,290	32,022	32,260	32,576	33,425	34,650	34,100
Accommodation and food services	16,635	17,153	17,727	18,259	18,775	19,554	20,516
Other services, except public administration	28,046	28,670	29,445	30,225	31,081	32,268	33,749
Government and government enterprises	45,255	46,057	46,392	47,106	48,155	50,031	51,407

Table PA-10. Employment Characteristics by Family Type

(Number, percent.)

Family type and labor force status	2014		2015		2016	
	Total	Families with own children under 18 years	Total	Families with own children under 18 years	Total	Families with own children under 18 years
All Families..	3,173,379	1,256,610	3,204,295	1,252,169	3,150,563	1,229,437
FAMILY TYPE AND LABOR FORCE STATUS						
Married-Couple Families..............................	2,352,767	841,562	2,366,755	830,337	2,341,561	828,926
Both husband and wife in labor force................	53.0	70.0	52.1	69.7	51.7	70.0
Husband in labor force, wife not in labor force	19.8	24.7	20.0	24.8	19.4	24.0
Wife in labor force, husband not in labor force.......	8.4	3.8	8.3	3.7	8.4	4.0
Both husband and wife not in labor force............	18.9	1.5	19.0	1.6	19.7	1.6
Other Families	820,612	415,048	837,540	421,832	809,002	400,511
Female householder, no husband present.............	72.6	75.1	72.8	75.0	71.7	74.2
In labor force......................................	49.2	59.6	48.6	60.0	49.6	62.2
Not in labor force..................................	23.4	15.5	24.2	15.0	22.0	12.0
Male householder, no wife present...................	27.4	24.9	27.2	25.0	28.3	25.8
In labor force......................................	20.5	22.2	20.7	22.6	21.3	23.0
Not in labor force..................................	6.9	2.7	6.5	2.4	7.0	2.8

Table PA-11. School Enrollment and Educational Attainment, 2016

(Number, percent.)

Item	State	U.S.
Enrollment		
Total population 3 years and over, enrolled in school	2,975,685	81,572,277
Enrolled in nursery school or preschool (percent).............................	6.2	6.0
Enrolled in kindergarten (percent)..	4.7	5.0
Enrolled in elementary school, grades 1-8 (percent)..........................	39.8	40.3
Enrolled in high school, grades 9-12 (percent)...............................	21.2	21.0
Enrolled in college or graduate school (percent).............................	28.1	27.7
Attainment		
Total population 25 years and over	8,921,975	218,475,480
Less than ninth grade (percent)..	3.2	5.4
9th to 12th grade, no diploma (percent)......................................	6.6	7.2
High school graduate, including equivalency (percent)........................	35.1	27.2
Some college, no degree (percent)...	16.0	20.6
Associate's degree (percent)...	8.2	8.4
Bachelor's degree (percent)...	18.8	19.3
Graduate or professional degree (percent)...................................	12.0	11.9
High school graduate or higher (percent).....................................	90.1	87.5
Bachelor's degree or higher (percent)..	30.8	31.3

Table PA-12. Public School Characteristics and Educational Indicators

(Number, percent; data derived from National Center of Education Statistics.)

Item	State	U.S.
Public Schools, 2015–2016 (except where noted)		
Number of school districts...	784	18,328
Number of schools..	3,019	98,456
Number of students...	1,717,414	50,327,015
Number of teachers...	120,893	3,151,497
Student-teacher ratio...	14.2	16.0
Expenditures per student (dollars), 2014-2015................................	14,405	11,445
Four-year adjusted cohort graduation rate (ACGR)[1,2]	86.1	84.1
Students eligible for free or reduced-price lunch (percent), 2014-2015.........	45.6	51.8
English language learners (percent), Fall 2015...............................	3.1	9.5
Students age 3 to 21 served under IDEA, part B (percent).....................	17.7	13.2

Public Schools by Type	Number	Percent of state public schools
Total number of schools...	3,019	100.0
Regular	2,925	96.9
Special education...	4	0.1
Vocational education..	84	2.8
Alternative education...	6	0.2

NOTE: Every school is assigned only one school type based on its instructional emphasis.
[1] ACGR data represents a new method of calculating high-school completion rates and may not be comparable to previous years' data for Averaged Freshmen Graduation Rates (AFGR).
[2] The United States 4-year ACGRs were estimated using both the reported 4-year ACGR data from 49 states and the District of Columbia and using imputed data for Idaho. The estimate for American Indian/Alaska Native students also includes imputed data for Virginia.

Table PA-13. Reported Voting and Registration of the Voting-Age Population, November 2016

(Numbers in thousands, percent.)

Item	Total population	Total citizen population	Registered			Voted		
			Total registered	Percent registered (total population)	Percent registered (total citizen population)	Total voted	Percent voted (total population)	Percent voted (total citizen population)
U.S. Total	245,502	224,059	157,596	64.2	70.3	137,537	56.0	61.4
State Total.............................	9,980	9,596	6,909	69.2	72.0	6,008	60.2	62.6
Sex								
Male	4,808	4,589	3,199	66.5	69.7	2,793	58.1	60.9
Female	5,172	5,007	3,709	71.7	74.1	3,215	62.2	64.2
Race								
White alone........................	8,435	8,203	5,916	70.1	72.1	5,153	61.1	62.8
White, non-Hispanic alone	8,022	7,884	5,716	71.3	72.5	4,991	62.2	63.3
Black alone.........................	1,071	1,007	751	70.1	74.5	637	59.5	63.2
Asian alone........................	311	223	138	44.4	61.8	135	43.3	60.3
Hispanic (of any race)........................	544	443	279	51.2	62.9	229	42.1	51.7
White alone or in combination	8,524	8,292	5,958	69.9	71.9	5,190	60.9	62.6
Black alone or in combination...........	1,152	1,088	805	69.9	74.0	692	60.1	63.6
Asian alone or in combination...........	325	238	147	45.2	61.8	144	44.2	60.4
Age								
18 to 24 years.....................	1,193	1,130	720	60.4	63.7	581	48.7	51.4
25 to 34 years.....................	1,649	1,525	1,026	62.2	67.3	837	50.8	54.9
35 to 44 years.....................	1,425	1,351	983	69.0	72.8	865	60.7	64.1
45 to 64 years.....................	3,471	3,382	2,536	73.1	75.0	2,294	66.1	67.8
65 years and over	2,243	2,208	1,643	73.3	74.4	1,431	63.8	64.8

Table PA-14. Crime

(Number, rate per 100,000. Data are derived from the FBI Uniform Crime Reports.)

Item	State			U.S. [1,2,3,4]		
	2015	2016	Percent change	2015	2016	Percent change
TOTAL POPULATION [5]	12,802,503	12,784,227	-0.1	321,418,820	323,127,513	0.5
VIOLENT CRIME						
Number..............................	40,339	40,447	0.3	1,231,566	1,248,185	1.3
Rate	315.1	316.4	0.4	383.2	386.3	0.8
Murder and Nonnegligent Manslaughter						
Number..............................	658	661	0.5	15,696	17,250	9.9
Rate	5.1	5.2	2.0	4.9	5.3	8.2
Rape [6]						
Number..............................	4,305	4,433	3.0	124,047	130,603	5.3
Rate	33.6	34.7	3.3	38.6	40.4	4.7
Robbery						
Number..............................	13,003	12,326	-5.2	327,374	332,198	1.5
Rate	101.6	96.4	-5.1	101.9	102.8	0.9
Aggravated Assault						
Number..............................	22,373	23,027	2.9	764,449	803,007	5.0
Rate	174.8	180.1	3.0	237.8	248.5	4.5
PROPERTY CRIME						
Number..............................	232,085	222,795	-4.0	7,993,631	7,919,035	-0.9
Rate	1,812.8	1,742.7	-3.9	2,487.0	2,450.7	-1.5
Burglary						
Number..............................	39,664	35,520	-10.4	1,579,527	1,515,096	-4.1
Rate	309.8	277.8	-10.3	491.4	468.9	-4.6
Larceny-Theft						
Number..............................	180,287	174,228	-3.4	5,706,346	5,638,455	-1.2
Rate	1,408.2	1,362.8	-3.2	1,775.4	1,745.0	-1.7
Motor Vehicle Theft						
Number..............................	12,134	13,047	7.5	707,758	765,484	8.2
Rate	94.8	102.1	7.7	220.2	236.9	7.6

NOTE: Although arson data are included in the trend and clearance tables, sufficient data are not available to estimate totals for this offense. Therefore, no arson data are published in this table.
X = Not applicable.
- = Zero or rounds to zero.
[1] The crime figures have been adjusted.
[2] The data collection methodology for the offense of forcible rape used by the Minnesota state Uniform Crime Reporting (UCR) Program (with the exception of Minneapolis and St. Paul, Minnesota) does not comply with national UCR Program guidelines. Consequently, its figures for forcible rape and violent crime (of which forcible rape is a part) are not published in this table.
[3] Includes offenses reported by the Zoological Police and the Metro Transit Police.
[4] Because of changes in the state's reporting practices, figures are not comparable to previous years' data.
[5] Populations are U.S. Census Bureau provisional estimates as of July 1 of each year.
[6] The figures shown for the offense of rape were estimated using the revised Uniform Crime Reporting (UCR) definition of rape.

Table PA-15. State Government Finances, 2016

(Dollar amounts in thousands, percent distribution.)

Item	Dollars	Percent distribution
Total Revenue	90,792,145	100.0
General revenue	79,737,894	87.8
Intergovernmental revenue	26,240,030	28.9
Taxes	37,394,589	41.2
General sales	10,221,593	11.3
Selective sales	9,062,781	10.0
License taxes	2,159,170	2.4
Individual income tax	11,932,232	13.1
Corporate income tax	2,456,231	2.7
Other taxes	1,562,582	1.7
Current charges	11,410,663	12.6
Miscellaneous general revenue	4,692,612	5.2
Utility revenue	0	-
Liquor stores revenue	1,937,885	2.1
Insurance trust revenue [1]	9,116,366	10.0
Total Expenditure	96,439,652	100.0
Intergovernmental expenditure	20,050,597	20.8
Direct expenditure	76,389,055	79.2
Current operation	52,170,583	54.1
Capital outlay	8,045,415	8.3
Insurance benefits and repayments	12,163,270	12.6
Assistance and subsidies	2,503,716	2.6
Interest on debt	1,506,071	1.6
Exhibit: Salaries and wages	9,995,674	10.4
Total Expenditure	96,439,652	100.0
General expenditure	82,457,161	85.5
Intergovernmental expenditure	20,050,597	20.8
Direct expenditure	62,406,564	64.7
General expenditure, by function:		
Education	25,179,057	26.1
Public welfare	27,933,780	29.0
Hospitals	4,991,927	5.2
Health	3,229,043	3.3
Highways	8,685,049	9.0
Police protection	1,045,151	1.1
Correction	2,101,822	2.2
Natural resources	660,210	0.7
Parks and recreation	342,281	0.4
Governmental administration	2,772,823	2.9
Interest on general debt	1,506,071	1.6
Other and unallocable	4,009,947	4.2
Utility expenditure	1602	-
Liquor stores expenditure	1,817,619	1.9
Insurance trust expenditure	12,163,270	12.6
Debt at End of Fiscal Year	47,099,314	X
Cash and Security Holdings	111,235,292	X

X = Not applicable.
- = Zero or rounds to zero.
[1] Within insurance trust revenue, net earnings of state retirement systems is a calculated statistic (the item code in the data file is X08), and thus can be positive or negative. Net earnings is the sum of earnings on investments plus gains on investments minus losses on investments. The change made in 2002 for asset valuation from book to market value in accordance with Statement 34 of the Governmental Accounting Standards Board is reflected in the calculated statistics.

Table PA-16. State Government Tax Collections, 2017

(Dollars in thousands, percent.)

Item	Dollars	Percent distribution
Total Taxes	37,853,091	100.0
Property taxes	43,360	0.1
Sales and gross receipts	19,629,437	51.9
General sales and gross receipts	10,509,734	27.8
Selective sales and gross receipts	9,119,703	24.1
Alcoholic beverages	386,816	1.0
Amusements	1,406,354	3.7
Insurance premiums	808,250	2.1
Motor fuels	3,143,576	8.3
Pari-mutuels	10,381	-
Public utilities	1,235,942	3.3
Tobacco products	1,401,259	3.7
Other selective sales	727,125	1.9
Licenses	2,240,809	5.9
Alcoholic beverages	34,222	0.1
Amusements	12,672	-
Corporations in general	18,752	-
Hunting and fishing	74,991	0.2
Motor vehicle	928,512	2.5
Motor vehicle operators	70,067	0.2
Public utilities	83,718	0.2
Occupation and business, NEC	997,941	2.6
Other licenses	19,934	0.1
Income taxes	14,408,126	38.1
Individual income	12,063,782	31.9
Corporation net income	2,344,344	6.2
Other taxes	1,531,359	4.0
Death and gift	931,908	2.5
Documentary and stock transfer	577,586	1.5
Severance	X	-
Taxes, NEC	21,865	0.1

X = Not applicable.
- = Zero or rounds to zero.

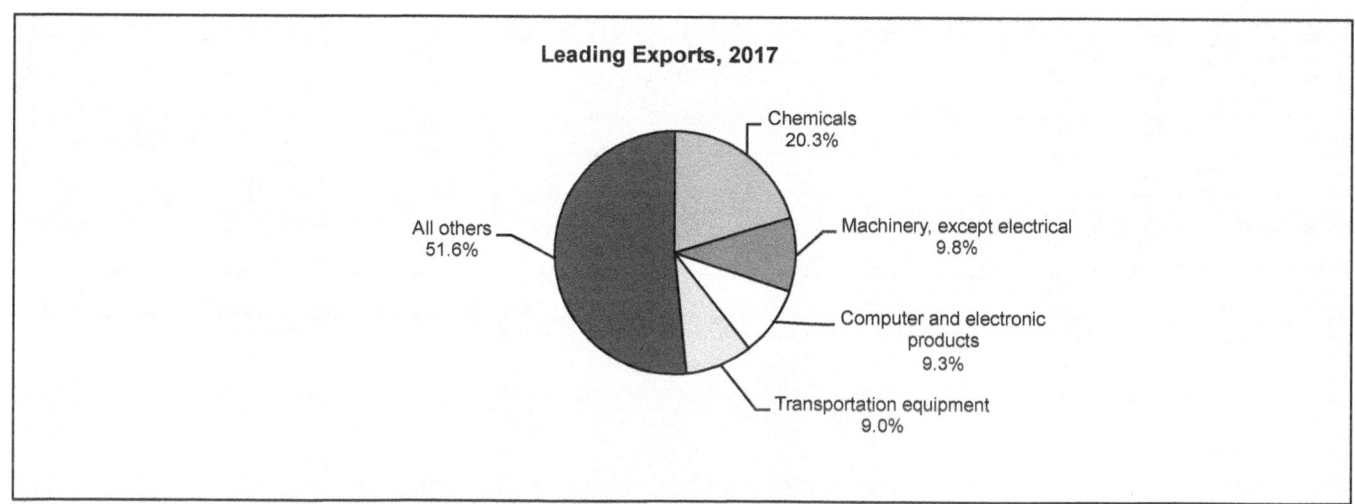

Leading Exports, 2017

Chemicals 20.3%
Machinery, except electrical 9.8%
Computer and electronic products 9.3%
Transportation equipment 9.0%
All others 51.6%

RHODE ISLAND

Facts and Figures

Location: Eastern United States; bordered on the N by Massachusetts, on the E by Massachusetts and the Atlantic Ocean, on the S by Block Island Sound and the Atlantic Ocean, and on the W by Connecticut

Area: 1,545 sq. mi. (4,002 sq. km.); rank—50th

Population: 1,059,639 (2017 est.); rank—43rd

Principal Cities: capital—Providence; largest—Providence

Statehood: May 29, 1790; 13th state

U.S. Congress: 2 senators, 2 representatives

State Motto: Hope

State Song: "Rhode Island"

State Nickname: The Ocean State

Abbreviations: RI; R.I.

State Symbols: flower—violet; tree—red maple; bird—Rhode Island red

At a Glance

- With an increase in population of 0.6 percent, Rhode Island ranked 45th among the states in growth from 2010 to 2017.

- In 2016, 4.3 percent of Rhode Islanders did not have health insurance, compared to 8.6 percent of the total U.S. population.

- Rhode Island's violent crime rate in 2016 was 238.9 per 100,000 population, compared to 386.3 for the entire nation.

- The state's median income in 2016 was $60,596, and 12.8 percent of its residents lived below the poverty level.

- In 2017, 19.6 percent of Rhode Island's population was under 18 years old, and 16.8 percent of its population was 65 years or older, compared to the national averages of 22.6 percent and 15.6 percent respectively.

Table RI-1. Population by Age, Sex, Race, and Hispanic Origin

(Number, percent, except where noted.)

Sex, age, race, and Hispanic origin	2000	2010	2017 [1]	Average annual percent change, 2010–2017
Total Population...	1,048,319	1,052,567	1,059,639	0.7
Percent of total U.S. population	0.4	0.3	0.3	X
Sex				
Male...	503,635	508,400	514,991	1.3
Female	544,684	544,167	544,648	0.1
Age				
Under 5 years..	63,896	57,448	54,761	-4.7
5 to 19 years...	218,720	204,310	187,447	-8.3
20 to 64 years..	613,301	638,928	639,476	0.1
65 years and over...	152,402	151,881	177,955	17.2
Median age (years)	36.7	39.4	39.9	1.3
Race and Hispanic Origin				
One race				
White	891,191	910,253	890,883	-2.1
Black...	46,908	75,073	87,261	16.2
American Indian and Alaska Native	5,121	9,173	10,948	19.4
Asian...	23,665	31,768	39,014	22.8
Native Hawaiian or Other Pacific Islander	567	1,602	2,015	25.8
Two or more races...	28,251	24,698	29,518	19.5
Hispanic (of any race)..	90,820	137,169	164,004	19.6

X = Not applicable.
- = Zero or rounds to zero.
[1] Population figures for 2017 are July 1 estimates. The 2010 estimates are taken from the 2010 Census.

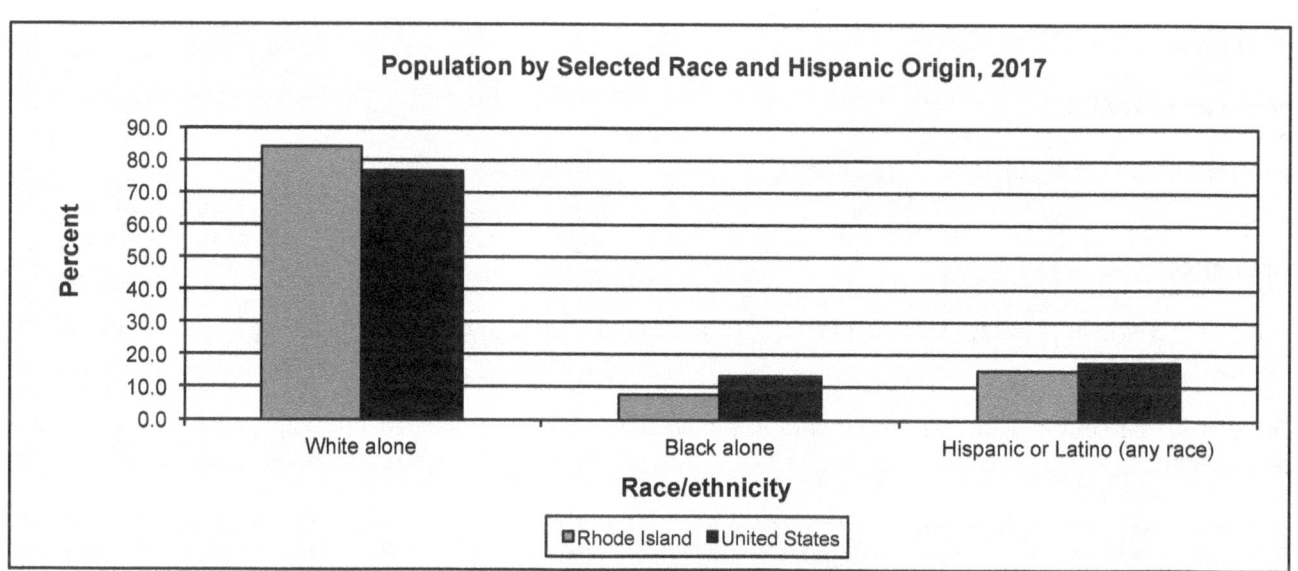

Population by Selected Race and Hispanic Origin, 2017

Table RI-2. Marital Status

(Number, percent distribution.)

Sex, age, and marital status	2000	2010	2016
Males, 15 Years and Over	396,396	414,628	424,571
Never married	32.5	39.8	40.1
Now married, except separated.....................................	54.9	45.2	44.8
Separated...	1.5	1.6	1.0
Widowed..	3.0	3.1	2.5
Divorced..	8.0	10.3	11.4
Females, 15 Years and Over	445,107	456,425	461,862
Never married	27.1	32.4	34.5
Now married, except separated.....................................	48.5	41.8	40.7
Separated...	2.3	2.4	2.0
Widowed..	11.5	10.4	9.6
Divorced..	10.7	13.0	13.2

Table RI-3. Households and Housing Characteristics

(Number, percent, dollars.)

Item	2000	2010	2016	Average annual percent change, 2010–2016
Total Households..	408,424	402,295	408,239	0.2
Family households..	265,398	246,028	247,448	0.1
Married-couple family....................................	196,757	173,848	172,506	-0.1
Other family..	68,641	72,180	74,942	0.6
Male householder, no wife present.................	16,032	17,525	18,027	0.5
Female householder, no husband present.........	52,609	54,655	56,915	0.7
Nonfamily households	143,026	156,267	160,791	0.5
Householder living alone.............................	116,678	125,371	131,879	0.9
Householder not living alone........................	26,348	30,896	28,912	-1.1
Housing Characteristics				
Total housing units.......................................	439,837	463,416	462,598	-
Occupied housing units	408,424	402,295	408,239	0.2
Owner occupied..	245,156	244,516	236,882	-0.5
Renter occupied...	163,268	157,779	171,357	1.4
Average household size..................................	2.47	2.51	2.48	-0.2
Financial Characteristics				
Median gross rent of renter-occupied housing	553	868	948	1.5
Median monthly owner costs for housing units with a mortgage	1,205	1,837	1,740	-0.9
Median value of owner-occupied housing units	133,000	254,500	247,700	-0.4

- = Zero or rounds to zero.

Table RI-4. Migration, Origin, and Language

(Number, percent.)

	State			U.S.		
Characteristic	2015	2016	Percent change	2015	2016	Percent change
Residence 1 Year Ago						
Population 1 year and over	1,045,062	1,045,691	0.1	317,635,720	319,361,956	0.5
Same house	86.2	85.9	X	85.3	85.4	X
Different house in the U.S.	13.0	13.3	X	14.1	13.9	X
Same county	7.8	8.4	X	8.5	8.3	X
Different county	5.3	4.9	X	5.6	5.6	X
Same state	1.6	1.8	X	3.2	3.2	X
Different state	3.7	3.1	X	2.4	2.4	X
Abroad	0.7	0.7	X	0.7	0.7	X
Place of Birth						
Native born	913,974	907,946	-0.7	278,128,449	279,388,170	0.5
Male	48.3	48.3	X	49.3	49.3	X
Female	51.7	51.7	X	50.7	50.7	X
Foreign born	142,324	148,480	4.3	43,290,372	43,739,345	1.0
Male	49.3	49.2	X	48.6	48.5	X
Female	50.7	50.8	X	51.4	51.5	X
Foreign born; naturalized U.S. citizen.............	77,381	81,710	5.6	20,697,103	21,238,372	2.6
Male	44.8	46.1	X	45.9	45.9	X
Female	55.2	53.9	X	54.1	54.1	X
Foreign born; not a U.S. citizen.................	64,943	66,770	2.8	22,593,269	22,500,973	-0.4
Male	54.5	53.1	X	51.1	51.0	X
Female	45.5	46.9	X	48.9	49.0	X
Entered 2010 or later	16.9	19.6	X	15.6	18.6	X
Entered 2000 to 2009	22.4	23.5	X	27.9	26.7	X
Entered before 2000................................	60.6	56.9	X	56.5	54.7	X
World Region of Birth, Foreign						
Foreign-born population, excluding population born at sea	142,324	148,480	4.3	43,289,646	43,738,901	1.0
Europe	21.9	24.3	X	11.1	10.9	X
Asia..	19.1	18.2	X	30.6	30.8	X
Africa..	12.6	12.9	X	4.8	4.9	X
Oceania..	0.2	0.5	X	0.6	0.6	X
Latin America	43.8	42.2	X	51.1	51.0	X
North America	2.4	2.0	X	1.9	1.8	X
Language Spoken at Home and Ability to Speak English						
Population 5 years and over...........................	1,001,905	1,002,282	-	301,625,014	303,328,961	0.6
English only	77.8	77.2	X	78.5	78.4	X
Language other than English........................	22.2	22.8	X	21.5	21.6	X
Speaks English less than "very well".............	8.2	8.4	X	8.6	8.6	X

NA = Not available.
X = Not applicable.
- = Zero or rounds to zero.

Table RI-5. Median Income and Poverty Status, 2016

(Number, percent, except as noted.)

Characteristic	State Number	State Percent	U.S. Number	U.S. Percent
Median Income				
Households (dollars)...	60,596	X	57,617	X
Families (dollars)	77,940	X	71,062	X
Below Poverty Level (All People)	129,932	12.8	44,268,996	14.0
Sex				
Male	58,976	12.0	19,760,056	12.8
Female	70,956	13.6	24,508,940	15.2
Age				
Under 18 years...	35,106	17.0	14,115,713	19.5
Related children under 18 years.........................	33,451	16.3	13,805,435	19.1
18 to 64 years..	79,642	12.4	25,723,818	13.2
65 years and over..	15,184	9.1	4,429,465	9.2

X = Not applicable.

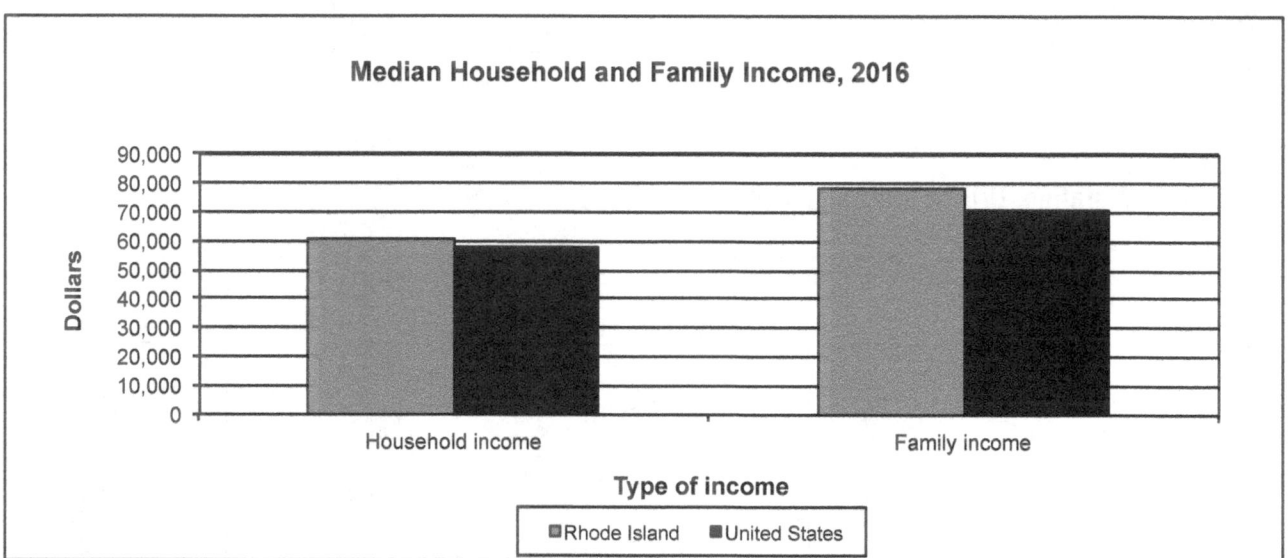

Median Household and Family Income, 2016

Table RI-6. Health Insurance Coverage Status for the Civilian Noninstitutionalized Population and Children Under 18 Years of Age

(Number, percent.)

Item	2008	2009	2010	2011	2012	2013	2014	2015	2016
Civilian Noninstitutionalized Population	1,030,284	1,035,366	1,036,743	1,035,117	1,034,895	1,036,046	1,039,789	1,041,268	1,040,259
Covered by Private or Public Insurance									
Number...	922,459	918,668	910,559	923,283	920,030	915,586	962,670	981,858	995,293
Percent...	89.5	88.7	87.8	89.2	88.9	88.4	92.6	94.3	95.7
Not Covered									
Number...	107,825	116,698	126,184	111,834	114,865	120,460	77,119	59,410	44,966
Percent...	10.5	11.3	12.2	10.8	11.1	11.6	7.4	5.7	4.3
Percent in the U.S. not covered................................	15.1	15.1	15.5	15.1	14.8	14.5	11.7	9.4	8.6
Children Under 18 Years of Age	228,072	226,681	223,970	218,624	216,675	212,430	212,271	211,397	208,268
Covered by Private or Public Insurance									
Number...	215,146	214,388	211,480	209,952	206,885	200,866	205,164	204,137	204,269
Percent...	94.3	94.6	94.4	96.0	95.5	94.6	96.7	96.6	98.1
Not Covered									
Number...	12,926	12,293	12,490	8,672	9,790	11,564	7,107	7,260	3,999
Percent...	5.7	5.4	5.6	4.0	4.5	5.4	3.3	3.4	1.9
Percent in the U.S. not covered................................	9.9	8.6	8.0	7.5	7.2	7.1	6.0	4.8	4.5

Table RI-7. Employment Status by Demographic Group, 2017

(Numbers in thousands, percent.)

Characteristic	Civilian noninstitutional population	Civilian labor force		Employed		Unemployed	
		Number	Percent of population	Number	Percent of population	Number	Percent of population
Total..	860	555	64.5	531	61.7	25	4.4
Sex							
Male..	412	288	69.7	272	65.8	16	5.6
Female...	448	268	59.7	259	57.8	9	3.2
Race, Sex, and Hispanic Origin							
White...	742	475	64.1	456	61.4	20	4.1
Male..	357	246	69.0	233	65.3	13	5.3
Female...	385	229	59.5	222	57.8	7	2.9
Black or African American.....................	60	39	66.3	37	61.5	3	7.0
Male..	30	20	66.9	18	61.4	2	8.1
Female...	30	20	65.7	18	62.0	1	6.0
Hispanic or Latino ethnicity[1]..............	117	77	65.4	71	60.7	6	7.1
Male..	55	40	73.5	37	67.4	3	8.4
Female...	62	36	58.3	34	55.0	2	5.8
Age							
16 to 19 years......................................	50	23	45.2	19	38.6	3	14.6
20 to 24 years......................................	65	46	70.8	44	67.6	2	4.5
25 to 34 years......................................	151	126	83.4	122	80.9	4	2.9
35 to 44 years......................................	133	115	86.5	110	82.5	6	4.8
45 to 54 years......................................	129	102	79.4	99	76.7	4	3.5
55 to 64 years......................................	152	103	67.5	98	64.6	4	4.3
65 years and over.................................	179	40	22.3	38	21.1	2	5.0

NOTE: Data in Table 7 are from the Current Population Survey (CPS) and do not match the estimates in Table 8. See notes and definitions for further information.
[1] May be of any race.

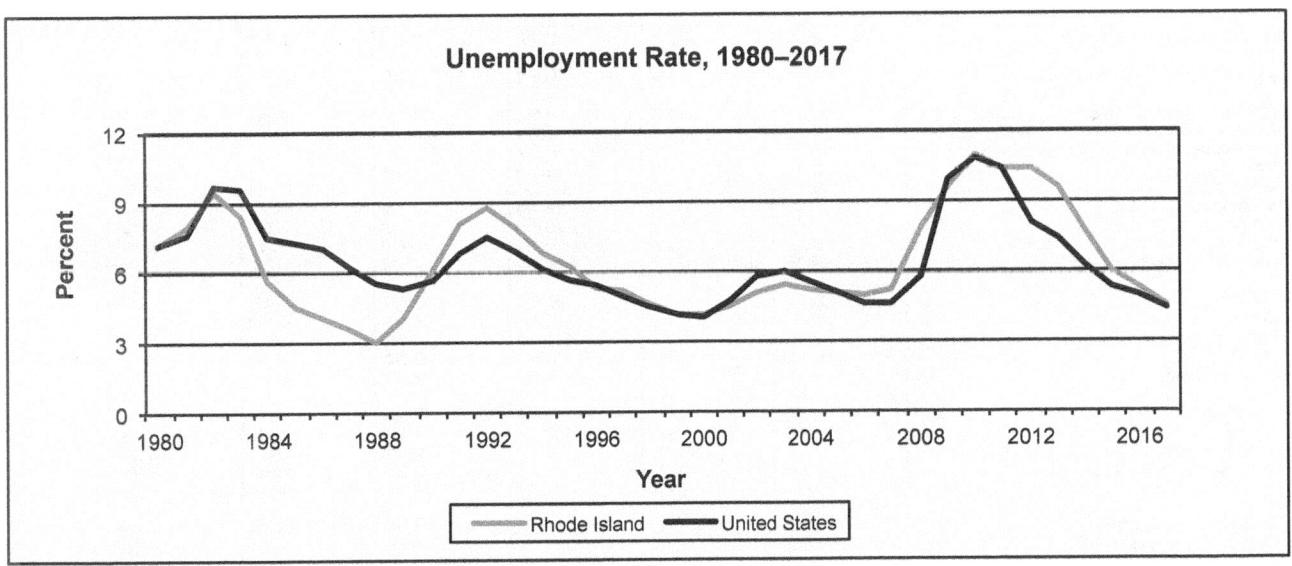

Unemployment Rate, 1980–2017

Table RI-8. Employment Status of the Civilian Noninstitutional Population Age 16 Years and Over

(Number, percent.)

Year	Civilian labor force	Civilian participation rate	Employed	Unemployed	Unemployment rate
2009..	567,280	67.4	504,951	62,329	11.0
2010..	566,704	67.3	503,216	63,488	11.2
2011..	560,056	66.4	498,248	61,808	11.0
2012..	558,487	66.0	500,434	58,053	10.4
2013..	556,926	65.6	505,370	51,556	9.3
2014..	555,909	65.2	513,121	42,788	7.7
2015..	554,486	64.8	521,255	33,231	6.0
2016..	553,555	64.5	524,745	28,810	5.2
2017..	554,658	64.3	529,867	24,791	4.5

Table RI-9. Employment and Average Wages by Industry

(Estimates through 2010 are based on the 2007 *North American Industry Classification System* [NAICS]. Estimates from 2011 onward are based on the 2012 NAICS.)

Industry	2010	2011	2012	2013	2014	2015	2016
	Number of jobs						
Wage and Salary Employment by Industry	474,551	476,085	477,784	484,147	491,907	498,383	502,729
Farm Wage and Salary Employment	503	550	536	614	615	613	572
Nonfarm Wage and Salary Employment	474,048	475,535	477,248	483,533	491,292	497,770	502,157
Private wage and salary employment	400,945	403,274	405,810	411,806	419,463	426,262	430,321
Forestry, fishing, and related activities	(D)	(D)	554	(D)	(D)	(D)	(D)
Mining	(D)	(D)	188	(D)	(D)	(D)	(D)
Utilities	1,129	1,077	1,058	1,060	1,057	1,082	1,080
Construction	16,521	16,174	16,499	16,584	16,948	17,431	18,634
Manufacturing	40,396	40,424	39,708	40,128	40,911	41,242	40,519
Durable goods manufacturing	25,810	25,856	25,343	25,595	26,120	26,032	25,257
Nondurable goods manufacturing	14,586	14,568	14,365	14,533	14,791	15,210	15,262
Wholesale trade	15,882	16,237	16,897	16,768	16,918	17,021	16,733
Retail trade	47,320	47,336	47,323	46,934	47,576	48,449	48,581
Transportation and warehousing	9,138	9,628	9,776	9,780	9,962	10,282	10,383
Information	10,009	10,169	9,597	9,096	8,872	8,631	8,087
Finance and insurance	24,082	23,896	24,199	24,722	25,069	25,544	25,569
Real estate and rental and leasing	5,801	5,814	5,919	6,050	6,072	6,138	6,233
Professional, scientific, and technical services	21,116	21,166	21,673	22,174	23,007	24,036	24,594
Management of companies and enterprises	9,331	9,858	10,536	11,343	12,015	12,574	13,394
Administrative and waste services	23,405	23,676	24,326	25,565	26,292	27,317	28,086
Educational services	24,973	25,627	24,316	24,266	25,324	25,856	26,594
Health care and social assistance	79,709	79,212	79,609	81,445	81,281	81,345	81,058
Arts, entertainment, and recreation	7,695	7,609	7,725	8,489	8,923	9,066	9,511
Accommodation and food services	42,246	42,849	44,369	45,426	46,617	47,528	48,462
Other services, except public administration	21,449	21,779	21,538	21,264	21,821	21,901	21,998
Government and government enterprises	73,103	72,261	71,438	71,727	71,829	71,508	71,836
	Dollars						
Average Wages and Salaries by Industry	45,317	46,299	47,464	48,458	49,946	51,321	53,543
Average Farm Wages and Salaries	26,113	20,902	31,032	27,930	29,517	27,189	32,114
Average Nonfarm Wages and Salaries	45,338	46,328	47,483	48,484	49,971	51,351	53,567
Average private wages and salaries	43,685	44,682	45,921	47,067	48,719	50,042	52,473
Forestry, fishing, and related activities	(D)	(D)	41,554	(D)	(D)	(D)	(D)
Mining	(D)	(D)	51,410	(D)	(D)	(D)	(D)
Utilities	86,734	93,879	92,194	96,742	97,839	98,657	106,956
Construction	52,554	53,804	54,496	55,199	56,067	57,703	59,916
Manufacturing	51,041	52,632	53,620	55,338	56,682	57,835	59,705
Durable goods manufacturing	52,539	54,280	55,210	56,999	58,021	58,862	61,888
Nondurable goods manufacturing	48,391	49,708	50,815	52,413	54,318	56,076	56,093
Wholesale trade	64,825	65,422	67,073	69,417	70,389	70,935	75,060
Retail trade	28,172	27,725	28,214	28,639	29,806	31,076	32,520
Transportation and warehousing	39,818	40,412	41,144	41,924	43,009	43,499	44,756
Information	62,978	65,805	68,741	67,782	70,540	71,955	53,647
Finance and insurance	75,615	80,297	84,148	86,563	93,574	93,640	114,161
Real estate and rental and leasing	38,977	40,027	41,607	42,631	44,237	46,459	48,674
Professional, scientific, and technical services	65,445	66,415	67,376	69,320	72,313	74,481	79,045
Management of companies and enterprises	104,262	106,265	114,488	116,746	122,375	124,016	120,588
Administrative and waste services	31,604	32,214	33,175	34,543	35,355	36,108	38,162
Educational services	39,490	39,443	40,698	42,279	42,584	42,798	43,589
Health care and social assistance	42,326	43,277	43,680	44,101	45,144	47,026	47,783
Arts, entertainment, and recreation	27,019	28,049	28,795	29,425	31,261	33,890	37,850
Accommodation and food services	18,208	18,761	19,364	19,968	20,667	21,764	23,741
Other services, except public administration	28,887	28,995	29,803	31,003	31,970	33,285	34,585
Government and government enterprises	54,401	55,518	56,353	56,621	57,285	59,153	60,124

D = Not shown to avoid disclosure of confidential information, but the estimates for this item are included in the total.

Table RI-10. Employment Characteristics by Family Type

(Number, percent.)

Family type and labor force status	2014		2015		2016	
	Total	Families with own children under 18 years	Total	Families with own children under 18 years	Total	Families with own children under 18 years
All Families..	256,077	108,359	250,262	105,051	247,448	99,442
FAMILY TYPE AND LABOR FORCE STATUS						
Married-Couple Families............................	178,127	66,035	174,967	65,193	172,506	61,174
Both husband and wife in labor force....................	56.9	74.2	56.7	74.9	54.0	71.2
Husband in labor force, wife not in labor force	16.5	19.2	17.2	18.2	17.8	21.0
Wife in labor force, husband not in labor force	9.0	4.7	7.8	4.3	8.9	5.3
Both husband and wife not in labor force................	17.6	1.8	17.2	2.2	17.8	1.6
Other Families	77,950	42,324	75,295	39,858	74,942	38,268
Female householder, no husband present..................	74.0	77.7	75.7	80.1	75.9	77.4
In labor force	52.9	64.8	54.9	67.1	55.1	65.3
Not in labor force	21.1	12.9	20.8	13.0	20.9	12.1
Male householder, no wife present........................	26.0	22.3	24.3	19.9	24.1	22.6
In labor force	20.6	19.8	19.9	18.6	19.2	20.0
Not in labor force	5.3	2.5	4.4	1.3	4.9	2.6

Table RI-11. School Enrollment and Educational Attainment, 2016

(Number, percent.)

Item	State	U.S.
Enrollment		
Total population 3 years and over, enrolled in school	264,768	81,572,277
Enrolled in nursery school or preschool (percent)........................	5.8	6.0
Enrolled in kindergarten (percent)......................................	3.5	5.0
Enrolled in elementary school, grades 1-8 (percent)......................	34.8	40.3
Enrolled in high school, grades 9-12 (percent)...........................	19.9	21.0
Enrolled in college or graduate school (percent).........................	36.1	27.7
Attainment		
Total population 25 years and over	734,045	218,475,480
Less than ninth grade (percent)	5.2	5.4
9th to 12th grade, no diploma (percent)	6.2	7.2
High school graduate, including equivalency (percent)....................	27.8	27.2
Some college, no degree (percent)	18.4	20.6
Associate's degree (percent)..	8.2	8.4
Bachelor's degree (percent)...	20.6	19.3
Graduate or professional degree (percent)...............................	13.5	11.9
High school graduate or higher (percent)	88.5	87.5
Bachelor's degree or higher (percent)...................................	34.1	31.3

Table RI-12. Public School Characteristics and Educational Indicators

(Number, percent; data derived from National Center of Education Statistics.)

Item	State	U.S.
Public Schools, 2015–2016 (except where noted)		
Number of school districts...	64	18,328
Number of schools...	313	98,456
Number of students	142,014	50,327,015
Number of teachers	10,631	3,151,497
Student-teacher ratio	13.4	16.0
Expenditures per student (dollars), 2014-2015............................	15,797	11,445
Four-year adjusted cohort graduation rate (ACGR)[1,2]	82.8	84.1
Students eligible for free or reduced-price lunch (percent), 2014-2015....	46.8	51.8
English language learners (percent), Fall 2015	7.4	9.5
Students age 3 to 21 served under IDEA, part B (percent).................	16.6	13.2

Public Schools by Type	Number	Percent of state public schools
Total number of schools...	313	100.0
Regular	297	94.9
Special education	1	0.3
Vocational education	10	3.2
Alternative education...	5	1.6

NOTE: Every school is assigned only one school type based on its instructional emphasis.
[1] ACGR data represents a new method of calculating high-school completion rates and may not be comparable to previous years' data for Averaged Freshmen Graduation Rates (AFGR).
[2] The United States 4-year ACGRs were estimated using both the reported 4-year ACGR data from 49 states and the District of Columbia and using imputed data for Idaho. The estimate for American Indian/Alaska Native students also includes imputed data for Virginia.

Table RI-13. Reported Voting and Registration of the Voting-Age Population, November 2016

(Numbers in thousands, percent.)

Item	Total population	Total citizen population	Registered			Voted		
			Total registered	Percent registered (total population)	Percent registered (total citizen population)	Total voted	Percent voted (total population)	Percent voted (total citizen population)
U.S. Total	245,502	224,059	157,596	64.2	70.3	137,537	56.0	61.4
State Total............................	836	766	538	64.4	70.3	464	55.5	60.6
Sex								
Male	404	369	253	62.7	68.6	213	52.8	57.8
Female	432	397	285	66.0	71.8	251	58.1	63.2
Race								
White alone.............................	699	664	467	66.7	70.3	403	57.7	60.7
White, non-Hispanic alone	599	588	417	69.5	70.9	363	60.5	61.7
Black alone..............................	63	58	42	(B)	(B)	34	(B)	(B)
Asian alone	37	16	9	(B)	(B)	9	(B)	(B)
Hispanic (of any race).....................	132	98	67	(B)	(B)	57	(B)	(B)
White alone or in combination	707	672	472	66.8	70.3	407	57.6	60.6
Black alone or in combination...........	69	64	47	(B)	(B)	38	(B)	(B)
Asian alone or in combination..........	39	18	10	(B)	(B)	10	(B)	(B)
Age								
18 to 24 years............................	81	69	43	(B)	(B)	34	(B)	(B)
25 to 34 years............................	148	137	93	62.7	67.6	74	49.7	53.6
35 to 44 years............................	145	125	95	65.1	75.9	78	53.4	62.2
45 to 64 years............................	284	263	184	64.8	69.9	169	59.5	64.2
65 years and over	178	172	124	69.7	72.0	111	62.4	64.4

B = Base is less than 75,000 and therefore too small to show the derived measure.

Table RI-14. Crime

(Number, rate per 100,000. Data are derived from the FBI Uniform Crime Reports.)

Item	State			U.S. [1,2,3,4]		
	2015	2016	Percent change	2015	2016	Percent change
TOTAL POPULATION [5]	1,056,298	1,056,426	-	321,418,820	323,127,513	0.5
VIOLENT CRIME						
Number...	2,562	2,524	-1.5	1,231,566	1,248,185	1.3
Rate	242.5	238.9	-1.5	383.2	386.3	0.8
Murder and Nonnegligent Manslaughter						
Number...	29	29	-	15,696	17,250	9.9
Rate	2.7	2.7	-	4.9	5.3	8.2
Rape[6]						
Number...	459	442	-3.7	124,047	130,603	5.3
Rate	43.5	41.8	-3.9	38.6	40.4	4.7
Robbery						
Number...	556	540	-2.9	327,374	332,198	1.5
Rate	52.6	51.1	-2.9	101.9	102.8	0.9
Aggravated Assault						
Number...	1,518	1,513	-0.3	764,449	803,007	5.0
Rate	143.7	143.2	-0.3	237.8	248.5	4.5
PROPERTY CRIME						
Number...	20,043	20,058	0.1	7,993,631	7,919,035	-0.9
Rate	1,897.5	1,898.7	0.1	2,487.0	2,450.7	-1.5
Burglary						
Number...	3,947	3,788	-4.0	1,579,527	1,515,096	-4.1
Rate	373.7	358.6	-4.0	491.4	468.9	-4.6
Larceny-Theft						
Number...	14,707	14,674	-0.2	5,706,346	5,638,455	-1.2
Rate	1,392.3	1,389.0	-0.2	1,775.4	1,745.0	-1.7
Motor Vehicle Theft						
Number...	1,389	1,596	14.9	707,758	765,484	8.2
Rate	131.5	151.1	14.9	220.2	236.9	7.6

NOTE: Although arson data are included in the trend and clearance tables, sufficient data are not available to estimate totals for this offense. Therefore, no arson data are published in this table.
X = Not applicable.
- = Zero or rounds to zero.
[1] The crime figures have been adjusted.
[2] The data collection methodology for the offense of forcible rape used by the Minnesota state Uniform Crime Reporting (UCR) Program (with the exception of Minneapolis and St. Paul, Minnesota) does not comply with national UCR Program guidelines. Consequently, its figures for forcible rape and violent crime (of which forcible rape is a part) are not published in this table.
[3] Includes offenses reported by the Zoological Police and the Metro Transit Police.
[4] Because of changes in the state's reporting practices, figures are not comparable to previous years' data.
[5] Populations are U.S. Census Bureau provisional estimates as of July 1 of each year.
[6] The figures shown for the offense of rape were estimated using the revised Uniform Crime Reporting (UCR) definition of rape.

Table RI-15. State Government Finances, 2016

(Dollar amounts in thousands, percent distribution.)

Item	Dollars	Percent distribution
Total Revenue	8,201,456	100.0
General revenue	7,430,240	90.6
Intergovernmental revenue	2,518,206	30.7
Taxes	3,265,727	39.8
General sales	973,585	11.9
Selective sales	691,853	8.4
License taxes	120,936	1.5
Individual income tax	1,236,194	15.1
Corporate income tax	144,269	1.8
Other taxes	98,890	1.2
Current charges	798,457	9.7
Miscellaneous general revenue	847,850	10.3
Utility revenue	22,692	0.3
Liquor stores revenue	0	-
Insurance trust revenue [1]	748,524	9.1
Total Expenditure	8,625,101	100.0
Intergovernmental expenditure	1,236,874	14.3
Direct expenditure	7,388,227	85.7
Current operation	5,051,293	58.6
Capital outlay	459,024	5.3
Insurance benefits and repayments	1,272,050	14.7
Assistance and subsidies	166,674	1.9
Interest on debt	439,186	5.1
Exhibit: Salaries and wages	1,285,467	14.9
Total Expenditure	8,625,101	100.0
General expenditure	7,189,986	83.4
Intergovernmental expenditure	1,236,874	14.3
Direct expenditure	5,953,112	69.0
General expenditure, by function:		
Education	2,164,098	25.1
Public welfare	2,701,788	31.3
Hospitals	67,065	0.8
Health	182,258	2.1
Highways	315,809	3.7
Police protection	81,380	0.9
Correction	201,516	2.3
Natural resources	53,335	0.6
Parks and recreation	45,791	0.5
Governmental administration	389,303	4.5
Interest on general debt	439,149	5.1
Other and unallocable	548,494	6.4
Utility expenditure	163,065	1.9
Liquor stores expenditure	0	-
Insurance trust expenditure	1,272,050	14.7
Debt at End of Fiscal Year	9,052,017	X
Cash and Security Holdings	16,638,914	X

X = Not applicable.
- = Zero or rounds to zero.
[1] Within insurance trust revenue, net earnings of state retirement systems is a calculated statistic (the item code in the data file is X08), and thus can be positive or negative. Net earnings is the sum of earnings on investments plus gains on investments minus losses on investments. The change made in 2002 for asset valuation from book to market value in accordance with Statement 34 of the Governmental Accounting Standards Board is reflected in the calculated statistics.

Table RI-16. State Government Tax Collections, 2017

(Dollars in thousands, percent.)

Item	Dollars	Percent distribution
Total Taxes	3,266,663	100.0
Property taxes	2,633	0.1
Sales and gross receipts	1,691,782	51.8
General sales and gross receipts	996,390	30.5
Selective sales and gross receipts	695,392	21.3
Alcoholic beverages	20,873	0.6
Amusements	X	-
Insurance premiums	120,587	3.7
Motor fuels	90,990	2.8
Pari-mutuels	1,122	-
Public utilities	97,711	3.0
Tobacco products	140,074	4.3
Other selective sales	224,035	6.9
Licenses	110,461	3.4
Alcoholic beverages	143	-
Amusements	222	-
Corporations in general	5,281	0.2
Hunting and fishing	1,691	0.1
Motor vehicle	26,788	0.8
Motor vehicle operators	4,589	0.1
Public utilities	2,454	0.1
Occupation and business, NEC	64,367	2.0
Other licenses	4,926	0.2
Income taxes	1,368,660	41.9
Individual income	1,238,928	37.9
Corporation net income	129,732	4.0
Other taxes	93,127	2.9
Death and gift	70,601	2.2
Documentary and stock transfer	22,526	0.7
Severance	X	-
Taxes, NEC	0	-

X = Not applicable.
- = Zero or rounds to zero.

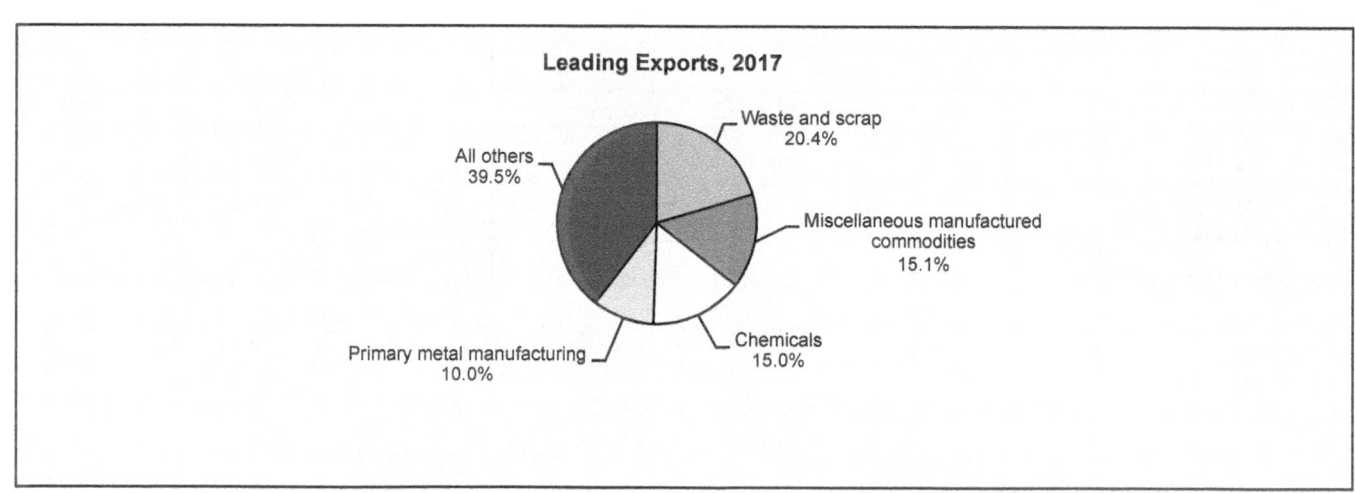

Leading Exports, 2017

Waste and scrap 20.4%
All others 39.5%
Miscellaneous manufactured commodities 15.1%
Primary metal manufacturing 10.0%
Chemicals 15.0%

SOUTH CAROLINA

Facts and Figures

Location: Southeastern United States; bordered on the N by North Carolina, on the E by the Atlantic Ocean, on the S by the Atlantic Ocean and Georgia, and on the W by Georgia

Area: 32,020 sq. mi. (82,932 sq. km.); rank—40th

Population: 5,024,369 (2017 est.); rank—23rd

Principal Cities: capital—Columbia; largest—Columbia

Statehood: May 23, 1788; 8th state

U.S. Congress: 2 senators, 7 representatives

State Mottoes: *Animis opibusque parati* ("Prepared in mind and resources"); *Dum spiro, spero* ("While I breathe, I hope")

State Songs: "Carolina"; "South Carolina on My Mind"

State Nickname: The Palmetto State

Abbreviations: SC; S.C.

State Symbols: flower—yellow jessamine; tree—cabbage palmetto; bird—Carolina wren

At a Glance

- With an increase in population of 8.4 percent, South Carolina ranked 11th among the states in growth from 2010 to 2017.

- South Carolina's median household income in 2016 was $49,501, and 15.3 percent of the population lived below the poverty level.

- South Carolina's violent crime rate in 2016 was 501.8 incidents per 100,000 population, which ranked 11th in the nation.

- In 2016, 10.0 percent of South Carolinians did not have health insurance, compared to 8.6 percent of the total U.S. population.

- South Carolina once again had the highest rate of traffic fatalities in the U.S. in 2016, with 1.88 deaths per 100 million vehicle miles driven.

Table SC-1. Population by Age, Sex, Race, and Hispanic Origin

(Number, percent, except where noted.)

Sex, age, race, and Hispanic origin	2000	2010	2017 [1]	Average annual percent change, 2010–2017
Total Population...	4,012,013	4,625,364	5,024,369	8.6
Percent of total U.S. population	1.4	1.5	1.5	X
Sex				
Male..	1,948,929	2,250,101	2,437,687	8.3
Female..	2,063,083	2,375,263	2,586,682	8.9
Age				
Under 5 years..	264,679	302,297	293,653	-2.9
5 to 19 years..	871,099	922,128	943,928	2.4
20 to 64 years...	2,390,901	2,769,065	2,922,211	5.5
65 years and over	485,333	631,874	864,577	36.8
Median age (years)...	35.4	37.9	39.4	4.0
Race and Hispanic Origin				
One race				
White	2,695,560	3,164,143	3,440,141	8.7
Black...	1,185,216	1,302,865	1,372,547	5.3
American Indian and Alaska Native	13,718	24,665	27,373	11.0
Asian...	36,014	61,247	85,665	39.9
Native Hawaiian or Other Pacific Islander	1,628	3,957	4,949	25.1
Two or more races	39,950	68,487	93,694	36.8
Hispanic (of any race)..	95,076	243,923	286,382	17.4

X = Not applicable.
[1] Population figures for 2017 are July 1 estimates. The 2010 estimates are taken from the 2010 Census.

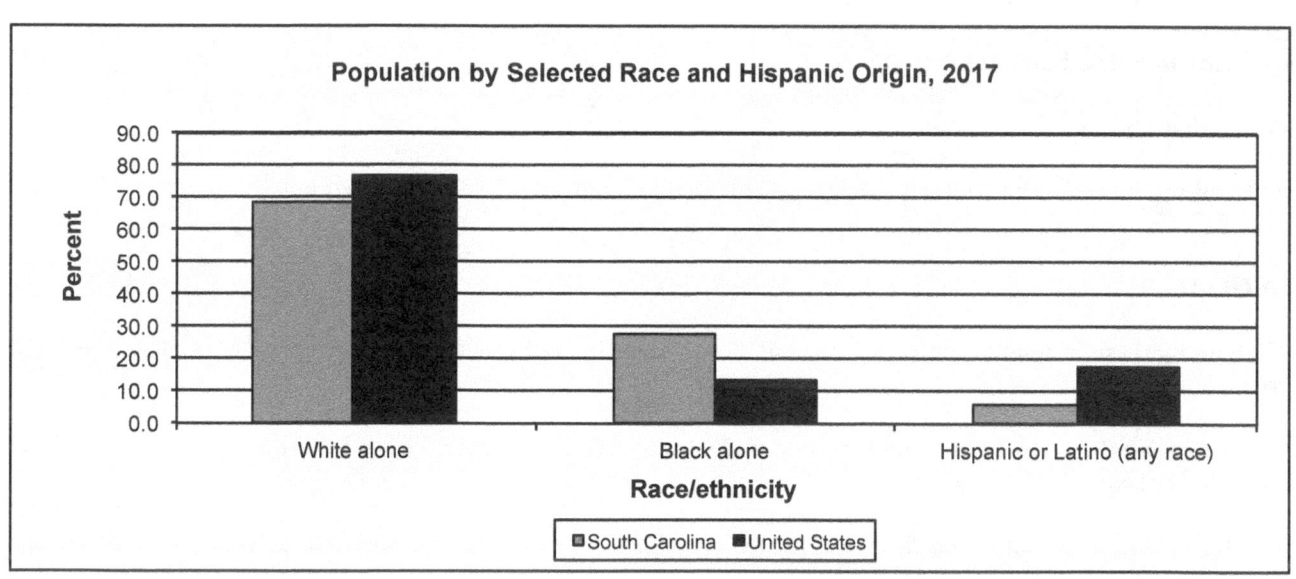

Population by Selected Race and Hispanic Origin, 2017

Table SC-2. Marital Status

(Number, percent distribution.)

Sex, age, and marital status	2000	2010	2016
Males, 15 Years and Over	1,516,125	1,797,441	1,937,011
Never married	28.8	35.2	35.6
Now married, except separated...	57.3	49.4	48.2
Separated..	2.8	3.0	2.4
Widowed..	2.7	2.8	3.2
Divorced...	8.3	9.5	10.5
Females, 15 Years and Over	1,652,793	1,939,054	2,109,514
Never married	23.4	29.1	30.0
Now married, except separated...	51.4	45.2	44.3
Separated..	3.8	3.9	3.4
Widowed..	11.5	10.6	10.5
Divorced...	9.9	11.2	11.7

Table SC-3. Households and Housing Characteristics

(Number, percent, dollars.)

Item	2000	2010	2016	Average annual percent change, 2010–2016
Total Households..	1,533,854	1,761,393	1,877,887	1.1
Family households	1,072,822	1,180,687	1,224,695	0.6
Married-couple family	783,142	827,387	872,181	0.9
Other family	289,680	353,300	352,514	-
Male householder, no wife present............................	62,722	77,062	85,039	1.7
Female householder, no husband present.......................	226,958	276,238	267,475	-0.5
Nonfamily households	461,032	580,706	653,192	2.1
Householder living alone...	383,142	489,995	550,907	2.1
Householder not living alone..	77,890	90,711	102,285	2.1
Housing Characteristics				
Total housing units..	1,753,670	2,140,337	2,236,262	0.7
Occupied housing units	1,533,854	1,761,393	1,877,887	1.1
Owner occupied	1,107,617	1,210,160	1,288,871	1.1
Renter occupied	426,237	551,233	589,016	1.1
Average household size..	2.53	2.55	2.57	0.1
Financial Characteristics				
Median gross rent of renter-occupied housing	510	728	841	2.6
Median monthly owner costs for housing units with a mortgage	894	1,177	1,182	0.1
Median value of owner-occupied housing units	94,900	138,100	153,900	1.9

Table SC-4. Migration, Origin, and Language

(Number, percent.)

Characteristic	State 2015	State 2016	State Percent change	U.S. 2015	U.S. 2016	U.S. Percent change
Residence 1 Year Ago						
Population 1 year and over	4,839,984	4,903,788	1.3	317,635,720	319,361,956	0.5
Same house..	84.8	85.2	X	85.3	85.4	X
Different house in the U.S.	14.7	14.4	X	14.1	13.9	X
Same county	8.1	7.7	X	8.5	8.3	X
Different county	6.7	6.8	X	5.6	5.6	X
Same state	3.1	3.4	X	3.2	3.2	X
Different state	3.5	3.4	X	2.4	2.4	X
Abroad	0.4	0.4	X	0.7	0.7	X
Place of Birth						
Native born..	4,663,397	4,723,155	1.3	278,128,449	279,388,170	0.5
Male	48.6	48.4	X	49.3	49.3	X
Female	51.4	51.6	X	50.7	50.7	X
Foreign born	232,749	237,964	2.2	43,290,372	43,739,345	1.0
Male	51.4	49.6	X	48.6	48.5	X
Female	48.6	50.4	X	51.4	51.5	X
Foreign born; naturalized U.S. citizen.......................	92,001	94,759	3.0	20,697,103	21,238,372	2.6
Male	46.5	45.5	X	45.9	45.9	X
Female	53.5	54.5	X	54.1	54.1	X
Foreign born; not a U.S. citizen.............................	140,748	143,205	1.7	22,593,269	22,500,973	-0.4
Male	54.5	52.4	X	51.1	51.0	X
Female	45.5	47.6	X	48.9	49.0	X
Entered 2010 or later	18.1	20.2	X	15.6	18.6	X
Entered 2000 to 2009	34.9	31.7	X	27.9	26.7	X
Entered before 2000..	47.0	48.1	X	56.5	54.7	X
World Region of Birth, Foreign						
Foreign-born population, excluding population born at sea	232,749	237,964	2.2	43,289,646	43,738,901	1.0
Europe...	15.8	18.7	X	11.1	10.9	X
Asia..	25.1	24.2	X	30.6	30.8	X
Africa	3.8	3.1	X	4.8	4.9	X
Oceania	1.0	0.3	X	0.6	0.6	X
Latin America...	51.0	50.2	X	51.1	51.0	X
North America..	3.4	3.5	X	1.9	1.8	X
Language Spoken at Home and Ability to Speak English						
Population 5 years and over....................................	4,608,658	4,671,107	1.4	301,625,014	303,328,961	0.6
English only	93.2	93.2	X	78.5	78.4	X
Language other than English.................................	6.8	6.8	X	21.5	21.6	X
Speaks English less than "very well"....................	2.7	2.7	X	8.6	8.6	X

NA = Not available.
X = Not applicable.
- = Zero or rounds to zero.

Table SC-5. Median Income and Poverty Status, 2016

(Number, percent, except as noted.)

Characteristic	State		U.S.	
	Number	Percent	Number	Percent
Median Income				
Households (dollars)..	49,501	X	57,617	X
Families (dollars)	61,535	X	71,062	X
Below Poverty Level (All People)	735,960	15.3	44,268,996	14.0
Sex				
Male	321,692	13.9	19,760,056	12.8
Female	414,268	16.6	24,508,940	15.2
Age				
Under 18 years...	248,595	23.0	14,115,713	19.5
Related children under 18 years.......................	244,530	22.7	13,805,435	19.1
18 to 64 years...	417,227	14.3	25,723,818	13.2
65 years and over	70,138	8.6	4,429,465	9.2

X = Not applicable.

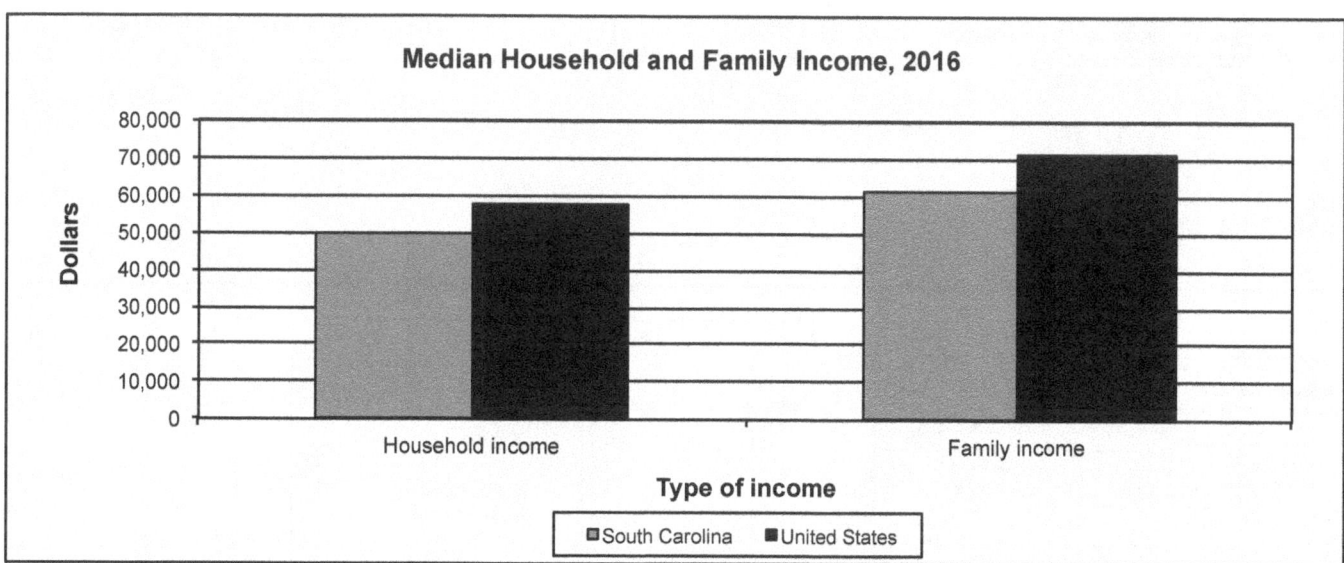

Table SC-6. Health Insurance Coverage Status for the Civilian Noninstitutionalized Population and Children Under 18 Years of Age

(Number, percent.)

Item	2008	2009	2010	2011	2012	2013	2014	2015	2016
Civilian Noninstitutionalized Population	4,373,390	4,454,344	4,536,835	4,579,231	4,623,171	4,678,122	4,733,742	4,801,301	4,861,188
Covered by Private or Public Insurance									
Number..	3,612,365	3,704,507	3,741,560	3,812,927	3,844,990	3,939,270	4,092,185	4,278,073	4,375,282
Percent...	82.6	83.2	82.5	83.3	83.2	84.2	86.4	89.1	90.0
Not Covered									
Number..	761,025	749,837	795,275	766,304	778,181	738,852	641,557	523,228	485,906
Percent...	17.4	16.8	17.5	16.7	16.8	15.8	13.6	10.9	10.0
Percent in the U.S. not covered...........................	15.1	15.1	15.5	15.1	14.8	14.5	11.7	9.4	8.6
Children Under 18 Years of Age	1,064,430	1,078,199	1,078,477	1,079,476	1,078,022	1,076,621	1,080,779	1,086,607	1,097,385
Covered by Private or Public Insurance									
Number..	930,776	970,760	976,620	988,285	988,908	1,004,026	1,020,796	1,042,427	1,053,682
Percent...	87.4	90.0	90.6	91.6	91.7	93.3	94.5	95.9	96.0
Not Covered									
Number..	133,654	107,439	101,857	91,191	89,114	72,595	59,983	44,180	43,703
Percent...	12.6	10.0	9.4	8.4	8.3	6.7	5.5	4.1	4.0
Percent in the U.S. not covered...........................	9.9	8.6	8.0	7.5	7.2	7.1	6.0	4.8	4.5

Table SC-7. Employment Status by Demographic Group, 2017

(Numbers in thousands, percent.)

Characteristic	Civilian noninstitutional population	Civilian labor force		Employed		Unemployed	
		Number	Percent of population	Number	Percent of population	Number	Percent of population
Total...	3,942	2,287	58.0	2,187	55.5	100	4.4
Sex							
Male......................................	1,860	1,200	64.5	1,146	61.6	54	4.5
Female....................................	2,082	1,087	52.2	1,041	50.0	46	4.2
Race, Sex, and Hispanic Origin							
White......................................	2,789	1,641	58.8	1,590	57.0	51	3.1
Male....................................	1,346	901	66.9	876	65.1	25	2.8
Female.................................	1,444	740	51.3	714	49.4	26	3.5
Black or African American................	1,031	576	55.9	529	51.3	48	8.2
Male....................................	458	266	58.0	238	51.9	28	10.6
Female.................................	573	310	54.2	291	50.8	19	6.2
Hispanic or Latino ethnicity[1]............	144	98	67.8	94	64.9	4	4.3
Male....................................	NA	NA	NA	NA	NA	NA	NA
Female.................................	NA	NA	NA	NA	NA	NA	NA
Age							
16 to 19 years.............................	281	96	34.3	84	29.8	13	13.2
20 to 24 years.............................	278	208	74.7	190	68.2	18	8.7
25 to 34 years.............................	582	458	78.7	435	74.8	23	5.0
35 to 44 years.............................	649	526	81.2	506	78.1	20	3.8
45 to 54 years.............................	623	468	75.0	456	73.2	12	2.5
55 to 64 years.............................	667	389	58.2	379	56.7	10	2.6
65 years and over........................	862	143	16.6	138	16.0	5	3.4

NOTE: Data in Table 7 are from the Current Population Survey (CPS) and do not match the estimates in Table 8. See notes and definitions for further information.
[1] May be of any race.

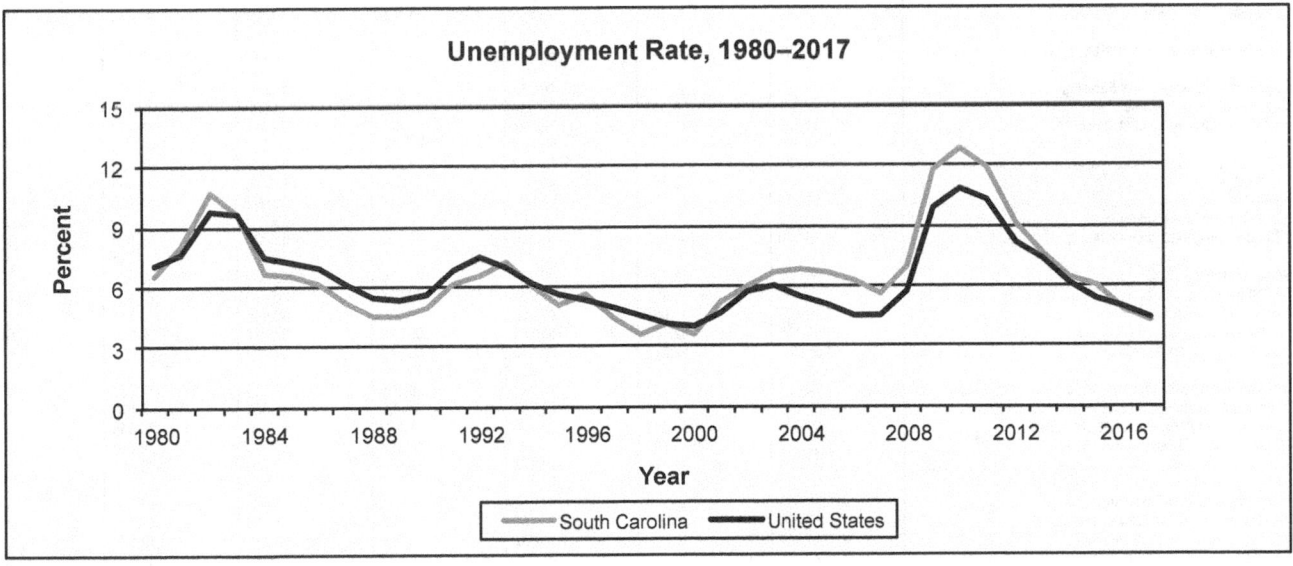

Unemployment Rate, 1980–2017

Table SC-8. Employment Status of the Civilian Noninstitutional Population Age 16 Years and Over

(Number, percent.)

Year	Civilian labor force	Civilian participation rate	Employed	Unemployed	Unemployment rate
2009..	2,152,745	61.7	1,910,670	242,075	11.2
2010..	2,155,668	60.5	1,915,045	240,623	11.2
2011..	2,175,523	60.2	1,945,900	229,623	10.6
2012..	2,186,878	59.8	1,985,618	201,260	9.2
2013..	2,190,968	59.2	2,023,642	167,326	7.6
2014..	2,222,978	59.2	2,079,565	143,413	6.5
2015..	2,269,339	59.4	2,134,244	135,095	6.0
2016..	2,293,666	59.0	2,179,521	114,145	5.0
2017..	2,312,651	58.6	2,213,894	98,757	4.3

Table SC-9. Employment and Average Wages by Industry

(Estimates through 2010 are based on the 2007 *North American Industry Classification System* [NAICS]. Estimates from 2011 onward are based on the 2012 NAICS.)

Industry	2010	2011	2012	2013	2014	2015	2016
	\multicolumn{7}{c}{Number of jobs}						
Wage and Salary Employment by Industry	1,893,730	1,914,988	1,948,461	1,986,153	2,033,961	2,089,696	2,135,524
Farm Wage and Salary Employment	6,516	6,818	6,839	7,785	6,085	7,511	7,270
Nonfarm Wage and Salary Employment	1,887,214	1,908,170	1,941,622	1,978,368	2,027,876	2,082,185	2,128,254
Private wage and salary employment	1,489,053	1,516,171	1,546,120	1,579,045	1,627,358	1,676,529	1,720,801
Forestry, fishing, and related activities	6,969	6,956	6,788	6,985	7,090	7,217	7,282
Mining	1,244	1,233	1,194	1,141	1,157	1,237	1,463
Utilities	12,045	11,919	12,134	12,212	12,349	12,348	12,371
Construction	82,725	79,200	79,917	82,269	84,960	89,140	97,150
Manufacturing	208,218	216,506	221,565	225,157	230,606	236,292	238,546
Durable goods manufacturing	114,252	121,053	126,092	129,343	133,648	137,664	139,600
Nondurable goods manufacturing	93,966	95,453	95,473	95,814	96,958	98,628	98,946
Wholesale trade	64,002	64,839	65,968	66,736	68,475	71,098	72,054
Retail trade	225,247	227,520	228,228	232,852	238,915	243,483	248,471
Transportation and warehousing	46,695	48,112	50,228	52,711	56,561	60,751	63,429
Information	25,849	25,898	25,782	26,431	26,468	26,961	27,025
Finance and insurance	68,631	68,662	69,519	70,593	70,410	70,805	72,141
Real estate and rental and leasing	26,555	26,246	25,968	26,808	27,841	28,730	29,859
Professional, scientific, and technical services	75,363	79,777	80,404	82,512	85,644	88,999	94,375
Management of companies and enterprises	14,302	15,060	15,890	16,489	17,042	16,678	17,954
Administrative and waste services	128,991	136,229	141,908	144,982	153,489	158,091	158,929
Educational services	29,068	29,771	30,408	30,766	32,094	32,623	33,521
Health care and social assistance	172,670	174,493	177,766	181,144	186,040	193,152	198,606
Arts, entertainment, and recreation	26,104	26,540	26,925	27,467	28,178	29,154	30,015
Accommodation and food services	182,600	185,411	191,160	196,777	202,176	211,109	219,014
Other services, except public administration	91,775	91,799	94,368	95,013	97,863	98,661	98,596
Government and government enterprises	398,161	391,999	395,502	399,323	400,518	405,656	407,453
	\multicolumn{7}{c}{Dollars}						
Average Wages and Salaries by Industry	38,744	39,660	40,568	41,030	42,032	43,223	45,776
Average Farm Wages and Salaries	22,862	18,819	27,893	19,497	23,973	26,451	21,519
Average Nonfarm Wages and Salaries	38,799	39,734	40,613	41,115	42,086	43,284	45,859
Average private wages and salaries	37,874	38,899	39,852	40,326	41,353	42,565	45,197
Forestry, fishing, and related activities	31,339	31,412	32,821	33,417	35,096	35,973	40,084
Mining	48,069	50,693	53,295	55,280	57,723	69,375	77,192
Utilities	78,467	80,476	81,359	84,787	87,517	92,254	93,526
Construction	41,966	42,924	44,652	45,391	47,206	48,854	56,864
Manufacturing	51,213	52,826	54,010	54,946	56,942	58,320	60,559
Durable goods manufacturing	53,305	55,296	56,367	57,308	59,783	60,779	62,407
Nondurable goods manufacturing	48,670	49,693	50,895	51,759	53,025	54,888	57,951
Wholesale trade	56,032	58,169	60,469	61,250	63,889	65,479	68,743
Retail trade	25,444	25,493	25,932	26,208	26,480	27,170	28,169
Transportation and warehousing	40,407	41,085	41,985	41,871	42,405	43,345	45,872
Information	52,156	52,169	53,764	55,522	57,917	59,102	61,934
Finance and insurance	55,040	57,379	59,410	60,478	61,779	64,839	69,163
Real estate and rental and leasing	34,622	36,197	37,772	39,105	40,789	42,333	45,294
Professional, scientific, and technical services	59,895	61,264	63,738	64,093	65,665	67,613	72,691
Management of companies and enterprises	66,808	69,614	72,730	71,579	71,896	74,345	90,214
Administrative and waste services	32,834	33,706	33,429	32,883	33,536	34,096	35,578
Educational services	27,885	28,713	29,372	29,990	30,565	30,885	30,997
Health care and social assistance	41,315	42,285	43,250	43,661	44,820	46,285	48,708
Arts, entertainment, and recreation	20,290	20,964	21,158	21,022	21,380	22,454	23,134
Accommodation and food services	16,917	17,364	18,005	18,275	18,578	19,273	20,674
Other services, except public administration	27,468	28,051	28,366	29,633	30,307	31,604	33,435
Government and government enterprises	42,256	42,964	43,588	44,234	45,064	46,254	48,653

Table SC-10. Employment Characteristics by Family Type

(Number, percent.)

Family type and labor force status	2014		2015		2016	
	Total	Families with own children under 18 years	Total	Families with own children under 18 years	Total	Families with own children under 18 years
All Families..	1,197,456	463,567	1,220,885	475,168	1,224,695	473,087
FAMILY TYPE AND LABOR FORCE STATUS						
Married-Couple Families................................	843,169	284,325	867,390	299,238	872,181	297,386
Both husband and wife in labor force...........................	47.5	66.6	47.1	66.4	47.4	67.2
Husband in labor force, wife not in labor force..............	21.8	27.5	21.7	27.6	21.4	26.8
Wife in labor force, husband not in labor force.............	8.5	4.4	8.4	3.7	8.7	3.9
Both husband and wife not in labor force.....................	22.2	1.5	22.3	2.1	21.8	1.7
Other Families	354,287	179,242	353,495	175,930	352,514	175,701
Female householder, no husband present...................	76.5	79.5	76.8	79.5	75.9	78.6
In labor force..	50.8	65.6	52.3	65.8	52.0	66.4
Not in labor force	25.7	13.9	24.5	13.8	23.9	12.2
Male householder, no wife present............................	23.5	20.5	23.2	20.5	24.1	21.4
In labor force..	17.5	18.4	17.2	18.6	16.7	18.0
Not in labor force	6.1	2.0	5.9	1.8	7.4	3.4

Table SC-11. School Enrollment and Educational Attainment, 2016

(Number, percent.)

Item	State	U.S.
Enrollment		
Total population 3 years and over, enrolled in school	1,209,286	81,572,277
Enrolled in nursery school or preschool (percent)...........................	5.3	6.0
Enrolled in kindergarten (percent)...	5.9	5.0
Enrolled in elementary school, grades 1-8 (percent)........................	41.6	40.3
Enrolled in high school, grades 9-12 (percent)...............................	20.9	21.0
Enrolled in college or graduate school (percent)............................	26.4	27.7
Attainment		
Total population 25 years and over	3,388,476	218,475,480
Less than ninth grade (percent)...	4.4	5.4
9th to 12th grade, no diploma (percent)......................................	9.0	7.2
High school graduate, including equivalency (percent).....................	29.0	27.2
Some college, no degree (percent)..	21.0	20.6
Associate's degree (percent)..	9.4	8.4
Bachelor's degree (percent)...	17.4	19.3
Graduate or professional degree (percent)..................................	9.8	11.9
High school graduate or higher (percent).....................................	86.6	87.5
Bachelor's degree or higher (percent)..	27.2	31.3

Table SC-12. Public School Characteristics and Educational Indicators

(Number, percent; data derived from National Center of Education Statistics.)

Item	State	U.S.
Public Schools, 2015–2016 (except where noted)		
Number of school districts..	102	18,328
Number of schools...	1,248	98,456
Number of students..	763,533	50,327,015
Number of teachers..	50,237	3,151,497
Student-teacher ratio..	15.2	16.0
Expenditures per student (dollars), 2014-2015.............................	9,831	11,445
Four-year adjusted cohort graduation rate (ACGR)[1,2]	82.6	84.1
Students eligible for free or reduced-price lunch (percent), 2014-2015...	55.9	51.8
English language learners (percent), Fall 2015.............................	5.6	9.5
Students age 3 to 21 served under IDEA, part B (percent).................	13.3	13.2

Public Schools by Type	Number	Percent of state public schools
Total number of schools...	1,248	100.0
Regular	1,185	95.0
Special education..	9	0.7
Vocational education...	42	3.4
Alternative education..	12	1.0

NOTE: Every school is assigned only one school type based on its instructional emphasis.
[1] ACGR data represents a new method of calculating high-school completion rates and may not be comparable to previous years' data for Averaged Freshmen Graduation Rates (AFGR).
[2] The United States 4-year ACGRs were estimated using both the reported 4-year ACGR data from 49 states and the District of Columbia and using imputed data for Idaho. The estimate for American Indian/Alaska Native students also includes imputed data for Virginia.

Table SC-13. Reported Voting and Registration of the Voting-Age Population, November 2016

(Numbers in thousands, percent.)

Item	Total population	Total citizen population	Registered			Voted		
			Total registered	Percent registered (total population)	Percent registered (total citizen population)	Total voted	Percent voted (total population)	Percent voted (total citizen population)
U.S. Total	245,502	224,059	157,596	64.2	70.3	137,537	56.0	61.4
State Total	3,733	3,598	2,575	69.0	71.6	2,233	59.8	62.1
Sex								
Male	1,774	1,709	1,145	64.6	67.0	992	55.9	58.0
Female	1,959	1,889	1,430	73.0	75.7	1,241	63.4	65.7
Race								
White alone	2,621	2,516	1,760	67.1	70.0	1,529	58.3	60.8
White, non-Hispanic alone	2,477	2,459	1,736	70.1	70.6	1,513	61.1	61.5
Black alone	975	964	720	73.8	74.6	628	64.4	65.2
Asian alone	62	48	35	(B)	(B)	29	(B)	(B)
Hispanic (of any race)	175	76	39	(B)	(B)	31	(B)	(B)
White alone or in combination	2,662	2,557	1,795	67.4	70.2	1,554	58.4	60.8
Black alone or in combination	997	986	735	73.8	74.6	640	64.3	65.0
Asian alone or in combination	62	48	35	(B)	(B)	29	(B)	(B)
Age								
18 to 24 years	341	332	185	54.5	55.9	146	42.7	43.9
25 to 34 years	635	585	366	57.7	62.6	288	45.4	49.3
35 to 44 years	642	587	409	63.7	69.7	346	53.9	58.9
45 to 64 years	1,301	1,281	951	73.1	74.2	860	66.1	67.1
65 years and over	815	812	663	81.3	81.6	594	72.9	73.1

B = Base is less than 75,000 and therefore too small to show the derived measure.

Table SC-14. Crime

(Number, rate per 100,000. Data are derived from the FBI Uniform Crime Reports.)

Item	State			U.S. [1,2,3,4]		
	2015	2016	Percent change	2015	2016	Percent change
TOTAL POPULATION [5]	4,896,146	4,961,119	1.3	321,418,820	323,127,513	0.5
VIOLENT CRIME						
Number	24,700	24,896	0.8	1,231,566	1,248,185	1.3
Rate	504.5	501.8	-0.5	383.2	386.3	0.8
Murder and Nonnegligent Manslaughter						
Number	399	366	-8.3	15,696	17,250	9.9
Rate	8.1	7.4	-8.6	4.9	5.3	8.2
Rape[6]						
Number	2,297	2,387	3.9	124,047	130,603	5.3
Rate	46.9	48.1	2.6	38.6	40.4	4.7
Robbery						
Number	3,931	4,035	2.6	327,374	332,198	1.5
Rate	80.3	81.3	1.2	101.9	102.8	0.9
Aggravated Assault						
Number	18,073	18,108	0.2	764,449	803,007	5.0
Rate	369.1	365.0	-1.1	237.8	248.5	4.5
PROPERTY CRIME						
Number	161,245	160,928	-0.2	7,993,631	7,919,035	-0.9
Rate	3,293.3	3,243.8	-1.5	2,487.0	2,450.7	-1.5
Burglary						
Number	34,551	32,976	-4.6	1,579,527	1,515,096	-4.1
Rate	705.7	664.7	-5.8	491.4	468.9	-4.6
Larceny-Theft						
Number	113,724	114,032	0.3	5,706,346	5,638,455	-1.2
Rate	2,322.7	2,298.5	-1.0	1,775.4	1,745.0	-1.7
Motor Vehicle Theft						
Number	12,970	13,920	7.3	707,758	765,484	8.2
Rate	264.9	280.6	5.9	220.2	236.9	7.6

NOTE: Although arson data are included in the trend and clearance tables, sufficient data are not available to estimate totals for this offense. Therefore, no arson data are published in this table.

X = Not applicable.

- = Zero or rounds to zero.

[1] The crime figures have been adjusted.

[2] The data collection methodology for the offense of forcible rape used by the Minnesota state Uniform Crime Reporting (UCR) Program (with the exception of Minneapolis and St. Paul, Minnesota) does not comply with national UCR Program guidelines. Consequently, its figures for forcible rape and violent crime (of which forcible rape is a part) are not published in this table.

[3] Includes offenses reported by the Zoological Police and the Metro Transit Police.

[4] Because of changes in the state's reporting practices, figures are not comparable to previous years' data.

[5] Populations are U.S. Census Bureau provisional estimates as of July 1 of each year.

[6] The figures shown for the offense of rape were estimated using the revised Uniform Crime Reporting (UCR) definition of rape.

Table SC-15. State Government Finances, 2016

(Dollar amounts in thousands, percent distribution.)

Item	Dollars	Percent distribution
Total Revenue	28,937,828	100.0
General revenue	24,904,905	86.1
Intergovernmental revenue	8,272,305	28.6
Taxes	9,555,900	33.0
General sales	3,268,415	11.3
Selective sales	1,352,392	4.7
License taxes	499,053	1.7
Individual income tax	3,869,342	13.4
Corporate income tax	440,489	1.5
Other taxes	126,209	0.4
Current charges	4,960,870	17.1
Miscellaneous general revenue	2,115,830	7.3
Utility revenue	1,864,592	6.4
Liquor stores revenue	0	-
Insurance trust revenue [1]	2,168,331	7.5
Total Expenditure	31,630,447	100.0
Intergovernmental expenditure	6,393,932	20.2
Direct expenditure	25,236,515	79.8
Current operation	18,389,556	58.1
Capital outlay	1,623,607	5.1
Insurance benefits and repayments	3,423,167	10.8
Assistance and subsidies	1,145,397	3.6
Interest on debt	654,788	2.1
Exhibit: Salaries and wages	3,939,086	12.5
Total Expenditure	31,630,447	100.0
General expenditure	26,639,772	84.2
Intergovernmental expenditure	6,393,932	20.2
Direct expenditure	20,245,840	64.0
General expenditure, by function:		
Education	9,558,397	30.2
Public welfare	7,429,108	23.5
Hospitals	1,803,684	5.7
Health	1,147,908	3.6
Highways	1,664,188	5.3
Police protection	184,010	0.6
Correction	502,322	1.6
Natural resources	223,364	0.7
Parks and recreation	135,457	0.4
Governmental administration	566,480	1.8
Interest on general debt	369,191	1.2
Other and unallocable	3,055,663	9.7
Utility expenditure	1,567,508	5.4
Liquor stores expenditure	0	-
Insurance trust expenditure	3,423,167	10.8
Debt at End of Fiscal Year	16,228,097	X
Cash and Security Holdings	40,744,272	X

X = Not applicable.
- = Zero or rounds to zero.
[1] Within insurance trust revenue, net earnings of state retirement systems is a calculated statistic (the item code in the data file is X08), and thus can be positive or negative. Net earnings is the sum of earnings on investments plus gains on investments minus losses on investments. The change made in 2002 for asset valuation from book to market value in accordance with Statement 34 of the Governmental Accounting Standards Board is reflected in the calculated statistics.

Table SC-16. State Government Tax Collections, 2017

(Dollars in thousands, percent.)

Item	Dollars	Percent distribution
Total Taxes..	9,828,825	100.0
Property taxes..	37,518	0.4
Sales and gross receipts	4,637,349	47.2
General sales and gross receipts	3,285,007	33.4
Selective sales and gross receipts	1,352,342	13.8
Alcoholic beverages..	177,317	1.8
Amusements..	38,814	0.4
Insurance premiums..	228,259	2.3
Motor fuels...	583,476	5.9
Pari-mutuels...	X	-
Public utilities	28,278	0.3
Tobacco products...	26,383	0.3
Other selective sales	269,815	2.7
Licenses..	518,886	5.3
Alcoholic beverages..	13,601	0.1
Amusements..	6,918	0.1
Corporations in general...	68,181	0.7
Hunting and fishing...	17,907	0.2
Motor vehicle..	229,898	2.3
Motor vehicle operators	6,770	0.1
Public utilities	10,268	0.1
Occupation and business, NEC	146,152	1.5
Other licenses	19,191	0.2
Income taxes..	4,517,931	46.0
Individual income..	4,142,276	42.1
Corporation net income	375,655	3.8
Other taxes...	117,141	1.2
Death and gift...	X	-
Documentary and stock transfer	117,141	1.2
Severance	X	-
Taxes, NEC	0	-

X = Not applicable.
- = Zero or rounds to zero.

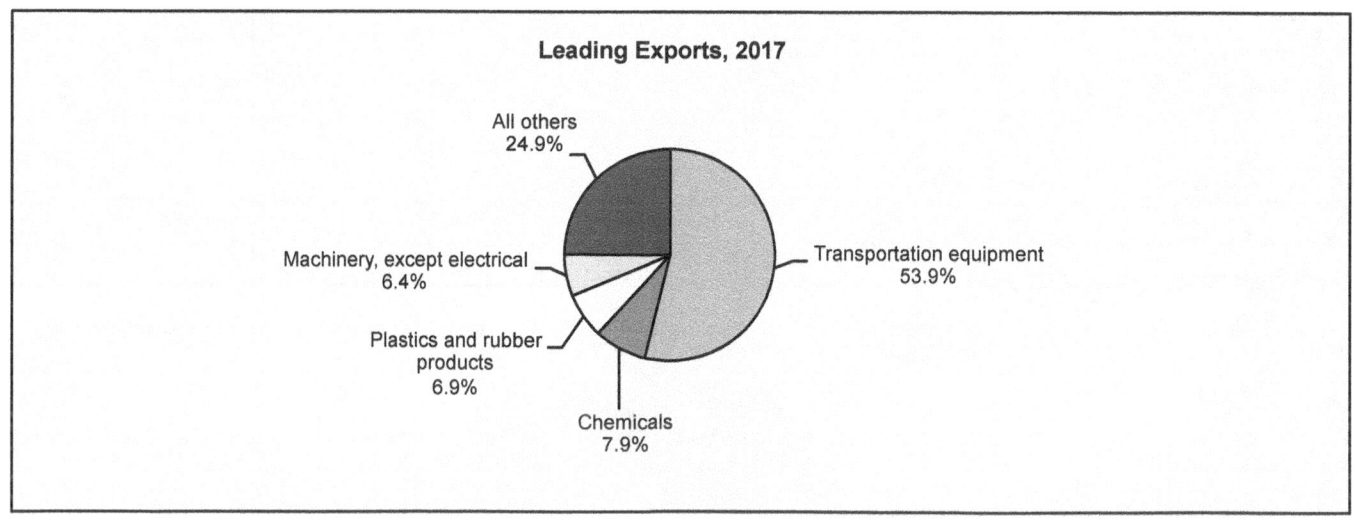

Leading Exports, 2017

All others
24.9%

Machinery, except electrical
6.4%

Plastics and rubber products
6.9%

Chemicals
7.9%

Transportation equipment
53.9%

SOUTH DAKOTA

Facts and Figures

Location: North central United States; bordered on the N by North Dakota, on the E by Minnesota and Iowa, on the S by Nebraska, and on the W by Wyoming and Montana

Area: 77,117 sq. mi. (199,731 sq. km.); rank—17th

Population: 869,666 (2017 est.); rank—46th

Principal Cities: capital—Pierre; largest—Sioux Falls

Statehood: November 2, 1889; 40th state

U.S. Congress: 2 senators, 1 representative

State Motto: Under God the People Rule

State Song: "Hail, South Dakota"

State Nickname: The Mount Rushmore State

Abbreviations: SD; S.D.; S. Dak.

State Symbols: flower—pasqueflower; tree—Black Hills spruce; bird—ring-necked pheasant

At a Glance

- With an increase in population of 6.5 percent, South Dakota ranked 16th among the states in growth from 2010 to 2017.

- In 2016, 8.7 percent of South Dakotans did not have health insurance, compared to 8.6 percent of the total U.S. population.

- South Dakota's violent crime rate in 2016 was 418.4 incidents per 100,000 population, compared to 386.3 for the entire nation.

- South Dakota's median income in 2016 was $54,467, and 13.3 percent of its residents lived below the poverty level.

- In 2017, South Dakota's unemployment rate was 3.3 percent, compared to the national unemployment rate of 4.4 percent.

Table SD-1. Population by Age, Sex, Race, and Hispanic Origin

(Number, percent, except where noted.)

Sex, age, race, and Hispanic origin	2000	2010	2017 [1]	Average annual percent change, 2010–2017
Total Population...	754,844	814,180	869,666	6.8
Percent of total U.S. population	0.4	0.3	0.3	X
Sex				
Male..	374,558	407,381	438,960	7.8
Female	380,286	406,799	430,706	5.9
Age				
Under 5 years..	51,069	59,621	61,759	3.6
5 to 19 years..	176,412	167,119	176,350	5.5
20 to 64 years..	419,232	470,859	489,933	4.1
65 years and over	108,131	116,581	141,624	21.5
Median age (years)	35.6	36.9	37.1	0.5
Race and Hispanic Origin				
One race				
White	669,404	706,690	738,554	4.5
Black...	4,685	10,533	18,479	75.4
American Indian and Alaska Native	62,283	72,782	78,456	7.8
Asian...	4,378	7,775	12,901	65.9
Native Hawaiian or Other Pacific Islander	261	517	719	39.1
Two or more races	10,156	15,883	20,557	29.4
Hispanic (of any race)..	10,903	23,699	32,811	38.4

X = Not applicable.
[1] Population figures for 2017 are July 1 estimates. The 2010 estimates are taken from the 2010 Census.
- = Zero or rounds to zero.

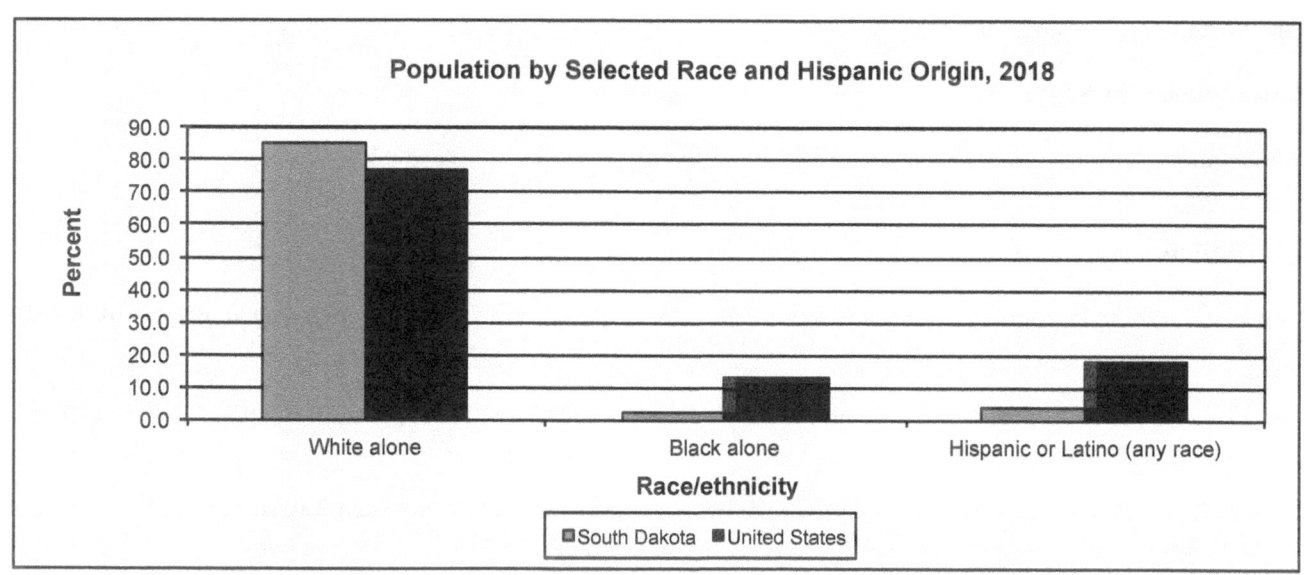

Population by Selected Race and Hispanic Origin, 2018

Legend: South Dakota, United States
X-axis: White alone, Black alone, Hispanic or Latino (any race) — Race/ethnicity
Y-axis: Percent

Table SD-2. Marital Status

(Number, percent distribution.)

Sex, age, and marital status	2000	2010	2016
Males, 15 Years and Over	289,858	322,689	342,764
Never married	29.8	33.5	35.6
Now married, except separated...	58.2	52.5	50.9
Separated..	1.0	0.9	1.2
Widowed..	2.4	2.8	2.4
Divorced..	8.5	10.3	9.9
Females, 15 Years and Over	299,754	325,640	341,957
Never married	22.5	26.0	28.0
Now married, except separated...	55.9	52.1	50.1
Separated..	1.1	1.0	1.0
Widowed..	11.4	9.5	9.9
Divorced..	9.0	11.4	11.0

Table SD-3. Households and Housing Characteristics

(Number, percent, dollars.)

Item	2000	2010	2016	Average annual percent change, 2010–2016
Total Households...	290,245	318,955	334,003	0.8
Family households	194,330	204,029	209,986	0.5
Married-couple family	157,391	161,534	164,515	0.3
Other family	36,939	42,495	45,471	1.2
Male householder, no wife present..............	10,734	12,526	14,431	2.5
Female householder, no husband present......	26,205	29,969	31,040	0.6
Nonfamily households	95,915	114,926	124,017	1.3
Householder living alone.............................	80,040	95,610	103,434	1.4
Householder not living alone.......................	15,875	19,316	20,583	1.1
Housing Characteristics				
Total housing units.......................................	323,208	364,031	383,827	0.9
Occupied housing units	290,245	318,955	334,003	0.8
Owner occupied	197,940	216,821	224,459	0.6
Renter occupied	92,305	102,134	109,544	1.2
Average household size................................	2.50	2.45	2.49	0.3
Financial Characteristics				
Median gross rent of renter-occupied housing	426	591	706	3.2
Median monthly owner costs for housing units with a mortgage	828	1,151	1,239	1.3
Median value of owner-occupied housing units......	79,600	129,700	160,700	4.0

Table SD-4. Migration, Origin, and Language

(Number, percent.)

Characteristic	State			U.S.		
	2015	2016	Percent change	2015	2016	Percent change
Residence 1 Year Ago						
Population 1 year and over	848,285	853,832	0.7	317,635,720	319,361,956	0.5
Same house	82.8	84.4	X	85.3	85.4	X
Different house in the U.S................................	16.9	15.2	X	14.1	13.9	X
Same county	8.7	7.8	X	8.5	8.3	X
Different county	8.2	7.3	X	5.6	5.6	X
Same state	5.1	3.6	X	3.2	3.2	X
Different state	3.2	3.7	X	2.4	2.4	X
Abroad	0.3	0.5	X	0.7	0.7	X
Place of Birth						
Native born	830,624	834,528	0.5	278,128,449	279,388,170	0.5
Male	50.3	50.3	X	49.3	49.3	X
Female	49.7	49.7	X	50.7	50.7	X
Foreign born	27,845	30,926	11.1	43,290,372	43,739,345	1.0
Male	49.7	51.7	X	48.6	48.5	X
Female	50.3	48.3	X	51.4	51.5	X
Foreign born; naturalized U.S. citizen.................	10,426	10,982	5.3	20,697,103	21,238,372	2.6
Male	41.4	48.0	X	45.9	45.9	X
Female	58.6	52.0	X	54.1	54.1	X
Foreign born; not a U.S. citizen.........................	17,419	19,944	14.5	22,593,269	22,500,973	-0.4
Male	54.7	53.8	X	51.1	51.0	X
Female	45.3	46.2	X	48.9	49.0	X
Entered 2010 or later	26.6	42.1	X	15.6	18.6	X
Entered 2000 to 2009	40.1	30.1	X	27.9	26.7	X
Entered before 2000...	33.3	27.8	X	56.5	54.7	X
World Region of Birth, Foreign						
Foreign-born population, excluding population born at sea	27,845	30,926	11.1	43,289,646	43,738,901	1.0
Europe	17.5	13.7	X	11.1	10.9	X
Asia..	38.6	33.2	X	30.6	30.8	X
Africa	18.7	21.6	X	4.8	4.9	X
Oceania	0.5	0.2	X	0.6	0.6	X
Latin America...	20.2	25.8	X	51.1	51.0	X
North America..	4.4	5.5	X	1.9	1.8	X
Language Spoken at Home and Ability to Speak English						
Population 5 years and over................................	798,872	804,562	0.7	301,625,014	303,328,961	0.6
English only	93.4	93.5	X	78.5	78.4	X
Language other than English.............................	6.6	6.5	X	21.5	21.6	X
Speaks English less than "very well".................	2.4	2.3	X	8.6	8.6	X

NA = Not available.
X = Not applicable.
- = Zero or rounds to zero.

Table SD-5. Median Income and Poverty Status, 2016

(Number, percent, except as noted.)

Characteristic	State		U.S.	
	Number	Percent	Number	Percent
Median Income				
Households (dollars)...	54,467	X	57,617	X
Families (dollars)	70,853	X	71,062	X
Below Poverty Level (All People)	110,962	13.3	44,268,996	14.0
Sex				
Male	48,953	11.6	19,760,056	12.8
Female	62,009	14.9	24,508,940	15.2
Age				
Under 18 years..	35,460	16.9	14,115,713	19.5
Related children under 18 years.....................................	34,530	16.5	13,805,435	19.1
18 to 64 years...	61,182	12.3	25,723,818	13.2
65 years and over	14,320	10.9	4,429,465	9.2

X = Not applicable.

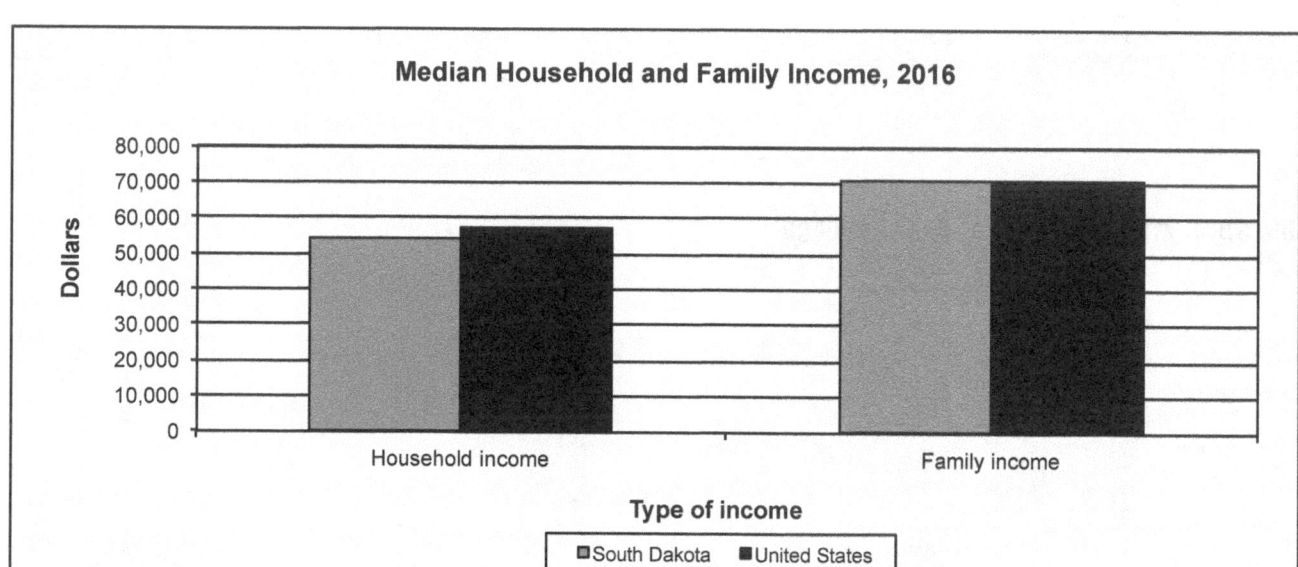

Table SD-6. Health Insurance Coverage Status for the Civilian Noninstitutionalized Population and Children Under 18 Years of Age

(Number, percent.)

Item	2008	2009	2010	2011	2012	2013	2014	2015	2016
Civilian Noninstitutionalized Population	783,531	792,969	798,141	805,505	816,425	827,039	835,403	841,363	848,774
Covered by Private or Public Insurance									
Number..	691,861	689,058	699,255	709,597	722,292	733,713	753,472	755,448	774,556
Percent...	88.3	86.9	87.6	88.1	88.5	88.7	90.2	89.8	91.3
Not Covered									
Number..	91,670	103,911	98,886	95,908	94,133	93,326	81,931	85,915	74,218
Percent...	11.7	13.1	12.4	11.9	11.5	11.3	9.8	10.2	8.7
Percent in the U.S. not covered...........................	15.1	15.1	15.5	15.1	14.8	14.5	11.7	9.4	8.6
Children Under 18 Years of Age	196,191	194,825	200,893	200,704	203,033	207,264	209,586	208,580	212,981
Covered by Private or Public Insurance									
Number..	179,673	180,074	184,198	188,665	191,198	194,142	197,674	194,544	203,436
Percent...	91.6	92.4	91.7	94.0	94.2	93.7	94.3	93.3	95.5
Not Covered									
Number..	16,518	14,751	16,695	12,039	11,835	13,122	11,912	14,036	9,545
Percent...	8.4	7.6	8.3	6.0	5.8	6.3	5.7	6.7	4.5
Percent in the U.S. not covered...........................	9.9	8.6	8.0	7.5	7.2	7.1	6.0	4.8	4.5

Table SD-7. Employment Status by Demographic Group, 2017

(Numbers in thousands, percent.)

Characteristic	Civilian noninstitutional population	Civilian labor force		Employed		Unemployed	
		Number	Percent of population	Number	Percent of population	Number	Percent of population
Total..	662	460	69.4	443	66.9	17	3.6
Sex							
Male..	331	244	73.7	235	71.1	9	3.6
Female.....................................	332	216	65.1	208	62.7	8	3.6
Race, Sex, and Hispanic Origin							
White.......................................	574	405	70.5	396	68.9	9	2.2
Male..	291	217	74.6	213	73.1	4	2.0
Female.....................................	283	187	66.2	183	64.6	4	2.3
Black or African American.............	NA	NA	NA	NA	NA	NA	NA
Male..	NA	NA	NA	NA	NA	NA	NA
Female.....................................	NA	NA	NA	NA	NA	NA	NA
Hispanic or Latino ethnicity[1].........	NA	NA	NA	NA	NA	NA	NA
Male..	NA	NA	NA	NA	NA	NA	NA
Female.....................................	NA	NA	NA	NA	NA	NA	NA
Age							
16 to 19 years...........................	NA	NA	NA	NA	NA	NA	NA
20 to 24 years...........................	67	53	78.5	49	73.2	3	6.5
25 to 34 years...........................	106	91	86.3	87	82.1	5	5.0
35 to 44 years...........................	92	80	86.9	77	84.2	3	3.3
45 to 54 years...........................	95	82	86.5	80	84.1	2	2.8
55 to 64 years...........................	118	93	78.6	92	77.6	1	1.2
65 years and over.......................	NA	NA	NA	NA	NA	NA	NA

NOTE: Data in Table 7 are from the Current Population Survey (CPS) and do not match the estimates in Table 8. See notes and definitions for further information.
[1] May be of any race.
NA = Not available.
… = Fewer than 500 persons

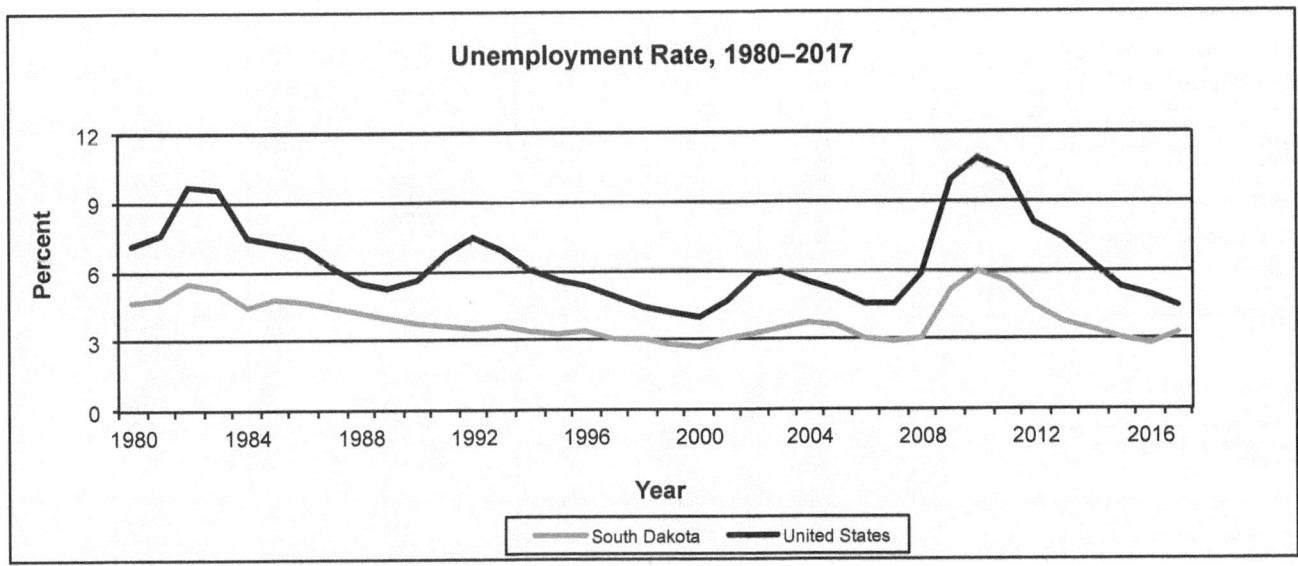

Table SD-8. Employment Status of the Civilian Noninstitutional Population Age 16 Years and Over

(Number, percent.)

Year	Civilian labor force	Civilian participation rate	Employed	Unemployed	Unemployment rate
2009.........................	446,010	72.2	423,993	22,017	4.9
2010.........................	441,339	71.3	419,355	21,984	5.0
2011.........................	440,934	70.7	420,054	20,880	4.7
2012.........................	442,442	70.1	423,501	18,941	4.3
2013.........................	443,079	69.4	426,284	16,795	3.8
2014.........................	446,475	69.4	431,139	15,336	3.4
2015.........................	449,408	69.4	435,450	13,958	3.1
2016.........................	451,934	69.2	438,377	13,557	3.0
2017.........................	455,175	69.0	440,028	15,147	3.3

Table SD-9. Employment and Average Wages by Industry

(Estimates through 2010 are based on the 2007 *North American Industry Classification System* [NAICS]. Estimates from 2011 onward are based on the 2012 NAICS.)

Industry	2010	2011	2012	2013	2014	2015	2016
	Number of jobs						
Wage and Salary Employment by Industry........................	423,507	427,833	435,383	438,456	444,762	447,859	451,683
Farm Wage and Salary Employment................................	4,943	5,557	6,845	6,298	6,367	4,908	4,622
Nonfarm Wage and Salary Employment...........................	418,564	422,276	428,538	432,158	438,395	442,951	447,061
Private wage and salary employment...............................	332,795	337,194	344,515	348,091	353,955	358,641	361,812
Forestry, fishing, and related activities..........................	2,098	2,269	2,397	2,471	2,430	2,427	2,455
Mining..	818	833	850	846	816	837	849
Utilities..	2,091	2,071	1,969	1,950	1,967	1,996	2,019
Construction..	20,828	20,785	20,749	21,090	21,854	22,767	23,447
Manufacturing..	37,011	39,268	41,233	41,574	42,447	42,652	42,233
Durable goods manufacturing.................................	24,021	25,887	27,217	27,515	28,482	28,537	27,593
Nondurable goods manufacturing............................	12,990	13,381	14,016	14,059	13,965	14,115	14,640
Wholesale trade..	18,663	19,061	19,589	19,978	20,899	21,215	21,280
Retail trade...	49,973	50,646	51,489	51,641	52,252	53,312	54,176
Transportation and warehousing.................................	10,333	10,479	10,515	10,534	11,247	11,524	11,380
Information...	6,544	6,398	6,208	6,025	6,060	5,885	5,770
Finance and insurance...	26,042	25,503	26,149	27,134	27,137	26,905	26,515
Real estate and rental and leasing.............................	3,462	3,517	3,543	3,626	3,729	3,811	3,864
Professional, scientific, and technical services	11,272	11,266	11,652	12,545	12,484	12,610	13,019
Management of companies and enterprises...................	3,625	3,768	4,146	4,235	4,572	4,936	5,079
Administrative and waste services..............................	12,884	13,812	13,622	13,100	13,386	13,317	13,383
Educational services	7,865	7,997	8,104	8,055	8,063	8,306	8,114
Health care and social assistance...............................	57,069	57,510	59,106	59,945	60,068	60,908	62,281
Arts, entertainment, and recreation.............................	6,504	6,413	6,341	6,190	6,402	6,610	6,645
Accommodation and food services..............................	36,847	37,315	38,241	38,703	39,290	39,787	40,424
Other services, except public administration.................	18,866	18,283	18,612	18,449	18,852	18,836	18,879
Government and government enterprises......................	85,769	85,082	84,023	84,067	84,440	84,310	85,249
	Dollars						
Average Wages and Salaries by Industry	33,919	35,003	36,217	36,833	38,260	39,658	41,865
Average Farm Wages and Salaries	37,203	36,398	44,444	39,940	40,978	38,828	42,755
Average Nonfarm Wages and Salaries	33,880	34,985	36,085	36,788	38,220	39,667	41,856
Average private wages and salaries.............................	33,657	34,925	36,128	36,967	38,521	40,056	42,013
Forestry, fishing, and related activities........................	24,440	25,071	25,315	26,679	25,863	27,415	31,169
Mining..	49,593	55,685	57,316	55,965	58,808	60,777	61,529
Utilities..	64,924	67,059	69,450	73,256	74,710	76,286	77,233
Construction..	38,080	38,984	39,931	40,942	42,886	44,987	45,513
Manufacturing..	39,903	41,466	42,175	42,447	44,511	45,441	48,670
Durable goods manufacturing.................................	40,469	42,403	42,836	43,536	45,259	45,996	48,324
Nondurable goods manufacturing............................	38,856	39,654	40,891	40,316	42,986	44,319	49,320
Wholesale trade..	46,650	48,908	51,352	52,927	54,992	56,262	57,587
Retail trade...	23,091	23,733	24,552	25,168	26,198	27,030	27,250
Transportation and warehousing.................................	39,275	41,193	42,125	42,862	43,978	44,955	46,585
Information...	39,903	41,823	42,780	43,368	44,834	45,799	45,635
Finance and insurance	45,799	48,149	49,764	50,336	52,962	56,374	59,382
Real estate and rental and leasing.............................	26,755	28,105	29,600	30,639	32,329	34,785	35,570
Professional, scientific, and technical services	46,507	49,104	51,609	49,921	52,681	56,395	60,751
Management of companies and enterprises...................	88,726	88,046	89,076	91,577	92,716	93,532	94,540
Administrative and waste services..............................	25,307	25,533	26,958	27,166	29,194	29,969	31,991
Educational services	24,601	24,242	24,522	24,861	25,031	24,814	23,952
Health care and social assistance...............................	40,059	41,621	43,112	44,281	45,810	47,772	51,797
Arts, entertainment, and recreation.............................	17,705	17,929	17,945	18,285	18,834	19,718	20,274
Accommodation and food services..............................	13,964	14,396	14,984	15,522	16,076	17,297	18,230
Other services, except public administration.................	23,597	25,062	25,613	27,009	28,115	29,510	31,532
Government and government enterprises......................	34,746	35,224	35,908	36,047	36,958	38,015	41,188

Table SD-10. Employment Characteristics by Family Type

(Number, percent.)

Family type and labor force status	2014		2015		2016	
	Total	Families with own children under 18 years	Total	Families with own children under 18 years	Total	Families with own children under 18 years
All Families..	210,903	88,396	217,013	94,326	209,986	92,357
FAMILY TYPE AND LABOR FORCE STATUS						
Married-Couple Families................................	165,397	59,765	170,511	64,388	164,515	64,612
Both husband and wife in labor force....................	61.7	78.8	61.1	78.4	61.4	79.8
Husband in labor force, wife not in labor force..........	16.2	17.2	16.2	18.3	15.7	15.8
Wife in labor force, husband not in labor force..........	7.0	2.7	6.5	1.9	6.7	2.8
Both husband and wife not in labor force................	15.1	1.3	15.8	1.3	15.8	1.1
Other Families	45,506	28,631	46,502	29,938	45,471	27,745
Female householder, no husband present................	68.7	73.3	69.5	70.4	68.3	69.1
In labor force..	51.7	61.6	53.7	62.3	48.2	55.6
Not in labor force	17.0	11.7	15.8	8.1	20.1	13.5
Male householder, no wife present.......................	31.3	26.7	30.5	29.6	31.7	30.9
In labor force..	26.8	26.0	26.2	27.6	25.1	28.2
Not in labor force	4.5	0.7	4.3	2.0	6.7	2.7

Table SD-11. School Enrollment and Educational Attainment, 2016

(Number, percent.)

Item	State	U.S.
Enrollment		
Total population 3 years and over, enrolled in school	218,239	81,572,277
Enrolled in nursery school or preschool (percent)..	6.6	6.0
Enrolled in kindergarten (percent)...	5.9	5.0
Enrolled in elementary school, grades 1-8 (percent)...	42.0	40.3
Enrolled in high school, grades 9-12 (percent)..	20.9	21.0
Enrolled in college or graduate school (percent)..	24.7	27.7
Attainment		
Total population 25 years and over	565,894	218,475,480
Less than ninth grade (percent)..	3.2	5.4
9th to 12th grade, no diploma (percent)...	5.6	7.2
High school graduate, including equivalency (percent)......................................	29.0	27.2
Some college, no degree (percent)...	21.8	20.6
Associate's degree (percent)...	11.5	8.4
Bachelor's degree (percent)	19.6	19.3
Graduate or professional degree (percent)..	9.2	11.9
High school graduate or higher (percent)	91.2	87.5
Bachelor's degree or higher (percent)...	28.9	31.3

Table SD-12. Public School Characteristics and Educational Indicators

(Number, percent; data derived from National Center of Education Statistics.)

Item	State	U.S.
Public Schools, 2015–2016 (except where noted)		
Number of school districts..	168	18,328
Number of schools..	698	98,456
Number of students..	134,253	50,327,015
Number of teachers	9,638	3,151,497
Student-teacher ratio	13.9	16.0
Expenditures per student (dollars), 2014-2015..	9,103	11,445
Four-year adjusted cohort graduation rate (ACGR)[1,2]	83.9	84.1
Students eligible for free or reduced-price lunch (percent), 2014-2015....................	39.5	51.8
English language learners (percent), Fall 2015	3.4	9.5
Students age 3 to 21 served under IDEA, part B (percent)...................................	14.5	13.2

Public Schools by Type	Number	Percent of state public schools
Total number of schools...	698	100.0
Regular	651	93.3
Special education..	12	1.7
Vocational education..	3	0.4
Alternative education..	32	4.6

NOTE: Every school is assigned only one school type based on its instructional emphasis.
[1] ACGR data represents a new method of calculating high-school completion rates and may not be comparable to previous years' data for Averaged Freshmen Graduation Rates (AFGR).
[2] The United States 4-year ACGRs were estimated using both the reported 4-year ACGR data from 49 states and the District of Columbia and using imputed data for Idaho. The estimate for American Indian/Alaska Native students also includes imputed data for Virginia.

Table SD-13. Reported Voting and Registration of the Voting-Age Population, November 2016

(Numbers in thousands, percent.)

Item	Total population	Total citizen population	Registered			Voted		
			Total registered	Percent registered (total population)	Percent registered (total citizen population)	Total voted	Percent voted (total population)	Percent voted (total citizen population)
U.S. Total	245,502	224,059	157,596	64.2	70.3	137,537	56.0	61.4
State Total...............................	631	612	437	69.3	71.4	362	57.3	59.1
Sex								
Male	314	304	213	68.0	70.3	171	54.6	56.5
Female	318	309	224	70.6	72.6	191	60.0	61.7
Race								
White alone..............................	560	551	406	72.5	73.6	340	60.7	61.6
White, non-Hispanic alone..........	546	543	402	73.6	74.0	336	61.6	61.9
Black alone...............................	11	8	4	(B)	(B)	3	(B)	(B)
Asian alone...............................	9	2	-	(B)	(B)	-	(B)	(B)
Hispanic (of any race)......................	21	15	8	(B)	(B)	7	(B)	(B)
White alone or in combination	565	557	410	72.6	73.7	343	60.7	61.6
Black alone or in combination...........	12	9	6	(B)	(B)	5	(B)	(B)
Asian alone or in combination...........	9	2	-	(B)	(B)	-	(B)	(B)
Age								
18 to 24 years...........................	84	81	41	(B)	(B)	26	(B)	(B)
25 to 34 years...........................	103	98	63	(B)	(B)	50	(B)	(B)
35 to 44 years...........................	94	90	61	(B)	(B)	52	(B)	(B)
45 to 64 years...........................	230	224	177	76.7	78.8	147	63.7	65.4
65 years and over	119	119	95	79.9	79.9	88	73.9	73.9

- = Zero or rounds to zero.
B = Base is less than 75,000 and therefore too small to show the derived measure.

Table SD-14. Crime

(Number, rate per 100,000. Data are derived from the FBI Uniform Crime Reports.)

Item	State			U.S. [1,2,3,4]		
	2015	2016	Percent change	2015	2016	Percent change
TOTAL POPULATION [5]	858,469	865,454	0.8	321,418,820	323,127,513	0.5
VIOLENT CRIME						
Number..	3,289	3,621	10.1	1,231,566	1,248,185	1.3
Rate..	383.1	418.4	9.2	383.2	386.3	0.8
Murder and Nonnegligent Manslaughter						
Number..	32	27	-15.6	15,696	17,250	9.9
Rate..	3.7	3.1	-16.2	4.9	5.3	8.2
Rape [6]						
Number..	495	509	2.8	124,047	130,603	5.3
Rate..	57.7	58.8	1.9	38.6	40.4	4.7
Robbery						
Number..	216	272	25.9	327,374	332,198	1.5
Rate..	25.2	31.4	24.6	101.9	102.8	0.9
Aggravated Assault						
Number..	2,546	2,813	10.5	764,449	803,007	5.0
Rate..	296.6	325.0	9.6	237.8	248.5	4.5
PROPERTY CRIME						
Number..	16,680	17,141	2.8	7,993,631	7,919,035	-0.9
Rate..	1,943.0	1,980.6	1.9	2,487.0	2,450.7	-1.5
Burglary						
Number..	2,960	3,000	1.4	1,579,527	1,515,096	-4.1
Rate..	344.8	346.6	0.5	491.4	468.9	-4.6
Larceny-Theft						
Number..	12,532	12,639	0.9	5,706,346	5,638,455	-1.2
Rate..	1,459.8	1,460.4	-	1,775.4	1,745.0	-1.7
Motor Vehicle Theft						
Number..	1,188	1,502	26.4	707,758	765,484	8.2
Rate..	138.4	173.6	25.4	220.2	236.9	7.6

NOTE: Although arson data are included in the trend and clearance tables, sufficient data are not available to estimate totals for this offense. Therefore, no arson data are published in this table.
X = Not applicable.
- = Zero or rounds to zero.
[1] The crime figures have been adjusted.
[2] The data collection methodology for the offense of forcible rape used by the Minnesota state Uniform Crime Reporting (UCR) Program (with the exception of Minneapolis and St. Paul, Minnesota) does not comply with national UCR Program guidelines. Consequently, its figures for forcible rape and violent crime (of which forcible rape is a part) are not published in this table.
[3] Includes offenses reported by the Zoological Police and the Metro Transit Police.
[4] Because of changes in the state's reporting practices, figures are not comparable to previous years' data.
[5] Populations are U.S. Census Bureau provisional estimates as of July 1 of each year.
[6] The figures shown for the offense of rape were estimated using the revised Uniform Crime Reporting (UCR) definition of rape.

Table SD-15. State Government Finances, 2016

(Dollar amounts in thousands, percent distribution.)

Item	Dollars	Percent distribution
Total Revenue	4,537,220	100.0
General revenue	4,250,719	93.7
Intergovernmental revenue	1,475,385	32.5
Taxes	1,747,550	38.5
General sales	968,787	21.4
Selective sales	471,254	10.4
License taxes	268,227	5.9
Individual income tax	0	-
Corporate income tax	32,684	0.7
Other taxes	6,598	0.1
Current charges	438,008	9.7
Miscellaneous general revenue	589,776	13.0
Utility revenue	0	-
Liquor stores revenue	0	-
Insurance trust revenue [1]	286,501	6.3
Total Expenditure	5,059,935	100.0
Intergovernmental expenditure	775,059	15.3
Direct expenditure	4,284,876	84.7
Current operation	2,778,061	54.9
Capital outlay	765,877	15.1
Insurance benefits and repayments	538,569	10.6
Assistance and subsidies	90,801	1.8
Interest on debt	111,568	2.2
Exhibit: Salaries and wages	750,526	14.8
Total Expenditure	5,059,935	100.0
General expenditure	4,521,366	89.4
Intergovernmental expenditure	775,059	15.3
Direct expenditure	3,746,307	74.0
General expenditure, by function:		
Education	1,464,173	28.9
Public welfare	1,046,368	20.7
Hospitals	23,145	0.5
Health	191,043	3.8
Highways	726,472	14.4
Police protection	46,310	0.9
Correction	126,395	2.5
Natural resources	171,797	3.4
Parks and recreation	42,006	0.8
Governmental administration	211,150	4.2
Interest on general debt	111,568	2.2
Other and unallocable	360,939	7.1
Utility expenditure	0	-
Liquor stores expenditure	0	-
Insurance trust expenditure	538,569	10.6
Debt at End of Fiscal Year	3,366,459	X
Cash and Security Holdings	15,527,699	X

X = Not applicable.
- = Zero or rounds to zero.
[1] Within insurance trust revenue, net earnings of state retirement systems is a calculated statistic (the item code in the data file is X08), and thus can be positive or negative. Net earnings is the sum of earnings on investments plus gains on investments minus losses on investments. The change made in 2002 for asset valuation from book to market value in accordance with Statement 34 of the Governmental Accounting Standards Board is reflected in the calculated statistics.

Table SD-16. State Government Tax Collections, 2017

(Dollars in thousands, percent.)

Item	Dollars	Percent distribution
Total Taxes	1,828,543	100.0
Property taxes	X	-
Sales and gross receipts	1,517,973	83.0
General sales and gross receipts	1,065,361	58.3
Selective sales and gross receipts	452,612	24.8
Alcoholic beverages	16,933	0.9
Amusements	8,853	0.5
Insurance premiums	66,496	3.6
Motor fuels	189,133	10.3
Pari-mutuels	319	-
Public utilities	3,103	0.2
Tobacco products	61,809	3.4
Other selective sales	105,966	5.8
Licenses	269,481	14.7
Alcoholic beverages	1,166	0.1
Amusements	6,573	0.4
Corporations in general	5,049	0.3
Hunting and fishing	29,866	1.6
Motor vehicle	82,947	4.5
Motor vehicle operators	5,410	0.3
Public utilities	X	-
Occupation and business, NEC	114,821	6.3
Other licenses	23,649	1.3
Income taxes	30,728	1.7
Individual income	X	-
Corporation net income	30,728	1.7
Other taxes	10,361	0.6
Death and gift	X	-
Documentary and stock transfer	185	-
Severance	10,176	0.6
Taxes, NEC	0	-

X = Not applicable.
- = Zero or rounds to zero.

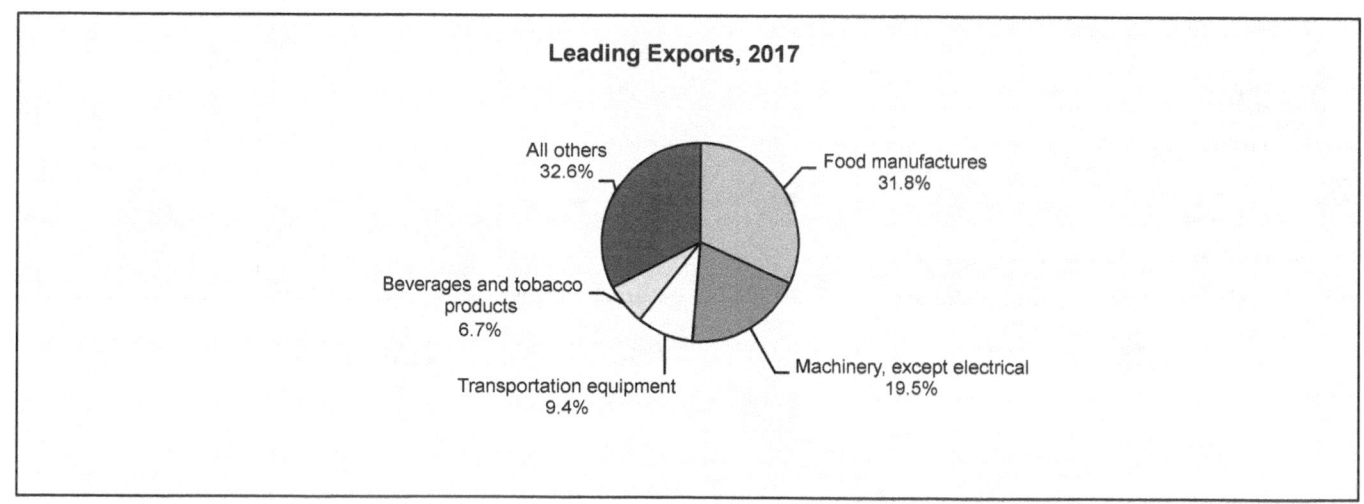

Leading Exports, 2017

All others 32.6%

Food manufactures 31.8%

Beverages and tobacco products 6.7%

Transportation equipment 9.4%

Machinery, except electrical 19.5%

TENNESSEE

Facts and Figures

Location: South central United States; bordered on the N by Kentucky and Virginia, on the E by North Carolina, on the S by Georgia, Alabama, and Mississippi, and on the W by Arkansas and Missouri

Area: 42,143 sq. mi. (109,151 sq. km.); rank—36th

Population: 6,715,984 (2017 est.); rank—16th

Principal Cities: capital—Nashville; largest—Nashville

Statehood: June 1, 1796; 16th state

U.S. Congress: 2 senators, 9 representatives

State Motto: Agriculture and Commerce

State Song: "The Tennessee Waltz"

State Nickname: The Volunteer State

Abbreviations: TN; Tenn.

State Symbols: flower—iris; tree—yellow poplar (tulip poplar); bird—mockingbird

At a Glance

- With an increase in population of 5.7 percent, Tennessee ranked 19th among the states in growth from 2010 to 2017.

- Tennessee's median household income in 2016 was $48,547, and 15.8 percent of the population lived below the poverty level.

- In 2016, 9.0 percent of Tennesseans did not have health insurance, compared to 8.6 percent of the total U.S. population.

- Tennessee's violent crime rate in 2016 was 632.9 per 100,000 population, compared to 386.3 for the entire nation; this was the 5th highest rate in the country.

- Tennessee's unemployment rate of 3.7 percent ranked 34th among the states in 2017 and was slightly lower than the national rate of 4.4 percent.

Table TN-1. Population by Age, Sex, Race, and Hispanic Origin

(Number, percent, except where noted.)

Sex, age, race, and Hispanic origin	2000	2010	2017 [1]	Average annual percent change, 2010–2017
Total Population................................	5,689,283	6,346,105	6,715,984	5.8
Percent of total U.S. population	2.0	2.1	2.1	X
Sex				
Male................................	2,770,275	3,093,504	3,275,966	5.9
Female	2,919,008	3,252,601	3,440,018	5.8
Age				
Under 5 years................................	374,880	407,813	408,644	0.2
5 to 19 years................................	1,186,152	1,268,308	1,264,469	-0.3
20 to 64 years................................	3,424,940	3,816,522	3,966,269	3.9
65 years and over	703,311	853,462	1,076,602	26.1
Median age (years)	35.9	38.0	38.7	1.8
Race and Hispanic Origin				
One race				
White	4,563,310	5,056,311	5,276,748	4.4
Black	932,809	1,068,010	1,148,218	7.5
American Indian and Alaska Native	15,152	26,256	30,876	17.6
Asian................................	56,662	93,897	125,244	33.4
Native Hawaiian or Other Pacific Islander	2,205	5,426	6,428	18.5
Two or more races	63,109	96,205	128,470	33.5
Hispanic (of any race)................................	123,838	301,090	366,554	21.7

X = Not applicable.
[1] Population figures for 2017 are July 1 estimates. The 2010 estimates are taken from the 2010 Census.

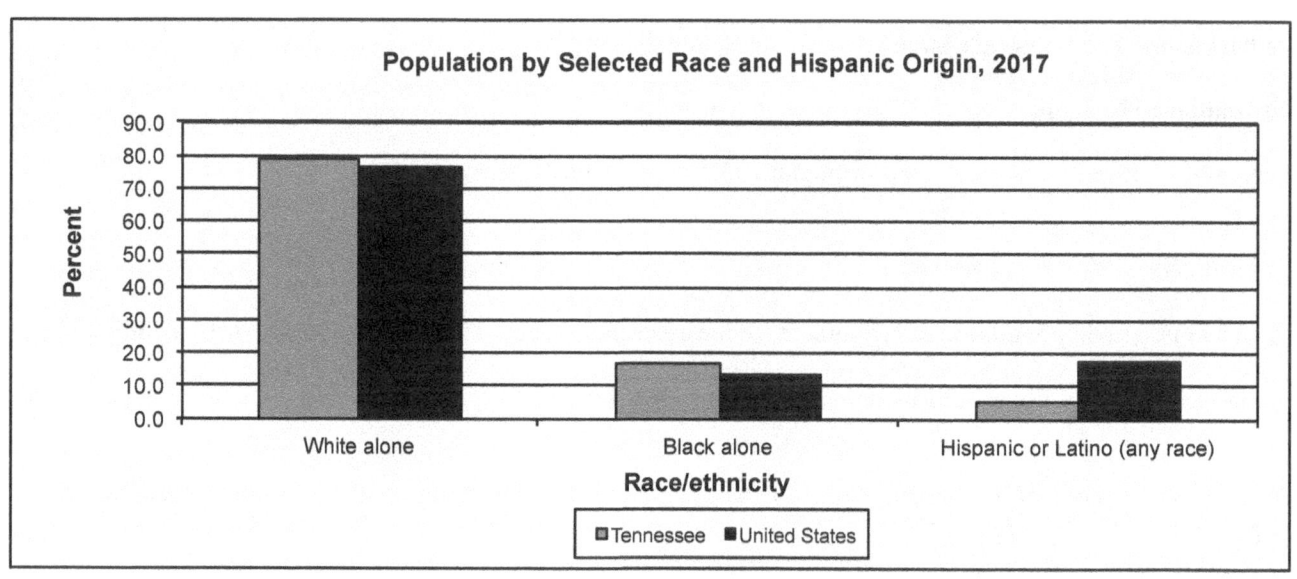

Population by Selected Race and Hispanic Origin, 2017

Table TN-2. Marital Status

(Number, percent distribution.)

Sex, age, and marital status	2000	2010	2016
Males, 15 Years and Over................................	2,169,327	2,461,573	2,608,425
Never married	26.6	31.4	33.4
Now married, except separated................................	58.9	52.2	50.1
Separated................................	1.7	2.1	2.1
Widowed................................	2.5	2.7	3.1
Divorced................................	10.4	11.7	11.4
Females, 15 Years and Over................................	2,353,303	2,652,823	2,797,265
Never married	20.7	25.3	27.5
Now married, except separated................................	53.6	47.9	46.7
Separated................................	2.3	2.7	2.4
Widowed................................	11.2	10.3	9.4
Divorced................................	12.2	13.7	13.9

Table TN-3. Households and Housing Characteristics

(Number, percent, dollars.)

Item	2000	2010	2016	Average annual percent change, 2010–2016
Total Households..	2,232,905	2,440,663	2,556,332	0.8
Family households	1,547,835	1,644,896	1,670,605	0.3
Married-couple family	1,173,960	1,195,406	1,223,193	0.4
Other family	373,875	449,490	447,412	-0.1
Male householder, no wife present.......................	85,976	106,616	114,687	1.3
Female householder, no husband present................	287,899	342,874	332,725	-0.5
Nonfamily households	685,070	795,767	885,727	1.9
Householder living alone....................................	576,401	675,565	734,646	1.5
Householder not living alone...............................	108,669	120,202	151,081	4.3
Housing Characteristics				
Total housing units..	2,439,443	2,815,087	2,919,698	0.6
Occupied housing units	2,232,905	2,440,663	2,556,332	0.8
Owner occupied	1,561,363	1,662,768	1,664,018	-
Renter occupied	671,542	777,895	892,314	2.5
Average household size.......................................	2.48	2.54	2.54	-
Financial Characteristics				
Median gross rent of renter-occupied housing	505	697	806	2.6
Median monthly owner costs for housing units with a mortgage	882	1,161	1,172	0.2
Median value of owner-occupied housing units	93,000	139,000	157,700	2.2

- = Zero or rounds to zero.

Table TN-4. Migration, Origin, and Language

(Number, percent.)

Characteristic	State 2015	State 2016	State Percent change	U.S. 2015	U.S. 2016	U.S. Percent change
Residence 1 Year Ago						
Population 1 year and over	6,522,259	6,580,953	0.9	317,635,720	319,361,956	0.5
Same house	84.9	85.8	X	85.3	85.4	X
Different house in the U.S.	14.8	13.9	X	14.1	13.9	X
Same county	8.6	8.3	X	8.5	8.3	X
Different county	6.2	5.6	X	5.6	5.6	X
Same state	3.2	3.0	X	3.2	3.2	X
Different state	3.0	2.6	X	2.4	2.4	X
Abroad	0.4	0.4	X	0.7	0.7	X
Place of Birth						
Native born	6,268,729	6,331,173	1.0	278,128,449	279,388,170	0.5
Male	48.6	48.7	X	49.3	49.3	X
Female	51.4	51.3	X	50.7	50.7	X
Foreign born	331,570	320,021	-3.5	43,290,372	43,739,345	1.0
Male	51.6	50.7	X	48.6	48.5	X
Female	48.4	49.3	X	51.4	51.5	X
Foreign born; naturalized U.S. citizen......	120,762	117,924	-2.4	20,697,103	21,238,372	2.6
Male	46.4	45.8	X	45.9	45.9	X
Female	53.6	54.2	X	54.1	54.1	X
Foreign born; not a U.S. citizen...........	210,808	202,097	-4.1	22,593,269	22,500,973	-0.4
Male	54.6	53.6	X	51.1	51.0	X
Female	45.4	46.4	X	48.9	49.0	X
Entered 2010 or later	22.7	25.1	X	15.6	18.6	X
Entered 2000 to 2009	36.3	34.3	X	27.9	26.7	X
Entered before 2000......................	41.0	40.5	X	56.5	54.7	X
World Region of Birth, Foreign						
Foreign-born population, excluding population born at sea	331,513	320,021	-3.5	43,289,646	43,738,901	1.0
Europe	9.7	11.1	X	11.1	10.9	X
Asia......................................	30.0	30.7	X	30.6	30.8	X
Africa	11.4	8.4	X	4.8	4.9	X
Oceania	0.4	0.6	X	0.6	0.6	X
Latin America............................	44.7	46.7	X	51.1	51.0	X
North America	3.9	2.6	X	1.9	1.8	X
Language Spoken at Home and Ability to Speak English						
Population 5 years and over................	6,201,062	6,247,026	0.7	301,625,014	303,328,961	0.6
English only	93.1	93.0	X	78.5	78.4	X
Language other than English..............	6.9	7.0	X	21.5	21.6	X
Speaks English less than "very well"......	2.9	2.9	X	8.6	8.6	X

NA = Not available.
X = Not applicable.
- = Zero or rounds to zero.

Table TN-5. Median Income and Poverty Status, 2016

(Number, percent, except as noted.)

Characteristic	State		U.S.	
	Number	Percent	Number	Percent
Median Income				
Households (dollars)...	48,547	X	57,617	X
Families (dollars)	60,659	X	71,062	X
Below Poverty Level (All People)	1,023,177	15.8	44,268,996	14.0
Sex				
Male	453,858	14.4	19,760,056	12.8
Female	569,319	17.1	24,508,940	15.2
Age				
Under 18 years...	334,238	22.6	14,115,713	19.5
Related children under 18 years..	329,494	22.4	13,805,435	19.1
18 to 64 years...	598,352	15.0	25,723,818	13.2
65 years and over	90,587	8.9	4,429,465	9.2

X = Not applicable.

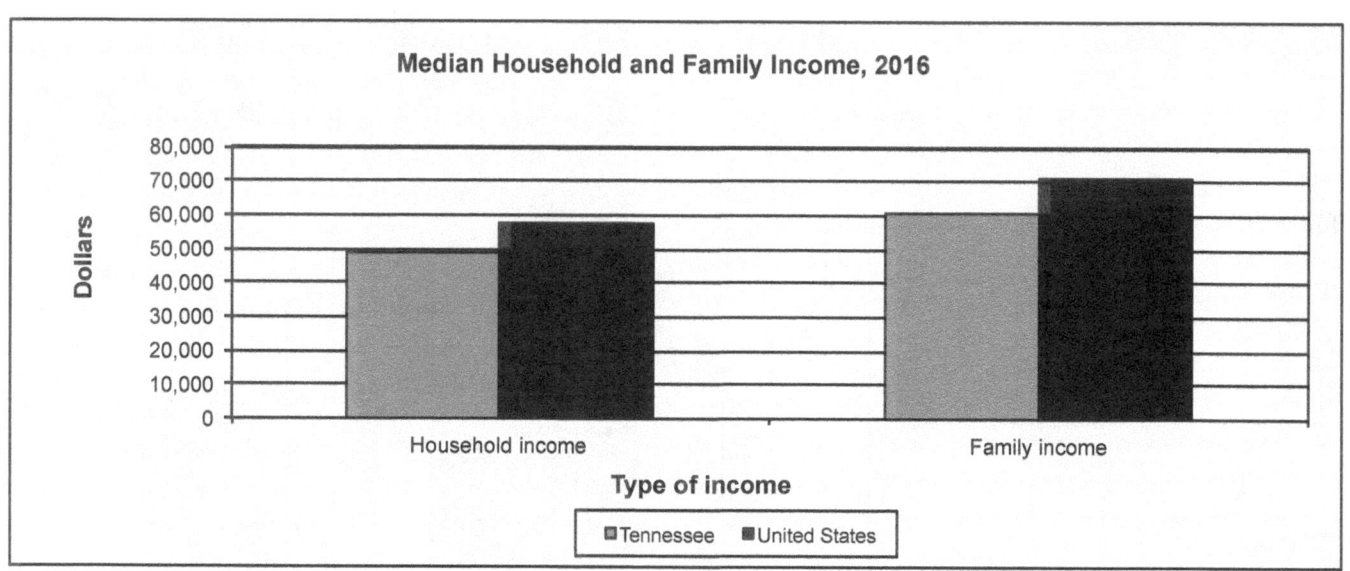

Median Household and Family Income, 2016

Table TN-6. Health Insurance Coverage Status for the Civilian Noninstitutionalized Population and Children Under 18 Years of Age

(Number, percent.)

Item	2008	2009	2010	2011	2012	2013	2014	2015	2016
Civilian Noninstitutionalized Population	6,113,391	6,188,118	6,259,546	6,302,351	6,354,629	6,394,644	6,448,737	6,496,300	6,546,914
Covered by Private or Public Insurance									
Number..	5,279,074	5,304,803	5,360,985	5,379,701	5,472,509	5,507,982	5,672,418	5,828,883	5,954,604
Percent...	86.4	85.7	85.6	85.4	86.1	86.1	88.0	89.7	91.0
Not Covered									
Number..	834,317	883,315	898,561	922,650	882,120	886,662	776,319	667,417	592,310
Percent...	13.6	14.3	14.4	14.6	13.9	13.9	12.0	10.3	9.0
Percent in the U.S. not covered.........................	15.1	15.1	15.5	15.1	14.8	14.5	11.7	9.4	8.6
Children Under 18 Years of Age	1,476,111	1,487,977	1,493,097	1,487,779	1,490,249	1,489,574	1,489,620	1,490,949	1,500,902
Covered by Private or Public Insurance									
Number..	1,369,798	1,400,671	1,413,853	1,402,852	1,405,719	1,404,287	1,412,007	1,428,845	1,447,865
Percent...	92.8	94.1	94.7	94.3	94.3	94.3	94.8	95.8	96.5
Not Covered									
Number..	106,313	87,306	79,244	84,927	84,530	85,287	77,613	62,104	53,037
Percent...	7.2	5.9	5.3	5.7	5.7	5.7	5.2	4.2	3.5
Percent in the U.S. not covered.........................	9.9	8.6	8.0	7.5	7.2	7.1	6.0	4.8	4.5

Table TN-7. Employment Status by Demographic Group, 2017

(Numbers in thousands, percent.)

Characteristic	Civilian noninstitutional population	Civilian labor force		Employed		Unemployed	
		Number	Percent of population	Number	Percent of population	Number	Percent of population
Total..	5,274	3,195	60.6	3,076	58.3	120	3.7
Sex							
Male..	2,517	1,690	67.1	1,627	64.6	63	3.7
Female	2,756	1,505	54.6	1,449	52.6	57	3.8
Race, Sex, and Hispanic Origin							
White..	4,162	2,487	59.7	2,405	57.8	82	3.3
Male..	2,008	1,341	66.8	1,295	64.5	46	3.4
Female	2,153	1,146	53.2	1,109	51.5	36	3.2
Black or African American..............	854	538	62.9	505	59.1	33	6.1
Male..	385	258	67.1	244	63.2	15	5.8
Female	469	279	59.5	262	55.8	18	6.3
Hispanic or Latino ethnicity[1]	220	151	68.8	148	67.2	4	2.4
Male..	124	107	86.7	105	84.7	2	2.3
Female	NA	NA	NA	NA	NA	NA	NA
Age							
16 to 19 years.............................	308	111	35.9	96	31.3	14	12.8
20 to 24 years.............................	418	299	71.5	279	66.8	20	6.6
25 to 34 years.............................	917	768	83.8	736	80.3	33	4.2
35 to 44 years.............................	823	670	81.4	652	79.2	18	2.7
45 to 54 years.............................	834	632	75.8	614	73.6	18	2.9
55 to 64 years.............................	891	535	60.0	522	58.6	13	2.4
65 years and over	1,083	180	16.6	176	16.3	4	2.2

NOTE: Data in Table 7 are from the Current Population Survey (CPS) and do not match the estimates in Table 8. See notes and definitions for further information.
[1] May be of any race.

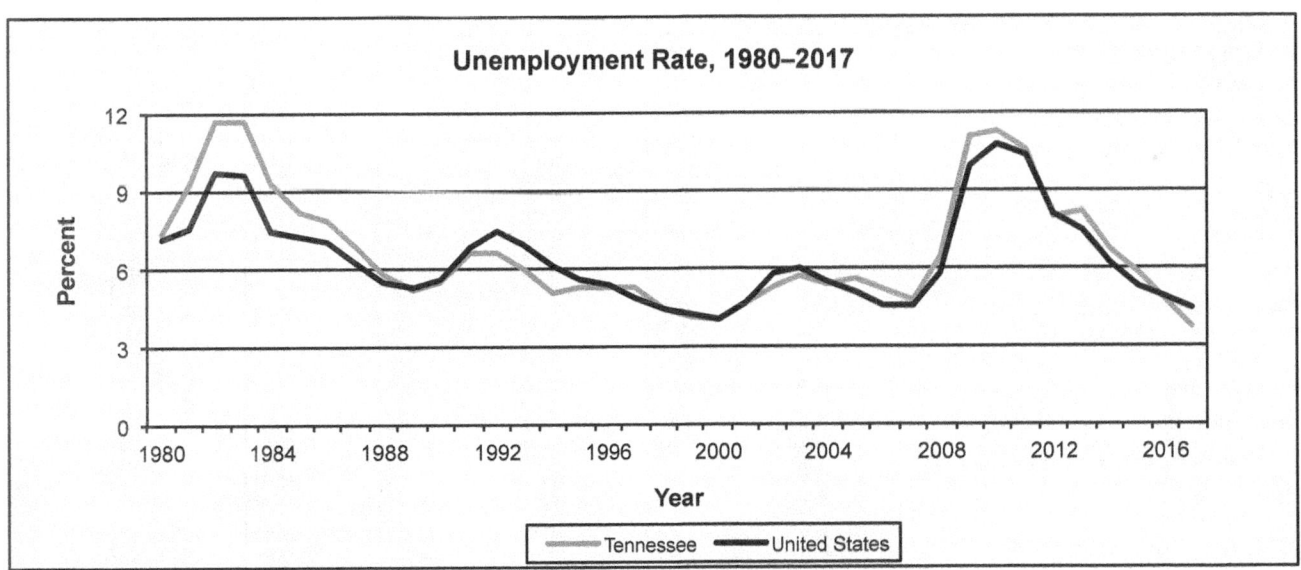

Table TN-8. Employment Status of the Civilian Noninstitutional Population Age 16 Years and Over

(Number, percent.)

Year	Civilian labor force	Civilian participation rate	Employed	Unemployed	Unemployment rate
2009...	3,052,678	62.7	2,733,113	319,565	10.5
2010...	3,090,795	62.8	2,792,063	298,732	9.7
2011...	3,125,307	62.9	2,844,662	280,645	9.0
2012...	3,100,671	61.8	2,857,945	242,726	7.8
2013...	3,067,431	60.6	2,828,479	238,952	7.8
2014...	3,022,927	59.2	2,824,016	198,911	6.6
2015...	3,062,706	59.4	2,890,640	172,066	5.6
2016...	3,134,725	60.1	2,987,074	147,651	4.7
2017...	3,198,767	60.6	3,080,210	118,557	3.7

Table TN-9. Employment and Average Wages by Industry

(Estimates through 2010 are based on the 2007 *North American Industry Classification System* [NAICS]. Estimates from 2011 onward are based on the 2012 NAICS.)

Industry	2010	2011	2012	2013	2014	2015	2016
	Number of jobs						
Wage and Salary Employment by Industry.........................	2,711,898	2,757,216	2,807,608	2,848,078	2,905,771	2,976,108	3,040,781
Farm Wage and Salary Employment.................................	8,430	9,323	9,901	9,150	9,927	11,141	9,177
Nonfarm Wage and Salary Employment............................	2,703,468	2,747,893	2,797,707	2,838,928	2,895,844	2,964,967	3,031,604
Private wage and salary employment.................................	2,246,595	2,294,109	2,348,606	2,390,888	2,450,409	2,522,162	2,586,474
Forestry, fishing, and related activities..............................	4,540	4,605	4,727	4,878	5,037	5,081	4,985
Mining...	3,549	3,594	3,427	3,424	3,430	3,458	3,060
Utilities..	3,357	3,317	3,356	3,342	3,380	3,366	3,394
Construction..	104,531	107,959	107,909	106,798	109,475	115,678	118,234
Manufacturing..	300,059	304,299	313,975	318,867	325,265	332,827	344,143
Durable goods manufacturing....................................	177,816	183,657	194,398	198,948	205,407	210,733	219,286
Nondurable goods manufacturing...............................	122,243	120,642	119,577	119,919	119,858	122,094	124,857
Wholesale trade..	117,444	118,044	121,161	122,872	123,754	121,607	120,444
Retail trade...	309,757	312,756	315,571	317,385	323,501	328,403	336,287
Transportation and warehousing..................................	130,188	135,002	140,699	144,274	147,394	155,455	163,491
Information...	44,369	43,265	42,797	43,474	43,353	43,450	45,007
Finance and insurance..	108,367	107,288	108,421	106,845	109,228	111,170	113,459
Real estate and rental and leasing...............................	32,875	31,812	32,379	33,608	35,193	37,211	38,864
Professional, scientific, and technical services	108,118	110,449	111,968	115,065	120,947	129,212	133,074
Management of companies and enterprises.......................	26,059	28,992	31,563	35,228	37,312	41,472	44,077
Administrative and waste services................................	171,006	186,036	195,552	204,974	217,073	224,684	229,050
Educational services	53,094	53,946	55,170	56,295	57,628	58,633	59,966
Health care and social assistance................................	329,629	336,314	343,825	347,917	350,658	361,027	367,592
Arts, entertainment, and recreation...............................	30,079	30,218	30,709	31,688	32,875	34,819	36,403
Accommodation and food services...............................	234,262	238,955	248,139	256,131	265,373	274,947	285,531
Other services, except public administration....................	135,312	137,258	137,258	137,823	139,533	139,662	139,413
Government and government enterprises...........................	456,873	453,784	449,101	448,040	445,435	442,805	445,130
	Dollars						
Average Wages and Salaries by Industry	41,009	41,873	43,404	43,573	44,701	46,176	48,475
Average Farm Wages and Salaries	20,674	16,362	21,339	23,808	23,229	19,002	25,431
Average Nonfarm Wages and Salaries	41,072	41,960	43,482	43,637	44,774	46,278	48,544
Average private wages and salaries................................	41,447	42,358	44,051	44,113	45,214	46,831	49,117
Forestry, fishing, and related activities.............................	23,088	23,885	24,682	24,951	25,878	26,590	29,183
Mining...	63,573	61,486	64,423	63,487	67,906	68,225	73,210
Utilities..	61,568	63,014	63,793	65,517	67,999	70,791	75,534
Construction	44,279	45,586	47,136	47,570	49,914	52,820	57,685
Manufacturing...	51,858	52,863	54,730	54,673	56,301	57,325	59,447
Durable goods manufacturing....................................	50,735	51,742	54,263	53,212	55,136	56,255	58,708
Nondurable goods manufacturing...............................	53,491	54,569	55,490	57,097	58,299	59,172	60,745
Wholesale trade..	57,520	59,664	62,067	61,572	64,264	67,281	70,915
Retail trade...	27,018	27,724	28,107	27,882	28,633	29,520	30,527
Transportation and warehousing..................................	48,093	49,515	50,159	50,675	51,270	52,516	55,223
Information...	54,019	57,049	59,041	58,964	61,817	62,876	65,785
Finance and insurance..	66,041	68,054	72,399	72,250	74,927	76,002	80,080
Real estate and rental and leasing...............................	38,115	39,888	42,139	42,655	44,668	46,651	50,520
Professional, scientific, and technical services	64,655	66,004	70,898	70,550	72,036	75,723	77,275
Management of companies and enterprises.........................	82,130	83,137	99,412	98,318	97,015	100,532	102,308
Administrative and waste services	31,373	31,170	32,675	33,174	32,317	33,064	34,846
Educational services	33,449	34,279	35,343	35,917	36,262	36,289	38,670
Health care and social assistance................................	44,813	45,546	46,389	46,669	47,777	49,686	51,623
Arts, entertainment, and recreation...............................	40,000	41,602	44,197	44,140	47,206	53,703	56,842
Accommodation and food services................................	17,692	18,050	18,452	18,329	18,862	19,571	21,359
Other services, except public administration.....................	28,128	28,797	30,223	30,632	32,000	33,365	36,238
Government and government enterprises.............................	39,227	39,947	40,502	41,093	42,356	43,128	45,219

Table TN-10. Employment Characteristics by Family Type

(Number, percent.)

Family type and labor force status	2014		2015		2016	
	Total	Families with own children under 18 years	Total	Families with own children under 18 years	Total	Families with own children under 18 years
All Families...	1,655,480	684,060	1,675,678	675,024	1,670,605	668,357
FAMILY TYPE AND LABOR FORCE STATUS						
Married-Couple Families................................	1,198,174	447,165	1,213,001	438,614	1,223,193	437,507
Both husband and wife in labor force...................	48.0	64.3	48.6	65.9	47.6	64.4
Husband in labor force, wife not in labor force.........	23.2	29.2	22.8	27.3	22.7	28.8
Wife in labor force, husband not in labor force........	9.1	4.2	8.5	4.5	8.3	4.3
Both husband and wife not in labor force..............	19.8	2.3	19.6	2.2	20.8	2.2
Other Families	457,306	236,895	462,677	236,410	447,412	230,850
Female householder, no husband present...............	74.9	77.9	74.2	75.9	74.4	76.0
In labor force..	49.8	61.8	49.6	61.5	49.3	61.2
Not in labor force....................................	25.1	16.2	24.5	14.4	25.0	14.8
Male householder, no wife present....................	25.1	22.1	25.8	24.1	25.6	24.0
In labor force..	18.2	19.5	18.7	20.8	18.4	20.6
Not in labor force....................................	7.0	2.6	7.1	3.3	7.3	3.3

Table TN-11. School Enrollment and Educational Attainment, 2016

(Number, percent.)

Item	State	U.S.
Enrollment		
Total population 3 years and over, enrolled in school	1,578,309	81,572,277
Enrolled in nursery school or preschool (percent).....................................	5.7	6.0
Enrolled in kindergarten (percent)...	5.1	5.0
Enrolled in elementary school, grades 1-8 (percent)...................................	42.1	40.3
Enrolled in high school, grades 9-12 (percent)..	21.9	21.0
Enrolled in college or graduate school (percent)......................................	25.1	27.7
Attainment		
Total population 25 years and over	4,527,198	218,475,480
Less than ninth grade (percent)...	4.8	5.4
9th to 12th grade, no diploma (percent)...	8.3	7.2
High school graduate, including equivalency (percent).................................	32.4	27.2
Some college, no degree (percent)..	21.2	20.0
Associate's degree (percent)...	7.3	8.4
Bachelor's degree (percent)..	16.7	19.3
Graduate or professional degree (percent)..	9.4	11.9
High school graduate or higher (percent)	87.0	87.5
Bachelor's degree or higher (percent)...	26.1	31.3

Table TN-12. Public School Characteristics and Educational Indicators

(Number, percent; data derived from National Center of Education Statistics.)

Item	State	U.S.
Public Schools, 2015–2016 (except where noted)		
Number of school districts...	146	18,328
Number of schools..	1,859	98,456
Number of students...	1,001,235	50,327,015
Number of teachers...	66,488	3,151,497
Student-teacher ratio...	15.1	16.0
Expenditures per student (dollars), 2014-2015..	8,776	11,445
Four-year adjusted cohort graduation rate (ACGR)[1,2]	88.5	84.1
Students eligible for free or reduced-price lunch (percent), 2014-2015................	55.9	51.8
English language learners (percent), Fall 2015	4.1	9.5
Students age 3 to 21 served under IDEA, part B (percent).............................	12.9	13.2

Public Schools by Type	Number	Percent of state public schools
Total number of schools...	1,859	100.0
Regular	1,806	97.1
Special education...	16	0.9
Vocational education..	15	0.8
Alternative education...	22	1.2

NOTE: Every school is assigned only one school type based on its instructional emphasis.
[1] ACGR data represents a new method of calculating high-school completion rates and may not be comparable to previous years' data for Averaged Freshmen Graduation Rates (AFGR).
[2] The United States 4-year ACGRs were estimated using both the reported 4-year ACGR data from 49 states and the District of Columbia and using imputed data for Idaho. The estimate for American Indian/Alaska Native students also includes imputed data for Virginia.

Table TN-13. Reported Voting and Registration of the Voting-Age Population, November 2016

(Numbers in thousands, percent.)

Item	Total population	Total citizen population	Registered			Voted		
			Total registered	Percent registered (total population)	Percent registered (total citizen population)	Total voted	Percent voted (total population)	Percent voted (total citizen population)
U.S. Total	245,502	224,059	157,596	64.2	70.3	137,537	56.0	61.4
State Total.............................	5,057	4,872	3,251	64.3	66.7	2,630	52.0	54.0
Sex								
Male	2,418	2,316	1,505	62.2	65.0	1,218	50.4	52.6
Female	2,639	2,556	1,746	66.2	68.3	1,412	53.5	55.3
Race								
White alone......................	4,014	3,893	2,640	65.8	67.8	2,176	54.2	55.9
White, non-Hispanic alone.............	3,808	3,783	2,601	68.3	68.7	2,148	56.4	56.8
Black alone.......................	814	800	519	63.8	64.9	402	49.4	50.3
Asian alone......................	132	82	42	(B)	(B)	29	(B)	(B)
Hispanic (of any race)......................	221	125	40	18.0	31.8	27	12.3	21.7
White alone or in combination	4,093	3,972	2,679	65.5	67.4	2,199	53.7	55.4
Black alone or in combination.............	828	814	525	63.4	64.5	404	48.8	49.7
Asian alone or in combination.............	148	98	48	(B)	(B)	32	(B)	(B)
Age								
18 to 24 years......................	523	503	235	45.0	46.8	156	29.9	31.1
25 to 34 years......................	971	903	520	53.5	57.6	379	39.1	42.0
35 to 44 years......................	777	741	513	66.0	69.2	411	52.9	55.5
45 to 64 years......................	1,720	1,674	1,187	69.0	70.9	1,008	58.6	60.2
65 years and over......................	1,065	1,052	797	74.8	75.7	676	63.4	64.2

B = Base is less than 75,000 and therefore too small to show the derived measure.

Table TN-14. Crime

(Number, rate per 100,000. Data are derived from the FBI Uniform Crime Reports.)

Item	State			U.S. [1,2,3,4]		
	2015	2016	Percent change	2015	2016	Percent change
TOTAL POPULATION [5]	6,600,299	6,651,194	0.8	321,418,820	323,127,513	0.5
VIOLENT CRIME						
Number.........................	40,400	42,097	4.2	1,231,566	1,248,185	1.3
Rate.........................	612.1	632.9	3.4	383.2	386.3	0.8
Murder and Nonnegligent Manslaughter						
Number.........................	406	486	19.7	15,696	17,250	9.9
Rate.........................	6.2	7.3	17.7	4.9	5.3	8.2
Rape[6]						
Number.........................	2,676	2,714	1.4	124,047	130,603	5.3
Rate.........................	40.5	40.8	0.7	38.6	40.4	4.7
Robbery						
Number.........................	7,474	7,813	4.5	327,374	332,198	1.5
Rate.........................	113.2	117.5	3.8	101.9	102.8	0.9
Aggravated Assault						
Number.........................	29,844	31,084	4.2	764,449	803,007	5.0
Rate.........................	452.2	467.3	3.3	237.8	248.5	4.5
PROPERTY CRIME						
Number.........................	193,796	189,835	-2.0	7,993,631	7,919,035	-0.9
Rate.........................	2,936.2	2,854.1	-2.8	2,487.0	2,450.7	-1.5
Burglary						
Number.........................	43,247	40,312	-6.8	1,579,527	1,515,096	-4.1
Rate.........................	655.2	606.1	-7.5	491.4	468.9	-4.6
Larceny-Theft						
Number.........................	137,679	134,404	-2.4	5,706,346	5,638,455	-1.2
Rate.........................	2,086.0	2,020.7	-3.1	1,775.4	1,745.0	-1.7
Motor Vehicle Theft						
Number.........................	12,870	15,119	17.5	707,758	765,484	8.2
Rate.........................	195.0	227.3	16.6	220.2	236.9	7.6

NOTE: Although arson data are included in the trend and clearance tables, sufficient data are not available to estimate totals for this offense. Therefore, no arson data are published in this table.
X = Not applicable.
- = Zero or rounds to zero.
[1] The crime figures have been adjusted.
[2] The data collection methodology for the offense of forcible rape used by the Minnesota state Uniform Crime Reporting (UCR) Program (with the exception of Minneapolis and St. Paul, Minnesota) does not comply with national UCR Program guidelines. Consequently, its figures for forcible rape and violent crime (of which forcible rape is a part) are not published in this table.
[3] Includes offenses reported by the Zoological Police and the Metro Transit Police.
[4] Because of changes in the state's reporting practices, figures are not comparable to previous years' data.
[5] Populations are U.S. Census Bureau provisional estimates as of July 1 of each year.
[6] The figures shown for the offense of rape were estimated using the revised Uniform Crime Reporting (UCR) definition of rape.

Table TN-15. State Government Finances, 2016

(Dollar amounts in thousands, percent distribution.)

Item	Dollars	Percent distribution
Total Revenue	31,427,933	100.0
General revenue	28,984,418	92.2
Intergovernmental revenue	11,238,782	35.8
Taxes	13,386,169	42.6
General sales	7,006,376	22.3
Selective sales	2,697,871	8.6
License taxes	1,516,966	4.8
Individual income tax	323,952	1.0
Corporate income tax	1,538,649	4.9
Other taxes	302,355	1.0
Current charges	2,234,205	7.1
Miscellaneous general revenue	2,125,262	6.8
Utility revenue	0	-
Liquor stores revenue	0	-
Insurance trust revenue [1]	2,443,515	7.8
Total Expenditure	32,459,124	100.0
Intergovernmental expenditure	7,617,664	23.5
Direct expenditure	24,841,460	76.5
Current operation	19,138,728	59.0
Capital outlay	1,565,050	4.8
Insurance benefits and repayments	2,618,534	8.1
Assistance and subsidies	1,253,017	3.9
Interest on debt	266,131	0.8
Exhibit: Salaries and wages	3,962,154	12.2
Total Expenditure	32,459,124	100.0
General expenditure	29,839,161	91.9
Intergovernmental expenditure	7,617,664	23.5
Direct expenditure	22,221,497	68.5
General expenditure, by function:		
Education	10,267,929	31.6
Public welfare	12,327,422	38.0
Hospitals	405,191	1.2
Health	669,897	2.1
Highways	1,552,187	4.8
Police protection	260,921	0.8
Correction	954,903	2.9
Natural resources	357,678	1.1
Parks and recreation	99,007	0.3
Governmental administration	865,952	2.7
Interest on general debt	266,131	0.8
Other and unallocable	1,811,943	5.6
Utility expenditure	1,429	-
Liquor stores expenditure	0	-
Insurance trust expenditure	2,618,534	8.1
Debt at End of Fiscal Year	6,075,745	X
Cash and Security Holdings	53,131,756	X

X = Not applicable.
- = Zero or rounds to zero.
[1] Within insurance trust revenue, net earnings of state retirement systems is a calculated statistic (the item code in the data file is X08), and thus can be positive or negative. Net earnings is the sum of earnings on investments plus gains on investments minus losses on investments. The change made in 2002 for asset valuation from book to market value in accordance with Statement 34 of the Governmental Accounting Standards Board is reflected in the calculated statistics.

Table TN-16. State Government Tax Collections, 2017

(Dollars in thousands, percent.)

Item	Dollars	Percent distribution
Total Taxes	13,893,728	100.0
Property taxes	X	-
Sales and gross receipts	10,010,965	72.1
General sales and gross receipts	7,260,193	52.3
Selective sales and gross receipts	2,750,772	19.8
Alcoholic beverages	187,125	1.3
Amusements	X	-
Insurance premiums	912,324	6.6
Motor fuels	915,858	6.6
Pari-mutuels	X	-
Public utilities	7,398	0.1
Tobacco products	256,762	1.8
Other selective sales	471,305	3.4
Licenses	1,635,495	11.8
Alcoholic beverages	1,644	-
Amusements	240	-
Corporations in general	871,205	6.3
Hunting and fishing	37,869	0.3
Motor vehicle	306,047	2.2
Motor vehicle operators	61,268	0.4
Public utilities	5,087	-
Occupation and business, NEC	343,298	2.5
Other licenses	8,837	0.1
Income taxes	1,976,200	14.2
Individual income	249,977	1.8
Corporation net income	1,726,223	12.4
Other taxes	271,068	2.0
Death and gift	14,904	0.1
Documentary and stock transfer	236,169	1.7
Severance	1,261	-
Taxes, NEC	18,734	0.1

X = Not applicable.
- = Zero or rounds to zero.

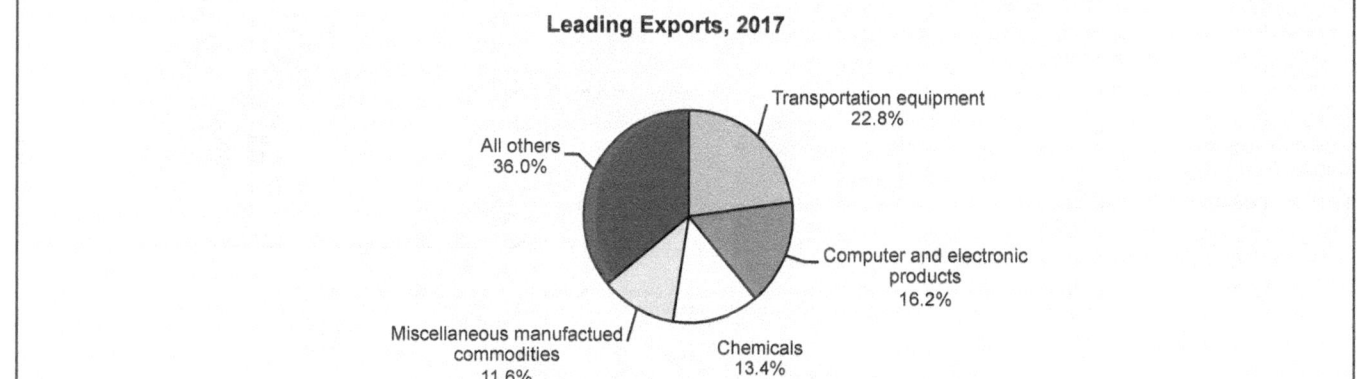

Leading Exports, 2017

Transportation equipment 22.8%

All others 36.0%

Computer and electronic products 16.2%

Miscellaneous manufactued commodities 11.6%

Chemicals 13.4%

TEXAS

Facts and Figures

Location: West South Central United States; bordered on the N by Oklahoma, on the E by Arkansas and Louisiana, on the S by Mexico and the Gulf of Mexico, and on the W by Mexico and New Mexico

Area: 268,581 sq. mi. (695,621 sq. km.); rank—2nd

Population: 28,304,596 (2017 est.); rank—2nd

Principal Cities: capital—Austin; largest—Houston

Statehood: December 29, 1845; 28th state

U.S. Congress: 2 senators, 36 representatives

State Motto: Friendship

State Song: "Texas, Our Texas"

State Nickname: The Lone Star State

Abbreviations: TX; Tex.

State Symbols: flower—bluebonnet; tree—pecan; bird—mockingbird

At a Glance

- With an increase in population of 12.1 percent, Texas ranked 2nd among the states in growth from 2010 to 2017.

- In 2017, Texas ranked 2nd for the highest percent of its population under 18 years old (26.0 percent).

- Texas's median household income in 2016 was $56,565, and 15.6 percent of the population lived below the poverty level.

- In 2016, 16.6 percent of Texans did not have health insurance, making it the state with the highest percent of uninsured residents.

- Texas ranked 18th among states for its violent crime rate and 19th for its property crime rate in 2016, which were 434.4 and 2,759.8 per 100,000 population respectively.

Table TX-1. Population by Age, Sex, Race, and Hispanic Origin

(Number, percent, except where noted.)

Sex, age, race, and Hispanic origin	2000	2010	2017 [1]	Average annual percent change, 2010–2017
Total Population..	20,851,820	25,145,561	28,304,596	12.6
Percent of total U.S. population	7.4	8.1	8.7	X
Sex				
Male...	10,352,910	12,472,280	14,061,793	12.7
Female..	10,498,910	12,673,281	14,242,803	12.4
Age				
Under 5 years...	1,625,628	1,928,473	2,031,625	5.3
5 to 19 years..	4,291,608	5,693,241	6,111,318	7.3
20 to 64 years..	12,233,052	14,921,961	16,688,941	11.8
65 years and over	2,072,532	2,601,886	3,472,712	33.5
Median age (years)	32.3	33.6	34.6	3.0
Race and Hispanic Origin				
One race				
White	14,799,505	20,389,793	22,404,118	9.9
Black	2,404,566	3,070,440	3,593,048	17.0
American Indian and Alaska Native	118,362	251,209	287,312	14.4
Asian	562,319	1,000,473	1,417,555	41.7
Native Hawaiian or Other Pacific Islander	14,434	31,242	40,740	30.4
Two or more races	514,633	402,404	561,823	39.6
Hispanic (of any race)...	6,699,666	9,578,505	11,156,514	16.5

X = Not applicable.

[1] Population figures for 2017 are July 1 estimates. The 2010 estimates are taken from the 2010 Census.

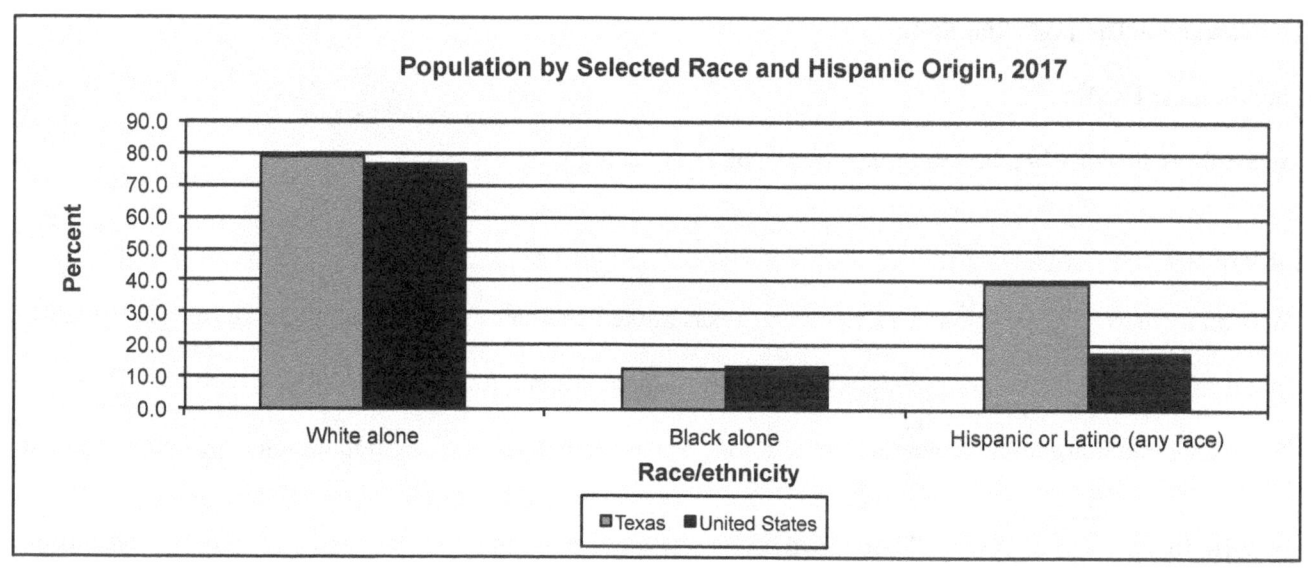

Population by Selected Race and Hispanic Origin, 2017

Table TX-2. Marital Status

(Number, percent distribution.)

Sex, age, and marital status	2000	2010	2016
Males, 15 Years and Over	7,820,248	9,587,343	10,719,917
Never married	28.6	34.6	36.3
Now married, except separated...	58.8	51.6	50.2
Separated..	2.0	2.3	2.0
Widowed..	2.1	2.2	2.4
Divorced..	8.5	9.4	9.1
Females, 15 Years and Over	8,117,395	9,903,147	11,053,027
Never married	22.6	27.6	30.1
Now married, except separated...	54.3	48.5	47.2
Separated..	2.9	3.3	2.9
Widowed..	9.1	8.1	7.8
Divorced..	11.0	12.5	12.0

Table TX-3. Households and Housing Characteristics

(Number, percent, dollars.)

Item	2000	2010	2016	Average annual percent change, 2010–2016
Total Households..	7,393,354	8,738,664	9,535,612	1.5
Family households...	5,247,794	6,091,590	6,602,215	1.4
Married-couple family.....................................	3,989,741	4,386,996	4,757,297	1.4
Other family...	1,258,053	1,704,594	1,844,918	1.4
Male householder, no wife present.................	320,464	436,727	497,765	2.3
Female householder, no husband present........	937,489	1,267,867	1,347,153	1.0
Nonfamily households..	2,145,560	2,647,074	2,933,397	1.8
Householder living alone.................................	1,752,141	2,166,469	2,399,930	1.8
Householder not living alone...........................	393,419	480,605	533,467	1.8
Housing Characteristics				
Total housing units...	8,157,575	9,996,209	10,754,268	1.3
Occupied housing units......................................	7,393,354	8,738,664	9,535,612	1.5
Owner occupied..	4,716,959	5,555,903	5,825,471	0.8
Renter occupied...	2,676,395	3,182,761	3,710,141	2.8
Average household size......................................	2.74	2.82	2.86	0.2
Financial Characteristics				
Median gross rent of renter-occupied housing........	574	801	956	3.2
Median monthly owner costs for housing units with a mortgage........	986	1,402	1,469	0.8
Median value of owner-occupied housing units........	82,500	128,100	161,500	4.3

Table TX-4. Migration, Origin, and Language

(Number, percent.)

Characteristic	State			U.S.		
	2015	2016	Percent change	2015	2016	Percent change
Residence 1 Year Ago						
Population 1 year and over...........................	27,092,848	27,472,626	1.4	317,635,720	319,361,956	0.5
Same house..	83.9	84.1	X	85.3	85.4	X
Different house in the U.S........................	15.3	15.0	X	14.1	13.9	X
Same county..	9.3	9.2	X	8.5	8.3	X
Different county...................................	6.0	5.8	X	5.6	5.6	X
Same state.......................................	4.0	3.9	X	3.2	3.2	X
Different state...................................	2.0	1.9	X	2.4	2.4	X
Abroad..	0.8	0.9	X	0.7	0.7	X
Place of Birth						
Native born...	22,797,819	23,132,676	1.5	278,128,449	279,388,170	0.5
Male...	49.5	49.5	X	49.3	49.3	X
Female..	50.5	50.5	X	50.7	50.7	X
Foreign born...	4,671,295	4,729,920	1.3	43,290,372	43,739,345	1.0
Male...	50.1	50.3	X	48.6	48.5	X
Female..	49.9	49.7	X	51.4	51.5	X
Foreign born; naturalized U.S. citizen...........	1,673,484	1,748,614	4.5	20,697,103	21,238,372	2.6
Male...	47.2	48.1	X	45.9	45.9	X
Female..	52.8	51.9	X	54.1	54.1	X
Foreign born; not a U.S. citizen...................	2,997,811	2,981,306	-0.6	22,593,269	22,500,973	-0.4
Male...	51.7	51.5	X	51.1	51.0	X
Female..	48.3	48.5	X	48.9	49.0	X
Entered 2010 or later................................	16.3	19.4	X	15.6	18.6	X
Entered 2000 to 2009................................	30.4	28.3	X	27.9	26.7	X
Entered before 2000..................................	53.3	52.3	X	56.5	54.7	X
World Region of Birth, Foreign						
Foreign-born population, excluding population born at sea........	4,671,295	4,729,920	1.3	43,289,646	43,738,901	1.0
Europe..	4.1	4.1	X	11.1	10.9	X
Asia..	21.1	21.1	X	30.6	30.8	X
Africa..	4.7	5.0	X	4.8	4.9	X
Oceania...	0.3	0.3	X	0.6	0.6	X
Latin America...	68.7	68.6	X	51.1	51.0	X
North America..	1.2	0.9	X	1.9	1.8	X
Language Spoken at Home and Ability to Speak English						
Population 5 years and over........................	25,502,406	25,855,685	1.4	301,625,014	303,328,961	0.6
English only...	64.6	64.4	X	78.5	78.4	X
Language other than English......................	35.4	35.6	X	21.5	21.6	X
Speaks English less than "very well"...........	14.3	14.0	X	8.6	8.6	X

NA = Not available.
X = Not applicable.
- = Zero or rounds to zero.

Table TX-5. Median Income and Poverty Status, 2016

(Number, percent, except as noted.)

Characteristic	State		U.S.	
	Number	Percent	Number	Percent
Median Income				
Households (dollars)	56,565	X	57,617	X
Families (dollars)	67,025	X	71,062	X
Below Poverty Level (All People)	4,261,337	15.6	44,268,996	14.0
Sex				
Male	1,909,827	14.2	19,760,056	12.8
Female	2,351,510	17.0	24,508,940	15.2
Age				
Under 18 years	1,619,026	22.4	14,115,713	19.5
Related children under 18 years	1,596,051	22.2	13,805,435	19.1
18 to 64 years	2,300,868	13.7	25,723,818	13.2
65 years and over	341,443	10.5	4,429,465	9.2

X = Not applicable.

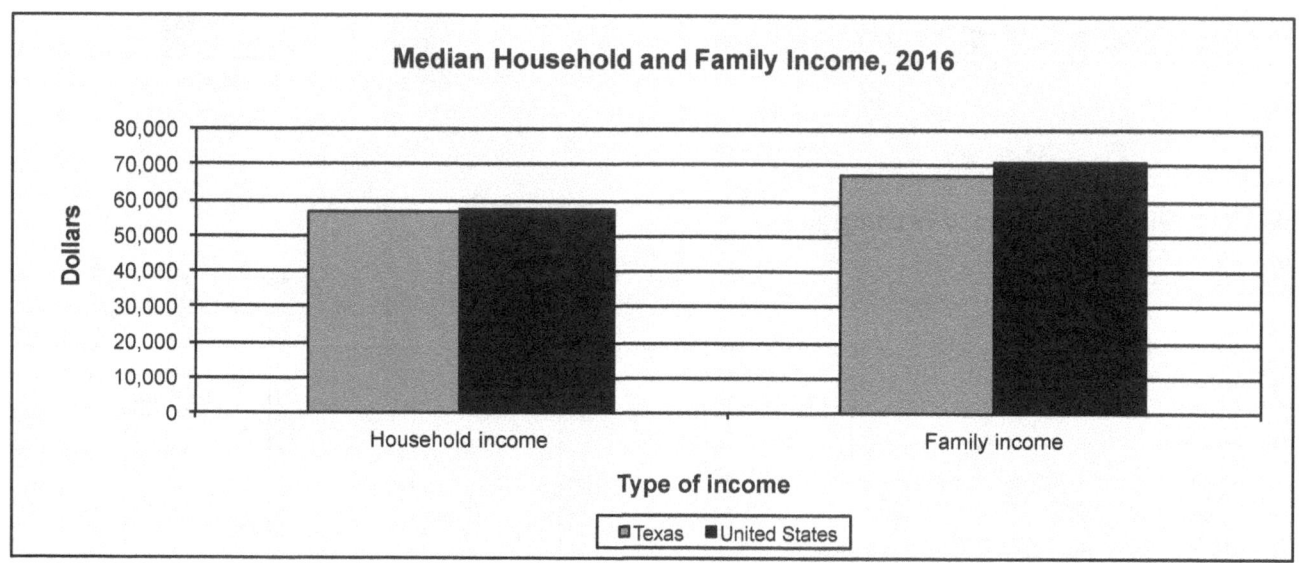

Table TX-6. Health Insurance Coverage Status for the Civilian Noninstitutionalized Population and Children Under 18 Years of Age

(Number, percent.)

Item	2008	2009	2010	2011	2012	2013	2014	2015	2016
Civilian Noninstitutionalized Population	23,827,328	24,291,561	24,779,450	25,197,453	25,584,499	25,976,562	26,485,838	26,990,435	27,386,023
Covered by Private or Public Insurance									
Number	18,082,042	18,508,305	18,903,976	19,407,607	19,822,141	20,228,395	21,438,361	22,375,210	22,840,643
Percent	75.9	76.2	76.3	77.0	77.5	77.9	80.9	82.9	83.4
Not Covered									
Number	5,745,286	5,783,256	5,875,474	5,789,846	5,762,358	5,748,167	5,047,477	4,615,225	4,545,380
Percent	24.1	23.8	23.7	23.0	22.5	22.1	19.1	17.1	16.6
Percent in the U.S. not covered	15.1	15.1	15.5	15.1	14.8	14.5	11.7	9.4	8.6
Children Under 18 Years of Age	6,714,046	6,877,730	6,876,022	6,946,969	6,971,878	7,028,782	7,106,727	7,197,853	7,282,033
Covered by Private or Public Insurance									
Number	5,518,072	5,758,045	5,879,529	6,030,447	6,108,588	6,140,477	6,322,789	6,515,730	6,611,211
Percent	82.2	83.7	85.5	86.8	87.6	87.4	89.0	90.5	90.8
Not Covered									
Number	1,195,974	1,119,685	996,493	916,522	863,290	888,305	783,938	682,123	670,822
Percent	17.8	16.3	14.5	13.2	12.4	12.6	11.0	9.5	9.2
Percent in the U.S. not covered	9.9	8.6	8.0	7.5	7.2	7.1	6.0	4.8	4.5

Table TX-7. Employment Status by Demographic Group, 2017

(Numbers in thousands, percent.)

Characteristic	Civilian noninstitutional population	Civilian labor force		Employed		Unemployed	
		Number	Percent of population	Number	Percent of population	Number	Percent of population
Total...	21,216	13,491	63.6	12,908	60.8	583	4.3
Sex							
Male......................................	10,312	7,434	72.1	7,120	69.0	314	4.2
Female...................................	10,904	6,056	55.5	5,788	53.1	269	4.4
Race, Sex, and Hispanic Origin							
White.....................................	16,859	10,633	63.1	10,217	60.6	416	3.9
Male.................................	8,243	5,975	72.5	5,751	69.8	224	3.8
Female..............................	8,616	4,658	54.1	4,466	51.8	192	4.1
Black or African American...........	2,620	1,742	66.5	1,622	61.9	121	6.9
Male.................................	1,209	839	69.4	777	64.2	63	7.5
Female..............................	1,411	903	64.0	845	59.9	58	6.4
Hispanic or Latino ethnicity[1]........	7,659	4,894	63.9	4,665	60.9	229	4.7
Male.................................	3,858	2,936	76.1	2,807	72.8	129	4.4
Female..............................	3,801	1,958	51.5	1,858	48.9	100	5.1
Age							
16 to 19 years........................	1,663	532	32.0	471	28.3	61	11.5
20 to 24 years........................	1,904	1,310	68.8	1,215	63.8	94	7.2
25 to 34 years........................	4,036	3,230	80.0	3,087	76.5	143	4.4
35 to 44 years........................	3,602	2,959	82.2	2,843	78.9	116	3.9
45 to 54 years........................	3,354	2,716	81.0	2,643	78.8	73	2.7
55 to 64 years........................	3,183	2,079	65.3	2,006	63.0	72	3.5
65 years and over	3,475	666	19.2	642	18.5	24	3.6

NOTE: Data in Table 7 are from the Current Population Survey (CPS) and do not match the estimates in Table 8. See notes and definitions for further information.
[1] May be of any race.

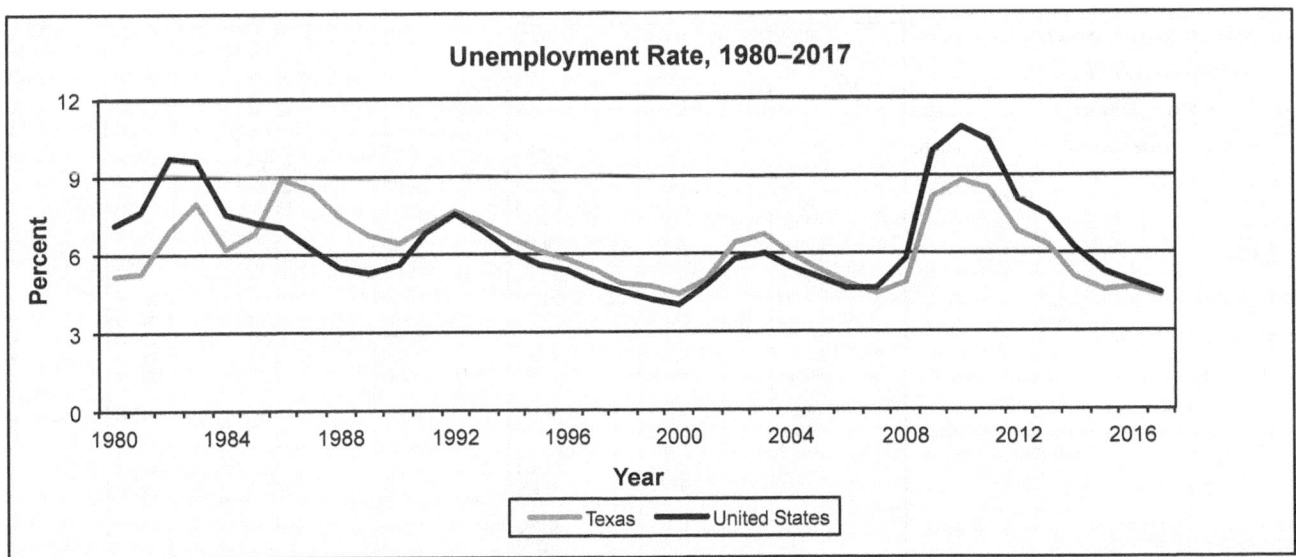

Table TX-8. Employment Status of the Civilian Noninstitutional Population Age 16 Years and Over

(Number, percent.)

Year	Civilian labor force	Civilian participation rate	Employed	Unemployed	Unemployment rate
2009..	11,910,799	65.8	11,008,903	901,896	7.6
2010..	12,241,970	65.9	11,244,632	997,338	8.1
2011..	12,504,498	65.9	11,535,095	969,403	7.8
2012..	12,670,455	65.6	11,818,675	851,780	6.7
2013..	12,857,595	65.3	12,052,646	804,949	6.3
2014..	13,024,701	64.9	12,360,368	664,333	5.1
2015..	13,074,570	63.8	12,493,197	581,373	4.4
2016..	13,317,176	63.7	12,702,122	615,054	4.6
2017..	13,538,385	63.7	12,960,595	577,790	4.3

Table TX-9. Employment and Average Wages by Industry

(Estimates through 2010 are based on the 2007 *North American Industry Classification System* [NAICS]. Estimates from 2011 onward are based on the 2012 NAICS.)

Industry	2010	2011	2012	2013	2014	2015	2016
	Number of jobs						
Wage and Salary Employment by Industry	10,790,781	11,042,608	11,367,650	11,670,732	12,028,094	12,305,468	12,456,932
Farm Wage and Salary Employment	43,326	41,977	43,718	47,503	47,110	49,030	50,699
Nonfarm Wage and Salary Employment	10,747,455	11,000,631	11,323,932	11,623,229	11,980,984	12,256,438	12,406,233
Private wage and salary employment	8,727,604	9,009,609	9,353,987	9,648,041	9,995,823	10,241,726	10,359,139
Forestry, fishing, and related activities	31,560	31,740	32,099	32,346	33,114	33,427	33,718
Mining	202,972	233,875	268,335	287,841	304,031	268,425	218,777
Utilities	48,301	49,010	48,693	48,981	49,022	49,455	49,763
Construction	585,279	583,161	602,678	631,784	669,947	701,478	720,921
Manufacturing	811,201	837,535	864,226	875,064	888,537	879,369	846,768
Durable goods manufacturing	515,892	543,773	569,119	578,553	589,975	577,702	541,667
Nondurable goods manufacturing	295,309	293,762	295,107	296,511	298,562	301,667	305,101
Wholesale trade	499,769	517,723	542,974	564,650	581,723	599,154	583,542
Retail trade	1,146,645	1,171,735	1,197,956	1,227,715	1,264,248	1,307,146	1,332,173
Transportation and warehousing	374,170	390,327	406,563	417,198	433,783	452,799	471,981
Information	195,789	195,887	197,235	201,252	203,279	201,054	202,246
Finance and insurance	463,249	476,380	492,851	507,099	517,398	533,924	545,920
Real estate and rental and leasing	175,546	178,925	183,940	192,392	200,908	205,205	208,460
Professional, scientific, and technical services	573,982	593,233	627,780	653,097	683,752	713,867	733,231
Management of companies and enterprises	79,375	83,406	89,976	93,917	111,745	116,664	119,308
Administrative and waste services	633,308	675,365	707,501	727,828	762,307	775,548	786,297
Educational services	153,578	159,028	162,971	165,827	169,692	173,531	179,316
Health care and social assistance	1,195,195	1,225,814	1,263,159	1,295,178	1,325,805	1,378,404	1,425,631
Arts, entertainment, and recreation	111,953	111,488	113,104	118,658	125,667	131,343	139,192
Accommodation and food services	903,182	938,896	981,693	1,028,314	1,070,233	1,117,385	1,160,078
Other services, except public administration	542,550	556,081	570,253	578,900	600,632	603,548	601,817
Government and government enterprises	2,019,851	1,991,022	1,969,945	1,975,188	1,985,161	2,014,712	2,047,094
	Dollars						
Average Wages and Salaries by Industry	46,505	48,285	50,075	50,665	52,660	53,769	55,637
Average Farm Wages and Salaries	26,295	32,493	31,875	26,301	31,683	38,167	30,509
Average Nonfarm Wages and Salaries	46,587	48,345	50,146	50,764	52,743	53,832	55,740
Average private wages and salaries	47,138	49,063	51,115	51,698	53,775	54,801	56,610
Forestry, fishing, and related activities	24,942	25,081	26,051	26,238	27,442	28,611	33,506
Mining	117,497	122,069	120,617	119,742	123,979	125,100	125,762
Utilities	89,996	90,259	98,762	97,642	100,436	104,051	112,450
Construction	49,192	50,919	54,213	55,702	58,586	60,534	62,821
Manufacturing	63,180	65,894	68,245	68,525	71,113	72,802	75,272
Durable goods manufacturing	65,431	68,311	70,111	70,295	73,116	74,113	77,558
Nondurable goods manufacturing	59,247	61,421	64,647	65,071	67,153	70,291	71,212
Wholesale trade	67,898	71,407	74,567	74,148	77,185	78,398	79,917
Retail trade	27,147	27,896	28,850	29,084	30,004	30,722	31,437
Transportation and warehousing	53,307	55,297	58,744	58,285	60,022	61,536	64,222
Information	67,351	70,676	73,399	75,305	76,706	79,783	81,230
Finance and insurance	68,427	71,429	74,499	75,762	79,571	82,471	87,702
Real estate and rental and leasing	46,074	49,458	52,884	53,963	57,305	58,296	64,271
Professional, scientific, and technical services	76,558	79,513	81,892	83,831	86,530	88,414	92,850
Management of companies and enterprises	99,994	106,975	114,364	113,568	123,477	124,005	139,123
Administrative and waste services	36,050	36,958	38,354	38,964	40,653	41,799	43,325
Educational services	35,885	36,896	37,520	38,686	39,025	39,859	41,084
Health care and social assistance	40,936	41,703	42,343	42,564	43,910	45,407	47,527
Arts, entertainment, and recreation	31,561	32,486	33,892	32,989	33,657	35,550	38,567
Accommodation and food services	18,279	18,876	19,569	19,879	20,539	21,233	22,472
Other services, except public administration	28,025	28,847	30,041	31,114	32,325	33,405	35,432
Government and government enterprises	44,204	45,096	45,543	46,202	47,547	48,904	51,337

Table TX-10. Employment Characteristics by Family Type

(Number, percent.)

Family type and labor force status	2014		2015		2016	
	Total	Families with own children under 18 years	Total	Families with own children under 18 years	Total	Families with own children under 18 years
All Families	6,386,885	3,036,494	6,520,909	3,076,309	6,602,215	3,112,730
FAMILY TYPE AND LABOR FORCE STATUS						
Married-Couple Families	4,582,954	2,049,534	4,709,478	2,092,503	4,757,297	2,118,877
Both husband and wife in labor force	49.9	59.2	49.3	58.6	49.9	60.0
Husband in labor force, wife not in labor force	28.7	36.0	28.5	36.0	28.0	35.0
Wife in labor force, husband not in labor force	6.7	3.2	6.9	3.5	6.6	3.2
Both husband and wife not in labor force	14.7	1.6	14.7	1.5	14.8	1.5
Other Families	1,803,931	986,960	1,811,431	983,806	1,844,918	993,853
Female householder, no husband present	73.5	77.4	73.0	76.6	73.0	76.9
In labor force	53.1	63.6	52.9	63.4	52.8	64.1
Not in labor force	20.4	13.8	20.1	13.2	20.2	12.8
Male householder, no wife present	26.5	22.6	27.0	23.4	27.0	23.1
In labor force	21.3	20.7	22.2	21.7	22.1	21.5
Not in labor force	5.1	1.8	4.8	1.8	4.9	1.6

Table TX-11. School Enrollment and Educational Attainment, 2016

(Number, percent.)

Item	State	U.S.
Enrollment		
Total population 3 years and over, enrolled in school	7,603,170	81,572,277
Enrolled in nursery school or preschool (percent)	6.0	6.0
Enrolled in kindergarten (percent)	5.2	5.0
Enrolled in elementary school, grades 1-8 (percent)	43.4	40.3
Enrolled in high school, grades 9-12 (percent)	21.1	21.0
Enrolled in college or graduate school (percent)	24.3	27.7
Attainment		
Total population 25 years and over	17,775,280	218,475,480
Less than ninth grade (percent)	8.6	5.4
9th to 12th grade, no diploma (percent)	8.5	7.2
High school graduate, including equivalency (percent)	25.2	27.2
Some college, no degree (percent)	21.8	20.6
Associate's degree (percent)	7.1	8.4
Bachelor's degree (percent)	18.9	19.3
Graduate or professional degree (percent)	10.0	11.9
High school graduate or higher (percent)	82.9	87.5
Bachelor's degree or higher (percent)	28.9	31.3

Table TX-12. Public School Characteristics and Educational Indicators

(Number, percent; data derived from National Center of Education Statistics.)

Item	State	U.S.
Public Schools, 2015–2016 (except where noted)		
Number of school districts	1,232	18,328
Number of schools	8,826	98,456
Number of students	5,301,477	50,327,015
Number of teachers	347,329	3,151,497
Student-teacher ratio	15.3	16.0
Expenditures per student (dollars), 2014-2015	9,081	11,445
Four-year adjusted cohort graduation rate (ACGR)[1,2]	89.1	84.1
Students eligible for free or reduced-price lunch (percent), 2014-2015	58.8	51.8
English language learners (percent), Fall 2015	16.8	9.5
Students age 3 to 21 served under IDEA, part B (percent)	8.7	13.2

Public Schools by Type	Number	Percent of state public schools
Total number of schools	8,826	100.0
Regular	7,872	89.2
Special education	14	0.2
Vocational education	0	-
Alternative education	940	10.7

NOTE: Every school is assigned only one school type based on its instructional emphasis.
[1] ACGR data represents a new method of calculating high-school completion rates and may not be comparable to previous years' data for Averaged Freshmen Graduation Rates (AFGR).
[2] The United States 4-year ACGRs were estimated using both the reported 4-year ACGR data from 49 states and the District of Columbia and using imputed data for Idaho. The estimate for American Indian/Alaska Native students also includes imputed data for Virginia.

Table TX-13. Reported Voting and Registration of the Voting-Age Population, November 2016

(Numbers in thousands, percent.)

Item	Total population	Total citizen population	Registered			Voted		
			Total registered	Percent registered (total population)	Percent registered (total citizen population)	Total voted	Percent voted (total population)	Percent voted (total citizen population)
U.S. Total	245,502	224,059	157,596	64.2	70.3	137,537	56.0	61.4
State Total...............................	20,172	17,378	11,724	58.1	67.5	9,626	47.7	55.4
Sex								
Male	9,775	8,325	5,479	56.0	65.8	4,465	45.7	53.6
Female	10,397	9,053	6,245	60.1	69.0	5,162	49.6	57.0
Race								
White alone..............................	16,095	13,909	9,306	57.8	66.9	7,700	47.8	55.4
White, non-Hispanic alone.............	9,534	9,383	6,822	71.6	72.7	5,905	61.9	62.9
Black alone..............................	2,458	2,358	1,724	70.2	73.1	1,349	54.9	57.2
Asian alone..............................	1,110	715	418	37.7	58.5	338	30.4	47.3
Hispanic (of any race).................	6,923	4,781	2,654	38.3	55.5	1,938	28.0	40.5
White alone or in combination	16,291	14,101	9,436	57.9	66.9	7,807	47.9	55.4
Black alone or in combination..........	2,576	2,473	1,812	70.3	73.3	1,417	55.0	57.3
Asian alone or in combination..........	1,135	736	440	38.7	59.7	356	31.3	48.3
Age								
18 to 24 years..........................	2,542	2,175	1,036	40.8	47.6	694	27.3	31.9
25 to 34 years..........................	3,950	3,186	1,918	48.6	60.2	1,483	37.5	46.5
35 to 44 years..........................	3,764	3,008	2,033	54.0	67.6	1,617	42.9	53.7
45 to 64 years..........................	6,450	5,743	4,181	64.8	72.8	3,579	55.5	62.3
65 years and over	3,465	3,265	2,556	73.7	78.3	2,254	65.0	69.0

Table TX-14. Crime

(Number, rate per 100,000. Data are derived from the FBI Uniform Crime Reports.)

Item	State			U.S. [1,2,3,4]		
	2015	2016	Percent change	2015	2016	Percent change
TOTAL POPULATION [5]	27,469,114	27,862,596	1.4	321,418,820	323,127,513	0.5
VIOLENT CRIME						
Number..	113,227	121,042	6.9	1,231,566	1,248,185	1.3
Rate...	412.2	434.4	5.4	383.2	386.3	0.8
Murder and Nonnegligent Manslaughter						
Number..	1,316	1,478	12.3	15,696	17,250	9.9
Rate...	4.8	5.3	10.4	4.9	5.3	8.2
Rape[6]						
Number..	12,250	13,367	9.1	124,047	130,603	5.3
Rate...	44.6	48.0	7.6	38.6	40.4	4.7
Robbery						
Number..	31,934	33,317	4.3	327,374	332,198	1.5
Rate...	116.3	119.6	2.8	101.9	102.8	0.9
Aggravated Assault						
Number..	67,727	72,880	7.6	764,449	803,007	5.0
Rate...	246.6	261.6	6.1	237.8	248.5	4.5
PROPERTY CRIME						
Number..	777,739	768,947	-1.1	7,993,631	7,919,035	-0.9
Rate...	2,831.3	2,759.8	-2.5	2,487.0	2,450.7	-1.5
Burglary						
Number..	153,054	148,740	-2.8	1,579,527	1,515,096	-4.1
Rate...	557.2	533.8	-4.2	491.4	468.9	-4.6
Larceny-Theft						
Number..	557,200	551,151	-1.1	5,706,346	5,638,455	-1.2
Rate...	2,028.5	1,978.1	-2.5	1,775.4	1,745.0	-1.7
Motor Vehicle Theft						
Number..	67,485	69,056	2.3	707,758	765,484	8.2
Rate...	245.7	247.8	0.9	220.2	236.9	7.6

NOTE: Although arson data are included in the trend and clearance tables, sufficient data are not available to estimate totals for this offense. Therefore, no arson data are published in this table.

X = Not applicable.

- = Zero or rounds to zero.

[1] The crime figures have been adjusted.

[2] The data collection methodology for the offense of forcible rape used by the Minnesota state Uniform Crime Reporting (UCR) Program (with the exception of Minneapolis and St. Paul, Minnesota) does not comply with national UCR Program guidelines. Consequently, its figures for forcible rape and violent crime (of which forcible rape is a part) are not published in this table.

[3] Includes offenses reported by the Zoological Police and the Metro Transit Police.

[4] Because of changes in the state's reporting practices, figures are not comparable to previous years' data.

[5] Populations are U.S. Census Bureau provisional estimates as of July 1 of each year.

[6] The figures shown for the offense of rape were estimated using the revised Uniform Crime Reporting (UCR) definition of rape.

Table TX-15. State Government Finances, 2016

(Dollar amounts in thousands, percent distribution.)

Item	Dollars	Percent distribution
Total Revenue	144,218,813	100.0
General revenue	122,794,738	85.1
Intergovernmental revenue	43,750,542	30.3
Taxes	52,132,817	36.1
General sales	32,131,385	22.3
Selective sales	14,239,389	9.9
License taxes	3,414,335	2.4
Individual income tax	0	-
Corporate income tax	0	-
Other taxes	2,347,708	1.6
Current charges	15,102,385	10.5
Miscellaneous general revenue	11,808,994	8.2
Utility revenue	0	-
Liquor stores revenue	0	-
Insurance trust revenue [1]	21,424,075	14.9
Total Expenditure	148,449,673	100.0
Intergovernmental expenditure	31,763,445	21.4
Direct expenditure	116,686,228	78.6
Current operation	83,146,762	56.0
Capital outlay	11,166,336	7.5
Insurance benefits and repayments	17,890,912	12.1
Assistance and subsidies	2,966,373	2.0
Interest on debt	1,515,845	1.0
Exhibit: Salaries and wages	18,568,924	12.5
Total Expenditure	148,449,673	100.0
General expenditure	130,548,688	87.9
Intergovernmental expenditure	31,763,445	21.4
Direct expenditure	98,785,243	66.5
General expenditure, by function:		
Education	56,423,563	38.0
Public welfare	37,548,331	25.3
Hospitals	7,649,451	5.2
Health	2,783,419	1.9
Highways	9,522,307	6.4
Police protection	1,038,324	0.7
Correction	4,093,657	2.8
Natural resources	990,514	0.7
Parks and recreation	243,623	0.2
Governmental administration	2,236,670	1.5
Interest on general debt	1,515,845	1.0
Other and unallocable	6,500,984	4.4
Utility expenditure	10073	-
Liquor stores expenditure	0	-
Insurance trust expenditure	17,890,912	12.1
Debt at End of Fiscal Year	49,357,183	X
Cash and Security Holdings	341,957,347	X

X = Not applicable.
- = Zero or rounds to zero.
[1] Within insurance trust revenue, net earnings of state retirement systems is a calculated statistic (the item code in the data file is X08), and thus can be positive or negative. Net earnings is the sum of earnings on investments plus gains on investments minus losses on investments. The change made in 2002 for asset valuation from book to market value in accordance with Statement 34 of the Governmental Accounting Standards Board is reflected in the calculated statistics.

Table TX-16. State Government Tax Collections, 2017

(Dollars in thousands, percent.)

Item	Dollars	Percent distribution
Total Taxes	53,612,926	100.0
Property taxes	X	-
Sales and gross receipts	46,897,352	87.5
General sales and gross receipts	32,490,144	60.6
Selective sales and gross receipts	14,407,208	26.9
Alcoholic beverages	1,228,641	2.3
Amusements	29,745	0.1
Insurance premiums	2,325,941	4.3
Motor fuels	3,585,179	6.7
Pari-mutuels	6,321	-
Public utilities	614,565	1.1
Tobacco products	1,467,486	2.7
Other selective sales	5,149,330	9.6
Licenses	3,432,901	6.4
Alcoholic beverages	68,608	0.1
Amusements	18,492	-
Corporations in general	140,776	0.3
Hunting and fishing	103,550	0.2
Motor vehicle	2,237,042	4.2
Motor vehicle operators	140,863	0.3
Public utilities	21,556	-
Occupation and business, NEC	537,912	1.0
Other licenses	164,102	0.3
Income taxes	X	-
Individual income	X	-
Corporation net income	X	-
Other taxes	3,282,673	6.1
Death and gift	X	-
Documentary and stock transfer	X	-
Severance	3,282,673	6.1
Taxes, NEC	0	

X = Not applicable.
- = Zero or rounds to zero.

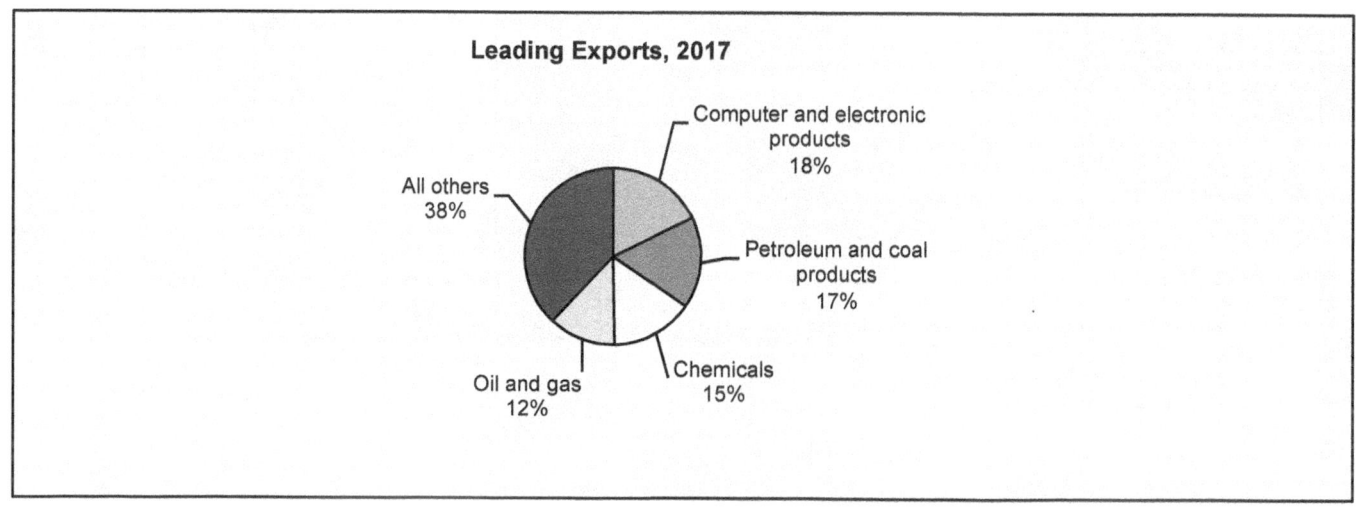

Leading Exports, 2017

Computer and electronic products 18%

Petroleum and coal products 17%

Chemicals 15%

Oil and gas 12%

All others 38%

Facts and Figures

Location: Western United States; bordered on the N by Idaho and Wyoming, on the E by Colorado, on the S by Arizona, and on the W by Nevada; Utah is one of the Four Corner states—at its SE corner it touches Arizona, Colorado, and New Mexico

Area: 84,899 sq. mi. (219,887 sq. km.); rank—13th

Population: 3,101,833 (2017 est.); rank—31st

Principal Cities: capital—Salt Lake City; largest—Salt Lake City

Statehood: January 4, 1896; 45th state

U.S. Congress: 2 senators, 4 representatives

State Motto: Industry

State Song: "Utah, We Love Thee"

State Nickname: The Beehive State

Abbreviations: UT

State Symbols: flower—sego lily; tree—blue spruce; bird—California seagull

At a Glance

- With an increase in population of 11.8 percent, Utah ranked 4th among the states in growth from 2010 to 2017.

- Utah's violent crime rate in 2016 was 242.8 per 100,000 population, compared to 386.3 for the entire nation.

- Of all the states, Utah had the highest percent of children in 2017, with 29.9 percent of its population under age 18.

- Utah also has the highest birth rate among states in 2016, at a rate of 16.5 births per 1,000 population.

- In 2016, 8.8 percent of Utahns did not have health insurance, compared to 8.6 percent of the total U.S. population.

Table UT-1. Population by Age, Sex, Race, and Hispanic Origin

(Number, percent, except where noted.)

Sex, age, race, and Hispanic origin	2000	2010	2017 [1]	Average annual percent change, 2010–2017
Total Population..	2,233,169	2,763,885	3,101,833	12.2
Percent of total U.S. population	0.8	0.9	1.0	X
Sex				
Male..	1,119,031	1,388,317	1,561,688	12.5
Female	1,114,138	1,375,568	1,540,145	12.0
Age				
Under 5 years..	209,378	263,924	255,200	-3.3
5 to 19 years...	601,599	698,613	763,484	9.3
20 to 64 years...	1,231,970	1,551,886	1,747,577	12.6
65 years and over	190,222	249,462	335,572	34.5
Median age (years)	27.1	29.2	30.9	5.8
Race and Hispanic Origin				
One race				
White	1,992,975	2,547,328	2,820,387	10.7
Black...	17,657	33,864	43,230	27.7
American Indian and Alaska Native	29,684	40,729	47,581	16.8
Asian..	37,108	57,800	79,393	37.4
Native Hawaiian or Other Pacific Islander	15,145	26,049	32,429	24.5
Two or more races	47,185	58,114	78,813	35.6
Hispanic (of any race)..	201,559	370,870	434,288	17.1

X = Not applicable.
[1] Population figures for 2017 are July 1 estimates. The 2010 estimates are taken from the 2010 Census.

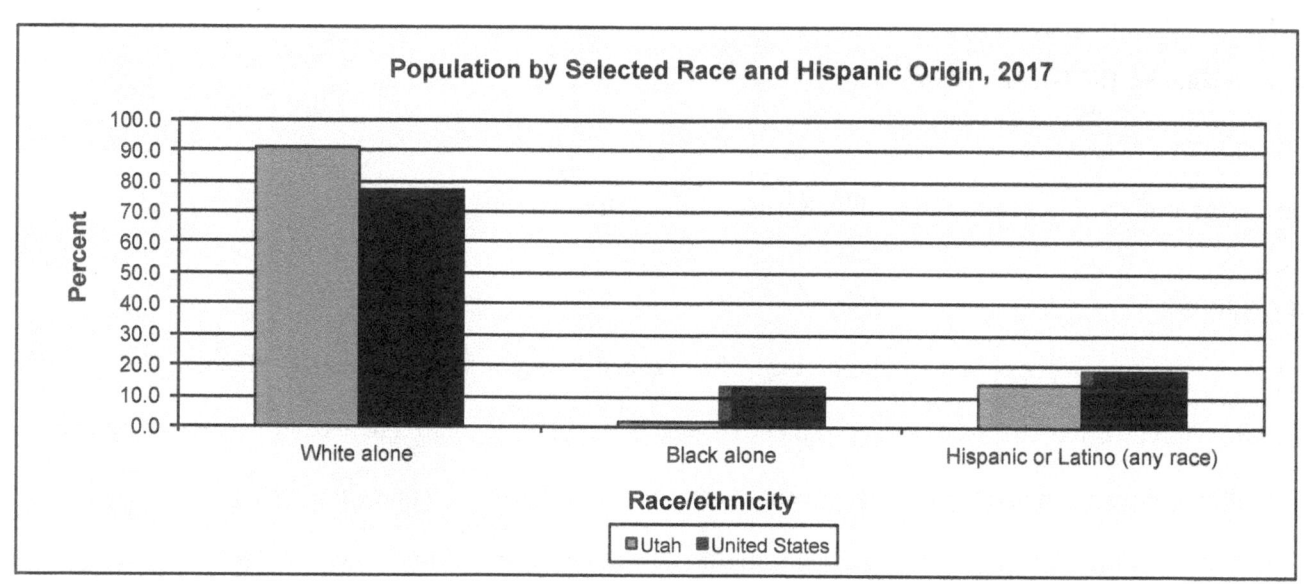

Table UT-2. Marital Status

(Number, percent distribution.)

Sex, age, and marital status	2000	2010	2016
Males, 15 Years and Over	813,693	1,014,706	1,139,070
Never married	30.6	31.3	34.0
Now married, except separated..	59.5	58.0	55.0
Separated...	1.1	1.3	1.4
Widowed..	1.6	1.8	1.6
Divorced..	7.3	7.6	8.1
Females, 15 Years and Over	852,995	1,019,010	1,137,690
Never married	25.2	25.8	27.5
Now married, except separated..	58.0	56.6	54.9
Separated...	1.4	1.6	1.9
Widowed..	6.6	5.8	5.6
Divorced..	8.8	10.1	10.2

Table UT-3. Households and Housing Characteristics

(Number, percent, dollars.)

Item	2000	2010	2016	Average annual percent change, 2010–2016
Total Households...................................	701,281	880,025	943,147	1.2
Family households...................................	535,294	665,964	711,124	1.1
Married-couple family...........................	442,931	543,212	578,132	1.1
Other family	92,363	122,752	132,992	1.4
Male householder, no wife present...........	26,422	37,258	42,803	2.5
Female householder, no husband present...	65,941	85,494	90,189	0.9
Nonfamily households	165,987	214,061	232,023	1.4
Householder living alone........................	124,756	164,863	176,449	1.2
Householder not living alone..................	41,231	49,198	55,574	2.2
Housing Characteristics				
Total housing units................................	768,594	981,821	1,054,242	1.2
Occupied housing units	701,281	880,025	943,147	1.2
Owner occupied	501,547	615,142	659,266	1.2
Renter occupied	188,734	264,883	283,881	1.2
Average household size............................	3.13	3.10	3.19	0.5
Financial Characteristics				
Median gross rent of renter-occupied housing	597	796	954	3.3
Median monthly owner costs for housing units with a mortgage	1,102	1,433	1,437	-
Median value of owner-occupied housing units...................	146,100	217,200	250,300	2.5

- = Zero or rounds to zero.

Table UT-4. Migration, Origin, and Language

(Number, percent.)

Characteristic	State			U.S.		
	2015	2016	Percent change	2015	2016	Percent change
Residence 1 Year Ago						
Population 1 year and over	2,947,423	3,002,244	1.9	317,635,720	319,361,956	0.5
Same house	82.6	82.4	X	85.3	85.4	X
Different house in the U.S.	16.6	16.8	X	14.1	13.9	X
Same county	10.2	9.7	X	8.5	8.3	X
Different county	6.3	7.1	X	5.6	5.6	X
Same state	3.0	3.5	X	3.2	3.2	X
Different state	3.3	3.6	X	2.4	2.4	X
Abroad	0.8	0.8	X	0.7	0.7	X
Place of Birth						
Native born	2,751,452	2,798,884	1.7	278,128,449	279,388,170	0.5
Male	50.5	50.5	X	49.3	49.3	X
Female	49.5	49.5	X	50.7	50.7	X
Foreign born	244,467	252,333	3.2	43,290,372	43,739,345	1.0
Male	48.0	49.5	X	48.6	48.5	X
Female	52.0	50.5	X	51.4	51.5	X
Foreign born; naturalized U.S. citizen........	95,513	93,582	-2.0	20,697,103	21,238,372	2.6
Male	46.2	46.7	X	45.9	45.9	X
Female	53.8	53.3	X	54.1	54.1	X
Foreign born; not a U.S. citizen...............	148,954	158,751	6.6	22,593,269	22,500,973	-0.4
Male	49.2	51.2	X	51.1	51.0	X
Female	50.8	48.8	X	48.9	49.0	X
Entered 2010 or later	14.7	21.5	X	15.6	18.6	X
Entered 2000 to 2009	31.6	31.3	X	27.9	26.7	X
Entered before 2000.............................	53.7	47.2	X	56.5	54.7	X
World Region of Birth, Foreign						
Foreign-born population, excluding population born at sea	244,413	252,333	3.2	43,289,646	43,738,901	1.0
Europe	9.3	10.3	X	11.1	10.9	X
Asia...	20.0	21.0	X	30.6	30.8	X
Africa...	3.4	3.1	X	4.8	4.9	X
Oceania	3.4	3.6	X	0.6	0.6	X
Latin America	60.5	58.9	X	51.1	51.0	X
North America	3.3	3.0	X	1.9	1.8	X
Language Spoken at Home and Ability to Speak English						
Population 5 years and over......................	2,745,950	2,797,795	1.9	301,625,014	303,328,961	0.6
English only	85.2	84.7	X	78.5	78.4	X
Language other than English.....................	14.8	15.3	X	21.5	21.6	X
Speaks English less than "very well"...........	4.8	4.9	X	8.6	8.6	X

NA = Not available.
X = Not applicable.
- = Zero or rounds to zero.

Table UT-5. Median Income and Poverty Status, 2016

(Number, percent, except as noted.)

Characteristic	State		U.S.	
	Number	Percent	Number	Percent
Median Income				
Households (dollars)..	65,977	X	57,617	X
Families (dollars)	74,181	X	71,062	X
Below Poverty Level (All People)	306,902	10.2	44,268,996	14.0
Sex				
Male	139,903	9.3	19,760,056	12.8
Female	166,999	11.2	24,508,940	15.2
Age				
Under 18 years..	100,801	11.1	14,115,713	19.5
Related children under 18 years......................................	97,800	10.8	13,805,435	19.1
18 to 64 years..	185,008	10.4	25,723,818	13.2
65 years and over	21,093	6.7	4,429,465	9.2

X = Not applicable.

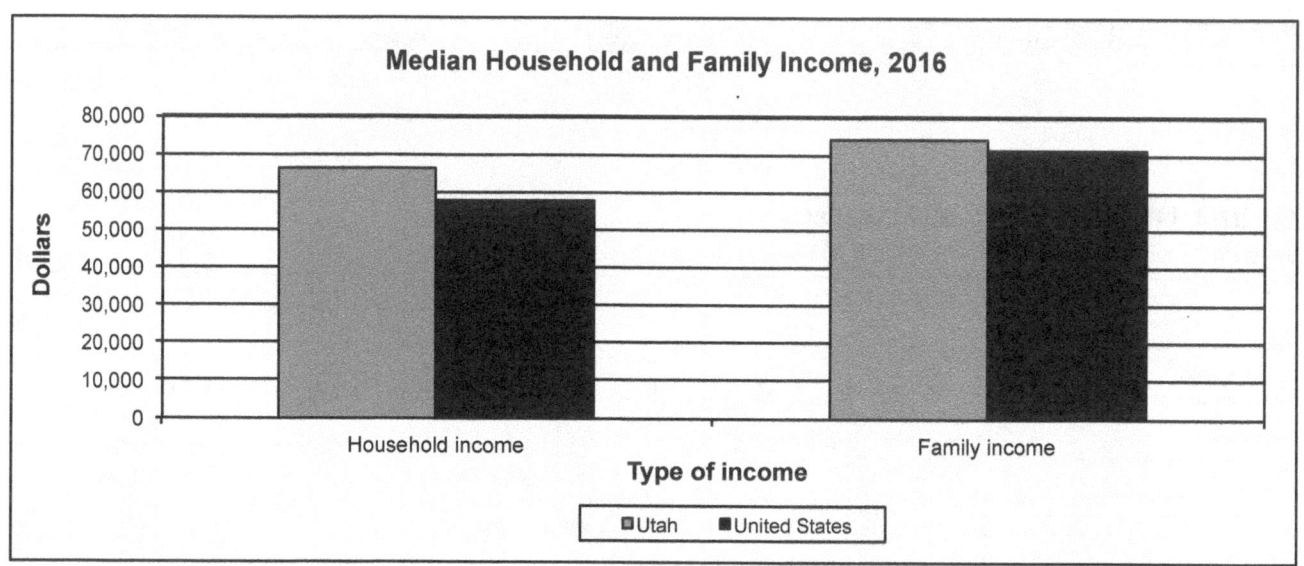

Table UT-6. Health Insurance Coverage Status for the Civilian Noninstitutionalized Population and Children Under 18 Years of Age

(Number, percent.)

Item	2008	2009	2010	2011	2012	2013	2014	2015	2016
Civilian Noninstitutionalized Population	2,704,865	2,755,284	2,750,354	2,789,648	2,829,001	2,874,213	2,916,303	2,971,003	3,024,767
Covered by Private or Public Insurance									
Number..	2,286,154	2,354,207	2,328,430	2,363,584	2,419,830	2,472,089	2,550,780	2,659,662	2,759,960
Percent...	84.5	85.4	84.7	84.7	85.5	86.0	87.5	89.5	91.2
Not Covered									
Number..	418,711	401,077	421,924	426,064	409,171	402,124	365,523	311,341	264,807
Percent...	15.5	14.6	15.3	15.3	14.5	14.0	12.5	10.5	8.8
Percent in the U.S. not covered......................................	15.1	15.1	15.5	15.1	14.8	14.5	11.7	9.4	8.6
Children Under 18 Years of Age	849,122	868,873	870,383	877,812	884,012	893,685	902,311	909,285	918,971
Covered by Private or Public Insurance									
Number..	737,791	779,741	775,692	780,570	794,321	808,794	817,543	844,090	865,371
Percent...	86.9	89.7	89.1	88.9	89.9	90.5	90.6	92.8	94.2
Not Covered									
Number..	111,331	89,132	94,691	97,242	89,691	84,891	84,768	65,195	53,600
Percent...	13.1	10.3	10.9	11.1	10.1	9.5	9.4	7.2	5.8
Percent in the U.S. not covered......................................	9.9	8.6	8.0	7.5	7.2	7.1	6.0	4.8	4.5

Table UT-7. Employment Status by Demographic Group, 2017

(Numbers in thousands, percent.)

Characteristic	Civilian noninstitutional population	Civilian labor force		Employed		Unemployed	
		Number	Percent of population	Number	Percent of population	Number	Percent of population
Total...	2,250	1,570	69.8	1,516	67.4	53	3.4
Sex							
Male...	1,121	875	78.1	849	75.8	26	3.0
Female......................................	1,129	694	61.5	667	59.1	27	3.9
Race, Sex, and Hispanic Origin							
White..	2,082	1,448	69.6	1,403	67.4	45	3.1
Male..	1,036	807	77.9	785	75.8	22	2.7
Female.....................................	1,047	641	61.3	618	59.1	23	3.6
Black or African American................	NA	NA	NA	NA	NA	NA	NA
Male..	NA	NA	NA	NA	NA	NA	NA
Female.....................................	NA	NA	NA	NA	NA	NA	NA
Hispanic or Latino ethnicity[1]...........	304	232	76.3	222	72.8	11	4.6
Male..	157	132	84.1	128	81.1	5	3.6
Female.....................................	147	100	67.9	94	63.9	6	5.8
Age							
16 to 19 years.............................	183	100	54.8	90	48.9	11	10.7
20 to 24 years.............................	259	214	82.3	205	78.9	9	4.1
25 to 34 years.............................	449	366	81.5	354	78.8	12	3.4
35 to 44 years.............................	421	347	82.5	339	80.6	8	2.3
45 to 54 years.............................	294	248	84.5	240	81.8	8	3.1
55 to 64 years.............................	305	223	73.2	220	71.9	4	1.7
65 years and over........................	339	71	21.0	69	20.5	2	2.3

NOTE: Data in Table 7 are from the Current Population Survey (CPS) and do not match the estimates in Table 8. See notes and definitions for further information.
[1] May be of any race.
NA = Not available.

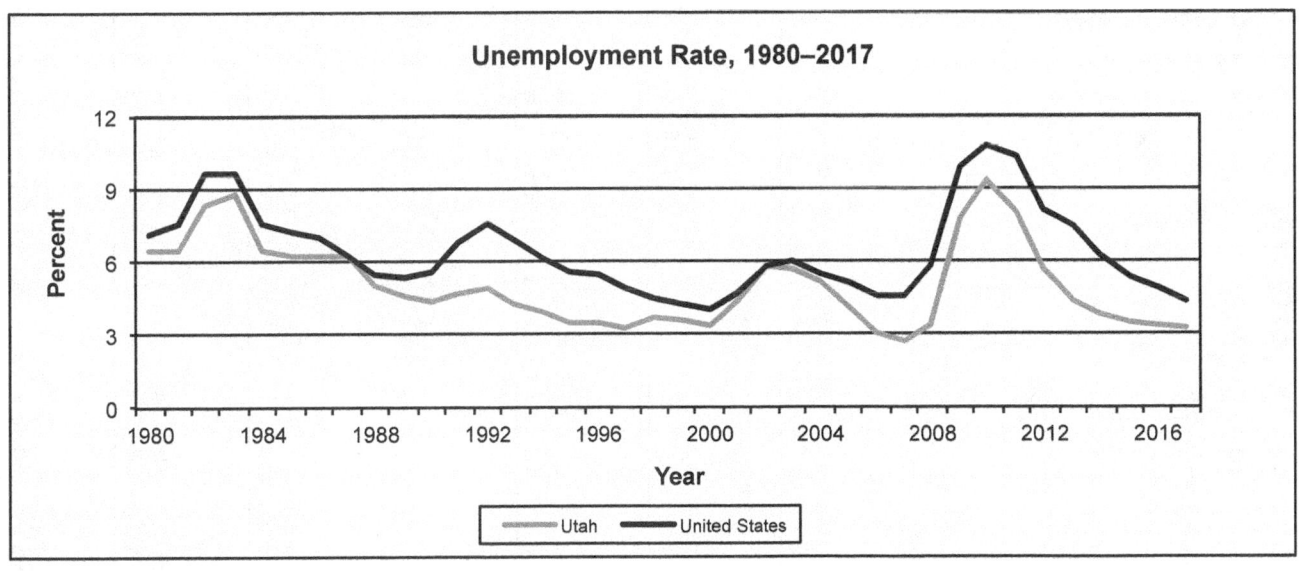

Table UT-8. Employment Status of the Civilian Noninstitutional Population Age 16 Years and Over

(Number, percent.)

Year	Civilian labor force	Civilian participation rate	Employed	Unemployed	Unemployment rate
2009..	1,365,850	69.2	1,266,009	99,841	7.3
2010..	1,356,097	68.8	1,249,814	106,283	7.8
2011..	1,350,444	67.8	1,259,337	91,107	6.7
2012..	1,372,971	67.8	1,298,807	74,164	5.4
2013..	1,405,630	68.1	1,341,192	64,438	4.6
2014..	1,428,293	68.0	1,373,801	54,492	3.8
2015..	1,464,173	68.3	1,411,194	52,979	3.6
2016..	1,511,279	68.8	1,459,309	51,970	3.4
2017..	1,560,846	69.4	1,510,208	50,638	3.2

Table UT-9. Employment and Average Wages by Industry

(Estimates through 2010 are based on the 2007 *North American Industry Classification System* [NAICS]. Estimates from 2011 onward are based on the 2012 NAICS.)

Industry	2010	2011	2012	2013	2014	2015	2016
	Number of jobs						
Wage and Salary Employment by Industry.......................	1,236,311	1,264,381	1,304,870	1,343,013	1,382,315	1,430,866	1,479,019
Farm Wage and Salary Employment...............................	4,745	4,476	4,495	4,798	4,502	4,373	4,618
Nonfarm Wage and Salary Employment...........................	1,231,566	1,259,905	1,300,375	1,338,215	1,377,813	1,426,493	1,474,401
Private wage and salary employment............................	997,121	1,020,488	1,059,033	1,097,208	1,135,166	1,181,597	1,224,280
Forestry, fishing, and related activities........................	1,382	1,411	1,399	1,457	1,532	1,557	1,620
Mining..	10,369	11,591	12,491	12,129	12,175	10,329	8,463
Utilities..	4,062	4,019	4,019	3,908	3,888	3,912	3,856
Construction...	67,530	67,266	71,313	75,629	80,837	86,806	94,094
Manufacturing...	110,393	113,016	115,985	118,052	120,017	123,008	125,292
Durable goods manufacturing................................	71,733	74,019	76,623	77,818	79,018	81,630	82,524
Nondurable goods manufacturing...........................	38,660	38,997	39,362	40,234	40,999	41,378	42,768
Wholesale trade...	44,172	46,251	47,996	48,477	48,862	50,204	50,117
Retail trade..	139,248	139,834	144,940	148,947	152,841	159,333	166,035
Transportation and warehousing...............................	43,080	44,833	46,519	47,197	48,666	51,519	53,423
Information..	28,116	28,416	30,228	31,306	32,174	33,246	35,726
Finance and insurance...	53,446	54,102	55,221	57,640	59,449	63,161	65,502
Real estate and rental and leasing............................	16,682	17,015	17,167	18,063	18,630	19,007	19,549
Professional, scientific, and technical services	65,836	68,730	73,021	79,029	83,621	88,701	92,780
Management of companies and enterprises....................	16,754	16,750	17,283	17,408	18,137	18,333	18,497
Administrative and waste services...........................	69,047	73,449	76,498	80,362	82,675	86,436	90,576
Educational services	39,457	40,824	41,897	42,774	44,094	45,945	48,990
Health care and social assistance...........................	119,309	121,459	124,302	130,157	132,733	138,848	145,088
Arts, entertainment, and recreation..........................	17,730	18,097	19,338	19,689	20,240	21,327	23,449
Accommodation and food services............................	93,791	96,180	100,007	104,624	108,629	113,101	116,150
Other services, except public administration................	56,717	57,245	59,409	60,360	65,966	66,824	65,073
Government and government enterprises....................	234,445	239,417	241,342	241,007	242,647	244,896	250,121
	Dollars						
Average Wages and Salaries by Industry	40,162	41,133	42,235	42,720	43,836	45,204	48,339
Average Farm Wages and Salaries	31,728	33,979	38,508	40,724	41,817	40,873	43,091
Average Nonfarm Wages and Salaries	40,195	41,158	42,248	42,727	43,843	45,217	48,355
Average private wages and salaries...........................	40,267	41,399	42,717	43,172	44,368	45,751	48,979
Forestry, fishing, and related activities.....................	26,643	27,033	28,332	30,161	31,581	31,815	35,212
Mining..	70,891	73,980	77,015	78,053	79,323	80,526	77,578
Utilities..	87,123	87,897	86,758	88,995	91,002	93,356	94,768
Construction...	42,905	43,829	44,926	44,270	45,690	47,279	51,603
Manufacturing...	50,928	51,694	52,677	53,225	54,527	56,223	58,915
Durable goods manufacturing................................	54,659	55,543	56,039	56,348	57,749	59,120	62,547
Nondurable goods manufacturing...........................	44,005	44,389	46,134	47,184	48,318	50,509	51,907
Wholesale trade...	55,801	58,745	60,119	62,397	62,829	64,047	68,032
Retail trade..	26,845	27,289	28,418	28,798	29,775	31,210	33,303
Transportation and warehousing...............................	43,785	44,554	45,251	46,443	47,482	48,633	52,964
Information..	53,734	58,043	60,623	61,454	65,104	69,360	73,605
Finance and insurance...	56,012	58,663	62,936	63,491	66,093	69,895	72,589
Real estate and rental and leasing............................	36,755	38,877	40,301	40,685	42,834	46,283	49,741
Professional, scientific, and technical services	60,901	62,894	63,719	63,512	66,872	67,970	74,129
Management of companies and enterprises....................	80,450	78,821	86,187	85,400	84,967	86,489	90,639
Administrative and waste services...........................	28,844	29,670	30,448	31,387	32,174	32,993	36,527
Educational services	27,428	28,027	28,354	28,946	29,823	30,566	31,623
Health care and social assistance...........................	38,540	39,328	40,169	40,556	41,403	42,109	46,398
Arts, entertainment, and recreation..........................	25,106	25,161	25,039	26,527	26,838	27,698	32,421
Accommodation and food services............................	16,480	16,968	17,597	17,738	18,393	19,404	21,177
Other services, except public administration................	40,191	41,259	43,246	43,927	43,383	44,831	48,545
Government and government enterprises....................	39,884	40,135	40,190	40,699	41,383	42,640	45,303

Table UT-10. Employment Characteristics by Family Type

(Number, percent.)

Family type and labor force status	2014 Total	2014 Families with own children under 18 years	2015 Total	2015 Families with own children under 18 years	2016 Total	2016 Families with own children under 18 years
All Families	688,140	351,950	693,181	346,662	711,124	357,341
FAMILY TYPE AND LABOR FORCE STATUS						
Married-Couple Families	563,526	281,444	564,803	278,527	578,132	286,278
Both husband and wife in labor force	51.8	57.5	50.3	56.3	50.9	57.5
Husband in labor force, wife not in labor force	29.7	39.5	30.3	40.0	29.3	38.8
Wife in labor force, husband not in labor force	5.3	2.3	5.0	2.0	5.1	2.4
Both husband and wife not in labor force	13.2	0.8	13.9	1.4	14.1	0.8
Other Families	124,614	70,506	128,378	68,135	132,992	71,063
Female householder, no husband present	69.7	72.9	69.0	71.4	67.8	69.8
In labor force	50.2	61.8	49.3	60.7	49.8	59.8
Not in labor force	19.5	11.1	19.7	10.6	18.0	10.1
Male householder, no wife present	30.3	27.1	31.0	28.6	32.2	30.2
In labor force	24.7	25.1	25.7	26.4	27.2	28.6
Not in labor force	5.6	2.0	5.3	2.2	5.0	1.6

Table UT-11. School Enrollment and Educational Attainment, 2016

(Number, percent.)

Item	State	U.S.
Enrollment		
Total population 3 years and over, enrolled in school	973,643	81,572,277
Enrolled in nursery school or preschool (percent)	6.1	6.0
Enrolled in kindergarten (percent)	5.6	5.0
Enrolled in elementary school, grades 1-8 (percent)	42.1	40.3
Enrolled in high school, grades 9-12 (percent)	20.6	21.0
Enrolled in college or graduate school (percent)	25.6	27.7
Attainment		
Total population 25 years and over	1,783,244	218,475,480
Less than ninth grade (percent)	2.9	5.4
9th to 12th grade, no diploma (percent)	5.4	7.2
High school graduate, including equivalency (percent)	22.7	27.2
Some college, no degree (percent)	26.5	20.6
Associate's degree (percent)	10.0	8.4
Bachelor's degree (percent)	21.4	19.3
Graduate or professional degree (percent)	11.2	11.9
High school graduate or higher (percent)	91.7	87.5
Bachelor's degree or higher (percent)	32.6	31.3

Table UT-12. Public School Characteristics and Educational Indicators

(Number, percent; data derived from National Center of Education Statistics.)

Item	State	U.S.
Public Schools, 2015–2016 (except where noted)		
Number of school districts	152	18,328
Number of schools	1,033	98,456
Number of students	647,870	50,327,015
Number of teachers	28,348	3,151,497
Student-teacher ratio	22.9	16.0
Expenditures per student (dollars), 2014-2015	6,751	11,445
Four-year adjusted cohort graduation rate (ACGR)[1,2]	85.2	84.1
Students eligible for free or reduced-price lunch (percent), 2014-2015	36.9	51.8
English language learners (percent), Fall 2015	6.6	9.5
Students age 3 to 21 served under IDEA, part B (percent)	12.3	13.2

Public Schools by Type	Number	Percent of state public schools
Total number of schools	1,033	100.0
Regular	935	90.5
Special education	64	6.2
Vocational education	6	0.6
Alternative education	28	2.7

NOTE: Every school is assigned only one school type based on its instructional emphasis.
[1] ACGR data represents a new method of calculating high-school completion rates and may not be comparable to previous years' data for Averaged Freshmen Graduation Rates (AFGR).
[2] The United States 4-year ACGRs were estimated using both the reported 4-year ACGR data from 49 states and the District of Columbia and using imputed data for Idaho. The estimate for American Indian/Alaska Native students also includes imputed data for Virginia.

Table UT-13. Reported Voting and Registration of the Voting-Age Population, November 2016

(Numbers in thousands, percent.)

Item	Total population	Total citizen population	Registered			Voted		
			Total registered	Percent registered (total population)	Percent registered (total citizen population)	Total voted	Percent voted (total population)	Percent voted (total citizen population)
U.S. Total	245,502	224,059	157,596	64.2	70.3	137,537	56.0	61.4
State Total................................	2,096	1,969	1,398	66.7	71.0	1,234	58.9	62.7
Sex								
Male	1,043	983	700	67.1	71.3	613	58.7	62.4
Female	1,053	986	698	66.3	70.8	621	59.0	63.0
Race								
White alone................................	1,955	1,852	1,339	68.5	72.3	1,181	60.4	63.8
White, non-Hispanic alone............	1,737	1,731	1,265	72.8	73.0	1,115	64.2	64.4
Black alone................................	20	16	8	(B)	(B)	7	(B)	(B)
Asian alone................................	44	27	19	(B)	(B)	19	(B)	(B)
Hispanic (of any race).................	245	148	94	38.5	63.8	86	35.0	58.1
White alone or in combination	1,977	1,874	1,348	68.2	71.9	1,190	60.2	63.5
Black alone or in combination...........	32	27	13	(B)	(B)	12	(B)	(B)
Asian alone or in combination...........	49	32	19	(B)	(B)	19	(B)	(B)
Age								
18 to 24 years................................	342	326	171	50.0	52.4	142	41.6	43.6
25 to 34 years................................	416	388	243	58.5	62.7	201	48.3	51.8
35 to 44 years................................	416	373	276	66.3	73.9	243	58.5	65.2
45 to 64 years................................	586	549	432	73.7	78.7	393	67.0	71.5
65 years and over	336	333	276	82.0	82.9	255	75.8	76.6

B = Base is less than 75,000 and therefore too small to show the derived measure.

Table UT-14. Crime

(Number, rate per 100,000. Data are derived from the FBI Uniform Crime Reports.)

Item	State			U.S. [1,2,3,4]		
	2015	2016	Percent change	2015	2016	Percent change
TOTAL POPULATION [5]	2,995,919	3,051,217	1.8	321,418,820	323,127,513	0.5
VIOLENT CRIME						
Number................................	7,071	7,407	4.8	1,231,566	1,248,185	1.3
Rate................................	236.0	242.8	2.9	383.2	386.3	0.8
Murder and Nonnegligent Manslaughter						
Number................................	54	72	33.3	15,696	17,250	9.9
Rate................................	1.8	2.4	33.3	4.9	5.3	8.2
Rape [6]						
Number................................	1,645	1,520	-7.6	124,047	130,603	5.3
Rate................................	54.9	49.8	-9.3	38.6	40.4	4.7
Robbery						
Number................................	1,326	1,541	16.2	327,374	332,198	1.5
Rate................................	44.3	50.5	14.0	101.9	102.8	0.9
Aggravated Assault						
Number................................	4,046	4,274	5.6	764,449	803,007	5.0
Rate................................	135.1	140.1	3.7	237.8	248.5	4.5
PROPERTY CRIME						
Number................................	89,278	90,058	0.9	7,993,631	7,919,035	-0.9
Rate................................	2,980.0	2,951.5	-1.0	2,487.0	2,450.7	-1.5
Burglary						
Number................................	12,468	12,836	3.0	1,579,527	1,515,096	-4.1
Rate................................	416.2	420.7	1.1	491.4	468.9	-4.6
Larceny-Theft						
Number................................	68,103	67,834	-0.4	5,706,346	5,638,455	-1.2
Rate................................	2,273.2	2,223.2	-2.2	1,775.4	1,745.0	-1.7
Motor Vehicle Theft						
Number................................	8,707	9,388	7.8	707,758	765,484	8.2
Rate................................	290.6	307.7	5.9	220.2	236.9	7.6

NOTE: Although arson data are included in the trend and clearance tables, sufficient data are not available to estimate totals for this offense. Therefore, no arson data are published in this table.
X = Not applicable.
- = Zero or rounds to zero.
[1] The crime figures have been adjusted.
[2] The data collection methodology for the offense of forcible rape used by the Minnesota state Uniform Crime Reporting (UCR) Program (with the exception of Minneapolis and St. Paul, Minnesota) does not comply with national UCR Program guidelines. Consequently, its figures for forcible rape and violent crime (of which forcible rape is a part) are not published in this table.
[3] Includes offenses reported by the Zoological Police and the Metro Transit Police.
[4] Because of changes in the state's reporting practices, figures are not comparable to previous years' data.
[5] Populations are U.S. Census Bureau provisional estimates as of July 1 of each year.
[6] The figures shown for the offense of rape were estimated using the revised Uniform Crime Reporting (UCR) definition of rape.

Table UT-15. State Government Finances, 2016

(Dollar amounts in thousands, percent distribution.)

Item	Dollars	Percent distribution
Total Revenue	18,164,518	100.0
General revenue	16,441,022	90.5
Intergovernmental revenue	4,233,941	23.3
Taxes	7,082,961	39.0
General sales	2,083,671	11.5
Selective sales	948,148	5.2
License taxes	290,426	1.6
Individual income tax	3,374,535	18.6
Corporate income tax	333,358	1.8
Other taxes	52,823	0.3
Current charges	4,008,310	22.1
Miscellaneous general revenue	1,115,810	6.1
Utility revenue	0	-
Liquor stores revenue	361,199	2.0
Insurance trust revenue [1]	1,362,297	7.5
Total Expenditure	19,630,299	100.0
Intergovernmental expenditure	3,511,958	17.9
Direct expenditure	16,118,341	82.1
Current operation	11,859,866	60.4
Capital outlay	1,511,457	7.7
Insurance benefits and repayments	1,787,517	9.1
Assistance and subsidies	719,439	3.7
Interest on debt	240,062	1.2
Exhibit: Salaries and wages	3,336,454	17.0
Total Expenditure	19,630,299	100.0
General expenditure	17,585,122	89.6
Intergovernmental expenditure	3,511,958	17.9
Direct expenditure	14,073,164	71.7
General expenditure, by function:		
Education	8,600,936	43.8
Public welfare	3,405,959	17.4
Hospitals	1,699,785	8.7
Health	388,627	2.0
Highways	835,995	4.3
Police protection	151,844	0.8
Correction	342,621	1.7
Natural resources	189,265	1.0
Parks and recreation	47,016	0.2
Governmental administration	615,522	3.1
Interest on general debt	240,062	1.2
Other and unallocable	1,067,490	5.4
Utility expenditure	0	-
Liquor stores expenditure	257,660	1.3
Insurance trust expenditure	1,787,517	9.1
Debt at End of Fiscal Year	7,013,698	X
Cash and Security Holdings	33,763,037	X

X = Not applicable.
- = Zero or rounds to zero.
[1] Within insurance trust revenue, net earnings of state retirement systems is a calculated statistic (the item code in the data file is X08), and thus can be positive or negative. Net earnings is the sum of earnings on investments plus gains on investments minus losses on investments. The change made in 2002 for asset valuation from book to market value in accordance with Statement 34 of the Governmental Accounting Standards Board is reflected in the calculated statistics.

Table UT-16. State Government Tax Collections, 2017

(Dollars in thousands, percent.)

Item	Dollars	Percent distribution
Total Taxes	7,832,889	100.0
Property taxes	X	-
Sales and gross receipts	3,530,809	45.1
General sales and gross receipts	2,533,961	32.4
Selective sales and gross receipts	996,848	12.7
Alcoholic beverages	50,002	0.6
Amusements	X	-
Insurance premiums	130,122	1.7
Motor fuels	487,731	6.2
Pari-mutuels	X	-
Public utilities	24,351	0.3
Tobacco products	116,158	1.5
Other selective sales	188,484	2.4
Licenses	321,715	4.1
Alcoholic beverages	5,900	0.1
Amusements	X	-
Corporations in general	466	-
Hunting and fishing	30,622	0.4
Motor vehicle	203,980	2.6
Motor vehicle operators	16,602	0.2
Public utilities	X	-
Occupation and business, NEC	55,350	0.7
Other licenses	8,795	0.1
Income taxes	3,950,776	50.4
Individual income	3,621,199	46.2
Corporation net income	329,577	4.2
Other taxes	29,589	0.4
Death and gift	X	-
Documentary and stock transfer	X	-
Severance	29,589	0.4
Taxes, NEC	0	-

X = Not applicable.
- = Zero or rounds to zero.

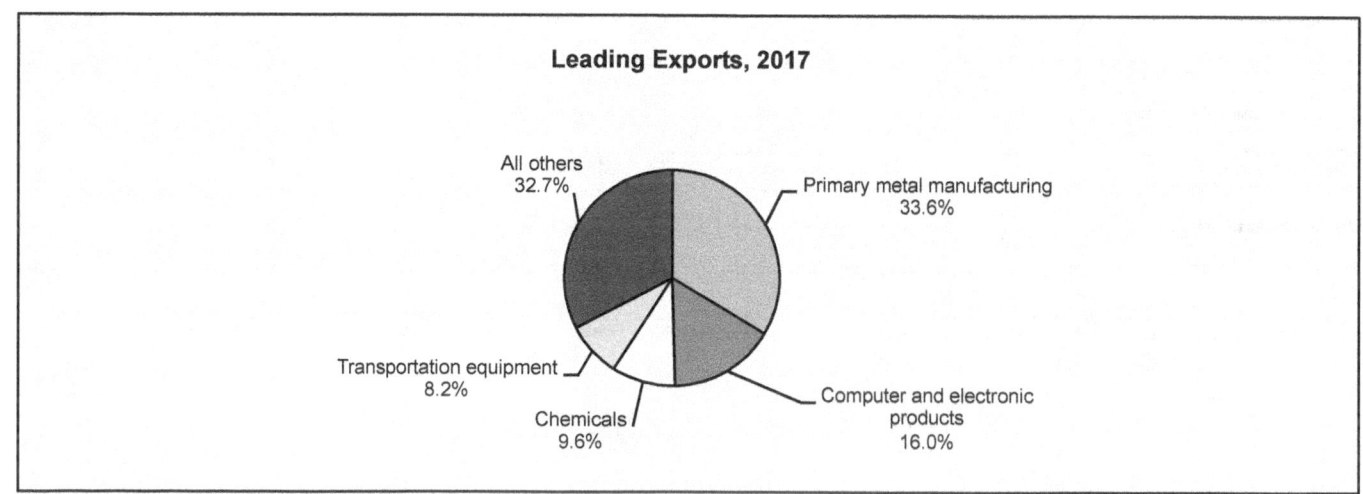

Leading Exports, 2017

All others 32.7%

Primary metal manufacturing 33.6%

Transportation equipment 8.2%

Chemicals 9.6%

Computer and electronic products 16.0%

VERMONT

Facts and Figures

Location: Northeastern United States; bordered on the N by Canada (Quebec), on the E by New Hampshire, on the S by Massachusetts, and on the W by New York

Area: 9,614 sq. mi. (24,901 sq. km.); rank—45th

Population: 623,657 (2017 est.); rank—50th

Principal Cities: capital—Montpelier; largest—Burlington

Statehood: March 4, 1791; the 14th state

U.S. Congress: 2 senators, 1 representative

State Motto: Freedom and Unity

State Song: "These Green Mountains"

State Nickname: The Green Mountain State

Abbreviations: VT; Vt.

State Symbols: flower—red clover; tree—sugar maple; bird—hermit thrush

At a Glance

- Vermont's was one of three states that experienced a decrease in population between 2010 and 2017, with a drop of 0.3 percent.

- Vermont's median household income in 2016 was $57,677, and 11.9 percent of the population lived below the poverty level.

- Vermont's violent crime rate in 2016 was the 2nd lowest in the nation at 158.3 per 100,000 population.

- In 2016, 3.7 percent of Vermonters did not have health insurance, which was the 3rd lowest percent in the country.

- Vermont had the 2nd lowest percent of its population under age 18 in 2017, with 18.7 percent of its residents in this age group. It also had the lowest birth rate in 2016, with 9.2 births per 100,000 population.

Table VT-1. Population by Age, Sex, Race, and Hispanic Origin

(Number, percent, except where noted.)

Sex, age, race, and Hispanic origin	2000	2010	2017 [1]	Average annual percent change, 2010–2017
Total Population...	608,827	625,741	623,657	-0.3
Percent of total U.S. population	0.2	0.2	0.2	X
Sex				
Male..	298,337	308,206	308,256	-
Female	310,490	317,535	315,401	-0.7
Age				
Under 5 years..	33,989	31,952	30,035	-6.0
5 to 19 years..	132,268	118,323	107,339	-9.3
20 to 64 years..	365,060	384,388	369,414	-3.9
65 years and over	77,510	91,078	116,869	28.3
Median age (years)..	37.7	41.5	42.9	3.4
Race and Hispanic Origin				
One race				
White	589,208	598,592	589,163	-1.6
Black	3,063	6,456	8,475	31.3
American Indian and Alaska Native	2,420	2,308	2,413	4.5
Asian..	5,217	8,069	11,348	40.6
Native Hawaiian or Other Pacific Islander	141	175	233	33.1
Two or more races	7,335	10,141	12,025	18.6
Hispanic (of any race)..	5,504	9,962	12,060	21.1

X = Not applicable.
- = Zero or rounds to zero.
[1] Population figures for 2017 are July 1 estimates. The 2010 estimates are taken from the 2010 Census.

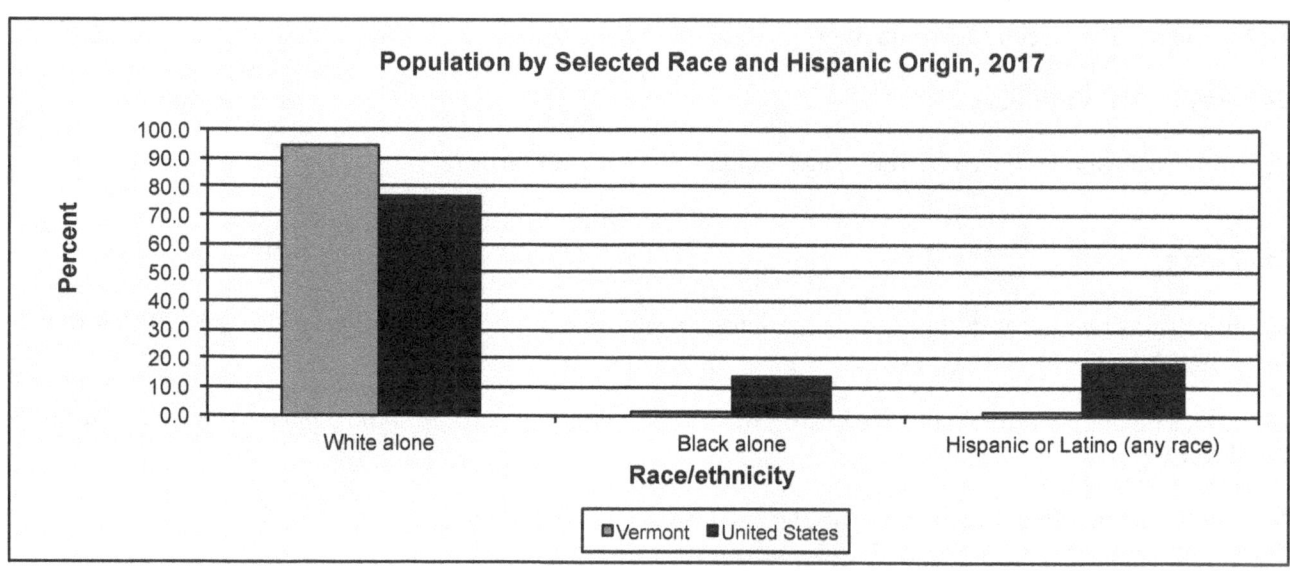

Table VT-2. Marital Status

(Number, percent distribution.)

Sex, age, and marital status	2000	2010	2016
Males, 15 Years and Over	236,517	254,288	257,638
Never married	29.7	34.2	34.8
Now married, except separated..	57.1	51.3	49.7
Separated..	1.2	1.3	1.1
Widowed..	2.4	2.5	2.9
Divorced..	9.6	10.7	11.5
Females, 15 Years and Over	251,764	266,860	269,436
Never married	23.9	27.7	28.5
Now married, except separated..	53.3	49.7	46.1
Separated..	1.4	1.4	1.0
Widowed..	10.0	8.2	9.7
Divorced..	11.5	13.0	14.7

Table VT-3. Households and Housing Characteristics

(Number, percent, dollars.)

Item	2000	2010	2016	Average annual percent change, 2010–2016
Total Households.....................	240,634	256,922	254,851	-0.1
Family households..........................	157,763	159,846	154,421	-0.6
Married-couple family...................	126,413	125,678	120,302	-0.7
Other family..............................	31,350	34,168	34,119	-
Male householder, no wife present.........	9,078	10,887	11,099	0.3
Female householder, no husband present....	22,272	23,281	23,020	-0.2
Nonfamily households	82,871	97,076	100,430	0.6
Householder living alone................	63,112	75,243	77,045	0.4
Householder not living alone............	19,759	21,833	23,385	1.2
Housing Characteristics				
Total housing units........................	294,382	322,698	329,539	0.4
Occupied housing units....................	240,634	256,922	254,851	-0.1
Owner occupied	169,784	180,847	177,772	-0.3
Renter occupied........................	70,850	76,075	77,079	0.2
Average household size....................	2.44	2.34	2.35	0.1
Financial Characteristics				
Median gross rent of renter-occupied housing	553	823	925	2.1
Median monthly owner costs for housing units with a mortgage	1,021	1,445	1,507	0.7
Median value of owner-occupied housing units	111,500	216,800	223,700	0.5

- = Zero or rounds to zero.

Table VT-4. Migration, Origin, and Language

(Number, percent.)

Characteristic	State			U.S.		
	2015	2016	Percent change	2015	2016	Percent change
Residence 1 Year Ago						
Population 1 year and over	619,952	619,387	-0.1	317,635,720	319,361,956	0.5
Same house..............................	85.9	86.4	X	85.3	85.4	X
Different house in the U.S.	13.4	13.2	X	14.1	13.9	X
Same county..........................	7.6	7.6	X	8.5	8.3	X
Different county	5.8	5.7	X	5.6	5.6	X
Same state.........................	2.4	2.2	X	3.2	3.2	X
Different state......................	3.4	3.4	X	2.4	2.4	X
Abroad	0.7	0.3	X	0.7	0.7	X
Place of Birth						
Native born..............................	597,795	596,371	-0.2	278,128,449	279,388,170	0.5
Male	49.3	49.7	X	49.3	49.3	X
Female	50.7	50.3	X	50.7	50.7	X
Foreign born.............................	28,247	28,223	-0.1	43,290,372	43,739,345	1.0
Male	48.8	41.5	X	48.6	48.5	X
Female	51.2	58.5	X	51.4	51.5	X
Foreign born; naturalized U.S. citizen....	15,464	16,364	5.8	20,697,103	21,238,372	2.6
Male	47.8	42.5	X	45.9	45.9	X
Female	52.2	57.5	X	54.1	54.1	X
Foreign born; not a U.S. citizen	12,783	11,859	-7.2	22,593,269	22,500,973	-0.4
Male	50.1	40.0	X	51.1	51.0	X
Female	49.9	60.0	X	48.9	49.0	X
Entered 2010 or later	21.9	22.0	X	15.6	18.6	X
Entered 2000 to 2009	24.6	18.4	X	27.9	26.7	X
Entered before 2000......................	53.6	59.5	X	56.5	54.7	X
World Region of Birth, Foreign						
Foreign-born population, excluding population born at sea	28,247	28,223	-0.1	43,289,646	43,738,901	1.0
Europe	32.3	29.7	X	11.1	10.9	X
Asia...................................	29.0	29.4	X	30.6	30.8	X
Africa	9.3	10.3	X	4.8	4.9	X
Oceania	1.4	1.1	X	0.6	0.6	X
Latin America..........................	10.8	9.4	X	51.1	51.0	X
North America	17.3	20.1	X	1.9	1.8	X
Language Spoken at Home and Ability to Speak English						
Population 5 years and over................	595,870	594,130	-0.3	301,625,014	303,328,961	0.6
English only...........................	93.9	94.5	X	78.5	78.4	X
Language other than English............	6.1	5.5	X	21.5	21.6	X
Speaks English less than "very well".....	1.5	1.3	X	8.6	8.6	X

NA = Not available.
X = Not applicable.
- = Zero or rounds to zero.

Table VT-5. Median Income and Poverty Status, 2016

(Number, percent, except as noted.)

Characteristic	State		U.S.	
	Number	Percent	Number	Percent
Median Income				
Households (dollars)...	57,677	X	57,617	X
Families (dollars)	74,805	X	71,062	X
Below Poverty Level (All People)	71,329	11.9	44,268,996	14.0
Sex				
Male	33,218	11.2	19,760,056	12.8
Female	38,111	12.5	24,508,940	15.2
Age				
Under 18 years..	17,167	14.8	14,115,713	19.5
Related children under 18 years..	16,580	14.4	13,805,435	19.1
18 to 64 years..	44,525	11.9	25,723,818	13.2
65 years and over	9,637	8.7	4,429,465	9.2

X = Not applicable.

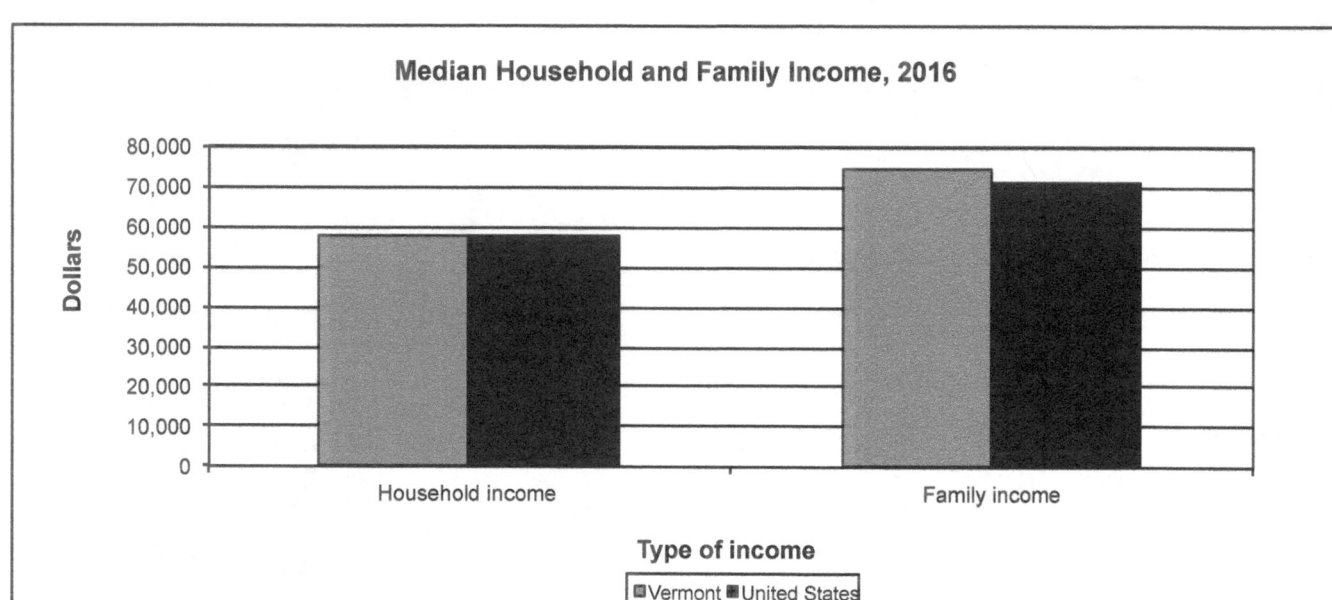

Table VT-6. Health Insurance Coverage Status for the Civilian Noninstitutionalized Population and Children Under 18 Years of Age

(Number, percent.)

Item	2008	2009	2010	2011	2012	2013	2014	2015	2016
Civilian Noninstitutionalized Population	615,089	615,376	619,886	620,159	619,928	620,896	620,453	620,107	618,622
Covered by Private or Public Insurance									
Number..................................	559,129	562,184	570,006	578,950	579,875	575,992	589,737	596,431	595,628
Percent..................................	90.9	91.4	92.0	93.4	93.5	92.8	95.0	96.2	96.3
Not Covered									
Number..................................	55,960	53,192	49,880	41,209	40,053	44,904	30,716	23,676	22,994
Percent..................................	9.1	8.6	8.0	6.6	6.5	7.2	5.0	3.8	3.7
Percent in the U.S. not covered..........................	15.1	15.1	15.5	15.1	14.8	14.5	11.7	9.4	8.6
Children Under 18 Years of Age	128,844	126,482	129,661	125,599	123,563	123,812	121,472	119,828	118,351
Covered by Private or Public Insurance									
Number..................................	123,678	122,493	127,034	122,580	120,072	119,930	118,832	118,577	116,493
Percent..................................	96.0	96.8	98.0	97.6	97.2	96.9	97.8	99.0	98.4
Not Covered									
Number..................................	5,166	3,989	2,627	3,019	3,491	3,882	2,640	1,251	1,858
Percent..................................	4.0	3.2	2.0	2.4	2.8	3.1	2.2	1.0	1.6
Percent in the U.S. not covered..........................	9.9	8.6	8.0	7.5	7.2	7.1	6.0	4.8	4.5

Table VT-7. Employment Status by Demographic Group, 2017

(Numbers in thousands, percent.)

Characteristic	Civilian noninstitutional population	Civilian labor force		Employed		Unemployed	
		Number	Percent of population	Number	Percent of population	Number	Percent of population
Total..	515	345	67.0	335	64.9	11	3.1
Sex							
Male..	253	179	71.1	174	68.8	6	3.1
Female..	263	166	63.0	161	61.1	5	3.0
Race, Sex, and Hispanic Origin							
White...	489	328	67.2	319	65.2	10	2.9
Male..	239	170	71.1	165	69.0	5	3.0
Female	250	158	63.3	153	61.5	5	2.9
Black or African American................	NA	NA	NA	NA	NA	NA	NA
Male..	NA	NA	NA	NA	NA	NA	NA
Female	NA	NA	NA	NA	NA	NA	NA
Hispanic or Latino ethnicity[1]	NA	NA	NA	NA	NA	NA	NA
Male..	NA	NA	NA	NA	NA	NA	NA
Female	NA	NA	NA	NA	NA	NA	NA
Age							
16 to 19 years...............................	33	16	47.2	15	43.4	1	8.1
20 to 24 years...............................	40	33	82.0	31	77.2	2	5.5
25 to 34 years...............................	72	63	87.6	61	84.5	2	3.5
35 to 44 years...............................	78	66	85.7	65	84.0	1	2.1
45 to 54 years...............................	78	66	85.4	65	83.5	2	2.3
55 to 64 years...............................	95	69	72.6	68	71.2	1	2.0
65 years and over	120	32	26.3	31	25.5	1	3.2

NOTE: Data in Table 7 are from the Current Population Survey (CPS) and do not match the estimates in Table 8. See notes and definitions for further information.
[1] May be of any race.
NA = Not available.

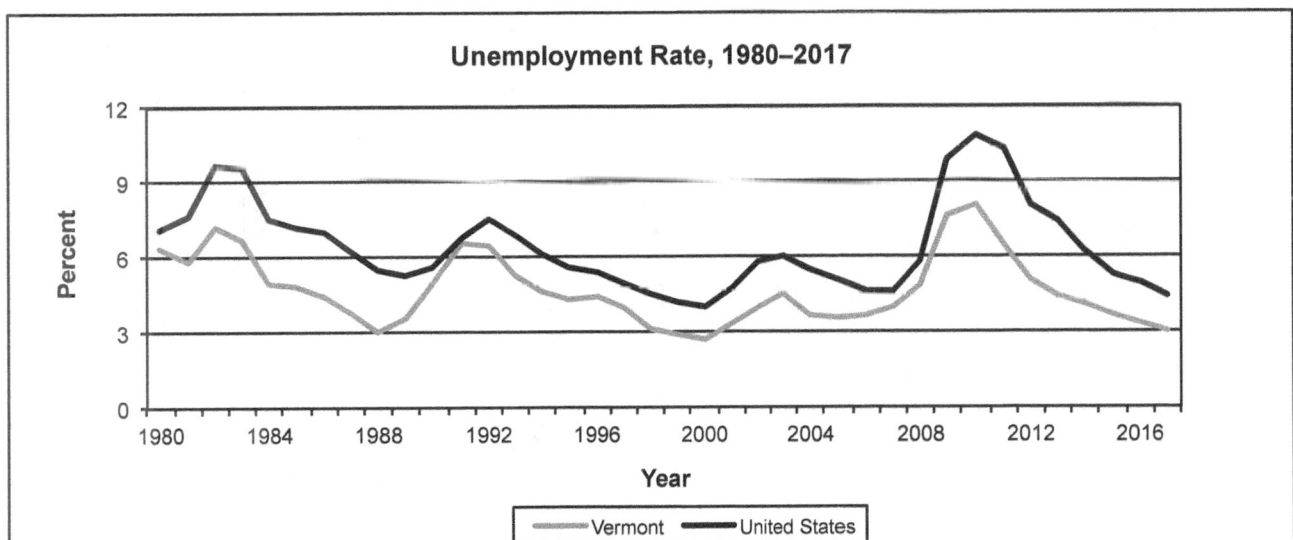

Table VT-8. Employment Status of the Civilian Noninstitutional Population Age 16 Years and Over

(Number, percent.)

Year	Civilian labor force	Civilian participation rate	Employed	Unemployed	Unemployment rate
2009...	359,836	71.0	336,104	23,732	6.6
2010...	359,402	70.8	337,488	21,914	6.1
2011...	358,108	70.3	338,463	19,645	5.5
2012...	354,857	69.5	337,284	17,573	5.0
2013...	350,447	68.4	334,964	15,483	4.4
2014...	347,172	67.6	333,438	13,734	4.0
2015...	344,520	67.0	332,199	12,321	3.6
2016...	344,572	67.0	333,399	11,173	3.2
2017...	344,760	66.9	334,378	10,382	3.0

Table VT-9. Employment and Average Wages by Industry

(Estimates through 2010 are based on the 2007 *North American Industry Classification System* [NAICS]. Estimates from 2011 onward are based on the 2012 NAICS.)

Industry	2010	2011	2012	2013	2014	2015	2016
	Number of jobs						
Wage and Salary Employment by Industry	310,614	313,625	318,425	320,279	323,603	325,821	326,373
Farm Wage and Salary Employment	2,249	2,458	2,581	2,953	2,961	2,950	2,753
Nonfarm Wage and Salary Employment	308,365	311,167	315,844	317,326	320,642	322,871	323,620
Private wage and salary employment	250,945	253,909	258,182	259,517	262,235	264,593	265,476
Forestry, fishing, and related activities	916	917	861	884	923	923	902
Mining	594	611	648	621	600	645	639
Utilities	1,800	1,801	1,828	1,790	1,727	1,548	1,342
Construction	14,031	14,524	14,625	14,508	15,192	15,544	15,698
Manufacturing	30,832	30,939	31,968	31,743	31,231	30,967	30,023
Durable goods manufacturing	21,781	21,618	21,753	21,221	20,382	19,696	18,778
Nondurable goods manufacturing	9,051	9,321	10,215	10,522	10,849	11,271	11,245
Wholesale trade	9,592	9,647	9,244	9,256	9,289	9,339	9,515
Retail trade	38,351	38,366	37,945	38,053	38,284	38,237	38,443
Transportation and warehousing	6,808	7,139	7,073	6,994	7,005	6,882	6,829
Information	5,357	4,962	4,671	4,680	4,765	4,637	4,640
Finance and insurance	9,324	9,360	9,294	9,187	9,250	9,235	9,202
Real estate and rental and leasing	3,027	3,031	3,065	3,138	3,149	3,016	3,029
Professional, scientific, and technical services	13,698	13,780	14,182	14,190	13,974	14,310	14,436
Management of companies and enterprises	893	1,418	1,962	1,949	2,081	2,219	2,085
Administrative and waste services	8,803	9,682	10,243	10,483	10,754	11,065	11,443
Educational services	13,742	14,048	14,245	14,195	14,526	14,778	15,094
Health care and social assistance	47,666	47,776	48,899	49,598	50,049	50,851	51,637
Arts, entertainment, and recreation	3,887	3,934	4,038	4,084	4,260	4,184	4,346
Accommodation and food services	28,708	28,910	29,585	30,459	31,086	32,079	32,133
Other services, except public administration	12,916	13,064	13,806	13,705	14,090	14,134	14,040
Government and government enterprises	57,420	57,258	57,662	57,809	58,407	58,278	58,144
	Dollars						
Average Wages and Salaries by Industry	38,739	39,484	40,197	41,244	42,193	43,360	45,047
Average Farm Wages and Salaries	26,127	20,925	31,010	27,945	29,501	27,185	32,117
Average Nonfarm Wages and Salaries	38,831	39,630	40,272	41,368	42,310	43,507	45,157
Average private wages and salaries	38,150	39,033	39,764	40,835	41,771	42,969	44,434
Forestry, fishing, and related activities	28,238	29,029	29,085	29,719	31,189	32,038	34,411
Mining	55,712	54,218	52,637	54,477	55,887	57,352	56,108
Utilities	92,310	92,697	95,712	98,065	104,387	123,178	95,246
Construction	42,686	43,298	43,671	45,399	46,231	46,949	48,525
Manufacturing	53,101	53,794	54,254	54,663	55,294	55,947	56,501
Durable goods manufacturing	57,389	58,377	58,802	59,099	59,234	59,899	59,798
Nondurable goods manufacturing	42,783	43,164	44,568	45,715	47,892	49,041	50,995
Wholesale trade	52,495	54,632	56,324	56,590	56,468	59,013	60,786
Retail trade	25,962	26,746	26,590	27,460	28,385	29,426	30,082
Transportation and warehousing	37,165	37,737	38,143	38,703	40,308	40,465	41,939
Information	45,131	49,247	48,895	51,420	53,809	56,210	54,017
Finance and insurance	62,199	64,146	66,034	67,665	69,790	73,157	77,983
Real estate and rental and leasing	33,341	34,480	36,126	37,860	38,495	39,637	42,157
Professional, scientific, and technical services	63,900	64,654	65,961	68,812	70,897	73,590	78,032
Management of companies and enterprises	78,473	78,311	77,929	81,898	87,230	86,152	86,215
Administrative and waste services	28,713	29,240	31,724	34,536	36,631	36,087	42,524
Educational services	30,534	30,781	31,171	32,382	33,235	33,487	35,055
Health care and social assistance	38,416	39,199	40,066	41,161	42,031	43,513	45,320
Arts, entertainment, and recreation	23,383	23,538	23,915	25,252	25,695	25,139	27,253
Accommodation and food services	19,782	20,617	21,093	21,812	22,626	23,743	25,698
Other services, except public administration	25,538	26,040	26,778	27,775	28,382	29,808	29,907
Government and government enterprises	41,806	42,280	42,549	43,761	44,729	45,951	48,461

Table VT-10. Employment Characteristics by Family Type

(Number, percent.)

Family type and labor force status	2014		2015		2016	
	Total	Families with own children under 18 years	Total	Families with own children under 18 years	Total	Families with own children under 18 years
All Families...............	160,392	65,545	152,379	58,593	154,421	58,887
FAMILY TYPE AND LABOR FORCE STATUS						
Married-Couple Families...............	124,116	42,593	123,509	41,961	120,302	39,099
Both husband and wife in labor force...............	59.5	76.6	57.1	75.8	56.4	75.7
Husband in labor force, wife not in labor force	15.3	17.7	15.2	17.7	15.6	18.0
Wife in labor force, husband not in labor force	8.5	3.6	9.1	4.2	8.9	4.7
Both husband and wife not in labor force...............	16.8	2.1	16.6	1.5	17.7	0.9
Other Families	36,276	22,952	28,870	16,632	34,119	19,788
Female householder, no husband present...............	68.4	70.6	70.1	68.6	67.5	70.5
In labor force...............	49.1	58.0	50.8	57.8	46.8	53.9
Not in labor force...............	19.3	12.6	19.2	10.9	20.7	16.6
Male householder, no wife present...............	31.6	29.4	29.9	31.4	32.5	29.5
In labor force...............	25.4	26.4	21.9	25.3	26.2	24.8
Not in labor force...............	6.2	2.9	8.1	6.0	6.3	4.7

Table VT-11. School Enrollment and Educational Attainment, 2016

(Number, percent.)

Item	State	U.S.
Enrollment		
Total population 3 years and over, enrolled in school	143,386	81,572,277
Enrolled in nursery school or preschool (percent)...............	6.9	6.0
Enrolled in kindergarten (percent)...............	4.7	5.0
Enrolled in elementary school, grades 1-8 (percent)...............	37.4	40.3
Enrolled in high school, grades 9-12 (percent)...............	19.1	21.0
Enrolled in college or graduate school (percent)...............	31.8	27.7
Attainment		
Total population 25 years and over	439,563	218,475,480
Less than ninth grade (percent)...............	2.5	5.4
9th to 12th grade, no diploma (percent)...............	5.3	7.2
High school graduate, including equivalency (percent)...............	29.3	27.2
Some college, no degree (percent)...............	17.3	20.6
Associate's degree (percent)...............	9.2	8.4
Bachelor's degree (percent)...............	21.1	19.3
Graduate or professional degree (percent)...............	15.2	11.9
High school graduate or higher (percent)...............	92.1	87.5
Bachelor's degree or higher (percent)...............	36.4	31.3

Table VT-12. Public School Characteristics and Educational Indicators

(Number, percent; data derived from National Center of Education Statistics.)

Item	State	U.S.
Public Schools, 2015–2016 (except where noted)		
Number of school districts...............	357	18,328
Number of schools...............	314	98,456
Number of students...............	87,866	50,327,015
Number of teachers...............	8,338	3,151,497
Student-teacher ratio...............	10.5	16.0
Expenditures per student (dollars), 2014-2015...............	18,769	11,445
Four-year adjusted cohort graduation rate (ACGR)[1,2]...............	87.7	84.1
Students eligible for free or reduced-price lunch (percent), 2014-2015...............	39.1	51.8
English language learners (percent), Fall 2015...............	1.6	9.5
Students age 3 to 21 served under IDEA, part B (percent)...............	15.8	13.2

Public Schools by Type	Number	Percent of state public schools
Total number of schools...............	314	100.0
Regular	298	94.9
Special education...............	0	-
Vocational education...............	15	4.8
Alternative education...............	1	0.3

NOTE: Every school is assigned only one school type based on its instructional emphasis.

[1] ACGR data represents a new method of calculating high-school completion rates and may not be comparable to previous years' data for Averaged Freshmen Graduation Rates (AFGR).

[2] The United States 4-year ACGRs were estimated using both the reported 4-year ACGR data from 49 states and the District of Columbia and using imputed data for Idaho. The estimate for American Indian/Alaska Native students also includes imputed data for Virginia.

- = Zero or rounds to zero.

Table VT-13. Reported Voting and Registration of the Voting-Age Population, November 2016

(Numbers in thousands, percent.)

Item	Total population	Total citizen population	Registered			Voted		
			Total registered	Percent registered (total population)	Percent registered (total citizen population)	Total voted	Percent voted (total population)	Percent voted (total citizen population)
U.S. Total	245,502	224,059	157,596	64.2	70.3	137,537	56.0	61.4
State Total.................................	500	488	351	70.2	71.9	305	61.0	62.5
Sex								
Male	246	241	166	67.6	69.0	144	58.4	59.7
Female	254	248	185	72.8	74.7	161	63.6	65.2
Race								
White alone................................	468	464	339	72.5	73.0	293	62.7	63.2
White, non-Hispanic alone	464	460	336	72.4	73.0	290	62.6	63.1
Black alone................................	5	4	2	(B)	(B)	1	(B)	(B)
Asian alone...............................	13	7	4	(B)	(B)	4	(B)	(B)
Hispanic (of any race)......................	5	4	3	(B)	(B)	3	(B)	(B)
White alone or in combination	479	476	344	71.8	72.3	298	62.3	62.8
Black alone or in combination...........	7	6	3	(B)	(B)	2	(B)	(B)
Asian alone or in combination...........	15	9	5	(B)	(B)	5	(B)	(B)
Age								
18 to 24 years.............................	57	55	34	(B)	(B)	26	(B)	(B)
25 to 34 years.............................	77	75	43	(B)	(B)	35	(B)	(B)
35 to 44 years.............................	72	70	50	(B)	(B)	42	(B)	(B)
45 to 64 years.............................	181	177	133	73.7	75.3	118	65.0	66.5
65 years and over	112	111	91	81.0	82.2	85	75.9	77.1

B = Base is less than 75,000 and therefore too small to show the derived measure.
- = Zero or rounds to zero.

Table VT-14. Crime

(Number, rate per 100,000. Data are derived from the FBI Uniform Crime Reports.)

Item	State			U.S. [1,2,3,4]		
	2015	2016	Percent change	2015	2016	Percent change
TOTAL POPULATION [5]	626,042	624,594	-0.2	321,418,820	323,127,513	0.5
VIOLENT CRIME						
Number..........................	739	989	33.8	1,231,566	1,248,185	1.3
Rate	118.0	158.3	34.2	383.2	386.3	0.8
Murder and Nonnegligent Manslaughter						
Number..........................	10	14	40.0	15,696	17,250	9.9
Rate	1.6	2.2	37.5	4.9	5.3	8.2
Rape[6]						
Number..........................	136	178	30.9	124,047	130,603	5.3
Rate	21.7	28.5	31.3	38.6	40.4	4.7
Robbery						
Number..........................	101	106	5.0	327,374	332,198	1.5
Rate	16.1	17.0	5.6	101.9	102.8	0.9
Aggravated Assault						
Number..........................	492	691	40.4	764,449	803,007	5.0
Rate	78.6	110.6	40.7	237.8	248.5	4.5
PROPERTY CRIME						
Number..........................	8,806	10,602	20.4	7,993,631	7,919,035	-0.9
Rate	1,406.6	1,697.4	20.7	2,487.0	2,450.7	-1.5
Burglary						
Number..........................	1,968	2,103	6.9	1,579,527	1,515,096	-4.1
Rate	314.4	336.7	7.1	491.4	468.9	-4.6
Larceny-Theft						
Number..........................	6,660	8,217	23.4	5,706,346	5,638,455	-1.2
Rate	1,063.8	1,315.6	23.7	1,775.4	1,745.0	-1.7
Motor Vehicle Theft						
Number..........................	178	282	58.4	707,758	765,484	8.2
Rate	28.4	45.1	58.8	220.2	236.9	7.6

NOTE: Although arson data are included in the trend and clearance tables, sufficient data are not available to estimate totals for this offense. Therefore, no arson data are published in this table.
X = Not applicable.
- = Zero or rounds to zero.
[1] The crime figures have been adjusted.
[2] The data collection methodology for the offense of forcible rape used by the Minnesota state Uniform Crime Reporting (UCR) Program (with the exception of Minneapolis and St. Paul, Minnesota) does not comply with national UCR Program guidelines. Consequently, its figures for forcible rape and violent crime (of which forcible rape is a part) are not published in this table.
[3] Includes offenses reported by the Zoological Police and the Metro Transit Police.
[4] Because of changes in the state's reporting practices, figures are not comparable to previous years' data.
[5] Populations are U.S. Census Bureau provisional estimates as of July 1 of each year.
[6] The figures shown for the offense of rape were estimated using the revised Uniform Crime Reporting (UCR) definition of rape.

Table VT-15. State Government Finances, 2016

(Dollar amounts in thousands, percent distribution.)

Item	Dollars	Percent distribution
Total Revenue	6,488,122	100.0
General revenue	6,121,318	94.3
Intergovernmental revenue	2,139,158	33.0
Taxes	3,085,865	47.6
General sales	371,365	5.7
Selective sales	659,892	10.2
License taxes	117,328	1.8
Individual income tax	729,986	11.3
Corporate income tax	98,336	1.5
Other taxes	1,108,958	17.1
Current charges	601,037	9.3
Miscellaneous general revenue	295,258	4.6
Utility revenue	0	-
Liquor stores revenue	61,926	1.0
Insurance trust revenue [1]	304,878	4.7
Total Expenditure	6,763,948	100.0
Intergovernmental expenditure	1,771,590	26.2
Direct expenditure	4,992,358	73.8
Current operation	4,033,417	59.6
Capital outlay	324,808	4.8
Insurance benefits and repayments	378,098	5.6
Assistance and subsidies	153,332	2.3
Interest on debt	102,703	1.5
Exhibit: Salaries and wages	906,270	13.4
Total Expenditure	6,763,948	100.0
General expenditure	6,325,029	93.5
Intergovernmental expenditure	1,771,590	26.2
Direct expenditure	4,553,439	67.3
General expenditure, by function:		
Education	2,735,875	40.4
Public welfare	1,769,967	26.2
Hospitals	20483	0.3
Health	387,363	5.7
Highways	454,280	6.7
Police protection	88,203	1.3
Correction	139,482	2.1
Natural resources	103,741	1.5
Parks and recreation	19,420	0.3
Governmental administration	168,125	2.5
Interest on general debt	102,703	1.5
Other and unallocable	335,387	5.0
Utility expenditure	1,159	-
Liquor stores expenditure	59,662	0.9
Insurance trust expenditure	378,098	5.6
Debt at End of Fiscal Year	2,492,083	X
Cash and Security Holdings	5,641,250	X

X = Not applicable.
- = Zero or rounds to zero.
[1] Within insurance trust revenue, net earnings of state retirement systems is a calculated statistic (the item code in the data file is X08), and thus can be positive or negative. Net earnings is the sum of earnings on investments plus gains on investments minus losses on investments. The change made in 2002 for asset valuation from book to market value in accordance with Statement 34 of the Governmental Accounting Standards Board is reflected in the calculated statistics.

Table VT-16. State Government Tax Collections, 2017

(Dollars in thousands, percent.)

Item	Dollars	Percent distribution
Total Taxes	3,127,523	100.0
Property taxes	1,056,635	33.8
Sales and gross receipts	1,058,569	33.8
General sales and gross receipts	375,870	12.0
Selective sales and gross receipts	682,699	21.8
Alcoholic beverages	26,028	0.8
Amusements	X	-
Insurance premiums	59,895	1.9
Motor fuels	81,020	2.6
Pari-mutuels	X	-
Public utilities	8,589	0.3
Tobacco products	76,686	2.5
Other selective sales	430,481	13.8
Licenses	127,049	4.1
Alcoholic beverages	485	-
Amusements	26	-
Corporations in general	3,894	0.1
Hunting and fishing	7,394	0.2
Motor vehicle	76,905	2.5
Motor vehicle operators	8,914	0.3
Public utilities	X	-
Occupation and business, NEC	25,169	0.8
Other licenses	4,262	0.1
Income taxes	825,025	26.4
Individual income	743,630	23.8
Corporation net income	81,395	2.6
Other taxes	60,245	1.9
Death and gift	16,670	0.5
Documentary and stock transfer	38,857	1.2
Severance	X	-
Taxes, NEC	4,718	0.2

X = Not applicable.
- = Zero or rounds to zero.

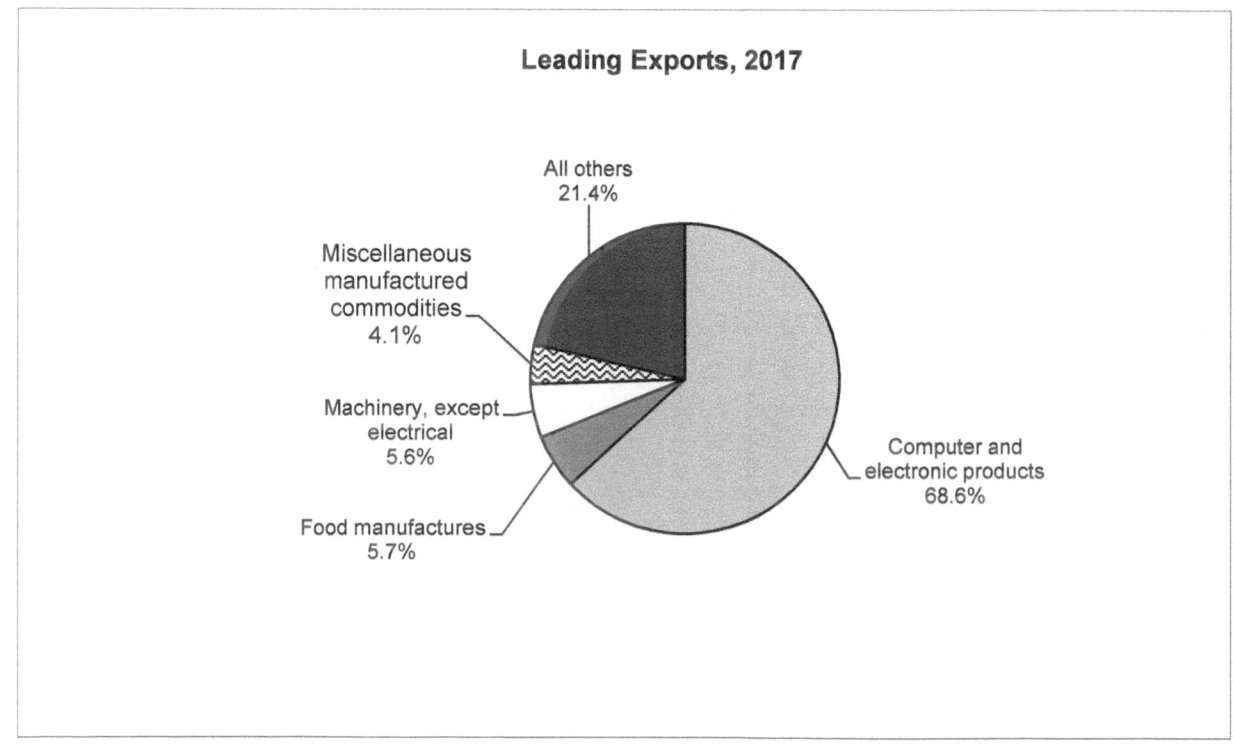

Leading Exports, 2017

All others
21.4%

Miscellaneous
manufactured
commodities
4.1%

Machinery, except
electrical
5.6%

Food manufactures
5.7%

Computer and
electronic products
68.6%

VIRGINIA

Facts and Figures

Location: Eastern United States; bordered on the N and NE by Maryland and the District of Columbia, on the E by the Atlantic Ocean, on the S by North Carolina and Tennessee, and on the W by Kentucky and West Virginia

Area: 42,774 sq. mi. (110,785 sq. km.); rank—35th

Population: 8,470,020 (2017 est.); rank—12th

Principal Cities: capital—Richmond; largest—Virginia Beach

Statehood: June 25, 1788; 10th state

U.S. Congress: 2 senators, 11 representatives

State Motto: *Sic semper tyrannis* ("Thus always to tyrants")

State Song: "Our Great Virginia" and "Sweet Virginia Breeze"

State Nickname: The Old Dominion State

Abbreviations: VA; Va.

State Symbols: flower—flowering dogwood; tree—flowering dogwood; bird—cardinal

At a Glance

- With an increase in population of 5.5 percent, Virginia ranked 20th among the states in growth from 2010 to 2017.

- Virginia's violent crime rate (217.6 incidents per 100,000 population) was the 4th lowest in the country in 2016.

- In 2017, 3.8 percent of Virginians were unemployed, compared to 4.4 percent of the total U.S. population.

- Virginia's median household income in 2016 was $68,114, and 11.0 percent of the population lived below the poverty level.

- In 2017, 6.8 percent of Virginians identified as "Asian alone," ranking it 8th among the states in this category.

Table VA-1. Population by Age, Sex, Race, and Hispanic Origin

(Number, percent, except where noted.)

Sex, age, race, and Hispanic origin	2000	2010	2017 [1]	Average annual percent change, 2010–2017
Total Population..	7,078,515	8,001,024	8,470,020	5.9
Percent of total U.S. population	2.5	2.6	2.6	X
Sex				
Male..	3,471,895	3,925,983	4,166,727	6.1
Female	3,606,620	4,075,041	4,303,293	5.6
Age				
Under 5 years...	461,982	509,625	511,674	0.4
5 to 19 years...	1,475,104	1,574,060	1,579,630	0.4
20 to 64 years...	4,349,096	4,940,402	5,107,288	3.4
65 years and over	79,233	976,937	1,271,428	30.1
Median age (years)	35.7	37.5	38.2	1.9
Race and Hispanic Origin				
One race				
White	5,120,110	5,725,432	5,904,472	3.1
Black...	1,390,293	1,579,414	1,680,680	6.4
American Indian and Alaska Native	21,172	41,525	45,889	10.5
Asian..	261,025	449,149	575,117	28.0
Native Hawaiian or Other Pacific Islander	3,946	8,201	9,601	17.1
Two or more races	143,069	197,303	254,261	28.9
Hispanic (of any race)..	329,540	660,501	795,323	20.4

X = Not applicable.

[1] Population figures for 2017 are July 1 estimates. The 2010 estimates are taken from the 2010 Census.

- = Zero or rounds to zero.

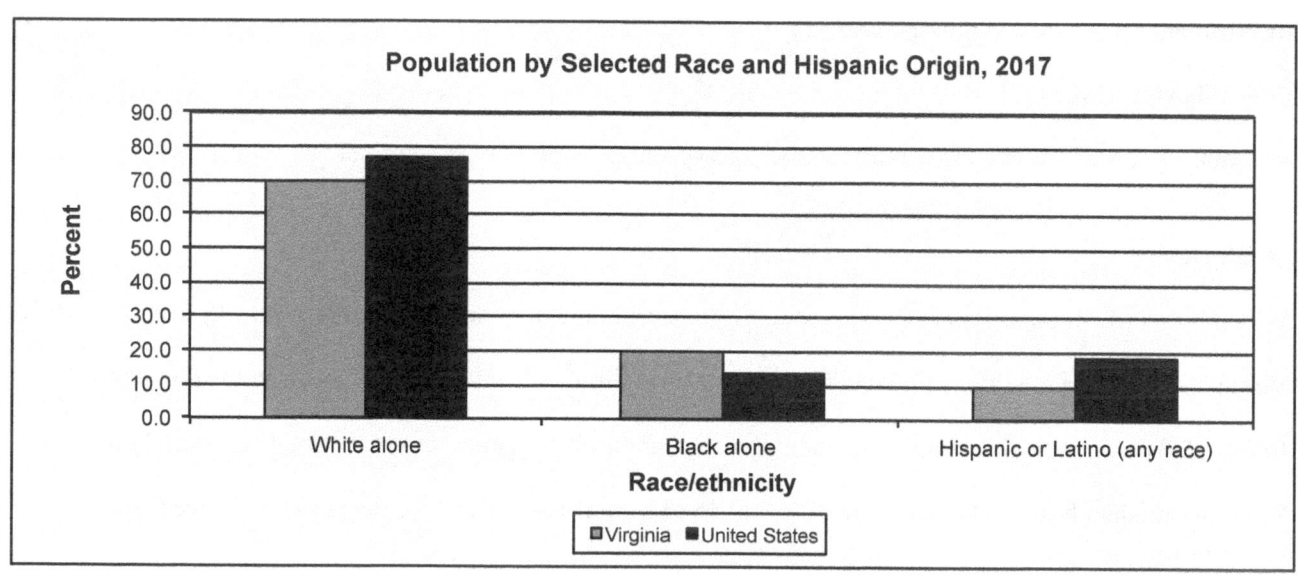

Table VA-2. Marital Status

(Number, percent distribution.)

Sex, age, and marital status	2000	2010	2016
Males, 15 Years and Over	2,724,334	3,156,115	3,344,431
Never married	29.1	34.2	35.6
Now married, except separated...	58.2	52.6	51.2
Separated...	2.6	2.3	2.1
Widowed...	2.3	2.3	2.5
Divorced...	7.9	8.5	8.7
Females, 15 Years and Over	2,899,294	3,331,264	3,516,410
Never married	23.5	28.0	29.6
Now married, except separated...	53.4	49.0	47.7
Separated...	3.2	2.9	2.7
Widowed...	9.9	8.7	8.4
Divorced...	10.0	11.4	11.5

Table VA-3. Households and Housing Characteristics

(Number, percent, dollars.)

Item	2000	2010	2016	Average annual percent change, 2010–2016
Total Households..	2,699,173	2,992,732	3,120,692	0.7
Family households..	1,847,796	2,013,520	2,063,049	0.4
Married-couple family..	1,426,044	1,517,627	1,557,536	0.4
Other family..	421,752	495,893	505,513	0.3
Male householder, no wife present....................	101,462	124,273	135,880	1.6
Female householder, no husband present..........	320,290	371,620	369,633	-0.1
Nonfamily households	851,377	979,212	1,057,643	1.3
Householder living alone......................................	676,907	794,535	853,868	1.2
Householder not living alone................................	174,470	184,677	203,775	1.7
Housing Characteristics				
Total housing units...	2,904,192	3,368,674	3,491,185	0.6
Occupied housing units	2,699,173	2,992,732	3,120,692	0.7
Owner occupied..	1,837,939	2,025,240	2,037,641	0.1
Renter occupied..	861,234	967,492	1,083,051	2.0
Average household size...	2.54	2.60	2.62	0.1
Financial Characteristics				
Median gross rent of renter-occupied housing	650	1,019	1,159	2.3
Median monthly owner costs for housing units with a mortgage	1,144	1,728	1,692	-0.3
Median value of owner-occupied housing units	125,400	249,100	264,000	1.0

Table VA-4. Migration, Origin, and Language

(Number, percent.)

Characteristic	State			U.S.		
	2015	2016	Percent change	2015	2016	Percent change
Residence 1 Year Ago						
Population 1 year and over	8,283,737	8,312,297	0.3	317,635,720	319,361,956	0.5
Same house	83.9	84.3	X	85.3	85.4	X
Different house in the U.S.	15.2	14.7	X	14.1	13.9	X
Same county	6.8	6.5	X	8.5	8.3	X
Different county	8.4	8.2	X	5.6	5.6	X
Same state	5.1	5.0	X	3.2	3.2	X
Different state	3.4	3.2	X	2.4	2.4	X
Abroad	0.8	0.9	X	0.7	0.7	X
Place of Birth						
Native born	7,364,367	7,380,639	0.2	278,128,449	279,388,170	0.5
Male	49.4	49.3	X	49.3	49.3	X
Female	50.6	50.7	X	50.7	50.7	X
Foreign born	1,018,626	1,031,169	1.2	43,290,372	43,739,345	1.0
Male	48.0	48.3	X	48.6	48.5	X
Female	52.0	51.7	X	51.4	51.5	X
Foreign born; naturalized U.S. citizen..........................	519,086	530,624	2.2	20,697,103	21,238,372	2.6
Male	46.1	46.8	X	45.9	45.9	X
Female	53.9	53.2	X	54.1	54.1	X
Foreign born; not a U.S. citizen....................................	499,540	500,545	0.2	22,593,269	22,500,973	-0.4
Male	50.0	49.9	X	51.1	51.0	X
Female	50.0	50.1	X	48.9	49.0	X
Entered 2010 or later	18.2	20.7	X	15.6	18.6	X
Entered 2000 to 2009	31.1	31.9	X	27.9	26.7	X
Entered before 2000...	50.7	47.5	X	56.5	54.7	X
World Region of Birth, Foreign						
Foreign-born population, excluding population born at sea	1,018,626	1,031,169	1.2	43,289,646	43,738,901	1.0
Europe	10.1	9.8	X	11.1	10.9	X
Asia	42.0	43.2	X	30.6	30.8	X
Africa	10.4	10.4	X	4.8	4.9	X
Oceania	0.2	0.3	X	0.6	0.6	X
Latin America	35.8	35.2	X	51.1	51.0	X
North America	1.5	1.2	X	1.9	1.8	X
Language Spoken at Home and Ability to Speak English						
Population 5 years and over...	7,872,076	7,908,026	0.5	301,625,014	303,328,961	0.6
English only	84.1	83.8	X	78.5	78.4	X
Language other than English..	15.9	16.2	X	21.5	21.6	X
Speaks English less than "very well"........................	5.9	6.0	X	8.6	8.6	X

NA = Not available.
X = Not applicable.
- = Zero or rounds to zero.

Table VA-5. Median Income and Poverty Status, 2016

(Number, percent, except as noted.)

Characteristic	State		U.S.	
	Number	Percent	Number	Percent
Median Income				
Households (dollars)	68,114	X	57,617	X
Families (dollars)	83,306	X	71,062	X
Below Poverty Level (All People)	896,440	11.0	44,268,996	14.0
Sex				
Male	394,203	9.9	19,760,056	12.8
Female	502,237	12.0	24,508,940	15.2
Age				
Under 18 years	261,817	14.3	14,115,713	19.5
Related children under 18 years	253,513	13.9	13,805,435	19.1
18 to 64 years	540,912	10.6	25,723,818	13.2
65 years and over	93,711	7.8	4,429,465	9.2

X = Not applicable.

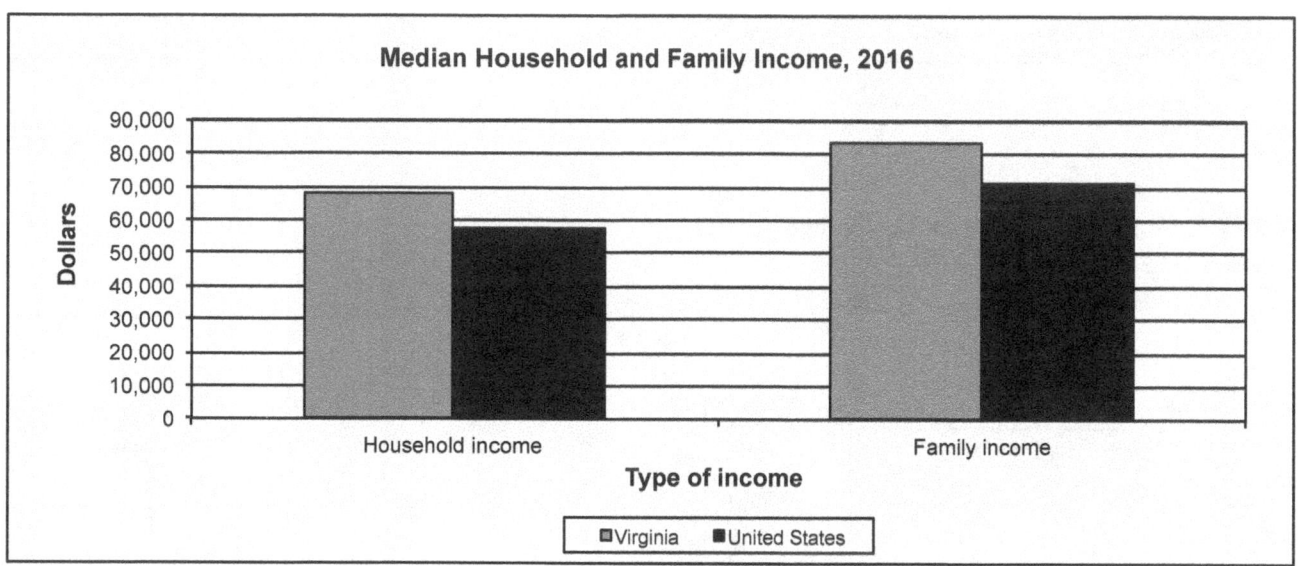

Table VA-6. Health Insurance Coverage Status for the Civilian Noninstitutionalized Population and Children Under 18 Years of Age

(Number, percent.)

Item	2008	2009	2010	2011	2012	2013	2014	2015	2016
Civilian Noninstitutionalized Population	7,520,250	7,643,783	7,807,416	7,887,164	7,973,466	8,054,191	8,114,884	8,162,517	8,199,576
Covered by Private or Public Insurance									
Number	6,621,496	6,736,026	6,787,286	6,904,303	6,973,731	7,063,565	7,231,248	7,416,224	7,484,692
Percent	88.0	88.1	86.9	87.5	87.5	87.7	89.1	90.9	91.3
Not Covered									
Number	898,754	907,757	1,020,130	982,861	999,735	990,626	883,636	746,293	714,884
Percent	12.0	11.9	13.1	12.5	12.5	12.3	10.9	9.1	8.7
Percent in the U.S. not covered	15.1	15.1	15.5	15.1	14.8	14.5	11.7	9.4	8.6
Children Under 18 Years of Age	1,815,340	1,842,559	1,849,665	1,849,081	1,851,845	1,861,658	1,864,738	1,867,092	1,864,852
Covered by Private or Public Insurance									
Number	1,676,909	1,720,976	1,728,285	1,740,598	1,747,907	1,760,407	1,757,636	1,776,406	1,775,840
Percent	92.4	93.4	93.4	94.1	94.4	94.6	94.3	95.1	95.2
Not Covered									
Number	138,431	121,583	121,380	108,483	103,938	101,251	107,102	90,686	89,012
Percent	7.6	6.6	6.6	5.9	5.6	5.4	5.7	4.9	4.8
Percent in the U.S. not covered	9.9	8.6	8.0	7.5	7.2	7.1	6.0	4.8	4.5

Table VA-7. Employment Status by Demographic Group, 2017

(Numbers in thousands, percent.)

Characteristic	Civilian noninstitutional population	Civilian labor force		Employed		Unemployed	
		Number	Percent of population	Number	Percent of population	Number	Percent of population
Total..	6,584	4,294	65.2	4,134	62.8	160	3.7
Sex							
Male..	3,155	2,244	71.1	2,162	68.5	82	3.7
Female.......................................	3,430	2,051	59.8	1,973	57.5	78	3.8
Race, Sex, and Hispanic Origin							
White...	4,617	2,956	64.0	2,867	62.1	89	3.0
Male.......................................	2,239	1,586	70.8	1,540	68.8	46	2.9
Female....................................	2,378	1,369	57.6	1,327	55.8	43	3.1
Black or African American.................	1,257	835	66.4	783	62.3	52	6.2
Male.......................................	573	388	67.6	363	63.4	24	6.3
Female....................................	684	447	65.4	420	61.4	28	6.2
Hispanic or Latino ethnicity[1]...........	554	411	74.1	392	70.8	18	4.5
Male.......................................	283	221	78.1	212	74.7	10	4.3
Female....................................	271	189	69.9	180	66.6	9	4.7
Age							
16 to 19 years.............................	419	156	37.2	138	32.9	18	11.5
20 to 24 years.............................	552	393	71.2	362	65.6	31	7.9
25 to 34 years.............................	1,114	943	84.6	898	80.6	45	4.8
35 to 44 years.............................	1,050	890	84.7	867	82.5	23	2.6
45 to 54 years.............................	1,125	934	83.0	911	81.0	23	2.5
55 to 64 years.............................	1,099	733	66.7	718	65.4	14	2.0
65 years and over..........................	1,225	247	20.1	242	19.7	5	2.0

NOTE: Data in Table 7 are from the Current Population Survey (CPS) and do not match the estimates in Table 8. See notes and definitions for further information.
[1] May be of any race.

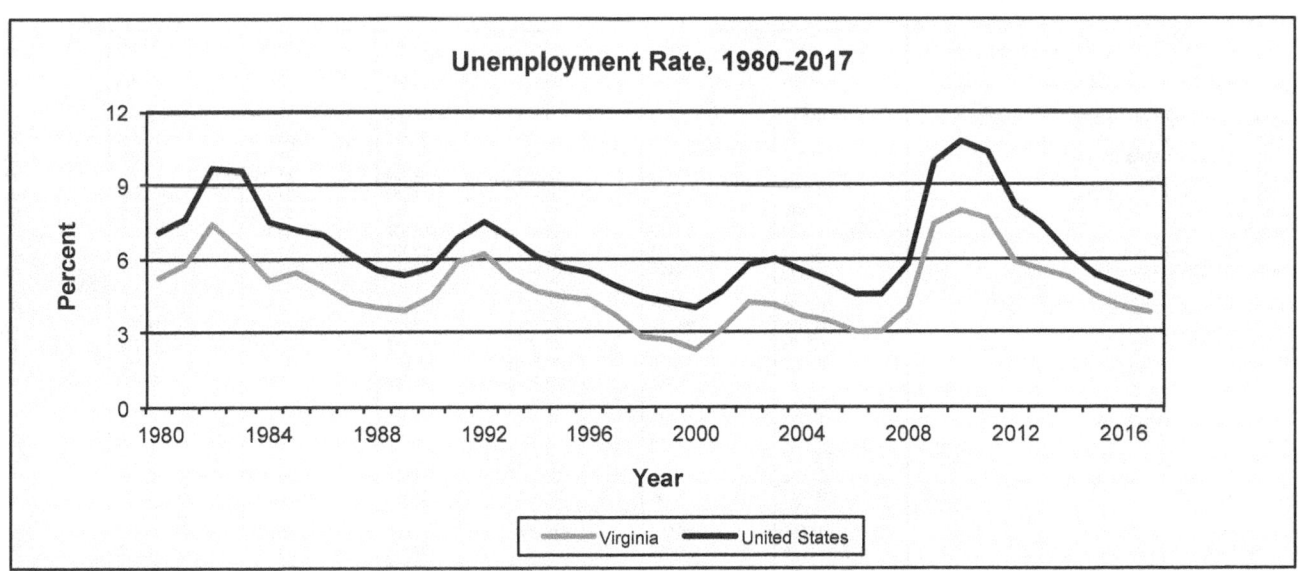

Table VA-8. Employment Status of the Civilian Noninstitutional Population Age 16 Years and Over

(Number, percent.)

Year	Civilian labor force	Civilian participation rate	Employed	Unemployed	Unemployment rate
2009..	4,118,171	68.6	3,842,516	275,655	6.7
2010..	4,157,658	67.7	3,860,386	297,272	7.1
2011..	4,211,802	67.4	3,934,326	277,476	6.6
2012..	4,223,844	66.8	3,967,987	255,857	6.1
2013..	4,237,277	66.3	3,995,182	242,095	5.7
2014..	4,244,109	65.9	4,022,160	221,949	5.2
2015..	4,216,974	64.9	4,029,043	187,931	4.5
2016..	4,242,650	64.8	4,069,139	173,511	4.1
2017..	4,307,753	65.2	4,146,134	161,619	3.8

Table VA-9. Employment and Average Wages by Industry

(Estimates through 2010 are based on the 2007 *North American Industry Classification System* [NAICS]. Estimates from 2011 onward are based on the 2012 NAICS.)

Industry	2010	2011	2012	2013	2014	2015	2016
	Number of jobs						
Wage and Salary Employment by Industry.........................	3,856,908	3,887,761	3,929,899	3,948,870	3,974,046	4,050,089	4,099,417
Farm Wage and Salary Employment.................................	13,123	10,306	10,499	11,678	14,301	12,948	11,968
Nonfarm Wage and Salary Employment.............................	3,843,785	3,877,455	3,919,400	3,937,192	3,959,745	4,037,141	4,087,449
Private wage and salary employment.................................	2,969,478	3,006,948	3,047,333	3,069,001	3,091,552	3,165,120	3,213,459
Forestry, fishing, and related activities..............................	5,595	5,590	5,734	5,966	6,101	6,751	6,999
Mining..	8,590	9,056	9,035	8,071	7,463	6,845	5,773
Utilities..	10,913	10,889	10,636	10,536	10,646	10,786	10,865
Construction..	189,854	184,070	182,079	182,178	183,419	189,695	193,515
Manufacturing..	230,597	230,796	231,785	231,357	232,063	233,733	232,727
Durable goods manufacturing..	132,359	134,326	136,484	136,575	137,524	138,405	135,487
Nondurable goods manufacturing.....................................	98,238	96,470	95,301	94,782	94,539	95,328	97,240
Wholesale trade..	110,633	112,724	111,825	111,819	111,416	111,356	111,531
Retail trade...	401,843	406,083	409,506	414,124	417,390	421,952	423,729
Transportation and warehousing.......................................	102,637	104,716	105,616	106,079	108,540	115,856	119,748
Information..	76,295	74,414	71,794	71,229	71,691	69,824	68,305
Finance and insurance..	124,280	128,507	131,529	134,049	135,871	139,122	142,123
Real estate and rental and leasing....................................	53,022	52,239	52,751	53,091	52,792	53,915	54,019
Professional, scientific, and technical services.................	386,006	394,529	399,057	397,523	392,570	402,634	414,055
Management of companies and enterprises........................	74,000	73,350	76,427	75,619	73,985	74,229	73,315
Administrative and waste services....................................	196,706	203,608	207,894	210,367	216,813	226,963	232,426
Educational services...	70,756	72,872	73,093	73,593	72,336	73,998	74,833
Health care and social assistance.....................................	381,213	388,288	397,629	406,261	410,904	423,331	434,049
Arts, entertainment, and recreation...................................	47,530	47,976	49,187	50,403	50,174	53,486	56,216
Accommodation and food services....................................	296,559	303,457	312,039	318,214	323,633	334,819	345,566
Other services, except public administration......................	202,449	203,784	209,717	208,522	213,745	215,825	213,665
Government and government enterprises............................	874,307	870,507	872,067	868,191	868,193	872,021	873,990
	Dollars						
Average Wages and Salaries by Industry	50,987	52,049	53,011	53,314	54,329	55,663	58,010
Average Farm Wages and Salaries	18,204	20,289	28,277	25,881	22,657	22,975	27,401
Average Nonfarm Wages and Salaries	51,098	52,133	53,077	53,396	54,443	55,768	58,099
Average private wages and salaries..................................	50,172	51,348	52,428	52,813	53,766	55,124	57,336
Forestry, fishing, and related activities..............................	27,991	28,521	29,317	30,037	31,513	32,892	36,284
Mining..	67,459	70,589	68,526	69,184	71,090	69,102	73,210
Utilities..	100,102	100,708	101,456	101,266	105,964	105,655	106,906
Construction	47,616	48,596	49,022	49,649	50,994	52,508	57,143
Manufacturing..	53,483	54,522	55,473	56,302	58,491	59,829	59,584
Durable goods manufacturing..	55,240	57,124	57,996	59,101	61,896	63,453	63,336
Nondurable goods manufacturing.....................................	51,117	50,900	51,859	52,268	53,537	54,568	54,355
Wholesale trade..	69,186	72,261	72,571	73,653	75,497	78,101	80,582
Retail trade...	26,508	26,802	27,384	27,695	28,229	28,979	29,768
Transportation and warehousing.......................................	47,035	47,866	49,864	51,111	52,060	51,762	54,437
Information..	80,769	81,830	84,358	88,040	92,779	97,560	96,822
Finance and insurance	75,393	78,453	83,257	83,606	86,021	89,639	96,408
Real estate and rental and leasing....................................	45,318	46,814	48,776	49,590	51,442	53,928	57,900
Professional, scientific, and technical services.................	93,389	96,078	97,683	98,141	99,125	100,999	105,361
Management of companies and enterprises........................	103,180	107,477	112,182	112,749	114,579	121,621	122,060
Administrative and waste services....................................	37,015	37,811	38,668	38,574	39,291	40,546	43,070
Educational services...	39,811	38,189	38,461	38,861	39,158	38,965	39,875
Health care and social assistance.....................................	44,698	45,820	46,634	47,036	48,030	49,060	51,218
Arts, entertainment, and recreation...................................	27,246	26,488	27,248	27,179	28,275	28,855	28,696
Accommodation and food services....................................	18,492	18,883	19,446	19,736	20,299	21,053	22,171
Other services, except public administration......................	35,138	35,612	36,167	36,908	37,792	39,125	41,408
Government and government enterprises............................	54,245	54,845	55,344	55,456	56,853	58,105	60,905

Table VA-10. Employment Characteristics by Family Type

(Number, percent.)

Family type and labor force status	2014		2015		2016	
	Total	Families with own children under 18 years	Total	Families with own children under 18 years	Total	Families with own children under 18 years
All Families.............................	2,051,042	901,080	2,054,857	882,330	2,063,049	880,662
FAMILY TYPE AND LABOR FORCE STATUS						
Married-Couple Families.............................	1,536,661	635,484	1,549,808	620,930	1,557,536	620,079
Both husband and wife in labor force........................	54.8	67.2	54.0	67.4	53.6	67.7
Husband in labor force, wife not in labor force	22.2	27.8	22.1	27.5	21.7	26.6
Wife in labor force, husband not in labor force	7.5	3.5	7.5	3.5	7.7	4.1
Both husband and wife not in labor force....................	15.5	1.5	15.7	1.3	16.3	1.2
Other Families	514,381	265,596	505,049	261,400	505,513	260,583
Female householder, no husband present.........................	74.1	76.6	73.2	76.5	73.1	75.8
In labor force.............................	53.6	64.3	53.2	64.9	52.4	62.8
Not in labor force	20.5	12.3	20.0	11.6	20.7	13.0
Male householder, no wife present...........................	25.9	23.4	26.8	23.5	26.9	24.2
In labor force.............................	20.7	21.8	21.6	21.6	21.3	22.4
Not in labor force	5.3	1.6	5.2	1.9	5.6	1.8

Table VA-11. School Enrollment and Educational Attainment, 2016

(Number, percent.)

Item	State	U.S.
Enrollment		
Total population 3 years and over, enrolled in school	2,146,237	81,572,277
Enrolled in nursery school or preschool (percent)...........................	5.8	6.0
Enrolled in kindergarten (percent)...........................	4.9	5.0
Enrolled in elementary school, grades 1-8 (percent)...........................	39.1	40.3
Enrolled in high school, grades 9-12 (percent)...........................	20.3	21.0
Enrolled in college or graduate school (percent)...........................	29.9	27.7
Attainment		
Total population 25 years and over	5,721,173	218,475,480
Less than ninth grade (porcent)...........................	4.3	5.4
9th to 12th grade, no diploma (percent)...........................	6.4	7.2
High school graduate, including equivalency (percent)...........................	24.0	27.2
Some college, no degree (percent)...........................	19.5	20.6
Associate's degree (percent)...........................	7.7	8.4
Bachelor's degree (percent)...........................	21.7	19.3
Graduate or professional degree (percent)...........................	16.4	11.9
High school graduate or higher (percent)...........................	89.3	87.5
Bachelor's degree or higher (percent)...........................	38.1	31.3

Table VA-12. Public School Characteristics and Educational Indicators

(Number, percent; data derived from National Center of Education Statistics.)

Item	State	U.S.
Public Schools, 2015–2016 (except where noted)		
Number of school districts...........................	222	18,328
Number of schools...........................	2,133	98,456
Number of students...........................	1,283,590	50,327,015
Number of teachers...........................	90,255	3,151,497
Student-teacher ratio	14.2	16.0
Expenditures per student (dollars), 2014-2015...........................	11,235	11,445
Four-year adjusted cohort graduation rate (ACGR)[1,2]	86.7	84.1
Students eligible for free or reduced-price lunch (percent), 2014-2015...........................	40.2	51.8
English language learners (percent), Fall 2015	8.5	9.5
Students age 3 to 21 served under IDEA, part B (percent)...........................	12.8	13.2

Public Schools by Type	Number	Percent of state public schools
Total number of schools...........................	2,133	100.0
Regular	1,864	87.4
Special education...........................	53	2.5
Vocational education...........................	89	4.2
Alternative education...........................	127	6.0

NOTE: Every school is assigned only one school type based on its instructional emphasis.
[1] ACGR data represents a new method of calculating high-school completion rates and may not be comparable to previous years' data for Averaged Freshmen Graduation Rates (AFGR).
[2] The United States 4-year ACGRs were estimated using both the reported 4-year ACGR data from 49 states and the District of Columbia and using imputed data for Idaho. The estimate for American Indian/Alaska Native students also includes imputed data for Virginia.

Table VA-13. Reported Voting and Registration of the Voting-Age Population, November 2016

(Numbers in thousands, percent.)

Item	Total population	Total citizen population	Registered			Voted		
			Total registered	Percent registered (total population)	Percent registered (total citizen population)	Total voted	Percent voted (total population)	Percent voted (total citizen population)
U.S. Total	245,502	224,059	157,596	64.2	70.3	137,537	56.0	61.4
State Total...............................	6,343	5,829	4,399	69.4	75.5	3,973	62.6	68.2
Sex								
Male	3,026	2,778	2,023	66.9	72.8	1,806	59.7	65.0
Female	3,317	3,052	2,376	71.6	77.9	2,168	65.3	71.0
Race								
White alone................................	4,459	4,172	3,218	72.2	77.1	2,891	64.8	69.3
White, non-Hispanic alone	3,976	3,885	3,009	75.7	77.5	2,702	68.0	69.6
Black alone................................	1,189	1,136	817	68.7	71.9	738	62.0	64.9
Asian alone................................	462	300	219	47.4	73.0	210	45.4	69.9
Hispanic (of any race)......................	606	342	240	39.5	70.1	219	36.2	64.2
White alone or in combination	4,571	4,285	3,298	72.1	77.0	2,967	64.9	69.2
Black alone or in combination...........	1,256	1,203	851	67.8	70.8	768	61.2	63.9
Asian alone or in combination...........	513	351	261	50.9	74.3	251	49.1	71.7
Age								
18 to 24 years.............................	819	737	501	61.1	67.9	447	54.6	60.7
25 to 34 years.............................	1,118	993	640	57.2	64.4	549	49.1	55.3
35 to 44 years.............................	982	833	651	66.3	78.1	573	58.3	68.8
45 to 64 years.............................	2,144	2,023	1,612	75.2	79.7	1,500	70.0	74.2
65 years and over.........................	1,279	1,244	996	77.8	80.0	903	70.6	72.6

Table VA-14. Crime

(Number, rate per 100,000. Data are derived from the FBI Uniform Crime Reports.)

Item	State			U.S. [1,2,3,4]		
	2015	2016	Percent change	2015	2016	Percent change
TOTAL POPULATION [5]	8,382,993	8,411,808	0.3	321,418,820	323,127,513	0.5
VIOLENT CRIME						
Number..	16,399	18,302	11.6	1,231,566	1,248,185	1.3
Rate...	195.6	217.6	11.2	383.2	386.3	0.8
Murder and Nonnegligent Manslaughter						
Number..	383	484	26.4	15,696	17,250	9.9
Rate...	4.6	5.8	26.1	4.9	5.3	8.2
Rape [6]						
Number..	2,340	2,737	17.0	124,047	130,603	5.3
Rate...	27.9	32.5	16.5	38.6	40.4	4.7
Robbery						
Number..	4,441	4,803	8.2	327,374	332,198	1.5
Rate...	53.0	57.1	7.7	101.9	102.8	0.9
Aggravated Assault						
Number..	9,235	10,278	11.3	764,449	803,007	5.0
Rate...	110.2	122.2	10.9	237.8	248.5	4.5
PROPERTY CRIME						
Number..	156,470	156,412	-	7,993,631	7,919,035	-0.9
Rate...	1,866.5	1,859.4	-0.4	2,487.0	2,450.7	-1.5
Burglary						
Number..	21,340	20,018	-6.2	1,579,527	1,515,096	-4.1
Rate...	254.6	238.0	-6.5	491.4	468.9	-4.6
Larceny-Theft						
Number..	127,019	126,606	-0.3	5,706,346	5,638,455	-1.2
Rate...	1,515.2	1,505.1	-0.7	1,775.4	1,745.0	-1.7
Motor Vehicle Theft						
Number..	8,111	9,788	20.7	707,758	765,484	8.2
Rate...	96.8	116.4	20.2	220.2	236.9	7.6

NOTE: Although arson data are included in the trend and clearance tables, sufficient data are not available to estimate totals for this offense. Therefore, no arson data are published in this table.
X = Not applicable.
- = Zero or rounds to zero.
[1] The crime figures have been adjusted.
[2] The data collection methodology for the offense of forcible rape used by the Minnesota state Uniform Crime Reporting (UCR) Program (with the exception of Minneapolis and St. Paul, Minnesota) does not comply with national UCR Program guidelines. Consequently, its figures for forcible rape and violent crime (of which forcible rape is a part) are not published in this table.
[3] Includes offenses reported by the Zoological Police and the Metro Transit Police.
[4] Because of changes in the state's reporting practices, figures are not comparable to previous years' data.
[5] Populations are U.S. Census Bureau provisional estimates as of July 1 of each year.
[6] The figures shown for the offense of rape were estimated using the revised Uniform Crime Reporting (UCR) definition of rape.

Table VA-15. State Government Finances, 2016

(Dollar amounts in thousands, percent distribution.)

Item	Dollars	Percent distribution
Total Revenue	51,655,912	100.0
General revenue	45,425,587	87.9
Intergovernmental revenue	10,227,735	19.8
Taxes	21,219,757	41.1
General sales	3,931,717	7.6
Selective sales	2,954,661	5.7
License taxes	826,306	1.6
Individual income tax	12,237,996	23.7
Corporate income tax	752,689	1.5
Other taxes	516,388	1.0
Current charges	9,732,266	18.8
Miscellaneous general revenue	4,245,829	8.2
Utility revenue	0	-
Liquor stores revenue	736,558	1.4
Insurance trust revenue [1]	5,493,767	10.6
Total Expenditure	53,747,025	100.0
Intergovernmental expenditure	12,466,977	23.2
Direct expenditure	41,280,048	76.8
Current operation	30,497,524	56.7
Capital outlay	3,034,096	5.6
Insurance benefits and repayments	4,870,598	9.1
Assistance and subsidies	1,772,716	3.3
Interest on debt	1,105,114	2.1
Exhibit: Salaries and wages	7,427,466	13.8
Total Expenditure	53,747,025	100.0
General expenditure	48,163,633	89.6
Intergovernmental expenditure	12,466,977	23.2
Direct expenditure	35,696,656	66.4
General expenditure, by function:		
Education	16,743,484	31.2
Public welfare	11,248,106	20.9
Hospitals	4,789,221	8.9
Health	1,452,591	2.7
Highways	4,900,426	9.1
Police protection	577,499	1.1
Correction	1,806,022	3.4
Natural resources	264,467	0.5
Parks and recreation	126,753	0.2
Governmental administration	1,560,825	2.9
Interest on general debt	1,105,114	2.1
Other and unallocable	3,589,125	6.7
Utility expenditure	119,165	0.2
Liquor stores expenditure	593,629	1.1
Insurance trust expenditure	4,870,598	9.1
Debt at End of Fiscal Year	28,628,254	X
Cash and Security Holdings	96,236,952	X

X = Not applicable.
- = Zero or rounds to zero.
[1] Within insurance trust revenue, net earnings of state retirement systems is a calculated statistic (the item code in the data file is X08), and thus can be positive or negative. Net earnings is the sum of earnings on investments plus gains on investments minus losses on investments. The change made in 2002 for asset valuation from book to market value in accordance with Statement 34 of the Governmental Accounting Standards Board is reflected in the calculated statistics.

Table VA-16. State Government Tax Collections, 2017

(Dollars in thousands, percent.)

Item	Dollars	Percent distribution
Total Taxes	22,213,025	100.0
Property taxes	31,232	0.1
Sales and gross receipts	6,916,097	31.1
General sales and gross receipts	3,970,133	17.9
Selective sales and gross receipts	2,945,964	13.3
Alcoholic beverages	224,426	1.0
Amusements	84	-
Insurance premiums	479,192	2.2
Motor fuels	997,561	4.5
Pari-mutuels	X	-
Public utilities	118,088	0.5
Tobacco products	171,198	0.8
Other selective sales	955,415	4.3
Licenses	856,649	3.9
Alcoholic beverages	14,115	0.1
Amusements	104	-
Corporations in general	62,961	0.3
Hunting and fishing	28,762	0.1
Motor vehicle	481,146	2.2
Motor vehicle operators	41,186	0.2
Public utilities	X	-
Occupation and business, NEC	223,721	1.0
Other licenses	4,654	-
Income taxes	13,879,848	62.5
Individual income	13,052,887	58.8
Corporation net income	826,961	3.7
Other taxes	529,199	2.4
Death and gift	8202	-
Documentary and stock transfer	385,278	1.7
Severance	2,583	-
Taxes, NEC	133,136	0.6

- = Zero or rounds to zero.

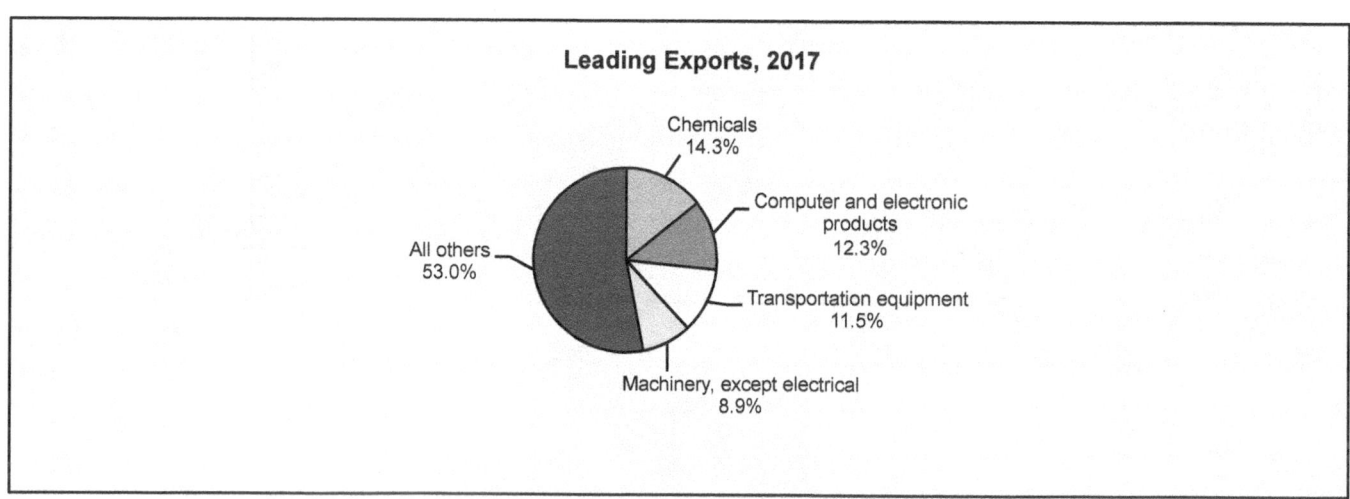

Leading Exports, 2017

Chemicals 14.3%

Computer and electronic products 12.3%

Transportation equipment 11.5%

Machinery, except electrical 8.9%

All others 53.0%

WASHINGTON

Facts and Figures

Location: Northwestern United States; bordered on the N by Canada (British Columbia), on the E by Idaho, on the S by Oregon, and on the W by the Pacific Ocean

Area: 71,300 sq. mi. (184,665 sq. km.); rank—18th

Population: 7,405,743 (2017 est.); rank—13th

Principal Cities: capital—Olympia; largest—Seattle

Statehood: November 11, 1889; 42nd state

U.S. Congress: 2 senators, 10 representatives

State Motto: *Alki* ("By and by")

State Song: "Washington, My Home"

State Nickname: The Evergreen State

Abbreviations: WA; Wash.

State Symbols: flower—coast rhododendron; tree—Western hemlock; bird—willow goldfinch

At a Glance

- With an increase in population of 9.9 percent, Washington ranked 8th among the states in growth from 2010 to 2017.

- Washington's median household income in 2016 was $67,106, and 11.3 percent of the population lived below the poverty level.

- In 2016, 6.0 percent of Washingtonians did not have health insurance, compared to 8.6 percent of the total U.S. population.

- Washington had the 3rd highest property crime rate in the country in 2016 (3,494.1 incidents per 100,000 population).

- Approximately 35.1 percent of Washingtonians had a bachelor's degree or more in 2016, compared to 31.3 percent of all U.S. residents.

Table WA-1. Population by Age, Sex, Race, and Hispanic Origin

(Number, percent, except where noted.)

Sex, age, race, and Hispanic origin	2000	2010	2017 [1]	Average annual percent change, 2010–2017
Total population...	5,894,121	6,724,540	7,405,743	10.1
Percent of total U.S. population	2.1	2.2	2.3	X
Sex				
Male..	2,934,300	3,349,707	3,703,473	10.6
Female	2,959,821	3,374,833	3,702,270	9.7
Age				
Under 5 years..	394,306	439,657	458,213	4.2
5 to 19 years..	1,288,713	1,330,238	1,361,249	2.3
20 to 64 years...	3,548,954	4,126,968	4,471,239	8.3
65 years and over..	662,148	827,677	1,115,042	34.7
Median age (years)...	35.9	37.3	37.7	1.1
Race and Hispanic origin				
One race				
White	4,821,823	5,535,262	5,887,060	6.4
Black...	190,267	252,333	310,425	23.0
American Indian and Alaska Native	93,301	122,649	141,535	15.4
Asian...	322,335	491,685	660,928	34.4
Native Hawaiian or Other Pacific Islander	23,953	43,505	56,953	30.9
Two or more races..	213,519	279,106	348,842	25.0
Hispanic (of any race).......................................	441,509	776,539	940,792	21.2

X = Not applicable.
[1] Population figures for 2017 are July 1 estimates. The 2010 estimates are taken from the 2010 Census.

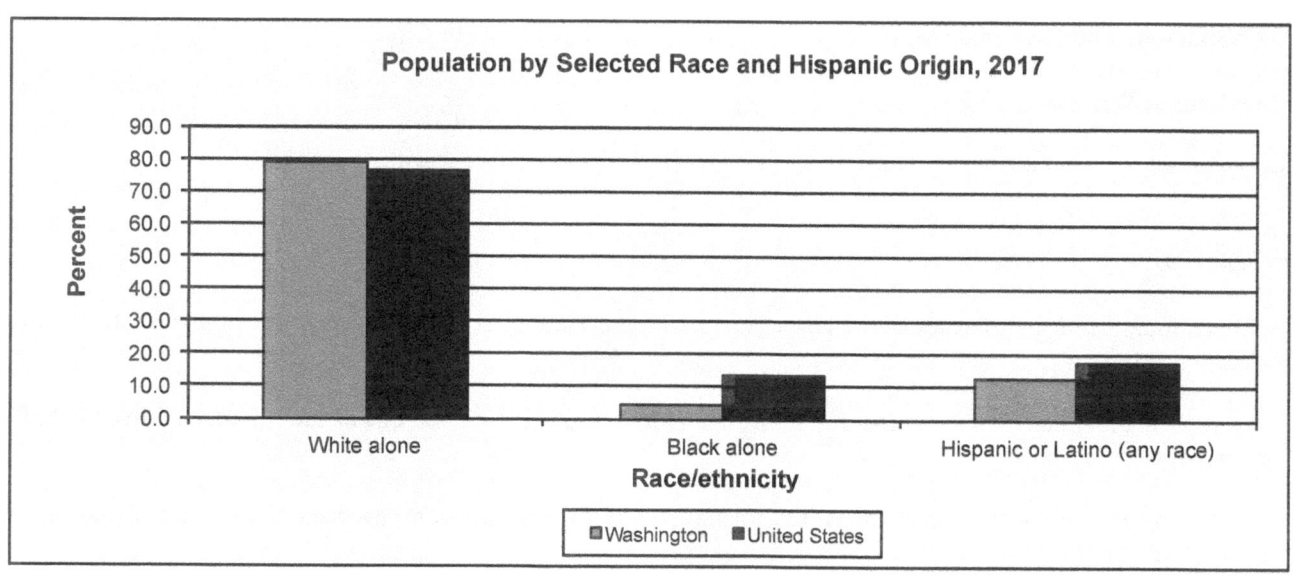

Population by Selected Race and Hispanic Origin, 2017

Table WA-2. Marital Status

(Number, percent distribution.)

Sex, age, and marital status	2000	2010	2016
Males, 15 Years and Over	2,287,431	2,686,801	2,943,737
Never married	29.8	33.8	35.1
Now married, except separated................................	56.6	52.0	51.2
Separated..	1.4	1.6	1.4
Widowed..	2.1	2.1	2.2
Divorced...	10.1	10.5	10.1
Females, 15 Years and Over	2,352,091	2,746,158	2,985,538
Never married	22.8	26.4	27.6
Now married, except separated................................	54.1	50.6	49.5
Separated..	1.8	2.1	1.7
Widowed..	8.6	7.8	7.6
Divorced...	12.7	13.2	13.6

Table WA-3. Households and Housing Characteristics

(Number, percent, dollars.)

Item	2000	2010	2016	Average annual percent change, 2010–2016
Total Households	2,271,398	2,606,863	2,768,076	1.0
Family households	1,499,127	1,681,386	1,784,043	1.0
Married-couple family	1,181,995	1,297,240	1,388,872	1.2
Other family	317,132	384,146	395,171	0.5
Male householder, no wife present	92,514	114,187	124,975	1.6
Female householder, no husband present	224,618	269,959	270,196	-
Nonfamily households	772,271	925,477	984,033	1.1
Householder living alone	594,325	731,452	747,815	0.4
Householder not living alone	117,946	194,025	236,218	3.6
Housing Characteristics				
Total housing units	2,451,075	2,888,594	3,025,802	0.8
Occupied housing units	2,271,398	2,606,863	2,768,076	1.0
Owner occupied	1,467,009	1,644,939	1,729,320	0.9
Renter occupied	804,389	961,924	1,038,756	1.3
Average household size	2.53	2.53	2.58	0.3
Financial Characteristics				
Median gross rent of renter-occupied housing	663	908	1,135	4.2
Median monthly owner costs for housing units with a mortgage	1,268	1,736	1,727	-0.1
Median value of owner-occupied housing units	168,300	271,800	306,400	2.1

- = Zero or rounds to zero.

Table WA-4. Migration, Origin, and Language

(Number, percent.)

Characteristic	State			U.S.		
	2015	2016	Percent change	2015	2016	Percent change
Residence 1 Year Ago						
Population 1 year and over	7,089,143	7,202,119	1.6	317,635,720	319,361,956	0.5
Same house	81.5	82.3	X	85.3	85.4	X
Different house in the U.S.	17.6	16.9	X	14.1	13.9	X
Same county	10.9	10.2	X	8.5	8.3	X
Different county	6.7	6.7	X	5.6	5.6	X
Same state	3.4	3.1	X	3.2	3.2	X
Different state	3.3	3.6	X	2.4	2.4	X
Abroad	0.9	0.9	X	0.7	0.7	X
Place of Birth						
Native born	6,190,193	6,267,606	1.3	278,128,449	279,388,170	0.5
Male	50.3	50.3	X	49.3	49.3	X
Female	49.7	49.7	X	50.7	50.7	X
Foreign born	980,158	1,020,394	4.1	43,290,372	43,739,345	1.0
Male	48.4	47.6	X	48.6	48.5	X
Female	51.6	52.4	X	51.4	51.5	X
Foreign born; naturalized U.S. citizen	458,313	482,135	5.2	20,697,103	21,238,372	2.6
Male	45.5	44.9	X	45.9	45.9	X
Female	54.5	55.1	X	54.1	54.1	X
Foreign born; not a U.S. citizen	521,845	538,259	3.1	22,593,269	22,500,973	-0.4
Male	51.0	50.0	X	51.1	51.0	X
Female	49.0	50.0	X	48.9	49.0	X
Entered 2010 or later	17.5	20.9	X	15.6	18.6	X
Entered 2000 to 2009	28.4	28.6	X	27.9	26.7	X
Entered before 2000	54.1	50.5	X	56.5	54.7	X
World Region of Birth, Foreign						
Foreign-born population, excluding population born at sea	980,158	1,020,359	4.1	43,289,646	43,738,901	1.0
Europe	15.4	14.4	X	11.1	10.9	X
Asia	42.4	42.5	X	30.6	30.8	X
Africa	5.0	6.2	X	4.8	4.9	X
Oceania	1.8	2.1	X	0.6	0.6	X
Latin America	30.9	30.2	X	51.1	51.0	X
North America	4.4	4.6	X	1.9	1.0	X
Language Spoken at Home and Ability to Speak English						
Population 5 years and over	6,725,680	6,838,056	1.7	301,625,014	303,328,961	0.6
English only	80.7	80.7	X	78.5	78.4	X
Language other than English	19.3	19.3	X	21.5	21.6	X
Speaks English less than "very well"	7.5	7.7	X	8.6	8.6	X

NA = Not available.
X = Not applicable.
- = Zero or rounds to zero.

Table WA-5. Median Income and Poverty Status, 2016

(Number, percent, except as noted.)

Characteristic	State		U.S.	
	Number	Percent	Number	Percent
Median Income				
Households (dollars)..	67,106	X	57,617	X
Families (dollars)	81,234	X	71,062	X
Below Poverty Level (All People)	805,691	11.3	44,268,996	14.0
Sex				
Male	367,685	10.3	19,760,056	12.8
Female	438,006	12.2	24,508,940	15.2
Age				
Under 18 years...	219,668	13.7	14,115,713	19.5
Related children under 18 years.................................	211,212	13.2	13,805,435	19.1
18 to 64 years..	505,116	11.2	25,723,818	13.2
65 years and over	80,907	7.6	4,429,465	9.2

X = Not applicable.

Median Household and Family Income, 2016

Table WA-6. Health Insurance Coverage Status for the Civilian Noninstitutionalized Population and Children Under 18 Years of Age

(Number, percent.)

Item	2008	2009	2010	2011	2012	2013	2014	2015	2016
Civilian Noninstitutionalized Population	6,428,235	6,546,149	6,638,081	6,716,822	6,793,078	6,864,149	6,954,806	7,066,812	7,184,110
Covered by Private or Public Insurance									
Number..	5,586,238	5,668,541	5,692,492	5,764,192	5,848,307	5,904,158	6,312,152	6,598,845	6,756,018
Percent..	86.9	86.6	85.8	85.8	86.1	86.0	90.8	93.4	94.0
Not Covered									
Number..	841,997	877,608	945,589	952,630	944,771	959,991	642,654	467,967	428,092
Percent..	13.1	13.4	14.2	14.2	13.9	14.0	9.2	6.6	6.0
Percent in the U.S. not covered......................................	15.1	15.1	15.5	15.1	14.8	14.5	11.7	9.4	8.6
Children Under 18 Years of Age	1,540,488	1,569,540	1,582,936	1,578,179	1,583,595	1,594,503	1,601,029	1,610,562	1,627,304
Covered by Private or Public Insurance									
Number..	1,410,093	1,462,000	1,481,322	1,480,971	1,492,516	1,499,708	1,526,102	1,568,043	1,585,868
Percent..	91.5	93.1	93.6	93.8	94.2	94.1	95.3	97.4	97.5
Not Covered									
Number..	130,395	107,540	101,614	97,208	91,079	94,795	74,927	42,519	41,436
Percent..	8.5	6.9	6.4	6.2	5.8	5.9	4.7	2.6	2.5
Percent in the U.S. not covered......................................	9.9	8.6	8.0	7.5	7.2	7.1	6.0	4.8	4.5

Table WA-7. Employment Status by Demographic Group, 2017

(Numbers in thousands, percent.)

Characteristic	Civilian noninstitutional population	Civilian labor force		Employed		Unemployed	
		Number	Percent of population	Number	Percent of population	Number	Percent of population
Total..	5,821	3,718	63.9	3,546	60.9	173	4.6
Sex							
Male..	2,863	2,012	70.3	1,916	66.9	96	4.8
Female...	2,958	1,707	57.7	1,630	55.1	77	4.5
Race, Sex, and Hispanic Origin							
White...	4,710	2,986	63.4	2,855	60.6	131	4.4
Male..	2,314	1,621	70.1	1,549	66.9	72	4.5
Female...	2,396	1,365	57.0	1,306	54.5	59	4.3
Black or African American.....................	220	151	68.8	143	65.0	8	5.6
Male..	124	91	73.3	86	69.5	5	5.1
Female...	NA	NA	NA	NA	NA	NA	NA
Hispanic or Latino ethnicity[1]	687	493	71.7	468	68.0	25	5.1
Male..	345	282	81.8	268	77.9	13	4.7
Female...	343	211	61.7	199	58.1	12	5.7
Age							
16 to 19 years....................................	340	144	42.4	121	35.6	23	16.1
20 to 24 years....................................	495	346	70.1	328	66.2	19	5.4
25 to 34 years....................................	1,080	872	80.7	820	75.9	51	5.9
35 to 44 years....................................	920	772	83.9	741	80.6	31	4.0
45 to 54 years....................................	927	741	79.9	721	77.7	21	2.8
55 to 64 years....................................	953	625	65.7	605	63.5	21	3.3
65 years and over................................	1,107	218	19.7	210	19.0	8	3.5

NOTE: Data in Table 7 are from the Current Population Survey (CPS) and do not match the estimates in Table 8. See notes and definitions for further information.
[1] May be of any race.

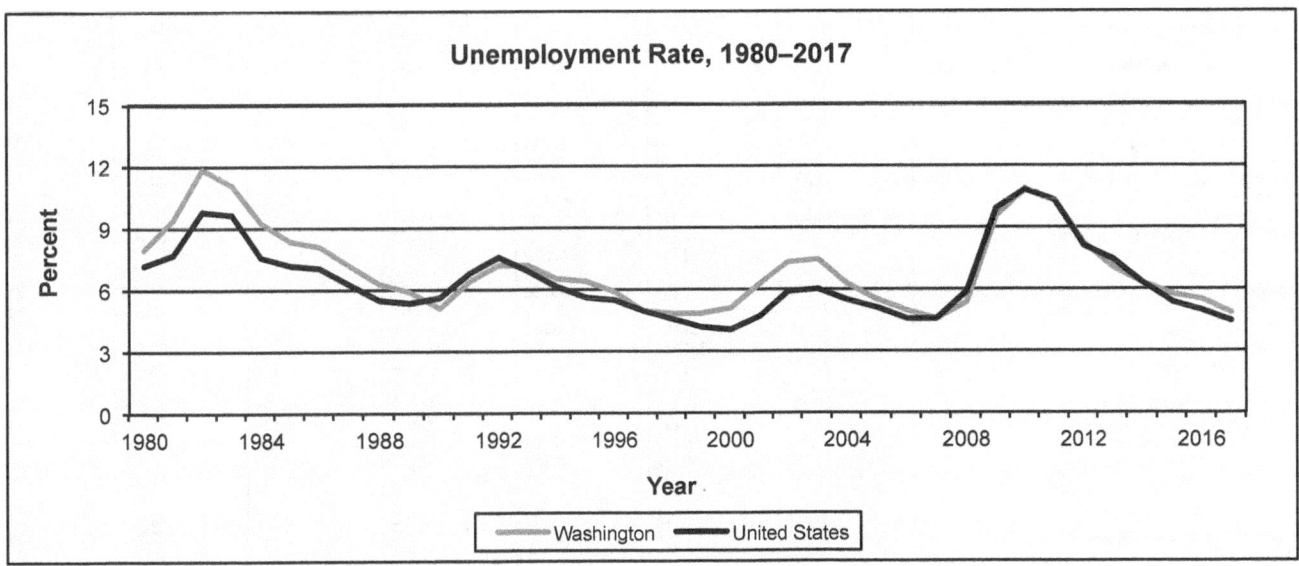

Table WA-8. Employment Status of the Civilian Noninstitutional Population Age 16 Years and Over

(Number, percent.)

Year	Civilian labor force	Civilian participation rate	Employed	Unemployed	Unemployment rate
2009..	3,535,200	68.3	3,211,649	323,551	9.2
2010..	3,511,326	67.0	3,160,544	350,782	10.0
2011..	3,461,428	65.2	3,140,190	321,238	9.3
2012..	3,471,282	64.6	3,189,271	282,011	8.1
2013..	3,463,869	63.7	3,219,842	244,027	7.0
2014..	3,489,666	63.3	3,275,753	213,913	6.1
2015..	3,545,904	63.2	3,345,496	200,408	5.7
2016..	3,635,200	63.6	3,444,126	191,074	5.3
2017..	3,724,722	63.9	3,547,430	177,292	4.8

Table WA-9. Employment and Average Wages by Industry

(Estimates through 2010 are based on the 2007 *North American Industry Classification System* [NAICS]. Estimates from 2011 onward are based on the 2012 NAICS.)

Industry	2010	2011	2012	2013	2014	2015	2016
	Number of jobs						
Wage and Salary Employment by Industry........................	2,999,842	3,032,727	3,131,758	3,199,080	3,283,925	3,361,613	3,452,409
Farm Wage and Salary Employment................................	48,035	47,192	56,397	53,379	53,512	51,721	52,492
Nonfarm Wage and Salary Employment...........................	2,951,807	2,985,535	3,075,361	3,145,701	3,230,413	3,309,892	3,399,917
Private wage and salary employment..............................	2,319,349	2,360,090	2,454,780	2,526,500	2,609,307	2,679,466	2,758,758
Forestry, fishing, and related activities..........................	28,107	28,654	30,087	30,879	31,534	31,914	31,779
Mining...	2,202	2,203	2,157	2,162	2,245	2,402	2,436
Utilities..	4,862	4,869	4,913	4,823	4,838	4,943	4,647
Construction...	144,998	140,274	142,919	153,393	165,274	179,164	192,199
Manufacturing..	258,156	269,066	280,497	286,551	288,598	291,104	289,794
Durable goods manufacturing......................................	183,710	193,099	204,382	209,168	209,511	211,158	207,354
Nondurable goods manufacturing.................................	74,446	75,967	76,115	77,383	79,087	79,946	82,440
Wholesale trade...	120,709	122,227	124,439	127,634	131,104	133,708	133,456
Retail trade..	310,747	315,418	322,037	332,130	345,814	358,991	372,666
Transportation and warehousing....................................	84,401	86,962	89,112	90,314	94,277	97,985	101,105
Information	102,749	104,479	105,441	106,435	109,617	114,400	121,064
Finance and insurance	93,514	93,666	94,470	96,354	98,163	98,968	100,082
Real estate and rental and leasing	46,258	45,605	45,786	47,274	48,640	50,306	51,515
Professional, scientific, and technical services	163,696	169,212	173,025	176,928	184,576	190,071	197,614
Management of companies and enterprises.....................	31,808	33,264	36,318	38,894	39,998	41,936	43,163
Administrative and waste services.................................	133,747	139,790	142,804	147,555	152,226	159,775	164,893
Educational services	50,092	51,661	52,465	53,533	54,958	56,510	57,158
Health care and social assistance.................................	333,346	336,277	380,054	393,137	402,753	398,868	411,383
Arts, entertainment, and recreation...............................	45,930	46,035	46,361	46,967	47,823	48,657	51,461
Accommodation and food services.................................	222,720	226,645	232,731	242,327	252,306	263,402	275,002
Other services, except public administration....................	141,307	143,783	149,164	149,210	154,563	156,362	157,341
Government and government enterprises	632,458	625,445	620,581	619,201	621,106	630,426	641,159
	Dollars						
Average Wages and Salaries by Industry	49,331	51,102	52,427	53,356	55,333	57,057	62,418
Average Farm Wages and Salaries	25,207	24,384	26,968	29,471	28,663	33,953	35,807
Average Nonfarm Wages and Salaries	49,724	51,525	52,894	53,761	55,775	57,418	62,828
Average private wages and salaries................................	49,670	51,765	53,256	54,099	56,218	57,910	63,588
Forestry, fishing, and related activities...........................	32,454	33,778	35,280	34,955	35,237	35,557	39,294
Mining..	56,234	59,754	60,992	63,154	64,057	68,084	74,343
Utilities..	77,220	81,842	83,774	85,783	87,781	93,343	95,006
Construction	51,797	52,850	53,666	54,405	55,720	57,744	65,115
Manufacturing..	65,248	68,424	69,790	71,735	75,443	74,884	73,327
Durable goods manufacturing......................................	72,098	75,726	76,892	79,341	84,325	83,308	80,430
Nondurable goods manufacturing.................................	48,344	49,864	50,720	51,176	51,912	52,635	55,461
Wholesale trade	64,372	66,787	69,458	69,087	71,004	73,213	77,633
Retail trade..	31,524	32,583	34,579	36,211	38,857	42,109	53,940
Transportation and warehousing....................................	49,501	51,800	53,517	54,373	55,207	56,618	61,271
Information...	111,515	121,687	135,539	137,016	150,328	150,847	173,331
Finance and insurance	70,271	73,164	77,437	79,404	81,918	85,473	90,303
Real estate and rental and leasing.................................	38,891	40,355	42,764	44,171	46,135	47,881	53,689
Professional, scientific, and technical services	76,310	77,843	80,651	82,598	85,689	86,010	94,741
Management of companies and enterprises........................	100,074	104,038	107,164	106,965	109,022	108,957	111,557
Administrative and waste services.................................	41,750	43,187	43,627	43,553	44,649	46,207	50,062
Educational services	28,476	28,921	29,735	30,523	30,843	31,095	32,197
Health care and social assistance.................................	45,373	46,623	43,923	43,892	44,860	48,238	52,207
Arts, entertainment, and recreation...............................	27,651	27,570	27,851	30,575	32,714	33,550	35,664
Accommodation and food services.................................	20,105	21,133	22,729	22,703	23,026	23,944	27,127
Other services, except public administration....................	30,477	31,963	32,568	33,818	33,669	34,844	37,738
Government and government enterprises............................	49,919	50,617	51,460	52,382	53,913	55,329	59,561

Table WA-10. Employment Characteristics by Family Type

(Number, percent.)

Family type and labor force status	2014 Total	2014 Families with own children under 18 years	2015 Total	2015 Families with own children under 18 years	2016 Total	2016 Families with own children under 18 years
All Families..........................	1,712,570	739,472	1,760,593	760,914	1,784,043	761,244
FAMILY TYPE AND LABOR FORCE STATUS						
Married-Couple Families..........................	1,316,747	521,639	1,363,817	539,460	1,388,872	552,273
Both husband and wife in labor force..........................	50.7	61.5	50.0	61.8	49.6	61.6
Husband in labor force, wife not in labor force..........................	23.8	32.7	23.2	31.9	23.2	31.5
Wife in labor force, husband not in labor force..........................	7.9	4.2	7.7	4.3	8.0	4.7
Both husband and wife not in labor force..........................	17.6	1.7	18.0	1.6	17.9	1.8
Other Families	395,823	217,833	396,776	221,454	395,171	208,971
Female householder, no husband present..........................	69.6	70.4	69.1	70.6	68.4	69.0
In labor force..........................	50.2	56.9	48.7	57.0	47.8	56.1
Not in labor force..........................	19.4	13.5	20.4	13.7	20.5	12.9
Male householder, no wife present..........................	30.4	29.6	30.9	29.4	31.6	31.0
In labor force..........................	24.2	27.0	24.8	26.9	25.8	28.1
Not in labor force..........................	6.2	2.6	6.1	2.5	5.8	2.9

Table WA-11. School Enrollment and Educational Attainment, 2016

(Number, percent.)

Item	State	U.S.
Enrollment		
Total population 3 years and over, enrolled in school	1,744,806	81,572,277
Enrolled in nursery school or preschool (percent)..........................	6.3	6.0
Enrolled in kindergarten (percent)..........................	4.7	5.0
Enrolled in elementary school, grades 1-8 (percent)..........................	41.4	40.3
Enrolled in high school, grades 9-12 (percent)..........................	20.8	21.0
Enrolled in college or graduate school (percent)..........................	26.7	27.7
Attainment		
Total population 25 years and over	4,996,555	218,475,480
Less than ninth grade (percent)..........................	3.8	5.4
9th to 12th grade, no diploma (percent)..........................	5.3	7.2
High school graduate, including equivalency (percent)..........................	22.3	27.2
Some college, no degree (percent)..........................	23.6	20.6
Associate's degree (percent)..........................	9.8	8.4
Bachelor's degree (percent)..........................	22.0	19.3
Graduate or professional degree (percent)..........................	13.2	11.9
High school graduate or higher (percent)..........................	90.8	87.5
Bachelor's degree or higher (percent)..........................	35.1	31.3

Table WA-12. Public School Characteristics and Educational Indicators

(Number, percent; data derived from National Center of Education Statistics.)

Item	State	U.S.
Public Schools, 2015–2016 (except where noted)		
Number of school districts..........................	330	18,328
Number of schools..........................	2,427	98,456
Number of students..........................	1,087,030	50,327,015
Number of teachers..........................	57,942	3,151,497
Student-teacher ratio	18.8	16.0
Expenditures per student (dollars), 2014-2015..........................	10,684	11,445
Four-year adjusted cohort graduation rate (ACGR)[1,2]	79.7	84.1
Students eligible for free or reduced-price lunch (percent), 2014-2015..........................	46.0	51.8
English language learners (percent), Fall 2015	10.4	9.5
Students age 3 to 21 served under IDEA, part B (percent)..........................	12.5	13.2

Public Schools by Type	Number	Percent of state public schools
Total number of schools..........................	2,427	100.0
Regular	1,998	82.3
Special education..........................	96	4.0
Vocational education..........................	20	0.8
Alternative education..........................	313	12.9

NOTE: Every school is assigned only one school type based on its instructional emphasis.
[1] ACGR data represents a new method of calculating high-school completion rates and may not be comparable to previous years' data for Averaged Freshmen Graduation Rates (AFGR).
[2] The United States 4-year ACGRs were estimated using both the reported 4-year ACGR data from 49 states and the District of Columbia and using imputed data for Idaho. The estimate for American Indian/Alaska Native students also includes imputed data for Virginia.

Table WA-13. Reported Voting and Registration of the Voting-Age Population, November 2016

(Numbers in thousands, percent.)

Item	Total population	Total citizen population	Registered			Voted		
			Total registered	Percent registered (total population)	Percent registered (total citizen population)	Total voted	Percent voted (total population)	Percent voted (total citizen population)
U.S. Total	245,502	224,059	157,596	64.2	70.3	137,537	56.0	61.4
State Total................................	5,592	5,104	3,906	69.9	76.5	3,382	60.5	66.3
Sex								
Male	2,765	2,497	1,852	67.0	74.2	1,525	55.2	61.1
Female	2,827	2,607	2,055	72.7	78.8	1,857	65.7	71.2
Race								
White alone..............................	4,628	4,353	3,403	73.5	78.2	3,027	65.4	69.5
White, non-Hispanic alone............	4,059	3,965	3,164	77.9	79.8	2,842	70.0	71.7
Black alone................................	201	184	116	57.7	63.2	78	38.8	42.6
Asian alone................................	426	239	190	44.6	79.6	165	38.7	69.0
Hispanic (of any race)......................	656	465	292	44.6	62.9	219	33.4	47.2
White alone or in combination	4,775	4,500	3,503	73.4	77.8	3,093	64.8	68.7
Black alone or in combination...........	239	222	137	57.4	61.9	85	35.5	38.3
Asian alone or in combination...........	470	283	224	47.7	79.4	188	40.1	66.7
Age								
18 to 24 years..............................	646	594	351	54.4	59.1	273	42.2	45.9
25 to 34 years..............................	987	848	587	59.4	69.2	460	46.5	54.2
35 to 44 years..............................	1,014	876	676	66.7	77.2	564	55.6	64.4
45 to 64 years..............................	1,986	1,859	1,523	76.7	81.9	1,366	68.8	73.5
65 years and over	958	927	769	80.3	83.0	720	75.1	77.6

Table WA-14. Crime

(Number, rate per 100,000. Data are derived from the FBI Uniform Crime Reports.)

Item	State			U.S. [1,2,3,4]		
	2015	2016	Percent change	2015	2016	Percent change
TOTAL POPULATION [5]	7,170,351	7,288,000	1.6	321,418,820	323,127,513	0.5
VIOLENT CRIME						
Number..	20,394	22,023	8.0	1,231,566	1,248,185	1.3
Rate...	284.4	302.2	6.3	383.2	386.3	0.8
Murder and Nonnegligent Manslaughter						
Number..	211	195	-7.6	15,696	17,250	9.9
Rate...	2.9	2.7	-6.9	4.9	5.3	8.2
Rape [6]						
Number..	2,705	3,077	13.8	124,047	130,603	5.3
Rate...	37.7	42.2	11.9	38.6	40.4	4.7
Robbery						
Number..	5,449	5,651	3.7	327,374	332,198	1.5
Rate...	76.0	77.5	2.0	101.9	102.8	0.9
Aggravated Assault						
Number..	12,029	13,100	8.9	764,449	803,007	5.0
Rate...	167.8	179.7	7.1	237.8	248.5	4.5
PROPERTY CRIME						
Number..	248,369	254,653	2.5	7,993,631	7,919,035	-0.9
Rate...	3,463.8	3,494.1	0.9	2,487.0	2,450.7	-1.5
Burglary						
Number..	50,993	49,180	-3.6	1,579,527	1,515,096	-4.1
Rate...	711.2	674.8	-5.1	491.4	468.9	-4.6
Larceny-Theft						
Number..	170,509	173,187	1.6	5,706,346	5,638,455	-1.2
Rate...	2,378.0	2,376.3	-0.1	1,775.4	1,745.0	-1.7
Motor Vehicle Theft						
Number..	26,867	32,286	20.2	707,758	765,484	8.2
Rate...	374.7	443.0	18.2	220.2	236.9	7.6

NOTE: Although arson data are included in the trend and clearance tables, sufficient data are not available to estimate totals for this offense. Therefore, no arson data are published in this table.
X = Not applicable.
- = Zero or rounds to zero.
[1] The crime figures have been adjusted.
[2] The data collection methodology for the offense of forcible rape used by the Minnesota state Uniform Crime Reporting (UCR) Program (with the exception of Minneapolis and St. Paul, Minnesota) does not comply with national UCR Program guidelines. Consequently, its figures for forcible rape and violent crime (of which forcible rape is a part) are not published in this table.
[3] Includes offenses reported by the Zoological Police and the Metro Transit Police.
[4] Because of changes in the state's reporting practices, figures are not comparable to previous years' data.
[5] Populations are U.S. Census Bureau provisional estimates as of July 1 of each year.
[6] The figures shown for the offense of rape were estimated using the revised Uniform Crime Reporting (UCR) definition of rape.

Table WA-15. State Government Finances, 2016

(Dollar amounts in thousands, percent distribution.)

Item	Dollars	Percent distribution
Total Revenue	50,774,856	100.0
General revenue	43,629,247	85.9
Intergovernmental revenue	13,704,988	27.0
Taxes	22,280,088	43.9
General sales	13,560,382	26.7
Selective sales	4,075,649	8.0
License taxes	1,461,200	2.9
Individual income tax	0	-
Corporate income tax	0	-
Other taxes	3,182,857	6.3
Current charges	4,912,580	9.7
Miscellaneous general revenue	2,731,591	5.4
Utility revenue	452	-
Liquor stores revenue	0	-
Insurance trust revenue [1]	7,145,157	14.1
Total Expenditure	53,463,325	100.0
Intergovernmental expenditure	11,871,289	22.2
Direct expenditure	41,592,036	77.8
Current operation	28,576,812	53.5
Capital outlay	2,951,903	5.5
Insurance benefits and repayments	6,987,148	13.1
Assistance and subsidies	1,636,435	3.1
Interest on debt	1,439,738	2.7
Exhibit: Salaries and wages	7,982,436	14.9
Total Expenditure	53,463,325	100.0
General expenditure	46,237,656	86.5
Intergovernmental expenditure	11,871,289	22.2
Direct expenditure	34,366,367	64.3
General expenditure, by function:		
Education	18,876,836	35.3
Public welfare	12,654,033	23.7
Hospitals	2,724,044	5.1
Health	1,961,839	3.7
Highways	2,797,191	5.2
Police protection	397,980	0.7
Correction	1,037,432	1.9
Natural resources	991,954	1.9
Parks and recreation	148,780	0.3
Governmental administration	1,239,726	2.3
Interest on general debt	1,439,738	2.7
Other and unallocable	1,968,103	3.7
Utility expenditure	238,521	0.5
Liquor stores expenditure	0	-
Insurance trust expenditure	6,987,148	13.1
Debt at End of Fiscal Year	33,059,765	X
Cash and Security Holdings	102,578,538	X

X = Not applicable.
- = Zero or rounds to zero.
[1] Within insurance trust revenue, net earnings of state retirement systems is a calculated statistic (the item code in the data file is X08), and thus can be positive or negative. Net earnings is the sum of earnings on investments plus gains on investments minus losses on investments. The change made in 2002 for asset valuation from book to market value in accordance with Statement 34 of the Governmental Accounting Standards Board is reflected in the calculated statistics.

Table WA-16. State Government Tax Collections, 2017

(Dollars in thousands, percent.)

Item	Dollars	Percent distribution
Total Taxes	23,997,592	100.0
Property taxes	2,097,507	8.7
Sales and gross receipts	19,170,768	79.9
General sales and gross receipts	14,509,841	60.5
Selective sales and gross receipts	4,660,927	19.4
Alcoholic beverages	354,939	1.5
Amusements	X	-
Insurance premiums	603,963	2.5
Motor fuels	1,812,646	7.6
Pari-mutuels	1,805	-
Public utilities	504,117	2.1
Tobacco products	430,022	1.8
Other selective sales	953,435	4.0
Licenses	1,453,628	6.1
Alcoholic beverages	150,772	0.6
Amusements	0	-
Corporations in general	39,776	0.2
Hunting and fishing	41,287	0.2
Motor vehicle	551,517	2.3
Motor vehicle operators	120,953	0.5
Public utilities	22,401	0.1
Occupation and business, NEC	357,846	1.5
Other licenses	169,076	0.7
Income taxes	X	-
Individual income	X	-
Corporation net income	X	-
Other taxes	1,275,689	5.3
Death and gift	167,972	0.7
Documentary and stock transfer	1,072,649	4.5
Severance	35,055	0.1
Taxes, NEC	13	-

X = Not applicable.
- = Zero or rounds to zero.

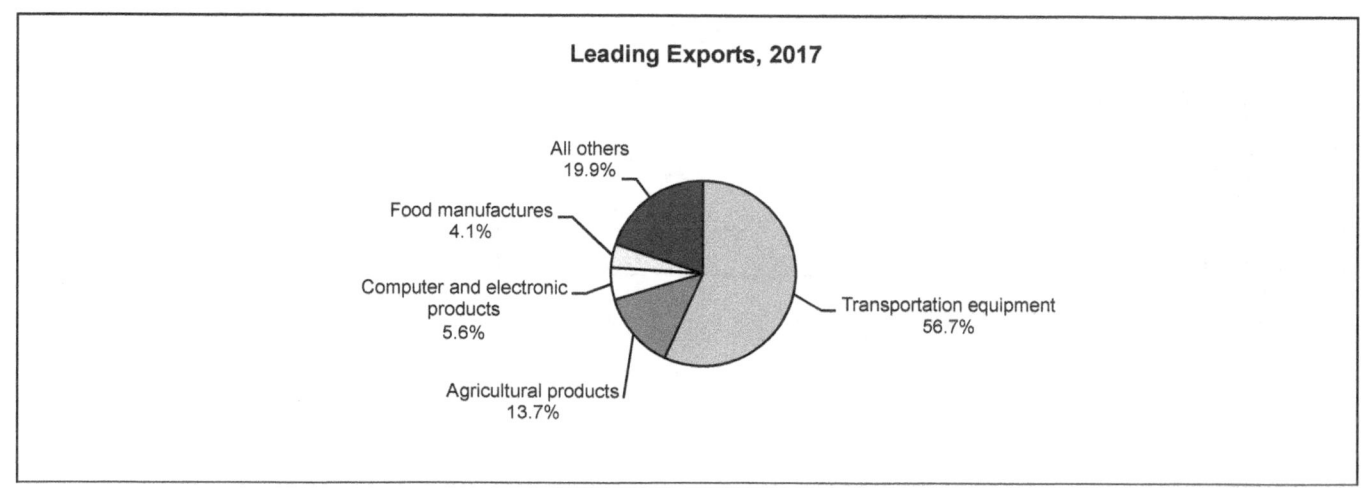

Leading Exports, 2017

All others 19.9%
Food manufactures 4.1%
Computer and electronic products 5.6%
Agricultural products 13.7%
Transportation equipment 56.7%

WEST VIRGINIA

Facts and Figures

Location: East central United States; bordered on the N by Ohio and Pennsylvania, on the E by Pennsylvania, Maryland, and Virginia, on the S by Virginia and Kentucky, and on the W by Kentucky and Ohio

Area: 24,230 sq. mi. (62,755 sq. km.); rank—41st

Population: 1,815,857 (2017 est.); rank—38th

Principal Cities: capital—Charleston; largest—Charleston

Statehood: June 20, 1863; 35th state

U.S. Congress: 2 senators, 3 representatives

State Motto: *Montani semper liberi* (Mountaineers are always free)

State Songs: "West Virginia Hills"; "This Is My West Virginia"; "West Virginia, My Home Sweet Home"

State Nickname: The Mountain State

Abbreviations: WV; W. Va.

State Symbols: flower—rhododendron (great laurel); tree—sugar maple; bird—cardinal

At a Glance

- West Virginia experienced the largest population decline among the states from 2010 to 2017, with its population falling 2.1 percent.

- West Virginia's median household income was $43,385 in 2016, the 2nd lowest among the states, and 17.9 percent of the population lived below the poverty level.

- At a rate more than twice the national average, West Virginia had the highest rate of drug overdose deaths in 2016 (52.0 deaths per 100,000 residents).

- West Virginia tied with Maine for the lowest percent of residents that self-identified as "Hispanic or Latino" in 2017, with just 1.6 percent of its population in this category.

- West Virginia had the highest homeownership rate of all the states in 2017, with 75.1 percent of residents owning homes.

Table WV-1. Population by Age, Sex, Race, and Hispanic Origin

(Number, percent, except where noted.)

Sex, age, race, and Hispanic origin	2000	2010	2017 [1]	Average annual percent change, 2010–2017
Total Population..	1,808,344	1,852,994	1,815,857	-2.0
Percent of total U.S. population	0.6	0.6	0.6	X
Sex				
Male..	879,170	913,586	898,620	-1.6
Female	929,174	939,408	917,237	-2.4
Age				
Under 5 years..	101,805	104,060	98,484	-5.4
5 to 19 years...	352,910	335,153	314,854	-6.1
20 to 64 years...	1,076,734	1,116,377	1,050,920	-5.9
65 years and over	276,895	297,404	351,599	18.2
Median age (years)..	38.9	41.3	42.5	2.9
Race and Hispanic Origin				
One race				
White	1,718,777	1,746,513	1,699,266	-2.7
Black	57,232	63,885	64,951	1.7
American Indian and Alaska Native	3,606	3,975	4,451	12.0
Asian...	9,434	12,637	15,071	19.3
Native Hawaiian or Other Pacific Islander	400	485	533	9.9
Two or more races..	15,788	25,499	31,585	23.9
Hispanic (of any race)..	12,279	23,679	29,065	22.7

X = Not applicable.
- = Zero or rounds to zero.
[1] Population figures for 2017 are July 1 estimates. The 2010 estimates are taken from the 2010 Census.

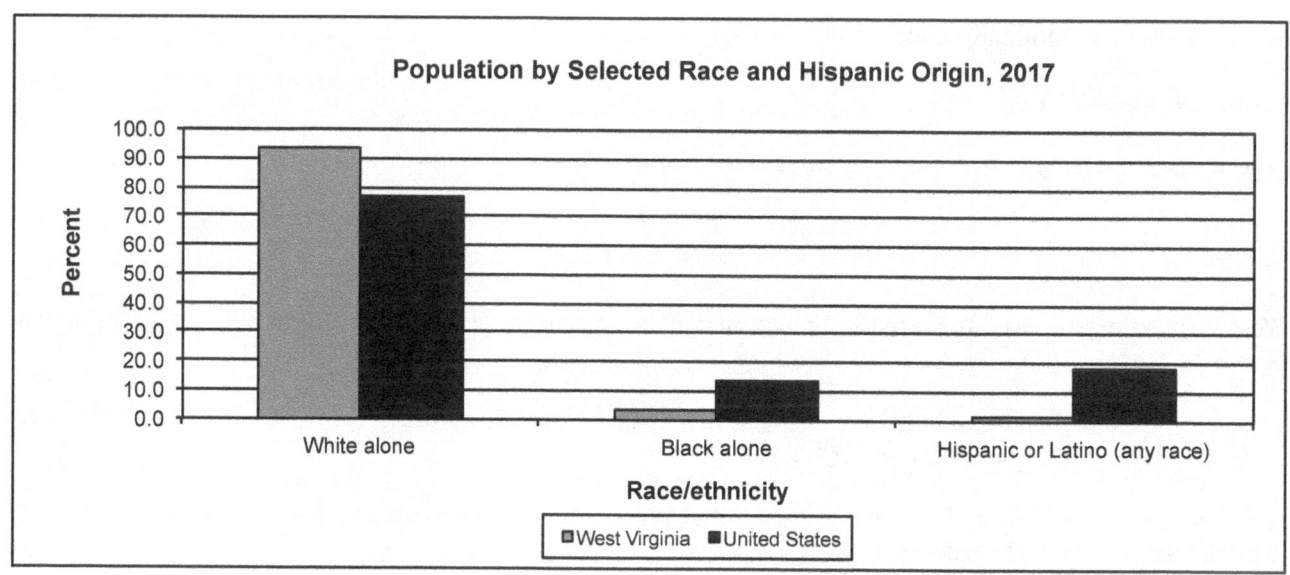

Table WV-2. Marital Status

(Number, percent distribution.)

Sex, age, and marital status	2000	2010	2016
Males, 15 Years and Over	710,443	750,542	742,920
Never married	25.4	30.3	32.3
Now married, except separated..	59.9	52.1	50.0
Separated..	1.3	1.6	1.5
Widowed..	3.2	3.4	3.6
Divorced..	10.1	12.6	12.7
Females, 15 Years and Over	768,858	785,182	776,940
Never married	19.1	22.6	24.0
Now married, except separated..	54.7	49.7	47.5
Separated..	1.6	1.7	1.8
Widowed..	13.9	12.8	11.6
Divorced..	10.8	13.2	15.0

Table WV-3. Households and Housing Characteristics

(Number, percent, dollars.)

Item	2000	2010	2016	Average annual percent change, 2010–2016
Total Households...	736,481	741,940	722,125	-0.4
Family households	504,055	485,652	467,396	-0.6
Married-couple family	397,499	372,301	347,095	-1.1
Other family	106,556	113,351	120,301	1.0
Male householder, no wife present......................	27,436	28,515	33,159	2.7
Female householder, no husband present...............	79,120	84,836	87,142	0.5
Nonfamily households	232,426	256,288	254,729	-0.1
Householder living alone...................................	199,587	219,848	214,380	-0.4
Householder not living alone..............................	32,839	36,440	40,349	1.8
Housing Characteristics				
Total housing units..	844,623	882,213	886,710	0.1
Occupied housing units	736,481	741,940	722,125	-0.4
Owner occupied	553,699	553,429	523,078	-0.9
Renter occupied	182,782	188,511	199,047	0.9
Average household size.......................................	2.40	2.43	2.47	0.3
Financial Characteristics				
Median gross rent of renter-occupied housing	401	571	682	3.2
Median monthly owner costs for housing units with a mortgage	713	918	997	1.4
Median value of owner-occupied housing units	72,800	95,100	117,900	4.0

Table WV-4. Migration, Origin, and Language

(Number, percent.)

Characteristic	State 2015	State 2016	State Percent change	U.S. 2015	U.S. 2016	U.S. Percent change
Residence 1 Year Ago						
Population 1 year and over	1,823,753	1,810,709	-0.7	317,635,720	319,361,956	0.5
Same house	88.3	87.4	X	85.3	85.4	X
Different house in the U.S.	11.5	12.4	X	14.1	13.9	X
Same county	6.3	7.0	X	8.5	8.3	X
Different county	5.2	5.4	X	5.6	5.6	X
Same state	2.9	2.7	X	3.2	3.2	X
Different state	2.3	2.6	X	2.4	2.4	X
Abroad	0.2	0.2	X	0.7	0.7	X
Place of Birth						
Native born	1,814,606	1,799,332	-0.8	278,128,449	279,388,170	0.5
Male	49.2	49.2	X	49.3	49.3	X
Female	50.8	50.8	X	50.7	50.7	X
Foreign born	29,522	31,770	7.6	43,290,372	43,739,345	1.0
Male	50.7	47.0	X	48.6	48.5	X
Female	49.3	53.0	X	51.4	51.5	X
Foreign born; naturalized U.S. citizen..................	15,430	15,066	-2.4	20,697,103	21,238,372	2.6
Male	43.6	38.0	X	45.9	45.9	X
Female	56.4	62.0	X	54.1	54.1	X
Foreign born; not a U.S. citizen.......................	14,092	16,704	18.5	22,593,269	22,500,973	-0.4
Male	58.5	55.1	X	51.1	51.0	X
Female	41.5	44.9	X	48.9	49.0	X
Entered 2010 or later	27.0	26.3	X	15.6	18.6	X
Entered 2000 to 2009	17.9	21.5	X	27.9	26.7	X
Entered before 2000..................................	55.2	52.2	X	56.5	54.7	X
World Region of Birth, Foreign						
Foreign-born population, excluding population born at sea	29,522	31,770	7.6	43,289,646	43,738,901	1.0
Europe	26.0	18.9	X	11.1	10.9	X
Asia..	43.3	41.1	X	30.6	30.8	X
Africa..	4.1	10.1	X	4.8	4.9	X
Oceania...	0.8	1.8	X	0.6	0.6	X
Latin America...	22.0	24.2	X	51.1	51.0	X
North America...	3.9	3.8	X	1.9	1.8	X
Language Spoken at Home and Ability to Speak English						
Population 5 years and over.............................	1,742,174	1,729,434	-0.7	301,625,014	303,328,961	0.6
English only	97.4	97.5	X	78.5	78.4	X
Language other than English...........................	2.6	2.5	X	21.5	21.6	X
Speaks English less than "very well".................	0.7	0.8	X	8.6	8.6	X

NA = Not available.
X = Not applicable.
- = Zero or rounds to zero.

Table WV-5. Median Income and Poverty Status, 2016

(Number, percent, except as noted.)

Characteristic	State		U.S.	
	Number	Percent	Number	Percent
Median Income				
Households (dollars)...	43,385	X	57,617	X
Families (dollars)	56,703	X	71,062	X
Below Poverty Level (All People)	319,063	17.9	44,268,996	14.0
Sex				
Male	143,200	16.4	19,760,056	12.8
Female	175,863	19.4	24,508,940	15.2
Age				
Under 18 years..	88,351	24.0	14,115,713	19.5
Related children under 18 years..	86,693	23.6	13,805,435	19.1
18 to 64 years...	198,829	18.5	25,723,818	13.2
65 years and over..	31,883	9.5	4,429,465	9.2

X = Not applicable.

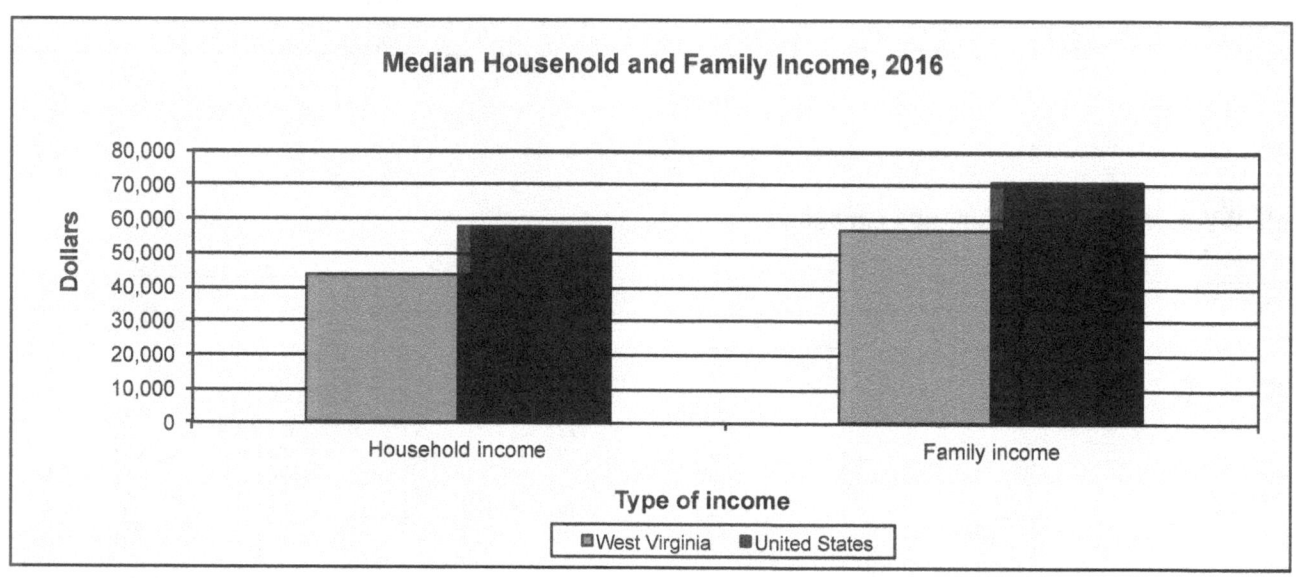

Median Household and Family Income, 2016

Type of income

☐ West Virginia ■ United States

Table WV-6. Health Insurance Coverage Status for the Civilian Noninstitutionalized Population and Children Under 18 Years of Age

(Number, percent.)

Item	2008	2009	2010	2011	2012	2013	2014	2015	2016
Civilian Noninstitutionalized Population	1,787,710	1,793,105	1,823,372	1,826,485	1,826,512	1,824,821	1,820,836	1,815,505	1,802,572
Covered by Private or Public Insurance									
Number..	1,504,531	1,539,190	1,557,211	1,554,198	1,562,703	1,569,752	1,664,746	1,707,423	1,706,690
Percent..	84.2	85.8	85.4	85.1	85.6	86.0	91.4	94.0	94.7
Not Covered									
Number..	283,179	253,915	266,161	272,287	263,809	255,069	156,090	108,082	95,882
Percent..	15.8	14.2	14.6	14.9	14.4	14.0	8.6	6.0	5.3
Percent in the U.S. not covered...	15.1	15.1	15.5	15.1	14.8	14.5	11.7	9.4	8.6
Children Under 18 Years of Age	384,815	382,883	385,274	385,302	382,980	381,156	382,225	378,396	375,790
Covered by Private or Public Insurance									
Number..	359,067	361,750	367,756	368,308	367,957	360,851	370,788	367,613	368,007
Percent..	93.3	94.5	95.5	95.6	96.1	94.7	97.0	97.2	97.9
Not Covered									
Number..	25,748	21,133	17,518	16,994	15,023	20,305	11,437	10,783	7,783
Percent..	6.7	5.5	4.5	4.4	3.9	5.3	3.0	2.8	2.1
Percent in the U.S. not covered...	9.9	8.6	8.0	7.5	7.2	7.1	6.0	4.8	4.5

Table WV-7. Employment Status by Demographic Group, 2017

(Numbers in thousands, percent.)

Characteristic	Civilian noninstitutional population	Civilian labor force		Employed		Unemployed	
		Number	Percent of population	Number	Percent of population	Number	Percent of population
Total..	1,469	782	53.2	741	50.5	41	5.2
Sex							
Male..	716	417	58.2	393	54.9	24	5.8
Female.....................................	752	365	48.5	348	46.3	17	4.6
Race, Sex, and Hispanic Origin							
White.......................................	1,386	736	53.1	698	50.4	38	5.1
Male......................................	676	394	58.2	371	54.9	22	5.7
Female....................................	710	342	48.2	327	46.1	15	4.5
Black or African American...............	49	28	56.3	26	52.7	2	6.7
Male......................................	25	14	57.7	14	54.2	1	5.7
Female....................................	NA	NA	NA	NA	NA	NA	NA
Hispanic or Latino ethnicity[1]............	NA	NA	NA	NA	NA	NA	NA
Male......................................	NA	NA	NA	NA	NA	NA	NA
Female....................................	NA	NA	NA	NA	NA	NA	NA
Age							
16 to 19 years.............................	102	29	28.5	25	23.9	5	16.3
20 to 24 years.............................	108	73	68.2	67	61.9	7	9.3
25 to 34 years.............................	211	162	76.5	152	71.9	10	6.1
35 to 44 years.............................	205	155	75.7	146	71.2	9	6.0
45 to 54 years.............................	240	173	72.1	168	70.1	5	2.7
55 to 64 years.............................	259	138	53.3	134	51.8	4	2.8
65 years and over..........................	343	51	14.9	50	14.5	2	2.9

NOTE: Data in Table 7 are from the Current Population Survey (CPS) and do not match the estimates in Table 8. See notes and definitions for further information.
[1] May be of any race.
NA = Not available.

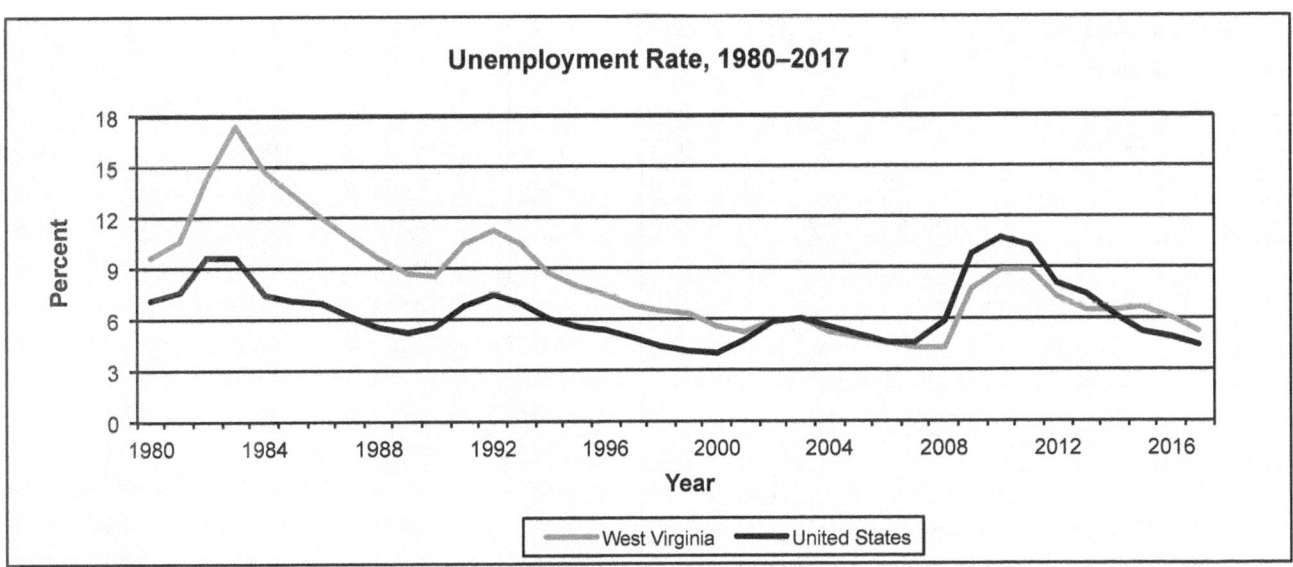

Unemployment Rate, 1980–2017

West Virginia —— United States

Table WV-8. Employment Status of the Civilian Noninstitutional Population Age 16 Years and Over

(Number, percent.)

Year	Civilian labor force	Civilian participation rate	Employed	Unemployed	Unemployment rate
2009..................................	814,027	56.0	751,165	62,862	7.7
2010..................................	811,125	54.9	740,910	70,215	8.7
2011..................................	807,021	54.3	741,972	65,049	8.1
2012..................................	807,917	54.4	747,384	60,533	7.5
2013..................................	798,530	53.8	744,410	54,120	6.8
2014..................................	787,845	53.1	735,511	52,334	6.6
2015..................................	780,428	52.8	727,758	52,670	6.7
2016..................................	781,600	53.1	733,980	47,620	6.1
2017..................................	778,821	53.3	738,309	40,512	5.2

Table WV-9. Employment and Average Wages by Industry

(Estimates through 2010 are based on the 2007 *North American Industry Classification System* [NAICS]. Estimates from 2011 onward are based on the 2012 NAICS.)

Industry	2010	2011	2012	2013	2014	2015	2016
	Number of jobs						
Wage and Salary Employment by Industry.........................	734,594	742,909	751,541	743,781	740,524	734,428	721,887
Farm Wage and Salary Employment.............................	1,289	1,425	1,699	1,570	1,703	1,911	1,574
Nonfarm Wage and Salary Employment.........................	733,305	741,484	749,842	742,211	738,821	732,517	720,313
Private wage and salary employment..........................	570,952	580,200	587,347	583,874	582,102	577,336	563,628
Forestry, fishing, and related activities...................	1,366	1,275	1,371	1,368	1,412	1,476	1,507
Mining..	29,238	32,888	32,729	30,876	29,192	24,956	19,313
Utilities...	5,630	5,438	5,307	5,178	5,204	5,051	5,167
Construction...	33,900	34,056	36,717	35,394	34,732	33,265	30,893
Manufacturing..	49,150	49,573	49,157	48,409	47,828	47,718	46,888
Durable goods manufacturing..........................	29,639	29,957	29,582	29,090	28,882	28,642	28,022
Nondurable goods manufacturing.....................	19,511	19,616	19,575	19,319	18,946	19,076	18,866
Wholesale trade	23,047	23,386	23,612	23,020	22,742	22,329	21,257
Retail trade..	87,389	87,872	88,416	88,334	87,541	87,427	87,603
Transportation and warehousing..........................	19,153	19,728	19,289	20,228	20,882	21,581	20,567
Information..	10,314	10,386	9,633	9,515	9,589	9,555	9,675
Finance and insurance	20,642	20,409	20,236	19,946	19,652	19,282	19,125
Real estate and rental and leasing......................	7,123	6,885	6,843	6,812	6,970	6,954	6,776
Professional, scientific, and technical services.......	24,682	25,270	25,744	26,145	26,368	26,086	25,186
Management of companies and enterprises............	5,471	5,696	6,687	6,490	6,382	6,407	6,293
Administrative and waste services......................	30,861	32,270	32,721	32,763	34,663	35,002	34,604
Educational services.......................................	8,730	8,931	9,136	8,936	8,882	8,905	8,948
Health care and social assistance.......................	108,948	110,492	113,227	114,116	114,068	115,680	115,561
Arts, entertainment, and recreation.....................	9,566	7,278	7,643	7,715	7,759	7,686	7,703
Accommodation and food services......................	63,160	65,983	67,086	67,316	66,962	67,298	67,071
Other services, except public administration..........	32,582	32,384	31,793	31,313	31,274	30,678	29,491
Government and government enterprises.................	162,353	161,284	162,495	158,337	156,719	155,181	156,685
	Dollars						
Average Wages and Salaries by Industry	37,130	38,527	39,193	39,658	40,641	41,172	42,488
Average Farm Wages and Salaries	20,673	16,368	21,335	23,806	23,230	19,006	25,440
Average Nonfarm Wages and Salaries	37,159	38,569	39,234	39,692	40,681	41,230	42,526
Average private wages and salaries.........................	36,907	38,525	39,316	39,591	40,603	41,090	42,507
Forestry, fishing, and related activities...................	25,908	26,776	27,804	27,808	28,998	29,534	29,752
Mining..	73,366	78,870	79,263	80,149	80,892	78,837	85,652
Utilities...	77,026	80,493	80,681	81,299	85,137	88,959	91,683
Construction	47,228	46,985	50,851	51,951	53,528	53,370	58,075
Manufacturing..	49,970	51,707	52,779	53,068	55,054	55,835	57,209
Durable goods manufacturing..........................	46,545	48,413	49,993	49,653	51,395	51,596	53,486
Nondurable goods manufacturing.....................	55,174	56,737	56,990	58,210	60,632	62,200	62,738
Wholesale trade	49,830	51,241	51,732	52,206	54,973	55,912	57,066
Retail trade..	23,164	23,730	24,146	24,414	24,668	25,658	25,632
Transportation and warehousing..........................	46,766	48,622	50,359	48,905	50,275	50,004	52,773
Information..	46,260	48,484	48,644	47,613	48,779	51,167	43,859
Finance and insurance	42,460	46,724	46,077	47,647	49,382	50,868	53,347
Real estate and rental and leasing......................	34,944	34,984	36,326	36,530	37,814	37,925	38,208
Professional, scientific, and technical services.......	50,523	50,654	53,053	53,754	55,169	56,109	60,645
Management of companies and enterprises............	67,657	81,774	70,876	69,869	72,385	73,950	76,561
Administrative and waste services......................	26,578	28,499	29,063	29,582	31,296	31,906	33,982
Educational services.......................................	23,401	24,330	24,583	24,743	24,673	24,855	26,713
Health care and social assistance.......................	37,127	37,833	38,796	39,617	40,985	42,623	45,535
Arts, entertainment, and recreation.....................	22,179	19,387	19,334	19,102	19,319	19,999	20,452
Accommodation and food services......................	15,907	17,203	17,656	17,665	18,039	18,865	19,682
Other services, except public administration..........	25,371	26,040	26,813	27,722	28,218	28,972	30,447
Government and government enterprises.................	38,045	38,728	38,937	40,066	40,972	41,752	42,591

Table WV-10. Employment Characteristics by Family Type

(Number, percent.)

Family type and labor force status	2014		2015		2016	
	Total	Families with own children under 18 years	Total	Families with own children under 18 years	Total	Families with own children under 18 years
All Families..	471,865	167,580	471,947	172,703	467,396	171,163
FAMILY TYPE AND LABOR FORCE STATUS						
Married-Couple Families...	354,686	108,911	351,328	112,219	347,095	111,119
Both husband and wife in labor force..............................	41.6	61.6	39.5	60.7	41.4	62.1
Husband in labor force, wife not in labor force	22.2	28.2	22.1	30.0	20.1	26.4
Wife in labor force, husband not in labor force	9.9	5.5	10.7	5.3	10.5	6.1
Both husband and wife not in labor force............................	26.3	4.6	27.1	3.6	27.6	5.0
Other Families	117,179	58,669	120,619	60,484	120,301	60,044
Female householder, no husband present...........................	71.6	70.4	70.3	70.5	72.4	73.7
In labor force..	41.6	51.1	40.9	52.1	43.1	55.4
Not in labor force	30.0	19.3	29.4	18.4	29.3	18.3
Male householder, no wife present..................................	28.4	29.6	29.7	29.5	27.6	26.3
In labor force..	17.5	23.7	18.2	23.8	17.6	23.3
Not in labor force	10.9	5.9	11.5	5.7	9.9	3.0

Table WV-11. School Enrollment and Educational Attainment, 2016

(Number, percent.)

Item	State	U.S.
Enrollment		
Total population 3 years and over, enrolled in school	394,881	81,572,277
Enrolled in nursery school or preschool (percent)............................	5.0	6.0
Enrolled in kindergarten (percent)...	5.4	5.0
Enrolled in elementary school, grades 1-8 (percent).........................	42.5	40.3
Enrolled in high school, grades 9-12 (percent)	21.0	21.0
Enrolled in college or graduate school (percent).............................	26.3	27.7
Attainment		
Total population 25 years and over	1,291,757	218,475,480
Less than ninth grade (percent)..	4.4	5.4
9th to 12th grade, no diploma (percent)	9.6	7.2
High school graduate, including equivalency (percent)........................	39.7	27.2
Some college, no degree (percent)...	18.1	20.6
Associate's degree (percent)...	7.4	8.4
Bachelor's degree (percent)..	12.6	19.3
Graduate or professional degree (percent)....................................	8.2	11.9
High school graduate or higher (percent)	86.0	87.5
Bachelor's degree or higher (percent)..	20.8	31.3

Table WV-12. Public School Characteristics and Educational Indicators

(Number, percent; data derived from National Center of Education Statistics.)

Item	State	U.S.
Public Schools, 2015–2016 (except where noted)		
Number of school districts..	57	18,328
Number of schools..	744	98,456
Number of students...	277,452	50,327,015
Number of teachers...	19,664	3,151,497
Student-teacher ratio...	14.1	16.0
Expenditures per student (dollars), 2014-2015...............................	11,512	11,445
Four-year adjusted cohort graduation rate (ACGR)[1,2]	89.8	84.1
Students eligible for free or reduced-price lunch (percent), 2014-2015.......	46.1	51.8
English language learners (percent), Fall 2015	1.0	9.5
Students age 3 to 21 served under IDEA, part B (percent).....................	16.3	13.2

Public Schools by Type	Number	Percent of state public schools
Total number of schools..	744	100.0
Regular	682	91.7
Special education...	3	0.4
Vocational education..	30	4.0
Alternative education...	29	3.9

NOTE: Every school is assigned only one school type based on its instructional emphasis.
[1] ACGR data represents a new method of calculating high-school completion rates and may not be comparable to previous years' data for Averaged Freshmen Graduation Rates (AFGR).
[2] The United States 4-year ACGRs were estimated using both the reported 4-year ACGR data from 49 states and the District of Columbia and using imputed data for Idaho. The estimate for American Indian/Alaska Native students also includes imputed data for Virginia.

Table WV-13. Reported Voting and Registration of the Voting-Age Population, November 2016

(Numbers in thousands, percent.)

Item	Total population	Total citizen population	Registered			Voted		
			Total registered	Percent registered (total population)	Percent registered (total citizen population)	Total voted	Percent voted (total population)	Percent voted (total citizen population)
U.S. Total	245,502	224,059	157,596	64.2	70.3	137,537	56.0	61.4
State Total................................	1,434	1,425	913	63.6	64.1	723	50.4	50.8
Sex								
Male	695	688	428	61.5	62.1	335	48.2	48.7
Female	739	736	485	65.6	65.9	388	52.5	52.7
Race								
White alone..............................	1,350	1,347	865	64.0	64.2	682	50.5	50.7
White, non-Hispanic alone	1,340	1,339	860	64.2	64.2	679	50.7	50.7
Black alone...............................	48	47	27	(B)	(B)	24	(B)	(B)
Asian alone	10	7	4	(B)	(B)	3	(B)	(B)
Hispanic (of any race)................	13	9	4	(B)	(B)	3	(B)	(B)
White alone or in combination	1,371	1,368	880	64.2	64.3	695	50.7	50.8
Black alone or in combination...........	55	55	30	(B)	(B)	25	(B)	(B)
Asian alone or in combination...........	14	11	8	(B)	(B)	6	(B)	(B)
Age								
18 to 24 years...........................	155	153	78	50.3	50.7	50	32.2	32.5
25 to 34 years...........................	226	225	141	62.3	62.7	98	43.5	43.8
35 to 44 years...........................	206	204	116	56.3	57.1	96	46.6	47.2
45 to 64 years...........................	513	509	329	64.2	64.7	268	52.2	52.6
65 years and over	334	334	249	74.3	74.5	211	63.1	63.3

B = Base is less than 75,000 and therefore too small to show the derived measure.

Table WV-14. Crime

(Number, rate per 100,000. Data are derived from the FBI Uniform Crime Reports.)

Item	State			U.S. [1,2,3,4]		
	2015	2016	Percent change	2015	2016	Percent change
TOTAL POPULATION [5]	1,844,128	1,831,102	-0.7	321,418,820	323,127,513	0.5
VIOLENT CRIME						
Number..	6,231	6,557	5.2	1,231,566	1,248,185	1.3
Rate..	337.9	358.1	6.0	383.2	386.3	0.8
Murder and Nonnegligent Manslaughter						
Number..	70	81	15.7	15,696	17,250	9.9
Rate..	3.8	4.4	15.8	4.9	5.3	8.2
Rape[6]						
Number..	672	657	-2.2	124,047	130,603	5.3
Rate..	36.4	35.9	-1.4	38.6	40.4	4.7
Robbery						
Number..	760	720	-5.3	327,374	332,198	1.5
Rate..	41.2	39.3	-4.6	101.9	102.8	0.9
Aggravated Assault						
Number..	4,729	5,099	7.8	764,449	803,007	5.0
Rate..	256.4	278.5	8.6	237.8	248.5	4.5
PROPERTY CRIME						
Number..	37,251	37,487	0.6	7,993,631	7,919,035	-0.9
Rate..	2,020.0	2,047.2	1.3	2,487.0	2,450.7	-1.5
Burglary						
Number..	9,170	9,301	1.4	1,579,527	1,515,096	-4.1
Rate..	497.3	507.9	2.1	491.4	468.9	-4.6
Larceny-Theft						
Number..	25,842	25,677	-0.6	5,706,346	5,638,455	-1.2
Rate..	1,401.3	1,402.3	0.1	1,775.4	1,745.0	-1.7
Motor Vehicle Theft						
Number..	2,239	2,509	12.1	707,758	765,484	8.2
Rate..	121.4	137.0	12.9	220.2	236.9	7.6

NOTE: Although arson data are included in the trend and clearance tables, sufficient data are not available to estimate totals for this offense. Therefore, no arson data are published in this table.
X = Not applicable.
- = Zero or rounds to zero.
[1] The crime figures have been adjusted.
[2] The data collection methodology for the offense of forcible rape used by the Minnesota state Uniform Crime Reporting (UCR) Program (with the exception of Minneapolis and St. Paul, Minnesota) does not comply with national UCR Program guidelines. Consequently, its figures for forcible rape and violent crime (of which forcible rape is a part) are not published in this table.
[3] Includes offenses reported by the Zoological Police and the Metro Transit Police.
[4] Because of changes in the state's reporting practices, figures are not comparable to previous years' data.
[5] Populations are U.S. Census Bureau provisional estimates as of July 1 of each year.
[6] The figures shown for the offense of rape were estimated using the revised Uniform Crime Reporting (UCR) definition of rape.

Table WV-15. State Government Finances, 2016

(Dollar amounts in thousands, percent distribution.)

Item	Dollars	Percent distribution
Total Revenue	13,928,479	100.0
General revenue	12,867,298	92.4
Intergovernmental revenue	4,868,024	35.0
Taxes	5,127,970	36.8
General sales	1,286,833	9.2
Selective sales	1,279,857	9.2
License taxes	128,478	0.9
Individual income tax	1,845,711	13.3
Corporate income tax	144,680	1.0
Other taxes	442,411	3.2
Current charges	1,677,667	12.0
Miscellaneous general revenue	1,193,637	8.6
Utility revenue	2,397	-
Liquor stores revenue	92,744	0.7
Insurance trust revenue [1]	966,040	6.9
Total Expenditure	14,562,503	100.0
Intergovernmental expenditure	2,385,622	16.4
Direct expenditure	12,176,881	83.6
Current operation	9,175,032	63.0
Capital outlay	915,138	6.3
Insurance benefits and repayments	1,497,137	10.3
Assistance and subsidies	303,896	2.1
Interest on debt	285,678	2.0
Exhibit: Salaries and wages	1,847,312	12.7
Total Expenditure	14,562,503	100.0
General expenditure	12,977,549	89.1
Intergovernmental expenditure	2,385,622	16.4
Direct expenditure	10,591,927	72.7
General expenditure, by function:		
Education	4,436,847	30.5
Public welfare	4,452,460	30.6
Hospitals	167,639	1.2
Health	324,640	2.2
Highways	1,164,023	8.0
Police protection	84,441	0.6
Correction	301,364	2.1
Natural resources	261,594	1.8
Parks and recreation	52,408	0.4
Governmental administration	493,325	3.4
Interest on general debt	285,678	2.0
Other and unallocable	953,130	6.5
Utility expenditure	11,834	0.1
Liquor stores expenditure	75,983	0.5
Insurance trust expenditure	1,497,137	10.3
Debt at End of Fiscal Year	7,223,531	X
Cash and Security Holdings	20,182,053	X

X = Not applicable.

- = Zero or rounds to zero.

[1] Within insurance trust revenue, net earnings of state retirement systems is a calculated statistic (the item code in the data file is X08), and thus can be positive or negative. Net earnings is the sum of earnings on investments plus gains on investments minus losses on investments. The change made in 2002 for asset valuation from book to market value in accordance with Statement 34 of the Governmental Accounting Standards Board is reflected in the calculated statistics.

Table WV-16. State Government Tax Collections, 2017

(Dollars in thousands, percent.)

Item	Dollars	Percent distribution
Total Taxes	5,092,275	100.0
Property taxes	7248	0.1
Sales and gross receipts	2,672,887	52.5
General sales and gross receipts	1,334,168	26.2
Selective sales and gross receipts	1,338,719	26.3
Alcoholic beverages	17,782	0.3
Amusements	38,958	0.8
Insurance premiums	120,163	2.4
Motor fuels	383,874	7.5
Pari-mutuels	2,611	0.1
Public utilities	107,719	2.1
Tobacco products	194,647	3.8
Other selective sales	472,965	9.3
Licenses	148,951	2.9
Alcoholic beverages	1,038	-
Amusements	3,432	0.1
Corporations in general	632	-
Hunting and fishing	11,691	0.2
Motor vehicle	4,329	0.1
Motor vehicle operators	114,005	2.2
Public utilities	406	-
Occupation and business, NEC	9,761	0.2
Other licenses	3,657	0.1
Income taxes	1,930,171	37.9
Individual income	1,813,866	35.6
Corporation net income	116,305	2.3
Other taxes	333,018	6.5
Death and gift	X	
Documentary and stock transfer	11,987	0.2
Severance	321,031	6.3
Taxes, NEC	0	-

- = Zero or rounds to zero.
X = Not applicable.

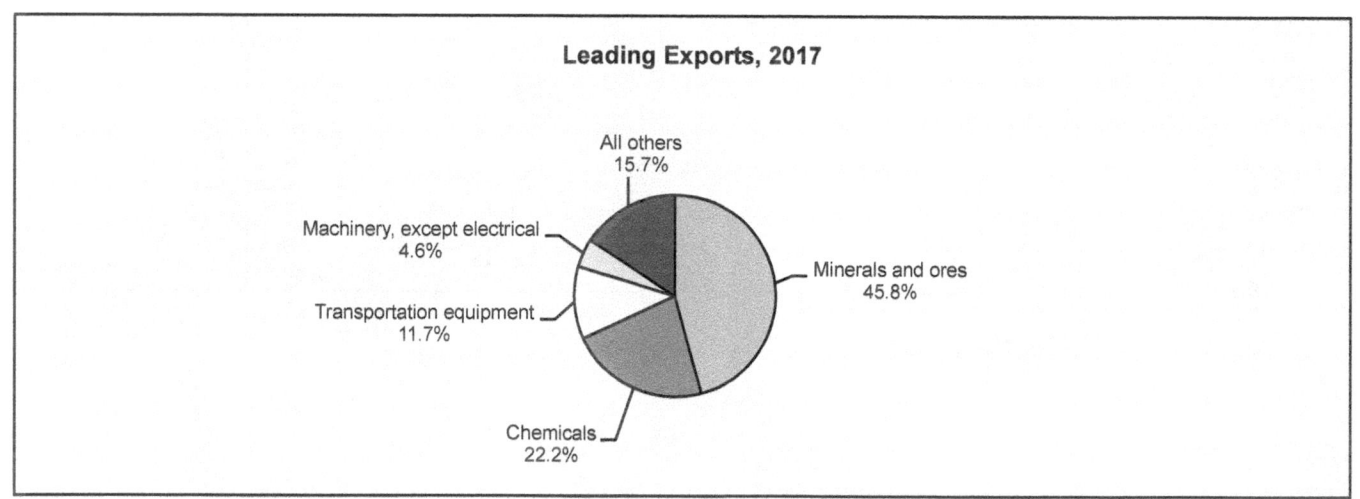

Leading Exports, 2017

- All others 15.7%
- Machinery, except electrical 4.6%
- Transportation equipment 11.7%
- Chemicals 22.2%
- Minerals and ores 45.8%

WISCONSIN

Facts and Figures

Location: North central United States; bordered on the N by Michigan and Lake Superior, on the E by Lake Michigan, on the S by Illinois, and on the W by Iowa and Minnesota

Area: 65,498 sq. mi. (169,639 sq. km.); rank—23rd

Population: 5,795,483 (2017 est.); rank—20th

Principal Cities: capital—Madison; largest—Milwaukee

Statehood: May 29, 1848; 30th state

U.S. Congress: 2 senators, 8 representatives

State Motto: Forward

State Song: "On, Wisconsin!"

State Nickname: The Badger State

Abbreviations: WI; Wis.; Wisc.

State Symbols: flower—wood violet; tree—sugar maple; bird—robin

At a Glance

- With an increase in population of 1.8 percent, Wisconsin ranked 40th among the states in growth from 2010 to 2017.

- Wisconsin's violent crime rate in 2016 was 305.9 per 100,000 population, compared to 386.3 for the entire nation.

- Wisconsin's median household income in 2016 was $56,811, and 11.8 percent of the population lived below the poverty level.

- In the November 2016 election, 68.7 percent of Wisconsin's eligible voters cast ballots, making it 3rd in the nation for voter turnout.

- The unemployment rate in Wisconsin in 2017 was 3.3 percent, compared to the national rate of 4.4 percent.

Table WI-1. Population by Age, Sex, Race, and Hispanic Origin

(Number, percent, except where noted.)

Sex, age, race, and Hispanic origin	2000	2010	2017 [1]	Average annual percent change, 2010–2017
Total Population..	5,363,675	5,686,986	5,795,483	1.9
Percent of total U.S. population	1.9	1.8	1.8	X
Sex				
Male..	2,649,041	2,822,400	2,882,738	2.1
Female..	2,714,634	2,864,586	2,912,745	1.7
Age				
Under 5 years...	342,340	358,443	335,888	-6.3
5 to 19 years...	1,189,753	1,143,753	1,102,188	-3.6
20 to 64 years..	3,129,029	3,407,476	3,402,850	-0.1
65 years and over	702,553	777,314	954,557	22.8
Median age (years)	36.0	38.5	39.4	2.3
Race and Hispanic Origin				
One race				
White..	4,769,857	5,036,923	5,060,891	0.5
Black..	304,460	367,021	385,451	5.0
American Indian and Alaska Native	47,228	60,100	66,752	11.1
Asian..	88,763	131,828	168,435	27.8
Native Hawaiian or Other Pacific Islander	1,630	2,505	3,209	28.1
Two or more races	66,895	88,609	110,745	25.0
Hispanic (of any race).....................................	192,291	349,366	398,780	14.1

X = Not applicable.
[1] Population figures for 2017 are July 1 estimates. The 2010 estimates are taken from the 2010 Census.

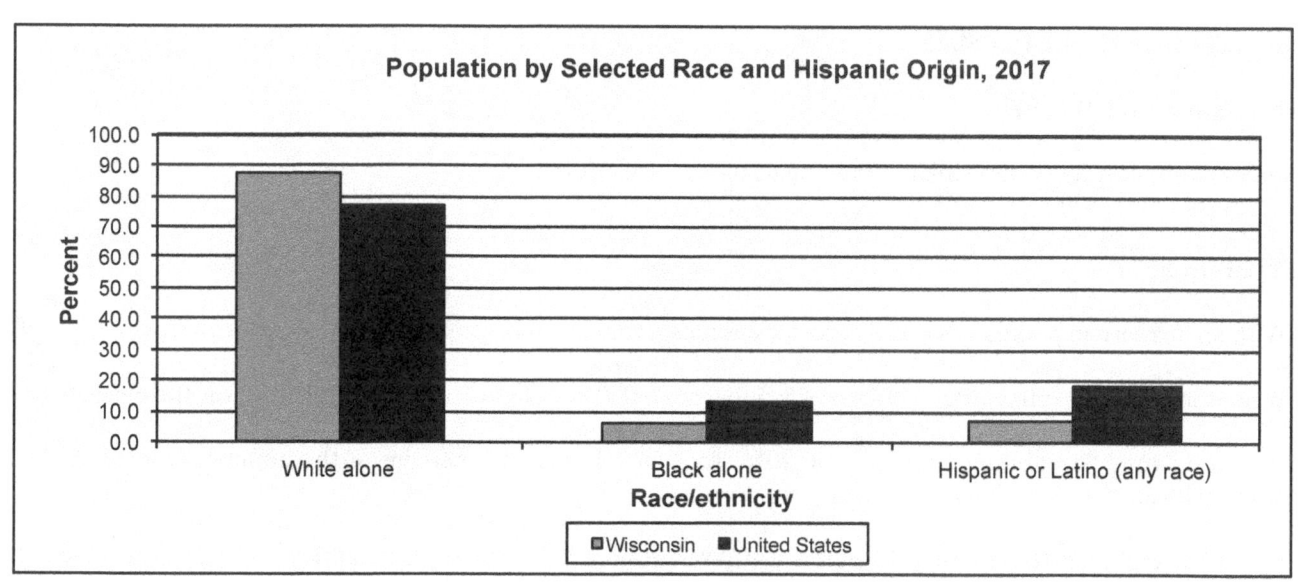

Population by Selected Race and Hispanic Origin, 2017

Table WI-2. Marital Status

(Number, percent distribution.)

Sex, age, and marital status	2000	2010	2016
Males, 15 Years and Over	2,072,397	2,261,022	2,330,764
Never married	30.2	34.1	35.7
Now married, except separated...............................	57.9	52.1	50.7
Separated..	1.1	1.0	0.9
Widowed..	2.4	2.6	2.5
Divorced...	8.4	10.2	10.2
Females, 15 Years and Over	2,167,164	2,328,733	2,388,042
Never married	24.3	28.1	29.5
Now married, except separated...............................	54.6	50.1	49.4
Separated..	1.3	1.2	1.0
Widowed..	10.2	9.2	8.5
Divorced...	9.7	11.4	11.6

Table WI-3. Households and Housing Characteristics

(Number, percent, dollars.)

Item	2000	2010	2016	Average annual percent change, 2010–2016
Total Households...	2,084,544	2,279,532	2,326,998	0.3
Family households	1,386,815	1,453,332	1,460,922	0.1
Married-couple family	1,108,597	1,125,314	1,129,359	0.1
Other family	278,218	328,018	331,563	0.2
Male householder, no wife present.........................	77,918	96,237	105,214	1.6
Female householder, no husband present................	200,300	231,781	226,349	-0.4
Nonfamily households	697,729	826,200	866,076	0.8
Householder living alone......................................	557,875	669,106	692,954	0.6
Householder not living alone..................................	139,854	157,094	173,122	1.7
Housing Characteristics				
Total housing units..	2,321,144	2,625,477	2,668,443	0.3
Occupied housing units	2,084,544	2,279,532	2,326,998	0.3
Owner occupied	1,426,361	1,566,039	1,551,232	-0.2
Renter occupied	658,183	713,493	775,766	1.5
Average household size..	2.50	2.43	2.42	-0.1
Financial Characteristics				
Median gross rent of renter-occupied housing	540	715	802	2.0
Median monthly owner costs for housing units with a mortgage	1,024	1,404	1,348	-0.7
Median value of owner-occupied housing units	112,200	169,400	173,200	0.4

Table WI-4. Migration, Origin, and Language

(Number, percent.)

Characteristic	State			U.S.		
	2015	2016	Percent change	2015	2016	Percent change
Residence 1 Year Ago						
Population 1 year and over	5,708,201	5,712,104	0.1	317,635,720	319,361,956	0.5
Same house	85.7	85.4	X	85.3	85.4	X
Different house in the U.S.	14.0	14.3	X	14.1	13.9	X
Same county	8.6	8.5	X	8.5	8.3	X
Different county	5.3	5.8	X	5.6	5.6	X
Same state	3.5	3.7	X	3.2	3.2	X
Different state	1.9	2.1	X	2.4	2.4	X
Abroad	0.3	0.3	X	0.7	0.7	X
Place of Birth						
Native born	5,492,356	5,490,165	-0.0	278,128,449	279,388,170	0.5
Male	49.7	49.7	X	49.3	49.3	X
Female	50.3	50.3	X	50.7	50.7	X
Foreign born	278,981	288,544	3.4	43,290,372	43,739,345	1.0
Male	49.9	50.7	X	48.6	48.5	X
Female	50.1	49.3	X	51.4	51.5	X
Foreign born; naturalized U.S. citizen	126,745	131,355	3.6	20,697,103	21,238,372	2.6
Male	46.8	47.0	X	45.9	45.9	X
Female	53.2	53.0	X	54.1	54.1	X
Foreign born; not a U.S. citizen	152,236	157,189	3.3	22,593,269	22,500,973	-0.4
Male	52.5	53.9	X	51.1	51.0	X
Female	47.5	46.1	X	48.9	49.0	X
Entered 2010 or later	17.4	21.8	X	15.6	18.6	X
Entered 2000 to 2009	30.9	29.1	X	27.9	26.7	X
Entered before 2000..	51.7	49.1	X	56.5	54.7	X
World Region of Birth, Foreign						
Foreign-born population, excluding population born at sea	278,943	288,544	3.4	43,289,646	43,738,901	1.0
Europe	15.7	16.3	X	11.1	10.9	X
Asia..	36.1	37.0	X	30.6	30.8	X
Africa	4.2	5.4	X	4.8	4.9	X
Oceania	0.5	0.2	X	0.6	0.6	X
Latin America..	41.1	38.4	X	51.1	51.0	X
North America..	2.4	2.6	X	1.9	1.8	X
Language Spoken at Home and Ability to Speak English						
Population 5 years and over..................................	5,434,494	5,444,618	0.2	301,625,014	303,328,961	0.6
English only	91.3	91.2	X	78.5	78.4	X
Language other than English.................................	8.7	8.8	X	21.5	21.6	X
Speaks English less than "very well"........................	3.1	3.2	X	8.6	8.6	X

NA = Not available.
X = Not applicable.
- = Zero or rounds to zero.

Table WI-5. Median Income and Poverty Status, 2016

(Number, percent, except as noted.)

Characteristic	State Number	State Percent	U.S. Number	U.S. Percent
Median Income				
Households (dollars)....................	56,811	X	57,617	X
Families (dollars)	72,891	X	71,062	X
Below Poverty Level (All People)	661,565	11.8	44,268,996	14.0
Sex				
Male	297,596	10.7	19,760,056	12.8
Female	363,969	12.8	24,508,940	15.2
Age				
Under 18 years....................	198,480	15.7	14,115,713	19.5
Related children under 18 years...................	192,004	15.3	13,805,435	19.1
18 to 64 years	394,619	11.4	25,723,818	13.2
65 years and over	68,466	7.6	4,429,465	9.2

X = Not applicable.

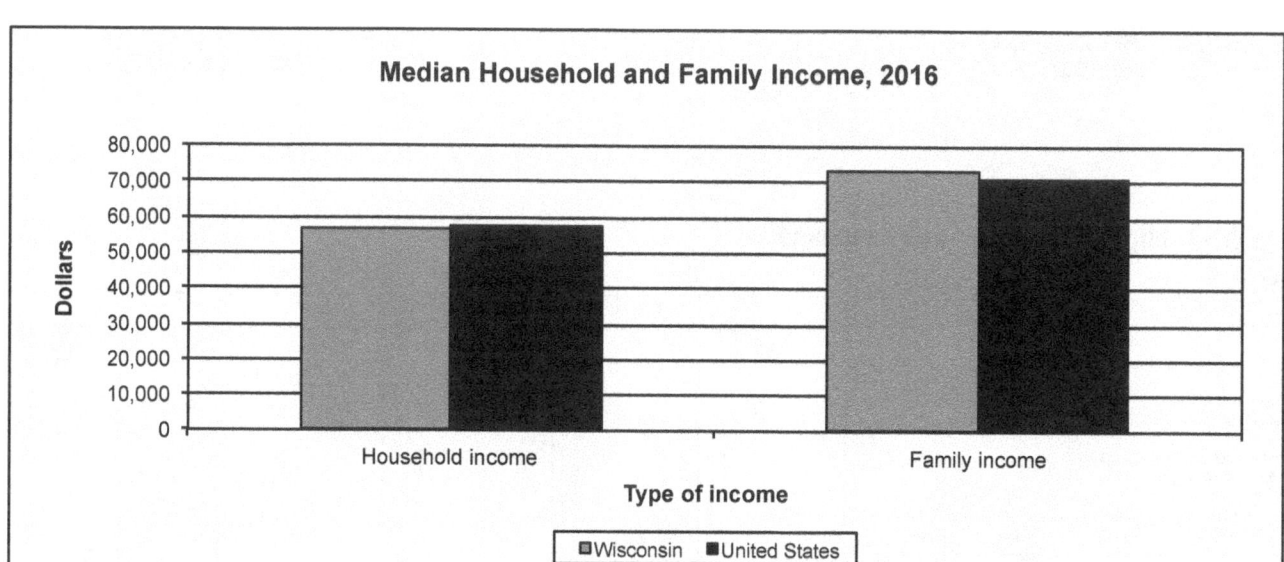

Table WI-6. Health Insurance Coverage Status for the Civilian Noninstitutionalized Population and Children Under 18 Years of Age

(Number, percent.)

Item	2008	2009	2010	2011	2012	2013	2014	2015	2016
Civilian Noninstitutionalized Population	5,540,009	5,566,055	5,613,402	5,634,063	5,652,085	5,669,266	5,684,725	5,698,995	5,706,681
Covered by Private or Public Insurance									
Number....................	5,033,698	5,045,182	5,084,202	5,127,389	5,146,087	5,151,470	5,267,002	5,376,379	5,406,475
Percent....................	90.9	90.6	90.6	91.0	91.0	90.9	92.7	94.3	94.7
Not Covered									
Number....................	506,311	520,873	529,200	506,674	505,998	517,796	417,723	322,616	300,206
Percent....................	9.1	9.4	9.4	9.0	9.0	9.1	7.3	5.7	5.3
Percent in the U.S. not covered........................	15.1	15.1	15.5	15.1	14.8	14.5	11.7	9.4	8.6
Children Under 18 Years of Age	1,309,167	1,302,837	1,334,158	1,322,921	1,315,276	1,304,781	1,297,792	1,290,350	1,283,539
Covered by Private or Public Insurance									
Number....................	1,241,272	1,237,430	1,267,048	1,264,685	1,253,719	1,243,493	1,240,181	1,244,122	1,238,131
Percent....................	94.8	95.0	95.0	95.6	95.3	95.3	95.6	96.4	96.5
Not Covered									
Number....................	67,895	65,407	67,110	58,236	61,557	61,288	57,611	46,228	45,408
Percent....................	5.2	5.0	5.0	4.4	4.7	4.7	4.4	3.6	3.5
Percent in the U.S. not covered........................	9.9	8.6	8.0	7.5	7.2	7.1	6.0	4.8	4.5

Table WI-7. Employment Status by Demographic Group, 2017

(Numbers in thousands, percent.)

Characteristic	Civilian noninstitutional population	Civilian labor force		Employed		Unemployed	
		Number	Percent of population	Number	Percent of population	Number	Percent of population
Total...	4,590	3,168	69.0	3,068	66.8	100	3.2
Sex							
Male..	2,259	1,665	73.7	1,609	71.2	57	3.4
Female...	2,332	1,503	64.5	1,459	62.6	43	2.9
Race, Sex, and Hispanic Origin							
White...	4,084	2,808	68.7	2,729	66.8	78	2.8
Male..	2,036	1,498	73.6	1,451	71.3	47	3.2
Female.....................................	2,049	1,309	63.9	1,278	62.4	31	2.4
Black or African American...................	236	163	68.9	148	62.6	15	9.1
Male..	NA	NA	NA	NA	NA	NA	NA
Female.....................................	NA	NA	NA	NA	NA	NA	NA
Hispanic or Latino ethnicity[1]	252	188	74.4	178	70.5	10	5.3
Male..	127	100	78.9	93	73.4	7	6.9
Female.....................................	NA	NA	NA	NA	NA	NA	NA
Age							
16 to 19 years................................	314	177	56.3	163	52.1	13	7.5
20 to 24 years................................	374	309	82.7	290	77.5	19	6.2
25 to 34 years................................	756	664	87.9	645	85.3	20	3.0
35 to 44 years................................	661	590	89.3	578	87.4	12	2.1
45 to 54 years................................	751	661	88.1	642	85.6	19	2.8
55 to 64 years................................	832	594	71.4	581	69.8	14	2.3
65 years and over	903	172	19.1	169	18.7	4	2.0

NOTE: Data in Table 7 are from the Current Population Survey (CPS) and do not match the estimates in Table 8. See notes and definitions for further information.
[1] May be of any race.
NA = Not available.

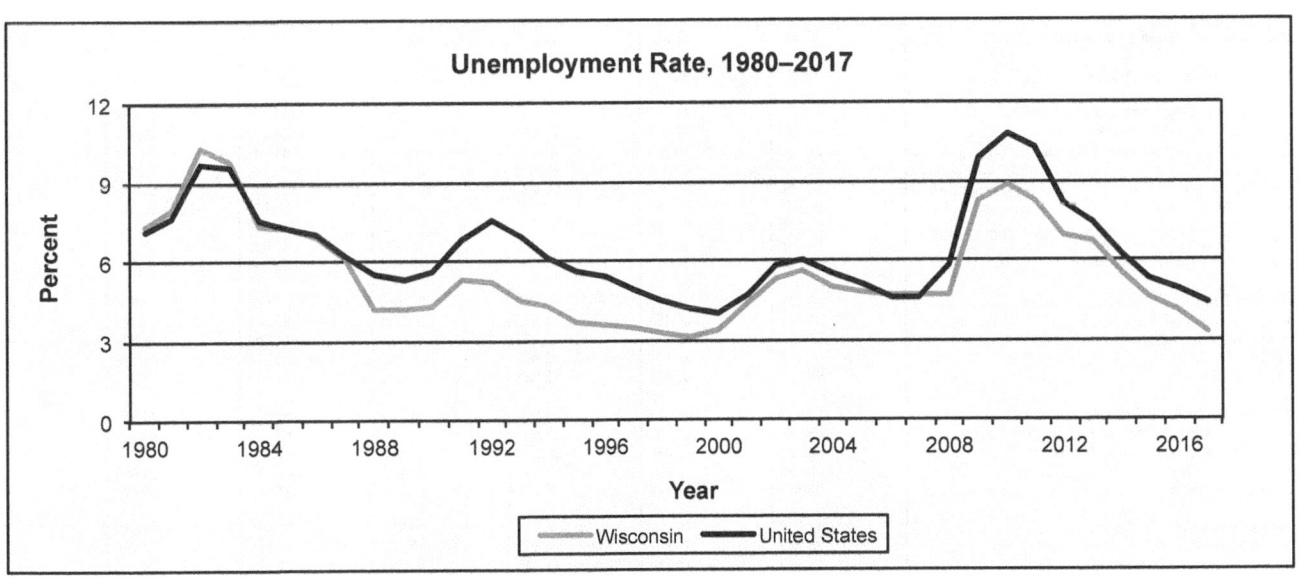

Table WI-8. Employment Status of the Civilian Noninstitutional Population Age 16 Years and Over

(Number, percent.)

Year	Civilian labor force	Civilian participation rate	Employed	Unemployed	Unemployment rate
2009..	3,100,348	70.2	2,834,335	266,013	8.6
2010..	3,081,512	69.5	2,814,393	267,119	8.7
2011..	3,079,759	69.1	2,840,996	238,763	7.8
2012..	3,073,981	68.6	2,857,418	216,563	7.0
2013..	3,079,305	68.4	2,871,997	207,308	6.7
2014..	3,082,564	68.1	2,915,848	166,716	5.4
2015..	3,094,351	68.1	2,953,622	140,729	4.5
2016..	3,130,520	68.6	3,005,478	125,042	4.0
2017..	3,151,909	68.6	3,048,242	103,667	3.3

Table WI-9. Employment and Average Wages by Industry

(Estimates through 2010 are based on the 2007 *North American Industry Classification System* [NAICS]. Estimates from 2011 onward are based on the 2012 NAICS.)

Industry	2010	2011	2012	2013	2014	2015	2016
	Number of jobs						
Wage and Salary Employment by Industry	2,783,755	2,812,907	2,842,635	2,876,051	2,914,062	2,945,802	2,981,103
Farm Wage and Salary Employment	23,031	24,276	21,305	25,245	24,495	22,635	22,732
Nonfarm Wage and Salary Employment	2,760,724	2,788,631	2,821,330	2,850,806	2,889,567	2,923,167	2,958,371
Private wage and salary employment	2,323,123	2,355,343	2,387,430	2,416,575	2,453,303	2,489,111	2,521,023
Forestry, fishing, and related activities	5,557	5,578	5,712	5,854	5,911	6,135	6,563
Mining	2,227	2,304	2,752	3,009	3,407	3,452	3,001
Utilities	11,109	10,915	10,898	10,707	10,418	10,536	9,701
Construction	98,034	95,771	96,380	101,451	106,427	112,357	115,706
Manufacturing	431,403	445,485	456,419	458,076	465,418	468,191	464,944
Durable goods manufacturing	258,744	270,621	279,646	279,725	283,711	284,991	280,152
Nondurable goods manufacturing	172,659	174,864	176,773	178,351	181,707	183,200	184,792
Wholesale trade	113,409	115,044	117,367	119,588	121,021	122,799	124,244
Retail trade	296,621	297,919	297,985	301,047	305,283	307,550	311,610
Transportation and warehousing	89,378	91,362	91,784	91,793	93,509	96,697	99,933
Information	46,788	47,127	46,684	47,297	48,071	49,034	49,137
Finance and insurance	130,118	130,001	130,577	129,039	126,733	127,244	127,718
Real estate and rental and leasing	25,428	24,964	24,840	25,079	25,044	25,489	26,030
Professional, scientific, and technical services	94,602	96,965	99,420	100,689	102,189	105,573	108,425
Management of companies and enterprises	47,160	50,751	53,040	55,773	59,407	62,436	68,690
Administrative and waste services	130,961	138,846	140,724	144,528	148,097	146,861	147,623
Educational services	54,201	54,618	54,899	55,696	55,892	56,337	56,242
Health care and social assistance	361,709	362,986	368,624	374,464	379,807	385,226	393,446
Arts, entertainment, and recreation	35,260	35,476	36,233	36,490	37,121	38,334	40,549
Accommodation and food services	218,215	218,718	222,340	226,413	228,614	233,982	237,274
Other services, except public administration	130,943	130,513	130,752	129,632	130,934	130,878	130,187
Government and government enterprises	437,601	433,288	433,900	434,231	436,264	434,056	437,348
	Dollars						
Average Wages and Salaries by Industry	40,422	41,602	42,664	43,375	44,399	45,966	47,796
Average Farm Wages and Salaries	28,870	25,615	37,348	32,305	36,210	37,100	43,138
Average Nonfarm Wages and Salaries	40,519	41,741	42,704	43,473	44,468	46,035	47,832
Average private wages and salaries	40,625	41,946	43,123	43,899	44,919	46,556	48,422
Forestry, fishing, and related activities	29,792	30,804	32,071	33,101	34,280	36,341	39,252
Mining	56,983	60,082	61,402	61,606	67,119	63,706	76,631
Utilities	92,556	95,991	98,022	103,598	101,366	103,197	102,711
Construction	50,045	51,184	52,695	54,210	56,128	58,012	62,261
Manufacturing	51,880	53,186	54,179	54,822	55,956	57,097	58,563
Durable goods manufacturing	53,644	55,199	55,979	56,508	57,686	58,391	59,994
Nondurable goods manufacturing	49,236	50,072	51,331	52,178	53,254	55,085	56,394
Wholesale trade	55,134	57,417	59,268	60,139	61,663	63,697	67,562
Retail trade	23,777	24,195	24,580	24,931	25,502	26,674	27,529
Transportation and warehousing	39,590	40,775	42,488	42,927	44,533	45,205	46,155
Information	54,116	56,217	58,850	61,297	65,520	69,686	70,843
Finance and insurance	59,726	62,547	65,831	67,041	69,144	72,939	75,662
Real estate and rental and leasing	33,052	34,178	34,946	35,699	37,055	39,361	43,364
Professional, scientific, and technical services	59,580	61,708	64,035	64,974	67,233	70,029	73,434
Management of companies and enterprises	84,527	87,346	89,600	91,843	93,649	97,060	94,567
Administrative and waste services	26,420	27,198	27,341	28,127	28,554	29,933	31,604
Educational services	32,839	34,248	35,117	35,728	35,963	36,475	38,226
Health care and social assistance	42,772	43,881	44,684	45,321	45,242	46,844	48,826
Arts, entertainment, and recreation	28,018	29,107	28,451	29,872	30,760	29,996	32,302
Accommodation and food services	13,830	14,314	14,945	15,187	15,746	16,585	17,860
Other services, except public administration	26,280	26,949	27,640	28,432	29,368	30,746	32,788
Government and government enterprises	39,956	40,622	40,399	41,103	41,936	43,048	44,428

Table WI-10. Employment Characteristics by Family Type

(Number, percent.)

Family type and labor force status	2014		2015		2016	
	Total	Families with own children under 18 years	Total	Families with own children under 18 years	Total	Families with own children under 18 years
All Families...	1,481,237	633,240	1,469,666	618,822	1,460,922	608,206
FAMILY TYPE AND LABOR FORCE STATUS						
Married-Couple Families................................	1,128,553	416,204	1,137,483	422,095	1,129,359	412,090
Both husband and wife in labor force......................	57.3	75.6	56.8	75.1	56.3	76.3
Husband in labor force, wife not in labor force	16.5	19.6	16.1	19.2	16.1	18.7
Wife in labor force, husband not in labor force	8.2	3.7	8.2	4.0	8.1	3.6
Both husband and wife not in labor force..................	18.1	1.2	18.4	1.4	18.9	1.1
Other Families	352,684	217,036	332,183	196,727	331,563	196,116
Female householder, no husband present...................	67.7	69.4	68.8	69.6	68.3	69.4
In labor force.......................................	50.1	58.1	51.1	59.2	51.6	59.5
Not in labor force	17.6	11.3	17.6	10.3	16.7	9.9
Male householder, no wife present......................	32.3	30.6	31.2	30.4	31.7	30.6
In labor force.......................................	26.6	27.9	25.5	27.9	26.2	28.8
Not in labor force	5.7	2.7	5.7	2.5	5.6	1.8

Table WI-11. School Enrollment and Educational Attainment, 2016

(Number, percent.)

Item	State	U.S.
Enrollment		
Total population 3 years and over, enrolled in school	1,428,041	81,572,277
Enrolled in nursery school or preschool (percent)	5.3	6.0
Enrolled in kindergarten (percent)...	5.7	5.0
Enrolled in elementary school, grades 1-8 (percent)...	40.3	40.3
Enrolled in high school, grades 9-12 (percent)	21.0	21.0
Enrolled in college or graduate school (percent)..	27.8	27.7
Attainment		
Total population 25 years and over	3,933,329	218,475,480
Less than ninth grade (percent)	2.7	5.4
9th to 12th grade, no diploma (percent)	5.4	7.2
High school graduate, including equivalency (percent)...	31.1	27.2
Some college, no degree (percent)	20.7	20.0
Associate's degree (percent)	10.7	8.4
Bachelor's degree (percent)	19.3	19.3
Graduate or professional degree (percent)...	10.2	11.9
High school graduate or higher (percent)	91.9	87.5
Bachelor's degree or higher (percent)..	29.5	31.3

Table WI-12. Public School Characteristics and Educational Indicators

(Number, percent; data derived from National Center of Education Statistics.)

Item	State	U.S.
Public Schools, 2015–2016 (except where noted)		
Number of school districts..	465	18,328
Number of schools...	2,255	98,456
Number of students	867,800	50,327,015
Number of teachers	58,185	3,151,497
Student-teacher ratio	14.9	16.0
Expenditures per student (dollars), 2014-2015..	11,538	11,445
Four-year adjusted cohort graduation rate (ACGR)[1,2]	88.2	84.1
Students eligible for free or reduced-price lunch (percent), 2014-2015..............................	41.5	51.8
English language learners (percent), Fall 2015	5.3	9.5
Students age 3 to 21 served under IDEA, part B (percent)..	13.9	13.2

Public Schools by Type	Number	Percent of state public schools
Total number of schools...	2,255	100.0
Regular	2,147	95.2
Special education..	12	0.5
Vocational education...	6	0.3
Alternative education..	90	4.0

NOTE: Every school is assigned only one school type based on its instructional emphasis.
[1] ACGR data represents a new method of calculating high-school completion rates and may not be comparable to previous years' data for Averaged Freshmen Graduation Rates (AFGR).
[2] The United States 4-year ACGRs were estimated using both the reported 4-year ACGR data from 49 states and the District of Columbia and using imputed data for Idaho. The estimate for American Indian/Alaska Native students also includes imputed data for Virginia.

Table WI-13. Reported Voting and Registration of the Voting-Age Population, November 2016

(Numbers in thousands, percent.)

Item	Total population	Total citizen population	Registered			Voted		
			Total registered	Percent registered (total population)	Percent registered (total citizen population)	Total voted	Percent voted (total population)	Percent voted (total citizen population)
U.S. Total	245,502	224,059	157,596	64.2	70.3	137,537	56.0	61.4
State Total...............................	4,465	4,354	3,323	74.4	76.3	3,068	68.7	70.5
Sex								
Male	2,193	2,132	1,584	72.2	74.3	1,468	66.9	68.8
Female	2,272	2,222	1,739	76.5	78.3	1,600	70.4	72.0
Race								
White alone...............................	4,079	3,998	3,130	76.7	78.3	2,897	71.0	72.5
White, non-Hispanic alone	3,792	3,776	3,009	79.4	79.7	2,796	73.7	74.0
Black alone................................	205	197	101	49.3	51.2	92	45.1	46.8
Asian alone	118	95	50	(B)	(B)	45	(B)	(B)
Hispanic (of any race)	329	260	136	41.2	52.1	111	33.8	42.8
White alone or in combination	4,129	4,049	3,165	76.6	78.2	2,923	70.8	72.2
Black alone or in combination...........	241	233	122	50.5	52.2	104	43.4	44.8
Asian alone or in combination...........	129	106	62	48.0	58.3	57	43.8	53.3
Age								
18 to 24 years............................	547	530	269	49.2	50.7	249	45.6	47.1
25 to 34 years............................	704	678	436	62.0	64.3	370	52.6	54.6
35 to 44 years............................	724	701	573	79.1	81.8	527	72.7	75.2
45 to 64 years............................	1,520	1,479	1,236	81.3	83.5	1,169	76.9	79.0
65 years and over	970	966	809	83.4	83.8	753	77.6	77.9

B = Base is less than 75,000 and therefore too small to show the derived measure.

Table WI-14. Crime

(Number, rate per 100,000. Data are derived from the FBI Uniform Crime Reports.)

Item	State			U.S. [1,2,3,4]		
	2015	2016	Percent change	2015	2016	Percent change
TOTAL POPULATION [5]	5,771,337	5,778,708	0.1	321,418,820	323,127,513	0.5
VIOLENT CRIME						
Number......................................	17,647	17,679	0.2	1,231,566	1,248,185	1.3
Rate	305.8	305.9	-	383.2	386.3	0.8
Murder and Nonnegligent Manslaughter						
Number......................................	240	229	-4.6	15,696	17,250	9.9
Rate	4.2	4.0	-4.8	4.9	5.3	8.2
Rape[6]						
Number......................................	1,780	1,979	11.2	124,047	130,603	5.3
Rate	30.8	34.2	11.0	38.6	40.4	4.7
Robbery						
Number......................................	5,232	4,706	-10.1	327,374	332,198	1.5
Rate	90.7	81.4	-10.3	101.9	102.8	0.9
Aggravated Assault						
Number......................................	10,395	10,765	3.6	764,449	803,007	5.0
Rate	180.1	186.3	3.4	237.8	248.5	4.5
PROPERTY CRIME						
Number......................................	113,924	111,720	-1.9	7,993,631	7,919,035	-0.9
Rate	1,974.0	1,933.3	-2.1	2,487.0	2,450.7	-1.5
Burglary						
Number......................................	19,554	19,425	-0.7	1,579,527	1,515,096	-4.1
Rate	338.8	336.1	-0.8	491.4	468.9	-4.6
Larceny-Theft						
Number......................................	83,385	82,337	-1.3	5,706,346	5,638,455	-1.2
Rate	1,444.8	1,424.8	-1.4	1,775.4	1,745.0	-1.7
Motor Vehicle Theft						
Number......................................	10,985	9,958	-9.3	707,758	765,484	8.2
Rate	190.3	172.3	-9.5	220.2	236.9	7.6

NOTE: Although arson data are included in the trend and clearance tables, sufficient data are not available to estimate totals for this offense. Therefore, no arson data are published in this table.
X = Not applicable.
- = Zero or rounds to zero.
[1] The crime figures have been adjusted.
[2] The data collection methodology for the offense of forcible rape used by the Minnesota state Uniform Crime Reporting (UCR) Program (with the exception of Minneapolis and St. Paul, Minnesota) does not comply with national UCR Program guidelines. Consequently, its figures for forcible rape and violent crime (of which forcible rape is a part) are not published in this table.
[3] Includes offenses reported by the Zoological Police and the Metro Transit Police.
[4] Because of changes in the state's reporting practices, figures are not comparable to previous years' data.
[5] Populations are U.S. Census Bureau provisional estimates as of July 1 of each year.
[6] The figures shown for the offense of rape were estimated using the revised Uniform Crime Reporting (UCR) definition of rape.

Table WI-15. State Government Finances, 2016

(Dollar amounts in thousands, percent distribution.)

Item	Dollars	Percent distribution
Total Revenue	36,854,453	100.0
General revenue	34,643,763	94.0
Intergovernmental revenue	9,319,175	25.3
Taxes	17,607,733	47.8
General sales	5,058,789	13.7
Selective sales	2,662,918	7.2
License taxes	1,151,656	3.1
Individual income tax	7,486,676	20.3
Corporate income tax	986,785	2.7
Other taxes	260,909	0.7
Current charges	4,516,598	12.3
Miscellaneous general revenue	3,200,257	8.7
Utility revenue	0	-
Liquor stores revenue	0	-
Insurance trust revenue [1]	2,210,690	6.0
Total Expenditure	39,241,416	100.0
Intergovernmental expenditure	9,601,077	24.5
Direct expenditure	29,640,339	75.5
Current operation	21,405,632	54.5
Capital outlay	1,201,561	3.1
Insurance benefits and repayments	5,325,699	13.6
Assistance and subsidies	778,645	2.0
Interest on debt	928,802	2.4
Exhibit: Salaries and wages	4,272,164	10.9
Total Expenditure	39,241,416	100.0
General expenditure	33,837,914	86.2
Intergovernmental expenditure	9,601,077	24.5
Direct expenditure	24,236,837	61.8
General expenditure, by function:		
Education	12,542,898	32.0
Public welfare	10,756,805	27.4
Hospitals	2,156,040	5.5
Health	467,675	1.2
Highways	1,706,689	4.3
Police protection	147,775	0.4
Correction	1,111,132	2.8
Natural resources	636,683	1.6
Parks and recreation	58,878	0.2
Governmental administration	757,452	1.9
Interest on general debt	928,802	2.4
Other and unallocable	2,567,085	6.5
Utility expenditure	77,803	0.2
Liquor stores expenditure	0	-
Insurance trust expenditure	5,325,699	13.6
Debt at End of Fiscal Year	23,052,389	X
Cash and Security Holdings	108,721,147	X

X = Not applicable.
- = Zero or rounds to zero.
[1] Within insurance trust revenue, net earnings of state retirement systems is a calculated statistic (the item code in the data file is X08), and thus can be positive or negative. Net earnings is the sum of earnings on investments plus gains on investments minus losses on investments. The change made in 2002 for asset valuation from book to market value in accordance with Statement 34 of the Governmental Accounting Standards Board is reflected in the calculated statistics.

Table WI-16. State Government Tax Collections, 2017

(Dollars in thousands, percent.)

Item	Dollars	Percent distribution
Total Taxes	18,133,496	100.0
Property taxes	132,022	0.7
Sales and gross receipts	7,972,959	44.0
General sales and gross receipts	5,223,935	28.8
Selective sales and gross receipts	2,749,024	15.2
Alcoholic beverages	61,203	0.3
Amusements	227	-
Insurance premiums	202,387	1.1
Motor fuels	1,044,996	5.8
Pari-mutuels	131	-
Public utilities	357,757	2.0
Tobacco products	644,478	3.6
Other selective sales	437,845	2.4
Licenses	1,179,054	6.5
Alcoholic beverages	1,902	-
Amusements	467	-
Corporations in general	22,546	0.1
Hunting and fishing	67,571	0.4
Motor vehicle	496,295	2.7
Motor vehicle operators	40,053	0.2
Public utilities	83,830	0.5
Occupation and business, NEC	465,569	2.6
Other licenses	821	-
Income taxes	8,752,242	48.3
Individual income	7,792,543	43.0
Corporation net income	959,699	5.3
Other taxes	97,219	0.5
Death and gift	1733	-
Documentary and stock transfer	70,786	0.4
Severance	10,151	0.1
Taxes, NEC	14,549	0.1

- = Zero or rounds to zero.

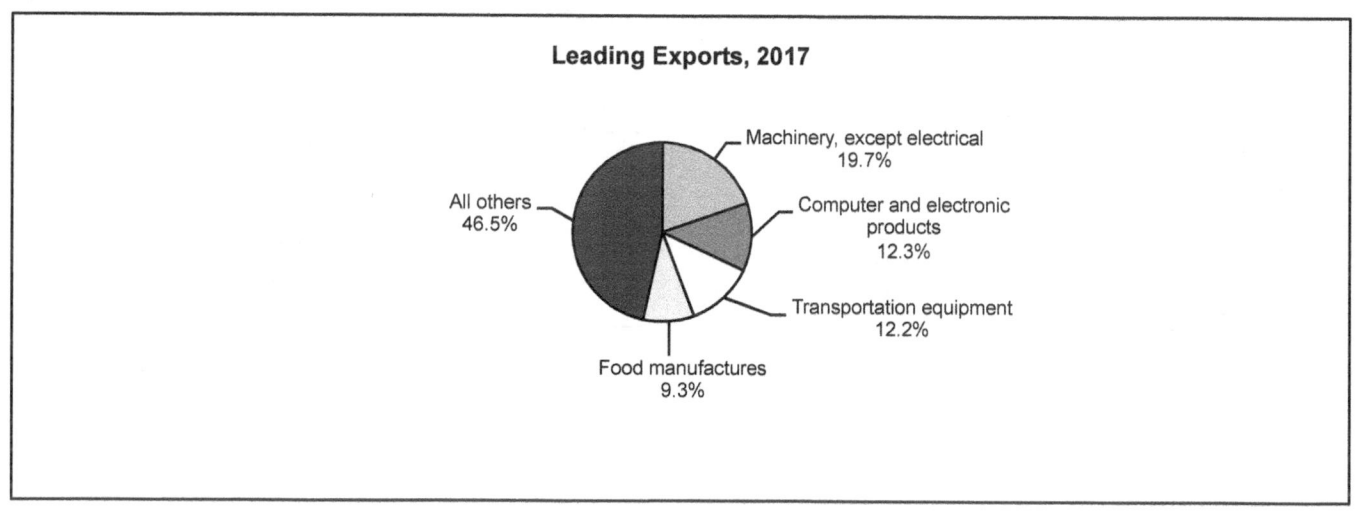

Leading Exports, 2017

- Machinery, except electrical 19.7%
- Computer and electronic products 12.3%
- Transportation equipment 12.2%
- Food manufactures 9.3%
- All others 46.5%

WYOMING

Facts and Figures

Location: Western United States; bordered on the N by Montana, on the E by South Dakota and Nebraska, on the S by Colorado and Utah, and on the W by Utah and Idaho

Area: 97,814 sq. mi. (253,336 sq. km.); rank—10th

Population: 579,315 (2017 est.); rank—51st

Principal Cities: capital—Cheyenne; largest—Cheyenne

Statehood: July 10, 1890; 44th state

U.S. Congress: 2 senators, 1 representative

State Motto: Equal Rights

State Song: "Wyoming"

State Nicknames: The Equality State; The Cowboy State

Abbreviations: WY; Wyo.

State Symbols: flower—Indian paintbrush; tree—cottonwood; bird—Western meadowlark

At a Glance

- With an increase in population of 2.6 percent, Wyoming ranked 32nd among the states in growth from 2010 to 2017.

- Wyoming's violent crime rate in 2016 was 244.2 per 100,000 population, compared to the U.S. rate of 386.3 per 100,000 population.

- Wyoming's median household income in 2016 was $59,882, and 11.3 percent of the population lived below the poverty level.

- Wyoming had the 3rd lowest childhood poverty rate in the country in 2016, with 11.1 percent of children under 18 years of age living in poverty.

- In 2016, 11.5 percent of Wyoming residents did not have health insurance, compared to 8.6 percent of total U.S. residents.

Table WY-1. Population by Age, Sex, Race, and Hispanic Origin

(Number, percent, except where noted.)

Sex, age, race, and Hispanic origin	2000	2010	2017 [1]	Average annual percent change, 2010–2017
Total Population................................	493,782	563,626	579,315	2.8
Percent of total U.S. population	0.2	0.2	0.2	X
Sex				
Male..	248,374	287,437	295,438	2.8
Female......................................	245,408	276,189	283,877	2.8
Age				
Under 5 years................................	30,940	40,203	37,031	-7.9
5 to 19 years................................	114,406	111,310	113,748	2.2
20 to 64 years...............................	290,743	342,023	336,929	-1.5
65 years and over............................	57,693	70,090	91,607	30.7
Median age (years)..........................	36.2	36.8	37.7	2.4
Race and Hispanic Origin				
One race				
White.......................................	454,670	529,110	537,396	1.6
Black.......................................	3,722	5,135	7,445	45.0
American Indian and Alaska Native	11,133	14,457	15,743	8.9
Asian.......................................	2,771	4,649	5,880	26.5
Native Hawaiian or Other Pacific Islander	302	521	579	11.1
Two or more races............................	8,883	9,754	12,272	25.8
Hispanic (of any race).......................	31,669	52,112	58,122	11.5

X = Not applicable.
- = Zero or rounds to zero.
[1] Population figures for 2017 are July 1 estimates. The 2010 estimates are taken from the 2010 Census.

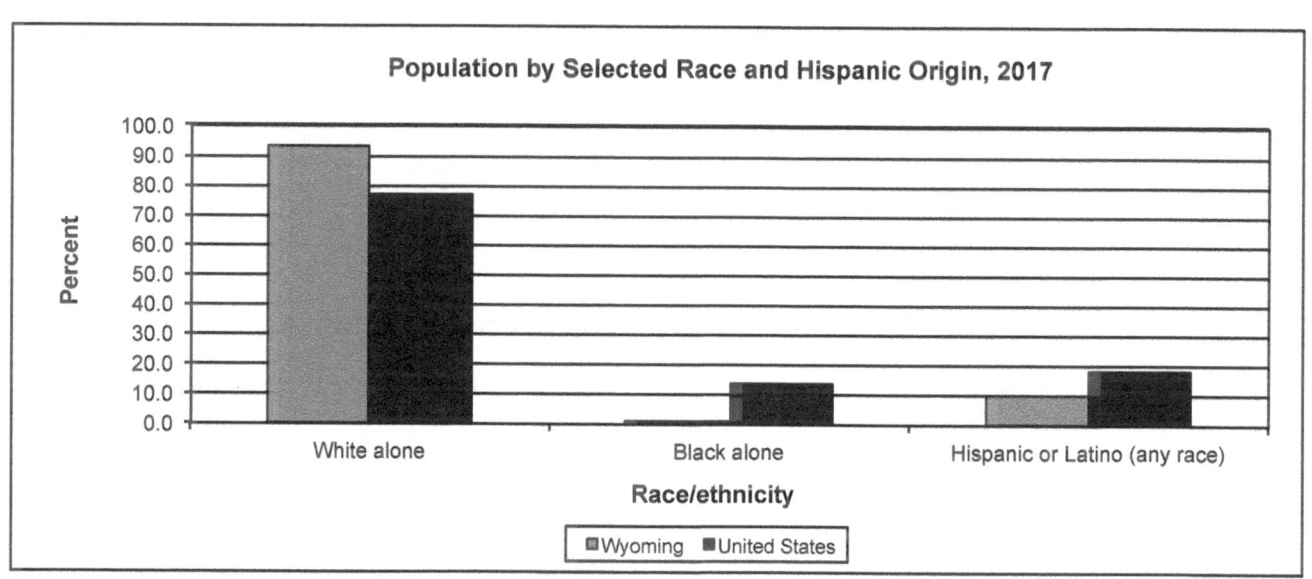

Population by Selected Race and Hispanic Origin, 2017

Table WY-2. Marital Status

(Number, percent distribution.)

Sex, age, and marital status	2000	2010	2016
Males, 15 Years and Over........................	195,412	228,725	237,253
Never married	26.6	29.0	30.2
Now married, except separated...................	58.8	56.2	53.2
Separated.......................................	1.0	1.3	1.6
Widowed...	2.3	2.4	2.4
Divorced..	11.3	11.2	12.5
Females, 15 Years and Over......................	195,433	220,169	229,148
Never married	20.0	20.7	24.7
Now married, except separated...................	57.5	55.1	52.8
Separated.......................................	1.3	2.0	1.3
Widowed...	9.2	8.6	7.9
Divorced..	12.0	13.6	13.2

Table WY-3. Households and Housing Characteristics

(Number, percent, dollars.)

Item	2000	2010	2016	Average annual percent change, 2010–2016
Total Households	193,608	222,803	223,619	0.1
Family households	130,497	147,394	145,524	-0.2
Married-couple family	106,179	119,756	117,038	-0.4
Other family	24,318	27,638	28,486	0.5
Male householder, no wife present	7,481	7,804	10,954	6.7
Female householder, no husband present	16,837	19,834	17,532	-1.9
Nonfamily households	63,111	75,409	78,095	0.6
Householder living alone	50,980	61,775	61,964	0.1
Householder not living alone	12,131	13,634	16,131	3.1
Housing Characteristics				
Total housing units	223,854	262,286	270,625	0.5
Occupied housing units	193,608	222,803	223,619	0.1
Owner occupied	135,514	155,278	153,894	-0.1
Renter occupied	58,094	67,525	69,725	0.5
Average household size	2.48	2.47	2.55	0.5
Financial Characteristics				
Median gross rent of renter-occupied housing	437	693	840	3.5
Median monthly owner costs for housing units with a mortgage	825	1,300	1,367	0.9
Median value of owner-occupied housing units	96,600	180,100	209,500	2.7

Table WY-4. Migration, Origin, and Language

(Number, percent.)

Characteristic	State			U.S.		
	2015	2016	Percent change	2015	2016	Percent change
Residence 1 Year Ago						
Population 1 year and over	579,102	577,567	-0.3	317,635,720	319,361,956	0.5
Same house	82.0	81.9	X	85.3	85.4	X
Different house in the U.S.	17.5	17.7	X	14.1	13.9	X
Same county	8.4	10.7	X	8.5	8.3	X
Different county	9.1	7.1	X	5.6	5.6	X
Same state	2.9	2.5	X	3.2	3.2	X
Different state	6.2	4.6	X	2.4	2.4	X
Abroad	0.5	0.4	X	0.7	0.7	X
Place of Birth						
Native born	564,108	566,645	0.4	278,128,449	279,388,170	0.5
Male	50.7	51.1	X	49.3	49.3	X
Female	49.3	48.9	X	50.7	50.7	X
Foreign born	21,999	18,856	-14.3	43,290,372	43,739,345	1.0
Male	42.0	46.5	X	48.6	48.5	X
Female	58.0	53.5	X	51.4	51.5	X
Foreign born; naturalized U.S. citizen	8,500	7,396	-13.0	20,697,103	21,238,372	2.6
Male	43.4	44.9	X	45.9	45.9	X
Female	56.6	55.1	X	54.1	54.1	X
Foreign born; not a U.S. citizen	13,499	11,460	-15.1	22,593,269	22,500,973	-0.4
Male	41.1	47.6	X	51.1	51.0	X
Female	58.9	52.4	X	48.9	49.0	X
Entered 2010 or later	16.7	21.0	X	15.6	18.6	X
Entered 2000 to 2009	36.2	34.3	X	27.9	26.7	X
Entered before 2000	47.1	44.7	X	56.5	54.7	X
World Region of Birth, Foreign						
Foreign-born population, excluding population born at sea	21,999	18,856	-14.3	43,289,646	43,738,901	1.0
Europe	12.4	18.2	X	11.1	10.9	X
Asia	18.9	24.2	X	30.6	30.8	X
Africa	5.3	6.8	X	4.8	4.9	X
Oceania	0.6	0.5	X	0.6	0.6	X
Latin America	58.8	46.9	X	51.1	51.0	X
North America	4.1	3.5	X	1.9	1.8	X
Language Spoken at Home and Ability to Speak English						
Population 5 years and over	547,957	547,628	-0.1	301,625,014	303,328,961	0.6
English only	92.5	92.4	X	78.5	78.4	X
Language other than English	7.5	7.6	X	21.5	21.6	X
Speaks English less than "very well"	2.5	2.0	X	8.6	8.6	X

NA = Not available.
X = Not applicable.
- = Zero or rounds to zero.

Table WY-5. Median Income and Poverty Status, 2016

(Number, percent, except as noted.)

Characteristic	State		U.S.	
	Number	Percent	Number	Percent
Median Income				
Households (dollars)..	59,882	X	57,617	X
Families (dollars)	73,574	X	71,062	X
Below Poverty Level (All People)	64,663	11.3	44,268,996	14.0
Sex				
Male...	30,401	10.5	19,760,056	12.8
Female	34,262	12.2	24,508,940	15.2
Age				
Under 18 years..	15,367	11.1	14,115,713	19.5
Related children under 18 years..	14,154	10.3	13,805,435	19.1
18 to 64 years	42,055	12.1	25,723,818	13.2
65 years and over	7,241	8.5	4,429,465	9.2

X = Not applicable.

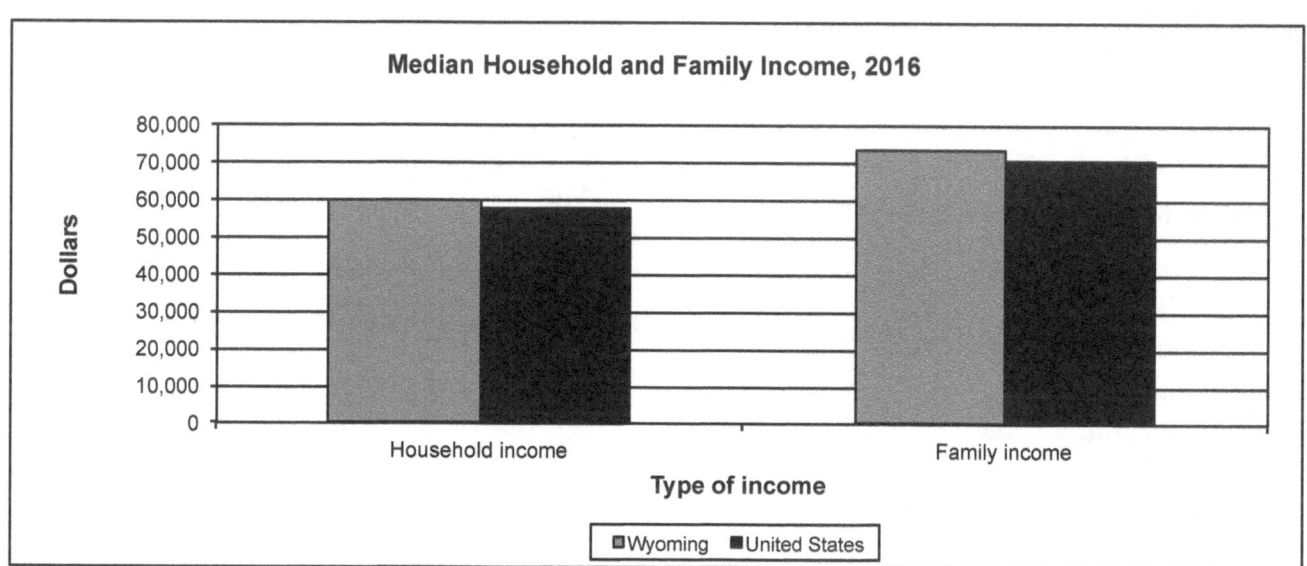

Table WY-6. Health Insurance Coverage Status for the Civilian Noninstitutionalized Population and Children Under 18 Years of Age

(Number, percent.)

Item	2008	2009	2010	2011	2012	2013	2014	2015	2016
Civilian Noninstitutionalized Population	523,428	533,716	555,010	558,832	567,082	573,210	574,798	576,557	576,027
Covered by Private or Public Insurance									
Number..	450,566	452,788	472,174	473,001	479,998	496,182	506,050	510,063	509,514
Percent...	86.1	84.8	85.1	84.6	84.6	86.6	88.0	88.5	88.5
Not Covered									
Number..	72,862	80,928	82,836	85,831	87,084	77,028	68,748	66,494	66,513
Percent...	13.9	15.2	14.9	15.4	15.4	13.4	12.0	11.5	11.5
Percent in the U.S. not covered.............................	15.1	15.1	15.5	15.1	14.8	14.5	11.7	9.4	8.6
Children Under 18 Years of Age	127,415	128,421	136,229	134,594	136,132	139,291	137,296	138,953	140,464
Covered by Private or Public Insurance									
Number..	116,288	116,924	125,461	122,956	123,417	131,357	129,159	128,097	128,136
Percent...	91.3	91.0	92.1	91.4	90.7	94.3	94.1	92.2	91.2
Not Covered									
Number..	11,127	11,497	10,768	11,638	12,715	7,934	8,137	10,856	12,328
Percent...	8.7	9.0	7.9	8.6	9.3	5.7	5.9	7.8	8.8
Percent in the U.S. not covered.............................	9.9	8.6	8.0	7.5	7.2	7.1	6.0	4.8	4.5

Table WY-7. Employment Status by Demographic Group, 2017

(Numbers in thousands, percent.)

Characteristic	Civilian noninstitutional population	Civilian labor force		Employed		Unemployed	
		Number	Percent of population	Number	Percent of population	Number	Percent of population
Total..	450	294	65.3	282	62.5	13	4.3
Sex							
Male..	228	160	70.5	153	67.2	8	4.7
Female..	223	134	60.0	129	57.8	5	3.7
Race, Sex, and Hispanic Origin							
White..	424	278	65.6	267	63.0	11	3.9
Male..	215	152	70.9	146	68.0	6	4.2
Female..	209	126	60.1	121	58.0	5	3.6
Black or African American............................	NA	NA	NA	NA	NA	NA	NA
Male..	NA	NA	NA	NA	NA	NA	NA
Female..	NA	NA	NA	NA	NA	NA	NA
Hispanic or Latino ethnicity[1]	40	28	68.4	26	63.7	2	6.7
Male..	21	16	76.3	15	71.5	1	6.2
Female..	19	11	59.4	10	55.1	1	7.5
Age							
16 to 19 years..	32	14	42.4	12	36.6	2	13.4
20 to 24 years..	36	27	74.8	25	68.6	2	8.2
25 to 34 years..	73	59	81.0	56	77.5	3	4.3
35 to 44 years..	76	66	87.6	64	84.8	2	3.2
45 to 54 years..	65	54	83.0	52	80.5	2	2.8
55 to 64 years..	83	56	67.0	54	65.0	2	3.2
65 years and over.......................................	86	19	22.1	18	21.3	1	3.7

NOTE: Data in Table 7 are from the Current Population Survey (CPS) and do not match the estimates in Table 8. See notes and definitions for further information.
[1] May be of any race.
NA = Not available.

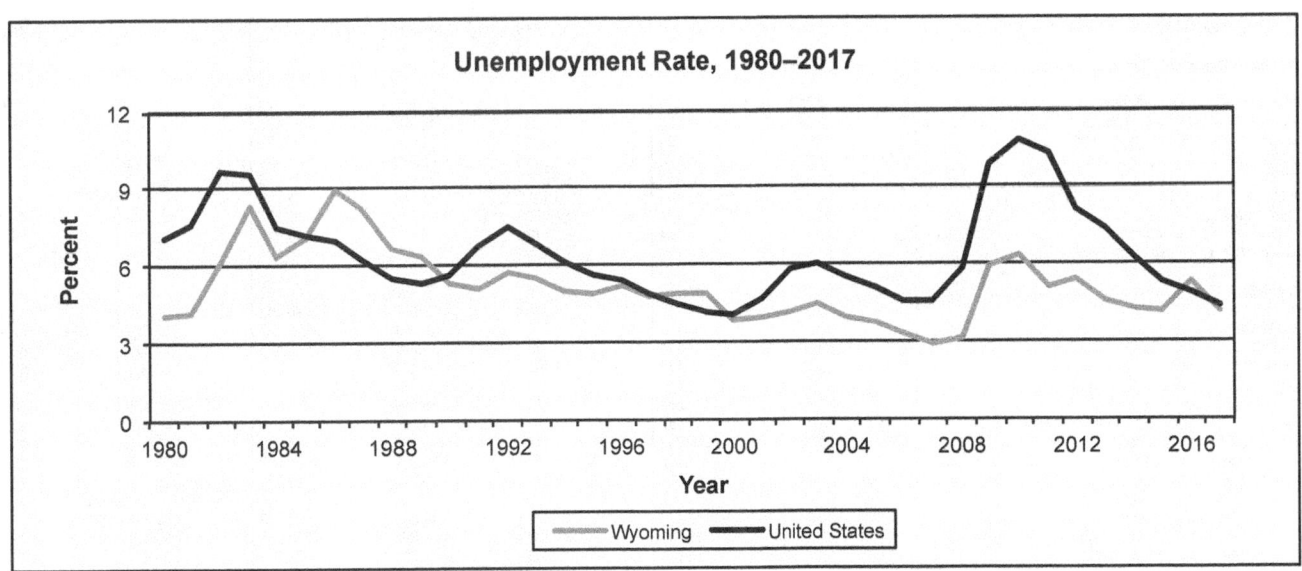

Unemployment Rate, 1980–2017

Table WY-8. Employment Status of the Civilian Noninstitutional Population Age 16 Years and Over

(Number, percent.)

Year	Civilian labor force	Civilian participation rate	Employed	Unemployed	Unemployment rate
2009..	300,120	71.8	281,150	18,970	6.3
2010..	303,297	70.4	283,744	19,553	6.4
2011..	306,815	70.2	289,019	17,796	5.8
2012..	307,267	69.2	290,932	16,335	5.3
2013..	306,608	68.4	292,131	14,477	4.7
2014..	306,331	68.1	293,657	12,674	4.1
2015..	304,775	67.5	291,686	13,089	4.3
2016..	300,922	66.7	285,052	15,870	5.3
2017..	293,347	65.5	281,017	12,330	4.2

Table WY-9. Employment and Average Wages by Industry

(Estimates through 2010 are based on the 2007 *North American Industry Classification System* [NAICS]. Estimates from 2011 onward are based on the 2012 NAICS.)

Industry	2010	2011	2012	2013	2014	2015	2016
	Number of jobs						
Wage and Salary Employment by Industry.........................	290,162	294,099	298,341	299,528	304,005	302,286	291,331
Farm Wage and Salary Employment.................................	2,837	3,271	3,711	3,688	3,566	3,822	3,871
Nonfarm Wage and Salary Employment...........................	287,325	290,828	294,630	295,840	300,439	298,464	287,460
Private wage and salary employment...............................	212,271	215,770	218,950	220,076	225,068	222,723	211,429
Forestry, fishing, and related activities.............................	1,007	1,059	1,100	1,136	1,170	1,165	1,167
Mining...	24,908	27,207	27,550	26,461	27,112	23,737	18,707
Utilities..	2,483	2,488	2,471	2,484	2,489	2,536	2,541
Construction...	23,172	21,733	22,172	22,472	24,447	23,843	21,710
Manufacturing...	8,724	9,185	9,362	9,474	9,818	9,765	9,235
Durable goods manufacturing................................	4,265	4,615	4,734	4,704	4,873	4,711	4,148
Nondurable goods manufacturing...........................	4,459	4,570	4,628	4,770	4,945	5,054	5,087
Wholesale trade..	8,497	8,868	9,199	9,291	9,541	9,538	8,535
Retail trade...	29,755	29,460	29,699	30,026	30,036	31,015	30,891
Transportation and warehousing................................	11,385	12,016	12,111	12,294	13,076	13,079	11,803
Information...	3,886	3,859	3,916	3,801	3,779	3,770	3,745
Finance and insurance..	7,152	7,105	7,094	7,180	7,197	7,231	7,249
Real estate and rental and leasing..............................	4,033	4,076	4,153	4,426	4,528	4,366	4,070
Professional, scientific, and technical services...............	9,232	9,166	9,313	9,330	9,604	9,442	8,946
Management of companies and enterprises.....................	857	866	956	1,032	1,014	1,025	901
Administrative and waste services..............................	7,278	7,909	7,909	7,916	7,954	8,135	8,083
Educational services...	2,142	2,083	2,030	2,123	2,133	2,158	2,223
Health care and social assistance...............................	23,870	24,044	24,111	24,393	24,476	24,645	25,146
Arts, entertainment, and recreation.............................	2,793	2,801	2,853	2,923	3,033	3,177	3,355
Accommodation and food services..............................	30,043	30,447	31,241	31,863	32,486	33,106	32,712
Other services, except public administration..................	11,054	11,398	11,710	11,451	11,175	10,990	10,410
Government and government enterprises.......................	75,054	75,058	75,680	75,764	75,371	75,741	76,031
	Dollars						
Average Wages and Salaries by Industry	42,637	44,004	45,367	45,834	47,357	47,173	46,542
Average Farm Wages and Salaries	35,261	30,896	35,050	39,813	39,672	35,142	38,631
Average Nonfarm Wages and Salaries	42,710	44,151	45,497	45,909	47,449	47,327	46,649
Average private wages and salaries..............................	42,521	44,285	45,815	46,227	47,973	47,482	46,294
Forestry, fishing, and related activities.........................	22,578	23,634	23,854	24,601	25,896	26,707	30,211
Mining...	77,942	80,828	83,346	85,574	88,929	88,771	91,606
Utilities..	81,406	84,357	84,537	85,601	88,845	92,220	85,889
Construction...	48,358	48,404	50,107	51,132	52,293	51,843	47,106
Manufacturing...	53,031	56,164	57,207	58,905	62,321	64,635	67,057
Durable goods manufacturing................................	47,162	48,594	50,149	50,915	53,648	53,945	55,949
Nondurable goods manufacturing...........................	58,645	63,809	64,428	66,785	70,869	74,599	76,114
Wholesale trade..	55,487	57,547	59,035	59,490	64,165	61,140	59,641
Retail trade...	25,986	26,741	28,026	27,857	28,552	28,941	28,446
Transportation and warehousing................................	53,371	55,223	56,910	56,493	58,529	58,028	59,432
Information...	40,008	41,844	43,088	44,294	45,875	47,071	46,106
Finance and insurance..	49,407	51,114	54,107	55,111	57,847	59,963	60,768
Real estate and rental and leasing..............................	38,945	43,084	45,350	46,634	48,924	47,468	46,629
Professional, scientific, and technical services...............	53,947	55,967	58,626	59,364	62,471	61,884	62,502
Management of companies and enterprises.....................	103,484	105,253	114,444	113,453	100,090	103,578	95,613
Administrative and waste services..............................	29,010	32,106	31,829	31,912	32,603	33,492	35,655
Educational services...	27,347	29,051	29,993	29,549	29,735	28,065	28,135
Health care and social assistance...............................	39,342	40,526	42,027	41,543	42,549	43,872	44,052
Arts, entertainment, and recreation.............................	21,410	21,486	21,420	22,086	23,813	23,897	27,059
Accommodation and food services..............................	18,516	18,991	19,883	20,713	21,215	21,847	22,736
Other services, except public administration..................	31,360	31,613	32,806	33,459	33,200	34,036	33,462
Government and government enterprises.......................	43,246	43,766	44,576	44,985	45,884	46,872	47,636

Table WY-10. Employment Characteristics by Family Type

(Number, percent.)

Family type and labor force status	2014		2015		2016	
	Total	Families with own children under 18 years	Total	Families with own children under 18 years	Total	Families with own children under 18 years
All Families.........................	148,660	63,332	145,470	63,698	145,524	59,042
FAMILY TYPE AND LABOR FORCE STATUS						
Married-Couple Families...............	116,668	45,397	117,245	45,664	117,038	41,342
Both husband and wife in labor force...........	57.7	68.0	56.4	68.9	52.9	70.2
Husband in labor force, wife not in labor force..........	19.8	26.8	20.3	26.3	20.0	25.6
Wife in labor force, husband not in labor force.........	7.2	4.5	6.7	3.5	8.3	3.7
Both husband and wife not in labor force................	15.3	0.6	16.3	1.1	18.2	0.4
Other Families	31,992	17,935	28,225	18,034	28,486	17,700
Female householder, no husband present................	62.0	64.0	58.1	56.7	61.5	61.3
In labor force......................	45.4	51.7	45.0	49.4	47.2	56.7
Not in labor force.................	16.6	12.3	13.1	7.3	14.4	4.6
Male householder, no wife present................	38.0	36.0	41.9	43.3	38.5	38.7
In labor force......................	30.2	32.8	35.8	40.4	34.3	37.5
Not in labor force.................	7.8	3.2	6.1	3.0	4.1	1.2

Table WY-11. School Enrollment and Educational Attainment, 2016

(Number, percent.)

Item	State	U.S.
Enrollment		
Total population 3 years and over, enrolled in school	151,204	81,572,277
Enrolled in nursery school or preschool (percent)	5.6	6.0
Enrolled in kindergarten (percent)..........	5.3	5.0
Enrolled in elementary school, grades 1-8 (percent)...........	43.9	40.3
Enrolled in high school, grades 9-12 (percent)...........	19.0	21.0
Enrolled in college or graduate school (percent)...........	26.3	27.7
Attainment		
Total population 25 years and over	390,794	218,475,480
Less than ninth grade (percent)..........	1.5	5.4
9th to 12th grade, no diploma (percent)...........	5.4	7.2
High school graduate, including equivalency (percent)...........	29.3	27.2
Some college, no degree (percent)...........	25.1	20.6
Associate's degree (percent)...........	11.7	8.4
Bachelor's degree (percent)...........	17.4	19.3
Graduate or professional degree (percent)...........	9.7	11.9
High school graduate or higher (percent)...........	93.2	87.5
Bachelor's degree or higher (percent)...........	27.1	31.3

Table WY-12. Public School Characteristics and Educational Indicators

(Number, percent; data derived from National Center of Education Statistics.)

Item	State	U.S.
Public Schools, 2015–2016 (except where noted)		
Number of school districts..........	60	18,328
Number of schools..........	370	98,456
Number of students..........	94,717	50,327,015
Number of teachers	7,653	3,151,497
Student-teacher ratio..........	12.4	16.0
Expenditures per student (dollars), 2014-2015..........	16,047	11,445
Four-year adjusted cohort graduation rate (ACGR)[1,2]	80.0	84.1
Students eligible for free or reduced-price lunch (percent), 2014-2015..........	37.6	51.8
English language learners (percent), Fall 2015..........	3.1	9.5
Students age 3 to 21 served under IDEA, part B (percent)..........	16.5	13.2

Public Schools by Type	Number	Percent of state public schools
Total number of schools..........	370	100.0
Regular	361	97.6
Special education..........	3	0.8
Vocational education..........	0	-
Alternative education..........	6	1.6

NOTE: Every school is assigned only one school type based on its instructional emphasis.
[1] ACGR data represents a new method of calculating high-school completion rates and may not be comparable to previous years' data for Averaged Freshmen Graduation Rates (AFGR).
[2] The United States 4-year ACGRs were estimated using both the reported 4-year ACGR data from 49 states and the District of Columbia and using imputed data for Idaho. The estimate for American Indian/Alaska Native students also includes imputed data for Virginia.
- = Zero or rounds to zero.
NA = Not available.

Table WY-13. Reported Voting and Registration of the Voting-Age Population, November 2016

(Numbers in thousands, percent.)

Item	Total population	Total citizen population	Registered			Voted		
			Total registered	Percent registered (total population)	Percent registered (total citizen population)	Total voted	Percent voted (total population)	Percent voted (total citizen population)
U.S. Total	245,502	224,059	157,596	64.2	70.3	137,537	56.0	61.4
State Total..............................	436	427	304	69.7	71.1	277	63.5	64.8
Sex								
Male	223	218	154	69.1	70.6	139	62.4	63.7
Female	213	209	150	70.3	71.7	138	64.7	66.0
Race								
White alone..............................	405	399	284	70.2	71.2	260	64.3	65.3
White, non-Hispanic alone............	374	373	270	72.2	72.3	249	66.6	66.8
Black alone..............................	5	5	4	(B)	(B)	3	(B)	(B)
Asian alone..............................	6	4	3	(B)	(B)	3	(B)	(B)
Hispanic (of any race).................	32	26	15	(B)	(B)	12	(B)	(B)
White alone or in combination	409	404	289	70.5	71.6	264	64.6	65.5
Black alone or in combination..........	6	6	6	(B)	(B)	4	(B)	(B)
Asian alone or in combination..........	7	4	3	(B)	(B)	3	(B)	(B)
Age								
18 to 24 years..........................	57	55	33	(B)	(B)	30	(B)	(B)
25 to 34 years..........................	75	73	47	(B)	(B)	42	(B)	(B)
35 to 44 years..........................	70	68	46	(B)	(B)	40	(B)	(B)
45 to 64 years..........................	151	148	110	72.9	74.2	102	67.4	68.6
65 years and over......................	83	83	68	(B)	(B)	63	(B)	(B)

- = Zero or rounds to zero.
B = Base is less than 75,000 and therefore too small to show the derived measure.

Table WY-14. Crime

(Number, rate per 100,000. Data are derived from the FBI Uniform Crime Reports.)

Item	State			U.S. [1,2,3,4]		
	2015	2016	Percent change	2015	2016	Percent change
TOTAL POPULATION [5]	586,107	585,501	-0.1	321,418,820	323,127,513	0.5
VIOLENT CRIME						
Number..	1,302	1,430	9.8	1,231,566	1,248,185	1.3
Rate...	222.1	244.2	10.0	383.2	386.3	0.8
Murder and Nonnegligent Manslaughter						
Number..	16	20	25.0	15,696	17,250	9.9
Rate...	2.7	3.4	25.9	4.9	5.3	8.2
Rape [6]						
Number..	173	205	18.5	124,047	130,603	5.3
Rate...	29.5	35.0	18.6	38.6	40.4	4.7
Robbery						
Number..	59	59	-	327,374	332,198	1.5
Rate...	10.1	10.1	-	101.9	102.8	0.9
Aggravated Assault						
Number..	1,054	1,146	8.7	764,449	803,007	5.0
Rate...	179.8	195.7	8.8	237.8	248.5	4.5
PROPERTY CRIME						
Number..	11,151	11,460	2.8	7,993,631	7,919,035	-0.9
Rate...	1,902.6	1,957.3	2.9	2,487.0	2,450.7	-1.5
Burglary						
Number..	1,762	1,771	0.5	1,579,527	1,515,096	-4.1
Rate...	300.6	302.5	0.6	491.4	468.9	-4.6
Larceny-Theft						
Number..	8,797	8,889	1.0	5,706,346	5,638,455	-1.2
Rate...	1,500.9	1,518.2	1.2	1,775.4	1,745.0	-1.7
Motor Vehicle Theft						
Number..	592	800	35.1	707,758	765,484	8.2
Rate...	101.0	136.6	35.2	220.2	236.9	7.6

NOTE: Although arson data are included in the trend and clearance tables, sufficient data are not available to estimate totals for this offense. Therefore, no arson data are published in this table.
X = Not applicable.
- = Zero or rounds to zero.
[1] The crime figures have been adjusted.
[2] The data collection methodology for the offense of forcible rape used by the Minnesota state Uniform Crime Reporting (UCR) Program (with the exception of Minneapolis and St. Paul, Minnesota) does not comply with national UCR Program guidelines. Consequently, its figures for forcible rape and violent crime (of which forcible rape is a part) are not published in this table.
[3] Includes offenses reported by the Zoological Police and the Metro Transit Police.
[4] Because of changes in the state's reporting practices, figures are not comparable to previous years' data.
[5] Populations are U.S. Census Bureau provisional estimates as of July 1 of each year.
[6] The figures shown for the offense of rape were estimated using the revised Uniform Crime Reporting (UCR) definition of rape.

Table WY-15. State Government Finances, 2016

(Dollar amounts in thousands, percent distribution.)

Item	Dollars	Percent distribution
Total Revenue	5,914,028	100.0
General revenue	5,090,453	86.1
Intergovernmental revenue	2,143,281	36.2
Taxes	1,913,607	32.4
General sales	641,495	10.8
Selective sales	178,651	3.0
License taxes	157,086	2.7
Individual income tax	0	-
Corporate income tax	0	-
Other taxes	936,375	15.8
Current charges	201,623	3.4
Miscellaneous general revenue	831,942	14.1
Utility revenue	0	-
Liquor stores revenue	113,914	1.9
Insurance trust revenue [1]	709,661	12.0
Total Expenditure	6,351,534	100.0
Intergovernmental expenditure	1,867,516	29.4
Direct expenditure	4,484,018	70.6
Current operation	3,127,364	49.2
Capital outlay	419,898	6.6
Insurance benefits and repayments	827,223	13.0
Assistance and subsidies	74,265	1.2
Interest on debt	35,268	0.6
Exhibit: Salaries and wages	719,723	11.3
Total Expenditure	6,351,534	100.0
General expenditure	5,373,518	84.6
Intergovernmental expenditure	1,867,516	29.4
Direct expenditure	3,506,002	55.2
General expenditure, by function:		
Education	1,982,651	31.2
Public welfare	824,960	13.0
Hospitals	4,665	0.1
Health	265,145	4.2
Highways	503,698	7.9
Police protection	47,640	0.8
Correction	145,404	2.3
Natural resources	363,685	5.7
Parks and recreation	24,038	0.4
Governmental administration	340,247	5.4
Interest on general debt	35,268	0.6
Other and unallocable	836,117	13.2
Utility expenditure	52,648	0.9
Liquor stores expenditure	98,145	1.5
Insurance trust expenditure	827,223	13.0
Debt at End of Fiscal Year	775,568	X
Cash and Security Holdings	29,340,747	X

X = Not applicable.
- = Zero or rounds to zero.
[1] Within insurance trust revenue, net earnings of state retirement systems is a calculated statistic (the item code in the data file is X08), and thus can be positive or negative. Net earnings is the sum of earnings on investments plus gains on investments minus losses on investments. The change made in 2002 for asset valuation from book to market value in accordance with Statement 34 of the Governmental Accounting Standards Board is reflected in the calculated statistics.

Table WY-16. State Government Tax Collections, 2017

(Dollars in thousands, percent.)

Item	Dollars	Percent distribution
Total Taxes	1,649,550	100.0
Property taxes	274,005	16.6
Sales and gross receipts	762,588	46.2
General sales and gross receipts	588,866	35.7
Selective sales and gross receipts	173,722	10.5
Alcoholic beverages	1,878	0.1
Amusements	X	-
Insurance premiums	24,762	1.5
Motor fuels	114,140	6.9
Pari-mutuels	3,191	0.2
Public utilities	3,999	0.2
Tobacco products	22,683	1.4
Other selective sales	3,069	0.2
Licenses	161,973	9.8
Alcoholic beverages	X	-
Amusements	X	-
Corporations in general	13,949	0.8
Hunting and fishing	34,543	2.1
Motor vehicle	71,657	4.3
Motor vehicle operators	2,318	0.1
Public utilities	X	-
Occupation and business, NEC	39,506	2.4
Other licenses	0	-
Income taxes	X	-
Individual income	X	-
Corporation net income	X	-
Other taxes	450,984	27.3
Death and gift	1	-
Documentary and stock transfer	X	-
Severance	446,410	27.1
Taxes, NEC	4,573	0.3

X = Not applicable.
- = Zero or rounds to zero.

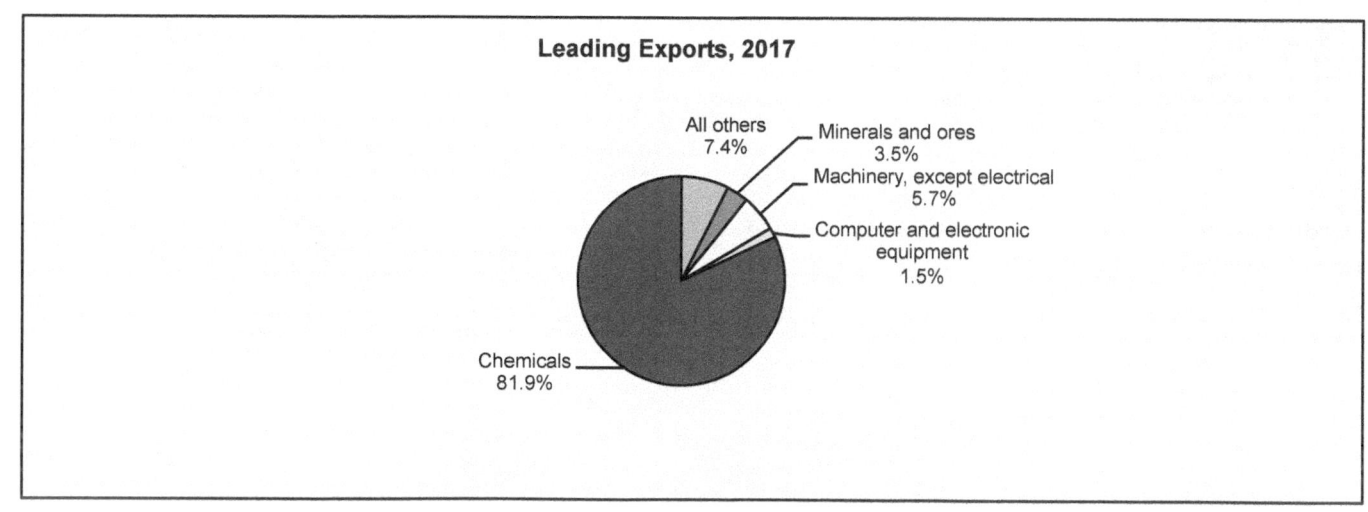

Leading Exports, 2017

All others 7.4%
Minerals and ores 3.5%
Machinery, except electrical 5.7%
Computer and electronic equipment 1.5%
Chemicals 81.9%

NOTES AND DEFINITIONS

The state chapters in this book follow a standard plan of organization, and the same data sources are used for the tables and figures found in each chapter. These notes describe the standard data sources, which are presented by topic in the order in which they appear in each chapter. Definitions, brief descriptions of methodology, and sources of additional information are also provided.

Symbols used are included in the footnotes of the tables.

Table 1.
Source: U.S. Department of Commerce. U.S Census Bureau. 2000 and 2010 Decennial Census. Census statistics, 2017.
<http://factfinder.census.gov/>.

Population estimates data are accessed through American FactFinder from the U.S. Census Bureau, as well as from the Census Bureau itself. The data for average annual percent change, 2010–2017, were calculated by the editor.

Population estimates and the decennial census. Population data are estimates produced by the Census Bureau. The Bureau's Population Estimates Program (PEP) produces estimates of the population as of July 1 for each year following the most recently published decennial census (the actual physical count of the population made every ten years, which is described below). Existing data on births, deaths, and domestic and international immigration are used to update the decennial census basc. PEP cstimates are used to set federal funding allocations, update national surveys, and monitor recent demographic changes.

Noncitizens residing in the United States are included, regardless of their immigration status.

Persons temporarily away from their usual residence on Census Day (April 1), for reasons such as vacation or business trips, were counted as being at their usual residence. People who live at more than one residence during the week, month, or year were counted as being at the place in which they lived most of the year. However, people without a usual residence were counted as being where they were staying on Census Day.

Age, sex, race, and ethnicity. While estimates of the age and sex of the population are straightforward, estimates of race and ethnicity are not. Decennial census data on race and ethnicity are based on self-identification by the respondent, and the same respondent may answer differently on separate occasions. On the 2000 decennial census, respondents could report more than one race; in previous censuses, respondents had to identify themselves as belonging to only one race.

The Census Bureau treats Hispanic or Latino origin as a separate and distinct concept from race. Beginning with the 2000 census, a separate self-identification question was asked regarding Hispanic or Latino origin. Persons of Hispanic or Latino origin are those who classified themselves as belonging to one of the specific categories listed on the questionnaire—Mexican, Puerto Rican, Cuban, or Other Spanish/Hispanic origin (including those whose origins are from Spain, the Spanish-speaking countries of Central and South America, or the Dominican Republic). People who are Hispanic may be of any race, and people in each race group may be Hispanic. The overlap of race and Hispanic origin is a major comparability issue, because Hispanics may be of any race. For a further discussion of this issue, see: U.S. Census Bureau. *U.S. Census Bureau Guidance on the Presentation and Comparison of Race and Hispanic Origin Data.* (June 12, 2003.) <http://www.census.gov/population/www/socdemo/compraceho.html>.

Table 2.
Source: U.S. Department of Commerce. U.S Census Bureau. 2000 Decennial Census. American Community Survey, 2000, 2010, and 2016.
<http://factfinder.census.gov/>.

Data on marital status were tabulated for persons 15 years and over. Marital status was reported for each person as either "now married," "widowed," "divorced," "separated," or "never married." Individuals who were living together (unmarried people, people in commonlaw marriages) reported the marital status they considered most appropriate.

Now Married, Except Separated. Includes people whose current marriage has not ended through widowhood, divorce, or separation (regardless of previous marital history). The category may also include couples who live together or people in common-law marriages if they consider this category the most appropriate. In certain tabulations, currently married people are further classified as "spouse present" or "spouse absent."

Separated. Refers to people who were not living with their spouse due to marital discord.

Divorced. Indicates people who reported being divorced and had not remarried.

Widowed. Refers to people whose last marriage ended with the death of their spouse and who had not remarried.

Never married. The term applies to those who had never been legally married or people whose only marriage ended in an annulment.

Table 3.
Source: U.S. Department of Commerce. U.S Census Bureau. 2000 Decennial Census. American Community Survey, 2000, 2010, and 2016.
<http://factfinder.census.gov/>.

The annual data were obtained from the Census Bureau. The data for average annual percent change, 2010–2016, were calculated by the editor.

Households. A household comprises one or more persons occupying a single housing unit, such as a house, apartment, or a room occupied as separate living quarters. A household may consist of a person living alone, a single family, two or more families living together, or any other group of unrelated individuals sharing a housing unit.

Householder. The person, or one of the people, in whose name the home is owned, being bought, or rented. If there is no such person present, any household member 15 years old and over can serve as the householder for the purposes of the census.

Two types of householders are distinguished: a family householder and a nonfamily householder. A family householder is a householder living with one or more people related to him or her by birth, marriage, or adoption. The householder and all people in the household related to him are family members. A nonfamily householder is a householder living alone or with nonrelatives only.

Housing unit. A house, an apartment, a mobile home or trailer, a group of rooms, or a single room occupied as separate living quarters, or if vacant, intended for occupancy as separate living quarters.

Median gross rent. The monthly amount of contract rent plus the estimated average monthly cost of utilities (electricity, gas, water, and sewer) and fuels (oil, coal, kerosene, wood, etc.).

Median monthly owner costs for housing units with a mortgage. The sum of payments for mortgages, deeds of trust, contracts to purchase, or similar debts on the property (including payments for the first mortgage, second mortgages, home equity loans, and other junior mortgages); real estate taxes; fire, hazard, and flood insurance on the property; utilities (electricity, gas, water, and sewer); and fuels (oil, coal, kerosene, wood, etc.). It also includes, where appropriate, the monthly condominium fee for condominiums and mobile home costs (installment loan payments, personal property taxes, site rent, registration fees, and license fees). Selected monthly owner costs were tabulated for all owner-occupied units, and usually are shown separately for units "with a mortgage" and for units "not mortgaged.

Median value of owner-occupied housing units. Data for the median value of owner-occupied housing units are respondents' estimates of how much their property would sell for if it was currently on the market.

Table 4.
Source: U.S. Department of Commerce. U.S Census Bureau. American Community Survey, 2015 and 2016.
<http://factfinder.census.gov/>.

The annual data derives from Census estimates. The data for percent change were calculated by the editor.

Residence 1 year ago. The data on residence 1 year ago were derived from answers to Question 15, which were asked of the population 1 year and older. For the American Community Survey, people who had moved from another residence in the United States or Puerto Rico 1 year earlier were asked to report the exact address (number and street name); the name of the city, town, or post office; the name of the U.S. county; and the ZIP Code where they lived 1 year ago. People living outside the United States and Puerto Rico were asked to report the name of the foreign country or U.S. Island Area where they were living 1 year ago.

Native born. The native population includes anyone who was a U.S. citizen or a U.S. national at birth. This includes respondents who indicated they were born in the United States, Puerto Rico, a U.S. Island Area (such as Guam), or abroad of an American (U.S. citizen) parent or parents.

Foreign born. The foreign-born population includes anyone who was not a U.S. citizen or a U.S. national at birth. This includes respondents who indicated they were a U.S. citizen by naturalization or not a U.S. citizen.

Respondent's ability to speak English. Respondents who reported speaking a language other than English were asked to indicate their English-speaking ability based on one of the following categories: "Very well," "Well," "Not well," or "Not at all." Those who answered "Well," "Not well," or "Not at all" are sometimes referred as "Less than 'very well.'" Respondents were not instructed on how to interpret the response categories in this question. Households in which no one 14 and over speaks English only or speaks a language other than English at home and speaks English "very well" identifies households that may need English language assistance. This arises when no one 14 and over meets either of two conditions: (1) they speak English at home or (2) even though they speak another language, they also report that they speak English "very well".

Table 5.
Source: U.S. Department of Commerce. U.S Census Bureau. American Community Survey.
<http://factfinder.census.gov/>.

Median household income. Includes the income of the householder and all other individuals 15 years old and over in the household, whether they are related to the householder or not. Because many households consist of only one person, average household income is usually less than average family income. Total income is the sum of the amounts reported separately for wage or salary income; net self-employment income; interest, dividends, or net rental or royalty income or income from estates and trusts; Social Security or railroad retirement income; Supplemental Security Income (SSI); public assistance or welfare payments; retirement, survivor, or disability pensions; and all other income. Receipts from the following sources are not included as income: capital gains, money received from the sale of property (unless the recipient was engaged in the business of selling such property); the value of income "in kind" from food stamps, public housing subsidies, medical care, employer contributions for individuals, etc.; withdrawal of bank deposits; money borrowed; tax refunds; exchange of money between relatives living in the same household; gifts; and lump-sum inheritances, insurance payments, and other types of lump-sum receipts.

Median family income. The incomes of all members 15 years old and over related to the householder are summed and treated as a single amount.

Poverty. Following the Office of Management and Budget standards that have been in use since the late 1960s, the Census Bureau uses a set of money income thresholds that vary by family size and composition to determine the proportion of Americans in poverty. If a household's total income is less than the threshold for the applicable family size, age of householder, and number of children present

in the family under 18 years of age, every individual in that household is considered to be living in poverty.

Table 6.
Source: U.S. Department of Commerce. U.S. Census Bureau. American Community Survey.
<http://factfinder.census.gov/>.

The data on health insurance coverage were derived from answers to Question 16 in the American Community Survey (ACS), which was asked of all respondents. Respondents were instructed to report their current coverage and to mark "yes" or "no" for each of the eight types of private and public insurance listed. Health insurance coverage in the ACS and other Census Bureau surveys define coverage to include plans and programs that provide comprehensive health coverage. Plans that provide insurance for specific conditions or situations such as cancer and long-term care policies are not considered coverage. Likewise, other types of insurance like dental, vision, life, and disability insurance are not considered health insurance coverage.

Private health insurance. Coverage through an employer or union, a plan purchased by an individual from a private company, or TRICARE or other military health care.

Public health insurance. Coverage includes the federal programs Medicare, Medicaid, and VA Health Care (provided through the Department of Veterans Affairs); the Children's Health Insurance Program (CHIP); and individual state health plans.

Table 7.
Source: U.S. Department of Labor. Bureau of Labor Statistics. Current Population Survey.
<http://www.bls.gov/cps/>.

Annual data on the labor force, employment, and unemployment for state and local areas are available from two major sources: the Current Population Survey (CPS) and the Local Area Unemployment Statistics (LAUS) program. In Table 7, the data are obtained from the CPS. The CPS is a monthly survey of approximately 60,000 households conducted by the Census Bureau for the Bureau of Labor Statistics. It provides comprehensive data on topics such as the labor force, employment, unemployment, and persons not in the labor force. The data for 2017 in Table 7 are preliminary, so the data may differ slightly from the final table when it is released, but it should be little changed.

Civilian noninstitutional population included are persons 16 years of age and older residing in the 50 States and the District of Columbia who are not inmates of institutions (for example, penal and mental facilities, homes for the aged), and who are not on active duty in the Armed Forces.

Civilian labor force includes all persons classified as employed or unemployed who are not inmates of institutions (for example, penal and mental facilities, homes for the aged), and who are not on active duty in the Armed Forces. Civilians 16 years of age and over in the noninstitutional population who are not classified as employed or unemployed are defined as not in the labor force.

Employment includes persons 16 years and over in the civilian noninstitutional population who, during the reference week, (a) did any work at all (at least 1 hour) as paid employees; worked in their own business, profession, or on their own farm, or worked 15 hours or more as unpaid workers in an enterprise operated by a member of the family; and (b) all those who were not working but who had jobs or businesses from which they were temporarily absent because of vacation, illness, bad weather, childcare problems, maternity or paternity leave, labor-management dispute, job training, or other family or personal reasons, whether or not they were paid for the time off or were seeking other jobs.

Unemployed persons. All civilians who were not employed (according to the above definition) during the reference week, but who were available for work—except for temporary illness—and who had made specific efforts to find employment sometime during the previous four weeks. Persons who did not look for work because they were on layoff are also counted as unemployed.

Unemployment rate. The number of unemployed as a percentage of the civilian labor force.

Table 8.
Source: U.S. Department of Labor. Bureau of Labor Statistics. Local Area Unemployment Statistics.
<http://www.bls.gov/lau/home.htm>.

The Local Area Unemployment Statistics (LAUS) program is a Federal-State cooperative effort in which monthly estimates of total employment and unemployment are prepared for approximately 7,300 areas.

The concepts and definitions underlying LAUS data come from the Current Population Survey (CPS), the household survey that is the official measure of the labor force for the nation. State monthly model estimates are controlled in "real time" to sum to national monthly labor force estimates from the CPS. These models combine current and historical data from the CPS, the Current Employment Statistics (CES) program, and State unemployment insurance (UI) systems. Estimates for seven large areas and their respective balances of State are also model-based. Estimates for the remainder of the substate labor market areas are produced through a building-block approach known as the "Handbook method." This procedure also uses data from several sources, including the CPS, the CES program, State UI systems, and the decennial census, to create estimates that are adjusted to the statewide measures of employment and unemployment. Below the labor market area level, estimates are prepared using disaggregation techniques based on inputs from the decennial census, annual population estimates, and current UI data.

Table 9.
Source: U.S. Department of Commerce. Bureau of Economic Analysis. <http://www.bea.gov/regional>.

In this table, the data by industry reflect the North American Industry Classification System (NAICS), a supply- or production-based system that replaced the Standard Industrial Classification (SIC) system in January 2003. Estimates of state employment and earnings by industry use NAICS. NAICS was adopted to more fully reflect the current composition of U.S. businesses and to establish a standard measure of industry classification throughout the United States, Canada, and Mexico, in accordance with the North American Free Trade Agreement, to enhance cross-border comparisons among these trading partners.

Wage and salary employment, also referred to as wage and salary jobs, measures the average annual number of full-time and part-time jobs in each area by place-of-work. All jobs for which wages and salaries are paid are counted. Full-time and part-time jobs are counted with equal weight. Jury and witness service, as well as paid employment of prisoners, are not counted as wage and salary employment; the payments for these activities are classified as "other labor income" in the personal income measure. Corporate directorships are counted as self-employment. This concept of employment differs from that in the Current Population Survey (CPS), which is the source of the employment data in the table on population and labor force. The CPS is a household survey. It counts each individual only once, no matter how many jobs the person holds, and it includes only civilian employment.

Wages and salaries consist of the monetary remuneration of employees, including corporate officer salaries and bonuses, commissions, pay-in-kind, incentive payments, and tips. It reflects the amount of payments disbursed, but not necessarily earned during the year. Wage and salary disbursements are measured before deductions, such as social security contributions and union dues. In recent years, stock options have become a point of discussion. Wage and salary disbursements include stock options of nonqualified plans at the time that they have been exercised by the individual. Stock options are reported in wage and salary disbursements. The value that is included in wages is the difference between the exercise price and the price that the stock options were granted. Average annual wages and salaries were calculated by the editor by dividing total wages and salaries paid during the year in each sector by total wage and salary employment in that sector.

Table 10.
Source: U.S. Department of Commerce. U.S. Census Bureau. American Community Survey, 2014, 2015, 2016.
<http://factfinder.census.gov/>.

Civilian labor force. (See definition under Table 7.)

Employment. (See definition under Table 7.)

Family. A family consists of a householder and one or more other people living in the same household who are related to the householder by birth, marriage, or adoption. All people in a household who are related to the householder are regarded as members of his or her family. A family household may contain people not related to the householder, but those people are not included as part of the householder's family in tabulations. Thus, the number of family households is equal to the number of families, but family households may include more members than do families. A household can contain only one family for purposes of tabulations. Not all households contain families since a household may be comprised of a group of unrelated people or of one person living alone – these are called nonfamily households. Families are classified by type as either a "married-couple family" or "other family" according to the sex of the householder and the presence of relatives. The data on family type are based on answers to questions on sex and relationship that were asked of all people.

Married-couple family. A family in which the householder and his or her spouse are listed as members of the same household.

Other family:

Male householder, no wife present. A family with a male householder and no spouse of householder present.

Female householder, no husband present. A family with a female householder and no spouse of householder present.

Table 11.
Source: U.S. Department of Commerce. U.S. Census Bureau. American Community Survey, 2016.
<http://www.census.gov/programs-surveys/acs.html>.

Data on school enrollment and educational attainment were derived from a sample of the population. Persons were classified as enrolled in school if they reported attending a "regular" public or private school (or college) during the year. The instructions were to "include only nursery school, kindergarten, elementary school, and schooling which would lead to a high school diploma or a college degree" as regular school. The Census Bureau defines a public school as "any school or college controlled and supported by a local, county, state, or federal government." Schools primarily supported and controlled by religious organizations or other private groups are defined as private schools.

Data on educational attainment are tabulated for the population 25 years old and over. The data were derived from a question that asked respondents for the highest level of school completed or the highest degree received. Persons who had passed a high school equivalency examination were considered high school graduates. Schooling received in foreign schools was to be reported as the equivalent grade or years in the regular American school system.

Vocational and technical training, such as barber school training; business, trade, technical, and vocational schools; or other training for a specific trade are specifically excluded.

High school graduate or more. This category includes persons whose highest degree was a high school diploma or its equivalent, and those who reported any level higher than a high school diploma.

Bachelor's degree or more. This category includes persons who have received bachelor's degrees, master's degrees, professional school degrees (such as law school or medical school degrees), and doctoral degrees.

Graduate degree or more. This category includes persons who have a master's degree, including the traditional MA and MS degrees and field-specific degrees, such as MSW, MEd, MBA, MLS, and MEng., or a professional school degree: medicine, dentistry, chiropractic, optometry, osteopathic medicine, pharmacy, podiatry, veterinary medicine, law, and theology.

Table 12.
Source: U.S. Department of Education, National Center for Education Statistics. *Common Core of Data.*
<http://nces.ed.gov/ccd/>.

The data are from the Common Core of Data (CCD), which is made up of a set of five surveys sent to state education departments. Most of the data are obtained from administrative records maintained by the state education agencies (SEAs). Statistical information is collected annually from approximately 100,000 public elementary and secondary schools and approximately 18,000 public school districts (including supervisory unions and regional education service agencies) in the 50 states, the District of Columbia, Department of Defense Schools, and the outlying areas. The SEAs compile CCD requested data into prescribed formats and transmit the information to NCES.

A **school district** or Local Education Agency (LEA) is the agency at the local level whose primary responsibility is to operate public schools or to contract for public school services.

The primary grades include pre-kindergarten through grade 4. Middle school grades included grades 5 through 8. High school grades include grades 9 through 12. Ungraded students are included in the total but are not separately listed. Some states have no ungraded students.

The **student-teacher ratio** is calculated by dividing the number of students in all schools by the number of full-time equivalent teachers employed by all schools and agencies.

Current expenditures per student are derived by dividing total current expenditures by the fall student membership count from the CCD. Current expenditures are comprised of expenditures for the day-to-day operation of schools and school districts for public elementary and secondary education, including expenditures for staff salaries and benefits, supplies, and purchased services. They exclude expenditures for construction, equipment, property, debt services, and programs outside of public elementary and secondary education, such as adult education and community services. Student membership consists of the count of students enrolled on or about October 1 and is comparable across all states. Data are for FY 2013; please see the NCES Web site for the exact beginning and ending dates of fiscal years for each state.

The 4-year adjusted cohort graduation rate (ACGR) is the number of students who graduate in 4 years with a regular high school diploma divided by the number of students who form the adjusted cohort for the graduating class. From the beginning of 9th grade (or the earliest high school grade), students who are entering that grade for the first time form a cohort that is "adjusted" by adding any students who subsequently transfer into the cohort and subtracting any students who subsequently transfer out, emigrate to another country, or die.

Students are eligible for **free and reduced-price lunch** under the National School Lunch Program, which was established by President Truman in 1946. The program is a federally assisted meal program operated in public and private nonprofit schools and residential child care centers and provides cash subsidies for free or reduced-price meals to students based on family size and income criteria. Participation in the National School Lunch Program depends on income, and eligibility is often used to estimate student needs.

An **English language learner** is an individual who, due to any of the reasons listed below, has enough difficulty speaking, reading, writing, or understanding the English language that it affects their ability to learn in an English-speaking classroom. Such an individual (1) was not born in the United States or has a native language other than English; (2) comes from environments where a language other than English is dominant; or (3) is an American Indian or Alaska Native and comes from environments where a language other than English has had a significant impact on the individual's level of English language proficiency.

Individuals with Disabilities Education Act (IDEA) is a federal law requiring services to children with disabilities throughout the nation. IDEA governs how states and public agencies provide early intervention, special education, and related services to eligible infants, toddlers, children, and youth with disabilities. Infants and toddlers with disabilities (birth–age 2) and their families receive early intervention services under IDEA, Part C. Children and youth (ages 3–21) receive special education and related services under IDEA, Part B.

Public School Types

A **regular school** provides instruction and education services that does not focus primarily on special education, vocational/technical education, or alternative education, or on any of the particular themes associated with magnet/special program emphasis schools.

A **special education school** focuses primarily on special education—including instruction for students with any of the following conditions: autism, deaf-blindness, developmental delay, hearing impairment, mental retardation, multiple disabilities, orthopedic impairment, serious emotional disturbance, specific learning disability, speech or language impairment, traumatic brain injury, visual impairment, and other health impairments—and that adapts curriculum, materials, or instruction for students served.

A **vocational education school** focuses primarily on providing formal preparation for semiskilled, skilled, technical, or professional occupations for high school-age students who have opted to develop or expand their employment opportunities, often in lieu of preparing for college entry.

An **alternative education school** is an elementary/secondary school that (1) addresses needs of students that typically cannot be met in a regular school, (2) provides nontraditional education, (3) serves as an adjunct to a regular school, or (4) falls outside the categories of regular, special education, or vocational education.

Table 13.
Source: U.S. Department of Commerce. U.S. Census Bureau. November Supplement to the Current Population Survey (CPS). *Voting and Registration in the Election of November 2016.*
<https://www.census.gov/topics/public-sector/voting/data/tables.html >

Voter participation data are obtained from additional questions regarding voting and voter registration, which are added to the Current Population Survey each November. Because these data are from a sample of the noninstitutional population, they differ from the "official" tally of voter participation reported by the Clerk of the U.S. House of Representatives.

Voting, people eligible to register. The population of voting age includes a considerable number of people who meet the age requirement but cannot register and vote. People who are not citizens are not eligible to vote. Among citizens of voting age, some people are not permitted to vote because they have been committed to penal institutions, mental hospitals, or other institutions, or because they fail to meet state and local resident requirements for various reasons. The eligibility to register is governed by state laws, which differ in many respects.

Registration is the act of qualifying to vote by formally enrolling on a list of voters. People who have moved to another election district must take steps to have their names placed on the voting rolls in their new place of residence.

In a few states or parts of states, no formal registration is required. Voters merely present themselves at the polling place on Election Day with proof that they are of age and have met the appropriate residence requirements. Therefore, in these areas people who are citizens and of voting age, and who meet the residence requirement, would be considered as being registered.

Voter, reported participation. Voter participation data are derived from replies to the following question asked of people (excluding noncitizens) of voting age: "In any election some people are not able to vote because they are sick or busy, or have some other reason, and others do not want to vote. Did (this person) vote in the election held on November (date varies)?"

Those of voting age were classified as "voted" or "did not vote." In most tables, this "did not vote" class includes those reported as "did not vote," "do not know," noncitizens, and nonrespondents. Nonrespondents and people who reported that they did not know if they voted were included in the "did not vote" class because of the general over-reporting by respondents in the sample.

Voter, reported registration. The data on registration were obtained by tabulating replies to the following question for those people included in the category "did not vote." "Was (this person) registered to vote in the November (date varies) election?"

All people reported as having voted were assumed to have been registered. Therefore, the total registered population is obtained by combining the number of people who voted and people included in the category "did not vote," but who had registered.

Table 14.
Source: U.S. Department of Justice. Federal Bureau of Investigation. Uniform Crime Reports. *Crime in the United States, 2016.*
<https://ucr.fbi.gov/crime-in-the-u.s/2016/crime-in-the-u.s.-2016 >

The Uniform Crime Reports (UCR) Program, administered by the Federal Bureau of Investigation (FBI), was created in 1929 and collects information on the following crimes reported to law enforcement authorities: murder and nonnegligent manslaughter, rape, robbery, aggravated assault, burglary, larceny-theft, motor vehicle theft, and arson. Law enforcement agencies also report arrest data for 21 additional crime categories.

The UCR Program compiles data from monthly law enforcement reports and from individual crime incident records transmitted directly to the FBI or to centralized state agencies that report to the FBI. The program thoroughly examines each report it receives for reasonableness, accuracy, and deviations that may indicate errors. Large variations in crime levels may indicate modified records procedures, incomplete reporting, or changes in a jurisdiction's boundaries. To identify any unusual fluctuations in an agency's crime counts, the program compares monthly reports to previous submissions of the agency and to those for similar agencies.

The FBI annually publishes its findings in a preliminary release in the spring of the following calendar year, followed by a detailed annual report, *Crime in the United States*, issued in the fall. (The printed copy of *Crime in the United States* is published by Bernan Press.) In addition to crime counts and trends, this report includes data on crimes cleared, persons arrested (age, sex, and race), law enforcement personnel (including the number of sworn officers killed or assaulted), and the characteristics of homicides (including age, sex, and race of victims and offenders; victim-offender relationships; weapons used; and circumstances surrounding the homicides). Other periodic reports are also available from the UCR Program. Any deviations from UCR standard data are noted in the table.

Note for Users

Since crime is a sociological phenomenon influenced by a variety of factors, the FBI discourages data users from ranking agencies and using the data as a measurement of the effectiveness of law enforcement. Until data users examine all the variables that affect crime in a town, city, county, state, region, or college or university, they can make no meaningful comparisons.

Violent crime is composed of four offenses: murder and nonnegligent manslaughter, rape, robbery, and aggravated assault. According to the UCR Program's definition, violent crimes involve force or threat of force.

Murder and nonnegligent manslaughter is the willful (nonnegligent) killing of one human being by another. Deaths caused by negligence, attempts to kill, assaults to kill, suicides, and accidental deaths are excluded. The program classifies justifiable homicides separately and limits the definition to (1) the killing of a felon by a law enforcement officer in the line of duty; or (2) the killing of a felon, during the commission of a felony, by a private citizen.

Rape is defined as: penetration, no matter how slight, of the vagina or anus with any body part or object, or oral penetration by a sex organ of another person, without the consent of the victim. The FBI UCR Program's definition of rape, formerly "forcible rape," was revised in 2013. Attempts or assaults to commit rape are also included; however, statutory rape (no force used—victim is under the age of consent) and incest are excluded. Due to the revised definition, figures for rape in 2013 and later are not comparable to data from previous years.

Robbery is the taking or attempted taking of anything of value from the care, custody, or control of a person or persons by force or threat of force or violence and/or by putting the victim in fear.

Aggravated assault is an unlawful attack by one person upon another for the purpose of inflicting severe or aggravated bodily injury. This type of assault usually is accompanied by the use of a weapon or by means likely to produce death or great bodily harm. Attempted aggravated assaults that involve the display of—or threat to use—a gun, knife, or other weapon is included in this crime category because serious personal injury would likely result if the assault were completed. When aggravated assault and larceny-theft occur together, the offense falls under the category of robbery. Simple assaults are excluded.

Property crime includes the offenses of burglary, larceny-theft, motor vehicle theft, and arson. The object of the theft-type offenses is the taking of money or property, but there is no force or threat of force against the victims. The property crime category includes arson because the offense involves the destruction of property; however, arson victims may be subjected to force.

Burglary (breaking or entering) is the unlawful entry of a structure to commit a felony or a theft. The use of force to gain entry need not have occurred. The Program has three subclassifications for burglary: forcible entry, unlawful entry where no force is used, and attempted forcible entry. The UCR definition of "structure" includes, for example, apartment, barn, house trailer or houseboat when used as a permanent dwelling, office, railroad car (but not automobile), stable, and vessel (i.e., ship).

Larceny-theft (except motor vehicle theft) is the unlawful taking, carrying, leading, or riding away of property from the possession or constructive possession of another. Examples are thefts of bicycles or automobile accessories, shoplifting, pocket-picking, or the stealing of any property or article that is not taken by force and violence or by fraud. Attempted larcenies are included. Embezzlement, confidence games, forgery, worthless checks, and the like, are excluded.

Motor vehicle theft is the theft or attempted theft of a motor vehicle. It includes the stealing of automobiles, trucks, buses, motorcycles, snowmobiles, and the like. The taking of a motor vehicle for temporary use by persons having lawful access is excluded from this definition. A motor vehicle is self-propelled and runs on land surface and not on rails. Motorboats, construction equipment, airplanes, and farming equipment are specifically excluded from this category.

Table 15.
Source: U.S. Department of Commerce. U.S Census Bureau.
<http://www.census.gov/govs/index.html>.

The Census Bureau conducts an annual survey covering a range of government finance activities carried out by all state and local governments in the United States, including revenue, expenditures, debt, and assets. The data in this volume relate to state revenues and expenditures only, with the exception of the District of Columbia, for which local government data was used. Data generally reference state government fiscal year 2016, but data for the District of Columbia is for fiscal year 2015. General revenue comprises all revenue except utilities, liquor store, and insurance trust revenue. Intergovernmental revenue is funds from other governments (mainly the federal government), including general support, grants, shared taxes, and loans or advances. Other data on government finance by state, not shown in this volume, include federal government expenditures, obligations, contract awards, and insurance programs.

Table 16.
Source: U.S. Department of Commerce. U.S. Census Bureau.
<http://www.census.gov/govs/statetax/>.

State tax data include all required taxes taken by government for public purposes, except for employer and employee assessments for Social Security and unemployment compensation. The data are shown in this volume are for each state's and the District of Columbia's fiscal year 2017.

INDEX

A

AGE, POPULATION BY
Alabama, 16
Alaska, 26
Arizona, 36
Arkansas, 46
California, 56
Colorado, 66
Connecticut, 76
Delaware, 86
District of Columbia, 96
Florida, 106
Georgia, 116
Hawaii, 126
Idaho, 136
Illinois, 146
Indiana, 156
Iowa, 166
Kansas, 176
Kentucky, 186
Louisiana, 196
Maine, 206
Maryland, 216
Massachusetts, 226
Michigan, 236
Minnesota, 246
Mississippi, 256
Missouri, 266
Montana, 276
Nebraska, 286
Nevada, 296
New Hampshire, 306
New Jersey, 316
New Mexico, 326
New York, 336
North Carolina, 346
North Dakota, 356
Ohio, 366
Oklahoma, 376
Oregon, 386
Pennsylvania, 396
Rankings by state
    percent 65 years and over, 4
    percent under 18 years old, 3
    poverty levels, 11, 12
Rhode Island, 406
South Carolina, 416
South Dakota, 426
Tennessee, 436
Texas, 446
Utah, 456
Vermont, 466
Virginia, 476
Washington, 486
West Virginia, 496

Wisconsin, 506
Wyoming, 516
ALABAMA
Age, population by, 16
Crime, 22
Education and school enrollment, 21
Employment status and characteristics, 19–21
Exports of goods, 24
Facts and figures, 15
Health insurance coverage, 18
Hispanic or Latino origin, population by, 16
Households and housing characteristics, 17
Income, 18
Marital status, 16
Migration, origin, and language, 17
Poverty status, 18
Race, population by, 16
Rankings by state, 3
Sex, population by, 16
State government finances, 23
State government tax collections, 24
Unemployment rate, 19
Voting and registration, 22
Wages by industry, 20
ALASKA
Age, population by, 26
Crime, 32
Education and school enrollment, 31
Employment status and characteristics, 29–31
Exports of goods, 34
Facts and figures, 25
Health insurance coverage, 28
Hispanic or Latino origin, population by, 26
Households and housing characteristics, 27
Income, 28
Marital status, 26
Migration, origin, and language, 27
Poverty status, 28
Race, population by, 26
Rankings by state, 3
Sex, population by, 26
State government finances, 33
State government tax collections, 34
Unemployment rate, 29
Voting and registration, 32
Wages by industry, 30
ALASKAN NATIVES
    see **RACE, POPULATION BY**
AMERICAN INDIANS
    see **RACE, POPULATION BY**
ARIZONA
Age, population by, 36
Crime, 42
Education and school enrollment, 41
Employment status and characteristics, 39–41

Exports of goods, 44
Facts and figures, 35
Health insurance coverage, 38
Hispanic or Latino origin, population by, 36
Households and housing characteristics, 37
Income, 38
Marital status, 36
Migration, origin, and language, 37
Poverty status, 38
Race, population by, 36
Rankings by state, 3
Sex, population by, 36
State government finances, 43
State government tax collections, 44
Unemployment rate, 39
Voting and registration, 42
Wages by industry, 40

ARKANSAS
Age, population by, 46
Crime, 52
Education and school enrollment, 51
Employment status and characteristics, 49–51
Exports of goods, 54
Facts and figures, 45
Health insurance coverage, 48
Hispanic or Latino origin, population by, 46
Households and housing characteristics, 47
Income, 48
Marital status, 46
Migration, origin, and language, 47
Poverty status, 48
Race, population by, 46
Rankings by state, 3
Sex, population by, 46
State government finances, 53
State government tax collections, 54
Unemployment rate, 49
Voting and registration, 52
Wages by industry, 50

ASIANS
see **RACE, POPULATION BY**

B
BIRTH RATES
Rankings by state, 7
BLACK RACE
see **RACE, POPULATION BY**

C
CALIFORNIA
Age, population by, 56
Crime, 62
Education and school enrollment, 61
Employment status and characteristics, 59–61
Exports of goods, 64
Facts and figures, 55
Health insurance coverage, 58
Hispanic or Latino origin, population by, 56
Households and housing characteristics, 57
Income, 58

Marital status, 56
Migration, origin, and language, 57
Poverty status, 58
Race, population by, 56
Rankings by state, 3
Sex, population by, 56
State government finances, 63
State government tax collections, 64
Unemployment rate, 59
Voting and registration, 62
Wages by industry, 60

COLLECTIONS
see **STATE GOVERNMENT TAX COLLECTIONS**
COLLEGE GRADUATES
Education and school enrollment
see **EDUCATION AND SCHOOL ENROLLMENT**
Rankings by state, 8
COLORADO
Age, population by, 66
Crime, 72
Education and school enrollment, 71
Employment status and characteristics, 69–71
Exports of goods, 74
Facts and figures, 65
Health insurance coverage, 68
Hispanic or Latino origin, population by, 66
Households and housing characteristics, 67
Income, 68
Marital status, 66
Migration, origin, and language, 67
Poverty status, 68
Race, population by, 66
Rankings by state, 3
Sex, population by, 66
State government finances, 73
State government tax collections, 74
Unemployment rate, 69
Voting and registration, 72
Wages by industry, 70

CONNECTICUT
Age, population by, 76
Crime, 82
Education and school enrollment, 81
Employment status and characteristics, 79–81
Exports of goods, 84
Facts and figures, 75
Health insurance coverage, 78
Hispanic or Latino origin, population by, 76
Households and housing characteristics, 77
Income, 78
Marital status, 76
Migration, origin, and language, 77
Poverty status, 78
Race, population by, 76
Rankings by state, 3
Sex, population by, 76
State government finances, 83
State government tax collections, 84
Unemployment rate, 79

Voting and registration, 82
Wages by industry, 80

CRIME
Alabama, 22
Alaska, 32
Arizona, 42
Arkansas, 52
California, 62
Colorado, 72
Connecticut, 82
Delaware, 92
District of Columbia, 102
Florida, 112
Georgia, 122
Hawaii, 132
Idaho, 142
Illinois, 152
Indiana, 162
Iowa, 172
Kansas, 182
Kentucky, 192
Louisiana, 202
Maine, 212
Maryland, 222
Massachusetts, 232
Michigan, 242
Minnesota, 252
Mississippi, 262
Missouri, 272
Montana, 282
Nebraska, 292
Nevada, 302
New Hampshire, 312
New Jersey, 322
New Mexico, 332
New York, 342
North Carolina, 352
North Dakota, 362
Ohio, 372
Oklahoma, 382
Oregon, 392
Pennsylvania, 402
Rankings by state, 8
Rhode Island, 412
South Carolina, 422
South Dakota, 432
Tennessee, 442
Texas, 452
Utah, 462
Vermont, 472
Virginia, 482
Washington, 492
West Virginia, 502
Wisconsin, 512
Wyoming, 522

D
DELAWARE
Age, population by, 86
Crime, 92

Education and school enrollment, 91
Employment status and characteristics, 89–91
Exports of goods, 94
Facts and figures, 85
Health insurance coverage, 88
Hispanic or Latino origin, population by, 86
Households and housing characteristics, 87
Income, 88
Marital status, 86
Migration, origin, and language, 87
Poverty status, 88
Race, population by, 86
Rankings by state, 3
Sex, population by, 86
State government finances, 93
State government tax collections, 94
Unemployment rate, 89
Voting and registration, 92
Wages by industry, 90

DISTRICT OF COLUMBIA
Age, population by, 96
Crime, 102
Education and school enrollment, 101
Employment status and characteristics, 99–101
Exports of goods, 104
Facts and figures, 95
Health insurance coverage, 98
Hispanic or Latino origin, population by, 96
Households and housing characteristics, 97
Income, 98
Local government finances, 103
Marital status, 96
Migration, origin, and language, 97
Poverty status, 98
Race, population by, 96
Rankings by state, 3
Sex, population by, 96
Unemployment rate, 99
Voting and registration, 102
Wages by industry, 100

DRUG OVERDOSE DEATHS
Rankings by state, 7

E
EDUCATION AND SCHOOL ENROLLMENT
Alabama, 21
Alaska, 31
Arizona, 41
Arkansas, 51
California, 61
Colorado, 71
Connecticut, 81
Delaware, 91
District of Columbia, 101
Florida, 111
Georgia, 121
Hawaii, 131
Idaho, 141
Illinois, 151
Indiana, 161

Iowa, 171
Kansas, 181
Kentucky, 191
Louisiana, 201
Maine, 211
Maryland, 221
Massachusetts, 231
Michigan, 241
Minnesota, 251
Mississippi, 261
Missouri, 271
Montana, 281
Nebraska, 291
Nevada, 301
New Hampshire, 311
New Jersey, 321
New Mexico, 331
New York, 341
North Carolina, 351
North Dakota, 361
Ohio, 371
Oklahoma, 381
Oregon, 391
Pennsylvania, 401
Rankings by state
    college graduates, 8
Rhode Island, 411
South Carolina, 421
South Dakota, 431
Tennessee, 441
Texas, 451
Utah, 461
Vermont, 471
Virginia, 481
Washington, 491
West Virginia, 501
Wisconsin, 511
Wyoming, 521

EMPLOYMENT STATUS AND CHARACTERISTICS
Alabama, 19–21
Alaska, 29–31
Arizona, 39–41
Arkansas, 49–51
California, 59–61
Colorado, 69–71
Connecticut, 79–81
Delaware, 89–91
District of Columbia, 99–101
Florida, 109–111
Georgia, 119–121
Hawaii, 129–131
Idaho, 139–141
Illinois, 149–151
Indiana, 159–161
Iowa, 169–171
Kansas, 179–181
Kentucky, 189–191
Louisiana, 199–201
Maine, 209–211

Maryland, 219–221
Massachusetts, 229–231
Michigan, 239–241
Minnesota, 249–251
Mississippi, 259–261
Missouri, 269–271
Montana, 279–281
Nebraska, 289–291
Nevada, 299–301
New Hampshire, 309–311
New Jersey, 319–321
New Mexico, 329–331
New York, 339–341
North Carolina, 349–351
North Dakota, 359–361
Ohio, 369–371
Oklahoma, 379–381
Oregon, 389–391
Pennsylvania, 399–401
Rhode Island, 409–411
South Carolina, 419–421
South Dakota, 429–431
State rankings, nonfarm payrolls, 9
Tennessee, 439–441
Texas, 449–451
Utah, 459–461
Vermont, 469–471
Virginia, 479–481
Washington, 489–491
West Virginia, 499–501
Wisconsin, 509–511
Wyoming, 519–521

ENERGY CONSUMPTION
Rankings by state, 12

EXPORTS OF GOODS
Alabama, 24
Alaska, 34
Arizona, 44
Arkansas, 54
California, 64
Colorado, 74
Connecticut, 84
Delaware, 94
District of Columbia, 104
Florida, 114
Georgia, 124
Hawaii, 134
Idaho, 144
Illinois, 154
Indiana, 164
Iowa, 174
Kansas, 184
Kentucky, 194
Louisiana, 204
Maine, 214
Maryland, 224
Massachusetts, 234
Michigan, 244
Minnesota, 254

Mississippi, 264
Missouri, 274
Montana, 284
Nebraska, 294
Nevada, 304
New Hampshire, 314
New Jersey, 324
New Mexico, 334
New York, 344
North Carolina, 354
North Dakota, 364
Ohio, 374
Oklahoma, 384
Oregon, 394
Pennsylvania, 404
Rhode Island, 414
South Carolina, 424
South Dakota, 434
Tennessee, 444
Texas, 454
Utah, 464
Vermont, 474
Virginia, 484
Washington, 494
West Virginia, 504
Wisconsin, 514
Wyoming, 524

F
FACTS AND FIGURES
        see **INDIVIDUAL STATES**
FINANCES
        see **STATE GOVERNMENT FINANCES**
FLORIDA
Age, population by, 106
Crime, 112
Education and school enrollment, 111
Employment status and characteristics, 109–111
Exports of goods, 114
Facts and figures, 105
Health insurance coverage, 108
Hispanic or Latino origin, population by, 106
Households and housing characteristics, 107
Income, 108
Marital status, 106
Migration, origin, and language, 107
Poverty status, 108
Race, population by, 106
Rankings by state, 3
Sex, population by, 106
State government finances, 113
State government tax collections, 114
Unemployment rate, 109
Voting and registration, 112
Wages by industry, 110

G
GEORGIA
Age, population by, 116
Crime, 122
Education and school enrollment, 121
Employment status and characteristics, 119–121
Exports of goods, 124
Facts and figures, 115
Health insurance coverage, 118
Hispanic or Latino origin, population by, 116
Households and housing characteristics, 117
Income, 118
Marital status, 116
Migration, origin, and language, 117
Poverty status, 118
Race, population by, 116
Rankings by state, 3
Sex, population by, 116
State government finances, 123
State government tax collections, 124
Unemployment rate, 119
Voting and registration, 122
Wages by industry, 120
GOVERNMENT FINANCES
        see **STATE GOVERNMENT FINANCES**
GROSS DOMESTIC PRODUCT
State rankings, 10

H
HAWAII
Age, population by, 126
Crime, 132
Education and school enrollment, 131
Employment status and characteristics, 129–131
Exports of goods, 134
Facts and figures, 125
Health insurance coverage, 128
Hispanic or Latino origin, population by, 126
Households and housing characteristics, 127
Income, 128
Marital status, 126
Migration, origin, and language, 127
Poverty status, 128
Race, population by, 126
Rankings by state, 3
Sex, population by, 126
State government finances, 133
State government tax collections, 134
Unemployment rate, 129
Voting and registration, 132
Wages by industry, 130
HAWAIIAN NATIVES
        see **RACE, POPULATION BY**
HEALTH INSURANCE COVERAGE
Alabama, 18
Alaska, 28
Arizona, 38
Arkansas, 48
California, 58
Colorado, 68
Connecticut, 78
Delaware, 88
District of Columbia, 98
Florida, 108

Georgia, 118
Hawaii, 128
Idaho, 138
Illinois, 148
Indiana, 158
Iowa, 168
Kansas, 178
Kentucky, 188
Louisiana, 198
Maine, 208
Maryland, 218
Massachusetts, 228
Michigan, 238
Minnesota, 248
Mississippi, 258
Missouri, 268
Montana, 278
Nebraska, 288
Nevada, 298
New Hampshire, 308
New Jersey, 318
New Mexico, 328
New York, 338
North Carolina, 348
North Dakota, 358
Ohio, 368
Oklahoma, 378
Oregon, 388
Pennsylvania, 398
Rankings by state
    percent of population not covered by insurance, 13
Rhode Island, 408
South Carolina, 418
South Dakota, 428
Tennessee, 438
Texas, 448
Utah, 458
Vermont, 468
Virginia, 478
Washington, 488
West Virginia, 498
Wisconsin, 508
Wyoming, 518

HIGH SCHOOL GRADUATES
Education and school enrollment
    see **EDUCATION AND SCHOOL ENROLLMENT**
HISPANIC OR LATINO ORIGIN, POPULATION BY
Alabama, 16
Alaska, 26
Arizona, 36
Arkansas, 46
California, 56
Colorado, 66
Connecticut, 76
Delaware, 86
District of Columbia, 96
Florida, 106
Georgia, 116
Hawaii, 126

Idaho, 136
Illinois, 146
Indiana, 156
Iowa, 166
Kansas, 176
Kentucky, 186
Louisiana, 196
Maine, 206
Maryland, 216
Massachusetts, 226
Michigan, 236
Minnesota, 246
Mississippi, 256
Missouri, 266
Montana, 276
Nebraska, 286
Nevada, 296
New Hampshire, 306
New Jersey, 316
New Mexico, 326
New York, 336
North Carolina, 346
North Dakota, 356
Ohio, 366
Oklahoma, 376
Oregon, 386
Pennsylvania, 396
Rankings by state
    percent Hispanic or Latino, 6
Rhode Island, 406
South Carolina, 416
South Dakota, 426
Tennessee, 436
Texas, 446
Utah, 456
Vermont, 466
Virginia, 476
Washington, 486
West Virginia, 496
Wisconsin, 506
Wyoming, 516
HOMEOWNERSHIP RATES
State rankings, 12
HOUSEHOLDS AND HOUSING CHARACTERISTICS
Alabama, 17
Alaska, 27
Arizona, 37
Arkansas, 47
California, 57
Colorado, 67
Connecticut, 77
Delaware, 87
District of Columbia, 97
Florida, 107
Georgia, 117
Hawaii, 127
Idaho, 137
Illinois, 147
Indiana, 157

Iowa, 167
Kansas, 177
Kentucky, 187
Louisiana, 197
Maine, 207
Maryland, 217
Massachusetts, 227
Michigan, 237
Minnesota, 247
Mississippi, 257
Missouri, 267
Montana, 277
Nebraska, 287
Nevada, 297
New Hampshire, 307
New Jersey, 317
New Mexico, 327
New York, 337
North Carolina, 347
North Dakota, 357
Ohio, 367
Oklahoma, 377
Oregon, 387
Pennsylvania, 397
Rhode Island, 407
South Carolina, 417
South Dakota, 427
State rankings, 13
Tennessee, 437
Texas, 447
Utah, 457
Vermont, 467
Virginia, 477
Washington, 487
West Virginia, 497
Wisconsin, 507
Wyoming, 517

I
IDAHO
Age, population by, 136
Crime, 142
Education and school enrollment, 141
Employment status and characteristics, 139–141
Exports of goods, 144
Facts and figures, 135
Health insurance coverage, 138
Hispanic or Latino origin, population by, 136
Households and housing characteristics, 137
Income, 138
Marital status, 136
Migration, origin, and language, 137
Poverty status, 138
Race, population by, 136
Rankings by state, 3
Sex, population by, 136
State government finances, 143
State government tax collections, 144
Unemployment rate, 139

Voting and registration, 142
Wages by industry, 140
ILLINOIS
Age, population by, 146
Crime, 152
Education and school enrollment, 151
Employment status and characteristics, 149–151
Exports of goods, 154
Facts and figures, 145
Health insurance coverage, 148
Hispanic or Latino origin, population by, 146
Households and housing characteristics, 147
Income, 148
Marital status, 146
Migration, origin, and language, 147
Poverty status, 148
Race, population by, 146
Rankings by state, 3
Sex, population by, 146
State government finances, 153
State government tax collections, 154
Unemployment rate, 149
Voting and registration, 152
Wages by industry, 150
INCOME
Alabama, 18
Alaska, 28
Arizona, 38
Arkansas, 48
California, 58
Colorado, 68
Connecticut, 78
Delaware, 88
District of Columbia, 98
Florida, 108
Georgia, 118
Hawaii, 128
Idaho, 138
Illinois, 148
Indiana, 158
Iowa, 168
Kansas, 178
Kentucky, 188
Louisiana, 198
Maine, 208
Maryland, 218
Massachusetts, 228
Michigan, 238
Minnesota, 248
Mississippi, 258
Missouri, 268
Montana, 278
Nebraska, 288
Nevada, 298
New Hampshire, 308
New Jersey, 318
New Mexico, 328
New York, 338
North Carolina, 348

North Dakota, 358
Ohio, 368
Oklahoma, 378
Oregon, 388
Pennsylvania, 398
Rankings by state
    median family income, 11
    median household income, 11
    per capita personal income, 10
    poverty levels, 11, 12
Rhode Island, 408
South Carolina, 418
South Dakota, 428
Tennessee, 438
Texas, 448
Utah, 458
Vermont, 468
Virginia, 478
Wages by industry
    see **WAGES BY INDUSTRY**
Washington, 488
West Virginia, 498
Wisconsin, 508
Wyoming, 518

INDIANA
Age, population by, 156
Crime, 162
Education and school enrollment, 161
Employment status and characteristics, 159–161
Exports of goods, 164
Facts and figures, 155
Health insurance coverage, 158
Hispanic or Latino origin, population by, 156
Households and housing characteristics, 157
Income, 158
Marital status, 156
Migration, origin, and language, 157
Poverty status, 158
Race, population by, 156
Rankings by state, 3
Sex, population by, 156
State government finances, 163
State government tax collections, 164
Unemployment rate, 159
Voting and registration, 162
Wages by industry, 160

INSURANCE
Health insurance coverage
    see **HEALTH INSURANCE COVERAGE**

IOWA
Age, population by, 166
Crime, 172
Education and school enrollment, 171
Employment status and characteristics, 169–171
Exports of goods, 174
Facts and figures, 165
Health insurance coverage, 168
Hispanic or Latino origin, population by, 166
Households and housing characteristics, 167

Income, 168
Marital status, 166
Migration, origin, and language, 167
Poverty status, 168
Race, population by, 166
Rankings by state, 3
Sex, population by, 166
State government finances, 173
State government tax collections, 174
Unemployment rate, 169
Voting and registration, 172
Wages by industry, 170

K
KANSAS
Age, population by, 176
Crime, 182
Education and school enrollment, 181
Employment status and characteristics, 179–181
Exports of goods, 184
Facts and figures, 175
Health insurance coverage, 178
Hispanic or Latino origin, population by, 176
Households and housing characteristics, 177
Income, 178
Marital status, 176
Migration, origin, and language, 177
Poverty status, 178
Race, population by, 176
Rankings by state, 3
Sex, population by, 176
State government finances, 183
State government tax collections, 184
Unemployment rate, 179
Voting and registration, 182
Wages by industry, 180

KENTUCKY
Age, population by, 186
Crime, 192
Education and school enrollment, 191
Employment status and characteristics, 189–191
Exports of goods, 194
Facts and figures, 185
Health insurance coverage, 188
Hispanic or Latino origin, population by, 186
Households and housing characteristics, 187
Income, 188
Marital status, 186
Migration, origin, and language, 187
Poverty status, 188
Race, population by, 186
Rankings by state, 3
Sex, population by, 186
State government finances, 193
State government tax collections, 194
Unemployment rate, 189
Voting and registration, 192
Wages by industry, 190

L
LANGUAGE
    see **MIGRATION, ORIGIN, AND LANGUAGE**
LATINO ORIGIN
    see **HISPANIC OR LATINO ORIGIN,**
        POPULATION BY
LOUISIANA
    Age, population by, 196
    Crime, 202
    Education and school enrollment, 201
    Employment status and characteristics, 199–201
    Exports of goods, 204
    Facts and figures, 195
    Health insurance coverage, 198
    Hispanic or Latino origin, population by, 196
    Households and housing characteristics, 197
    Income, 198
    Marital status, 196
    Migration, origin, and language, 197
    Poverty status, 198
    Race, population by, 196
    Rankings by state, 3
    Sex, population by, 196
    State government finances, 203
    State government tax collections, 204
    Unemployment rate, 199
    Voting and registration, 202
    Wages by industry, 200

M
MAINE
    Age, population by, 206
    Crime, 212
    Education and school enrollment, 211
    Employment status and characteristics, 209–211
    Exports of goods, 214
    Facts and figures, 205
    Health insurance coverage, 208
    Hispanic or Latino origin, population by, 206
    Households and housing characteristics, 207
    Income, 208
    Marital status, 206
    Migration, origin, and language, 207
    Poverty status, 208
    Race, population by, 206
    Rankings by state, 3
    Sex, population by, 206
    State government finances, 213
    State government tax collections, 214
    Unemployment rate, 209
    Voting and registration, 212
    Wages by industry, 210
MARITAL STATUS
    Alabama, 16
    Alaska, 26
    Arizona, 36
    Arkansas, 46
    California, 56
    Colorado, 66

    Connecticut, 76
    Delaware, 86
    District of Columbia, 96
    Florida, 106
    Georgia, 116
    Hawaii, 126
    Idaho, 136
    Illinois, 146
    Indiana, 156
    Iowa, 166
    Kansas, 176
    Kentucky, 186
    Louisiana, 196
    Maine, 206
    Maryland, 216
    Massachusetts, 226
    Michigan, 236
    Minnesota, 246
    Mississippi, 256
    Missouri, 266
    Montana, 276
    Nebraska, 286
    Nevada, 296
    New Hampshire, 306
    New Jersey, 316
    New Mexico, 326
    New York, 336
    North Carolina, 346
    North Dakota, 356
    Ohio, 366
    Oklahoma, 376
    Oregon, 386
    Pennsylvania, 396
    Rhode Island, 406
    South Carolina, 416
    South Dakota, 426
    Tennessee, 436
    Texas, 446
    Utah, 456
    Vermont, 466
    Virginia, 476
    Washington, 486
    West Virginia, 496
    Wisconsin, 506
    Wyoming, 516
MARYLAND
    Age, population by, 216
    Crime, 222
    Education and school enrollment, 221
    Employment status and characteristics, 219–221
    Exports of goods, 224
    Facts and figures, 215
    Health insurance coverage, 218
    Hispanic or Latino origin, population by, 216
    Households and housing characteristics, 217
    Income, 218
    Marital status, 216
    Migration, origin, and language, 217
    Poverty status, 218

Race, population by, 216
Rankings by state, 3
Sex, population by, 216
State government finances, 223
State government tax collections, 224
Unemployment rate, 219
Voting and registration, 222
Wages by industry, 220
MASSACHUSETTS
Age, population by, 226
Crime, 232
Education and school enrollment, 231
Employment status and characteristics, 229–231
Exports of goods, 234
Facts and figures, 225
Health insurance coverage, 228
Hispanic or Latino origin, population by, 226
Households and housing characteristics, 227
Income, 228
Marital status, 226
Migration, origin, and language, 227
Poverty status, 228
Race, population by, 226
Rankings by state, 3
Sex, population by, 226
State government finances, 233
State government tax collections, 234
Unemployment rate, 229
Voting and registration, 232
Wages by industry, 230
MEDIAN INCOME
see **INCOME**
MICHIGAN
Age, population by, 236
Crime, 242
Education and school enrollment, 241
Employment status and characteristics, 239–241
Exports of goods, 244
Facts and figures, 235
Health insurance coverage, 238
Hispanic or Latino origin, population by, 236
Households and housing characteristics, 237
Income, 238
Marital status, 236
Migration, origin, and language, 237
Poverty status, 238
Race, population by, 236
Rankings by state, 3
Sex, population by, 236
State government finances, 243
State government tax collections, 244
Unemployment rate, 239
Voting and registration, 242
Wages by industry, 240
MIGRATION, ORIGIN, AND LANGUAGE
Alabama, 17
Alaska, 27
Arizona, 37
Arkansas, 47

California, 57
Colorado, 67
Connecticut, 77
Delaware, 87
District of Columbia, 97
Florida, 107
Georgia, 117
Hawaii, 127
Idaho, 137
Illinois, 147
Indiana, 157
Iowa, 167
Kansas, 177
Kentucky, 187
Louisiana, 197
Maine, 207
Maryland, 217
Massachusetts, 227
Michigan, 237
Minnesota, 247
Mississippi, 257
Missouri, 267
Montana, 277
Nebraska, 287
Nevada, 297
New Hampshire, 307
New Jersey, 317
New Mexico, 327
New York, 337
North Carolina, 347
North Dakota, 357
Ohio, 367
Oklahoma, 377
Oregon, 387
Pennsylvania, 397
Rhode Island, 407
South Carolina, 417
South Dakota, 427
Tennessee, 437
Texas, 447
Utah, 457
Vermont, 467
Virginia, 477
Washington, 487
West Virginia, 497
Wisconsin, 507
Wyoming, 517
MINNESOTA
Age, population by, 246
Crime, 252
Education and school enrollment, 251
Employment status and characteristics, 249–251
Exports of goods, 254
Facts and figures, 245
Health insurance coverage, 248
Hispanic or Latino origin, population by, 246
Households and housing characteristics, 247
Income, 248
Marital status, 246

Migration, origin, and language, 247
Poverty status, 248
Race, population by, 246
Rankings by state, 3
Sex, population by, 246
State government finances, 253
State government tax collections, 254
Unemployment rate, 249
Voting and registration, 252
Wages by industry, 250

MISSISSIPPI
Age, population by, 256
Crime, 262
Education and school enrollment, 261
Employment status and characteristics, 259–261
Exports of goods, 264
Facts and figures, 255
Health insurance coverage, 258
Hispanic or Latino origin, population by, 256
Households and housing characteristics, 257
Income, 258
Marital status, 256
Migration, origin, and language, 257
Poverty status, 258
Race, population by, 256
Rankings by state, 3
Sex, population by, 256
State government finances, 263
State government tax collections, 264
Unemployment rate, 259
Voting and registration, 262
Wages by industry, 260

MISSOURI
Age, population by, 266
Crime, 272
Education and school enrollment, 271
Employment status and characteristics, 269–271
Exports of goods, 274
Facts and figures, 265
Health insurance coverage, 268
Hispanic or Latino origin, population by, 266
Households and housing characteristics, 267
Income, 268
Marital status, 266
Migration, origin, and language, 267
Poverty status, 268
Race, population by, 266
Rankings by state, 3
Sex, population by, 266
State government finances, 273
State government tax collections, 274
Unemployment rate, 269
Voting and registration, 272
Wages by industry, 270

MONTANA
Age, population by, 276
Crime, 282
Education and school enrollment, 281
Employment status and characteristics, 279–281

Exports of goods, 284
Facts and figures, 275
Health insurance coverage, 278
Hispanic or Latino origin, population by, 276
Households and housing characteristics, 277
Income, 278
Marital status, 276
Migration, origin, and language, 277
Poverty status, 278
Race, population by, 276
Rankings by state, 3
Sex, population by, 276
State government finances, 283
State government tax collections, 284
Unemployment rate, 279
Voting and registration, 282
Wages by industry, 280

MOTOR VEHICLE ACCIDENTS
State rankings, 13

N
NATIVE AMERICANS
  see **RACE, POPULATION BY**
NEBRASKA
Age, population by, 286
Crime, 292
Education and school enrollment, 291
Employment status and characteristics, 289–291
Exports of goods, 294
Facts and figures, 285
Health insurance coverage, 288
Hispanic or Latino origin, population by, 286
Households and housing characteristics, 287
Income, 288
Marital status, 286
Migration, origin, and language, 287
Poverty status, 288
Race, population by, 286
Rankings by state, 3
Sex, population by, 286
State government finances, 293
State government tax collections, 294
Unemployment rate, 289
Voting and registration, 292
Wages by industry, 290

NEVADA
Age, population by, 296
Crime, 302
Education and school enrollment, 301
Employment status and characteristics, 299–301
Exports of goods, 304
Facts and figures, 295
Health insurance coverage, 298
Hispanic or Latino origin, population by, 296
Households and housing characteristics, 297
Income, 298
Marital status, 296
Migration, origin, and language, 297
Poverty status, 298

Race, population by, 296
Rankings by state, 3
Sex, population by, 296
State government finances, 303
State government tax collections, 304
Unemployment rate, 299
Voting and registration, 302
Wages by industry, 300

NEW HAMPSHIRE
Age, population by, 306
Crime, 312
Education and school enrollment, 311
Employment status and characteristics, 309–311
Exports of goods, 314
Facts and figures, 305
Health insurance coverage, 308
Hispanic or Latino origin, population by, 306
Households and housing characteristics, 307
Income, 308
Marital status, 306
Migration, origin, and language, 307
Poverty status, 308
Race, population by, 306
Rankings by state, 3
Sex, population by, 306
State government finances, 313
State government tax collections, 314
Unemployment rate, 309
Voting and registration, 312
Wages by industry, 310

NEW JERSEY
Age, population by, 316
Crime, 322
Education and school enrollment, 321
Employment status and characteristics, 319–321
Exports of goods, 324
Facts and figures, 315
Health insurance coverage, 318
Hispanic or Latino origin, population by, 316
Households and housing characteristics, 317
Income, 318
Marital status, 316
Migration, origin, and language, 317
Poverty status, 318
Race, population by, 316
Rankings by state, 3
Sex, population by, 316
State government finances, 323
State government tax collections, 324
Unemployment rate, 319
Voting and registration, 322
Wages by industry, 320

NEW MEXICO
Age, population by, 326
Crime, 332
Education and school enrollment, 331
Employment status and characteristics, 329–331
Exports of goods, 334
Facts and figures, 325

Health insurance coverage, 328
Hispanic or Latino origin, population by, 326
Households and housing characteristics, 327
Income, 328
Marital status, 326
Migration, origin, and language, 327
Poverty status, 328
Race, population by, 326
Rankings by state, 3
Sex, population by, 326
State government finances, 333
State government tax collections, 334
Unemployment rate, 329
Voting and registration, 332
Wages by industry, 330

NEW YORK
Age, population by, 336
Crime, 342
Education and school enrollment, 341
Employment status and characteristics, 339–341
Exports of goods, 344
Facts and figures, 335
Health insurance coverage, 338
Hispanic or Latino origin, population by, 336
Households and housing characteristics, 337
Income, 338
Marital status, 336
Migration, origin, and language, 337
Poverty status, 338
Race, population by, 336
Rankings by state, 3
Sex, population by, 336
State government finances, 343
State government tax collections, 344
Unemployment rate, 339
Voting and registration, 342
Wages by industry, 340

NORTH CAROLINA
Age, population by, 346
Crime, 352
Education and school enrollment, 351
Employment status and characteristics, 349–351
Exports of goods, 354
Facts and figures, 345
Health insurance coverage, 348
Hispanic or Latino origin, population by, 346
Households and housing characteristics, 347
Income, 348
Marital status, 346
Migration, origin, and language, 347
Poverty status, 348
Race, population by, 346
Rankings by state, 3
Sex, population by, 346
State government finances, 353
State government tax collections, 354
Unemployment rate, 349
Voting and registration, 352
Wages by industry, 350

NORTH DAKOTA
   Age, population by, 356
   Crime, 362
   Education and school enrollment, 361
   Employment status and characteristics, 359–361
   Exports of goods, 364
   Facts and figures, 355
   Health insurance coverage, 358
   Hispanic or Latino origin, population by, 356
   Households and housing characteristics, 357
   Income, 358
   Marital status, 356
   Migration, origin, and language, 357
   Poverty status, 358
   Race, population by, 356
   Rankings by state, 3
   Sex, population by, 356
   State government finances, 363
   State government tax collections, 364
   Unemployment rate, 359
   Voting and registration, 362
   Wages by industry, 360

O
OHIO
   Age, population by, 366
   Crime, 372
   Education and school enrollment, 371
   Employment status and characteristics, 369–371
   Exports of goods, 374
   Facts and figures, 365
   Health insurance coverage, 368
   Hispanic or Latino origin, population by, 366
   Households and housing characteristics, 367
   Income, 368
   Marital status, 366
   Migration, origin, and language, 367
   Poverty status, 368
   Race, population by, 366
   Rankings by state, 3
   Sex, population by, 366
   State government finances, 373
   State government tax collections, 374
   Unemployment rate, 369
   Voting and registration, 372
   Wages by industry, 370
OKLAHOMA
   Age, population by, 376
   Crime, 382
   Education and school enrollment, 381
   Employment status and characteristics, 379–381
   Exports of goods, 384
   Facts and figures, 375
   Health insurance coverage, 378
   Hispanic or Latino origin, population by, 376
   Households and housing characteristics, 377
   Income, 378
   Marital status, 376
   Migration, origin, and language, 377

   Poverty status, 378
   Race, population by, 376
   Rankings by state, 3
   Sex, population by, 376
   State government finances, 383
   State government tax collections, 384
   Unemployment rate, 379
   Voting and registration, 382
   Wages by industry, 380
OREGON
   Age, population by, 386
   Crime, 392
   Education and school enrollment, 391
   Employment status and characteristics, 389–391
   Exports of goods, 394
   Facts and figures, 385
   Health insurance coverage, 388
   Hispanic or Latino origin, population by, 386
   Households and housing characteristics, 387
   Income, 388
   Marital status, 386
   Migration, origin, and language, 387
   Poverty status, 388
   Race, population by, 386
   Rankings by state, 3
   Sex, population by, 386
   State government finances, 393
   State government tax collections, 394
   Unemployment rate, 389
   Voting and registration, 392
   Wages by industry, 390
ORIGIN
   see **MIGRATION, ORIGIN, AND LANGUAGE**

P
PACIFIC ISLANDERS
   see **RACE, POPULATION BY**
PENNSYLVANIA
   Age, population by, 396
   Crime, 402
   Education and school enrollment, 401
   Employment status and characteristics, 399–401
   Exports of goods, 404
   Facts and figures, 395
   Health insurance coverage, 398
   Hispanic or Latino origin, population by, 396
   Households and housing characteristics, 397
   Income, 398
   Marital status, 396
   Migration, origin, and language, 397
   Poverty status, 398
   Race, population by, 396
   Rankings by state, 3
   Sex, population by, 396
   State government finances, 403
   State government tax collections, 404
   Unemployment rate, 399
   Voting and registration, 402
   Wages by industry, 400

POPULATION
Rankings by state, 3
POPULATION, PERCENT CHANGE
Rankings by state, 3
POVERTY STATUS
Alabama, 18
Alaska, 28
Arizona, 38
Arkansas, 48
California, 58
Colorado, 68
Connecticut, 78
Delaware, 88
District of Columbia, 98
Florida, 108
Georgia, 118
Hawaii, 128
Idaho, 138
Illinois, 148
Indiana, 158
Iowa, 168
Kansas, 178
Kentucky, 188
Louisiana, 198
Maine, 208
Maryland, 218
Massachusetts, 228
Michigan, 238
Minnesota, 248
Mississippi, 258
Missouri, 268
Montana, 278
Nebraska, 288
Nevada, 298
New Hampshire, 308
New Jersey, 318
New Mexico, 328
New York, 338
North Carolina, 348
North Dakota, 358
Ohio, 368
Oklahoma, 378
Oregon, 388
Pennsylvania, 398
Rankings by state
    persons below poverty level, 11, 12
Rhode Island, 408
South Carolina, 418
South Dakota, 428
Tennessee, 438
Texas, 448
Utah, 458
Vermont, 468
Virginia, 478
Washington, 488
West Virginia, 498
Wisconsin, 508
Wyoming, 518

PROPERTY CRIME
see **CRIME**

R
RACE, POPULATION BY
Alabama, 16
Alaska, 26
Arizona, 36
Arkansas, 46
California, 56
Colorado, 66
Connecticut, 76
Delaware, 86
District of Columbia, 96
Florida, 106
Georgia, 116
Hawaii, 126
Idaho, 136
Illinois, 146
Indiana, 156
Iowa, 166
Kansas, 176
Kentucky, 186
Louisiana, 196
Maine, 206
Maryland, 216
Massachusetts, 226
Michigan, 236
Minnesota, 246
Mississippi, 256
Missouri, 266
Montana, 276
Nebraska, 286
Nevada, 296
New Hampshire, 306
New Jersey, 316
New Mexico, 326
New York, 336
North Carolina, 346
North Dakota, 356
Ohio, 366
Oklahoma, 376
Oregon, 386
Pennsylvania, 396
Rankings by state
    percent American Indian and Alaska Native alone, 5
    percent Asian alone, 5
    percent black alone, 4
    percent Hispanic or Latino, 6
    percent Native Hawaiian and Pacific Islander alone, 5
    percent two or more races, 6
    percent white alone, 4, 6
Rhode Island, 406
South Carolina, 416
South Dakota, 426
Tennessee, 436
Texas, 446
Utah, 456

Vermont, 466
Virginia, 476
Washington, 486
West Virginia, 496
Wisconsin, 506
Wyoming, 516

RANKINGS BY STATE
Birth rates, 7
Crime, 8
Drug overdose deaths, 7
Employment, nonfarm payrolls, 9
Energy consumption per capita, 12
Gross domestic product, 10
Homeownership rates, 12
Households and housing characteristics, 13
Income
    median family income, 11
    median household income, 11
    per capita personal income, 10
    persons below poverty level, 11, 12
Motor vehicle accidents, 13
Percent 65 years and over, 4
Percent black alone, 4
Percent college graduates, 8
Percent Hispanic or Latino, 6
Percent of persons below the poverty level, 11, 12
Percent population change, 3
Percent two or more races, 6
Percent under 18 years old, 3
Percent white alone, 4, 6
Population, 3
Population, percent change, 3
Poverty levels, 11, 12
Property crime rates, 8
Race, population by, 4–6
Traffic fatalities, 13
Unemployment rates, 9
Violent crime rates, 8
Voting population, 7

REAL GROSS DOMESTIC PRODUCT
State rankings, 10

RHODE ISLAND
Age, population by, 406
Crime, 412
Education and school enrollment, 411
Employment status and characteristics, 409–411
Exports of goods, 414
Facts and figures, 405
Health insurance coverage, 408
Hispanic or Latino origin, population by, 406
Households and housing characteristics, 407
Income, 408
Marital status, 406
Migration, origin, and language, 407
Poverty status, 408
Race, population by, 406
Rankings by state, 3
Sex, population by, 406
State government finances, 413

State government tax collections, 414
Unemployment rate, 409
Voting and registration, 412
Wages by industry, 410

S
SALARIES
Income
    see **INCOME**
Wages by industry
    see **WAGES BY INDUSTRY**
SCHOOL ENROLLMENT
    see **EDUCATION AND SCHOOL ENROLLMENT**
SEX, POPULATION BY
Alabama, 16
Alaska, 26
Arizona, 36
Arkansas, 46
California, 56
Colorado, 66
Connecticut, 76
Delaware, 86
District of Columbia, 96
Florida, 106
Georgia, 116
Hawaii, 126
Idaho, 136
Illinois, 146
Indiana, 156
Iowa, 166
Kansas, 176
Kentucky, 186
Louisiana, 196
Maine, 206
Maryland, 216
Massachusetts, 226
Michigan, 236
Minnesota, 246
Mississippi, 256
Missouri, 266
Montana, 276
Nebraska, 286
Nevada, 296
New Hampshire, 306
New Jersey, 316
New Mexico, 326
New York, 336
North Carolina, 346
North Dakota, 356
Ohio, 366
Oklahoma, 376
Oregon, 386
Pennsylvania, 396
Rhode Island, 406
South Carolina, 416
South Dakota, 426
Tennessee, 436
Texas, 446
Utah, 456

Vermont, 466
Virginia, 476
Washington, 486
West Virginia, 496
Wisconsin, 506
Wyoming, 516

SOUTH CAROLINA
Age, population by, 416
Crime, 422
Education and school enrollment, 421
Employment status and characteristics, 419–421
Exports of goods, 424
Facts and figures, 415
Health insurance coverage, 418
Hispanic or Latino origin, population by, 416
Households and housing characteristics, 417
Income, 418
Marital status, 416
Migration, origin, and language, 417
Poverty status, 418
Race, population by, 416
Rankings by state, 3
Sex, population by, 416
State government finances, 423
State government tax collections, 424
Unemployment rate, 419
Voting and registration, 422
Wages by industry, 420

SOUTH DAKOTA
Age, population by, 426
Crime, 432
Education and school enrollment, 431
Employment status and characteristics, 429–431
Exports of goods, 434
Facts and figures, 425
Health insurance coverage, 428
Hispanic or Latino origin, population by, 426
Households and housing characteristics, 427
Income, 428
Marital status, 426
Migration, origin, and language, 427
Poverty status, 428
Race, population by, 426
Rankings by state, 3
Sex, population by, 426
State government finances, 433
State government tax collections, 434
Unemployment rate, 429
Voting and registration, 432
Wages by industry, 430

STATE GOVERNMENT FINANCES
Alabama, 23
Alaska, 33
Arizona, 43
Arkansas, 53
California, 63
Colorado, 73
Connecticut, 83
Delaware, 93

District of Columbia, 103
Florida, 113
Georgia, 123
Hawaii, 133
Idaho, 143
Illinois, 153
Indiana, 163
Iowa, 173
Kansas, 183
Kentucky, 193
Louisiana, 203
Maine, 213
Maryland, 223
Massachusetts, 233
Michigan, 243
Minnesota, 253
Mississippi, 263
Missouri, 273
Montana, 283
Nebraska, 293
Nevada, 303
New Hampshire, 313
New Jersey, 323
New Mexico, 333
New York, 343
North Carolina, 353
North Dakota, 363
Ohio, 373
Oklahoma, 383
Oregon, 393
Pennsylvania, 403
Rhode Island, 413
South Carolina, 423
South Dakota, 433
Tennessee, 443
Texas, 453
Utah, 463
Vermont, 473
Virginia, 483
Washington, 493
West Virginia, 503
Wisconsin, 513
Wyoming, 523

STATE GOVERNMENT TAX COLLECTIONS
Alabama, 24
Alaska, 34
Arizona, 44
Arkansas, 54
California, 64
Colorado, 74
Connecticut, 84
Delaware, 94
Florida, 114
Georgia, 124
Hawaii, 134
Idaho, 144
Illinois, 154
Indiana, 164
Iowa, 174

Kansas, 184
Kentucky, 194
Louisiana, 204
Maine, 214
Maryland, 224
Massachusetts, 234
Michigan, 244
Minnesota, 254
Mississippi, 264
Missouri, 274
Montana, 284
Nebraska, 294
Nevada, 304
New Hampshire, 314
New Jersey, 324
New Mexico, 334
New York, 344
North Carolina, 354
North Dakota, 364
Ohio, 374
Oklahoma, 384
Oregon, 394
Pennsylvania, 404
Rhode Island, 414
South Carolina, 424
South Dakota, 434
Tennessee, 444
Texas, 454
Utah, 464
Vermont, 474
Virginia, 484
Washington, 494
West Virginia, 504
Wisconsin, 514
Wyoming, 524

STATE RANKINGS
　　see **RANKINGS BY STATE**

T
TAXATION
　　see **STATE GOVERNMENT TAX COLLECTIONS**
TENNESSEE
Age, population by, 436
Crime, 442
Education and school enrollment, 441
Employment status and characteristics, 439–441
Exports of goods, 444
Facts and figures, 435
Health insurance coverage, 438
Hispanic or Latino origin, population by, 436
Households and housing characteristics, 437
Income, 438
Marital status, 436
Migration, origin, and language, 437
Poverty status, 438
Race, population by, 436
Rankings by state, 3
Sex, population by, 436
State government finances, 443

State government tax collections, 444
Unemployment rate, 439
Voting and registration, 442
Wages by industry, 440
TEXAS
Age, population by, 446
Crime, 452
Education and school enrollment, 451
Employment status and characteristics, 449–451
Exports of goods, 454
Facts and figures, 445
Health insurance coverage, 448
Hispanic or Latino origin, population by, 446
Households and housing characteristics, 447
Income, 448
Marital status, 446
Migration, origin, and language, 447
Poverty status, 448
Race, population by, 446
Rankings by state, 3
Sex, population by, 446
State government finances, 453
State government tax collections, 454
Unemployment rate, 449
Voting and registration, 452
Wages by industry, 450
TRAFFIC FATALITIES
State rankings, 13

U
UNEMPLOYMENT RATES
Alabama, 19
Alaska, 29
Arizona, 39
Arkansas, 49
California, 59
Colorado, 69
Connecticut, 79
Delaware, 89
District of Columbia, 99
Florida, 109
Georgia, 119
Hawaii, 129
Idaho, 139
Illinois, 149
Indiana, 159
Iowa, 169
Kansas, 179
Kentucky, 189
Louisiana, 199
Maine, 209
Maryland, 219
Massachusetts, 229
Michigan, 239
Minnesota, 249
Mississippi, 259
Missouri, 269
Montana, 279
Nebraska, 289

Nevada, 299
New Hampshire, 309
New Jersey, 319
New Mexico, 329
New York, 339
North Carolina, 349
North Dakota, 359
Ohio, 369
Oklahoma, 379
Oregon, 389
Pennsylvania, 399
Rankings by state, 9
Rhode Island, 409
South Carolina, 419
South Dakota, 429
Tennessee, 439
Texas, 449
Utah, 459
Vermont, 469
Virginia, 479
Washington, 489
West Virginia, 499
Wisconsin, 509
Wyoming, 519
UNITED STATES RANKINGS
    see **RANKINGS BY STATE**
UTAH
    Age, population by, 456
    Crime, 462
    Education and school enrollment, 461
    Employment status and characteristics, 459–461
    Exports of goods, 464
    Facts and figures, 455
    Health insurance coverage, 458
    Hispanic or Latino origin, population by, 456
    Households and housing characteristics, 457
    Income, 458
    Marital status, 456
    Migration, origin, and language, 457
    Poverty status, 458
    Race, population by, 456
    Rankings by state, 3
    Sex, population by, 456
    State government finances, 463
    State government tax collections, 464
    Unemployment rate, 459
    Voting and registration, 462
    Wages by industry, 460

V
VERMONT
    Age, population by, 466
    Crime, 472
    Education and school enrollment, 471
    Employment status and characteristics, 469–471
    Exports of goods, 474
    Facts and figures, 465
    Health insurance coverage, 468
    Hispanic or Latino origin, population by, 466

Households and housing characteristics, 467
Income, 468
Marital status, 466
Migration, origin, and language, 467
Poverty status, 468
Race, population by, 466
Rankings by state, 3
Sex, population by, 466
State government finances, 473
State government tax collections, 474
Unemployment rate, 469
Voting and registration, 472
Wages by industry, 470
VIOLENT CRIME
    see **CRIME**
VIRGINIA
    Age, population by, 476
    Crime, 482
    Education and school enrollment, 481
    Employment status and characteristics, 479–481
    Exports of goods, 484
    Facts and figures, 475
    Health insurance coverage, 478
    Hispanic or Latino origin, population by, 476
    Households and housing characteristics, 477
    Income, 478
    Marital status, 476
    Migration, origin, and language, 477
    Poverty status, 478
    Race, population by, 476
    Rankings by state, 3
    Sex, population by, 476
    State government finances, 483
    State government tax collections, 484
    Unemployment rate, 479
    Voting and registration, 482
    Wages by industry, 480
VOTING AND REGISTRATION
    Alabama, 22
    Alaska, 32
    Arizona, 42
    Arkansas, 52
    California, 62
    Colorado, 72
    Connecticut, 82
    Delaware, 92
    District of Columbia, 102
    Florida, 112
    Georgia, 122
    Hawaii, 132
    Idaho, 142
    Illinois, 152
    Indiana, 162
    Iowa, 172
    Kansas, 182
    Kentucky, 192
    Louisiana, 202
    Maine, 212
    Maryland, 222

Massachusetts, 232
Michigan, 242
Minnesota, 252
Mississippi, 262
Missouri, 272
Montana, 282
Nebraska, 292
Nevada, 302
New Hampshire, 312
New Jersey, 322
New Mexico, 332
New York, 342
North Carolina, 352
North Dakota, 362
Ohio, 372
Oklahoma, 382
Oregon, 392
Pennsylvania, 402
Population by state, 7
Rhode Island, 412
South Carolina, 422
South Dakota, 432
Tennessee, 442
Texas, 452
Utah, 462
Vermont, 472
Virginia, 482
Washington, 492
West Virginia, 502
Wisconsin, 512
Wyoming, 522

W
WAGES BY INDUSTRY

Alabama, 20
Alaska, 30
Arizona, 40
Arkansas, 50
California, 60
Colorado, 70
Connecticut, 80
Delaware, 90
District of Columbia, 100
Florida, 110
Georgia, 120
Hawaii, 130
Idaho, 140
Illinois, 150
Income
    see INCOME
Indiana, 160
Iowa, 170
Kansas, 180
Kentucky, 190
Louisiana, 200
Maine, 210
Maryland, 220
Massachusetts, 230
Michigan, 240

Minnesota, 250
Mississippi, 260
Missouri, 270
Montana, 280
Nebraska, 290
Nevada, 300
New Hampshire, 310
New Jersey, 320
New Mexico, 330
New York, 340
North Carolina, 350
North Dakota, 360
Ohio, 370
Oklahoma, 380
Oregon, 390
Pennsylvania, 400
Rankings by state
    median family income, 11
    median household income, 11
    per capita personal income, 10
    poverty levels, 11, 12
Rhode Island, 410
South Carolina, 420
South Dakota, 430
Tennessee, 440
Texas, 450
Utah, 460
Vermont, 470
Virginia, 480
Washington, 490
West Virginia, 500
Wisconsin, 510
Wyoming, 520

WASHINGTON

Age, population by, 486
Crime, 492
Education and school enrollment, 491
Employment status and characteristics, 489–491
Exports of goods, 494
Facts and figures, 485
Health insurance coverage, 488
Hispanic or Latino origin, population by, 486
Households and housing characteristics, 487
Income, 488
Marital status, 486
Migration, origin, and language, 487
Poverty status, 488
Race, population by, 486
Rankings by state, 3
Sex, population by, 486
State government finances, 493
State government tax collections, 494
Unemployment rate, 489
Voting and registration, 492
Wages by industry, 490

WEST VIRGINIA

Age, population by, 496
Crime, 502
Education and school enrollment, 501

Employment status and characteristics, 499–501
Exports of goods, 504
Facts and figures, 495
Health insurance coverage, 498
Hispanic or Latino origin, population by, 496
Households and housing characteristics, 497
Income, 498
Marital status, 496
Migration, origin, and language, 497
Poverty status, 498
Race, population by, 496
Rankings by state, 3
Sex, population by, 496
State government finances, 503
State government tax collections, 504
Unemployment rate, 499
Voting and registration, 502
Wages by industry, 500

WHITE RACE
   see **RACE, POPULATION BY**

WISCONSIN
Age, population by, 506
Crime, 512
Education and school enrollment, 511
Employment status and characteristics, 509–511
Exports of goods, 514
Facts and figures, 505
Health insurance coverage, 508
Hispanic or Latino origin, population by, 506
Households and housing characteristics, 507
Income, 508
Marital status, 506

Migration, origin, and language, 507
Poverty status, 508
Race, population by, 506
Rankings by state, 3
Sex, population by, 506
State government finances, 513
State government tax collections, 514
Unemployment rate, 509
Voting and registration, 512
Wages by industry, 510

WYOMING
Age, population by, 516
Crime, 522
Education and school enrollment, 521
Employment status and characteristics, 519–521
Exports of goods, 524
Facts and figures, 515
Health insurance coverage, 518
Hispanic or Latino origin, population by, 516
Households and housing characteristics, 517
Income, 518
Marital status, 516
Migration, origin, and language, 517
Poverty status, 518
Race, population by, 516
Rankings by state, 3
Sex, population by, 516
State government finances, 523
State government tax collections, 524
Unemployment rate, 519
Voting and registration, 522
Wages by industry, 520